D1321040

A GRAMMAR OF THE GERMAN LANGUAGE

BY

GEORGE O. CURME

Second Revised Edition

FREDERICK UNGAR PUBLISHING CO.
NEW YORK

89476

Dedicated to

HERMANN COLLITZ and GEORG EDWARD

with gratitude and regard

TENTH PRINTING, 1970

ISBN 0-8044-0113-6

Printed in the United States of America

Die Sprache, in ihrem wirklichen Wesen aufgefaßt, ist etwas beständig und in jedem Augenblick Vorübergehendes . . . Sie selbst ist kein Werk, sondern eine Tätigkeit . . . Sie ist nämlich die sich ewig wiederholende Arbeit des Geistes, den artikulierten Laut zum Ausdruck des Gedankens fähig zu machen.

(W. von Humboldt)

"Dieser Mensch redet wie ein Buch," ist ein krankes Lob. Umgekehrt sei die Losung: "Dies Buch redet wie ein Mensch."

(Otto Schroeder)

PREFACE TO THE FIRST EDITION

THIS book is intended to furnish to students of the German language and literature an outline of German grammar, based not upon some ideal conception of how the language should be spoken, but upon the actual varying usage of the intelligent classes in the German Empire, Austria, and Switzerland. An earnest attempt has been made to make the work a valuable book of reference, so that the general student might find in it an impartial and rather full presentation of the facts of the language founded upon the works of scholars and also an independent study of the polite and colloquial literature itself. In order to attain to the greatest possible completeness in the given space, it was thought best, not to present the materials gathered in the course of the work on the subject, but only to give precise statements of results illustrated in most cases by a few apt examples. In this way a great many more points have been treated than in large scholarly works where the prominent aim is to present the materials gathered in long researches. The plan to make the book as complete as possible has been materially furthered by the slow development of the work thruout a period of over fifteen years. From year to year new points presented themselves and old ones appeared in fuller outline, so that continued search and occasional accidental finds have added much to the original draft of the work.

The full index will place the contents of the book at the disposal of the student.

This treatise often differs considerably from German works in subject matter and manner of presentation, as it is written entirely from the standpoint of the needs of English-speaking students. Hence considerable space is often devoted to points scarcely mentioned by German scholars, or not treated at all.

Thruout the book much attention has been paid to classification in order that the individual life of the grammatical categories might be carefully studied. It is hoped that the results of this course will prove to have not only a scientific but also a practical value. Thus, for instance, in order that both of these aims might be attained, the inflection of nouns is presented in the minutest detail. Here it is hoped that full treatment will lead to clearness. This part of German grammar is so inconsistent and confused that only a full picture can give an adequate idea of the inflection as it actually is. However clear the inflectional groups may appear to one versed in historical grammar who is familiar with the various causes that have produced the present forms, to the general student these groups are not entirely clear unless the list of words composing each group is complete, as there is often no formal sign by which one may be guided in assigning a word to its proper group. Here, indeed, the German himself constantly blunders, how then can a foreigner without the fullest light expect to see clearly? The confusion is often increased and natural tendencies arrested by learned men, who, looking at the questions from different standpoints, suggest different forms as the correct usage. Also the best authors of our time reflect in their works the general uncertainty with regard to form. Of course, final decisions cannot be given in such cases, and it only remains to record the fluctuations of usage. The dire confusion at this point will ultimately lead to considerable changes in the language itself, and indeed certain tendencies toward uniformity and simplicity are apparent. In treating this difficult subject the words of foreign origin have been included. The unscientific method of excluding such words, so generally followed by German scholars, has led to false impressions as to the real size and importance of the existing classes of German nouns.

Altho this book is designed as a study of the German of to-day, it was found necessary, in order to give a faithful picture of the living language in all its varied styles, to include to a certain extent a study of the earlier forms of the language. It is difficult to state the precise date when a certain form or expression can fairly be said to be dead. Colloquial language often preserves earlier forms that have elsewhere passed away. The master-pieces of earlier parts of the present period are still heard everywhere in the theaters, and otherwise still occupy the thought of the present generation, and thus still influence the language of poetry and higher diction in general. The language of Luther is still heard in the churches and has stamped itself upon the language of certain classes of people and styles of speech. Beautiful gems of thought in the form of proverbs have been handed down from earlier times like precious heir-looms unchanged. Literature now abounds in description of the language and customs of people in the out-of-the-way provinces, who speak quaint dialects which often faithfully preserve grammatical forms now no longer in general use. In the historical novel and drama we find a conscious or unconscious imitation of the peculiar language of older parts of the period. Among the earliest forms of the present period treated here the examples taken from Luther's translation of the Bible are especially frequent. Also as this translation is fairly available to all, many references to interesting constructions in it have been made by merely quoting chapter and verse after a short remark explaining the construction. The edition here used is that of 1545, the last published by Luther himself. The available editions which will probably be used by students are all largely modernized, but even from these imperfect texts general impressions can be obtained. The language of the N. H. G. period has been uniformly conformed in spelling to the new official orthography, as far as it could faithfully reproduce the original form of the words, with the exception of passages taken from Luther's translation of the Bible. These are given with Luther's spellings, capitalizations, and punctuation in the hope that they might prove interesting and instructive. Of course only the most general points in this important part of the period are touched upon. A word from a period earlier than N. H. G. is never introduced for its own sake, or to give a picture of an older state of things, but always solely for the purpose of throwing light upon some dark construction in present usage or the literature that is still generally studied. Thus there is not the slightest attempt to give a connected outline of earlier periods. However, in thus introducing glimpses of earlier forms of speech, a good deal is gained toward teaching the student to look at language in the true light, and he may thus in an easy and forcible way learn that grammar is not made up of the infallible decrees of book-makers, but that it is a growth, and has reached its present form by various evolutions, here piously preserving fossilized remnants of by-gone ages, there struggling toward uniformity out of a tangle of prehistoric conditions no longer understood, now enriched by the genius of the individual, and now by the rich quota of the different dialects, now working constructively along plain and simple lines not hitherto known.

Altho attention has thus been carefully directed to early N. H. G. and also to the language of the classical period and the conspicuous authors of the first half of the 19th century, the main stress lies in the direction of present usage. Seven hundred works of varied styles published since 1850 by authors from various parts of the German Empire, Austria, and Switzerland, have been carefully read. Representative newspapers from different parts of these same countries have been studied. In this work, however, the political lines that have been drawn across the map of Germany, dividing it up into Austria, Switzerland, etc., have in all points of a general nature been disregarded, and terms *North*, *South*, etc., have been used as designations of the different parts of *one* country—one at least in language. In little points, usage differs considerably, not only in different parts of this territory, but also in the same section, and the author has not been able to share the assurance of certain grammarians who are so positive that they have prescribed the correct forms. The plain fact is that there is considerable fluctuation in present usage, tho not so much as earlier in the period, and this fluctuation is found even in the highest forms of current literature. Everywhere thruout these pages will be found double and triple forms for the same thing, that is a picture of the language as it is. A table of many fluctuating forms has been kept by the author constantly before him, and data inserted from time to time. In some cases the prevailing form has become apparent, and has been recorded. In other cases the situation will not become clear until many minute investigations have been made by many scholars. In still other cases nothing can be fixed, as the language itself has not assumed final form. To prescribe forms at this point, as many German grammarians do, is quite pernicious, for the capricious decisions of different scholars, differing widely as they often do, add to the general confusion and arrest natural linguistic tendencies. However, between forms that fluctuated in Lessing's day a final decision has often been made, or both forms have been retained with different shades of meaning.

The usage of the best authors of our time has been taken in all cases as the highest authority. By this, however, poets and philosophers are not alone meant. The best authors in the different fields of literature, even the much maligned newspapers, have been taken as guides. The pessimistic views of certain scholars with regard to the language of the daily press are not supported by the facts. The German newspaper man fills his place worthily and furnishes additional evidence of the power and flexibility of the German language. Indeed, his influence is especially needed in these days of intense realism, when polite literature often abandons the literary language entirely, or intersperses into it copious samples of dialect from every part of two empires and the Swiss republic. It is, however, far from our intention to criticize these naturalistic tendencies in literature which are so truly characteristic of our time, for we are not indifferent to a movement which in such a marked manner has widened human sympathies and increased the interest in polite literature in general. This broadening of the sphere of literature has increased the burdens of the grammarian, and made it seem to the author of the present work quite necessary that at least the salient features of popular language should be treated. Still greater attention has been paid to colloquial speech, and this study has been made more easy by the extensive literature of the naturalistic school, which has consciously striven to reproduce the language of actual life. Indeed, an earnest attempt has been made to treat the different styles of speech and to define as carefully as possible their proper boundaries. Altho, in general, matters pertaining to style belong to rhetoric, a large number of the points in question belong strictly to grammar. Just as each locality has its particular dialect, so has each style its own individual grammatical forms. One style requires a genitive, another the accusative, one style a strong verb, another a weak one, &c. The conservative literary language clings to old grammatical forms, while colloquial speech prefers newer, more regular ones. Foreigners are particularly liable to stumble here and the native German grammarian in his quite uniform recommendation of the older more dignified inflection may lead English-speaking students astray. The conservative German grammarian may be pardoned for his zeal in defending the decaying forms of the language. To the foreigner, however, who is not able, as is a native, to discover the misguided enthusiasm of the grammarian, many of these lauded forms are very misleading, as they represent the language of the past, or of poetry, or elevated discourse. Even the great learned works of the best German scholars give the student only too often erroneous ideas of the present state of the language, so great is their zeal in unfolding the usage of earlier periods and so strong their apathy towards the questions of to-day. These decaying forms are thruout this work always treated as such and not recommended as models of present usage. To every people and every generation language is bequeathed, not as an article of antiquarian interest that must remain untouched and be carefully kept unchanged, but as the most useful and plastic of things, that which is connected with all that is interesting in life and which can be readily adapted to the new and changing needs of the generation. Also with regard to new forms and constructions, the usage of the best authors has been taken as authority rather than the dictum of conservative grammarians. A rich and plastic language like the German is capable of great and varied development if it remains the language of the nation and is not degraded to the position of the language of a few narrow-minded theorists. In the nation lie ever concealed countless hidden forces that are unceasingly at work on the strengthening, upbuilding, and beautifying of the language. In its present interesting period of linguistic growth, may the German language remain unchecked and free! However, for the sake of those who still believe in the dictatorial powers of the grammarian, in every instance there is a note after such new forms indicating that they are not approved by certain grammarians.

The conclusions with regard to the pronunciation are the result of the author's personal observations in different parts of Germany along with a study of the rich literature upon this subject. The signs of the time seem to point so decidedly to the Berlin pronunciation that it seems folly not to recognize it as the most representative form of the spoken language. The author, however, has not in other respects slighted the South, as can be seen in the book itself. The beautiful style of certain Swiss and Austrian authors was a great enticement to prolong unduly work in this direction.

The illustrative sentences used in this book are in most part taken directly from the literature of the language. In a number of cases where the cited sentence is long or intricate, parts not necessary to the thought of the sentence have been omitted. Thus sentences sometimes appear as complete which in the original are only parts of sentences. It is hoped, however, that this liberty will be pardoned on pedagogical grounds and for economic reasons, especially as otherwise not the slightest liberties have been taken with the authors' language, and great care has been employed to follow closely the text of the authorized prints, and wherever possible the latest editions, in order to avoid the danger of typographical errors or careless proof-reading. In a number of cases the examples have been taken from well-known grammatical and lexical sources, as the originals were not accessible. In a number of very common idioms no illustrative sentences could be found in the dictionaries, and in these cases they have been taken directly from the spoken language. It was not thought necessary to cite always the author in case of common usage, tho in many interesting sentences this is done. The authors' names are, however, given where the usage in question is disputed. In such cases only one or two sentences are usually quoted, as it was impossible in the given space to enter into elaborate discussion. The conclusions, however, rest usually upon an ample collection of facts. In other cases the facts were not entirely convincing, but seemed to offer the proposed solution. In a number of instances where general misconceptions prevail a fuller presentation of the facts was made, contrary to the general plan of the work. In a number of instances also three representative authors are cited, one from the early part, one from the middle, and one from the present part of the period, in order to show that the usage has not fluctuated thruout the period. This occurs especially where some particular usage is represented in grammars and dictionaries as obsolete, dialectic, or as belonging to some particular part of the period, while the facts of the language clearly show that the word has been in general and continual use. Also in a number of cases several authors from widely different parts of the country have been cited, in order to show that the form is not provincial as stated by certain scholars. Where usage is limited to a particular style, section of the country, or a part of the period, a short statement of the facts is always made and a representative author cited. In certain parts of the book, however, as in the treatment of the noun, the strong verb, and portions of the syntax, no authors could be cited, altho these portions rest upon a collection of facts as extensive as the others. These materials can only be used in a dictionary.

The great majority of quotations have been taken from common prose. The usual practice among grammarians of quoting so much poetry seems unsound in a book of this kind, especially as the unusual and exceptional forms here found may by the inexperienced student be taken for common forms of speech. The author recalls the smiles of his German friends of years ago who could not restrain the irresistible impulse to twitch the muscles of the face at the familiar-unfamiliar sound of his 'classic' language in a modern conversation. Their Goethe and Schiller seemed inexpressibly odd in the new environment. The object of a grammar should not only be to show the power of the language to express man's highest thoughts and deepest feelings, but also to show its manner of giving expression to the needs of human life in its varied aspects.

At the close of his labors the author confesses that the ideal which appeared to him in his first youthful conception of the work—that of giving a faithful picture of the language as it is written and spoken to-day—has not been completely realized. The linguistic phenomena presented by the language of a great people are too complex to be fully comprehended and faithfully described by one individual. However, the author has allowed the original title to stand upon his work, as it represents an ideal toward which he has constantly striven.

Altho the aim thruout was to build up this work out of the actual facts of the language as gathered in the free and independent study of its polite and colloquial literature, nevertheless much of that which is good in it is due directly to the labors of many scholars who have thrown light upon the different phases of the study, such as Grimm, Vernaleken, Andresen, Heyne, Sanders, Paul, Wilmanns, Matthias, Wunderlich, Behaghel, Sütterlin, Minor, Vietor, Engelien, Blatz, Heintze, Hempl, Valentine, and others. The school-grammars of Lyon, Weiße, Brandt, Thomas, Bierwirth, Eve, Aue, Beresford-Webb, Fasnacht, also the notes of Mr. Wolstenholme in his annotated school-texts, have furnished valuable assistance. The author feels himself especially indebted to the following scholars who have read all of the manuscript or parts of it, and by encouragement or fruitful criticism have contributed much toward making the book what it is: Professor Hermann Collitz, of Bryn Mawr; Professor H. C. G. von Jagemann, of

Harvard; Professor Gustav F. Gruener, of Yale; Professor George Hempl, of the University of Michigan; Professor C. H. Grandgent, of Harvard; Professor Camillo von Klenze, of the University of Chicago; Professor James T. Hatfield, of Northwestern University; Professors Ernst Voss and Edwin Roedder, of the University of Wisconsin; and Dr. Francis Wood, of the University of Chicago. The author finds it very difficult to define the full amount of his indebtedness to his colleague Mr. Georg Edward. For years Mr. Edward has by his accurate knowledge of his native language and literature assisted the author at critical points and kept him away from gross blundering. The author feels the same deep gratitude toward Professor Collitz, who gave encouragement and support at a time of great discouragement, when it appeared that the work could never be carried to a successful close.

In conclusion, the author recalls the helpful services of Mr. William Klingebiehl, of Clutier, Iowa, in the earlier draft of the grammar, also the kindness of the authorities of the Public Library of Chicago and the Public Library of Cincinnati, and last but not least the valuable aid rendered by the following scholars in the reading of the proofs: his colleagues Professor James T. Hatfield, Dr. Marcus Simpson, and Mr. Georg Edward; Professor Starr Willard Cutting and Dr. Francis Wood, of the University of Chicago; Professor William Wirtz, of Parsons College (Fairfield, Iowa); Dr. Fred. C. Hicks, of Monmouth College; Professor Charles R. Keyes, of Cornell College (Mt. Vernon, Iowa); Professor Elfrieda Hochbaum, of Wells College; the following students in Northwestern University: Mr. Walter E. Roloff, Mr. Friedrich Ruff, and Miss Hedwig H. Hochbaum. A number of their remarks upon the proofs have been embodied in the Grammar. The careful work of the Oxford University Press has rendered comparatively easy the efforts to present a faithful text.

EVANSTON, ILLINOIS,
April, 1904.

REVISED EDITION

This edition has been thoroly revised and considerably enlarged. It is especially gratifying to report that upon the basis of a careful reading of a large number of periodicals and books from recent German literature it has been possible in many cases to define more accurately present usage. In some instances it has been necessary to reverse the decisions of the first edition. The author has had but one aim before him, namely to present the facts of the language and not to collect facts for the purpose of trying to establish favorite grammatical theories. Hence he has not hesitated to change his position when the facts seemed to demand it. Wherever it was not possible to attain to certainty he has frankly indicated it, as he believes this attitude of doubt is better than the misleading confidence displayed by many grammarians. In a very large number of cases the language has not yet assumed final form and time alone will bring rhythm and harmony.

The book has been enlarged by the addition of new material, not by multiplying the examples of the first edition. Indeed, on the other hand, much of the original illustrative material has been removed. Moreover, just before the manuscript of the new edition was put into the hands of the printer much of the new illustrative matter was cut away. This procedure has the great disadvantage that it deprives the scholar of the evidence which has led to the conclusions reached, but it has brought nearer realization the original aim to present a comprehensive view of the forms of German expression. On the other hand, the views presented in the original edition have been greatly modified, for seventeen years of further intensive study under the beneficent influence of maturer years and a wider range of observation have changed the author and his work considerably, at least he feels the new issue as quite a different book. It is a record of striking inner change and development. May it be as stimulating and helpful to the reader as the experiences involved in its making have been to the author!

This edition, as also the first, rests upon a study of books and periodicals representing the different styles of literature. It might seem at the first glance that the novelists and dramatists are more fully represented than the writers on history, science, philology, theology, law, etc. A more careful inspection, however, will show that these works have not been slighted. They appear less in these pages for the simple reason that they best represent the higher unity of speech and present few irregularities. In the novel and drama we find the irregular beat of common life varying widely in different provinces and social strata and moreover often disturbed by the exciting influences of passionate feeling. It would be folly to attempt to give an absolutely complete picture of these linguistic phenomena along with the countless forces involved. Hence it should not be surprising if the author's hand has often failed him, but the study has been to him a pleasing one and he has never tired in the struggle to draw the outlines so that they might give at least a faint idea of this complex life.

Differing from his attitude in the first edition, the author in the present edition after another tour of investigation in Germany itself is inclined to recommend the stage pronunciation rather than choice North German or the choice pronunciation of any one section, as the feeling is slowly but surely gaining ground that the standard of the stage represents the best German of our time.

In the preparation of this edition the recent philological literature has been carefully studied. The author desires to add to the list of scholars mentioned in the preface of the first edition as the sources of much valuable material the following names which will suggest at least in part his increased indebtedness: Jespersen, Bremer, Wundt, Marty, Schuchardt, Brugmann, Wegener,

Joseph Schatz, Sommer, Luick, Erdmann-Mensing, Jellinek, Gustav Krüger, Sweet, Sattler, Poutsma, J. Franck, Aug. Fritsch, Franz Saran, Blümel, Deutschbein, Pollak, Molz, John Ries, Aug. Vogel, Kluge, Siebs, Göransson, Ehrismann, W. Kurrelmeyer, Aron, and a very large number of others, who in one way or another have contributed valuable materials to the book. Much assistance has also been received from the recent publications of scholars mentioned in the preface of the first edition.

For personal assistance thanks are principally due to Mr. Georg Edward, the author's old friend and former colleague. The traces of his influence are abundantly manifest everywhere thruout the book. It is difficult for the author to state his exact indebtedness here to a man who for twenty-three years was almost daily and at periods almost hourly a source of valuable information. The records of scholarship offer few such cases of sacrificing friendship and disinterested learning. Mr. Edward, tho not a philologist, possesses as a native German that which is lacking to the author—an *inborn* feeling for the meaning of German words and constructions, which has been rendered extraordinarily keen by a long and intimate acquaintance with the literature of the language in its varied phases. A large number of fine observations have been contributed by Professor Edwin C. Roedder of the University of Wisconsin, which have greatly enriched the book. The work also owes much to Professor Gustav E. Karsten, the late editor of the Journal of English and Germanic Philology, who has rendered valuable assistance at many places. Useful contributions and criticisms have also been received from Professors H. C. G. von Jagemann and H. C. Bierwirth of Harvard; Professor B. J. Vos of Indiana University; Professors Julius Goebel and O. E. Lessing of the University of Illinois; Professor Eduard Prokosch of Bryn Mawr; Professor Francis Wood of the University of Chicago; Doctors F. A. Bernstorff and Hans Kurath of Northwestern University. Dr. Kurath has contributed a large number of valuable observations which have been embodied in the Phonology. The author wishes to express here his feeling of gratitude to Dr. Kurath without desiring to hold him responsible for other things in the Phonology which he does not indorse. The author, of course, has the same attitude to all who have helped him in his studies. The author also desires to express his thanks here in general for the many suggestions that have come to him by mail or in the form of book-reviews.

The following persons have rendered valuable assistance in the reading of the various proofs: Professor James T. Hatfield, and Doctors F. A. Bernstorff and Hans Kurath of Northwestern University; Professors Ernst Voss and Edwin C. Roedder of the University of Wisconsin; Professor Charles R. Keyes of Cornell College, Mt. Vernon, Iowa; Mr. Georg Edward; Professor Francis Wood of the University of Chicago; Mr. William Michaelis, proof-reader of the Lakeside Press, to whose intelligent watchfulness and skill much credit is due for the accurate text.

Evanston, Illinois,
March, 1922.

TABLE OF CONTENTS

PART III

WORD-FORMATION

PART IV

SYNTAX

INTRODUCTION

THE GERMAN LANGUAGE

THE Germanic group of languages belongs to the Indo-European family, i. e. is descended from the same original language with the Indo-Iranic (Sanskrit, Persian, etc.), Baltic (Lithuanian, Lettish), Slavic (Russian, Polish, Bohemian or Czech, Servian, Bulgarian, etc.), Celtic, Greek, and Latin, from the last of which have come modern Italian, French, Spanish and Portuguese. The language of the Germanic people before its final breaking up into different tribes speaking languages all closely related but more or less differentiated is usually called pre-Germanic. No written documents in this language have come down to us, but for scientific purposes its grammar has been theoretically reconstructed by a comparison of the existing Germanic languages in connection with their older literature and the written documents of related languages now extinct. These Germanic tongues are divided into three groups. Of the first group, the East Germanic, only Gothic, now extinct, is well known to us. The second group, the North Germanic, includes modern Danish-Norwegian, Swedish, and Icelandic. The third group, the West Germanic, embraces High German and Low German, to the latter of which belong English (in its oldest stage called Old English or Anglo-Saxon), Dutch (the literary language of Holland and a large part of Belgium), and Low German in the narrow sense, i. e. the dialect of North Germany, in its oldest known stage called Old Saxon. Of these Germanic languages Gothic has aside from a few Old Norse inscriptions the oldest literary documents, reaching back into the fourth century A. D., and thus, by reason of its age and highly developed grammatical structure, is much studied by all who desire to obtain an idea of the oldest Germanic language known to us. High German, usually for the sake of brevity called German, is the language of Germany, Austria, a large part of Switzerland, and sections of other countries that touch or lie near Germany on the East, South, and West. Tho divided by political forces this territory is linguistically one and in this book is treated as such, so that the terms North, South, etc., refer not to Germany but to the North, South, etc., of the German-speaking territory. German is characterized among the Germanic languages by its richness in inflectional forms. However, in earlier periods these forms were still richer. Upon the basis of its sounds and inflectional forms German is divided into the following three periods.

1. O(ld) H(igh) G(erman) begins with the eighth century and extends to 1100. In this period Latin was the language usually employed in official documents and all literary and scientific productions, and hence comparatively little in the way of literature proper is found in the German of this period. From the early part of this period, only a few individual words and a few meager fragments are preserved. Further on, poems and connected discourse appear. The center of the literary life of this period is in the South.

O.H.G. was distinguished by rich, full vowels in its inflectional endings, such as *a*, *o*, *u*: (pl. of tag *day*) N. taga, G. tago, D. tagum, A. taga.

2. M(iddle) H(igh) G(erman) is the period from 1100-1350. In this period Latin still prevails as the leading literary language, but there is also a rich literature in German, which is much used, especially in poetry. Between 1180 and 1250 this literature culminated in the first classical period of German poetry. German was used also to some extent in prose, especially in writings of a religious character. Since 1221 legal documents occasionally appear in German, first in the Southwest, which later gradually led to its use as the official language of the empire. The center of literary life is still in the South, but the middle part of the empire also begins to play an important rôle.

M.H.G. is distinguished by the decay of the full, rich vowels *a*, *o*, *u* in the inflectional endings to the monotonous *e*: (pl. of tag *day*) N. tage (O.H.G. taga), G. tage (O.H.G. tago), D. tagen (O.H.G. tagum), A. tage (O.H.G. taga). This reduction of the vowels in the inflectional endings was due to the tendency already discernible in O.H.G. to pronounce the vowels of the root syllables more forcibly and give them relatively much greater length than the vowels of the other syllables, which thus lost their fulness and richness. These are marked features of the Germanic languages as compared with such languages as French and Italian.

3. N(ew) H(igh) G(erman) is the period from 1350 to the present time. In general the period of N.H.G. may, from the standpoint of language, be divided into three parts. The first part, from 1350-1750, which may be called *early N.H.G.*, is a period of considerable change and growth. The second part, from 1750-1810, may be called the *classical period*, by reason of the classical beauty and strength of the works of the great masters Lessing, Goethe, and Schiller, and in less measure of other writers of this time. Language questions had already in the latter part of the early N.H.G. period been earnestly discussed, and greater uniformity of usage had gradually been coming about. The great literary monuments of the classical period established in large measure a firm standard of speech. The third part, from 1810 to the present, which may be called *late N.H.G.*, has no marked peculiarity, but shows everywhere a tendency to level away little inequalities, and bring about greater simplicity and uniformity. The language is, however, still far from having a *complete* standard of usage either in grammar or pronunciation.

The center of literary life shifts within the course of the early N.H.G. period towards the middle of Germany, and one man, Martin Luther, plays a very important rôle in the development of the language. Latin is still much used, but the stirring questions of the Reformation brought the mother-tongue into prominent use, and gradually Latin retired to the rear. The year 1691 was the last one in which more Latin books appeared than German. Luther's bold stand for German has had far-reaching effects. His translation of the Bible into German, final edition in 1545, was his most valuable contribution in this direction. This great and successful task, however, was not an easy one. Latin had so long been the medium of communication in the higher forms of literature that the native language was left largely to the common people. Thus under this neglect it fell more and more into dialects. The books that were published in German before Luther's time bore strong dialectic traces. The only common language in Germany was the official language as found in laws, legal documents, decrees, etc. The oldest law-book, der Sachsenspiegel, appeared in Low German in 1230, der Schwabenspiegel in 1260, a High German work modeled upon the Sachsenspiegel. The High German official language gradually came into wide use in official life and in business. Thus the native language, tho neglected by the best thinkers, had now long been used by jurists, government officials, and tradesmen. This official language was now also quite generally used by those who wrote in German for a general public, but it was strongly modified everywhere under local influences. The confusion was increased by the fact that the people of North Germany spoke a form of Low German, a quite different language indeed. Luther desired to be generally understood, and wrote in the High German official language. He employed a somewhat modified form of the official language used in Saxony, which, tho High German and thus closely related to the speech of the South, has a distinctly Middle German character. In Luther's writings this official language shows traces of the influence of the neighboring Middle German chanceries, particularly those of the northeastern section of his homeland of Thuringia, but it also has a few distinctly South German features as found in the imperial chancery and a few signs of Low German influences received from the common people of Wittenberg. Thus the language in which Luther wrote was largely Middle German with a few South German features and a few Low German elements, and was accordingly without the extremes of either the South or the North, and had something in common with both, altho it was much nearer that of the South. Luther's translation was in general well received, and became with respect to its language the basis of modern German. As it was essentially the language of Protestantism it helped to extend the use of High German into the northern Low German countries, which were Protestant, and for the same reason was opposed in the Catholic South, which regarded the language of the imperial chancery as a better standard. It is easy, however, to exaggerate the influence of Luther and the Reformation. The growing cultural and trade relations of the North with the Midland were very important factors in spreading High German in the low lands. Luther's form of German, altho in large part a South German language, met in some sections of the South, especially in Switzerland, strong resistance on account of its great divergence from the native dialect. But on account of the evident necessity of a literary standard, and the leadership of Middle Germany in the mental and literary life of the nation, Luther's language, modified at many points by Middle, South, and even Low German influences, gradually spread over all parts of the country, slowly assuming a more uniform character until about two hundred years after Luther's time it attained in general its present form. The Low German (Plattdeutsch) of our own time is a mere dialect or a group of dialects, and tho used by several talented authors in their best works, it has in general relinquished to High German the pulpit, school, and press. Low German writers, however, who at present occupy a commanding place in literature, are fond of interspersing into the literary language words of Low German origin with High German inflection, or rather they allow their characters to do this in accordance with actual usage in everyday life. On the other hand, South German authors are contributing to the wealth of this same literary language by introducing words from the rich stores of the South German dialects.

In a part of the N.H.G. period, especially in the eighteenth century, High German was threatened by French, which was much used at the different princely courts and by the upper classes of people in general. The phenomenal achievements, however, of Goethe in literature, of German scholars in science, of German business men in large enterprises, the struggles upon the bloody battlefields of the last two centuries, have greatly increased and solidified the feeling of nationality and thoroly established German speech in all the strata of society and in all forms of literature. There is at present a lively interest manifested by Germans in the process of the purification of their native language from foreign words which remind them of their former dependence. This movement, which was begun in the sixteenth century, was carried on with great enthusiasm in the seventeenth century, and off and on ever since has experienced periods of revival of active interest, is not merely an expression of superficial pride, but is a general and deep joy in the development of the mother-tongue in its purity and strength. The naturalistic school of literature has also introduced into literary speech the fresh tones of life, of which it stood in such great need. The Germans of Austria and Switzerland are taking part in these movements, and are contributing their full share.

N.H.G. is in general distinguished from M.H.G. by the following changes. **(1)** The most far-reaching change was the lengthening of all short vowels in open syllables: M.H.G. *dĭser*, N.H.G. **dieser**. This development first appeared in the North in the twelfth century and later spread southward, but has not even yet affected the native speech of the extreme Southwest: **Grä̆-ber**, Swiss dialect for the present literary form **Grä̆'ber**. For fuller discussion see **4.** 1. *b. Note*; **4.** 2. B. *b. Note* **(1)**; **198.** *Historical Note*; **199.** *Historical Note.* **(2)** The change of the long M.H.G.

vowels *ī, ū, iu* (pro. y:) into the diphthongs **ei, au, eu**: M.H.G. *zīt, hūs, hiute* have become N.H.G. **Zeit, Haus, heute.** This diphthongation began in the twelfth century in the Southeast and is intimately connected with the spread of Austrian and Bohemian law northward from the year 1350 on. This diphthongation has also taken place in English in case of *ī* and *ū*, of course quite independently: wife (waif) from O.E. wīf; house from O.E. hūs. In Germany the old long vowels are still preserved in Low German, also in dialects of the Southwest except before a strongly articulated consonant, where they are shortened: (L.G.) **Hūs, hūser, sūr** (=**sauer**), **Tīd** (=**Zeit**); (Swiss) **Hūs, Hüser, sūr**, but **Zĭt, hŭt**, (=heute), etc., as the vowel stands before **t.** **(3)** The change of the M.H.G. diphthongs *ie, uo, üe* into the long vowels **ie** (=ī), **ū, ǖ**: M.H.G. *diep, huof, grüene* have become **Dieb, Huf, grün.** This monophthongation began in the thirteenth century in Middle Germany, but did not become established in the literary language until Middle German much later had become paramount. The old diphthongs *ie, uo, üe* are still preserved in S.G. dialect, usually in altered forms: *ie, ue, üe* (or *ie*). Bavarian dialect sectionally has *a* as a final element in these diphthongs: *ia, ua, üa* (or *ia*). These dialect forms occur of course in popular songs: **Behüet** (for **behüt'**) **dich Gott! es wär' zu schön gewesen** (Scheffel's *Trompeter*, Lieder jung Werners, XII). **(4)** The development of the M.H.G. diphthongs *ei, ou, öu* into the N.H.G. diphthongs **ei** or **ai** (both=ae), **au, eu** or **äu** (both=ɔø): M.H.G. *bein, meie, troum, vröude, tröumen* have become **Bein, Mai, Traum, Freude, träumen.** Altho M.H.G. *ei* is still written **ei** the first element of the diphthong has in fact developed into **a.** The new diphthongs first appeared in Bavarian toward the close of the thirteenth century and gradually became established in the literary language. In the dialects we find a different development here. **(5)** M.H.G. *e* and *i* have become rounded in a number of cases: **(a)** e sometimes becomes ö in the neighborhood of l, sch, w: **Hölle** (M.H.G. helle), **schöpfen** (M.H.G. schepfen), **zwölf** (M.H.G. zwelf), etc. In a few cases also elsewhere: **ergötzen** (M.H.G. ergetzen). **(b)** i sometimes becomes ü, especially after w: **Würde** (M.H.G. wirde). Earlier in the period, forms with e and i are still found. In dialect the opposite feature is found, i. e. the unrounding of ö and ü. See **12.** 1. *a*, **8.** 1. *a*, and **26.** *A*. **(6)** M.H.G. *u* and *ü* have under Middle German influence in most cases become N.H.G. **o** and **ö** before **n** or **nn**, and in a number of instances before **m** or **mm**: **Sohn** (M.H.G. sun), **Sonne** (M.H.G. sunne), **gesponnen** (M.H.G. gespunnen), **König** (M.H.G. künec); **Sommer** (M.H.G. sumer), **geschwommen** (M.H.G. geswummen). **(7)** S in the beginning of a word before l, m, n, and w, and sometimes medially after r, has become **sch**: M.H.G. slāf, smërze, snël, swërt, hërsen, have become N.H.G. **Schlaf, Schmerz, schnell, Schwert, herrschen.** Initial **s** has become **sch** also before **p** and **t**, as in **sprechen, stehen,** but this development has not yet found expression in the orthography. See also **40.** 2. *g*. **(1)**. **(8)** There has arisen a change of vowel in the singular of the present tense in certain strong verbs: **ich nehme, du nimmst, er nimmt.** See **201.** *f*.

Since Luther's day many more or less important changes have appeared in the literary language and orthography, as the language has been constantly growing and developing, and stricter and more scientific principles now obtain in the orthography. Only a few of the points where Luther's language and orthography differ from present usage are here given, as they are treated more fully in the Grammar: **(1)** In the inflection of nouns Luther's language diverges little from M.H.G. and thus differs widely from the present literary standard. **(2)** The difference of vowel which existed between the singular and plural of strong verbs has been leveled away and now only one vowel is found thruout singular and plural. Thus **ich fand, wir funden** of Luther's day have become **ich fand, wir fanden.** For other changes in the strong verb see **201.** *f*. **(3)** Unmutation (see **208.** 1. *a*) has under South German influence disappeared in a few verbs, the vowel of the infinitive now standing in all the forms of the verb. Thus Luther's **ich setze,** past **ich satzte,** have become **ich setze, ich setzte.** **(4)** Unaccented **e** has dropped out in a multitude of words. Luther's **höreten, sorget,** have become **hörten, sorgt.** On the other hand Luther drops *final* **e** very freely, where it must now stand: **der erst(e), dasselbig(e), Tag** (acc. pl. instead of **Tage**), **Stimm** (instead of **Stimme**), etc. Luther here often fluctuates between the full form in **-e** and the shorter form without it, just as there was fluctuation here in the Midland itself, the northern portion usually employing the fuller, the southern portion preferring the shorter forms. Later the fuller forms gained the ascendency. **(5)** In Luther's language M.G. unshifted **d** and **pp** occasionally occur instead of the regular High German **t** and **pf**, but in the later literary language the S.G. forms prevailed: **Widwe, schnuppen,** now **Witwe, schnupfen.** **(6)** Middle German was inclined to mutate more than the South, hence in the days of M.G. influence this usage was followed in a number of cases where later S.G. forms gained the victory. See **26.** A (3rd par.) for examples. **(7)** The East Middle German **qu** is occasionally found in Luther's language where **zw** is now employed. See **40.** 2. *c* (3rd par.) for an example. **(8)** At points, under S.G. influence, **haben** in compound tenses has been replaced by **sein.** See **191.** II. 3 A and *Note*. A number of minor changes have taken place. Initial **u** is now always written **u,** not **v** as formerly: **vnd,** now **und.** We now write uniformly **au** and **eu** where Luther often has **aw** and **ew**: **bawm, trew;** now **Baum, treu.** We now write **ä** where Luther has **e**: **hende** now **Hände.** The doubling of consonants, which is so frequent in Luther's writings, is now limited to the one case that double consonants are used to show shortness of vowel. This difference can be noticed by comparing, in the present revised editions of the Bible, Mark iv. 26-27 with the following from the edition of 1545: **VND er sprach | Das reich Gottes hat sich also | als wenn ein Mensch samen auffs land wirfft | vnd schlefft | vnd stehet auf | nacht vnd tag | Vnd der Same gehet auff vnd wechset | das ers nicht weis.** It will also be noticed in the preceding passage that capitals were not as now uniformly used in the beginning of nouns, and that a perpendicular line could be used instead of a comma or colon. Luther used to write especially the more emphatic nouns with capitals. In the learned literature of our day, there is an attempt being made to restore the usage of a still older period, when capitals were used only in the case of proper nouns and at the beginning of stanzas. This learned literature usually, however, makes one exception, namely that sentences begin with capitals. There does not seem to be at present much outlook for a triumph of this usage.

The orthography, which has gradually developed since Luther's day, has had since 1880 a formidable rival. In that year Prussia, the largest German state, issued a little book containing rules for a reform of the orthography. Also other states had adopted a reformed spelling, but the Prussian orthography naturally found the widest support. School-books followed closely the proposed reforms; books, newspapers, and periodicals designed for the general public held more or less conservatively to the old order of things; scholars dissatisfied with the lack of thoroness in the reforms went still further in the direction of conforming the orthography to the spoken language. In 1901 a few additional changes in the direction of simplicity were proposed by an orthographical conference, which were approved by the governments of the German Empire, Austria, and Switzerland, and appeared in the Prussian rules of 1902. Thus these movements for reform culminated in an official orthography for the German-speaking peoples. The newspapers and other periodicals responded to this united effort of the governments more readily than to the first independent movements. They now quite generally employ the official orthography and support cordially the minor further simplifications which have sprung up almost spontaneously out of the official rules of 1902 and have found a place in the editions of the official orthography published later by the different states and in the widely used handy manual **Duden, Rechtschreibung der deutschen Sprache und der Fremdwörter.**

The little confusion that still remains in the orthography will gradually disappear, but there still continues a difference of usage with respect to the style of the letters. The so-called German alphabet, which gradually arose in early times among the monks thruout Europe as a modified form of the Latin alphabet, was continued after printing was invented, but was later dropped by other nations, who returned to the Latin letters. In the German-speaking territory the German alphabet is still in general use in literature intended for a wide public, such as the daily press and popular books and periodicals. On the other hand, in scientific literature and advanced studies in general, where all mental work is felt as a contribution to the thought of the world, the Latin characters find growing favor as a symbolic tie which binds all men together and as an alphabet with eminent practical advantages by reason of its universality. Curiously enough the Latin alphabet is also widely used in advertisements and the market reports, stock quotations, and other commercial items in the newspapers and popular periodicals.

In our time, another interesting process is going on. The North has at last gained the political and literary ascendency in Germany, and it in its turn, after South and Middle Germany have each in their turn had their day, is moulding and fashioning the language. Maritime terms from the Low German coasts and other North German speech-forms are finding their way into the literature and, what is much more important, the pronunciation of the North, which is in general characterized by a pronounced tendency to ignore more and more older phonetic conditions and conform as closely as possible to the *printed form*, is gradually making itself felt, indeed has become the most representative form of the spoken language, as the pronunciation of the stage, the only generally recognized standard, is in large measure based upon it. Thus the literary German of our day is the product of all three parts of Germany. South and Middle Germany created it, and North Germany is modifying its sounds, and is enriching its vocabulary.

German Type	German Script.	German Name	German Type	German Script.	German Name
A a	A a	a:	N n	N n	ɛn
B b	B b	be:	O o	O o	o:
C c	C c	tse:	P p	P p	pe:
D d	D d	de:	Q q	Q q	ku:
E e	E e	e:	R r	R r	ɛʀ
F f	F f	ɛf	S ſ, s*	S ſ, s	ɛs
G g	G g	ge:	T t	T t	te:
H h	H or H h	ha:	U u	U u	u:
I i	I i	i:	V v	V v	fao
J j	J or J j	jɔt	W w	W w	ve:
K k	K k	ka:	X x	X x	ɪks
L l	L l	ɛl	Y y	Y or Y y	ʏpsi·lɔn
M m	M m	ɛm	Z z	Z z	tsɛt

Modified Vowels†

Ä ä Ö ö Ü ü Äu äu

Ä ä Ö ö Ü ü Äu äu

Compound Consonants

ch	ck	ph	th	tz	sch	St	st	ſſ‡	ß‡
tse:-ˈha:	tse:-ˈka:	pe:-ˈha:	te:-ˈha:	te:-ˈtsɛt	ɛs-tse:-ˈha:	ɛs-ˈte:	ɛs-ˈte:	ɛs-ˈɛs	ɛs-ˈtsɛt
ch	ck	ph	th	tz	sch	St or St	st	ſſ	ß

*s at the end, ſ at the beginning and middle, in Roman letters both represented by s.

†In naming the modified vowels say ɛ:, ɵ:, y:, or say mutated ɑ, &c.

‡For use of ſſ and ß see **4.** 2. D. *a.* In Roman letters ß is represented by ß. Some use **ss for** both ſſ and ß.

O Wunder sondergleichen, wie im Laut
Sich der Gedanke selbst das Haus gebaut!
O zweites Wunder, wie dem Blick die Schrift
Den Schall versinnlicht, der das Ohr nur trifft!
Nicht Willkür schuf das Wort, sonst wär es hohl;
Es ist des Geistes notwendiges Symbol.

(Geibel.)

Es gibt eine formelle Technik ohne inneren Gehalt. Doch wo wertvoller Gehalt in einer Künstlerseele wohnt, da ringt er auch nach Gestaltung in technisch vollendeter Form. Das Ringen kommt dem Gehalt wiederum zu gute und erhält den Brunnen der Sprachkraft im Fluß, während es ihn zu erschöpfen scheint.

(Schroeder.)

PART I.

PHONOLOGY AND ORTHOGRAPHY.

1. *Best Pronunciation.* In Germany there is no standard of pronunciation that is acknowledged and absolutely followed by the mass of intelligent people. The German stage has established fixed rules for pronunciation which many scholars and enthusiasts regard as a standard that may some day be generally recognized as the ideal and thus become to the spoken language what the literary language is now to colloquial speech. There is no doubt that this standard has influenced the choice pronunciation of different sections and that it will continue to exert its influence, but it has not yet acquired such a commanding position as to indicate that it will soon supplant the living language. The sectional differences in the pronunciation of the living language are very marked, but in general there is a North German and a South German pronunciation. The following short treatise takes into account the pronunciation of different sections, but deals principally with colloquial North German as spoken by the mass of intelligent people, as nearly as such a common standard can be ascertained under the existing circumstances. Many Germans may differ in particulars as to this standard. The stage pronunciation is also treated here for the benefit of those who prefer an ideal standard that rises above sectional usage. In most particulars it is quite near to choice North German.

Sounds of the Letters and their Classification.

2. A. *Sounds of the Letters.* The growth of letters has not kept pace with that of sounds, hence one letter may represent several sounds. Phonetic symbols are used in the following treatise to distinguish the different sounds of the letters. In the following table only an approximate equivalent is given for each German sound, the more accurate description being reserved for fuller treatment in the succeeding articles. The first number after the phonetic symbol refers to an article which gives a more accurate description of the sound. The second number refers to an article which gives the various spellings for the sound. Wherever comparisons are made with English without further qualification the pronunciation of the northern states is meant. S. E. indicates the Southern English of England.

Spellings	Phonetic Symbols	English Equivalents
ă	a (**16.** 2. (*a*); **16.** 2. (*b*))	as a in father, but shorter.
ā, aa, ah	a: (**16.** 1. (*a*); **16.** 1. (*b*))	as a in father.
ae = ä (**26.** A); in Dutch names = **ā** (**16.** 1. *b.* (**7**)); elsewhere = **a** + **e**: **Michael** (mɪça·ɛl), **Hexaeder** (hɛksa·'e:dəʀ), **Aeronaut** (a·e·ʀo·'naot), etc.		
ai	ae (**23.** 1)	as i in wife.
ai = **a**+**i** (**23.** 1. *Note*); in French words = **ǟ** (**13.** 1. (*b*). (**4**)) and **ä̆** (**14.** (*b*)).		
ain in French words . . .	ɛ̃: nasalized ɛ: on the stage, in the North pronounced as ɛŋ. See **25**.	

am, an in French words . .	ã: nasalized a: on the stage, in the North pronounced as aŋ. See **25.**	
au	ao (**23.** 2)	as ou in loud.
au=ō (**18.** 1. (*b*). (8)); =**a**+**u** (**23.** 2. *Note*).		
aw=ā in Shawl; **33.** 4. (**4**).		
ay=**ai**; see **23.** 1. (**4**).		
ä	**ɛ** (**14.** *a*; **14.** *b*) .	as e in let.
ä, äh	**ɛ:** (**13.** 1. (*a*); **13.** 1. (*b*))	a prolonged ɛ.
äu	**ɔø** (**23.** 3)	as oy in boy.
äu=**ä**+**u** (**23.** 3. *Note* 3).		
b or **bb**	**b** (**29; 30.** 4).	**as b in bat.**
b final or next a voiceless consonant=**p.**		
c before front vowels (see **6. 1.** (*a*)) =**z** (ts).		
c in some French words= **s** (s); see **33.** 2. (**8**).		
ç=**s** (s).		
c in some Italian words=tʃ (**33.** 4. (**5**)).		
c elsewhere=**k.**		
ch after **au** or a back vowel (see **6.** 1. (*b*)).	**x** (**32.** 3. *b*).	
ch after other vowels or after consonants in German words.	**ç** (**32.** 3. *a*).	
ch in foreign words; **32.** 3. *a.* *Note.*		
chs(=𝔠𝔥ſ and 𝔠𝔥𝔰)=**ks;** see **30.** 3. (**2**).		
ck after short vowels=**k.**		
d or **dd**	**d** (**29; 30.** 5).	**as d in day.**
d final or next a voiceless consonant=**t.**		
ĕ=**ă.**		
ē, ee, eh	**e:** (**11.** 1. (*a*); **11.** 1. (*b*))	as American a in dictate (ˈdiktet, but in S. E. ˈdikteit).
e unaccented	**ə** (**21**)	**as a in sofa.**
ê in French words= **ẽ.**		
eau in French words=**ō.**		
ee in English words=**ī**; see **7.** 1. (*b*). (**7**).		
ei=**ai**; in a number of foreign words = **e** + **i**: **Atheˈist, Deˈismus,** &c.; in **Jockei** =**e** or **ae**; see **35.** 5. (**4**).		
ein in French words=ɛ̃: or ɛŋ; see **25.**		
em, en in French words=ã: or aŋ; see **25.**		
eo=**e**+**o**: **Theorie** (te·o·ˈʀi:) **Theodor** (te:o·do:ʀ)		
eu=**äu**; final or before a single consonant in French		

Spelling	Symbol	Sound
words=**ȫ** (**12.** 1. (*b*). (**5**)); elsewhere in French words =**ö̆** (**15.** (*b*). (**2**)); in certain foreign words=**e**+**u** (**23.** 3. *Note* 2).		
ey in proper names=**ai**; see **23.** 1. (**3**).		
f	f (**32.** 1; **33.** 1)	as f in fine.
g initial	ɡ (**29**; **30.** 6)	as g in good.
g medial after front vowels= **j**; see **35.** 3. (**2**). The stage requires ɡ here.		
g medial after back vowels . The stage requires ɡ here.	ɡ (**34.** 4; **35.** 4).	
g after front vowels finally or before a consonant in a suffix or an inflectional ending=**ch** in **ich**; see **29.** The stage requires k here.		
g after back vowels finally or before a consonant in a suffix or an inflectional ending=**ch** in **ach**; see **29.** The stage requires k here.		
g after **n** is silent; see **36.** *b*.		
g in some French words before **e** or **i**	ʒ (**34.** 5; **35.** 5. (**2**)) . .	as g in rouge.
g in some English words =dʒ (see **39.** 4).		
ge before back vowels in French words=ʒ; see **35.** 5. (3).		
gg medial after short vowel =ɡ-ɡ; see **30.** 6. (**3**).		
gg final=**k.**		
ggi in some Italian words= dʒ; see **35.** 5. (**4**).		
gh=**g.**		
gn in foreign words=ŋn, ɡn, and nj; see **36.** *c*. (**5**).		
gu before front vowels in foreign words=ɡ; see **30.** 6. (**4**).		
gy=dj in Hungarian words; see **39.** 8.		
h initial	h (**28**)	as h in hat.
h elsewhere silent.		
ĭ	ɪ (**9.** (*a*); **9.** (*b*))	as i in pin.
ī, ih	iː (**7.** 1. (*a*); **7.** 1. (*b*)). .	as e in react.
i unaccented before a vowel	ĭ (**7.** 2. (2nd par.)) . . .	as American i in famil*i*ar.
ie, ieh=**ī.**		
ie and **iè** in foreign words; see **7.** 1. (*b*). *Note* 1.		
ier in French words=jeː or iːʀ; see **7.** 1. (*b*). *Note* 1.		
ier unaccented=ĭəʀ as in **Spanier** (ˈʃpaːˎnĭəʀ).		

ieu = ĭə: as in **adieu**; = **eu** **23.** 3. (**5**).		
il, ill in French words; see **39.** 5.	l' (**39.** 5).	
im, in in French words = ɛ̃: or ɛŋ; see **25.**		
j	j (**34.** 3; **34.** 3)	as y in yes.
j in French words = French **g** before **e** or **i**; see **34.** 5; **35.** 5. (**1**).		
j in English words = dʒ; see **39.** 4.		
k	k (**29**; **30.** 3)	as k in kind.
l	l (**37.** 1)	as l in let.
m	m (**36.** *a*)	as m in man.
n except before **c, g, k, q, x** .	n (**36.** *a*)	as n in no.
n before **c, g, k, q**; see **36.** *c*.(**3**)	ŋ (**36.** *b*; **36.** *c*. (**2**), (**3**)) .	as ng in singer.
ng = ŋ; see **36.** *b*.		
ŏ	ɔ (**17.** *a*; **17.** *b*).	as American o in obey, potat*o* or S. E. o in rob.
ō, oh, oo	o: (**18.** **1.** *a*; **18.** **1.** *b*) . .	as American o in poetic or S. E. o in obey.
oa in **Toast** = **ō**; elsewhere = **o**+**a**: **Klo′āke**, &c.		
oe = **ö** (**26.** A); in L.G. names = **ō** (**18.** 1. (*b*). (**5**)); in Dutch words = **ū** (20. 1. (*b*). (**8**)); elsewhere = **o**+**e**: **Po′ēt**, &c.		
oey = **ȫ** in **Oeynhausen** (**12.** 1. *b*. (**4**)).		
oi in L.G. names = **ō** (18. 1. (*b*). (**6**)); in L.G. words = **eu** (**23.** 3. (**3**)); in French words = o·a· or o·a (**16.** **1.** (*b*). (**5**) and 2. (*b*)); elsewhere = o·′i: as in **Trapezo′id**, &c.		
om, on in French words = ɔ̃: or ɔŋ; see **25.**	ɔ̃: nasalized ɔ: (**25**).	
ou in French words = **ū** (**20.** 1. (*b*). (**7**)); = **ŭ** (**19.** (*b*). (**3**)).		
ow in L.G. and Eng. words = **ō** (**18.** 1. (*b*).(**7**)); in Slavic words = ɔv medially and ɔf finally or before a consonant; see **33.** **1.** (**6**).		
oy in foreign words = o·a·j (**35.** 3. (**4**)); = **eu** (**23.** 3. (**4**)).		
ö̆	ɵ rounded ɛ; see **15.** (*a*); **15.** (*b*).	
ȫ, öh	ɵ: rounded e:; see **12.** **1.** *a*; **12.** 1. (*b*).	
p	p (**29**; **30.** 1)	as p in pen.

pf=**p**+**f**; **39. 1.**		
ph, pph=f; see **33. 1. (4), (5).**		
qu=**kw** and **k**; see **39. 7.**		
r	ʀ (**34.** 6) or r (**37.** 2).	
s (=𝔰 and ſ), **ss** (=ſſ), **ß** (=ß); see **33.** 2	s (**32.** 2; **33.** 2)	as s in sit.
s initial and medial; **35. 2. (1), (2).**	z (**34.** 2; **35.** 2)	as s in rose.
sch	ʃ (**32.** 4; **33.** 4)	as sh in shave.
sh in English words=**sch.**		
sp, st initial in stem syllable =ʃp, ʃt; **33. 4. (2)**; =sp, st; see **33.** 2 **(4).**		
t, th, tt, dt	t (**29; 30.** 2)	as t in ten.
ti=tsĭ; see **39. 3. (10).**		
tz=**z**; see **39. 3. (2), (3).**		
ŭ	ʊ (**19.** *a*; **19.** *b*)	as u in put.
ū, uh	u: (**20. 1.** (*a*); **30. 1.** (*b*))	as o in unstressed who, only longer.
u=**v** (**35. 1. (5), (6), (7)**); in French words=**ü.**		
ue=**ü** (**26.** A); in the name **Kotzebue**=**ū**; in French words=**ǖ** (**8. 1.** (*b*).**(6)**); elsewhere=**u**+**e**:**Du'ell.**		
ui=**ǖ** (**8. 1.** (*b*).**(4)**); =**eu** (**23.** 3. **(6)**); =vi: (**35. 1. (7)**); =the rising diphthongs ŭi:, ŭɪ; see **20.** 2; elsewhere=**u**+**i**: **Luise** (lu·'i:zə), **Luitpold** (lu:ɪtpɔlt)		
um, un in French words= ɵ̃: or ɵŋ; see **25.**	ɵ̃: nasalized ɵ: **(25).**	
uo=u:o in **Kuoni** (name).		
ü̆	ʏ rounded ɪ; see **10.** *a*; **10.** *b*.	
ǖ, üh	y: rounded i:; see **8. 1.** (*a*); **8. 1.** (*b*).	
v=**f**; see **33. 1. (2), (3).**		
v medial in Low German words=**w**; see **35. 1.(4).**		
v initial and medial in foreign words=**w**; see **35. 1. (3).**		
w	v (**34. 1; 35. 1**)	as v in very.
x=**ks**; see **39. 2.**		
y̆, ȳ= **ĭ, ī** or **ü̆, ǖ** (see **9. 1.** (*b*).**(6)**; **10.** (*b*).**(3)**; **7. 1.** (*b*).**(5), (6)**; **8. 1.** (*b*). **(5).** *Note*).		
y in some foreign words= **j**; see **35. 3. (4).**		
y in some Dutch words= **ai**; see **23. 1. (5).**		
z=**ts**; see **39. 3. (1).**		
z=s (z); see **35. 2. (3).**		

B. *Classification of German Sounds.*

I. *Vowels.*

Vowels may be classified from different points of view. The vowels are here classified according to the horizontal movement (see **3.** 1. *a* below) of the tongue in forming them. The various modifications of these sounds are treated later under each vowel.

SIMPLE VOWELS

Front Vowels

i:, y:, ɪ, ʏ, e:, ɵ:, ɛ, ɛ̃:, ɘ, ɘ̃:

Back Vowels

a:, ã:, a, ɔ, ɔ̃:, o:, ʊ, u:

Mixed Vowel

ə (see **21**)

DIPHTHONGS

Falling (**22, 23**)

ao, ɔɵ (**eu** or **äu**), ae (**ei** or **ai**), ui

Rising (**24**)

ĭa:, ĭə, ĭo:, etc.

II. *Consonants.*

Front		Labials	Dentals	Palatals	Velars	Uvular	Glottals	Back
	Stops	p **b**	t **d**		k **g**		ʔ (**38**)	
	Nasals	**m**	**n**		**ŋ**			
	Spirants	f v	s z	ç (**32.** 2. *a*) **j** ʃ (**32.** 4) **ʒ** (**34.** 5)	x (**32.**3.*b*) **g** (**34.** 4)	ʀ(**34.** 6)	h	
	Liquids		**l, r** (**37.**2)					

Sounds marked by heavy type are voiced, others are voiceless.

Note. The sounds have here been divided into the two usual classes of vowels and consonants upon the basis of the function usually performed by the various sounds. A vowel can form of itself a syllable. A consonant does not of itself form a syllable, but is only used in conjunction with vowels to form syllables. Hence the above classification does not always hold good. The consonants **l, m, n, ŋ, r,** are sometimes in one sense used as vowels in that they become syllabic, forming of themselves syllables. See **41.** 4. The vowels found as the less sonorous element of diphthongs are in fact consonants. The vowel i often becomes a consonant in certain positions, i. e. becomes unsyllabic, forming the less sonorous part of a rising diphthong. See **7.** 2 (2nd par.). These points indicate clearly that the qualification of a syllable-forming sound is a prominent degree of sonority and not the manner of its formation. Sounds are now syllable-forming and now a mere subordinate element according as they are relatively prominent by means of their sonority or relatively inconspicuous. Sometimes a sound which has a low degree of sonority may become a syllable-forming element when it is surrounded by less sonorous sounds, as **s** in **pst!** The classification of sounds upon the basis of function does not always help us in gaining a correct conception of the nature or formation of the various sounds. Thus **l, m, n,** and lingual **r** (r) do not differ in any essential point from vowels in their formation, tho upon the basis of function they must in most cases be classified as consonants. Thus also **h** does not materially differ in formation from the simple vowels **a, o, u,** &c., except that the vocal chords do not vibrate, but it is here classified as a consonant, as it always produces the acoustic effect and performs the function of a spirant. See **28,** *Note.*

FORMATION OF SOUNDS.

3. 1. In forming a vowel the mouth remains more or less open, and the vocal chords vibrate. Each new position of the tongue produces a new vowel, which may again be modified in various ways. The tongue movements and various modifications can only be briefly treated here.

a. Tongue Movements. The tongue moves horizontally and vertically—backwards and forwards, upwards and downwards. The horizontal movement results in three general classes of sounds, *back* vowels formed by the back part of the tongue, *front* vowels formed by the front part of the tongue, *mixed* vowels formed by allowing the tongue to drop into a neutral position, in which neither articulation predominates. The vertical movement of the tongue results in three general classes, *high* vowels formed by raising the tongue close to the roof of the mouth, *mid* vowels by raising the tongue moderately, *low* vowels by lowering the tongue. These positions will be discussed later with each vowel.

b. Rounding. Vowels are rounded by protruding the lips as in whistling. Thus by rounding, iː, ɪ, eː, ɛ, become yː, ʏ, øː, ɵ. See **8, 10, 12, 15.**

c. Narrowness, Wideness. A sound is said to be 'narrow' when the muscles of the tongue become tense and bulge up, and thus narrow the resonance chamber. When a sound is formed without this tenseness it is said to be 'wide.' The difference between eː and ɛ is that the former is narrow and the latter wide. In North German all long vowels except **ǟ** (ɛː) are narrow and all short ones wide. This explains the strong tendency to pronounce **ǟ** as eː instead of ɛː. These modifications will be given later in connection with each vowel.

d. Nasality. In forming nasal vowels the breath passes thru the nose as well as the mouth. Nasality is the characteristic of vowels in many words from the French. See **25.**

2. In forming consonants the mouth is either closed as in the case of stops and nasals, or narrowed as in the case of spirants. The distinguishing feature of a consonant is the friction, or stopping of the breath in some part of the mouth or throat. If voice enters into the formation of a consonant, that is, if the vocal chords vibrate in producing it, it is said to be voiced, otherwise it is voiceless. The formation of the different consonants is described later.

Quantity of Vowels.

4. 1. General rules.

a. Accented vowels are long when final, or before a vowel or one consonant: **dā, Sē-en, Māl, mā-len.** Notice that, if a vowel follows the stem, the final consonant is always carried over, and the stem syllable becomes open, i. e. terminates with a vowel.

The quantity of the vowel must be ascertained from the simple stem of the word, the inflectional endings that may be added not counting: **der Hūt, des Hūts; lōben, du lōbst, gelōbt.**

Note. To the, in general, very reliable rule that the vowel of the simple stem gives the quantity to the derivative forms, there are exceptions: (**1**) Exceptions among weak verbs are limited to the following cases: **ich hābe, du hăst, er hăt, er hătte, gehābt**; in loose colloquial North and Middle German **ich kriege** (kʀiːjə) *I get*, but **du kriegst** (kʀɪçst), **er kriegt** (kʀɪçt), **er kriegte** (kʀɪçtə), **gekriegt** (gə'kʀɪçt), as explained in **201.** *f* and **209**, but in more careful language ɪç kʀiːgə, duː kʀiːkst, er kʀiːkt, etc.; the isolated adjective participle **berĕdt** (in choice language **berēdt**) *eloquent* from **rēden.** (**2**) A difference of vowel or consonant sometimes makes the quantity irregular in strong or irregular verbs: **ich nēhme, du nĭmmst.** See also **201.** *f.* The special cases are noted under the strong verbs. (**3**) The monosyllabic forms of the nouns ending in **b, d, f, g, s** are often in N.G. short instead of long, since the difference in the pronunciation of these consonants finally and medially has prevented the spreading of the long vowel from the open lengthened forms to the closed monosyllabic forms: **der Tāg** or **Tăg**, but always **des Tā'ges.** See **2.** B. *b. Note* (**1**) below. (**4**) The adverbs **weg** (vɛk) and in colloquial language **flugs** (flʊks) have retained the old short vowel, as they are always in a closed syllable, while in **Wēg** and **Flūg** it has become long after the analogy of the lengthened forms **Wē'ges** and **Flū'ges.** See **2.** B. *b. Note* (**1**) below. In **flugs,** however, after the analogy of **des Flūgs** the **u** is now in choice language pronounced uː. (**5**) A difference may arise from the absence of the feeling of the original connection of the words: **Heer,** but **Hĕrzog; Fāhrt,** but **fĕrtig,** &c.

b. An accented vowel standing before a double consonant (double **k** usually written **ck**) or two or more consonants is usually short and the syllable is closed, i. e. terminates in a consonant, but it is long in the special cases (see **2.** A. *d.* (**2**) (**3**), below) where the syllable is open: **Ball, er'schrecken** (ɛʀ'ʃʀɛk-kən), **Halt, sin-ken, fas-ten,** but **Hȳ'drā.** Thus a vowel in an accented open syllable is always long, whether it stands before one consonant or more: **mā'len, Mē'trik,** &c. Compare **41.** 1, 2.

A vowel is short in a few words before *one* consonant, and the syllable is closed: **Fi'ăker** (also **'Fiaker**), **Gra'mmătik, gra'mmătisch, Ho'tĕl, Ka'pĭtel, 'Lĭtera'tūr, Me'tăpher (ph=f), Re'liĕf** (ʀe·'lĭɛf), **'Săphir, 'Zĭther (th=t),** &c.

Note on Historical Development. The great majority of the long vowels of the language have corresponding short ones in M.H.G. At the beginning of the present period all short vowels became long in open syllables, i. e. where the final consonant of the stem was carried over to the next syllable. Before one consonant the syllable was usually open and the vowel became long except often before **t, m,** and sometimes **l, n.** Thus M.H.G. bă-nen, gĕ-ben, hŏ-nec, gĭ-bel became **bāh'nen, gē'ben, Hō'nig, Gie'bel,** but in M.H.G. gerĭ-ten, gŏ-tes, gŏ-ter, vrŏ-men, as explained below, the syllable before t and m became closed, which resulted in the retention of the short vowel: gerit-ten, Got-tes, Göt-ter, from-men. Before a M.H.G. double consonant or a combination of consonants the syllable was already closed, so that in N.H.G. the short vowel here remained short: M.H.G. vŭllen, hălten, N.H.G. **fŭllen, hălten.** Tho **ng** and **sch** are now simple sounds, ŋ, ʃ, they each in M.H.G. represented two sounds, i. e. a combination of consonants, which after a short vowel closed the syllable, so that in N.H.G. the short vowel remained short, as in **singen** (zɪŋ-ŋən), **waschen** (vaʃ-ʃən). Compare **32.** 4. *Note* (**2**). Where, however, the sound before **sch** was a long vowel or a diphthong it remained a long vowel or a diphthong: **wūsch, Fleisch.** The long vowel here remained long as **sch** (sx, later ʃ) in the lengthened forms in accordance with the general tendency after long vowels was carried over to the next syllable, which thus left the root syllable open and kept the long root vowel long: **wū'schen.** As **ng** (ŋg), on the other hand, could not be thus easily carried over to the next syllable, the long vowel before it naturally became short in accordance with the general tendency of long vowels to become short in a closed syllable before a combination of consonants, as described in **2.** A. *d. Note* below: **fingen** (fɪŋ-gən, now fɪŋ-ŋən) from older **fiengen** (fi:ŋ-gən). The syllable before **ch** (i. e. **ch-ch,** divided **ch,** from older **kch,** from older aspirated **k** as still preserved in Eng. spea*k*) was originally closed as it stood before a combination of consonants, hence a short vowel before **ch** has remained short, but where the sound before **ch** was a long vowel or a diphthong it has remained a long vowel or a diphthong: **sprĕchen** (early O.H.G. sprehhan, i. e. sprex-xan), **sprā'chen** (early O.H.G. sprah-hun, i. e. spra:x-xʊn), **rauchen** (early O.H.G. rouh-han, i. e. roux-xan). As can be seen in the old forms in parentheses **ch** was in early O.H.G. a divided sound even after a long vowel or a diphthong. A little later the **ch** after a long vowel or a diphthong was carried over to the next syllable as a single sound in accordance with the general tendency here to carry over all consonants to the next syllable. This left the root syllable open and kept the long root vowel long. Tho **sch, ng, ch** are now simple sounds and are divided after a short vowel, from an aversion to heaping up too many unsightly letters they are never doubled in the written language.

The double consonants treated in the preceding paragraph all stand between vowels and are real divided sounds. After the analogy of doubling the consonant here it has become the custom after a short vowel to double the consonant when it stands in the final position or before a consonant, but this double consonant does not represent a divided sound. It is a mere orthographical device to indicate the shortness of the preceding vowel: **komm** and **kommt** after the analogy of **kommen.** As the characters **ng, sch, ch** from an aversion to heaping up too many unsightly letters are not doubled after a short vowel when they stand between vowels, they are of course not doubled after a short vowel when they stand in the final position or before a consonant: **făngen, făng, făngt; wăschen, wăsch, wăscht; sprĕchen, sprĭch, sprĭcht.** In older periods the character representing a consonant was only doubled when the sound was divided: M.H.G. balles (N.H.G. **des Balles**), O.H.G. sprăh-hun (N.H.G. **sie sprā'chen**), but in the final position M.H.G. bal (N.H.G. **Ball**), O.H.G. sprăh (N.H.G. **er sprāch**) as the sound is undivided. The older usage of only doubling the character when the sound is divided is still observed for voiceless s, but two characters are used here, ss for the divided sound and ß for undivided s: **wissen, er weiß, er wußte.** See also **2.** D. *a* below. The old orthographical principle of only doubling a consonant when it is a divided sound is still in wide use in English: *thinner* but *thin, runner* but *run, ran.*

In a few words a long vowel stands in a closed syllable before two consonants: **Kēbsweib, Krēbs, Māgd, Ōbst, Vōgt.** In older German an e stood after the consonant which follows the stem vowel, so that the stem vowel stood in an open syllable before one consonant: M.H.G. ke-beswīp, kre-beʒ, ma-get, o-beʒ, vo-get. In this older form the stem vowel became long. The following vowel later disappeared, but the stem vowel remained long.

Wherever a vowel became long in an open syllable the same quantity was usually later extended for the sake of uniformity to the closed syllables of the same inflectional system. See **2.** B. *b. Note* (**1**) below. On the other hand, the inflectional system was sometimes leveled by the short vowel of the closed syllables, i. e. before *t, m,* and sometimes *l* and *n* the open syllables were closed by doubling or dividing the consonant in order to make the vowel short and thus keep it in harmony with the short vowels in the same system. M.H.G. vă-ter, nă-me, &c., became N.H.G. **Vā'ter, Nā'me,** &c., but leveling by the short vowel of the closed syllable is more common here: M.H.G. să-tel, gerĭ-ten, gŏ-ter, vĕ-ter, hă-mer, dŏ-ner became **Sattel, geritten, Götter, Vetter, Hammer, Donner,** as the e of the unaccented syllable often dropped out in colloquial speech before l, m, n, r, as in **Sătl, gerĭtn, Gŏtr, Vĕtr, Hămr, Dŏnr,** which resulted in bringing the root vowel before two consonants thus closing the syllable and keeping it short and usually also in the spreading of the short vowel to the fuller forms, which are now written with double consonants to indicate the closedness of the syllable and the shortness of the vowel, **Sattel,** etc. In a few monosyllabics, as M.H.G. snĭt, trĭt, &c., the short vowel of the closed nominative and accusative spread to the fuller forms, **Schnitt, Schnittes,** &c., **Tritt, Trittes,** &c.

The above described lengthening of short vowels in open syllables did not take place in the extreme part of the S. W., which still preserves here the old historic short sound. See **2.** B. *b. Note* (**1**) below.

c. Unaccented simple vowels are short, except when final: **glaubĕn, Fürstĭn, Frühlĭng,** &c. Unaccented final vowels except **e** are long or half-long. See **2.** B. *c.* and *Note* thereunder.

2. Rules for Quantity in Detail.

A. The following are long:—

a. A diphthong: **Gaul, Gäule.**

b. Doubled vowels and **ie**: **Paar, Heer, Boot, bieten.** Only **a, e, o** can be doubled. They must, however, be written single when mutated: **Paar,** but **Pärchen.** Vowels are now written double only in the following words: **Aal, Aar (Adler), Aas, Haar, Paar, paar, Saal, Saat, Staat; Beere, Beet, Geest, Heer, verheeren, Klee, Kra'keel, Lee, leer, leeren, Meer, Reede, scheel, Schnee, See, Seele, Speer, Teer; Boot, Moor, Moos.**

c. Simple accented vowels when final, or before a vowel or one consonant: **dā, Sēen, bāden, Mikro'skōp.** Exceptions: **A'prĭl, grŏb** (but long in open syllables, as in **grō-ber,** &c.) or in choice language **grōb** (long as in **grōber**), **Ka'pĭtel, Lŭther, Zĭther,** &c.

The length of the vowel may also be indicated by a silent **h: Wahl, ihm, ihn,** &c. For the use of **h** here see **28.**

d. Simple accented vowels are sometimes long before more than one consonant:

(**1**) The vowels **a, e,** and less frequently other vowels, are long before **r**+ a dental (**d, t, z, s, sch**): **wērden, Schwērt, Quārz,** &c. Thus these vowels are long, altho they stand in closed syllables; see B. *b. Note* (**2**) below. This pronunciation is a new development, and is not yet universally recognized.

(2) Vowels are sometimes long before **st, bst, pst, tsch, chs** (=**ks**), **z** (=**ts**), and in still other cases. The words will be given later under the respective vowels. In all these cases the consonants should be carried over to the next syllable wherever it is possible, so that the accented syllable may be open: **Ō\`stern, dū\`ster,** &c.

In a few cases short vowels have become long before these combinations of consonants, usually under the influence of analogy. Thus as M.H.G. dŭ became **dū** as the vowel stood in an open syllable, M.H.G. dŭzen naturally became **dū\`zen** under the influence of **dū**.

Long vowels—both those originally long and those that have in N.H.G. become long—cannot usually be distinguished as long when they stand before these combinations of consonants, but within the present period a simple device has been found to distinguish the quantity of the vowel before ts. Before **z** the sound is uniformly a long or half-long vowel or a diphthong, while before **tz** it is always a short vowel: **siezen**: (zi:\`tsən), **dū\`zen, Akazie** (a·ˈka:\`tsĭə), **inspizieren** (ɪnspi·ˈtsi:ʀən), **Kauz** (kaots), but **Katze** (katsə, the syllabic division being in the t). After a consonant, **z**—not **tz**—is used, as the two consonants mark the preceding vowel as short: **Herz.**

Note. Most of these vowels were long or were diphthongs in earlier periods of the language, and hence their length has nothing to do with the process of lengthening explained in **1.** *b. Note*, above. In general, long vowels have come down to us long, but in the present period there has long been busily at work a new force—the tendency to shorten a long vowel in a closed syllable before a combination of consonants—which already in many words has reduced a long stem vowel to a short one, as illustrated here by a few characteristic examples: **brăchte** (M.H.G. brāhte), **dĭcht** (M.H.G. dīhte), **Lĭcht** (M.H.G. lieht, M.G. of the same period līcht, from which the present literary form comes), **stund** (M.H.G. stuont, M.G. of the same period stūnt, from which **stund** (see **203**) comes); **fĭng, gĭng, hĭng** from older **fieng, gieng, hieng,** which until 1903 were required by the official Austrian rules; older **Mūter, Fūter,** now **Mŭtter, Fŭtter,** as the **e** often dropped out in colloquial speech and the root syllable thus became closed and the vowel became short; **Lĕrche** (M.H.G. lērche), **Gĕrtrud** (M.H.G. gēr); **vier** (fi:ʀ), but short ɪ in **vierzehn, vierzig, Viertel**; **wāhr** but usually **wăhrlich**; **hat** (M.H.G. hāt) with a short vowel as it often stands in a closed syllable before a combination of consonants, as in **er hat gesagt** and **hat er** (the **e** often dropping out in colloquial speech) **gesagt.**

In a few words an old long vowel stands in a closed syllable before a combination of consonants, thus apparently forming exceptions to the rule just described: **Pāpst** (M.H.G. bā-best), **Prōpst** (M.H.G. prō-best), etc. As can be seen by the old forms in parentheses an **e** once stood after the consonant which follows the stem vowel, so that the stem vowel stood in an open syllable before one consonant, which preserved the long quantity of the vowel until it had become firmly associated with the word. Sometimes the force of analogy has preserved the old long vowel in a closed syllable before a combination of consonants. Thus tho we often hear **wuchs** (vʊks) as **u** here stands in a closed syllable before a combination of consonants we more frequently hear long **u** here after the analogy of the lengthened forms where **u** stands in an open syllable, as in **wūchsen** (vu:\`ksən), and after the analogy of the other past tense forms in the same class, as **wūsch, schūf,** etc. Likewise **hōchst** remains long after the analogy of **hōher, hōher,** etc. In the unstressed preposition **nāch** (M.H.G. nāch) we often hear in colloquial speech short **a** instead of the long vowel as found in choice language, while the stressed adverb **nāch** invariably retains its old long vowel: **năch Háuse** (instead of the more choice **nāch Háuse**), but regularly **nắchgèhen.**

(3) In many words from the Latin or Greek, the consonants between vowels, especially a stop (**p, t, k, b, d, g**) + **r** or **l,** are carried over to the next syllable, as in the original. This leaves the preceding syllable open, which according to German usage (see 1. *b* above) becomes long: **Mī\`tra, Mē\`trŭm,** &c., half-long in words with secondary stress, as in **\`Mī-kroˈskōp,** &c.

B. Short:—

a. Simple vowels before double consonants, or two or more different consonants: **Gatter, Hunde.**

b. Simple vowels before one consonant in some uninflected forms, and in a few inflected monosyllabics that do not form open syllables in the course of inflection: **an, in, ab, um, weg, mit, von, ob, bis, das, daß, was, bin, bist, ist,** the article **der, des,** &c. (in careful speaking and declaiming pronounced dɛʀ, dɛs, &c., or sometimes even de:ʀ, de:m, de:n, not however de:s, but ordinarily dəʀ, dəs, &c., with weak stress). Such monosyllabics are, however, always long if they contain a **h,** final **r** (except in the article), or accented **-em, -en**: **ihm, ihn, wer** (ve:ʀ), **vor, für, emˈpor,** the demonstrative and relative **der** (de:ʀ), **dem** (de:m), **den** (de:n), &c. The personal pronoun **er** is pronounced e:ʀ, but it often, when weakly stressed, becomes ɛʀ, or even əʀ. On the stage **zum** and **zur** are pronounced tsu·m and tsu·ʀ, but in colloquial speech they become tsʊm and tsʊʀ.

Note. **(1)** The reason that the vowel of most of the above words is short is that it always stands in a closed syllable. Formerly the vowel of monosyllabic nouns ending in a single consonant could also be short, as in **Grăm, Stĭl.** At the beginning of the present period these same vowels became long in all lengthened forms in accordance with the new law that lengthened all short vowels in open syllables: **Grā-mes, Stie-les.** See 1. *b*. above and *Note* thereunder. The long vowel of the lengthened forms, following the general trend toward uniformity thruout the same inflectional system, spread later to the closed syllables. Thus **Grăm, Stĭl** became **Grām, Stiel.** For several little irregularities see **1.** *a. Note* **(3)** and **1.** *b. Note*, above. As the above-mentioned short closed forms were never inflected, or never became open in the course of their inflection, they remained short. In dialects of the extreme Southwest we find the opposite development—a lengthened vowel in a closed syllable before a weakly articulated consonant or certain combinations of consonants, while the original short vowel survives in open syllables: **Grāb, Rād, Sārg, wārm, Bārt, Lāmpe, wērden, gērn,** etc., but **Grā-ber, Rā-der,** &c. In dialects of the Southeast there is a development somewhat similar but much narrower in scope—a lengthened vowel in a closed final syllable before two consonants or before a simple sound that developed out of two consonants, while the old short vowel survives in all syllables which originally were not final as now: **Kōpf,** but pl. **Kŏpf(e); Fīsch (sch** originally = s + x), but pl. **Fĭsch(e).**

(2) Final **r** has in the literary language an effect upon a preceding accented vowel differing from that of other final consonants. It usually lengthens the vowel, altho it closes the syllable, as in **vōr, wēr,** &c. It also has the same effect medially in certain cases. See A. *d.* **(1)** above.

c. Unaccented simple vowels are short except when final: **haltĕn, Gĕfängnĭs, Herrĭn,** &c. Unaccented final vowels except **e** are long or half-long. Long or half-long unaccented final vowels occur in a few isolated words, as **Uhū, Schuhū,** and in a number of names, as **Ottō, Brunō, Fridā, Hertā,** &c. Aside from these words, the prefix **miß-,** and suffixes, such as **-lich, -in, -ling,** &c., which have secondary accent, **e** is now the only German vowel found outside the accented root syllable, as the various fuller vowels of earlier periods have, under the effect of weak stress, been all reduced to this one form. This unaccented **e** is almost uniformly pronounced ə except in the prefixes **be-, emp-, ent-, er-, ge-, ver-, zer-,** where it is treated differently in the different forms. In **be-** and **ge-** it is almost always pronounced ə. In **emp-, ent-, er-, ver-,** and **zer-,** it is usually sounded ɛ in careful speaking but often in colloquial speech in accordance with the general tendency in unaccented syllables becomes ə in **er-, ver-,** and **zer-.** Of course compounds deviate from the general rule, as the components retain the quantity which they have as independent words: **Schlittschūh, Schiffāhrt,** &c. Also the heavy suffixes **āt, jān, bār, sāl, tūm, ūt,** usually also **sām,** which were in part once independent words, form exceptions to the rule: **Heirāt, hörbār,** &c.

Note. Quality of Unaccented Vowels in Foreign Words. Other vowels than **e** are, however, often found in unaccented syllables in foreign words, and it should be noted that they do not, except in final syllables, conform to the German rule for quantity. Foreign vowels except **e** are long or half-long when final: **'Annā, 'Salomō, 'Alibī,** &c. Also final **e** is long in a few words: **A'thenē, Fak'similē, 'Lethē,** &c., unaccented final vowels in the first component of foreign compounds, however, are half-long before a stressed syllable: **Telegraph** (te·le·'ɢʀa:f), **Periskop** (pe·ʀi·'sko:p). Elsewhere unaccented **a, ä, e, i, o, ö, u, ü,** which stand in an open syllable before a vowel, a single consonant, or the following combinations of consonants, **ti** (tsĭ), **z** (ts), **qu** (kv), or a stop (**p, t, k, b, d, g**) + **r** or **l**, vary from half long to short. They are, however, unlike the usual short vowels in *quality*, but in this respect are all, except ä, narrow (see **3.** 1. *c*), i. e. are exactly like the usual long narrow vowels a:, e:, i:, o:, ɵ:, u:, y:, only pronounced a little more quickly, and hence to distinguish them from the usual short wide (see **3.** 1. *c*) sounds a, ɛ, ɪ, ɔ, ɵ, ʊ, ʏ the usual character for the long narrow sounds will hereafter be employed except that the lower dot in the colon, the mark of length, is dropped: a·, e·, i·, o·, ɵ·, u·, y·. Unaccented ä in these foreign words is a half-long wide ɛ indicated by ɛ·. Examples: **Patient** (pa·'tsĭent), **Akazie** (a·'ka:'tsĭə), **Frequenz** (fʀe·'kvents), **Mikrobe** (mi·'kʀo:'bə), **Duplik** (du·'pli:k), **Kinematograph** ('ki·ne·'ma·to·''ɢʀa:f), **Etymologie** ('e·ty·'mo·lo·''gi:), **Eumeniden** ('ɔøme·'ni:'dən), **Schokolade** ('ʃo·ko·'la:'də), **Böotien** (bɵ·'o:'tsĭən), **Mänade** (mɛ·'na:'də), &c. There is in long words considerable difference in the length of these vowels. Those that have secondary accent are longer than those without stress. The length increases in proportion to the strength of the accent.

On the other hand, these unaccented vowels are pronounced wide, i. e. as short German vowels, where they stand before a combination of consonants other than **ti** (tsĭ), **z** (ts), **qu** (kv), or a stop (**p, t, k, b, d, g**) + **r** or **l**, for the syllable is closed as the consonants are not usually carried over to the next syllable: **Kultivator** (kʊlti·'va:'toʀ), **Hektograph** (hɛkto·'gra:f), **Despot** (dɛs'po:t), **historisch** (hɪs'to:'ʀɪʃ), **Magistrat** (magɪs'tʀa:t), etc. In the languages from which such words were taken the first syllable is closed and this is the case in German as attested by the wide quality of the vowel, altho in native words some of these combinations, as **sp, st, gn,** are usually carried over to the next syllable. In many of these foreign words **sp, st, gn** are carried over as in German, especially before a stressed syllable, where in native words the tendency is strong, but in all these cases it seems probable that in careful speaking the first consonant of the combination is divided and pronounced also with the preceding syllable in order to keep it closed and short: **Aspekt** (as-'spɛkt), **Estrade** (ɛs-'stʀa:də), **Signal** (zɪg-'gna:l), &c. In the usual rapid flow of speech, however, the first unstressed part of the divided consonant disappears, so that the syllable becomes open, but the vowel keeps its original wide quality: **Aspekt** (a'spɛkt), **Estrade** (ɛ'stʀa:də), **Signal** (zɪ'gna:l). Also a vowel in an unaccented final syllable ending in a consonant is pronounced wide, i. e. as a short German vowel, as the syllable is always closed: **Botanik** (bo·'ta:'nɪk), **Metrum** (me:'tʀʊm), &c. Furthermore the unaccented vowel preceding an accented syllable is pronounced wide, i. e. as a short German vowel, when it stands before a double consonant, but the syllable is usually open and the consonant is carried over to the next syllable as an undivided sound: **Kollege** (kɔ'le:'gə), **Kommode** (kɔ'mo:'də), **korrekt** (kɔ'ʀɛkt), &c. Such words are compounds and the first component ending as it does in a consonant is in a slow distinct enunciation a closed syllable as attested by the wide quality of the vowel, but in the usual rapid flow of speech the syllable becomes open in accordance with the general German law of carrying over the consonant where the following syllable is accented.

In a large number of foreign words **e** becomes ə in unaccented syllables just as in native German words, especially in words from the French where in the original it is weakly articulated: **Cholera** (ko:ləʀa:), **Literatur** (lɪtəʀa·'tu:ʀ), **Kamera** ('ka:məʀa:), **Kamerad** (kamə'ʀa:t), etc.

d. Long vowels become short in words which by reason of their lack of logical importance in the sentence remain entirely without accent, but such vowels retain the *quality* they originally had as long vowels, and to distinguish them from the usual short vowels they are marked by dropping the lower dot in the colon, the sign of length: **Mir íst, als ốb ich die** (di·) **Hánde | Aufs Háupt dir légen sóllt'. Ich háb dich gelíebet so** (zo·) **mánches Jáhr.**

C. *Rules for Doubling to Show that the Vowel is Short.* A single consonant must be doubled after a short vowel, but in the following cases variations occur:—

a. The final consonant in the suffixes **nis, in, as, es, is, os,** and **us** remains single when no inflectional ending follows, but when an additional syllable is added, the **s** and **n** are doubled: **das Gefängnĭs,** but **des Gefängnĭsses,** pl. **die Gefängnĭsse; die Königĭn,** pl. **die Königĭnnen.**

b. Instead of double **z** the combination **tz** is used: **die Kătze.**

c. Instead of double **k** the combination **ck** is used; **schrĕcken,** but **erschrāk** with only one **k** as the vowel is long.

d. The combinations **ng, sch, ch** are never doubled after a short vowel like the other characters representing simple consonantal sounds. Doubling does not take place here from an aversion to heaping up too many unsightly letters. Before **ng** and **sch** a simple vowel is usually short, as explained in **4.** 1. *b. Note.* Before **ch** the vowel is sometimes short, sometimes long, as will be noted below under the different vowels. See also **4.** 1. *b. Note.*

e. When from a verbal stem containing a double consonant a derivative word is formed by means of the suffixes **d, t,** or **st,** the double consonant becomes single: **Gespinst** from **spinnen; Gewinst** from **gewinnen; Geschäft** from **schaffen; kund** from **kennen; Gestalt** from **stellen,** &c.

f. When a vowel in the suffix is dropped, bringing doubled consonants and a following consonant together, one of the doubled consonants is dropped, as there will still be two consonants left to show that the preceding vowel is short: **Grumt, Kumt, Samt, Taft,** &c., for **Grummet, Kummet, Sammet, Taffet,** &c. Similarly in compounds: **Schiffahrt,** &c., for **Schifffahrt,** &c.

D. *Quantity Unascertainable from Position:*

a. Before **ss** the vowel is always short: **essen,** &c. The written form of the **s** sound here clearly indicates that it is divided, i. e. belongs to both syllables. Of course, this character can only be used when it stands between vowels. Before **ß** the vowel is long, if a vowel follows **ß**: **āßen.** The written form of the **s** sound here clearly indicates that it is an undivided sound. Double **s** is always written **ß** at the end of a word or before a consonant, as the sound here is undivided, so that in these positions the quantity of the vowel cannot be ascertained: **biß, aßt, Fluß, Fuß.** The quantity can be ascertained when a vowel follows in the inflectional ending: **des Flŭsses, des Fūßes; ich biß, du bĭssest; ihr āßt, sie āßen.**

b. Before **ch** the vowel is sometimes short, sometimes long: **brĕchen, brāch, gebrŏchen.** Compare **4.** 1. *b. Note.*

Pronunciation of the Different Vowels.

5. The following description of the vowels is only approximately correct. Even the most scientific analysis cannot take the place of *viva voce* pronunciation of sounds. The pronunciation given is for *accented* vowels unless otherwise stated. Wherever comparisons are made with English without further qualification the pronunciation of the northern states is meant. S.E. indicates the Southern English of England.

6. 1. Classification:

(*a*). The *front* vowels, so called because in their formation the tongue is advanced to the front part of the mouth, are **ī, ǖ, ĭ, ǚ, ē, ȫ, ǟ, ä̆, ĕ, ö̆** in the order of the positions of the tongue, beginning in the front of the mouth and moving backward.

(b). The *back* vowels in the order of the positions of the tongue, beginning a little behind the middle of the mouth and moving backward, are **ă, ā, ŏ, ō, ŭ, ū.**

(*c*). There is a vowel in which neither front nor back articulation prevails. This is the unaccented **e** (ə), which from its manner of articulation is called mixed **e.** See **21.**

2. *Relations to each other.* The following diagram will give a general idea of the relations of the German vowels to each other with regard to the point of articulation in the mouth.

High

Front | iy | ɪʏ | eɵ | ɛɛ̃əə̃ | ə | o | ʊ | u | ɔ ɔ̃ | a ã | Back

Low

The point of articulation is highest in i, y, u, of which i and y are front and u is back. The lowest point of articulation is in a, which is back but is near the forward articulations.

Front Vowels.

The sounds of the front vowels follow in their order:

7. 1. (*a*). iː (ī), the high-front-narrow vowel (see **3.** 1. *a* and *c*), is pronounced like e in react, but the English sound is shorter as it is in an unaccented syllable. The corresponding long English sound is the diphthong ɪi, as ee in seed (sɪid). It is found in accented open syllables and in closed ones before **h** and **r**: **Lie-be, ihm, mir;** also in other closed syllables which become open when an inflectional ending follows: **Stiel, des Stie-les.** See **4.** 2. B. *b. Note* (**1**).

(*b*). iː is written: (**1**) **ie** (or **ieh**) in all German words except **mīr, dīr, wīr, īhm, īhn, īhnen, īhr, īhrer, īhrig, Īgel, Īsegrim, Bīber, Līd, wīder, gīb, gībst, gībt** (also **gĭb, gĭbst, gĭbt**; see **201.** *f*, 2nd par.), and in many names of persons ending in unaccented **-īn**: **Balduin** (balduˑiːn), **Edwin** (ɛtviːn), **Alwin, Böcklin,** etc.; (**2**) **ie** also in foreign words that have become thoroly naturalized, as in **Brief, Para'dies,** &c.; (**3**) **i** or **ie** in accented syllables before one consonant, or finally in many foreign words, written **i** or **ie** according as they were spelled in the language from which they were taken, as in **Ma'schine, Nische** (niːʃə), **Ber'lin, Ste'ttin, Artille'rie,** &c., but written **ie** uniformly in foreign verbs, as in **stu'dieren**; (**4**) **y** (representing **ij** = **ī** in an older orthography, and hence different in origin and sound from the **y** in **8.** 1. *b*. (**5**)) before one consonant in proper names, as **Schwyz, Sybel**; (**5**) **y** before one consonant in words from the Greek as in **Ana'lyse,** &c., where, however, in choice pronunciation yː is usually heard, as explained in **8.** 1. *b*. (**5**) and the *Note* thereunder, except in **Ysop** ('iːzɔp), **Zylinder** (tsiˑ'lɪndəʀ); (**6**) **y** final in other foreign words, as in **Jury, Willy,** &c.; (**7**) **ee** in a few words from the English, as in **Spleen, Yankee** ('jɛŋkiː); (**8**) **ea** in English words, as in **Lear.**

Note 1. Foreign words in **ie** present many difficulties: (**1**) Words in **-ier** fall into two groups, which have been introduced into the language at different periods and have developed a different pronunciation. The older group is pronounced iːʀ, the younger group jeː: **Offizier** (ɔfiˑ'tsiːʀ), **Rentier** (ʀɛnt'jeː). No safe rule can be given to distinguish these groups except that the verbs uniformly have the pronunciation iːʀ, as in **stu'dieren.** Elsewhere the dictionary must be consulted. (**2**) Final accented **ie** = iː, as in **Ma'rie, So'phie, Kolo'nie,** etc., but = iː'ə in lengthened forms, as maˑ'ʀiː'əns, koˑloˑ'niː'ən, etc. Also notice the difference between the French **Marie** (maˑ'ʀiː), **Sophie** (zoˑ'fiː) and the Latin forms **Marie** (maˑ'ʀiː'ə), etc. Also under secondary stress final **ie** is pronounced iː, as in **Sellerie** ('zɛlə'ʀiː), etc. Final **ie** immediately after a stressed syllable is pronounced ĭə (see **2** below, 2nd par.): **Akazie** (aˑ'kaː'tsĭə). (**3**) French *iè* = iˑɛː, as in **Karriere** (kaʀiˑ'ɛːʀə), **Piece** (piˑ'ɛːsə). (**4**) Non-final accented **ie** elsewhere in nouns = iˑeː or ĭeː before one consonant and iˑɛ or ĭɛ before more than one: **Hygiene** (hyˑgiˑ'eːnə or hyˑ'gĭeːnə), but **Serviette** (zɛʀviˑ'ɛtə or zɛʀ'vĭɛtə). (**5**) **ie** = iˑeˑ in unstressed non-final syllables: **Hiero'glyphen, Piedestal** (piˑeˑdeˑ'staːl).

Note 2. In German words **ie** was originally a diphthong, and hence both vowels were pronounced. Later **ie** became merely long **i,** the **e** serving as a sign of the length of the preceding vowel, and words which originally had no **e** after the **i** took it to show that the **i** was long. For example see **4.** 2. B. *b. Note* (**1**). In the S.G. dialects **ie** is still pronounced as a diphthong in words that had it originally.

2. In unaccented open non-final syllables **i** (also **y**) before a consonant has the same sound, only pronounced a little more quickly and must not be confounded with **i** in closed syllables described in **9.** (*a*): **Militär** (miˑliˑ'tɛːʀ). See **4.** 2. B. *c. Note.*

Unaccented **i** followed by a vowel usually becomes unsyllabic, i. e. does not form a syllable. This **i,** here indicated by ĭ, forms a diphthong with a following unaccented vowel, as also American ĭ in familiar (fə'mɪlĭər, but in S.E. fə'mɪljə): **Akazie** (a'kaː'tsĭə), **Lilie** ('liː'lĭə), **Fuchsie** ('fʊksĭə), **mordio** (mɔʀdĭoː), &c. It also forms a diphthong with a following accented vowel, as American ĭ in refuse (rɪ'fĭʊuz, but in S.E. rɪ'fju:z): **Relief** (ʀe·'lĭɛf), **Promotion** (pʀo·mo·'tsĭo:n), **Addition** (adi·'tsĭo:n), **Milieu** (mi·'lĭɵ:). In consonantal combinations difficult to unite with ĭ, namely a stop (**p, t, k, b, d, g**) + **r** or **l**, the **i** becomes syllabic, i. e. forms an independent syllable: **Allotria** (a'lo:'tʀi·a:), **Kabrio'lett, Kambrien, Anglia,** &c. The stage prescribes syllabic i in all these cases: a'ka:'tsi·ə, &c., but ĭ for **g** in **'ge**, as in **ew'ge** ('e:'vĭə), **freud'ge** ('frɔə'dĭə), &c.

8. 1. (*a*). y: (ṻ), the high-front-narrow-round vowel, does not exist in English speech. It is formed by placing the tongue into the position for i: (or, more accurately, by drawing in and lowering the front part slightly more than in the position for i:, at the same time hollowing it, thus enlarging the resonance-chamber back of the teeth), and then pronouncing with lips protruded and rounded as for u:. The hollowing of the front part of the tongue seems to result from the natural inclination of the tongue to participate in the rounding. As the lip-rounding is usually less energetic than for u: there is a tendency here to unround. Hence instead of y: we often hear i: in Middle and South Germany, and in parts of the North, especially among the lower classes. See **26.** A (last par.).

(*b*). This y: is written: (**1**) **ü** before one consonant, as in **hüten**; also in **Rüsche,** the plurals **Bücher, Flüche, Tücher**; (**2**) **ü** in certain words before more than one consonant, especially **st,** as in **hüsteln, düster, wüst,** and usually in **Nüster, Rüster,** also in **Rübsen,** and the proper names **Ülzen, Üchtritz**; (**3**) **üh,** as in **Pfühl,** &c.; (**4**) **ui** in a few proper names, as **Duisburg**; (**5**) **y** in Greek words (see *Note*) before one consonant, as in **Asyl**; (**6**) **u** in open syllables, sometimes followed by a silent **e,** in words from the French: **Aper'çu, Re'vue, Tuilerien** (ty·i·lə'ʀi:ən).

Note. In colloquial speech **y** is often pronounced **i:** in words from the Greek, but in choice language **y:** is the usual pronunciation in most words. In a few words it is pronounced i: or i·. See **7. 1.** *b*. (**5**).

2. In unaccented open syllables **ü** and **y** have this same sound, **only** pronounced a little quicker: **Bureau** (by·'ʀo:, often written **Büro**). See **4.** 2. B. *c. Note.*

9. (*a*). ɪ (ĭ), the high-front-wide vowel, is pronounced **much as i in pin.** It is found only in closed syllables, as in **mit, Irrtum,** &c.

(*b*). It is written: (**1**) usually **i** before two or more consonants: **bitter**; (**2**) **i** in monosyllabic words which never form open syllables: **bin, in,** &c., see **4.** 2. B. *b*; (**3**) **i** in suffixes, as **ig, nis, in,** &c.; (**4**) **i** also in **A'pril, Clique** (klɪkə), **Ka'pitel, Zither**; (**5**) **ie** in **Viertel, vierzehn, vierzig,** often in **kriegst, kriegt, kriegte, gekriegt** (but only in the meaning *to get*, where however in choice language i: is preferred); (**6**) **y** before two or more consonants in native German names, as in **Hyrtl, Kyffhäuser,** and often also before two or more consonants in foreign words, as in **lynchen** (lɪnçən or lɪntʃən) of English origin and in some words from the Greek, as **Myrte, Ä'gypten,** but in other Greek words the usual pronunciation is ʏ. See **10.** *b*. (**3**).

10. (*a*). ʏ (ŭ̈), the high-front-wide-round vowel, is not heard in English. It is formed by placing the tongue into the position for ɪ (or, more accurately, by drawing in and lowering the front part slightly more than in the position for ɪ, at the same time hollowing it, thus enlarging the resonance-chamber back of the teeth), and then pronouncing with lips protruded and rounded as for ʊ. The hollowing of the front part of the tongue seems to result from the natural inclination of the tongue to participate in the rounding. This sound is found only in closed syllables, as in **Hütte.** As the lip-rounding is less energetic than for ʊ there is a tendency here to unround. Hence instead of ʏ we often hear ɪ in Middle and South Germany, especially among the lower classes. We also hear ɪ in the popular German of the North. See **26.** A. (last par.).

(*b*). ʏ is written: (**1**) **ü** before more than one consonant or a double consonant, as in **Fürst, Hütte,** &c.; (**2**) **ü** also before **ch** in **brüchig, Küche, Sprüche** (pl. of **Spruch**), and the proper name **Blücher**; (**3**) **y** before more than one consonant or before one consonant in a final unaccented syllable, in Greek words, as in

Ypsilon, Si'bylle, Mystik, Sympa'thie, Satyr, &c., but in several words the usual pronunciation is ɪ. See **9.** *b.* (**6**); (**4**) **u** in short, usually closed syllables in French words, as in **Surtout** (syʀ'tu:), etc.; **Budget** (bʏ'dʒe:).

11. 1. (*a*). e: (ē), the mid-front-narrow vowel, is much like American a in dictate (dɪktet, but in S.E. dɪkteit), but the American sound is shorter as it is in an unaccented syllable. The corresponding long American sound is the diphthong ɛe (S.E. ei), as *a* in late (lɛet, S.E. leit).

(*b*). e: is written: (**1**) **e** before a vowel or single consonant, also in some foreign words when final: **Theodor, Rede, Fak'simile**; (**2**) **e** also before more than one consonant in certain words: before **rd** in **Be'schwerde, Erde, Herd, Herde, Pferd, werden,** and in proper names, as in **Verden, Werdau, Werden,** but **Hĕrder, Wĕrder, Wĕr'dohl**; before **rt**(**h**) in **Schwert, Wert,** and in proper names, as in **Kaiserswerth,** but **'Hĕrta**; also in **beredt** (bə'ʀe:t), **Brezel** (also **Prezel**), **erst, Erz, Kebsweib,** and **Krebs** (**4.** 1. *b. Note*), **nebst, stets,** and in the proper names **Dresden** (but **Brĕslau**), **Estland, Esten, estnisch, Mecklenburg, Quedlinburg** (kve:dli:nbʊʀk), **Schleswig, Schwedt, Schwetz** (but **Schwĕtzingen**), **Teplitz** (on the stage, but in the city itself **Tĕplitz**), **Trebnitz** (tʀe:pnɪts), **Gerhard** (but **Gĕbhard, Gĕrtrud**), **Hedwig**; (**3**) **ee,** as in **Beet, Beere,** &c.; (**4**) **eh,** as in **Reh, Fehde,** &c.; (**5**) **ei** in **Jockei**; see **35.** 5. (**4**); (**6**) **é** in French words, as in **Café**; (**7**) **hee** in **Thee,** now better written **Tee**; (**8**) **er** in some French words, as **Bankier** (baŋ'kĭe:); (**9**) **ai** in English **Plaid** (ple:t).

2. In unaccented open non-final syllables, **e** has the same sound, only pronounced a little quicker: **Sekretär** (ze·kʀe·'tɛ:ʀ).

12. 1. (*a*). ø: (ō̈), the mid-front-narrow-round vowel, is not found in English speech. It is formed by placing the tongue into the position for e: (or, more accurately, by drawing in and lowering the front part slightly more than in the position for e:, at the same time hollowing it, thus enlarging the resonance-chamber back of the teeth), and then pronouncing with lips protruded and rounded as for o:. The hollowing of the front part of the tongue seems to result from the natural inclination of the tongue to participate in the rounding. The lip aperture is larger than in y:. It is usually found in accented open syllables: **Höh-le, Tö-ne.** In an unaccented syllable in **Bischöfe, bischöflich, Herzöge.** As the lip-rounding is less energetic than for o: there is a tendency here to unround. Hence instead of ø: we often hear e: in Middle and South Germany and in parts of the North, especially among the lower classes. See **26.** A (last par.).

(*b*). ø: is written: (**1**) **ö** when final, or before a vowel or a single consonant, as in **Bö, Diarrhöe** (di·a'ʀø:), **Epo'pöe, tönen**; **Böschung, Flöz, Höschen, Flöße** (sing. **Flöß**); (**2**) **ö** also before more than one consonant in **höchst, Gehöft, Vögte** (sing. **Vōgt**), **Behörde, Börde, Börse, rösten, trösten, tröstlich,** and the proper names **Mörs, Österreich, Wörth, Lötzen,** and those in **-förde, -vörde**; (**3**) **öh,** as in **Höhle, Höhe,** &c.; (**4**) **oey** in the bathing resort **Oeynhausen** and **oi** in the city **Loitz**; (**5**) **eu** in words from the French when final or before one consonant, as in **adieu** (a'dĭø:)), **Queue** (kø:), **Messieurs** (mɛ'sĭø:), **Ingenieur** (ɪnʒe·'nĭø:ʀ); (**6**) **oeu** in French words when final or before one consonant, as in **Cœur,** &c.

2. In unaccented open non-final syllables **ö** has the same sound, only pronounced a little quicker: **Böotien** (bø·'o:`tsĭən). See **4.** 2. B. *c. Note.*

13. 1. (*a*). ɛ: (ā̈), a prolonged ɛ (see **14.** *a*). It sounds very much like American *ea* in *pear* (pɛ:r, but in S.E. pɛə). Instead of ɛ: we often hear e:, as there is a tendency in North German to make long sounds narrow and short ones wide. See **3.** 1. *c.* In choice language, however, North Germans endeavor to pronounce ā̈ as ɛ: and ē as e: in order to conform the pronunciation to the printed characters. This is also the pronunciation required by the stage. South Germans pronounce ā̈ and ē in accordance with their historical values, which are not indicated by the printed form. Thus in S.G. ē is often wide, as in **geben** (gɛ:bən), while ā̈ is often narrow, as in **zählen** (tse:lən). The intricate

S.G. pronunciation, which often differs in different parts of the South, is not discussed here.

(*b*). ɛ: is written: (**1**) **ä** when final, or before a vowel or a single consonant, as in **Pylä, säen, wäre**; also before **ch** in **bräche** (past subj.), **spräche** (past subj.), **Gemächer, Gespräch**; in **gemäß**; before **dt** in the plural **Städte** (also ʃtɛtə); (**2**) **ä** also before more than one consonant in certain words: before **tsch** in **grätschen, hätscheln, Kar'dätsche, Kar'tätsche, tätscheln**; before **rt** in **Bärte, zärtlich, verzärteln**; in **Gebärde, Gemälde, Rätsel, nämlich**; before **chst** in **nächst**; before **tz** (ts) in proper names, as in **Königgrätz**; frequently in Latin and Greek words, as in **Äschylus, He'phästus,** &c.; (**3**) **äh**, as in **mähen,** &c.; (**4**) **ai** in French words in open syllables, as in **Palais** (pa'lɛ:), **Affaire** (a'fɛ:'ʀə) or better **Affäre**; (**5**) **e** before **r** (not silent **r**, but only when pronounced) in French words, as in **Dessert** (dɛ'sɛ:ʀ), also elsewhere in certain French words as **Enquete** (ã·'kɛ:'tə), **Tete** (tɛ:'tə).

2. **ä** or **ai** in unaccented, open syllables has the same sound, but is pronounced a little quicker: **plädieren** or **plaidieren** (plɛ·'di:ʀən), **Renaissance** (rənɛ·'sã:s), &c. See **4.** 2. B. *c. Note.*

14. (*a*). ɛ (ĕ or ă), the short mid-front-wide vowel, is the same sound as American *e* in *let* (lɛt), but is wider than S.E. *e* in *let* (let). This sound is found (**1**) In accented closed syllables: **fett, Hände, Hermann, Herzog, Stephan** (stɛfan), **Chef** (ʃɛf), **Billett** (bɪl'jɛt), **Ho'tel** (**4.** 1. *b*); (**2**) In unaccented closed syllables in a few groups of words: **ver-** (**4.** 2. B. *c*), **der** (**4.** 2. B. *b*); in the final syllable of proper names, as in **Robert, Hubert, Wilhelm,** &c.; in the final syllable of foreign names, as in **Sokrates, Elisabeth** (e·'li:za·bɛt); in **Elen, Elend, elend**; (**3**) In unaccented open syllables in **he'rab, he'runter, he'raus,** &c.

(*b*). ɛ is written: **e**, as in **Netz**; **ä**, as in **hämmern, gemächlich;** in the North **ai** in some French words, as in **Terrain** (tɛ'ʀɛŋ), but in the South and on the stage **ain** is pronounced ɛ̃: (tɛ'ʀɛ̃:).

15. (*a*). ɘ (ŏ), the mid-front-wide-round vowel, is the rounded form of ɛ, produced by placing the tongue in the position for ɛ, (or, more accurately, by drawing in and lowering the front part slightly more than in the position for ɛ, at the same time hollowing it, thus enlarging the resonance-chamber back of the teeth), and then pronouncing with lips protruded and rounded as for ɔ. The hollowing of the front part of the tongue seems to result from the natural inclination of the tongue to participate in the rounding. The lip aperture is larger than for ʏ. As the lip-rounding is usually less energetic than for ɔ there is a tendency here to unround. Hence instead of ɘ we often hear ɛ in Middle and South Germany and in parts of the North, especially among the lower classes. See **26.** A. (last par.).

(*b*). ɘ is written: (**1**) **ö** in German words before a double consonant, or two or more consonants, as in **Hölle, Hölzer**; (**2**) **eu** in French words before the combination **ill** or **il**: **Feuilleton** (fɘjə'tõ:), **Fauteuil** (fo·'tɘi).

Back Vowels.

16. 1. (*a*). a: (ā), the long low-back-narrow vowel, is pronounced as *a* in *father*, which, however, must not be rounded (see **3.** 1. *b.*) as is often heard in different German dialects and in the pronunciation of sections of our own country.

(*b*). a: is written: (**1**) **a** when final (except in **dă, jă, nă** in exclamations), or before a vowel or a single consonant, as in **Ānnā, Baal** (ba:'al), **baden, Wal**; before **ch** in **brach** (adj. and past tense of **brechen**), **Brache, Ge'mach, ge'mach** (but **ge'măchlich**), **nach** (prep. and adv.), **Schmach, sprach, Sprache, stach**; before **sch** in **drasch** (also dʀaʃ); (**2**) or before more than one consonant in certain words: before **r** + consonant in **Art, Arzt, Barsch, Bart, Harz, Quarz, Schwarte, Start, zart**; also in **Ā'dler, Magd** (**4.** 1. *b. Note*), **Papst** (**4.** 2. A. *d. Note*); **Bratsche, Kar'bätsche, Kladdera'dätsch, latschen, watscheln,** and the proper names **Glatz, der Harz**; (**3**) **aa,** as in **Aal**; (**4**) **ah**, as in **Ahle**; (**5**) in French words accented **i** (except when final sound) after **o,** as in **Boudoir** (bu:do·ˈa:ʀ) and unaccented **i** or **y** after **o** in half-long syllables, as in **Toilette** (to·a·ˈlɛtə), **oktroyieren** (ɔktʀo·a·ˈji:ʀən); notice that **j** is inserted between a· and a following vowel; **(6) aw** in the English word **Shawl** (ʃa:l), better **Schal; (7) ae** in Dutch proper names, as in **Laeken.**

2. (*a*). a (ă), the short-low-back-wide vowel, is pratically the same sound as long a, only shorter and a trifle wider. It is heard in accented closed syllables: **alt, Ball, barsch, Garten, hart, hast, Karte, Klatsch, Mărschăll, Marter, platschen, schwarz, Tartsche, wahrlich** (but **wāhr**), **warten,** often in closed syllables before one consonantal sound: **ab, an, das, hat, man, was (4.** 2. B. *b*), **ach, Amsterdam, As, Bamberg, Claque** (klakə), **Damhirsch, Fiˈaker (4.** 1. *b*), **Gala** (gala:), **Grammatik** (gʀaˈmatɪk), **Hamburg, Kap, Paletot** (paləto:), **Tram, Walfisch, Walnuß, Walroß;** in unaccented syllables: **Eidam, Kaˈnone, Paˈpā, Paˈpier, Walˈküre** (on the stage **ˈWālküre**), &c., but usually **ˈBalsām, ˈSultān.**

(*b*). It is always written **a** except as the second element of the diphthong **oi** in some French words when it is the final sound: **Octroi** (ɔktʀoˈa).

17. (*a*). ɔ (ŏ), the mid-back-wide-round vowel, is somewhat like final *o* in potato or *o* in obey as pronounced in the northern states, or the first element in the American diphthong *o* found in note (nɔot, but in S.E. pronounced nout). It sounds somewhat like S.E. *o* in rob but is not so wide and low. The short *o* heard in New England in such words as 'coat,' 'road,' &c., is also very near the German sound. The German **o** must not be pronounced as *o* in American *not,* which is a low and very wide vowel, and hence has a lower position of the tongue than the German vowel. Moreover, in American English the *o* in *not* is over a wide area spoken without rounding of the lips. Be careful to give short German **o** its full sound in final unaccented syllables, and not to slur it as in unaccented syllables in English in such words as *cannon.*

(*b*). It is written: **(1) o** before a double consonant, or two or more consonants, as in **Groll, Sorte; (2) o** before a single consonant in **Brombeere, Don, grob** (in uninfl. form; see **4.** 2. A. *c*), **Grog, Hochzeit, Jot, Log, Lorbeer, Monsieur** (mɔˈsǐø:), **Mob, von, Vorteil,** in final unaccented syllables, as in **ˈDoktor** (but in plural **Dokˈtōren), Bischof** (bɪʃɔf or bɪʃo:f, pl. always bɪʃø:fə), &c.; **(3) e** or **ä** in the diphthong **eu** or **äu,** as in **heute** (hɔøtə), **Bäume** (bɔømə).

18. 1. (*a*). o: (ō), the mid-back-narrow-round vowel, is like the American *o* in poetic (poˈɛtɪk, but in S.E. pronounced pouˈɛtɪk), but the American sound is short as it is in an unaccented syllable. It is also like the second element in the American diphthong *o* or the first element in the S.E. diphthong *o* in *note* (nɔot, in S.E. nout). In German the tongue is somewhat further back and higher and the lips are much more rounded.

(*b*). It is written: **(1) o** when final or before a single consonant, as in **so, Noah, Rose; o** before **ch** in **hoch,** but short in **Hochzeit;** long in open syllables in **Oˋbacht, beˈoˋbachten,** but short in closed syllables in **Obˋdach, obˋsiegen,** &c. **(2)** also **o** before more than one consonant in certain words: before **st** in **Kloˋster, Oˋstern, Trost,** and the name **Jost,** but short in closed syllables in **Osten, Posten,** &c.; before **bst, pst** in **Obst (4.** 1. *b. Note*), **Propst (4.** 2. A. *d. Note*), also in **Lotse, Mond, Vogt** (see **4.** 1. *b. Note*), **Oˋbrigkeit,** and the proper name **Thorn;** before **rt** (silent **t**) in words from the French, as in **Fort, Reˈssort;** in **Koks; (3) oo,** as in **Boot,** &c.; **(4) oh,** as in **roh; (5) oe,** in Low German names, as **Soest; (6)** also as **oi** in Low German names, as **Troisdorf,** &c., except **Boitzenburg,** where **oi** is pronounced as ɔø; **(7) ow** in many Low German (for the most part originally Slavic) proper names and some English nouns: **Bredow** (name), **Treptow** (city), **Bowle; (8) au** in French words, as in **Sauce** (zo:ˋsə); **(9) eau** in French words, as in **Plaˈteau; (10) oa** in English words, as in **Toast.**

2. In unaccented open non-final syllables it has the same sound, only pronounced a little quicker. See **4.** 2. B. *c. Note.*

19. (*a*). ʊ (u), the high-back-wide-round vowel, is like u in *put*, but in German **u** the lips are more rounded. It is only found in closed syllables: **bunt, Kunst.**

(*b*). It is written: **(1) u** before a double consonant, or two or more consonants, as in **Mutter, Gruft; (2)** also **u** before one consonant in **Luther** (but u·

in **lu'thērisch**), **Ulrich** (name), **Huß** (name), **Rußland, bugsieren,** (bʊk'si:ʀən), **um, zum, zur** (**4.** 2. B. *b*), **Urteil** (but u: in other words with **Ur-**, as **Ursache,** &c.), **Jus, ka'put, Klub, plus, Rum,** and in Latin suffixes, as in **Metrum, Fiskus;** (**3**) **ou** in French words in closed syllables, as in **Ressource** (ʀɛ'sʊʀsə).

20. 1. (*a*). u: (ū), the high-back-narrow-round vowel, is much as *o* in who when unstressed. It is the second element in the American diphthong oe in shoe (ʃʊu). In S.E. *oe* in shoe is usually a long u as in German. In German the sound is made slightly further back.

(*b*). u: is written: (**1**) **u** when final, or before a single vowel or consonant, as in **du, Duo** (du:'o but pronounced u in **hui** hui, **pfui** pfui; see **23.** 4), **Bude, Ur-** (as in **Urlaub,** &c., but pronounced ʊʀ in **Urteil**), **Ludwig,** also in a final closed syllable in **Beelzebub** (be·'ɛltsəbu:p or more commonly 'bɛltsəbu:p, also written **Belzebub**); (**2**) **u** in the suffixes **tum** and **ut,** as in **Reichtum, Armut;** (**3**) **u** before **ch** in **Bruch** (*bog*, but short in **Bruch** break, fracture), **Buch, Buche, Fluch, Kuchen, suchen, Tuch, Wucher, juchzen, ruchbar, ruchlos, verrucht;** (**4**) **u** before a combination of consonants in **Wuchs, wuchs, husten, pusten, Schuster, Wust, Ge'burt** (but ǖ in **ge'bürtig**), **flugs, duzen** (du:tsən), **Uz** (u:ts), **uzen** (u:'tsən), and the proper name **Gū'drūn;** (**5**) **uh,** as in **Kuh,** &c.; (**6**) **ue** in the name **Kotzebue;** (**7**) **ou** before a single consonant or when final in French words, as in **Tour, Rendezvous** (ʀɑ̃·de·'vu:); (**8**) **oe** in Dutch words, as in **Boer** (more commonly written **Bur**), &c.

2. In unaccented open non-final syllables, **u** has the same sound, only pronounced a little more quickly: **Mulatte** (mu·'latə). See **4.** 2. B. *c. Note.* When preceded by **g** and followed by a stressed vowel unaccented **u** forms with the vowel a rising (**22**) diphthong in a few foreign words; **Linguist** (lɪŋ'gŭɪst), **Pinguin** (pɪŋ'gŭi:n), **sanguinisch** (zaŋ'gŭi:nɪʃ).

The Mixed Vowel e (ə).

21. ə (unaccented **e**), the mid-mixed-wide vowel, is a sound somewhat like the *a* in *sofa*, but it is a little higher. It is only found in unaccented syllables, as in **'lieben, 'gebe, 'Spindel, ge'liebt, be'liebt;** in the proclitics (see **57.** C) **der, des, dem, den,** &c. In the final unaccented syllables **el, em, en, er,** the **e** often naturally drops out in ordinary language: **rittn** for **ritten,** &c. On the other hand, in dignified or solemn language it approaches the sound of e in open and ɛ in closed syllables: **Liebe** (li:be), **lieben** (li:bɛn). In singing it resembles ɵ, conforming however more or less to the preceding vowel. In S.G. e is widely used instead of ə also in common speech, in some sections finally or before a consonant, in other sections only finally. In the emphatic language of a contrast ə quite generally becomes e in open and ɛ in closed syllables: **nicht verkauft** (fɛ́ʀkaoft), **sondern gekauft** (gé:kaoft).

Diphthongs.

22. Diphthongs are divided into falling and rising. In the former class there is a decline of sonority in the second element. In the latter class there is an increase of sonority in the second vowel.

23. The falling diphthongs are: **ei, au, eu** or **äu, ui.**

1. ei is pronounced much as i in wife, or more accurately ae, also ai. The German sound is nearer i in wife than the i in mine. It is written: (**1**) **ei,** as in **Ei, Stein;** (**2**) **ai,** as in **Mai;** (**3**) **ey** in proper names, as in **Meyer;** (**4**) **ay** in proper names, as in **Bayern;** (**5**) **y** in Dutch names, as in **Yssel.**

Note. In a few foreign words **ai** represents two vowels each forming a syllable: **Mosa'ik, mo'sa'isch, Kain** (ka:'ɪn), &c.

2. au is pronounced much as ou in *loud* (laʊd), or more accurately ao, also au. It is always written **au.**

Note. In some foreign words **au** represents two vowels each forming a syllable: **Ka'pernaum, Mene'läus,** &c.

3. eu is pronounced much as oy in *boy*, or more accurately ɔɵ, also ɔy and ɔi. The diphthong ɔɵ is written: (**1**) **eu,** as in **Heu, Zeus, Theseus,** but for exceptions see *Note* 2 below; (2) **äu,** as in **gläubig,** but see *Note* 3 for exceptions; (3) **oi** in a few Low German words, as **Boi, a'hoi, Boitzenburg,** &c., and the foreign word **Lev'koie** (lɛf'kɔeə or **Levkoje** (lɛf'ko:jə); (4) **oy** in Low German names and a few foreign words, as **Hoyers'werda, Mis'droy; Troygewicht, Sa'voyen;** (5) **ieu** in **Lieutenant** (lɔɵtnant), better **Leutnant;** (6) **ui** in Dutch words, as in **Zuidersee.**

Note 1. Eu and äu are pronounced ae in S.G. and M.G. dialects. See **26.** A (last par.).
Note 2. In some words **eu** represents two vowels each forming a syllable: **Te'dēum, Bakka'laureus,** &c.
Note 3. In some foreign words **äu** represents two vowels each forming a syllable: **Jubi'läum, Mat'thäus,** &c.

4. ui is pronounced ui. The second element is almost as sonorous as the first. It only occurs in the exclamations **hui** and **pfui.**

24. The rising diphthongs are ĭə, ĭɔ, ĭʊ, ĭa:, ĭo:; 'ĭa:, 'ĭɛ, 'ĭe:, 'ĭo:, ĭɵ:; 'ŭi:, 'ŭɪ. For examples see **7.** 2 (2nd par.) and **20.** 2.

Nasal Vowels.

25. In many of the later loan-words from the French, nasal vowels, which are indicated by a following **m** or **n,** are pronounced as in the original with the modification that in German the sound is always long as it stands in an open syllable, i. e. **am, an, em, en** = ã: (nasal a); **ain, ein, im, in** = ɛ̃:; **om** and **on** = ɔ̃:; **um** and **un** = ɵ̃:, when the **m** or **n** is not doubled or followed by a vowel: **Chance** (ʃã:'sə), **Entree** (ã·'tʀe:), **Bassin** (ba'sɛ̃:), **Ballon** (ba'lɔ̃:), **Verdun** (vɛʀ'dɵ̃:). This pronunciation prevails on the stage, in the South, and in parts of the Midland. In the North ã:, ɛ̃:, ɔ̃:, ɵ̃: are quite generally replaced by the nearest native sounds, aŋ, ɛŋ, ɔŋ, ɵŋ, i. e. a, ɛ, ɔ, ɵ, followed by ŋ (see **36.** *b*): **Chance, Entree, Bassin, Ballon, Verdun,** pronounce 'ʃaŋsə, aŋ'tʀe:, ba'sɛŋ, ba'lɔŋ, vɛʀ'dɵŋ. The vowel is always short as it stands in a closed syllable. In a few thoroly naturalized words these endings are pronounced as in German: **Bataillon** (batal'jo:n), **Balkon** (bal'kɔ̃: or bal'ko:n), **Garnison** (gaʀni·'zo:n), **Ballon** (now often ba'lo:n instead of ba'lɔ̃:), &c.

Mutation (Umlaut) of Vowels.

26. A. *Mutation of the Back Vowels.* The vowels **a, o, u,** and the diphthong **au,** are modified or mutated, as it may be called, when an **i** or **j** follows in the next syllable, or in the second succeeding syllable: **Stunde, stündlich; Mutter, mütterlich; Raum, räumlich.** The cause of mutation, which in German began to develop about the middle of the eighth century, cannot usually be seen in the present period of the language, as the **i** or **j** which formerly stood in the following syllable has disappeared or decayed to the form of **e: Gäste** (pl. of **Gast**), but O.H.G. gesti; **nähren,** but O.H.G. nerian. This is not specifically a German development but is found in all Germanic languages except those which like Gothic disappeared at an early period. The mutation of **a** was in earlier times written **e,** which is in part still preserved: **brennen, brannte,** &c. The mutated vowels have in different periods been designated in different ways. In earlier N.H.G. it was common to write an **e** over or alongside of the vowels, but at present the usual sign of mutation is two dots above the vowels, which are the remnants of the **e** of former times. Older usage survives in a few names: **Goethe,** &c. Also sometimes after capitals: **Ae, Oe, Ue,** usually **Ä, Ö, Ü.** In recent periodicals and books we sometimes find **e** written above the vowel as formerly, especially in poems and books of a poetic character and in reprints of older works where archaic tendencies are natural, sometimes however in advertisements merely to attract attention.

The pronunciation of these mutated sounds has been treated above. When the **i** or **j,** which are pronounced in the front part of the mouth, followed the back vowels **a, o, u,** and the diphthong **au,** the result was that the back sounds were modified, i. e. in part assimilated to frontal **i** or j, the tongue shifting more to the front in unconscious anticipation of the following **i** or **j.**

Physiological (see *Note*) mutation is oldest and most wide-spread in the North. It is most recent and least used in the South. It is a conspicuous feature of the literary language, which was largely formed in the mutating territory of the Midland. In S.G. the mutation of **u** did not take place before **l, m, n, r** + another consonant, or before **ck, pf, tz.** Moreover, **au** was not mutated in S.G. before a labial and **a** was not uniformly mutated before **l** or **r** + another consonant. S.G. forms have become established in a number of cases in the literary language: **geduldig** and **schuldig** (in contrast to Luther's **gedültig** and **schüldig**), **Innsbruck** (the Austrian city, in contrast to the N.G. **Osnabrück**), **nutzen** or **nützen** (originally M.G.), **glauben** (in contrast to Luther's **gleuben**), **gewaltig** (in Luther's earlier writings also **geweltig**), &c. Other S.G. forms occur occasionally in the literary language, or were formerly used: **hupfen** (Goethe's *Faust,* **l.** 4337, now **hüpfen**), **Zahnluck** (Scheffel's *Trompeter,* Drittes Stück, here for the sake of the meter, usually **Zahnlücke**), &c. Sometimes both the mutated M.G. and the unmutated S.G. forms have survived as they have become differentiated in meaning: **drücken** *to press* and **drucken** *to print*, **zücken** (**das Schwert**) *to draw* (*the sword*) and **zucken** *to twitch, wince.*

For centuries there has been a tendency to unround here, i. e. not to round or protrude the lips, so that, as is described more accurately under the separate vowels, **ö** becomes **e**, **ü** becomes **i**, **eu** becomes **ei**. As can be seen by the rimes of Goethe and Schiller, **können: verbrennen, müde: Friede, bereuen: befreien,** unrounding was in the classical period the rule even in the literary language. Later the N.G. rounded sounds, **ö, ü, eu** replaced here unrounded **e, i, ei** in the literary language. Except in the North, in East Franconian, and in the larger part of Switzerland unrounded sounds still prevail here in dialect.

Note. Mutation is still an active force, but its spread is brought about by quite a different cause. The cause of mutation in former times was the physiological forces mentioned above, the present cause of mutation is the psychological one of analogy. Thus certain grammatical groups which from physiological reasons suffered mutation in former periods have so influenced other groups that they too have assumed mutated form. For an example of mutation by analogy see **72.** *a.*

B. *A-Mutation.* This is also a change of sound in the stem under the influence of the following vowel, resulting in a partial assimilation of the stem vowel to the vowel in the following syllable. In West Germanic, i. e. the German period before separation into High German and Low German, *i* and *u* developed into *e* and *o* when an *a, e,* or *o* followed in the next syllable. This change of vowel is called *a*-mutation from the frequency of the mutation under the influence of a following *a*. Illustrative examples are given in **198**, 1. Division, *d*; 2. Division, *d*; **199**, 1. Division, *d*; **201.** *e*. The change of *i* to *e* in both English and German took place in only comparatively few cases and quite irregularly, so that the vowels do not correspond in the two languages: **Leber** (O.H.G. lebara, with *a*-mutation), Eng. liver (without *a*-mutation). The *u* mutated to *o* here quite regularly except before a nasal + consonant, or before *i* (*j*). Thus the perf. participle **geholfen** (O.H.G. giholfan) has the mutated **o**, while in **gebunden,** perf. participle of **binden,** a word belonging to the same gradation class, the mutation did not take place, as it was hindered by the **nd** following the vowel of the stem. Thus also **Huld,** but **hold** (original stem holda); **Fülle** (O.H.G. fullī), **füllen** (Gothic fulljan), but **voll** (original stem folla). Later unmutated **u** became **ü** according to A, above, when an **i** or **j** followed, as in the examples **Fülle** and **füllen.**

C. *Mutation of* **e.** In West Germanic, i. e. in the German period before separation into High German and Low German, the vowel **e** was changed to **i** before a nasal + a consonant, or if an **i** or **j** followed in the next syllable. Thus the stem vowel in **binden** is **i**, while in some other verbs belonging to the same class it is **e**, as in **helfen.** Thus also the **e** of **Erde** has become **i** in **irdisch,** as it is followed by **i.** Thus also **Werk** becomes **wirklich,** &c. Sometimes the force at work can only be seen in its effects, as the following **i** has become **e**, or has dropped out: **Berg,** but **Gebirge** (O.H.G. gibirgi); **recht,** but **Gericht** (O.H.G. girihti). The change of **e** to **i** under the influence of a following **i** is closely related to the mutation of back vowels under the influence of a following **i.** The tongue shifts from the position of the front vowel **e** a little further forward under the influence of the following **i** until **e** becomes **i.** As this mutation, like *a*-mutation, belongs to the West Germanic period it is older than the mutation of the back vowels. In O.H.G. *e* became *i* if an *u* followed in the next syllable: Latin *septem*, but **sieben** (O.H.G. sibun). This is called *u*-mutation. See also **197.** C. *b.* for further examples of i-, nd-, and *u*-mutation. The different forces at work in these changes are no longer felt, but they have played an important part in shaping the present forms of the language.

D. *Vowel Gradation* (Ablaut). A difference of accent in different forms of the same word developed in early times vowel gradation, that is, a difference of vowel: compare λείπω, but ἔλιπον.—In English vowel gradation often exists, altho it is not indicated by the orthography: historian (hɪsˈtɔːrɪən), history (ˈhɪstərɪ). As can be seen from the examples, loss of accent is accompanied by a reduction of the vowel element. This force can now often be seen only in its effects, as the difference of accent has in most part disappeared: ˈcapio, acˈcipio (formerly ˈaccipio, hence reduction of stem vowel). Vowel gradation is now most clearly to be observed in strong verbs, and for practical reasons this subject is discussed under that head. See **197. A.**

Consonants.

27. *General Rules:*

1. *Change of Sound.* Unlike vowels, which do not change their quantity and pronunciation from the addition of inflectional endings, consonants may change considerably their sound in certain positions, as noted below (in articles **29-37**) under the different consonants: **lesen** (leːzən) to read, **du liest** (liːst); **liegen** (liːgən) to lie, **du liegst** (liːkst); here the **s** and **g** in the different words have different sounds.

2. *Quantity.* In general, consonants in German are always short, while in English they are short after a long vowel or a diphthong and long after a short vowel: short in **soll, Kamm, Mann, lang** (laŋ), **Kuß, Flasche, Rat,** feet, need, &c., but long in bell, ham, man, tongue, kiss, smash, rat, &c. Divided consonants are short in both German and English: **Männer,** manner, &c.

THE GLOTTAL SPIRANT h.

28. **H** is pronounced like *h* in *hand,* only more forcibly. Only the initial **h** of a stem syllable, be it a simple word, a compound, or a suffix, has this pronunciation: **Halt, Anhalt, Weisheit.** The **h** is pronounced medially in **Oheim** and **Ahorn,** as they are compounds, or are felt as compounds. The **h** is still sounded in **Wilhelm,** &c., but in some compound names, as **Walther** (now usually written **Walter**), **Mathilde** (also written **Matilde**), &c., it is silent, as the names are not vividly felt as compounds. The medial **h** is naturally pronounced in the onomatopœic forms **Uhu, Schuhu,** also the exclamations **aha, oho.** Medial **h** is also pronounced in foreign words: **Jehovah, Alkohol, Sahara, kontrahieren,** &c. Declaimers and singers, following the printed form, sometimes pronounce medial **h** in German words, as in **gehen,** but this practice is not based on actual usage in the usual literary language. In all simple German words medial and final **h** have become silent except in the Southwest (especially in Switzerland and Tyrol), where in certain dialects it can still be heard medially between vowels, as in **sehen.** It must, indeed, have thus been pronounced medially thruout a large part of Germany up to a comparatively recent date, or it would not have come down to us so well preserved here in the orthography. Even after medial **h** had become silent it was felt as having a meaning. As it was originally the initial sound of its syllable and hence usually stood after an open syllable it usually in N.H.G., as in **sē'hen,** followed a long vowel, so that even after it had become silent it was felt as indicating the length of the preceding vowel. Since the fifteenth century, however, **h** often does not possess an etymological value, as many new unhistorical **h**'s have from time to time been inserted merely as a sign to show that the preceding vowel is long. This tendency became strong toward the end of the sixteenth century. As the **h** was often used where the preceding vowel would be clearly marked as long without its assistance, the new official rules require here its omission in many cases, as **Rat** instead of **Rath,** while in others they inconsistently allow it to stand. This inconsistency is easily justified in those cases where the **h** is not a mere sign to show the length of the preceding vowel, but is an etymological part of the stem which has in course of time become silent, altho in other words of the same origin the **h** appears in the older form of a pronounced **ch**: **sehen** (pro. ze:'ən) *to see*, but **Sicht** *sight.* The silent **h** has been especially allowed to stand before **l, m, n, r** when the final element of the stem and after a vowel before **e,** in all of which cases however there does not seem in most words to be any good reason for using it: **Ahle, rühmen, sühnen, führen, nähen, gehen,** &c.

An h is in N.G. often pronounced after **p, t, k** (as also in English), altho no printed character here represents it. See **29.** *a.*

Note. According to its formation **h** is a vowel, differing, however, from other vowels in that it is voiceless. It always has the mouth position of the following vowel. Thus **hu** is a voiceless **u** followed by a voiced **u**, and **ha** is a voiceless **a** followed by a voiced **a**, &c. The one character **h** stands thus, not for one sound, but for a number of different voiceless vowels. **H** is classed here as a consonant because it is invariably used as a consonant and also has the acoustic effect of a consonant, namely, that of a voiceless spirant, except between voiced sounds, where it is voiced.

STOPS: voiceless p, t, k; voiced b, d, g.

29. The voiceless stops **p, t, k** are pronounced much as in English. The voiced stops **b, d, g** are, according to the standard of the stage, pronounced as in English, when they stand at the beginning of a word, or elsewhere before a vowel or voiced consonant, i. e. initially in word or syllable, but when final (end of word or syllable) or next to a voiceless consonant they become voiceless **p, t, k**: (voiced) **bieten, das, gut, Ne-bel, e-del, Ta-ge**; but final **b, d, g** in **ob, Hund, Tag,** and **Hedwig,** and final **b', d', g'** (see also *c* below) in **hab', wurd', sag'** are pronounced voiceless, as ɔp, hʊnt, ta:k, he:tvɪç, ha:p, vʊʀt, za:k; also **b, d, g** in **Abt,** (**des**) **Eids, liegt** are pronounced voiceless, as apt, aets, li:kt. Distinguish carefully between **b, d, g** that stand as the final sound of a syllable or before a consonant in a suffix or an inflectional ending and **b, d, g** that stand as the initial sound of a medial syllable where it is immediately followed by the final **l, n, r** of the stem: **Knäblein** (knɛ:p'laen), **liebt** (li:pt), but **neblig** (ne:'blɪç, stem **Nebel**); **redlich** (ʀe:t'lɪç), but **Redner** (ʀe:'dnəʀ, stem **reden**); **reglos** (ʀe:k'lo:s or ʀe:ç'lo:s), but **regnen** (ʀe:'gnən, stem **Regen**). The stage prescribes a slight difference of pronunciation between **b, d, g** and **p, t, k** when they follow a long vowel, either in the final position as in **Grāb, lāg, tāt,** &c., or before a consonant as in **lēbt, wāgt, spūkt,** &c. Here **p, t, k** are pronounced forcibly, while in case of **b, d, g** the inception is pronounced as a weak **p, t, k** and the close is uttered forcibly. The vowel before the **p, t, k** is spoken steadily, while the vowel before **b, d, g** is spoken decrescendo gradually vanishing as the following weak **p, t, k** is begun. The stage also prescribes that **b, d, g** before the voiced suffixes **-lich, -lein, -los, -nis, -bar, -sam, -sal, -sel** be pronounced as unaspirated p, t, k: **lieblich** 'li:p'lɪç, i. e. with unaspirated p, &c.

The change of sound from **b** to **p** and **d** to **t** at the end of a syllable, or next to a voiceless consonant, is well established in the North, but that of **g** to **k** has, altho supported by the stage and many scholars, not yet become general usage. The **g** in these positions is in the North still usually a spirant and is pronounced as the voiceless spirants **ch** in **ich** and **ach** (see **32.** 3. *a* and *b*). The general pronunciation of medial **g** is still j or g as described in **34.** 3 and 4 and **35.** 3 and 4. Good usage in the North has, however, decided for the stage pronunciation g initially and the tendency to medial g instead of j or g is at present so strong in *choice* language as to point to the ultimate victory of g here. In the final position and next to a voiceless consonant ç and x are still widely used, but in choice language the tendency is to pronounce k, the pronunciation of the stage. On the other hand, the stage itself recognizes the pronunciation of ç for **g** in the suffix **-ig** when final or before a consonant, except where a **ch** occurs in the next syllable: **König** kø:nɪç, **Königs** kø:nɪçs, but **Königreich** kø:nɪkraeç, **königlich** kø:nɪklɪç, &c., g however medially: **Könige** kø:nɪgə, &c. For the stage pronunciation of **'ge** (= **ige**) see **7.** 2. (2nd par.).

In the South the **g** in all the positions described above is pronounced as an unaspirated k. See *a*.

For the pronunciation of **g** after **n,** as in **singen,** see **36.** *b*.

a. Sectional and Dialectic Peculiarities. In Middle and South Germany **b, d, g** lack voice element, and hence it is often difficult for us to distinguish in these sections between **b** and **p, d** and **t, g** and **k.** There is usually, however, a real difference between M.G. and S.G. voiceless **b, d, g** and **p, t, k,** namely, the former are pronounced with *relaxed*, the latter with *tense* muscles. In the best pronunciation of these sections initial **p, t, k** before a stressed vowel are further distinguished by an explosion, i. e. are followed by an h sound. Actual usage here, however, often varies from this standard in diverse ways, especially in that **p** and **t** are here often unaspirated, i. e. not followed by an h sound. The stage differentiates these two groups much more clearly. The **b, d, g** are voiced, the **p, t, k** voiceless and initially in word or syllable before a vowel and in the final position aspirated. When final, **b, d, g** are pronounced **p, t, k** and hence aspirated. The stage even insists upon aspiration in the initial position in an unstressed syllable, as in **Lum-pen.** In general a **p, t,** or **k** is not aspirated before a consonant as aspiration here is often difficult: **ab** ap', **Pack** p'ak', &c., but **abbiegen** ap-bi:gən, **nackt** nakt', **gibt** gi:pt', **Apfel** apfəl, &c. Before certain suffixes, as described above, final **b, d, g** are not aspirated. On the other hand, **p** is aspirated before **l** or **r,** as in **platt, Pracht, t** is aspirated before **r,** as in **treu,** and **k** is in general aspirated before non-aspirated consonants, as in **Quelle** (k'vɛlə), **Knie,** &c. This pronunciation represents the best N.G. usage, but in colloquial speech **p, t, k** are not aspirated in an unstressed syllable, as in **Lum-pen, Wol-ken,** &c. Also **p** in the combination **sp** is not aspirated, as in **spät, sprechen,** likewise medial **t** in the combinations **ft, st, cht, ts, tz,** as in **heftig, stehen, Gäste** (but **Gast** gast'), **Nichte, nichts, sitzen** (zɪt-tsən). The dialect of the extreme South is characterized by a very strong articulation of **k,** which often becomes kx or x (from older kx). See **40.** 1. *c. Note* 6. Medial **b** between vowels and after **l** or **r** is pronounced in the dialects of the Midland, Southeast, and in sections of the North as a voiced spirant, in the Midland and Southeast as the bilabial *v* described in **34.** 1, in the North as the labio-dental spirant **w,** i. e. v: (M.G. and Southeast G.) **Liebe** li:*v*ə, **Farbe** faʀ*v*ə, &c.; (N.G.) **Liebe** li:və, &c. Compare **40.** 1. *a. Note* 3. In the North the popular pronunciation of **g** is that of a spirant; initially j, ç, g, or x; medially and finally according to the general usage described above, with the exception that it often becomes voiceless medially in the Midland.

b. In derivatives and compounds these stops are pronounced voiceless if they stand at the end of either component: **Abart** (apa:ʀt). In that case (see **41.** 3. *a*), however, where the final **stop** is carried over to the next syllable, it is pronounced voiced: **be'-o-bachten.**

c. The **b, d, g,** that become final by the elision of **e** are usually voiceless: **hab' Dank** ha:p daŋk, **Leid und Freud'** laet unt fʀɔøt, **sag' mir** za:k mi:ʀ. In case of a stressed word before an enclitic beginning with a vowel, however, these consonants are voiced: **hab' ich** ha:ˎbɪç, **Freud' und Leid** ˈfʀɔøˎdʊnt laet.

How the Stops are written.

30. 1. The p sound is written **p** or **pp** (after a short vowel), as in **Paar, Rappe; b** finally and also medially before a consonant in the stem, suffix, or inflectional ending, or **bb** before an inflectional ending: **ab** (ap), **ob** (ɔp), **Subskription** (ˎzʊpskʀɪpˈtsĭo:n), **Abt** (apt), **leiblich** (laepˎlɪç, but **neblich** ne:ˎblɪç; see **29**), **bebt** (be:pt), **ebbt** (ɛpt).

2. The t sound is written **t** or **tt** (after a short vowel), as in **Tau, fett; th** in German names, as **Goethe,** but Christian names **Herta** rather than **Hertha,** &c.; **th** in many foreign words, as in **Thema, Themse,** &c.; **d** finally and also medially before a consonant in the suffix, as in **Mund** (mʊnt), **Ludwig** (lu:tvɪç), **Adjektiv** (atjɛkˈti:f), **Kindlein** (kɪntlaen), but only d in **Handlung** (han-dlʊŋ, &c., where the l is a part of the stem **Handel;** see **29**); **dt** in a few words, as in **Stadt, sandte, berēdt,** &c.

3. The k sound is written: **(1) k** or **ck** (after a short vowel), as in **kahl, dick; (2) ch** in a number of words where it is followed by an **s** (= ẞ or ſ) which forms a part of the stem, as in **Ochs** (= Ochs), **Ochsen** (= Ochſen), but not in **(des) Buchs, wach-sam,** &c.; **(3) ch** initially in some German names, **Chemnitz, Chlodwig,** &c., also in many foreign words, as in **Chor,** see **32.** 3. *a. Note.* **(2)**; **(4) q** before **u,** as in **Quelle** (kvɛlə); **(5) g** finally or before a consonant in a suffix or an inflectional ending = k upon the stage, as in **Tag, täglich, tagt,** but = g where the following consonant is a part of the stem, as in **reˎgnen;** see **29; g** also quite generally as well as upon the stage in a few isolated words, as **bugsieren** (bʊkˈsi:ʀən), **flugs** (flu:ks), **Gig** (gɪk), **Grog** (gʀɔk), **Log** (lɔk), and the proper names **Augsburg** (aoksˎbʊʀk) and **Jagst** (jakst); **(6)** in sections of the North **g** after ŋ when final or before a voiceless consonant, as in **ging** (gɪŋk), **bringst** (bʀɪŋkst), where on the stage and in choice language in the North the **g** is silent; **(7) gg** finally, or medially before a consonant, as in **Brigg, flaggt; (8) c** in many foreign words, as in **Cognac** (kɔnjak, now better in German spelling **Kognak**), also in some German names, **Campe,** &c.; **(9)** also **cc** in some foreign words, as in **A'ccord,** now better in German spelling **A'kkord.**

4. The b sound is written: **(1) b** as initial sound in word or syllable: **Bahn, Liebe, nēˎblig** (see **29**), **Abraham** (a:bʀa·ham), **sublim** (zu·ˈbli:m), but of course pronounced p when it is the final sound in the syllable, as in **Gelübde** (gəˈlʏpdə), **Subordination** (zʊpˀɔʀdi·na·ˈtsĭo:n); **(2) bb** after a short vowel when followed by a vowel, as in **Ebbe; b** as a final sound in the syllable in a number of foreign words, as **Bobsleigh** (bɔbˎsle:), **Oblate** (ɔb-ˈla:tə, on the stage o·ˈbla:tə), **obli'gat,** &c., but pronounced p after German fashion in very common words, as **Subjekt** (zʊpˈjɛkt), &c., of course, sometimes fluctuating between German and foreign pronunciation, as in **Ablativ** (ap-laˈti:f, ab-laˈti:f, on the stage a-blaˈti:f), &c.

5. The d sound is written: **(1) d** as initial sound in word or syllable: **du, 'Rēˎdner (29), 'Āˎdler, or-dnen** (but pronounced t in **wid-men** as **d** is the final sound of the syllable), **Budget** (bʏˈdʒe:); **(2) dd** or **ddh** after a short vowel when followed by a vowel: **Kladde, Buddha** (bʊda:), &c.

Note. The d is silent in a few words from the French: **Fonds** (fɔ̃:), **Plafond** (plaˈfɔ̃:), &c.

6. The g (voiced stop as in English g in *go*) sound is written: **(1) g** initially as in **gut; (2) g** also medially when followed by a vowel and preceded by a vowel or consonant (for colloquial N.G. pronunciation here see **34.** 4, **35.** 3. **(2)**): **Sage, Ziege, Berge;** also written **g** as the initial sound of a medial syllable, where it is usually followed by the final **l, n,** or **r** of the stem, but if these consonants do not form a part of the stem the pronunciation of **g** here is ç or x in colloquial N.G. or according to the stage k, as the **g** is the final sound of the syllable: **Vöglein** fø:ˎglaen (stem **Vogel**), **regnen** ʀe:ˎgnən (stem **Regen**), **Wagner** va:ˎgnəʀ (stem **Wagen,** or sometimes in colloquial N.G. with a different syllabic division va:x'nəʀ), but **möglich** mø:ç'lɪç, or better mø:k'lɪç, **fraglich** fʀa:x'lɪç, **or** better fʀa:k'lɪç; for the colloquial N.G. pronunciation of **Vöglein, regnen** see **35.** 3. **(3)**; furthermore written **g** medially in foreign words before **l, m, n, r,** both when it is the initial sound of the medial syllable and contrary to usage in native German words also when it is the final sound: **Reglement** (ʀe·glə'mã:), **Geographie** (ge·o·gʀa·'fi:), **Signal** (zɪ'gna:l); (as final sound in syllable) **Dogma** (dɔg-ma:), but often here in German fashion dɔk-ma: or dɔx-ma:, often with different pronunciation according to syllabic division: **Signal** zɪ'gna:l (**4.** 2. B. *c. Note*), or zɪk'na:l, zɪç-'na:l, or zɪŋ-'na:l (**36.** *c*). **(3) gg** medially after a short vowel when followed by a vowel, as in **Flagge; (4) gu** before a front vowel in foreign words, as in **Gui'tarre,** or now better in German spelling **Gi'tarre, Guerilla** (ge·'ʀɪlja:), **Guillotine** (gɪljo·'ti:nə); **(5) gh** in foreign words, as in **Ghibe'lline, Ghetto,** or better in German spelling **Gibelline, Getto.**

Spirants.

31. Voiceless **f, s (s, ss, ß), ch, g, sch**; voiced **w, s, j, g, r.**

Spirants like stops vary in part in pronunciation according to their position, as will be noted in the following articles.

32. Voiceless spirants—**f, s (s, ss, ß), ch, g, sch.**

1. f is pronounced as f in *fine*: **fünf,** &c. Compare **33.** 1. *Note.*

2. s sounds nearly like ss in *moss*, but is narrower in its tongue articulation, that is, has a somewhat smaller air-channel between the tongue and the teeth-roots, which gives the hiss a higher pitch: **Haus, Eis,** &c. See also **34.** 2. *a.*

3. The spirants **ch** and **g** are not found in English. Their pronunciation depends upon their position:

a. Medially and finally after a front vowel (see **6.** 1. *a* above) or any consonant, initially in some foreign words (see *Note* below), and always in the diminutive suffix **chen, ch** is a voiceless j, thus closely resembles English or American y in *yes* spoken without voice or the American voiceless spirant that follows c in *cure* (kçʊ:r), but it is much stronger: **stechen, ich, Lerche, Chi'rurg, Mädchen.** The phonetic symbol for this sound is ç. Also **g** final or before a consonant has in colloquial North German the same sound when it follows a front vowel or any consonant: **Steg, legt, Berg.** The stage demands that **g** here be pronounced k.

Note. In foreign words **ch** can also form the initial sound of a syllable. Its pronunciation in this position depends in part upon the origin of the word: **(1)** In Greek words it is pronounced ç before a front vowel and sometimes before a consonant: **Che'mie, Chrie** (çʀi:ə), &c. **(2)** In Greek words before a back vowel and also before a consonant it is usually pronounced k: **Cha'rakter, Cholera, Chor, Christ,** &c. **(3)** In Greek words between vowels **ch** is pronounced as in German words, i. e. ç after front vowels and all consonants, and **x** after back vowels: **Mechanik** (me:-'ça:nɪk), **Arche, Or'chester** (on the stage ɔʀ'kɛstəʀ), **Hypochondrie** (hy·po·xɔn'dʀi:). In **Melancho'lie** and **Mar'chese** however, it is pronounced as k. **(4)** In French words it is pronounced ʃ initially and medially: **Chi'cane** (now better written **Schikane**), **Choko'lade** (Span. but with French pronunciation of **ch**; better **Schokolade**), **Branche,** &c. **(5)** In English words = ʃ (French) or tʃ (Eng.): **Check** (now **Scheck**), **chartern** (tʃaʀtəʀn), &c.

b. After back vowels (see **6.** 1. *b*, above) **ch** becomes a velar spirant, as in **ach, A'chat, A'chill.** It is heard from Scotchmen for ch in *loch.* It is formed by raising the back part of the tongue towards the middle of the soft palate, a little higher than in the position for short **u,** and then forcing thru this space between the tongue and palate a broad current of air, which produces a rough rasping sound. In a few foreign words **cch** has this same sound: **Bacchus,** &c. In colloquial North German **g** is also thus pronounced, when it stands after a back vowel and is not followed by a vowel: **Tag tagt.** The phonetic symbol for this sound is x.

Note. In older German **ch** was always a velar sound, i. e. was pronounced **x** after front as well as back vowels, as it originally developed out of the velar sound k as described in **40.** 1. *b* and *c*. This older usage still survives in the dialects of the extreme South and in isolated sections farther north as in parts of Westphalia: **sicher** (sɪxəʀ) (in Tyrol, Switzerland).

4. sch something like sh in *shy*, but in German the lips are protruded more, and the point of the tongue is less raised: **scharf, Schiff,** &c. Tho usually represented by three letters (**sch**), this sound is a simple one, the phonetic symbol of which is ʃ.

Note. This sound has come from two quite different sources: **(1)** In many words, as described in **40.** 2. *g.* **(1)**, it developed out of **s. (2)** In many other words it corresponds to O.H.G. sk, hence was originally a combination of two sounds s and k. This older order of things survives medially and finally, as in **Disk** (= H.G. **Tisch**), &c., in certain dialects of the western half of the Low German territory. In the extreme western part of this territory **sk** developed in the final position into **sch**, i. e. s+x and at present is pronounced s as the s has assimilated to itself the **x**. The pronunciation s+x arose in late O.H.G. and survives in Westphalian dialect in the initial position. The present simple sound was general in the South about 1300. The older pronunciation with two distinct sounds has left traces behind in the literary language in that it has kept the preceding short vowel short. See **4. 1.** *b. Note.*

How Voiceless Spirants are written.

33. 1. The f sound is written: **(1) f** or **ff** (after short vowel), as in **Fall, Schiff,** &c.; **(2) v** in a few German words, as in **Vater, Vetter, Gevatter, Vehme** (better **Feme**), **ver-, Vieh, viel, vier, Vlies (Vließ), Vogel, Volk, voll, vom, von, vor, vorder, zu'vörderst, vorn, Frevel;** initially in a number of German, Low German, and Dutch proper names, as **Vilmar, Virchow,** (fɪʀço:), **Voß, Vischer, Veldeke, Vērden, Bremer'vörde,** medially only in **Havel, Bremer'haven, Kux'haven, Wilhelms'haven;** in a few L.G. words, finally and before a consonant, as in **Luv, luvwärts, luvt** (but **luven** lu:vən); **(3) v** finally in all foreign words, as in **passiv,** medially in **Pulver,** and regularly before a consonant, as in **Evchen** (but **Eva** e:va:), **Lev'koje,** initially in **van** (before Dutch names), **Veit, Vers, Vogt, Veilchen, Vesper; (4) ph** in foreign words, as in **Philo'soph, Dĭph'thong,** &c.; **(5) pph** in the Greek name **Sappho; (6)** often **w** finally or before a consonant in many Slavic words, as **Boleslaw, Kiew** (ki:ef), **Asow** (a:zɔf), **Asowsches Meer,** &c., where however the stage requires **w** (i. e. v), bo:ləslav, &c.

Note. In oldest German we find the German f-sound sometimes expressed by v, as the monks of that time seem to have pronounced Latin v as f. Thus there arose two characters for the f-sound. In M.H.G., v was used to indicate the weakly articulated old Germanic f, as found in M.H.G. visch (N.H.G. **Fisch**), Eng. *fish*, and f was employed to indicate the strongly articulated sound developed in the second shifting out of Germanic p (see **40. 1.** *c*), as in hel*f*en, Eng. hel*p*. This old distinction between the weak and the strong f is still in large part preserved in Swiss dialects. This distinction had probably disappeared in the final position even in oldest literary German and in M.H.G. this change found a formal expression in the orthography by the uniform use of f at the end of a word, which clearly indicates that the weaker sound was here supplanted by the stronger one: M.H.G. wol*f*, but in the genitive wol*v*es. Later the stronger articulation spread to all positions, and hence f replaced v in all positions except in the few words given above, where the older orthography survives as a fossil. The pronunciation of v as f in the words from the Latin **Vers, Vesper, Veilchen, Veit, Vogt,** &c., indicates the older German way of pronouncing Latin v. In **Brief** (Latin bre*v*e), **Käfig** (Latin ca*v*ea), &c., the character f is used. The f in **prüfen** (Old French pro*v*er) indicates that the Germans substituted the nearest sound in their language for the French v, which at that time was unknown in German. See **35. 1.** *Note.*

2. The s sound is written: **(1) s(=ꞩ)** at the end of a word, as in **Moos, Stuhls** (ʃtu:ls, not ʃtu:lz as English-speaking students usually pronounce), **Tals,** &c.; ks in the Latin form of **x** in a few foreign and native words, as **Marx, nix** (dialect for **nichts**), &c.; **(2) s** (=ſ) medially before consonants, as in **Liste,** also before vowels if it is preceded by a consonant other than **l, m, n, ng** (ŋ), **r**: **Erbse** ('ɛʀpsə), but the **s** is voiced in **Linse** as it follows **n;** ks in the Latin form of **x** in a few foreign and native words, as in **Xaver** (ksa:vəʀ or ksa·'ve:ʀ), **exakt** (ɛks-'ʔakt), **Hexe,** &c.; **(3) S** or **s** (=ſ) initially in foreign words before a consonant other than **p** or **t,** as in **Skizze, Smaragd, Szene** (stse:nə); **(4) s** (=ſ) initially before **p** or **t** in many foreign words that are still vividly felt as foreign, as in **spon'tan, Spaa, Spleen** (spli:n), **ste'ril, Stenogra'phie, Stuart,** &c., also medially after a prefix, as in **ab'strakt, In'stinkt, konstru'ieren, 'Konstanz** (city) &c.; **(5) ss** (=ſſ) between vowels when a short vowel, and **ß** (=ſꞩ) when a long vowel precedes, as in **Flüsse, Füße; ß** at the end, or medially before a consonant in all words which require ss or **ß** between vowels, as in **Fluß,** G. **Flusses, Fūß,** G. **Fūßes, müssen, du mußt, stōßen, du stōßt; (6)** heard as the latter element in the double sound ts (written **z, tz, t** before **i, c** before front vowels; see **39.** 3) even before vowels, as in **Katze, heizen, Patient, aszetisch** (as'tse:tɪʃ, also written **ascetisch,** but more commonly **asketisch,** pronounced with a **k**); **(7) ç** in words from the French, as in **Façon** (fa'sɔ̃:); **(8) c** in some French words, especially before ə, as in **Annonce** (a'nɔ̃:sə); **(9) z** in **Bronze** (bʀɔ̃:sə, also pronounced with z), and in the Spanish words **Kadiz** (ka:dɪs), **Cortez** (kɔʀtɛs), **Gomez** (go:mɛs), &c.

3. ç is written **ch** in some words and **g** in others, as described in **32. 3.** *a.* It is written **x** in the name **Xi'mēnā.**

Also x is written **ch** in some words and **g** in others. See **32. 3.** *b.*

4. ʃ is written: **(1) sch** as in **scharf,** &c., but **sch** in the Italian word **Scherzo** (skɛʀtso:) is pronounced **sk,** as **h** here has only been added to **c** before the front vowel **e** to give the **c** the hard sound of k; **(2) s** initially before **p** or **t** in all stem syllables: **sprechen, stehen, verstehen, Ziegelstein;** also in a large number of very common foreign words which are felt as native words, as in **spa'zieren, Spi'on, Stu'dent,** &c.; **(3) ch** in French and other foreign words; see **32.** 3. *a. Note* **(4)**, **(5)**; **(4) sh** in English words, as in **Shakespeare, Shawl** (better **Schal**), **(5)** contained in **c** (before **e** and **i**) and cci = tʃ in Italian words, as **Cello** (tʃɛlo:), **Violoncell** (vi·o·lɔn'tʃɛl), **Cicerone** (tʃi·tʃə'ʀo:nə), **Boccaccio** (bɔ'katʃo:); **(6) x** in **Don Quixote** (according to the French dɔ̃:ki'ʃɔt, more commonly in French spelling **Don Quichotte,** the former form, the old Spanish spelling, sometimes with Spanish pronunciation dɔn ki'xo:te); **(7)** contained in **ch** in English words (see **32.** 3. *a. Note* **(5)**) and also in **Guttapercha** (gʊta'pɛʀtʃa:, also gʊta'pɛʀça:); **(8)** contained in the Slavonic **tsch** or **cz** (= tʃ), as in **Tscheche** or **Czeche** (tʃɛçə).

a. In Hanover, Holstein, Friesland, and Mecklenburg, initial **s** before **p** and **t** is pronounced as voiceless *s* instead of ʃ: staen instead of ʃtaen (**Stein**).

b. In the Southwest **st, sp** are pronounced ʃt, ʃp also finally and medially; not only so in dialect, but often also by the educated classes: kʊnʃt, bʏʀʃtə, haʃpəl instead of kʊnst, bʏʀstə, haspəl. In some M.G. dialects ʃ is heard for **z** after **r**: bø:ʀʃə instead of **Börse.** In the dialect of Berlin ʃ is heard after **r** for s and ʒ for z: **Durst** (dʊʀʃt), **Hirse** (hɪʀʒə).

Voiced Spirants—w, s, j, g, j or g (both = ʒ), r.

34. 1. w (v) is much like v in *very*. It was originally a bilabial sound pronounced with both lips just as English w, but in the North and upon the stage it is now the labio-dental v sound, i. e. is formed with the lips and teeth, but is not quite as distinctly buzzed as English v. In South and Middle Germany it is a bilabial sound, *v*, pronounced with both lips, which are nearly parallel, so that there results a very narrow passage along almost their entire length, while our bilabial English w is pronounced with lips closed at the sides but protruded in the center forming a round opening. S.G. bilabial *v* also differs from English w in that the tongue is not, as in English, raised to the position of **u.** The S.G. **w** is not accompanied by a buzz as in the North. N.G. **w** is sometimes still bilabial after a consonant, or when written **u** after **q**, as in **Schwester, zwei, Quelle.** It is here more commonly the usual labio-dental sound.

Note. In O.H.G. the u sound as a vowel was written u or v, both characters with the same u sound, but as a consonant it appeared as uv, vu, uu, or vv until toward the end of the period when it began to become usual to represent the consonantal sound by writing the last combination together as one character, w, double v (i. e. double u), just as it is still written in both German and English. Modern English preserves not only the old character and the old name, but also the old u sound. In German the old character has been preserved, but its name ve: indicates that the old sound has been replaced by another. S.G. w is nearer to the original pronunciation.

2. Voiced s (z) is pronounced like s in *rose*: **senden, Rose.** This sound is not the original Germanic s but a North German development. See **40.** 2. *g.* **(2)**.

a. In all the positions (see **35.** 2) where **s** in N.G. is voiced, it is in S.G. voiceless. See also **35.**2. *b.* In German, s, especially when divided, is more strongly articulated after a short vowel than after a long one or a diphthong. By this means South Germans can distinguish between the s in **Haß, hassen** (has, hasən, in both N.G. and S.G. pronounced with strongly articulated s) and the s in **Besen** (S.G. be:sən, N.G. be:zən), but they cannot distinguish between the s in **reißen** (S.G. and N.G. ʀaesən) and the s in **reisen** (S.G. ʀaesən, N.G. ʀaezən).

3. j (j) has much the same sound as y in *yes*: **ja, jagen,** &c. The articulation is closer in German than in English y, and hence in German there is a gentle buzz, caused by the friction of the air in passing thru the narrowed space. This friction is more marked in the North than in the South.

Note. Originally **j** was only a consonantal **i** and until the fifteenth century was written **i.** The printed form for German capital **i** and **j** are still the same. The new character **j** arose in the fifteenth century but was at first used also for **i**, especially in the initial position: (Luther) **jr, jn = ihr, ihn.** In the seventeenth century the consonantal character of consonantal **i** had become so pronounced by reason of the distinct buzz that accompanied it that the North German grammarian Schottel insisted upon the employment of **i** for the vowel and **j** for the consonant, and gradually this usage became established. In the South the consonantal character is not so clearly developed as in the North.

4. g is in colloquial North German a voiced spirant after back vowels, when also followed by a vowel: **wagen, nagen, Fugen.** The phonetic symbol is g. The English *g* is here a stop, but this German sound is a spirant, the breath continuing and not suddenly stopped as in English. Germans in the South pronounce this **g** as in English, except that it is voiceless. On the stage and in choice North German it is spoken as in English.

5. ʒ, the voiced sound corresponding to voiceless **sch,** not found in German words but in many foreign ones, is somewhat like s in *pleasure*: **Journalist,** &c. For spellings see **35.** 5. This sound is replaced in S.G. and M.G. by ʃ.

6. German **r** has an entirely different sound and is formed differently from the English. It is produced by the uvula, the little fleshy conical body suspended from the middle of the lower border of the soft palate. The uvula is set in vibration by the current of escaping air pushing against it. To form this **r** the back of the tongue must be quite tightly closed in around the uvula, forming a little groove in which it hangs, so that the escaping air must of necessity push it out to pass beyond. The tongue is kept drawn back and remains *motionless.* This **r** is not usually trilled, but is pronounced quite softly, and often in colloquial speech passes over into a or ə in final syllables, or before certain consonants: **mehr** (me:a), **Mutter** (mʊta), **starben** (ʃtaəbən), **Wurm** (vʊəm), &c. Sometimes it disappears altogether before consonants, in which case the preceding vowel is lengthened: **Warze** (va:tsə), &c. On the other hand it is in some sections pronounced as x: **warten** (vaxtən), **Pforte** (pfɔxtə), &c. There is also another **r**, the tongue **r,** which prevailed in earlier periods of the language and is still heard in certain localities and is required by the stage. See **37.** 2.

How Voiced Spirants are written.

35. 1. The v sound is usually written: **(1) w,** as in **wohl; (2) f** dialectically in sections of the North when the **f** stands before a vowel of an inflectional ending, in case of nouns and adjectives whose simple stem ends in **f,** as in **(des) Briefes** (bʀi:vəs), **steifer** (ʃtaevəʀ), &c., where however in choice language f is spoken; **(3) v** initially and medially in foreign words, as in **Vase, Pa'ssiva,** but never when final, as in **passiv** (pa'si:f); **(4) v** medially in Low German words, as in **luven,** and a large number of proper names, as **Kleve** (city), **Ha'nnover, Trave** (river), **Dove** (family name), **Sievers** (zi:fəʀs or zi:vəʀs, family name), **Beethoven; (5) u** after **q,** as in **Qual** (kva:l); **(6) u** after **k** in **Bis'kuit; (7) u** after s (s), as in **Suade, Suite,** &c.

Note. In Middle and South Germany **v** in foreign words is pronounced thruout as f as there is no **v**-sound in the native speech of these sections, while North Germans can pronounce it initially and medially as they have the sound here in their native speech. Of course, foreign words that have come into the literary language thru S.G., as in case of **prüfen** (Old French *prover*) have the f-sound. Compare **33. 1.** *Note.*

2. The z sound is represented in print by the following characters: **(1) s** initially before vowels, as in **sieben, Absicht, ratsam, Trübsal,** but not in case of **-sel** (as in **Rätsel** ʀɛ:tsəl), which is no longer vividly felt as a suffix with a distinct meaning; **(2) s** also medially before vowels (expressed or understood), when it itself is preceded by a vowel or consonantal vowel (**l, m, n, ng** (ŋ), **r**), as in **leise, weis(e)re, Linse, Mengsel,** pronounced with voiced **s,** but the **s** is voiceless in **Erbse, schnapsen, Häcksel,** as it is preceded by a consonant other than **l, m, n, ng, r; (3) z** initially in Low German and Dutch proper names, as in **Zuidersee,** (zɔødəʀ'ze:), also in a few other foreign words, as **Gaze, Ha'zard, Ba'zar, Ve'zier,** &c., now better written **Hasard, Basar, Wesir,** but **Gaze.**

a. The **s** that becomes final by the elision of **e** is usually voiceless: (imperative) **blase** (bla:zə) or **blas** (bla:s); **leise** (laezə) or **leis** (laes), but in the first person of verbs usually written **s'** altho it is voiceless: **Ich les'** (le:s) **das oft.** In case of a verb and a following enclitic beginning with **a** vowel the **s** is usually voiced: **Das les' ich** (le:'zɪç) **oft.** In a few cases of syncope the **s,** when the initial sound of the syllable, is voiced before a following consonant, only however where the full form with voiced **s** is also used: **eis'ge** (ae'zǐə) or **eisige** (ae'zɪgə), **gewesner** (gə've:'znəʀ) or **gewesener** (gə've:'zənəʀ), **Basler** (ba:'zləʀ) or **Baseler** (ba:'zələʀ), but **Klausner** (klaos'nəʀ), &c. If in a contracted word voiced **s** comes to stand before a suffix, it is voiceless: **z** in **Hase,** but s in **Häschen.**

b. In all the above positions s is voiceless in the South, as can be seen in the rhymes of the poets from this section: **Und wie mit des fernen Donners Getose | entstürzt es brüllend dem finstern Schoße** (Schiller). See also **34.** 2. *a.*

3. j is written: **(1) j** initially, as in **ja, Jesus,** also medially in Low German and foreign words, as **Boje, Ma'jor; (2) g** medially in colloquial North German when followed by a vowel and preceded by a front vowel or by a consonant, as in **Siege, Berge; (3)** also written **g** in colloquial N.G. as the initial sound of a medial syllable, where it is usually followed by the final **l, n,** or **r** of the stem, but if these consonants do not form a part of the stem the pronunciation of **g** here is ç or according to the stage k, as the **g** is the final sound of the syllable: **Vöglein** fø:ˈjlaen (stem **Vogel**), **regnen** ʀe:ˈjnən (stem **Regen**), but **möglich** mø:çˈlɪç or better mø:kˈlɪç; medial **g** in all the cases given in (**2**) and (**3**) is pronounced g instead of j in choice N.G. and upon the stage; (**4**) **y** in some foreign words, as in **Yankee** (jɛŋki:), in French words after **o,** where **y** is equal to a·j wherever a vowel follows, as in **loyal** (lo·a·ˈja:l), **Royalist** (ʀo·a·ja·ˈlɪst); (**5**) also contained in the combinations **ll, ill,** and **gn** in French (and in the last case also Italian) words, also in Spanish ñ: **Bouteille** (bu·ˈtɛljə), **Campagne** (kamˈpanjə), Mignon (mɪnˈjɔ̃:), **Bologna** (bo·ˈlɔnja:), **Coruña** (ko·ˈʀʊnja:). See also **39.** 5 and 6.

4. There is but one way of writing g, namely, **g** after back vowels when followed by a vowel, as in **Wagen.** The pronunciation g is used here on the stage.

5. ʒ (voiced **sch**) is written: (**1**) **j** in French and some other foreign words, as in **Journal, Jury** (ʒy:ʀi:), **Don Juan** (dɔ̃:ʒu·ã: in the sense of *seducer*, but dɔn ju·ˈa:n or according to the Spanish dɔn xu·ˈa:n as a proper name); (**2**) **g** (before **e** or **i**) in French or Italian words, as in **geˈnieren, Logis** (lo:ˈʒi:), **Agio** (a:ʒĭo:), **Genie** (ʒe·ˈni:, French), but **Genius** (ge:nĭʊs, from the Latin); (**3**) **ge** before back vowels in French words, as in **Sergeant** (zɛʀˈʒant); (**4**) contained in **j** or **g** in some English words and in **g** (before **e** and **i**) and **ggi** in some Italian words, where **j, g, ggi** are pronounced dʒ, as in **Jockei** (dʒɔke: or dʒɔkae), **Gentleman** (dʒɛntəlmən), **Michelangelo** (mi·kelˈandʒe·lo:), **Arpeggio** (aʀˈpɛdʒo:), &c., where however in S.G. and M.G. tʃ is spoken instead of dʒ.

6. The ʀ sound is written: **r,** as in **rot; rr** after a short vowel, as in **harren; rh** in German proper names and in Greek words, as in **Rhein, Rhapˈsode; rrh** in Greek words, as in **Kaˈtarrh.**

Nasals.

36. *a.* The labial and dental nasals **m** and **n** are pronounced as English *m* and *n* in *mad* and *nag*: **Magd, Hand.** They are always written **m, n,** or after a short vowel **mm, nn.**

b. The velar nasal **n** (ŋ) is pronounced as *ng* in English *singer*. The character **n** that represents this velar nasal is the same as the one that represents the dental **n,** but they can easily be distinguished from each other, as the velar **n** is always followed by **g, k, ck, c, x:** in **Hand** the dental nasal, but in **Gang** and **sinken** the velar. After the velar **n, g** has become ŋ, having become assimilated to the preceding velar: older **singen** zɪŋgən, now zɪŋən with a double or divided ŋ, a part being spoken with each syllable, graphically zɪŋ-ŋən. When, however, this double ŋ is not followed by a vowel, but is final or stands before a consonant as in **sang** zaŋ, **singt** zɪŋt, it, like all other double sounds, becomes single, so that ŋ here differing from ŋ elsewhere is not followed by another velar. Thus in the final position and before a consonant all trace of g has in choice language disappeared, except the ŋ itself, which in a very early period had become velarized from dental n under the influence of the following velar g: O.H.G. sɪŋgan from older sɪngan. Thus, tho the g is here absolutely silent, it actually lives on in the preceding velar ŋ. Sectionally, however, the old g is still heard. When final or before **s, t, st,** it is pronounced in parts of the North as **k: gingen** (gɪŋən), but often in N.G. **ging** (gɪŋk), **längs** (lɛŋks), **bringt** (brɪŋkt), **Angst** (aŋkst). Provincially the **g** that follows ŋ is pronounced g in the North when followed by a vowel: **des Ganges** (gaŋgəs instead of gaŋəs). In M.G. and S.G., prevailingly in N.G., and also upon the stage, the **g** after ŋ is *always* assimilated or silent. Be careful in speaking German not to follow the English practice of pronouncing the **g** after this palatal nasal when the **g** is followed by the vowel **e**: say **Fing-er** (fɪŋəʀ, not fɪŋgəʀ). In foreign words, however, the **g** is usually pronounced, except before ə: **Ganges** gaŋgɛs (river), **lingual** (lɪŋˈgŭa:l), &c., but **Dschungel** (dʒʊŋəl). The **n** at the end of a prefix does not in a choice pronunciation become ŋ before **k** or **g: ankommen** (ˈankɔmən), **angreifen** (ˈangʀaefən).

c. ŋ is written: (**1**) usually **ng,** as in **singen;** (**2**) **n** in native words before **k** or **ck,** as in **winken, Vincke** (name); (**3**) **n** medially and finally before **c, g, k, x,** in foreign words, as in **Salamanca** (zalaˈmaŋka:), **Ungarn** (ʊŋgaʀn), **Albalonga** (albaˈlɔŋga:), **Sphinx** (sfɪŋks), &c. However, in the Latin and Greek prefixes **en, in, kon, syn** the **n** is also pronounced n, usually however with the distinction that ŋ is spoken in a stressed syllable and n in an unaccented syllable: **Synkope** (zʏŋko·pe:), but **enklitisch** (ɛnˈkli:tiʃ), &c.; (**4**) in colloquial North German **n** or **m** in French words in the combinations **an** or **en, in, on, un** or **um,** &c., as illustrated in **25,** where however on the stage instead of ŋ the preceding vowel is nasalized as explained in **25;** (**5**) **g** before **n** in foreign words, however, only in foreign words other than French and Italian, as in **Agnes** (ˈaŋ-nɛs), **Signal** (ziŋ-ˈna:l). Instead of the ŋ sound, x and ç are often heard here: ˈax-nɛs, ziç-ˈna:l. In choice language, however, **gn** here is pronounced gn, as in **Agnes** (agnɛs). In French and Italian words **gn** is pronounced nj, as in **Chamˈpagner, Camˈpagna.**

Liquids.

37. The liquids **l** and **r** are sounds differing somewhat from the English **l** and **r.**

1. In forming German **l** the back part of the tongue is not raised as in making English l, but is lowered and brought farther forward than in English and pressed against the teeth, while the front part of the tongue assumes a convex form, so that the space between its surface and the roof of the mouth is more narrow than in the position for English l, and hence the resultant sound is clearer and lighter. In making German **l** the opening of the lips in the corners of the mouth is much more marked than in English l.

2. The old **r** (r) is pronounced with the tip of the tongue with a distinct trill. It is now, on the one hand, confined to provinces and small towns, or, on the other hand, elevated to use upon the stage on account of its forcible sound. It is disappearing despite its adoption by the stage and certain enthusiasts. The more common r is the uvular. See **34.** 6.

Glottal Stop.

38. There is in German a consonant that is not represented by any sign in the written language, namely, the glottal stop. Phonetists represent this sound by ʔ. It resembles a very faint cough. The glottis is closed and then suddenly opened, the air thus escaping with a slight explosion. It is usually found before all strongly accented initial vowels, i.e. before pronouncing a stressed initial vowel the *breath is stopped for a moment.* This is one of the most characteristic features of German speech and hence is rarely lacking, except dialectically in sections of the South. Thus Germans who speak the glottal stop do not run words together, as we often do in those cases where a word ending in a consonant precedes one beginning with a vowel, since there is really in the German a consonant between the words. Thus we say *notatall,* but the Germans say **ein ʔApfel.** This glottal stop is most clearly perceptible in strongly accented syllables, and hence often entirely disappears in rapid conversation in enclitics and proclitics: **da habʼ ích** (ha:pˈʔɪç), or more commonly **da hábʼ ich** (ˈha:ˋbɪç); **es** (ʔɛs) **zappelt ja noch,** when spoken distinctly, but **es** (əs) **zappelt ja noch,** when spoken rapidly, the proclitic **es** losing its identity and becoming a part of the following word. As a rule it is heard in the second element of compounds, if that element begins with a vowel: **WindesʔEile.** It is not, however, heard in the second element of the following classes of compounds, as the separate elements are not distinctly felt and thus blend together: (**1**) in compound particles, as **daran** (da·ˈʀan), **hinab** (hɪˈnap), **herein** (hɛˈʀaen), **vorüber** (fo·ˈʀy:bəʀ), **woraus** (vo·ˈʀaos), &c.; (**2**) in **Ōˋbacht, beˈōˋbachten, eiˈnander,**

vollenden (fɔ'lɛndən), **vollends** (fɔlənts), **allein** (a'laen), &c.; **(3)** in foreign compounds, as **Sy'node, Inte'resse,** &c.

The glottal stop is not especially indicated in this treatise.

Consonantal Combinations.

39. The following consonantal combinations are discussed here, as they may present some difficulties:

1. **pf** represents a compound of the simple sounds **p** and **f**, the **p** passing over into **f** before the closure is fully exploded. The greater volume of breath is expended upon the **f** so that it is lengthened and strengthened. This is the natural pronunciation of the South, and is also found upon the stage and in choice North German, but the people in a large part of the North and Midland pronounce only **f** in the initial position and after **m**: **Ferd** (fe:ʀt) instead of **Pferd** (pfe:ʀt), **Damf** instead of **Dampf.**

2. **x** represents a compound of the two simple consonants **k** and **s**. **ks** is written: **(1) x,** as in **Axt, exakt** (ɛks'ˀakt), **Xaver** (ksa:vəʀ or ksa·'ve:ʀ); **(2) chs,** as in **Ochs, Ochsen;** **(3) ks,** as in (des) **Werks;** **(4) cks,** as in **klecksen, Klecks;** **(5) gs,** as in **flugs, Jagst (Jaxt), Augsburg.**

3. **z** represents a compound of the simple consonants **t** and **s**. ts is written: **(1) z** initially, also after a long or half long vowel or a diphthong and after a consonant, as in **zehn, dū'zen, A'kāzie, inspizieren** (inspi'tsi:ʀən), **Kauz, Herz;** see **4. 2.** A. *d.* (2), 3rd par.; (2) **tz** after a long vowel in a few proper names, as **Grātz** (now usually **Graz**), &c.; (3) **tz** regularly after a short vowel, as in **Katze** (katsə); **(4) ts,** as in **Rätsel** (ʀɛ:'tsəl), (des) **Hochmuts;** **(5) tts,** as in (des) **Tritts;** **(6) dts,** as in **Bodenstedts** (gen. of a proper name); **(7) ths,** as in **Freiligraths** (gen. of a proper name); **(8) ds,** as in (des) **Bads;** **(9) c,** or often better **z** in foreign words before front vowels, as in **Cäsar, Ac'cent** or better **Akzent** (ak'tsɛnt); **(10) t** before an **i** that stands before a vowel, as in **Patient** (pa'tsĭɛnt), but not in French words, where ie = i:, as in **Partie** (paʀ'ti:); **(11) zz** in words from the Italian: **Gran'dezza, Skizze,** &c.

4. The compound sound dʒ, which is like *g* in *gentleman*, is represented in print by **j** or **g** in words taken from the English and by **g** (before **e** or **i**) and **ggi** in Italian words. See **35. 5. (4).**

5. In the popular language of the North **ll** after **i,** and **il** and **ill** after another vowel not initial, are pronounced lj medially and lç in the final position in all words taken from the French: **Billet** (bil'jɛt), **Medaille** (me:'daljə), **Fauteuil** (fo·'tølç). Medial **lj** is also spoken in S.G. popular speech, but finally or before a consonant the usual S.G. pronunciation here is l: **Fauteuil** (fo·'tøl or fo·'tɛl), **Fauteuils** (fo·'tøls or fo·'tɛls). The pronunciation of the medial lj has become established also in the literary language in a number of common words, as, **Bataillon** (batal'jo:n), **Billet** (bɪl'jɛt), **Bouillon** (bʊl'jɔ̃:), **Kanaille** (ka'naljə), **Medaille** (me·'daljə), **Patrouille** (pa'tʀʊljə), **Postillon** (pɔstɪl'jo:n), **Reveille** (ʀe·'vɛljə), &c., but the final lç or l finds little favor. Aside from the list just mentioned, most educated people prefer to pronounce these sounds more in accordance with the French, j in the medial, i in the final position: **Feuilleton** (føjə'tɔ̃:), **Fauteuil** (fo·'tøi), **Detail** (de·'tai), &c. The stage here recommends a pronunciation which is more conformed to popular S.G. speech but which as yet has not come into wide use in the literary language. It prescribes l', i. e. an l blended with j by assuming at the inception of l the mouth position of j: **Detail** (de·'tael'), **Details** (de·'tael's). A distinct j is heard after this sound when a vowel follows: **Feuilleton** (føl'jətɔ̃:).

6. In French and Italian words **gn** is pronounced nj: **Champagner** (ʃam'panjəʀ), &c. For **gn** in other foreign words see **36.** *c.* **(5).**

7. **qu** and **ku** represent a compound of the two simple consonants **k** and **v,** of which the latter is more commonly labio-dental than bilabial (see **34. 1**), both in German and foreign words: **Quelle** (kvɛlə), **Quadrat** (kva·'dʀa:t), **Biskuit** (bɪs'kvi:t), &c. In a number of words from the French, however, **qu** is

pronounced k: **Quarantäne** (ka·ʀɑ̃·ˈtɛːnə), **Queue** (køː), **Bouquet** or better **Bu'kett, Marquis** (maʀˈkiː), **Mar'quise,** &c. These words are still felt as French words and follow more or less closely the French pronunciation, but in case of older loan-words the pronunciation has become German, as in **quitt** (kvɪt).

8. gy is pronounced dj in words from Hungarian: **Magyar** (madˈjaːʀ) or better **Mad'jar** Magyar, Hungarian.

BRIEF HISTORY OF GERMAN CONSONANTS.

Their Relation to those of other Languages.

40. 1. Consonants form in every language the strong enduring trunks of linguistic growth, and thus remain tolerably constant thruout the centuries, both in the original language and in related tongues, also in words which have passed from one people to another. Thus the consonants in German and English are much the same. Altho consonants in general have thus not changed radically their nature as have vowels, a number of them have nevertheless a clearly marked development, which furnishes important data for determining the relation of languages to each other. There are three distinct periods of development. The first period, which represents the original order of things, is found in a large measure preserved in Latin, Greek, and other older languages, and their modern forms such as modern Greek, Italian, French, Russian, &c. The second period appears in Gothic, Scandinavian, Low German, and hence also in English, which in its original stock of words is Low German. This first shifting took place in prehistoric Germanic. The detailed account of these sound changes is given in *a, b, c* below. The third period appears in High German. This second shifting began in the sixth century and was completed in the tenth. It is described in detail below.

A brief history of the more difficult and characteristic consonantal changes and their relations to the different dialects and kindred languages is here given in the hope that it may prove helpful to the student in increasing his appreciation of the language.

a. Indo-European bh, dh, gh. Where we have in the parent language (Indo-European) bh (developing later in Latin into f- or -b-), dh (in Latin f-, -d-, or -b-), gh (in Latin h-, g-, -g-, or -h-) we have in Gothic, Low German and English b (in English, however, appearing as b initially, v medially, and f finally), d, g (in English also written y initially before front vowels, y, i, w, medially or finally), and in High German **b, t** (sometimes written **th**), **g.** In passing from the second to the third period, bb (now written b in English) and gg (often appearing as dg in English) usually become **pp, ck.**

EXAMPLES.

First Period		Second Period First Shifting		Third Period Second Shifting
Early Stage	Latin	Early Stage	English	German
bh	(1) *f*rater, (2) lu*b*et	ƀ	(1) *b*rother, (2) lo*v*e, (3) gra*v*e, (4) cal*f*, (5) ri*b* (O.E. ri*bb*)	(1) **Bruder,** (2) **lieben,** (3) **graben,** (4) **Kalb,** (5) **Rippe**
dh	(1) *f*ores, (2) vi*d*ua, (3) ver*b*um	đ	(1) *d*oor, (2) wi*d*ow, (3) wor*d*, (4) bi*d* (O.E. bi*dd*an)	(1) **Tür,** (2) **Witwe,** (3) **Wort,** (4) **bitten**
gh	(1) *h*ortus, (2) *h*elvus, (4) lon*g*us, (6) ve*h*ere	ǥ	(1) *y*ard (O.E. *g*eard), (2) *y*ellow, (3) *g*rass, (4) lon*g*, (5) to st*y*, (6) wa*y* (O.E. we*g*), (7) wa*i*n, (8) ha*i*l, (9) borro*w*, (10) we*dg*e	(1) **Garten,** (2) **gelb,** (3) **Gras,** (4) **lang,** (5) **steigen,** (6) **Weg,** (7) **Wagen,** (8) **Hagel,** (9) **borgen,** (10) **Weck**

Note 1. We often find in literary German **bb, gg** instead of **pp, ck: Krabbe** (Eng. crab), **flügge** (Eng. fledge). Such words have been borrowed from the Low German, which in general has much influenced the literary language.

Note 2. Within the third period the t that had developed from Germanic d became voiced after nasals, and thus regained its former sound: (O.H.G.) bintan, hunta, &c.; (N.H.G.) **binden, Hunde,** &c. In a few words, however, the t remained: **hinter, hinten, unter, unten, munter,** also in the conjugation of verbs, as **nannte, konnte,** &c., after the analogy of **liebte,** &c.

Note 3. The characters b, d, g do not represent the same sounds in different periods and different parts of the same territory. In Germanic in the early stage of the first shifting they were voiced spirants, ƀ, đ, ǥ. In prehistoric High German they developed into voiced stops, b, d, g, and still later in oldest South German appear as voiceless stops. The present literary language recognizes this development in case of Germanic đ by employing the character t, which in the North is pronounced t', i.e. as an aspirated t, in the South also t' in choice language but in colloquial speech and dialect as an unaspirated t or a voiceless d. In case of the sounds that have developed out of

Germanic ƀ and g the literary language uses the letters **b** and **g**, which in the South are pronounced as voiceless b and ɡ, in the choice language of the North initially and medially as voiced b and ɡ, finally or before a consonant b as p and g as ç or x, or on the stage k (details in **29**). In English the Germanic spirants ƀ, đ, g, except g before front vowels, became voiced stops, b, d, ɡ initially and đ also elsewhere (for exception see *Note* 4) and also g sometimes elsewhere, especially after a nasal and in a number of cases when doubled: gold, longer, frog (O.E. frogga). Initial spirant g survives before front vowels, as in *yellow* (German **gelb**). Where initial g is found here as a stop, as in *give, guest* (gest), it is usually explained as the result of Scandinavian influence. In N.G. and M.G. popular speech g is still in most positions a spirant. For full explanation see **29** and also *a* thereunder. In Old English, g remained a spirant medially and finally. Later it developed into a w, y, or i, and still later had also other developments, so that the original sound is no longer felt: borgian (O.E.), borrow (N.E.); weg (O.E.), way (N.E.); hagol (O.E.), hail (N.E.). In a few German words medial g has developed in much the same way: **Getreide** (M.H.G. getregede, all that which has resulted from bearing, i.e. grain, from **tragen** to bear), **Hain** (contracted from **Hagen** forest, grove, now entirely replaced by the shorter form), **Maid** (from older maget, N.H.G. **Magd**), &c. As described in **29.** *a* there is a voiced spirant b in wide use medially in the dialects of the Midland, Southeast, and in sections of the North. This voiced spirant is in the North and parts of the Midland the old Germanic spirant ƀ as it is found in the oldest documents of these sections, while the voiced spirant spoken further south in the Midland and Southeast has developed out of a weakly articulated voiceless stop, which in the oldest historic period was a strongly articulated voiceless stop, which thru the intermediate stage of voiced stop had developed out of the Germanic spirant ƀ, as described above. Thus thru several intermediate stages this modern spirant has back-developed into the original Germanic spirant ƀ. The group of b's which developed after l and r, as described in **40.** 2. *c*, has joined this group of ƀ's. In the literary language they are pronounced as the stop b but in the dialects of the Midland, the Southeast, and sections of the North they are still spoken as the spirant **w**, as in older German, i.e. with the same pronunciation as the spirant ƀ just described. In English we have the survivals of Germanic spirant ƀ in medial v and final f, as in calves, calf.

For another group of b's, d's, g's which has joined this one, and had the same development see **2.** *a* below.

Note 4. In a number of English words, *d* (including the *d*'s which resulted from *th* in accordance with Verner's Law; see **2.** *a* below) has in comparatively recent times developed into a voiced *th* before (e)r, and found a corresponding expression in the orthography: father (O.E. fæder), **Vater**; mother (O.E. modor), **Mutter**; weather, **Wetter**, &c.

b. *Indo-European* p, t, k. Where in Latin we have the voiceless stops p, t, k (c, q), we find in Gothic, Low German, and English the voiceless spirants f, th (d in *modern* L.G.), h (in English also written gh), and in High German **f, d, h** (**ch**). The character h does not represent the same sound in the different periods. Early in the second period, immediately after the first shifting, it was pronounced as **ch.** Even as early as the Gothic period it had become h, at least initially. It is in the German of our time always pronounced as h initially, and elsewhere is silent, except when final or before a **t** or **st,** where the older pronunciation is still sometimes preserved, and is indicated by the character **ch: hoher,** but **hoch, höchst; näher** but **nächst; schmähen,** but **Schmach; sehen,** but **Gesicht;** **(er) flieht,** but in poetic or archaic language **(er) fleucht.** Usually, however, final **ch** has been leveled to **h** under the influence of medial **h** that stands in other forms of the same word. Thus older **Schuch** (still preserved in the proper name **Schuchardt** (= M.H.G. schuochworhte *shoe-worker*, i.e. *shoe-maker*) has become **Schuh** after the analogy of **des Schuhes.** In isolated words where this analogy does not present itself the old final **ch** is preserved: **doch, durch, nach, noch.** In oldest German double h was pronounced **ch.** It survives in **lachen** (lax-xən), **Zeche** (tsɛç-çə), **zechen** (tsɛç-çən), altho the doubling or dividing is not indicated by the orthography. See also *Note* 7 below. Also in English, h has become h initially, elsewhere it has disappeared, or is represented by gh, which is now silent or pronounced as f.

The various changes of p, t, k (c, q) in the different periods are illustrated by the following examples:

First Period, Latin.	Second Period, English (First Shifting).	Third Period, German (Second Shifting).
*p*es	*f*oot	**Fuß**
*t*res	*th*ree	**drei**
*c*or, se*qu*or	*h*eart, si*gh*t and see,	**Herz, Gesicht** and **sehen,**
	hi*gh*, rou*gh*	**hoch, rauh**

While it is true as above stated and illustrated that p, t, k of the first period developed into the spirants f, th, h (= **ch**) in the second period, these new sounds very soon even before the time of historic records experienced a further development. In the initial position and after a stressed vowel, f, th, h (= **ch**) remained f, th, h (= **ch**), but after an unaccented vowel between voiced sounds these voiceless spirants became voiced spirants, ƀ, đ, g as described and illustrated in 2. *a* below. These ƀ's, đ's, g's joined the large group of ƀ's, đ's, g's in *a* above and developed later along with them.

The f, th (i.e. þ), h (originally x) of the second period developed out of the strengthening of the articulation of the p, t, k of the first period, i.e. aspiration (**29.** *a*) developed after p, t, k, expressed phonetically by p‘, t‘, k‘, and later became so strong that it developed into an independent spirant, so that p‘, t‘, k‘ became pf, tþ, kx. Later the second sound in each combination assimilated to itself the first sound, so that pf, tþ, kx became f, þ, x. Still later x lost the velar articulation and became the h sound as we hear it to-day in English. Altho the first stages of this development are not disclosed by historic records they may be regarded as assured, for we see almost the same development repeated later in historic times, as described in *c* below, last par.

Note 1. The consonants p, t, k, did not shift when the final sound in the combinations sp, st, sk, pt, kt: spuo (L.), spew (E.), **speien** (G.); hostis (L.), gasts (Gothic), guest (E.), **Gast** (G.); piscis (L.), fisc (O.E.), fisc (O.H.G.), N.H.G. **Fisch,** Mod. Eng. fish; captus (L.), hæft (O.E.), **Haft** (G.); octo (L.), eahta (O.E.), eight (Mod. E.), **acht** (G.). While the final sound p, t, k of these combinations remained unchanged thruout the two shiftings the aspirated p before t developed in the first shifting into f, and the aspirated k before t into h (i.e. x), as in the last two examples. It is evident here that aspiration, now a marked feature of the Germanic languages, had not reached its full development yet. The consonant before final p,t, k, prevented the development of aspiration after p, t, k and consequently the formation of a spirant here. In late O.H.G. the k after s. as in fisc, developed into x, so that fisc became fısx and still later fıʃ, as described in **32.** 4. *Note.* (**2**). The late O.H.G. development of k here into x indicates clearly that after the second shifting aspiration had developed after k. In our own time there has been a further development of aspiration after p, t, k in combination with other consonants, but in certain combinations, as described in **29.** *a*, it has not yet appeared.

The ft's and ht's have been increased from another source. In Germanic before a t all labials appear as f, and velars as h (=**ch**): give, gift; **geben, Gift;** may (O.E. mæg), might (O.E. miht); **mögen, Macht;** think, thought (O.E. đohte); **denken, dachte.** This movement began in pre-Germanic, and is so complicated that it cannot be explained here.

Note 2. In the earliest history of English, th developed into *d* after or before *l*, so that we here find *d* in both English and German: wild, **wild;** gold, **Gold;** needle, **Nadel,** &c. In the eleventh century Low German th began to develop into d in all positions, thus shifting to d as High German had already done, so that modern Low German, differing from English, now has the same sound here as High German: **dat** (L.G.), **das,** that.

Note 3. Indo-European p, t, k have been seemingly preserved in Germanic where they stood before an accented syllable with initial n. The Indo-European p, t, k became, according to rule, f, th, h (**ch**), which according to Verner's Law (see 2. *a* below) developed into b, d, g, as the preceding vowel was unaccented. By assimilation the bn, dn, gn became bb, dd, gg. Simple b, d, g were spirants, but bb, dd, gg developed into stops, and later became voiceless pp, tt, ck, perhaps at the same time that Indo-European b, d, g became p, t, k, as described in *c* below. In the second shifting pp, tt, ck became, according to *c*, below, **pf, tz, ck,** so that in case of k there is no difference of sound in the three periods: du*c*o (L.), tu*ck* (Eng.), **zucken.** Related words will have different sounds here, according as Indo-European p, t, k were originally simple sounds or were followed by an accented n: **schnauben** (regular Germanic f having developed into b according to Verner's Law), **schnupfen; schneiden, schnitt** (Germanic th having developed into d according to Verner's Law and later in H.G. shifting to t), **schnitzen; ziehen, zog, Zug** (the regular Germanic h having developed into **g** according to Verner's Law), **zucken,** compare English tie (O.E. tiegan), tuck; **biegen, bücken; schmiegen, schmücken.**

Note 4. Corresponding to English *thousand* we should expect **Dausend** and in O.H.G. the form with **d** is found. After much fluctuation the form with **t** has become established. In older German **teutsch** was often used for the correct **deutsch,** but it has disappeared.

Note 5. In Low German f before **t** goes over into **ch,** which is also found in the literary language in a few words from L.G.: **sacht** (= H.G. **sanft**), **Schlucht** (H.G. **Schluft,** now little used in plain prose, but not infrequent in poetry and even in prose in S.G. writers, as in Hermann Hesse's *Peter Camenzind*, p. 2), **Nichte** (H.G. form **Niftel,** now only archaic). For the dropping out of **n** in **sacht** see 2. *e* below.

Note 6. In M.G. dialects **nd** becomes **ng.** Luther introduced this form into the language in **schlingen** *to swallow.* The original form survives in the related word **Schlund.**

Note 7. The old final **ch** is often better preserved in southern dialects than in the literary language: **Viech** instead of the literary form **Vieh.** This old **ch** often spreads in these dialects to the medial position: **Viecher,** pl. of **Viech.** In the literary language the opposite development usually takes place, medial **h** leveling out final **ch: Schuh** instead of older **Schuch,** as it follows the analogy of **des Schuhes.**

c. Indo-European b, d, g. Where in Latin we find the voiced stops b, d, g, we find in Gothic, Low German, and English p, t, k (c, q, in English also ch, tch), and in High German two different groups, according to their position in the word—**pf, z, k,** on the one hand, and **f, s** (**ss, ß**), **ch** on the other. In passing from the second to the third period, p remained **p** before **p,** it became **pf** initially, also after **m** and **p** but elsewhere became **f;** **t** remained **t** before **t,** it became **z** (**tz**) initially, also after **t** or another consonant, but elsewhere, i.e. medially and finally after a vowel, became **ss, ß,** or **s; k** remained unchanged initially, after another consonant, or when doubled (written **ck**), but a single **k** developed into **ch** medially and finally after a vowel. Thus as explained below, **p** remained unchanged before **p, t** unchanged before **t, k** unchanged before **k,** also initially and after **k** or another consonant. As a modification of this statement it should be noted that **p** and **t** remained unchanged after **s,** and **t** unchanged after **f** and **ch,** as explained in *b. Note* 1. Also for the peculiar development of **k** after **s** see *b. Note* 1. The various changes described above may be illustrated by the following examples:

First Period, Latin.	Second Period, English (First Shifting).	Third Period, German (Second Shifting).
du*b*ùs (Lithuanian* word corresponding to (4))	(1) *p*ool, (2) stum*p*, (3) a*pp*le, (4) dee*p*, (5) hel*p*	(1) **Pfuhl,** (2) **Stumpf,** (3) **Apfel,** (ap-pfəl), (4) **tief,** (5) **helfen**
*d*ecem, cor (cor*d*is)	*t*en, hear*t*, si*tt*an (O.E.; now sit), ea*t*, a*t*e, i*t*	**zehn, Herz, sitzen** (zɪt-tsən), **essen, aß, es**
jugum	yo*k*e, ba*k*e, *c*old, drin*k*, mil*k*, li*ck* (*Note* 4); ben*ch*, stre*tch*	**Joch, bachen** or **backen** (*Note* 5), **kalt, trinken, melken, lecken, Bank, strecken**

Pf and **z** or **tz** (both = ts) in German are the result of the strengthening of the aspiration (**29.** *a.*) found in the p and t of the second period, which is still preserved in English. While **pf** thus developed out of the aspirated **p** after a **p,** and **z** after the aspirated **t** after a **t,** the **p** before the aspirated **p** and the **t** before the aspirated **t** remained unchanged, as **p, t, k** then as now (see **29.** *a*) were not aspirated before an aspirated sound: **Apfel** (ap-pfəl), **sitzen** (zɪt-tsən). German **pf** and **z** (ts) further developed in certain positions into **f** and **ss** or **ß,** as the first sound in these combinations was assimilated to the second. Hence we should naturally expect to find the strong aspiration of the k of the second period developed into **kch** and we should expect to find this new combination in certain positions developed by assimilation into **ch.** All these changes have actually taken place and are still clearly discernible in the extreme South as described in *Note* 6 below. In the literary language only the final stage of this development has been preserved, namely the **ch** which developed out of the **kch** which had developed out of the aspirated k of the second period, as in **Joch,** from older **Jokch,** which is from an older form with aspirated k, which is still preserved in English yo*k*e. This development is found in the literary language only after vowels, but it is old. Later it spread in the extreme South to other positions. The development here of pʻ, tʻ, kʻ to **f, ß** (i.e. s), **ch** (i.e. x) is almost identical with that described in

*As b was a rare sound in the original language it is difficult to find apt examples. Lithuanian is used for the illustration here as Latin does not serve the purpose so well.

b (last par.) above, where the p, t, k of the first period became aspirated and developed into the f, th (i.e. þ, a lisped s), h (in its oldest stage = x) of the second period.

Note 1. As Germanic p, except before p, became either **pf** or **f**, we should not expect to find any **p's** in German except the **p's** before **pf**, which are not indicated by the orthography, as in **Apfel** (ap-pfəl), and those that came from Germanic bb and sp according to *a* and *b* (*Note* 1) above, but in fact we find a considerable number of other **p's** and **pp's**. They are not exceptions to the rule, but are loan-words in large part from the Low German: **picken, puffen, Pumpe, humpeln, Knüppel, schuppen** (N.G., but in S.G. **schupfen**), **Lippe** (a L.G. and M.G. word introduced by Luther, now more common than the H.G. **Lefze**), &c. Also from other languages: **Pakt** (L.), **Parade** (Fr.), &c. There is another list of words containing **p** from another source: In oldest S.G. b was often strongly articulated and hence was written p. Later the articulation except in certain positions was weakened to voiceless b and hence was often written b. Still later in the Midland in Saxony and Thuringia we find both b and p pronounced as voiceless **b**, so that b in Luther and other M.G. writers from this section was very often written p. Thus for many centuries there was considerable fluctuation, so that often in the same word historic b, whether of German or foreign origin, was written b or p, or both forms occur. On the other hand, historic p often appeared as b. Later, scholars in many cases regulated here the orthography in accordance with historic principles and Midlanders from the Rhine region and North Germans worked unconsciously in the same direction as they distinguished in their native speech between b and p. In some words, however, historical b, whether of German or foreign origin, is still written **p: Polster** (Luther, but in O.H.G. bolstar or polstar, Eng. bolster), **Panier** (Luther, Fr. bannière), **gepott** (Luther, but later changed by him to its present form **Gebot**), &c. On the other hand, in a few words Low German and foreign p appears as **b: Bremse** (Middle Low German premese), **Birne** (L. pira), &c. Luther under S.G. influence wrote **Bapst** (Old French papes, from L. papa), which later under learned influence became **Papst** in order that it might better indicate its origin.

Note 2. Tt (or t) before er (older r) did not shift in the change from the second to the third period: baitrs (Gothic), bitter (Eng.), **bitter** (G.); **wintrus** (Gothic), winter (Eng.), **Winter** (G.); otter (Eng.), **Otter** (G.); true (Eng.), **treu** (G.).

Note 3. The student might naturally think there should be no double **t's** in German aside from those in the words given in *Note* 2, as the others shifted to **tz**. There are, however, a number of **tt's**, not exceptions to the rule but a modern development. In M.H.G. a short vowel was often found in an open syllable before a single consonant: **vĕ-ter**, hă-mer, &c. In early N.H.G. the vowel here usually became long, as illustrated in **4. 1.** *b*. *Note*, but often before **t** and **m** the syllable became closed, so that the vowel remained short and the consonant was doubled to indicate the closedness of the syllable and the shortness of the vowel: M.H.G. **vĕ-ter, hă-mer**, but N.H.G. **Vet-ter, Ham-mer.** See also **4. 1.** *b*. *Note*.

Note 4. English lick and German **lecken**, which belong here, are related to Latin lingere *to lick*, which comes from the Indo-European stem ligh and hence belongs to group *a* as confirmed by Gothic laigōn *to lick*, which is the corresponding Germanic form of the second period. The Germanic stem lig- had another form, lign-, which was formed by adding the accented suffix n. Later this form became ligg- by assimilation. Double b, d, g did not remain spirant b, d, g thruout the early Germanic period as did the simple sounds, but developed, as described in *b*. *Note* 3, above, along with the original Indo-European voiced stops b, d, g into voiceless stops, i.e. pp, tt, **kk** (ck). In this way *liggōn became lecken, and passed out of the group *a* and joined the words in this group (*c*), which had developed a **k** out of Indo-European g.

Note 5. As the simple and double sounds had a different development, we find different consonants in related words or related languages, according as the sounds were simple or double: **wachen, wecken**; bake, batch; **bachen** (early N.H.G. and still in S.G.; see **203.** 1), **backen** (literary word).

Note 6. Corresponding to the H.G. change of **t** and **p** to **tz** and **pf** is the change of **k** to **kch** (kx) found in certain positions in certain dialects of the extreme South: (Tyrol) **Kchind** for **Kind, Finkch** for **Fink**, but **ch** (x, from older kx) after l and **r**, as in **Pirche** (from older **Pirkche**) for **Birke.** *Initial* **ch** from older **kch** is found further west in most parts of Switzerland: **Chopf** for **Kopf.** This **ch** from older **kch** is widely found in different positions in Swiss dialects. Where, however, Germanic **k** stood after **n** or where it was doubled it did not in most dialects develop further than **kch: Finkch** for **Fink, tekche** for **decken** (dek-kən). Instead of **kch** in these two positions we find simple **k** in certain sections of eastern Switzerland where there was a large Romance population at the time of the original occupation of the country by the Germans. The Romance people in speaking the language of the invaders substituted for the difficult German combination **kch** their native **k**, which finally became established in the dialect. In loan-words from the literary language and in foreign words we find in the different Swiss dialects **kch** for foreign **k** instead of the native sound **ch** as an attempt is made to approach the foreign pronunciation: **kchriegen** for literary **kriegen** *to get*, **Kchamerad** for **Kamerad**, &c.

All these changes of **k** to **kch** and the further development to **ch** are, except after vowels, of much later date than the change of **t** to **tz** and that of **p** to **pf.** The change of **k** thru **kch** to **ch** *after vowels*, however, as in **Joch** (Eng. yoke) belongs to the *early* period of the first High German consonantal changes and took place over the entire territory, hence is not only found in Switzerland and Tyrol but everywhere in High German.

Note 7. In many words we find t instead of **z** and **ß**. They are for the most part introductions from Low German: **Talg, Teer, Boot, Beute,** &c.

2. OTHER CONSONANTAL CHANGES.

The above consonantal changes, the main points of which were in part discovered by Jacob Grimm, in part formulated by him from the older discoveries of Rask and then published in 1822, in part presented to scholars later by other investigators, have been sketched only in their roughest outlines. There are many exceptions and also additional changes. Attention is here called to a few of the more important:

a. *Verner's Law*. In 1876 the Danish scholar K. Verner published his discovery that the cause of the deviation of a certain group of words from the laws given in the preceding articles lay in a difference of accent in the prehistoric period. From this discovery it becomes evident that in the pre-Germanic period at the time that Indo-European p, t, k shifted to the spirants f, th (pronounced as in English), h (= **ch**) the accent did not rest regularly upon the first syllable of a word as to-day but often rested upon another and often even fell upon different syllables in the same inflectional system, so that pre-Germanic accent must have been in general the same free stress as that originally found in the Indo-European family of languages and still preserved in part in Sanskrit and Greek. In this prehistoric period, as can be later seen in Gothic and less perfectly in Old English and other Germanic languages, the voiceless spirants **f**, th, h (= **ch**), s, remained voiceless only initially and after an accented vowel, but between voiced sounds after an unaccented vowel became voiced b, d, g, z (voiced s): 'kle*p*tō (Greek), hli*f*an (Gothic) *to steal*, but he*p*'ta (Greek), si*b*un (Gothic) *seven*; 'frā*t*er (Latin), brō*th*ar (Gothic), but pa'*t*ēr (Greek), fa*d*ar (Gothic) *father*; 'de*c*em (Latin), tai*h*un (Gothic) *ten*, but de'*k*u (pre-Germanic), ti*g*us (Gothic) *decade*; qui*s* (Latin) *some one or other*, hwa*z*uh (Gothic) *any one at all, every one*. Also the unaccented prefix ge (cognate with Latin *c*o-, *c*on-, *c*um) shows a voiced form of an originally voiceless consonant, i.e. **ch.** English should also in general show the same consonants here as the Gothic, but in the course of their development b, d, g have changed considerably, as described for the b's, d's, g's in **1.** *a*, above, and also *Notes* 3 and 4 thereunder.

Both of these groups—the b's, d's, g's from Indo-European bh, dh, gh and the b's, d's, g's from Germanic f, th, h (= **ch**) according to Verner's Law—which had come from originally quite different sources merged into one in prehistoric Germanic. From then on, the b's, d's, g's from both of these sources had the same development. Germanic z became r in English, and all the other members of the German family before the period of the second shifting: Eng. was, were; **was** (15th century, later leveled to **war** by the plural form), **waren.** The r from older z is found in the pronouns **er, ihr, mir, wir, ihr, wer,** in the plural ending **-er,** in the comparative ending **-er,** in the inseparable prefix **er-,** &c.

After the second shifting of the consonants had taken place in High German, the b, d, g, which resulted from f, th, h (**ch**) according to Verner's Law, appear as **b, t, g,** while the f, th, h (**ch**) which followed the accented vowel appear as **f, d, h (ch).** Germanic z had already become **r** previous to this shifting, while Germanic s remained **s.** Hence different consonants may still be found in the different grammatical forms of the same word or in related words, owing to the original difference of accent. Thus we find an occasional change of **f** to **b, d** to **t, h** to **g, s** to **r: Hof** and **hübsch, schneiden** and **schnitt, ziehen** and **zog, zehn** and **zwanzig, Frost** and **frieren.** The English consonants here as elsewhere did not participate in the second shift. Low German differing from English suffered also the change of *th* to *d,* but the change took place much later than in High German.

Note. A force somewhat similar to Verner's Law was again at work in English at the close of the Middle English period, especially in the final position after a vowel: *oath* with voiceless *th* after a stressed vowel, but the unstressed preposition *with* with voiced *th*; stressed *off* with voiceless *f,* but unstressed *of* with voiced f, i.e. v; voiced *s* after an unstressed vowel, as in kisses (kɪsɪz), &c.

b. The labialized velars g^wh, k^w, g^w of the parent Indo-European language shifted irregularly in different languages, altho they in general followed the laws described in the preceding articles. They consisted of a velar and a labial element. In the course of their development they lost by assimilation sometimes one of these elements, sometimes another, and were otherwise variously affected. The following table presents a general view of these changes:

I.-E. g^wh	Lat. f, gu, v	Germanic gw, g, w.
,, k^w	,, qu	,, hw, h; gw, g, w.
,, g^w	,, v, gu	,, qu (i.e. kw).

The Germanic g's in the second line are the result of development from h (= **ch**) under the operation of Verner's Law (see *a* above) and hence once followed an unaccented vowel. Only a few examples can be given here: angustus (L.), aggwus (Goth.), **eng** (G.); quis (L.), who (Eng.), **wer** (G.); linquo (L.), leihwan (Goth.), loan (Eng.), **leihen** (G.); tranquillus (L.), hweila (Goth.), while (Eng.), **Weile** (G.); aqua (L.), ahwa (Goth.), **-ach** (G.; see **245.** I. 18. *a*), as in **Salzach** (river), where the older sound of Germanic *h* is preserved; vivus (L.), quick (Eng.), **Quecksilber** (G.), **erquicken** (G.). It will be seen by a glance at the table that it does not contain consonants that were usually affected by the second shifting, so that in general we find the Germanic consonants still surviving in both English and German. In the individual life of the two languages, however, these consonants have here developed somewhat differently, as can be seen by the examples.

c. Germanic thw has developed peculiarly. It went over regularly into dw in O.H.G., and later in M.H.G. developed into tw, and still later in that period into zw: thwingan (Old Saxon), dwingan (O.H.G.), twingen (M.H.G.), zwingen (late M.H.G. and N.H.G.).

Germanic dw has had a similar development: dwarf (Eng.), twerg (O.H.G.), twerc (M.H.G.), **Zwerg** (N.H.G.).

High German tw, whether derived from Germanic thw or dw, has developed into **zw** or **qu.** A number of words fluctuate between the two forms, and in other cases independent differentiated forms have become established: **Zwerg** (literary German), **Querg** (East Middle German); **Quinger** (Lamentations II. 8) in modern editions **Zwinger; Zwerchfell** diaphragm, **quer** across.

Also **lw** and **rw** have had a peculiar development. In O.H.G. in the final position the **w,** at that time bilabial like English w (**34.** 1. *Note*), became o or u, which later was reduced to *e* and at the close of the M.H.G. period disappeared, but medially the **w** in late M.H.G. developed into **b,** at that time the bilabial spirant *v* (**34.** 1), a sound closely resembling the **w** but later developing into the stop **b** (**29**), altho it is still widely heard in the dialects of the Midland and the Southeast, also in sections of the North as a spirant: **Mehl** (O.H.G. melo), but **Schwalbe** (O.H.G. swalawa, Eng. swallow); **gar** (O.H.G. garo), but **gerben** (O.H.G. garawen). In case of inflected words we should expect to find a form without **b** in the final position and a form with **b** when a vowel follows in the inflectional ending, but usually leveling takes place, so that the one or the other form is extended thruout the inflectional system. In case of M.H.G. val, gen. valwes both forms survive as **fahl** and **falb,** sometimes without differentiation, sometimes slightly differentiated. This group of b's, the stop as well as the spirant b's, has joined the group of b's in 1. *a. Note* 3 above.

d. In the M.H.G. period, final **m** in an unaccented syllable developed into **n: Busen** boso*m*, **Faden** fatho*m*, &c. **Atem** forms an exception as the original final **m** has been retained after the analogy of the verb **atmen** (M.H.G. atemen), which naturally keeps the **m** as it is not the final sound.

e. Suppression of **n.** In the literary language **n** has disappeared in the combination **-ing** in those words the stems of which ended in an **n: König** for older **Köning,** &c. The form **Pfenning** was still in limited use in the classical period.

In dialect final **n** has disappeared in large parts of the Midland and South, especially in unaccented syllables. Occasionally such forms appear in books which reflect colloquial usage: **Fräulein, wie gefällt es Ihne** (for **Ihnen**) **denn in Schwaben?** (Raabe's *Pechlin*, chap. 12).

The opposite tendency, the insertion of an **n,** appears occasionally in the literary language as well as in dialect: **genung** (Goethe, Schiller, &c.) for **genug,** &c.

Notice that the m and n which preceded Germanic f, th, s have disappeared in English, while they still remain in German in the form of **n:** soft (O.E. sōfte), but **sanft** (O.H.G. semfti adj., samfto adv.); other, but **ander;** tooth, but **Zahn** (O.H.G. zand and zan); goose, but **Gans;** us, but **uns.** Of course, also in Low German, the parent of English, consequently also in literary German wherever Low German words with such a development have become established: **sacht** (from older L.G. sāfto, High German **sanft;** see *Note* 5 under 1. *b* above), English soft.

f. The older tongue **r** has been replaced by a uvular sound. See **34.** 6 and **37.** 2.

g. *The Origins and Developments of the S Sound*:

(1). *Germanic S.* The original Germanic s was a sound between s and ʃ. In the prehistoric period in accordance with Verner's Law (*a* above) it became voiced between vowels after an unaccented syllable and later developed into **r.** For examples see *a* above. In other positions it was in older periods a voiceless s. In North Germany this voiceless sound survived only in the positions described in **33.** 2. (**1**), (**2**). Initially before a vowel and medially between vowels it became voiced, i.e. became z: **Sohn** (zo:n), **lesen** (le:zən). Initially before **l, m, n, w, p, t,** as illustrated below, it developed into ʃ. In the South the old voiceless s remained intact except initially before **l, m, n, w, p, t,** where it developed into ʃ. This change to ʃ began in the South and in dialect has gone much farther there, taking place sometimes also before vowels and in the final position in case of the genitive ending **s.**

The development of s into ʃ has affected a large number of words. The present orthography reflects this change of sound in case of **schl, schm, schn, schw,** but not in case of initial **sp** (= ʃp) and **st** (= ʃt): sleht (O.H.G.), but **schlecht** (N.H.G.); smuz (O.H.G.), but **Schmutz** (N.H.G.); sprehhan (O.H.G.) and **sprechen** (N.H.G.). The beginning of this change cannot be accurately assigned to any definite time. It was a gradual development. It began in the South at the close of the thirteenth century and then spread. The orthography was slow to recognize these changes. As late as the sixteenth century we still find instances of **sl, sm,** &c., even in the South. This movement has not yet come to a close, for **sp** and **st** are still pronounced sp and st in Hanover, Holstein, Friesland, and Mecklenburg. The general pronunciation ʃp and ʃt has not yet found expression in the orthography as the pronunciation developed after the spelling had been well established in the usage of the printers. The sound changed, but the orthography remained.

Medial and final s became **sch** in a number of cases after **r: Bursche** (M.H.G. burse), **herrschen** (M.H.G. hērsen), &c., but **Durst, Ferse,** &c.

(2). *S from Germanic T.* In the second half of the thirteenth century the number of voiceless s's in German was increased by accessions from a new source. In the High German shifting of consonants Germanic t, corresponding to t in English bi*t*e, developed after a vowel thru ts into a voiceless lisped s. This sound is written z in O.H.G. and M.H.G. manuscripts but in learned works of to-day is represented by ʒ in order to indicate this pronunciation and distinguish it from the z = ts, which stood in other positions than after a vowel: M.H.G. **zwei** (tsvae), English two; biz (in M.H.G. manuscripts, but in modern learned works biʒ), English bite. In the second half of the thirteenth century ʒ fell together with Germanic s, but it must have been a little more strongly articulated because it did not later become voiced between vowels as Germanic s: **reisen** (ʀaezən, from M.H.G. reisen), but **reißen** (ʀaesən, from M.H.G. rīʒen). When final, before a consonant, or doubled they both still have the same voiceless sound, i.e. s, as at the close of the thirteenth century: **Kuß** (kʊs, from M.H.G. kus), **küßte** (kʏstə, from M.H.G. kuste), **küssen** (kʏs-sən, from M.H.G. küssen); **aß** (a:s, from M.H.G. aʒ), **es** (ɛs, now representing both the M.H.G. neut., nom., and acc. eʒ and gen. es (see **140.** *c*)), **gutes** (gu:təs, from M.H.G. guoteʒ), **ißt** (ɪst, from M.H.G. iʒʒet), **essen** (ɛs-sən, from M.H.G. eʒʒen). Initial s before a vowel is always the old Germanic s, but it is now voiced in the North: **Sohn** (zo:n), &c.

h. Foreign words of course form exceptions to the general rules for the development of German consonants and their relation to kindred languages. Recently adopted loan-words usually have the same form as they have in the language from which they were taken, sometimes, however, conforming to German orthography: **Chaussee** (Fr. chaussée), **Fabrik** (Fr. fabrique), &c. The older the words the more of course they have changed and taken on German form. If the words were borrowed before the period of the second shifting they developed in the same manner as German words: **Pflaume** (L. prūnum), **Kelch** (O.H.G. kelich, from the L. calicem), **Kerker** (from L. carcerem; **Karzer,** derived from the same word, was introduced into the language later by those acquainted with the form of the Latin but employing the modern pronunciation of it), **Kreuz** (from the L. crucem; a later introduction than **Kerker,** as can be seen by the modern pronunciation of the c), &c.

Syllables in Individual Words.

41. A word has as many syllables as it contains separate vowels or diphthongs: **Se'en, bau'en.** In dividing words into syllables when there are consonants at the close of the syllable, the division is based upon the following principles:

1. As in English a single consonantal sound between vowels belongs after a long vowel or diphthong to the following syllable, which is uniformly dynamic, i. e. begins with an increase of breath impulse: **hō\`len, ʹSprā\`che, ʹhei\`lig.** After a short vowel it is in the North as in English divided equally between the two syllables: **hassen, alle, erʹschrecken, lachen** (laxən), **singen** (zɪŋən). Such divided consonantal sounds are usually represented by double consonants (double **k** usually written **ck**) except in case of **ch** and **ng.** Altho the written language in these two cases does not by doubling indicate that the syllabic divide is *within* the consonant this division regularly takes place in the spoken language. In case of explosive consonants the explosion takes place in the second syllable at the end of the sound, as in **t** in **Hütte** (hytə). Wherever, as in all these cases, the double consonant is in a simple word the second syllable is static, i. e. begins without an increase of breath impulse so that the articulation glides along almost evenly and the two syllables are thus not separated by any appreciable mark. Where, however, the double consonant is in a compound the second syllable is dynamic, as in **mittun** (mɪt\`tu:n, or better míttù:n, as explained in **2** below). For convenience to indicate the kind of syllable the consonant is written single in the phonetic transcript to show that the second syllable is static and double when it is dynamic. Sometimes, however, when it is desirable to call especial attention to the fact that a consonant before a static syllable is divided it is written twice with a hyphen between the two characters: **al-le, has-sen,** &c., but **mit\`tun,** &c. with the sign for secondary stress to indicate that the syllable is dynamic.

In the Southwest there is often quite a different system of syllabic division. There it is usual to carry over the consonant to the next syllable wherever it can be easily done, not only after a long vowel but also after a short one: **holen** (ho:\`lən), **fassen** (fa-sən), &c. This syllabic division is not a modern development but a survival of older usage. See **4.** 1. b. *Note* and **4.** 2. B. *b. Note.* (1).

2. In common German words two or more consonantal sounds are after a long vowel or a diphthong carried over, wherever it can be easily done, to the following syllable, which is uniformly dynamic: **hū\`sten, Au\`ster, rē\`gnen, Rē\`dner, duzen** (du:\`tsən), **hā\`tscheln,** &c. The consonants, however, must be conveniently divided up between the syllables if it is difficult to carry them over: **sagte** (za:k\`tə), **rauchte** (ʀaox\`tə), &c. After a short vowel the second syllable is static, i. e. begins without a marked increase of breath impulse, so that the articulation glides along almost evenly and the two syllables are thus not separated by any appreciable divide: **fasten,** etc.

In case of compounds the second element, of course, begins with an increase of breath impulse as in a dynamic syllable in a simple word, but the impulse is much stronger and there is a slight pause between the two components: **táufèucht** *wèt with dêw.* The stress mark over the vowel indicates that the accent is group-stress (**50.** A. 6) rather than word-stress, for compounds originated in a group of words in a sentence and are still felt as groups as can be clearly seen in English, where a large number of Old English compounds are to-day represented by modern groups. Similarly in English we distinguish *bee\`stings* (first milk from a cow after calving) from *bêestìngs* and *selfish* (without an increase of breath in the second syllable) from *shéllfìsh.*

Note. Syllabic Division in Foreign Words. In foreign words where the vowel stands before a single consonant, **ti** (tsĭ), **z** (ts), **qu** (kv), a stop (**p, t, k, b, d, g**) + **r** or **l**, or a double consonant which is followed by an accented vowel, the syllable is open, i.e. terminates in a vowel and this vowel is long or half long except before a double consonant, where it is short: **Etymologie** (ʹe·ty·\`mo·lo·ʺgi:), **Bibliographie** (\`bi·bli·o·\`gʀa·ʺfi:), **Nation** (na·ʹtsĭo:n), **Akazie** (a·ʹka:\`tsĭə), **reziprok** (ʀe·tsi·ʹpʀo:k), **konsequent** (kɔnze·ʹkvɛnt), **Metrum** (me:\`tʀʊm), **Kommode** (kɔʹmo:\`də), **Kollege** (kɔʹle:\`gə). The accents indicate the beginning of a dynamic syllable and probably also the dots after the vowels indicate a faint increase of breath impulse. In all these cases the consonants are carried over to the next syllable. Notice how differently we pronounce these words in English: \`ɛtɪʹmɔlə\`dʒɪ, \`bɪblɪʹɔgrə\`fɪ, &c. As these vowels are in large measure short the syllables are closed, i.e. terminate in a consonant, which leads to the formation of static syllables. There is thus a tendency to form the syllables into groups of two or three, where only the first syllable in each group is dynamic. The German only forms static syllables after a double consonant which is not followed by an accented syllable and after a combination of consonants other than a stop + **r** or **l**: **Kollation** (kɔla·ʹtsĭo:n), **Kolportage** (kɔlpɔʀʹta:ʒə), **Zirkus** (tsɪʀkʊs). Notice that the first vowel here is short and that the syllable is closed. Compare **4.** 2. B. *c. Note.*

3. Compound words form exceptions to the above rules, as the syllabic division is made on etymological principles, and hence falls between the components: **Haus'tür, ent'äußern.**

a. Exceptions are **dar, war, her, hin,** when they stand before a vowel in compounds: **da'rüber, wa'rum, he'rum, hi'nein.** In the pronunciation of ordinary conversation other exceptions occur, as the distinct etymological elements are not always in the consciousness of the speaker: **be'ō'bachten, Ō'bacht, vo'llenden** (fɔ'lɛndən), **a'llein, Au-fent'halt,** &c., especially where the etymology has become obscured by sound changes, as in **em'pfangen** (**p** for older **t**), &c.

4. In unaccented **el, em, en, er,** the **e** in rapid talking often drops entirely out, and the consonants **l, m, n, r** become syllabic, i. e. form of themselves syllables, which is indicated by phonetists by the sign ₀ under the letter: **Hügel, liebem, lieben,** pro. hy:gl̥, li:bm̥, li:bn̥. In careless speech the front nasal, i. e. the dental nasal n, when syllabic, often becomes the labial nasal m after the labials **b, p, m,** and becomes the velar nasal ŋ after the velars ŋ and k and the uvular ʀ, i. e. becomes a back nasal after a back consonant: li:bm̥, lɪpm̥, na:mm̥ instead of **lieben, Lippen, Namen**; zɪŋŋ̥, daŋkŋ̥, va:ʀŋ̥ instead of **singen, danken, waren.**

All syllabic consonants fill out about the full time required to pronounce an unaccented syllable, and hence words containing them cannot form good rhymes with words containing unsyllabic consonants: thus **Karren** (kaʀn̥) should not rhyme with **Garn.**

Syllables in Connected Discourse.

42. In ordinary language, words often lose their etymological identity in our consciousness and different words blend together, and are often treated in actual practice as one word with different syllables, in which case the rules given above for separating syllables apply also here: **Heute nahm er das Buch mit** is pronounced **Heute nā-mer das Buch mit.**

Separation of Syllables at the End of a Line.

43. The separation of long words at the end of a line usually takes place according to the natural laws of separation in the spoken language as given above, but a few variations occur, and hence the complete rules are given as follows:

1. A consonant between two vowels belongs to the following syllable: **hü-ten, Le-ben,** &c.

2. If several consonants stand between vowels usually only the last one is carried over: **Rit-ter, Sperlin-ge** (pro. 'ʃpɛʀlɪŋə, i.e. ŋ being pronounced as any double consonant with both syllables), **klir-ren, Klemp-ner, Ach-sel, krat-zen, Städ-te, Verwand-te, kämp-fen, Karp-fen.**

3. **ß, ch, sch, ph, st, th** are never separated: **Bu-ße, Be-cher, Hä-scher,** (but **Häus-chen**; see 6 below), **Geogra-phie, La-sten, Klo-ster, Ma-thilde.**

4. **ck** is separated into **k-k: Dek-kel.**

5. In foreign words all combinations of **b, p, d, t, g, k** with **l** or **r** are carried over: **Pu-blikum, Me-trum, Hy-drant.**

6. Compound words are separated first into the different elements of which the compound consists, and within each element the rules given above are observed: **Fürsten-schloß, Tür-an-gel** (pro. aŋəl), **Häus-chen.** Notice **Schiffahrt,** &c. but at the end of the line separated **Schiff-fahrt,** &c.

a. This separation at the end of the line of compound words into their component elements will not always be the same as the pronunciation: **darum** (= **dar** + **um**) is separated **dar-um,** but pronounced **da'rum; Inter-esse** (= L. inter + esse), but pronounced **Inte'resse.**

Accent.

44. Particular syllables in a word or particular words in a sentence may be made prominent above others and distinguished by especial stress. Thus there is a *word accent* and a *sentence accent,* the latter of which is usually called group-stress, as the sentence falls into groups of words, each with a chief stress.

I. Word Accent.

45. In polysyllabic words there may be not only the principal accent, but also a secondary accent, and even a third, besides the unaccented syllables. The principal accent in the following articles will be marked by ′, or, if there are three accents, by ″, the secondary by ‵, or, if there are three, by ′, the third accent by ‵, the unaccented syllable by ˘: **Ber′lin, ′Luther, lu′the‵risch, ′Eigen‵tum, ′Vorur‵teil, ″Un‵ebĕn′heit.** The mark of accent is placed immediately *before* the stressed syllable. Where the principal accent is upon the first syllable the mark is usually omitted as the place of the accent is self-evident. When the marks of accent, as in the preceding examples, are placed before the accented syllables of a word the desire is to indicate the word-stress, the usual stress that the syllables of a word have. When the mark is placed *over* the vowel the desire thruout this book is to indicate group-stress, the stress which the word has when it stands as a component in a syntactical group of words, as in **der Àufgang der Sónne.** As such words often, as explained in **247. 2,** assume a oneness of meaning and hence are then written as one word, as in **Sónnenàufgang** *sûn-rise,* the mark is still often placed above the vowel to indicate that the word was originally a group of words and has retained its original group-stress.

Accent must not be confounded with quantity. A syllable may be long, i.e. contain a long vowel, or diphthong, or a short vowel followed by two or more consonants, and yet have weaker accent than a short syllable, as in **′Ab‵grund.**

The placing of the accent in German is regulated by the following principles:

1. *Normal accent.* Some particular syllable in a word, usually the root syllable in a simple word or a derivative and the modifying component element (see **248**) in a compound, receives the principal accent: **′singen, Ge′sang, ′Schulhaus.**

In words of more than one syllable a secondary stress often becomes necessary. If the word is a compound, that syllable in the basal component receives secondary accent, which would have principal accent if the component were an independent word: **′Durch‵messer, ′Fahr‵wasser, ′Haus‵herren.**

It will be noticed from these examples that this normal accent usually brings the chief stress upon the first syllable. This principle of accenting words is the leading one, but deviations occur, as described in 2, 3, 4 below.

Note. The results of the operation of Verner's Law (**40. 2.** *a*) make it plain that in the prehistoric period of the Germanic languages at the time of the shifting of the Indo-European stops p, t, k to the spirants f, th, h (= ch) the accent had not yet become fixed upon the first syllable of a simple word as we find it to-day. The original causes that later in this prehistoric period led to the fixing of the stress upon the first syllable of simple words are not known. As becomes probable, however, from **215.** 3. *Historical Note* and **247.** 2 the first member of a syntactical group of words was in the prehistoric period regularly stressed. A large number of compounds formed directly from these old syntactical groups have come down to us with their old stress. It seems quite probable that in the prehistoric period the stress of simple words gradually conformed to this old type, found not only in compounds but everywhere in the normal syntactical groups of the sentence. This seems all the more probable, as in our own time, as seen in **47.** 3. A. *e* and *g*, a very large number of modern formations, **an′statt, he′rab, berg′auf,** &c. have the new group-stress of our day, which now has the accent upon the second member of the group, and many old formations, as seen in **47.** 3. D. *a*, are giving up their older accent and are now conforming their stress to the new group-stress.

2. *Emphatic Accent.* The speaker may for some emotional reason place unusual stress upon some particular word, but he is then not content with accenting the syllable which usually has the stress, but also puts equal or perhaps a little stronger stress upon some other syllable, even tho it is usually unaccented, and thus arises a double accent: **′undank′bares Kind! eine ′ausge′sprochene Schönheit, ′end′loser Gram, ′wunder′licher Gedanke, ′gē′rechter Himmel! Er ist ein ′abge′feimter Schurke! Wir sind ′furcht′bar zurück! ′Unter′steh dich!** The tendency here is to make the second stress slightly stronger in order to preserve the unity of the word. Words that have this double accent are indicated in this treatise by a chief stress upon each of the two strongly accented syllables, altho the second stress is probably slightly stronger.

This emphatic stress is most commonly found in exclamations, especially in words that stand in the attributive relation: **ein ′unge′zogenes Betragen!,** but usually in the predicate: **Sein Betragen ist ′ungezogen** (Th. Ameis in Herrig's

Archiv, **49**, p. 231). Exclamations, which are among the oldest forms of speech, have had from earliest times the old attributive type of sentence structure, as explained in **252.** 1. *b. Note*, and do not even yet conform readily to the newer normal type of sentence which requires the predicate adjective to stand after the copula.

In a number of cases this emphatic stress has become so intimately associated with certain words which are often spoken with emphasis that the stronger of the two stresses, i.e. the one which rests upon the syllable that originally did not have the chief stress, often or in some cases even regularly remains in normal speech as the principal accent of the word: **ab'scheulich, all'mählich, aus'drücklich, ausge'zeichnet, außer'ordentlich, eigen'tümlich** (in the meaning *peculiar*, but **'eigentümlich** in the sense *as one's own property*, as in **etwas 'eigentümlich an sich bringen** to purchase something so that it becomes one's own property), **glück'selig, haupt'sächlich, über'schwenglich, un'endlich, unge'heuer, un'sterblich, ur'sprünglich, vor'züglich, wahr'haftig, wahr'scheinlich, zu'künftig.**

3. *Rhythmical Accent.* For physiological reasons it is difficult to pronounce two strongly accented syllables in succession. Therefore in such a case the accent is divided so that there will be a rhythmical succession of strong and weak syllables. This rhythmical principle is quite an important one in German and often disturbs the normal accent. Thus it is more common to-day to say **'Endur'teil, 'Schwimman'stalt, 'unab'hängig, 'unacht'sam,** than **'End'urteil, 'Schwimm'anstalt, 'un'abhängig, 'un'achtsam.**

4. *Foreign Accent.* In many foreign words the German principle of accenting is entirely abandoned in favor of the original accent of the foreign word, and hence in many words from the French and Latin the chief stress is found upon the last, or less frequently upon the next to the last, syllable: **Ele'fant, Initia'tive.** The accent upon the last syllable is, however, for rhythmical reasons *sometimes* removed to the first when the final syllable is followed by an accented syllable in the next word: **'General 'Blücher** instead of **Gene'ral 'Blücher; So'fie,** but **'Sofie 'Krause; der Rentier** (ʀɛn'tĭe:), but **der 'Rentier 'Schmidt.** This rhythmical accentuation has not yet become so well established in German that it *usually* displaces the regular stress upon the last syllable.

The secondary accent in these foreign words is usually upon the first syllable: **'Aktivi'tät, akkompagnieren** ('akɔmpan'ji:ʀən). Here again the rhythmical tendency to distribute the accented syllables so as to make a succession of strong and weak syllables sometimes disturbs the usual position of the secondary accent: a'kɔmpan'ji:ʀən instead of 'akɔmpan'ji:ʀən. In long words there may be a third stress: **Respektabilität** ('ʀe·spɛk'ta·bi·li·''tɛ:t or ʀe·'spɛkta·'bi·li·''tɛ:t), **Etymologie** ('e·ty·'mo·lo·''gi:). A marked peculiarity of German stress in these long foreign words is that the accents are distributed over the whole word, so that the different vowels do not suffer much in quantity or quality, while in English one strong stress carries two or more weak syllables, so that the weakly stressed vowels suffer in quantity and quality. A fuller discussion is found in **4.** 2. B. *c. Note* and **41.** 2. *Note.*

II. Sentence Accent.

46. Logical and emphatic stress prevail in sentence accent. All that seems to the speaker logically more important or as weightier from the standpoint of his own feeling is made prominent by accent. The number of shades in stress is here much greater than in word accent, some being more or less marked, others very fine and scarcely perceptible. The short sentence **Wo wollt ihr denn hin?** may be read with the following accentuations according as the one or the other word becomes logically more important: $\overset{1}{\textbf{Wo}}$ $\overset{4}{\textbf{wollt}}$ $\overset{2}{\textbf{ihr}}$ $\overset{5}{\textbf{denn}}$ $\overset{3}{\textbf{hin?}}$ or $\overset{4}{\textbf{Wo}}$ $\overset{3}{\textbf{wollt}}$ $\overset{1}{\textbf{ihr}}$ $\overset{5}{\textbf{denn}}$ $\overset{2}{\textbf{hin?}}$ or $\overset{4}{\textbf{Wo}}$ $\overset{2}{\textbf{wollt}}$ $\overset{3}{\textbf{ihr}}$ $\overset{5}{\textbf{denn}}$ $\overset{1}{\textbf{hin?}}$ The lower numbers here denote stronger, the higher numbers weaker accent.

DETAILS CONCERNING ACCENT.

I. Word Accent.

Principal Accent.

47. 1. *Accent in Simple Stem Words.* The root syllable has here the accent: **'Sprache, 'gingen, 'gutem.**

2. *Accent in Derivative Words.* Words with suffixes and prefixes are often differently accented.

A. *Accent of Words with Suffixes.* In words with suffixes the principal accent rests upon the root syllable: **'Bäcker, 'hei'lig, 'traum'haft.**

The following exceptions occur:

a. Words ending in the suffix **-lei** have fluctuating stress with the principal accent now upon the root syllable, now on the suffix. See **47.** 3. A. *b. cc.*

b. A few words have from various causes shifted their accent from the root syllable: the verbs in **178.** 2. A. *b.* (**3**) so far as they are of German origin, as **schar'wenzeln, schma'rotzen, kla'bastern, kar'nüffeln,** &c.; **Hor'nisse** (also **'Hornisse**), **le'bendig** (in the eighteenth century also the older form **'lebendig**), **Wa'cholder, Ho'lunder;** sometimes **offen'bar, unmittel'bar** (or more commonly **'offenbar, 'unmittelbar**), and regularly a number of other similar words given in **45.** 2; **Fo'relle, Herme'līn, Wal'küre** (on the stage **'Walküre**); a few feminine Christian names, the second component of which ends in an unaccented syllable, as **Ger'trude** (but **'Gertrud**), **Kuni'gunde,** &c.; in the North often names in **-līn,** as **Böck'līn** (instead of the more correct S.G. **'Böcklīn**).

Note. The origin of many of the German verbs in **178.** 2. A. *b.* (**3**) referred to above is not clearly understood. Some see in the first syllable an arbitrary insertion of a vowel and a consonant, so that the accent remains in fact upon the root syllable: **schar'wenzeln** from **schwänzeln,** &c. In many cases it seems more probable that these verbs are onomatopœic formations and hence naturally in accordance with **47.** 3. A. *e.* (**11**) are accented on the last element. In some words, as **will'fahren,** where the syntactical relation of the components is not clear, there is a natural tendency to stress the second element and thus conform to normal group-stress (**50.** A. 6), which requires accent upon the second member. The accent in **le'bendig, Ho'lunder, Wa'cholder, Fo'relle,** &c. is usually explained by the weight of the second syllable, but there may be other factors involved. The stress **le'bendig** may be the result of emphatic stress, as in **45.** 2, for it is often used in emphatic language, as in **Er ist ein 'le'bendiger Beweis dafür!** The same is true of **offen'bar, unmittel'bar. Fo'relle, Hor'nisse, Herme'līn, Ho'lunder, Wa'cholder** may have developed their present stress from the resemblance of their form to foreign words of similar appearance, as **Li'belle, Nar'zisse, Ber'līn, Ka'lender, Ole'ander.**

c. A very large number of foreign words have the accent upon the last or next to the last syllable: **Infini'tiv, Initia'tive,** &c. There is a tendency for those accented upon the last syllable to shift it upon the first in accordance with German fashion: **'Infinitiv,** &c.; especially in case of contrast, as in **'Singular** in contrast to **'Plural, 'Objekt** in contrast to **'Subjekt,** &c. Some, as **'Kompaß,** have become thoroly naturalized and have the accent upon the first syllable. Those in **-ik** have the accent upon the stem where they are derived directly from the Latin but receive the stress upon the suffix where they have entered the language thru the French: **Ar'senīk, Bo'tanīk, 'Chronīk, Gra'mmatīk, 'Metrīk, Po'ētīk, Rhe'torīk, 'Taktīk, 'Technīk; Fa'brīk, Katho'līk** (but **ka'tholisch**), **Poli'tīk, Phy'sīk,** formerly **'Musīk** with Latin accent, now in French form **Mu'sīk;** sometimes with fluctuating stress: **Arithme'tīk** or **Arith'metīk, Meta'physīk** or **Metaphy'sīk, Mathema'tīk** or **Mathe'matīk,** &c. Notice especially the accented ending **īn,** as in **Ber'līn,** &c.

Foreign names of nationalities in **-er** accent the next to the last syllable, if that syllable is long, otherwise the first syllable: **He'brāer, Kar'thāger,** but **'Arāber, 'Itāler.**

A number of accented foreign suffixes are also now added to German words, especially **'āge, 'ālie, 'āner, 'ant, 'ei, 'eien** (infinitive ending), **'enser, 'ieren** (infinitive ending), **'ierung, 'ist, 'ös: La'ppālie, Weima'rāner,** inhabitant of Weimar, **Bäcke'rei, kas'teien, Je'nenser** inhabitant of Jena, **stol'zieren, schaude'rös** (slang) frightful, **pe'chös** (slang) unfortunate.

d. In adding the German suffix **isch** to words, foreign adjectives have the accent upon the syllable preceding **isch,** while German words accent the root syllable: **a'rabisch, ä'therisch,** but **'klopstockisch** or **'klopstocksch.** Only **lu'therisch** *Lutheran* among German words, as **in die lu'therische Kirche,** has here foreign accent. This word has also a regular German accent, but with a different shade of meaning: **'Luther(i)sch** *Luther's, coming from Luther,* as **die 'luther(i)sche Bibelübersetzung.** Catholics and often Protestants pronounce this word **'lutherisch** in both of these meanings.

B. *Accent of Words with Prefixes.* Prefixes are differently accented, as follows:

a. Adjectives or substantives with the prefix **ge-** are accented upon the root syllable, those with **ant-, et-, miß** upon the prefix, those with **un-** sometimes upon the root syllable, sometimes upon the prefix: **Ge'sang, 'Antwort, 'etwas, 'Mißmut; 'Unhold,** but **unüber'sehbar.** Nouns with **un-** and monosyllabic and also polysyllabic adjectives with **un-,** provided they do not end in **-lich, -bar,** or **-sam,** accent usually the prefix, while perfect participles with **un-,** and polysyllabic adjectives with **un-** and at the same time the suffixes **-lich, -bar,** or **-sam,** take usually the stress upon the root syllable, the last group, however, only when the words have passive force: **'Unmensch, 'Ursprung, 'unpaß, 'unabhängig, 'unvorteilhaft, 'unvermögend; unent'wegt, unge'logen, unver'dient, unbe'schäftigt; uner'forschlich, unaus'führbar, unauf'haltsam,** but **'unerfreulich, 'untauglich,** &c., as they have active force. The passive idea naturally suggests verbal force and leads to the stressing of the verbal stem. A few in **-lich** have the accent upon the root syllable, altho they do not have passive force, as they have emphatic accent (see **45.** 2 above): **un'möglich, un'endlich, un'sterblich, unver'züglich,** &c. Even where the meaning is passive we find the accent upon the prefix if the idea is that of actuality rather than mere possibility: **'unausführlich** *not carried out in detail,* but **unaus'führlich** or **unaus'führbar** *impracticable.* The **un-** is stressed in the first example as the idea of actuality, a finished condition of things, suggests adjective force, while the idea of possibility suggests verbal force, hence stress upon the verb in the second and third examples. Usage fluctuates with regard to the accent of the participle with the prefix **un-**, but there is a marked tendency to place the accent upon the root syllable in the predicate relation and upon **un-** in attributive function: **Der Brief ist unge'öffnet,** but **der 'ungeöffnete Brief.** The **un-** is stressed in the attributive relation standing before the governing noun, as the adjective force in this form is vividly felt. On the other hand, the verbal stem is stressed in the predicate relation as the verbal force is here distinctly felt, while the **un-** naturally loses its accent as the negative with verbs is usually unstressed. See also **246.** I. 9. *a* (2nd par.). The strong stress on **un-** in adjectives often causes a following accented syllable to lose its stress. See **45.** 3. Participles, however, in which **un-** stands before an accented prefix take the chief stress upon **un-** in the attributive relation but have it usually upon the following accented prefix in the predicate relation: **eine ganz 'unange\`brachte Sparsamkeit,** but **Sparsamkeit ist hier ganz un'ange\`bracht.** With reference to **un-** it should not be forgotten that here as elsewhere logic is sovereign and may disturb all these rules: **ein 'unfeines Benehmen, ein 'unkluges Benehmen,** but **ein un'feines und zugleich un'kluges Benehmen. Der Leib des Menschen ist 'sterblich, seine Seele aber ist 'unsterblich.**

b. The verbal prefixes **be, emp, ent, er, ge, ver, zer,** and usually **miß,** are unaccented: **be'fehlen, zer'schlagen.** For the explanation of the lack of accent in these prefixes see *c* below and **215.** I. 3. *Historical Note.* The accent of verbal prefixes is treated at length in articles **215.** I and II and **246.** II. 8.

c. Nouns and adjectives on the one hand and verbs on the other are sometimes differently treated with regard to accent. Derivative and compound nouns and adjectives have the accent upon the first component, while firm derivative and compound verbs with the same components have the stress upon the second component: **'Durchstich,** but **durch'stechen.** This difference is explained by prehistoric conditions. In the prehistoric period nouns and adjectives readily formed compounds as attested by the large number that have come down to us. At that time as to-day a compound was made up of a group of words that stand in a syntactical relation to each other: **'Haustür** (= **die Tür des Hauses**). In this book such a compound is often called a group-word. See **247.** 2 for fuller information. In these oldest compounds or group-words the modifying component regularly preceded the governing component and in accord with its importance regularly received the principal stress. In the later development of the language the modifier usually followed the governing word but retained its old stress, so that in these modern groups the second member has the principal accent: **die Mùtter des Júngen.** When such a modern group was felt as a unit and thus became a modern compound or group-word it retained its modern group-stress: **die Mùttergóttes** *the picture of the Virgin Mary.* Thus there are two types of compounds or group-words, the older group with the stress upon the first component, the modern group with the stress upon the second member. The older type, however, is still a powerful factor in the language and sometimes influences the modern compounds, as described in **249.** II. 2, and often leads to the formation of new compounds and group-words with the form and accent of the old type. Compare 3. B. *a* below.

On the other hand, firm verbal compounds with the stress upon the first component have not had such a rich development. Few such firm verbal compounds have come down to us from the prehistoric period and these few soon disappeared, as explained in **215.** I. 3. *Historical Note.* Even to-day verbs cannot enter into firm compounds with the stress upon the first component. Thus tho there are a very great number of such adjective and substantive compounds there is not a single firm compound verb of this type. In oldest German, however, just as to-day, we find verbs that have entered into firm relations with weakly stressed adverbs which stand before them and modify somewhat their meaning or serve as prepositions to indicate the direction of the activity: ir'teilen, duruh'faran, modern **er'teilen, durch'fahren.** Some of these adverbs have lost much of their older form thru loss of stress, as **er-** (from older *ur*), **ver-** (= Gothic *faur, fra, fair* in the fourth century), &c. If such adverbs are also found as the first component in compound nouns they have a fuller form, as their strong stress in nouns has preserved their older fuller form, as in **'Urteil** (corresponding in etymology tho not in meaning to **er'teilen**). See also **215.** I. 3. *Historical Note.*

This difference of development in derivative and compound nouns and verbs has left the following traces behind:

aa. **Ant** and **ur,** prefixes of nouns, are accented, and have thus with the aid of accent retained their full vowels, while the same prefixes have in verbs, by reason of their weak accent, lost their fullness of vowel and been reduced to the forms **ent** and **er: 'Urteil,** but **er'teilen; 'Antwort,** but **ent'sprechen.** When nouns are formed with **ent** and **er,** they are not direct compounds, but are derived from verbs: **Ent'schuldigung** from **ent'schuldigen, Er'werbung** from **er'werben. Antworten, urteilen** are derived from the nouns **Antwort, Urteil.**

In oldest German also **be-** and **ver-** were stressed when used as prefixes of nouns, just as at present **ant-** and **ur-.** Later they lost their accent as they were so much used in verbs with weak stress that this stress became uniform. A few isolated examples of stressed **be-** in its older form **bi-** survive, as the present form is so different from **be-** that it is not felt as the prefix **be-: 'bieder,** from M.H.G. 'biderbe; **'Beichte** from M.H.G. bīht, from older 'bijiht.

bb. In nouns and adjectives the prefix **miß** is usually accented, while in verbs it is usually unaccented: **'Mißbrauch, 'mißbräuchlich,** but **miß'brauchen.** In verbs, however, there is at present a marked tendency to shift the accent upon the prefix: **'mißbrauchen** instead of **miß'brauchen.** For explanation of this shifting of the accent see **246.** II. 8. Nouns derived directly from verbs have verb accent: **Miß'handlung** from **miß'handeln.** Sometimes the same word has verb or noun accent according as the influence of the verb or noun is felt: **das Miß'trauen in die** (the acc. showing the direction of an activity toward) **Bevölkerung** *distrust in the people,* but **das 'Mißtrauen in der Bevölkerung** *the distrust that prevails among the people.*

cc. The difference in the accent of *compound* nouns and verbs is treated in 3. B. *a* below.

3. *Accent of Compounds.* The compound formations of the different periods, which in 2. B. *c* above and in **247.** 2. *a, b, c* are distinguished more accurately as old, younger, and modern group-words, are here for sake of brevity called compounds. The rules here given refer uniformly to the older formations except where otherwise expressly stated.

A. *Accent of Compound Nouns and Adjectives.* The modifying component usually takes the principal accent: **'Hauptmann, 'Lesebuch.** This brings the accent usually upon the first syllable.

There are a number of exceptions:—

a. A number of compound adjectives and adverbs in **-ig, -lich, -los,** have the accent upon the stem of the second component: **not'wendig, ab'sichtlich, heil'los.** This accent is the result of the emphatic stress which they often have in forcible language. See **45.** 2. The regular accent upon the modifying component is also common: **'notwendig,** &c. A number of other common compounds much used in emphatic language take emphatic stress: **ausge'zeichnet** excellent, &c.

In a number of other compounds the accent upon the second component seems to result from the tendency to follow the rhythm of the sentence, i. e. to conform to normal group-stress (**50.** A. 6), which requires accent upon the second member of a group: **barm'herzig, drei'einig, leib'haftig, leib'eigen, teil'haftig,** &c. In all these words there is an unaccented syllable after the second root syllable. Compare 3. D. *a* below. Also the strong descriptive force in these compounds tends to favor the stress upon the second component. See **247.** 2. *b.*

b. In some compounds the accent has not yet settled down definitely upon either element, since the logical force of neither is strongly pronounced. In this case the accent fluctuates according to the position of the word in the sentence. At the end of the sentence or within the sentence wherever no strongly stressed word immediately follows, the word is accented upon the second element, within the sentence, when an accented word follows, the first element is accented: **Der Mensch ist noch blut'jung,** but **ein 'blutjunger Mensch.** Words that have this fluctuating accent are indicated in this treatise by a chief stress upon each element: **'blut'jung.** This must, however, not be construed as equality of stress, for the one or the other of the elements is usually stressed with a little more force to indicate the unity of the group. There is a tendency here, as elsewhere in modern groups with descriptive force (**247.** 2. *b.*), toward a stronger stress upon the second element: **'schnee'weiß,** but **Schnee'weißchen** or **Schnee'wittchen** (name), etc. Many of these words are used in emphatic language and the stress is then the emphatic stress described in **45.** 2.

These words are:—

aa. Compounds of which the first element is a substantive that does not contain an essential modification of the basal component, but only strengthens it by giving a concrete illustration of the general idea already contained in it: **'haar'scharf, 'mause'tot, 'blut'rot, 'pech'schwarz, 'baum'stark, 'wunder'schön, 'feder'leicht, 'sonnen'klar, 'stock'blind, 'gras'grün,** &c.

Similar to these formations are the compounds the first component of which does not have its literal meaning but contains mere strengthening force, such as often the prefixes **erz-, un-, ur-** and nouns like **Hunde-, Mords-,** &c.: **'Erzbe'trüger, 'erz'dumm, 'Un'summen, 'ur'alt, 'Hunde'kälte, 'hunde'müde, 'Mords'kerl,** &c.

bb. Thus also compounds of which the first element is an adjective or adverb that does not contain an essential modification, but only strengthens or defines more definitely the general idea contained in the second element: **'hell'gelb, 'dunkel'gelb, 'wild'fremd, 'schreiend 'rot, 'vielge'nannt, 'klein'winzig,** &c.

cc. A number of uninflected compounds: **'aller'hand, 'aller'lei, 'der'lei, 'einer'lei, 'meines'gleichen,** &c.; certain adverbs, as **'aller'orts,** &c.

c. Sometimes there is a difference of meaning in connection with a difference of accent: **'steinreich** *stony,* but **'stein'reich** *very rich;* **'Erzbischof** *archbishop,* but **'Erz'schelm** *arrant knave;* **'Unmensch** *inhumane creature,* but **'Un'summen** *enormous sums;* **ein 'außerordentlicher Professor** *an assistant professor,* but **ein 'außer'ordentlicher Professor** *a professor of extraordinary merit;* **'Donnerwetter** *thunderstorm,* but **'Donner'wetter** (exclamation or oath); **'ausgezeichnet** (participle) *distinguished,* but **ausge'zeichnet** (adj.) *splendid.* The accent upon the first syllable marks the element as a modifying one, while the double accent indicates fluctuating (*b*) or emphatic (**45.** 2) stress and the lack of stress upon the first element shows the result of emphatic stress, as in **45.** 2.

d. The adjectives and adverbs **all, groß,** and especially words that have intensifying force, as **hoch, wohl,** &c., usually have chief stress in compound nouns, while they have secondary or fluctuating (see *b. aa* and *bb* above) stress in adjective compounds: **'Allmacht, 'Großmacht, 'Hochdeutsch, 'Wohlstand,** but **all'mächtig, 'groß'mächtig, 'hoch'weise, wohl'edel, 'hoch'fein,** &c. It must be noticed, however, that nouns made from these adjectives also have the accent of the adjectives: **allge'mein** and **Allge'meinheit.** Notice **'Alltag** *week-day,* **'alltäglich** *on week* *days*, but **all'täglich** *daily*. The difference in accent usually found between nouns and adjectives comes from the fact that the modifying force of the component is felt in nouns, while in adjectives it is destroyed by emphatic accent, or the first component has only strengthening force, as in *b. aa* and *bb* above. Also in adjectives the first component must have accent when it really contains an essential modification of the basal component: **'allseitig, 'großmütig, 'hochdeutsch, 'wohlgeboren.** Notice, however, that the second component in other compounds may take the accent for quite a different reason from that given for the above-mentioned adjectives, namely, because it becomes logically emphatic: **alt'indisch** in contrast to **alt'nordisch,** but **'altenglisch** in contrast to **'neuenglisch.**

e. Accent of Modern Compounds. A large number of compounds, called modern compounds (**247.** 2. *c*), have the stress of a modern group. In spoken language a sentence is not a unit, but is made up of groups of words. The unity of each group is usually indicated by a stress upon the last member of the group. A few illustrations of this modern group-stress may serve to explain many deviations from the rules given above for accent in compounds: (**1**) Adjectives compounded with a substantive have usually the accent, but, as adjectives standing before nouns in the syntactical structure of a sentence shift the accent upon the noun, so may such syntactical constructions retain their original group-stress when they are written together and spoken as one word, i.e. as a modern compound: **'Jungfrau, 'Graubart,** but **der Hohe'priester, Geheime'rat** (but **Ge'heimrat,** when the syntactical structure is broken and an old compound is formed). Compare **50.** A. 6. *b*. (**2**) The articles in modern compounds remain unaccented as in a modern group: **der'selbe, des'gleichen, ein'mal** (but **'einmal** *once*, as **ein** is a numeral and not an article) *once upon a time*, but **'derjenige,** as the demonstrative force is felt. (**3**) An attributive genitive in modern compounds takes, as in a modern group, the accent if it follows the dependent noun: **Mutter'gottes, zeit'lebens.** If the governing noun follows, it is accented in case of compounds denoting a period of time, as in **Tages'anfang,** thus retaining here also the original modern group-stress, while other compounds of this form are usually old compounds and take the accent upon the first component. (**4**) A name of a material or something measurable when compounded with some word denoting a measure, quantity, or weight takes the accent as in a modern group: **Viertel'stunde, Viertel'jahr,** but **'Halbjahr,** as it is an old compound. (**5**) Prepositions in modern compounds remain unaccented, as in a modern group: **ab'handen, ab'seiten.** (**6**) Numeral compounds take the accent upon the last element, except in the attributive relation, where the first element is accented: **fünfund'zwanzig, drei'hundert, dritte'halb,** but **'fünfundzwanzig Mann, 'dreihundert Mann, 'drittehalb Liter.** (**7**) The last part of the name of an individual takes the accent as in a modern group: **Hans'wurst** (also **'Hanswurst**) jack-pudding. (**8**) When a whole sentence becomes a compound, the accent varies according as it is felt as a modern or an old compound: **Lebe'hoch, gott'lob,** but **'Kehraus, 'Saufaus, 'Packan.** Compare carefully **249.** II. 2. Modern group stress is very common in a large number of fragments of sentences, as **berg'an, berg'auf, nach'dem,** &c. (**9**) Points of the compass have accent upon the last element: **Nord'ost, Süd'ost, Nord'west.** (**10**) Co-ordination is indicated by a strong accent upon each element but with a little stronger stress upon the last one to indicate the unity of the group, as in **schwarzweiß'rot, deutschfran'zösisch, Schleswig-'Holstein.** (**11**) In a very large number of words, especially onomatopœic formations and compounds in which the original meaning of the components is no longer clear and in which there is no essential modification of the basal component felt, the unity of the different elements of the word is indicated as in a group of words in a sentence by placing the accent upon the last member of the group: **kladdera'datsch, par'dauz, piff'paff, kla'bastern** (see **47.** 2. A. *b. Note*), **Schla'fittchen, Schla'raffe, das Ab'c,** &c.

f. The following modern formations have the accent upon the second element as that element distinguishes them from other words of similar formation: **Jahr'hundert, Jahr'tausend, Jahr'zehnt.**

g. Accent of Compound Proper Names. No absolute rules can be given for the accent of names of places, as there are two different types without fixed rules for their use. In most words the place is pointed out by a strong logical stress upon the first member to distinguish it from other places with the same basal component: **'Altenburg** in contrast to **'Neuenburg; 'Königsberg** in contrast to **'Fürstenberg, 'Wittenberg, 'Friedberg,** &c. In many words, on the other hand, the evident aim is not to *distinguish* one place from another, but rather to point it out by *describing* it in normal language, i.e. with the stress upon the second component as in a modern group (**247.** 2. *b*, *c* and **249.** II. 2.): **'Neuen'teich** (=**zum nèuen Téich**), **'Witten'berge, 'Hohen-'zollern, 'Hohen'staufen, 'Schön'brunn, 'Neu'york, 'Großber'lin, 'Zwei'brücken, 'Friedrichs-'hafen, 'Wilhelms'höhe, 'Ludwigs'lust, 'Königs'hütte,** &c. In many words where the first component cannot possibly be construed as having logical distinguishing force it is natural to put the stress upon the second member as in a modern group: **'Österreich-'Ungarn, 'Elsaß-'Lothringen, 'Schleswig-'Holstein.** Compare *e.* (**10**) above. The first component, however, must in all cases take the accent when it becomes essential to the thought, as for instance to make a contrast: **'Alt'strelitz, 'Neu'strelitz,** but **Ich wohne nicht in 'Neu'strelitz, sondern in 'Alt'strelitz.** There is considerable fluctuation in stress in different sections of the country, as to one section descriptive stress is sufficiently clear, while to another distinguishing stress seems necessary in order to keep the place distinct from an other name with the same basal component. See **249.** II. 2. Compare **247.** 2. *b*, *c*.

B. *Accent of Compound Verbs.* The accent here depends upon whether the parts are separable or firmly united: (**1**) If the modifying component is separable, it is accented: **'aufstehen, 'untergehen, 'ausgehen.** (**2**) If the modifying component is inseparable, it is unaccented:

über'setzen, voll'ziehen. The adjective **voll'kommen** *complete, perfect,* belongs here, as it is in fact the perf. participle of the lost inseparable **voll'kommen.** The adjective participle **will-'kommen** *welcome* has been influenced in its accent by **voll'kommen.** (**3**) If the verbal compound is not directly compounded, but has been formed from a compound noun, it has noun accent: **'frühstücken.** This subject is treated at length in articles **215–218.** For the historical explanation of the accent of compound verbs see 2. B. *c* above and **215.** I. 3. *Historical Note.*

a. Nouns formed from these verbs retain the accent of the verb: **voll'ziehen, Voll'zug; 'vorfallen, 'Vorfall.**

However, here, as in 2. B. *c. aa* above, we find in one group of words a different treatment of noun and verb. Nouns in composition with **durch, hinter, über, um, unter, wider,** have uniformly the accent upon the prefix, altho the corresponding verb is accented upon the verbal stem: **'Widerspruch,** but **wider'sprechen; 'Durchstich,** but **durch'stechen; 'Überschlag,** but **über'schlagen; 'Unterhalt,** but **unter'halten.** Many of these nouns are modern formations, as **'Überschlag,** and tho formed from verbs with the accent upon the second component of the compound, they have the stress upon the first component after the analogy of the many old compound nouns of the language which have this stress, as described in 2. B. *c* above. This is true, however, only when they are felt vividly as nouns. Whenever the noun has an ending which has strong verbal force, such as **-ung** and the **-en** of the infinitive, they have the stress of verbs: **der 'Durchstich** the cut, excavation that has been made thru a dike, hill, &c., but **beim Durch-'stechen** or **bei der Durch'stechung des Deiches,** where the idea of verbal activity is prominent.

b. In older periods of the language the perfect participle like other adjectives took the accent upon the first syllable and hence upon the prefix, while in case of verbs compounded with a proclitic adverb (i.e. an inseparable prefix) the pure verbal forms had group-stress, i.e. accent upon the verbal stem, as explained in 2. B. *c* above. The old manner of accenting the participle may still survive in the one participial adjective **'untertan** *subject to,* participle of the now obsolete **unter'tun** (still found in early N.H.G.; see 1 Cor. xv. 27). It is quite possible here, however, that the present accent of the adjective participle is modern, the accent shifting from the verbal stem to the prefix, as the word was felt as an adjective and noun, and all relation to the lost **unter'tun** was forgotten. Aside from this isolated example the accent of the participle now follows that of the verb: **voll'zogen,** part. of **voll'ziehen.**

C. *Accent of Compound Adverbs and Interjections.* The accent here rests usually upon the last syllable as modern group-stress prevails here (see 3. A. *e.* (**8**) and (**11**) above): **berg'auf, strom'ab, hi'nüber, her'vor, da'rauf, vie'lleicht, viel'mehr, juch'hei!** The logical importance of some other syllable often causes exceptions to this rule: **da'durch, da'rin,** &c. become **'dadurch, 'darin** when the demonstrative force is felt. See **141.** 5. A. *b.*

D. *Accent of Decomposite Words.* Altho a compound may consist of two words or several, it can as a rule have only two component elements—the *basal component,* which contains the more general idea, and the *modifying component,* which contains an essential modification. Either component may be a compound. The stress of the modifying component of decomposites is regulated by the principles given in A and B above for simple compound nouns, adjectives, and verbs: **'Bundestagsbeschluß** (**'Bundestag + Be'schluß**), **'vorurteilsfrei** (**'Vorurteil + frei**), **über'vorteilen** (**über + 'vorteilen**), and many compounds (see **245.** IV. 3. B) which are not yet generally written as one word, such as **in'stand setzen, zu'grunde legen.** Nouns made from this last class of verbs retain the verb accent and are usually written as true compounds in one word: **In'standsetzung, Zu'grundelegung.** If the compound has more than two components it is usually a modern compound, i.e. a whole sentence or a syntactical fragment of a sentence which is written as one word, or it may be a mere co-ordination of words. Such a modern compound has in some cases group-stress upon the last member and in others accent upon the first syllable after the manner of an old compound: **Einmal'eins, sechshundertund'dreißig, schwarz-rot'goldene Fahne,** but **'Stelldichein, 'Springinsfeld.** For fuller discussion see **249.** II. 2.

a. Many exceptions are found to the above general rules. There is an evident tendency in long words, which in reality consist of a group of words, to shift the accent from the first component to the second, if the latter is compound, in accordance with the natural impulse to conform to the usual law observed in stressing groups of words in the sentence, namely in a group consisting of two distinct components to stress the second component, as described in **50.** A. 6. This occurs especially in case of: (**1**) The names of certain church festivals or holidays: **Palm-'sonntag, Kar'freitag, Ascher'mittwoch,** &c. (**2**) Many titles or official positions: **Feld'zeugmeister, Vize'feldwebel, General'postmeister,** especially those in **ober-** and **unter-,** as **Ober-'staatsanwalt, Unter'staatssekretär.** Many other words of this form but with different meaning, as **Kriegs'schauplatz,** &c., often have this stress, as it is a question of form not meaning. The longer the compound the stronger the tendency to conform to the normal group-stress of the sentence. In the North, where we often hear **Vor'mittag, Nach'mittag,** &c., instead of the regular **'Vormittag,** &c., this tendency is more widespread than in the South, is found sometimes even in compounds with a simple basal component, as in **Bürger'meister, Rats'keller** (in Bremen), **Lebens'mittel,** &c. This stressing of the basal component has become generally established in the words in **47.** 3. A. *a* (2nd par.) with a dissyllabic basal component, as **leib'haftig,** also in certain names ending in an unaccented syllable, as **Ger'trude, Ma'thilde,** &c., but not **Ger'trud.** The hesitation to follow this tendency where the accent would fall on the last syllable is observable elsewhere. Many words like **Landge'richtsrat** with a compound modifying component and a simple basal component often have the chief stress upon the second member of the modifying component instead of the regular stress upon the first member and thus conform in general to the normal group-stress of the sentence in that the stronger stress follows the weaker. Such words cannot take the stress upon the monosyllabic basal component and thus conform closely to the normal group-stress of the sentence, for the stress upon the final syllable of a word would give the impression of foreign origin. A modern *group* takes the stress upon the final member but a native German *word* is only stressed on the last syllable when it originated in a modern group: **Neuen'teich (zum neuen Téich), Schön'bronn, an'statt, Viertel'jahr,** &c.

E. *Accent of Derivatives formed from Compounds and Compounds formed from Derivatives.* A derivative formed from a compound is accented as a derivative, but a compound in which the basal component is a derivative is accented as a compound: **Liebhabe'rei ('Liebhaber + ei),** but **'Stadtpolizei (Stadt + Poli'zei); Schriftstelle'rei ('Schriftsteller + ei),** but **'Paßschererei (Paß + Schere'rei).**

4. *Pronunciation of Foreign Words.* The accent here depends upon whether the word is still distinctly felt as a foreign or as a German word. Many foreign words have been thoroly naturalized and have received German accent, many others are sometimes pronounced as foreign words sometimes as German words; the greater number, however, still retain the accent of the language, from which they were borrowed. Some words which are now accented as German words had foreign accent in earlier periods of the language. In view of the great irregularity that here prevails, this subject cannot be treated in a grammar, and the student must be referred to his lexicon. The German dictionaries in use in Germany avoid these foreign words, but they are usually treated in a separate work called **Fremdwörterbuch.**

Secondary Accent.

48. Secondary accent is not bound so closely to certain syllables as is the principal accent, but is often under different circumstances shifted from one syllable to another. There are two factors involved in determining secondary accent, the *normal* stress and a *physiological* principle. Sometimes both unite in fixing the accent upon a certain syllable, sometimes one principle gains the victory over the other.

1. *Normal Secondary Accent.* The normal stress in compound and derivative words is as follows:

A. In compound words, that syllable receives secondary accent which would receive principal accent if the component were an independent word; **'Fahr\`wasser, 'Haus\`herrin, 'aus\`merzen.** In decomposites, altho there may be a number of different words, there will be usually only two components, so that the principal accent falls upon the principal syllable of the modifying component and the secondary accent upon the principal syllable of the basal component: **'Vaterlands\`liebe ('Vaterland + 'Liebe), 'Feld\`diebstahl.** The accent here is, however, often disturbed by the tendency (described in 2 below) to distribute the accents so as to make a regular and rhythmical succession of accented and unaccented syllables: **'Voran\`zeigĕ, 'Endur\`teilĕ** instead of **'Vor\`anzeige, 'End\`urteile.** Compare **45.** 3.

B. *Accent of Suffixes.* After a root syllable which contains the principal meaning and chief accent, certain suffixes from their logical force as modifying elements take secondary accent, some of which are the remnants of once independent words. These suffixes are:

a. Substantive suffixes: **āt, ūt, ōd, heit, ĭn, keit, lein, lĭng, nĭs, sāl, schăft, tūm: 'Hei\`maten, 'Klei\`node, 'Köni\`gin, 'Ewig\`keit.**

b. Adjective suffixes: **băr, hăft, ĭcht, ĭg, ĭsch, lĭch, sām, sēlig: 'brauch\`bar, 'leb\`haft.**

2. *Physiological Principle in Secondary Accent.* For physiological reasons it is difficult to pronounce two accented syllables one after the other. It is easier and at the same time more rhythmical to place an unaccented syllable between the first and second accent. Thus to avoid the clashing of principal and secondary accent the latter is often removed from the syllable logically important to one of minor importance: **'Voran\`zeige** instead of **'Vor\`anzeige.** On the other hand it is difficult to pronounce more than two unaccented syllables one after the other, and hence the natural tendency is to give one of several unaccented syllables a secondary accent, provided, however, that it will not clash with another accent of the same strength: **'besse\`re Gestalt,** but the secondary accent upon a final syllable must be suppressed or shifted when it would stand before another accent: **sie er'wartete \`Mari'annen; das 'Endur\`teil ĕr'folgt,** but **das 'End\`urteil 'spricht.** Thus secondary accent depends largely upon the accents in the preceding or following syllables. The following details should be noted:

a. In polysyllabic words the secondary accent depends upon the logical value or the position of the syllable. The important syllables as described in 1 above are accented if their position admits of it. Also a short logically unimportant syllable receives an accent if it is at a distance of two or more syllables from the principal accent, providing it is not followed by an accent: **'heite\`re Gĕ'sellschaft.**

The intensity of all secondary accents increases with their distance from the principal accent, and sometimes becomes stronger than the accent upon a logically more important syllable: in **''Auf\`sehe'rinnen** the suffix **in** has a stronger accent than the root syllable **seh.** Similarly in **''mit\`teil'sam, ''wirt\`schaft'lich,** &c. Here, however, as elsewhere, the secondary accent is influenced by the accent of the following word, as two accents must not come together: **'Hoffnu\`ngen er'weckt,** but **'Hoff\`nungen 'täuscht.**

b. A single syllable between two accents is unaccented: **Das 'Altĕr 'schützt vŏr 'Torhĕit 'nicht.**

c. If there are two syllables between two accents, they are both unaccented if short, but the first may be accented if it is long: **'Widĕrlĭch\`keit,** but **''Un\`ēbĕn'heit, ''selt\`sāmĕ 'Art.** The second of the two syllables standing between accents can be accented only when the word stands before a pause in the sentence or at the end of the sentence, in which cases it does not really stand between two accents, but between an accent and a pause: **Dem ′Glücklĭchĕn ′kann es an ′nichts ge′brechen**, or **Dem ′Glücklĭ‵chen | ′kann es an ′nichts ge′brechen. Dem ′wechsĕlndĕn ′Leben,** but **Gar wechselnd ist des Mannes rascher Sinn, dem Leben untertan, dem ′wechseln‵den.**

d. If there are three syllables between two accents, the middle syllable usually takes the secondary accent unless it be considerably lighter and shorter than the first syllable, in which case the first syllable is accented: **ein ′undank‵bāres ″Kind,** but **eine ′un‵glücklĭchĕ ″Liebe.** The third of these syllables can never have the accent, as it would bring it immediately before the principal accent (see *e*).

e. A secondary accent can stand *before* the principal accent, but never immediately before it: **‵wider′legen, ‵Theolo′gie.** Here as elsewhere the intensity of the secondary accent increases with its distance from the principal stress. Thus the secondary accent is much stronger in the second of the two preceding examples.

f. For secondary accent in foreign words see **45.** 4 (2nd par.).

Unaccented Syllables.

49. The limitation of the principal accent in the main to the root syllable is now a principle quite generally observed thruout the Germanic family of languages, including both English and German. This system has not always obtained, as fossil remnants still show, but since its adoption has been of great influence in shaping the form of the German language. Since the principal syllable, which is usually the root syllable, receives the main accent, the inflectional endings, many suffixes, and the prefixes **be, emp, ent, er, ge, ver, zer,** are neglected in accenting, and hence they have lost the full vowel forms which they once had. The various vowels and diphthongs of the languages, as **a, o, u, au,** &c., have been preserved only in the accented syllables, while in the unaccented syllables the same vowels and diphthongs have all been reduced quite uniformly to **e**: **er′füllen** (Gothic usfulljan). In words like **′Eigĕn‵tümĕr** the secondary accent has preserved the vowels from decay, while the unaccented vowels have been reduced to **e.** Many words have lost their fulness of sound, many vowels have disappeared for ever. The process of decay has not yet ceased. Sometimes the vowel **e** is now of so little importance that it can be pronounced or omitted: **gerade** or **grad, bange** or **bang.** Sometimes the **e,** altho it has dropped out in comparatively recent times, is no longer felt at all. No one thinks any more of the **e** once after **g** in **Glaube, Glück,** &c. In the different inflectional systems, **e** is often in familiar language entirely suppressed, while in a more choice style it can be skilfully dropped or employed according to the rhythmical requirements of the sentence. See **62.** F. *b.* It will also in this connection be noticed thruout the Grammar that the German is especially fond of the trochee (–́ ⏑) or the falling spondee (–́ –̀) as a word foot, and is now often disposed to change longer feet into these favorite shorter feet by dropping an unaccented **e,** if it can be conveniently done. Thus –́ ⏑ ⏑, –́ –̀ ⏑, –́ ⏑ –̀, become –́ ⏑, –́ –̀: **′Königs,** not **′Königĕs; ′Mon‵tags,** often instead of **′Mon‵tagĕs; ′himm‵lisch,** not **′himmĕ‵lisch.** It must be noticed that the dropping of **e** here is solely a question of accent, for in dissyllabic forms the same words retain the **e:** (des) **Tages,** (der) **Himmel.** Also in words closely united by thought we can notice the tendency to divide up the syllables into dissyllabic feet: **heute,** but **′heutzŭ′tagĕ.** Thus also trisyllabic rising feet become disyllabic: **bĕ′gleiten,** from **be + geleiten; bĕ′gnügen,** from **be + genügen.** Compare **62.** *C. Note* and D. It should be noticed, however, that the literary form of speech is averse to all these changes of feet, if the clearness of the thought could thereby be endangered. Thus we must say **wandelte** (past indic.) and not **wandelt,** for the latter form would be the same as the pres. indic., and would thus endanger the thought. In the **e**-less plural class of strong nouns, however, even the literary language has endorsed this dropping of **e,** altho the plural became thereby identical in form with the sing. See **68.** Dialect goes much farther in suppressing unaccented sounds than the written language. In S.G. dialect also unaccented final **n** has disappeared: **Du muscht** (**mußt**) **bei mir bleibe** (for **bleiben**)—Auerbach.

In many words full vowels have been preserved in the unaccented syllable, but such words are quite uniformly of foreign origin: **Mu′latte, ′Doktor, Mi′nute,** &c. Only in such words as **′Uhu,** and in a number of names, as **Otto, Herta,** &c., has the unaccented vowel been preserved in German words.

II. Sentence Accent.

50. Just as a word may have different *syllables* with different degrees of stress so has a sentence *words* with different degrees of stress, which in long sentences form definite groups each with its principal and secondary accent. Just as logic and emotion may influence the stress of a word so do they often in a sentence change the character of a group of words. The different forces at work in the accentuation of a sentence are discussed in the following articles.

A. *Grammatical or Group Accent.*

As certain syllables of a word take accent, so also are certain grammatical elements in a sentence stressed. The factors that enter into stress are largely mechanical. Just as words are usually distinguished as separate units in speech by a heavy stress upon the first syllable of each word different grammatical groups are usually distinguished as larger units by a strong accent upon the *last* member of each group, as illustrated in 6 below. There are, however, many variations from this simple principle, for which general rules can be laid down, but it must be remembered that they are only general rules and are set aside whenever the logically important idea shifts to other elements. As will be seen below, the question of accent is sometimes intimately connected with that of word-order. The marks denoting accent are placed above the vowels and indicate not word-stress but group-stress, i.e. the stress which the word receives when it stands in a syntactical group of words.

The following general hints on grammatical or group stress may be useful:

1. In general the predicate as the most important thing to be communicated is more strongly accented than the subject: **Der Hund béllt.**

2. *Stress of Predicate Word and Copula or Auxiliary.* The predicate adjective or noun, the dependent infinitive or participle, the separable prefix of a separable verb, are of more importance than the copula, auxiliary, or finite verb which bind them to the subject, and hence receive the accent, and according to German usage stand at the end of the sentence: **Er ìst réich. Er ìst sícher àngekommen** (compare 3. *a* below). **Er ìst ein tüchtiger Mánn. Er ìst ein tüchtiger Mánn gewòrden.** For this important point, see **215.** II. 1. A and **285.** II. B. *b. gg.*

a. Auxiliary or Copula Stressed. The copula or auxiliary is more strongly stressed than the participle or infinitive wherever it is desired to emphasize the idea of actuality or non-actuality of an act: **„Und ich wette, Sie haben wieder einen Eierkuchen gebacken." „Háb ich auch."** Many examples of stressed auxiliaries are given in **190.** 1. A. *c*, **190.** 2, **252.** 1. *b.* (2nd par.).

b. Stress in Threatening Language. Utterances spoken in a threatening tone usually have the strongest stress upon the first word even tho it be logically unimportant, so that the predicate words which are usually strongly accented have here less stress than the first word: **Wíllst du aufmerken!** Do you intend to pay attention?! **Géhst du gleich her!** (verb stressed more heavily than the prefix **her**) Don't you intend to come at once?! **Dáß du mir aufmerkst! Ób du hergehst! Wénn du das noch einmal tust!** (Albert Debrunner in *Deutsche Literaturzeitung*, 1919, p. 739). **Dás tust du mir nicht mehr!** (id.). **Láß mir das ein andermal bleiben!** (id.). **Nímm dich in acht, daß das nicht mehr vorkommt!** (id.).

3. *Stress of Verb and Adverb.* If the predicate verb has an object or adverbial modifier, these usually in normal or inverted word-order take a stronger accent than the verb itself, except in case of a reciprocal, reflexive, or personal pronoun: **Das Werk lobt den Méister. Er spricht láut. Sie reden zusámmen** (*at the same time*), but **Sie réden zusammen** (= **miteinander**). **Er fréut sich.**

a. Modal adverbs, i.e. such as modify not the verb but the thought of the whole sentence, are usually stressed less than the verb: **Er géht nicht. Du kénnst ihn ja.** The use of such weakly accented adverbs in connection with heavy stress on the verb is the characteristic German way of emphasizing the activity expressed by the verb: **Ich árbeite ja** (unstressed) I dó work. See also **185.** B. I., 2. *e.* (**2**) and **223.** XI. A. *a.* The unstressed adverb **nur** placed after the stressed verb indicates that the subject engages only in the activity expressed by the verb: **Blinder Eifer schádet nur.** Stress upon an object or an adverb calls attention to some detail in the statement. Stress upon the verb emphasizes not only the verbal activity but the statement as a whole. Hence when the attention is called to the thought as a whole the verb is more strongly stressed than an adverb or an object: **Er gèht sícher** *He is pursuing the proper course*, but **Er géht sìcher** He'll be sure to go. **Er wird sìcher géhen. Er ist sìcher ángekommen** (compare 2). **Er rácht sìcher diese Kränkung. Er wird diese Krànkung rácheh.** In most principal propositions with normal or inverted word-order the attention is directed to some detail expressed by an object or an adverbial element, so that the verb is usually stressed less than its modifiers, but when as in these examples, the attention is directed to the thought as a whole and the question of achievement is involved the verb is more heavily stressed than its modifiers. See also *b.*

b. As in a subordinate clause or an utterance with transposed word-order the attention is usually directed to the thought as a whole the simple verb is usually distinctly stressed, so that the simple verb of the subordinate clause has for the most part a distinctly stronger stress than the simple verb in a principal proposition with normal or inverted word-order: **Er kòmmt mórgen,** but **Ich möchte gern wissen, ob er mòrgen kómmt, ob er mórgen oder ǘbermorgen kòmmt. Wie sie ihn líebte, líebte, líebte!** (Wildenbruch's *Schwesterseele*, chap. VII). For further treatment see **284.** I. 3. *a* (toward end). Where, however, in the principal proposition the attention is called to the thought as a whole the verb is distinctly stressed. See *a.*

The stress of the simple verb in English is much the same as in German in both the principal proposition and the subordinate clause. English no longer has the verb at the end in the subordinate clause, but the stronger stress of the verb still usually distinguishes the subordinate clause from the principal proposition: He èntered the róom and nòticed the condítion of things, *but* As soon as he éntered the ròom, he nòticed the condítion of things.

c. A simple verb in the initial position is always stressed just as other important words that stand in the first place: **Réiche mir das Búch! Réisen Sie dieses Jáhr wieder nach Kárlsbad? Sáh ein Knáb' ein Rṓslein stéhn** (Goethe's *Heidenröslein*). Compare **284. I. 2.** *a.*

d. The stress of the verbal elements in compound tense forms is discussed in **215. II. 1. A; 285.** II. B. *b. aa, bb, cc*; **237.** 1. B. *a. Note.*

4. If there are a number of objects or adverbial modifiers, the logically more important are accented and stand toward the end of the sentence, especially an adverb of place: **Columbus fuhr am 3. August 1492 von Pálos ab.** The order here is treated in detail in **285.** II. B. *c, d, e.*

5. Pronouns, articles, prepositions, conjunctions, auxiliaries receive less stress than other parts of speech. These classes of words often become enclitics or proclitics, when an accented syllable *immediately* precedes or follows, that is, they here lose their accent and are treated as if they were

a part of the preceding or following word: (enclitics) **hást du** (pro. **hástu**), **die Nácht durch,** &c.; (proclitics) **durch Líebe, es íst, er wéiß,** but **èr běkénnt** because the pronoun is followed by an unaccented syllable. Often monosyllabic pronouns or articles become enclitics after prepositions, and are sometimes even contracted and thoroly fused into one word with the preposition: **mít euch, béi ihm, áuf das** or **aufs, ín dem** or **im.** See also **57.** B and C, and **58.** B. *b, c.*

6. *Different Kinds of Group-stress.* When two or more elements are closely related, there is often a marked tendency to form a unit, i.e. to bind the parts closely together by one principal accent, which rests upon the last element. The strong stress upon the last member of the group marks the *unity* of the group, indicating the end of one group and distinguishing it from the next one if the discourse is continued. This is normal or descriptive (**247.** 2. *b.*) group-stress. The strong stress that is occasionally found on the first member calls attention to the logical importance that it has assumed under the special circumstances, hence it is often used to distinguish one person or thing from another. This is logical, or distinguishing or classifying stress. It is not only employed in the usual syntactical groups of a sentence, but is very common in group-words (**247.** 2). Examples are given in **247.** 2. *b* and **255.** II. 1. Descriptive stress and distinguishing or classifying stress are also characteristic of English, which, however, has developed a more uniform, consistent use of the two principles. Compare **255.** I. *b* (2nd par.). In German a sharp discrimination here has been prevented: (**1**) by the survival of an older descriptive stress upon the first member in certain attributive adjective groups (**247.** 2. *a*); (**2**) by the development of a new normal or descriptive group-stress with the accent upon the first member at the end of sentences or clauses which have a compound tense. This new normal or descriptive stress is in this treatise called end-stress. It is discussed more at length in **215.** II. 1. A (3rd par.).

The following groups of normal or descriptive stress are common:

a. The adverb is less stressed than the following adjective, participle, or adverb: **Das Buch ist ungewȍhnlich réichhaltig und interessánt.** Of course, the logical importance may shift upon the preceding adverb: **Das Buch ist ungewóhnlich rèichhaltig und interessànt.** Thus the chief stress upon either the first or the last element of the group does not destroy the grammatical relations, but an *equal* stress upon the preceding adverb and the two following adjectives may, as here, entirely destroy the grammatical relations: **Das Buch ist ungewóhnlich, réichhaltig und interessánt.** Here **ungewöhnlich** is an adjective on a par with the two adjectives that follow it.

Emphatic descriptive stress is very common here in strong excited language. The adverb is accented strongly but just a *little less* strongly than the following adjective: **Das Buch ist zű dúmm!**

b. An adjective usually receives less stress than the noun which it limits: **das Dèutsche Réich.** If, however, a numeral precedes a noun denoting a weight or measure and its dependent substantive the adjective numeral has a heavier stress than the following noun: **dréi Pfȕnd Zúcker.** Here as in *h* below **Pfȕnd Zúcker** forms a group. Now when this group enters as a unit into the larger group **dréi Pfȕnd Zúcker** the first member **drei** must have a stronger stress than **Pfund** or else it would be felt as forming a group with **Pfund** instead of with the larger unit **Pfȕnd Zúcker.** The strongest stress upon **Zucker** in **dréi Pfȕnd Zúcker** clearly shows that the end of the group is **Zucker,** not **Pfund.** Of course, the logical importance often shifts from the noun upon the preceding adjective: **Gib mir das bráune Pfèrd.** This logical or distinguishing stress is also found in group-words and compounds: **Júngfràu,** &c. See also **247.** 2. *a, b, c,* and **249.** II. 1. A. This logical stress which is stronger than the accent upon the governing noun must be distinguished from emphatic descriptive stress, which is also strong but just a *little less* strong than that of the governing noun: **O allzu rȁscher Mánn!, díeser Schúft!, Der Jörg** (pet name for **Georg**) **ist éin Sȁufer!** Logical stress distinguishes one person or thing from another. Emphatic stress describes *one* person or thing and often indicates strong feeling or shows an emotional interest in the statement. For another form of descriptive stress see **111.** 9.

c. When the second word stands as an appositive to the first: **Mȕtter Natúr. Wer soll dein Hüter sein, Vàter Rhéin? Schíller der Díchter, der Dìchter Schíller.** Also *d* contains this appositional construction. In older German the appositive was stressed as to-day, but it preceded the governing noun. This older usage survives in compounds and group-words: **der Rhéinstrȍm.** See **255.** II. 1. G. *a* (2nd par.).

d. When a title and a proper name form one idea: **Kàiser Wílhelm;** but **Kȍnig Kàrl, nicht Hérzog Kàrl.**

e. In case of Christian and surname: **Jàkob Grímm;** but **Érich Schmìdt, nicht Johánnes Schmìdt.**

f. Usually in case of a noun and its modifying genitive, generally with clear descriptive force: **Er wird die Schwèlle meines Háuses nicht übertreten,** or **Er wird meines Hàuses Schwélle nicht übertreten. Gȍethes Váter,** or **der Vàter Góethes.** See **255.** II. 1.

Of course, the logical importance often shifts from the second member to the first and we then have *logical stress*: **Selbst die Kräuter und Wurzeln miß' ich ungern, wenn auch der Wért der Wàre nicht groß ist. Das ist Wílhelms Bȕch, nicht méines.** This logical stress is very common in compounds and group-words (**247.** 2): **Knábenàrt, Fráuenhànd, Mánneswòrt, Lúngenentzȕndung, Áugenentzȕndung,** &c. Also often in old group-words (**247.** 2. *a*), where the genitive relation as in the older period of uninflected speech is not marked by an ending: **Kópfverlètzung, Hérzklȍpfen,** &c.

Quite different from this logical accent is *emphatic stress,* which calls attention to the important member of the group: (Johannes) **Was führt Dich denn zu uns?** (Vockerat) **Gȍttes Wílle, tja! Der Wílle Góttes führt mich zu Euch** (Hauptmann's *Einsame Menschen,* V). **Sie sagte**

neulich: Wir Frauen lebten in einem Zùstand der Entwûrdigung (id. II). Where the emphasis, as in these examples, rests upon the second member the stress can be as strong as desired without disturbing the modern group-stress. If, however, the emphatic member precedes, it is strongly stressed, but its force must be a *little* less than that of the second member, so that the modern group-stress is preserved: **Es gibt vielleicht Dinge zu verrichten, die augenblicklich wichtiger sind als sämtliche Maleréien und Schreiberéien der Wélt** (id.). If the first member were more strongly stressed it would be felt as logical stress.

Logical stress distinguishes one object from another or classifies it. Emphatic stress describes *one* object and shows an interest in it praising or censuring it.

Of course, if two groups with emphatic stress stand in contrast to each other the stress becomes logical: **Die Flèxion der Nómina hat sich nicht so reich entfaltet wie die der Vérba** (Wilmanns's *Deutsche Grammatik*, III, p. 317).

g. Usually in case of a noun with its modifying prepositional phrase, when they together form one idea: **Das Bùch auf dem Tísch.**

h. When a noun denoting a weight or measure and the following noun denoting a material or something measurable together form the idea of a complete whole: **ein Stùck Túch, ein Glàs Wéin.**

i. In case of several words which are connected by a preposition or conjunction and form together one idea: **Zwèig auf Zwéige** *one branch upon the other*, i.e. all upon one pile, **wèit und bréit, Grùnd und Bóden** *property, real estate*; **jùng und ált, gròß und kléin, àrm und réich.** The unity of the idea arises here from the fact that the words are either synonyms, and thus represent the same thing from two different standpoints, or are opposites or complements, and thus show the whole range of the idea from the two extremes. Of course the logical importance of the first word may sometimes require it to be accented: **Zwéig auf Zwéig** (compare with first example above) *one branch at a time.* The accent upon the first word here shows that it is to be taken separately.

j. Co-ordination: **Hàns, Màx und Wílhelm waren da.**

B. *Logical and Emphatic Accent.*

Logical accent is sovereign and can set aside all the preceding rules, disturbing both the group and word accent. Any word or syllable can for logical reasons receive the accent: **Der Mánn** (the *man*, not the *woman*) **ist nicht alt. Der Mann íst alt. Der Mann ist nícht** (contradicting) **alt. Der Mann ist nicht ált, sondern júng. Dér** (that) **Mann ist nicht alt.** Thus also that syllable or, in a compound, that component may for logical reasons take the principal accent, which under normal conditions uniformly has the secondary accent, or remains unaccented: **Der Hase ist nicht furchtbár, sondern furchtsám. Er hat nicht eine Brénnerei, sondern eine Bráuerei angelegt. Ich habe das mir nicht érbeten, sondern vérbeten. Aufgeschóben ist nicht aufgehóben. Nicht die Gartentúr, sondern die Gartenmáuer ist beschädigt.** One says in correcting an incorrect grammatical form: **gebén, nicht gebé.**

Emphatic stress results from emotion. Its effect on words is described in **45. 2**, its effect on groups of words in A. 6. *a*, *b*, *f* above.

51. *Sentence Accent affected by the Rhythm.* Words that are comparatively unimportant to the meaning, and hence do not absolutely demand stress, may be with or without accent, according to the requirement of the natural rhythm of the sentence. They remain unaccented if their accentuation would bring two accented syllables together; but when they are preceded or followed by other less important unaccented syllables they may receive accent in order to make an easy and rhythmical succession of accented and unaccented syllables. Thus in the following sentences the predicate verb, which in general is weakly accented when it has modifiers, has in the one instance no accent, because it is followed by an accent, while in the other it is accented, as it is followed by an unaccented syllable: **Bórgen macht Sórgen,** but **Kléider màchen Léute.** However, when the logical force of the words becomes strong, they must receive accent, even tho the accent disturbs the rhythm. Thus we answer an inquiry after the number and sex of the children that a man has with the words: **Er hat dréi Tóchter.**

52. *Sentence Accent affected by the Tempo.* Aside from the points mentioned above, there are other factors which influence the accent. Among these the tempo plays an important rôle. As the movement in the sentence increases in speed, the number of accents decreases, and their intensity becomes greater. Also at the beginning and end of a sentence or before a pause the accent becomes more pronounced.

Pitch, or Tone.

53. 1. The pitch in which something is spoken indicates the attitude of the mind or the state of the feelings. In a foreign language pitch is one of the most subtle of things, but in English and German, so closely related by a common origin, it is for the most part the same. There are, however, differences. A number of scholars have observed in the English of England that pitch is considerably lower than in German, which indicates that the people of England give to their feelings a more restrained expression marked by less variation in tone. On the other hand, pitch differs somewhat in different parts of the same country, also in individuals according to health, age, and sex. In spite of these differences the tone in which something is spoken is usually understood quite clearly by men and often even animals, and hence there must be fixed rules which underlie these phenomena. This subject, however, cannot be discussed here.

2. *Falling and Rising Intonation.* Falling intonation is indicated by a period, rising intonation by a raised period. Attention is here called to only a few important fundamental points, which in general correspond to English usage:

a. Falling intonation usually indicates completeness, hence is employed at the end of a statement: **Karl· ist· krank· ge.we.sen.**

b. Rising intonation usually indicates incompleteness, expectancy, hence is used at the close of a question that is to be answered by yes or no: **Ist. er. hier. ge·we·sen·?** In other kinds of questions the voice usually falls at the end of the sentence as there is no state of expectancy or suspense as to the outcome of a decision or an act but a mere demand for information: **Wer· hat· das· ge·tan.?** If, however, one *repeats* the interrogative pronoun or adverb with emphasis in impatient tone the voice rises at the end of the sentence to indicate that one expects an answer: **Wér. hat· das· ge·tan·?**

The voice rises at the end of a clause which precedes another clause and falls at the end of the sentence: **Er ruft mich·, wenn ihr fertig seid. Wenn ihr fertig seid·, ruft er mich.** In a sentence containing a direct quotation the principal proposition closes with rising intonation if it precedes the quotation, but if it follows the quotation it has the intonation of the syllable which immediately precedes it: **Er. sag·te·: „Ge·hen· Sie· mit.!" „Ge·hen· Sie· mit.!," sag.te. er. „Ist. er. hier. ge·we·sen·?", frag·te· er·** (Siebs's *Bühnenaussprache*, p. 87). Compare **269. 1.** *b* and **164** (toward end).

Use of Capital Letters.

54. The use of capital letters in German differs from the English in several points. The following are begun with a capital:

1. Every complete sentence in prose, and in poetry every verse.

2. Every direct quotation: **Der Bettelsack sagt nie: „Ich habe genug."**

3. Every noun and any word used as a noun, if it can take the definite article, an adjective, or any other modifying word before it: **der Mann, der Alte, der Junge,** but **alt und jung** *old and young*, because no article can stand before these words in this set expression; **das Weinen; das trauliche Du; Schönes, etwas Schönes.**

a. Pronominal adjectives, indefinite pronouns and numerals, tho often used substantively, are written with a small letter: **mancher, niemand, man, einer, ein wenig,** &c.

b. Also many nouns in certain set expressions, used adverbially, are written with a small letter: **zuliebe tun; zustatten kommen, von alters her, anfangs.**

4. Adjectives and ordinals preceded by the article, when they stand after proper names, forming with the name the designation of one individual: **Friedrich der Große** or **der Zweite.**

5. Adjectives and possessives in titles: **Seine Majestät; das Königliche Zollamt; der Wirkliche Geheimrat; die Norddeutsche Schulzeitung.**

6. Certain pronouns in direct address, as explained in **138. 1**, and also those referring to the speaker in the proclamations and words of emperors and kings. Also other pronouns, pronominal adjectives, and the numeral **ein** sometimes take a capital to indicate emphasis, but more commonly are written with a small letter with an accent above the vowel, as **éin,** or are spaced, as **e i n.** If, however, groups of words or whole sentences are to be emphasized the letters are spaced in German, or they appear in heavier type. Differing from English, the pronoun of the first person, **ich** *I*, is written with a small letter, unless it begins a sentence or direct quotation.

7. Adjectives in **sch** derived from names of persons and those in **-er** from names of places: **die Grimmschen** or **Grimm'schen Märchen; der Kölner** (sometimes also **kölner**) **Dom.**

a. But adjectives made from proper names, whether of persons, peoples, or countries, are written with a small letter when used, not with reference to one person or thing, but in a general universal sense: **die lu'therische Kirche; römisch, preußisch, kölnisch,** &c.

8. Usually only the first element of compound nouns is written with a capital, but sometimes other elements take a capital, especially in the following cases: (1) When a misunderstanding might arise from the use of small characters: **Erd-Rücken** to keep it from being confounded with **Er-drücken; der Z-Laut,** &c. (2) Proper names and adjectives: **Schleswig-Holstein, Niederschlesisch-Märkische Eisenbahn.** (3) The last component element in long compounds: **Dampfschiffahrts-Gesellschaft, Appellationsgerichts-Präsident.** (4) Common class nouns in compounds containing a prep. phrase: **das In-die-Höhe-Kommen,** but with a small letter where the thought is clear: **das Imamtbleiben.** Notice that in the above cases a hyphen (-) must be used when an element within the compound has a capital.

Apostrophe.

55. An apostrophe is used as in English to indicate that a sound which can be pronounced is suppressed: **wen'ge** for **wenige; er redet'** for **redete.**

The exceptions are as follows:

1. An apostrophe is not used in the common contractions of the article with a previous preposition: **am, ans,** &c. for **an dem, an das,** &c.

2. It is not now usual to place an apostrophe before **s** in the gen.: **Schillers, Goethes,** &c. Older usage: **Schiller's,** &c.

3. If a proper name ends in a sibilant **s, ß, tz,** &c., no additional **s** appears in the printed or written form of the gen., altho an additional s is actually spoken. In the printed and written form the apostrophe is usually employed here to indicate the case: **Voß'** (now sometimes **Voß's**) **Luise.** See also **86. 2. *a.***

PART II.

THE PARTS OF SPEECH.

THEIR GRAMMATICAL FORMS, USE, NATURE.

PRELIMINARY.

Number, Case, Gender.

56. *a.* There are in German two numbers, the singular and plural.

b. There are four cases: the *nominative*, the *genitive*, the *dative*, the *accusative.* The meaning and uses of these cases are treated in the Syntax.

c. There are three genders, *masculine*, *feminine*, and *neuter*. The general rule for the gender of nouns denoting living beings is that the noun is masculine or feminine according to the natural sex of the object represented by it, but there are many exceptions to the rule. The gender of nouns denoting things destitute of sex is not always neuter as in English, but is masc., fem., or neut., regulated in part by the meaning or the form of the word. Some rules for gender are given in **98** and **99,** but in general the gender of each word must be learned, as there is much irregularity. The gender of the noun is usually indicated by the form of the preceding article or other modifying word.

INFLECTION OF THE ARTICLES.

DEFINITE ARTICLE.

57. A. The *definite* article has in the development of the language become ever more and more a necessary accompaniment of the noun. It stands immediately before the noun, and thus not only indicates its gender, but also, as it is richer in forms, marks its case more distinctly.

	SINGULAR.				PLURAL.
	Masc.	Fem.	Neut.		M., F., and N. alike.
Nom. . . .	**der**	**die**	**das**	. . .	**die** *the.*
Gen.. . . .	**des**	**der**	**des**	. . .	**der** *of the.*
Dat.. . . .	**dem**	**der**	**dem**	. . .	**den** *to* (or *for*) *the.*
Acc.	**den**	**die**	**das**	. . .	**die** *the.*

B. The definite article is an enclitic, i.e. it leans upon a preceding word, the voice passing rapidly over it, as if it were a part of the preceding word. For this reason the article suffers many contractions with a preceding preposition or other word, especially the contraction of **dem** (neut. and masc. dat.) and **das** (acc.) with a preceding monosyllabic preposition. **Zur** for **zu der** is the only fem. contraction allowed. The more common contractions are **am, ans, aufs, beim, fürs, im, ins, vom, zum,** for **an dem, an das, auf das, bei dem, für das, in dem, in das, von dem, zu dem;** sometimes in the familiar language of every day: **aufm, hinterm, gegens, übern,** &c., for **auf dem, hinter dem, gegen das, über den,** &c. In the spoken language contraction with a preceding verb is also very common: **Er hat's** (**hat das**) **große Los gewonnen.**

a. In the classics we find the contractions **zun** for **zu den** (dat. pl.), **an** (pronounce **an'n**) for **an den** (acc. sing. masc. and dat. pl.), and **in** (pronounce **in'n**) for **in den** (acc. sing. masc. and dat. pl.), which have since disappeared from the literary language: **vom Kopf bis zun Füßen** (Schiller's *Räuber*, 2, 3). **Ihr warft sie dem Feind an Kopf** (Goethe's *Götz*, 1, 2). **Und setz' dich in Sessel!** (id., *Faust*, l. 2428). **Er fabelte gewiß in letzten Zügen** (ib., l. 2962). Such contractions are still common in colloquial and popular language.

b. Contraction is the rule in all the above cases in the numerous *set phrases* where the article loses its demonstrative (see D) force entirely, and hence its importance, pointing to no concrete object in particular which thus needs to be pointed out or described, in order to be identified, but to one which has taken on abstract and general force: **Er schlug die Gegner aufs Haupt** He defeated his opponents (lit. hit them upon the head). **Er faßte ihn scharf ins Auge** He looked at him sharply. **Er geht zur Schule** (no reference to a particular school, but, in general, to the place where one learns).

Outside of these set expressions the article is also, on the same general principle, very often contracted when it has no demonstrative force, especially in familiar language where the relations of the persons and objects to each other are perfectly clear and need not be pointed out. However, when the least demonstrative force enters into the article, it cannot be contracted, especially in choice language: **Ich habe im guten Glauben gehandelt** *I acted in good faith*, but **Ich habe in dem guten Glauben gehandelt, daß ich in meinem Rechte wäre.**

c. Instead of being contracted the article is sometimes lengthened. The lengthened gen. and dat. forms **derer** (for **der**) and **denen** (for **den**) are found more or less frequently up to the beginning of the nineteenth century: **die Befolgung derer Gesetze** (Klopstock). **Vielleicht daß Gott denen Großen die Augen auftut** (Goethe). Occasionally still in language colored by dialect: **Aber geholfen hat er schon vielen, weil er mir die Wissenschaft von denen Kräutern gegeben hat** (Wilhelm Fischer's *Sonnenopfer*, I).

C. The definite article is also a proclitic (i.e. leans upon the following word), the voice passing rapidly over it and resting upon the next word: **Der Ménsch ist sterblich.** Hence the article is often contracted or written as a part of the following word: **'s Morgens = des Morgens** *of mornings*, **der'selbe** *the same*. The article is a proclitic or enclitic according as it precedes or follows a stronger accent to which it naturally attaches itself.

D. The definite article is in fact only the unaccented and shorter form of the demonstrative adjective **der** *that* (see **129.** 1), and still, tho in greatly reduced degree, retains its demonstrative force. Owing to its enclitic nature the pronunciation of the def. article differs according to circumstances just as the English *the*, tho always more or less short and obscure, thus differing from the demon. adjective **der**, which has a strong accent.

Indefinite Article.

58. A. Its declension is as follows:

	Singular.			Plural.
	Masc.	Fem.	Neut.	M., F., and N.
Nom. . . .	**ein**	**eine**	**ein** *a*	. . . **meine** *my*
Gen. . . .	**eines**	**einer**	**eines** *of a*	. . . **meiner** *of my*
Dat. . . .	**einem**	**einer**	**einem** *to (for) a*	. . . **meinen** *to (for) my*
Acc. . . .	**einen**	**eine**	**ein** *a*	. . . **meine** *my*

B. Of course there can be no plural of **ein**, but as all the other words declined like **ein** have a plural, **mein** is declined as a model for the whole group in the plural. The words declined like **ein** are: **kein** *no* and all the possessive adjectives, **mein** *my*, **unser** *our*, **dein** *thy*, **euer** *your*, **sein** *his*, *its*, **ihr** *her*, **ihr** *their*. Notice that this group *has no ending to show gender in nom. sing. of the masc.* and *nom.* and *acc. sing. of the neut.* Of these words **ein** is the only one that is an enclitic, and hence is the only one that can suffer apheresis (see *b*).

a. The indefinite article like the definite is an enclitic or proclitic, being the unaccented form of the accented numeral adjective **ein** *one*, which is sometimes distinguished from the indef. article by being written with a capital or, more commonly by an accent, or by spaced letters: **Ein, éin, e i n.**

b. Owing to its enclitic or proclitic nature the indef. article is often contracted after or before a word, forming in the familiar language of every day a complete shorter declension as follows:

	Singular.		
	Masc.	Fem.	Neut.
Nom.	**'n**	**'ne**	**'n**
Gen.	**'nes**	**'ner**	**'nes**
Dat.	**'nem** (or **'m**)	**'ner**	**'nem** (or **'m**)
Acc.	**'nen** or **'n** (=**n'n**)	**'ne**	**'n**

Example: **Es war 'ne furchtbare Zeit** (M. Dreyer's *Drei*, I).

c. This group of words had in early N.H.G. other abbreviated forms, as **eins** (gen. masc. and neut.) for **eines, eim** or **em** for **einem, einn** or **ein'** for **einen,** &c. These forms are often found in the language of Luther and occasionally in the works of Goethe: **Es ist besser wonen im wüsten Lande | Denn bey eim zenckischen vnd zornigen Weibe** (Proverbs 21. 19). **Mit eim leidlich Geld** (Goethe's *Urfaust,* l. 258). **Wenn ich so saß bei 'em Gelag** (ib., l. 1372). In the careless spoken language of every-day life these contractions still continue to take place: **Mit eim Mal?** (M. Dreyer's *In Behandlung,* I.) In the same manner we find earlier in the period contracted forms of the other words inflected like **ein,** namely, **kein** and the possessive adjectives, and in poetry and popular language such contractions still appear: **König Sifrid liegt in seim roten Blute!** (Uhland's *Die drei Lieder*).

d. In more choice language the indefinite article is pronounced in full, but with weak accent.

USE OF THE ARTICLES.

I. General Statement.

59. A. The indefinite article **ein** *a,* in form the unaccented numeral **éin** *one,* true to its origin singles out one object, action, or quality from among a number. It designates an individual object in different ways:

a. It points to an individual person or thing without fixing its identity: **Ein Kind begegnete uns. Ein Buch liegt auf dem Tisch.** If the individual introduced by the indefinite article is afterwards referred to, it is designated by the definite article, since it is considered as known: **Es war einmal ein König. Der König hatte kein Kind.**

b. In its more indefinite sense, **ein** is equal to **irgend ein** *any,* designating no individual in particular: **Nie ist ein Kaiser so reich gewesen.**

c. The indefinite article can usually stand before a proper name in only two cases: (**1**) to designate one member of a family: **Ich habe einen Schmidt gekannt** I knew a man by the name of Schmidt; (**2**) to convert a proper name into a common class noun: **Für einen Knaben stirbt ein Posa** (*a man like Posa*) **nicht** (Schiller's *Don Carlos,* 5, 9). **Ein Goethe kommt nicht alle Jahrzehnte vor.** Compare *d.*

d. **Ein** always indicates individualization, but usually without definite reference. In M.H.G., however, there are abundant evidences of a tendency toward definite reference as **ein** often assumes the force of a weak demonstrative or determinative. (**130.** 2): wer was ein maget, diu den gral truoc? (*Parzival,* 500. 24) = **Wer war die Jungfrau, die den Gral trug?,** *lit.* Who was a certain maiden, who carried the grail? In early N.H.G. the weak demonstrative force of **ein** is still common: **Geitz ist eine** (now **die**) **wurtzel alles vbels** (1. Tim. vi. 10). In a few instances it still survives in official language: **An ein hohes Ministerium** instead of the now more common: **An das hohe Ministerium.** This old demonstrative force is still sometimes used where in English we may render **ein** by *such a man as, such men as, such distinguished*: **Die Erhebung des deutschen Volkes im Befreiungskriege ward von den poetischen Klängen eines Körner, Arndt, Eichendorff begleitet. Die Darstellung und Inszenierung war eines Burgtheaters würdig** (Dr. Hans Hartmeyer in *Hamburger Nachrichten,* Feb. 13, 1906, describing the presentation of a play in the Burgtheater, Vienna). **Zum zweiten Male will man vom Deutschen Reich zwei Provinzen** (**Elsaß und Lothringen**) **losreißen, die ständig zu Deutschland gehörten bis zu den Raubzügen eines Ludwig XIV** (definite person) (*Lokalanzeiger,* Jan. 12, 1917). This **ein** is quite different from the **ein** described in *c.* (**2**) above, altho it is sometimes impossible to distinguish them by reason of insufficient context. Here the reference is to definite individuals, while in *c.*(**2**) the name denotes, not a definite individual but **any** member of a certain class of persons or things.

In colloquial language the old determinative force of **ein** is still quite common where it has the meaning of **ein solcher**: **Es war eine Nacht, in der man nicht gern einen Hund hinausjagt. Er hat eine Freude, es ist kaum zu glauben.**

B. *Definite Article with Individualizing Force.* The definite article **der** *the,* in form the unaccented demonstrative **der** *that,* true to its origin, points out a definite object or thing, not directly by a gesture, as the demon. **der**, but by implication, referring to a person or thing which has already been brought before the mind by previous mention, or which is clearly indicated by the context, and hence is either a weak demonstrative or a weak determinative (**130.** 2): **Trudchen hatte eine arme Mutter. Aber die Mutter war sehr fromm und gottesfürchtig. Der damalige Kaiser von Deutschland; die zwei letzten Kaiser von Deutschland; das Buch auf dem Tische; das Buch, das auf dem Tische liegt.** The definite article individualizes persons and things, i.e. it points, not to a class but to a definite individual or to definite individuals within a class.

Altho originally the definite article pointed out a definite individual within a class, the idea of a definite individual often so overshadows that of a class that the idea of a class in part or entirely disappears: (the idea of a class still felt) **der Montag, der Januar, der Merkur,** &c.; (the idea of a class almost or entirely absent) **der Erlöser** the Redeemer, **Friedrich der Große** Frederick the Great, **der Grunewald** (forest near Berlin), **die Vereinigten Staaten** the United States, &c. Thus for many centuries common class nouns have been developing into proper names, so that a large number of these strong individualizations of the new type with the definite article now stand over against the strong individualizations of the old type, the articleless proper names in D. A number of the words of the new type have already dropped or occasionally drop the definite article and have joined or occasionally join the older group: **Deutschland** (formerly **das deutsche Land**), etc. On the other hand, this new group has been greatly increased by accessions from the older group, as illustrated in II. B, C, D, E, G, H, I. (**1**).

C. *Both Articles with Generalizing Force.* Both **ein** and **der** have individualizing force, both indicating individualization within a class. Hence in general statements, i.e. where there is no reference to a definite individual, **ein** and **der** both assume generalizing force, i.e. the representative idea becomes more prominent than the conception of a sharp individualization, one individual representing a whole class. Here **ein** corresponds in general to English *a*, both **ein** and *a* representing a less definite, a less vivid form of individualization than **der.** In general, **der** corresponds to the articleless form in English, as *man* in *Man is mortal* but is much more widely used, the German form with **der** representing the new type of individualization described in B (2nd par.), the English form of expression representing the old style of individualization as found in proper names. The new type of individualization with **der,** so common in German, is also often found in English with the definite article where the idea of a class is strongly pronounced. Examples: **Das weiß ein Kind. Eine Ratte ist größer als eine Maus** A rat is larger than a mouse, or **Die Ratte ist größer als die Maus** The rat is larger than the mouse. **Ein Mensch ist in seinem Leben wie Gras** As for man his days are as grass. **Ein Dieb ist furchtsam, ein Löwe stark. Der Mensch ist sterblich** Man is mortal. **Der afrikanische Elefant ist größer als der indische. Der Tisch ist ein Hausgerät. Du bist doch die geborene alte Jungfer** (Fontane's *Effi*, chap. i) You are, indeed, a regular old maid. **War er nicht der Generalbösewicht?** (Kröger's *Leute eigener Art*, p. 117) Wasn't he a consummate villain? **Das ist die reine Lüge** That is a downright lie. The plural of the article is also used: **Beide waren ja noch die reinen Kinder** (R. Voss's *Psyche*, XIII) Both were still mere children. **Der Blinde erregt** or **die Blinden erregen unser Mitleid.**

D. *Omission of Article.* Proper names do not usually take an article, as the name itself points out clearly the object in question: **Hans ist angekommen.** This is the survival of a once much wider usage. In oldest Germanic the definite article was little used with nouns, not even with common class nouns. All things living and lifeless were conceived of as individuals. Gradually the old idea of individuality became much restricted. It is now common only with proper names, in a much less degree with names of materials and abstract nouns, sometimes in names of planets, ships, &c., and in a few accessions from the new type, such as titles, as discussed below in II. C, D, E. *c*, *g*. *Note*. It is most restricted in the genitive, where it is now little used except with proper names as the idea of a living personality has become closely associated with the articleless genitive: **Gold** (II. C. *b*) **schmilzt bei 1064°**, but **das Atomgewicht des Goldes ist 197,2.** See also II. E. *g. Note.* On the other hand, the absence of the definite article to-day is often felt as a contrast to its presence and hence indicates an indefinite portion, amount, or extent, as illustrated below in II. C, D, or a class or kind in contrast to a definite object, as illustrated in E below and III. *f.* Also words which in the sing. usually require the article often drop it in the *plural*, as the reference is not to definite individuals but only in a general way to a class or indefinite number: **Kinder und Narren sagen die Wahrheit.** In all these cases when the reference becomes a definite one the article must stand.

E. *Use of the Article with Modified Nouns.* Nouns which do not usually take an article require it at once when they become modified by an adjective, a genitive, a phrase, or relative clause, provided the modifier thus with the aid of the article marks the noun as a definite and distinct thing, but, of course, a modified noun is without the definite article if the reference is to something indefinite or to the general conception of a class or kind: **Wilhelm** *William*, **Frankreich** *France*, but **der kleine Wilhelm** *little William*, **das sonnige Frankreich** *sunny France*, as German contrary to modern English usage requires, except in direct address, the article before modified proper names as before other modified nouns wherever the reference is to a definite individual, i.e. as in older English usage, often still surviving in poetic or choice language, modern German still employs here regularly the new type of individualization described in B (2nd par.), while modern English drops the article after the analogy of usage with the unmodified proper name. Aside from proper names usage is here in general the same in both languages. The absence of the article suggests something indefinite or the general conception of class or kind with only a general characterization, while the definite article points to something definite or to a definite individual: **Sie hat nervösen Kopfschmerz** (idea of class or kind, not the idea of a definite attack), **heftige Kopfschmerzen** (indefinite number), but **Sie hat den gestrigen Kopfschmerz** (definite attack) **noch nicht überwunden. Schwarze Tinte** (idea of class, kind) **sieht hier besser aus als rote. China produziert schwarzen und grünen Tee** (idea of class or kind and indefinite quantity). **Feines Weizenmehl** fine wheat flour (general indication of class or kind), **das feinste Weizenmehl zu dem billigsten Preise** the finest wheat flour at the lowest market price (the superl. in both cases with the art. as a definite quality and price are stated), but **feinstes Weizenmehl zu billigstem Preise** very fine flour at a very low price (not entirely definite); **in hohem Alter** at an advanced age (indefinite), but **im hohen Alter von 78 Jahren** (definite); **Gott sei Dank!** thanks be to God! but **dem Gotte Israels** to the God of Israel. **Der Gott, der Eisen wachsen ließ, der wollte keine Knechte** (Arndt's *Vaterlandslied*). The article is of course dropped in case of persons when the identity of the individual is perfectly clear and the modifier is added only to call attention to some particular fact, not to point out the individual: **Gott, der uns bisher beigestanden hat, wird uns auch in der Zukunft nahe sein.**

F. The article must often be used on merely formal grounds to make clear the case: **Er zieht den Rosen Nelken vor,** but when the substantive clearly shows the case, the article in such instances drops out, as the reference is an indefinite one: **Er zieht Äpfeln Pfirsiche vor. Gold** (II. C. *b*) **schmilzt bei 1064°,** but to indicate the dative clearly: **Dieses Metall gleicht dem Golde.** Likewise **Er studiert Mathematik** (II. H), but **Er hat sich der Mathematik gewidmet. Zinn ist dem Zink ähnlich. Er läuft der Ehre nach.** In the genitive: **Die Geschichte der Mathematik, ein ganzer Tag der Arbeit** a whole day of work; **in Prima** or **in der Prima,** but **der deutsche Unterricht der Prima; der Glanz des Goldes. Er liebt Ruhe** or **die Ruhe,** but only **Er bedarf der Ruhe,** even tho the reference is to an indefinite amount, where there is usually no article. The use of the articles is especially frequent before names of persons to bring out clearly the case: **Ich ziehe Homer dem Virgil vor.**

II. Detailed Statement of the Uses of the Articles.

A. Common class nouns take the article both in the sing. and pl., when they are the names of definite objects, or stand as representatives of their class or genus, but drop it in all cases where they express an indefinite number or an abstract, general idea: **Die Blätter sind der Schmuck der Bäume,** but **Der Baum treibt Blätter. Das Buch auf dem Tisch,** but **Jeder Kaufmann muß gehörig Buch führen** Every merchant must keep his book account (no definite book, but his accounts in general) properly. **Das ist der Welt Lauf** *That is the way of the world,* but **Aus jedem ihrer Worte sprach die Dame von Welt** *From every word that she spoke it was clear that she was a lady familiar with the ways of* POLITE SOCIETY (= **Welt,** here used in its abstract application). **Der Mensch ist sterblich** *Man* (as the representative of his race) *is mortal,* but **Mensch sein heißt Kämpfer sein** *To be a man* (here = *alive to all that is of human interest*) *means to be a fighter in life's battles.* **Gläser zerschmettern wäre Wirtshaus gewesen** (*the way they do it in a* **Wirtshaus,** i.e. *coarse and vulgar*). In the last two sentences **Mensch** and **Wirtshaus** neither refer to definite individuals nor do they picture a man or a tavern as the representatives of their kind, but are used in a general abstract sense almost with the force of a predicate adjective. See III. *a.*

a. If a genitive precedes its governing noun, the latter must drop the definite article, as the genitive points out definitely the particular object, and hence must itself require the article: **Der Herr des Hauses,** or **des Hauses Herr.**

Note. In an earlier period the gen. which preceded its governing noun often did not, as to-day, have an article of its own, as the genitive did not point to a definite individual but to a class and its characteristics, so that it often had almost or quite the force of an adjective. Many survivals of this construction occur in the form of compound nouns: **Manneswort** *the word of a man,* **Freundesherz** *the heart of a friend,* **Menschenherz** *the human heart,* and thus also many fem. compounds ending in **en,** the old weak gen. form for the singular as well as the plural (see **76.** II. 1): **Frauenstimme** *the voice of a woman,* **eine Mahnung aus Frauenmund** *an exhortation from the mouth of a woman,* &c. Compare **249.** II. 1. B. *Note.*

b. The definite article stands very frequently for a possessive adjective when no ambiguity could thus arise, especially before parts of the body or articles of clothing, often accompanied by the dat. of the pronoun or noun referring to the person affected: **Der Kopf tut mir so weh** My head aches so badly. **Man nahm den Besiegten die Waffen ab. Er steckt die Nase in alles. Er schloß ihm die Augen** He closed his (a friend's) eyes. **Er schloß die Augen** He closed his (own) eyes. **Er verlor das Leben. Er kam herein mit dem Hut in der Hand. Er rieb sich die Augen.**

c. In a distributive sense the definite article in German often corresponds to the English indefinite *a* (in last example not the indef. art. *a,* but a form of the prep. *on*): **Dieses Tuch kostet 90 Pfennig(e) die Elle** This cloth costs 90 pfennigs a yard. **Er ruft Hosenträger aus, das Dutzend zu einer Mark** He is offering suspenders for a mark a dozen. **Fünfmal das Jahr** five times a year. The definite article used here in German and the indefinite in English except in the last example is the generalizing article described in I. *C.*

d. A title in the form of an attributive gen. takes the indef. art. in German, while in English no article at all is used: **Wilhelm I. nahm den Titel eines Kaisers an** William I. accepted the title of emperor.

e. The indefinite article in German is used in many idiomatic expressions: **ein jeder** or **ein jeglicher** each, everybody, **ein solcher (Mann,** &c.) such a (man, &c.), **so ein (großes Land),** or **ein so (großes Land)** such a (large country), &c.

B. *Collective nouns* are treated as common class nouns, as they point to definite groups of persons or things: **die Armee** the army, pl. **die Armeen, die Mannschaft** the crew, pl. **die Mannschaften,** &c. Many are felt as strong individualizations of the new type described in I. B (2nd par.): **das Parlament** parliament, **der Kongreß** congress, **das Altertum** antiquity, **das Mittelalter** the middle ages, **die Natur** nature, **die Menschheit** mankind, **die Gesellschaft** society, **die Wissenschaft** science, &c. Notice that in English the noun is usually, as in the older type of individualization, unaccompanied by the article, as it is felt as representing something single in kind, like a proper name. Compare I (**1**) below.

If the collective noun is felt as a common noun denoting a definite thing the article is used if the reference is to the entire body, but dropped when the reference is to an indefinite portion: **Nach dem Treffen erschien das Pappenheimsche Fußvolk** *After the engagement Pappenheim's infantry came up,* but **Es erschien Pappenheimsches Fußvolk** *Some of Pappenheim's infantry came up.*

C. *Names of materials* usually, differing from English, have the article as they are felt as individualizations of the new type described in I. B (2nd par.) above, but as in the old type of individualization, so common in English, the noun is still often unaccompanied by an article as it is felt as representing something single in kind, like a proper name: **Gold** or perhaps more commonly **das Gold gehört nächst dem Silber zu den besten Leitern der Elektrizität und der Wärme.** Compare I (**1**) below. The article is often dropped because the idea of an indefinite mass or of a class is present: **Man schlägt, spaltet Holz. Kohlenstaub deckt Weg und Gras. Trinken Sie Tee oder Kaffee? Bänke, Stühle von Holz; grünes, dürres, faules Holz.** Of course, an article is used if a definite portion or mass of the material is indicated: **Der Tee auf dem Tische, ein** (or **das**) **Tuch** a shawl, **ein** (or **das**) **Glas** a glass (drinking utensil), **ein Stein** a stone, **ein Eisen** a horse-shoe.

a. The indefinite article is often placed directly before a noun indicating a food or drink where in English such nouns are commonly preceded by some other noun or an indefinite pronominal adjective indicating the usual amount of the substance served at one time to one person, or the usual amount prepared at one time in one mass: **eine Suppe** a dish of soup, **ein Butterbrot** a piece of bread and butter, **eine Kartoffel** some potatoes, a dish of potatoes, **ein Bier** a glass of beer, **ein Bitterer** a glass of bitters, **ein Brot** a loaf of bread. **Meine Frau bringt mir einen Kaffee mit einem Rum** My wife is bringing me a cup of coffee with rum. **Mylord bereitete sich einen Tee** My lord made himself some tea.

b. Origin of the Article with Names of Materials and Abstract Nouns. As the names of materials and abstract nouns in older periods had no article, whenever it was desired, on the one hand, to give expression to the idea of a strong individualization of the old type and, on the other hand, to the idea of a class, an indefinite mass, extent, amount it was often unclear from the language used which of these ideas the speaker intended to convey. It gradually became the custom to prefix the definite article to express individualization. As this idea, however, is most forcibly expressed in the old style as in case of proper names, it is still quite common to employ the old style: **Gold schmilzt bei 1064°. Redlichkeit ist die Lebensluft alles guten Stils** (Engel's *Deutsche Stilkunst*, p. 23).

D. *Abstract nouns*, differing from English, usually have the definite article as they are felt as strong individualizations of the new type described in I. B (2nd par.), but as in the old type of individualization, so common in English, the noun is still often unaccompanied by an article as it is felt as something single in kind, like a proper name: **Der Geiz ist die Wurzel alles Übels**, but in 1. Tim. vi. 10 **Geitz ist eine wurtzel alles vbels. Der Mut verlernt sich nicht, wie er sich nicht lernt** (Goethe's *Götz*, 4, 3). **Nu aber bleibt Glaube | Hoffnung | Liebe | diese dry | Aber die Liebe ist die grössest vnter jnen** (1. Cor. xiii. 13). The simple noun without the article is still often preferred as a more vivid form of individualization: **Kleinmut erzieht nicht, Glaube erzieht** (Cauer). **Eine Reformation ist ein gesellschaftliches Werk, und als solches bedarf sie des Zusammenwirkens von Führung und Masse** (F. Wieser in *Deutsche Rundschau*, March 1920, p. 352). **Zeit ist Geld.** Very common in old saws: **Ehrlichkeit währt am längsten. Müßiggang ist aller Laster Anfang. Zeit bringt Rosen. Kommt Zeit, kommt Rat.** See C. *b* above and I. (**1**) below. On the other hand, abstract nouns regularly appear without the article when the idea of amount, extent, degree, or kind of the quality, condition, or activity is defined in only a general way, but they at once demand an article or a pronominal adjective when the idea is individualized, that is, when the extent or kind becomes definite, or the attention is directed to some particular case or cases, or when the abstract noun is used in the singular in a generalizing sense to represent the idea in all its entirety, in its widest sense, and not as limited to one individual case or several: **Der Mensch muß Ruhm und Tadel ertragen lernen** Man must learn to bear both praise and censure. **Glück macht Mut. Er trägt alles mit Geduld. Ich fange nur mit freier Hand, aber Gelenkigkeit gehört dazu** I catch fish with my hands, but it takes some skill. **Der Alte versank in Nachsinnen. Jammern ist unnütz.** But: **Ich finde dazu die Zeit nicht** I have not the time (for this particular task). **Dén Ärger möcht' ich sehen!** *Who ever saw such an aggravation?*, or simply **Dér Ärger! Eine Geduld, welche nichts erschüttern kann; der Friede der Seele, die Liebe Gottes, die öffentliche Meinung** public opinion, **diese Meinung. Solche Ungerechtigkeiten sind unerhört. Das Jammern ist unnütz** Your lamenting will do no good. **Das war ein guter Rat** That was good advice *or* a piece of good advice. **Geben Sie mir einen guten Rat** Give me some good advice. **Er war ganz liebevoller Sohn, die Rücksicht und Ehrerbietung selbst** He was quite an affectionate son, *the very personification of consideration and respect.* **Ist denn das die Möglichkeit?** Is it possible, within the range of the possible?! or in shorter, weaker form: **Ist's die Möglichkeit?** You don't say so!

E. The *names of persons* in general need no article, as the name itself indicates with sufficient clearness the individual. This is the old style of individualization described in I. D. The definite article, however, is often found here in the following cases:

a. When the reference is to a person already mentioned, or one that is explicitly designated by some adjective modifier: **Das ist der Karl** That is Carl (of whom we were speaking). **Friedrich der Große, or der große Friedrich, der dicke Wilhelm, der alte Herr Schmidt.** Since the sixteenth century it has been quite common to place the definite article before a name not designated by any modifier, as the name is felt as a strong individualization of the new type described in I. B (2nd par.), i.e. an individualization within a class, so that the person is felt as being a definite member of a definite class or circle: **Wenn die Kinder ihn nur von weitem sahen, so riefen sie schon: Mutter, der Brezelkaspar kommt!** Whenever the children saw him even afar off, they cried out: Mother, Jasper the brezel-seller is coming! **Mit dem Theodor** (member of the same class at school) **will ich gar nicht mehr umgehen. Ich mag und will's nicht glauben, daß mich der Max verlassen kann** (Schiller's *Wallensteins Tod*, 3, 18, where Wallenstein speaks of his friend Max). In familiar language the definite article sometimes takes the place of **Herr** *Mr.* and **Frau** *Mrs.* or **Fräulein** *Miss* before surnames, when the persons spoken of are individualized, are felt as being definite members of a definite circle of acquaintances or friends: **Der Schmidt or Herr Schmidt, die Schmidt or Frau Schmidt.** It is quite common to use the article before the name of a celebrated writer, statesman, &c., who has become distinguished in his class: **die Marlitt, die Ebner (Frau Baronin Marie von Ebner-Eschenbach), die Elliot,** &c.; **der Bismarck,** &c.

Note. Origin of the Article with Names of Persons. The definite article before names of persons and animals is more common in the spoken than written language, and very much more common in the South than in the North: **der Karl** instead of **Karl, der Pluto** (name of a dog). The use of the article with names of persons comes from the fondness of Germans to individualize within a class, a tendency already perceptible in M.H.G., as illustrated in *b* below: **Ich wundere mich, warum des Doktors** (**93. 1.** *a*) **nicht kommen . . . des Löwenwirts haben mir's sogar versprochen** (Auerbach's *Edelweiß*, xi). Thruout the story the latter character is called not by his name but **der Lö-**

wenwirt and his wife is **die Löwenwirtin.** Likewise within the family circle **der Vater, die Mutter** are often used instead of **Vater, Mutter** as names. This usage is especially firm with diminutives, which according to **245.** I. 8. **1.** *f. Note* 3 originally meant *the son or the daughter* of the person mentioned in the stem of the word and still are widely used as terms of endearment within the family and even elsewhere and hence are felt as individualizations within a definite group. As the use of diminutives is more deeply rooted in the South than in the North the use of the article with names in general is more common in the South than in the North. On the other hand, in both North and South the custom of using proper nouns without the article is often extended to common class nouns when used as familiar names just as in English: **Mutters Kleid** mother's dress. See **90.**

b. In direct address the name or title is usually without the definite article as the old style of individualization has in this category gained a complete victory: **Otto, tue das nicht!** Thus also in letters: **Teuerste Luise! Geehrter Herr! Lieber** (or **Liebster**) **Schmidt!** My dear friend Schmidt. In conversation the manner of address is as in English: **Herr Schmidt** Mr. S., **Frau Schmidt** Mrs. S., **Fräulein Schmidt** Miss S., &c., but **Guten Morgen, Herr Doktor!** Good morning, Doctor. Boys are addressed by their Christian names for short, and men in familiar language call each other by their surnames, or **-chen** is added to the surname, as **Stengelchen** my dear Stengel. In M.H.G. as in oldest German a proper name has in direct address as elsewhere no definite article before it, but a title or a common class noun used in direct address takes the definite article or sometimes the indefinite article (in M.H.G. *ein* = *der*; see I. A. *d*), as the noun is felt as a strong individualization of the new type described in I. B (2nd par.), i.e. an individualization within a class, so that the person is felt as being a definite member of a definite class: Ich wil dich warnen, Hagene, daz Adrianes kint (*Nibelungenlied*, aventiure 25). Sit willekomen Sifrit, ein (= der) künic uz Morlande. Ich sol gehorsam iu nu sin, | swester sun unt der herre min (*Parzival*, 789, 9–10). The idea of a class gradually became dim here and disappeared almost entirely at the close of the fifteenth century, so that each noun in direct address together with its modifiers is now felt as representing a definite person like a proper name and as a proper name drops the article but often takes a possessive adjective, which serves to bring the speaker into close relation to the person addressed: **O Hagen, Kind Adrians** or **Adrians Kind!, lieber Freund!, mein bester Freund!, mein Herr!, meine Herren!, meine Damen und Herren!** The only survival of older usage with the definite article is the employment of **der** after **Herr** in early N.H.G., as in **Herr der Wirt!** (Hans Sachs) = **Herr Wirt!** In English, however, the old usage lasted much longer and still lingers on in poetic style: The last of all the Romans, fare thee well! (*Jul. Cæsar*, 5, 3). What ho! The Captain of our Guard! Give the offender fitting ward (Scott's *Lady of the Lake*, V. 26).

At the close of the sixteenth century it became common according to **140.** *a. Note* (4th par.) to address persons indirectly instead of directly, i.e. instead of employing the articleless form of the noun or the personal pronoun of the second person, the forms which are usually employed in direct address, it became common to use a noun with the definite article and the third person of the verb, if a verb was used, the forms which are usually employed when speaking indirectly: **Was wollen die Herr'n?** (close of sixteenth century) = **Was wollt ihr? Gott grüß den Wirt und die weisen Herr'n!** (Hans Sachs) = **Gott grüße Euch, Herr Wirt, und Euch, weise Herren!** The definite article here in direct address is thus of entirely different origin from that described in the preceding paragraph. This old usage lingers on in provincial speech: **Guten Abend, die Herren!** Good evening, gentlemen! In the literary language in archaic style: **Gott zum Gruß, die Herr'n!** (Wildenbruch's *Die Quitzows*, 2, 1). Also in deferential language: **Der Herr Hauptmann wird gewiß die Güte haben usw.** Captain, you surely will be so kind, etc. The article is often dropped after the analogy of the usual form of direct address: **Ach, Fräulein sind (253.** I. 1. *a*) **so gut!** O, Miss, you are so good! The use of an article in the indirect form of address is also employed in colloquial English: How's the Captain? = How do you do, Captain? That's a good boy.

c. Also titles in the third person which precede names of individuals, whether persons or things, usually have no article, as they are felt as a part of the name: **Professor Müller** Professor Müller, **Herr Schmidt** Mr. Schmidt, **König Wilhelm, Schloß Walferdingen** Castle Walferdingen, **Kap Skagen** Cape Skagen. In an earlier period the omission of the article here was not so common, and still usage fluctuates in certain cases. In the nom. the omission of the article is decidedly more common than its retention, and also common in the acc., but not so much so as in the nom.; in the gen. the article is retained if the gen. follows the governing substantive, but is dropped if the governing noun follows. **Advokat Müller hat eine große Praxis. Ich habe das Vergnügen, Herrn Doktor Wespe zu sprechen?** Have I the honor of addressing Dr. Wespe? **Die Praxis des Advokaten Müller,** but **Advokat Müllers Praxis.** The omission of the article is here not common in the dat. except after prepositions, where the title sometimes has the article and sometimes drops it: **Die italienischen Truppen unter Oberst Arimandi. Der König und die Königin von Schweden und Norwegen nebst dem Prinzen Eugen. Nach Kap Flora** (*Beilage zur Allgemeinen Zeit.*, Aug. 26, 1905, p. 383), **am Kap Flora** (id.). In all the above cases when the title is felt in its full force and not as a part of the usual name the article must be used. In the plural all such titles naturally take the article, as they are felt in their full force: **Doktor B. meint** *Doctor B. thinks, &c.*, but **die Doktoren B. und D. meinen** Doctors B. and D. think, &c.

Designations of relationship before a name are sometimes treated like titles, so that we occasionally find the article before the designation of relationship: **Die Tante Löckchen, wie sie in der ganzen Stadt hieß** (Wildenbruch's *Schwester-Seele*, chap. I). But much more commonly the two nouns are felt as a name, so that the article is usually omitted, even when the name is in the genitive and follows the governing noun: **Der Liebling Tante Löckchens** (ib.).

d. Aside from the previous logical reasons, the article is also often used on formal grounds **to** distinguish the different cases. The article is much more frequently used in the gen., dat., and acc. than in the nom., and is avoided also in the dat. and acc. if the colloquial weak ending **-en** be used: **Die Werke des Praxiteles,** but where an s can be easily added **die Werke Schinkels. Karl sagt es dem Fritz** or **sagt es Fritzen. Karl lobt den Fritz** or **lobt Fritzen.** Also in case of a preceding title which usually has no article or inflection, being felt as one with the name, the article must stand if the name itself resists inflection by reason of its sibilant ending, and the case relation is not otherwise made clear: **das Leben Kaiser Wilhelms I.,** but **das Leben des Kaisers Tiberius.** But occasionally the title is inflected, but is without the art. See **92. 1.** *a.*

e. Proper names of course take an article when they are used as common nouns. This is the case when a proper name, which has become noted for some one thing, is applied to any individual who has distinguished himself similarly, or when by way of metonymy the name of an individual is applied to one of his works or creations, or a work of art is named from the person it represents: **Wilhelm der Stille weiht sich, ein zweiter Brutus, dem großen Anliegen der Freiheit. Die Gottsched sind zahlreicher als die Goethe** Men like Gottsched are more numerous than those like Goethe. **In Tertia lesen die Schüler den Ovid. Ich habe den Goethe** I have the works of Goethe. **Ich bringe ihr den Ho'mēr** I'll bring her a copy of Homer ('s poems). **Der Raphael in der Dresdener Galerie** the painting by Raphael in the Dresden gallery, **der kleine Sanders** the smaller edition of Sanders's German dictionary, **der Herkules** the statue of Hercules, **Die Minna von Barnhelm** (play named from its heroine), **der Faust** (play named from its leading character). On the contrary, however, in case of names of books, plays, &c. the article is often dropped after the analogy of proper nouns in general: **Und hier habe ich Gerok—Palmblätter** (Hauptmann's *Einsame Menschen*, 2, p. 47) And here I have Gerok, namely his *Palmblätter*. Frequently **Minna von Barnhelm, Faust,** &c., but usually with the article in the genitive: **Der erste Teil des Faust.**

f. A proper name takes the article as any common class noun when the reference is to one, a definite group, or the entire number of individuals who have the same origin, and hence a name in common: **ein Bourbon** a Bourbon, **die Bour'bonen** the Bourbons. This is the rule in case of illustrious or well-known houses, but in case of private families the article is more commonly omitted, as according to **93. 1.** *a* the form was originally a genitive singular, not a plural: **Brauns sind nicht reich** The Browns are not rich. Illustrious names must of course drop the article when they are used partitively: **Die deutschen Kaiser des achtzehnten Jahrhunderts waren Habsburger.**

g. Names of planets, ships, hotels usually take the definite article as they are felt as strong individualizations of the new type described in I. B. (2nd par.), i.e. each name is felt as an individualization within a class, so that the object is felt as being a definite member of a definite class: **der Mars, der Jupiter, die Viktoria** (name of a ship), **der Polarstern** Polar Star (ship), **der Coriolan** (newspaper), **die Union** (newspaper), **im Blauen Stern** at the Blue Star (hotel).

Note. In lively language the names of planets and ships are often, as in the old style of individualization, unaccompanied by the article as each name is felt as representing something single in kind, like a proper name, usually however only in the nominative, less commonly in the dative, rarely in the genitive: **Von den Planeten ist Merkur nur noch in den ersten Tagen des Februar am Morgenhimmel sichtbar** (*Hamburger Nachrichten*, Feb. 2, 1905), but **die Monde des Jupiter. Hannover** (ship) **ist gestern Kap Henry passiert** (*Hamburgischer Correspondent*, May 30, 1901). **Die Arbeiten auf „Brandenburg" gehen ihrer Vollendung entgegen** (*Hamb. Nachr.*, Oct. 28, 1904). German periodicals sometimes treat the names of newspapers in the same way, especially foreign words: **„Daily Telegraph" meldet usw.** (*Allgemeine Zeit.*, June 14, 1905). **Trotz ihres hohen Alters besitzt aber Tante Voß** (familiar name of **die Vossische Zeitung**) **noch immer eine ziemliche Lebenskraft** (*Hamb. Nachr.* Oct. 29, 1904). **World berichtet usw.** (*Neue Freie Presse*, Oct. 3, 1919).]

F. *Geographical names* fall into two distinct classes, one with the article, the other without it:

1. The *names of the natural divisions* of the earth's surface, such as rivers, lakes, seas, oceans, mountains, forests, peninsulas, deserts, plains, valleys, groups of islands, &c., except the names of individual islands and the names of continents, take the article, as they were originally common class nouns, or are designations of familiar objects (see E. *a* above) and hence are strong individualizations of the new type described in I. B (2nd par.): **der Rhein** (Gallic Rēnos *river*) the Rhine, **die Salzach** (ach related to Latin aqua *water*) tributary of the Inn, **der Brocken** or **Blocksberg** (peak in the Harz Mts.), **das Matterhorn** (Mt.), **der** (or **das**) **Wasgau** or **die** (pl.) **Vogesen** (vo'geːzən) the Vosges (Mountains), **die Eifel** (highlands in the extreme western part of Prussia), **der Grunewald** (forest near Berlin), **der Pelopo'nnēs** the Peloponnesus, **die Sa'hara** the Sahara, **die Campagna** (kam'panja:), **das Enga'dīn** the Engadine, **das Veltlin** (vɛlt-'liːn), **die Zy'kladen** the Cyclades, but **Kreta** Crete, **Eu'ropa** Europe, &c.

a. The article may drop out before words in a list or when connected by **und: Das Schicksal des Luthertums an Donau, Moldau und Elbe** (Lamprecht's *Deutsche Geschichte*, 7. 2., p. 532); **der nördliche Westerwald, durchströmt von Wied und Nister** (Emil Hommer's *Studien zur Dialektgeographie*, p. 1).

2. The *neuter names of the political divisions* of the earth, such as cities, countries, and minor divisions of countries, usually have no article when they are unmodified as they are individualizations of the old type, each noun being felt as representing, like a name of a person, something single in kind, but they require the definite article when modified by an adjective, a gen., or a relative clause: **Berlin** Berlin, **Deutschland** Germany, but **das schöne Deutschland** beautiful Germany, &c., Compare I. E. Many names of places had an article in an older period, as they were originally common class nouns, or had for their final element a common class noun, and hence were individualizations of the new type, i.e. individualizations within a class. Compare I. B (2nd par.) and **88. 1.** In most cases all feeling for the origin of such words is lost, but a few groups of words and a few isolated names still retain the article in accordance with older usage:

a. Only one town or city, **der Haag** The Hague (lit. the hedge), takes the article: **im Haag,** but also after the analogy of other towns **in Haag.**

b. All feminine and masculine names of countries and districts take the article: a number of fem. in **-ei** or **-ie,** as **die Lombar'dei** Lombardy (i.e. land of the Lombards), **die Tür'kei** Turkey, **die Tschechoslowa'kei** Czecho-Slovakia, **die Norman'die** Normandy (i.e. land of the Normans); some fem. in **-au,** as **die Moldau** Moldavia; fem. in **-mark** *march,* as **die Altmark;** a few isolated fem., as **die Schweiz** Switzerland, **die Pfalz** the Palatinate, **die Lausitz** Lusatia, **die Le'vante** the Levant, **die Bretagne** (bʀə'tanjə) Brittany, **die Gaskogne** (gas'kɔnjə), **die Riviera** (ʀi·'vie:ʀa:) &c.; masc. in **-gau** *district,* which are also sometimes neut. in accordance with the earlier gender of the word, as **der (das) Rheingau; der Su'dan** the Sudan; **der** or more commonly **das Elsaß** (sometimes like other neuters without the article: **durch Elsaß**—*Hamburger Nachrichten,* Jan. 10, 1905) Alsace. Notice also **die Vereinigten Staaten** *the United States* according to I. B (2nd par.) above.

Note. The poet sometimes takes liberties with these words and drops the article, thus vividly treating them as real proper nouns instead of common nouns according to their origin: **Weil wir es satt sind, daß Mark Brandenburg jedem geldgier'gen Schuft aus Böhmerland verschachert wird** (Wildenbruch's *Die Quitzows,* 2). The article usually drops out before these words in common prose when they stand in a list: **Mit je einem Studierenden sind vertreten: Schweiz, Frankreich, Griechenland, Türkei** (*Beilage zur Allg. Zeit.,* Dec. 20, 1906).

c. Neuter names of places quite uniformly are used without the article, except the few in b and those in **-land,** where the **-land** is felt in some cases as a common noun, and thus requires the article, or in most cases drops it in accordance with the general rule that neuter names do not take the article: **im Hessenland(e)** or **in Hessenland** in Hesse (lit. land of the Hessians), **das Vogtland** section in Saxony (lit. land under a governor), once a bulwark against the Slavs, **das Wendland** section in Hanover, originally *land of the Wends,* **die Niederlande** the Netherlands, &c., but **Deutschland** Germany, **Ermeland** and **Samland,** sections along the Baltic, &c. Notice the isolated neuter **das Ba'nat** the Banat.

G. The *names of streets, squares,* and *city-wards* naturally take the article, as the final component element is a common noun: **die Friedrichstraße, der Schillerplatz** Schiller Square, **das Spandauerviertel** (part of Berlin). These are strong individualizations of the new type described in I. B (2nd par.) above. Compare I. (**1**) below. In adverbial expressions indicating street and number the article is often omitted. **Wo wohnst du? Halbdorfstraße fünfzehn.**

H. The *names of the seasons, months* (see also **94.** 3. A. *b*), *days, parts of the day, the meals, the classes* (in school), and *the sciences* usually require the article: **im Sommer, zu Anfang des August, am Sonntag. Der Morgen graut. Ist das Frühstück fertig? Die Prima** (highest class in a secondary school), **die Se'kunda, die Bo'tanik** botany, **die Che'mie** chemistry, **die organische Chemie** organic chemistry, **die Astrono'mie** astronomy, **die Mathema'tik** mathematics, &c. The nouns with the article in all these groups are individualizations of the new type described in I. B (2nd par.) above. Compare I. (**1**) below. The names of the classes at school and the sciences, however, are often felt as each representing something single in kind like a proper name and hence like proper names they often drop the definite article: **Hans sitzt in Prima, kommt nach Prima. Die reine Mathematik zerfällt in die Arithme'tik, die Algebra und die Geome'trie,** but **Mathematik ist die Wissenschaft der Größen** and **Er studiert Mathematik.** In lively style also elsewhere in this category: **Der Winter verging, Frühling zog ein in die flandrischen Lande** (Prof. Hans von Hayek in *Velhagen und Klasings Monatshefte,* Jan. 1916, p. 38). **Um die Mitte Dezembers** (Mörike).

I. A difference of development or conception in some cases leads to a different use of the article in the two languages: (**1**) From a glance at B, C, D, E it becomes apparent that English has preserved much better than German the old simple form of the noun without the definite article wherever it represents a person or thing single in kind, like a proper name. In German after the definite article had become firmly associated with common class nouns the idea of individualization—inherent in the definite article from the very start, at first however only individualization within a class—became so strong that often the idea of class entirely disappeared. Thus the new form with the definite article often has the same force as the old simple articleless noun and represents a person or a thing single in kind like a proper name, only perhaps with a little more concrete force and a little less vivid individualization: **das Schicksal** destiny, **der Tod** death, **die Vorsehung** Providence, **der Himmel** heaven, **die Hölle** hell, **das Para'dies** paradise, **das E'lysium** elysium, **die Ehe** matrimony, **die Nachwelt** posterity, **das Christentum,** &c. See also B,C,D,E and I. B (2nd par). (**2**) On the other hand the article is often dropped in German even tho used in English, to indicate that the thing or idea is not conceived of with a definite extent or intensity: **Ich habe Kopfweh** I have a headache. **Er hat Familie** He has a family. **Er geriet in großen Zorn** He fell into a great rage. **Bekanntschaft mit jemandem machen** to form an acquaintance with someone. **Er hatte bei guten Leuten Wohnung** (a place to board) **gefunden.** (**3**) German often uses the definite article where English employs the indefinite: **einem das Leben zur Last machen** to make life a burden to someone, **im Augenblick, im Nu** in a moment, **im Galopp** in a gallop, **im Schritt** at a foot-pace, **im Trab** at a trot, **in der Lage sein, Gutes zu tun** to be in a position to do good, **zur Abwechselung** for a change, &c.

III. Omission of the Article.

The article in general is omitted: (**1**) sometimes when the noun contains an abstract idea and regularly when it contains the general conception of a class or kind and hence does not designate a definite object; (**2**) when, as in case of proper nouns or common class nouns used as proper nouns, the object is already sufficiently defined, also when the noun is felt as representing something single in kind, like a proper name; and (**3**) in many set expressions and proverbs coined in an early period when the article was little used.

The article is omitted in the following common cases:

a. In the predicate when the noun does not designate a definite individual but something abstract, such as a quality, relation, condition, calling, or capacity of any kind, moreover, any fact or idea in a broad general sense, also indefinite time: **Der Mensch ist ein Gott, sobald er Mensch ist** Man is a god when he is humane. **Ich bin Partei** I am biased. **Beispiel** (= illustrative of) **einer lebenden flexivisch reich ausgebildeten Sprache ist das Russische. Ich bin Braut** I am betrothed. **Sie fühlt sich Mutter. Thu'kydides war ganz und gar ein Kind der Sophistenzeit wie Hero'dot, dessen Werk ihm Vorbild war. Es war doch etwas anderes, als letzten Winter auf dem Regimentsballe in Königsberg, aber freilich Königsberg ist Provinz** (provincial). **Und doch war er** (the artist Menzel) **treuester Diener, Idealbild eines Beamten, ja Verkörperung des urpreußischen Begriffs Soldat; aber sein König war die Kunst** (Karl Storch in *Der Türmer*, March 1905). **Er wurde preußischer Untertan. Sie ist noch Kind. Im Grunewald** (forest near Berlin) **ist Holzauktion. Es ist Aufgabe des Staates, strenge darüber zu wachen, daß usw.** it is the business of the state, etc. **Es ist Tatsache, daß usw.** It is a fact that, etc. **Das ist fast Gewißheit** That amounts to almost a certainty. **Er ist nur Anfänger** He is a mere beginner. **Er ist Baumeister, Witwer, Junggeselle, Bürgermeister von Berlin, Professor an der Universität Berlin, Inhaber des eisernen Kreuzes, Vater vieler Kinder. Er kam als Retter in der Not. Die Überproduktion an Staatsnoten ist gewöhnlich Folge eines Krieges. Es war Eckzimmer des Hauses. Es wurde Abend. Es wurde Winter.** The adjective nature of the predicate noun is sometimes clearly indicated by the use of the singular with reference to a plural subject: **Er sagte, jeder Friedensfreund werde herzlich wünschen, daß die dem Senate vorliegenden Schiedsgerichtsverträge Gesetz würden** (*Hamburger Nachrichten*, Jan. 31, 1905). Sometimes the predicate substantive assumes almost pure adjective force and can be modified by an adverb: **Ich bin nicht Kenner genug** (adv.). Aside from this common group of abstract meanings it is usual to employ the indefinite article in the predicate: **Er ist ein Esel, ein Schafskopf, ein Dieb, ein Verräter, ein Verächter der Weiber. Der Walfisch ist ein Säugetier.** Of course, the slightest approach to definiteness calls for the definite article: **Das ist der Baumeister** That is the architect (of whom we were just talking).

Note. This omission of the article in the predicate is especially frequent in appositional and parenthetical phrases, which are often contracted clauses in which the appositional substantive is the real predicate, and hence the omission of the article is natural, but the omission often thus occurs even when in a complete sentence the same word in the predicate would require the article: **Als Anfänger** (= **Obgleich er Anfänger ist**) **behandelt er die Sache doch mit Meisterschaft. Ich Esel, dreifacher Esel verscherze auf diese Weise meinen Freund**, but **Ich bin ein Esel. Unter der Regierung des Königs Siegmund, Sohn des deutschen Kaisers Karls IV.** (*National-Zeitung*). **Ich schreibe Ihnen in Aix (ehemalige Hauptstadt der Provinz).**

b. If a genitive precedes its governing noun, the latter must drop its article. See II. A. *a.*

c. The article is often dropped when a singular noun is used by way of synecdoche, to designate more than one or a regular succession, as the idea is that of a class or kind, not the designation of a definite object: **Er trug sie mit starkem Arm. In tiefem Tal, auf schneebedeckten Höhen war stets dein Bild mir nah. Mit scharfem Schritt** with a quick step.

d. In prepositional phrases the indefinite article can be omitted when the reference is evidently to only *one* object: **ein Gebäude mit flachem Dach. Ein auf bewaldetem Berge liegendes Schloß. Auf hagerem Halse hob sich ein blasses vergilbtes Frauenantlitz.**

e. The article is dropped before a noun as in English when it introduces a formal definition of itself, as it represents something single in kind, like a proper noun: **Kunst ist** (or **heißt**) **die Darstellung des Schönen.**

f. The article is dropped before a noun which does not represent a definite object or thing but is used in a broad, general sense to indicate a class or kind: **Blutigel ist Blutigel** A leech is a leech wherever you find it. **Ende gut, alles gut** If the end is good, all is good. **Kinder, ihr kommt offenbar von der Arbeit, ihr riecht frisch nach Palette** (Wilbrandt's *Die Maler*, 1, 1). **Seehauch geht durch alles hellenische Leben, seine Schönheit und Poesie** (Prof. Dr. Ed. Heyck in *Velhagen und Klasings Monatshefte*, May 1905, p. 275). **Nur Leute mit jungen Herzen könnten wir gebrauchen, und junges Herz hat Mut und faßt schnell Vertrauen** (Paul Keller's *Das letzte Märchen*, p. 10). **Eigener Herd ist Goldes wert. Altklug** (**111.** 7. *h.* (**2**). (*a*)) **lebt nicht lang.** Examples with modifying adjective are given in I. E. The article is absent thus in many pithy sayings some of which date back to a time when the article was little used, and thus bear the stamp of an earlier coinage. Older usage has survived in such expressions, as their general meaning and the idea of a class or kind contained in them precluded the use of the article with its definite, individual force. This old type has also influenced modern expression considerably.

The article is frequently omitted before the absolute superlative to express a high degree in a general way without reference to any particular comparison: **Einfachste, tiefste Harmonie ist im Sturm, wie in der Windstille** (Raabe). **Auf fadeste Dummköpfe machte er Eindruck, auf Arnold nicht** (G. Hauptmann).

g. The article is dropped in an enumeration of things or particulars, for now as in oldest German the idea of unit, sovereign individuality, separate item, something single in kind usually overshadows all other conceptions, but of course the article is used if for any reason it is desired to individualize certain objects within a class: **Bei der Ausfüllung der Frachtbriefrubrik „Art**

der Verpackung" hat der Versender einen möglichst bezeichnenden Ausdruck (Faß, Sack, Kiste, Kasten, Ballen, u. dgl.) zu wählen. Die falsche, aber bisher landläufige Ansicht, daß Rhein, Reuß, Rhône und Tessin am St. Gotthard entspringen, gab auch zu einer irrigen Auffassung der Straßenverhältnisse Anlaß. Herr Schreiber Witthoff, Topfmarktecke, Hinterhaus, vierte Etage links. Zürich am Ausfluß der Limmat aus dem Züricher See, jetzt die volkreichste Stadt der Schweiz, Mittelpunkt einer großartigen Industrie in Seide, Baumwolle, Maschinen u. a., bedeutender Handel, Eisenbahnknotenpunkt und lebhafter Fremdenverkehr. But the article is used in the following sentence, as the objects are individualized within a class: **Da (unter dem Christbaume) lag ein braunes Müffchen, ein schwarzer Samthut, ein buntes Kleid, ein Märchenbuch, ein Bilderbuch, sechs Schreibebücher, Federn und Schieferstifte, Strickgarn und auch eine wunderschöne Puppe.**

h. Similar to the above is the very common use of dropping the article of each of a pair of words connected by **und**, or **weder — noch** neither — nor, **nicht — noch** not — or, for the idea of unit, sovereign individuality, something single in kind is still prominent here as in oldest German: **Tag und Nacht, Leib und Seele, Eingang zu Garten und Kegelbahn, der Blick des Pastors von Kanzel und Altar, auf Sofa und Stühlen, zwischen Friedrichsdenkmal und Brandenburger Tor. Da wächst weder Baum noch Strauch. In blinder Hast jagte Kaspar dahin, achtete nicht auf Stock noch Stein, nicht auf Zaun noch Graben.**

Note. This omission of the article is not limited to set expressions, as stated in some grammars, but is permissible before all words thus coupled together, except in the gen. case, where as yet the omission does not uniformly occur: **Vater und Mutter sind heimgekehrt. Liebe Vater und Mutter. Gehorche Vater und Mutter,** but **Gedenke des Vaters und der Mutter. Trotz Sträubens und Stemmens.**

i. The article is dropped before nouns which are used twice, once before and again after a prep.: **Woge auf Woge, von Tag zu Tage, Schritt vor Schritt, Auge um Auge,** &c.

j. The article is dropped in a very large number of set expressions, most of which have this in common—that they either indicate sovereign individuality or something single in kind, or on the other hand have a broad general meaning, and do not refer to definite objects or things. These expressions are survivals of a very old period when the article was not as now required with nouns. Later the demonstrative **der** became attached to the noun as an article, weakened in accent but still with enough of its former force to point out something definite. Older usage survived in many expressions where the original idea of singleness in kind was still distinctly felt and the absence of the article was thus felt as natural and on the other hand where the *general* meaning naturally precluded the use of the *definite* article. The following groups of expressions are thus used without the article, tho in some cases the newer form with the article can also be found:

aa. The adverbial gen. of time, place, manner, condition: **morgens** or **des Morgens** of mornings, **sommers** in the summer time, **bei erster Gelegenheit, höheren Orts** before a higher authority, **flugs** quickly, **schlimmstenfalls** if the worst happens, in the worst event, &c.

bb. The acc. as object of a verb, or the dat. or acc. after preps. in numerous set expressions in which the substantive does not retain its literal meaning, but enters into close relations with the verb, forming with the latter *one* idea, usually of a general or figurative application: **reinen Mund halten** to remain mum, **Hand anlegen** to put one's hand to, to go to work, **teilnehmen** to take part in; **zu Berge fahren** to ride up hill, or sail up stream, **zu Kreuze kriechen** to become humbled. See **245.** IV. 3. B.

cc. The dat. or acc. in numerous prep. phrases in which the substantive retains its separate meaning, independent of the verb, but has a general or indefinite application. The more common cases are the following:

(1) In general statements of time: **vor Mittag** before noon, **nach Tisch** after meal-time. **Tag über** all day, &c. **Nach getaner Arbeit ist gut ruhn.**

(2) In adverbial phrases of manner and reason: **zu Fuß, zu Wasser gehen** to go on foot, by water, &c.; **vor Angst beben** to tremble on account of anxiety, **aus Liebe handeln** to act prompted by love, &c.

k. The article is dropped before certain adjectives or adjective-substantives (see **111.** 3. *a* and 7. *h*): (1) **folgender kleine Roman,** &c.; (2) **Alt und jung waren da.** In the first group the article contrary to English usage is omitted as the adjective, such as **folgender, erwähnter,** &c., is felt as having demonstrative force, like **dieser, jener,** &c., pointing to a following definite person or thing. This is often clearly shown by the weak form of the following descriptive adjective. In the second group the adjective has no article before it as the reference is indefinite or general.

l. The indefinite article is not usually used before **hundert** hundred and **tausend** thousand: **hundert Schüler** one hundred pupils.

m. The article is dropped in short, concise commands or warnings: **Augen links! Kopf zurück!**

n. The article is often dropped before abstract or collective nouns and names of materials when they represent something single in kind, like a proper name, or on the other hand when they indicate an indefinite portion, amount, or extent. The details are given in II. B. C. D.

Also any noun which usually has concrete meaning loses the article if it assumes abstract meaning: **Der Oberst hatte in seiner kurzen, etwas militärischen Art und Weise gesprochen, aus der jedoch Herz klang, das zum Herzen ging.**

o. The article is almost always dropped before proper names or common class nouns used as proper names in direct address, and as a rule elsewhere, but there are many exceptions, as enumerated in II. E and the sub-articles. Also the following points come under this head:

aa. In familiar language, titles and designations of relationship are often used as proper names and as proper names, of course, have no definite article before them, and in poetry and folk-lore also the names of familiar objects, may, in order to impart vividly the idea of personality drop the definite article and assume the force of proper names (see II. E. *a. Note* and **90**): **nach Hoheits Befehl** according to the command of your Highness. **Herrschafts sind heute ganz unter sich** (words of a hired girl) My employer and his family are to-day entirely to themselves. **Gnädiges Fräulein ist in ihrem Recht!** (Hans Hoffmann's *Iwan der Schreckliche*, chap. IV, where the speaker is speaking of a young lady whom in direct speech he addresses as **gnädiges Fräulein**). **Tantes Kleid** Aunt's dress. **Mutter hat's erlaubt. Knabe sprach: ich breche dich, Röslein sprach: ich steche dich** (Goethe's *Heidenröslein*). Individualization of the new type described in I. B (2nd par.), i.e. the form with the definite article, is also common here: **Du kommst doch her, um den Papa zu bitten, daß er dir heraushelfen soll** (Wildenbruch's *Schwester-Seele*, II, chap. XVII).

bb. In official language or a familiar style, definite persons or organizations are called not by their proper name but by some common noun that represents the capacity in which the person or thing appears. This common noun like a proper name drops the article: **Beklagter trete vor** Let the defendant step forth. **Schreiber dieser Zeilen** the writer of these lines, **Verfasser** the author, &c.

cc. Names of books, firms, and headings and addresses like proper names in general drop the article: **Geschichte der Völkerwanderung** History of the Migration of the Nations, **Vorwort** Preface, **Einleitung** Introduction, **Eisengießerei von R. M., Artikel bei Stoffnamen** The Use of the Article before Names of Materials (heading of an article in a German Grammar). **Mein Geschäft befindet sich S.W., Friedrichst. 160** My place of business is in the southwest part of the city, Frederick Street, No. 160.

Inflection of Common Nouns.

60. 1. *Classification.* Nouns are divided into three declensions, the Strong, Weak, and Mixed. The different cases and numbers in all these declensions are formed by adding certain vowel or consonant endings to the stem of the noun and sometimes by modifying (indicated below by ¨) the stem vowel. The following is the general outline of the different systems of terminations and different methods of treating the stem vowel:—

Strong.					Weak.	Mixed.	
E-Plural Type				Er-Plural Type			
Singular.					Singular.	Singular	
Unmutated	Mutated		E-less Form				
—	—	Nom.	—	—	— (e)	—	
— (e)s	— (e)s	Gen.	—s	— (e)s	— (e)n	— (e)s	
— (e)	— (e)	Dat.	—	— (e)	— (e)n	— (e)	
—	—	Acc.	—	—	— (e)n	—	
Plural.					Plural.	Plural. 1st Cl.	2nd Cl.
—e	¨e	Nom.	(¨)	¨er	— (e)n	— (e)n	—s
—e	¨e	Gen.	(¨)	¨er	— (e)n	— (e)n	—s
—en	¨en	Dat.	(¨)n	¨ern	— (e)n	— (e)n	—s
—e	¨e	Acc.	(¨)	¨er	— (e)n	— (e)n	—s

The declensions are distinguished by the case ending in the gen. sing. and nom. pl.

A. The Strong declension has **s** or **es** in the gen. sing.: **der Spaten** spade, gen. **des Spatens.** It subdivides into four *classes* in the plural according to the formation of the nom. plural:

a. The Unmutated E-Plural Type adds **e** in the nom. pl. without modification of the root vowel: **der Arm** arm, pl. **die Arme.** Such a noun is here for short called an unmutated e-plural.

b. The Mutated E-Plural Type adds **e** in the plural and modifies the root vowel: **der Fuß** foot, pl. **die Füße.**

c. The E-less Form of the E-Plural Type drops the regular plural ending **e** in the nom. pl., but sometimes modifies the root vowel: **der Spaten, pl. die Spaten; der Vater,** father, pl. **die Väter.** A noun in this class is here called an e-less plural and is further distinguished as an unmutated **e**-less plural or a mutated **e**-less plural according to its form in the plural.

d. The **Er**-Plural Type adds **er** to form the nom. pl. and modifies the root vowel: **das Buch** book, pl. **die Bücher.** Such a noun is here for short called an **er**-plural.

B. The Weak declension has **n** or **en** in every case sing. and pl. except nom. sing.: **der Knabe** boy, gen. **des Knaben,** dat. **dem Knaben,** acc. **den Knaben,** pl. nom. **die Knaben,** &c.

C. The Mixed declension is *strong* (i.e. takes **s** or **es** in gen.) in the sing. and falls into two groups in the pl.

a. The first group takes the weak pl., i.e. ends in **n** or **en** thruout the pl.: **der Staat** state, gen. **des Staat(e)s,** pl. **die Staaten.**

b. The second group has the foreign ending *s* thruout the pl.: **das Echo** echo, gen. **des Echos,** pl. **die Echos.**

D. In any of these declensions where the case ending of the noun is deficient the article (which is ever playing a more important rôle) marks distinctly the case: **der Omnibus, des Omnibus,** &c. See 2 below.

2. Present Fluctuations and Tendencies. There is at present considerable confusion in German declension in case of many individual words. Grammars and dictionaries differ very much in the types of inflection which they recommend for these individual words, according as their authors are looking conservatively into the past or hopefully into the future. In the language itself there is evidently a marked tendency in the direction of uniformity, a movement away from the complexity of older inflection with its many groups toward a greater simplicity which manifests itself by a gradual gravitation of many words toward the largest groups with the most common inflectional forms. Two types of inflection are gaining the ascendency—for feminines the weak inflection, for masculines and neuters the unmutated **e**-plural with the **e**-less form after **-el, -en, -er, -chen, -lein, Ge___e.** Words from the different groups are slowly finding their way into these two living groups. Foreign words accented upon the last syllable are following these same lines of development with the exception of masculines representing living beings. These masculines denoting living beings still cling to their old historic inflection, the weak declension, as the conception of life has, in case of masculines, become intimately associated with the weak declension since it now contains very few masculines which denote lifeless things: **der Ban'dit** bandit, **des Ban'diten,** pl. **die Ban'diten,** but **der Gra'nit** granite, **des Gra'nits,** pl. **die Gra'nite.** Also here, however, there is a trend toward the unmutated **e**-plural, as masculines ending in accented **-al, -an, -än, -ar, -är, -eur** (ɵːʀ), **-ier, -on, -or** are usually **e**-plurals even when they represent living beings: **der Ma'jor** *major,* **des Ma'jors,** pl. **die Ma'jore.**

Earlier in the period there developed a tendency to drop the **s** of the genitive singular, especially in case of proper nouns preceded by the definite article, as the feeling prevailed that the preceding inflected article marked the case with sufficient clearness. At the present time usage is still somewhat unsettled here, but there is a tendency to restore the **s** in certain categories, especially in titles, as is described in the proper places below. With foreign nouns, common and proper, the **s** has never been securely fixed, but there is at present a marked tendency to treat foreign class nouns as far as possible exactly as native words.

General Rules for all Declensions.

61. *a.* Feminine nouns never vary in the singular, the article or context alone showing case. Thus feminines belong to their respective classes and declensions only in the plural. Occasionally traces of inflection in the sing. can still be found, indicating a different state of things in earlier periods. See **76. II. 1.**

b. Nouns ending in unaccented **ar, e, el, em, en, er, chen, il, ir, lein, sel, ul,** always lose the **e** of the case ending: **der Flügel** wing, gen. **des Flügels,** dat. pl.

den Flügeln, not **des Flügeles, den Flügelen; die Feder** pen, pl. **die Federn; der Ungar** Hungarian, pl. **die Ungarn,** but **der Ta'tar** Tartar, pl. **die Ta'taren.**

c. Usually the last noun of compound substantives is alone declined, and also gives the gender to the compound. Certain modern compounds, however, are inflected differently. See **80. 2.**

STRONG DECLENSION.

General Rules.

62. A. In every strong masc. or neut. (for fem. see **61.** *a*) noun the nom. and acc. sing. of the respective genders are the same, and in nouns of all genders the nom., gen., and acc. plural of the respective genders are alike, the accompanying article or adjective alone marking case relations.

B. Every strong noun ends in **en** or **n** (see **61.** *b*) in the dat. pl.

C. The case ending **e** according to **61.** *b* is dropped after the suffixes **-e, -el, -em, -en, -er, -chen, -lein, -sel: der Engel** angel, **des Engels** (not **Engeles**), **dem Engel** (not **Engele**), &c. In case of those ending in **n,** no additional **n** is added in the dat. pl.: **der Spaten** spade, gen. **des Spatens,** dat. pl. **den Spaten; das Fräulein** *young lady*, dat. pl. **den Fräulein.**

Note. The rule of dropping **e** after the above-mentioned suffixes is a special application of the old law that required the suppression of the most weakly stressed vowel or vowels in words of more than two syllables. This old law which began to operate in M.H.G. and was still at work in early N.H.G., has produced marked results in the form and inflection of words: **Händler** (from older **'Hande'ler**), **Wagner** (M.H.G. 'wage'ner), **Gärtner** (M.H.G. 'garte'nære), **himmlisch** (M.H.G. 'hime'lisch), &c. Likewise in a group of words the components of which are so closely related that they are felt as one word: hèr Párzival! (*Parzival*, **315.** 26) in direct address, but elsewhere herre, now always **Herr;** similarly **Graf** and **Fürst,** which have been shortened from older **Grafe, Fürste** as the words are much used in titles before names, where they have weak stress: **Gràf Álbrecht, Fùrst Bísmarck.** For the effects of this law in the inflection of nouns see **68.** As the tendency increased to pronounce the vowel of the root syllable more forcibly and give it relatively much greater length than the vowels of the other syllables the vowels that were the least stressed gradually lost their fulness and finally disappeared. Thus as a result of this old law the trochaic foot (⏊ ⏑) has gained a great victory over the dactylic (⏊ ⏑ ⏑): pl. **die 'Wagĕn** for older **die 'Wagĕnĕ.** Altho this law under S.G. influence has after the suffixes **-el, -em, -en, -er** prevailed in the inflection of nouns and in part elsewhere, it usually yields to the M.G. usage of retaining the inflectional endings in order that the grammatical relations may be clearly indicated: past tense **er dienete** (Luther), later **diente,** not **dienet** or **dient;** pl. **die 'Käfĭge,** not **die Käfĭg.** Compare **110.** A. *a*, *b*, *c* and **178.** 1. B. *a*.

D. The gen. sing. takes **es** when it ends in some sound difficult to unite with the **s** of the case ending without the aid of **e,** just as *es* in English is added to form the pl. when *s* alone would be difficult to pronounce: one glass, two glasses. Usually **es** stands after final **b, d, ld, nd, mpf, s, ß, ss, z, sch, st,** or after a final vowel or diphthong: **der Fisch** fish, **des Fisches; der Bau** building, **des Baues.** In case of a final vowel or diphthong, even tho in print the **e** (as in **des Baus**) be suppressed, it is nevertheless slightly heard.

Also in the other cases **es** is usually employed in monosyllabic forms, especially in choice language, but simple **s** is also widely used, in familiar speech even after some of the above-mentioned consonants. Simple **s,** on the other hand, is used in the following cases: (**1**) According to the old law described in C. *Note* regularly in the **e**-less plural class and also elsewhere in order to avoid a dactyl (⏊ ⏑ ⏑), in less measure also to avoid an antibacchius (⏊ ⏊ ⏑), that is, when the final syllable of the uninflected form of the word is unaccented or has only secondary accent: **der Vogel, des Vogels,** not **des 'Vogĕlĕs; der Käfig** cage, **des Käfigs,** not **des 'Käfĭgĕs; des Hōfes, des Mōndes,** but usually **des 'Kirch'hōfs, des 'Voll'mōnds,** not infrequently however also **des 'Kirch'hōfĕs, des 'Voll'mōndĕs,** as we feel that the inflected genitives **-hofes, -mondes** are not fixed forms but living genitives and ought to have the full ending **-es** in accordance with present general usage outside of compounds. On the other hand, we *must* say **Schafskopf** blockhead, **Kindskopf** childish person, **Blutsfreund** kindsman, &c., as they were coined earlier in the period when the old law described in C. *Note* was in full force and are now felt as set forms. But we say **'Tages'anbruch, 'Tages'presse, 'Jahres'zeit, 'Kindes'pflicht** as they are modern formations and stand in close touch with the genitive groups of a modern sentence which prefer a genitive in **-es** to one in simple **-s.** In such common cases as **im Anfang des zweiten 'Kriegs'jahres** (*Neues Wiener Journal*, Oct. 12, 1919), **&c.** we find groups in which there are two genitives, as in **Kriegsjahres,** the first a set form, the second a genitive in close touch with the genitive groups of a modern sentence. Thus where we find traces of the old law, as in the first component of numerous old compounds of older coinage, in the **e**-less plural class, and in nouns abbreviated from older dactyl form, as in **des Käfigs** (from older **Käfiges**), it is preserved rather than observed, i.e. it has become fixed in these set types. (**2**) Also in the adverbial genitive: **tags drauf** on the next day, **hierorts** at this place, **falls, flugs,** &c., all set expressions and hence not in close touch with the genitive groups of a normal sentence, which prefer a genitive in **-es** to one in simple **-s**; likewise in **nichts** (**145.** *g. Note* 2), **Dings** (**83**), &c., which are no longer felt as genitives. (**3**) Usually in foreign words except after sibilants: **des Lords, des Klubs,** &c., but **des Kompasses.** The **-es**, however, is not infrequent after an accented syllable in very common foreign words, which naturally assume the **-es** that is now so common in German words: **die Prüfung des gesamten Materiales** (Wolf von Unwerth in *Anzeiger für deutsches Altertum* xxxv, p. 115). (**4**) In proper names **-es** is now not used at all. In case of names of persons the genitive usually ends in **-s**, even after sibilants, for as explained in **86.** 2. *a* an additional *s* is actually *spoken* after a sibilant, altho in print we find here only an apostrophe: **Wilhelms, Max'** (maks's). Names of persons ending in a sibilant, however, *may* take **-ens** in the genitive: **Maxens.** Names of places take **-s** in the genitive, except those ending in a sibilant, which take a **von** before the name instead of a genitive ending: **Ber'lins,** but **die Straßen von Pa'ris.**

E. The dative sing. ending **e** is still widely used in choice language, but it is much disregarded in familiar language, especially in words of more than one syllable. In certain cases it is not used at all, even in choice language.

It is not usually found: (*a*) in the **e**-less plural class: **mit dem Spaten;** (*b*) in the word **Gott** *God* when no article stands before it: **Gott sei Dank!,** but **dem Gotte Israels;** (c) in proper names: **in Frankreich** in France; (*d*) usually after an unaccented syllable when it would form a dactyl (⏗ ⏑ ⏑) or antibacchius (⏗ ⏗ ⏑): **mit dem 'Kōnĭg, vor einem 'Mōnāt,** but it is also often found here, as many with a sensitive grammatical conscience feel that the dative sign ought not to be suppressed: **dem Könige, dem Monate;** (*e*) after words ending in a vowel: **in dem See;** (*f*) in the names of winds: **dem Nord** (but in gen. **des Nordes**) **ausgesetzt** exposed to the north-wind; (*g*) in case of nouns without an article or adjective modifier in prepositional phrases, either in the attributive or the adverbial relation, especially in case of names of materials and abstract nouns used in a general or indefinite sense and in case of prepositional phrases connected by a conjunction: **ein Tisch von Holz, ein Ring von Gold, der Ankauf von Land, Zufuhr von Fleisch, eine Art von Haus, ein Mann von Geist; zu Fuß** on foot, **von Jahr zu Jahr, von Ort zu Ort, aus Neid, mit Ernst, mit Weib und Kind, mit Mann und Maus, von Haus und Hof, mit Rat und Tat;** but with an article or adjective modifier the **e** may appear: **das Ende vom Lied(e), ein Ring von gediegenem Gold(e);** (*h*) in nouns which are preceded by a name of a weight or measure: **mit einem Liter Wein;** (*i*) usually in foreign words: **dem Senat, dem Problem,** &c.

Note. The large group of words referred to in **245.** IV. 3. B occurring in set adverbial expressions form often a very noteworthy exception to the rule that the dative drops the **e** in case of nouns without the article in prepositional phrases. The **e** was attached to these words in an earlier period when an **e** was common here, and now it remains in a complete state of fossilization, and hence cannot always be used and dropped at will, as is the case with other words: **Er zieht sein Wörterbuch zu Rate** (perhaps more common than **Rat**) *He consults his dictionary*, but **Er gehört zum Rate** or **Rat.** In some cases this **e** is very firm in these adverbial expressions: **Er geht zugrunde** He is going to rack and ruin.

F. The using or dropping of **e** in the gen. and dat. is often a matter of euphony:

a. The poet feels quite free to drop **e** in the dative: **Die Axt im Haus erspart den Zimmermann** (Schiller's *Tell*, 3, 1). The suppression of **e** in **Hause** here is rather for the sake of rhythm than to avoid a hiatus, for in German a hiatus here does not seem to give offense either in poetry or in prose: **mit dem Schwerte in der Faust** (*id.* 2, 2). **Er ist dem Geize ergeben.** Compare **178.** 1. B.

b. The **e** is much used both in prose and poetry to avoid two accented syllables coming together, and thus standing between accented syllables it causes a rhythmic succession of accented and unaccented syllables: **Năch Góldĕ drăngt, ăm Góldĕ hăngt doch alles!**

Unmutated E-Plural Type of the Strong Declension.

63. To this class, which forms its plural by adding **e** without mutation of the root vowel, belong:—

1. Masculine monosyllabics:

a. Almost all masculine monosyllabics not capable of mutation in the plural, that is, those monosyllabics not containing one of the vowels **a, o, u, au: der Weg** way, **der Dienst** service, **der Preis** prize, **der Plüsch** plush. This is a very large group, but the words need not be enumerated, as they are easily recognized by their form.

b. The following masculine monosyllabics containing one of the vowels **a, o, u, au,** but forming their plural without mutation. Those marked with * have sometimes a mutated plural, only occasionally in the North, but in the South quite frequently or even regularly earlier in the period, those marked with † fluctuate in the plural everywhere between mutated and unmutated form, but mutation is much more common in the South. ***Aal** eel, **Aar** eagle, **Akt** act, **Alk** (also wk.) auk, **Alp** incubus, **Ar** (see 5. *c* below), **Arm** arm, **Ban** ban, ruler of a banat, **Barsch** perch, **Bas** master, ***Bast** bast, **Bau** (pl. **Baue** dwellings of animals, pl. **Bauten** buildings) building, **Blaff** bark (of a dog), **Bold** fellow, dwarf, **Bord** (rarely neut.) edge, **Bord** (see 5. *c* below), ***Born** fount, ***Borst** crack, fissure, **Buchs** box-tree, **Bums** low beer-saloon, **Butt** (pl. usually wk.; also a wk. fem. **die Butte**) turbot, **Clan** (pl. also **Clans**) clan, ***Dachs** badger, **Dank** (pl. rarely **Danke** or **Dänke**, usually **Danksagungen;** see **96.** 5. B), **Docht** wick, **Dolch** dagger, **Dom** cathedral, ***Dorn** (see **83**), ***Dorsch** torsk, **Drall** (also a wk. fem. **die Dralle**) groove in the bore of a rifle, **Drost** (also wk.) magistrate, **Druck** (see **83**), **†Drusch** thrashing, **Duns** (pl. also wk.) dunce, **Falz** groove, ***Fant** coxcomb, **Farn** fern, **Faun** (sometimes wk.) faun, ***Fjord** (pl. also sometimes **Fjords, Fjorden**) fiord, **Flachs** flax, **Flaps** boor, ***Flaus** or ***Flausch** tuft, **Flor** (pl. rare) bloom, blossom, **Flur** (sometimes a wk. fem.) entrance hall, **Forst** (**79.** 1. *a*), ***Fund** find, **Fuß** (**83**), **Gau** (pl. sometimes **Gauen,** especially, however, in poetry in the second meaning; sometimes neut.) district, field, **Golf** gulf (of sea), **Grad** degree, **Gran** (see 5. *c* below), **Grand** coarse sand, ***Grat** ridge, **Groll** (pl. rare) resentment, **Grunz** groan (sign of disapproval), **Guck** look, **Gurt** girth, belt, **Hack** stroke with a hoe, ***Haft** (pl. sometimes wk.) clasp, **Hag** enclosure, fence, grove, **Hall** sound, clang, **Halm** (pl. sometimes wk.) blade (of grass), **Halt** halt, **Harst** (prov.) troop, **Haß** (pl. rare) hate, **Hau** place where timber is being or has been cut down, blow, often in the pl. with the meaning *flogging*, **Hauch** breath, **Holm** holm, **Hops** hop, **Horst** aerie, **Hort** safe retreat, treasure, ***Huf** (pl. sometimes wk.) hoof, **Hulk** (pl. also **Hulks**; sometimes fem.) hulk (naut.), **Hund** dog, **Hupf** jump, **Jux** (pl. sometimes wk.) joke, **Kalk** lime, ***Karst** mattock, **Khan** (pl. sometimes **Khans**) khan, **Klapp** or **†Klaps** slap, **Klatsch** clash, slap, lash, **Klonz** wedge, **Kloon** ball of spun yarn, **Klopf** knock, **Klops** cooked meat-ball, **Knack** or **Knacks** crack, break, injury, ***Knall** crack, loud sound, **Knast** knot, ***Knorz** knot, **Knups** thump, **Kohl** cabbage, ***Kolk** deep pool, whirlpool, ***Kork** cork, **Kral** (sometimes neut.) kraal, **Krach** (pl. also **Krachs**) crash, panic (in business), **Kran** (pl. also **Kräne;** sometimes wk.; nom. sometimes **Kranen**) crane (machine), **Kratz** scratch, **Kulm** peak, **Kult** or **Kultus** (pl. **Kulte**) cult, **†Kumpf** or **Kump** (N.G.) basin, **Kurs** exchange, course, **Kux** share in a mine, ***Lachs** salmon, **Lack** lac, **Lahn** plate-wire, **†Latz** breast-cloth, **Lauch** leek, **Laut** sound, **Lolch** cockle, **Lorch** or **Lork** (N.G.) toad, ***Luchs** lynx, **Lump** (often also wk.) worthless fellow, **Lunch** (pl. also **Lunches**) lunch, **Lurch** batrachian, **Lurks** (colloq.) awkward fellow, fumbler, **Maat** mate (naut. term), **Mahr** nightmare, **Mast** (**79.** 1. *a*), **†Matz** Mat, little fool, **Mohn** poppy, **Mohr** moreen, **Molch** salamander, **Mond** (see **83**), **Mord** (pl. **Morde** *kinds of murder*, pl. **Mord-**

taten, *cases of murder*), **Most** unfermented wine, **Muck** or **Mucks** half-audible sound, **Muff** (sometimes a wk. fem. **die Muffe**) muff, ***Mund** (pl. also **Münder**) mouth, **Murks** (pop.) dirty or contemptible fellow, **Mutz** (sometimes wk.) bobtail, bear, stupid fellow, short coat, **Nord** north-wind, **Ohm** (also neut.) aam, **Olm** proteus, **Ort** (**83**), **Ost** east-wind, †**Pacht** (see **70.** 1. *a*), †**Pack** pack, bundle, **Paff** report (of a gun), whiff or puff (in smoking), **Pakt** (pl. sometimes wk., especially in **Ehepakten** marriage-contract) agreement, **Park** (pl. also **Parks**) park, **Part** (also neut.) part, †**Pasch** doublets, **Pfad** path, **Pfau** (**76.** I. 3), †**Pfropf** (nom. also **Pfropfen**, an unmut. **e**-less pl.), cork, stopper, ***Pfuhl** pool, **Plan** (**70.** 1. *a*), **Poch** rap, **Pol** pole (north and south), **Port** port, **Prahm** (also a wk. fem. **die Prahme**) flat-bottomed boat, **Prall** shock, **Puls** pulse, **Punkt** point, ***Punsch** punch, **Putsch** revolutionary attempt, **Putz** (pl. rare except in compounds, as **Kopfputze** different styles of head-dress) adornment, ***Qualm** vapor, thick smoke, **Quarz** quartz, ***Quast** (more commonly a wk. fem. **die Quaste**) tassel, **Ratz** polecat, ***Rost** grate (of a stove), ***Ruck** jerk, **Ruf** call, **Rutsch** land- or snow-slide, **Salm** (sometimes wk.) young salmon, **Samt** velvet, **Sand** (see **83**), †**Schacht** shaft (in mine), ***Schalk** rogue, wag, †**Schall** sound, ***Schaub** bundle of straw, **Schlāks** (colloq.) ungainly fellow, long-shanks, **Schlamp** (pop.) feast, train (of a dress), untidy man, **Schlaps** lout, ***Schlot** chimney, ***Schluck** swallow (of water, &c.), **Schlump** (pop. N.G.) lucky chance, †**Schmatz** smack, **Schmuck** (pl. more commonly **Schmucksachen**) ornament, **Schof** flock (of teals), **Schorf** scab, ***Schŏß** shoot, branch, **Schrat** sylvan spirit, **Schrot** (5. *c* below), ***Schuft** scamp, **Schuh** shoe, **Schupp** (N.G.) or **Schupf** (S.G.) shove, ***Schurz** apron (for men), **Schwalch** opening (in a furnace), **Schwof** (colloq.) dance, hop, **Shawl**, better **Schal** (pl. usually **Schals**) shawl, **Skalp** scalp, **Sod** (pl. sometimes **Söde**, **Söder**) boiling, **Sog** wake (of a ship), **Spalt** split, **Spann** instep, **Spat** spar, **Sporn** (**79.** 1. *a*), **Sprŏß** (also wk. **der Sprosse**) shoot, offspring, **Spuk** ghost, **Spunt** (naut. term; sometimes neut.) a small piece of timber, **Stahl** (see *Note*), **Stāks** (N.G.) lean and awkward person, **Star** (sometimes wk.) starling, **Start** (pl. usually **Starts**) start, **Stock** story (of a house), **Stoff** stuff, **Stopf** stopper, darned place, **Strand** strand, **Strauß** (usually here in first meaning, sometimes however wk., pl. usually **Sträuße** in the second meaning, pl. always **Sträuße** or in pop. language **Sträußer** in the last meaning) ostrich, combat, bouquet, **Strolch** vagabond, **Stups** (colloq. N.G.) or **Stupf** (colloq. S.G.) prick, punch, blow, ***Sud** brewing, **Sund** sound, strait, **Taft** taffeta, **Tag** (pl. sometimes **Täge** in S.G.) day, **Takt** time, measure (in music), **Talg** tallow, **Talk** talc, **Tang** tang, **Tank** (pl. also **Tanks**) tank, **Taps** clumsy fellow, **Tăß** (N.G.) heap (of sheaves), **Thron** throne, **Toast** toast, health, **Tod** (pl. **Tode** *kinds of death*, but **Todesfälle** *cases of death*) death, **Ton** clay, **Topp** (**79.** 1. *b*), **Trakt** tract, stretch, **Tran** train-oil, **Trăß** trass, **Trauch** crank, **Troll** hobgoblin, boor, **Trosch** crest of feathers, **Troß** crowd, gang, **Trupp** (**83**), **Tuff**, tuff, **Tupf** (nom. also **Tupfen**) dot, spot, **Tusch** flourish of trumpets, **Ulk** joke, **Ur** urus, **Wal** whale, **Walm** hipside (of a roof), **Warl** swivel-hook, **Warp** kedge, **Wart** warder, **Wau** weld, **Zapp** bald-coot, **Zoll** inch, **Zuck** jerk, twitch, **Zulp** sucking-bag.

Note. This list can be increased by adding (**1**) other nouns denoting materials, plants, and animals; (**2**) a large number of technical and provincial words; (**3**) a few more foreign monosyllabics. The plurals of nouns in the first group do not usually denote different pieces or plants, but different varieties or grades of the material, or different varieties of the species: **der Quarz** quartz, pl. **Quarze** different kinds of quartz.

Differentiation of meaning takes place sometimes in the plural between the mutated and unmutated form: **Stahl** *steel*, pl. **Stähle** *butcher's steels*, pl. **Stahle** *different kinds of steel*. See also **96.** 2.

2. Masculine dissyllabics and polysyllabics:

a. A number of derivatives, the first component of which is a prefix and the second a monosyllabic noun which is rarely found as an independent word, or as such does not belong to this class: **Be'fehl** command, **Be'gehr** (also neut.) demand, desire, **Be'huf** purpose, **Be'lang** (in the first meaning without a pl., in the second meaning with the pl. **Belange** or sometimes **Belangen**) importance, interest, **Be'richt** report, **Be'scheid** answer, information, **Be'such** visit, **Be'weis** proof, **Er'folg** success, ***Erlaß** (**Ablaß** *indulgence* granted by the church, **Aderlaß** *bleeding*, **Anlaß** *cause, occasion*, always with mutation in the pl.; **Auslaß** outlet, **Durchlaß** *culvert*, **Einlaß** *entrance*, more commonly with mutation, **Nachlaß** *bequest, that which is left behind after death*, sometimes with, sometimes without mutation in the pl.) decree, **Er'werb** acquisition, gain, **Ge'mahl** (also neut. in the meanings *husband, wife*, especially the latter) husband, **Ge'span** (sometimes wk.) comrade, **Ge'span** in Hungary a count, high official, **Ge'spons** (also wk.; also neut., especially in the meanings *bride, wife*; now rare, usually employed in humorous language) bridegroom, husband, **Ge'wahrsam** safe keeping, **Ge'winn** or **Ge'winst** gain, **Urlaub** leave of absence, **Ver'ein** society, **Ver'gleich** comparison, **Ver'hack** or **Ver'hau** abatis, ***Ver'lust** loss, **Ver'such** attempt, experiment, **Ver'weis** reproof, **Ver'zicht** renunciation.

b. A few compounds the last component of which is rarely found as an independent word or as such does not belong to this class: ***Aufruhr** uproar, revolt, †**Hans'wurst** (sometimes wk.) buffoon, **-jan** (pl. sometimes **-jans**) in compounds (as **Dummerjan**; see **245**. I. 16. *b*), **Mischmasch** hodgepodge, **Mittwoch** Wednesday, **Nachweis** proof, **Pausback** chubby-faced child, **Unart** mischievous little fellow, **Unhold** mischievous being, fiend, **Unterschlupf** shelter, **Vielfraß** glutton, **-zack** in compounds (as **Dreizack** trident), **Zwieback** (pl. also **Zwiebäcke**) pieces of cold toast.

c. A number of dissyllabic or polysyllabic nouns with accent upon the first syllable which do not have component elements of an appreciable meaning, but are made up of elements not distinctly felt, whether it be from the fact that they have been in the course of time corrupted, or because they are of an origin that is not clearly felt, including a number of foreign words: **Abend** evening, **Ahorn** maple-tree, **Alfanz** tom-fool, **Ambŏß** anvil, **Atlas** (pl. **Atlasse**, also **At'lanten** in the second meaning) satin, atlas, **'Balsam** (pl. also **Bal'same**) balm, **Barchent** fustian, **Bastard** (pop. **Bastert**, pl. **Basterte**) and **Bankert** (vulg.) bastard, **Bräutigam** intended, **Bussard** buzzard, **Derwisch** dervish, **Eidam** (poetic) son-in-law, **Fetisch** fetish, **Firlefanz** foolishness, fool, windbag, **Hagestolz** (also wk.) bachelor, **Harnisch** armor, **Heiland** Savior, Christ, **Herold** herald, **Herzog** (see **70**. 1. *c*. (2)), **Klimax** (see 4 below), **Kobalt** cobalt, **Kobold** (see **245**. I. 16. *a*.) hobgoblin, **Kodex** (**des Kodexes** or **Kodex**, pl. **Kodexe** or **Kodizes** ko:di·tses) code, **Leichnam** corpse, **Oheim** or **Ohm** uncle, **Pallasch** heavy cavalry sword, **Popanz** bugbear, **Scharlach** scarlet (cloth), **Stieglitz** (sometimes wk.) goldfinch, **'Tabak** (also **Ta'băk**) tobacco, **Talisman** talisman, **Tolpatsch** awkward fellow, **Transit** (pl. sometimes **Transits**) transit, **Ukas** (**des Ukases** or **Ukas**, pl. **Ukase** or **Ukas**) ukase, **Wallach** (also wk.) gelding, **Wiedehopf** hoopoe.

d. A few onomatopœic formations: **Kiebitz** lapwing, **Kuckuck** (pl. also **Kuckucks**) cuckoo, **Uhu** or **Schuhu** (pl. also **Uhus, Schuhus**) horn-owl, **Wauwau** (pl. also **Wauwaus**) doggie.

e. A small but growing number of modern compounds (see **249**. II. 2), as **Springinsfeld** romp, **Guckindiewelt** greenhorn, &c.: **Guckindiewelte** (Storm's *Viola tricolor*, II. p. 71). Most compounds of this kind still prefer non-inflection: **alle Pharisäer und Gernegroß** (Fontane's *Stechlin*, XXXII. p. 398). See also **80**. 2.

3. Masculine derivatives formed by the aid of unaccented suffixes other than those employed in the e-less plural class and **-tum** of the er-plural class, namely, those in **-at**, **-(i)ch**, **-icht**, **-ig**, **-ing**, **-ling**, **-is**, **-rich**, &c.: **Monat**, **Zierat** (**79**. 1. *b*), **Rettich, Habicht, Frühling, Wegerich,** &c.

Also usually unaccented masculine foreign suffixes, as **-al**, **-ian**, **-iv**, **-ol**, &c., except those in **79**. 2. and **70**. 4: **'Plural** (also **Plu'ral**), **'Grobian**, **'Superlativ** (also **Superla'tiv**), **'Alkohol**, &c. Also some of those in **79**. 2 are trending in this direction. See **79**. 2. *d*.

4. A few feminines: a number in **-nis** and **-sal**, as **Betrübnis, Drangsal,** &c.; **Maid** (poetic) maiden; the foreign words **Ananas** (pl. **-sse** or uninfl.) pineapple, **Klimax** (also masc.) climax, **Salpinx** salpinx, **Sphinx** sphinx.

a. Earlier in the period the feminines in **-nis** and **-sal** were also inflected weak after the analogy of other feminines that do not suffer mutation in the plural: **Verstehet jr diese gleichnissen** (now usually neut.) **nicht?** (Mark iv. 13). **Warum fliehe ich Trübsalen?** (Lessing).

5. Neuters:

Historical Note. In early N.H.G. neuters might have their nom. and acc. pl. exactly like the nom. sing.: **meine grawe** (**graue**) **Har** (= **Haare,** acc. pl.; Gen. xlii. 38). This former manner of inflecting the pl. is still very common in one construction, namely, where nouns are used as weights and measures, as **sechs Pfund** *six pounds.* See **96.** 4. 1. Here, however, the uninflected forms of the nom. and acc. pl. have spread to the gen. and dat.

The present plural ending **e** of the following neuter groups is after the analogy of the masculines in this same class. This new development was at an end at the beginning of the seventeenth century in case of monosyllabics, which led in this movement, followed soon by the longer neuter forms. See also *b. Note* below and **68.**

The following neuters belong here:

a. All ending in **-icht, -nis, -sal: Dickicht,** thicket, **Ereignis event, Schicksal,** fate.

Note. Neuters in **-nis** had earlier in the period, like the present neuters of the form **Ge — e** as **Gemälde,** an **-e** in both singular and plural, which was later dropped in the sing. but retained in the plural, so that these neuters like the neuter groups in *b* and *c* might be conformed to the masc. **e**-plural type of inflection. Neuters in **-icht** and **-sal** conformed to this type by simply assuming **-e** in the plural.

b. All beginning with **ge-** and not ending in **-e, -el, -er,** as **Ge'setz** *law,* except the few in **74.** 4.

Note. Nouns in this group had earlier in the period both in the nom. sing. and pl. an **e,** which was originally not a case ending but a part of the stem. Thus this group was once identical with the words of the form **Ge — e** (as in **Gebirge**) in the **e**-less plural class. The words in this group were separated from the others by dropping the **e** of the nom. sing., so that the **e** which remained in the nom. pl. was construed as a pl. ending. This new development became quite strong in the seventeenth century after the monosyllabic neuters had assumed **-e** in the plural, as described in *Historical Note* above, and the **e**-plural had thus become a common feature of neuter nouns as well as masculines. The words whose root syllable ended in **b, d, g,** and **s,** usually retained the **e** in the sing., the others dropped it: **Gebäude, Gebirge,** but **Gebell,** &c. Contrary to this rule a few words still retain more or less frequently the older form with **e: Gefäll(e), Geläut(e), Gelüst(e),** usually **Gesenke,** and regularly **Gerippe.** The **e** which is still in the sing. of these words or was once there was originally an **i,** and hence the mutation in most of these words: **Gespräch** (O.H.G. gisprâchi).

c. The majority of monosyllabic neuters. Among these words are many names of materials the plurals of which we translate by *kinds* or *grades of.* See **1.** *b. Note* above. The list is as follows: **Ar** (also masc.) are, **As** (des **Asses,** pl. **die Asse**) ace, **Beer** (in early N.H.G. and still in dialects as in the works of Rosegger; now a wk. fem. in the form of **die Beere,** which is in fact the old pl.) berry, **Beet** (pl. sometimes wk.) bed (in a garden), **Beil** axe (with short handle), **Bein** leg, **Bett** (**83**), **Bier** beer, **Blei** lead, **Boot** (pl. sometimes **Böte**) boat, **Bord** (also masc.) shelf, **Bräu** brand of beer (**Löwenbräu, Spatenbräu,** &c.), **Brot** (pl. sometimes **Bröte**) loaf of bread, **Bund** bundle, bunch, **Deck** deck, **Ding** (**83**), **Dock** (pl. more commonly **Docks**) dock, **Eck** (in use earlier in the period and still occasionally found; now usually restricted to compounds such as **Dreieck** triangle, &c.; elsewhere now replaced by the wk. fem. **Ecke**) corner, **Erz** ore, **Fell** hide, **Fenn** fen, **Fest** festival, **Fett** fat, **Fjäll** (or **Fjeld**) elevated plain (in Scandinavia), **Flach** flat bottom of a boat, **Flet** (N.G.) navigable canal, **Flöz** horizontal stratum, **Frett** ferret, **Garn** yarn, **Gas** gas, **Gift** poison, **Gleis** track, **Glück** happiness, **Gold** gold, **Gramm** gram, **Gran** (also masc.) grain (weight), **Gros** (des **Grosses,** pl. **die Grosse**) gross, **Haar** hair, **Haff** (pl. also **Haffs**) fresh water bay (along the Baltic), **Harz** gum (of tree), **Heck** stern, **Heer** army, **Heft** note-book, **Heil** happiness, salvation, **Hirn** brain, **Jahr** year, **Joch** yoke, **Kap** (pl. also **Kaps**) cape, **Kar** bowl, dish, pocket (in the mountains), **Kinn** chin, **Knie** knee, **Kreuz** cross, **Kumt** hame, **Land** (**83**), **Laub** (earlier in period with the plurals **Läuber** or **Laube** in the first meaning, now usually in the second meaning without pl.) leaf, foliage, **Leck** (also masc.) leak, **Liesch** flowering rush, **Lob** (pl. usually **Lobeserhebungen** or **Lobsprüche**) praise, **Log** (ship's) log, **Los** lot, **Lot** plumb-line, **Maar** kind of crater, **Mahl** (pl. also **Mähler,** usually so in **Gastmähler**) repast, **Mal** (pl. more commonly **Mäler,** especially in **Denkmäler** or **Denkmale, Muttermäler,** but now always **Merkmale** characteristics, **Wundenmale** or **Wundmale** scars, **Nägelmale** marks of nails) mole, mark, sign, **Mal** time (two, three times, &c.), **Malz** malt, **Maß** measure, **Meer** sea, **Mehl** flour, **Moor** moor, **Moos** (pl. **Möser** swamps) moss, **Mus** (pl. sometimes **Müser**) marmalade, **Netz** net, **Niet** (also masc.; also wk. fem. **die Niete**) rivet, **Nock** yard-arm, **Öhr** eye (of a needle), **Öl** oil, **Paar** pair, **Pech** pitch, **Pferd** horse, **Pfund** pound, **Pult** desk, **Quart** quart, **Recht** right, **Reck** horizontal bar, **Reep** rope (naut. term), **Reff** reef (in a sail), **Reh** doe, **Reich** empire, **Ried** (pl. sometimes **Rieder**) reed, swampy land, **Ries** ream, **Riff** reef (of rocks), **Rohr** reed, pipe, **Roß** (pl. in early N.H.G. **Rösser,** as in Deut. xvii. 16; still so in Austria, as in Rosegger's *Martin der Mann*, p. 80) horse, steed, **Rund** (sometimes masc.) circle, **Salz** salt, **Schaf** sheep, **Scheit** (**83**), **Schiff** ship, **Schilf** (sometimes masc.) reed, **Schock** three-score, **Schott** (pl. also wk.; also a wk. fem. **die Schotte**) bulkhead, **Schrot** (also masc.) cylindrical block, coarse-ground grain, **Schwein** hog, **Seil** rope, **Sieb** sieve, **Siel** (also masc.) sewer, drain, **Spiel** play, **Spill** capstan, **Spind** (sometimes masc., also a wk. fem. **die Spinde**) case for clothes, books, &c., **Spriet** sprit, **Stag** stay (naut. term; pl. also **Stags**), **Stück** (pl. sometimes **Stücken**) piece, **Tau** heavy rope, **Teil** (**83**) share, **Tief** deep channel, canal, **Tier** animal, **Tor** gate, **Tuch** cloth, **Vieh** (**74.** 1), **Vlies** fleece, **Watt** (**79.** 1. *b*), **Wehl** (also masc.; also fem. **Wehle**) deep place wrought by the waves, water-gall, **Wehr** dam, **Werft** (more commonly a wk. fem.) wharf, **Werk** work, **Wort** (**83**), **Wrack** (pl. also **Wracks**) wreck, **Zelt** (pl. sometimes **Zelten, Zelter**) tent, **Zeug** (in early N.H.G. also masc.) stuff, troop or army (early N.H.G.), **Ziel** goal, **Zink** (sometimes masc.) zinc, **Zinn** tin, and a few more names of materials and a few technical terms.

d. A few derivatives and compounds the final component of which does not exist as an independent noun, or as such does not belong to this class: **Antlitz** (poetic) face, **Augenmerk** aim, **Be'steck** (pl. often **Be'stecks**) knife and fork, **Darlehn** (now usually **Darlehen, e**-less plural) loan, **Eiland** (**83** under **Land**), **Elend** (pl. rare) misery, **Ge'bot** commandment, **Hundert** hundred, **Kleinod** (**79.** 1. *b*), **Rückgrat** backbone, **Tausend** thousand, **Urteil** judgment, **Ver'bot** prohibition, **Ver'lies** dungeon, **Ver'steck** (sometimes masc.) hiding-place, **Vielflach** polyhedron, **Vollblut** (pl. also **Vollblut**) thorobred (horse, &c.).

e. A few dissyllabics and trisyllabics the component parts of which do not have an appreciable meaning, among them a number of foreign words: **Defizit** (pl. also **Defizits**) deficit, **Dutzend** dozen, **Fazit** (pl. also **Fazits**) sum, result, **Mammut** (pl. also Mammuts) mammoth, **Messing** brass, **Petschaft** seal, **Tesching** (sometimes masc.; pl. also **Teschings**) a gun of very small bore.

6. A few modern compounds (see **80.** 2): **Vergißmeinnicht** forget-me-not, **Lebewohl** farewell. Non-inflection or a form in **-s** is more common here in the plural, and non-inflection is also found sometimes in the singular. See **80.** 2.

7. A large number of foreign words accented upon the last syllable. The striking feature of these words is the very strong preponderance of neuters. Almost all the neuters in the language accented upon the last syllable belong here, except a few in **74.** 5 and **79.** 2. *e* and *f*, and a number of words in these groups are trending in this direction.

In some of these foreign words there is a tendency to shift the accent upon the first syllable after the manner of German words. Some take occasionally the plural in **-s** instead of the regular ending **-e,** as **die Gra'veurs** instead of the more common **Gra'veure.** In general, however, there is now a strong tendency in choice language to discard **-s** in favor of the German ending **e.**

To this group belong:

a. Masculines and neuters ending in accented **ag, ast, at, ct** (**kt**), **et, il, ist, it, ith, ll, ng, og, om, op, ost, ot, ph, pt, tt, ut,** only, however, when they represent things, for nouns which have these same endings are weak when they represent persons or other living beings: **der Appa'rat** apparatus, **des Appa'rats,** pl. **die Appa'rate,** but **der Ag'nat** agnate, **des Ag'naten,** pl. **die Ag'naten; das Ven'til** valve, **des Ven'tils,** but **Ä'dil** edile, **des Ä'dilen; der Gra'nit** granite, **des Gra'nits,** but **der Ban'dit** bandit, **des Ban'diten; der Epi'dot** epidote, **des Epi'dots,** but **der Idi'ot** idiot, **des Idi'oten;** &c. For exceptions see **76.** I. 4. *a. Note.* Also **das Kroko'dil,** inflected according to the **e**-plural type and a few other neuters in **-'il** (**79.** 2. *e*) inflected according to the **e**-plural type or the mixed declension form exceptions to this rule. These neuters in **-'il** are trending toward *b* below.

The list of the above endings is not complete, but in general it holds good that masc. and neut. nouns accented upon the last syllable belong here if they represent lifeless objects.

b. Masc. and neut. nouns representing either beings or things ending in accented **al** (see *Note* 1), **an** (see *Note* 2), **än, ar** (see *Note* 2), **är, äst, em, ert, eur** (pronounce ör), **ier, iv, lt, mm, ol, on** (see *Note* 2), **or,** and the sibilants **s, ß, x, z: O'pal** opal, **Pe'nnal** pen-case, **Admi'ral, Aeroplan** (a·e·RO·'pla:n; = **Flugzeug**) aeroplane, **De'kan** dean, **Klis'tier** clyster, **Offi'zier** officer, &c. Occasionally the accent shifts upon the first syllable after **German** fashion: **der 'Kompaß, des 'Kompasses,** &c. But if the sibilant was originally unaccented the word does not belong here: **der Kon'sens** consent, **des Kon'senses,** but **'Musikus (82)** musician, **des Musikus.**

Note 1. A few foreign nouns in **-'al** belong to the mutated **e**-plural class, and several, as **Admi'ral,** fluctuate between the two classes, but the tendency is toward non-mutation. See **70.** 4.

Note 2. A few nouns representing living beings are weak: **Autoch'thon** (also **Autoch'thone**) autochthon, **Bar'bar** barbarian, **Dia'kon** (also an e-pl.) deacon, **Hospo'dar** (also an e-pl.) hospodar, **Hu'sar** hussar, **Ka'waß** (or **Ka'wasse**) kavass, **Koä'tan** one of the same age, **Kor'sar** pirate, **Pro'fōs** or **Profōß** (both forms also e-plurals) provost, **Ri'val** (also an e-pl.) rival, **Scho'lar** (archaic) pupil, **Ti'tan** (also **Ti'tane**) titan, **U'lan** uhlan, **Vete'ran** veteran.

Note 3. **Pas'tor** and **Te'nor** form the irregular plural **Pas'töre, Te'nöre,** the latter of which is, perhaps, even more common than the regular plural **Te'nore.** See **70.** 4. If **Pastor** is accented upon the first syllable, which is more common, it does not belong here at all, but to the group in **79.** 2. *a.* **Pas'tor** is sometimes weak.

c. The isolated masc. **Cha'rakter** character has the accent upon the final syllable of the stem only in the pl., **Charak'tere,** but in the language of the common people the pl. is **Cha'rakter,** and the word with them has thus passed over into the **e**-less plural class. This plural was formerly also sometimes used in the literary language: **die verschiedenen Charakter der verschiedenen Bücher** (Goethe).

General Note. It will be observed by even a glance at the preceding groups that some of them, especially the masc. monosyllabics and, to a less extent, masc. dissyllabics and polysyllabics, stand under the influence of the mutated **e**-plural class, the mutation in the pl. spreading from that class by analogy to this. Thus a number of words are uncertain in their pl., and it cannot easily be determined whether the regular pl. without mutation or the new one with mutation is the more common, but at present the tide has turned and in general the drift is toward the unmutated forms. See **70.** 1. *a. Note.* Earlier in the period a number of the words now belonging to 7 were entirely or partially weak: **der Roman** (pl. wk.; sing. str. except in compounds: **des Romans,** but **Romanenheldin**), **Monolog** (wk.), **Baron** (wk.), **Spion** (wk.), **Koloß** (wk.); **das Atom** (wk.), **Epigramm** (str. in sing., wk. in pl.), **Phantom** (str. in sing., wk. in pl.), &c., all now in the unmutated **e**-plural class.

64. Models of Inflection for the Unmutated **E**-Plural Type:

Singular.

Arm, *arm,* m.	**Gefängnis,** *prison,* n.	**Drangsal** *distress,* f.
N. **der Arm**	**das Gefängnis**	**die Drangsal**
G. **des Arm(e)s**	**des Gefängnisses**	**der Drangsal**
D. **dem Arm(e)**	**dem Gefängnis (or -nisse)**	**der Drangsal**
A. **den Arm**	**das Gefängnis**	**die Drangsal**

Plural.

N. **die Arme**	**die Gefängnisse**	**die Drangsale**
G. **der Arme**	**der Gefängnisse**	**der Drangsale**
D. **den Armen**	**den Gefängnissen**	**den Drangsalen**
A. **die Arme**	**die Gefängnisse**	**die Drangsale**

Note. Words in **s** preceded by a *short* vowel double the **s** when a vowel follows; see the inflection of **Gefängnis** above. Thus also **der Iltis, des Iltisses; der Atlas, des Atlasses,** &c. See also **4.** 2. C. *a,* p. 17.

Unmutated E-less Plural Type of the Strong Declension.

65. To this class, which has no additional ending in the nom. plural and never has an **e** in a case ending, belong:

a. Masc. and neut. nouns ending in unaccented **-el, -en** (always contracted to **n** after **-el** and **-er** in verbal nouns: **das Handeln** acting, **das Stottern** stuttering), **-er, -chen, -lein, -sel: der Spaten** spade, **der Vater** father, &c. In popular language the plural here is often weak. See **79.** 1. *a. Note.*

Also the diminutives in **-erl** and **l,** which have been borrowed from the Bavarian and Austrian dialects, belong here when used in the literary language: **der Gīgerl** fop, **des Gīgerls,** pl. **die Gīgerl.** In certain dialects the words of this group are weak in the plural and this inflection is often found in the literary language. See **79.** 1. *b. Note.*

b. All neuter nouns beginning with the prefix **ge-** and ending in **-e: das Gemälde** oil painting, &c.

c. The isolated masculine **Käse** cheese, and two neuter verbal nouns, **Tun** doing and **Sein** being.

d. Diminutives in **-le** in the Swabian and Alsatian and **-li** in Swiss dialects: **das Herrle** the little man, **des Herrles,** pl. **die** (, **der, den, die**) **Herrle.** Some Swiss dialects lengthen the stem in the plural: **das Äugli** (= **Äuglein**), pl. N. **Äugli**, G. (lacking), D. **Äuglene,** A. **Äugli.** The **n** drops out in all these dialects in the dat. pl. of this group.

66. Models of Inflection for the Unmutated **E**-less Plural Type:

Singular.

N. **der Spaten**	**das Hündchen**	**das Gemälde**
G. **des Spatens**	**des Hündchens**	**des Gemäldes**
D. **dem Spaten**	**dem Hündchen**	**dem Gemälde**
A. **den Spaten**	**das Hündchen**	**das Gemälde**

Plural.

N. **die Spaten**	**die Hündchen**	**die Gemälde**
G. **der Spaten**	**der Hündchen**	**der Gemälde**
D. **den Spaten**	**den Hündchen**	**den Gemälden**
A. **die Spaten**	**die Hündchen**	**die Gemälde**

67. Notice that: (**1**) if the noun ends in **en** it does not add another **n** in the dative plural. (**2**) Neuter nouns of the form **Ge——e**, as **Gebäude,** often (full explanation in *Note* below and in **83.** *b*) modify the root vowel, and usually so the diminutive endings **-chen** and **-lein**, as **das Hündchen** or **Hündlein** *little dog* (fuller statement in **245. I. 8. 1.** *c*). This mutation is not a sign of the plural, but goes thruout the sing. and pl. (**3**) Words of the forms **Ge—e, ‥—chen, ‥—lein** are usually neuter: **der Hund,** but **das Hündchen,** &c.

Note. Words of the form **Ge — e** or **Ge —** (ending in **el, er,** as **Gefieder,**) often have modification of the stem vowel by mutation (see **26.** A and C), as they once had after them an **i**, which has become **e** or dropped out: **Gedränge** (O.H.G. gidrengi), **Gefilde** (O.H.G. gifildi) derived from **Feld, Gefieder** (O.H.G. presumably gifidari or gifidiri) derived from **Feder.** However, a large number of verbal nouns, usually new formations formed from the infinitive stem, do not mutate: **das Gelaufe.** When the mutated form and the unmutated form exist side by side there is often a little shade of difference in meaning. See **83.** *b*.

68. This class is historically only a modified form of the **e**-plural type. The old rule that did not allow **e** to stand after **-el, -em, -en, -er,** caused as early as M.H.G. many words that were formerly in the unmutated **e**-plural class to drop the plural ending **e**: (O.H.G.) engil *angel*, pl. engila; M.H.G. engel, pl. engel(e). This movement has thus given rise to a new class of nouns not found in O.H.G. The neuters with these endings passed over into this new class very easily and naturally, as they already as neuters in general had no plural ending in the nom. and acc. as early as O.H.G., and hence needed only to drop the **e** in the other case endings. The fact that only words of more than one syllable came over into this **e**-less plural class indicates that the cause of dropping the **e** lies entirely in the accent. This reduction of form is the result of the older tendency to suppress the most weakly stressed vowel in words of more than two syllables—the old law described in **62.** C. *Note*. The masculines and neuters in **-e, -el, -em, -en, -chen, -er** went over entirely into the new class. This development is essentially South German. Middle German inclined to retain the **e** in the plural after masculines in **-el, -en, -er,** as in **Hügele, Meistere,** &c. Luther sometimes followed this M.G. usage, but in general adopted the S.G. tendency to drop **e** here. Masculines and neuters with heavier suffixes, such as **-at, -ich, -ig, -ing, -ling, -rich, -nis, -sal,** did not participate in this movement. The old law described in **62.** C. *Note*, which required the suppression of the unaccented vowel in the third syllable, did not work so uniformly after a secondary accent as after a lightly stressed **-el, -en, -er.** Moreover the general tendency of the literary language was in the direction of developing a distinctive plural ending, so that many neuters instead of dropping endings assumed the clear plural ending **e** after the analogy of masculines, as described in **63.** 5. *Historical Note* and the *Notes* under *a* and *b* of the same article. Neuter diminutives in **-lein,** however, did not add **-e** in the plural but remained unchanged after the analogy of diminutives in **-chen.**

The words in the new **e**-less plural class were later greatly increased by accessions from the weak declension: M.H.G. balke *beam*, G. balken, D. balken, &c., but N.H.G. **Balken,** G. **Balkens,** D. **Balken,** &c. This new trend of weak nouns toward the **e**-less class of the strong declension began to manifest itself at the close of the fourteenth century. The new development first appeared in the South in the plural of nouns denoting lifeless objects in the form of mutation to distinguish the plural more clearly: **schäden** instead of **schaden.** About the same time nouns denoting lifeless objects, much less commonly nouns denoting living beings, began to appear with the strong genitive **-s** added to their regular weak genitive as there had arisen a feeling that the strong ending, so widely used in the language, was a more characteristic sign of the genitive: **des schadens, des knabens** instead of **des schaden, des knaben.** Later the genitive **-s** was dropped in case of the nouns denoting living beings as the feeling prevailed that the weak genitive, so closely associated with many very common nouns denoting living beings, was characteristic of the genitive of these words. The words which have thus come from the weak declension are almost wholly the names of lifeless objects, which fact accounts for their change of declension. The most common case form of names of living beings is the nom., since a living being is naturally thought of as acting, while the most common case forms of names of lifeless objects are the acc. and dat., since we think of them as things we use, as the objects of an activity or a preposition. Hence after the strong genitive **-s** had become established in the weak nouns representing lifeless objects their frequent dat. and acc. form in **-en** soon became fixed in the mind as the usual form, and gradually displaced the less familiar nom. form in **-e**. On the other hand, the frequent use of the nominative in the nouns denoting living beings, as **knabe,** preserved the old weak ending **-e** there. Also most of the nouns denoting lifeless objects in **69,** such as **Glaube, Name, Wille,** &c., on account of their frequent use in the nominative kept their old weak ending **-e** as in case of nouns denoting living beings, but there was never any tendency here as in case of nouns denoting living beings to restore their old weak genitive, as the new strong ending **-s** that had been added to their old weak genitive was in harmony with the genitive of most other nouns representing lifeless things. As the nom. form remained firm in case of designations of living beings, and the acc. form supplanted the nom. form in case of names of things, the same word was split into two forms if it had two meanings, one the name of a person, one the name of a thing: **der Franke** Frank (race), **der Franken** (in Switzerland) franc (coin); **der Knote** low, vulgar, coarse fellow, **der Knoten** knot; **der Lump** (formerly **Lumpe**) ragged beggar, good-for-nothing fellow, **der Lumpen** rag; **der Rappe** black horse, originally *raven*, and still so in S.G. dialect, **der Rappen** (in Switzerland a coin upon which is a picture of a raven) $\frac{1}{100}$ franc; **der Tropf** (formerly **Tropfe**) simpleton, **der Tropfen** drop.

The change of words from the **e**-plural class and weak declension to this class was a gradual one, and the former order of things can still be seen in Luther's works in a number of cases: **der kuche** (Hosea VII. 8) old wk. nom., now **Kuchen.** On the other hand, a large number of feminines which in early N.H.G. had their sing. and pl. in most part alike, and hence properly belonged here, especially those in **-e, -in,** and **-ung,** passed over later into the weak declension, following the general tendency of feminines towards the weak declension: (dat. sing.) **sünde** (2 Cor. v. 21), (acc. pl.) **sünde** (1 Cor. xv. 3); (nom. sing. of **Löwin**) **die Lewinne** (Ezek. xix. 2), (nom. pl.) **Lewinne** (Joel i. 6); (nom. sing.) **wonunge** (only in the earlier editions of Luther's Bible, later **wonung**), (acc. pl.) **wonunge** (Ps. lxxxvii. 2).

69. *Irregularities in the Declension of the Unmutated* **E**-*less Plural Type.* Tho usually deficient in the nominative singular ending **en,** the following masculine nouns may now be put into the unmutated **e**-less plural class: **Funke** spark, **Gedanke** thought, **Glaube** faith, **Haufe** heap, **Name** name, **Same** seed, and **Wille** will. **Buchstabe** letter (of the alphabet), which is usually a weak masculine, belongs here sometimes. All these words except **Buchstabe** (nom. **Buchstaben** still rare) sometimes have the singular nominative ending in **-en.** On the other hand, **der Gefallen** kind act, favor is more common than **der Gefalle** and **der Frieden** peace is perhaps a little more common than **der Friede** (see *a*). The plural of all these forms is entirely regular. For the peculiar fluctuation of form here see **68** (2nd par.).

	Singular.	Plural.
N.	**der Name(n)**	**die Namen**
G.	**des Namens**	**der Namen**
D.	**dem Namen**	**den Namen**
A.	**den Namen**	**die Namen**

a. **Friede** (O.H.G. fridu) was not originally weak but strong. It had in early N.H.G. the following inflection: **der Friede, des Friedes, dem, den Friede** alongside of the forms **der Friede, des Friedens, dem, den Frieden.** The forms in **-en** show that the nom. **e** had led to the conception that the noun was weak. The old strong gen. in **-es** is now obsolete, the nom. in **-e** is still quite common, and the old strong dat. and acc. forms in **-e** not infrequent in the classical period when no article precedes the noun, and still occurs so occasionally: **Und wie lange haben wir schon Friede?** (Lessing's *Minna*, 2. 1). **Ihm hatten | längst die stillen Schwarzwaldtannen | Friede ins Gemüt gerauscht** (Scheffel's *Trompeter*, 1). The **n** of the oblique cases has gradually become fixed in the nom., but has not yet displaced the old ending **e.**

Mutated E-Plural Type of the Strong Declension.

70. To this class, which mutate the root vowel in the plural and add **e,** belong:

1. The following masculine groups:

a. The following masc. monosyllabic nouns, which contain a mutatable vowel (**a, o, u, au**). Those marked with * have *sometimes* an unmutated plural, those marked with † fluctuate in the plural between mutated and unmutated form. **Abt** abbot, **Arzt** physician, **Ast** branch, **Bach** brook, **Balg** (**83**), **Ball** ball, **Band** volume, **Bart** beard, **Băß** bass, **Bauch** belly, **Baum** tree, **Bausch** bolster, pad, **Block** block, **Bock** he-goat, **Brand** fire, **Brauch** custom, **Bruch** fracture, **Brŭch** (also, perhaps however less commonly, a neut. **er**-pl.) bog, **Bug** bend, **Bund** alliance, **Busch** bush, **Chor** (see 3 below), **Damm** dam, **Dampf** vapor, **Darm** intestine, **Draht** wire, **Drang** (pl. rare) impulse, strong desire, †**Drusch** thrashing, **Duft** fragrant odor, **Dunst** vapor, **Fall** fall, **Fang** catch, tusk (of boar), tooth (of wolf), talon, claw, **Floh** flea, ***Flor** crape, gauze, **Flōß** (see 3 below), **Fluch** curse, **Flug** flight, **Fluß** river, **Frack** (pl. also **Fracks**) dress-coat, **Frosch** frog, **Frost** frost, **Fuchs** (S.G. sometimes also wk., sometimes wk. also elsewhere in the second and third meaning) fox, chestnut horse, Freshman (in a German university), **Fuß** (**83**) foot, **Gang** walk, **Gast** guest, ***Gauch** (pl. sometimes wk.) cuckoo, fool, ***Gaul** horse, nag, **Grund** ground, reason, **Grūß** greeting, **Gŭß** casting, **Hahn** (earlier in the period also wk.) cock, **Hals** neck, **Hang** declivity, **Hof** court, **Hub** lift, **Hut** hat, **Kahn** boat, **Kamm** comb, ***Kamp** enclosed field, **Kampf** combat, **Kauf** purchase, **Kauz** (earlier in the period also wk. and an unmut. **e**-pl.) brown owl, fellow, **Klang** sound, †**Klaps** slap, **Klōß** clod, dumpling, **Klotz** block, **Knauf** knob, **Knaus** (S.G.), or **Knaust** or **Knūst** (N.G.) heel (of a loaf of bread), **Knopf** button, **Knuff** cuff (blow), **Koch** cook, **Kog** land wrested from the sea, **Kopf** head, **Korb** basket, **Krampf** cramp, **Kran** (**63.** 1. *b*), **Kranz** wreath, **Kropf** craw, wen, **Krug** pitcher, †**Kumpf** (**63.** 1. *b*), **Kuß** kiss, **Lauf** (sometimes, especially earlier in the period, also **Lauft**) course, time, **Lohn** reward, **Markt** market, **Marsch** march, †**Matz** Mat, little fool, **Mops** pug dog, **Napf** bowl, †**Pacht** (more commonly a wk. fem.) lease, rental, †**Pack** (**63.** 1. *b*), **Papst** pope, †**Pasch** doublets, **Paß** pass, **Pfahl** stake, **Pflock** peg, **Pflug** plow, **Plan** (pl. earlier in the period **Plane,** which is still often used in the second meaning) plan, grass-plot, **Platz** place, **Propst** provost (of a church), rector, ***Puff** thump, **Ranft** crust, **Rang** rank, **Rat** councilor, **Raum** space, **Rausch** intoxication, **Rock** coat, **Rumpf** trunk, body, **Saal** room, **Sack** sack, **Saft** juice, **Sand** (**83**), **Sang** song, **Sarg** coffin, **Satz** sentence, **Saum** hem, †**Schacht** shaft (in mine), ***Schaft** shaft, **Schatz** treasure, **Schaum** foam, **Schlaf** (usually a wk. fem. **die Schläfe**) temple (on the head), **Schlag** blow, **Schlauch** leather bag, **Schlund** chasm, **Schlupf** hiding place, **Schlurf** gulp, **Schlŭß** close, †**Schmatz** smack, **Schmaus** feast, **Schnaps** whiskey, **Schopf** tuft (of hair, feathers), **Schōß** lap, **Schrank** case, press, **Schrund** (usually wk. fem. **die Schrunde**) cleft, **Schub** push, **Schurf** scratch, pit, opening (min.), **Schŭß** shot, **Schwamm** sponge, **Schwan** (**76. I.** 3. *b*) swan, **Schwang** swing, **Schwank** prank, farce, **Schwanz** tail, **Schwarm** swarm, crowd, **Schwung** flight, soaring, **Schwur** oath, **Sohn** son, **Span** shaving, **Spāß** joke, **Sprŭch** saying, saw, **Sprung** jump, **Spund** bung, **Stab** staff, **Stahl** (**63.** 1. *b. Note*), **Stahl** (pl. also **Stahle,** nom. sing. also **Stahlen,** an unmut. **e**-less pl.) sample, **Stall** stable, **Stamm** trunk, tribe, **Stand** stand, rank, station, **Stock** stick, cane, **Storch** (sometimes wk.) stork, **Stoß** push, pile, **Strang** rope, trace, **Strauch** (pl. now perhaps more commonly **Sträucher**) bush, shrub, **Strauß** (**63.** 1. *b*), **Strom** stream, **Strumpf** stocking, ***Strunk** stump, **Stuhl** chair, **Stumpf** short end, stump, **Sturm** storm, **Sturz** (earlier in the period unmut. in pl.) fall, **Sumpf** swamp, **Tanz** dance, **Ton** tone, **Topf** pot, **Trank** drink, **Traum** dream, **Trog** trough, **Tropf** (earlier in the period wk. and sometimes still so) simpleton, **Trumpf** trump, **Turm** tower, **Vōgt** governor, steward, **Wall** rampart, **Wanst** paunch, **Wolf** wolf, **Wūchs** growth, **Wulst** (also fem.; see 2 below) pad, bustle, roll, **Wunsch** wish, **Wurf** throw, **Zahn** tooth, **Zaum** bridle, **Zaun** hedge, fence, **Zoll** toll, **Zopf** plait of hair, cue, **Zug** train.

Note. This mutating group is a *little* smaller than the unmutating mutatable group in **63. 1.** *b*, but it may turn out to be *much* smaller, as the latter group may prove to be larger than the present enumeration shows, as explained in the *Note* under **63.** 1. *b*. The mutating group, however, contains a number of very common words, and has thus naturally from the earliest historic times attracted to itself words from the other group. It has thus been slowly increasing thruout the different periods almost up to our own time, and in dialect, especially in the South, may perhaps still be spreading, but at present in the literary language mutation in this group seems to be losing ground, and a number of words have gone over to the other group or fluctuate between them. Compare **63.** 1. *b*. It has also not the prospect of attracting foreign monosyllabics that seems to be before the non-mutating group. The former inflection of some of the words that have come from the non-mutating group to this class can still be seen in fossilized proper names: **Königshofen** (dat. pl.; see **88. 1**). The pl. of **Hof** is now elsewhere uniformly **Höfe.**

b. Several masculines of the form **Ge-**: **Gebrauch** custom, **Genŭß** enjoyment, **Gerŭch** odor, **Gesang** song, **Geschmack** (pl. sometimes **Geschmäcker**) taste, **Gestank** stench.

c. A few derivatives and compounds, the final component of which does not exist as an independent word, or as such does not have a mutated plural:

(1) Derivatives: **Bedacht** (pl. rare) consideration, **Belag** slice of meat for a sandwich, veneer, coating, **Bestand** amount on hand, **Betrag** amount, **Ertrag** yield, return, **Verdacht** (pl. rare) suspicion, **Verdruß** vexation, **Vertrag** contract.

(2) Compounds: **Ab-, Aus-, Ein-, Händedruck** (see **Druck** in **83**), **Ab-, Ader-, An-, Aus-, Durch-, Ein-, Nachläß** (**63.** 2. *a*), **Antrag** offer, ***Anwalt** attorney, **Beitrag** contribution, **Diebstahl** theft, **Einwand** objection, †**Hanswurst** (**63.** 2. *b*), **-hans** *Johnny* in compounds (as **Prahlhans** braggart), **Herzog** (earlier in the period wk., now with pl. **Herzoge,** still used in choice language, or more commonly **Herzöge;** still wk. in compound names of places, as **Herzogenbusch**) *duke*, earlier in the period in its original meaning *leader of an army*, *leader*, *captain*, **Lautschwund** suppression of a sound, **Marschall** (early N.H.G. **Marschalk;** pl. also **Marschalls**) marshal, **Vorwand** pretext, **Zwieback** (**63.** 2. *b*).

2. The following feminines: **Angst** (see *a* below) anxiety, †**Armbrust** (formerly a neut. or masc. from Latin *arcubalista*, still often with its old pl. **Armbruste,** now felt as a compound of **Arm** and **Brust,** which accounts for its new pl. **Armbrüste**) cross-bow, **Axt** ax, **Bank** bench, **Braut** bride, **Brunst** fire, heat, desire, lust, **Brust** breast, **Faust** fist, **-flucht** in the compounds **Ausflucht** evasion, **Zuflucht** (pl. rare) refuge, as a simple noun and elsewhere in compounds wk., **Fluh** (Swiss; see also *c* below) wall of rock, precipice, **Frucht** fruit, **Gans** goose, **Geschwulst** (less commonly **Schwulst**) swelling, **Gruft** vault, **Hand** hand, **Haut** skin, **Kluft** (sometimes wk.) cleft, **Kraft** strength, **Kuh** cow, **-kunft** in compounds (as in **Einkunft** income), **Kunst** art, **Laus** louse, **Luft** air, **Lust** pleasure, **Macht** might, **Magd** servant girl, **Maus** mouse, **Nacht** night, **Naht** seam, **Not** (see *a* below) need, necessity, strait, **Nŭß** nut, **Pracht** (pl. **Prachten** and **Prächte**) splendor, **Sau** (usually wk.; see **83**), **Schlucht** or the less common, rather poetic form **Schluft** (the former now usually wk.) defile, cleft, **Schnur** (pl. often wk., sing. sometimes **Schnure**) string, **Schnur** (obs. or bib.; pl. also wk.) daughter-in-law, **Stadt** city, **Sucht** (Hauptmann's *Heinrich*, 1, 1. p. 6; **meiner Eifersüchte Qual**—Sudermann's *Das ewige Männliche*, 2; **jahrelang gehegte Sehnsüchte**—Otto Ernst's *A. S. J.*, p. 268; usually wk.) malady, **Wand** wall (of a room), **Wulst** (also masc., pl. **Wülste**) pad, bustle, roll, **Wurst** sausage, **Zucht** (wk. in the first two meanings) breed, brood, modest act that shows good breeding, **Zunft** guild.

a. The regular dat. pl. **Nöten** is used in many idiomatic expressions, and its frequent use has led to the erroneous idea that the plural thruout is **Nöten,** which is thus sometimes used instead of the regular form **Nöte.** For the same reason we also find sometimes the pl. **Ängsten** instead of **Ängste.**

b. A few irregularities indicate a different declension in a former period: **ab'handen** (dat. pl.) *lost, mislaid*, **vor'handen sein** *to exist*, **bei Handen sein** *to be at hand*, and other such fossilized expressions; **Weihnachten** (dat. pl.) Christmas; **Macht** is regularly wk. in the two compounds, **Ohnmacht** *swoon*, **Vollmacht** *full power to act in all cases.* In Goethe's day the simple word could be wk.: **Mit Machten sprudle, Quell', aus deinen Höhlen** (Goethe).

c. In M.H.G. the sing. of these feminines was not uninflected as now, but the gen. and dat. added **e** and the vowel suffered mutation. This former inflection can still be seen in proper names, also in a few compounds in which the first component is a gen.: **Klaus von der Flüe** (dat. of **Fluh**) a character in Schiller's *Tell*; **Gänsefeder** *feather of a goose, goose-quill.* The old dative singular also survives in **be'hende** (= M.H.G. behende), i.e. literally **bei der Hănd** *at hand*, but usually employed as an adjective or an adverb with the meaning *nimble, nimbly.* In a few isolated cases both the nom. and dat. (or gen.) forms of a simple noun have been preserved, but they are not felt as nom. and dat., for they have become independent nouns with differentiated meanings: **Fahrt** *journey, drive*, **Fährte** *track, trace, scent*; **Stadt** *city*, **Stätte** *place.*

3. Two neuters: **Flŏß** (sometimes masc.) *raft* and **Chor** (neut. and masc., the former in the first meaning and the latter in the other meanings, both genders sometimes used indiscriminately; the neut. form perhaps more commonly w. pl. **Chore**) *part of the church where the choir sit*, also used for the *body of singers* and the *song* they sing, also *crowd, band, company.* Here belong sometimes the

neuters **Boot** *boat*, **Brot** *loaf of bread*, **Rohr** pipe, which are usually unmutated e-plurals.

4. A few masc. foreign words with accent upon the final syllable, but sometimes after German fashion upon the first: **Al'tar** (and in earlier N.H.G. **'Altar;** pl. also **Al'tare**) altar, **'Bischof** bishop, **Cho'ral** hymn, **Gene'ral** (pl. in choice language more commonly **Gene'rale**) general, **Ka'nal** canal, **Kap'lan** chaplain, **Kardi'nal** cardinal, **Mo'rast** (pl. also **Mo'raste**) morast, **Pa'last** and **'Palast** palace, **Te'nor** (pl. also **Te'nore**) tenor. In these words it is the second vowel that suffers the mutation: **der Al'tar**, pl. **die Al'täre.** Sometimes other foreign words, as **Admi'ral** admiral, **Korpo'ral** corporal, join this group, and earlier in the period the list was still larger, comprising such as **Bibliothe'kar, Po'kal,** &c., but present feeling is opposed to the mutation of foreign words.

71. Models of Inflection for the Mutated E-Plural Type:

	Singular.	
Sohn *son*, m.	**Floß** *raft*, n.	**Hand** *hand*, f.
N. **der Sohn**	**das Floß**	**die Hand**
G. **des Sohn(e)s**	**des Floßes**	**der Hand**
D. **dem Sohn(e)**	**dem Floß(e)**	**der Hand**
A. **den Sohn**	**das Floß**	**die Hand**
	Plural.	
N. **die Söhne**	**die Flöße**	**die Hände**
G. **der Söhne**	**der Flöße**	**der Hände**
D. **den Söhnen**	**den Flößen**	**den Händen**
A. **die Söhne**	**die Flöße**	**die Hände**

Mutated E-Less Plural Type of the Strong Declension.

72. To this class, which is an e-less plural type with the same inflection as the nouns in **65** with the additional feature of mutation in the plural, belong only a small number of words in **-el, -en, -er.** The unmutated e-less plural group in **65** is very much larger. Among those that suffer mutation in the plural can be safely counted: only one neuter, **Kloster** cloister, but also quite often **Wasser** (**Stille Wasser sind tief,** but **Mineralwässer, Industrieabwässer** waste water from factories, **Kanalisationsabwässer** sewage water, &c.) water, and sometimes **Lager** camp, warehouse, bed (of ore, &c.); two feminines, **Mutter** and **Tochter;** the following masculines: **Acker** field, **Apfel** apple, **Boden** (pl. also **Boden**) bottom, soil, **Bruder** brother, **Faden** (earlier in the period without mutation in the pl.) thread, **Garten** garden, **Graben** ditch, **Hafen** harbor, pot, **Hammer** hammer, **Handel** contention, **Laden** shutter, shop (in the first meaning, pl. also **die Laden**), **Mangel** lack, **Mantel** cloak, **Nabel** (pl. also **Nabel**) navel, **Nagel** nail, **Ofen** stove, **Sattel** saddle, **Schaden** damage, **Schnabel** beak, **Schwager** brother-in-law, **Vater** father, **Vogel** bird. In the expression **Es ist schade!** *It is too bad!* **Schaden** preserves an older nom. sing. form, just as the nouns in **69.**

a. Many other masculines also belong here sometimes: **Bogen** bow, **Hammel** wether, **Kasten** box, **Kragen** collar, **Magen** stomach, **Wagen** wagon, &c. Grammarians discourage the spread of mutation here, as these words were unmutated in earlier periods of the language. When this class was formed by dropping **e** in the plural, in accordance with the development described in **68** a number of words which entered the new class, **Apfel, Hafen** pot, **Hammer, Mantel, Nagel, Sattel, Schnabel,** were already mutated in the plural. **Mutter, Tochter,** and **Bruder** had no ending in the nom. and acc. plural as early as O.H.G. and a little later **Vater** joined this little group. In M.H.G. these four words had assumed mutation in the plural and, with the seven nouns with mutated **e**-less plurals mentioned above, established in the language the mutated **e**-less type of plural. This mutating group possessed a great advantage over the other words in the **e**-less class, as they had a plural form clearly distinct from the singular, and the economic instincts of the people, undisturbed by historical considerations, appreciated this advantage at once, and extended the mutation in the plural to other words. Even originally weak words were affected. In Luther's language **der Garten** is still weak as in M.H.G.: **des garten** (2. Kings ix. 27). Later it became an **e**-less plural like a number of other weak nouns as described in **68**

(2nd par.), and finally joined the above mutating group. The list given above represents the view of conservative grammarians. Literary men do not always confine themselves to it: **Schubkästen** (Gutzkow), **die Glaskästen** (Raabe's *Hungerpastor*, chap. iv), **die Köpfe, die Herzen und Mägen der Menschheit** (Raabe's *A. T.*, chap. 26), **preußische Mägen** (H. Hoffmann's *Rittmeister*, p. 141). South German authors use mutation here still more freely. There is evidently, however, in the North a tendency at present in choice language against the extension of mutation here as in general also elsewhere.

ER-Plural Type of the Strong Declension.

73. This class adds **er** to form the nominative plural and mutates the root vowel if it is capable of it: **das Buch** book, **des Buchs,** pl. **die Bücher.** Those ending in **-tum** mutate this suffix instead of the root vowel: **das Herzogtum** duchy, pl. **die Herzogtümer.**

a. The ending **-er** now found in the plural of these words was once **-ir,** and hence the mutation. This **-er,** however, is not a case ending, but a derivative suffix, and was in earlier periods also found in the sing. It finally disappeared in the sing. and was then felt as a plural ending. It is still found in the sing. in a few derivatives, where, however, its force is no longer felt. See **245.** II. 3. *a. Note.*

b. This **-er** as plural ending is a very popular one, and is often used in dialect or familiar humorous language with words of the mutated or the unmutated **e**-plural class instead of the regular ending of those classes, as **Steiner** for **Steine** stones, **Elender** (Schiller's *Wallensteins Lager*, l. 521; here for the sake of a pun on **Länder**), in diminutives (see **245.** I. 8. 1. *f. Note* 2), &c. A number of words fluctuate between the unmutated **e**-plural class and this class even in the literary language, as is mentioned in particular under each class. Perhaps the forms in **-e** are choicer than those in **-er,** even sometimes bordering upon the poetic, but they are often much less common: **Denkmale** and **Denkmäler, Gewande** and **Gewänder.** In a number of cases there is a differentiation of meaning between the form in **-e** and that in **-er.** See **83.** *a.* A number of words which now are firmly fixed in the **er**-plural class were in earlier periods and earlier in the present period in the unmutated **e**-plural class, lacking in earlier periods, however, endings in nom. and acc. pl. See **63.** 5. *Historical Note,* and **74.** 1. *a.*

Note. Historical Development. This group was small in the first half of the thirteenth century, the classical period of M.H.G. The spread of this type was largely due to South German influences. In M.H.G. the neuter nom. and acc. plural were the same as the nom. and acc. singular. In N.H.G. there arose a desire to distinguish the plural from the singular. Middle Germans began to extend to the endingless neuter plural form the **e**-plural of masculines. In South German this could not be done as final vowels were regularly suppressed. Hence South Germans began to use here the **er**-plural which had already become established in a few words. Middle Germans and the literary language, which in general rested upon Middle German, yielded in part to this S.G. movement, but later there arose a reaction against it guided by the feeling that the **e**-plural was in accord with the trend toward greater simplicity of form in the language. Present literary usage became fixed about the close of the sixteenth century. In dialect, however, especially in the South, the **er**-plural is still widely used.

74. To this class, which has no feminines, belong:

1. All other native German neut. monosyllabics not found in the unmutated **e**-plural group in **63.** 5. *c*, the mutated **e**-plural group in **70.** 3, and in the *mixed declension* in **79.** 1. *b*, namely: **Aas** (pl. also **Aase**) carcass, **Amt** office, **Bad** bath, **Balg** (**83**), **Band** (**83**), **Biest** (pop.) beast (of fleas, bedbugs, dogs, &c.), domestic animal, **Bild** picture, **Blatt** leaf, **Brett** board, **Brŭch** (see **70.** 1. *a*), **Bŭch** book, **Dăch** roof, **Daus** deuce, **Ding** (**83**), **Dorf** village, **Ei** egg, **Făch** compartment, **Făß** barrel, **Feld** field, **Geld** money, **Gicht** convulsion, **Glas** glass, **Glied** link, **Grab** grave, **Gras** grass, **Gut** property, **Haupt** head, **Haus** house, **Holz** wood, **Horn** horn, **Huhn** fowl, **Kalb** calf, **Kind** child, **Kleid** dress, **Korn** grain, **Kraut** herb, **Lamm** lamb, **Land** (**83**), **Licht** (**83**), **Lid** eyelid, **Lied** song, **Lŏch** hole, **Mahl** (**63.** 5. *c*), **Mal** (**63.** 5. *c*), **Maul** mouth (of animals), **Mensch** (**83**), **Moos** (**83**), **Mus** (**63.** 5. *c*), **Nest** nest, **Pfand** pledge, **Rad** wheel, **Reis** shoot, **Rind** beef, **Scheit** (**83**), **Schild** shop sign, **Schlŏß** castle, **Schwert** sword, **Stift** endowed institution, **Tal** (in poetic language sometimes an unmut. **e**-pl.) valley, **Tuch** (**83**), **Vieh** (collective noun, hence usually without pl.; sometimes referring to an individual, occasionally with pl. **Viehe,** but more commonly **Vieher** *animals*, fig. **Rindvieher** *stupid fellows*; colloq. and pop. S.G. pl. **Viecher** *beasts*, *'critters'*, see **40.** 1. *b. Note* 7) cattle, **Volk** people, **Wams** (pl. also **Wamse;** sometimes masc.) waistcoat, **Weib** woman, **Welf** (also a masc. **e**-pl., more commonly replaced by **das Junge, ein Junges**) cub, whelp, **Wort** (**83**). Here also belongs **Trumm** (also masc.) ruin, fragment. Its plural is usually **Trümmer,** and only rarely **Trümme** and **Trumme.** The sing. is very little used, and hence its form is not vividly felt. This has given rise to new formations in the sing. The usual plural form is sometimes taken for a sing. This new sing. is either fem.

or masc. The pl. formed from this new sing. is of course wk., i.e. **Trümmern,** if it is regarded as fem., and is an **e**-less pl., i.e. **Trümmer,** if it is felt as a masc.

a. In M.H.G. and even later in early N.H.G. a number of these words were inflected after the model of the unmutated **e**-plural class, as described for the early N.H.G. period in **63.5.** *Historical Note.* This can still be seen in many fossilized forms, as in **Feld, Haus, Haupt** in names of places, as **Rheinfelden** (dat. pl.; see **88.** 1), **Rheinhausen** (dat. pl.), **Berghaupten** (dat. pl.); also in the dat. pl. form **Häupten** in a few set expressions, as **zu Häupten (des Bettes,** &c.) *at the head* (*of the bed,* &c.). In early N.H.G. **Haupt** had as a rival the M.G. form **Häupt** (O.H.G. houbit, and hence mutation), which still in such expressions as the preceding survives in its early N.H.G. dat. pl. form **Häupten,** which, however, in meaning has now the force of the sing. The pl. form here is probably after the analogy of **zu Füßen,** where the plural has a real meaning.

2. All in **-tum,** of which two only are masc. (**Irrtum** *error* and **Reichtum** *wealth*) and the rest neut.: **das Christentum,** &c.

3. A few isolated masculines: **Bösewicht** (pl. now perhaps more commonly **Bösewichte**) rascal, **Dorn** (**83**), **Geist** spirit, **Gott** God, god, **Hundsfott** (pl. **Hundsfötter**) scoundrel, **Leib** body, **Mann** man, **Mund** (**63.** 1. *b*), **Ort** (**83**), **Rand** edge, **Ski** (ʃi: or ski·, pl. also **Skīs, Skī'e**) ski, **Strauch** (**70.** 1. *a*) bush, shrub, **Strauß** (**63.** 1. *b*), **Vormund** (in early N.H.G. wk. with form **Vormünd**(e), later str. with pls. **Vormünde,** more commonly **Vormunde,** most commonly **Vormünder**) guardian, **Wald** (see *b*) forest, **Wurm** (pl. rarely **Würme**; see **83**).

a. Masculines did not originally belong to this class. Some of these masculines, as **Ort, Gott** (M.H.G. der got *God,* but daȥ abgot *idol*), were once neut. as well as masc., and later retained the neut. pl. form, altho they dropped the neut. article in favor of the masc. Several masculines were attracted into this class, assuming the neut. pl. after the analogy of neut. nouns of a similar meaning: **Wälder** *woods* after the analogy of **Hölzer** *woods*; **Geister** *spirits* after the analogy of **Götter** *gods*; **Leiber** *bodies* after the analogy of **Geister,** with which it stands in contrast; **Männer** *men* after the analogy of **Weiber** *women.*

b. **Wald** was formerly an **e**-pl., as can still be seen in the fossilized proper name **Unterwalden** (dat. pl. = **unter den Wäldern**).

4. A few neuters, exceptions to the **e**-pl. cl. (**63.** 5. *b*): **Gehalt** (earlier and sometimes still masc. with pl. **Gehalte**) salary, **Gemäch** room (of a house), **Gemüt** disposition, **Geschlecht** (poet. pl. **Geschlechte**) generation, **Gesicht** (**83**), **Gespenst** ghost, **Gewand** (pl. sometimes **Gewande**) garments, **Gewölb** (usually **Gewölbe,** an **e**-less pl.) vault.

5. A few foreign words: (**1**) exceptions to the unmutated **e**-pl. class: **das Kapi'tell** or **Kapi'täl** (both forms usually **e**-pls.) capital of a pillar, **der Pe'nnal** (pl. sometimes **Pe'nnale, Pe'nnäle**; nom. sing. more commonly **Pe'nnäler,** an **e**-less pl.) gymnasium student, **das Prä'sent** (pl. usually **Prä'sente**) present, **das Regi'ment** regiment, **das Spi'tal** or **Hospi'tal** (pl. sometimes **Hospi'tale**) hospital; (**2**) **der Wiking** viking.

75. Models of Inflection for the **Er**-Plural Type:

Singular.

	Buch *book,* n.	**Irrtum,** *error,* m.	**Bild** *picture,* n.
N.	das Buch	der Irrtum	das Bild
G.	des Buch(e)s	des Irrtums	des Bild(e)s
D.	dem Buch(e)	dem Irrtum	dem Bild(e)
A.	das Buch	den Irrtum	das Bild

Plural.

N.	die Bücher	die Irrtümer	die Bilder
G.	der Bücher	der Irrtümer	der Bilder
D.	den Büchern	den Irrtümern	den Bildern
A.	die Bücher	die Irrtümer	die Bilder

Weak Declension.

76. I. *Present Literary Usage.*

The weak declension ends in **-n** or **-en** (see **61.** *b*) in every case sing. and pl. except the nom. sing., and never modifies the root vowel in the pl.: **der Knabe** boy, **des, dem, den,** pl. **die, der, den, die Knaben.** Feminines not being declined in the singular have only the plural of this declension. To the weak declension belong:—

1. All the native and foreign fem. nouns in the language, with the following few exceptions: (**1**) **Mutter** and **Tochter** in the *mutated* **e**-*less plural class*; (**2**) those ending in **-nis** and **-sal** in the *unmutated* **e**-*plural class*; (**3**) the list in the *mutated* **e**-*plural class* (see **70.** 2); (**4**) a few foreign words (see **80.** **1** and **63.** 4).

a. Foreign fem. in **-a** and **-is** drop these letters in the pl. and add **-en**: **die Firma** firm, pl. **die Firmen**; **die Basis**, pl. **die Basen.** All in **-in** double the **n** in the pl.: **Fürstin** princess, pl. **Fürstinnen.** The plural of **die 'Phalanx** phalanx is usually **die Pha'langen.**

2. All masculines of two or more syllables ending in unaccented **-e,** provided they represent persons or other living beings: **der Knabe** boy, **der Preuße** Prussian, **der Löwe** lion, &c. Also three names of lifeless things belong here: **der Buchstabe** (see **69**), **der Hirse** (usually str.; now more commonly fem. **die Hirse**) millet, **der Zehnte** tithe. The list of lifeless things was once much larger. In **68** and **78.** *Note* a description is given of the forces that have withdrawn from the weak declension the masculines and neuters representing lifeless things. Hence, of the many masculines and the smaller number of neuters which once belonged to the weak declension there remain only the masculines denoting living beings, so that the idea of life has become associated with weak masculine inflection.

3. The following list of masculines representing living beings, which, having no **-e** in the nom. sing., or having lost there the **e** which once belonged to them, cannot now be recognized by an ending and hence in a number of cases are now often felt as **e**-plurals, i.e. strong nouns with **-s** in the gen. sing. and **-e** in the plural: **Ahn** (often str. in sing.) ancestor; **Bär** bear; **Bauer** (also str. in sing.; always str. in the compounds **Ma'schinenbauer** machinist, **Orgelbauer** organ-builder, &c., where it is derived from **bauen** to build) peasant; **Bayer** (sometimes str. in sing.) Bavarian; **Bleß** (also a wk. fem. **die Blesse**) blazed horse; **Bursch** (pl. not infrequently **Bursche**) or **Bursche** young fellow, student, servant; **Christ** (but an **e**-pl. in the meaning *Christmas present*) Christian; **Dolmetsch** (sing. also uninflected, pl. also **Dolmetsche**; usually replaced by the str. **Dolmetscher**) interpreter; **Drost** (also an **e**-pl.) magistrate; **Ehehalt** (early N.H.G. and still used in the South) servant; **Elf** elf; **Farr** or more commonly **Farre** (earlier in the period, still in the Southwest) bull; **Faun** (usually an **e**-pl.) faun; **Fex** (more commonly an **e**-pl.) fool; **Fink** finch; **Fratz** silly fellow; **Fuchs** (**70.** 1. *a*), **Fürsprech** (also an **e**-pl.) attorney; **Fürst** ruling prince, prince; **Geck** (earlier in the period also an **e**-pl.) vain fellow; **Gesell** workman, fellow, and with the exception of **Gemahl** (**63.** **2.** *a*), **Gespan** (**63.** 2. *a*), and sometimes **Gespons** (**63.** 2. *a*) all other masculines of this form (i.e. beginning with **Ge-** and not ending in **-e**) representing persons; **Gnom** gnome; **Graf** count; **Greif** (also an **e**-pl.) griffin; **Held** hero; **Herr** (**des Herrn,** pl. **die Herren**) Mr., gentleman, lord, master; **Hirt** shepherd; **Hohenzoller** (the form **Hohenzollern** is also used as a collective noun inflected as a proper name: **Hohenzollerns Taten** [Wildenbruch's *Quitzows*, 3, 12] *the deeds of the* family of Hohenzollern) a member of the House of Hohenzollern; **Kaffer** (also str. in sing.) clod-hopper; **Kaffer** (also str. in sing.) Kafir; **Kakerlak** (see **79.** 1. *a*); **Kum'pan** (usually an **e**-pl.) companion; **Leu** (dat. and acc. sometimes **Leu;** poetic word for **Löwe**) lion; **Lump** (**63.** 1. *b*); **Mensch** human being; **Mohr** Moor; **Muselman** (or **Muselmann,** gen. **-s,** pl. **-männer**) Mussulman; **Nachfahr** (sing. sometimes str.) successor, descendant; **Narr** fool; **Oberst** (or more rarely **Obrist**; sometimes str. or uninflected in sing.) colonel; **Ochs** ox; **Pfaff** priest, parson (contemptuously); **Pfau** (often str. in sing., pl. sometimes **Pfaue**) peacock; **Pommer** Pomeranian; **Prinz** son of a **Fürst**; **Protz** vulgar, conceited man of wealth; **Scheck** dapple (horse); **Schelm** (earlier in the period wk. and sometimes so still; now usually an **e**-pl.) rogue; **Schenk** cup-bearer; **Schöps** (usually an **e**-pl.; only rarely wk. as a simple word, but regularly so in compounds, as in **Schöpsenfleisch**) wether; **Schultheiß** mayor (especially of a small place); **Spatz** (often str. in sing., pl. sometimes **Spatze**) sparrow; **Steinmetz** stone-cutter; **Tor** fool; **Tropf** (**70.** 1. *a*);

Truchseß (also an **e**-pl.) formerly one who placed food before his lord; **Untertan** (sing. also str.) subject (of a king, &c.), **Vorfahr** (sometimes str. in sing.) predecessor, ancestor; **Weih** (also an **e**-pl.) and **Weihe** (also a wk. fem.) kite (bird); **Welf** Guelph; **Zar** (sometimes an **e**-pl.) czar; also a few names of nationalities and famous families which are usually found only in the plural: **Angeln** Angles, **Zimbern** Cimbri, **Nibelungen** (pl. sometimes **Nibelunge** as in M.H.G.) Nibelungs, **Billungen** (pl. sometimes **Billunge**), &c. Most of the weak nouns denoting nationalities have **e** in the nom. sing. (as **der Däne** Dane, **der Russe** Russian, &c.), and hence belong to 2 above.

A few masculines not ending in **-e** representing lifeless objects are weak: **Frank** (**10 Frank[en]**; in Austria, also str. in sing.; in Switzerland entirely replaced by the unmut. **e**-less plural **Franken**) franc (coin); **Spitz** (Schiller's *Wallensteins Lager*, 6, now a weak fem. **die Spitze**, usually in this meaning found in the plural) lace; **Zeh** (also str. in sing., usually a wk. fem. **die Zehe**) toe. This list was once larger.

a. Also others sometimes drop the **e** of the nom. sing., as **der Schranz** or **Schranze,** &c. **Hirsch** *stag,* **Lenz** (poetic) *spring-time,* **Mai** *May,* **März** *March,* **Salm** *young salmon,* **Star** *starling,* and **Strauß** *ostrich,* are occasionally weak, but are more commonly **e**-plurals, **Mai** and **März** however, are still more commonly uninflected (see **85.** *a*).

b. Some of the words which used to belong here, especially names of living beings, after throwing off the **-e** which distinguished them as weak, drifted over into the strong declension, but still show their original weak inflection in compounds: **Greisenalter, Hahnenfuß, Schwanengesang, Sternenhimmel,** &c., from **Greis, Hahn, Schwan, Stern,** &c., all now mut. **e**-pls. except the first and last, which are unmut. **e**-pls. For fuller statement see **249.** II. 1. B. *a.* Provincially, especially in the S.W., some of these words which represent animals are still as simple nouns inflected weak when used as names of taverns: **„zu den drei Schwanen"** (on a sign) 'At the Three Swans,' **im Hirschen** (see *a* above), &c. The frequent use of the oblique case ending **-en** of these weak nouns after prepositions has left the impression that the words also in the nominative end in **en,** hence such forms as **der Hirschen, der Schwarze Bären, der Pfauen** (Spitteler's *Conrad,* p. 204), all names of taverns.

c. There is a tendency for some of the above list of weak nouns to become strong, which especially manifests itself in the acc.: **Da lauerte einst der wilde Urgermane auf den zottigen Bär** (instead of **Bären**) (Raabe's *A. T.*, chap. xiii). Less frequently in the gen., but sometimes also there: **mit des Markgrafs Weib** (Hauptmann's *Schluck und Jau,* p. 24), but **des jungen Markgrafen Weib** (ib.).

4. Many masc. foreign nouns:

a. Those ending in accented **ag, arch, ast, at, aur, ct** (**kt**), **et, ik, il, ist, it, ith, ll, ng, og, om, op, ost, ot, ph, pt, rd, tt, urg, ut, yst,** only, however, when they represent persons or other living beings: **Le′gāt** legate, **Pi′lōt** pilot, &c. Formerly **e** was added to a number of these endings. After **b, d, g** this older usage still in general prevails as the omission of **e** here would in the nom. sing. give **b, d, g** a different pronunciation from that found in the other cases: **E′phebe, Rhap′sode, Stra′tege, Philo′loge,** &c. After **nd** (see *c*), however, the **e** is dropped: **Vaga′bund,** &c. If the **e** is retained these words, of course, belong to 2 above.

Note. The following exceptions occur: **Pe′dell** (an **e**-pl. or wk.) beadle, **Hippo′gryph** (an **e**-pl. or wk.) hippogrif, **Leo′pārd** (sometimes an unmut. **e**-pl.) leopard, **Prä′fekt** (also an **e**-pl.) prefect; the following masculines, which are wk., tho they represent things: **Auto′mat** slot-machine, **Den′drīt** dendrite, **Diph′thōng** (usually an **e**-pl.) diphthong, **Ko′mēt** comet, **Ma′gnēt** (usually an **e**-pl.) magnet, **Mono′lith** (also an **e**-pl.) monolith, **Pla′nēt** planet, **Sate′llit** satellite; the plural **A′nnālen** annals.

b. Names of peoples having a consonantal ending which is accented upon the last syllable: **Ko′săk** Cossack, **Sara′zēn**(**e**) Saracen, **Bul′gār** Bulgarian, **Mag′yar** or better **Mad′jar** (sometimes str. in sing.) Magyar, Hungarian, **Ta′tar** Tartar, &c. A few which have the accent upon the first syllable (see **61.** *b*): **′Ungar** (sometimes str. in sing.) Hungarian, **′Kaffer** (see 3 above).

c. Masculines ending in accented **and, end, und, ant, ent, isk, graph** representing persons or things: **Multipli′kand** multiplicand, **Dokto′rand** one who is passing his doctor's examination, **Dia′mant** (wk. with poetic forms **′Demant** or **De′mant,** which are **e**-pls. or wk.), **Konso′nant** consonant, **Ok′tant** octant, **Stu′dent** student, **Quo′tient** quotient, **Obe′lisk** obelisk, **Tele′graph** telegraph, &c. There is one exception: **der Ama′rant** amaranth, **des Ama′rants,** pl. **Ama′rante** or **Ama′ranten.** Neuters having these endings are **e**-plurals: **Kompli′ment** &c.

d. The bird **der Papa'gei** (sometimes an unmut. **e**-plural) parrot.

Note. The above lists of endings are not complete, but in general all foreign nouns accented upon the last syllable which represent persons or living beings are weak except those with the endings listed in **63.** 7. *b.* The less common endings, however, have not become closely associated with a particular declension, so that there is here fluctuation: **der Ka'paun** capon, usually strong, sometimes weak, &c. The tendency toward the strong declension is more vigorous in colloquial speech than in the literary language, where the new association of weak inflection with the idea of life is now well established within the limits defined above.

II. *Older Usage and Modern Dialect.*

1. In an earlier period of the language and often as late as early N.H.G. the feminines were also inflected in the singular, and forms showing weak inflection here are often still found in poetry, in prose in a very few set expressions, such as **auf Erden** *upon earth,* and quite commonly in some dialects: **Ein verkeret Hertz findet nichts guts | Vnd der verkereter Zungen ist | wird in vnglück fallen** (Prov. xvii. 20). **Sah ein Knab' ein Röslein stehn, | Röslein auf der Heiden** (Goethe's *Heidenröslein*). In S.G. dialect the **n** of the oblique cases has spread to the nom., so that singular and plural end in **en: Scharf auf den Tisch fallen lassen muß er ja das Bügeleisen, sonst wird die Hosen nicht glatt** (Rosegger's *Der Bauernspöttler*), in the plural **sonst werden die Hosen nicht glatt.** The dropping of the weak endings in the singular of feminines, according to usage in the literary language, resulted from a desire for clearer expression. As the weak forms were alike in singular and plural in all the cases except the nominative the grammatical relations were not always clear. Hence it gradually became common to have weak feminines uninflected in the singular after the analogy of the group of strong feminines which after the loss of their distinctive vowel endings seemed in M.H.G. and early N.H.G. to be uninflected in the singular. Thus arose clear forms for singular and plural. In the same manner the strong feminines of the mutated **e**-plural class which were once inflected in the singular, as described in **71.** 2. *c.*, became uninflected there after the analogy of the other strong feminine group, and thus all feminines have become uninflected in the singular. On the other hand, of the large number of feminines which were originally in the strong declension the large majority have become weak in the plural, leaving in the strong declension only the few that have already been enumerated under the first three classes.

2. Earlier in the period strong masc. and neut. nouns have not infrequently in the gen. plural the seemingly weak case ending **-en: Das preisen die Schüler aller Orten** (Goethe's *Faust,* l. 1934). As this peculiar genitive plural was from the start most common in adverbial use where it had much the same force as the dative plural after a preposition, it seems quite probable that it is in fact only the extension of the dative form to the genitive in adverbial function: **aller Orten** after the analogy of **an allen Orten.** The common adverbial ending **-en**, as in **draußen, drüben,** &c. greatly facilitated this development. This peculiar pl. gen. ending for a time spread somewhat beyond the boundaries of the adverbial construction, as in **voller süßer Worten und Sittensprüchen** (Goethe), but it is now strictly confined to it and survives in only a few archaic expressions, such as **'aller'orten** everywhere, **'vieler'orten** in many places, **'aller'wegen** everywhere, always.

77. Models of Inflection for the Weak Declension:

Singular.

	Knabe *boy*, m.	**Graf** *count*, m.	**Frau** *woman*, f.	**Feder** *pen*, f.
N.	**der Knabe**	**der Graf**	**die Frau**	**die Feder**
G.	**des Knaben**	**des Grafen**	**der Frau**	**der Feder**
D.	**dem Knaben**	**dem Grafen**	**der Frau**	**der Feder**
A.	**den Knaben**	**den Grafen**	**die Frau**	**die Feder**

Plural.

N.	**die Knaben**	**die Grafen**	**die Frauen**	**die Federn**
G.	**der Knaben**	**der Grafen**	**der Frauen**	**der Federn**
D.	**den Knaben**	**den Grafen**	**den Frauen**	**den Federn**
A.	**die Knaben**	**die Grafen**	**die Frauen**	**die Federn**

MIXED DECLENSION.

78. This declension, which is a mixture of the strong and weak declensions or the strong and foreign declensions, falls into two groups—one strong in the sing. and weak in the pl., the other also strong in the sing. but with the foreign ending *s* in the pl.: **der Staat** state, **des Staat(e)s,** pl. **die Staaten; das Echo** echo, **des Echos,** pl. **die Echos.** There are but few native German words in the mixed declension, but a large number of foreign nouns in both groups, among which there is a tendency, not now so marked as earlier in the period, to drop sometimes the **s** of the gen. sing.: **das Drama, des Dramas,** or occasionally **Drama.** Foreign words in this declension do not so frequently take the accent upon the last syllable as in the other declensions.

Note. Historical Development. The mixed declension is made up of words from different sources. The nucleus of the group with the weak plural in **-en** consisted of weak neuter and masculine nouns. On account of their frequent use in the plural they were prevented from following the weak nouns described in **68.** into the strong declension. Their frequent use in the plural preserved their old weak plural form in **-en**, which in these words developed a peculiar plural meaning, namely the idea of a group of connected parts or closely related individuals: **Augen, Ohren, Wangen,** (wk. neut. in M.H.G.), **Waden** (wk. masc. in M.H.G.), **Schmerzen, Sporen, Strahlen, Vettern, Ahnen, Untertanen,** &c. As the **en**-plural became associated in these words with the idea of a group, the ending **-en** could not be used here in the singular to indicate a single individual as the **-en** in the other weak nouns in **68** which went over into the strong declension, as in **Balken** sing. and **Balken** pl. Thus the strong inflection came to be used here in the singular, which established a clear distinction, strong inflection in the singular to indicate an individual, and the weak **en**-plural to indicate a group: **das Auge, des Auges,** but in the plural **die Augen.** A number of words indicating living beings, however, fluctuated between strong and weak inflection in the singular as the idea of life was so closely associated with the weak declension that it often suggested weak inflection here. These fluctuations with the indication of present usage are given after the different nouns in **79. 1** and **76. I. 3.**

This association of the idea of a group of related individuals with the **en**-plural created a new masculine and neuter plural type, which became productive and thus attracted a number of strong nouns into this new plural: **Dornen, Stacheln, Zieraten, Forsten** (connected tracts of forest land), **Staaten** (first used in a collective sense of the States General of Holland), **Enden** (**beide Enden** after the analogy of **beide Augen**), **Betten** (at first with a collective idea of all the beds in the house), **Hemden** (at first with a collective idea, one's shirts), **Gliedmaßen** (in a collective sense of the limbs of the body), **Kleinodien, Unbilden.** A number of Low German and foreign words naturally gravitated into this declension under the influence of their meaning, which in the plural suggested the idea of a group of related parts or individuals: **Masten, Marsen, Toppen, Spanten, Watten, Muskeln, Nerven, Professoren, Konsuln, Dezemvirn, Insekten, Statuten, Interessen, Juwelen,** &c. In words representing living beings, however, there is some fluctuation, as the idea of life often suggests here weak inflection, as indicated below after the different words.

As these words are so frequently used in the plural and in some cases so little in the singular the gender is not firmly associated with the word, so that some nouns appear in the singular as feminine as the **en**-plural, which is the commonest plural for feminines, suggested the feminine gender: **die** but in M.H.G. **das Wange, die** but in M.H.G. **der Wade, der** or now also **die Forst, der Zins** but formerly also **die Zinse, die Unbill** or less commonly **die Unbilde** for M.H.G. **daz** unbilde, **der Nerv** or sometimes **die Nerve, das Juwel** or sometimes **die Juwele.** On the other hand, as in some words (**See,** &c.) the gender was either masculine or feminine the weak feminine form facilitated the entrance of the strong masculine into this declension by suggesting the **en**-plural.

In colloquial speech there is a tendency to inflect strong nouns in **-el** and **-er** according to the mixed declension, strong in the singular, weak in the plural, in order to distinguish the plural from the singular. See **79. 1.** *a. Note* and *b. Note.*

Many foreign words with unstressed suffixes are inflected according to this declension, strong in the singular, weak in the plural, as they fit in here best. As they in general denote lifeless objects they were naturally inflected strong in the singular, but as their foreign unstressed endings did not adapt them to strong inflection in the plural they were declined according to the weak declension, which earlier in the period was intimately associated with foreign words.

The rise of the mixed declension has greatly hindered the development of German inflection toward greater simplicity in form, toward one declension for all masculines and neuters, i.e. the **e**-plural class or in case of nouns in **-el, en, -er, -chen, -lein** its **e**-less form. There is to-day a strong reaction against the mixed declension among good writers and scholars. The plural **Sinnen,** common in the classical period, has made way for the regular form **Sinne.** Forms like **Stiefeln, Pantoffeln** are yielding to **Stiefel, Pantoffel.** Foreign words are manifesting a tendency to assume the inflection of **e**-plurals, as indicated below.

79. *Strong in the Singular, Weak in the Plural.* To the group that forms the sing. strong and the plural weak belong:

1. A few native German or naturalized words:

a. Masculines: **Bur** (also wk.) Boer, **Butt** (sometimes an **e**-pl., sometimes a wk. fem. **die Butte**) turbot, **Dorn (83), Forst** (older plural **Forste** still often used; sometimes a wk. fem.) forest, **Gevatter** godfather, **Hader** old rag, **Kakerlak** (sing. also wk.) albino, **Lorbeer** laurel, **Mars** (sometimes fem.) top (naut. term), **Mast** (pl. also **Maste**) mast, **Muskel** muscle, **Nachbar** (sometimes wk.) neighbor, **Nerv** (sometimes a wk. fem. **die Nerve**) nerve, **Psalm** psalm, **Schmerz** (**des Schmerzes,** &c.; earlier in the period nom. also **Schmerze** or **Schmerzen,** gen. **Schmerzens,** dat. **Schmerzen,** acc. **Schmerzen**) pain, **See** lake, **Sinn** (from early N.H.G. almost up to our time pl. **Sinne** and **Sinnen,** now usually the former) sense, **Sporn** (pl. usually **Sporen,** but also sometimes **Spornen** and **Sporne,** the latter always when it refers to persons, as **Heißsporne** *hot spurs*) spur, **Staat** state, **Stachel** sting, **Strahl** beam, ray, jet (of water, &c.), **Topp** (pl. sometimes **Toppe, Topps**) top part of the mast, **Vetter** (sometimes wk.) cousin, **Zierat** (sometimes an **e**-pl.; sometimes a wk. fem.) ornament, **Zins** (pl. earlier in the period **Zinse;** sometimes a weak fem. **die Zinse**) rent (in this meaning now usually **Mietzins**), interest (in this sense usually in the pl.).

Note. In the language of the common people many words that belong to the unmutated **e**-less plural class, especially those in **-el** and **-er,** are inflected according to this group. This arises from the feeling that the plural ought in some way to be distinguished from the sing. This tendency appears occasionally in good authors: **spitze Giebeln** (Goethe); **das einzige Gelaß, welches noch Fenstern hatte** (Immermann); **die schlimmsten Gewissensskrupeln** (Raabe's *A. T.,* chap. xxiii); **die Splittern | zerbrechender Schäfte** (Scheffel). **Klirrend flogen die Splittern des Wurfgeschosses** (Raabe). **Die neuen Onkeln und Tanten** (Ertl's *Freiheit,* p. **79**), **solche Trotteln** (ib. p. 259), **kuglige Dinge wie Klinkern und Marbeln** (W. A. Lay's *Experimentelle Didaktik,* p. 69), **seine Augen, voll blauer heimlicher Feuern** (Frenssen's *Bismarck,* p. 31). The plural **Stiefeln** *boots* is quite common, but not so much so as a little earlier in the period: **das Paar neuer Stiefeln** (Raabe), **ein Paar hoher Stiefeln** (Spielhagen's *Faustulus,* p. 45), **Reitstiefeln** (Hauptmann's *Und Pippa tanzt!,* 1). The plural **Pan'toffeln** is quite common, but is now yielding gradually to **Pan'toffel.**

b. Neuters: **Auge** eye, **Bett** bed, **Ende** end, **Gör** (N.G.; also a wk. fem. **die Göre**) a little child, urchin, brat, **Hemd** shirt, **'Kleinod** (pl. **Klei'nōdien,** also **'Kleinōde,** always when figurative) jewel, **Möbel** (pl. earlier in the period **Möbels** and **Möbeln,** of which the latter is still used, but is being gradually replaced by

Möbel) article or piece of furniture, **Ohr** ear, **Schott** (**63.** 5. *c*), **Spant** (used sometimes in the sing. in a collective sense as in **das Achterspant,** more commonly in the pl., **die Achterspanten**) frame (of ship), **Want** (used sometimes in the sing. in a collective sense: **Ich stieg ins Fockwant;** usually in the pl.; sometimes fem.) rigging, **Watt** (usually in the pl.; sometimes **e**-pl., sometimes a wk. fem. **die Watte**) shallow place bordering upon the shore only covered at high tide, and **Herz** heart, which inflects: N. and A. **das Herz,** G. **des Herzens,** D. **dem Herzen,** pl. **die, der, den, die Herzen.** Rarely with Dative **dem Herz: Schier wird's dem Herz zu enge** (Scheffel's *Trompeter*, Lieder jung Werners, v).

Note. In Austrian and Bavarian dialects, nouns with the diminutive suffix **-el** are declined according to this group: **das Hendel** chicken, pl. **die Hendeln; das Mandl** male fowl, pl. **die Mandeln; das Weibel** female fowl, pl. **die Weibeln; du armes Hascherl du!** (Halbe's *Rosenhagen*, p. 100) *you poor fellow!*, **ös** (= **ihr**; see **140.** *g*) **Hascherln** (Anzengruber's *Die Kreuzelschreiber*, 1, 4), &c. Often also in serious prose: **eines der launigsten Liedeln der Sammlung** (A. Bettelheim in *Beilage zur Allgemeinen Zeitung*, 29. Nov. 1901, p. 1), **arme Hascherln** (Ertl's *Freiheit*, p. 190). **Chiavacci stellt die Gigerln dem Gockel an die Seite, der auch stolz auf seine Federn am Mist einhersteigt** (Schranka's *Wiener Dialekt-Lexikon*, p. 59). Also outside of Austrian and Bavarian literature: **Ihr dummen Gösseln!** (Raabe's *Hastenbeck*, p. 15). **Die Mädeln gehören zu den Mädeln, und die Buben zu den Buben** (Isolde Kurz's *Nachbar Werner.*)

2. Many foreign nouns:

a. Masculines ending in unaccented **-or,** which is short and unaccented in the singular, but long and accented in the plural, thus conforming to the Latin, which shows a short and unaccented *o* in dissyllabic forms and a long and accented *o* when an additional syllable is added: **der 'Doktŏr** doctor, **des 'Doktŏrs, dem 'Doktŏr** (not **'Doktōre**), **den 'Doktŏr,** plural **die Dok'tōren,** &c.

Note. Of course, words in accented **-ōr** belong to the unmutated **e**-plural class: **der Ma'jōr** major, **des Ma'jōrs,** pl. **die Ma'jōre.**

b. Masculines in **-'ismus: der Kate'chismus, des Kate'chismus,** pl. **die Kate'chismen.** They do not add an additional **s** in the gen. sing., and they change in the pl. **-mus** to **-men.** Earlier in the period the words of this group were often in French form instead of the Latin: **Despotism,** &c., instead of **Despotismus,** &c.

c. Neuters in **-a,** which sometimes drop the **s** of the gen. sing. and usually change **-a** in the pl. to **-en: das Drama** drama, **des Dramas** or sometimes **des Drama,** pl. **die Dramen.** Sometimes **s** is added to form the pl.: **die Dramas.** The plural of **das Klima** climate is **die Klimate** or **Klimata, Klimas, Klimen, Klimaten.** The plural of **Komma** comma is **die Kommas, Kommata, Kommaten, Kommen.**

d. Neuters ending in **-'eum, -ium, -uum, -on** (unaccented) and masculines in unaccented **-us** and **-ius,** all of which take **s** (except those in **us** and **ius**) in the gen., or sometimes remain unchanged, and change in the pl. **-um, -on,** and **-us** to **-en: das Mu'sēum** museum, **des Mu'sēums,** pl. **die Mu'seen; das Parti'zipium** participle, **des Parti'zipiums,** pl. **die Parti'zipien; das Indi'viduum** individual, **des Indi'viduums,** pl. **die Indi'viduen; das Distichon** *distich*, **des Distichons,** pl. **die Distichen** (also **Disticha**), &c. Those in **-us** and **-ius** usually remain unchanged in the gen. sing.: **der Nunzius, des Nunzius,** pl. **die Nunzien.** A number of very common nouns in **-us** are manifesting a decided tendency to add the endings of the **e**-plural class to the foreign ending **-us,** more frequently, however, in the pl.: **der Krokus, des Krokus,** pl. **die Krokusse** or **Krokus; der Omnibus, des Omnibus** or **Omnibusses,** pl. **die Omnibusse** or **Omnibus; der Bambus, des Bambusses** or **Bambus,** pl. **die Bambusse** or **Bambus;** like **Krokus** also **Fokus, Kaktus,** (pl. also **Kak'teen**), **Globus** (pl. also **Globen**). This tendency is also marked in a number of proper names in **-us, -es, -as,** whether used as proper names or as common class nouns: **Brutus, Herkules, Judas,** pl. **die Brutusse, Herkulesse, Judasse.** A number of words may drop the foreign ending in the sing., and then add **s** in the gen. sing. and **ien** in the plural, or may be inflected according to the unmut. **e**-plural class: **das Parti'zip, des Parti'zips,** pl. **die Parti'zipien** or **die Parti'zipe; das Kon'zil** (more common than **Kon'zilium**), **des Kon'zils, die Kon'zilien** or more commonly **Kon'zile; das Prin'zip, des Prin'zips,** pl. **die Prin'zipe** or **Prin'zipien; der Typus** or **Typ, des Typus** or **des Typs,** pl. **die Typen.**

Some neuters in **-um** take **s** in the gen. and change **um** to **a** in the plural: **das Masku'linum, des Masku'linums,** pl. **die, der, den, die Masku'lina.** Some of these nouns often drop the **-um** of the sing., then take **s** in the gen., and change the **a** of the pl. to **en**: **das Verb** or **Verbum, des Verbs** or **Verbums,** pl. **die Verben** or **Verba.** A few of these neuters in **-um** take **s** in the pl.: **das Album, des Albums,** pl. **die Albums** (also **Alben, Album, Albume**).

e. Neuters formed from neuter adjectives which in the Latin end in *e* in the sing. and *ia* in the pl. The German nouns drop the *e* of the sing., thus ending usually in **-'īl** and **-'āl**, and change the Latin pl. *ia* into *ien*: **das Fo'ssil** fossil, **des Fo'ssils,** pl. **die Fo'ssilien; das Mine'ral** mineral, **des Mine'rals,** pl. **die Mine'ralien,** &c. A number of these words are drifting toward the unmut. **e**-pl. class: **das Rep'til** reptile, **des Rep'tils,** pl. **die Rep'tile** or **Rep'tilien; das Mine'ral, des Mine'rals,** pl. **die Mine'rale** or **Mine'ralien.**

f. A number of isolated foreign words: the masculines **A'spekt** aspect (astrol.), prospect, view, **'Augur** (pl. **'Augure** or **Au'guren;** also wk.) augur, **Cäsar** (pl. **Cä'saren**) Cæsar, emperor, **'Dämon** (des **'Dämons,** pl. **die Dä'monen**) demon, **De'zemvir** (pl. **De'zemvirn;** also wk.) decemvir, **Fa'san** (also an **e**-pl. and wk.) pheasant, **'Großmogul** (pl. **'Großmoguln, 'Großmogule,** or **Großmoguls**) Great Mogul, **Konsul** (pl. **Konsuln**) consul, **Pharao** (pl. **die Phara'onen**) Pharaoh, **Satyr** satyr, **Tri'bun** (also wk. and an unmutated **e**-pl.) tribune (magistrate), **Tri'umvir** (pl. **Tri'umvirn;** sometimes wk.) triumvir, **Zen'turio** (also wk. **des Zenturi'onen,** &c.; pl. **die Zenturi'onen**) centurion; the neuters: **Auto'graph** autograph, **In'sekt** insect, **Inte'resse** interest, **Ju'wel** (sometimes an **e**-pl.; often masc.; only rarely fem. **die Ju'wele**) jewel, **Kon'klave** conclave, **Sta'tut** statute.

g. A number of neuters in **-'ens** remain unchanged in the sing. and change in the pl. **-ens** to **enzien (entien): das Rea'gens** reagent, **des Rea'gens,** pl. **die Rea'genzien (Reagentien).**

h. A number in unaccented **-os** and **-as** remain usually unchanged in the sing. and change in the pl. the stem and shift the accent upon the suffix: **der 'Heros** hero, **des 'Heros,** pl. **die He'roen; der 'Kustos** custodian, **des 'Kustos,** pl. **die Kus'toden; der 'Atlas** atlas, **des 'Atlasses** or **des 'Atlas,** pl. **die 'Atlasse** or **At'lanten; der 'Primas** primate, **des 'Primas** (or **des Pri'maten**), pl. **die Pri'maten, 'Primas,** or **'Primasse; das Epos** epic, **des Epos,** pl. **die Epen,** but **das Rhi'noze'ros** rhinoceros, **des Rhi'noze'ro(sse)s,** pl. **die Rhi'noze'rosse.**

80. To the group that takes the **s** in the gen. sing. and thruout the pl. belong:

1. A large number of masc. and neut. words from the French, English, and other languages, ancient or modern, which are still felt as foreign on account of their foreign sound, accent, or endings (often **a, o, u, i;** the French nasal vowels, **ain, ein, im, in, om, on, um, un,** for which see **25**; a vowel before a silent final consonant) that cannot easily be fitted into the German declensions: **der Domino** domino, **des Dominos,** pl. **die, der, den, die Dominos; das** (also **der**) **Kinō** theater in which moving pictures are presented, in this sense = **Lichtspieltheater,** sometimes also kinetoscope or kinetograph, in this sense = **das Kineto'skop** or **der Kineto'graph** (or **Kinemato'graph**), **des Kinos,** pl. **die, der, den, die Kinōs; das Cha'mäleon** (k-) chameleon, **des Cha'mäleons,** pl. **die, der, den, die Chamäleons; das Restaurant** (rɛsto:'rã:) restaurant, **des Restau'rants,** pl. **die Restau'rants; der Paletot** (palə'to:), **des Pale'tots,** pl. **die Pale'tots.** Also a few feminines belong here: **die Lady,** pl. **die Ladys; die Ma'ma,** pl. **die Ma'mas; die Miß,** pl. **die Misses** or **Missen; die Villa,** pl. **die Villas** or **Villen; die Team** (ti:m; fem. after the analogy of the corresponding German word **die Mannschaft**) team (as in football team), pl. **die Teams.**

Since the eighteenth century there has been a marked tendency in choice language to replace the foreign plural ending **s** by German **e** in case of masculines and neuters, and thus place these words in the unmutated **e**-plural class, or in case of feminines to inflect according to the weak declension. A large number of these words are already entirely or partially naturalized: **das Kos'tüm, des Kos'tüms, die Kos'tüme; der** (sometimes **das**) **Lift** (usually masc. after the analogy of the corresponding German words **der Aufzug** or **Fahrstuhl**), **des Lifts, die Lifte** or **Lifts; der Kaftan, des Kaftans, die Kaftane** or **Kaftans; der Turban, des Turbans, die Turbane** or **Turbans; das Defizit, des Defizits, die Defizite** or **Defizits; der** (or **das**) **Schrap'nell, des Schrap'nells, die Schrap'nells** or **Schrap'nelle; der Kai, des Kais, die Kais** or **Kaie.** The words ending in a vowel sound or the French nasals offer the most stubborn resistance. Where, however, the nasal vowel has been replaced by a German vowel plus dental **n,** the words may be inflected according to the unmutating **e**-plural type: **das Bataillon** (batal'jo:n), pl. **die Bataillone** (batal'jo:nə). If the French pronunciation is retained or if the nasal has been replaced by a vowel + velar **n** (ŋ) the words resist German inflection: **das Bassin** (ba'sɛ̃: or ba'sɛŋ) basin, pl. **die Bassins** (ba'sɛ̃:s or ba'sɛŋs).

2. A few German words not really substantives may take an **s** in the gen. sing. and thruout the pl., such as letters of the alphabet, exclamatory particles, other parts of speech used as substantives, or the syntactical fragment of a sentence or a whole sentence used as a modern compound (see **249. II.** 2; for rule as to gender see **98.** 2. C. *e*): **das A** the letter a, **des As,** pl. **die As; das Ja** the word yes, **des Jas,** pl. **die Jas; das Ach** the exclamation Oh!, **des Achs,** pl. **die Achs. Mein früheres Ich** my former self; **entweder sind die Menschen von ihren Ichs und was damit Bezug hat, besessen usw.** (Schiller). **Ein ganzes Heer von Freilichs, Dennochs und Abers** (Gutzkow). **Da gibt's Gutentags und Gutenabends, daß kein Ende ist** (Goethe). **Der Schlagetot** ruffian, **des Schlagetots,** pl. **die Schlagetots, der Schubbejack** ragamuffin, **des Schubbejacks,** pl. **die Schubbejacks** or **Schubbejacke.**

Others prefer non-inflection here: **das A, des A,** pl. **die A. Wie so schal dünkt mich dies Leben! . . . Stets das Heute nur, des Gestern und des Morgen flaches Bild** (Grillparzer's *Der Traum ein Leben*, 1). **Das Bild eines frechen Tunichtgut** (Fontane's *Vor dem Sturm*, IV. 19); **alle Pharisäer und Gernegroß** (id., *Stechlin*, XXXII); **die Stellungnahme des Ich zu dem Volke** (Hugo Gaudig in *Zeitschrift für Pädagogische Psychologie*, Nov.-Dec. 1918, p. 360). **Sie (die Jugend) ist durchaus erfüllt von den Aussichten des Morgen und Übermorgen** (*Vossische Zeitung*, June 8, 1919).

In a number of cases there is a tendency more or less strong to inflect such formations according to the regular declensions: **mein reizendes Gegenüber (beim Tisch), meines Gegenübers,** pl. **meine Gegenüber; das Jelängerjelieber, des Jelängerjeliebers, die Jelängerjelieber; über uns deutsche Gernegroße** (W. Anz in *Zeit. des Allg. d. Sprachvereins*, 1906, p. 268), **lebhafte Hoche** (*Frankfurter Zeit.*, May 6, 1914; pl. also **Hochs** or **Hoch**), **Übersehen der anderen Iche** (*Zeit. für den D. Unterricht*, Jahrg. 25, p. 387), **Nichtsnutze** (nom. pl., quite common), **diese Nimmersatte** (nom. pl., quite common), **alle ihre Stelldicheine** (rare) (J. Paul), **Kehrauße** (pl. more commonly unchanged **Kehraus**), **Saufauße** (often in colloquial speech, usual pl. in literary language **Saufaus**), **Taugenichtse** (nom. pl.; very common), **die Tunichtgute** (Fontane's *Pog.*, VIII), **Vergißmeinnichte** (nom. pl.; quite common). See **63.** 2. *e* and 6.

3. Many words in the regular declensions, mostly words representing persons, take colloquially this **s** in the pl., especially so in N.G.: **die Kerls** the fellows, **die Mädchens** the girls, **die Fräuleins** the young ladies, and even in case of wk. nouns, which add the **s** to the regular weak plural: **die Herrens** the gentlemen, **die Jungens** young chaps.

a. This **s** was used in Gothic to form the pl. of all masc. and fem. words, but it had disappeared in H.G. before the O.H.G. period. It was, however, still preserved in Middle Low German in a few words representing persons, like **Herdes** (= **Hirten**), where the **s** was needed to distinguish the plural from the singular. After the analogy of these words it was employed in words in **-er** representing persons in order to distinguish the plural from the singular: **Borger** (= **Bürger**), pl. **Borgers.** This Low German plural in **s** was greatly favored by the growth of the plural in **s** for proper names, which was originally a genitive singular (see **93.** 1. *a*), as found also in High German in **Müllers haben Besuch.** As many Low German family names are diminutives, as **Gödeke, Rötteken,** their plural in **s** spread to the class of diminutives as a whole, so that this plural became common for many names of things. In the sixteenth century, furthered by strong Dutch influence, this plural spread in Low German and was extended to all masculines in **-el, -en, -er** to distinguish the plural from the singular. Altho this plural ending is now supported by universal usage in French and English and also by wide use in Low German, and is much used colloquially in the North by those speaking High German, it is carefully avoided in choice language.

81. Models of Inflection for Mixed Declension:

Singular.

	Staat *state*, m.	Drama *drama*, n.	Trupp *troop*, m.	Villa *villa*, f.
N.	der Staat	das Drama	der Trupp	die Villa
G.	des Staat(e)s	des Drama(s)	des Trupps	der Villa
D.	dem Staat(e)	dem Drama	dem Trupp	der Villa
A.	den Staat	das Drama	den Trupp	die Villa

Plural.

N.	die Staaten	die Dramen	die Trupps	die Villas
G.	der Staaten	der Dramen	der Trupps	der Villas
D.	den Staaten	den Dramen	den Trupps	den Villas
A.	die Staaten	die Dramen	die Trupps	die Villas

Foreign Words.

82. A few foreign words that, on account of the retention of their foreign endings (us, is, um, o, &c.), cannot be declined in any of the preceding declensions remain as they are found in their native language, the form of the nom. sing. being used thruout the sing., and the nom. pl. thruout the pl., the article alone marking the other cases: **der (des, dem, den) Musikus** musician, **pl. die (der, den, die) Musizi; der Kasus, pl. die Kasus,** &c.

Scholars, however, often prefer to decline Latin words thruout as in the original, more frequently so earlier in the period: **Imperfectum, Imperfecti,** &c. This is most common with grammatical terms.

a. Note the following irregular formations: **der Cherub, des Cherubs, pl. die 'Cherubīm (also Cherube, Cherubs, Cheru'binen); der Seraph, des Seraphs, pl. die Seraphe or Seraphīm.**

Differentiation of Substantive Forms.

83. Many nouns have two forms and may be declined according to the one or the other. This redundancy may assume one of four forms: **(1)** The noun may have two genders for the same form, as **der** or more commonly **die Hirse** *millet.* **(2)** There may be two forms for the same noun, each with a different gender, as **der Quast** *tassel* or **die Quaste.** **(3)** The noun may have only one form for the sing., but two in the pl., as **der Ort** *town*, pl. **Orte** or less commonly **Örter.** **(4)** The same word may have in different dialects the same gender, but different forms or declensions or both, which often pass from their respective dialects over into the literary language with or without differentiated meaning: **die Schluft** (H.G., but now little used) and **die Schlucht** (L.G., but now well established in the literary language) cleft, gorge; **der Brunnen** *well, fountain*, **Born** (L.G. and M.G.; poetic) fount, well-spring. Redundant forms occur often in the spoken and written language and it is frequently difficult to choose between them, and no harm will be done if the one or other be chosen, unless usage at last settles down upon one of the forms, as in **das Bündel** *bundle*, **der Docht** *wick*, **der Garaus** *finishing stroke*, **der Käfig** *cage*, &c. Double forms have always existed in the language and have resulted in good, for many of them have been put to use by the people who, led by an economic instinct, have given to each form a slightly different shade of meaning. Words also which have only one form for different meanings and applications tend to develop different forms for the different meanings and applications. Also nouns which are derived from the different forms of the same verb or other word tend toward a distinct differentiation in meaning.

Either the difference in gender or in the form of the noun in the singular or plural may cause the difference of meaning, as can be seen by the following illustrative examples:

Der Acker field, pl. **Äcker**; **der Acker** acre, pl. **Acker.**

Der Akt act (in a drama), pl. **Akte**; **die Akte** act (of parliament or some other authority), document, pl. **Akten.**

Der Antichrist antichrist, **des Antichrists, pl. die Antichriste; der Antichrist** enemy of Christianity, **des Antichristen, die Antichristen.**

Die (Goethe's *Egmont*, 5; this attempt at differentiation has not been generally sustained, now usually **das**) **Ärgernis** anger; **das Ärgernis** that which causes anger, i.e. offense.

Der Balg skin, pl. **Bälge**; in the meanings *child, thing* (in familiar language referring to a child, boy, or girl), also in a bad sense *brat*, **der Balg, pl. Bälge,** but now also frequently neuter with plural **Bälger,** following the analogy of **das Kind**; in the meaning *bellows* with the plural **Bälge** or **Balgen,** the latter usually in compounds: **Die Bälge or Balgen einer Orgel treten, Balgenschwengel,** &c.

Der Ball, pl. Bälle ball; **der Ballen** bale.

Der Band volume, **pl. Bände; das Band** ribbon, **pl. Bänder; das Band** tie (of friendship, &c.), fetter, **pl. Bande.**

Der Bau (see **63. 1.** *b*).

Der Bauer peasant; **der** (also **das**) **Bauer** bird cage.

Das Beet bed (in a garden), pl. **Beete; das Bett** bed (for sleeping), river-bed, pl. **Betten.** In the meaning *river-bed* the plural **Bette** is sometimes used: **längs der Flußbette** (Fr. König, Ingenieur und Hydrotekt, in *Deutsche Kolonialzeit.*, Feb. 16, 1905), **die Benützung der öffentlichen Gewässer bezw. ihrer Bette** (*Neue Zürcher Zeit.*, Aug. 31, 1905).

Der Brunnen *well, fountain,* ordinary prose word; **der Born** *well-spring, fount,* poetic word.

Der Buckel *hump,* in popular speech *back,* pl. **Buckel; die Buckel** *boss* (on a shield), pl. **Buckeln,** but in this meaning also **der Buckel,** pl. **Buckel.**

Der Bund alliance; **das Bund** bundle.

Der Chor song sung by the choir, or the choir itself; **das** (or **der**) **Chor** place in the church where the choir sits. See also **70. 3.**

Der Christ (pop.; also in *Faust,* Abend) Christmas present, **des Christes,** pl. **die Christe; der Christ** Christian, **des Christen,** pl. **Christen.**

Das Denkmal monument, pl. usually **Denkmäler,** but often **Denkmale** in choice language.

Der Dienstmann man on the streets who carries bundles for hire, vassal; pl. **Dienstmänner** in the first meaning; pl. **Dienstleute** servants of a house; pl. **Dienstmannen** vassals.

Das Ding thing, pl. **Dinge;** pl. **Dinger** when speaking in a tone of pity or playfully of the young of animals, birds, or of girls (as 'queer things'), or disparagingly and contemptuously of things; **das, der,** or **die Ding,** or more commonly **Dings** (a genitive used now for all cases; see **255.** II. 1. H. *c*) **da** (when memory fails to recall a thing or person) *what-you-may-call-it, what-you-may-call-him* or *-her.* The form **Dings** is also used of girls: **das kleine Dings** (Storm's *Ein Doppelgänger,* p. 215).

Der Dorn thorn; pl. **Dornen** used of the bush; pl. **Dorne** with reference to different varieties, as **Hage-, Kreuz-, Schwarz-, Weißdorne;** pl. **Dorne** and **Dörner** of the individual thorns, and also in the mechanical arts of a punch, tongue of a buckle, &c. Usage in all these points, however, is not yet firmly fixed. Compare **78.** *Note.*

Der Druck *print, pressure,* pl. of the simple form usually **Drucke;** pl. in compounds usually unmutated where the word is felt as belonging to **drucken** *to print,* as in **Nachdrucke** *pirated editions,* **Abdrucke** *reprints,* **Neudrucke** *reprints;* pl. in compounds usually mutated where the word is felt as belonging to **drücken** *to press,* as in **die Abdrücke** impressions (by stamping), proofs (of photos), copies (of books), **Ausdrücke** expressions, **Eindrücke** impressions (of the mind), **Händedrücke.**

Der Effekt effect, impression, pl. **Effekte;** pl. **Effekten** effects, movables, stocks.

Der Erbe heir; **das Erbe** inheritance.

Die Erkenntnis perception, comprehension; **das Erkenntnis** decision of a judge; **die Erkenntnis der Schuld geht dem Erkenntnis des Richters voran.**

Der Faden thread, pl. **Fäden; der Faden** fathom, pl. **Faden.**

Der Fleck and **der Flecken** both have the meanings *stain, spot, blemish, place,* and *large village,* but the tendency is to use **Flecken** in sense of *village* and **Fleck** or **Flecken** in the other meanings. **Fleck** more commonly in the literal meaning, as **Ölfleck,** &c., and **Flecken** in the moral sense of *blemish.* In the compound **Marktflecken** *market-town, borough* the form in **-en** is always used.

Der (sometimes **die**) **Flur** entrance hall of a house, pl. **Flure** if masc.; **die Flur** field (poetic), pl. **Fluren.**

Der Fuß foot (of a person), pl. **Füße; zwei Fuß** (see **96. 4. (1)**) **lang** two feet long; **Fuße verschiedener Länge** feet (standards of measurement) of different length.

Die Gans goose, pl. **Gänse; das Gans** word goose, pl. **die Gans** or **Ganses; Das erste Gans ist nicht so schön geschrieben wie das zweite.** Thus any noun of any gender becomes neut. when it stands not for a person or object but for the written word which represents it.

Der Gehalt intrinsic worth or value, also **der Salzgehalt des Wassers,** &c.; **das** (sometimes still **der,** in accordance with older usage) **Gehalt** salary, pl. **Gehälter** (sometimes as formerly **Gehalte**).

Das Geschrei cry, clamor; **das Geschreie** continued disagreeable screaming. See *b* below.

Das Gesicht face, pl. **Gesichter; das Gesicht** vision, pl. **Gesichte.**

Das Gewand garment; pl. **Gewänder;** pl. **Gewande** (poetic). See also **73.** *b.*

Die Gift (rare except in the compound **die Mitgift**) present; **das** (see **100. 1**) **Gift** poison.

Der Haft clasp; **die Haft** arrest.

Der Halt support, halt, halting-place, pl. **Halte; ein** (neut.) **Halt** a stop or end, as in **ein Halt gebieten** to put a stop to. This is a case of only seeming differentiation. The second form is in fact the imperative of the verb **halten,** which is here used as a noun, and hence is neut. according to rule (see **98.** 2. C. *e*).

Der Heide heathen; **die Heide** heath.

Das Horn horn, pl. **Hörner;** pl. **Horne** kinds of horn.

Der Hut hat; **die Hut** guard; **die Vorhut** vanguard.

Der Im'port import, pl. **Im'porte** (also **Importen**): **Der Wert der Importe** (*Hamburgischer Correspondent,* Apr. 20, 1905); **Die Importe** genuine imported Havana cigar, pl. **Im'porten: Die ersten Züge aus der eben angezündeten Importe** (W. v. Polenz's *Liebe ist ewig,* p. 27).

Der Jude Jew, in popular language **der Jüde** (Raabe's *Höxter und Corvey,* chap. xiv).

Das Korn corn, grain, pl. **Körner; der Korn** whiskey, pl. **Korne** or **Korns: feiner Korn** Dutch gin.

Der Kunde customer; **die Kunde** information.

Der Laden shutter, pl. **Laden** (also **Läden**); **der Laden** store, shop, pl. **Läden.**

Das Land land, pl. **Länder;** pl. **Lande,** the older pl. form, which still remains (**1**) in poetry, as in **über alle Lande** (in prose **Länder**); (**2**) in proper names, as in **die Niederlande** the Netherlands, **die Rheinlande, die Vierlande** (four islands in the Elb southeast of Hamburg); (**3**)to designate the different divisions of one political whole: **die deutschen Lande,** in recent usage, however, assuming more and more a general poetic meaning, being replaced in the exact meaning of the existing states by **die deutschen Länder** (Dr. Fritz Poetsch in *Die Woche*, Sept. 6, 1919, and so regularly in *Die Verfassung des Deutschen Reichs*, Aug. 11, 1919). See also *a* below. (**4**) in **Eilande** islands.

Das Licht light, candle; pl. **Lichter** lights; pl. **Lichte** candles.

Der Lump poor, ragged, worthless fellow, pl. **die Lumpe,** also **Lumpen; der Lumpen** rag.

Der Mai (month of) May; die (formerly **der**) **Maie** green bough (used for festive decorations in May), Maypole, pl. **Maien.**

Der Makler broker, agent; **der Mäkler** broker or more commonly faultfinder.

Der Mann man, pl. **Männer;** pl. **Mannen** warriors, vassals; pl. **Mann** (see **96. 4. (1)**); pl. **-leute** (see **96.** 9).

Der Mensch human being; **das Mensch** wench, strumpet, pl. **Menscher.** The neuter is sometimes used in a good sense in the meaning *woman*: **Es ist gut, daß ich altes Mensch noch bei wege bin, wenn ihr mich braucht** (Bernhardine Schulze-Smidt's *Im finstern Tal*, XII).

Der Mittag noon; **das** (also **der**) **Mittag** dinner.

Der Mo'ment moment (of time), **das Mo'ment** moment (consequence, weight).

Der Mond moon, satellite, month, now an unmutated e-plural, was also weak earlier in the period. The weak gen. still occurs in the first meaning in compounds in poetic style, as in **Mondenglanz.** In the last meaning **Mond** is still sometimes weak in poetic style, especially in the plural.

Das Moos moss, pl. **Moose; das Moos** (or **Ried**) swamp, pl. **Möser** (**Riede**).

Der Muff, pl. **Muffe,** or sometimes **die Muffe,** pl. **Muffen; die Muffe,** pl. **Muffen** sleeve (in mechanics).

Die Mutter mother, female screw: pl. **Mütter** mothers, **Muttern** (earlier here also **Mütter**) female screws.

Das or **der Nickel** nickel (metal); **der Nickel** ten pfennig piece.

Der (or **das**) **Ort** awl (from the original meaning *point*), pl. **Orte** (or **Örte**); **der Ort** place, town; pl. **Orte** *places*, as in **Man kann nicht an allen Orten zugleich sein;** pl. **Orte** or **Örter** *towns.* Many grammarians favor **Örter** in the last meaning, so as to distinguish between **Orte** *places* and **Örter** *towns.* Actual usage, however, favors **Orte** for both meanings.

Der Ost east wind, **Nord** north wind, **Süd** south wind, &c., all with a pl. in **e**; **der Osten** the East, **Westen** the West, **Norden** the North, **Süden** the South, all indicating a section of country. Both forms may also often be used for the points of the compass, the shorter forms especially in maritime expressions: **Der Wind kam rein aus Ost(en).** In plain prose it would be more common to say **der Ostwind, Westwind,** &c., for the winds, while in nautical language **der Ost, West,** &c., are much used.

Der (sometimes **das**) **Pack** or **Packen** pack, bundle; **das Pack** rabble.

Die Pfirsiche or more commonly **der Pfirsich** (pl. **die Pfirsiche**) peach (fruit); **der Pfirsich** peach-tree, more commonly **Pfirsichbaum.**

Das Pro'dukt production, pl. **die Pro'dukte** productions of the mind; pl. **die Pro'dukten** productions of the soil, produce. This distinction is common in familiar language, but the pl. **Produkte** is the only form used in the literary language for all these meanings except in compounds: **Produkte,** but **Produktenhändler, Produktenmarkt.**

Der Rest that which is left, ruin, pl. **die Reste,** pl. **die Rester** remnants of cloth in a dry goods store.

Der Sand sand, strand, sandy plain, sandbank; pl. **Sande** kinds of sand, in poetic style strands, sandy plains; pl. **Sände** sandbanks (in river or sea).

Die Sau *sow*, pl. **die Säue** (early N.H.G.) *sows, swine*, in the latter meaning still **Säue in expressions** following more or less accurately biblical utterances, as in **Man muß die Perlen nicht vor die Säue werfen** (G. Ompteda's *Eysen*, chap. xxxiii); (eighteenth century) pl. **die Säue** *sows, domestic swine*, **Sauen,** *wild swine*; now the wk. pl. is usually used for *domestic sows* and *wild swine*, altho **Säue** is sometimes in accordance with older usage employed for the former meaning.

Das Scheit piece of wood; pl. **Scheite** or **Scheiter** pieces cut for a purpose, as to **burn,** &c., pl. **Scheiter** pieces broken by violence: **das Schiff geht zu Scheitern.**

Der Scharlach scarlet (color, cloth); **der** and often **das Scharlach** scarlet-fever.

Der Schild shield; **das Schild** shop sign.

Die Schwulst swelling, or more commonly **die Geschwulst; der Schwulst** bombast.

Der Schurz apron for men, pl. **Schurze; die Schürze** apron for women and children.

Der See lake, pl. **die Seen; die See** sea.

Die Spalte (sometimes **der Spalt** in the first meaning) split, column (in a newspaper); **der Spalt** (pl. **die Spalte**) split in a figurative sense, contentious division, quarrel, especially common in the compound **Zwiespalt** dissension.

Der Stock stick, cane, story (of a house), pl. **die Stöcke** canes, pl. **Stocke** or **Stock** stories: **Spazierstöcke** *walking sticks*, but **ein Haus von drei Stocken** or **Stock** *a house of three stories*, and **Das Haus ist drei Stock hoch.**

Der Teil part; **das Teil** share.

Der Tropfen drop; **der Tropf** dull, stupid fellow.

Der Trupp gang, unorganized crowd, flock, pl. **die Trupps** (or **Truppe**), as **ein Trupp Arbeiter, Menschen, Kinder, Hühner, Gemsen; die Truppe** organized company or troop.

Das Tuch piece of cloth (handkerchief, shawl, &c.), pl. **die Tücher;** pl. **Tuche** kinds of cloth.

Eine Uhr a clock, watch, pl. **die Uhren; ein** (neut., uninflected) **Uhr** (uninflected) one o'clock, pl. **zwei Uhr** two o'clock, &c.

Der Verdienst wages; **das Verdienst** merit, desert.

Die Vesper vespers (see also **96.** 8); **das** also **die Vesper** afternoon meal: **Nachmittage lang hatten sie hier gespielt und zum Vesper rohe Rüben gegessen** (Hermann Hesse's *Unterm Rad*, p. 21).

Die Walnuß (pl. **Walnüsse**) walnut (fruit); **der Walnuß** (pl. **Walnüsse**) or more commonly **der Walnußbaum** walnut (tree).

Die Wehr defense; **das Wehr** dam (in a river).

Das Wort word with reference to meaning in connected discourse, pl. **die Worte;** pl. **die Wörter** words apart from their meaning: **Er sprach in beredten Worten,** but **Das Telegramm hat 16 Wörter.** This distinction is not yet universally observed, **Worte** seeming to be the favorite in both meanings.

Der Wurm worm; **das Wurm** helpless babe, 'poor thing' (man or woman).

Das Zeug material, substance, stuff, **das Zeugs** (gen. now used for all cases; see **255.** II. 1. H. *c*) *stuff* in a contemptuous sense.

The similarity in form is sometimes merely accidental: **das Tor** gate, **der Tor** fool; **die Mark** mark (coin), **das Mark** marrow, &c.

a. There is a tendency to make a difference between the neut. pl. in **-e** and that in **-er,** when they both occur with the same word. The former has in a number of cases collective force, denoting a number of connected parts or related individuals, the latter form has separating, individualizing force: **das Wort** word; pl. **Worte** words in connected discourse with reference to their meaning; pl. **Wörter** words as individuals without reference to their connection in one sentence, as **Wörterbuch,** lit. word-book, *dictionary*; **das Band** tie, ribbon, pl. **Bande** ties of affection which bind us together, pl. **Bänder** ribbons. Thus also **das Land** country; pl. **Lande** different divisions of one country, in a poetic style emphasizing the idea of inner unity, pl. **Länder** countries, also different states of one country, emphasizing the idea of their individual political rights. See also **Land** and **Dorn** in the above list. The idea of a number of connected parts or related individuals is also closely associated in many words with the plural ending **-en** of the mixed declension, as shown in **78.** *Note.* The difference between plurals in **-er** and **-e** is sometimes merely a matter of style. See **73.** *b.* The forms in **-e** are older than those in **-er,** and hence often naturally incline to use in poetical or less common expressions.

b. There is a tendency to distinguish between the meaning of words of the form **Ge — e** and on the other hand **Ge —̈**. The form **Ge — e** (never mutating the stem vowel) has a more abstract meaning, indicating a repetition or continuation of some action, or often implying contempt or dislike for the performance, and hence on account of its abstract nature without a pl., while the form **Ge —̈** (always mutating the stem vowel if capable of it) has a more concrete meaning, and admits thus of a plural: **das Quellengerausche** the noise of the murmuring spring (which unceasingly murmurs on), **das Geklirre der Tassen und Schüsseln** the rattling of the cups and dishes (in washing), **das Gesinge** tedious singing, **das Getue** an affected noisy manner that proceeds about doing something unimportant, as if it were of great importance (not always, however, in a disparaging sense: **Ihr Benehmen war ein wenig keck, das konnte er sich nicht verhehlen, aber wie so ganz frei von Dreistigkeit war diese Keckheit, wie so ganz ohne Gefallsucht ihr gefälliges Getue und Gehabe**—Wildenbruch's *Die heilige Frau*, p. 130), **das Geklopfe** a continual unpleasant knocking or hammering, **das Gelaufe** a continual unpleasant running to and fro, but **das Geräusch** the noise, pl. **die Geräusche,** &c. The form **Ge — e** is usually made directly from the stem of the verb without mutation, but if the verb itself is mutated the vowel of the derivative noun must of course also be correspondingly modified: **das Gehämmere,** &c. from **hämmern,** &c. The **-e,** however, sometimes distinguishes the one form from the other, altho the distinction cannot appear in the stem vowel: **das Geschreie** continued disagreeable screaming, but **das Geschrei** *a cry, clamor*, &c.

Note. But the distinction between these forms cannot be made thruout, as, according to present usage, **b, d, g,** and usually **s,** do not as a rule stand as a final letter in these formations, and hence **e** must be added, thus destroying in all words not capable of mutation the difference of form and hence the possibility of making a distinction in meaning: **Getreide** *grain* with **e** altho with concrete meaning, &c. On the other hand, the **e** of the abstract form usually drops out after **-el** and **-er,** according to the general rule that **e** cannot stand after **-el** and **-er,** and thus the abstract form cannot here be distinguished from the more concrete: **Geklimper** drumming (upon the piano). The **e,** however, is now often added here in spite of the rule, as it seems necessary to preserve the shade of meaning: **das Gewinsele** (Immermann), **Gehämmere** (Fontane); often also in case of nouns that clearly show this shade of meaning by the unmutated form of the stem-vowel: **Gedudele** (Paul Keller), &c.

c. There is a tendency to differentiate the meaning of words in **-nis** according to their gender, the feminines assuming more abstract, the neuters more concrete meaning: **das Hindernis** *obstacle*, but **die Befugnis** authority. Compare also **Erkenntnis** above. There is, however, much irregularity and fluctuation here.

Inflection of Proper Nouns.

84. Proper nouns as well as common nouns were once inflected strong and weak. In the seventeenth century both masculine and feminine names are sometimes still inflected weak thruout, but almost all traces of this older inflection have disappeared from the literary language except the plural ending **-en** of feminines (see **93.** **1.** *b.* (**2**)), the rather colloquial dat. and acc. ending **en** (see **87**), and the corrupted gen. **ens** (**86.** 2. *a*), which is in fact a str. gen. added to a wk. gen. Other weak forms are still occasionally found: **Was ist die ganze schleswig-holsteinische Geschichte neben der Geschichte des Alten Fritzen?** (Fontane's *Der Tunnel über der Spree*, chap. iv). **Mit des alten Fritzen eigenhändigem Krückstock** (id., *Vor dem Sturm*, III. chap. ii). **Mit des Herzogs Moritzen Obersten, dem Herrn Sebastian von Walwitz** (Raabe's *Unseres Herrgotts Kanzlei*, chap. vi). **Er redete auch den jüngsten Ursleuen, sein Paten- und Enkelkind, an in einer Weise, die mich besonders belustigte** (R. Huch's *Ludolf Ursleu*, chap. xi). The old weak gen. has also been preserved in a number of compounds: **Ottendorf, Luisenstraße.** Outside of these compounds the gen. of these names is **Ottos, Luise(n)s.** Other traces of weak inflection in the names of persons and families are given in **93.** **1.** *b.* (**2**) and (**6**). The ending **-en** is best preserved in the plural of feminine names. See **93.** **1.** *b.* (**2**). It is often found in the singular in the dat. and acc. of unmodified names. See **87.** Tho this singular form in **-en** is now felt as a weak case form, it was originally in all strong masculine proper names an ending borrowed from the acc. of the strong adjective declension, as in **diesen, guten.** Later it spread to the dat., as it was taken for a weak case ending, which is the same for the acc. and dat. This misconception was all the more natural, as many masculine and feminine proper names were originally weak and hence had **-en** in the dat. and acc. Thus this **-en,** now used uniformly in the dat. and acc. of masc. and fem. proper names, had a twofold origin.

The str. declension has also been much reduced, and there is, as will be seen below, much fluctuation in present usage. There is a general tendency in all classes of proper nouns and often in titles to drop the **s** of the gen. whenever preceded by an article or other modifying word that marks distinctly the case. With names of persons this can now be considered a rule.

85. Those proper nouns that have the article always before them—i.e. the names of natural divisions of the earth's surface (as rivers, lakes, seas, mountains, plains, forests, &c.), the names of countries of the fem. or masc. gender, names of newspapers, works of art, months, days of the week, nations, peoples, parties, dynasties—were originally, and in part are still, common class nouns, and hence are in general declined, as common class nouns of the same form would be: **der Rhein** the Rhine, **des Rheins,** &c.; **der Brocken** (peak in the Harz Mts.), **des Brockens,** &c.; **die Alpen** the Alps, **der Alpen,** &c.; **die Schweiz** Switzerland, **der Schweiz,** &c.; **in den letzten Tagen des Augusts** (Raabe); **der Preuße** the Prussian, **des Preußen,** &c.; **der Karolinger** Carlovingian, **des Karolingers,** &c.

a. The names of months, newspapers, works of art, literary productions, organizations, boats, ships, now more generally drop the **s** of the gen.: **Am Abend des 22. August** (*Beilage zur Allgemeinen Zeitung*, 18. Sept. 1901), **zu Ende des Februar** (Stilgebauer's *Götz Krafft*, I, p. 41), but in poetic language where the genitive precedes its governing noun inflection is preserved as in **des Maies Erwachen; der Redakteur des Coriolan, des Bund,** &c. editor of the Coriolan, Bund, &c.; **der Dichter des Faust** the author of Faust; **der Gruß des „Schubertbund"** the greeting from the Schubertbund (musical organization), **auf der Kommandobrücke des „Sperber"** (Dominik's *Kamerun*, p. 43) upon the conning-bridge of the "Sperber" (name of boat) (*Hamburger Nachrichten*, Dec. 15, 1905), &c. The names of days of the week are inflected when used adverbially, but when used after prepositions or after a governing noun non-inflection after the article is common: **Die Zusammenkunft ist des Dienstags,** but **während des ganzen Montag** (Rundschau, 2. 5, 278, quoted by Sanders in his *Ergänzungswörterbuch*, p. 547 and censured by him as careless, but to-day this dropping of the genitive ending **s** is quite common and natural in accordance with usage in case of names of months), **die Ereignisse des Donnerstag** (*Hamburgischer Correspondent*, May 5, 1905), **in den Morgenstunden des Montag** (*Frankfurter Zeit.*, May 19, 1920). Also foreign names of rivers and mountains as a rule drop the **s** in the gen.: **die Höhen des Monte Cavo** the heights of Monte Cavo, **das Tal des** (or **der** in accordance with German usage) **untern Rhône, im Wassergebiet des Po und des Rheins** (K. Bohnenberger in *Zeitschrift für deutsche Philologie*, 1913, p. 372), &c. This usage, tho strongly condemned by grammarians, is spreading even to German geographical names: **für einen Anwohner des Stechlin** (lake) (Fontane's *Stechlin*, III), **auf dem Gipfel des Hohenstaufen** (Raabe's *Pechlin*, chap. xiv), **am Westhang des Schratzmännle** (*Großes Hauptquartier*, Oct. 13, 1915), **die Gewässer des Rhein** (Kutzen and Steinecke's *Das deutsche Land*, p. 30), **diese Gegend des Main** (ib., p. 223), **die fernen**

Höhen des Spessart (Stilgebauer's *Götz Krafft*, I, 1, p. 30) the distant heights of the Spessart (a well-wooded mountainous district of Bavaria), &c.. Examples can even be found in textbooks on geography. It is a natural impulse towards uniformity, as all other proper nouns drop **s** in the gen. when preceded by an article (see **86.** 1).

b. The names of the months often drop the article and remain uninflected after **Anfang, Mitte, Ende: Ende Mai** the last of May. See **94.** 3. A. *b*.

c. The great mass of foreign names of peoples and tribes have been conformed to German inflection, but those which still retain endings (**a, i, o, u, oi,** &c.) which resist inflection according to German models take an **s** in the gen. sing. and thruout the plural, or perhaps more commonly remain uninflected, especially in the plural, the article alone indicating the case and number: **der Eskimo, des Eskimo**(**s**), pl. **die Eskimo**(**s**), **die Herero** (*Hamburger Nachrichten*, Oct. 18, 1904) found nine times in this issue and **die Hereros** in this same issue three times. If **s** becomes established in the genitive singular and the uninflected form in the plural the inflection will be conformed to that of the **e**-less plural type except in the dative plural, where the uninflected form or the form in **-s** must be used.

86. 1. Names of persons and all political divisions, as countries, states, counties, cities, and the like, do not in general take an article except when modified by an adjective. The proper name takes an **s** (never **es**) in the gen. sing. when it is not preceded by an article or limiting adjective, but takes no ending when preceded by an article, limiting adjective, or the genitive of a noun with which it stands in apposition: **Wìlhelms Hút,** but **der Hút des klèinen Wi̋lhelm; Ànnas Hút,** or **der Hùt der Ánna; die Universitä̀ten Déutschlands,** but **die Verfássung des republikànischen De̋utschland; die Éinwohner der Hàuptstadt Berli̋n; das Kínd des Schùhmachers Schmi̋dt.** In all these cases the proper name forms with the governing noun a group with the chief stress upon the last member.

If the person has two or more names, the last one only takes the **s: die Regierung Friedrich Augusts; Marie von Ebner-Eschenbachs gesammelte Schriften,** &c.

a. If a masculine noun in the genitive modified by a preceding article, limiting adjective, or the genitive of a noun with which it stands in apposition, precede the noun upon which it depends, it usually takes an **s: des großen Karls Taten** (but **die Taten des großen Karl**), **des Adolf Burgers Haus, des verratenen Arthurs Vater** (Lienhard's *König Arthur*, 5), **des Pastor Friedrichs Sohn, des Onkel Heinrichs Stimme.** Also the modified name preceding the preposition **wegen** takes the genitive ending **s,** as **wegen** is in fact the dative plural of the noun **Weg: des Rudolfs wegen** (Ernst Heilborn's *Zwei Kanzeln*, II). The retention of the genitive ending in all these cases results from the feeling that the case sign ought to be indicated at the point where the genitive comes in contact with the governing noun. Hence the **s** of the name is dropped when it stands after the governing noun as the grammatical relation is indicated by its article which stands in immediate contact with the preceding governing noun. We still, however, sometimes find the **s** in the genitive also when it follows the noun: **Er (der Mond) guckte mild in die Kutsche des zehnten Karls** (Charles X of France) (Raabe's *Hungerpastor*, chap. vi). **Der Streithengst des großen Alexanders** (Karrillon's *O Domina mea*, p. 134). The **s** in the genitive in all these cases is the survival of an older usage which always required an **s** in the genitive of strong masculine names (see **89**). Now, however, not even the above mentioned remnant of this rule is observed closely: **des Stabtrompeter Raßmann Blasen** (Scheffel's *Trompeter*, 6. Stück), **des Heinzl Mutter** (Meinhardt), **des alten Sparr Augen** (Wildenbruch), **des alten Petersen Tochter** (Fontane), **des alten Pastors Reiche Amtsnachfolger** (Fedor Sommer's *Ernst Reiland*, p. 27). These examples indicate that the law of *immediate contact*, referred to above and also in **92.** 1. *a*, is not yet firmly established. It is opposed by the feeling that a name ought not to be inflected if it is preceded by an article.

In case of neuter names of countries, continents, and cities the genitive ending is much better preserved, occurring not infrequently even when it follows the governing noun: **aus einer größeren Stadt des mittleren Deutschlands** (Storm's *Eine Malerarbeit*, vol. ii. p. 65), **die drei berühmtesten Genies des jetzigen Europas** (Lienhard's *Münchhausen*, 1). **Hier** (in *L'Adultera*) **betritt er** (Fontane) **den Boden des modernen Berlins** (A. Bartels's *Deutsche Dichtung*, p. 214.). **Den Eindruck des vielhunderttürmigen Moskaus zu schildern** (*Hamburger Nachrichten*, April 2, 1905).

b. If a proper name is used as a common class noun it may, like class nouns, be inflected in the sing. and pl.: **die Reden unseres Ciceros** the speeches of our great orator (lit. our Cicero), **die Ciceros, die Cromwelle und Bismarcke der Zukunft.** But like a proper noun it is often uninflected after an article: **eine alte Auflage des Baedeker** (Rodenberg's *Klostermanns Grund-*

stück, III). A proper noun cannot only be used as a common noun with reference to one of a class of individuals, but also to one individual in different stages of development as different characteristics are here compared: **Wiewohl diese Szene erst in der Ausgabe von 1808 hinzugekommen ist, hat sich hier Goethe völlig in den Charakter des Fausts seiner frühen Jugend hineinzufühlen vermocht** (Johannes Volkelt's *Zwischen Dichtung und Philosophie*, p. 7).

c. There is sometimes a shade of meaning between inflection and non-inflection after a preceding noun: **die Blûteperiode der Ôstseestädte Stettín, Dânzig, Kőnigsberg** *the period of greatest prosperity for the Baltic cities Stettin, Danzig, Königsberg*, but **Es ist die Blûteperiode vornehmlich der Ôstseestädte: Stettíns, Dânzigs, Kőnigsbergs** (Lamprecht's *Deutsche Geschichte*, zweiter Ergänzungsband, p. 459) *It is the period of greatest prosperity, especially for the cities along the Baltic, particularly for Stettin, Danzig, Königsberg.* In the first example **Stettin, Danzig, Königsberg,** appositives to **Ostseestädte,** stand in such a close grammatical relation to the two preceding nouns that they form with them a group and, as the last member of the group, receive the chief stress. In the second example the three appositives stand in a looser grammatical relation to the preceding nouns and hence form an independent group with independent stress and it becomes necessary to indicate the grammatical relation to the preceding group. Similarly **der Tŏd der zwei bedeutenden Fòrscher Mínor und Erich Schmídt,** but **mit dem Tòde zweier bedeutender Fórscher, Mínors und Erich Schmídts** (Jos. Körner in *Literaturblatt für germanische und romanische Philologie*, XXXIX. *Jahrg.*, p. 18).

2. For names of persons and places not preceded by an article, the following variations of the general rule for the formation of the gen. occur:

a. Names of persons ending in a sibilant **s, ß, sch, x, z,** may remain unchanged in the gen. sing., adding, usually, however, the apostrophe: **Voß' Gedichte, von Ines' kleinen kräftigen Händen** (Storm), **nach Pentz' Weisung** (Fontane), **die Stimmen von Felix' Kameraden, eine Anzahl von Lenz' Versen** (Hermann Grimm), **Agnes' Hochzeit** (G. Hirschfeld), **das Bildnis aus dem dunkeln Winkel der Studierstube Adam Olearius'** (Jensen), **Isolde Kurz, die Tochter Hermann Kurz'** (Bartels's *Deutsche Dichtung*, p. 202), **Brockhaus' Konversations-Lexikon, Professor Delitzsch' Hypothesen** (*Hamburger Nachrichten*, Feb. 11, 1905). Sometimes we find **s** after those in **s** and quite often after those in **sch: Voß's Luise** (Karl Erbe's *Wörterbuch der deutschen Rechtschreibung*, p. xvi), **Busch's Erzählung** (Minor), **beim Anblick Grobitzsch's** (Hartleben), **bei der Beliebtheit Ludwig Pietsch's** (*Neue Zürcher Zeit.*, Jan. 4, 1904), **die Vorträge Professor Delitzsch's** (*Hamb. Nachr.*, Feb. 11, 1905), **Äußerungen Busch's über seine eigenen Werke** (*Frankfurter Zeit.*, Sept. 21, 1913). Instead of **s** we rarely find **es: Meljanzes Vater** (Martin's *Wolframs von Eschenbach Parzival*, II, p. xxv). Some use in case of all sibilants the mixed gen. ending **ens,** a form once common, but apparently much less used to-day, more frequent, however, with Christian names than surnames: **an Ludwig Pietschens Seite, Köselitzens** (surname) **spärliche Meldungen** (Franz Overbeck in *Die neue Rundschau*, March 1906, p. 329), **auf Hansens Bitten** (G. Hauptmann), **Franzens Idee** (G. Hirschfeld), **Götzens Blicke** (Stilgebauer's *Götz Krafft*), **Luciussens** (surname) **Musik** (Hermann Hesse's *Unterm Rad*, p. 127).

Grammarians are, in general, eager to find a way out of the tangle of present usage here. A number urge the form in **-ens,** but it does not find a wide support outside of a few short names like **Hans, Max,** &c. The most common form—the one with the mere apostrophe—is in reality no genitive at all, as it cannot be distinguished in the spoken language from the nominative. Grammatical justice demands here a clear genitive ending, and it is quite probable that most people who write **Voß'** in fact speak **Voßs,** i.e. pronounce an **ß** with double pressure, thus making a slight syllabic division in the middle, so that a real double **s** is spoken. Likewise in case of the genitive **-sch',** as in **die Auflehnung Popowitsch'** (Jellinek's *Geschichte der neuhochdeutschen Grammatik*, p. 263), it is quite probable that an **s** is in fact spoken after **sch.** Careful observers even write the **s** here as can be seen by the examples given above. It would be desirable if this common usage of speaking an **s** after a sibilant should find an expression in the written language. It was once the rule to write **s** or **es:** Artuses hof (Wolfram's *Parzival*, **296**, 25), Artuss her (ib. **326**, 5). At one time the **'s** was in large measure lost also in English, but it seems to be the prevailing form to-day. Some South German grammarians avoid the difficulty here by recommending the use of the definite article, thus elevating here a common S.G.

colloquialism to the dignity of literary form: **der Bruder des Klaus** instead of **der Bruder Klaus'.**

In the eighteenth century the genitive in **-(e)ns** was not restricted to names ending in a sibilant but was widely used, especially with names in **-e**: **Karlens, Achillens, Fichtens** (nom. **Fichte**); **Adelheidens,** &c. This usage is still found with feminines in **-e** (see *b* below), sometimes with names ending in a sibilant, sometimes with names in **-eke,** as in **Meinekes** or in colloquial language sometimes **Meinekens,** sometimes with **Vater** and **Mutter** (see **90**).

Note. In case of names which follow the governing noun the gen. **s** is sometimes avoided by using the article: **die Bücher des Felix.** In general, however, the article is avoided before an unmodified name, altho it is regularly used if modified: **die Bücher des kleinen Felix.** In case of surnames the use of the article becomes natural, when a title or some descriptive noun is inserted between the article and the name: **die Reden des Altertumsforschers Curtius.** Compare **59.** II. E. *a.*

b. Fem. in **-e** may add **-s** or **-ens: Maries** or **Mariens Hut.**

c. Foreign nouns ending in a sibilant often prefer the article, and thus remain uninflected, as **die Germania des Tacitus** the Germania of Tacitus; or they may perhaps more frequently be treated as a German word: **Tacitus' Germania** (title of a book by E. Schwyzer, published in 1912), **Tacitus' Historien** (Stilgebauer's *Götz Krafft,* I, p. 206.), **Thoas' letzte Worte** (Hermann Grimm's *Fragmente,* I, p. 98), **Sophokles' Antigone** (ib. II, p. 29), **der ästhetische Wert Dickens'** (Paul Hensel's *Thomas Carlyle,* p. 113); or in case of a few, having thrown off their foreign ending, may take the apostrophe or **-ens: Ho′räz' Oden** or **Ho′räzens Oden** the odes of Horace, instead of **die Oden des Ho′rätius; Ä′ne‵as'** or **Ä′ne‵ens,** gen. of **Ä′ne‵as,** &c.

d. Foreign names of persons do not now retain their original Latin or Greek declension except in a few biblical names: N. **Jesus Christus,** G. **Jesu Christi,** D. **Jesu Christo,** A. **Jesum Christum; das Evangelium Matthäi** the gospel of Matthew, &c. Even here the rule for German nouns is often preferred: **Christus' Geburt,** &c.

e. As it is not customary for names of places to insert **en** before **s** of the gen., such names of places as end in a sibilant form no gen., but express this relation by the prep. **von** *of*: **die Straßen von Paris,** but **die Straßen Hamburgs,** or **Hamburgs Straßen.** In poetry, however, the apostrophe may be used after sibilants: **an Kolchis' Küste** (Grillparzer's *Argonauten,* 2), **für Hellas' Heil und Glück** (ib.), **Hellas' Dichter** (Wildenbruch's *Die Lieder des Euripides,* p. 13). Sometimes also in plain prose: **der Schwerpunkt der Verteidigung 'Tripolis'** (*Neue Zürcher Zeit.,* Dec. 8, 1911), **nicht ein kaum bekannter Fürst, der von der Gnade Paris' oder Londons lebt** (*Frankfurter Zeit.,* Nov. 23, 1915).

87. Names of places and persons take no sign for the dat. and acc. in choice language, but earlier and still in the classical period the ending **-en** for dat. and acc. sing. was quite common in case of unmodified names of persons. This **-en** survived in the colloquial language and has again become quite common in recent literature which reflects colloquial speech: **Die wär' die Rechte, dachte er sich, wenn er Adelen nachblickte** (Wilhelm Fischer's *Die Freude am Licht,* p. 148). **Das tranken wir immer bei Bismarcken** (Sudermann's *Es lebe das Leben,* p. 60). **Als Frau Imme öffnete, stand Rudolf auf dem kleinen Flur und sagte, daß er Vatern holen solle und Hedwigen auch** (Fontane's *Stechlin,* chap. xiv). For the origin of the forms in **-en** see **84.**

88. In a number of instances words which are in an oblique case are not felt as such, and are inflected as if they were simple stems:

1. The many geographical names in **-en** are in fact datives: **(zur) Neuenkirchen, Sachsen,** from older ze (= **zu**) der niuwen kirchen, ze den Sachsen. They originated in prepositional phrases, later the preposition and article disappeared and the dative became the stem of the new form: **die Hauptstadt Sachsens.**

2. Thus an original gen. is often not felt as such and treated as a simple stem: **Wir werden uns nächsten Johanni** (St. John's day) **wieder sprechen** (Spielhagen's *Was will das werden?,* II. ii). **Bis künftige Johannis.** Here **Johanni,** or **Johannis,** is a masc. gen. treated as an acc., the gender being masc. after the analogy of the word **Tag** understood or fem. after the analogy of **Weihnachtszeit** Christmas-time, **Pfingstzeit** pentecost. Compare **255.** II. 1. B. *g.*

89. Formerly and still in the classical period the gen. which was preceded by an article usually took an **s**: **Die Leiden des Jungen Werthers** *The Sufferings of Young Werther* (title of one of Goethe's works).

90. Colloquially masculine and feminine common nouns (the latter of which according to the general rule are not inflected in the sing.) are often treated as proper nouns, the substantive dropping the article and taking an **s** in the gen. and sometimes **(e)n** (see **87**) in the dat. and acc., when it refers to a definite person: **Vater kommt. Wenn sie Kaisers Geburtstag feiern** (Fontane's *Effi*, chap. vii). **Du bist Vaters Tochter** (Hauptmann's *Michael Kramer*, Act 1). **Ja, deine Tochter und Vaters bin ich** (ib.). **Nachbars Hänschen, Schusters Dortchen, Pastors Gustav, Mamas (Mutters, Tantes) Zimmer. Ich werde das Muttern sagen. Als Frau Imme öffnete, stand Rudolf auf dem kleinen Flur und sagte, daß er Vatern holen solle und Hedwigen auch** (Fontane's *Stechlin*, chap. xiv). **Ich werde Großmutter bitten.** Likewise fem. titles: **Majestäts Befehl** his Majesty's order. Of course these words, like proper names, may take **-(e)ns** instead of **-s** in the genitive if they end in a sibilant or **-e**, sometimes also in case of **Vater** and **Mutter: Exzellenz'** or **Exzellenzens Befehl, Tantes** or **Tantens Kleid, Mutterns Geburtstag** (Viktor von Kohlenegg's *Eckerlein* in *Velhagen und Klasings Monatshefte*, Dec. 1919, p. 373).

A title with a preceding article is sometimes treated as a name, if it is used as such: **des Dekan** (Marriot's *Der geistliche Tod*, chap. ii), **mit den Sachen des Doktor** (Hauptmann's *Friedensfest*, p. 15), but more commonly with inflectional **s: die Stimme des Doktors** (ib., p. 48), **des Doktors Hand** (ib., p. 52).

91. The residence of an individual is often written in one word with his name: **Herr Lammers-Bremen** Mr. Lammers from Bremen; **Direktor Wirth-Plötzensee bei Berlin** Director Wirth from Plötzensee near Berlin. Formerly **von** was placed before the name of the place. The **von** is not now used, as it might be construed as representing a title of nobility. Compare **94. 3. A.** *c* and **92. 5.**

Inflection of Titles.

92. A full treatment of the proper titles which must be given to people of different social standing can be obtained in any of the numerous **Briefsteller** which usually treat this delicate subject.

The leading points as to the inflection of these titles are as follows:

1. When a title (or titles) not preceded by an article stands before a name of a person, the title and name are now usually felt as a unit, i.e. as a compound name, and hence the second element, i.e. the name is alone inflected, except the one title **Herr** *Mr.*, which is always inflected: **Kàiser Wílhelms Schlốß, Professor Dr. A. Kuhns Vorlesungen, Reichskanzler Fürst Bismarcks Verdienste, Das Lében Hèrzog Bếrnhards. Er sprach von Präsidènt Gránt, von Grâf Réchberg.** But **Herrn Schmidts Hut, der Hut Herrn Schmidts, der Hut des Herrn Schmidt, der Sohn des Kaufmanns Herrn Schmidt.** Earlier in the period **Herr** could also be treated like other titles and was left uninflected when not preceded by an article: **Mache Er Herr Justen** (see **87**) **den Kopf nicht warm** (Lessing's *Minna*, 1, 2).

a. Exceptions occur not infrequently when a genitive follows its governing noun. Here the title often assumes the inflection, as the feeling prevails that the inflection of the dependent element should take place at the point of immediate contact with its governing word: **die Medaillen Papsts Clemens des Siebenten** (Goethe), **bis zum Monumente Königs Max II.** (Hans Hopfen), **die Schwester Königs Artus** (E. Martin's *Wolframs von Eschenbach Parzival*, II, p. 445), **einige Jahre im Hause Meisters Lorenz** (Wilhelm Fischer's *Die Freude am Licht*, p. 181), **neben der Grabstätte der Gattin Herzogs Konrad des Roten** (Steinhausen's *Geschichte der deutschen Kultur*, p. 111), **die Festrede Bürgermeisters Dr. Pauli** (*Hamburger Nachrichten*, March 23, 1905), **vom Tode Königs Christian tief erschüttert** (ib. Jan. 30, 1906), **nach Ansprachen Majors a. D. [außer Dienst] Badhauser, des katholischen und protestantischen Anstaltsgeistlichen** (*Allgemeine Zeit.*, April 12, 1905). The inflected title is often preceded by an inflected form of **Herr: vom Munde Herrn Majors Bennecke** (Wildenbruch's *Schwester-Seele*, chap. x).

b. The inflection of **Herr** in all positions is the survival of older usage, where weak titles did not, like strong ones, enter into close relations with a following name to form a unit: frouen Jeschuten muot (*Parzival*, 262. 25), mines hern Gawanes munt (id., 300. 21), der junge sun froun Uoten (*Nibelungenlied*, Aventiure 33), under den vanen hern Saules (quoted from Blatz, I, p. 349), but künec Artuses hof (Walther von der Vogelweide, p. 99, Paul's ed.). The idea of unity could arise more easily with strong nouns because they usually had no ending in the nominative and accusative and often in the dative, which facilitated the blending of title and name.

2. *a.* When the title standing before the name is preceded by an article or other modifying word, inflection or non-inflection results according to the meaning:

(1) If the title retains a degree of independence not entering into such close relations with the name as to form a unit with it, it is inflected: **der Sốhn des Pàstors Rếiche** or **des Pàstors Réiche Sốhn.** In the latter case the name is sometimes inflected as the feeling sometimes prevails that inflection ought to take place in the dependent word when it stands in direct contact with the governing word: **meines Freundes Papphoffs Regenschirm** (Raabe's *Frühling*, chap. IV). Inflection of the name here is rare when the governing word precedes: **auf der staubigen Chaussee des Vetters Wassertreters** (id. *Abu Telfan*, XXXVI).

(**2**) If title and name form a unit, both words remain uninflected when the governing noun precedes: **die Stímme des Ònkel Hĕinrich** or more commonly without the article: **die Stímme Ònkel Hĕinrichs.** Sometimes as in older usage with the inflection of the name: **der Klang der Hausglocke des Doktor Dachreiters** (Raabe's *Pechlin*, chap. XIX). If a common noun is used here instead of the name, inflection is quite common: **Die Meinung des Bruder Stadtrats** *his brother the alderman* (Raabe's *Abu Telfan*, p. 32), **im traulichen Forsthause Karls sowohl wie in dem Heim des Bruder Juristen** (*his brother the lawyer*) **am Rhein** (Hans Brand in *Westermanns Monatshefte*, May 1905, p. 245).

When the governing noun follows, the feeling usually prevails that inflection should take place at the point of immediate contact with the governing noun: **des Ònkel Héinrichs Stímme** or more commonly without the article: **Ònkel Héinrichs Stímme.** This is the common usage of the M.H.G. period: des künec Gahmuretes kint (*Parzival*, 301, 5). Inflection of also the title here is quite rare in case of strong nouns: in des küneges Ezeln lant (*Nibelungenlied*, Aventiure 24). To-day both title and name sometimes remain uninflected as they are together felt as a name, which in the position before the governing noun is not only inflected but sometimes remains uninflected: **des Stabtrompeter Raßmann Blasen** (Scheffel's *Trompeter*, 6. Stück).

(**3**) Weak titles are in general treated as strong ones, but they manifest a reluctance, as in older usage (see 1. *b*), to enter into close unity with the following name, especially after the article. Thus we often find such expressions as **die Truppen des Generaloberst von Woyrsch** (*Großes Hauptquartier*, July 2, 1915), **dem Generaloberst von Hindenburg** (*Der Völkerkrieg*, IV, p. 154), but inflection in choice language is more common: **die Offensive der Armee des Generalobersten von Woyrsch** (*Großes Hauptquartier*, July 18, 1915, also July 19, &c.); **der Sohn des Grafen Rechberg, des Grafen Rechbergs Sohn,** or **des Grafen Rechberg Sohn.** Close union, however, is more common in case of things: **an Bord des „Prinz Waldemar“** (boat). Likewise in case of persons when the article drops out: **Graf Rechbergs Sohn.**

Note. In the rare case where a title in the gen. is preceded by a dependent gen. which is modified by an article or pronominal adjective, the governing title must of course drop its article. In this case usage does not commonly require a gen. ending on the governing gen., as the force of the article or pronominal adjective before the preceding dependent gen. is felt, but more conscientious writers use the gen. ending here: **an Bord Seiner Majestät Schiff** (instead of **Schiffs**) **Möwe, der liebenswürdige Kommandant S.**[einer] **M.**[ajestät] **Kreuzers Falke** (*Kölnische Zeitung*). Others prefer here to replace the governing gen. by a dat. after **von: an Bord von Seiner Majestät Schiff Möwe.**

b. If several titles preceded by an article stand before a name, often only the first title is inflected, or in case **Herr** is used both **Herr** and the following title are inflected, but there is here much fluctuation in usage, the tendency, however, being towards inflection, especially in case of weak nouns: **die Vorlesungen des Professors Hofrat Schmidt; des Herrn Staatsministers von Stein; die Mitteilung unseres verehrten Herrn Direktors Doktor Rosenberg** (Hirschfeld); **des Herrn Professor Niedermöller** (M. Dreyer); **die Armee des Generals Graf Bothmer** (*Großes Hauptquartier*, Oct. 10, 1915). The second and third title are usually felt as standing in apposition with the first. Where non-inflection is employed as in the preceding examples this grammatical relation does not find a formal expression, hence it is becoming more common to indicate this grammatical relation by appending an inflectional ending to the second title as the one that stands in immediate contact with the governing word: **das großherzige Entgegenkommen des Geheimen Medizinalrats Professors Dr. Külz** (*Weser-Zeitung*); **des Feldmarschalls Prinzen Eugen** or **des Feldmarschalls Prinz Eugen** (both forms given in Nagl's *Deutsche Sprachlehre*, p. 167); **die Truppen des Generals Grafen Bothmer** (*Großes Hauptquartier*, Sept. 1, 1915); **im Beisein des Oberbefehlshabers, Feldmarschalls Erzherzog Friedrich** (ib., May 3, 1915).

Often the last title and name are considered as a compound noun and hence the inflectional ending is added only to the second element: **der Empfang Seiner Majestät Kaiser Wilhelms** (*Hamburger Nachrichten*, Nov. 9, 1904); **aus der Kunstkammer des fürstlichen Mä'zens Herzog Albrechts V. von Bayern** (Dr. Ph. M. Halm in *Beilage zur Allgemeinen Zeit.*, June 6, 1905); **die Feier des ersten**

Geburtstages unseres jüngsten Hohenzollern, Prinz Wilhelms (*Daheim*, 1907, Nr. 41). Compare this last example with the first one from Nagl's *Deutsche Sprachlehre* given above.

If a second or later title is preceded by the article it must of course be inflected: **die Freude Seiner Majestät des Kaisers.**

3. An appended title is in case of persons inflected whether the preceding name is declined or not: **die lange Regierung Friedrichs** or **König Friedrichs des Großen,** or **die lange Regierung des Königs Friedrich des Großen; Heinrichs des Finklers Name; Max' I.** (read **des Ersten**) **Gemahlin;** but non-inflection in case of names of ships: **zu Ehren der Offiziere des deutschen Linienschiffes „Kaiser Karl der Große"** (*Hamburger Nachrichten*, July 27, 1905), **die Entsendung des Kaiser Karl der Große** (*Neue Zürcher Zeit.*, July 28, 1905). Some prefer to drop **s** in the first example, as the inflection of the appended title clearly marks the case relation: **der Bruder Friedrich des Großen** (Fontane's *Vor dem Sturm*, II. 14), **bald nach dem Regierungsantritt Friedrich Wilhelm I.** (*Hamb. Nachr.*, Oct. 29, 1904). This usage, however, seems in general to be yielding to the tendency to mark grammatical relations clearly in both elements. The title alone may be inflected in case of **junior, senior: auf dem Bette Butzemann juniors** (Raabe's *Deutscher Adel*, chap. xx), **Raabe juniors Stimme** (Halbe's *Mutter Erde*, p. 157). We also often hear: **die Stimme Raabes junior.** If the name is preceded by an article the title here remains uninflected: **das Hochzeitsgeschenk des Herrn Eckhart senior** (Baumbach's *Der Schwiegersohn*, chap. xi).

4. Such words as **Freund, Vater,** &c., are often treated as titles: **Das ist Freund Müllers Frau.**

5. The word following **von** in names originally marked the residence or locality. As the use of **von** became in the seventeenth century the prerogative of nobility the word after **von** became fixed and gradually lost its force so that it is now felt as a part of the name, and hence the **s** is appended to it: **Otto von Bismarcks Reden.** Some inflect the name here according to the principle described in 1. *a* and 2. *b* above. The genitive **-s** is appended to that part of the name that stands in direct contact with the governing noun. Thus if the name precedes the governing noun, the ending is appended to the end of the name, as in the example just given. If the name follows the governing noun the ending is added to that part of the name that stands before the **von,** as it is in immediate contact with the governing noun: **die Reden Ottos von Bismarck, das Leben Götzens von Berlichingen** (Goethe), **die Braut Friedrichs von Glimmern** (Raabe's *A. T.*, chap. xii), **ein Jugendporträt Wilhelms von Oranien** (*Kölnische Zeitung*, No. 1, 1895), **Leben und Bildnis Friedrichs von Hagedorn** (title of a book by Hubert Stierling, published in 1911). Present usage, however, seems to prefer here inflection at the end of the entire name as it is felt as a unit, a compound, and like a compound takes inflection at the end: **der jüngere Bruder Friedrich von Hagedorns** (Daniel Sanders's *Deutsche Literaturgeschichte*, p. 81), **im Zeitalter Otto von Bismarcks** (Fontane's *Cécile*, XIII), **zwei Briefe Wilhelm von Humboldts** (*Beilage zur Allgemeinen Zeitung*, 1901, No. 84). **Das ist eine Beleidigung des Andenkens unseres Väterchens und Professor von Rangenhofens** (G. Ompteda). Thus in accordance with this conception the name always has inflection at the end, whether it precedes or follows the governing noun. The other type with the inflection of the word before the **von** is now rarely generalized so that it is also employed when the name precedes the governing noun: **Alberts von Köstnitz Vater** (Wilhelm Fischer's *Die Freude am Licht*, II, p. 52). Of course, this type is not infrequent in learned literature dealing with older periods where historic names occur in which the word after the **von** is a real dative, a name of an actual place: **Wolframs von Eschenbach Parzival und Titurel** (name of a book by Ernst Martin, Halle 1903). This type is still in full force where the word after **von** is the name of an actual place or country: **Friedrich Wilhelms III.** (read **des Dritten**) **von Preußen lange Regierung.**

In our own time it is again common to distinguish individuals by mentioning the place where they live, which is now placed after the name as an appositive to it: **Schmidt-Berlin.** A little earlier in the period **von** was placed before the name of the place as in older German: **Hoffmann von Fallersleben,** &c. This usage has been abandoned as the **von** here easily creates the false impression that it indicates a title of nobility.

6. The title **Frau** is placed before the name and rank of the husband, and **Frau** or **Fräulein** before a designation of relationship, and usually alone has inflection, if the article or a pronominal precedes: **(die) Frau Schmidt,** gen. **der Frau Schmidt,** &c., but **Frau Schmidts Sohn; (die) Frau Professor, (die) Frau Doktor, (die) Frau Oberst,** &c.; **Ihre Frau Mutter, Ihre Frau Tante, Ihr (Ihre) Fräulein Tante,** &c. Earlier in the period **-in** was often added to the title and still occasionally occurs: **die Frau Professorin** (Goethe). In a number of cases the old ending **-in** is still usually employed: **(die) Frau Rätin** or **Rat, (die) Frau Geheime Rätin, (die) Frau Senatorin, die Gräfin** or **die Frau Gräfin, die Herzogin** or **die Frau Herzogin, die Königin** or **die Frau Königin, die Kaiserin Friedrich** the wife of Emperor Frederick, &c.; **Ihre Frau Gemahlin, Ihre Frau Schwägerin, Ihr (Ihre) Fräulein Schwägerin,** &c. If the title is preceded by an adjective, or is itself an adjective, the adjective must be inflected: **Frau Geheime Rätin, Frau Abgeordnete Zeitz** (name).

Instead of **Frau** or **Fräulein** the fem. article is often placed before the name, which in popular language often adds **in** (usually corrupted to **en**) and in N.G. dialect also **sche** (see **245. I. 6. 1.** *c.*): **die Marlitt** Miss Marlitt (the pseudonym of a well-known authoress), **die Schulzen** (corruption of **Schulzin**) Mrs. Schulz, **die Beckerin** or **Beckersche** Mrs. Becker, **die Frau Pastorsche** (Raabe's *Odfeld,* chap. xxii). Formerly **in** was added to the name also in the literary language: **die Gottschedin** (authoress, 1713-62), **die Karschin** (poetess, 1722-91).

In case of males **Herr** is placed before the designation of relationship or rank, and is always inflected: **Ihr Herr Vater, Ihres Herrn Vaters; Ihr Herr Bruder,** &c.; **Ihr Herr Gemahl,** &c.; **Ihr Herr Chef** your employer; **der Herr Oberst,** &c., **Herr Oberst** (direct address); **der Herr Professor,** &c., **Herr Professor** (direct address).

Plural of Names of Persons and Places.

93. There is considerable diversity of usage in the formation of the plural of names of persons and places:

1. The favorite formation in familiar language is either to add **s ('s,** or **ens** after sibilants) to the name or title used as a name, or less frequently to leave the name undeclined in all the cases: **Müllers haben Besuch** The Müllers have company. **Kurz darauf traten Lehweß's ein** (Ernst Heilborn's *Kleefeld,* X). **Wir gehen zu Schulzens, zu Doktors** We are going to Schulze's, to the family of the doctor. **Zwei Wolfs, zwei Maries** (or very commonly **Marien** according to *b.* (**2**) below), two persons by the name of Wolf, Mary; **die beiden Elisabeths** or **Elisabeth** (or often **Elisabethen** and sometimes **Elisabethe** according to *b.* (**2**)), but usually **die beiden Agnes, Ines** with non-inflection, to avoid the repetition of the sibilant, non-inflection being also more common here than the form in **-en** according to *b.* (**2**); **die vielen Ludwig in der französischen Geschichte, im Familienhause der Weyland** (Raabe's *Wunnigel,* chap. i), **die beiden Sarasin** (*Neue Zürcher Zeit.*, Oct. 26, 1906) the two Sarasins (well-known scientists and travelers).

Geographical names especially remain uninflected in the plural: **die beiden Frankfurt** the two cities of Frankfurt, **die beiden Mecklenburg** (or **Mecklenburgs**) the two Mecklenburgs.

If the title used as a name is weak, the plural is formed by adding **ens: Präsidentens treten heute eine kleine Reise ins Gebirge an** The family of the president starts out on a little trip into the mountains to-day. **Exzellenzens machen umgehend ihren Gegenbesuch** (Hans Arnold's *Nicht Lügen*). **Bei Kronprinzens** (*Frankfurter Zeit.*, May 1, 1914). The regular plural in **s** is also used: **Ich kann doch in diesem Aufzug nicht zu Oberpräsidents gehen** (Arnold's

Nicht Lügen). Titles in the mixed declension add **s** in the plural: **Pro'fessors lassen bitten** (*ib.*). **Zu 'Pastors** (*ib.*). The accent in the last two nouns indicates that these forms are in fact genitives. See *a*. Compare **59.** II. E. *f*.

a. In such examples as **Wir gehen zu Schulzes** the **es** is now felt as a plural ending, altho the noun originally was a gen. sing. dependent upon a governing noun understood such as **Angehörige.** In S.G. popular language the gen. of the sing. article in the reduced form of **'s** is here still placed before the name, even tho the verb plainly shows that the noun is felt as a plural: **'s Hartmanns begleiteten uns.** In other cases, however, as in **die beiden Bertas** the **s** is a real plural ending.

b. Many prefer to inflect names of persons according to the regular declension for common nouns, as follows: **(1)** Most of the masculines end in the plural in **e**: **die Wolfe, Friedriche,** der **letzte der Weylande** (Raabe's *Wunnigel*, chap. ii) *the last of the Weylands*, &c. Earlier in the period the plural of **Hans** John was weak, but it is now usually **Hanse,** or when used as a common class noun **Hänse** (see **70.** 1. *c* (**2**)). Sometimes the plural of the proper name is **Hänse**: **In „Westermühlen" waren wir beiläufig mitunter sechs oder sieben Hänse beisammen und es gehörte Übung dazu, um nicht in Konfusion zu geraten** (Storm an Mörike, Nov. 1854). **(2)** Most feminines take the weak plural ending **en** except those in **a** and **y**, which take **s** quite uniformly: **die Marien, Mathilden, Adelheiden,** but **die Bertas, Nannys,** &c. Those ending in a consonant have sometimes a strong plural according to the unmutated **e**-plural class: **die Elisabethe** instead of the more common wk. form **Elisabethen.** Diminutives in **-chen** and **-el** form the plural according to the **e**-less plural class: **die Hannchen, Marthel.** **(3)** Those masculines ending in **-e, -el, -en, -er,** also all diminutives in **-chen** and **-el,** take no ending in the plural: **die Luther, Schlegel, Karlchen** &c. **(4)** Foreign nouns may remain uninflected, but may also add **-s** or **-e,** and some in **-o** may add **-nen** or **-ne**: **die Noah, Alba,** &c.; **die Cagliostros** (ka·'liɔstRo:s), &c.; **die Vir'gile,** &c.; for those in **-as, -es, -us,** see **79.** 2. *d*; **die Scipi'onen, weltberühmte Cice'rone** (*Paulsen's Geschichte des gelehrten Unterrichts*, 2nd ed. p. 51), &c. **(5)** As a rule names of persons are not inflected according to the mutated **e**-plural and **er**-plural classes of the strong declension, as there is at least in the literary language an aversion to mutation here, but in colloquial speech mutated plurals can also be found after the analogy of common nouns: **die Wölfe in der Schule, die Quäste** (pl. of **Quast**) (Fontane's *Wanderungen*, vol. I, chap. **Garz**). These mutated plurals are not infrequently used in a sarcastic or humorous sense: **Es wird gewünscht, daß sämtliche Kortmänner** (pl. of **Kortmann**) **in Zukunft ihre unverschämten Zudringlichkeiten gefälligst unterlassen** (Stader). **Sie ist eine Grünebaum, und die Grünebäume können im Notfall die Zähne zusammenbeißen** (Raabe's *Hungerpastor*, chap. i). **(6)** Only the names of nationalities and a few famous families are inflected weak. See **76.** I. 3 (toward end). Raabe in his *Eulenpfingsten*, chap. ix, has formed the plural of the family name **Nebelung** weak, perhaps facetiously after the analogy of the mythical dynasty **die Nibelungen** (see **76.** I. 3, toward end). Fontane in his *Vor dem Sturm* forms the plural of the family name **Vitzewitz** according to the **e**-plural class, but in one place (I.1) we find a weak plural where it is represented as a part of an inscription upon a house of the year 1634: **Das ist der Vitzewitzen Haus.** Some N.G. authors employ the weak plural quite commonly: **Leonie des Beaux! Wie klingt dir das von einer Schneidertochter hier im Lande der Fritzen und Karlinen?** (Raabe's *Die Akten des Vogelsangs*, p. 71). **Und wenn wir hier noch drei Dierksen hätten** (Otto Ernst's *Flachsmann als Erzieher*, 3, 1). **Das war die Sippschaft der Uhlen** (Frenssen's *Jörn Uhl*, chap. i, and often elsewhere). **Die Ursleuen der alten Zeit waren vielleicht religiöse Schwärmer** (R. Huch's *Ludolf Ursleu*, chap. ii).

c. The names of countries and places usually form their plural with **s** or remain uninflected. The plural of **die Schweiz,** however, takes **e**: **Die Schweize werden immer kleiner** (Fontane's *Wanderungen*, vol. I, chap. *Die Ruppiner Schweiz*).

2. Some make a shade of difference in meaning between the uninflected plural form and the plural in **s**. In the sense of *men like*, all proper names remain uninflected in the plural, while they end in **s** to designate all or several members of a family: **die Scherer, die Grimm** men like Scherer, Grimm, but **Brauns sind nicht reich** The Browns (a definite family) are not rich. Here again we find a difference of usage. In the former meaning we now more commonly find proper names inflected according to the regular declension for common nouns, as described in 1. *b* above: **die Goethe** the men like Goethe, **die Luther, die Bismarcke, die Sokratesse, die Scipionen, die Shakespeares,** &c. Sometimes, however, we find uniformly **-s** here even with German names: **kleine Lindaus und Blumenthals** (A. Bartels) little Lindaus and Blumenthals.

Some add **s** to indicate different members of the same family and inflect the name according to the regular declensions, to distinguish different families of the same name: **die Schmidts** the different members of a definite family by the name of Schmidt. **Es gibt viele Schmidte** (or **Schmidt**) There are many families of the name of Schmidt.

3. Two or more names are often found in the singular after one plural article, which indicates the case of each of the proper names and by its plural form

shows that all are included in the statement: **Goethe war menschlich und dichterisch den Fielding und Smollet überlegen. Eichhorn war aus der Zeit der Befreiungskriege her bekannt als ein Freund der Arndt, Schleiermacher, Perthes, Reimer. Die Lindau und Genossen** Lindau and his literary following; **die Schmidt, Vater und Sohn; die beiden Stechlins, Vater und Sohn** (Fontane's *Stechlin*, chap. ii); and also without the article: **Stradnitz Vater und Sohn** (Marriot's *Seine Gottheit*, chap. vii), **von Arnstein Söhnen, Wien** (H. von Hofmannsthal's *Der Abenteurer*, p. 161).

Sometimes we find not only a plural article but also a plural adjective, both of which show by their plural form that they apply to all the proper names: **Bei Steinau zwang er die völlig überraschten Thurn und Bubna zu schimpflicher Kapitulation.**

The article in each of the above cases has collective force, and hence when the names are to be taken separately the article must be dropped: **Nachkommen von Geschlechtern, deren Namen mit den Tagen Karl Augusts, Amalias, Goethes für immer verknüpft sind, wollten die neuerfrischte Goethearbeit fördern.**

Instead of the definite article before a number of names we often find the indefinite with the force of *such men* (*women*) *as*: **Zu den Dorfgeschichtenerzählern stellen wir schließlich auch noch einen Dichter, der mit seinen Natur- und Landschaftsschilderungen einen gewissen Gegensatz zu den Kultur- und Sittengemälden eines Auerbach, Rank und Rosegger bildet, Adalbert Stifter** (L. Salomon). **Auf der anderen Seite wollen wir aber auch nicht vergessen, daß in dem Land eines Albert Bitzius, eines Gottfried Keller und eines Konrad Ferdinand Meyer der deutsche Geist mit seine herrlichsten Blüten getrieben hat** (*Hamb. Correspondent*, July 5, 1902). Compare **59. I. A.** *d*.

4. If a title or other noun stands before an appositive name, the plural form depends upon the relation of the title to the name. If title and name are usually found together and are thus felt as *one* name, the combination is accordingly treated as a single name, and hence the plural ending is added to the last word of the combination: **die Fräulein Schmidts** *the Miss Schmidts*; **ihr Vogel Strauße** (Wildenbruch's *Unter der Geißel*, Werke, IV, p. 7). Usage here, however, fluctuates as in **263. I. 1.** *a* and also in English, and hence we also find **die Fräulein Schmidt** *the Misses Schmidt*, especially where no ambiguity can arise, as in case of a modifying word or a plural verb: **die beiden Fräulein Schmidt. Die Fräulein Schmidt sind krank.** But even where there is no ambiguity we also find the pl. in **s**: **die beiden Fräulein Felgentreus** (Fontane's *Frau J. T.*, iv). In **die Frau Mutter** the second word usually takes the pl. form: **von den Frau Müttern** (Raabe's *Deutscher Adel*, chap. iii). In case of **Herr,** however, both words are inflected: **meine lieben, verehrten Herrn Leutnants** (Hartleben's *Rosenmontag*, 2. 3). Also in case of **Frau: mit den Frauen Müttern** (Raabe's *Gutmanns Reisen*, chap. iv).

If the title or other noun does not necessarily form a part of the appositive name, but is felt as containing a definite important modification of it, it is inflected, while the name itself remains uninflected: **die Forschungen der beiden Vettern Sarasin, die Gebrüder Grimm, bei den Schwestern Fröhlich** (Marie v. Najmájer in *Jahrbuch der Grillparzer-Gesellschaft*, XIV, p. 141). Both words are often inflected: **Meine Vettern Rambergs** (Hartleben's *Rosenmontag*, 3. 5). **Grafen Basedows habe es im Lande gegeben, solange Menschen zurückdenken könnten** (Spielhagen's *Herrin*, p. 209).

Peculiarities in the Inflection of Nouns.

94. 1. Many nouns, especially those that have no article or other modifying word before them, often remain uninflected. Non-inflection usually results because the person or thing is conceived abstractly without concrete relations, or the noun stands for a definite individual, as in the cases in *d*, and hence, as proper names in general, resists inflection after the definite article. **Inflection,**

however, also often occurs in most of these categories, as the person or thing is conceived with concrete relations, especially in the plural, which is always concrete, or the writer becomes conscious of the case relation and in a mere mechanical way employs inflection. The following categories are common:

a. Unmodified nouns connected by **und**: **die Grenze zwischen Affe und Mensch, das Verhältnis von Herr und Sklave, ein Mann von Herz und Mut. Nun setze dich dahin zwischen Herr und Frau Dörr** (Fontane). Sometimes also with inflection: **Dort verabschiedete er sich sofort von Herrn und Frau Lehmann** (Hirschfeld's *Das grüne Band*, viii). **Die Kluft zwischen Fürsten** (here Kaiser Wilhelm II.) **und Volk** (*Hamburger Nachrichten*, Sept. 3, 1910).

Non-inflection is also common in case of unmodified nouns connected by **weder – noch**: **Du meinst, du brauchst weder Gott noch Mensch** (Frenssen's *Hilligenlei*, p. 530). In both of the two cases here discussed, however, a plural assumes its proper ending: **zwischen Herr und Gesinde, zwischen Hausvater und Familienmitgliedern** (Lamprecht's *Deutsche Geschichte*, zweiter Ergänzungsband, p. 360).

b. In a list of unmodified words: **die Stufen von Lehrling, Gesell und Meister** the different stages of apprentice, journeyman, and master. Inflection is also found here: **diese Mischung von Pedanten, Halbkünstler und Gesellschaftsmenschen** (Carl Busse in *Velhagen und Klasings Monatshefte*, July 1914, p. 470.) Adjective-substantives must always be inflected: **die Errettung von Schiff, Mannschaft und Reisenden.**

c. As an unmodified objective predicate (**262.** III. 2. A): **Der Wirt nannte mich Graf und dann Exzellenz** (Immermann). Sometimes inflection occurs here: **Es war ungefähr so, wie wenn Sie auf der Durchreise nach einem andern Stern wären oder von einem andern kämen. Kurz was man so Idealisten nennt** (Wilbrandt's *Franz*, III). For fluctuation of usage after reflexive verbs see **218.** 2. *b*. Except in case of reflexive constructions an objective predicate after **als** is usually inflected, as it is usually necessary to show the case: **Er besang den Kaiser als Helden** (not **Held** as the form could be construed as a nom. agreeing with the subject.). Where the thought is perfectly clear the uninflected form may be used: **Besonders die Zentrumspresse gibt sich geflissentlich Mühe, es als Wille des Kaisers hinzustellen, daß usw.** (*Neue Zürcher Zeit.*, Sept. 4, 1910). The abstract meaning of **Wille** here suggested non-inflection, but where the meaning is more concrete inflection is common even where non-inflection would not impair the thought: **Eine blonde junge Dame hat ihr Söhnchen als Husaren gekleidet** (Eugen Zabel's *Europäische Fahrten*, p. 4).

d. As an unmodified appositive: **das Gebell des knurrischen Hofhunds Gewissen** (Goethe's *Götz*, 2, 1). **Dem Ausgestoß'nen seine Tochter geben, heißt s e l b s t sich um den Namen Jude bringen** (Gutzkow's *Uriel Acosta*, 3, 4). **Und doch war er** (the artist Menzel) **ja Verkörperung des preußischen Begriffs Soldat** (K. Storck in *Der Türmer*, March 1905). The noun which the appositive explains may in German be suppressed: **Was verstehen Sie unter Engel? Aber kommen Sie mir nicht mit [dem Wort] Flügel** (Fontane's *Frau Jenny*, chap. ix). The appositive in all these cases is seemingly a common class noun, but it has the force of a proper noun, as explained in **255.** III. 1. B. A proper noun is still more common here: **der Sohn des Pastors Schmidt.**

e. Modified or unmodified nouns that have become so closely associated with a verb as to form one idea with it, especially in the predicate relation: **Wir sind nicht mehr Herr über das, was entsprungen ist, aber wir sind Herr, es unschädlich zu machen** (Goethe's *Wahlverw.* 2, 12). **Unter Umständen können wir alle Modell sein** (Hauptmann's *Michael Kramer*, Act 2, p. 58). **Aber wir wurden Zeuge eines zweiten Vorfalls** (Ompteda's *Der Doppelgänger*). **Nach einigen Wochen schon waren sie gut Freund mit mir** (Marriot's *Seine Gottheit*, chap. ii). Sometimes also in the accusative relation. For an example see **257.** 2. A, last two sentences.

f. In case of an unmodified noun that stands before a preposition and is repeated again after it: **Sie ruhten Herz an Herz.** Also in case of a single unmodified noun following a preposition, where the meaning is abstract: **Was für 'ne Sorte von Graf ist das?** (Sudermann's *Die Ehre*, 2, 6). **Er war zwar wunderlich, ein Stück von Eremit** (Timm Kröger's *Ein geistlich Armer*).

g. Neut. and masc. nouns used in a collective sense after expressions of weight, measure, extent, or quantity. See **96**. 4. (**1**).

2. An unmodified noun in the singular following **von** in a phrase which stands as an appositive to a preceding noun usually remains uninflected in the singular: **ein armer Teufel von Philologe** (Schücking), **ein Juwel von Herzensmensch** (F. Lienhard), **eine Seele von Mensch** (Gustav Krüger), **als Sohn eines Prachtmenschen von Vater** (*Frankfurter Zeit*., May 31, 1914). **Schaudern würde ich vor dem Ungeheuer von Mensch, das solches vermöchte** (Engel's *Ein Tagebuch*, I. p. 11). Sometimes inflection in the oblique cases: **Er schalt „den Lümmel von Jungen", der von „Tuten und Blasen nichts wüßte"** (Frenssen's *Jörn Uhl*, chap. xviii). **Lieber wollte er untergehen, lieber seine Kinder vor seinen Augen sterben sehen, als seine oder ihre Rettung einem elenden Kerl von Bauern danken zu müssen** (Ebner-Eschenbach's *Jokob Szela*, p. 104). In the plural the dative form is required: **Und meine Hunde von Reitern!** (Goethe's *Götz*, 3, 13); **wir beiden dummen Jungen von Medizinern** (Hartleben's *Das Kalbscôtelette*). If an article precedes, the dative is also required in the sing.: **ein Schurke von einem Soldaten** (Lessing's *Minna*, **3. 11**). See also **104**. 1. A. *a* and B. *c*.

3. A. When a noun modifies a noun or pronoun denoting weight, measure, extent, quantity, or kind, and forms together with it the idea of one complete whole, it stands in the gen. only in choice language, while in the ordinary language of every day it more commonly stands in apposition with the preceding noun of weight, measure, extent, or quantity, except when that preceding noun is in the gen. sing., in which case it more commonly takes the form of the nominative: **ein Pfund Fleisch** (instead of **Fleisches,** which is now obsolete), **ein Glas guter Wein** (or in choice language **guten Weins,** as the genitive is here preserved when it is modified), **der Preis des Pfundes Fleisch** (instead of **Fleisches**), **mit einem Dutzend guten Äpfeln** (or often **guter Äpfel**), **Vasen aus** (made out of) **einer Art schönem Marmor, zehn Grad Kälte** ten degrees of frost, i.e. below the freezing-point, **zehn Grad Wärme** ten degrees above the freezing-point, **(Er gab mir) ein Wörtchen Antwort** an answer of a word or so, a short answer, **ein Stab von 40 Zentimeter Länge, ein weißer Bau mit fünf Fenster Front, zerrissen von Tausenden Geschossen, vielen Tausend Deutschen bekannt, 2000 Mark Anfangsgehalt, 200 Mark Zulage, zwanzig Prozent Ersparnis, fünf Prozent Rabatt, fünf Prozent Dividende, drei Prozent Zinsen, dreitausend Mark Schulden, 300 Mark Kassenvorrat, drei Jahre Balkan** three years in the Balkans, **drei Jahre Elend** or **des Elends, drei Jahre Krankheit, (Er bat um) eine Minute gnädiges Gehör, nach einem Augenblick Nachdenken** or **des Nachdenkens, nach einer Stunde Rast, nach einer Stunde Marsch, nach drei Wochen Warten** or **des Wartens, nach vier Jahren Frist** after a period of four years, **6 Tage bis 1** (read **einen**) **Monat Gefängnis** from six days to one month's imprisonment, **zu sechs Jahren Zuchthaus verurteilt, in einem halben Hundert Häusern, in Millionen Köpfen, seit Milliarden Jahren, seit einem halben Dutzend Jahren, mit einem schön gebundenen Band Goethe, eine Partie Schach. Er kauft ein Dutzend gute Stahlfedern. Dem Rackold** (name) **war dann der Zuwuchs der Waise allerdings eine harte Sache zu seinen eigenen sieben Stück Kindern** (Walther Siegfried's *Um der Heimat willen*, III). **Kartal ist eine Stunde Eisenbahn von Konstanti'nopel entfernt** Cartal is an hour's ride by rail from Constantinople. **In Ostafrika hat man in acht Jahren 128** km. **(Kilometer) Bahn gebaut** (*Deutsche Kolonialzeit*. Jahrg. 21, No. 23, p. 224). **Wer einmal über 4000 Spalten Wörterbuch hinter sich gebracht hat usw.** (Hermann Fischer in *Zeitschrift für deutsche Wortforschung*, 1910, p. 134) whoever has already published over 4000 columns of a dictionary, &c.

The gen. ending **s** of the noun denoting the weight or measure is often suppressed, while the dependent word has the regular gen. form: **zum Ankauf eines**

Stück Viehs (Raabe's *Die Innerste*, chap. i). **Wir sollen uns des kleinen Stückchen festen Bodens freuen** (Hans Dragendorff in *Deutsche Monatsschrift*, April 1906, p. 41). The gen. ending **s** of the noun denoting the weight or measure is sometimes suppressed, while the following noun is without inflection: **die Hälfte des halben Schoppen Apfelwein** (Raabe's *Eulenpfingsten*, chap. x).

It must be noticed that in case of a pl. noun of weight, measure, or quantity, the following noun in apposition can sometimes alone show the case, as the noun denoting weight, &c. has the same form for sing. and pl. and cannot distinguish case relations in the pl.: **mit zwei Dutzend Äpfeln, mit drei Schock Eiern, ein Viehstand von 50–60 Haupt Rindern.**

The noun or pronoun denoting weight, measure, &c. sometimes follows the dependent noun and may even be separated from it by one or more words, in which case words modified by a limiting adjective (see B) can also take the appositional construction: **Harmonisches Getön war wenig dabei** (Raabe's *Horn von Wanza*, chap. xvi). **Sonst bot es (i.e. das Gedicht) angreifbare Punkte die Menge** (Fontane's *Vor dem Sturm*, I. chap. xvii). **Einfache Zahladverbia gibt es nur wenige** (Braune's *Althochdeutsche Grammatik*, p. 202). **Solche Fehler können die Menge im Plinius sein.** For historical explanation see **255.** II. 1. H. *a*, 2nd par.

a. Instead of the appositional construction the dependent noun often in colloquial speech prefers the nom. form of each number thruout that number, except in the masc. acc. sing. and the dat. pl., where the appositional construction is the rule: **der Preis eines Fuders österreichischer Wein** the price of a fuder (a measure) of Austrian wine, **samt einem Fuder österreichischer Wein, ein Fuder** (acc.) **österreichischen Wein, der Preis eines Paars wollene Strümpfe, mit einem Paar wollenen Strümpfen.** Titles, however, remain uniformly in the nominative: **Dreißig Jahre deutscher Schulverein** the activities of the German School Association during a period of thirty years. **Ich habe die zwei Bände Grüner Heinrich gelesen.**

In Austrian authors the dative is sometimes found instead of the appositional construction: **Aber auch ein gut Stück menschlicher Schwäche und echt österreichischem Behagen an guter Speise, am Wein, am Lachen lächelte aus ihm** (R. H. Bartsch's *Die Haindlkinder*, p. 148). For the Austrian tendency to use the dative instead of the appositional construction see **255.** III. 1. A. *k*).

b. With names of streets, months, and seasons the article often drops out and the gen. then gives way to the appositional construction, or more commonly retains the nom. form thruout: **Ecke Hoher Steinweg** on the corner of the High Causeway, **mit dem Anfang Juli** or **Anfang Juli** with the beginning of July, **Ende Dezember, Ausgangs Sommer,** and always so in naming the day of the month: **der erste** [Tag understood] **Mai** the first of May. In a more careful style also inflection: **an der Ecke der Buckowerstraße und des Luisenufers, am Ende des Dezember.**

c. The gen. also gives way to the appositional construction in certain cases of proper nouns where possession is not to be emphasized, but where it is desired to show that the proper name is closely identified with the thing expressed by the preceding noun: **das Porträt W. Zimmermann** the portrait of (i.e. representing) W. Zimmermann, **zehn Grad Fahrenheit, Celsius, Reaumur** ten degrees Fahrenheit, Celsius, Reaumur, **der Antrag Rümelin** the motion made by Rümelin, **im Verlage der bekannten Kunstanstalt Rudolf Schuster, Berlin** published in the well-known art institution conducted by Rudolph Schuster, Berlin, **die Leipziger Maschinenfabrik Karl Krause** the machine works of K. K. in Leipzig, **der Prozeß Reinsdorff** the law suit carried on by or against Reinsdorff, **das vor einigen Tagen vorgekommene Duell Kotze-Schrader** the duel which took place a few days ago between Messrs. Kotze and Schrader, **Ferdinand Schmidt Nachfolger** (on a sign) Ferdinand Schmidt, now followed by a successor, **der gräfliche Zweig Eysen** (G. Ompteda) the branch of the Eysens that has the rank of counts, **die Arche Noah** Noah's ark, **die Villa Schirmacher** the villa of Mr. S. **Sie fuhren in den Bahnhof Kassel** (into the railroad station at Cassel) **ein und, ebenfalls glücklicherweise, bald weiter** (Raabe's *Gutmanns Reisen*, chap. iv). **Methode Schliemann zur Erlernung der englischen Sprache** Schliemann's method of learning English, **das Ministerium Windischgrätz** the ministry formed by prime minister Windischgrätz, **die Armeegruppe Mackensen** (*Großes Hauptquartier*, May 8, 1915). And often by Luther where we should expect a gen.: **die Tochter Pharao, die Zedern Libanon.** This idiom is also very common with geographical names: **Das Elsässische erstreckt sich von einer Linie Zabern, Weißenburg, Seltz südwärts bis usw.** The Alsatian dialect extends from a line passing thru Zabern, Weißenburg, Seltz, southward to, &c. **Der Plan einer Bahn Posen-Warschau, im Abendschnellzug Breslau-Gleiwitz, beim Überlandflug Berlin-München, Hansen-Dresden** Hansen who lives in Dresden, to distinguish one man from another of the same name, and similarly **Hansen-Bonbon** Hansen the manufacturer of bonbons, coined facetiously to distinguish this Hansen from others of the same name.

B. The gen. alone can be used in all the above cases if the dependent noun is modified by an article or a limiting adjective: **ein Pfund guter Tee** or **besserer**

Tee, but **des besten Tees, ein Pfund unseres Tees,** &c. The dat. after **von** here often takes the place of the gen.: **einer von diesen Männern.** For an important exception to the general rule see last part of A.

4. Titles of books, &c. are inflected, or more commonly uninflected: **in Hauptmanns „Einsamen Menschen,“ in „Der Fleck auf der Ehre.“** See also **255.** III. 1. A. *g.*

5. The inflectional ending is sometimes affixed only to the second of two nouns connected by **und,** to emphasize their oneness of meaning (see **249.** II. 2. F. *a*): **der Besitz eigenen Grund und Bodens; von Gott und Rechts wegen** by rights; **trotz Sturm und Regens; aus der Mitte seines energischen Tun und Treibens** (Raabe's *P.M.*, xviii); **Verlust ihres Hab und Gutes; ein unbändiger Geselle mit einem Tropfen des Marloweschen Sturm und Dranges** (*Neue Zürcher Zeit.*, Feb. 11, 1905), but also with the inflection of both words: **von seiten unseres neuesten Sturms und Drangs in der deutschen Literatur** (Konrad Falke in *Deutsche Monatsschrift,* Sept. 1906, p. 862). The inflection of the second of a pair of words connected by **und** was employed freely in early N.H.G.: **vmb Korn vnd Mosts willen** (Luther), **mit geschenck vnnd gabenn** (id.), or also with inflection of the first word, **mit gesetzen oder werck** (id.). This usage is still not infrequent in the classical period: **mit mancherlei Mängel und Gebrechen** (Goethe); **an Tier und Vögeln fehlt es nicht** (id., *Faust,* l. 238). **Von Sonn und Welten weiß ich nichts zu sagen** (ib., l. 279). With the exception of a few set expressions, as those given above, it is now rare: **Dann hört man sie auf Trepp und Gängen stöhnen** (Storm's *Im Nachbarhause links*).

6. When compound nouns have been formed by *writing as one word* a noun and a preceding modifying adjective which enters the compound with its inflected form, the adjective is declined thruout as if it stood apart from the noun: **der Hohepríester** the high priest, **des Hohenpríesters, ein Hoherpríester.** If such a compound enter again into a new compound of which it is itself the first component element and another noun the second, the inflected adjective of the first component element usually agrees illogically with the second component element: **der àrme Sǘnder** *the condemned criminal,* but **ein bleiches Àrmessǘndergesícht** *a pale face of a condemned criminal,* **das bleiche Àrmesǘndergesícht, zu den Àrmensǘnderfrühstücken; das Schwàrze Méer** *the Blàck Séa,* but **die übrigen Schiffe der Schwàrzen-Mḗer-Flótte** (*Neue Zürcher Zeit.* July 1, 1905); **Tàusend und èine Nácht** *The Arabian Nights,* but **wie ein Abend aus dem Tàusendundèinennáchtbúch** (Raabe's *Zum Wilden Mann,* chap. vii). Such compounds are mere syntactical fragments struggling toward the estate of a true compound. The adjective is inflected, since it is customary for adjectives to be inflected, and usage here as elsewhere requires adjective inflectional forms to follow the last component. A more logical system of inner inflection is to construe as often as possible the first noun of the compound as nominative singular or plural and allow the adjective of the compound to agree with it: **in der Max II.-Kaserne** (read **Màx der Zwḗite Kasérne**), **Meuterei auf der Schwàrze-Mḗer-Flótte** (*Allgemeine Zeit.*, June 30, 1905; the first element of the compound **Schwarze-Meer** in the nom. with the weak inflection of the adjective, as the adjective in this combination is outside of compounds usually preceded by the definite article), **ein Àrmesǘndergesícht** a face such as poor condemned criminals have. **Von Àrmelḗutemaleréi als kunsthistorischem Begriffe ist in einem eben erschienenen Hefte die Rede.** Instead of the nominative sing. or pl. we often in the South find in a few words like **Armesündergesicht,** &c. the gen. pl. of the first noun preceded by the weak gen. pl. of its modifying adjective: **das Armensünderglöckchen** (Gottfried Keller's *Dietegen* in *L. v. S.* II, p. 192). A still more logical way of declining such compounds, bound to triumph tho in many cases not as yet employed or not so common as the above, is to form them into genuine compounds and dispense with the inflection of the adjective of the first element: **das bleiche Àrmsǘndergesícht, die Schwàrzmḗerflótte** the Blàck Sḗa fléet, &c. still with their original group-stress, while others have the principal stress upon the

first component after the manner of old compounds: **Kúrzwàren** *hard-ware,* &c. Compare **249.** II. 2 and also A thereunder.

In many cases such compounds are not written together as forming one word, altho they are entitled to such recognition as well as the preceding: **der silberne Kreuzbund** Society of the Silver Cross, &c. A number of similar formations, as **ein geräucherter Fischhändler, reitende Artilleriekaserne** (inscription formerly upon the barracks near the 'Oranienburger Tor' in Berlin), **ein ausgestopfter Tierhändler, ein wohlriechender Wasserfabrikant, ein dreistöckiger Hausbesitzer,** &c., are capable of a comical construction, *a smoked fishdealer*, instead of *a smoked-fish dealer*, &c. The comical feature of this clumsy construction has helped to bring it into disrepute and facilitate the movement toward the form of a genuine compound, mentioned above.

7. In a few modern compounds (**249.** II. 2), which in reality are each only a fragment of a sentence written together as one word, that element of the compound may be inflected which in the syntactical structure of the sentence would be inflected, or the compounds may remain wholly uninflected: **die Handvoll** handful, pl. **zwei Hände voll** or **Handvoll.** Some of these compounds are now felt more or less as old compounds and hence are treated as such, the final element alone being inflected: **der Springinsfeld** romp, **des Springinsfeld(es),** pl. **Springinsfelde.** See **80.** 2 and **249.** II. 2.

8. A fossil noun in an oblique case may not be felt as such and hence construed as a simple stem: M.H.G. ze den wîhen nahten (dat. pl.) *on the holy nights*, now **Weihnachten** construed as a fem., neut., or masc. sing. See **96.** 1. Compare **88.**

9. Feminine nouns are not now in general inflected in the sing., but the following exceptions occur:

1. The following groups of feminines take an s in the gen. sing. after the manner of strong masculines and neuters:

a. Feminine names. See **86.** 1 and 2. *b.*

b. Names of relationships and feminine titles when used as names. See **90.**

c. Some articleless feminines depending upon a preposition, prep. phrase, or an adjective which governs the genitive: **an Zahlungs Statt** *instead of payment*, after the model of **an Kindes Statt; von Obrigkeits wegen** *by order of the authorities*, after the model of **von Amts wegen** *officially*; **krankheitshalber** after the model of **Feiertags halber. Antworts** (now **Antwort**) **genug** (Lessing) after the analogy of **Brots genug** (Luther). The s of **Antworts** may also be explained according to **102.** *c.*

2. Feminines show weak inflection in the singular only rarely in simple forms, but quite frequently in compounds. See **76.** II. 1 and **249.** II. 1. B. *a.*

10. If it is desired to call attention to the word itself, not to the thing represented by the word the case form is not the case required by the grammatical construction but the *nominative*, the form usually employed in naming a substantive when it is simply cited, lit. the *naming* case, a usage which has given the name to this case, altho it has other more common functions: **Ungewöhnlich ist der Plural von Haß** (nom., not **vom Hasse**). **Stuhl ist der Singular zu** (or **von**) **Stühle** (not **Stühlen**).

Declension of the Adjective-Substantive.

95. Nouns made from adjectives are only rarely declined according to any of the regular declensions for nouns. See **111.** 10. A few substantives made from adjectives have no inflection. See **111.** 7. *h.* They are usually inflected just as the adjective would be in the same position, but like nouns are written with a capital letter: **der Alte** the old man; **die Alte** the old woman; **das Schöne** the beautiful. For declension in full see **109.** For survivals of older usage see **111.** 10. *Note.*

Peculiarities of Number in Nouns.

96. 1. While in general the sing. denotes one and the plural more than one, in certain cases the opposite, namely, that one denotes many and many one, may be true. A number of objects may be divided into groups, each one of which may be looked at as a unit, a whole: **ein Tausend Zigarren** a thousand cigars; **ein Dutzend** a dozen; **ein Schock** a numerical whole consisting of 60 units; **eine Mandel** a numerical whole consisting of 15 units. Thus also collective nouns, as **die Herde** herd, **die Armee** army, &c., are nouns in the sing. denoting many. These words can usually form a plural as naturally as any common noun, but some, as **das Vieh** *cattle*, **das Gesinde** *servants taken collectively*, cannot form a plural, since they are conceived of in a *general* way and not as divisible into *distinct* groups. Thus as the mind can conceive of individual units as a whole and give expression to this conception in language, the form of the word does not always distinguish between sing. and pl., and colloquially and in popular language we can even find pl. words with a sing. article: **ein zehn Mark** the sum of ten marks, **ein** (also **eine**) **8 Tage** a period of a week, **eine zehn Jahre nach den andern** (Fedor Sommer's *Ernst Reiland*, p. 129), **am Ende der zweiten acht Tage** (Wildenbruch) at the end of the second week. Thus also **Ostern** Easter, **Pfingsten** Pentecost, **Weihnachten** Christmas, tho originally dative plurals, dative after the preposition **zu** and plural on account of these festivals each lasting several days, may also be regarded as singulars, fem. (under the influence of the pl. **die**), masc. (under the influence of **der Tag**), or perhaps more commonly neut. (under the influence of **das Fest**): **So waren wieder Pfingsten gekommen, aber wie waren es diesmal andere Pfingsten!** (Stifter's *Stud.*, 1. 154). **Die ewigen Ostern des Herzens** (Keller's *Seldwyla*), **vorige Weihnachten** (Fontane's *Effi*, chap. xi); **jede Weihnachten** (Lewald). **Gedenkst du noch an einen Weihnachten?** (Storm's *Unter dem Tannenbaum*, vol. I, p. 180). **Auf ein frohes Weihnachten** (Fontane's *Unwiederbringlich*, chap. vii). **Ostern fällt** (or **die Ostern fallen**) **dieses Jahr spät. Pfingsten ist** (or **die Pfingsten sind**) **vorüber. Was ist Weihnachten** (or **Was sind die Weihnachten**) **ohne Kinder?** In case of the conception of the form as plural notice the peculiar use of the plural of the ordinal: **Kein fröhliches Fest im Sinne harmloser Freude sind diese zweiten Kriegsweihnachten** (*Frankfurter Zeit.*, Dec. 25, 1915). The singular of these three festivals is usually only preserved in compounds: **Osterferien, Pfingstmontag, Weihnachtsabend.** The simple singular feminine form **Weihnacht** is sometimes found instead of **Weihnachten.**

Sometimes the name of a foreign newspaper is treated as a singular, as in English, altho the form is distinctly plural: **Der „Times" meldet man aus Petersburg, daß usw.** (*Neue Zürcher Zeit.*, June 8, 1905). **Wenigstens wird der „Times" gemeldet usw.** (*Hamburger Nachrichten*, Jan. 2, 1907). See also **253. I. 2. *g*.**

Thus also **Buch** *book*, literally *letters*, now always sing., for one object, was in Gothic and O.H.G. in the pl. to designate *one* book.

On the other hand, the pl. is so associated with the original sing. form **Geschwister** (in Lessing's *Nathan*, 1, 2, still used in sing.), a collective noun meaning *brothers and sisters*, that the pl. article is now used (**die Geschwister**), while we in other cases use the sing. article before collective nouns of the same form: **das Gedränge** throng, **das Gebirge** mountain-system, &c.

2. Names of materials do not from their very nature admit of a plural in the usual sense, but may take a plural to designate different species, varieties, or grades of the same thing: **der Wein** wine, pl. **Weine** different kinds of wine, **Rheinweine** Rhine wines, **Rotweine; das Holz** wood, pl. **Hölzer** different kinds of wood; **die Baumwolle** cotton, pl. **die amerikanischen Baumwollen** American varieties of cotton; **feine Bleie** fine grades of lead (for pencils, &c.).

a. This simple pl. is often replaced by compound plurals, formed by adding to the name of the material the substantive **Art** for the species of life or growth, or kinds of manufactured articles, and **Sorte** for different varieties of the same species of life or growth, or for different brands or sorts of manufactured articles, or by adding **Stoffe** (or **Zeuge** or **Gewebe**) to the name of textile goods: **Getreidearten** different kinds of grain, **Holzarten** different kinds of wood, **Stahlarten** different kinds of steel; **Kaffeesorten** different sorts of coffee, **Kohlarten** or **Kohlrassen, Branntweinsorten** different sorts of brandy; **Seidenstoffe** or **Seidenzeuge** silks, **Atlasgewebe** satin fabrics.

b. Of course when the names of materials denote a definite portion of the material a plural can be formed, which in a number of cases (see **83**) has developed a different pl. from the form indicating different kinds of the material: **das Brot** bread, loaf, pl. **die Brote** loaves; **das Horn** horn, pl. **Hörner** pieces of horn, horns (of an animal), pl. **Horne** kinds of horn; **das Tuch** cloth, pl. **Tücher** pieces of cloth, shawls, pl. **Tuche** kinds of cloth.

3. Names of persons do not take a pl. except when they indicate that a number of persons enjoy a common name, or when they assume the force of common nouns: **Goethes** the Goethes (family), **die Goethe** great poets like Goethe.

4. **(1).** An important group of words have an uninflected pl., in form exactly like the nom. sing., when they are used in a collective sense to express weight, measure, extent, and quantity—namely, all neut. and masc. nouns, and the feminines **Faust** or **Hand** hand, **Handvoll** handful, **Last** two tons, **Mandel** (pl. also **Mandeln**) a numerical whole consisting of 15 units, **Mark** mark (coin): **zwei Fässer** *two separate casks,* but **zwei Faß Wein** two casks (as a measure) of wine; **zwei Biere** *two kinds* of *beer,* but **zwei Bier** two glasses of beer, **mit zwei Glas Bier; zwei Säcke** *two* (empty) *sacks,* but **zwei Sack Mehl** two sacks of flour; **in einer Hitze von 80 Grad Reaumur; ein Gewicht von 140 Kilogramm** (or **Kilo**) a weight of 140 kilograms; **ein weißer Bau mit fünf Fenster Front; 400 Mann Infanterie** 400 men of infantry (who move as *one* man under the command of one man), but **4 Männer** four men (taken individually); **zehn Pfennig** ten pfennigs in *one* piece, but **zehn Pfennige** ten one-pfennig pieces; **einige Dutzend Kadetten** several dozen cadets in one group, but **Dutzende solcher Fälle** dozens of such cases; **mit zwei Drittel von ihnen** (Marie von Bunsen's *Das alltägliche Paar* in *Deutsche Rundschau,* May 1898, p. 282) or **mit zwei Dritteln von ihnen; zwei Mark, ein Pferd 15 Faust hoch, die drei Handvoll Erde, ein Schiff von 200 Last. Vier Mandel geben ein Schock.** The same construction occurs in English in certain expressions, as forty head of cattle, ten yoke of oxen, three score and ten, &c., but the construction as far as lifeless objects are concerned is waning and often sounds provincial. See *a* below.

In case of other feminines be sure to place the noun in the pl.: **zwei Flaschen Wein, zwei Tassen Kaffee.**

If it is not a question of weight or measurement, but of a mode of weighing or measuring, the regular pl. form is used: **Ein Kilo hat zwei Pfund und das Pfund 500 Gramm** *A kilogram contains two pounds and a pound 500 grams,* but **Bei uns wiegt man nach Pfunden** *In our country we weigh by pounds.*

a. This usage of leaving nouns in the sing. form in the pl. when used collectively started with the neuters, which in an earlier period had their regular pl. like the sing., as in English *one sheep, two sheep.* Later this plural, which in form was like the sing., did not seem to suffice, and hence alongside of the old form a new plural was formed in one of two ways, either by adding **ir,** which still later changed to the present form **er,** or the word took on the common masc. pl. ending **e,** and thus for each word there arose two pl. forms, as **Glas** and **Gläser** glasses; **Pfund** and **Pfunde** pounds. Later both of these forms were put to a good use in that a different shade of meaning was given to each. The form in **er** or **e** was applied to objects taken separately, the one that took no pl. ending, in accordance with its apparently sing. form, was invested with collective force to express weight, measure, extent. This usage was found so convenient that it spread to masculines and to the few feminines above mentioned. We follow this usage in case of certain living beings: *two little fishes, two large herrings,* but *a boatload of fish, herring.* In case of a number of gregarious animals the idea of mass is now so firm in English that the singular is used for both singular and plural, as in carp, perch, pike, salmon, trout, &c., sheep, deer, moose, &c. It is characteristic of the English development that this construction is almost entirely limited to living beings. In German, on the other hand, it is largely confined to lifeless objects, so that for all the English examples given above German usually has a plural form: **zwei Hechte** *two pike,* &c. Only in case of **das Wild** *game, deer* and **das Vieh** *cattle* has the singular collective force: **ein Rudel Wild** *a herd of deer,* **zwanzig Stück Vieh** *twenty head of cattle.*

(2) There are exceptions to the rule stated above:

a. Foreign and native nouns take sometimes their regular pl. ending to express weight, measure, and extent, or may remain uninflected, apparently without any difference in meaning between the different forms: **zehn Talente** 10 talents, **eine Summe von 30 Taler** or **Talern, 10 Pfennige** or **Pfennig, zehn Schritte** or **Schritt, bei drei Metern Entfernung** (Walther Siegfried's *Um der Heimat willen,* IV). The plural form is used especially to give individualizing force and thus often to add emphasis, even in case of native words of all genders: **ganze Händevoll** entire handfuls. **Fritz stürzt zwei Gläser Wasser hinunter** (Sudermann's *Fritzchen*). **Er hatte mehr als einmal viele Tausende Beitrag gezahlt, wenn es galt, das Fortbestehen irgend einer Wohltätigkeitseinrichtung zu sichern** (G. Ompteda's *Eysen*, chap. ix).

b. Nouns expressing measure of *time* may be inflected, or remain undeclined after numerals except in the gen. and dat. pl., where they are always inflected: **zwei Monat** or **Monate** *two months*, but **in zwei Monaten** in two months.

5. A. Abstract nouns, especially neut. adjective-substantives and neut. infinitive-substantives, do not admit of a plural as a rule: **das Schöne** that which is beautiful, **das Stehen** standing, **die Weisheit** wisdom, **die Schönheit** beauty, **die Freiheit** freedom, **die Größe** greatness, &c.

a. Abstract nouns, however, take a plural when they take on concrete meaning by representing concrete objects or indicating a number of kinds and distinct actions: **das Schreiben** *writing*, in the abstract, without a pl., but **das Schreiben** letter, pl. **die Schreiben; das Andenken** *memory*, without a pl., but **das Andenken** present, a token of remembrance, pl. **die Andenken;** thus also **Schönheiten** beauties, **Freiheiten** liberties, **Größen** sizes; to express kinds: **die Krankheit** sickness, pl. **die Krankheiten** different kinds of sickness; to express different acts: **der Sprung** jump, pl. **die Sprünge** jumps, &c.

Note. Fossilized remnants point to a more liberal use of the plural here in an earlier period to give emphasis to the meaning of the abstract idea or to indicate a number of concrete manifestations of it at one time or at different times: **in Gnaden bei jemand stehen** to be in favor with some one, to be recipients of repeated favors, **zu Ihren Diensten** at your service, **Offizier in preußischen Diensten** an officer in Prussian service. **Die Salbe hat mir gute Dienste geleistet** The salve has rendered me good service. In some such expressions the pl. force can scarcely be felt, and is in fact a fossil: **mit Ehren** with honor, **zugunsten** in favor of, **zu meinen Ungunsten oder Gunsten, zuschanden machen** to destroy, **zuschulden kommen lassen** to make oneself guilty of, &c. This old plural is especially a favorite with the poet and hence is sometimes called the poetical plural. So fond is the poet of this old construction that he sometimes coins a plural form in case of words which have never had a plural form: **die Jubel, die Schlummer,** &c. Sometimes this plural is retained in English where the sing. is found in German: **Man hegt Hoffnung, Verdacht** Hopes, suspicions, are entertained.

b. The plural of abstract nouns sometimes expresses a part of a whole, hence has less extensive meaning than the sing.: **Der Fürst verlieh dem Volke statt des Rechts Rechte** The prince gave the people instead of justice certain rights. Thus also **die Wahrheit** *truth* is broader in meaning than the pl. **Wahrheiten** truths. In similar contrasts even concrete nouns take on real abstract sense in the sing. with broad generalizing force, while the pl. is more concrete and of narrower application: **Wüstlinge rühmen sich stolz und mit Recht, sie kennten die Weiber, zarte Gemüter allein kennen und ehren das Weib. „Da gibt's ja Wissen und Wissenschaften die Fülle!" „Ja wohl!" lachte Schmidt auf. „Nur keine Wissenschaft!"** (Fedor Sommer's *Ernst Reiland*, p. 149).

B. A few abstract and collective nouns can form no pl. in the usual way, but borrow a form from some kindred derivative, or enter into a compound to form a pl., which of course in the case of abstract nouns must have a more distinctly concrete meaning than the sing., as no strictly abstract noun admits of a pl., or in case of collective nouns must have individualizing force:

Singular.	Plural.
der Atem breath,	**Atemzüge.**
das Bestreben effort,	**Bestrebungen.**
der Betrug deceit, fraud,	**Betrüge'reien.**
der Bund league,	**Bündnisse.**
der Dank thanks, gratitude; **vielen Dank!** many thanks!	**Danksagungen,** expressions of gratitude.
das Erbe inheritance,	**Erbschaften.**
das Feuer fire, conflagration,	**Feuersbrünste.**
der Friede peace,	**Friedensschlüsse, Friedensverträge** treaties of peace.
die Furcht fear,	**Befürchtungen.**
die Gewalt force, violence,	**Gewalttätigkeiten.**
das Glück luck, fortune,	**Glücksfälle** pieces of good fortune.
die Gunst favor,	**Gunstbezeigungen.**

der Kohl (N.G.), **das Kraut** (S.G.) cabbage, **der Kohlkopf, das Krauthaupt** head of cabbage, — **Kohle, Kräuter,** or **Kohl-** or **Krautarten** kinds of cabbage, **Kohlköpfe, Krauthäupter** cabbages.

der Kummer sorrow, — **Kümmernisse.**

das Land land, — **Lände'reien** estates, broad acres.

das Leben life, — **Menschenleben** lives.

das Leid grief, — **Leiden** (pl. of **das Leiden**).

die Liebe love, — **Liebschaften** amours.

das Lob praise, — **Lobeserhebungen, Lobsprüche.**

der Lohn reward, — **Belohnungen.**

Lug und Trug lying, — **Lüge'reien und Betrüge'reien.**

der Mord (see **63. 1.** *b*) murder, — **Mordtaten.**

die Not necessity, distress, — **Notwendigkeiten** necessities, necessary things, **Nöte** distress.

Obst fruit (collectively), **Frucht** fruit (collect. or a single specimen), — **Obstsorten** fruits (i.e. kinds of), **Früchte** fruit (single specimens of, as in **Früchte zum Nachtisch, eingemachte Früchte** *preserves*).

der Rasen turf, grass-plot, — **Rasenplätze.**

der Rat advice, — **Ratschläge** counsels.

der Raub robbery, — **Räube'reien.**

der Regen rain, — **Niederschläge, Regenfälle.**

der Same seed, — **Samen** seeds (of the same kind), **Samen** or more commonly **Säme'reien** seeds (of different kinds as found in different packets).

der Schmuck ornament, — **Schmucksachen.**

der Schnee snow, — **Schneemassen** heaps of snow, **Schneefälle** falls of snow.

der Segen blessing, — **Segnungen.**

der Streit dispute, — **Streitigkeiten.**

der Tod death, — **Todesfälle** cases of death.

der Trost consolation, — **Tröstungen.**

die (sometimes **der, das**) **Unbill,** less commonly **die** (**das**) **Unbild, die Unbilde** wrong, injury, inclemency, — **Unbilden.**

das Unglück misfortune, — **Unglücksfälle** unhappy accidents.

der Verdruß vexation, — **Verdrießlichkeiten.**

der Verrat treason, — **Verräte'reien** treacherous acts.

die Verteidigung defense, — **Verteidigungswerke** fortifications.

der Verzug delay, — **Verzögerungen.**

die Vorsicht caution, — **Vorsichtsmaßregeln** precautionary measures.

der Wahn illusion, — **Wahnvorstellungen.**

der Zank quarrel, — **Zänke'reien.**

das (**der, die**) **Zubehör** all that belongs to a thing: **Tee mit Zubehör. Er kaufte die Wirtschaft mit allem Zubehör. Komplimente sind das Zubehör der Bewillkommnung.** — **Zubehöre** (neut. and masc. pl.), **Zubehören** (fem. pl.): **Er führte mich in allen Zubehören seiner Wirtschaft herum.** In most cases the sing. form of expression is more common.

It should be carefully noted, however, that most of the above plural derivatives or compounds can also be used in the singular, usually of course with more concrete force than the corresponding form that can only be used in the sing.: **der Verrat** *treason*, **die Verräterei** *treacherous act*.

Note. **Der Bau** building, tho not an abstract noun, forms also its plural with a borrowed form, **die Bauten.** See also **63. 1.** *b*.

6. A few nouns have no plurals at all: **der Adel** nobility, **die Asche** ashes, **die glühende Asche** glowing embers, **die Beute** or **der Raub** booty, **der Bodensatz** sediment, dregs, **das Einkommen** income, **das Elend** (pl. rare) misery, **der Ersatz** indemnification, substitute, **das Geschlinge** or often **Gekröse** heart and lungs of an animal, **der Hafer** oats, **der Hopfen** hops, **die Infante'rie** or **das Fußvolk** infantry, **der Inhalt** contents, **die Kavalle'rie** or **die Reite'rei** cavalry, **der Klerus** clergy, **die Poli'zei** police, **das Publikum** the public, a course of free university lectures (in this meaning with the pl. **Publika**), **der Putz** (see **Staat** below, sometimes with pl., see **63. 1.** *b*) ornament, **der Staat** finery, attire (**Sie sind in ihrem besten Staate** or **Putze** They are in their best attires or clothes), **das Vieh** (sometimes with pl., see **74.** 1) cattle, **das Wild** deer, and the names of sciences ending in **ik: die Germa'nistĭk** Germanics, **die Mathema'tĭk** mathematics, **die Meta'physĭk** metaphysics, **die Poli'tĭk** politics, **die Taktĭk** tactics, **die Sta'tistĭk** statistics, &c.

7. Some nouns are used only in the plural:

a. Certain words which were originally conceived of as plural: **Ferien** vacation, holidays, **Fasten** lent; sometimes **Ostern, Pfingsten, Weihnachten,** for which see 1 of this article. Also a number of Roman festivals usually occur in the pl.: **die Baccha'nalien** bacchanalia, **Flo'ralien** festival of Flora, **Satur'nalien** festival of Saturn, &c.

b. A number of words which contain the idea of a group of distinctly different but related individuals or of connected parts have usually only the pl. form, tho occasionally a sing. occurs: **Aktien** (sing. **eine Aktie** one share of stock) stock, **Ali'mente** financial support required by law to be given to certain persons under certain circumstances, alimony, &c., **A'nnalen** annals, **die Auslagen** outlay (**Welches sind Ihre Auslagen für mich?**), **Au'spizien** auspices, **Beinkleider** or **Hosen,** or sing. **das Beinkleid** or **die Hose** trousers, **Briefschaften** letters, papers, **Chemi'kalien** chemicals, **in Chiffern** in cipher, **E'ffekten** movable goods, "traps," **Eingeweide** intestines, **Einkünfte** income, **Eltern, Großeltern** parents, grand-parents, **E'xequien** obsequies, **Fisima'tenten** (colloq. **Das sind Fisima'tenten**) pretense, subterfuge, humbug, **Frieseln** purples, **Gebrüder** brothers (as partners in some business: **zu haben bei Gebrüder Müller,** but **Ich habe zwei Brüder**), **in Gedanken versunken** lost in thought, **Gefälle** duties, revenue, income, **Gerätschaften** implements, tools, **Geschwister** brother and sister, or the children of a family, **Gliedmaßen** (replaced in the sing. by **das Glied,** or the name of the particular limb) limbs, **Hämorrho'iden** piles, **Händel** (**Er sucht Händel bei mir**) quarrel, **Haue** (see also *Note* 2 below) flogging, lit. blows, **Honorati'oren** people of rank or high station, notabilities, "the big guns," **Hosenträger** (pl., or sometimes sing. **der Hosenträger**) suspenders, **Iden** the ides, **In'signien** insignia, **Inte'ressen** interests, **Kal'daunen** tripe, **Kollek'taneen** collectanea, **Kosten** costs, expenses, expense (**auf Kosten seiner Gesundheit** at the expense of, &c.), **meine Kräfte** my strength (**Meine Kräfte verlassen mich**), **Kriegsläufte** warlike times, **Kurzwaren** hard-ware, **Kutteln** (S.G.) = **Kaldaunen, Laren** Lares, **Lebensmittel** victuals, provisions, **Leute** (see 9 below) people, **Machenschaften** machinations, **Manen** manes, **Masern** measles, **Molken** whey, **Musi'kalien** (pieces of) music, **Natu'ralien** productions of nature, **Noten** music (**Haben Sie Ihre Noten mit?**), **Perso'nalien** short description of a person, **Pe'naten** Penates, **Pocken** or **Blattern** small-pox, **Prälimi'narien** preliminaries, **Preti'osen** valuable articles, such as precious stones, jewelry, **Ränke** intrigues, **gute Ratschläge** good advice, **Röteln** German measles, **Schlacken** dross, **Schmerzen** often pain (**Ich hatte solche Schmerzen, daß usw.** I was in such pain that &c., but He took great pains **Er gab sich redliche Mühe**), **Skrofeln** scrofula (**Er leidet an Skrofeln**), **Spesen** or **Unkosten** transportation charges and all expenses connected with a shipment of goods, **Spitzen** lace, **Sporteln** fees, perquisites, **Stoppeln** stubble, **Treber** or **Trester** draff, **Trümmer** (see this word, **74.** 1) ruins, **Überhosen** overalls, **keine Umstände machen** not to stand on ceremony, **Umtriebe** machinations, **Unterhosen** drawers, **Uten'silien** utensils, **Zeitläufte** times, **Zinsen** interest (money, but sing. **der Zins** in the meaning rent);

also geographical names just as in English: **die Alpen** the Alps, **die Zy'kladen** the Cyclades, **die Darda'nellen** the Dardanelles, **die He'briden** the Hebrides, **die Niederlande** the Netherlands, **die Pyre'näen** the Pyrenees, **die Vo'gesen** the Vosges, &c., but these plurals do not correspond in every case in the two languages, as **das Felsengebirge** the Rockies; **die Vereinigten Staaten als ein ganz anderes Land als das heutige** an entirely different U. S. from that of to-day; &c.

Note 1. Besides the more common words in the above list, there are many others, especially those scientific terms which designate classes of animal or plant life: **die Herbi'voren** herbivorous animals, **Orchi'deen** orchids, &c.

Note 2. The sing. is often used, in order to indicate an individual of a class or group, or a fragment or portion of a whole, or to express a collective idea: **die Alpe** a single range of the Alps. **Diese Haue** (pl. used as a sing. in a collective sense) **erfolgte** (Langenscheidt Berl. 55). **Unter diesen Worten waren sie bis in den Garten gekommen, an eine Stelle, wo viel Buchsbaum** (sing. used in a collective sense) **stand** (Fontane's *Stechlin*, chap. vi). **„Wenn also das Schiff — apropos, was kann es geladen haben?“ „Jedenfalls Hering, Herr Doktor, salzen und frischen“** (Spielhagen's *Faustulus*, p. 60). The singular is often used in English of fish in a collective sense where the plural is used in German: perch **Barsche**, pike **Hechte**, trout **Fo'rellen**, smoked fish **geräucherte Fische**, &c. Do you like fish? **Essen Sie gerne Fische?**

8. A number of very common words are singular in German (and hence often also capable of a plural) which are only plural in English: **das Almosen** alms, pl. **die Almosen** different items of alms, **die A'postelgeschichte** Acts (in the Bible), **Aufwartung** respects, (**einem seine Aufwartung machen**), **ein Bitterer** bitters (**Er trinkt einen Bitteren**), **der Bodensatz** settlings, lees, dregs, grounds, sediment, **die Brille** spectacles, pl. **die Brillen** the pairs of spectacles, **in Buntstift** in crayons (**ein Bild in Buntstift**), **das Dam(en)spiel** or **Dambrett(spiel)** draughts, checkers (**Spielen Sie Dambrett** or **Damen?**), **das Domino** dominoes, **die Drehkrankheit** staggers (disease), **die Druse** the strangles (disease), **der Erlös** the proceeds, **Erspartes** savings, **das Feuerwerk** the fireworks, **die Fleischbank** the shambles (meat-market), **die Flügeltür** the folding doors, **die Gasanstalt** or **das Gaswerk** the gas-works, **der Gewinn** winnings, **die Golfbahn** or **das Golffeld** the links, **das 'Hauptquar'tier** the headquarters, **das Hirschgeweih** the antlers, **im schottischen Hochland** in the Highlands of Scotland, **die Hochzeit** the nuptials, **die Ka'serne** the barracks, **das** (or **der**) **Kehricht** the sweepings, **die Kneifzange** nippers, **die Lichtputze** snuffers, **der Lohn** (pl. **die Löhne**) wages (**Der Arbeitgeber bestimmt den Lohn für den Arbeiter,** but **Er zahlt seinen Leuten die Löhne aus**), **die Lunge** the lungs, lights, **die Mauke** the scratches (disease), **das einzige Mittel** the only means, remedy, **vielerlei Mittel** many different kinds of means, remedies, **im Mittelalter** in the Middle Ages, **die Nachricht** (piece of) news, **die neuesten Nachrichten** the latest items of news, **das Proto'koll** the minutes, **der Reichtum** riches (**Reichtum entflieht** *riches fly away*, but also in the plural: **Er besitzt Reichtümer**), **mit der Miete im Rückstande sein** to be in arrears with the rent, **Schadenersatz** damages, **die Schere** scissors, **das Seifenwasser** the soapsuds, **die Sittlichkeit** the morals, **die Traube** the bunch of grapes, **Treff** clubs (**Treff ist Trumpf** clubs are trumps), **sein Treiben** his doings, **die Treppe** stairs, pl. **die Treppen** the flights of stairs, **Trumpf** trumps (see **Treff**), **das Uhrwerk** the works of a clock or watch, **das Unkraut** weeds (**Unkraut vergeht nicht**), pl. **Unkräuter** weeds of different varieties, **einen zur Vernunft bringen** to bring one to his senses, **die Vesper** (**zur Vesper gehen**) vespers, **der Wald** the woods, forest, **die Wasserleitung** waterworks, water-pipes, water-supply, **West'indien** the West Indies, **eine oftmalige Wiederkehr des Tages** many happy returns of the day, **im rechten Winkel** at right angles (**Diese Linien schneiden sich im rechten Winkel**), **diese Wirtschaft** these goings-on, **das Zahnfleisch** the gums, **die Zange** the tongs, **pl. die Zangen** the pairs of tongs, **der Ziegenpeter** the mumps, **der Zirkel** pair of compasses.

A number of words are in German used in both numbers where in English the singular is employed: **die Auskunft** information, pl. **die Auskünfte, der Fortschritt** progress, pl. **die Fortschritte, das Geschäft** business, pl. **die Geschäfte, das Haar** hair, pl. **die Haare, die Kenntnis** knowledge, pl. **die Kenntnisse: Er ist bereit, Auskunft** or **Auskünfte zu erteilen,** the plural when different matters are involved, so that the plural idea becomes prominent. **Die Partei des Fortschritts** the party of progress, but **Meine Schüler machen große Fort-**

schritte My pupils are making great progress. **Er hat ein sehr ausgedehntes Geschäft** He has a very extensive business, but **Die Geschäfte gehen langsam** Business (i.e. sales, &c.) is slow. **Sie hat schwarze Augen und dunkles Haar** or **dunkle Haare. Etwas kommt mir zur Kenntnis** Something comes to my knowledge, but **ein Mann von vielen Kenntnissen** a man of great knowledge.

9. The pl. of **-mann** in compounds is usually **-leute,** which, however, does not mark sex as **-mann** does in the sing., but may include both sexes, and thus represent people not as individuals, but as belonging to a distinct class, or profession, or trade: **der Edelmann** nobleman, pl. **Edelleute** people of noble birth; **der Hauptmann** captain, pl. **Hauptleute; der Kaufmann** merchant, pl. **Kaufleute.** Thus many such plurals: **Bergleute** miners, **Fuhrleute** drivers, &c. The regular pl. is, however, used when the sex becomes prominent: **der Ehemann** married man, pl. **die Ehemänner** married *men*, but **Eheleute** married people. Thus also when the persons designated are not so much thought of as belonging to a *class*, but rather are conceived of as *individuals* who embody the idea of inner, personal, manly worth: **der Ehrenmann** man of honor, pl. **die Ehrenmänner; der Kraftmann** man of power, genius, pl. **Kraftmänner; der Ersatzmann** substitute, pl. **Ersatzmänner.** Thus also **Biedermänner** honest men, **Staatsmänner** statesmen, **Hauptmänner** *leading men*, but **Hauptleute** captains. Thus sometimes, as in the last example, the same word forms a plural either in **-männer** or **-leute,** according to the meaning. The plural in **-männer** is also used with reference to the exterior form of men, as in **Hampelmänner** jumping-jacks, **Schneemänner** snow-men, **Strohmänner** men of straw (lit. or fig.), &c.

Note. Synonymous with **Leute** is the collective noun **das Volk** *people* and **die Menschen** *people.* **Volk,** as its use in the sing. would indicate, expresses strongly the collective idea with many shades, as **das deutsche Volk** the German people, **das literarische Volk** literary people, **verliebtes Volk** people in love, **das gemeine Volk** the common people, **das Landvolk** the rural population. **Es ist schlechtes Volk** They are a bad set, &c. In dialect **Leut** can also be thus used as a neuter noun in accordance with older usage in the literary language: **Unter lauter altes Leut soll ich mich vergraben?** (Marriot's *Menschlichkeit*, p. 184). In present literary usage the plural **Leute** may also refer to a crowd or class of people, but rather as individuals, and thus the collective idea in it is much weaker than in **Volk: die Leute in diesem Hause** the people in this house, **arme, reiche, alte Leute** poor, rich, old people, **fremde Leute** strangers, **meine Leute** my servants, factory men. **Es waren nur zwei Leute im Zimmer, als ich kam. Die Leute sagen's** People say so. **Kleider machen Leute** Clothes make the man. **Unsere Väter waren Leute!** (Goethe's *Egmont*, 2) Our fathers were men of sterling qualities. As can be seen in the last example under **Volk** and the last two under **Leute,** the former often expresses contempt and the latter honor and importance. **Menschen** differs from **Leute** in that it lacks entirely collective force and thus refers to individuals only. **Alle Menschen** (every individual) **müssen sterben,** but **Alte Leute** (as a class) **müssen sterben, junge Leute können sterben. Menschen** differs from **Männer** only in that it includes males and females, while **Männer** refers only to the former.

Note that **Volk** in the sense of *nation* has a pl. **Völker.** The colloquial pl. of the corresponding English word has quite a different meaning: my folks = **meine Angehörigen, meine Leute.**

10. If a noun is modified by two numeral adjectives, the first indeclinable with pl. force, the second declinable with sing. force, added to the first to complete and make more exact the statement, the noun may be either sing. or pl. If the sing. form of the noun be chosen, then the second adjective must agree with it, but if the pl. form be preferred, which is more common, then the second adjective like the first remains uninflected: **Tausend und eine Nacht** The Thousand and One Nights ('The Arabian Nights'), **hundert und ein Kamel** one hundred and one camels, **in zwei und einem halben Jahr** in two and a half years, **drei und eine achtel Meile** three and one-eighth miles, or more commonly (except in the first example in this one meaning) **in zweiundeinhalb Jahren, dreiundeinachtel Meilen.** For a case where the noun must be in the pl. see **121.** 2. *d. Note.*

11. In German the singular is used where in English the plural is employed, in that case where a plural noun refers to as many different things as it has modifying adjectives, as **die englische und die deutsche Sprache** the English and German languages, but **die französischen und die deutschen Universitäten** the French and German universities, i.e. the French universities and the German universities. **Die schwarze und die weiße Kuh** the black cow and the white one, **die schwarzen und die weißen Kühe** the black cows and the white ones; **die schwarz und weiße Kuh** the black and white cow, i.e. the cow which is part black, part white, **die schwarz und weißen Kühe** the cows which are part black, part white. The article can be used only once where there is only one person or thing or one group of persons or things, as in the last two examples. The article is also used only once where there are two objects which are parts of a whole: **der erste und zweite Band** the first and second volumes (of a set), **die ersten und zweiten Bände der beiden Reihen** the first and second volumes of the two series. Similarly where two distinct units are merged into one for a common purpose, or where two distinct parties are struggling against one another in a common contest for the mastery: **die englische und französische Flotte** or **die englisch-französische Flotte** the English and French fleet or the Anglo-French fleet; **der deutsch-französische Krieg,** &c.

12. The Germans often use the sing. in a distributive sense (where we use the pl.) when the reference is to a *single* thing or respect which applies alike to a number of persons: **Viele haben das Leben verloren** Many lost their lives. **Alle hoben die rechte Hand auf** All raised their right hands. **Der Henker hieb den Verurteilten den Kopf ab. Ihr müßt den Kopf gerade halten.** See also **263.** II. 3.

13. The sing. is much used with generalizing force both in German and English, but in the former to a greater extent than in the latter: **Der Mensch wird zum Unglück geboren** Man is born unto trouble. Often this generalizing sing. takes on real abstract force, as is described in 5. A. *b* above.

14. For the words which have different plurals with differentiated meanings, see **83.**

Gender of Nouns.

97. Gender in German is not, as in English, determined by sex or non-sex, but is either natural or grammatical.

The gender of nouns is natural when it is based upon sex. Natural gender is confined to names of animate beings. Such nouns are masculine if they denote males, and are feminine if they denote females.

Grammatical gender is determined, not by sex, but by the meaning and form of the word. It is of three kinds—masculine, feminine, neuter. By grammatical gender even nouns denoting things and abstract ideas are often masculine or feminine by virtue of their meaning or form: **der Herbst** autumn, **der Fluß** river, **die Fahrt** drive, **die Reife** ripeness. The origin of grammatical gender and its original relation to natural gender is not clearly understood. Some think that the basis of all gender is the natural sex of man and beast, which originally in the lively play of the imagination was also ascribed to lifeless objects. Others with greater probability think the question more a matter of form and meaning. The idea of masculine or feminine sex could attach itself to certain suffixes which occurred in certain nouns and pronouns denoting males or females. Many nouns which denoted lifeless objects or abstract ideas had the same ending as the nouns denoting animate beings, and thus became intimately associated with them and were treated *grammatically* in exactly the same way, their modifiers being required to assume a masc. or a fem. form. Also many words which did not have an ending that suggested the masc. or the fem. gender had a *meaning* similar to certain masc. or fem. nouns and hence were similarly treated, their modifiers being required to assume a masc. or a fem. form. All the pronouns referring to these nouns that had become masc. or fem. upon the basis of mere form or meaning were masc. or fem., so that a large number of lifeless objects had become thoroly associated with the idea of sex and had thus been brought into relation to life, but it does not seem probable that a vivid idea of sex and animate life was ever associated with these things in ordinary language. From the very beginning the ideas of form and general meaning were the principal factors. In a limited number of words, however, masc. and fem. forms have led to the vivid idea of sex. Thus popular fancy pictured to itself the moon as a shepherd among his sheep (stars), starting from the grammatical gender of (**der**) **Mond.** The imagination may also in a limited number of words have directly personified things, assigning gender to them on the basis of some fanciful resemblance to animate beings.

The neuter (i.e. neither) gender denoted originally, as its name signifies, absence of gender, and has arisen to the dignity of a third gender only by its difference in grammatical form from that of the other two genders. In Indo-European, from which Germanic has come, the masculine and feminine had a different form for the nominative and the accusative as the nouns were felt as representing living beings who act and are acted upon, while neuter nouns did not have a different form for the two cases as they were felt as representing an inert mass that could neither act nor suffer when acted upon. Even in oldest German this old order of things had in a large measure disappeared. To-day the feminine as well as the neuter has under all circumstances the same form for the nominative and the accusative. Thus language has grown less picturesque, more matter-of-fact.

It is now only possible by the aid of philology to determine the different forces at work in gender, and that only imperfectly. The following detailed treatment is intended only as a practical guide to the use of gender as it is to-day.

Gender according to Meaning.

98. 1. The gender of nouns indicating animate beings is, as in English, masc. or fem. according to sex: **der Vater** father, **die Mutter** mother; **der Mann** man, **die Frau** woman; **der Bruder** brother, **die Schwester** sister; **der Knecht** servant, **die Magd** maid-servant; **der Bock** male goat, **die Ziege** female goat; **der Ochse** ox, **die Kuh** cow.

There are a few exceptions:

a. A few isolated words: **das Weib** and **Frauenzimmer** woman, **das Mensch** wench, in the language of the common people **das Mannsen** man, **das Weibsen** woman.

b. Nouns representing not an individual but a species or class are not of uniform gender, some being masc., some fem., some neuter: **der Mensch** man, **der Adler** eagle, **die Person** person, **die Waise** orphan, **die Schwalbe** swallow, **das Pferd** horse, &c.

c. In nouns denoting tne young of animals and also of human offspring the idea of sex is not prominent, and hence the gender is usually neuter: **das Kalb** calf, **das Füllen** colt, **das Junge eines Schafes, ein ganz Kleines** baby, &c.

d. All nouns representing living beings become neut. when they take a neut. suffix: **Fräulein** Miss, young lady, **liebes süßes Tantchen** dear good Auntie.

2. The gender of nouns indicating lifeless objects is difficult for the foreigner to detect, but may be learned in part by the following rules:

A. Masculines are:

The names of the days of the week, months, seasons, winds, points of the compass, mountains, stones, and foreign rivers (see B. *a*): **der Montag** Monday, **der Januar** January, **der Winter** winter, **der Pa'ssat** the 'trade-wind,' **der Norden** the north, **der Brocken** the Brocken, **der Dia'mant** diamond, **der Don** the Don (river). Of course if such names are compounds they are not necessarily masc., but are governed by their last component: **das Frühjahr** Spring, **das Matterhorn** (peak of the Alps), &c.

B. Feminines are:

(**1**) The names of most German rivers, most trees, plants, flowers, fruits (except **der Apfel** and **der Pfirsich,** the latter of which also has a fem. form, **die Pfirsiche**), cigars (see *b* below), postage stamps (see *b* below), and cardinal numerals used as substantives: **die Weser** the Weser river, **die Elbe** the Elbe river, **die Eiche** oak, **die Rose** rose, **die Kar'toffel** potato, **die Traube** grape, **die Henry Clay** (name of a cigar), **die Porto'riko** the Porto Rico postage stamp, **die Eins** the figure 1. For more concerning the gender of numerals see **121.** 3. *Note.*

a. The prevailing gender for German rivers is fem., as a number were originally compounded with a fem. suffix -aha related to the Latin aqua *water*: **Werra** from Werraha. A few German rivers, as **der Bober, Eisack, Elbing, Inn, Kocher, Lech, Main, Neckar, Pregel, Regen,** and

Rhein, are masc., as are also American rivers and foreign streams in general excepting those ending in a fem. suffix, as **e, a,** and often these are masc.: **der Mississippi, Don, Columbia,** &c., but **die Themse** Thames, **Wolga,** &c. Some foreign rivers have double gender, sometimes according to the languages from which they were taken, as **der Rhone, der Tiber,** sometimes fem. after German fashion, as **die Rhone, die Tiber.**

b. The names of cigars and postage stamps are fem., as the mind supplies the words **Zigarre, Marke.** In the same manner other words may take the gender of some word supplied by the mind: **ein** (neut.) **Stahl,** for **Stahlpulver; das** (see also **83**) **Scharlach** (with gender of **Fieber**) scarlet-fever; **feiner Korn** (with the gender of **Branntwein**) Dutch gin; **beim Blindekuh** (with the gender of **Spiel**) (Fontane's *L'Adultera*, chap. viii) *in the play of blindman's-buff*; **die Blickensderfer** (name of **eine Schreibmaschine**).

(**2**) The gender of the names of ships is usually that of the original word, but there is a tendency to employ the feminine gender in case of ships named after persons or places: **der Kaiser Wilhelm, die Luise, die Möwe,** but **die Deutschland, an Bord der „Moltke"** (*Hamburgischer Correspondent*, June 24, 1903), **auf der „Hohenzollern"** (ib.), **die Hamburg** (ib., June 29, 1903), **die Navahoe** (ib.), **die Emden** (official German report of Sept. 25, 1914), **die Rückkehr der Bodensee** (*Das Berliner Tageblatt*, Nov. 5, 1919) the return of the Bodensee (passenger airship). In case of ships named after persons or places many avoid the feminine as an anglicism and employ the masculine after the analogy of **der Dampfer: an dem Untergang des „Maine"** (*Neue Zürcher Zeitung*, March 23, 1898), **der Caracas** (*Hamburgischer Correspondent*, Dec. 24, 1902), **unser tapferer Emden** (Engel's *Ein Tagebuch*, II, p. 387). In case of ships named after persons and places some writers employ the gender of the original word, dropping the article when the word is unmodified, but using it when modified: **Scharnhorst,** but **der stolze Scharnhorst; Emden** but **das tapfere Emden. Bodensee benötigte (auf der Fahrt von Friedrichshafen nach Berlin) nur 3¾ Stunden** (*Hamburger Nachrichten*, Nov. 22, 1919).

C. Neuters are:

a. The names of minerals except: **der Stahl** steel, **der Tombak** (sometimes neut.) tombac, **der Kobalt** (sometimes neut.) cobalt; and **Nickel** (masc. in the meaning **Zehnpfennigstück**) nickel, **Wismut** bismuth, **Zink** zinc, which are either neut. or masc., but more commonly the former.

b. The names of countries, islands, provinces, cities, and places except those that always take the article (**59.** II. F. 2. *a* and *b*).

Note. In poetic style cities are often personified and treated as fem., as a survival of a once more general usage: **die rege Zürich** (Schiller), **die goldene Augsburg** (Frenssen's *Bismarck* p. 52).

c. Certain abstract nouns, especially abstract adjective-substantives, as **das Schöne** *the beautiful*, and infinitive-substantives, as **das Singen** singing.

d. The letters of the alphabet, as **das A** the a, **das Abc** the A-B-C.

e. Modern compounds and nouns formed from other parts of speech (see **80.** 2), except those that denote persons, or other living beings, which also sometimes take the neut. but usually the natural gender: **ein Vergißmeinnicht** forget-me-not, **ein Mehr** a majority, **ein Plus** that which is above and beyond, **ein unbekanntes Etwas** an unknown something, **das bessere Ich in uns** (Goethe's *Wilhelm Meisters Lehrjahre*, II. chap. xi). Oswald: **Du heiraten? Wen?** Simpson: **Eben dieses Wen wollte ich dir unterbreiten.** (Wilbrandt's *Die Maler*, 3, 3). You marry? Whom? – It is just this question of the whom that I was about to lay before you. **Ich hasse dieses pedantische allerdevoteste deutsche Sie** (id., *Franz*, III). **„Entweder Sie erklären augenblicklich, daß Sie meinen würdigen Vater mit Ihrem Gelächter nicht kränken wollten, oder wir verzichten auf die Ehre Ihrer Gegenwart". „Wer ist das Wir?" schrie sie kirschbraun vor Zorn dem Doktor zu** (Baumbach's *Der Schwiegersohn*, VIII). **Hier gibt's kein Rückwärts, sondern nur ein Vorwärts. Bei Tische hatte ich ein reizendes Gegenüber** At the table a charming young lady sat opposite me. **Wenn sie mich wollte – Sie! Welche Sie?** (Wilbrandt's *Maler*, 3, 4) If she would have me–She! What She? **Es ist kein Er; es ist eine Sie** (Raabe's *Frau Salome*, chap. xi) It (here the thief) is no male person; it is a girl. **Ein** (masc.) **Springinsfeld** romping boy or girl, **ein** (masc.) **Saufaus** toper, &c.; **das Kikeri'ki** *crowing of the cock*, but **der Kikeri'ki** cock, and hence also **der**

Kikeri'ki, name of a comic paper. Some formations of this kind used as names of newspapers and periodicals, as **der Vorwärts** and **der Über'all,** are masc. as they are conceived as having the qualities of men, i.e. are the representatives of certain principles or the embodiments of certain ideas, but others, as **Über Land und Meer** and **Vom Fels zum Meer,** are neuter in accordance with the general rule. Substantives derived from interjections denoting noises are not neut. but usually masc. after the analogy of other names of noises, which are largely monosyllabic derivatives from verbal stems and hence are naturally masc.: **der Knack, der Klatsch, der Paff, der Kladdera'datsch** *great noise, row,* and hence **der Kladdera'datsch,** name of a satirical paper in Berlin. **Luginsland** watch-tower is masc. after the analogy of **Turm.**

A sentence or a part of a sentence is often used as a neut. noun: **Wie schmerzlich, nach und nach hinter der eigenen Leistung zurückzubleiben . . . , ein ungestümes „Mach' Platz!" zu hören** (Erich Schmidt's *Charakte'ristiken,* II, p. 233). **Er war dann später mit einem kurzen „gute Nacht" in seine Kammer gegangen** (Storm's *In St. Jürgen*).

The gender of modern compounds is sometimes regulated by the first word. See **102.** *h* (toward end).

Gender according to Form.

99. To some of the rules of formal gender there are many exceptions. In the following articles only the general outline of present usage can be given:

1. Masculines are:

a. Most monosyllabics by gradation (**197.** A. *a*), showing in many cases the same vowel as the past tense of the strong verbs from which they are derived: **der Band** *volume,* from **binden** *to bind*; **der Biß** *bite,* from **beißen** *to bite*; **der Sproß** *sprout,* from **sprießen** *to sprout*; **der Schluß** *close,* from **schließen** *to close.* A few monosyllabics show another vowel than that of the past: **der Tritt** *step,* from **treten** *to step*; **der Befehl** *order,* from **befehlen** *to order,* &c. A few are neuter: **das** (sometimes **der**) **Floß** raft, **das Schloß** lock, castle. A few are feminine. See 2. *a* below.

Examples of this class of words with the peculiarities of their formation are mentioned in articles **198–205** under each class of strong verbs, where they should be studied carefully.

b. Most monosyllabics formed from the stem of wk. verbs or the stem of the present tense of strong verbs: **der Tanz** *dance,* from **tanzen** *to dance*; **der Fall,** from **fallen** *to fall,* &c.

c. Nouns having the following suffixes: **-er, -ler, -ner,** denoting agents, as **der Schreiber** clerk, **der Künstler** artist, **der Pförtner** door-keeper, **der Wecker** alarm clock, literally awakener; those in **-el** denoting an instrument, as **der Hebel** crow-bar; those in **-em, -ich, -ig, -ing, -ling, -rich,** as **der Atem** breath, **der Fittich** wing, **der König** king, **der Hering** herring, **der Frühling** Spring, **der Gänserich** gander, &c.

2. Feminines are:

a. Dissyllabics by gradation ending in **-e,** showing in many cases the same vowel as the past tense of the strong verbs from which they are derived: **die Sprache** *language,* from **sprechen** to speak, &c.; (with another vowel than that of the past tense) **die Fliege** *fly,* from **fliegen** *to fly,* &c.

Most monosyllabics by gradation are masculine, but a few are feminine: **Schur** shearing, **Fuhr** (usually in compounds, as **Ausfuhr** exportation). See close of 1. *a.*

b. Nouns having the following suffixes: **-e** (in abstract nouns and names of lifeless objects); many in **-t**; all in **-ei** (accented), **-in, -ung, -heit, -keit, -schaft;** a few in **-ut** and **-at**; a number in **-nis** and **-sal**: **die Größe** greatness, size, **die Stube** room, **die Macht** might, **die Necke'rei** teasing, **die Gräfin** countess, **die Heizung** heating, **die Vermessenheit** audacity, **die Frömmigkeit** piety, **die Landschaft** landscape, **die Armut** poverty, **die Heimat** native place, **die Bangnis** state of fear, **die Bedrängnis** distress, **die Besorgnis** apprehension, **die Betrübnis** sadness, **die Düsternis** darkness, **die Fährnis** (Koser's *König Friedrich der Große*, II, p. 333) danger, **die Kenntnis** knowledge, **die Unkenntnis** ignorance, **die Kümmernis** sorrow, **die Trocknis** (Raabe, Frenssen) dryness, **die Wildnis** wilderness, **die Wirrnis** chaotic condition, **die Trübsal** (see 3. *c* below).

3. Neuters are:

a. Nouns having diminutive suffixes (see **245. I. 8. 1.** *f*), and those in **-icht** denoting a collective idea: **das Kindchen** little child, **Dickicht** thicket, but **der** or **das Kehricht** sweepings.

b. All in **-tum** (except **der Reichtum** wealth, and **der Irrtum** error) and those in **-tel** (from **Teil** part): **das Fürstentum** principality, **das Viertel** fourth.

c. The majority of those in **-nis, -sal, -sel**: **das Gefängnis** prison, **das Schicksal** fate, **das Rätsel** riddle, &c. A goodly number in **-nis** are fem. See 2. *b* above. A few fluctuate between fem. and neut. with a preference in most cases for the former: **die** (formerly also **das**) **Befugnis** authorization, **die** (or **das**) **Beschwernis** trouble, burden, **die** (also **das**) **Bitternis** bitterness, **die** (**das**) **Ersparnis** economy, saving, **Erkenntnis** (see **83**), **die** (**das**) **Säumnis** delay, **die** (**das**) **Verderbnis** corruption, **die** (**das**) **Versäumnis** delay, **das** (**die**) **Wagnis** *bold venture*, &c. Four in **-sal** are usually fem., sometimes neut.: **Drangsal** distress, **Mühsal** drudgery, **Saumsal** slothfulness, **Trübsal** affliction. A few in **-sal** are generally neut., sometimes, especially earlier in the period, masc.: **Rinnsal** channel, **Scheusal** monster, &c.

d. All of the form **Ge—e**, or **Ge-** (without e), except the strong masculines **Gebrauch** use, **Gedanke** thought, **Gedeih** (now obsolete) prosperity, **Gefalle(n)** favor, **Gehalt** (see **83**), **Gehorsam** obedience, **Genuß** enjoyment, **Geruch** odor, **Gesang** song, **Geschmack** taste, **Gestank** stench, **Gewahrsam** (earlier in the period fem., sometimes neut.) custody, **Gewinn** or **Gewinst** gain; the masculines **Gesell(e)** companion and all other masculines of this form (**Ge—e** or **Ge-**) which represent persons; the feminines **Gebärde** gesture, **Gebühr** due, fee, **Geburt** birth, **Geduld** patience, **Gefahr** danger, **Gefährde** fraud, danger, **Gemeinde** community, **Genüge** satisfaction, **Gerechtsame** privilege, **Geschichte** history, **Geschwulst** swelling, **Gestalt** form, **Gewähr** guarantee, **Gewalt** power.

Fluctuation in Gender.

100. The gender of nouns is now much better established in the language than earlier in the period, but it is still unsettled in many words. The following points may be of service:

1. The following substantives have double gender with a preference, perhaps, for the first mentioned form: **das** and **der Abteil** compartment (in a railway car), **der** and **das Al'tar** altar, **die** and in early N.H.G. and classical period **der Angel** fishing-hook, **das** and **der Ar** are, **das** and **der Ar'senik** arsenic, **das** and **der A'tom** atom, **der** and **das Bauer** bird-cage, **der** and **das Begehr** wish, demand, **der** and **das Bereich** domain, **der** and **das Breisgau** (section in Baden), **der** and **das Brūch** swampy land, **das** and **der Bündel** bundle, **der** and **das Büschel** bunch, tuft, **das** and **der** (rare) **Datum** date, **die** and **das Drangsal** trouble, perplexity, **das** and **der Elsaß** Alsace, **der** and **das Episko'pat, Pri'mat,** &c. (see **245.** I. 19), **das** and **der Euter** udder, **der** and **das Ex'trakt** extract, **das** and **der Fi'asko** failure, **das** and **der Filter** filter, **das** and **der Flōß** raft, **die** and **der Geisel** hostage, **das** (with Goethe and Schiller also **der** and still occasionally so; in early N.H.G. **die**) **Gift** poison, **das** and **der Gran** grain (weight), **der** and **das Grat** ridge, **das** and **der Gummi** rubber, **der** and **die Haspel** reel, **das** and **der Hehl** secrecy, **die** and **der Hirse** millet, **das** and **der Ju'wel** jewel, **der** and **das Ka'min** fire-place, **der** and **das Karzer** school prison, **der** and **das Ka'theder** teacher's desk, chair in a university, **der** and **das Kies** gravel, **das** and **der Kino** moving picture theater, **der** and formerly also **die Kleinmut** faintheartedness, **der** and perhaps as frequently **die Klimax** climax, **das** and often **der Knäuel** (ball of yarn, &c.), **das** and often **der Kompro'miß** compromise, **der** and **das Kris'tall** crystal, **das** and perhaps as frequently **der Leck** leak, **das** and **der** (rare) **Lexi'kon** lexicon, **das** and **der Liter** liter, **das** and **der Lob** praise, **der** and **das Lohn** wages, **das** and **der Mete'or** meteor, **das** and **der Meter** meter, always masc. however in **Trimeter, He'xameter,** and **Gaso'meter, das** or **der** (for a boy or a girl), also **die** (for a girl) **Mündel** ward, **das** and **der** (after the analogy of **der Dom**) **Münster** cathedral, **der** and **die Muskel** muscle, **das** and **die Neunauge** lamprey, **das** and **der Nickel** nickel, **der** and formerly also **das Ort** place, **der** and **das Ort** (83) awl, **der** and often **die Otter** otter, **die** and **der Pacht** lease, **das** and **der Pathos** pathos, solemn or often high-sounding, bombastic language, **das** and often **der Pendel** pendulum, **das** and **der Perpen'dikel** plumb-line, pendulum, **der** and **das Pfühl** pillow, **die** and formerly also **der Phalanx** phalanx, **der** and **das Plaid** (ple:t) shawl, **das** and **der Polster** cushion, pillow, **das** and **der Pult** desk, **die** and **der Quader** square dressed

block of stone, **die** and **der Reling** breast-rail, **die** and formerly also **der Reve'renz** bow, curtsy, **das** and **der Rückgrat** back-bone, **der** and formerly also **die Scheitel** crown (of the head), **der** and **die Schneid** snap, courage, **das** and **der** (rare) **Se'mester** semester, **das** and **der Siel** sewer, **der** and **das Spek'takel** noise, racket, **das** and often **der Spittel** old people's home, **das** and **der Tesching** gun of a small bore, **der** and **das Ungestüm** vehemence, **das** and **der Versteck** hiding-place, **die** and formerly also **der Waise** orphan, **die** and **das Wiek** little bay, **der** and **das Ze'ment** cement, **das** and often especially earlier in the period **der Zepter** scepter, **der** and **die Zierat** ornament, **das** and **der Zink** zinc, **das, die, der Zubehör** belongings, **die** and formerly also **der Zwiebel** onion, and others.

a. In dialect many deviations from the literary language occur in the gender of words: **die** (for **der**) **Bach, der** (for **die**) **Butter, das** (for **der**) **Monat,** &c.

2. The following have not only double gender, but also double forms, with perhaps a preference for the first mentioned at least in ordinary language, and in some cases a leaning to the second in elevated diction: **die Backe** and **der** (as a rule earlier in the period) **Backen** cheek, **der Karren** and (especially in N.G.) **die Karre** cart, **der Muff** (**83**) and **die Muffe** muff, **der Nerv** and **die Nerve** nerve, **das** (or **der**) **Niet** or **die Niete** rivet, **die Peri'ode** or formerly also **der Peri'od(e), der Pfirsich** and **die Pfirsiche** peach, **der Pfosten** and **die Pfoste** post, **der Pfriem** or **Pfriemen** and **die Pfrieme** awl, **die Quaste** and **der Quast** tassel, **die Quelle** and in poetic language **der Quell** spring (of water), **die Ritze** and **der Ritz** chink, **die Schläfe** and **der Schlaf** temple (on the forehead), **die Scherbe** and **der** (S.G.) **Scherben** shard, **der Sparren** and **die Sparre** rafter, **die** (and **das**) **Werft** and **die Werfte** dock-yard, **die Zehe** and **der Zeh** toe, and others. The different dialects and sections often diverge here widely.

3. For nouns which have different genders and forms with differentiation of meaning see **83.**

Gender of Foreign Nouns.

101. Foreign nouns retain the gender which they had in the language from which they were borrowed: **der Kerker** from the Latin *carcer*, m.; **das Kloster** from the Latin *claustrum*, n.

a. A number of foreign words, however, have changed their gender in accordance with the rules for German words, influenced in some cases by their meaning and in other cases by their ending: **das Karzer** (Schiller's *Lager*, 7) *school prison* (L. carcer, m.) on account of **das Gefängnis** *prison*, now more commonly **der Karzer**; **der Marmor** *marble* (L. marmor, n.) on account of **der Stein** *stone*; **das Banner** and **Panier** *banner, standard* (from the French bannière, f.) under the influence of **das Feldzeichen** *banner*; names of foreign countries usually neuter after the analogy of German geographical names, as **das alte Europa** (in Latin fem.) *old Europe*; **der Keller** *cellar* (L. cellarium, n.) after the analogy of German words in **-er**; **die Etage** (masc. in French) *story* (of a house) after the analogy of German words in **-e**; **die Kanzel** and **die Bibel,** as they are in fact plurals (the Latin pl. cancelli altaris *the railing of the altar* and the Greek and Latin pl. biblia), which here, as often elsewhere, are used as feminine singulars. Words from the English, which no longer has grammatical gender, take their gender from some resemblance in meaning or form to German words: **das Beefsteak** after the analogy of **das Rindfleisch, der Streik** after the analogy of **der Streich.** As the French has no neut., names of things which in it are masc. often become neut. in German: **das Porträt** from *le portrait*, **das Resultat** from *le résultat*, &c. On the other hand, words which originally in the Latin are neut. have become masc. influenced by the French, which has converted the neut. into the masc.: **der Palast** from Latin *palatium*, n. thru French *palais*, m.

b. In quoting from a foreign language, if it is not possible to avoid placing an article before a foreign word or the first word of a quoted phrase, the gender is commonly conformed to the gender of the corresponding word in German: **Sweet in seiner History (die Geschichte)** of English Sounds, **der Korrespon'dent der „Daily Mail" (die Post).**

Gender of Compound Nouns.

102. Compound nouns have the gender of the last component: **die Haustür** door of the house, **der Hausflur** entrance-hall of a house, **das Haustier** domestic animal.

The exceptions are:

a. A number of words having for their final component **Mut,** namely, **Demut, Langmut, Sanftmut, Anmut, Großmut** (sometimes masc.), **Schwermut, Wehmut,** are fem., while others, as **Freimut, Gleichmut, Hochmut, Jagdmut, Kleinmut** (sometimes fem.), **Mißmut, Übermut, Unmut,** &c., are masc. Here the fem. words have a different origin from the masc. words, being originally abstract nouns derived from adjectives formerly in use and having in M.H.G. the fem. ending **e** and mutating the stem vowel, while the masculines are compounded with the masc. substantive **Mut** and are according to rule masc. At length the final **e** of the fem. nouns entirely disappeared, and dropping mutation under the influence of the masculines they became identical in form with them, but retained the fem. article. However, the meaning of the word has also exercised some influence over the gender of these words, for, after the masc. and fem.

forms had become identical, some masc. became fem., and some fem. became masc., and of words of modern coinage some took on the masc., some the fem. article. At present the feminines, as can be seen from the above complete list, express the milder virtues and qualities, while the masculines denote the more vigorous or violent traits or feelings, or their opposites.

b. **Abscheu** *disgust,* **Vogelscheu** (Goethe's *Egmont,* act 4, Straße; now **die Vogelscheuche)** *scarecrow,* are masc., but other compounds of **Scheu** are fem., as **die Wasserscheu,** &c.

c. **Die Antwort** *answer,* but **Wort** and its compounds are neut. **Antwort** is in fact not a compound of **Wort,** but a derivative from it, and had in M.H.G. a different form: **antwürte** (later changed to **Antwort,** as its form was influenced by that of **Wort**), neut. or fem. In early N.H.G. **Antwort** is still neut., and a few survivals of this usage still occur in the classical period: **ein richtiges antwort** (Prov. xxiv. 26). **Ich glaubte, das sei Antworts genug** (Lessing's *Emilia,* 4, 3). The **s** of **Antwort** may in the sentence from Lessing be also explained according to **94. 9. 1.** *c.*

d. **Teil** is now usually masc., but it is still neut. in accordance with older usage in certain set expressions: **der letzte Teil des Buches, der vierte Teil des Landes** (but in early N.H.G. **das zehende teil der Stad fiel**—Rev. xi. 13). It is still neut. in the meanings *allotted portion, portion* (in certain set expressions), and sometimes *a good deal*: **Sie haben ihr Teil dahin** They have their portion (i.e. reward). **Du hast das beßre Teil erwählt** (Schiller's *Maria,* 5, 6; compare Luke x. 42). **Ein gut Teil Leichtsinn, um ein gut Teil reicher** a good deal richer. Also its compounds are usually masc., except: the contracted and uncontracted form in fractions, as **das Drittel** or **Dritteil** third, &c.; **das** (also **der**) **Abteil** *compartment* (in a railroad car), **das Gegenteil** opposite, **Hinterteil** (perhaps more commonly masc.) *back part,* **Vorderteil** (perhaps more commonly masc.) *forepart,* **Pflichtteil** (more commonly masc.) *that which necessarily falls to a legal heir, whether the testator will or no,* **Erbteil** *inheritance,* **Mutterteil** *inheritance from the mother,* **Vaterteil** *patrimony,* **Altenteil** (perhaps less commonly masc.) reservation made by an old person in making over his estate to an heir. **'Urteil** (n.) is not a compound of **Teil,** but is derived from the corresponding verb **er'teilen** (**ur-** reduced to **er-** by reason of loss of accent), which formerly also had the meaning *to pass sentence* or *judgment* besides its present significations. This old meaning is now expressed by **'urteilen,** which is a derivative of **Urteil.**

e. **Mittwoch** *Wednesday* is masc. after the analogy of the other days of the week.

f. **Heirat** *marriage* is fem. altho **Rat** is masc., since the origin of the word was forgotten and the force of **Rat** was no longer felt. The abstract nature of the present meaning led to its use as a fem.

g. Compounds which are the names of places are neut. even tho the last component is of some other gender, since they follow the general rule for the gender of places: **das schöne Hamburg** *beautiful Hamburg,* but **die Wartburg** (a single castle).

h. A number of compounds, which are in fact each a syntactical fragment of a sentence or a whole sentence written as one word, are neut., or if they represent persons have natural gender without reference to the gender of the last component: **das Vergißmeinnicht** forget-me-not, **der Springinsfeld** romping boy, **der Taugenichts** a good-for-nothing fellow, &c. See **98. 2. C.** *e.*

In other cases where the natural gender is not pronounced, the gender of such a syntactical fragment is sometimes regulated by that of the first word: **die Handvoll** handful, **der Löffelvoll** spoonful, **der Fußbreit** the width of a foot.

INFLECTION OF THE ADJECTIVES.

103. Adjectives may be divided into two general classes—*descriptive* and *limiting* (see **118**) adjectives.

Descriptive Adjectives and Participles.

104. 1. *Inflection.* A descriptive adjective is one that expresses some quality or attribute of the object designated by the noun. Also the two participles usually have descriptive force when used adjectively. Contrary to English usage these adjectives and participles are, except in the predicate, inflected, forming two distinct declensions—the *strong* and the *weak.* The leading points as to their inflection are as follows:—

A. The *strong* declension, which has by far the fuller inflection (see **106**), is employed when the descriptive adjective or participle is not preceded by a limiting adjective, or when there stands before the descriptive adjective or participle a limiting adjective which has no ending to show gender and case: N. **guter Wein; mein kleiner Bruder; ein schlafendes Kind; zwei kleine Brüder.** Hence the strong adjective not only modifies the meaning of its noun, but it also marks its case and gender in the absence of the article or some other limiting adjective that has full endings to show case and gender.

a. A descriptive adjective which is not preceded by an article and follows **von** in a phrase that stands as an appositive to a preceding noun often agrees in case with the article of the preceding noun and is also regulated in its inflection by it, and hence is strong if the article has no form to show gender and case: **so ein Esel von alter** (or better **altem**) **Freund!** Compare B. *c* below and also **109.** *c.*

B. The **weak** declension, which has only two endings, **e** for the nom. sing. of all genders and for the acc. sing. of the fem. and neut., and **en** for all other cases of the different genders, sing. and pl., is employed when there stands before the descriptive adjective or participle some limiting adjective such as the def. article or other limiting adjective with strong inflection which can show the case and gender: N. **der gute Knabe,** G. **des guten Knaben;** N. **der erquickende Schlummer.**

a. Sometimes the limiting adjective is understood, having already been previously used in the same sentence, in which case the descriptive adjective or participle is weak: **der Erbfeind unseres Reiches und heiligen Glaubens.**

Sometimes in colloquial language the article is omitted even where there has been no previous use of one: Lotte: **Ich denk' mir das gar nicht so schön, aus dem großen Leben wieder zurück in die Einsamkeit.** Döring: **Im Gegenteil! Einzig Richtige** (Halbe's *Die Heimatlosen*, p. 37).

b. Earlier in the period the strong forms are often found after str. limiting adjectives in accordance with an older usage: **unsre eigne Weiber** (Lessing), **diese einzelne Stücke** (id.).

c. A descriptive adjective which is not preceded by an article and follows **von** in a phrase that stands as an appositive to a preceding noun often agrees in cases with the article of the preceding noun and is also regulated in its inflection by it, and hence is weak if the article has a form which shows the gender and case: **durch eine Versäumnis von zwei Monaten, die ich einem Esel von alten** (or better **altem**) **Freund danke** (Schwind an Mörike).

C. If the descriptive adjective is preceded by two limiting adjectives with different inflection, its declension is controlled by that of the second limiting adjective: **Dieser mein guter Freund.**

D. Two or more descriptive adjectives which modify the same noun take the same inflection: **guter alter Wein; ein guter alter Mann; dieser gute alte Mann.**

2. *Non-inflection.* Descriptive adjectives and participles were in older German much more widely used without distinctive case endings than to-day, as explained in E. *a* below. At present they are not declined in the following cases:

A. In the *predicate* in the positive and comparative, but they are inflected here in the superlative (see **112. 1**). In the predicate relation the adjective or participle is used:

a. As the *predicate complement* of intransitives of incomplete predication (as **sein** to be, **bleiben** to remain, **scheinen** to seem, **werden** to become, &c.; see **252.** 2. B. *a*) or of passive verbs: **Er ist alt. Das Wetter scheint besser. Er ist der älteste. Er wird glücklich genannt.** Here also belongs the past participle in the compound tenses of such intrans. verbs as are conjugated with **sein: Er ist gekommen.**

b. As *predicate appositive* (see **252. 1.** *c*): **Sie kamen glücklich an. Sie saß weinend am Bette ihrer Mutter. Der Wind bläst kalt.**

c. As *objective predicate*, i.e. when the adjective or participle predicates a quality or state of the object. This predication is not represented as absolute, but as limited and modified by the idea contained in the verb: **Er glaubt sich krank** (= **Er ist, nach seiner Meinung, krank**). **Sie weinte sich krank** (= **Sie wurde durch Weinen krank**). **Wir fanden ihn sehr leidend** (= **Er litt sehr, gemäß unsrer Wahrnehmung**). **Ich betrachte dies als überflüssig** (= **Meiner Meinung nach ist dies überflüssig**). **Ich halte die Sache für abgemacht. Ich sehe dich gegürtet und gerüstet** (= **Du bist, wie ich sehe, gegürtet und gerüstet**). But in the superlative: **Man preist diesen Mann den glücklichsten. Ich fühle mich heute am schwächsten.**

Here also belongs the past participle in the compound tenses of transitive verbs: **Er hat den Brief geschrieben.**

The copula **sein,** which in case of predicate adjectives and participles usually formally announces the predication, is here in accordance with older usage still not expressed, as explained in **252. 1.** *b. Note* and **262.** III. **2.** B.

Note. The objective predicate often indicates the result of the action of the verb upon its object, and hence is in this use by some called the *factitive predicate*: **Er schlug ihn tot.**

B. After the noun which it modifies, but only in the positive and comparative, never in the superlative:

a. Instead of standing attributively before a noun, an adjective or participle often follows it in the relation of an appositive. A single adjective or participle rarely stands after the noun, as **Röslein rot,** except in poetry, but it *usually* takes this position when it is itself modified by an elliptical clause or by a phrase which is limited by a clause, also sometimes if it is merely modified by another word or words, or if there are several adjectives or participles separated from each other by commas or by **und: eine Rose rot wie Blut [ist], ein Mann älter als ich [bin]. Ein panischer Schreck, vermehrt durch das falsche Gerücht, daß vor den Toren sich Cäsars Reiter gezeigt hätten, kam über die vornehme Welt. Und küßte sie an** (now usually **auf**) **den Mund so bleich** (Uhland). **Eine Stange drei Meter hoch. Endlich erscheint ein weibliches Ding, flüchtig, unbedachtsam, wild, witzig bis zur Unverschämtheit, lustig bis zum Tollen. Der Himmel nah und fern, er ist so klar und feierlich. Ein Edelknecht sanft und keck.**

But in the superlative: **Dieser Mann, der älteste unter allen.**

The adjectives in **111. 7.** *c* can only in this position be used attributively.

Note 1. With the exception of the cases mentioned above which usually require the adjective or participle to stand after the noun, this position of an adjective and participle is peculiarly adapted to poetic style, and in prose is often replaced by the usual attributive position before the noun, an arrangement of words which often is markedly different from the English, as is nicely illustrated by the following sentence: [In her revery which carried her back to her youthful days] **Sie sah sich heranwachsen im Hause ihres Vaters, des alten, reichen Kaufherrn, ein von Luxus umgebenes, durch Schmeicheleien verwöhntes und doch inmitten alles Reichtums ein armes, weil von keiner Mutter behütetes Mädchen** (Helene Stökl's *Am heiligen Abend*).

Note 2. The non-inflection of these adjective or participial appositives is readily explained by the fact that they are not real attributive adjectives, but stand in elliptical clauses of which they are felt as predicate: **Sie hat einen Nacken [,der] weißer [ist,] als Schnee.**

Note 3. For exceptions to the rule that the adjective is here uninflected see **111. 9.**

Note 4. If the adjective or participial appositive have an article, which is especially the case in poetic style, where for emphasis an epithet instead of preceding follows the noun, it is always inflected: **Auf dem Teich, dem regungslosen, weilt des Mondes holder Glanz.** Also in prose in case of titles: **Friedrich der Große, Karl der Fünfte.**

Note 5. In M.H.G. the postpositive adjective could be inflected, and this older usage survives in rare instances in poetry: **Ich habe einen solchen Baum jüngst gesehen, gebogenen über eines Baches Saum und schwankenden in Frühlingslüfte Wehen** (Rückert). A little more common is the inflection here of **selig** *deceased*: **Mein Mann seliger war bei Jahren und nicht leicht zu rühren** (Goethe). The nom. masc. form **seliger** has become a mere fossil, as it is also used in the oblique cases: **Ich habe die Sache von meinem Vater seliger ererbt** (Immermann). Non-inflection here, however, is the rule: **mein Vater selig** (or still more commonly **mein seliger Vater**).

b. In case of those nouns (see **96.** 4. (**1**)) which remain uninflected when used in a collective sense to express weight, measure, extent, the modifying qualifying adjective follows the noun, and hence is not inflected: **fünf Pfund flämisch, zehn Fuß rheinisch.**

C. Uninflected adjectives or participles often stand in the relation of a predicate appositive to a following or preceding noun or pronoun, when the adjective or participle represents a subordinate adverbial clause of which it would be the predicate complement or verbal predicate: [weil sie] **Froh** [war], **ganz allein und jeder lästigen Beobachtung entrückt zu sein, hatte sie sich in die Ecke zurückgelehnt und die Augen geschlossen. Dies hörend** (= **als er dies hörte**), **brach er in Tränen aus. Er grüßte, sich tief verbeugend** (= **indem er sich tief verbeugte**). **Allzustraff gespannt** (= **wenn er allzustraff gespannt wird**), **zerspringt der Bogen.** Often introduced by **als: Mein Freund hat als enterbt** (= **da er enterbt worden ist**) **keine Mittel mehr.** The appositional construction here is much older than the fuller clause forms which are given in parentheses. See **268.** 4.

Note. The adjective or participle usually refers to the subject of the sentence, as in the above examples, but it is also used as objective predicate: **Der Arzt hat den Kranken als geheilt** (=**da er geheilt war**) **entlassen. Dieses Gericht ißt man warm** (=**während es warm ist**). This construction may become ambiguous: **Ich verließ ihn, sein Unglück beklagend.** Here **beklagend** may refer to **ich** or **ihn.** The participial construction should be avoided here, but of course is unobjectionable where no ambiguity is liable to arise: **Ich fand ihn seine Bücher ordnend.**

D. In the absolute construction, where the participle or adjective is not in apposition with any word in the main clause, non-inflection is the uniform rule. This absolute construction is treated at length in **265.** B. By comparing **265.** B. *a*, *b*. (**1**) it will become evident that the participle here was originally a predicate appositive and hence this construction once belonged to C.

E. Sometimes non-inflection of adjectives and participles occurs in the attributive relation, in poetry, dialect, familiar language, and in many set expressions that have come down to us from an earlier period when non-inflection here was more common. In all of these cases, however, non-inflection is now usually limited to the nom. and acc. neut. sing. in the strong declension: **Ein unnütz Leben ist ein früher Tod** (Goethe's *Iphigenie*, I. 115). **Kein größer Glück als ein vertrauend Herz** (Dahn's *Jugendgedichte*, 190). **Lieb Weib, lieb Kind, auf gut Glück** at random, **auf baldig Wiedersehen** I hope to see you again soon. Especially frequent in old maxims: **Bar Geld kauft wohlfeil.** The uninflected attributive form occurs only rarely elsewhere: **Das Alter ist ein höflich Mann** (Goethe). **Lieb Knabe** (Schiller's *Tell*, 1, 1), **der gleißend Wolf** (Uhland). **Sinnend sprach zu ihm jung Werner** (Scheffel's *Trompeter*, Sechstes Stück). **Lieder jung Werners** (ib., p. 212). **Und ich weiß ein ander Lied von | einem jung jung Zimmergesellen** (ib., Zweites Stück).

a. History of the Uninflected Form. Luther was much freer in the use of uninflected forms than even elevated discourse allows to-day. He often dropped the strong masc. nom. sing. ending and also final **e** both in the strong and weak declensions in any gender, case, or number: **manch frum** (= **frommer**) **priester, ein zornig man, weltlich gewalt, die weltlich gewalt, etlich gotlich vnd Christlich artickel.** This older usage survives in compounds: **Edelmann, Großstadt,** &c.

A historical view of the case is at this point helpful. The so-called uninflected form is here in a number of cases the natural historic form. The adjective followed in earlier periods the inflection of nouns, as can also be seen in Latin. In course of time the endings of the nouns became much weather-beaten, so that they seem to-day endingless in the nom. and acc. sing. of masculines and neuters, and in case of neuters (see **69. 5.** *Historical Note*) also in the plural: **der, den Tag, das Wort, zehn Pfund.** The adjective should here also be endingless, and the uninflected forms we find in Luther's writings are in part the correct historic forms. Even in Gothic, however, the oldest Germanic language, we often find in descriptive adjectives instead of their old endingless case forms the distinctive case endings of the demonstrative adjective **der,** an evident indication of the desire to mark gender and case more clearly, and these new endings and those borrowed still later from the same source have in large measure displaced the correct historic endingless forms. On the other hand, in the predicate relation, where adjective and noun have exactly the same grammatical function, namely that of predication, the old endingless form has supplanted the inflected forms in the positive and comparative, so that here noun and adjective have, as originally, the same form, now however only in the singular, as in the plural nouns still have a plural form as it is essential to the thought, while adjectives have here the same form as in the singular, since the idea of number is not now felt as essential in the predication of a quality. In certain pronominal adjectives we still find both old and new forms, but with differentiated function: **mein Buch,** but **sein Buch und meines.**

105. *General Rules.* The fem. and neut. have each their respective acc. sing. like the nom., the nom. and acc. of all genders are alike in the pl., also the gen. and dat. sing. of the fem. are always identical.

106. Strong declension of **gut** *good.*

	Singular			Plural.
	Masc.	Fem.	Neut.	Common form for all genders.
N.	**guter**	**gute**	**gutes**	**gute**
G.	**guten(es)**[1]	**guter**	**guten(es)**[1]	**guter**
D.	**gutem**	**guter**	**gutem**	**guten**
A.	**guten**	**gute**	**gutes**	**gute**

Note 1. The strong descriptive adjective is now really weak in the gen. of the masc. and neut. sing., as the old strong form **-es** is usually replaced here by the weak **-en** except in a few set expressions, as **reines Herzens** *of a pure heart,* &c., which have come down to us from earlier periods unchanged. The weak form began to appear in the fifteenth century and became common in the seventeenth and eighteenth centuries. J. Grimm and other grammarians have sought to bring the strong gen. into favor again, and a few recent authors as von Sybel have followed their example, but in general the weak form is very firm in present usage. *Limiting* adjectives (the numeral **ein,** the articles, and pronominal adjectives), however, still retain as a rule strong inflection in the gen.: **dieses Buches, welches Buches.** But the new weak gen. is now also often found in limiting adjectives, especially in adverbial expressions: **allenfalls** and **jedenfalls** *in any event,* **keinesfalls** or **keinenfalls, jedenorts** everywhere, &c. Also occasionally and perhaps with growing frequency elsewhere: **Wimmelte es doch . . . von Kindern . . . jeden Alters!** (Spielhagen's *Was will das werden?*, I, chap. iv). **Die vier Werke, die er so selbst als einen Geistes empfand** (Otto Brahm in *Die neue Rundschau*, Dec. 1906, p. 1433).

Note 2. In early N.H.G. the strong ending **es** (masc. and neut. gen., and neut. nom. and acc.) was often in both descriptive and limiting adjectives contracted to **s**: **Vnd er thet Abram guts vmb jren willen** (Gen. xii. 16). This contraction is still found in Goethe's time, and even up to the present day in poetry and dialect: **Um Guts zu tun, braucht's keiner Überlegung** (Goethe's *Iphigenie*, l. 1989). **Hast du kein freundlichs Wort, du Gute** (Grillparzer's *Die Argonauten*, Act 2). **Schöns Schätzle, vergiß du nit mein** (Auerbach). In general this contraction is now rare in descriptive adjectives except in a few set expressions, such as **was Rechts** (also **Rechtes**) *something fine,* **und so was Guts** (Hauptmann's *Michael Kramer*, Act 1) *and such good things.* However, in the neut. nom. and acc. sing. substantive forms **eins** (see **121.** 1. D) and **keins** (as in **keins von beiden** *neither one*) this contraction is still quite common even in literary German. In colloquial language it is also common in the neut. nom. and acc. sing. substantive possessive forms **meins, deins,** &c., and also in the substantive demonstrative **jens**: **Ein fremdes Kind ist sehr nett so**

[1] For full explanation of this form, see *Note* 1.

von weitem, aber wenn man es als seins betrachten soll . . . (Ompteda's *Cäcilie von Sarryn*, chap. xx). **Man lernt ja von manchem so das und jen's** (Hauptmann's *Michael Kramer*, Act 1).

Note 3. The strong ending **-em**, masc. and neut. dat. sing., is in different periods sometimes replaced in careless language by the more convenient **-en**, which gives the word the appearance of a weak form. Weinhold, in his *Mittelhochdeutsche Grammatik*, p. 560, gives examples for M.H.G. In early N.H.G. this seemingly weak form is quite frequent: **von den Romischen reuber** (Luther), **von einen Bischoff** (Luther), **vor anbrechenden Morgen** (*Fausibuch des Christlich-Meynenden*, 1725). It occurs occasionally in the classical period and still later: **von weiten** (Lessing), **daß ich mich kaum vor jemanden sehen lassen konnte** (Lessing), **welche Sprache niemanden von der Familie fremd war** (Goethe). **Sie traueten niemanden mehr, nicht dem Nachbar, nicht dem Verwandten, ja kaum noch dem Herrgott** (Raabe's *Else von der Tanne*). **Sie möchte von niemanden abhängen** (Wilhelm Fischer's *Die Freude am Licht*, II, p. 42). **Was er sonst niemanden sagte usw.** (Anna Schieber's *Alle guten Geister*, p. 235, and also frequently elsewhere). It is most common in **jemanden, niemanden,** but even here it is not so common as the strong form. Elsewhere it now rarely occurs in the literary language, but is often found in popular speech: **Sie elender, undankbarer Mensch, ist das der Lohn, daß wir Ihnen in unsern Haus ein Jahr und sechs Monat' Geld hab'n verdienen lassen?** (Anzengruber's *Das vierte Gebot*, 1, 8).

Note 4. In Low German, where the nom. and acc. neut. sing. was in earlier periods without an ending we now often find under the influence of the literary language the ending **-et**, the Low German form corresponding to High German **-es: Een janzet, schönet, richtiget Tannenbäumken!** (= **Bäumchen**) (Friebe in G. Hauptmann's *Friedensfest*, 1).

107. Weak declension of **gut**:

	Singular			Plural for all genders.
	Masc.	Fem.	Neut.	
N.	**der gute**	**die gute**	**das gute**	**die** } **guten**
G.	**des guten**	**der guten**	**des guten**	**der** } **guten**
D.	**dem guten**	**der guten**	**dem guten**	**den** } **guten**
A.	**den guten**	**die gute**	**das gute**	**die** } **guten**

For the origin of this declension see **111.** 10. *Note.*

Note. In early N.H.G. the acc. fem. sing. sometimes ended in **en** instead of **e**, thus occasionally preserving here the M.H.G. form: **vber die gantzen** (instead of **gantze**) **Erde** (Gen. I. 26).

108. *Mixed Declension.* It must be especially noted that after **ein** and the other limiting adjectives inflected like it, i.e. **kein** and the possessives (see **58.** A and B), the descriptive adjective is strong in the sing., in the nom. of the masc. and the nom. and acc. of the neut. because the preceding limiting adjective is here deficient in endings to show gender and case. Elsewhere in the singular and thruout the plural the descriptive adjective is weak because the preceding limiting adjective has here distinctive endings.

	mein guter Freund, *my good friend*	**meine gute Schwester,** *my good sister*	**mein gutes Buch,** *my good book*
		Singular.	
N.	**mein guter Freund**	**meine gute Schwester**	**mein gutes Buch**
G.	**meines guten Freundes**	**meiner guten Schwester**	**meines guten Buch(e)s**
D.	**meinem guten Freund(e)**	**meiner guten Schwester**	**meinem guten Buch(e)**
A.	**meinen guten Freund**	**meine gute Schwester**	**mein gutes Buch**
		Plural.	
N.	**meine guten Freunde**	**meine guten Schwestern**	**meine guten Bücher**
G.	**meiner guten Freunde**	**meiner guten Schwestern**	**meiner guten Bücher**
D.	**meinen guten Freunden**	**meinen guten Schwestern**	**meinen guten Büchern**
A.	**meine guten Freunde**	**meine guten Schwestern**	**meine guten Bücher**

a. In earlier periods the weak form of the adjective was also used here in the nom. sing. As a last survival of this older usage the weak form was earlier in the present period occasionally employed after the nom. **unser: unser nicht genug zu preisende Kapellmeister** (Goethe); **unser alte Vater** (Novalis, 4, 119).

109. *Adjective-substantives.* Nouns made from adjectives or participles (see *b*) are declined as adjectives, but are written with a capital:—

	the rich man	*a rich man*	*the rich*	*rich people*	*that which is good*
N.	**der Reiche**	**ein Reicher**	**die Reichen**	**Reiche**	**das Gute**
G.	**des Reichen**	**eines Reichen**	**der Reichen**	**Reicher**	**des Guten**
D.	**dem Reichen**	**einem Reichen**	**den Reichen**	**Reichen**	**dem Guten**
A.	**den Reichen**	**einen Reichen**	**die Reichen**	**Reiche**	**das Gute**

a. (1) The gender of adjective-substantives which do not represent living beings can often be explained by supplying some word understood: **die Linke,** short for **die linke Hand** *the left hand*; **der Bittere** for **der bittere Schnaps** *bitters*; **Gegenwärtiges** (referring to **das Schreiben** *letter*) **bezweckt Herrn E., Sohn eines unserer hiesigen Freunde, Ihnen bestens zu empfehlen.**

Zieh Dir rasch Dein Meergrünes (referring to **das Kleid**) **an.** The neut. form is used for the young of animals and for children (see **98.** 1. *c*): **ihr Junges** her (i.e. the cow's) calf, **ein ganz Kleines** a baby.

(**2**) The neut. adjective-substantive preceded by the definite article has a comprehensive, generalizing force: **das Schöne** the beautiful, all that is beautiful. The form without the article contains a collective idea: **Schönes** beautiful things. **Kleinstes wird an dem getadelt, der in Menge Größtes adelt** (Rückert) People censure very little things in him who puts nobility into many very great things. **Für Fräulein Dora war natürlich mehreres dabei** Among them were of course several things for Miss Dora.

The neuter adjective-substantive often has a meaning that cannot be embodied in one English word: **sein Äußeres** his exterior appearance; **ihr Innerstes** her inmost feelings. **Lange, lange tönte es nach in dem metallenen Reifen, als habe die Glocke nun aus Eigenem noch zu sprechen** For a long time, after the ringing of the bell ceased, it kept on resounding as if it had now something to say of its own initiative. **Morgen ein mehreres** I will write something additional tomorrow. **Er hat von einer Base ein weniges geerbt** He inherited a little property from a female relative. **Er tut nie ein übriges** He never does more than he must do.

b. Participles when used as substantives still retain their former verbal nature, and hence retain their adverbial modifiers and take direct objects: **etwas längst Bekanntes** something that has been known for a long while, **ein Medizin Studierender** a student of medicine (lit. one studying medicine). See **111.** 7. *d*.

c. The unmodified adjective-substantive following **von** in a phrase that stands as an appositive to a preceding noun is regulated in its inflection by the article of the preceding noun, and also agrees with it in case: **Der Schlingel von Bediente** the rogue of a servant, **ein alter Schelm von Lohnbedienter.** If the adjective-substantive is modified by an article, it is uniformly in the dat. instead of agreeing in case with the preceding noun: **der Hund von einem alten Bedienten.** Compare **104.** 1. A. *a* and B. *c*, also **94.** 2.

d. The inflection of adjective-substantives was originally weak. See **111.** 10. *Note.* There is one group of neuters, however, which were originally strong and are still inflected strong or are uninflected. See **111.** 7. *h*.

e. An adjective-substantive is inflected weak if it is preceded by a title or a noun denoting quantity which is modified by a strong limiting adjective: **Meine Herren Geschworenen!** (Ponten's *Jungfräulichkeit,* p. 396), **das Volk der 70 Millionen Deutschen** (Engel's *Ein Tagebuch,* I, p. xi).

110. Adjectives having a suffix sometimes vary from the regular inflection:

A. In colloquial speech the **e** of the unaccented suffixes **-el, -en, -er** often drops out before an **e** of the following case ending, or still often in accordance with older usage the **e** of the case ending **-en** and **-em** drops out after **-el** or **-er,** but in the literary language there is a tendency to prefer—except immediately after a diphthong— the full form, almost always so in case of adjectives in **-en** and **-er: der edle Mann, des edlen** or **edeln Manns, aus edlem** or **edelm Hause; die offne Tür, ein heitres Gesicht, eines heitren** or **heitern Gesichtes, mit heitrem** or **heiterm Sinne;** (in the literary language) **teurer** (sometimes **teuerer) Freund,** but often **der edele Mann, aus edelem Hause, mit heiterem Sinn** and usually **die offene Tür, ein heiteres Gesicht.** As the inflected forms of the comparative of such adjectives are so clumsy there is a natural tendency to replace these words by more euphonious ones wherever possible: **mit herberem** (rather than **bittererem, bittrerem,** or **bittererm) Schmerze.**

a. Nouns made from adjectives (see **111.** 10) with these suffixes do not follow this rule of contraction, but that in vogue for nouns (see **62.** C), and until recently also for adjectives (see *b*): **Das Übel** evil, **des Übels,** dat. pl. **den Übeln.** See *c*.

b. Goethe and also earlier writers usually contract the adjectives in **-el** and **-er** in harmony with verbs (**178.** 1. B. *a* and *c*) having the same suffix, as **edle, edler, edles, edelm, des (dem, den,** &c.) **edeln,** &c., thus dropping the **e** of the suffix before the case endings **-e, -er, -es,** but before other case endings the **e** of the case ending itself. This usage is still not infrequently found, but in general the new and natural trend of colloquial usage is to make the declension uniform and after the analogy of the nom. to inflect: **der edle, des, dem, den edlen,** &c. The noun and the adverb, however, are true to the older rule (see **62.** C), which requires the dropping of **e** after **-el, -en, -er,** and thus the new tendency of the adjective to retain the **e** of the case ending after these suffixes has isolated a few nouns and adverbs which are derived from such adjectives, so that their origin is not always felt: **der Jünger (des Jüngers,** dat. pl. **den Jüngern)** disciple, lit. *the younger* in contradistinction to the master (**Herr**), but **der jüngere** (dat. pl. **den jüngeren) Bruder** (dat. pl. **Brüdern)** the younger brother; thus also **die Eltern** parents, lit. older ones, but **die älteren Brüder** *the older brothers,* **das Dunkel (des Dunkels)** *darkness,* but **das dunk(e)le Zimmer** *the dark room,* gen. **des dunk(e)len Zimmers;** also **anders** (adv.) *otherwise,* but the adj. nom. neut. form **anderes; besonders** (adv.) *especially,* but the adj. nom. neut. form **besonderes.** See *c*.

c. Originally there was in most cases no vowel before the **l, n, r** in adjective and substantive suffixes. A vowel developed here in a later period which has ever since remained firm in nouns

However, in adjectives containing a diphthongal stem the vowel did not fully develop when a vowel followed in the next syllable, and we still say: **der teure** (or sometimes **teuere**). In other adjectives the **e** developed in the suffix and has remained up to our time, as described in A and *b.*

In M.H.G. the **e** of the inflectional endings was suppressed after the suffixes **-el, -en, er.** This older usage is still observed in nouns (see **62.** C), and survives also in verbs before **n** (see **178.** 1 . B. *a*) and often in adjectives before **n** and **m** (see A above). Present usage is not favorable to the mutilation of adjective inflectional endings. Thus the fluctuation described in the above articles represents the struggle of modern usage with older laws.

B. Adjectives ending in **-ig** often in N.G. colloquial speech lose in pronunciation and sometimes in print the **i** of the suffix before the case ending **es,** while in S.G. the **e** of the case ending **-es** is still sometimes suppressed: **mut**(**i**)**ges** (mu:tǐəs) **Roß** (N.G.); **mutigs Roß** (S.G.). South German here preserves older usage. See **106.** *Note* 2.

Peculiarities in the Declension of Descriptive Adjectives.

111. 1. Adjectives in the vocative (case of direct address) do not suffer an article before them, and hence are usually strong: **lieber Freund, liebe Freunde.** Not infrequently weak forms still occur in the plural, the survivals of a once common construction (see 10. *Note* below): **Guten Tag, jungen Leute!** (M. Dreyer's *Der Probekandidat,* p. 25). **Geht, lieben Leute** (Keyserling in *Der dumme Hans,* Aufzug 2).

a. In beginning letters an exclamation point is placed after the vocative: **Liebe Schwester! Liebster Bruder!**

2. Descriptive adjectives in the nom. and acc. pl. following the indefinite pronominal adjectives and indefinite numerals **ähnliche** similar, **andere** other, **beide** both, **einige** some, **einzelne** single, **etliche** some, **gewisse** certain, **manche** many, **mehrere** several, **sämtliche** all, whole, complete, **solche** such, **sonstige** other, the remaining, **verschiedene** different, **viele** many, **irgendwelche** any at all, **wenige** few, &c., are strong or weak but are, except after **beide, sämtliche, solche,** more commonly declined strong, altho the preceding limiting adjective is strong and shows the case: **beide gleiche Hälften** (Fontane), **einige gute Bücher, manche unbetonte Wörtchen** (Wilmanns's *Deutsche Grammatik,* I, p. 388), **sämtliche preußische Bataillone** (Koser's *König Friedrich der Große,* p. 145), **solche eindeutige Assoziationen** (Wundt's *Völkerpsychologie,* II, p. 81), **solche jüngere Bauten** (R. Zahn in *Velhagen und Klasings Monatshefte,* Nov. 1905, p. 296), **irgendwelche kulturkämpferische Allüren** (*Hamburger Nachrichten,* Jan. 20, 1907). Also in the gen. pl. the adjective is, perhaps, more commonly inflected strong but differing from the usage in the nom. and acc. the weak form is also quite common: **einiger guter** (or often also **guten**) **Bücher, der Optimismus gewisser deutscher Politiker** (*Hamb. Nachr.,* Nov. 11, 1905), **mit Ausnahme weniger unbedeutender Schiffe** (ib., May 31, 1905); **die berufsmäßigen Ausüber dieser und ähnlicher mimischen Künste** (Vogt and Koch's *Geschichte der deutschen Literatur,* 1st ed., p. 247), **sich einzelner vorgeschobenen Posten zu bemächtigen** (*Hamb. Nach.,* Nov. 28, 1904), **trotz mancher unvermeidlichen** (strong nom. form employed above by the same author) **Mängel** (Wilmanns's *D. G.,* I, p. viii), **die Deutung solcher kretischen** (strong nom. employed above by the same author) **Funde** (R. Zahn in *V. & K. M.,* Nov. 1905, p. 309). Weak forms occur sometimes also in the nom. and acc. pl. after some of these indefinites, rarely however after **einige, viele, wenige, andere: gewisse in der Sprache eine wichtige Rolle spielenden semantischen Gegensätze** (Brugmann's *Kurze vergleichende Grammatik,* p. 315), **über so manche seltsamen Begebenheiten** (G. von der Gabelentz's *Der Mönch,* IV), **auf irgendwelche englischen Zusicherungen hin** (*Hamb. Nachr.,* Oct. 24, 1905). In the singular, adjectives after most of these words are almost uniformly weak: **einiges frische Obst,** but occasionally strong, as in **solcher adnominaler Gebrauch** (Brugmann's *K. v. G.,* p. 434). **Darin ist einiges Wahres enthalten** (G. Hauptmann). Some of these words as **ähnlich, gewiß, sonstig, verschieden,** have not become so firmly established here as the others, and hence the strong inflection of the following descriptive adjective is often found after them, perhaps more commonly so: **längst widerlegte Legenden, Entstellungen und sonstiges krauses Zeug** (*Hamb. Nachr.,* Jan. 19, 1907). Earlier in the period the strong form of the adjective is not infrequent after **all-** or **kein-** either in the sing. or the pl., and survivals of this older usage still occur occasionally: **alles Gutes** (Lessing), **alle rechtschaffene Christen** (id.), **trotz aller angewandter Mühe** (Raabe's *Die Leute aus dem Walde,* II, chap. x), &c. **Solche, sämtliche** and **beide** seem to be about to follow the example of **alle** and **keine,** as they often require the weak inflection of the following adjective: **solche stillen Abende** (Fontane's *Schach von Wuthenow,* chap. iv), **solche lautlichen Elemente** (Brugmann's *K. v. G.,* p. 289), **Vertreter der Studentenschaft sämtlicher deutschen Hochschulen Österreichs** (*H. N.,* Nov. 5, 1904), **sämtliche englischen Schiffe** (ib., Nov. 15, 1904), **beide deutschen Mächte** (Lamprecht's *Deutsche Geschichte,* 7. 2., p. 731).

The weak form has become established after **alle** and **keine** because they possess more pronouncedly the character of a limiting adjective than the other words. The other words, like descriptive adjectives, often have a limiting adjective before them and hence are often felt as descriptive adjectives. As descriptive adjectives they do not influence the inflection of the adjective that follows them. In *meaning,* however, they resemble limiting adjectives. This doubleness of nature is confusing German feeling. While in most cases they are usually felt as descriptive adjectives, **solche, sämtliche,** and **beide** are gradually becoming established as limiting adjectives, as **sämtliche** and **beide** are closely related in thought to **alle** and **solche** to the demonstrative **diese.**

a. In the gen. pl. after **zweier** and **dreier** there is fluctuation: **das Zusammentreffen zweier gleicher** (or less frequently **gleichen) Konsonanten.**

3. If several adjectives limiting the same noun are co-ordinate they have the same declension: **frisches, klares Wasser.** But if the second or second and third adjective stand closer in meaning to the noun, forming with it *one* idea, the first adjective is inflected strong and the following adjectives may be inflected weak, to show that they do not stand in the same relation to the noun: **folgendes eigene Erlebnis.** The rule of showing subordination in the adjective by placing it in the wk. declension is new and not yet firmly established, and is as yet restricted to the following cases:

a. The following adjectives, which resemble in their nature limiting adjectives, may after the manner of limiting adjectives require a wk. adjective after them, but usually only in the sing. and much less commonly in the pl., tho the trend is in that direction: **beifolgend** or **beiliegend** enclosed, accompanying, **benannt** aforenamed, **besagt, erwähnt, vorerwähnt** aforementioned, **bewußt** the (point, matter, &c.) in question, **derartig** of this kind, **erster-** the former, **folgend** following, **gedacht, mehr gedacht** mentioned, several times mentioned, **letzter-** the latter, **nachstehend** following, **vorstehend** or **vorausgehend** preceding, **obig** abovementioned, &c., all of which, contrary to English idiom, may have no article before them: **folgender kleine Roman, bei der Besprechung von Harnacks erwähntem großen Werk, folgende wichtige** (or perhaps less commonly **wichtigen) Gründe, folgende eingehenderen Mitteilungen** *Hamburger Nachrichten*, Oct. 13, 1904), **folgende beiden Zahlen** (Otto Hötzsch in *Deutsche Monatsschrift*, Feb. 1906, p. 640). **Wir wissen bereits durch das Töchterlein, daß der Rat Nebelung nicht rauchte, sondern nur schnupfte, und letzteres harmlose Vergnügen hatten die Götter gleich benutzt,** &c. (Raabe's *Eulenpfingsten*, chap. iii). **Aus vorstehender kurzen Skizze** (A. Schröer in *Englische Studien*, 1907, vol. 38, p. 69), **bei vorausgehendem langen Vokal** (P. Lessiak in *Zeitschrift für deutsche Mundarten*, 1909, p. 4). The sing. form is sometimes strong: **bewußtes einziges Erbtöchterlein** (Voss's *Psyche*, IV), **folgender origineller Bericht** (*Hamb. Nachr.*, Dec. 14, 1904), **folgender treuer Auszug** (*Neue Zürcher Zeit.*, Jan. 7, 1914).

b. Also in the dat. sing. and less often in the fem. gen. sing. and the gen. pl. after any strong descriptive adjective a second descriptive adjective in the same way, to show subordination, *may* be weak: **in langem grauen Mantel; ein Mann von großem juristischen Wissen; mit vollendetem fünfzehnten Lebensjahre; zu nächster großen Messe; wegen eingetretener schlechten Beschaffenheit der Straße** (*Deutsche Rundschau*); **reiner französischen Weine; in Ermangelung neuer tatsächlichen Nachrichten** (*Hamb. Nachr.*, June 6, 1904): **das Zuströmen von neuem sprachlichen Material** (Dr. Sigmund Feist in *Zeitschrift für den deutschen Unterricht*, Jahrg. 28, p. 162) &c. The second adjective is often wk. simply from an aversion to the recurrence of the heavy endings **em** and **er**: **mit bleichem, verzerrten Gesicht** (Spielhagen). This usage is also found in older periods: mit reiner süeȥen hohen art (*Parzival*, 164. 15). It is probable that the aversion to the repetition of such endings as **em** and **er** first gave rise to the wk. forms here, and later the mind perceived that there also often existed here a difference in the relation of the different adjectives to the noun, and then for logical reasons began to distinguish regularly between them by their endings. There is at present considerable fluctuation of usage here, some authors preferring the weak form, others the strong, but there is in choice language a tendency to prefer here the strong form.

4. Adjective-substantives differ only rarely from the regular inflection of adjectives:

a. When an adjective-substantive follows one or more strong descriptive adjectives it is usually strong, as in **ein dreigliedriges Ganzes** (Wundt's *Völkerpsychologie*, II, p. 230) *a whole consisting of three members*, but earlier in the period it is often weak: **Betrogene Sterblichen!** (Hagedorn). **Ein ehrwürdiger Alte** (Lessing). **Welch ein glücklicher Sterbliche!** (Heine). **Das Eigentum weniger Sterblichen** (Schiller). **Ein hübsches Ganze** (Goethe). **Ein herbes Äußere** (Heine). The weak forms occur still instead of the more common strong ones in the neut. nom. and acc. and in the gen. pl., as in **sein innerstes Innere** (Bilbroth in Edward Hanslick's *Aus meinem Leben*, XXVIII), **ein häßliches Ganze** (Konrad Falke in *Deutsche Monatsschrift*, Aug. 1905, p. 621), **wertvolles, schwer gewonnenes Gute** (Prof. Theodor Siebs in *Literaturzeit.*, July 12, 1913, p. 1734), **die Töchter bärbeißiger Alten** (Wildenbruch's *Das Riechbüchschen*, p. 10), **das Verhältnis vieler Deutschen zu Schiller** (Kühnemann's *Schiller*, Vorwort), **kleine Überreste mohammedanischer Gläubigen** (*Deutsche Monatsschrift*, March 1904, p. 877). Sometimes also in the nom. and acc. pl.: **Ihr seid schöne Getreuen** (Frenssen's *Die drei Getreuen*, I). The weak forms here are the survivals of a once common construction which required the inflection of adjective-substantives to be weak. See 10. *Note* below.

b. Adjective-substantives not preceded by an article or inflected pronominal adjective are now quite uniformly strong, altho the older weak forms occasionally occur, especially in the words **Beamter** *official* and **Bedienter** *servant*: **Bedienten eilten ihm dienstfertig entgegen** (Temme). **Fünf neue Liebsten** (H. Hoffmann's *Wider den Kurfürsten*, chap. iv). In early N.H.G. weak forms were much more common here: **Und es giengen zu jm (ihm) Blinden vnd Lahmen (= Blinde und Lahme)**—Matth. xxi. 14. See 10. *Note* below.

In the masc. dat. sing., however, the weak form is not thus restricted, but is in general still quite common: **dem Herrn N. N., Gesandten** or **Gesandtem der Niederlande in Berlin. So blieb ihm als Mann, Held und Verliebten nichts übrig** (Raabe's *A. T.*, chap. xxix). The old wk. dat. of the neut. and fem. is also occasionally found: **nach genossenem Guten** (Raabe's *Höxter und Corvey*, chap. xv). **Aber ein sauberer Brei . . . roch nach Pech, Schwefel und noch**

viel Schlimmern (id., *Stopfkuchen*, p. 138). **Im ganzen war übrigens diese Art, unversehens zu einer Art Vertrauten** (used here with reference to a lady) **von wildfremden Menschen gepreßt zu werden, nicht behaglich** (S. Junghans in *Zwei Brüder*, p. 62). Sometimes in other cases when the form follows a dependent gen.: **aus Treue gegen den Bruder und dessen Angehörigen** (Ludwig's *Zwischen Himmel und Erde*, X). See 10. *Note* below.

5. A descriptive adjective which modifies a noun that stands in apposition with a preceding word is usually inflected regularly, but the following irregularities occur when the adjective is not preceded by an article:

a. The proper inflection of a descriptive adjective that is not preceded by an article and follows immediately in *close* connection a personal pronoun is not entirely clear to the German. As personal pronouns have neither an article nor the strong endings of the other pronouns to mark gender, it should seem natural for the descriptive adjective in a following appositional phrase to be inflected strong, which is also usually the case, except in the dat. sing. and nom. pl. and sometimes in the acc. pl., where according to present usage either str. or wk. forms may stand, in the case of the nom. pl. perhaps more commonly the wk., in the acc. pl. the str.: **ich armer Mann,** but **mir armem** or **armen Mann, mir armem Wurm** (Fontane), **von Dir jungem Schnaufer** (Raabe), **mit mir altem Hunde** (Hauptmann's *Fuhrmann Henschel*, 4), **mir kranken Sohn der Musen** (Heine), **mir armen Büblein** (Walther Siegfried's *Ein Wohltäter*), **mir jungen, ihr fast unbekannten Menschen** (Karl Hans Strobl in *Velhagen und Klasings Monatshefte*, Oct. 1905, p. 238); **mir armer** or perhaps more commonly **armen Frau, mit mir armen Fürstin** (Freytag), **mir alten erfahrenen Frau** (Hauptmann's *Einsame Menschen*, 2); **wir alten Juristen** (Raabe), **wir Deutsche** (Fontane), **wir Deutschen** (*Hamburger Nachrichten*, Aug. 27, 1913), **wir deutsche Schreiber** (Eduard Engel's *Deutsche Stilkunst*, p. 6), **wir zwei Einsamen** (Lienhard's *König Arthur*, 5); **O ihr närrischen Leute** (Raabe), less commonly strong after **ihr: Ihr hochwürdige Herren** (Anzengruber's *Der Schandfleck*, chap. ii), **ihr plumpe, rohe Menschen!** (Scheffel's *Trompeter*, Zehntes Stück), **ihr Auserwählte** (Halbe's *Das tausendjährige Reich*, p. 71); **für uns arme Frauen** (Fontane) rather than **uns armen Frauen,** to distinguish it from **uns** (dat.) **armen Frauen.** Fluctuation often occurs even in the same author: **Der junge Bursch mit dem Milchgesicht, er stellt uns Alte in Schatten** (Meinhardt). **Er schickt uns anderen in die Berge zur Erholung** (Meinhardt). The weak forms here are survivals of a construction common in earlier periods. See 10. *Note* below.

b. When a descriptive adjective that modifies an appositive noun or is itself an appositive is not preceded by an article and follows a noun or pronoun, it is usually str. except in the gen. and dat. sing. of the fem., where the wk. form is also found, and perhaps more frequently so: **von dem Herrn Erich Schmidt, ordentlichem Professor,** but **mit der schönen Baronesse Christine Arne, jüngsten Schwester seines Gutsnachbarn Arne** (Fontane's *Unwiederbringlich*, chap. i). **Man spricht jetzt von Frau Krescentia Rossel, geborenen Schopp** (P. Heyse). **Mit einer Art wilden Ironie** (Raabe's *Die Leute aus dem Walde*, III, chap. vii). **Aber wir huldigen dir, schönsten der Himmlischen, | reinsten, jungfräulichsten, Artemis, dir** (Wilamowitz-Moellendorff's *Griechische Tragödie*, I. p. 131). But also the strong form: **von . . . dessen . . . Weibe Anna, geborener Weibikin** (Raabe's *Meister Autor*, III). Occasionally wk. forms occur in the masc. and neut. dat.: **einem Stück gebacknen Fisch** (Goethe), **mit einem Stück brüchigen Eisen** (Raabe's *A. T.*, chap. xx), **an einem Schöppchen recht sauren Mosel** (H. v. Sp. in *Velhagen und Klasings Monatshefte*, Jan. 1907, p. 642), **kleine Vorteile, die ihm als ältesten Hauptmann eigentlich zukamen** (*Tägliche Rundschau*). The wk. forms in all these instances are survivals of a construction common in earlier periods. See 10. *Note* below.

6. The descriptive adjective following a gen., especially **dessen** or **deren,** gen. of the demonstrative or relative, is sometimes wk., tho the preceding word can in no way show their gender and case: **in der Natur balsam'schen Wohltat** (Goethe). **Es klang wie Erlösung aus Theas rasch hervorgestoßenen Frage** (from a recent novel). **Was in Preußen nur wenige, außerhalb Preußens niemand, auch nicht dessen besten Freunde, zu verlangen wagten, forderte nach kurzem Schwanken Treitschke** (name) **mit rückhaltloser Entschiedenheit: die Vereinigung Schleswig-Holsteins mit Preußen** (Bailleu in *Deutsche Rundschau*, 1896, Heft 1, p. 61). **Mit dessen adjektivischen Attribute** (Eugen Einenkel in *Anglia*, 1903, vol. xxvi, p. 483), **mit dem Kronprinzen Georg an dessen zehnten Geburtstage** (*Hamburger Nachrichten*, Feb. 11, 1905). **Ihre . . . Augen . . . , von deren ihm gehörenden Wunderreichtum er nichts wußte** (Raabe's *Die Akten des Vogelsangs*, p. 114). **Die Entwickelung des Zeitungszweikampfes, deren wesentlichsten Punkte Ihren Lesern bekannt sind** (*Hamb. Nachr.*, Jan. 7, 1908). Compare: von ir vil grimmen zorne (*Nibelungenlied*, Aventiure VI). This is the survival of a once common construction. See 10. *Note* below.

7. The adjective is not declined:

a. When it is derived from the name of a city and is formed by adding **er** to the proper name: **der alte Berliner Lehrer** the old Berlin teacher, **des alten Berliner Lehrers; der Verband Berliner Industrieller** (*Hamburger Nachrichten*, Nov. 6, 1904). When the substantive is understood, such adjectives are manifesting a tendency toward inflection, to the vexation of strict grammarians, who are mindful of the origin of the form (see *Note*): **Erzähle mir davon, aber nichts von den grönländischen Gespenstern; ich habe an unseren Hohen-Vietzern** (name of place **Hohen-Vietz**) **über und über genug** (Fontane's *Vor dem Sturm*, II. chap. xvi). Such adjectives are not usually employed in the predicative or substantive relation. See **245.** II. 10. 1. *b.*

Note. Here **Berliner** is felt as an indeclinable adjective, and hence written sometimes with a small letter, but it is in fact a noun in the gen. pl., and means *of the people of Berlin.* That it is now felt as an adjective can be seen from the adverb which is often placed before it instead of the originally more correct adjective: **echt Münchner Löwenbräu,** or **echtes Münchner Löwenbräu** genuine Munich beer of the lion brand.

b. If it is the first of two or more adjectives which together unite in forming *one* idea: **rot und weiße Kühe** cows spotted red and white, **die weiß und roten Dolden des Wasserliesch** (Fontane's *Stechlin*, chap. i), **der Eingang zum schwarz und weißen Zelte des Hohenzollern** (Wildenbruch's *Die Quitzows*, 3, Verwandlung), **in gäng und gäber Münze** in current coin. **Deutsche schmücken ihre Häuser mit schwarz, rot und goldenen Fahnen** Germans adorn their houses with the national flag consisting of black, red and gold stripes. In case of a number of uninflected adjectives in **-er** (see *a* above), the **-er** is only added to the last word: **der Berlin-Frankfurt-Charleviller Schlafwagen** (*Frankfurter Zeit.*, Feb. 23, 1915). The inflection of the first adjective in a number of cases would entirely change the sense: **rote und weiße Kühe** red cows and white cows. Instead of the uninflected forms we also find now quite commonly compound adjectives: **ein schwarzrotgoldenes Banner** (Treitschke's *Deutsche Geschichte*, II. 422), **die schwarzrotgoldenen Farben** (ib., III. 756). In some cases two adjectives form a real compound, the second element alone assuming the inflection, but are written as separate words: **die großherzoglich badische Regierung** the government of the *grand-duchy of Baden*, **die königlich preußische Flagge** the flag of the *kingdom of Prussia*.

Note. In the early N.H.G. literary language it was quite common to leave uninflected the first of two adjectives connected by **und**: **ein gros und mechtiges Volck** (Gen. xviii, 18). This usage continued thruout the classical period and even later in poetic language: **in klar und trüben Tagen** (Goethe). Also where **und** is omitted: **Das Wicht'ge wiegt nicht gleich in dein', in ihrem Munde** (Grillparzer's *Libussa*, 1). This usage survives only where the two adjectives form a real compound as in **rot und weiße Kühe**. In such compounds the language of our time prefers the outward form of a compound and drops the **und**: **schwarzweiße Fahnen.** This fondness for the compound form goes so far that the first of two adjectives is often left uninflected where they do not in a strict sense form a compound: **in schlicht** (instead of **schlichtem,**) **treuherzigem Tone.** This is also a survival of older usage: **vorhtlich süezer man** (Wolfram's *Parzival*, 748. 26) = **schrecklicher und lieblicher Mann.**

c. In the case of the following adjectives, since they are only used as predicate complement or objective predicate, or in some cases in the appositive relation following the noun (see **104.** 2. B):

(**1**) Adjectives which for the most part were formerly nouns and still resist adjective declension: **angst** uneasy, **brach** fallow, **feind** hostile, **freund** friendly disposed to, **not** necessary, **pleite** (colloq. from Jewish German) bankrupt, **schade** too bad, a pity, **schuld** at fault, to blame for, **sturm** (Southwest G.) out of one's senses, beside one's self, lit. a storm, **wett** even, quits: **Mir ist noch angst. Er ist den Lügen feind. Er wird mir feind, spinnefeind,** but in the attributive relation **der mir feindliche** or **feindlich gesinnte Mann,** with the form in **-lich** also in the predicate when the word is a compound, as in **Die Steuerreform ist weder mittelstandsfeindlich noch bauernfeindlich** (Dr. Wirth in the "Nationalversammlung," April 26, 1920). **Er ist mir nicht freund,** but in the attributive relation **der mir freundliche** or **freundlich gesinnte Mann,** with the form in **-lich** also in compounds, as in **Das Blatt ist regierungsfreundlich. Er ist mir gut Freund. Der Sache Feind, der Person Freund** adverse to the cause but friendly to the person who represents it. **Das ist nicht not. Ich habe das nicht not** (objective predicate). **Es ist ewig schade!** It's a thousand pities. **Es ist schade um die schöne Zeit!** It's a pity that so much valuable time should be wasted. **Es ist schade um ihn!** He's to be greatly pitied. **Aber für einen Nichtstuer ist meine Schwester mir zu schade!** (Wildenbruch's *Opfer*, 17) My sister is too good for, &c. **Es ist recht schade, daß du nicht gehen kannst! Aber Sie reden ein Zeug, daß man ganz sturm im Kopf könnt' werden** (Hermann Hesse's *Diesseits*, p. 221). The older substantive nature of these forms often leads to the use of capitals with some of them, but the absolute proof that these substantive forms are now felt as adjectives is the occasional comparative forms that occur: **Mir tät' ein Löffele[in] Warmes noch nöter** (H. Kurz's *Sonnenwirt*, 318).

Note. A number of substantives have thus first become predicate adjectives, and later were felt as genuine adjectives, and are now used attributively with full adj. inflection: **fromm** (from M.H.G. vrume *use*) good, pious, lit. useful. A number of nouns have not gone so far as the nouns in the above list, but have dropped their article in the predicate and now stand on the boundary line between adjective and noun: **Ich bin Braut** (= **verlobt**). **Er ist mehr Diplomat als Feldherr.**

(**2**) Also the following, which are usually confined to the predicate or appositional relation: **abhold** averse to, unfavorably inclined toward, **abspenstig** alienated from, **abwendig** alienated from, **allein** (from which comes the attributive form **alleinig** *single, sole*) alone, **anheischig** obligated, **ansichtig** with **werden** *to get a sight of*, **ausfindig** with **machen** *to find out*, **barfuß** (in attributive use usually **barfüßig**) bare-footed, **barhaupt** (attributively **barhäuptig**) bare-headed, **eingedenk** mindful of, **einig** or **eins** in the meaning *agreed*, **futsch** (colloq.) gone, disappeared (**Mein Stock ist futsch**), **gäng und gäbe** (sometimes inflected; see *b* above; similar formations, as **klipp und klar, null und nichtig, recht und billig,** also uninflected) current, **gar** done (of things cooking; but in other meanings inflected: **gares Leder** dressed leather, &c.), **gesonnen** willing, inclined, **getrost** of good cheer, cheerful (in this meaning sometimes inflected: **Seien Sie getrosten Mutes!**), **gewahr** aware of, with **werden** *to perceive*, **gewärtig** on the lookout for, expecting, **gewillt** willing, inclined, **gram** (old predicate adjective from which the substantive **der Gram** has come) filled with dislike toward, **habhaft** with **werden** *to get possession of*, **handgemein** engaged in close fight, **irre** astray, wrong, **ka'pores** (from Jewish German) and **ka'putt** (both colloq., the latter widely used) broken, done for, done up, **kund** known, **leid** sorry for, disagreeable (in this meaning inflected in early N.H.G. and still in S.G. dialect), **links** left-handed, wrong, mistaken, **lōs** free, rid of, off, **rechts** right-handed, **mausig** in **sich mausig machen** to show off, give one's self airs, **me'schugge** (colloq. from Jewish German) crazy, **mies** (colloq.) bad, intolerable (**Die Sache steht, wird mies, Mir ist mies darum** I don't want to hear anything about it, I am not interested in it), **nütze** or **nutz** (more common earlier in the period; in early N.H.G. both forms are inflected, now replaced attributively and in large measure predicatively by **nützlich,** altho the negative form **unnütz** is still quite common in both relations) of use, **quitt** rid of, even (with somebody), **schlüssig** resolved, with **werden** *to make up one's mind*, **teilhaftig** sharing in, **unpaß** unwell, **untertan** subject to, **verlustig** deprived of, (with verbs) to lose, forfeit, **zugetan** devoted: **Er ist mir abhold. Ich mache mich dazu anheischig** I pledge myself to do it. **Der Knabe, eingedenk der früher erlittenen Strafe, gehorchte.** These words are usually only used in the predicate because they have entered into such close relation with a verb like **sein, werden,** or **gehen** that the expression has become fixed. Where, however, there is need of an inflected attributive form there is a tendency in some cases, as mentioned above, to employ as in **245.** II. 9. 2. B a special attributive form rather than to use the form that has become associated with the verb and is felt as an adverb. In other cases the predicate form is occasionally used attributively and inflected: **der barfuße** (altho there is a special attributive form, namely **barfüßig) Knirps** (Heer's *Joggeli*, p. 16). **Leider blieb ich infolge der kaputten Füße liegen** (Feldpostbrief, Oct. 23, 1914). **Miese Sache!** (Feldpostbrief, Aug. 19, 1914). Also used sometimes substantively: **Bist du ein Linkser?** (left-handed) (Hesse's *Unterm Rad*, p. 264).

d. When adjectives or participles which are modified by an adverb are converted into adjective-substantives, the limiting adverb does not make the corresponding change into the state of an adjective, but still like an adverb remains uninflected, tho it modifies a substantive: **die geistig Armen** *those weak intellectually*, from the adjective expression **geistig arm; etwas längst Bekanntes.** The words **geistig** and **längst,** tho they apparently limit their respective substantives, do not take on adjective force and inflection, because the former still as an adverb limits the quality in the word **Armen,** and the latter modifies the verbal force in **Bekanntes** (perf. part.), and neither refer to the living being or the thing implied in the noun. However, if the word before the adjective-substantive limits the substantive as a whole, including both the quality (or action) and the individuals or things represented by the noun, it is inflected: **geizige Reiche** stingy rich people, **ein fleißiger Studierender** (pres. part.) a diligent student.

e. In the case of a very few foreign adjectives, especially those denoting colors: **prima Material** first-class material, **das rosa Kleid** the rose-colored dress, **lila Schleifen** lilac-colored bows. Thus also **karmesin** crimson, **pensee** (pã·'se:) pansy-colored, and a few others less common. In colloquial language we sometimes find inflection: Mutter: **Sieh mal! So ein Pech, Lotten ihre Tasse** [**habe ich zerbrochen**]. Hanni: **Ach?! die rosae?** (Beyerlein's *Dämon Othello*, 1, 4). They are of course inflected when compounded with the German words **farbig** or **farben** *colored*: **in lilafarbigen Kleidern, in orangefarbenem Hut.**

f. In a few geographical terms where adjective and noun together form one name: **in Russisch Polen,** or written together **Russisch-Polen** in Russian Poland, and many other similar expressions.

g. An apparent exception is the non-inflection of **eigen** *own*: **Das ist mein eigen.** Here, however, **eigen** is a neut. substantive, which, tho once in common use, is now so little used that it is quite usually felt as the common adjective **eigen,** and hence is written with a small letter.

h. *Adjective-substantives.* When an adjective now becomes a substantive it retains its adjective form: **der Gute, ein Gutes,** &c. In the prehistoric period adjectives had the same inflection as nouns. A few adjective-substantives still have the inflection of strong neuter nouns, often however dropping the **s** of the genitive and usually the **e** of the dative. As they usually have no plural they seem to be uninflected. These words have an abstract general meaning and hence have not followed the tendency of other adjective-substantives, which refer to definite persons and things and hence like adjectives have assumed distinctive endings. The neuter of the inflected adjective often conveys the same meaning as the endingless form of these old abstract nouns, as **in Unverhofft** (or also **das Unverhoffte**) **kommt oft,** but older usage persists tenaciously here in a very large number of pithy old sayings, preserved as it were by the charm of the terse apt expression and sometimes in part by the rime, as in this example. Some of these old words have acquired more concrete meaning and hence also plural forms: **Gut,** pl. **Güter; Recht,** pl. **Rechte;** &c. Compare **104.** 2. E. *a*.

The following groups occur:

(1) When no article precedes and they are mentioned in pairs, or occur in set prepositional expressions: **Der Abstand von reich und arm** (see **54.** 3), **von vornehm und gering** the contrast between rich and poor, genteel and humble, **gleich und gleich** 'birds of a feather,' **jung und alt** young and old, **schwarz auf weiß** in writing, **von klein auf** from early childhood, **der Unterschied zwischen Wahr und Freierfunden, Jenseits von Gut und Böse** (title of a book by Fr. Nietzsche). Also with the article: **von da an bis zu Shakespeare, Byron und dem übrigen Groß und Klein** (Raabe's *Die Akten des Vogelsangs*, p. 38). **Einer Entscheidung über das Falsch oder das Richtig, an der dem Rat Suchenden gerade gelegen ist, gehn sie** (i.e. **die Grammatiken**) **aus dem Wege** (Grunow's *Grammatisches Nachschlagebuch*, Vorwort). These combinations both with or without the article are, as explained in **249.** II. 2. F. *a*, modern compounds and naturally resist inflection within the compound and usually also at the end, as so often elsewhere in such compounds.

(2) When the adjective-substantive is used to indicate in a general way without definite reference a thing or a person briefly characterized by an articleless adjective or participle:

(*a*) As subject: **Gut ist gut und besser ist besser** A good thing is good, but a better thing is better yet. **Allzu scharf macht schartig** What is too sharp like a knife with too fine an edge will break off. **Ehrlich währt am längsten** Honesty is the best policy. **Vorschnell ist nicht Bauernart** To act overhastily is not the nature of the peasant. **Unversucht schmeckt nicht** That which has not been tried has no taste, i.e. you can't tell how it tastes until you try. **Geschehen** (adjective-substantive) **ist ein'mal geschehen** (verb). **Altklug nie Frucht trug,** or

Altklug lebt nicht lang = Was altklug ist, lebt nicht lang. Jung geheiratet (**183.** 1. B. *b*) **lebt lang,** but **Jung gefreit hat niemand gereut** is another construction as explained in **185.** B. II. *b.*

(*b*) As an object: **Wir haben frei** We have vacation. **Sie haben recht** You are right. **Er hält gut für böse** He considers good bad. **Er macht aus arg ärger** He makes a bad matter worse.

(**3**) Of colors when used in the abstract; but when a concrete meaning enters into the substantive, inflection according to the adjective declension takes place: **das Braun** brown, **Schwarz** black, **Grün** green, **das Blau des Himmels; verschiedene Purpur, Grau, Olivengrün** (Gustav Krüger's *Schwierigkeiten des Englischen*, II. p. 153). Instead of the indeclinable form often with an **-s** in the gen., except after sibilants, and sometimes with an **-e** in the plural: **des Blau(s), Braun(s), Schwarz, Grün(s). Dieses Grün entsteht aus der Mischung hellen Gelbs und dunklen Blaus. Bei chemischer Untersuchung vieler im Handel vorkommender Mineralblaue** (Karmarsch's *Tech.*, 2, 661). But with concrete meaning: **das Schwarze** the bull's-eye of a target, **der Braune** brown horse, **das Grüne** the green fields, **Grünes** greens, **ein Grüner** a greenhorn, a hunter (from color of his uniform), **das Weiße im Auge.**

(**4**) Of languages when used in the abstract with regard to their quality, their varying forms, their employment as a mode of personal expression, but when they take on more concrete meaning and become names of definite things, as the languages of nations or the definite distinct form that any one language assumes in a particular clearly marked period of its development or in a particular part of the territory they are declined according to the adj. declension: **ein schlechtes Deutsch** a bad German, **das Deutsch der heutigen Zeit, die Aneignung eines dialektfreien Deutsch, das Juristendeutsch, das Kaufmannsdeutsch, das Englisch der niederen Klassen, das Deutsch im Munde der Deutschen im Auslande, das Hochdeutsch im norddeutschen Munde, in markigem Deutsch** in pithy German. **Er übersetzte das Gedicht in sein geliebtes Deutsch** *He translated the poem into German, his favored mode of expressing himself*, but **Er übersetzte das Gedicht ins Deutsche** *He translated the poem into the German language.* **Er beschäftigt sich mit dem Deutschen** He is studying the German language. **Das Althochdeutsche, das Mittelhochdeutsche, das Neuhochdeutsche, das Bayrische, das Niederrheinische.** Of course, the same word may be uninflected or inflected according as it represents the language as varying from a standard or represents it as an organic whole with distinct laws of its own altho it may have relations to another kindred language: **das Deutsch der Schweiz,** or **Schweizerdeutsch** when we think of it as a variant form of German, but **die vollständige Sammlung aller im Schweizerdeutschen eingebürgerten Fremdwörter** when we think of it as a distinct dialect.

Sometimes as in (**3**) we find **-(e)s** in the genitive instead of the indeclinable form: **Gegen Auswüchse des Papierdeutschs** (E. Friedegg's *Deutsche Sprachsünder*, p. 5). **Statt des kraftvoll schönen Deutsches von Federer** (name) **springt einem ein eiliger, ohne Feingefühl und Liebe behandelter Stil entgegen** (Carl Busse in *Velhagen und Klasings Monatshefte*, Sept. 1913, p. 152).

8. The adjective in the predicate is now uninflected, but in M.H.G. was here inflected as elsewhere, as one or two fossilized remnants still show: **Er ist voller Tücke.** This strong masc. nom. sing. **voller** is still much used in the predicate before nouns not preceded by a modifier, but all feeling that it is a masc. nom. sing. is lost, as it is used of all genders and numbers as predicate complement, as objective predicate, or in the appositive relation: **Das Stück war voller Handlung. Die Finger sind voller Ringe,** but before an adjective modifier **voll von schönen Ringen. Wir werden das Haus voller Gäste haben. In letzter Zeit war die unglückliche Frau in Schulden und Not geraten, aus der sie, voller Verzweiflung, wohl keinen andern Ausweg sah als den Tod.** Sometimes also before modified nouns, where the adjective is usually strong, but sometimes also weak: **voller boshafter Schnurren** (Lessing), **voller tiefen Sorgen** (id.), **die Zukunft voller dunkler Wolken** (*Deutsche Kolonialzeit.*, April 29, 1905). **Man war voller peinlichen Erwartung** (*Beilage zur Allgemeinen Zeitung*, Jahrg. 1901, 9. Nov., p. 5). In the language of the common people **halber** and **aller** are also used like **voller: Die Nacht ist halber hin. Ich dächte, Sie** (i.e. **Mamsell Sophie**) **wäre so halber mit dem Herrn Sekretarius Knippscheer versprochen** (Lauf's *Frau Aleit*, p. 78). **Der Kaffee steht au aller noch da** (Anzengruber's *Fleck auf der Ehr*, 2, 14). In the last example **aller** may be a case of real predicate inflection, which still survived in early N.H.G. and may live on more or less intact in the dialects. In the neut. sing. and in the pl., predicate inflection of **all** is still common even in the literary language: **Das ganze Bild ist alles Licht** (Goethe). **Diese waren alle anwesend.** Elsewhere non-inflection in the predicate is now the rule: **Die Welt ist all ein flüchtig Scheinen** (Freiligrath). This uninflected **all,** sometimes in the form of **alle,** is also used sometimes for the neut. sing. **alles: Wie das Landvolk all herbeilief** (Goethe). **Wie das Zeug alle hieß** (id.).

The inflected pl. form **alle** has become a fixed form for all genders and numbers in the meaning *all gone*: **Der Wein ist alle. Meine Hyazinthen sind alle.** Also the uninflected form is used here: **Ihr kleines bißchen Brot ward nicht all** (Gebrüder Grimm).

In some Alemannic dialects the predicate adjective is inflected still as in earlier periods: **Herr Vetter, Ihr seid grobe** (= **grober,** here in rhyme with **lobe**)! (Scheffel's *Trompeter, Lieder jung Werners*, VII). **D' Nacht ist fïsteri** (= **finstere**) (Frei's *Schulgrammatik*, art. 67), **S' Wätter ist ugstüems** (= **ungestümes**) (ib.) The weather is stormy.

9. As explained in **104.** 2. B. *a. Note* 2, the adjective is not inflected when it follows its noun, because it is felt as the predicate adjective of an elliptical clause; but if such is not the case and it is felt as an attributive adjective it must be inflected here as elsewhere: **Zum dritten Male durchfurchten wir das tyrrhenische Meer, das wir nun in all seinen Launen, freundlichen und schlimmen, kennen gelernt hatten.** The inflected attributive adjective follows the noun especially in the vocative relation, in scolding or swearing, or on the other hand in expressions of

tenderness, in all of which cases the governing noun has a strong accent and the adjective an almost equally strong one, the emphatic descriptive stress described in **50.** 6. *b:* **Das ist nicht mein Fräulein, Scháf, dúmmes!** (Hartleben's *Rosenmontag*, p. 118). **Spión infámer!** (Lienhard's *Münchhausen*, 1). **Kannst du nicht ein bißchen nachhelfen, Mutterchen einzigstes?** (Marianne Mewis's *Mettes Kinder*). An inflected adjective often follows the governing noun in the market reports: **Tee, indischer, ruhig** (*Hamburgischer Correspondent*, June 22, 1903).

10. Some adjective-substantives cannot be either strong or weak like adjectives, but are inflected according to one of the regular declensions for common or proper nouns: **der Herr** (compar. of the adj. **hehr** august, honored) master, gentleman, **des Herrn,** pl. **die Herren; die Eltern** (compar. of **alt** old) parents; **der Junge** lad, **des Jungen,** pl. **die Jungen** (colloquially in N.G. **die Jungens**), **ein Junge** *a lad*, but the word applied to the young of animals has the regular adj. inflection, as **ein Junges,** pl. **die Jungen, zwei Junge; der Fürst** (M.H.G. vürste *the first*, wk. superlative) ruling prince, **des Fürsten,** &c.; **der Oberst** (superlative) colonel, **des Obersten,** &c.; **der Greis** old man, **des Greises,** pl. **die Greise**, earlier in the period wk. thruout and still so in compounds, as in **Greisenalter** *old age*; **der Jünger** disciple, lit. *the younger* in contradistinction to the master or teacher, **des Jüngers,** pl. **die Jünger; das Gut** estate, **des Guts,** pl. **die Güter,** but **das Gute** that which is good, **des Guten; das Übel** evil, **des Übels,** &c.; **das Recht** right, **des Rechts,** pl. **die Rechte,** and thus also **Unrecht** injustice; the fossil gen. **Rechtens** (in such common expressions as **das ist Rechtens** That is the law, in accordance with the law, &c.), the wk. gen. of the adj. **recht** to which a strong gen. has been added; **das Dunkel** darkness, **des Dunkels,** but still with adj. declension in certain set expressions: **ins Dunkle gehen** to go out into the dark, **im Dunkeln tappen** to grope in the dark; many names of persons, now inflected like other names of persons: **Herr Weiße, Rothe, Schwarze, Braune,** which still have their old weak nom. ending e altho no longer inflected weak. An old group of neuter adjective-substantives, which are declined like **e**-plurals or are uninflected, have been treated in **7.** *h* above.

Note. Origin of the Weak Inflection of Adjectives. Altho the adjective may now be inflected weak, the weak type of inflection originally belonged strictly to nouns. In the prehistoric period it was extended to adjectives, at first, however, only when used as nouns. The surviving representatives of this oldest type of adjective-substantives differ considerably from the common type of to-day in that the adjective has often suffered a change of meaning. The adjective in this oldest type was the *habitual* characterization of an individual, so that it often lost much of its original meaning and became a mere formal sign of individualization, a mere formal device to distinguish *permanently* one individual from others: **Braune** Brown, family name, lit. *brown one*, still with its old weak nominative ending, but now inflected strong; **Bruno** Bruno, Christian name which has come down from the O.H.G. period unchanged = modern **Braune,** hence also lit. *brown one*, still with its O.H.G. weak nom. ending o, but now inflected strong; **Eltern** parents, lit. *older ones*, still always weak as in older German; &c. At the beginning of the historical period a further development is already well established. We often find the adjective-substantive used with the full literal meaning of the adjective to distinguish *for the moment* one individual from others, i.e. used as a temporary individualization and hence weak after the analogy of the old habitual individualizations: Tho wihte siu ther alto, thar forna ju ginanto (Otfrid, I. 15. 25, ninth century) **Da weihte sie** (i.e. **Maria und Jesum**) **der alte, eben genannte,** where *alto* and *ginanto* are temporary individualizations here made for the purposes of the moment to make clear to the reader the person in question. These weak forms were felt by Otfrid with the full meaning and grammatical force of adjectives so that he often uses them elsewhere attributively before a noun wherever he desires to distinguish for the moment one individual from others, or very frequently thruout his book wherever he wishes to characterize a person by a term which expresses his feeling of the moment, as in line 9 of the same passage where he calls the same old man *ther saligo man* **der heilige Mann** and in line 12 where he calls him without the noun *ther guato* **der Gute.** Thus arose the weak type of adjective inflection, a type unknown in Latin and Greek. Weak inflection became associated in this new construction with the idea of *definite* individualization, but it was not necessarily associated with the definite article, as in these examples. Otfrid often uses weak forms without the definite article: fater unser guato! (ib., II. 21. 27), now strong, **Vater unser, du guter!,** as the weak form is no longer used in direct address in the singular, altho it is sometimes still used here in the plural as in **Guten Morgen, jungen Leute!** (Max Dreyer's *Der Probekandidat*, p. 25). Weak inflection without the definite article is sometimes still used in other forms of definite individualization described in 4. *b* (last example), 5. *a* and *b*, and 6 above, and in the ordinal compounds **selbdritt** (M.H.G. selbe dritte), &c. (see **126.** 2. *c* and *Note*), where the distinguishing weak ending has disappeared. The weak form in these newer formations rests entirely upon the definiteness of the idea. The older habitual individualizations differ from the newer type in that they are uniformly weak whether the reference is definite or indefinite. The first five weak nouns in 10 above still faithfully preserve the characteristics of this old type. It is also well preserved in compounds, where in spite of the general or indefinite reference the adjective-substantive is still always weak as in the prehistoric period. **Armenarzt** parish doctor, lit. doctor of poor people, **Gelehrtenversammlung** convention of learned men, &c. In M.H.G. and early N.H.G. weak inflection was thus often used in *simple* adjective-substantives, even where the reference was indefinite. Examples are given in 4. *a* above and also in the first paragraph of 4. *b*. This usage is still found in certain dialects, as in the neighborhood of Bern, Switzerland: **e Stumm** (M.H.G. ein stumme, now **ein Stummer**), &c. In the literary language both of the older types of individualization are now confined to the groups of survivals given above. The inflection of adjectives and adjective-substantives is now elsewhere regulated by a mere formal principle: Weak inflection is used if the form is preceded by the definite article or other strong limiting word, otherwise the form is strong.

COMPARISON OF ADJECTIVES.

Ascending Comparison.

112. Adjectives are compared by adding **-er** to form the comparative and **-st** to form the superlative:

Positive.	Comparative.	Relative Superlative.	Adverbial Superlative.
schlank slender	**schlanker**	**der, die, das schlankste**	**am schlanksten**
klein small	**kleiner**	**der, die, das kleinste**	**am kleinsten**

A few monosyllabics modify the stem vowel in the comparative and superlative. See **113.** 4.

1. *Inflection.* The above are, with the exception of the superlative, the simple uninflected forms as found when the adjective stands in the predicate: **Wilhelm ist klein, Karl ist kleiner.**

In the attributive relation the positive and comparative are declined by adding the regular strong or weak endings to the simple positive and compar.: **ein kleiner Knabe, ein kleinerer Knabe, der kleine Knabe, der kleinere Knabe,** &c.

The *relative* superlative adds **st** to the simple positive and is inflected strong or weak, both attributively and predicatively: **Mein kleinstes Buch. Hans ist der kleinste Knabe. Unter allen Bäumen ist dieser der kleinste.** For the real grammatical force of the last superlative form, however, see 3. A below.

The *adverbial* superlative always remains unchanged (see **231.** II, **an,** 1. A. (*b*)). For the use of this form see 3. B below.

2. *a. Relative Comparative.* Differing from English, German usually employs only one form here, the comparative in **-er: Marie ist schöner als Anna** Marie is more beautiful (i.e. relatively more beautiful) than Anna. The exceptions are given in **115.**

Note. Earlier in the period, even in the classical authors, the superlative was sometimes loosely used of two objects, from the desire of making the superior degree more prominent: **Wir wollen sehen, welcher Genius der stärkste** (instead of **der stärkere**) **ist, dein schwarzer oder mein weißer** (Goethe).

b. Absolute Comparative. The regular relative comparative form is often used absolutely, i.e. to indicate that the degree of the quality is not conceived with reference to any particular object or objects, but only in a general comparative sense: **Die ältere Dame** the comparatively old lady, the elderly lady, **neuere Sprachen** modern languages, **seit längerer Zeit** for some time, **in neuerer Zeit** in modern times, **ein Lehrling besserer Herkunft** an apprentice belonging to a good family. **Er gehört zu den bessern, wenngleich noch nicht zu den guten Schülern** He is a pretty good or comparatively good student, but not among the really good students. **Wir sind in diesen Zimmern gewöhnlich nur an kühleren Sommer- oder wärmeren Herbsttagen. Wenn die Brücke geschlossen ist, so kann kein größeres Schiff hindurch. Ich wünsche keine nähere Verbindung mit ihm. Wir machten einen längeren** (a tolerably long) **Spaziergang.** This comparative is used much more widely in poetry than in prose, and often where in the latter we would use a positive, especially in hexameter verse, where the compar. so readily forms a dactyl: **Ein fremder | Geist verbreitet sich schnell über die fremdere Flur** (Schiller's *Spaziergang*).

3. The different forms of the superlative and their use:

A. The *relative* superlative expresses only relatively the highest degree, and thus represents the highest degree attained by some person or thing as compared with other persons or things of the same class: **Hans ist der fléißigste** or a little more forcibly **der allerfléißigste Schüler in der Klasse** John is the most (unstressed) díligent pùpil in the class. The **aller-** of the superlative form sometimes takes the stress instead of the superlative itself just as *all* in English sometimes for emphasis assumes the accent: **der állerfleißigste Schüler** the most diligent of áll the pupils.

This superlative, even tho it stands alone in the predicate, is felt as an attributive form: **Hans ist der fleißigste (Knabe** or **Schüler).**

B. The *adverbial* superlative, like many other adverbs (see **222.** 2. A), is often used as a predicative adjective, as in *a* below. With certain adverbs denoting quantity, amount (see *b*) it is also used substantively just as adverbs denoting quantity, amount are in general used substantively as well as adverbially.

a. Predicate relation:

aa. It often represents the highest degree attained by some body or thing as compared with itself at different times, places, and under different circumstances, which are usually indicated by some accompanying adverbial element: **Der Sturm war am héftigsten gegen Morgen. Hier ist der See am tíefsten. Ich fühle mich am glúcklichsten, wenn ich allein bin.**

In English this superlative differs in form from the relative superlative in that it drops the definite article: The storm was móst violent (without stress, but according to C with quite a different meaning we say "most víolent") towards morning. The lake is deepest here.

bb. It is often used in the predicate in a relative sense in accordance with its literal meaning (see **231.** II, **an,** 1. A. (*b*)), whenever the attribute is felt distinctly as a real predicate form, no one particular noun being understood, and hence must always be employed when the objects or acts compared are not of one kind: **Karl ist der fleißigste** (understand **Schüler**), but **Wer ist im Schreiben am besten?** (lit. at that which is best, i.e. in the first place). **Am verlegensten war der Justizrat; aber er sammelte sich rasch** (Fontane's *Unterm Birnbaum,* XI). **Am ärmsten unter seinen Leidensgefährten sah wohl mein Vater aus** (Ebner-Eschenbach's *Meine Kinderjahre*). **Waren die Erdbeeren nicht besser als die Stachelbeeren? Ja, aber die Trauben waren am besten. Die Künstler waren so eitel und aufdringlich wie die Politiker, die Literaten noch eitler und aufdringlicher, und am eitelsten und aufdringlichsten waren die Weiber** (Hermann Hesse's *Peter Camenzind,* p. 127). **Am interessantesten ist in Härings** (author) **Erinnerungen vielleicht sein Beitrag zur Entstehungsgeschichte des „Münchhausen"** (book) (Prof. Dr. Werner Deetjen in *Zeitschrift für den deutschen Unterricht,* Jahrg. 28, p. 24). **Solche Leute sind immer am anspruchsvollsten** (Victor Fleischer's *Im Krug zum grünen Kranze*).

b. Substantive relation. The forms **am meisten** and **am wenigsten** are often used substantively, and hence can stand in any position where a substantive would be found: **Nichts bedürfen ist göttlich; und am wenigsten** (object) **bedürfen bringt der Gottheit am nächsten. Sie wissen, ich verliere selbst am meisten** (object) **dabei.** They are also, as any substantive indicating quantity, followed by a partitive gen., which now usually (see **94.** 3. A and B) goes over into the appositional construction: **Die Stedte . . . | in welchen am meisten** (subject) **seiner Thaten geschehen waren** (Matth. xi. 20). **Sie warteten die Zeit ab, in welcher am meisten** (subject) **Menschen** (in apposition with **am meisten**) **die Habsburgerstraße passierten. Am meisten Freude machten mir aber die Vorlesungen vor studentischem Publikum** (*Deutsche Rundschau,* 1911, p. 58).

C. There is also an *absolute* superlative (with the same form and inflection as the relative superl.), which expresses in and of itself a very high, not necessarily the highest, degree: **Dies Land war eine tréueste Búrg des Jesuitenordens** This land was a most fáithful strónghold of Jesuitism. **Ein hőchstes Gűt** a véry great posséssion, **eine dánkbarste Rőlle** a very effective róle, **ein gewándtester und klárster Rédner.** There is here a strong accent upon the superlative, but not quite so strong as the accent upon the following noun—the emphatic stress described in **50.** A. 6. *b.*

In English this superlative is usually marked by employing the periphrastic form and accenting the adjective more strongly than the preceding unstressed *most*: It is a most lóvely flőwer *or* a véry lovely flőwer. Sometimes the simple superlative is employed here, but it is usually distinguished from the relative superlative by a heavy and prolonged pronunciation: O, he made the rú—dest remárk! As can be seen by the examples emphatic stress prevails in English as in German.

a. This superlative is in English in general used quite freely attributively or predicatively, but it is not used in German at all in the predicate relation except in the one word **aller'liebst,** which is used, not only attributively but also as a real predicate with uninflected form: **eine allerlíebste Blűme** a most lóvely flőwer. **Die Blume ist allerlíebst.** In the attributive or substantive relation the absolute superlative is not infrequently used, but is usually confined to particular categories. It is employed especially:

aa. In direct address or at the close of a letter: **liebster Sohn** dear son, **teuerste Schwester** dear sister, **Ihr ergebenster Freund N. N.** Your most devoted friend N. N.

bb. In many prepositional phrases, used adverbially: **in tiefster Trauer** in the deepest sorrow, **in bester Stimmung** in the best humor, **mit größter Hochachtung** with very great respect.

cc. Before names of materials and other articleless nouns, to indicate in a general way a high degree: **feinstes Weizenmehl zu billigstem Preis** very fine flour at a very reasonable price, **erste Schriftsteller** authors of the first rank, **beste Sorten** brands **or** sorts that are among **the** best. **Es war lieblichster Frühling. Einfachste, tiefste Harmonie ist im Sturm, wie in der Windstille** (Raabe's *Leute aus dem Walde*, III. 5). **Auf fadeste Dummköpfe machte er Eindruck, auf Arnold nicht** (Hauptmann's *Michael Kramer*, Act 1). **Die Vorgänge, die hier nur an einzelnen wichtigsten Beispielen verfolgt werden konnten** (Lamprecht's *Deutsche Geschichte*).

dd. Often after **ein, kein, jeder, alle** (pl.), and other pronominal adjectives: **eine leiseste Spur** a very faint trace. **Nun wird sich gleich ein Gräulichstes eräugnen** (= **ereignen**; Goethe's *Faust*, II, l. 5917). **Es ist ein tiefster Zug** (one of the most vítal tráits) **der Unternehmungswirtschaft, einen endlos anwachsenden Markt für ihre Industrieerzeugnisse zu ersehen** (Lamprecht's *Deutsche Geschichte*). **Kein leisester Hauch regte sich** Not the faintest breath of wind stirred. **Jede leiseste Berührung** every touch, even the faintest, **alle bedeutendsten Züge aus der Heldensage** all of the most impórtant féatures of heroic legends. **Der Artikel ist von vielen ersten Autoritäten warm empfohlen** This article is warmly recommended by many of the very best authorities.

b. This idea is also expressed by placing **sehr, höchst, äußerst, über'aus,** or some such word having the general meaning of *very*, before the positive: **ein séhr** or **hőchst fruchtbares Lánd** a most fértile lánd. **Das Land ist séhr** or **hőchst frúchtbar.** In the literary language this positive form of statement is more common than the superlative in the attributive relation and in the predicate it is exclusively employed except in case of the one word **allerliebst** (see *a* above). In colloquial speech, however, it is frequently replaced by other forms of statement in both attributive and predicative relations:

aa. In colloquial language in German as also in English a high degree is often expressed, not by an adverb and the positive of an adjective, but by certain simple adjectives which have become very emphatic, such as **fa'mos** splendid, capital, **riesig** gigantic, very great, **pyrami'dal** very great, large, lit. pyramidal, **kolo'ssal** very great, &c.: **famoser Kerl, famoses Wetter, ein riesiges Vergnügen. Alles bricht in pyramidalen Jubel, in Fanatismus aus** (Gutzkow). **Die Rede war famos, kolossal.** Such words can also be used adverbially, like **sehr,** &c., to strengthen an adjective: **ein kolossal netter Mensch** a 'mighty' nice fellow, **riesig kalt,** &c.

bb. Instead of a simple adjective we often find, especially in colloquial speech, a compound in which the high degree is indicated by the first component: **'stock'blind** blind as a bat, **'blut'jung** quite, very young, **'mords'dumm** or **'kreuz'dumm** awfully stupid, **'hunds'elend** or **'hunde'elend** very miserable, sick as a dog, **'hunds'kalt** beastly cold. **Das steht bomben'fest** That is dead sure. **Das ist jammer'schade!** That is a great pity. **Es war eine stőckfinstere Nácht.** For the fluctuating accent here see **47.** 3. A. *b.*

4. The force of the comparative is often heightened by prefixing **weit** or **bei weitem** *by far*, and that of the superl. by **aller** (gen. pl.) *of all*: **Karl ist weit fleißiger als Emil. Gustav ist der allerfléißigste.** See A.

5. The proper conjunctions to be used with the different degrees are discussed in articles **239.** 1. *a*, *b* and 2. *a.*

113. The following variations from the regular comparison as given above occur:

1. *a.* Adjectives ending in **el, en, er** sometimes form their comparative by suppressing the **e** of the suffix as in the positive, and sometimes in addition also the **e** of the case ending before **n** and **m**: **der ed(e)lere, des, dem, den, die, der ed(e)leren** or **ed(e)lern; ed(e)lerem** or **ed(e)lerm.** See **110.** A.

b. The superlatives of adjectives ending in **el, en, er** retain the **e** of the suffix: **der heiterste Morgen.**

2. Monosyllabic adjectives ending in a sibilant, **s, ß, sch, st,** or in **d** and **t,** add **est** to form the superlative- **der älteste,** &c. Often, however, contraction takes place in familiar language: **der härtste, ältste, süßte,** &c., instead of **der härteste, älteste, süßeste,** &c., the hardest, oldest, sweetest, &c. The contraction of **größt** from **größest** is now the usual form even for the literary language. Grammarians generally give it as the only form, but **größest** is not infrequent: **mit dem größesten Vergnügen** (Raabe's *Alte Nester*, I. chap. xiv), **mit dem allergrößesten Eifer** (Wildenbruch's *Neid*, p. 90), &c. Adjectives of more than one syllable ending in **d** and **t** uniformly add **st** to form the superlative provided the syllable preceding the **st** is unaccented: **der blindeste,** but **blendendste.** Even after an unaccented syllable we find **est** here if otherwise a combination of consonants would arise which would be difficult to pronounce: **in der boshaftesten Gemütsverfassung** (Raabe).

Adjectives ending in **isch** may add **st: die kindischste Torheit.** Some recommend here **t** as a superlative ending, as the **s** is often absorbed in the preceding **sch: der bäu(e)rischte.** Our time, however, seems averse to the mutilation of grammatical forms, and hence we even find here the ending **est** as a way out of the difficulty: **das Praktischeste.**

a. Sometimes to avoid such and other clumsy forms writers and speakers prefix **am meisten** or **im höchsten Grade** to the positive to form the superlative: **als die am meisten praktische der drei Damen** (Roquette); **am meisten,** or **im höchsten Grade barbarisch.**

3. We often find the comparative repeated, the two forms being separated by **und: weiter und weiter** *farther and farther,* or *ever farther.* Instead of this form we also find the positive instead of the first comparative: **rot und röter** (Goethe), **nah und näher** (Johannes Scherr's *Schiller,* II. chap. iii). **Die Blicke der Mütter wurden kühl und kühler, die Händedrücke der Väter flüchtig und flüchtiger** (O. v. Leixner). In the language of the early part of the period the first member of such expressions is often a positive in form, but in fact a comparative, the suffix **-er** being understood in accordance with older usage, which often in case of two words separated by **und** expressed the suffix or case ending but once (see **111. 7.** *b. Note*): **Viel weiß und bleicher als der Mon** (Spee's *Trutznachtigal,* 38. 11). Thus also in case of the superlative: **in den allerschön und lustigsten Landschaften** (Zesen's *Adriat. Rosemund,* 154. 13).

4. *Mutation in Comparative and Superlative.* The following monosyllabics are mutated in the comparative and superlative: **alt** old, **arg** bad, **arm** poor, **grob** coarse, **groß** large, **hart** hard, **hoch** (see 5 below) high, **jung** young, **kalt** cold, **klug** wise, **krank** sick, **kurz** short, **lang** long, **nah**(e) (see 5 below) near, **oft** (**117.** 1. *a*), **scharf** sharp, **schwach** weak, **schwarz** black, **stark** strong, **sturm** (S.W. German) out of one's senses, beside one's self, **warm** warm. Example: **arm,** compar. **ärmer,** super. **der, die, das ärmste** or **am ärmsten.** The following are sometimes mutated and sometimes unmutated: **bang** anxious, **blank** bright, polished, **blaß** pale, **dumm** stupid, **fromm** pious, **gesund** healthy, **glatt** smooth, **karg** stingy, **knapp** close, tight, **krumm** crooked, **mager** (mutated in com. and superl. in S.G.) lean, **naß** wet, **rot** red, **sauber** clean, **schmal** narrow, **zart** tender, and a number of others, all of which mutate more or less frequently in the individual cases in familiar speech, tho not so commonly in the written language. Of these doubtful words **bang, blaß, dumm, fromm, gesund, glatt, karg, naß,** and **rot** are, perhaps, more commonly mutated, but the unmutated forms are not infrequent. **Rot** is usually unmutated in figurative meaning and in compounds, as in **die rotesten Gesinnungen** *the most extreme socialistic views,* **die dunkelroteste Rose** *the rose of the darkest red;* but sometimes with mutation: **der röteste Sozialdemokrat** (Telmann's *Was ist Wahrheit?,* V.). Also a number of other adjectives which usually mutate in simple forms usually remain unmutated in compounds, as in case of **rot: der klügste** *the wisest one,* but **auf die altklugste Weise** in the most precocious manner; **der jüngste,** but **der blutjungste, unerfahrenste Kiekindiewelt** (Sanders's *Hauptschwierigkeiten,* p. 288), &c. Also, however, with mutation: **Der lebensklügste** (Frenssen's *Hilligenlei,* XI).

Note. In a former period of the language the comparative and superlative had each two methods of formation: the comparative ended in *-ir* or *-ōr,* the superlative in *-ist* or *-ōst.* Those that had *-ir* and *ist* were of course mutated (see **26.** A), and the others did not suffer mutation. Later *-ir* and *-ōr* became *-er,* and *-ist* and *-ōst* became *-est,* mutation alone distinguishing still the former groups. Many words which were not entitled to mutation assumed it later after the analogy of the mutating group. Since the classical period, however, mutation has been slowly declining.

5. The two adjectives **hoch** *high* and **nah**(e) *near* are irregular: in **hōch** the **ch** becomes **h** when a vowel follows in the degree or case ending, as **der hohe, der höhere,** but **der hōchste; nah** becomes **nāchst** in the superlative. We sometimes find an unmutated absolute superl. of **nah** with **h** instead of **ch: das Noch-näher-bringen von zwei so allernahesten Herzen** (Suttner's *Die Waffen nieder!,* III, p. 270).

6. Sometimes words for especial emphasis or to convey a little different idea than is usually implied in them are compared when in their ordinary meaning they do not admit of comparison: **Du bist mein und nun ist das Meine meiner als jemals** (Goethe's *H. u. D.,* IX. 311). At the close of letters we sometimes find: **Der Deinigste, der Ihrigste.** We say **die eisernste Herrschaft ausüben** *to exercise the most oppressive* (lit. most iron) *authority,* altho in a literal sense **eisern** cannot be compared.

114. Comparison of Adverbs.

Adverbs have in the positive usually the uninflected form of adjectives, and also elsewhere have no inflection whatever. They are compared just as adjectives except in the superlative:—

Positive.	Comparative.	Relative Superlative.	Absolute Superlative.
hart hard	**härter**	**am härtesten**	**aufs härteste**
schön beautifully	**schöner**	**am schönsten**	**aufs schönste**

1. *a. Relative Comparative.* Differing from English usage German employs usually only one form here, the comparative in **-er: Hans schreibt schöner als Wilhelm** John writes more beautifully than William. The few exceptions are given in **115.**

b. Absolute Comparative. The regular relative comparative form is sometimes used absolutely: **des Herrn Seminardirektors** *Dr.* **Michael Geistbeck schon länger vergriffene, aber anhaltend begehrte „Elemente der wissenschaftlichen Grammatik der deutschen Sprache"** (Karl Credner in the Preface of his *Deutsche Grammatik*); **die für f, þ, s häufiger erscheinenden Schreibungen** b, d, z (Streitberg's *Gotisches Elementarbuch*, p. 91). **Wir entbehrten schon länger der Verpflegung** (aus dem Feldpostbrief eines Tiroler Arbeiters in the *Innsbrucker Volkszeitung*, 1914). **Nun besitzt für Deutschland nur ein länger dauerndes Wirtschaftsbündnis durchschlagenden Wert** (*Vossische Zeitung*, March 5, 1916).

2. The *relative* superlative (see **231.** II, **auf,** 2. G. *Note*) of the adverb expresses the relatively highest degree attained by somebody or something as compared with somebody or something else, or with itself at different times and under different circumstances: **Er schreibt am schönsten von all den Knaben. Die Sonne steht um Mittag am höchsten.**

a. For a few adverbs which form the relative superl. differently see 3. *a* and *c* below and also **117.** 2. *b*.

3. The *absolute* superlative (see **231.** II, **auf,** 2. G. *Note*) expresses in a general way a very high degree in and of itself without reference to that attained by anybody or anything else: **Er schreibt aufs** (or **auf das**) **schönste** *He writes mòst béautifully*, lit. *in the direction of that which is most beautiful.* In English the absolute superlative usually has the accent upon the adverb proper, while in the relative form the preceding *most* is stressed: John writes *mòst béautifully*, but Of the boys John writes *móst bèautifully* or quite regularly in American English *the móst bèautifully*, with an insertion of *the* before *most* after the analogy of the adjective form *the móst bèautiful.*

a. A few adverbs form the absolute superl. without the aid of prepositions by simply suffixing **st,** especially those in **-ig** and **-lich: baldigst** very soon, **innigst** very deeply, **höflichst** very politely, **gefälligst** be so kind, if you please, &c., and a few monosyllabics as **höchst, äußerst** very, **längst** for a long while, **allerliebst** very nicely, **meist** usually, almost, &c. The highest degree possible is expressed by placing this superlative of **möglich** or **tunlich** *before* a participle, adjective or adverb and *after* a verb: **möglichst genaue Auskunft** information as accurate as possible, **tunlichst bald** as soon as possible, **ich gehe ihm möglichst aus dem Wege** I go out of his way, avoid him, as much as possible.

The superlative in **-st** often has relative force before an attributive participle or adjective, never, however, with verbs: **die nächstfolgende Zeile, eines der höchsten, der schwierigst zu erreichenden Ziele, der Höchstbesteuerte** the highest taxpayer, **die dichtest bevölkerten Landstriche, die schwerst bewaffneten Truppen.** In all these cases the regular relative superlative form with **am** is also used: **die am schwersten bewaffneten Truppen,** &c.

Some of these words also have lengthened forms in **ens,** some of which are used relatively and some absolutely: (absolutely) **bestens** as best I can, **meistens** for the most part, **nächstens** presently, **schönstens** *as nicely as possible, very much*, as in **Ich danke schönstens;** (relatively) **erstens** in the first place, firstly, **höchstens** at the most, **längstens** or **spätestens** at the very latest, **frühestens** at the very earliest, **mindestens** or **wenigstens** at the very least, &c.: **Er ist mindestens zehn Jahre alt.**

b. A few absolute superlatives are formed with **im** (with dat. of the adj.) instead of **aufs,** usually in negative sentences: **nicht im geringsten** or **im mindesten** not in the least, **nicht im entferntesten** not even the most remotely, **nicht im leisesten** not in the slightest.

c. The absolute superl. is sometimes formed with **zum** (with dat. form of the adj.) instead of **aufs,** and sometimes this form with **zum** is used instead of the relative superl. with **am: Ich habe sie zum schönsten gebeten** I asked them as nicely as I could. **Nicht der, welcher zuerst, sondern zum (= am) sichersten auf den Feind trifft, hat sich dem Siege genähert.**

d. The absolute superlative is often replaced by the positive modified by another adverb denoting a high degree, such as **sehr, recht, höchst, äußerst, außerordentlich, ungemein: Sie tanzt sehr schön. Seine Gesundheit stellte sich wieder her, aber äußerst langsam.** In colloquial language, in German as also in English, a high degree is often expressed, not by **sehr,** &c. and the positive of another adverb, but by certain simple adverbs which have become very emphatic, such as **fa'mos** splendidly, **kolo'ssal** hugely, very greatly, **riesig** very greatly, very much, &c.: **Ich habe mich famos amüsiert. Ich habe mich kolossal gefreut. Ich langweile mich riesig:** See also **112.** 3. C. *b. aa.*

4. When an adverb modifies an adjective or participle, and it is a question of the higher or highest degree of the adverb and not the adjective or participle, the adverb should logically take the degree ending, but often the adjective or participle takes it instead, as the two are felt rather as one word than two, and the adjective or participle usually standing last naturally assumes the ending of the compound: **schlechtest ausgerüstet,** &c., and also in good authors **schlechtausgerüstetest,** &c. The compound form is most natural in set expressions which have developed a peculiar meaning: **schwerwiegendst, tiefgreifendst, tiefgefühltester Dank, wohlgemeinteste Ermahnungen, feinfühlendere Leute, die gutgeartetsten Kinder, die hochgestelltesten Männer, hochfliegendste Pläne, weitreichendste Verbindungen.** A natural tendency to exaggerate leads some to give both words degree endings: **größtmöglichst** for **möglichst groß,** &c.

Periphrastic Comparison.

115. Besides the case mentioned in **113.** 2. *a*, where the periphrastic form of comparison occurs, are the following:

1. When two qualities of one thing, or two adverbs or adverbial phrases modifying one verb, are compared with each other, the comparative is usually formed by placing **mehr**, also **eher**, before the simple positive instead of adding **-er: Das Zimmer ist mehr lang als breit. Er ist eher klein als groß** He is rather to be called small than large. **Er sprach mehr aufrichtig als klug. Sie drückte mich an den Busen mehr mit schmerzlicher als zärtlicher Bewegung. Er las eher laut als deutlich.**

The regular comparative suffix **-er** is also used here in the classical period, and not infrequently still: **Vielleicht hat er wahrer als klug und fromm gesprochen** (Goethe's *Egmont*, 1, Palast der Regentin). **Das zweifenstrige Gemach war bedeutend länger als breit** (Raabe's *Die Leute aus dem Walde*, chap. vii).

2. In comparing two objects as to the one quality which each possesses in an eminent degree, **mehr** may be placed before the positive of each adjective, or the comparative may also be formed regularly with **-er**, the former method, however, emphasizing the comparison of the predicates, the latter emphasizing the subjects: **Karl ist mehr klug, Wilhelm ist mehr schlau;** or **Karl ist klüger, Wilhelm ist schlauer. Mehr** is also used in the same manner in the attributive relation to call attention to the characteristic feature of some object: **Wüllersdorf war wieder darauf aus, das Gespräch auf mehr gleichgültige Dinge zu lenken** (Fontane's *Effi*, chap. xxviii). **Mehr praktische Ziele verfolgt die Broschüre, welche Prof. Dr. Hunziker in Aarau im Auftrage des Alldeutschen Vereins herausgab** (A. Büchi in *Anzeiger für Indo-Germanische Sprach- und Altertumskunde*, xiii. Band, p. 62). **Eine mehr nebensächliche Rolle spielen bei der Ablautfrage folgende zwei uridg. Lauterscheinungen** (Brugmann's *Lautlehre*, p. 145). **Er war sehr ruhig und benahm sich verständig und war in seinen Urteilen so befestigt, daß er die mehr theoretischen Ausführungen von Pastor Frisius und die mehr praktischen Anschauungen, die Lehrer Haller entwickelte, bei allem guten Willen, den er als höflicher Mann hatte, nicht verwenden konnte** (Frenssen's *Die drei Getreuen*, chap. iii).

Mehr is also used in the predicate with reference to one person or object when the question is raised as to which of two qualities is more characteristic of the subject: **Ich Euch um den Hals fa — [llen] — seid Ihr mehr närrisch oder mehr frech?!** (Lienhard's *Till Eulenspiegel*, Der Fremde).

3. If an attribute of one object, or an activity, is compared with itself under different circumstances or at different times, the comparative is formed with **mehr**, or also regularly: **Ich war früher mehr bekannt und vertraut** (or **bekannter und vertrauter**) **mit ihm. Die Sache wird immer bedenklicher,** or **wird mehr (und mehr) bedenklich. Im Antlitzausdruck eigentümlich halb der Psyche und halb dem Amor gleichend, nur wollte es den Fortgehenden bedünken, als sei sie während seiner Abwesenheit dem letzteren etwas mehr ähnlich geworden** (Jensen's *Das Bild im Wasser*, p. 335).

a. **Mehr** is often used in connection with the word **immer** *ever*, or in the form **mehr und mehr** *more and more*, to indicate a gradual increase of intensity: **Er wurde dadurch immer mehr,** or **mehr und mehr verlegen,** or **immer verlegener.**

4. Adjectives and participles which require after them an object in an oblique case or a prepositional object, and thus approach the nature of verbs, are compared either as regular adjectives, or by placing **mehr** before the positive and **am meisten** before the superlative: **Ludwig ist mir ähnlich; ich habe kein mir ähnlicheres** or **mehr ähnliches Kind** (Daniel Sanders); **keins meiner Kinder ist mir ähnlicher,** or **mehr ähnlich; er ist mir am meisten ähnlich,** or **am ähnlichsten. Dieser Beweis ist der älteste, kläreste** (now **klarste**) **und der gemeinen Menschenvernunft am meisten angemessene** (Kant). **Das mich am meisten Verdrießende.** Where the verbal nature of the participle, as in the last example, is distinctly felt, the compar. and superl. are more commonly formed by prefixing **mehr** and **am meisten** to the positive.

5. Adjectives (**111.** 7. *c.* (**1**)) or adverbs which are derived from substantives or other parts of speech and are not yet felt fully as adjectives or adverbs are usually compared with **mehr** in the compar. and **am meisten** in the superl.: **Ich bin ihm mehr gram als dir. Das tut mir mehr leid, als ich sagen kann. Dem jugendlich rastlosen Greise Blücher** (proper name) **wurde die Unentschiedenheit der Dinge zuerst und am meisten zuwider** (also preposition and adverb). The regular forms in **-er** and **-st** are sometimes found, tho rarely.

a. Thus also nouns and the pronoun **es** which stand in the predicate with the force of adjectives are compared: **Er ist mehr Diplomat als Feldherr. Es war mehr Spaß als Ernst. Schön bist du; wüßtest du's minder, du wärest es mehr.**

6. Some adverbs which denote a relative position with regard to the speaker or some other point form a comparative with **mehr** or **weiter** and a superlative with **am meisten** or **am weitesten: Er stand mehr links** He stood more to the left. See also **117.** 2. *b*, second paragraph.

A few adjectives which denote a relative position, such as **äußer, inner, äußerlich,** form a comparative with **mehr,** but their superlative with the regular **-st** ending: **Sonst ging die Entwicklung unserer Sprache dahin, die beiden Flexionsformen ganz unabhängig von Bedeutungsgruppen bei allen Adjektivis nach mehr äußeren Bedingungen zu regeln** (Wunderlich's *Der deutsche Satzbau*, 1st edition, p. 170). **Leute, die wenig oder gar kein Gewissen haben, würden auch allzu glücklich sein, wenn die ewige Gerechtigkeit es nicht so prächtig verstände, ihnen auch an mehr äußerlicher Stelle den Sachverhalt klar zu machen!** (Raabe's *Die Leute aus dem Walde*, II. chap. viii). See also **117.** 2. *a*.

7. **Es ist möglicher, daß,** &c., is not so common as **Es ist eher möglich,** &c.
8. Occasionally we find periphrastic comparison elsewhere, where we should expect the suffix **-er: Und dir ist Vaterland mehr als die Fremde fremd** (Goethe).
9. Double comparison is rare: **eine mehr schicklichere Ursache** (Lessing). **In den Donau-Fürstentümern ward die Lage des russischen Heeres mehr und mehr unhaltbarer** (*Volks-Zeitung*, 24. 267). See also **117. 1.** *b.*

Descending Comparison.

116. Descending comparison of adjectives and adverbs is formed by placing **weniger** or **minder** *less* before the positive to form the comparative, and **am wenigsten** or **am mindesten** to form the superlative: **hart** hard, **weniger** (or **minder**) **hart** *less hard*, **ein weniger** (or **minder**) **hartes Ei, eine weniger stark gewürzte Suppe, am wenigsten** (or **am mindesten**) **hart** least hard, **der am wenigsten** (or **am mindesten**) **fleißige Schüler, die am wenigsten stark gewürzte Suppe.** In case of adjectives or participles, especially in the attributive or substantive relation, it is also quite common to employ the uninflected superlative form **wenigst** or **mindest** instead of **am wenigsten** or **am mindesten,** now often writing the two words as one: **In diesen Dingen sind die klügsten Frauen die wenigst klugen** (Adele Gerhard's *Pilgerfahrt*, p. 51). **Das erleichtert den Skandinaviern, die mindestromantischen Germanen zu sein** (Prof. Ed. Heyck in *Velhagen und Klasings Monatshefte*, May 1905, p. 283).

Irregular and Defective Comparison.

117. 1. Irregular adjectives and adverbs (the simple stem only is here given):

Positive.	Comparative.	Superlative.
bald (adv.) soon	**eher** rather, sooner	**baldigst** as soon as possible.
früh (adj. & adv.) early, soon	**früher** (now less commonly **bälder** or **balder**) earlier, sooner	**frühest** (**bäldest, baldest**) earliest, soonest, first.
gern (adv.) willingly	**lieber** (see *e* below)	**liebst.**
ungern unwillingly, often regular,	more commonly, however, as	**gern.**
gut (adj. & adv.) good, well	**besser** (**baß,** adv.; see *d* below)	**best.** (**gutest;** see *f*).
wohl (adv.), sometimes used in the positive instead of **gut** (see *c* below).		
oft (adv.) *often* or	**öfter** (adj. & adv.; see *a*) **öfterer** (rare)	**öftest** (adv.) **öfterst** (rare)
oftmalig (adj.)		
häufig (adj. & adv.)	**häufiger** (adj. & adv.)	**häufigst** (adj. & adv.).
viel (adj. & adv.) much	**mehr** (uninfl.) **mehrer-** (see *b*)	**meist** **mehrst** (see *b*).
wenig (adj. & adv.) *little* (in amount or degree), pl. *few*	**weniger** (adj. & adv.) **minder** (adj. & adv.)	**wenigst** (adj. & adv.) **mindest** (adj. & adv.).

a. **Öfters,** comparative of **oft,** is often used adverbially in an absolute sense, and is to be distinguished from the relative comparative **öfter: Das begegnet mir öfters** That happens to me comparatively or quite often. **Versuchungen treten uns öfter nahe, als wir glauben** Temptations come near to us more often than we think. The comparative **öfter-** is also used in adjective function in an absolute sense *rather frequent*: **öftere Besuche, seine öftere Gegenwart.**

b. **Mehrer-** (due to double comparison) *greater* (before a sing. noun), *more* and **mehrst** (superl. formed from the compar. **mehr**) *most* are not infrequent earlier in the period: **Vnd da die Anfurt vngelegen war zu wintern | bestunden jr das mehrer teil auff dem Rat | von dannen zu faren** (Acts xxvii. 12). **Daß ein Aufenthalt in diesem Antikensaal dem studierenden Künstler mehrere Vorteile gewährte, als eine Wallfahrt . . . nach Rom** (Schiller, 3. 577). **Die mehresten dieser Unglücklichen** (id., Kab. 2, 2). This older usage is still occasionally found: **Zur Seite summte der heimliche Teekessel, und von Zeit zu Zeit füllte er die kleine chinesische Tasse mit der goldklaren Flüssigkeit, der er zu mehrerer Vergeistigung aus blanker Kristallflasche etwelchen Arrak zuzusetzen pflegte** (H. Seidel's *Der Luftballon*). **Solche Widersprüche in den Entschließungen des Königs zeigten sich nun bald immer mehrere und immer grellere** (Karl Biedermann's *Dreißig Jahre deutscher Geschichte*, I. p. 93). This older usage is most common in a few set expressions: **Davon künftig ein mehreres** *more about that some other time,* **des mehreren** *more in detail, more fully.* **Mehrere** (pl. of **mehrer-**), however, is still quite common as an indefinite numeral adjective in the sense of *several.* See **139. 1.** *h.*

c. **Wohl** is a predicative adjective which is only used in the meaning *well* with reference to the health or bodily comfort, and is entirely regular in comparison. It must not be confounded with **gut**, which besides its usual adjective meaning *good* is used as an adverb of manner with the meanings *well, nicely,* and also used as an adjective in the comparative and superlative with the force of **wohl: Er schreibt gut, besser, am besten,** but **Ihm ist heute wohl, wohler** or **besser. Er befindet sich wohl, wohler** or **besser, am wohlsten** or **am besten.** Historically considered, **wohl** was originally not an adjective as at present, but the adverbial form of the adjective **gut.** This original usage occurs frequently as late as the classical period, and is still retained in adjective, participial, and substantive compounds and in a number of set expressions: **wohlgemut, wohlschmeckend, wohlerhalten, wohlbekannt, Wohlklang, Wohlgeruch,** &c. **Wohl** is found before adjective participles also where they are not written as a part of a compound: **Sein Hinterstübchen war wohl geziert** (Raabe.). In set expressions: **Er will mir wohl. Er tut wohl daran. Ich wünsche Ihnen wohl zu schlafen** I wish you a good night's rest. **Möge es Ihnen wohl bekommen!** May it agree with you well! **Mir gefällt der Kerl ausnehmend wohl** (also **gut**) (Raabe's *Zum wilden Mann*, chap. x).

d. An old adverbial comparative of **gut** is **baß.** It is sometimes in antique style or dialect still used with the meanings *better, more, rather,* more frequently *very much, again, further*: **Eines Dieners mit Weisheitszähnen bin ich baß entraten** (Storm's *Pole Poppenspäler*) I am better rid of, &c. **Ich habe mich manchmal baß** (very much) **gewundert über dich** (Hauptmann's *Vor Sonnenaufgang*, 1). The adverb was not mutated in the compar. in older periods of the language as was the adj., as can be still seen in this fossilized form **baß** (adverb) in contradistinction to **besser** (adj.).

e. In earlier periods the comparison of **gern** was regular. It is also frequently regular in early N.H.G. and occasionally even later, and is still often so in popular language, which thus preserves here older usage.

f. The regular superlative of **gut** is not infrequent in colloquial speech, especially in comic or sarcastic language, only, however, in direct address: **Seh'n Sie, mein Gutester, das nennt man so Menschenliebe in den Tropen** (Schulze-Smidt's *O Tannebaum*, 1). **Nee, mein Gutester!** (Fulda's *Jugendfreunde*, 1, 7).

g. A regular superlative of **viel** occurs sometimes, always, however, an absolute superlative: **Vielste Grüße von Ihrem G. Keller** (G. Keller an T. Storm, May 19, 1883).

2. Defective adjectives with positive wanting, only used attributively or substantively:

Comparative.	Superlative.
Der, die das äußere outer	**der, die, das äußerste** outmost
erstere former	**erste** first
innere inner	**innerste** inmost
hintere hinder	**hinterste** hindmost
letztere latter	**letzte** last
mittlere middle	**mittelste** middlemost
obere upper	**oberste** uppermost
untere under	**unterste** undermost
{ **vordere** in front **vördere** (earlier in the period)	{ **vorderste** foremost **vörderste** (still surviving as an adverb; see *b* below)

a. Of these **erst** and **letzt** are superlatives treated as positives, from which compar. forms **erster-** and **letzter-** have been made. The compar. forms of the others have been made from adverbs and are in force really positives, and of the one word **mittel** all three degrees can sometimes be found without difference of meaning: **der mittele** (or **mittlere,** or **mittelste**) **Finger.** When it is desired to impart real comparative force to these comparatives, which does not often occur, it is necessary to prefix **mehr.** See **115. 6.**

Contrary to English usage the article is often, perhaps even more commonly, omitted before the comparative forms **erster-, letzter-: Er reichte mit freundlichem Morgengruß Heiding und danach Erwin Buchhoff die Hand und sagte zu letzterem, daß usw.** (Adolf Stern's *Der Pate des Todes*, II). In the masc. and neut. gen. sing., however, the form with the article **des ersteren, des letzteren,** is always used, as the form without the article, **ersteres, letzteres,** might be construed as a nom. or acc. neut. For the misuse of the form **letzter-** see *c* below.

b. Only the superl. of adverbs is formed from these adjectives: **zu äußerst** the farthest away, **zu hinterst** the farthest behind, **zu innerst** the farthest within, **zu mittelst** the farthest towards the middle, &c., and three in which **zu** and the adverb are written together, **zu'erst** first, **zu'letzt** last, **zu'vörderst** or **zu'vorderst** foremost, in the first rank, in front, before all (things), in the first place, first and foremost. In the case of **zuvörderst** and **zuvorderst** there is a tendency to differentiate, so that the former is used with regard to time and the latter with regard to place.

However, corresponding to these defective adjectives denoting a position are other adverbial forms of kindred origin, which with the aid of paraphrasing can form all three degrees: **außen** without, out of doors, **innen** within, **hinten** behind, **oben** above, **unten** below, **vorne** in front. Their comparatives are formed by placing before the adverb the comparatives **weiter** *farther* or **mehr** *more,* and their superlatives by the superlatives of the same adverbs: **oben, weiter oben, am weitesten oben; unten, mehr unten,** &c. Likewise in case of other adverbs denoting position: **links** *to the left,* **weiter links, am weitesten links.** In case of some of these adverbs we sometimes find here in facetious language the regular comparative ending **-er: Wenn wir sie erst links haben, dann ist's nicht mehr schwer: dann graulen wir sie ihm auch wohl immer linkser** (Wilbrandt's *Hermann Ifinger*, chap. iii).

c. The comparative form **letzter-** (see *a*) is a favorite in present usage and is even often employed to refer to the last of a number of persons or things, where it is grammatically incorrect, as it is a comparative and should indicate the latter of two persons or things: **Er konnte sich demnach mit seinem schwarzen Gesellschaftsrock, den neuen sandfarbenen Beinkleidern und einer glänzenden rotschottischen Atlaskrawatte schmücken, welch letztere er mit einer unechten Brillantnadel feststeckte** (M. Kossack's *Erste Liebe, Westermanns Monatshefte*, 1892, vol. 71, p. 782). It is also often used where a personal pronoun, a possessive, a demonstrative, or an adverb might be more tersely and appropriately employed: **Dessenungeachtet vergaß Herr Volker keinen Augenblick die dem Gaste schuldige Rücksicht. Er behandelte letzteren** (instead of **ihn**) **nur etwas von oben herab** (ib.). **Das Blumengärtchen stieß durch eine Lücke des Schloßgartens an den schattigsten Teil des letzteren** (instead of **an dessen schattigsten Teil**). **Der Statthalter und Herr v. H. haben neulich das vom Kaiser jüngst erworbene Gut Urville besichtigt, wie verlautet, weil der Kaiser auf letzterem** (instead of **dort**) **nächstes Frühjahr einige Tage zubringen will.** It is often entirely superfluous: **Daß die deutsche Ausgabe . . . auch durch verschiedene Zusätze des Herrn Übersetzers bereichert ist, welch letzterer** (instead of **welcher**) **zugleich einige Irrtümer berichtigt hat** (James Bryce, *Das heilige römische Reich*, Deutsche Ausgabe von Dr. A. Winckler, p. vi).

Limiting Adjectives.

118. A limiting adjective is one that merely defines or restricts the meaning of a noun.

Limiting adjectives differ in form or meaning from descriptive adjectives in that:

a. They do not stand uninflected in the predicate, and hence the masc. form for the nom. is usually, except in the case of uninflected words, given in the dictionary to represent the word instead of giving the simple stem, which only occurs in a few cases, as will be found recorded in the proper places. The simple stem of these latter words is often given to represent the word, as indeed these forms do sometimes occur.

b. They cannot all be inflected strong or weak. Some are always declined strong, even in the masc. and neut. gen. sing.; some are inflected str. or wk. according to circumstances. Thus the different groups of this class must be treated separately.

Note. The weak forms in this class of adjectives are in general of comparatively recent origin and have been gradually increasing, as they have been influenced by the declension of descriptive adjectives.

c. They cannot be compared, except a few which are treated under the head of comparison of descriptive adjectives. See **117**, and **113**. 6.

119. Limiting adjectives are divided into two classes—*numeral* and *pronominal* adjectives.

Numerals.

120. Cardinals:

0, null
1, ein, eine, ein, but **eins** in counting when no noun follows
2, zwei; early N. H. G. **zween** (masc.), **zwo** (fem.); see **121.** 2. *a. Note*
3, drei
4, vier
5, fünf or **funf** (early N.H.G.)
6, sechs
7, sieben
8, acht
9, neun
10, zehn
11, elf, eilf (now obsolete)
12, zwölf
13, dreizehn
14, vierzehn
15, fünfzehn (funfzehn, pop. **fufzehn)**
16, sechzehn
17, siebzehn, (siebenzehn)
18, achtzehn
19, neunzehn
20, zwanzig
21, einundzwanzig
22, zweiundzwanzig
23, dreiundzwanzig
30, dreißig
31, einunddreißig
40, vierzig
50, fünfzig (funfzig, pop. **fufzig)**
60, sechzig
70, siebzig (siebenzig)
80, achtzig
90, neunzig
100, hundert
101, (ein)hundertundeins
102, (ein)hundertundzwei
200, zweihundert
300, dreihundert

400, vierhundert **10,000, zehntausend**
1,000, tausend **100,000, hunderttausend**
1,001, (ein)tausendundeins

eine Milli'on a million, **zwei Milli'onen** two millions, **eine Milli'arde** a thousand millions, **eine Billi'on** a million millions.

121. Inflection:

1. **Ein** is inflected strong or weak as any descriptive adj. with several variations:

A. If it is used attributively and is not preceded by a limiting adjective, it is inflected exactly as the indefinite article, differing from it only in being more strongly accented: **e i n** (see **58.** B. *a*) **Mann nicht zwei, e i n Buch nicht zwei, ein guter Mann.**

a. Before numerals used as collective nouns, before fractions and the substantive **Uhr** *o'clock*, and also before certain pronominal adjectives and nouns denoting an indefinite quantity, **ein** is found uninflected: **mit ein** (i.e. *about a dozen*, but for an exact dozen we say **einem**) **Dutzend guten Äpfeln. Ein Sechstel von ein halb, bleibt ein Drittel** One-sixth from one-half leaves one-third. **20 multipliziert mit ein Viertel gibt 5. Nach ein Uhr** after one o'clock, **mit ein bißchen Mut** with a little courage, **in ein paar Tagen, mit ein wenig Geduld.**

b. The uninflected ein is found in a few set expressions connected by **und** and **oder** (see 2. *d* below): **Ich sah es ein und anderem Augenpaar an, daß hier geweint worden war. Franzerl** (proper name) **war sein ein** (or **eins**; see B below) **und alles. An einunddemselben** (also **einem und demselben**) **Tage; zu** (at) **dreiundeinhalb Prozent; ein oder zwei Wochen; in ein oder zwei Stunden,** or often inflected here and in similar expressions, as in **mit einem oder zwei Blumentöpfen** (Adele Gerhard's *Die Geschichte der Antonie van Heese, I*); in colloquial language **in ein Tager** (contracted from **Tag oder**) **sechs** in about six days, &c.

c. The singular form **ein** or **eine** is used in colloquial language to give a collective idea to nouns in the pl.: **Er bleibt noch wohl ein** (or **eine**) **8 Tage** He will probably remain yet about a week. **Vor ein 7, 8 Jahren** about 7 or 8 years ago. **So ein 2 bis 3 Jahre Zuchthaus wird er wohl bekommen. Wenn ich nur eine 2 oder 300 Taler hätte!** If I only had the sum of two or three hundred thalers! See also **96.** 1.

d. In colloquial language **ein** is often used in the plural in the expression **so ein.** See **131.** 1. *a. Note* 2.

B. If **ein** is preceded by some limiting word which cannot mark the gender and case of the noun, as the possessive gen. of a noun or pronoun, or the nom. masc. and nom. and acc. neut. of a possessive adjective, it is inflected strong: **Des Königs eines Schloß lag in Stuttgart, das andere in Ludwigsburg. Mein Freund und dessen einer Sohn** (or **eine Tochter** or **eines Kind**) **sind schon angekommen. Wir feiern heute einen tragisch doppeltfestlichen Tag. . . . Indem sich mein eines Auge für die Grabrede feuchtet, fängt das andere für die fröhliche Geburtsrede zu lachen an** (Wilbrandt's *Die Maler*, 2, 7).

C. Preceded by the definite article or some other limiting adjective which marks gender and case, **ein** is inflected weak: **der eine Knabe; der eine, der andere** the one, the other. In S.W.G. we find sometimes the form **der einte** instead of **der eine** when used in contrast to **der andere.**

a. The definite article may stand before the pl. of **ein,** referring collectively to one of two groups: **die einen . . . die andern** the persons in the one group . . . those in the other.

D. Used substantively, standing alone, **ein** is declined as a strong adj., the neut. nom. and acc. usually, however, in the contracted form **eins: einer von diesen Herren, ein(e)s von diesen Büchern, so einer** such a one.

a. The uninflected neut. form **eins** occurs in some very common idioms: **zwölf Minuten nach eins** twelve minutes after one o'clock, **mit eins** suddenly, **von eins bis hundert zählen** to count from one to one hundred.

b. In popular language **ein-** is often used in the plural: **Diese Knöpfe sind eine der besten = gehören zu den besten.** See also **134.** 2 (3rd par.).

2. The cardinals except **ein** are not now usually inflected: **zehn Finger, einige zwanzig Jahre** some twenty years, **einige hundert Jahre** several hundred years.

In case of the absence of some preceding article or pronominal adj. to show case, the prep. **von** marks the gen. relation of these indeclinable numerals: **der dritte Teil von sechs ist zwei.** In the other cases the context as in English shows the case.

a. Sometimes **zwei** and **drei** are in the attributive relation declined strong in the gen. and dat. pl., if there is no preceding word to show case: **Zweier Zeugen Mund tut alle Wahrheit kund** The testimony of two witnesses establishes the truth. The gen. **zweier, dreier,** occur more frequently than the dat. **zweien, dreien,** as some preceding preposition in the latter case usually makes the dative relation sufficiently clear without the aid of the case ending. If an adjective follow **zwei** or **drei** the numeral may remain uninflected leaving to the adjective the office of indicating the case, or it may itself assume this function: **Durch zwei unverdächtiger Zeugen Aussage** or **durch zweier unverdächtiger Zeugen Aussage.** Sometimes we find the strong gen. pl. form of other numerals, but non-inflection is much more common: **während zwölfer Tage** (Niendorf's *Gudrun,* 1 , 10).

The neuter of **drei,** and much more rarely of **vier,** has when used substantively developed strong sing. forms with collective force after the analogy of **beides** (see **139.** 1. *d*): **Ich will alles dreies merken** I will note all three points. **Alles dreies wirkte mächtig zusammen** All three things worked powerfully together. **Und ich bin eigentlich alles drei's** (i.e. **Kind, Narr, Poet**) (Fontane's *L'Adultera,* XXI) And I am really all three (of the things you have mentioned). In popular language the neut. of **zwei** is often used instead of **beides: dieses zweies nehme ich.**

Note. In early N.H.G. the forms **zween** (masc.), **zwo** (fem.), **zwei** (neut.), were much used for the nom. and acc. and still occur in poetry and S.G. dialects. In the eighteenth century and later they were not clearly understood and hence often confounded. The neuter form has at last crowded out the masc. and fem. forms.

In a few compounds the older form **zwie** is found instead of **zwei,** as **Zwielicht** twilight, **Zwietracht** dissension, &c.

b. The numerals in **-zig** lengthen this form to **-ziger** to show the decades of the century or of human life, and remain uninflected: **in den achtziger Jahren des vorigen Jahrhunderts** in the eighth decade of the last century, **die nachsiebziger Zeit** the period in Germany after the great political changes of 1871, **in der Mitte der vierziger Lebensjahre** in the middle of the forties. See also 5 below.

c. When these numerals stand alone, either substantively or with some noun understood, they are sometimes, especially in the dat. and least frequently in the gen., declined, usually with the inflection of nouns of the unmutated **e**-plural type; but in general this inflection is limited to certain set expressions, and should rather be considered as quaint, and hence avoided: **diese viere** these four (boys), **sechs** (more common than **sechse**) **kamen** six (people) came, **wir sind unser sechs** (or **sechse**) there are six of us, **der Rat der Vier** (*Vossische Zeitung,* June 7, 1919) Council of Four, "The Big Four" (in the peace treaty at Paris), **das Vorhaben der Drei** the intention of the three, **die obern Zehntausend** the upper ten thousand (as opposed to the masses). **Zu seinen Häupten der wolkenlose Himmel, zu seinen Füßen dieses Leben, dachte er der Tausend und Abertausend, die der Strudel der Weltstadt unbarmherzig in seine Tiefen reißen würde** (Stilgebauer's *Götz Krafft,* II, p. 446). **Die Dreie hocken wahrhaftig wieder da und spielen ihren Skat weiter** (Hans Weber in *Kriegschronik des Daheim,* vol. II, p. 289). **Mit einer kongenialen Begabung zum Geiz durchschaute sie rasch jeden Kniff der Dreie** (Walter Siegfried's *Ein Wohltäter*). **Ein Mann in den Sechzigen** (or **Sechzig**); **wenn einer, wie ich, über die Achtzig(e) hinaus ist; zu dreien** (or **drei**) **sitzen** to sit three together, **auf allen vieren kriechen, mit sechsen fahren** to go in a coach and six. **Er hat alle neune geworfen** He has knocked down all the nine (nine-pins). **Er kam mit fünfzig** (more common than **fünfzigen**). **Weniger Worte sind zwischen Zweien, die einander lieben, wohl nie gemacht worden und nie haben Zwei sich besser verstanden** (Ebner-Eschenbach's *Meine Kinderjahre*). **Allen vieren** (*to all four persons*) **sagte Onkel Gottfried zugleich guten Tag** (Ompteda's *Sylvester von Geyer,* XI).

Note. We sometimes find the substantive forms of numerals inflected strong or weak like adjectives instead of non-inflection or inflection according to the unmutated **e**-plural type: **Ich wil jnen nichts thun | vmb vierziger willen** (Gen. xviii, 29). **Las meine seele vnd die seele deiner Knechte dieser funffzigen fur dir etwas gelten** (2 Kings i. 13). **Zehn Schüler haben gearbeitet; dieses sind die Arbeiten vierer, achter — ebenso hunderter, tausender** (Wetzel's *Die deutsche Sprache,* p. 199, 12th ed.). **Das Schicksal aller vieren** (Blatz's *Neuhochdeutsche Grammatik,* I. p. 390, 3rd ed.), **das Leben tausender** (Grillparzer's *König Ottokar,* 4), **vor den Augen hunderttausender von Lesern** (Jensen's *Heimkunft,* VII), **die Augen tausender** (Heer's *Der König der Bernina,* chap. xv). **Der deutsche Gelehrte bedient sich hunderter, tausender von Fremdwörtern** (Eduard Engel's *Deutsche Stilkunst,* p. 206). **Dieses Elend vieler tausender deutscher Staatsangehöriger** (*Deutsche Zeit.,* Nov. 10, 1914). **Die Unkosten der Ansiedelungen vieler tausenden** (von Zeppelin in *Deutsche Monatsschrift,* April 1904, p. 68), **das Endresultat aller der tausenden von Beobachtungen** (Prof. E. Weichert in *Deutsche Rundschau,* Sept. 1907, p. 380). Where there is no article or other inflected limiting adjective to denote the case relation the strong form of the numeral is indispensable, unless recourse is had to prepositions. Hence strong inflection here is very common. Strong adjective inflection is also established in case of **drei** in the neut. sing. See *a* above. When the article is used substantive inflection can be employed in case of **Hundert, Tausend,** &c. See 4 below.

d. Also numerals which are capable of inflection remain usually uninflected when brought into connection with uninflected numerals by some conjunction or preposition, or sometimes the inflected numeral agrees with the noun in the sing. (**96.** 10): **in einer Höhe von ein bis zwei Meter(n), aus hundertundein triftigen Gründen,** or **aus hundert und einem triftigen Grunde** for a hundred and one good reasons, **dreihundert[und]ein Eier** or **300 und ein Ei, dreiundeinhalb** (or **drei und ein halbes**) **Prozent, in sechsundeinhalb Jahren,** or **in sechs und einem halben Jahr, ein für allemal** once for all, **in ein** (also **einem**; see 1. A. *b* above) **oder zwei Tagen.**

Note. If an article or inflected limiting adj. in the pl. precede such mixed numerals, the noun must be in the pl. and the numeral may remain entirely uninflected, or the declinable numeral, namely **ein,** may show the gender, not case or number, as it has no pl. forms, and hence no attempt ought to be made to make it agree with the governing noun in case and number: **aus diesen hundertundein triftigen Gründen, unter den fünfeinhalb** or **den fünf und eine halbe** (agreeing with the noun in gender only) **Millionen Sezessionisten** among the five and a half million Secessionists. **Ich habe mehr zu tun als eure tausend und eine Häkeleien zu schlichten. Den ein oder zwei sicheren Fällen seiner** (i.e. **Fritz Reuters**) **Abhängigkeit von Hoffmann können wir nämlich ein, vielleicht zwei Beispiele aus dem „Parlament zu Schnappel" gegenüberstellen, wo Hoffmann höchst wahrscheinlich von Reuter beeinflußt worden ist.** Some, however, make **ein** agree also in case, which sounds very harsh, as this attempt to make adj. and noun agree brings a sing. adj. before a pl. noun in the same case and brings about a clash instead of an agreement: **von den tausend und einem Mißgeschicken** (Sealsfield's *Transatlantische Reiseskizzen*, I. 64).

e. The numerals are especially uninflected in giving dates, numbers of houses (in the street), time of day, and often with suppression of the case form of the noun, the omission of articles, and even of nouns and prepositions: **Leipzig hatte 350,000 Einwohner in 1890** (in imitation of the French, or more commonly according to the German idiom **im Jahre 1890**, or simply **1890**) **gegen 170,000 in 1885. Er wohnte (im) Dezember (des Jahres) 76 Lindenstraße 74** (short for **im Hause 74 der Lindenstraße**). **Die Strecke Berlin-Potsdam, 1838 eröffnet, war die erste preußische Bahn** The line between Berlin and Potsdam was the first Prussian railroad, opened in 1838. **Ein Viertel (auf) eins** or **ein Viertel nach zwölf** a quarter after twelve, **halb (auf** understood) **zwei** half-past one, **drei Viertel auf drei,** or **ein Viertel vor** or **bis drei** a quarter to three, or in railroad language as in English: **zehn (Uhr) zwanzig** (written 10.20).

3. When used substantively as names of figures, all numerals are declined weak, as they are all fem.: **Die Eins ist nicht deutlich** the figure 1 is not plain. **Du hast die Fünf zu groß geschrieben** You have written the 5 too large. **Eine römische Zehn** a Roman X. The form in **-e** is less common: **So? und warum nennt Ihr | die Fünfe eine heilige Zahl** (Schiller's *Piccolomini*, 2, 1). The plural always has **-en: die Zahl 1881 enthält zwei Einsen und zwei Achten.**

Note. These numbers are also used as feminine substantives in various other applied relations: **eine schöne Drei von Freunden, eine böse Sieben** a vixen, **zwei Dreien** a pair-royal of treys. **So stellt sich endlich | die große Drei** (Jupiter, Venus, Mars) **verhängnisvoll zusammen** (Schiller's *Wallensteins Tod*, 1, 1). **Der einzig Eine bist du, doch du lenkst | als eine mystisch große Drei die Welt** (Platen).

Zwei and **Drei** are sometimes used as neuter substantives in a collective sense: **Liebe, menschlich zu beglücken, | nähert sie ein edles Zwei; | doch zu göttlichem Entzücken, | bildet sie ein köstlich Drei** (Goethe). **Das schwesterliche Drei** the three Graces (or the three Parcae or Fates).

4. **Hundert, Tausend, Million, Milliarde, Billion,** can be used substantively, and are then inflected as nouns, the first two according to the unmutated **e**-plural type and the others weak: **Das erste Hundert, ganze Hunderte von Menschen. Es geht in die Tausende** It reaches up into the thousands. **Man schätzt die Zahl sämtlicher Rumänen** (Roumanians) **auf 10 Millionen.**

5. Masc. substantives are formed from the numerals by adding **er,** all inflected according to the **e**-less plural type: **die Einer, Zehner, Hunderter** units, tens, hundreds, **ein Vierziger** a man of forty, **ein Achtundvierziger** one who took part in the stirring events of 1848, **die Achtundzwanziger** the troops of the 28th regiment, **ein Gläschen Dreiundachtziger** a nice glass of wine of the year '83, **ein Greis nahe den Achtzigern** (or **den achtziger Jahren,** or **den Achtzigen,** or **den Achtzig**) an old man near the eighties, **ein mittlerer Vierziger** (Fontane) a man in the middle of the forties, **ein Vierer** a boat with four rowers, **ein Siebener** a member of a body or committee of seven. Some of these formations are also common in compounds: **ein Viererzug** a team of four horses, **der Siebenerausschuß** the committee of seven men, **der Vichrerrat** the Council of Four (in the peace treaty at Paris in 1919).

122. Ordinals:

1. The ordinals except those for 'first,' 'third,' and 'eighth,' which are irregular, are formed by adding **t** to the numbers 2–19, and **st** from 20 on. They are declined strong and weak as adjectives. Only the last number is inflected if compound.

1st **der (die, das) erste**
2nd **der zweite**; earlier in the period also **der zweete, die** (fem.) **zwote**; also, **der, die, das ander** (still found in **anderthalb**—see **126.** 2. *b*— and in **am anderen Tage** *the next day*
3rd **der dritte**
4th **der vierte**
7th **der siebente,** or **siebte** (S.G.), early N.H.G. **siebende**
8th **der achte** (adds no **t**)
20th **der zwanzigste**
21st **der einundzwanzigste**
22nd **der zweiundzwanzigste**
101st **der hundertunderste,** sometimes **der hunderteinte** or **hunderteinste**
102nd **der hundertundzweite**
103rd **der hundertunddritte,** sometimes **der hundertdreite**
107th **der hundertundsieb(en)te**
108th **der hundertundachte**
200th **der zweihundertste**
300th **der dreihundertste**
1000th **der tausendste**

a. Ordinals are sometimes uninflected in the idiom **zu zweit, dritt,** &c., with the force of **zu zweien, dreien,** or **zu zwei, drei** *two* or *three together*: **Ich bin jetzt**

wahrlich nicht in der Stimmung, zu dritt zu sein Indeed I am not in a mood to have a third party with us. **Wir Göppinger sind zu zwölft** There are twelve of us from Göppingen.

b. Ordinal adverbs are formed by adding **ens** to the simple stem: **erstens** in the first place, **zweitens** in the second place, **zwanzigstens,** &c.

c. After the analogy of **der vierte** (&c.) and **der zwanzigste** are formed **der wievielte** and **der wievielste** *what date, what number, how many*: **Der wievielte ist heute?** or **Den wievielten haben wir heute?** *what is the day of the month?* **Der wievielte waren Sie im Examen?** What was your place in the examination? **Die wievielste Liebschaft ist dies wohl?** About how many love-affairs does this make that he has already had? Also other similar formations occur: **in der elfdreiviertelten Stunde** *in the last quarter-hour*, literally, in the last quarter-hour before twelve. See also **126.** 2. *b*.

2. The ordinals are often in certain set expressions replaced by cardinals, which in this case stand after the noun: **Kapitel sechs** chapter 6, **Band fünf** vol. 5, &c. **Das Stück ging bis Schluß Aktes III steigend empor—Akt III schlug am mächtigsten ein** (Wildenbruch to B. Litzmann, Nov. 25, 1881).

123. The ordinals all require an article or pronominal adj. before them, but **erst** often drops it and is then used in the sense of an absolute superl.: **erste Schriftsteller** *authors who are among the best*, but **die ersten Schriftsteller** *the best authors.*

124. *The days of the month.* As in English, the ordinal is used for the days of the month. Letters are usually dated after the following model: **Berlin, den 5.** (read **fünften**) **März 1894. Ihr Schreiben vom 19.** (read **neunzehnten**) **ds.** (**dieses Monats**), **am Abend des 20.** (read **zwanzigsten**), **vom 3.** (read **dritten**) **bis 14.** (read **den vierzehnten**) from the 3rd to the 14th, **bis mit den 1.** (read **ersten**) **Oktober,** or **bis und mit den 1. Oktober** up to and including October the first.

125. Distributive numerals are formed by prefixing **je** to cardinals or ordinals: **Er gab den Knaben je zehn Pfennig** He gave to each of the boys ten pfennigs. **Die Gefangenen wurden zu je zwei und zwei** (by twos) **zusammengebunden. Je der zehnte Bürger** every tenth citizen.

126. Compound numerals:

1. Numerals formed from cardinals are:

a. *Variative* numerals, which add **-erlei** to the simple cardinal, forming an uninflected compound: **einerlei** of one kind, **zweierlei** of two kinds, **dreierlei** of three kinds; **hunderterlei, allerlei** of all kinds, &c. The **lei** in these compounds is in reality a fem. noun in the gen., as can still be seen in the ending of the cardinal (**einer** fem. gen.), but it is felt and treated as an uninflected adjective: **allerlei gute Bücher** all kinds of good books, dat. **von allerlei guten Büchern, allerlei guter Wein** every kind of good wine, **Kinder beiderlei Geschlechts, die mancherlei Folterschrauben,** &c. Substantively: **mit hunderterlei solcher Vorsätze** (Hauptmann's *Friedensfest*, 3).

b. *Multiplicatives,* which add **-fach** and **-fältig** to the cardinal: **einfach** single, simple; **einfältig** simple (silly); **zweifach** and **zweifältig** twofold; **dreifach** and **dreifältig** threefold, &c. The inflection is strong and weak.

c. *Iterative* adverbs, which add **-mal** to the simple cardinal: **einmal** once, **zweimal** twice, **dreimal** three times, &c. Also with inflection: **das eine Mal, mit einem Male** all at once, **zu vier verschiedenen Malen,** &c. Also the ordinal is thus used: **das erste Mal** the first time, &c. See 2. *d* below.

Note 1. Adjectives are formed from iterative adverbs by adding the adj. ending **-ig** to **-mal: ein dreimaliger Angriff** a thrice-repeated attack.

Note 2. Observe the difference of accent between **'einmal** *once* and **ein'mal** *once upon a time.* In the former case **ein** is a numeral and hence is accented, while in the latter case it is an article, and hence is unaccented. The article in **einmal** is, however, accented when the word indicates future time and is used in the meaning **irgend 'einmal** *some time*: **Er wird doch 'einmal kommen** He will surely come *some time.*

2. Numerals formed from ordinals are found in:

a. The neut. substantives expressing fractions, formed by adding **-tel** (reduced form of **Teil** *part*) to the stem of the ordinals, suppressing, however, the final **t** of the ordinal before the **t** of the suffix: **ein Drittel** *a third*, **ein Viertel** (pro. fɪʀtəl) *a fourth,* **ein Siebentel** or **Siebtel** (S.G.), **sieben Achtel** = $\frac{7}{8}$, &c.,

but instead of **ein Zweitel** is used **ein halb** (**121.** 1. A. *a* and **139.** 2. *d*, *Notes* **1** and 2) or **die Hälfte** (except in the technical language of business and music, where **ein Zweitel** is also employed, as in **Zigarren in Zweitelkisten, eine Zweitelnote**); **vier Hundertfünftel** = $\frac{4}{105}$; **hundert und hundertvier Hundertfünftel** = $100+\frac{104}{105}$; **ein Hunderteintel** = $\frac{1}{101}$; **ein Hundertzweitel** = $\frac{1}{102}$; **ein Zwanzigstel** = $\frac{1}{20}$; **ein Hundertstel** = $\frac{1}{100}$. Sometimes **teil** is still used in full instead of the reduced form **tel,** especially after **hundert** (formerly also used as ordinal instead of **hundertst**) in the meaning *per cent.*: **ein Dritteil** *one-third*, **92 Hundertteile** 92 per cent.

Note. These substantives are often considered as indeclinable adjectives: **ein fünftel Kilometer, eine fünftel Meile, drei viertel Pfund, drei viertel Stunden.** The numeral may also be regarded as the first element of a modern compound, and hence both parts are then written as one word: **eine Viertel'stunde, ein Viertel'jahr.** The accent in such compounds still shows that they are not felt as old compounds. See **47.** 3. A. *e.* (**4**).

b. The compounds which add **halb** to the ordinal, which tho formerly declined are now usually uninflected: **dritthalb** or **drittehalb** two and a half, lit. (two and) half of the third, **vierthalb** or **viertehalb** three and a half, &c., but always **anderthalb** (for **anderehalb** half of the second; see **122. 1**; the **t** in place of **e** after the analogy of **vierthalb,** &c.) instead of **zweit(e)halb.** Exs.: **anderthalb Ellen. Das sind schon dritthalb Jahre** (Hebbel's *Agnes Bernauer*, 4, 3). **Um dritthalb Jahre** (Fontane's *Frau Jenny*, chap. ii), **durch dritthalb Jahrhunderte** (*Hamburger Nachrichten*, Dec. 16, 1904), **drittehalb Meter hoch** (*Westermanns Monatshefte*, Aug. 1905). This construction is still in use but is not so common as **zwei(und)einhalb** two and a half, **drei(und)einhalb** three and a half, **in sechs(und)einhalb Jahren,** or **in sechs und einem halben Jahre,** &c. **Anderthalb,** however, is much more common than the other words of the same formation.

When these words in **-halb** stand alone substantively they *may* be inflected strong: **Mein Vatter hett nur einen Arm, so hab' ich anderthalben** (Fischart, *Garg.*, 94 b). The original nature of this construction requires the sing. form, and this still occurs, but the plural is now more common: **auf einen Schelmen anderthalbe** (Goethe). **Für zwei essen oder wenigstens für anderthalbe** (Kurz, *W.*, 89). Inflection still occurs occasionally also in the attributive relation, but only in the old sing.: **Mehrere und zwar die erfolgreichsten dieser Dramen dauern nicht länger als einen vollen Tag, andere nur anderthalben Tag** (Eugen Zabel in *Velhagen und Klasings Monatshefte*, Aug. 1906, p. 612).

Corresponding inflected forms with a stem in **-t** and the force of ordinals occur occasionally: **noch in der zwölftehalbten Stunde** (*Mont.-Ztg.*, 17. 17) in the last half-hour (before twelve). Sometimes the form without **t** is used here: **in der zwölftehalben Stunde.**

c. In the following idiomatic compounds:

(1) Inflected: **der, die, das zweitbeste** the next to the best, **der drittbeste** the third from the best, **der vorletzte** the next to the last, **der drittletzte** the third from the last.

(2) Uninflected (see *Note*): **selbander** or **selbzweit** myself the second, i.e. myself along with another, **selbdritt** myself the third, **selbviert,** &c.: **Ich pflege selbander zu reiten. Dann schritten sie selbzweit dahin** (Anna Schieber's *Alle guten Geister*, p. 185). Inflection here also occurs: **selbzwanzigster gefangen** (Lessing's *Nathan*, 1, 5) taken prisoner along with nineteen others. The use of the cardinal here is less common, and from the strict standpoint of grammar is incorrect. It occurs, however, in the best authors: **selbfünfe** (Goethe's *Wanderjahre*, 2, 12), **selbst** (instead of **selb**) **funfziger** (Lessing's *Emilia Galotti* 3, 1).

Note. The apparently uninflected forms **selbdritt,** &c. are mutilated remnants of older weak forms, **selbe dritte,** &c. The force of the weak inflection is the same as described in **111.** 10. *Note.*

d. The ordinals can be compounded with **mals** to form adverbs and with **malig** to form adjectives: **erstmals** for the first time, **die erstmalige Zusammenkunft der deutschen Architekten in Leipzig** the first meeting of the German architects in Leipsic. Compare **1.** *c* above.

PRONOMINAL ADJECTIVES.

Demonstratives.

127. The demonstratives, which can be used either adjectively or substantively, are: **dieser, diese, dieses** this; **jener, jene, jenes** that; **der, die, das** this, that; **derjenige, diejenige, dasjenige** that; **welcher, welche, welches (130.** 3) that, that one; **solcher, solche, solches** such, such a, or **solch ein** (**eine, ein**), or **ein solcher, eine solche, ein solches,** or **so ein** (**eine, ein**), or simple **ein, eine, ein** (see **131.** 2. *a*); **der'selbe, die'selbe, das'selbe** the same; **selbiger, selbige, selbiges** the same; **der nämliche, die nämliche, das nämliche** the same; **derartiger, derartige, derartiges** of such a nature. The inflection of these pronominals is treated in the following articles. For the demonstratives or determinatives which are always uninflected see **161.** 2 and 3; **141.** 5. A. *b*; **143.**

128. A. **Dieser, diese, dieses** *this*, and **jener, jene, jenes** *that*, are inflected like the strong descriptive adjective except in the genitive of the masculine and neuter sing., where the regular strong ending **-es** is used instead of the weak **-en** (see **106.** *Note* 1). In the nom. and acc. neut. sing. **dieses** is often contracted to **dies.** In the masc. and neut. dative sing. we sometimes find instead of the correct strong form the weak ending **-en** after a strong limiting adjective after the analogy of descriptive adjectives: **in allem diesen Trubel** (Bismarck to his wife, Nov. 17, 1848), **allem diesen Jammer fern** (Marriot's *Der geistliche Tod*, p. 266, 5th edition), **von allem diesen aber nun abgesehen** (Adolf Bartels in *Deutsche Monatsschrift*, Dec. 1905, p. 409).

a. The forms **dieses** (or more commonly **dies**) and **jenes** remain uninflected when they are used in connection with the verb **sein** and a predicate noun, to indicate that the subject is identical with the predicate: **Erlauben Sie mir, Ihnen die Herren vorzustellen. Dies ist Herr Schmidt und jenes ist Herr Meyer. Dies ist eine schöne Blume. Dies sind schöne Blumen. Ist dies Ihre Feder?** Note in these sentences that the verb agrees with the predicate. The regular inflected form showing the proper gender and number can also be used: **Dieser** (or **der**) **ist der Schuldige.**

b. **Dies** is also uninflected when it is used as a subject or object referring to something that is introduced to one's attention by a gesture or explained by the context immediately preceding: **Wofür halten Sie dies?** What do you take this for? **Dieses alles geschah auf der Mittagsseite des Schlachtfeldes.**

B. **Dieser,** often strengthened by the adverb **hier,** refers to something near the speaker, while **jener,** often strengthened by some adverb as **da, dort** *there, yonder*, points to something more remote: **dieses Haus hier und jenes dort; in dieser und jener Welt** in this world and the one to come. Hence **dieser** is often translated by *the latter* and **jener** by *the former*: **Der Frühling und der Herbst hat seine Freuden: dieser gibt Früchte, jener Blumen.**

Both are used much more in the attributive than the substantive relation. The neut. sing., however, is often used substantively (see A. *a* and *b*). Also the other genders are frequently employed in the substantive relation in the meanings *the former, the latter*.

a. **Jener** is also much used to indicate something well known, either by referring backward to some definite person or thing already mentioned or by making reference to some well-known person or thing that is at once recognized by the accompanying description: **jene eben zitierten Stellen. Jene Blätter, nach denen Sie fragten, habe ich noch nicht gefunden. Es war jene Nacht, in der die dickbauchige, schwarzgeteerte Holländer Kuff gegen den Büsener Deich jagte** (Frenssen's *Die drei Getreuen*, III, 1). **Ada war nicht von jenen Puppen, die mit sich machen ließen, was man wollte. Flechten von jenem schönen Kastanienbraun, wie man es in Deutschland so selten findet. Ihm kam der Gedanke, sein Oheim müsse auch zu jenen Menschen gehören, die ein Verständnis für die Sprache der Naturdinge besäßen** (Jensen's *Das Bild im*

Wasser, p. 87). **Er meint jene Sorge, die uns zu furchtsamen Sklaven des Tages und der Dinge macht, jene Sorge, durch welche wir stückweise an die Welt verfallen** (Harnack's *Das Wesen des Christentums*, Fünfte Vorlesung).

b. Often, especially in popular ballads, **jener** is used in a quite indefinite sense, indicating a place well known to the speaker, but not in any way described so as to be clearly recognized by those addressed: **Da droben auf jenem Berge, | da steht ein feines Schloß** (Heine). **Die Sonne hebt sich noch einmal | leuchtend vom Boden empor, | und zeigt mir jene Stelle, | wo ich das Liebste verlor** (id.).

c. For determinative use of **jener** see **130**. 2. *a*.

129. 1. Der, die, das *that* are used either adjectively or substantively, but with somewhat different inflection for each use. Adjectively used, **der** is inflected exactly like the def. article, differing from it only in that it has a much stronger stress and has the stem vowel long before **m, n,** and **r.** To distinguish **it** from the article in print it is sometimes written with a capital, spaced letters, or furnished with an accent: **Der, d e r,** or **dér.** Used substantively it is declined as follows:

	Singular.			Plural.
	Masc.	Fem.	Neut.	Common form.
N.	**dēr**	**die**	**dăs**	**die**
G.	**dĕssen** **dĕs**	**dēren** **dēr** **dērer**	**dĕssen** **dĕs**	**dēren** **dēr** **dērer**
D.	**dēm**	**dēr**	**dēm**	**dēnen** or **dēn** (2. B)
A.	**dēn**	**die**	**dăs**	**die**

2. From the beginning of the N.H.G. period there has been considerable fluctuation in the use of the demonstrative forms, and usage is not yet entirely settled. The prevailing usage of our time seems to be as follows:

A. Genitive Forms. The form here depends upon the grammatical function:

If the demonstratives are used attributively before the noun the short forms are uniformly used: **der Name d e s** (that) **Knaben, der,** &c.; **die Namen d e r Knaben, die,** &c.

If the demonstratives are used substantively, the forms vary according to their grammatical function and fall into four groups:

First group. If they are used as pure demonstratives, or instead of personal pronouns (see **141.** 2) or possessives (see **138.** 2. *d*), the forms are quite uniformly: (sing.) **dessen** (masc.), **deren** (fem.), **dessen** (neut.); (pl.) **deren** (for all genders). Exs.: **Ich erinnere mich dessen nicht mehr** I do not remember that any more. **Sie empfing ihre Freundin und deren** (her) **Tochter. Es lagen Spanier hier; deren erinnere ich mich sehr wohl. Nimm die Trauben, ich habe deren** (of them) **genug.**

Second group. If they are used determinatively followed by a relative clause, the forms are: (sing.) **dessen** (masc.), **derer, deren,** or still more commonly **der** (fem.), **dessen** (neut.); (pl.) **derer** for persons, unless it stands before the governing noun, where the form is usually **deren** (sometimes **derer**); pl. for things **deren,** or **derjenigen,** sometimes **derer.** Exs.: **Es ist der Sohn dessen, den wir gestern gesehen haben. Das Glück derer, die fern von ihm war** (Ompteda's *Sylvester von Geyer*, LXXVIII). **Der Himmel hat durch die Hand derer, die du liebst, mich davor geschützt** (Jensen) (also **deren** and more frequently **der,** but better **der Dame.** It is often better in the gen. of the fem. to use a noun here, as the thought will otherwise be impaired, for the forms **derer** and **deren** are felt as plural, and **der** has not yet become fixed here as a sing. in contrast to the plurals **derer** and **deren**). **Das Schicksal deren, die ihn trug** (Auerbach's *Dorfgeschichten*, 1, 61). **Sich lächerlich zu machen in den Augen der, die ihn zu einem Gott erheben kann** (Spielhagen's *Selbstgerecht*, II, p. 45). **Der Herr vernichtet die Macht derer, die sich wider ihn auflehnen. Habe ich aber auch jemand übervorteilet durch déren** (in original ed. **der)**

ètliche, die ich zu euch gesandt habe (2 Cor. XII. 17, revised ed.). **Trockne die Tränen von déren Gesicht, die dann um mich weinen** (Kleist). **Bei dem Studieren der Wissenschaften, besonders deren, welche die Natur behandeln** (Goethe). **Die Waffen, einschließlich deren, die die Personen bei sich tragen, sollen an ihrem augenblicklichen Platze gelassen werden** (*Hamburger Nachrichten*, Jan. 4, 1905). **Das Jahrhundert | ist meinem Ideal nicht reif. Ich lebe | ein Bürger derer** (now more commonly **deren** or **derjenigen**), **welche kommen werden** (Schiller). **Reißt alle, alle [Blumen] ab, | sogar die Knospen derer** (now more commonly **deren** or **derjenigen**), **die erst kommen** (Hebbel's *Nibelungen*, II, V, 7).

Third group. If they are used determinatively followed by a gen. or a prepositional phrase, the forms are: (sing.) **dessen** or **des** (masc.), **der** (fem.), **dessen** or **des** (neut.); (pl.) **derer** for persons, **deren** (also **der** and sometimes **derer**) for things. Exs.: **Die Besprechungen meines Anwalts und dessen** (or **des**) **meines Gegners haben zu einem Vergleich geführt. Ich bin in Sorge nicht sowohl wegen deiner Angelegenheit, wie wegen der deines Bruders. Sie erinnert sich gern ihrer Freundinnen, besonders derer aus ihrer Schulzeit. Er fand neue Bundesgenossen statt derer aus frühern Zeiten. Sie erinnert sich gern ihrer frühern Erlebnisse, besonders deren** (or **der**) **aus den Schuljahren. Ihre Augen hatten nicht ganz das leuchtende Blau, auch nicht den tiefen Ernst derer Sophiens** (Perfall's *Der schöne Wahn*, p. 60). To this group also belongs **derer** before **von** in names of people of noble birth: **das Geschlecht derer von Logau.**

Fourth group. The following corrupted gen. forms, **dessent** (masc. and neut.), **derent** (**deret**) fem. gen. sing. and gen. pl. for all genders, are not infrequently found in composition with **wegen** *on account of*, **um — willen** *for the sake of*, **halb(en)** *on account of*: **derentwegen** *on account of these things*, &c. There is, however, a slight tendency in choice language to restore the correct form, especially in case of **um — willen: Wenigstens hoffe ich, daß sich Ihre Verrichtúngen in Braunschweig . . . werden so gehäuft haben, daß Sie wenigstens derenwegen bleiben müssen** (Lessing). **Ich will kein Geld von Euch; um dessen willen bin ich nicht gekommen** (Storm's *Im Brauer-Hause*, p. 102). **Ein mutmaßlich aus einem alten märkischen Herrenhause herstammender . . . Pfeilerspiegel . . . lieh der ärmlichen Einrichtung trotz ihres Zusammengesuchtseins oder vielleicht auch um dessen willen etwas von einer erlöschenden, aber doch immerhin 'mal dagewesenen Feudalität** (Fontane's *Poggenpuhls*, chap. i).

a. The short gen. form **des** is now quite rare aside from the use in the second and third groups given above and its employment in adverbial and conjunctional compounds, as **um 'deswillen** *on account of that* (with reference, not to a particular object, but to a thought: **„Wie kann ich jetzt auch an mein wirbelndes Dasein ein andres zu ketten wagen?" „Begreifst du nicht," flüsterte sie, „daß ich gerade um deswillen zu dir stehen will?"**—Telmann's *Wahrheit*, XXIV), *on this account* (introducing a clause of cause: **um 'deswillen, weil** *on this account, because, for the reason that*), **'deswegen** *on that account*, **'deshalb** (earlier in the period **deshalben**) *for that reason*, **in'des** and **unter'des** (or more commonly **in'dessen** and **unter'dessen**; for meaning see **240**), also in the combinations **des und des**, or **des und jenes** *of this one and that one*, and in poetic language and old sayings, as **Wes Brot ich esse, des Lied ich singe** I sing the praises of him whose bread I eat. Notice especially the frequent use of **um 'deswillen weil** (**272. D**): **Was endlich das von Professor Laband angeführte Beispiel, betreffend die Ausweisung der Engländer aus Hamburg, betrifft, so ist es um deswillen beweisunkräftig, weil der Hamburger Senat so wenig wie eine andere Bundesregierung solche Torheiten begehen wird** (*Hamburger Nachrichten*, June 7, 1906). All these cases are survivals of early N.H.G. usage, where the short gen. forms **der, des** (later also falsely written **deß**) were the rule. The short form **des** has become quite firm in the above-mentioned adverbial compounds **deswegen**, &c., where the reference is to a thought, less firm, however, in **indes** and **unterdes**, where the same idea is found. The long form **dessen** is also often used in **um dessen willen** instead of **um deswillen** *on account of that* with reference to a thought: **Der Urheber der Steuer nannte sich Bismarck, und dieser Bismarck wurde in den Stuben der Zigarrenarbeiter um dessen willen nicht geliebt** (O. Ernst's *Semper der Jüngling*, p. 103). The corrupted form **dessent** is sometimes used in the adverbial compounds **dessentwegen**, &c., where the reference is to a thought, but it is more commonly employed where the reference is to a definite antecedent. Either **des** or **dessen** is used in connection with **um willen** when a relative clause introduced by **was** follows: **Er** (T. Mommsen) **war seit langer Zeit in Wahrheit der Führer der Universität, nicht nur um des Glanzes seines Namens willen, sondern um deswillen, was er ihr leistete** (Adolf Harnack in *National-Zeitung*, 1903, No. 588).

Ich sage das aber, Kind, um dessen willen, was mir noch zu erzählen bleibt (Spielhagen's *Was will das werden?*, I, chap. xi). Sometimes also 'dessentwillen here: **Zwar nicht um dessentwillen was er getan** (Walther Siegfried's *Um der Heimat willen*, X).

The new lengthened forms **derer** (fem. gen. sing. and gen. pl.) and **denen** (dat. pl.) were formed by adding the regular strong adjective endings to the original short forms. The form **denen** begins to appear first in the Southwest about 1450, the form **derer** in Middle Germany about 1536. They both became established in prose about 1600. The forms **dessen** and **deren** lengthened from **des** and **der**, originated in the Southwest. The genitive plural form **deren** begins to appear about 1450 and becomes established about 1600. The singular forms **dessen** and **deren** appear later than the plural **deren** and come slowly into general use. The S.G. **deren** and the M.G. **derer** have not as yet, as stated above, become clearly differentiated.

In early N.H.G. also the M.H.G. forms **dere** and **dero** were used with the force of **deren**: **Denn welche diese Grewel thun dere seelen sollen ausgerottet werden von jrem volck** (Lev. xviii. 29). Of these **Dero** *your, his*, used in speaking to and of persons of high rank, were in the last days of monarchical Germany still lingering on in official style and in the language of the princely courts: **Dero Erlaubnis** the permission of your (or his) Highness.

b. Earlier in the period the distinction that the short forms should be used in the gen. for attributive and the long ones for substantive use was not known, and even in the classical period was not yet fully developed: **Ich habe oben gesagt, der Raum sei die Ordnung derer Dinge, die zugleich sind, die Zeit hingegen die Ordnung dessen, was auf einander folgete** (Chr. Wolff). **Kurze Übersicht derer Gaben, welche usw.** (Goethe). Present usage is nicely reflected in the following sentence from Wildenbruch: **Seine dunklen, blaugrünen Augen hatten den scharfen Blick d e r Menschen, die viel und aufmerksam mit der Natur verkehren, und seine hageren Gesichtszüge jenes nach innen gekehrte Lächeln derer, die viel erlebt haben, und deren (151. 1) Herz ein gutes Gedächtnis besitzt.** The lengthened forms are to-day found attributively only in antique or, as in the following sentence from Hans Hopfen's *Studiosus Taillefer*, p. 37, in comic style: **Es kam ihm vor, als sollt' er von ihm wie von dem Repräsentanten aller derer braven Burschen, die eben nicht vom gleichen Bande umschlungen gewesen waren, das ihrige aber in Ehren getragen hatten, gleichfalls gerührten Abschied nehmen.**

c. To give a clear formal expression to the idea of the dative relation the genitive forms **dessen** and **deren**, which are used instead of a possessive (see **138.** 2. *d*), are, tho they are genuine pronouns, sometimes still as occasionally also earlier in the period treated as adjectives and inflected like **sein** and **ihr**: **Minna blieb von ihrem Gatten bis zu dessem Tode getrennt** (Stahr's *Goethe's Frauengestalten*, 2. 286). This is as yet confined to the dat. of the masc. and neut. See also **151.** 1. *c*. In the same manner within historic times the possessive **ihr** *her, their* was developed out of the gen. of **sie**.

B. Dative Forms. The form depends upon the grammatical function in the dat. pl. The distinction is the same as for the gen., namely, the short form is used attributively before the noun, the lengthened form substantively: **von den Leuten, die, &c.**; **mit denen, die** with those who; **mit seinen Verwandten und denen seiner Frau.** If the dative plural is used determinatively followed by a genitive or a prepositional phrase, the form is usually **dēnen** as elsewhere in substantive use, but we still find here sometimes the older short form **dēn**: **Ob sich die Verhältnisse bei größeren Schiffsformen mit dēn der Versuchsobjekte decken werden, erscheint fraglich** (*Hamburger Nachrichten*, Nov. 27, 1904). The form **dēn** is also sometimes employed instead of **dēnen** when the demonstrative stands alone: **In dēn** (i.e. **in den Hunden**) **da steckt etwas** (Freytag's *Die verlorene Handschrift*, 1, 188). **Ginge es nach dēn** (i.e. **den Scharfmachern**), **so hätten wir nicht nur Attentate wie in Rußland, sondern auch längst den Bürgerkrieg** (*Der Türmer*, March 1905, p. 822).

a. Earlier in the period the lengthened form **deren** was also used in the fem. dat. sing.: **Hab deren zu Lieb ein neu's Liedlin gedicht, so Euer Gnad das begehrt zu hören, wollt' ich's deren zur Letzte singen** (Wickram's *Rollwagen*). Still in dialect in the form of **dere, deren,** or **derer**: **Wann ich nur von derer wegkimm!** (Anzengruber's *Kreuzelschreiber*, 2, 9). Also in adjective function: **Ich frag' dich nur, ob du glaubst, daß du in derer Weise was richt'st?** (id., *Schandfleck*, xiv).

b. Earlier in the period the distinction between attributive and substantive use of the double forms had not developed so sharply as to-day: **von denen** (now **den**) **Leuten, die, &c.** (Goethe). This usage is still preserved in S.G. and West M.G. dialect.

C. *The Neuter Singular*. The neuter singular forms, especially the nom. and acc. **dăs** (in dialect frequently spoken **des** or **dös**) and the dat. **dēm**, are much used without a change of form for reference to one or more objects or to things of different genders but always with the case required by the grammatical construction:

(1) Like **dies** (see **128.** A. *a*) the nom. is used to express identity: **Das ist meine Feder. Das sind meine Federn.** It is often very similar in meaning to **dies**: **Ist das** (or **dies**) **der Weg auf den Bahnhof?**

(2) It is often used as subject or object, a more emphatic form than **es**, referring without regard to the gender of the noun to some object at hand, some matter in hand, a condition of things, or an activity: **Wie heißt man das?** What do you call that? **Das geschieht ihm recht** That serves him just right. **Das geht bei mir nicht so** That won't do with me. **Das können wir nicht ruhig mit ansehen** We cannot tolerate that. **Dem kann ich nicht ruhig zusehen** I can't look on with indifference while such things are going on. **Das verwickelt sich** Matters are becoming complicated.

(3) **Das** with sing. verb is used to represent a class of people or beings as a whole: **Kinder leben sorglos dahin; das singt und spielt bei den ernstesten Lagen des Lebens. Was aber sich Mensch nennt, das lebt von dem Gedanken der alles schonenden und erhaltenden Liebe und ihres Gebotes** (Hermann von Blomberg in *Der Türmer*, March 1905, p. 824). A. **Sie sind Anarchisten.** B. **Was ist denn das?** A. **Das sind Leute, die usw.** Often also with reference to one or more in a contemptuous sense: **Will das** (referring to Riccaut) **zu uns?** (Lessing's *Minna*, 4, 2). **Aber das** (i.e. **die Arkebusiere**) **denkt wie ein Seifensieder** (Schiller's *Lager*, l. 1006).

(4) As a subject, predicate, or object, to refer emphatically to an idea already expressed in some preceding sentence, noun, adjective, or participle: **Er hat mich heute morgen barsch angefahren. Das** (subject) **darf nicht wieder geschehen,** or **das** (object) **darf er nicht wieder tun. Zwischen nicht geringen Teilen der Bevölkerung und der neu geschaffenen bewaffneten Macht hat sich eine Konfliktsstimmung eingestellt, die zu einer ernsten Gefahr werden kann. Es muß versucht werden, dem** (dat. object) **vorzubeugen** (*Vorwärts*, June 4, 1919). Often in the predicate relation: **Er ist ein Bettler,** or **Er ist arm. Das war er früher nicht. Dieses Frauenzimmer gibt sich für die Tochter des englischen Konsuls aus. Das ist sie auch in der Tat.**

Also **es** can be used here instead of **das** except in the dative relation, where **dem** is employed, as illustrated in the sentence from "Vorwärts" and in **141. 4** (2nd par.). Elsewhere **es** is employed much more frequently than **das**, differing, however, from it in that it is less emphatic and has not the freedom of word-order, in the object and predicate relation only standing *after* the verb: **Er hat mich heute morgen barsch angefahren. Es darf nicht wieder geschehen,** or **Er darf es** (or **das**) **nicht wieder tun. Er ist jetzt ein Bettler,** or **Er ist jetzt arm; er war es** (or **das**) **aber früher nicht. Dieses Frauenzimmer gibt sich für die Tochter des englischen Konsuls aus. Sie ist es auch in der Tat. Sie meint, du seist entflohen; und halb und halb bist du es schon.**

(5) It is also often used in a collective sense. See **153. 1. (1); 263. II. 4.** *c*.

D. Dative and Accusative after Prepositions. After prepositions the demonstrative usually takes the adverbial form, if it points to things. See **141. 5. A.** *b, c, d*.

Note. This adverbial form is, however, usually replaced by the inflected form of the demonstrative when it points to a following relative clause: **Der Minister hat die Kommissionsmitglieder gebeten, von dem** (instead of **davon**), **was er zur Begründung der Vorlage gesagt hat, nichts in die Öffentlichkeit kommen zu lassen.** This rule is not rigidly followed: **Auch wußten sie nichts davon** (instead of **von dem**), **was an diesem schönen Sonntage vorging** (G. Keller). **Und das Ergebnis davon, das sich in ihm noch immer dämmernd festsetzte, war: daß man, um der Stärkere zu sein, auch die Kraft des Geistes, nicht nur die des Leibes, besitzen müsse** (Wilhelm Fischer's *Die Freude am Licht*, p. 135).

3. **Der, die, das** *this, that*, are the most popular demonstrative forms, altho the least definite, as they are used in a general way for both **dieser** and **jener,** indicating the position of objects as near or distant only by the aid of a gesture or the context.

Der is used substantively more than attributively, yielding in large measure to **dieser** and **jener** in the latter function. In several substantive relations, however, **dieser** and **jener** are common. See **128. A.** *a* and *b*; **128. B.** Besides the meanings of **dieser** and **jener, der** has other meanings, often replacing the personal pronouns (see **141.** 2) and being used like **derjenige** (see **130.** 2) as a determinative followed by a genitive, prepositional phrase, or relative clause. In all these common substantive uses of **der** the primarily adjective forms **dieser** and **jener** are little used.

***a*.** **Der** is sometimes still omitted before a dependent gen., not only in poetry but also in plain prose: **Und welch ein Band ist sichrer als (das) der Guten?** (Goethe's *Tasso*, 3, 2). **Durch wessen Schuld ist sie so geworden, wenn nicht durch Ezards und Galeidens?** (R. Huch's *Ludolf Ursleu*, chap. xxiv). Earlier in the period this usage was much more common.

***b*.** In a few expressions **der** is rendered by *such, So and So*: **Wenn das sein Wunsch ist** if such (that) is his wish, **in dḗr und dḗr Stadt** in such and such a city, **an dḗm und dḗm Tage** on such and such a day. **Der und Der** (**Die und Die**) **hat es gesagt** Mr. (Mrs.) So and So said so.

130. 1. **Derjenige, diejenige, dasjenige** *that* are declined as if each element (**der** and **jenige**) were written apart and the latter element were a wk. adj. Used adjectively or substantively, their declension is as follows:

	Singular.			Plural.
	Masc.	Fem.	Neut.	Common form.
N.	**derjenige**	**diejenige**	**dasjenige**	**diejenigen**
G.	**desjenigen**	**derjenigen**	**desjenigen**	**derjenigen**
D.	**demjenigen**	**derjenigen**	**demjenigen**	**denjenigen**
A.	**denjenigen**	**diejenige**	**dasjenige**	**diejenigen**

a. Earlier in the period up to the close of the seventeenth century we find here the simple wk. form of **jen-**: **dem jenen, welcher . . .** (Opitz 1. 105). From the sixteenth century we find the lengthened form **jenig**. Earlier in the period it could be used without the def. art.: **ich verfluch alle jenige, die anderer Meinung sein** (Fischart).

b. The form **dieserjenige** *this one* (*here*) is used in popular speech: **Ich denke immer, der hat sich aus einer andern Welt in diesejenige verirrt and kann den Weg nicht wieder zurückfinden** (Raabe's *Schüdderump*, chap. ix).

2. **Derjenige,** unlike **der,** which is either a determinative or a pure demon., has only determinative force, i.e. is followed always by a gen., prep. phrase, or a relative clause: **derjenige, der** (or **welcher**) *that one who*; **nicht mein Hut, sondern derjenige meines Bruders; nicht dieses Buch, sondern dasjenige im roten Einband; derjenige Mann, der** (or **welcher**). There is no difference of meaning between the determinative **der** and **derjenige** except that the latter is a heavier and consequently more emphatic word. It is also in general much used in the written language in the attributive relation in preference to **der,** as the latter cannot in the printed form be distinguished from the definite article by a heavy accent as in the spoken word. Also in the precise phraseology of definition and law and of exact language in general it is a decided favorite: **Notwehr ist diejenige Verteidigung, welche erforderlich ist, um einen gegenwärtigen rechtswidrigen Angriff von sich oder einem anderen abzuwenden** (*Bürgerliches Gesetzbuch*, § 227). As **derjenige** is much used in print and is much employed by clumsy speakers to gain a little time, certain grammarians have felt themselves called to ridicule it as stilted and ungainly, at the same time failing to recognize the true province of the word. Recent literary usage is evidently tending to prefer it to **der** as a clearer expression for the determinative idea. The lengthened forms of **der,** however, especially **derer** (gen. pl.), are more common here than the monosyllabic forms, as they are clearer determinatives and not so liable to be confounded with the definite article or the demonstrative.

In early N.H.G. also **welch** and **solch** were used as determinatives. The four determinatives **der, jener, welcher,** and **solcher** were already in use in M.H.G. In the sixteenth century the new form **derjenige** came into use. Differentiation in meaning and function has been gradually developing. **Der** is more inclined to pure demonstrative function pointing to a definite person or thing, altho it is still widely used in determinative function to point forward to a person or thing described in a following relative clause or a genitive or prepositional phrase. For *definite* reference to a person or thing which is described in a following clause or phrase **derjenige** is now the favorite determinative, **Jener** is also still used here but with a little different shade of meaning. See ***a*** below near end and **128. B. *a*.** For indefinite and general reference **derjenige, welcher,** and **solcher** are employed. The use of **welcher** is given in 3 below. The boundaries between **derjenige** and **solcher** in present usage are drawn in **131.** 3 below.

a. Sometimes in accordance with older usage **jener** is still used determinatively instead of **der** or **derjenige** modified by a gen. or a relative clause. **Der hohe Adel zürnte über den politischen Einfluß des Bürgertums, welches im Reichsrat das Ansehn des Herrenhauses durch jenes der Abgeordneten in Schatten stellte** (von Sybel). **Mir dienen | als Zeugen jene, die's mit Augen sah'n** (Fulda's *Der Talisman*, 4. 6). **Nur gering ist die Zahl derjenigen, welche sich mit der Venus beschäftigt haben, noch geringer die Zahl jener, welche auf diesem Planeten etwas gesehen haben, und am allergeringsten die Zahl jener, deren Beobachtungen wirklich einen Wert besitzen** (Leo Brenner). **Wenn er von jenen Dingen sprach, die er der Welt und dem Leben abzuringen . . . hoffte, so war immer nur von inneren, seelischen Gewinnen die Rede** (Ganghofer's *Der Glücksucher*). Also in general usage **jener** or its governing word is followed by a relative clause, but it here differs in meaning from the determinatives **der** and **derjenige** in that it only points out somebody or something that has already been mentioned, or refers to some well-known person or thing that is at once recognized by the accompanying description. For examples and further explanation of this use of **jener** see **128.** B. *a.*

b. Instead of **der der** (or **welcher**) or **derjenige der** (or **welcher**) we sometimes still find in accordance with older usage simple **der: Aber die einen anderen Menschen brauchen, kommen selten zur Höhe** (Prof. D. Martin Schian in *Deutsche Rundschau*, 1911, vol. 146, p. 408). The relative pronoun after the determinative **der** is here not expressed in accordance with older usage. See **154.** *Note.* The reference in this example is general, but it has as in case of **derjenige der** a shade of meaning quite distinct from that found in **wer** as it has individualizing force. See **156.** Simple **der** more commonly points to definite or fairly definite individuals: **Die ich meine, heißt Frau Findeklee** (Hauptmann's *Versunkene Glocke*, l. 1047). **Jene, die am meisten in uns getötet und begraben haben, sind oft, die uns am nächsten standen** (Heyking's *Briefe, die ihn nicht erreichten*, New York, Dec. 1899). **Aber die das glaubten, waren doch nur wenige** (Prof. Dr. Ernst Vogt in *Frankfurter Zeit.*, Feb. 22, 1914).

3. *Indefinite and General Determinative.* The old general indefinite determinative **welcher** is still sometimes used: **In welche Unternehmung er sich auch einläßt, stets hat er Glück** *In whatever enterprise he enters upon*, &c., lit. *in that enterprise he enters upon*, &c. The adverb **auch** is now usually found here in connection with **welch,** which indicates that this older usage only survives in concessive clauses. In early N.H.G., however, it was not thus limited but was freely used where to-day **derjenige der,** or **wer** is employed: **Welcher Bawm (= derjenige Baum, der) nicht gute früchte bringet | wird abgehawen** (Matth. iii. 10). **Welchen (= wen) der HERR lieb hat | den züchtiget er** (Hebrews xii. 6). This **welch** is usually classified as a general indefinite relative adjective, but historically considered it is a general indefinite determinative. The definite or indefinite determinative **derjenige** is always followed by a relative pronoun. The indefinite determinative **welch** is followed by an asyndetic relative clause, i.e. one not introduced by a relative pronoun, a construction very common in English, as illustrated by the literal translation of the first German example given above. Compare **154.** *Note.* In early N.H.G. **welcher** began to take on definite meaning: **Welchen (= den** or **derjenige, den) ich küssen werde | der ist's** (Mark xiv. 44). In substantive clauses, as in this example and other varieties of the substantive clause, **welcher** with definite force has not become so common as **der** or **derjenige der,** but in attributive relative clauses it is now thoroly established and used interchangeably with **der,** where, however, it is now felt as a relative pronoun: **Das Buch, welches** (originally *that one*, an appositive to **Buch** pointing forward to the following explanatory clause, now only felt with the force of the relative *which*) **ich in der Hand halte, ist eine deutsche Grammatik.**

131. 1. **Solch** *such, such a* is strong or weak as any adjective, but is uninflected before **ein** and inflected or uninflected before a descriptive adjective. If strong, the gen. of the masc. and neut. sing. ends properly in **es,** but, as in the case of descriptive adjectives, a weak gen. is often found. Exs.: **solcher kleine Hund,** or **solch ein kleiner Hund,** or **solch kleiner,** or (perhaps the most common form) **ein solcher kleiner Hund; jedes solche geblümte Täßlein; solches** or **solchen Glückes ungewohnt.** *Not such* is translated by **kein solch: Ich bin kein solcher Narr. Keines solchen Narren, keine solchen Narren; in einzelnen solchen Fällen** in individual cases of this kind; **eine Mehrheit**

von beigeordneten solchen Einheiten a number of such units that have been coordinated; **viele solche** (or **solcher**) **Menschen. Es gab größere und kleinere solche Wagen** There were larger and smaller scales of this kind. **Es sind zwei solche da.** Substantively: **Ein solcher ist gefährlich** Such a man is dangerous. **Mußte nicht Christus solches leiden?** (Luke xxiv. 26). **Das sind ein Paar Ohrgehänge, wie der Herr keine zweiten solche findet in Venedig** (H. von Hofmannsthal's *Der Abenteurer und die Sängerin*, p. 171). The masc. and neut. gen. sing. is usually weak in substantive use: **In der Lebensform des Bürgers als solchen** (wk. gen.) **liegt etwas Tragisches** (Kühnemann's *Schiller*, p. 237). **In der Anschauung des Griechentums als solchen** (Ernst Heilborn in *Frankfurter Zeit.*, Dec. 23, 1913).

English *such* is sometimes rendered by **der.** See **129. 3. *b*.**

a. In colloquial language **solch** is very commonly replaced by **so ein,** negatively often in popular language in the form **so kein: Von so einem Manne spricht man Jahrhunderte. So einer** such a one, &c. **So kein Gesicht sah ich in meinem Leben!** (Goethe's *Faust*, 2808). **Ich habe einen Hunger, so hab' ich mein Lebtag keinen verspürt.** Instead of the neuter substantive form **solches** we now more commonly hear in colloquial speech **so etwas: Hat man je so etwas gehört? So etwas verlernt sich nicht so leicht. So etwas von** is often used instead of attributive **solch** or **so ein: Solchen,** or **so einen,** or **so etwas von Kot sieht man nicht alle Tage.** Instead of the attributive **solch** we often find the adverbial form **so** in popular language: **Es gibt so Gänschen** (i.e. girls), **die hübsch weiche Schnäbel haben** (H. Hoffmann's *Wider den Kurfürsten*, chap. i).

Note 1. **So ein** is often used referring to something so well known that there is no need of detailed description: **Er trägt auch so einen großen breitkrämpigen Hut** He also wears one of those large broad brimmed hats (which are now so commonly worn). **Ich möchte so ein Bilderbuch für ein kleines Kind haben** I should like to have a picture book such as would be suitable for a little child.

Note 2. **So ein** is often contracted to **so'n** and quite frequently takes a plural, altho simple **ein** has no form for the plural: **Ich dächte, wenigstens unsere streng gesitteten Kreise halten sich — so — nen — so'ne Sachen vom Halse** (Sudermann's *Heimat*, 1, 7).

b. Instead of **solch** we sometimes find in colloquial language **so welch-,** only, however, in the substantive relation: **Es sind Waldbeeren; so welche wachsen in den Gärten nicht** (Storm's *Unter dem Tannenbaum*, vol. I, p. 191.)

c. Notice especially the case where a qualifying adjective follows the demonstrative and the idea of the intensity of the quality is more prominent than the demonstrative idea. Here *such, such a* are usually translated by **so, ein so:** *such* bad weather **so schlechtes Wetter,** *such* a good man **ein so guter Mann.** Also **solch, so ein,** or **so etwas von** (example in *a* above) contains this idea of intensity, especially before a noun not modified by an adjective: **Dieses Schiff rannte mit solcher Heftigkeit gegen die Brücke, daß es sie auseinander sprengte. Solch ein, so ein** (in sing.), **solch—** (in pl.) are often used with disparaging force: **Mit solchen** (with such a meager stock of) **Kenntnissen wollen Sie sich zum Examen melden?**

2. **Solch** *as a Determinative.* **Solch** is also a determinative, followed by a relative clause, a genitive, or a prepositional phrase, but it differs from the determinatives **der** and **derjenige** in that it does not point to definite individuals but refers to a person or a thing as a member of a *class* of persons or things without fixing definitely the identity of the individual in question, variously translated, *one, such* (*as*), *that, those,* or by repeating the noun to which it refers: **Zur Begleitung eines Flügels sang dort eine angenehme weibliche Stimme ein leidenschaftliches Lied, ein solches, das Sturm und Aufruhr der heftigsten Gefühle darstellte** (H. Seidel's *Lorelei*). **Der weise Erzieher lehrt seinem Zögling solche Wahrheiten, die der Stufe seiner Erfahrung und seines Verstandes entsprechen** (Kuno Fischer). **Die Krankheit, welche eben vorwiegend eine solche des Willens gewesen war und nicht des Körpers** (Frenssen's *Die Sandgräfin*, chap. viii). **Bislang war es mir noch nie in den Sinn gekommen, daß mein Vater sich vielleicht mit noch anderen entscheidenderen Gedanken trug als nur mit solchen der Sorge und des Kummers** (R. Huch's *Ludolf Ursleu*, chap. xxii). **Wohl fehlte es weder an Ausdrücken des moralischen Entzückens, noch an solchen der ästhetischen Empörung** (Kühnemann's *Schiller*, p. 29). **Ebenso wichtig, wie ältere Nachweise für Tollwut sind mir natürlich solche für tollwütig** (Stosch in *Zeitschrift für deutsche Wortforschung*, I. Band, p. 374). **Der berühmte Mann einer kleinen Stadt zu sein ist etwas ganz anderes als ein solcher in einer großen** (Wildenbruch's *Schwester-Seele*, chap. xi) To be the famous man of a little town is something quite different from being the famous man of a large city. **Eigentümlichkeiten des Wortschatzes sowie solche der Syntax** (O. Tacke in *Zeitschrift für den deutschen Unterricht*, 1915, p. 776)

peculiarities of vocabulary as well as peculiarities of syntax. There is in **solch** always something indefinite, hence it must be replaced by **der** or **derjenige** when the reference becomes definite, even where the idea of class, kind, quality is clearly present: **Wie den Engländern eine gewisse Sentimentalität, die freilich ganz verschieden ist von derjenigen ihrer deutschen Vettern, durchaus nicht fremd ist** (Prof. Dr. Ernst Sieper in *Westermanns Monatshefte*, vol. 111, p. 189).

a. Accented **ein** is often used here like **solch: Es war eine** (= **eine solche**) **Nacht, in welcher man nicht gern einen Hund hinausjagt. Das Zenzl ist eine, die einen Mann glücklich machen kann** (Voss's *Psyche*, VIII).

3. **Solch** *Competing with Other Forms.* In the use of **solch** described in 2 to refer not to definite individuals but to persons or things of a particular class or kind the idea is always more or less general or indefinite. Hence there arose early, even in the M.H.G. period, the tendency to use **solch** for general or indefinite reference. In the sixteenth century the new form **derjenige** gradually became established as the determinative for more definite reference than that suggested by **solch.** The use of **solch** for indefinite reference, however, is at present in general confined to cases where **solch** refers to a noun which has already been used, as in the examples from Frenssen, Huch, Kühnemann, Stosch, Wildenbruch, and Tacke in 2 above, or where it itself stands before the noun and points to a following relative clause, as in the example from Fischer. If there is no such *noun* present, **derjenige** is usually employed, even tho the reference is general and indefinite: **Derjenige, der sich mit Einsicht für beschränkt hält, ist der Vollkommenheit am nächsten** (Goethe). **Wie sonst diejenigen, die im Herrn sterben** (Paul Heyse's *Marienkind*, p. 96). Compare **156.** In the plural, however, also **solch** is used here: **Für solche, denen die vergleichende Grammatik schon vertraut ist, ist es** (i.e. **dieses Werk**) **nicht bestimmt** (Meillet-Prinz's *Einführung in die vergleichende Grammatik*, Preface). Also the neuter sing. as it has indefinite force: **Wir können im Rahmen der Schule von zeitgenössischer Literatur nur eine Auswahl des Besten geben und nur solches, was entweder an andere Lektüre anzuknüpfen ist usw.** (*Zeitschrift für den deutschen Unterricht*, 1915, p. 447.) Instead of **solches** we might use **das** or **dasjenige** here, but **solches** stresses more the idea of class or kind.

In contrast to this use of **solch** is its employment to refer to definite persons and things: **Nunmehr fuhr der Kaiser bei dem Zelt an, betrat solches** (= **es**) **und usw.** (Goethe). **Ein Haufe Franktireurs überfiel die Brücke und sprengte solche** (= **sie**) **in die Luft.** (*Kölnische Zeitung*). This usage is not in accord with the indefinite nature of **solch** and in spite of its frequent employment by the great writers of the classical period is now gradually disappearing from choice language. Where, however, the personal pronouns are themselves not employed and are usually replaced by other words it is much used, competing here with **der** and **derselbe,** as described in **141.** 1, 2, 3, 5. B. *b. Note.*

Solch not only competes with **derjenige** and the personal pronouns, as described above, but is also used instead of the indefinite **welch** *some, any*: **Bei alledem verbrauchte er aber Geld, ohne solches** (= **welches**) **einzunehmen** (R. Huch's *Schlaraffis*, p. 140). This usage is in harmony with the indefinite nature of **solch.**

Grammarians have written a good deal upon the false use of **solch,** but their censure is often indiscriminate. In many instances present usage is not incorrect, as often claimed, but manifests a keen sense for a fine shade of meaning, the **solch** referring not to a definite person or thing, as in case of **er, sie, es, der, derjenige,** but rather to an object or objects of some particular kind, often described by the modifying element of the compound in case of a compound antecedent or by a modifying word following or preceding a simple antecedent: **Ich durfte den armen Studenten doch nicht für einen sechswöchigen Kursus ihre letzten Zwanzigmarkstücke aus der Tasche ziehen, wenn sie überhaupt solche besaßen** (H. Hoffmann). **Die bedeutendste Schrift über das Niederdeutsche ist Agathe Laschs mittelniederdeutsche Grammatik. Eine solche nach dem jetzigen Stande der Wissenschaft zu schreiben, war nicht leicht**

(Oskar Weise in *Zeitschrift für den deutschen Unterricht,* 1915, p. 520). **Ich danke Ihnen sehr dafür, daß Sie so gütig waren, dem Herzog in meinem Namen ein Exemplar der Horen zu überreichen. Es folgt solches** (= **dafür ein anderes Exemplar der Horen**) **hier zurück** (Schiller an Goethe, 1. 105). **Er erwartete von ihr unbedingt den ersten Brief und dieser Brief kam nicht, denn sie erwartete einen solchen von ihm** (Ompteda's *Frieden,* chap. xii). **Ich hatte mir . . . eingebildet . . . auf dem Bock säße der Tod in einem schwarzen, flatternden Mantel, auf seinem klappernden Schädel einen blanken niedrigen Hut, wie ich solche an unseren Droschkenkutschern zu sehen gewohnt war** (R. Huch's *Ludolf Ursleu,* chap. xxvi). Out of this common usage has arisen the common employment of **ein solcher** or simple **solcher** to point to something as a member of a class without definitely fixing its identity: **Unter den zahlreichen Telegrammen befindet sich auch ein solches aus New York** (*Kölnische Zeit.*). **U in du ist zweimal mit Längezeichen gedruckt, zweimal ohne solches** (Oskar Weise in *Zeitschrift für den deutschen Unterricht,* 1915, p. 430). Here **ein solcher** competes with **einer** *one,* but it is a clearer expression, for the idea of number is not prominent. **Eines** may be used instead of **ein solches** in the first example, but it could not be used at all in the second as the idea of class entirely overshadows the idea of number. **Solch** often refers similarly to a simple noun, where in English we use the word *mere* before the repeated noun: **Er meinte, sie wäre selbstsüchtig, sie gönne ihm das Vergnügen** (of studying Spanish dialects in Spain) **nicht, das ihm mehr als ein solches** (*mere pleasure*) **war** (Ompteda's *Frieden,* chap. xii).

132. 1. A. Der'selbe, die'selbe, das'selbe *the same* are inflected like **derjenige.** See **130. 1.** It is not only used adjectively, as in **derselbe Mann,** but also substantively: **Er ist derselbe, der** (subject) **uns gestern anbettelte. Unser Freund ist nicht mehr derselbe, der** (predicate) **er war,** or **als der** (predicate appositive) **er herkam.**

a. If contraction with a preceding preposition takes place the parts are separated: **am selben, zur selben,** &c.

b. Sometimes the article is dropped and **selb** is inflected strong: **um selbe Zeit** (Schiller). **Ich nehme meinen Kindern alle Bücher ab, sobald sie selbe nicht mehr brauchen, und lege sie in Verwahrung** (Rosegger).

c. Lengthened forms both with and without the article were common earlier in the period: **derselbige, selbiger.** With the article the form is weak, without it strong. The lengthened forms are little used to-day in plain prose, but still occur not infrequently in poetic language or in antique or solemn style. It is sometimes used as an emphatic form of **derselbe: Auch wenn man zweimal dasselbe tut, ist es gleichfalls nicht mehr dasselbige** (Raabe's *Alte Nester,* I. chap. x).

d. In S.G. dialects **derselbe** or **selbiger** have developed various forms, as **dersall, dersell, seller; deseb, seb.** These forms usually have demonstrative force = **der** or **jener.** See B. *a. Note* below. These dialects use **der nämliche** instead of the literary **derselbe.**

e. The form **dieser selbe** is occasionally found, usually with a slight shade of difference, in that it, as the English *this same* or *this very same,* has more distinctly demonstrative force and conveys more emphasis: **Diese plötzliche Frage setzte das Mädchen kaum in Erstaunen, das sich heute und gestern mit nichts anderem als nur mit diesem selben Gegenstande beschäftigt hatte** (K. F. Meyer).

f. The form **jener selbe** *that same* is occasionally found: **In jenem selben Jahre noch war es, wo usw.** It was in that very same year that, &c.

B. **Derselbe** has a wider range of meanings than the English *the same* as used in ordinary prose. Besides its primary meaning it is also used in the following derived meanings:

a. **Derselbe** is often used instead of a personal pronoun. See **141.** 2, 3, 4, 5. B. *b,* 6, 7. This use developed out of its employment as a demonstrative, which was common in early N.H.G. See *Note.*

Note. The demonstrative idea and that of identity approach each other at times very closely. In reply to the question **Sind Sie nicht Herr Waldfried, der Sohn des Bezirksförsters?** the answer may be: **Ich bin derselbe,** or **Der bin ich.** From such or similar cases **derselbe** had already in M.H.G. assumed demonstrative or determinative force, and hence was strongly stressed: **Weh aber dem Menschen | durch welchen des menschen Son verhaten wird | Es were dem selben Menschen besser | das er nie geboren were** (Mark xiv. 21). **Wenn du in einem ungewissen und zweifelhaften Werke, da du zweierlei für dir hast, begriffen, so erwehle** (**erwähle**) **denselben Teil, welcher am leichtesten zu thun ist** (Olearius, *Rosenthal*). Also used substantively: **vnd wenn du seinen Mund auffthust | wirstu einen Stater finden | Den selbigen nim vnd gib jn fur mich und dich** (Matth. xvii. 27). As can be seen in the first two sentences of this Note, both **der** and **derselbe** may have the force of emphatic personal pronouns. Both of them often lose their original force and are then used merely to replace personal pronouns, as described in **141. 1, 2, 3, 4, 5. B.** *b,* **6, 7.** The older use of **derselbe** as a demonstrative or determinative pure and simple has in a large measure disappeared in the literary language of our time, surviving only in dialect (see A. *d* above): **Aber ein neues Gewissen muß einer schon haben, wenn er so etwas auf sich nehmen kann, ein funkelnagelneues. Selb** (= **das**) **ist meine Meinung** (Voegtlin's *Das neue Gewissen*, p. 80). Its use, however, instead of the personal pronouns has increased. See **141. 7.** *Historical Note.*

b. In the language of monarchical Germany **derselbe** was used in connection with **allerhöchst, höchst, hoch** in addressing an emperor, king, and other potentates, and is still used in case of legislative bodies, to replace as a personal pronoun the title **Ew. Kaiserliche Majestät, Hoher Reichstag,** &c., after it has once been used. The exact form depends upon the title in question: **Allerhöchstdieselben** (to the emperor; pl. in form, also with pl. verb), **Hochderselbe** (to the Reichstag), &c.

NOTE. Wherever **derselbe** in the cases in *a* and *b* is used to replace a personal pronoun it is more weakly accented than in the primary demonstrative use.

2. **Der nämliche** *the same, the very same, the identical* is inflected like **derselbe;** the parts, however, are separated in writing. The parts of **derselbe** were also written separately early in the period. **Der nämliche** has a much narrower range of meanings than **derselbe,** not being used at all in the groups *a* and *b* under 1. B above. It is sometimes used with the primary meaning of **derselbe,** sometimes with a different shade in the sense of *identical*: **unter demselben Blau, über dem nämlichen Grün** (Schiller's *Spaziergang*, 199). **Wir gehen tausendmal den nämlichen** (identical) **Weg, aber nimmer wieder denselben** (Raabe's *Alte Nester*, I. chap. x).

133. Derartig *of such a nature,* strong or weak, or less frequently **derart** uninflected: **derart** or **derartige Beleidigungen** insults of such a nature. **Das Verhältnis war nicht derart** or **ein derartiges, daß es Johanna große Verlegenheit verursacht hätte. Eine derartige Schnelligkeit war bisher unerhört. Derartiges kommt nicht vor** Such things do not occur.

Note. The form **derart** or **der Art** should remain uninflected, as it is in fact a fem. noun in the gen. However, it is sometimes felt as a demon. adj. and accordingly inflected: **von derarten Maßnahmen** (*Volks-Zeitung*).

Interrogative and Relative Adjectives.

134. 1. The interrogative adjective **welcher, welche, welches** *which, what,* used adjectively or substantively, in questions direct or indirect, is always strong when declined, but must be uninflected before **ein,** and may be before a descriptive adjective and sometimes before a neut. noun in the nom. and acc. sing.: **welcher Schüler? welches edle Herz? Welch edlen** or more commonly **welches edlen Mannes Tat ist das? Ich möchte wissen, welcher Mann das gesagt hat** (indirect question). The uninflected form is especially frequent in exclamations: **Welch eine Torheit! Welch edler Mann! Welch schönes Fest! Welch** or more commonly **welches Glück!** What good fortune!

2. The parts of the interrogative **was für ein** (**eine, ein**) *what kind,* used in questions direct and indirect, are indeclinable except **ein,** which is declined as the indefinite article when used adjectively, and like strong adjectives when used substantively: **Was für ein Buch ist das? Ein deutsches. Was für eins?** What kind of book is that? A German book. What kind? **Ich möchte wissen, was für ein Buch Sie lesen** (indirect question).

The **ein** drops out before a noun denoting an abstract idea or a material and in the plural of the adjective use, but in the substantive use it is replaced thruout by the strong indefinite **welch** *some*: **Was für Torheit treibst du da? Was für Wein haben Sie getrunken? Wir haben starken Wein getrunken. Was für welchen?** *What kind?* **Was für Bücher sind das? Deutsche Bücher. Was für welche?** *What kind?* **Er hat Freunde, aber was für welche? Mit was für einem Bleistift schreibt er?,** but **Mit was für Bleistiften schreiben sie?** The **für** in these examples is not a preposition, but a particle introducing the following appositive. For the history of this construction and the relation in meaning between **was für ein** and **welch-** see *d* below.

The use of **welch-** in the substantive relation after names of materials and abstract ideas and in the plural, as found in the above examples, is wide-spread. Many, however, prefer to drop the **welch-: Wünschen Sie Butter? Was für**

haben Sie? (instead of **Was für welche haben Sie?**) **Gelehrsamkeit, aber was für?** (Goethe). **Ich kaufte zwei Bücher. Was für sind es?** (instead of **Was für welche sind es?**) **Bei der Kur erfuhr man gegenseitig alle Leiden und Schicksale und was für!** (Berlepsch's *Fortunats Roman*, 178). In popular language **eine** is often heard in the plural instead of **welche: In dem Park wachsen Bäume. Was für eine?**

When the reference is not to a material or an abstract idea, but to a single thing, **was für was** is used in the substantive relation: **„Wie heißt er denn?" „Tiberius." „Was für was?" frug er, und das Kind wiederholte das Wort** (Storm's *Bötjer Basch*, p. 27).

a. In the nom. and acc. **für** can be separated from **was: Was ist das für ein Vogel?**

b. **Was für ein** is often used like **welch-** in exclamations: **Was für ein schönes Haus!**

c. In questions direct and indirect, also in indefinite or general relative clauses, **was für**, often strengthened by the adverb **alles**, is used in the general indefinite sense of *what, what all, what different, all the various* (things, &c.) *which*: **Was ist das alles für ein Schreien und Toben? Was sind das nicht alles für Ausflüchte! Was du dir doch alles für Sorgen machst! Sie fing an, herzuzählen, was alles für gute Dinge und schöne Sachen im Hause seien, was sie selbst für Hauptsachen in einer kleinen Truhe besitze.**

d. In M.H.G. and early N.H.G. **was** with the partitive genitive was used, where we now find **was für ein: Was Nutzens hast du von mir?** (Steinhöwel) In what have you received any benefit from me? Here as elsewhere the genitive passed over into the appositional construction, later the appositive being usually introduced by **für** (see **252.** 2. A. *b.* (**2**). *Note*): **In was Land** [now **was für ein Land**] **ziehen nicht die Zigeiner (Zigeuner)?** (Fischart, 1590). **Ach, was ist's ein Mann!** (Goethe's *Egmont*, 1, Bürgerhaus). Now, and even in Goethe's time, the usual form is **Was ist's für ein Mann!** The simple appositional construction is, however, still common in colloquial language, especially in exclamations: **Ei was Gewissenhaftigkeit!** (Ludwig's *Zwischen Himmel und Erde*, XIX). **Was ein Gesicht!** (M. Dreyer's *Drei*, 3). **O was komische Sachen!** (id., *In Behandlung*, 1). For a fuller history of the construction see **147.** 1. E. In such sentences **was für ein** may be replaced by **welch** when it inquires after a particular thing: **Welchen Nutzen** (what particular benefit) **hast du von mir?** There is often, however, no difference between **was für ein** and **welch-**, but the growing tendency has been to differentiate the meanings of the two expressions, the former expressing an inquiry after a particular kind or sort, the latter an inquiry after a particular thing: **Was für ein Pferd ist das?** *What kind of horse is that?* but **Welches Pferd wollen Sie reiten? — Den Braunen** *Which horse are you going to ride? — The bay.* In some dialects **welcher** is not used here at all, **was für ein** still being used for **welcher: Was for en Mann is des?** (dialect of Mainz).

3. In indirect questions and exclamations the German has two adjective forms, **ein wie, eine wie, ein wie,** or **ein welch, eine welch, ein welch,** which correspond to English *what a*, which is also confined to indirect questions and exclamations: **Der Vorfall führt uns recht lebhaft vor Augen, eine wie gewaltige Wirkung die geistlichen Spiele zu ihrer Zeit auszuüben vermochten** (Vogt and Koch's *Geschichte der deutschen Literatur*, p. 248). **Es ist erstaunlich, ein welch intensives Leben aus diesem Wörterbuch hervorquillt** (*Jahresbericht der germanischen Philologie*, 33, 163).

4. The early N.H.G. form **waser** has been entirely replaced by **was für ein.** See **147.** 1. E.

135. The relative adj. **welcher, welche, welches** is declined like the interrogative: **Er sagte „guten Tag," welchen Gruß sie freundlich erwiderte**; with noun understood: **Die Bevölkerung Rumäniens besteht zu $^4/_5$ aus Rumänen, einem Mischlingsvolke aus lateinischen und slavischen Bestandteilen, welche letzteren** (the latter of which) **romanisiert wurden.**

a. **Welcher** is usually a pure pronoun with the additional function of a subordinate conjunction, and requires the verb at the end of its clause. Even as real adjectives, as in the preceding examples, enough of the pronominal and conjunctional nature is left to require the verb at the end.

Possessives.

136. The possessives are **mein** my, **dein** thy, your, **sein** his, its, **ihr** her, its their, **unser** our, **euer** your, **Ihr** your. These words are used either adjectively or substantively, but with different inflection for each use. For their use see **138.**

a. In S.G. dialects other possessives are in use: **enker = euer** *your*, **ihner** *their*, **söner** *their.*

Declension.

137. 1. Used adjectively the possessives are inflected exactly like the indefinite article in the sing. and like the strong adjective in the pl.: **mein Hut, meine Feder, mein Buch, dieser mein Sohn** *this my son*, pl. **meine Hüte, Federn, Bücher.** When a strong pronominal precedes, we sometimes find instead of the correct strong form weak inflection of the possessive after the analogy of descriptive adjectives: **in diesem unseren Phantasiestübchen** (Raabe's *Die Akten des Vogelsangs*, p. 90). **Bei allem seinen großen Ruhm** (Ebner-Eschenbach's *Glaubenslos*, chap. iii).

a. In poetry the uninflected form following the noun can still be found: **Steh auf, du Schwester mein** (Uhland). This word-order is also found in the first words of the Lord's Prayer, always when used as a noun: **Vater unser usw.** *Our Father*, &c., **das Vaterunser** *the Lord's Prayer*. Also the form **Euer** (sometimes found in the contracted form **Ew.**, which form is explained by the older spelling **ewer**) is still sometimes uninflected when used before a title in direct address: **Die Nachrichten aus Paris, welche Euer Excellenz durch das Auswärtige Amt mitgeteilt worden sind,** &c. (General Tresckow to General Roon); **das Schreiben Euer Hochwürden vom 25. v. M.** (*Graf von Bülow an den Missionsinspektor Herrn Haußleiter*, Dec. 8, 1904).

b. With reference to ruling princes and persons of high rank we often find in the language of monarchical Germany **höchst** before the possessive: **Euerer Hoheit und Liebden für Höchstihren heutigen Vortrag Meinen aufrichtigen Dank auszusprechen, ist Mir Herzensbedürfnis** (Herzog Johann Albrecht zu Mecklenburg an Herzog Adolf Friedrich zu Mecklenburg, Feb. 3, 1912).

2. A. Used substantively they agree in gender with the noun to which they refer and are inflected like a descriptive adjective, and hence have three forms — the *strong*, the *weak*, and in the predicate the *uninflected* form.

a. When standing alone without a preceding limiting adjective they are, especially in familiar language, inflected like strong adjectives, except in the gen. of the masc. and neut. sing., where they still have the strong form **es** instead of the wk. **en** (see **106.** *Note* 1): nom. **meiner, meine, meines,** &c. **Ist das Ihr Hut oder ist es meiner? Mein Bruder und seiner, unser Haus und Ihres.**

b. If preceded by the def. article, which form is now a favorite substitute for the simple possessive (see *a* above), they are declined exactly as the wk. adj.: **der meine, die meine, das meine; mein Bruder und der seine, meine Schwester und die seine, mein Buch und das seine.**

Often the stem **mein, dein,** &c. is lengthened by adding **ig** and then inflected in the same way: **der meinige, die meinige, das meinige; Unser Haus und das Ihrige.** These lengthened forms have gradually established themselves since the sixteenth century and have now, perhaps, become more common than the unlengthened ones. The latter, however, are in no wise felt as unusual, and are even favorites in choice prose or poetry: **Wenn Ihr Gesetz denn anders lautet als das meine, so kann ich nur dem meinen folgen. Lieber will ich ein gequälter Sünder bleiben als eine Puppe in der Hand meiner Mutter oder in der Ihren** (H. Hoffmann's *Rittmeister*).

Note. This possessive form with the article is now only used substantively, but this is only a modern differentiation. In M.H.G. it is also used attributively before the noun: die sine riche geste (*Nibelungenlied*, Aventiure 9).

c. These possessives, with the exception of **ihr** *her, their*, **Ihr** *your*, which are now usually inflected or replaced by some other construction, may like descriptive adjectives remain uninflected in the predicate after the intransitives **sein, werden, bleiben, scheinen,** and sometimes **gehören** (not only colloquially, as often stated, but occasionally even in elevated discourse), and as an objective predicate after **nennen, wissen, glauben, fühlen, empfinden, machen,** &c., if they express the abstract or general idea of ownership, authorship, but they are inflected strong or weak if it is simply desired to indicate that the thing represented by the predicate is identical with that represented by the subject: **Was euer ist, soll euer bleiben** What is yours shall remain yours. **Der Wagen ist nur halb mein. Das Geld ist sein. Der Tag ist unser** (Liliencron's *Kriegsnovellen*, battle of Vionville). **So lang das Schwert ich schwinge, | gehört, was ich besitze, Herr, auch dein!** (M. Greif's *Heinrich der Löwe*, 1, 2). **Dein g'hört alles da herum** (Ebner-Eschenbach's *Glaubenslos*, chap. vii). **Mein scheint die Schuld, doch weiß ich sie dein. Der Mensch hat nur sich selber sein zu nennen** (P. Heyse).

Earlier in the period also **ihr** was used predicatively, but it is also possible to construe this form in early N.H.G. as a gen. of the personal pronoun (see **140.** *b*), and later in the period, where the reference is to one woman, as a dative of the personal pronoun (see **258.** 1. A. *c*): **Selig sind | die da geistlich arm sind | Denn das Himmelreich ist jr** (Matth. v. 3). **Sagen Sie meinem Fränzchen, daß ich noch immer ihr bin** (Goethe to K. Fabricius, June 27, 1770). **Ihr bin ich, bildend soll sie mich besitzen** (id., *Tasso*, 2, 2). Instead of **Ihr** and **ihr** in the predicate we now often find **Ihre** and **ihrer** (see *Note* 2 below). Perhaps most people would avoid this construction here and use another.

But inflection for the expression of identity: **Mein Geschmack ist immer auch der seine** (Fulda's *Talisman*, 2, 6). **Er wollte Reilands Sache auch weiterhin die seine bleiben lassen** (Fedor Sommer's *Ernst Reiland*, p. 405). **Sein Los ist uns'res!** (Hebbel's *Nibelungen*, III, IV, 4). **Die Wünsche, die sie hegt, sind auch die meinen** (Fontane's *Vor dem Sturm*, III, 8). Compare these last examples with **Ihr habt mich auserwählt zu Eurem Führer, | mein wurde Euer Wille, Eure Tat** (Wildenbruch's *Die Quitzows*, 2).

Note 1. If the subject is **er, sie, es,** the uninflected form of the possessive is usually employed in the predicate; but if situation **es** (**141.** 9. *a*), which does not change form for gender and number, is made subject, the inflected substantive forms must be used: **Wem gehört der Hut — die Feder — das Buch?** Answer: **Er ist mein — sie ist mein — es ist mein;** or **es ist meiner** (**der meinige** or **der meine**) — **meine** (**die meinige** or **die meine**) — **meines** (**das meinige** or **das meine**), and in the pl.: **es** (speaking of hats, pens, books) **sind meine** (**die meinigen** or **die meinen**). The uninflected form emphasizes the idea of possession, and the inflected form that of identity. Even if the subject is **er, sie,** or **es,** the inflected form must be used if the idea of identity is prominent: **Dein Weg ist krumm, er ist der meine nicht** (Schiller's *Wallensteins Tod*, 2, 7). Also here the uninflected form emphasizes the idea of possession and the inflected form that of identity.

Note 2. In familiar conversation still, especially in the Midland and North, and also in the classics, there is an uninflected form in the predicate which in case of **ihr** *her*, **ihr** *their*, **Ihr** *your* ends in **e,** as **ihre, Ihre,** which is a survival of the M.H.G. form ire, employed in the Midland for the usual M.H.G. ir, the fem. gen. sing. and the gen. pl. of the personal pronoun si (**sie**): **Ich fürchte fast, daß dieses Frauenzimmer niemals Ihre wird** (Schiller). **Mein ist alles, was sonst ihre war** (Grillparzer's *Ottokar*, 2). **Das [das Kruzifix] ist nun Ihre** (Fontane's *Vor dem Sturm*, IV. 26). **Trud und Gerdt schritten langsam die lange Straße hinunter, bis an das Mindesche Haus, das nun ihre war** (id., *Grete Minde*, chap. vii). **Wir denka halt alle, das Mädchen wär' Ihre** (Hauptmann's *Fuhrmann Henschel*, Act 2). This is a survival of older periods when there was no possessive adjective for the fem. 3rd person and for the 3rd pers. pl., altho there were elsewhere regular adjective possessive forms. The possessive idea was in these places, where special forms were lacking, expressed by the gen. of the personal pronoun. The surviving pronominal forms **ihre, Ihre** were, however, after the formation of a possessive adjective for the 3rd pers. fem. and 3rd pers. pl., construed as a weak predicate adjective, and hence similar forms were sometimes made from the other possessives: **Sie doch wenigstens wissen, daß das, was meine ist, auch Ihre ist** (Lessing).

Instead of the colloquial **ihre** we find in choice language the form **ihrer,** the modern genitive of the personal pronoun **sie: Wir selbst, als Schwestern deiner Fürstin gleich, | gehorchen ihr, weil ihrer ward das Reich** (Grillparzer's *Libussa*, 3). **Denn ihrer** (i.e. **der Leidenschaften**) **ist ja das Reich und die Herrlichkeit der Welt** (Raabe's *Schüdderump*, chap. xii). **Ihrer ist die Schuld, — ganz allein ihrer!** (Telmann's *Wahrheit*, X).

B. These possessives can also be used as real substantives without antecedent, in which case they are written with capitals, with inflection as follows:

a. Referring to one's relatives, friends, party associates, and also, in neut. form, to one's property or duty, they are inflected weak: **Er lebt nur für die Seinigen** He only lives for his family. **Die Meinigen werden erfreut sein, die Ihrigen zu begrüßen** My folks will be glad to greet yours. **Die — Meinigen? Ich habe keine Meinen** (Wildenbruch's *König Laurin*, 3, 1). **Die drei verbündeten Herrscher hielten selbst auf einer Anhöhe in der Nähe und sahen die übermenschlichen Anstrengungen der Ihrigen.** In letters: **Ganz der Ihrige, die Deinige. Meine Schwester hat all das Ihrige verloren** My sister has lost all her property. **Ich habe das Meinige getan** I have done my duty.

Note. Provincially these substantives may be heard strong: **Meiner** my husband, my master, **Meine** my wife, my mistress. **Die hat eine Kusin, der Ihrer** (whose husband) **trifft nur alle vier Wochen einmal nach Haus** (Ebner-Eschenbach's *Rittmeister Brand*, V).

b. The short forms **Mein, Dein,** &c. are uninflected neut. substantives when used in the abstract or general sense of *possession, right of possession*: **Streit um Mein und Dein** contention as to what is mine and yours. **Dein und Mein bringt alles Unglück herein** Contention as to the right of possession of property brings about a good deal of misfortune.

Note. From the above it will be seen that aside from the special case in B. *b*, above, there are *four* substantive forms for the predicate, but only three for the subject, while there is only *one* form for the adj. use: **Das Buch ist mein, meines, das meine,** or **das meinige** (predicate). **Ihr** (adj.) **Buch ist neuer als meines, das meine,** or **das meinige** (subject.)

Use.

138. The following points as to the use of possessives may be of practical value:

1. As there are three forms corresponding to the three forms for the second person of the personal pronoun, care must be exercised as to their proper use. **Dein** *your, thy* is the form of the possessive, corresponding to the familiar form **du** (**140.** *a*): **Du wirst das Deine empfangen** You will get what is due you. **Ich habe mein Buch vergessen; leihe (du) mir deines.** The form of the possessive corresponding to **Sie,** the polite form of address, is **Ihr: Wo haben Sie Ihren Überrock gekauft?** The form of the possessive corresponding to **ihr,** the familiar address to two or more, is **euer: Ich rate euch, bekümmert ihr euch mit euren Angehörigen nicht um meine, sondern um eure Angelegenheiten.** Thus in familiar language **dein** or **euer** is used according as the address is to one or more persons, but each must agree in gender, number, and case with the following noun which it limits: **dein Buch** *your* (speaking to *one* friend) book, pl. **deine Bücher** your books; **euer Buch** your (speaking to several friends who own one book) book, pl. **eure Bücher** your books.

All pronouns and their corresponding possessives are written with capitals when employed in direct address in letters (not usually, however, elsewhere except in case of the polite form of address): **Lieber Bruder! Ich habe seit Deinem letzten Hiersein keine Nachricht von Dir erhalten.** The polite form of address **Sie** (with reference to one or more) and the corresponding possessive **Ihr** are always written with a capital, and usually also the other forms of conventional address explained in **140.** *a. Note,* namely **Er, Sie** (fem. sing.), **Ihr** (with reference to one or more) along with their corresponding possessives **Sein, Ihr, Euer.** Usage, however, fluctuates here at several points, some using capitals more freely, others more sparingly.

a. In the language of monarchical Germany in addressing potentates, dignitaries, kings, &c., the usual possessive is **Euer,** altho the corresponding personal pronoun is no longer **Ihr: Mein Herz weissagt, Ew. (= Euer) Durchlaucht werden die Erhaltung meines Lebens, das ganz Ihnen gehört, nicht verschmähen und mich auch in der Ferne als Ihren unveräußerten Untertanen betrachten wollen** (Voss to the Duke of Oldenburg, May 20, 1802). **Ich gebe mich gerne der Hoffnung hin, daß Eure Heiligkeit, wenn von der wahren Lage unterrichtet, Ihre Autorität werden anwenden usw.** (Kaiser Wilhelm an den Papst, Sept. 3, 1873). Notice here, however, that **Euer** is used only immediately before the title, and is elsewhere replaced by **Ihr. Sein, Ihr,** and **Ihro** (uninflected) were earlier in the period also used here like **Euer.** See **140.** *a. Note.*

2. There are two pronominals for the third person. Referring either to a masc. or neut. noun, **sein** is used and hence must be translated by *his, one's,* or *its*: **Er hat sein Schläfchen gemacht** He has taken his nap. **Man kennt nicht immer seine wahren Freunde** One does not always know one's true friends. **Jedes Land hat seine Vorzüge** Every land has its advantages. When the reference is to a neut. collective noun, the German possessive is **sein,** which must in some cases be translated by *their*: **Das Volk bestand auf seine Rechte** The people insisted upon their rights. The form **ihr** may mean in English *her, its, their.* If it refers to a female, it is to be translated by *her*: **Marie schreibt ihren Aufsatz** Mary is writing her essay. If it refers to a thing of fem. gender, it is translated by *its*: **Die Sache hat ihre gute Seite** The affair has its bright side. If it refers to more than one, it is translated by *their*: **Die Mädchen schreiben ihre Aufsätze** The girls are writing their essays.

a. The adverbial expression **seinerzeit** is used with reference to a word in the first, second, or third person, sing. or pl., masc., fem., or neut., with the meaning *in our* (*your, his, her, its*) *day* or *time, once upon a proper occasion* in connection with a past tense, and *in due time* or *season* in connection with a reference to a future time: **Wir waren seinerzeit auch rüstige Bergsteiger** We were also in our time (lit. in its time, in the time for it) sturdy mountain climbers. **Diese Kirche galt seinerzeit** (in its day) **für die schönste der Stadt. Seine Abhandlung über** Cynips scutellaris, **die Gallapfelwespe, machte seinerzeit** (at the time of publication) **in den betreffenden Kreisen Aufsehen** (Raabe's *Die Akten des Vogelsangs,* p. 10). **Meine Frau sagte seinerzeit** (once upon a proper occasion): **„Guter Gott, wie dankbar können wir doch sein, daß du nicht so warst wie die beiden anderen von euch"** (ib.). **Ich werde seinerzeit** (in due season) **auf die Sache zurückkommen. Das wirst du seinerzeit** (in due time) **erfahren.** Some prefer here to select the possessive according to the gender, person, and number of the word to which it refers: **Eine Geschichte des deutschen Volkes, welche an Stelle der ihrer Zeit tüchtigen . . . Geschichte der Teutschen von Pfitzer treten soll** (*Augsb. Allg.*). This is especially the case to bring out a contrast: **Auch Gärten, die aneinander grenzten . . . gab es da noch zu unserer Zeit, als die Stadt noch nicht das „erste Hunderttausend" überschritten hatte** (Raabe's *Die Akten des Vogelsangs*, p. 8).

b. The possessives, like the personal pronouns, may be used reflexively referring to the subject of the sentence, and when the subject is pl. may also be used reciprocally: **Ich fördere meine, du förderst deine, er fördert seine, sie fördert ihre Interessen** I further my, you further your, he furthers his, she furthers her interests. **Sie fördern ihre Interessen** They further their own interests, or it may mean their mutual interests.

In case of the third person of the reflexive possessive and the reciprocal possessive thruout, the reference cannot always be made clear by the use of the simple pronominal. It may not be clear whether **sein** *his* and **ihr** *her* refer to the subject or to another party, and whether **unser** *our*, **euer, Ihr** *your*, **ihr** *their*, are to be considered as personal, reflexive, or reciprocal pronominals, hence it is often necessary to add **eigen** *own* to the reflexive and **gegenseitig** *mutual* to the reciprocal possessive: **Er fördert seine eigenen Interessen. Sie fördern ihre gegenseitigen Interessen.**

Note. In careless and in popular language **sein** is sometimes found as a reflexive possessive, referring indifferently to a fem., masc., or pl. noun instead of the usual **sein** for the masc., **ihr** for the fem. and pl.: **Die Untersuchung wider Sonzognos Mörder geht seinen regelmäßigen Gang** (*Volkszeitung*, 23. 39). **Alle diese tendenziösen Stellen mußten seine fulminante Wirkung üben** (ib., 24, 56).

c. In M.H.G. and even as late as the classical period of N.H.G. we find a pleonastic possessive of the third person in conjunction with the gen. of a noun: **an des Illo** (name) **seinem Stuhl** (Schiller), **des Teufels sein Angesicht.** Often where in the literary language of to-day the genitive is dependent upon a form of the determinative **der**, or where some other construction must be used: **Da, nimm meinen Ring, verwahre ihn und gib mir des Majors seinen** (for **gib mir den des Majors**) **dafür** (Lessing's *Minna*, 4, 5). This construction is still found in colloquial and popular speech, but the dative which has also been in use for a long time and has been steadily gaining ground has become more common here than the genitive: **Da schlägt Fritz' seine Pendule elf Uhr** (Moltke in a letter). **Du bist meine Frau und nicht der Diplomaten ihre** (Bismarck's *Briefe an seine Braut und Gattin*, May 14, 1851). **Meiers** (gen. of a name) **ihr Haus ist schön. In Meiers ihrem Hause gefällt mir's gut. Gegen dem seine Weisheit** (Lessing). **Wem sein Hut ist das?** for the literary form **Wessen Hut ist das? Es ist dem Wilhelm seiner** for **Er gehört dem Wilhelm. Dem Vogel seine Federn, dem Hans sein Hut, dem sein Hut, der ihr Kind,** &c. **Für meinem Feldwebel seine Frau** (Auerbach's *Dorfgeschichten*). **Ich will dem Mathes** (name) **seine Kinder sehen** (ib.). **Du hast eine gute Stirn, ganz wie dem Väterchen seine** (Schulze-Smidt's *Denk' ich an Deutschland in der Nacht*, II).

The dative construction has arisen out of the dative of interest (**258.** 3. B). From **dem Vater ist sein Haus abgebrannt** has come **Dem Vater sein Haus ist abgebrannt.** The dative is now naturally the favorite in popular speech as the genitive is in general little used there.

d. The demon. genitives **dessen** *his*, **deren** *her, their*, are much used instead of the declined forms of **sein** and **ihr** to avoid ambiguity, **dessen, deren** referring to an oblique case, and **sein, ihr** to the subject: **Sie sprach viel von ihrer Schwester und erzählte viel von deren Schicksalen** She spoke much of her sister and related a good deal of her (i.e. the sister's) experiences. But if the reference is to her own experiences, it should read: **von ihren Schicksalen. Der Graf hat diesem Manne und dessen Sohne alles anvertraut** The count has entrusted all to this man and his (the latter's) son. But if the reference is to the count's own son, it must read: **seinem Sohne.** Also **derselbe** can be used instead of **dessen, deren** in such cases: **Der Graf hat diesem Manne und dem Sohn desselben alles anvertraut.**

Dessen, deren are also used in a following independent proposition instead of the possessive when the reference is to a nom. or an oblique case in a preceding independent or subordinate proposition: **Ablativ und Lokativ sind am frühesten untergegangen, schon in urgermanischer Zeit, und die übrig gebliebenen Kasus mußten deren frühere Aufgaben mit vertreten** (Behaghel's *Die deutsche Sprache*, p. 316, 2nd ed.). **Zuletzt trat Heinrich in diesem trauernden Hause fast ganz in die Stelle, die Rudolf eingenommen hatte. Er wohnte in dessen Stube, er benutzte dessen Bücher** (Raabe).

Dessen and **deren** are also used elsewhere instead of **sein** to avoid ambiguity: **die Gräfin, ihre Verwalterin und deren** (i.e. *the latter's*) **Tochter.**

Dessen and **deren** are often used of persons of high rank or position even where no ambiguity would arise by the use of **sein, ihr: der König und dessen Gemahlin.** The use of **dessen** and **deren** is not thus limited to persons of rank: **Es unterschreibt der Vater oder dessen Stellvertreter** (*Hamburger Nachrichten*, Feb. 19, 1905). In M.H.G. the use of the demonstrative was common where a possessive is now employed. Later a differentiation between possessive and demonstrative developed, as described above, but as in the last two German examples older undifferentiated usage still lingers on.

e. Instead of the possessive the demonstrative **der** or **derselbe** is much used if the reference is to things: **Sie legte die Hand auf den Stein und empfand dessen Wärme** or **die Wärme desselben** rather than **seine Wärme. Meine Absichten will ich verteidigen, nicht deren künstlerische Ausführung** (Fulda's *Die Kameraden*, Vorwort).

f. Earlier in the period **Ihr** or the uninflected **Ihro** was used instead of **Sein** *his*, when the reference was to a person with a high title, as it was thought proper to use a possessive which would accord with the fem. title or the plural form of the verb: **Ich bin kein Rebell, habe gegen**

Ihro Kaiserliche Majestät nichts verbrochen (Goethe's *Götz*, 4, 2). We now say here **Seine Majestät,** with reference to the queen or empress **Ihre Majestät.** With reference to a *preceding* fem. title, **Ihr** is still used to indicate males. See **263.** I. 3.

3. The possessive is often in German replaced by the article in connection with the dative of a personal pronoun. For examples of this usage see **258.** 3. B. *a.* The simple article without the personal pronoun is often employed instead of a possessive, provided no ambiguity could arise thereby: **Sie hatte die Blumen in der Hand** *She had the flowers in her hand.*

Also **dessen, deren,** and **derselben** may under certain circumstances replace the possessive, as explained in 2. *d* and *e* above.

On the other hand, the possessives are used in some expressions in German where they are omitted in English: **Meine Herren!** Gentlemen! **Meine Damen!** Ladies! **Sie werden Ihren Ärger mit ihm haben** You will have a good deal of trouble with him. **Er hat seine liebe Not mit dem Reden** He has a good deal of difficulty in speaking. In popular and colloquial language the possessive is a favorite and is often used even where it does not seem necessary: **Seine siebenzig Jahre hat er bald gut auf dem Nacken** (Raabe's *Meister Autor*, chap. xviii). **Der Ring ist seine 100 Mark wert.** This unnecessary use of the possessive is especially frequent in the popular constructions described **in 2.** *c* **above, and** in **258.** 3. B. *a.*

4. Notice the difference of idiom in the two languages in the following expressions: **ein Verwandter von Ihnen** *a relative of yours,* **ein Freund von mir** *a friend of mine.* **Die Sperlinge sind noch mein Tod** (H. Seidel's *Eine Sperlingsgeschichte*) *The sparrows will be the death of me yet.*

Indefinite Numerals.

139. The indefinites, which are used adjectively or substantively, may be divided into three groups:

1. The following contain the idea of number:

a. **'aller'hand** *all kinds of, every kind of,* uninflected: **allerhand gute Weine, mit allerhand guten Weinen, allerhand guter Wein, mit allerhand Flitter geschmückt, allerhand Unverständliches.** Substantively: **einem allerhand mitteilen.** See **161.** 4. The stress here is the same as that of the adjectives in **47.** 3. A. *b. cc.*

Note. This form is in fact a modern compound consisting of the noun **hand** *kind* in the gen. pl. and its modifying adjective, which in M.H.G. were written apart: **aller hande** *of all kinds.*

b. **'aller'lei** *all kinds of, every kind of,* uninflected: **allerlei gute Weine, mit allerlei guten Weinen, allerlei guter Wein, allerlei Unverständliches. Sie fuhren in allerlei Gefährt** (Ilse Frapan's *Mamsell Biene*). Substantively: **Sie sprechen von allerlei. Da hat man denn allerlei solchen Klatsches gehört, der dich vielleicht auch interessiert** (Frau von Thadden in a letter, March 23, 1863, *Deutsche Rundschau*, Dec. 1911, p. 373). See also **126. 1.** *a.* For accent see **47.** 3. A. *b. cc.*

c. **ander-** *other*, str. and wk.: **ein and(e)rer Mann; der and(e)re Mann; and(e)re Männer; ein and(e)rer** another (man); **eine and(e)re Frau; ein and(e)res Buch; am anderen** (see **122.** 1, '2nd') **Tage** the next day. **Wollen Sie noch eine** (not **eine andere**) **Tasse Tee haben?**

Note. Altho in the literary language **ander** in expressions of time points to the future, it may in dialect, as also in literary English, point to the past. Compare: I saw him the other day. This usage is also found in older literary German: **daz ist mir durch den knappen leit, | ders** *andern tages* (*the day before*) **mit züchten reit | und Gawan sagte mære** (*Parzival*, **381.** 4-7).

d. **beid-** *both*, str. and wk.: **beide Hände, or die beiden Hände, die** (or **meine, diese, jene**) **beiden Knaben** both of the (or my, these, those) boys. The neut. sing. is used collectively, embracing two nouns or the ideas contained in two verbs: **beides, Brief und Paket** both letter and package. **Er irrte sich in beidem** He was mistaken in both points. **Das beides ist richtig** Both points are correct. **Wir müssen büßen und wir können sühnen; diese Frau hat es beides getan** (Ompteda's *Frieden*, chap. xiii). Much used in idiomatic combinations: **wir beide,** or less commonly **beide wir** both of us, **diese beiden Knaben** more common than **diese Knaben beide,** or **beide diese Knaben,** the latter forms, however, being more emphatic; **keiner von beiden** neither of them, **alle beide** (or in popular and colloquial language **zwei beide,** or **alle zwei beide**) both of them, **welche beide** both of which.

Note 1. Following pronouns, the inflection of **beid-** is strong except after **wir** and **ihr,** where after the manner of descriptive adjectives we also find the weak inflection, and even more frequently so after **ihr: wir beide** (Raabe), **wir zwei beide** (P. O. Höcker's *Dodi*, 1), **wir beiden verlornen** (M. Halbe), **ihr beide** (Grillparzer's *König Ottokar*, 1), **ihr beiden Narren** (Raabe), **ihr beiden** (Hauptmann's *Michael Kramer*, 3), **dies beides** both of these, **das beides** both of those, **alles beides** both. **Sein Tod ist ein schwerer Schlag für die Gemahlin und für die Königin, die beide** (both of whom) **niedergeschmettert sind.**

Note 2. **Beide, alle,** and often **jeder** (see last example in 1st par. of *f* below) have a position in the sentence differing sometimes from English: (**1**) They usually follow pronouns, standing in the appositional construction, when *all* are embraced in the statement: **Ich kann nicht Ihnen allen helfen** I cannot help all of you (or as in German *you all*). **Sie schickten mir Handschuhe, welche mir alle zu groß sind** You sent me gloves all of which are too large for me. For examples of the position of **beide** see examples in *Note* 1 above. When a partitive idea is to be expressed, they usually stand in the dat. after **von: Einer von beiden kommt** One of the two will come. (**2**) They may for emphasis follow a noun: **Ich sah die Eltern beide** I saw both of the parents. **Er wandte sich von seinen Freunden allen ab.** (**3**) When they are modifiers of the subject they may for emphasis stand after the verb: **Die Schuldigen verstummten alle** Every one of the guilty ones became silent. **Deine Eltern sind beide wohl** *Both of your parents are well*, or as in German *Your parents are both well*. (**4**) For especial emphasis they may, when they are modifiers of the subject, also stand first in the sentence followed by the verb and later by the subject: **Alle wollen sie des Kaisers Antlitz sehen** (Wildenbruch's *Kaiser Heinrich*, 2, 2). **Beide standen wir am Fenster.** (**5**) **Beide** differing from **alle** now usually follows a gen., a possessive, or other pronominal: **all seines Vaters Gut** and **alle meine Bücher,** but **meines Vaters beide Güter** and **mit meinen beiden Augen.** Earlier in the period, however, **beid-** might also precede: **beiden seinen Frauen** (Luther), **von beiden diesen Punkten** (Lessing). This older word-order is still occasionally found and indeed Sanders in his *Hauptschwierigkeiten*, p. 67 recommends it for present usage where **beid-** is to be made emphatic. **Beid-** still regularly precedes the possessive when it is itself preceded by the article: **Meinert hatte überrascht die Hand seines Besuchers, die er bis dahin in den beiden seinen gehalten, losgelassen** (Telmann's *Wahrheit*, I). The first examples in (**5**) show how **beide** in a greater degree than **alle** is becoming more like attributive adjectives, in that it now usually follows the article and the pronominals. They were both originally predicate appositives, which accounts for their peculiar position in the sentence, as illustrated in (**1**)–(**5**).

e. **ein** *one, any, some*, often in connection with the adverb **irgend,** which gives the generalizing force in the sense of *any, some, any at all*, inflected like the indefinite article when used adjectively, and like a strong adjective when used substantively: **Wenn ich nur irgend ein Mittel dagegen wüßte!** If I only knew some remedy for it! Substantively: **irgend einer** any one; **jenes Buch oder irgend eines.**

The wanting plural of **irgend ein** is supplied by **irgend welche** or simple **welche** in declarative sentences, and in questions either by **irgend welche** or **irgend** alone: **Irgend eine Person hat,** or in the plural **irgend welche Personen haben es ihm verraten. Meiner Überzeugung nach richtet sich die Schwere der Silben weder nach der Klasse noch nach irgend welchen syntaktischen Funktionen** (Saran's *Deutsche Verslehre*, p. 45). **Die Fischlein waren . . . so schön, wie er noch nie welche gesehen hatte** (R. Huch's *Schlaraffis*, p. 94). **Haben irgend welche Personen** or **irgend Personen außer Ihnen darum gewußt?** In the substantive relation **welche** cannot be dropped here.

The wanting plural of **ein** in the meaning *several, a few* is supplied by **welch-** (used as a rule only substantively) or **einige** (used adjectively): **Hast du ein paar Pfennige? Ich habe welche,** but usually **Er ist schon einige Jahre tot.** Many prefer to omit **welch.** See 3. *k* below, last sentences. In popular and colloquial language **welch** is often used here adjectively: **Welche** (in choice language **einige**) **Menschen sind nicht zufrieden.** Other forms than **welche** and **einige** occur in dialect, such as **ere** (a partitive gen. = **ihrer**), **eine: Hast du ein paar Pfennige? Ich habe ere** or **eine.** With reference to materials **ein** is replaced in the singular by **welch-** in the substantive and by **etwas** in the attributive relation: **Wenn Sie Geld haben, so geben Sie mir welches. Geben Sie mir etwas Geld.**

So great a favorite is **welch-** that it is often used in the singular where **ein** might be used: **Kann ich und will ich früher abreisen, so kann ich ja am Donnerstag noch irgend welche mir triftig scheinende Ausrede nach Letzlingen senden** (Bismarck to his wife, Oct. 21, 1850). **Sie sind am allermächtigsten ohne irgend welchen Rang** (H. Hoffmann's *Wider den Kurfürsten*, chap. x).

f. **jed-** *every, each, any*, strong (see **106.** *Note* 1), or if preceded by the indefinite article mixed, used adjectively or substantively. The indefinite article *must* precede the genitive in the substantive relation. Exs.: **ein jeder rechtschaffene Bürger** (Goethe's *Egmont*, 2), or **jeder rechtschaffene Bürger; das Gefühl eines jeden,** but **das Gefühl jedes** or **eines jeden edlen Menschen. Ein jeder ist seines Glückes Schmied. Jede Feder ist gut genug** Any pen will do. **Jeder** (anybody) **kann Ihnen sagen, wo ich wohne. Jeder dieser Männer hat sein Verdienst,** or **diese Männer haben jeder ihr Verdienst. Wenn drei Konsonanten, die jeder gesprochen werden usw.** When three consonants each of which is pronounced, &c.

Earlier in the period **jed-** could be used in the plural with the force of **alle: jede andern Mittel** (Goethe's *Egmont,* 1, Palast der Regentin), **jede zehn Schritte** (Heine). Occasionally still: **Lustig rasselt über ein Räderwerk der Lotdraht in die Tiefe; bei jeden neuen 1000 m. steigt die Erwartung usw.** (F. Bidlingmaier in *Deutsche Rundschau,* July 1904, p. 69). **Mit anzusehen, wie unfehlbar Baldwin in allen** (with collective force) **und jeden** (with individualizing force) **Fragen ihre Einwände besiegte** (Walther Siegfried's *Um der Heimat willen,* VII).

Earlier in the period **jedwed-, jedweder-,** and **jeglich-,** all with the inflection and meaning of **jed-,** were frequently used, and with the exception of **jedweder-** still occur in choice language, especially in a solemn or dignified style: **jedwede Art von Sünde** (Ranke), **ein jeglicher wunderliche Vogel** (Raabe's *Unseres Herrgotts Kanzlei,* chap. v). The form **jeglich,** like **all,** is sometimes found uninflected before a possessive: **So zieht mit jeglich ihrer Habe die Seele des Kindes und kindhaft junger Völker in die ahnende Weite der Unerforschlichkeit hinaus** (Prof. Dr. Ed. Heyck in *Velhagen und Klasings Monatshefte,* May, 1905, p. 274).

Note. Instead of **ein jeder** we find **jed- ein-** in N.G. dialect, just as in English: **Damit kriegt man jeden einen mürbe** (M. Dreyer's *In Behandlung,* 2).

g. **manch** *many a, many, a number of,* strong and weak, but uninflected before **ein,** also often before a descriptive adjective: **mancher Mann, manche Frau, manches Kind, mancher** many a man. **Ich habe Ihnen so manches zu sagen** I have a number of things to tell you. **Manche gute Leute** a number of good people; **die manchen Stunden, die ich darauf verwendet habe.** But **manch ein starker Mann,** or **manch starker Mann,** or **mancher starke Mann; im Erinnerungsbilderbuch manch jetzigen Millionärs** (Heyking's *Briefe, die ihn nicht erreichten,* New York, Jan. 1900). It is rather uncommon in general to place the indefinite article before **manch-,** altho in some sections, as in the S.W., it occurs occasionally: **Ein mancher blieb haften** (Scheffel's *Ekkehard,* 13).

Manch differs from **viel** in that it denotes only number, while the latter denotes also quantity: **viel** (not **manch**) **Geld.** Both **viel** and **manch** denote number in the plural. The former denotes a large number and stands in contrast to **wenige** *few,* while **manche** indicates an indefinite number larger than **einige** *several.* Also in the singular in a collective sense with the same differentiation in meaning: **Von Gold und Silber starrt Euer Schatz: | mir fehlt's an manchem, fehlt's an vielem wohl** (Grillparzer's *Ottokar,* 3). **Manch** differs from **viel** also in having individualizing force, which explains its frequent use in the singular, just as *many a* in English. On account of its individualizing force, it cannot be used in questions asking after the number: **Wie viele** (not **manche**) **waren da?**

h. **mehrer-** (**117. 1.** *b*) *several,* strong and weak: **mehrere wichtige Dinge, mehreres Wichtige** *several important things.* **Wie sollte man die mehrern Wagen fortbringen?** (Goethe). A little earlier in the period the form **mehr** was not infrequent: **mit mehren Damen** (Bismarck to his betrothed, Feb. 1, 1847).

i. **ein paar** *a few, several,* uninflected (see **121. 1. A.** *a*): **mit ein paar Worten.** In colloquial language and dialect the **ein** is often suppressed: **Ich lebte paar Jahre in Berlin. Ich war nur paarmal da. Vor paar Täg'n** (Anzengruber's *G'wissenswurm*). The definite article or a limiting adjective may precede **paar: Aber diese paar archaistischen Abweichungen sind kaum von Belang** (Wackernagel's *Altindische Grammatik,* I. p. xlv). A. **Ich war nur 5 Tage in Berlin, aber in den paar Tagen habe ich die Stadt gründlich kennen gelernt.** B. (contemptuously) **Was? In dén paar Tagen** (or **in den páar**) **Tagen willst du Berlin gründlich kennen gelernt haben?** A. (contemptuously) **Mit déinen paar** (or

mit deinen páar) Groschen willst du dich durchschlagen? B. **Ja, mit meinen páar Groschen will ich schon fertig werden.** When **paar** is preceded by a strong limiting adjective and followed by a descriptive adjective the latter is sometimes strong instead of weak as the substantive origin of **paar** is still felt: **Diese paar unmögliche Wortstellungen** (Engel's *Deutsche Stilkunst*, p. 308). The definite article and the limiting adjectives are always inflected. When **Paar** is written with a capital and **ein** is inflected, the expression takes again its original meaning, i.e. *a pair*: **mit einem Paar Kanarienvögel.** See also **253. I. 1.** *g. Note* **1.**

2. The following contain the idea of *quantity*:

a. **bißchen** (S.G. **bissel**) *little, little bit*, more confined to the style of every day than **ein wenig,** and, moreover, implying a smaller amount. It is uninflected, but may be preceded by an inflected article, demonstrative, or possessive, which, however, does not agree in gender with the noun following **bißchen,** but is neuter, as is also the following relative, the article and relative agreeing not with the substantive but with **bißchen** itself, thus distinctively indicating its original substantive nature: **Die Johanniswürmchen sind um des bißchen Glanzes willen noch keine Sterne** Glow-worms are not by any means stars because of the little light they shed. **Darüber hinaus möchte ich fürs erste allerdings den verbleibenden Rest meines bißchen Kapitals nicht angreifen** (Boy-Ed). **Mit ihrem bißchen Kraft; das bißchen Armut, das Reiche** (name) **hinterließ** (Fedor Sommer's *Ernst Reiland*, p. 146); **das ganze bißchen Willensenergie, was (153. 1. (1)) ihr die Ohnmachtsanwandlung übrig ließ** (Boy-Ed's *Das ABC des Lebens*, p. 364). If there is a descriptive adjective before the noun it is sometimes strong as the article or limiting adjective before **bißchen** is not felt as belonging to the following noun: **Der Beobachtung wert ist hierbei die Grandezza, mit welcher . . . und wie sie** (the half-breeds of Central America) **in ihrem Wesen das bißchen „spanisches Blut," welches vielleicht in ihren Adern rollt, zur Geltung bringen wollen** (B. von Werner's *Ein deutsches Kriegsschiff in der Südsee*, p. 52). The weak form of the descriptive adjective is more common here: **das bißchen warme Mittagsessen** (Hermann Anders Krüger's *Kaspar Krumbholtz*, p. 27); **aber die Lumpen, in die das bißchen Eingeborene eingewickelt war** (Enking's *Momm*, p. 189).

The substantive following **bißchen** sometimes drops the **s** of the genitive in accordance with **94.** 3. A, 2nd par. as it is felt as an appositive to the noun **bißchen,** which denotes a measurement or amount: **„Mein Bruder ist Kaufmann geworden und gilt als das schwarze Schaf in der Familie." „Na, hören Sie, Sie werden ihn wegen des bißchen Farbenunterschied doch nicht anfeinden!"** (*Fliegende Blätter*, July 4, 1911). Compare with the first example from Boy-Ed given above.

Used substantively: **Die ganze Welt kommt mir mit einem Mal so dumm und unsinnig vor, daß auf das bißchen, was ich von der Sorte dazu gebe, wirklich nichts ankommt** (Raabe). **Nicht ein bißchen mehr!** Don't take the least bit more! Usually the indef. art. before **bißchen** remains uninflected after the analogy of **ein wenig, ein paar: mit ein bißchen Verstand.** The uninflected **wenig** can only be used after **ein,** and hence could not stand in the first four examples in the first paragraph above.

Note. Often **ein bißchen** is used adverbially: **Warten Sie ein klein bißchen. Er ist nicht ein bißchen eitel** He is not a bit (or not in the least) vain. Sometimes with suppressed **ein: Wir wollten Sie bißchen besuchen** (Anna Sommer's *Die zerbrochene Sonne*).

b. **etwas** *some*, uninflected: **etwas Wein, etwas Geld.** It is often used adverbially: **etwas sauer** somewhat sour.

Note. In early N.H.G. **etwas** was felt as a neut. substantive and could have a following gen. depending upon it: **etwas Trosts** (Luther). Later the gen. passed over into the appositional construction: **etwas Trost.** To-day **etwas** can in such cases be regarded as an uninflected adj. with the same general meaning as the inflected adj. **einig-,** with this modification, that **etwas** is now in general used with singular nouns for an indefinite *amount, mass*, while **einig-** may be used for an indefinite *amount*, but is more particularly used with pl. nouns or the singular of adjective-substantives for an indefinite *number*: **etwas Butter, etwas Ehre, etwas Mut, einiges Geld, einige Bücher, einiges Interessante** *several interesting things*. However, before abstract nouns in the sing., **einig-** is often used instead of **etwas: einige Zeit, einige Erfahrung, nach einigem Stolpern über allerhand Unebenheiten** (Raabe's *Finkenrode*, chap. ii). In the substantive relation **etwas** is replaced by **welch-.** See 1. *e* above. For **etwas** as a real substantive (with dependent noun) see **145.** *f. Note* 1.

c. **ganz** *all, whole, entire,* strong and weak, but may also be uninflected before names of countries and places which have no art. before them, when used in a figurative or inexact sense: **ein ganzer Apfel** a whole apple, **der ganze Apfel, ein ganzer Mann** a man every inch of him; **das ganze Deutschland** *the whole of Germany, Germany one and undivided,* but **Ganz Deutschland lag in Schmach und Schmerz** All Germany lay in disgrace and grief. **„Ganz Berlin" ist noch lange nicht „das ganze Berlin." Die begeisterten Wünsche ganz Frankreichs. Ich durchreiste ganz Deutschland.** But the ending cannot be dropped in case of those countries which always take the art.: **die ganze Schweiz** *all Switzerland,* not **ganz Schweiz.** It is much used in idiomatic expressions: **im ganzen** on the whole, **im ganzen einkaufen** to buy by wholesale, **im ganzen und großen überschlagen** to make a rough estimate, &c.

Ganz is often used in the plural, but it never denotes number, indicating also there entirety, i.e. the completeness of each whole. See 3. *d. Note,* below, toward end.

Note 1. The usual adverbial form is **ganz** *quite, entirely, very*: **ganz gut.** Formerly **gänzlich** was the usual adverbial form and is still sometimes used. This form is also used adjectively, only, however, before abstract nouns denoting an activity or a quality, where the original adverbial nature of the form is largely preserved (see **245.** II. 11. 2. A. *f*): **gänzliche Befreiung, gänzliche Verschiedenheit.**

Note 2. **Ganz** is also used as a neut. noun, but with its original adj. declension: **Zwei Halbe** (halves) **sind ein Ganzes** (a whole). **Vier Halbe sind zwei Ganze,** or **sind zwei Ganzen gleich** (equal to). **Ein harmonisch geordnetes Ganze** or **Ganzes** (see **111.** 4. *a*), **der dritte Teil eines Halben.** Also masc. referring to **Schoppen: einen Ganzen, einen Halben trinken** to drink a whole, a half-measure (of beer or wine).

d. **halb** *half,* strong and wk., and like **ganz** remains uninflected before names of countries and places which have no article before them, when used figuratively or in an inexact sense: **ein halber Apfel** half of an apple, **der halbe Apfel, die halbe Stadt, ein halber Mann, das halbe Paris** half of Paris, **das halbe Paris** or more commonly **halb Paris** half of the people of Paris, **durch halb Paris. Die französische Revolution erschütterte halb Europa.** But always **die halbe Schweiz.**

Note 1. It is uninflected in the form **ein halb** used as a fraction, also in the form **halb** when used adverbially, and in a few expressions substantively. **Zehn mit ein halb multipliziert gibt fünf. Die Stunde ist schon halb um** The hour is already half up. **Die Uhr schlägt die halbe Stunde,** or **schlägt halb. Es ist halb neun** (o'clock). Formerly and still in popular language inflected in the predicate: **Ich bin halber im Traum.** See **111.** 8.

Note 2. **Halb** is also used as a neut. or masc. noun, but with its original adj. declension. See *Note* 2, under *c.*

e. **ein wenig** *a little,* uninflected: **ein wenig Wasser** (in older German **ein wenig Wassers**—Gen. xviii. 4), **mit ein wenig Verstand.** Substantively: **Ich nehme ein wenig von dem Brot.** There is little or no difference between **ein wenig** here and **ein weniges** *a small amount, a little* in 3. *j* below. See also *a* above.

Note. **Ein wenig** is much used adverbially: **Sie haben die Sache ein wenig übereilt.**

3. The following contain the idea of *quantity* or *number,* according as the noun is in the sing. or pl.:

a. **aller, alle, alles** *all,* usually strong when inflected, but may remain uninflected before an article or pronominal, usually with the form **all,** but often in popular language **alle: alle Freude** all the joy, **alles Gute** all that is good, **all** or **alle der Wein, all** or **alle des Weins,** &c.; **all der Wein** *all the wine* (quantity), but **alle Schüler** all the pupils (number); **alles in allem** *all in all,* but **alle, Gute und Böse** all people, good and bad; **all der Schmerz** *all the pain,* but **Sie kamen alle** *They all came.* For further details concerning inflection see **111.** 8.

In referring to definite persons and things which are clearly indicated by the context, the definite article is not used so frequently after **all** as in English, being usually employed only when it has strong demonstrative or determinative force: **aller Wein, alle Butter** all the wine, butter (in the house, &c., according to the connection). **Alle Gäste verließen eiligst das Haus** All the guests left the house in great haste. But with demonstrative or determinative force: **All das Geld reicht nicht hin, ihn zufrieden zu stellen** All this money (which has been given him) does not suffice to satisfy him. **Bei all der Pracht ist er nicht glücklich** In the midst of all the splendor, which surrounds him, he is not happy. **All die** (or **alle die** or simply **alle**) **Gemälde, die er auf die Ausstellung gesandt hat, sind verkauft.**

For the position of **alle** in the sentence see 1. *d. Note* 2 above.

Note 1. Instead of the regular str. forms, **all** often has wk. forms in the gen. (see **106.** *Note* 1) sing. when not preceded by def. art., and, perhaps, still more frequently in the gen. and dat. sing. when preceded by the article: **trotz allen Vertrauens. Und fiel' ein Feind in unsre Gauen, | wir würden des allen die Früchte schauen** (Grillparzer's *Libussa*, 2). **Dabei läßt sich aber nicht leugnen, daß die Erreichung des allen durch die neuen Bestrebungen stark behindert wurde** (Dr. Hans Kleinpeter in *Beilage zur Allgemeinen Zeit.*, Sept. 10, 1905). **Mir ist so angst bei dem allen. Ich werde nichts von dem allen tun.**

Note 2. In the predicate in the sense of *out of* the invariable form **alle** is much used: **Der Wein ist alle** We are out of wine. Perhaps the form **alle** was originally a predicate appositive in the nom. pl., originating in such sentences as **die Kuchen sind alle** (**verzehrt**).

Note 3. Before the dat. neut. sing. the uninflected form **alle** is quite common: **trotz alle'dem** in spite of all that.

Note 4. In the classical authors **all-** is sometimes equal to **jed-**: **So schläft nun aller Vogel** (Goethe). In a few cases we can still use both **all-** and **jed-**, the former with general, the latter with individualizing force: **Aller** or **jeder Anfang ist schwer. Wir hatten allen Grund** (*every reason*, in a general sense) **zum Verdacht gegen ihn. Getragenes Zeug aller Art** (H. Seidel's *Das Atelier*, I). Usage now generally prefers here the sing. of **jed-** or the plural of **all-**, especially the latter, in a number of expressions: **alle paar Minuten** every few minutes, **alle Tage** every day, **alle drei Tage** every third day, **alle sieben Tage ein Heft** (on the outside cover of each number of *Die Woche*).

Note 5. After **ohne** we translate both **all-** and **jed-** by *any*: **ohne alle** (or **ohne jede**, or **ohne alle und jede**) **Ursache** *without any reason.*

Note 6. In the course of the present period **all-** has gradually been supplanted by **ganz-** in the meaning *whole, entire*, but the older usage still survives in poetic language: **durch all sein Leben** (Geibel, 2, 241), now usually **durch sein ganzes Leben.** Differentiation of meaning here has taken place in **alle Welt** *everybody* and **die ganze Welt** *the universe.* Compare **die ganze Nacht** all night; **ganz Deutschland** all Germany; **die ganze Familie** all the family.

Note 7. In dialect the neut. form **alles** is frequently contracted to **als**, which often by reason of this change of form becomes isolated from the original form, and takes on more general meaning, especially that of the adverb **immerfort: Da saugt mir das Mädel—weiß Gott, was als** (for **alles**) **für?—überhimmlische Alfanzereien ein** (Miller in Schiller's *Kabale und Liebe*, 1, 1). **Solltest nur die wunderhübsche Billeter auch lesen, die der gnädige Herr an deine Tochter als** (= **immerfort**) **schreiben tut** (ib., Frau Miller). **Er ist als** (= **immer**) **noch ledig** (*Wörterbuch der elsässischen Mundarten*, I, p. 28). Also with the force of **eben, gerade: Es ist als nach Ihrem Herrn Pastor geschickt** (C. Viebig's *Die Wacht am Rhein*, p. 448).

b. **einig-**, earlier in the period = O.H.G. einag *one, only, single*, later, in N.H.G. *harmonious* (in this meaning still in use), and O.H.G. einig = **irgend ein** (see 1. *e* above), from the latter of which come the common meanings of our day, *a few, some, several*, inflected strong and weak: **der einige Gott** (Matth. xix. 17), **ein einiger Son** (Tobit vi. 16). **Denn du vermagst nicht ein einigs Har weis und schwartz zu machen** (Matth. v. 36). **Kein Handwercksman einiges Handwercks** (Rev. xviii. 22), **aus Furcht des Todes oder sonst einiges Dinges** (Claudius) from fear of death or some other thing; **einiges frische Obst** some fresh fruit, **einige Schritte davon** several steps away, **in einiger Entfernung, einige Zeit darnach. In diesem Buche findet sich neben einigem Guten auch einiges Mittelmäßige und einiges Schlechte. Von diesen einigen 70 Bänden der** Tauchnitz Edition **gehören nur 20 den Jahren 1893 bis 1898 an** (Conrad's *Syntax der Englischen Sprache*, p. v). **Nur einige waren da** Only a few people were there. **Er besah die zwei Gespanne Ochsen, die Kühe, die einigen Schafe** (Stifter's *Witiko*, 1. 202). See also 2. *b. Note* and 1. *e* above.

aa. The forms **etlich-** (strong and weak = **einig-** and now being gradually displaced by it) and **etwelch-** (strong and weak = **irgend ein** or **irgend welch-**, or **einig-** in the sing. and **irgend welche** and **einige** in the pl.) still occur in the literary language. The former was very common in Luther's language and is still sometimes used, and quite frequently so in archaic and biblical style. The latter form was not common earlier in the period, but it still lingers on in choice language: **Etwelches kleine Geschenk mitzubringen sei immer empfehlenswert bei großen Herren** (H. Hoffmann's *Teufel vom Sande*, p. 174). **Zum Überfluß hatte er die Gewohnheit, jedesmal selbst gleichsam seine Visitenkarte abzugeben, vermöge etwelchen kleinen Unfugs, den er in dem betretenen Raume zu verüben für gut fand** (id., *Rohleders hohe Minne*). **Das anvertraute Gut war viel zu kostbar, um es etwelchen Gefahren auszusetzen** (id.). **Denn dieser pflegte an dergleichen niedlichen Geschöpfen Wohlgefallen zu haben, welche im Grunde doch mehr ihn verehrten, als er ihnen huldigte, da sein Alter und seine geistige Bedeutung eine Überlegenheit mit sich brachten, die nicht einmal durch etwelche Verliebtheit seinerseits auszugleichen war** (R. Huch's *Ludolf Ursleu*, chap. xv). **Dann etwelche Portionen Kaffee, sagen wir vorläufig fünf** (Fontane's *Frau Jenny*, chap. xi). **Auch setzte sie ihm ein Glas trinkbaren Weines vor . . . mit etwelchen Schnitten kalten Bratens** (Wilhelm Fischer's *Die Freude am Licht*, II, p. 40). In the language of Switzerland it is often preceded by **ein** and **der: Hierauf trat eine etwelche Besserung ein. Wegen der etwelchen Unsicherheit, in welcher die Männer die Welt halten** (Keller's *Seldw.*, 2. 311).

c. **g(e)nug** (sometimes **genung** earlier in the period and still in dialect and poetry) *enough*, uninflected, also used adverbially: **Er hat genug Geld,** or **Geld genug; genug Bücher.** It formerly governed the genitive, which is still sometimes used: **Es ist des Weins genug,** or **genug des Weins,** or **genug Wein,** or **Wein genug.** See *i. Note.*

d. **gesamt** and **sämtlich** *all, entire, complete*, both strong and weak: **die sämtlichen zwölf Kessel des Dampfschiffes waren im Betrieb. Schillers sämtliche Werke, die gesamte Familie, mit gesamter Heeresmacht, die gesamten Armen des Ortes; eine Arbeit, die ihre gesamten Geisteskräfte in Anspruch nahm.**

Note. Usually, as in the above examples, **gesamt,** in accordance with the force of its prefix **ge-**, denotes a union of homogeneous or integral parts into *one* whole, and even when used in the plural has the force of *one* mass or a corps of forces working as *one*, while **sämtlich** in the sing. or pl. indicates that there are different distinct units which form the whole. They both differ from the more common and general **all-** in that the latter simply indicates that the quantity or number is complete and lacks the distinct idea of a union of integral or homogeneous parts or individual forces working toward a common end. Different from the preceding is **ganz,** which does not refer at all to the parts that make up a whole, but represents in idea an undivided whole, or in the plural undivided wholes: **der ganze Körper** the whole body, **mit ganzem Herzen** with all my heart, **das ganze Haus** the whole house, **die ganze Familie, die einzige schöne Frau der ganzen Eysen** (G. Ompteda) the only beautiful woman in all the different branches of the Eysen family, **ganze Schuhe** shoes that are not rent. **Die Kriege der Gegenwart rufen die ganzen Völker zu den Waffen** (Moltke).

e. **kein** *no, none, not a, not* (see *Note*), *no one, not a one,* inflected like the indef. article **ein** when used adjectively in the sing., but like a strong adjective when standing alone (see **106.** *Note* 1) in the sing. or pl., or when used adjectively in the plural: **kein Buch. Ein Buch ist besser als kein(e)s. Das steht in keines** or **keines Menschen Macht. Keine Bücher.** For the genitive after **kein** see *Note* under *i* below.

Note 1. The adverb *no* is translated by **nein.** The adjective *no* is rendered by **kein,** but **kein** has a broader field than the English adjective *no,* as it also generally corresponds to *not a, not* (with intervening words) *a, not any,* and *not* (before a noun or a noun and its modifiers): **Das ist kein übler Einfall** That is not a bad idea. **Weiche keinen Fingerbreit von Gottes Wegen ab** Do not deviate a finger's breadth from God's ways. **Bitte, geben Sie mir Käse. Ich habe keinen im Hause** Please give me some cheese. I haven't any in the house. **Es ist noch keine sechs Uhr** (colloquial) It is not six o'clock yet. **Kein** is the negative of **ein,** but it has a broader field, as it can stand where **ein** usually cannot, namely, before names of materials, abstract nouns, and in the plural: **Ich habe kein Geld. Er kennt keinen Kummer. Das Kind hat keine Eltern. Kein** is replaced by **nicht** or **nicht ein** when it is desired to bring out especial emphasis or a contrast: **Ein Vater schuf die Welt, kein** (or emphatically **nicht ein**) **Gott des Strafgerichtes. Mich rettet nicht Gewalt, nicht List.**

Note 2. In early N.H.G. and still in dialect **kein** has also the meaning *any.* For example see **277. 1.** B. *a.* This double meaning of *no* and *any* comes from the fact that two different M.H.G. words dechein *any* and nechein *no* were confounded, so that the latter sometimes assumed the meaning of the former.

Note 3. Instead of **keiner** we find in N.G. dialect **kein ein** just as in English: **Das kann auch kein ein** (Kröger's *Leute eigener Art,* p. 232.)

f. **lauter** and now less commonly **eitel** *nothing but,* indeclinable: **lauter schöne Blumen. Natürlich ist das alles eitel Wind** (talk, wind)! **Es herrschte eitel Ruhe und Frieden.**

Note. These words are still inflected in early N.H.G.: **aus lauterm Haß** (Ezek. xxxv. 11).

g. **mehr** *more,* usually uninflected: **mehr Geld; mehr Leute.** See *i. Note.* For the form **mehrer-** see **117.** 1. *b.*

Note. Thruout the period attempts have been made by good authors to introduce inflection, and such forms still occur: **Ein Dutzend Häuser stehen schon in Brand, und es kommen ihrer noch sehr viel mehre dran** (H. Hoffmann's *Wider den Kurfürsten,* chap. xxviii). Inflection is most common in the adverb **mehrenteils =meistenteils.**

h. **übrig** *the rest, remaining, superfluous,* strong and weak: **Er tut nie ein übriges** He never does more than he has to do. **Im übrigen Europa** in the rest of Europe; **die übrigen Personen; im übrigen,** or **was das übrige betrifft** *as to the rest.*

i. **viel** *much,* pl. *many,* strong and weak, inflected or uninflected, but inflected always when preceded by the definite article or a pronominal adjective and almost always in the pl. when used substantively: **viele** or **viel Bücher, viele** (or **viel**) **gute Bücher, die vielen Bücher, viel Gutes** much that is good, **vieles Gute** many good things, **mit viel Gutem. Unter vielem Verhaßten ist mir das Schreiben das Verhaßteste** (Goethe's *Egmont,* 2). **Laß dein vieles Reden. Der viele Wein, den er trinkt; die viele Milch, die wir brauchen.** Substantively: **viele** many persons; **zum Besten vieler; die vielen, die hier sind; vieles** many things (see *Note* toward end).

German often distinguishes between the idea of *quantity* and that of *degree,* where in English no distinction is made: **Er ißt viel** He eats much, but **Ich liebe ihn sehr** I love him much. Formerly **viel** was used with the force of **sehr** before adjectives, and this older usage is still found in poetic and archaic style: **die vielschöne gnädige Frau** (Eichendorff's *Taug.* 8). It is still commonly used before a comparative or **zu: Er ist viel reicher. Er läuft viel schneller als Hans. Er ist viel zu reich, als daß usw.**

Note. **Viel, wenig, mehr, genug** are here for practical reasons classed as adjectives inflected or uninflected, but the following is a more scientific statement of the case. They were in earlier periods construed as indeclinable substantives, requiring a dependent partitive gen., and still admit of this construction, but take now usually the appositional construction after them, especially in the sing., or in case of **viel** and **wenig** are also used as inflected attributive adjectives: early in the period **viel Volcks** (Mark viii, 1), **viel falscher Propheten** (Matth. xxiv. 11); now **viel Geld, viel edle Männer** (in apposition with **viel**), or **viele** (adjective) **edle Männer.** When the article or a pronominal adjective precedes, **viel** and **wenig** are always inflected: **Er lebt von dem wenigen Vermögen, das ihm übrig geblieben ist.** In certain set expressions coined earlier in the period, the older construction of the indeclinable substantive with its dependent partitive gen. usually remains intact, and cannot be replaced by the newer one of attributive adj. before its substantive: **viel Aufhebens von etwas machen** to make a great fuss about something, **viel Wesens von etwas machen** to make much ado about something, but sometimes in modern form: **Was macht ihr so viel Aufheben | mit einem. der wie ich im Sande lag, | den ihr allda in Gnaden aufgelesen?** (Sudermann's *Die drei Reiherfedern,* **3, 5**).

There is little live feeling for the old partitive genitive here, for it is often construed as a word in the accusative or nominative limited by **ein, kein, einig, solch, kein** + descriptive adjective, or without a limiting word: **Kein Mensch hat davon ein Aufhebens** (acc.) **gemacht** (Bismarck's *Reden*, 2. 76) No one has made a fuss about it; but also with its correct form, **Ich meinte, Sie wären doch viel zu sehr von der Wissenschaft und Philosophie, um um solch 'ne Kleinigkeit so'n Aufheben zu machen** (Raabe's *Der Lar*, p. 23). **Er macht kein Federlesens** (acc.) He will make short work of it. **Die Jupiterstatue des Phidias, von der damals einiges Aufhebens** (nom.) **gemacht wurde** (Ebner-Eschenbach). **Mach' mir kein großes Aufhebens!** (acc.) Don't make a great fuss, I beg of you! **Ich weiß ja nicht, was antworten, wenn du solch ein Aufhebens** (acc.) **machst** (Walther Siegfried's *Ein Wohltäter*). Also without a limiting word: **ohne Rühmens** (acc.) (Grünebaum in Raabe's *Hungerpastor*, chap. vi), **ohne Aufhebens** (acc.) (Lauff's *Kärrekiek*, p. 107).

The words **viel, wenig, mehr, genug** are differently treated when they express the idea of number and stand alone or before a pronoun or a noun which is modified by an article or pronominal adj. In these cases **viel** and **wenig** are usually inflected, and if modified must be followed by the partitive gen., or by **von** or **unter** with dat., while **genug** and **mehr** are indeclinable here, but like **viel** and **wenig** are followed by the gen., or **von** with dat.: **viele waren da** many persons were there, **aber diesem Rufe folgten heute nur wenig** [as a survival of older usage; more commonly **wenige**] (Fontane's *Quitt*, chap. vi), **viele von ihnen, viele dieser Bücher**, or **viele von** (or **unter**) **diesen Büchern; genug waren da** enough people were there, **mehr solcher** (or **solche**) **Leute, mehr von ihnen, genug der Träume.**

Genug, mehr, viel, and **wenig** are all used as indeclinable substantives when they denote an indefinite mass or amount, in which case they may stand alone or be followed by the gen. or the dat. after the prep. **von: Ich habe genug davon. Genug des Geschwätzes** or **genug von dem Geschwätz. Du reichst mit wenig von dem bessern Stoff** (or **des bessern Stoffes**) **weiter als mit viel von dem schlechtern** You will accomplish more with a little of the better material than with much of the worse. See also **253.** I. 1. *g. Note* 2, with reference to the number of the verb after these words. The substantives **viel** and **wenig** may also be inflected, taking the neut. forms of the strong adjective, however, usually with a different shade of meaning from the uninflected forms. The former may, in accordance with the nature of the strong neut. form not preceded by an article, contain a collective idea, while the uninflected form or the strong form preceded by the indef. article emphasizes the idea of amount: **Ich meine nicht vieles, sondern viel: ein weniges, aber mit Fleiß** (Lessing's *Emilia*, 1, 2) I do not mean [that an artist should work on] many things, but much of one thing: a small amount, but thoroly. **Man kann vieles** (many things) **lernen und doch nicht viel** (much) **wissen.**

j. **wenig,** earlier in the period and in a few expressions still *little* in size, value, importance, now and thruout the period more commonly *little* in amount, pl. *few*; strong and weak, inflected or uninflected, but inflected always when preceded by the definite article or a pronominal adjective and almost always in the plural when used substantively: **Denn du bist das wenigst vnter allen völckern** (Deut. vii. 7). **Meine wenige Person** (Adelung); **wenig Gutes** little that is good, **weniges Gute** few good things, **mit wenig Gutem; wenige** or **wenig Bücher, von wenigen** or **wenig Büchern; mit seinem wenigen Gelde; das wenige Geld, was ich besaß** (Raabe). **Ich malte es mir aus mit der wenigen Phantasie, die mir gegeben** (Ompteda's *Frieden*, VI). **Die wenigen Bücher.** Substantively: **das wenige, was ich habe** the little that I have; **wenige** few persons; **die wenigen, die es gesehen haben.** The strong form here not preceded by the indef. article contains the idea of number: **ein weniges** a small amount, a little, but **Von den Menschen wüßte ich nur weniges** (*few things*) **und wenig** (*little*) **Erfreuliches zu sagen.** See also *i. Note.*

Note. The comparative form **weniger,** tho inflected in the earlier part of the period, now prefers decidedly noninflection except where ambiguity would arise therefrom: **Mit weniger Vergnügen. Es waren heute weniger Abgeordnete versammelt als gestern** There were fewer representatives present to-day than yesterday. But **weit wenigere Freisinnige** *much fewer Liberals* is clearer than **weit weniger Freisinnige,** which might mean *far less liberal-minded men*, as **weniger** can be construed as an adverb. As the positive is sometimes inflected and sometimes uninflected, the form **weniger** is sometimes ambiguous, as it may be construed as a fem. gen. or dat., or as the uninflected comparative. Thus in **mit weniger Mühe** the meaning may be *with little trouble* or *with less trouble*. The ambiguity can be avoided by dropping inflection in the former meaning and by substituting the inflected comparative of **gering** *little* for the uninflected comparative **weniger** or the rare inflected form **wenigerer: mit wenig Mühe** *with little trouble*, **mit geringerer Mühe** *with less trouble*. On the other hand, the uninflected form should be avoided in the positive when it would stand before an adjective, as it might be construed as an adverb: not **Er verkehrt mit wenig gebildeten Herren,** but **Er verkehrt mit wenigen gebildeten Herren** He associates with few educated men.

k. **welch** *some*, strong: **Haben Sie Zucker—Milch—Geld—Äpfel? Ich habe welchen—welche—welches—welche.** It serves as the plural of **ein** and is also used instead of the singular of **ein** when the reference is to materials. See 1. *e* above, also **134.** 2. Sometimes with the definite article: **Da (auf dem Wasser) sind sie (die Schiffer) was, un da haben sie'n weiten Blick — die welchen wenigstens, die welchen auch nich** (M. Dreyer's *In Behandlung*, 1). A number of grammarians are unfriendly to this word, but they are not supported by actual usage: **Wenn die Pferdchen nicht Geschäfte haben, so möchte ich Väterchen wohl bitten, daß er welche zu heut über acht Tage, 27. früh nach Schlawe oder Stolz schickte** (Bismarck to his wife, Oct. 21, 1850). **Je mehr Geld sie verloren, desto sehnsüchtiger wünschten sie welches zu haben** (G. Keller's *Romeo und Julie auf dem Dorfe*, p. 25). **Unanfechtbare Wahrheiten gibt es überhaupt nicht, und wenn es welche gibt, so sind sie langweilig** (Fontane's *Stechlin*, chap. i). **Auch setzte sie ihm ein Glas trinkbaren Weins vor mit Küchlein, wenn sie welche gebacken hatte** (Wilhelm Fischer's *Die Freude am Lichte*, II. p. 40). **„Rosen!" „Das sind mindestens für fünfzig Mark welche," meinte Marie, „so ein Haufen!"** (H. Böhlau's *Adam und Eva*, chap. vi). The examples could be indefinitely increased, as the word is a general favorite in colloquial language.

Often, especially in the South, the **welch** is omitted, and some grammarians recommend this form of statement: Elisabeth: **Weißt du noch, wie er das letzte Mal ausritt, da er dir Weck mitbrachte?** Karl: **Bringt er mir wieder mit?** (Goethe's *Götz*, 1, 3). **Ja, Geld, mein Freund, | Geld ist ein gutes Ding, wenn man nur hat** (Grillparzer's *Ottokar*, 3). **Dort standen allerlei Schächtelchen mit guten Hustenbonbons, die ich sonst sehr zu würdigen wußte. „Nimm Dir," sagte sie** (Ebner-Eschenbach's *Meine Kinderjahre*). **Jetzt hast du Ohrringe. Wart' einmal, ich hänge mir auch an** (Anna Schieber's *Alle guten Geister*, p. 52).

PRONOUNS.

PERSONAL PRONOUNS.

140. The personal pronouns are: **ich** *I*, **du** (familiar form) *thou* or *you*, **Sie** (polite form) *you*, **er** *he*, **sie** *she*, **es** *it*. These are declined as follows:

Singular.

	First Person. (for all Genders).	*Second Person.* (for all Genders). *Familiar.*	*Polite* (see *a*).	*Third Person.* Masc.	Fem.	Neut.
N.	**ich**	**du**	**Sie**	**er**	**sie**	**es**
G.	**meiner** (**mein**)	**deiner** (**dein**)	**Ihrer**	**seiner** (**sein**)	**ihrer** (**ihr**)	**seiner** (**sein, es**)
D.	**mir**	**dir**	**Ihnen**	**ihm**	**ihr**	**ihm**
A.	**mich**	**dich**	**Sie**	**ihn**	**sie**	**es**

Plural.

				For all Genders.
N.	**wir**	**ihr**	**Sie**	**sie**
G.	**unser** **uns(e)rer**	**euer** **eu(e)rer**	**Ihrer**	(**ihr**) **ihrer**
D.	**uns**	**euch**	**Ihnen**	**ihnen**
A.	**uns**	**euch**	**Sie**	**sie**

a. Form and Use of Pronouns in Direct Address. The polite form of the second person is in reality only the capitalized forms of the 3rd person pl. The pl. is exactly like the sing. This form is now used in all ordinary intercourse between people except in the familiar language of close friendship. Altho it is so common in actual life, it is almost unknown in poetic language and higher diction generally, as the air of conventionality associated with it ill accords with the spirit of poetry.

The familiar form **du** in the sing. and **ihr** in the pl. is used towards animals, children, parents, and close friends, also in lyrical poetry and in the solemn language of the Church and prayer, and stating general truths not directed to any person in particular, and occasionally in addressing individuals not as such, but as a mass or a class in an informal and general way, where it is not necessary to observe the formalities of polite society, and furthermore in polemical treatises in directing words directly to one's opponent, or in one's thoughts in directing words to one to whom one would aloud only use **Sie**: **Sage mir, mit wem du umgehst, und ich will dir sagen, wer du bist** (a proverb couched in familiar language, since the address is to no person in particular). **Darum, Bergleute, steigert weiter die Kohlenförderung, Landwirte, liefert Kartoffeln ab** (Proclamation of President Ebert, Nov. 4, 1919 to urge greater production, &c.). **Aber die Herren Journalisten haben Nerven, wie die Frauen. Alles regt euch auf, jedes Wort, das jemand gegen euch sagt, empört euch! Geht mir** (away with you), **ihr seid empfindliche Leute** (Freytag's *Journalisten*, 1, 1). In the last three sentences the speaker addresses in a general way several sharp remarks in the familiar form to journalists as a class, but he would not be so impolite as to use this form in speaking directly to any one person or a definite group of persons. **Kurzsichtigster aller Schullehrer, verknöchertster aller Pedanten, ist dir denn niemals davon eine Spur der Erkenntnis aufgegangen, daß gerade ihre unerschöpfliche Fruchtbarkeit der größte Vorzug der deutschen Sprache ist?** (the reply of Dr. Karl Kaerger to the lamentations of Dr. Gustav Wustmann over the decay of the German language). **Kommandant, du bist ein armer Mann** (Heer's *Felix Notvest*, p. 196, words directed in thought to one previously addressed by **Sie.**

Note. Historical Development. Of later origin than the editorial *we*, the Plural of Modesty discussed in *f.* (3) below, is the associative *we* used in imperial decrees in that period of Roman history when two or three rulers reigned together and hence were associated in the official proclamations. Later whenever the political power was centered in one emperor the old *we* was retained, so that altho often the associative force was present as the ruler included his advisors the associative *we* developed into royal *we*, the Plural of Majesty or the Plural of Dignity, as the ruler spoke of himself in his official announcements in the pl. instead of the sing., as 'We decree' instead of 'I decree.' This usage was imitated by German kings, dukes, &c., in their official decrees, and still in our own time the last German emperor writes (Oct. 28, 1893): **Wir Wilhelm, von Gottes Gnaden deutscher Kaiser, König von Preußen usw. verordnen usw.** A person of high rank speaking thus of himself in the 1st pers. pl. must use the possessive **unser** instead of **mein: Es ist uns zu Ohren gekommen, daß unsere getreuen lieben Untertanen usw.**

In the ninth century such persons in high standing who thus spoke of themselves in the 1st pers. pl. were by others addressed by **Ihr** (2nd pers. pl.) instead of the 2nd pers. sing. Later all persons of rank or even of good standing were addressed by **Ihr**, and thus **Ihr** became the universal polite form till the fifteenth century. In the Middle Ages children also addressed each of their parents by **Ihr**, which custom lingers still in places in the country: **Vater, das erste Reis, das Euch auf Eurem Heimweg an den Hut stößt, das brecht für mich ab** (from Grimm's *Märchen*). Likewise in Wolfram's "Parzival" Gahmuret addresses his elder brother by **Ihr** but is in return addressed by **du.** This usage still survived in the eighteenth century as seen in Gellert's comedy "Die zärtlichen Schwestern," where the younger sister respectfully addresses the elder sister by **Ihr.**

At the beginning of the fifteenth century arose a new form of address towards persons of high rank. From a feeling of hesitation to approach them directly they were addressed indirectly by their pompous titles, which caused the verb to be placed in the 3rd person, at first in the singular, later in the singular or plural, finally only in the plural: Ich thet was üwer gnad mich hieß (Hans von Bühel, A.D. 1400). **Wenn Euer Kurfürstliche Gnade glaubte, so würde Sie Gottes Herrlichkeit sehen** (Luther). **Wir wollen also tun wie Euer Fürstliche Gnaden schreiben** (id.). **Haben Euer Fürstliche Durchleuchtigkeit (Durchlauchtigkeit) auch Falken?** (1594, H. J. v. Braunschweig). The plural of the verb here is due to the plural subject **Gnaden**, an abstract plural much used also elsewhere as a more emphatic form than the singular, as in **von Gottes Gnaden** *by the grace of God.* The plural form of the verb was then extended by analogy to use with other titles. The plural form of the title itself, however, has become fixed only in **Eure** or **Euer** (**137. 1.** *a*) **Gnaden** (formerly an address to princes and rulers, now only to a **Graf, Reichsfreiherr,** and the highest orders of the clergy, as **Bischof**), **Eure Hochwürden** (the address used to a **Propst, Abt, Domherr, Ober-Konsistorialrat, Hofprediger**), **Eure Hochehrwürden** (address to a pastor), **Euer Liebden** (in the time of the empire the address used by one prince or ruler to another). They are now felt, however, as singulars in spite of the plural form: **Sr.** (**Seiner**) **Hochwürden dem Propst N. N.** (form of address upon the envelop). As in the examples given above from Luther the possessive **Euer**, which was used in connection with the old polite address **Ihr**, was inconsistently retained in connection with the new polite form in the third person, but there soon sprang up the third person possessives **Sein** with reference to a male (**Ihr** with reference to a female), **Ihr** with reference to either a male or a female: **Euer, Seine,** or **Ihre Gnaden.** The last mentioned form, i.e. **Ihr**, was used either because the title to which reference was made was usually feminine or plural, or it was thought that the plural form of the verb which was so often used with these titles required a possessive which referred to more than one. In the seventeenth century the uninflected possessive **Ihro** sprang up to vie with **Euer, Sein,** and **Ihr.** To-day only **Euer** is used immediately before the title, but elsewhere it is replaced by **Ihr.** See also **138. 1.** *a* and **2.** *f.*

Towards the close of the sixteenth century the direct address in the third person, so common with persons of rank, began to be used toward untitled persons as a polite form of address. The titles **Herr** Mr. and **Frau** Mrs., or often with the article **der Herr, die Frau,** were used and further on in the same sentence or following ones were replaced by the pronouns **Er** and **Sie: Ich bitt gantz freundlich, der Herr woll'** (instead of **du wollest** or the more polite **Ihr wollet**) **mir es nicht für übel deutn, das** (= **daß**) **ich ihn** (instead of **Dich** or **Euch**) **ansprech' bey den Leutn** (Herzog Heinrich Julius, A.D. 1593). Finally **Herr** and **Frau** dropped out, and **Er** and **Sie** with the 3rd pers. sing. of the verb were used in direct address: **Wohin geht Er?** Where are you going? (addressed to a gentleman). **Wohin geht Sie?** (to a lady). **Ihr** was the next polite form, and **du** was used toward friends.

Towards the close of the seventeenth century a new polite address arose, which began a struggle for supremacy with the polite forms **Er, Sie,** and **Ihr** already in use. The new polite form was **Sie**, the 3rd pers. pl. instead of the 3rd pers. sing. thus only having one form for the two genders. It was first used as a convenient substitute for **Euer Gnaden** after the full title had already been mentioned: **Ich bin oft vermahnet und gebeten von vielen, ich wollte und sollte Euer Kurfürstlichen und Fürstlichen Gnaden schreiben, daß Sie den Gefangenen H. ja nit wiederumb loslassen wollten** (Luther). Later its use was widened, so that it replaced **Er** and **Sie** (with the 3rd pers. sing. of the verb). This new form gained the final victory somewhere near 1740 and became firmly fixed by the rich prose literature which sprang up at this time. However, **Er, Sie, Ihr, du** still continued to be used with varying shades of meaning. Towards the third quarter of the eighteenth century, **Sie** (with the verb in the 3rd pers. pl.) was the very polite form used to persons of high rank or position, or as a special mark of respect. **Er** and **Sie** (with verb in 3rd. pers. sing.) were the ordinary polite forms for ordinary people not well acquainted, for older people in addressing respectfully those younger, for those in higher station in addressing in respectful tone those in lower station, or for young people who desired to be respectful to older people but not coldly formal. **Ihr** was still less formal, and **du** with its pl. **ihr** was used towards intimate friends or towards young people. This state of things can be seen in Lessing's play *Minna von Barnhelm*, and continued over into the nineteenth century, and even lingers still in the conservative country districts, as can be seen in recent authors who give us pictures of rural life, as in Ludwig's *Der Erbförster*, Ebner-Eschenbach's *Die Unverstandene auf dem Dorfe*, and Lauff's *Frau Aleit.* The student must remember, however, that this relation of **Sie, Ihr,** and **Er** to each other will not usually be found in the more stately language of the higher forms of the dramatic literature of this period, for **Sie** is here replaced by **Ihr.** Thus in Goethe's *Faust*, Margaret addresses her neighbor Martha by **Sie** (3rd sing. fem.), towards whom she desires to be at once respectful and cordial, while she addresses Faust at first by the more formal and dignified **Ihr.** Martha addresses Margaret by the familiar **du**, but usually uses **Ihr** to the stranger Mephistopheles. On the other hand, strict distinctions of rank often disappear and **du** is uniformly used or occasionally employed without regard to the station of the person addressed. This is especially true in dramas of a high ideal character where the petty distinctions of conventional society are naturally disregarded thruout or are for a moment forgotten. Thus with Greek simplicity Goethe uses **du** quite uniformly thruout his "Tasso." For our own time usage is given above. **Er** and **Sie** (with verb in sing.) once so polite, have sunk in rank even below **Ihr**, and are now very rarely used except in a half-jesting familiar tone, while **Ihr**, which was promoted to use in poetry and elevated discourse, especially in the more serious dramas of the classical period and the early part of the nineteenth century, has been relegated to use among peasants, where it is in sections still employed as a form of address to avoid the too familiar **du** and the too polite **Sie** (with verb in pl.), or is employed by children as a more respectful form of address to parents than **du.** The polite form **Sie** has in the drama of our day in large measure replaced the stately **Ihr** of the classical period, as the language of the drama has in general taken on to a greater extent than ever before the form and tone of the living spoken language. In the recent dramas, however, that are of a high ideal character, removed from the common scenes of every day, the traditions of the classical drama are faithfully preserved and the stately **Ihr** prevails.

For the peculiar use of pronouns in over-polite language see *f* below.

b. Genitive and Dative Forms. The short forms for the gen. sing. are now rarely found except in a few set expressions and in poetry. Tho grammarians concede that the long forms have gained the victory for the gen. sing., they still dispute the victory of all the long forms except **ihrer** for the pl. Of these short forms **ihr** (earlier spelling **jr**) for the gen. fem. and gen. pl. for all genders is now (except occasionally in the gen. pl. before **aller,** as in **Ihr aller Glückwünsche empfing ich**) entirely obsolete, altho used much in early N.H.G., and even occurring sometimes in poetry up to our own time: **Der HErr bedarf jr** (Matth. xxi. 3). **Da wurden jr beider Augen auffgethan** (Gen. iii. 7). **Allein je mehr die Seele wert, je mehr der Teufel ihr begehrt** (Uhland). But now **ihrer,** not only in the sing. but also in the pl.: **ihrer beider Augen.** Hence it is only natural that the plural gen. of the other pronouns often assumes the long form after the analogy of **ihrer.** In spite of the oft-repeated protests of the grammarians, these forms are quite common in every style of literature: **Ich erinnere mich Eurer nicht** (Goethe's *Götz,* 3, 6). **O meine Eltern! Muß ich erst jetzt, jetzt eurer mich erinnern!** (Grillparzer's *Sappho,* 2, 1). **Kein merkwürdigerer Gegensatz hätte unserer warten können** (G. Keller's *Nachgelassene Schriften,* 223). **So Ihr Euch nur wacker haltet, | wartet Eurer noch ein Stuhl im | hohen Reichsgericht zu Wetzlar** (Scheffel's *Trompeter,* zweites Stück). **So sind Eurer zu viel** (Freytag's *Rittmeister,* chap. iv). **So muß ich es tun statt eurer** (Fontane's *Schach von Wuthenow,* chap. iv). **So lachen wir eurer** (Raabe's *A.T.,* chap. xxiii). **Und laßt dies Bett statt Eurer mich besteigen** (M. Greif's *Heinrich der Löwe,* 2, 1). **Wir müßten unserer hundert sein, um das Erforderliche tun zu können** (Suttner's *Die Waffen nieder!,* III, p. 270). **Die Tafel wartet Eurer, Herr König** (Wildenbruch's *König Heinrich,* 1, 9). **Du hörst den Jubel aller Frühlingssänger, die unsrer warten** (Hauptmann's *Versunkene Glocke,* l. 1208). **Vor eurer aller Augen** (Fulda's *Talisman,* 1, 9). **Und dann wäre auch wohl mal die Zeit gekommen, daß du dich unserer geschämt hättest** (Ompteda's *Sylvester von Geyer,* XCI). **Aber ach, welche Enttäuschung harrte unserer** (Königsmarck's *Japan und die Japaner,* p. 4). **Um unserer selbst willen** (Felix Hollaender's *Der Weg des Thomas Truck,* II, p. 413), **eurer gedenkend** (Heer's *Joggeli,* p. 77). **Jetzt oder nie bedarf ich eurer** (H. von Hofmannsthal's *Die Hochzeit der Sobeide,* p. 97). **Die Frage, ob in der Zukunft ein neues Jena oder ein neues Sedan unserer harrt** (*Hamburger Nachrichten,* May 21, 1906).

The lengthened gen. forms **meiner, deiner, seiner, ihrer,** instead of older **mein, dein, sein, ihr,** have probably arisen under the influence of the ending **er** in the gen. pl. forms **unser** and **euer.** The lengthened forms began to appear in the fourteenth century and in prose in the singular gained the ascendency over the short forms by the end of the sixteenth century. The ascendency of the long forms in the plural has not yet been generally recognized. In the Southwest the lengthened singular forms **meinen, deinen,** &c., were in use in the sixteenth century instead of **meiner, deiner,** &c.

In Luther's earlier writings the old dat. pl. 3rd pers. **jn** (M.H.G. **in**) is still used. The weakened form **en** is still found in the language of the youthful Goethe: **Ich will 'en die Würme** (now **Würmer**) **schon aus der Nase ziehn** (*Urfaust,* p. 23). This weakened form is still in use in colloquial language, but is no longer written. Traces of the lengthened form **ihnen** began to appear in M.H.G. in the twelfth century. From there the long form slowly spread over the entire territory. It became the prevailing form about 1600 in prose and a little later also became established in poetry. The addition of **-en** is after the analogy of the dative plural in **-en** found in nouns and adjectives.

c. Old Genitive **es.** The old neut. gen. sing. **es** is still found in a few set expressions, but is in fact not felt as a genitive: **Ich bin es müde** I am tired of it. **Er will es nicht Wort haben** He will not acknowledge it. **Dann wird es jeder Dank wissen, wenn Preußens Regent und Preußens Heer bereit sind** (Raabe's *Gutmanns Reisen,* chap. xix). This **es** is now felt as a nom. or acc., and this false conception has led to the use of the nom. or acc. of other words, where the gen. should stand: **Es** (gen. construed as nom., hence also **das**) **nimmt mich**

Wunder It surprises me, lit. wonderment seizes me on account of it. **Es stand also wirklich schlimm; aber das** (acc.) **wollte er nicht Wort haben** (Spielhagen's *Freigeboren*, p. 264). **Ich weiß dir deine** (acc.; better **für deine**) **Freigebigkeit großen Dank** (Alex. König, *1001 Nacht*, II. p. 15). See also **260. 3.** *b*, and **262.** II. B. *b*).

d. **Meinetwegen, meinethalben.** The gen. of all genders and numbers in composition with the prepositions **wegen** *on account of*, **willen** *for the sake of*, **halben** (or **halb**) *on account of*, change the last letter of their long forms to **t**: **meinetwegen** on my account, for all I care; **meinetwillen** for my sake; **meinethalben** on my account; **deinetwegen,** &c.

Note 1. This is only a convenient way of stating this rule, for **et** in **meinet, deinet,** &c. is in reality not the gen. ending of the personal pronouns at all, but the corrupted form of a possessive adj. In compounds with **halben** (sometimes contracted to **halb**), the second element is in reality a noun in the dat. pl., used adverbially (see **223.** I. 10. *c*), the first element is the modifying possessive: **meinen halben,** lit. *upon my sides* (i.e. account). In the compounds with **wegen** the forms **meinetwegen, deinetwegen,** &c. represent older **von meinen Wegen** *on my account*, lit. *from my side.* The compounds with **willen** are in reality in the acc. sing. governed by the prep. **um**: (**um**) **ihre(n)twillen** = **um ihren Willen** (still in this form in Luther's Bible, Gen. xii. 16). In all these cases an excrescent **t** has forced its way into the words after the **n** of the possessive, followed by the dropping of **n**. However, by popular conception these possessives are construed as the genitive of the personal pronouns, and indeed often the real genitive of the personal pronouns can be heard: **Es tut mir leid, daß Ihr jetzt wegen meiner den weiten Weg macht** (Auerbach's *Dorfgeschichten*, 8, p. 11). **Wegen meiner lies!** (Hauptmann's *Michael Kramer*, Act I) Read for all I care! **Quälen Sie sich nicht wegen meiner** (Adele Gerhard's *Die Pilgerfahrt*, p. 207). The genitive forms are the rule when the pronoun is separated from the preposition by one or more words **meiner selbst und deinetwegen, deiner und der Mutter wegen, um seiner selbst willen,** but with different word-order: **nur der Mutter und meinetwegen,** &c.

Note 2. Instead of the ending **-et** or **-er** we often find **-s** in colloquial language after the analogy of the genitive of nouns in such expressions as **Rechts halben, Gesundheitswegen: Meinshalben redet doch, was ihr wollt** (Hauptmann's *Michael Kramer*, Act 1). **Meinswegen** (ib.; also Hirschfeld's *Agnes Jordan*, Act 3). We sometimes find the double ending **ts**: **mein'tswegen** (Anzengruber's *Schandfleck*, chap. xiii).

e. Reduction or *Change of Form.* On account of the enclitic or proclitic nature of the personal pronouns they often in colloquial language suffer apheresis, syncope, or a shortening of the vowel. If monosyllabic the initial vowel, if dissyllabic the unaccented **e**, may drop out, as in the following examples taken from Hauptmann's *Einsame Menschen*: **Und der Junge . . . na ja! Dem gibt man seine Milch, man hält'n** (for **ihn**) **sauber . . . aber das kann 'ne Magd auch machen, und später . . . später kann ich'm** (for **ihm**) **doch nichts mehr bieten. Ich muß Ihn'n sagen. Ich hab's** (for **es**) **schon lange bemerkt.** The one form **'s** (for **es**) is now common even in the literary form of speech. In colloquial language unaccented **Sie** often becomes **Se** (zə).

Note. In dialect the personal pronouns are often curiously deformed, as in the following: **mir** or **mer** (for **wir**), arising from assimilation to the final consonant of the preceding verb, as in **habm mir** (for **haben wir**); **dir** (or **der**) or **tir** (or **ter**) = **ihr**, arising from such forms as **sei dir** (for **seid ihr**); **ns** (for **sie**), from such forms as **habns** (for **haben sie**).

f. Peculiar Uses of Pronouns. In addition to the statement of usage given in *a* and *Note* thereunder, attention is here called to the following points:

(1). *Over-polite Speech.* In over-polite language, when the address is to a superior, the direct form **Sie** is avoided in the first instance and the title in the third person used instead. Later on in the sentence when the same person is again addressed, the third person pl. form of the personal pronoun is used and also the possessive corresponding to this form, both pronoun and possessive, however, being written with a capital letter to indicate direct address: **Dem Karl muß man gut sein, der ist so alert, wie was, Herr Amtsrat werden Ihre Freude haben** (Arnold). **Mein Herz weissagt, Ew. Durchlaucht werden die Erhaltung meines Lebens, das ganz Ihnen gehört, nicht verschmähen, und mich in der Ferne als Ihren unveräußerten Untertanen betrachten wollen** (J. H. Voss). In early N.H.G., however, the pronouns of the third person sing. could also be used here, as the verb could also be in the sing. (see *Note* under *a* above): **Da nun Ew. kurfürstliche Gnade begehrt zu wissen, was Sie tun soll in dieser Sache, zumal Sie meint, Sie habe viel zu wenig getan, so antworte ich untertänig, Ew. kurfürstliche Gnaden hat schon allzuviel getan, und sollte gar nichts tun** (Luther).

When the person is spoken *of* in the third person, the third person pl. form of the pronoun is now also used here, but is written with a small letter: **Der Herr Maler lassen sich empfehlen, und sie würden am Sonntag zum Diner erscheinen** (report of a servant to his mistress in Wildenbruch's *Eifernde Liebe*, chap. vi) The artist sends his compliments and begs to say that it will give him great pleasure to dine with you on Sunday.

(**2**). *The First Person Plural for the Second Person Singular.* This often takes place in colloquial language in a tone of stern censure: **Wo haben wir so lange gesteckt?** Where have you been all this time? Often also instead of the imperative. See **177.** I. B. *b.* (2nd par.). On the other hand often in a mild tone of familiarity: **Was haben wir Neues, Marinelli?** (Lessing's *Emilia,* **1, 6**) What news do you have for me, Marinelli?

(**3**). *The Editorial "We."* Just as in English the first person plural is often used by authors and speakers instead of the first person singular and the possessive **unser** instead of **mein,** the author or speaker thus modestly turning the attention away from himself by representing his readers or hearers as accompanying him in thought: **Wir wenden uns nun zunächst zur Zeit des 15. Jahrhunderts usw.** (Behaghel's *Der Gebrauch der Zeitformen,* p. 104.). **Ist unsere Ableitung der Nebensätze richtig usw.** (ib., p. 181). This Plural of Modesty is very old, for we find a quite similar usage in classical Latin.

g. In Gothic the personal pronouns have a dual, i.e. a form used in addressing two persons. Later the dual disappeared from the literary language, and the plural assumed its office in addition to its own. In Bavarian and Austrian dialects, however, the dual forms for the second person, **es** or **ös** (or, according to *e Note,* **des, dös**), **enker, enk, enk,** replaced the plural forms **ihr, euer, euch, euch,** and are still generally used, filling the office of both dual and plural: **Umkehren könnt's** (for **könnt es = könnt ihr**), **stieß der Bote hervor. Aus ist's. Der Anderl** (name) **laßt sagen: Mir** (for **wir**; see *e. Note*) **brauchen enk nicht** (Rosegger). From the frequent contraction of the verb with the following dual has arisen the idea that the 2nd pers. pl. ending of the indic. and imper. is **ts: Ös jung' Leut' kennts freilich nur 'n lustigen Steinklopferhanns** (Anzengruber's *Kreuzelschreiber,* 3, 1). **Gehts jetzt, Kinder, gehts ein wenig in den Hof 'naus** (Raimund's *Der Verschwender,* 3. 7).

141. Substitutes for the Personal Pronouns.

Personal pronouns have a much narrower range of usefulness in German than in English. The lack of accent and other defects cause them very often to be replaced by heavier or more explicit forms.

1. When the *third* person is emphasized, the demon. **der, die, das** very often takes the place of the personal pronoun: **Mit dem kann man nichts machen** You can't do anything with *him.* **Und ein Hut, ein Hut! Mit dem ging' ich nicht in der Wüste Sahara um Mitternacht** What a hat! I wouldn't wear it in the desert of Sahara at midnight. Formerly **er** often had strong demonstrative or determinative force as *he* in *he who* in English and **derjenige** in German. A survival of this older usage is given in **160.** 2. *a. Note.* It is still stressed in a contrast: **Ér ging von hinnen, aber dír ließ er als Erbe das halb zerstörte Reich** (Sudermann's *Teja,* 11).

When the reference is not to definite individuals but to things as members of a class of things without a definite fixing of their identity we usually find a form of **solch,** which is variously translated, *they, one, such,* or is often rendered by repeating the noun to which it refers: **Die Zahl der Abkürzungen im Bibeltexte ist gering. In den lateinischen Randbemerkungen begegnen dagegen solche häufig** (P. Pietsch and E. Thiele in Einleitung, p. xxi, vol. I, *Luthers Deutsche Bibel*) There are few abbreviations in the text of the Bible. On the other hand, in the Latin marginal notes they occur frequently. **Die bedeutendste Schrift über das Niederdeutsche ist Agathe Laschs mittelniederdeutsche Grammatik. Eine solche nach dem jetzigen Stande der Wissenschaft zu schreiben, war nicht leicht** (Oskar Weise in *Zeitschrift für den deutschen Unterricht,* 1915, p. 520) The most important work on Low German is Agathe Lasch's Middle Low German Grammar. To write one, or To write such, *or more smoothly* To write a Middle Low German Grammar in the present state of our knowledge of the subject was not an easy task. The use of **solch** in 2, 3, 5. B. *b. Note* below is based upon this principle. See also **131.** 3 (2nd par.) for incorrect use of **solch** for the personal pronouns **er, sie, es.**

2. The gen. sing. and pl. of pronouns representing things is usually replaced by the demon. genitives **dessen, deren, desselben, derselben,** or in the plural where the reference is a little more indefinite also **solcher** or **von solchen: Behalte dein Geld; ich bedarf dessen nicht** Keep your money; I am not in need of it.

Spare die Worte; es sind deren genug gewechselt Save your words; enough of them have already been spoken. **Sie, trotz eines languissanten Zuges, oder vielleicht auch um desselben willen, eine Schönheit ersten Ranges** (Fontane's *Cécile*, chap. ix). **Während der Winterabende war im Refektorium etwas Figurenzeichnen getrieben worden, und ich hatte mir, als ich eine Menge radierter, bekleideter Staffagefiguren kopierte, einige oberflächliche Übung im Entwerfen solcher erworben** (G. Keller's *Der grüne Heinrich*, p. 280). **Der logische Akzent ermöglicht bei abweichender Wortfolge die Bildung von Formeln, andererseits kann er aber auch bei normaler Wortstellung die Bildung von solchen hintertreiben** (Herbert Wenck in *Beiträge*, 1905, vol. 31, p. 233).

Except in the case of a collective idea or a general or indefinite reference there is a growing tendency to use here the regular genitive forms of the personal pronouns, especially wherever a thing is personified or is vividly pictured as having individual life or force: **„Sicherheiten für die Zukunft" hat der Reichskanzler wiederholt als das unerläßliche Ziel des Krieges für uns bezeichnet. Wir bedürfen ihrer gegen Rußland mindestens so sehr wie gegen eine andere Macht** (Prof. J. Haller in *Das größere Deutschland*, March 13, 1915, p. 356).

Note. The partitive gen. of personal pronouns representing either persons or things may often be replaced in the 3rd person not only by the gen. of **der** or **derselbe**, but also by the dat. of the personal pronoun after the prep. **von** in case of persons and the adverbial compound of the prep. with the demon. **da** (see 5 below) in case of things: **viele derselben, deren viele** many of them (persons or things according to the context), **sechs von ihnen** six (persons) of them, **sechs davon** six (things) of them. The dat. after **von** may also replace the gen. of the first and second persons: **sechs von uns.** Sometimes the prep. **unter** is used instead of **von**: **welcher unter euch** which of you, who among you.

3. The gen. of a pronoun which represents a thing and depends upon a noun preceded by the indefinite article or a pronominal adjective is usually replaced by the gen. of **derselbe**, not by the gen. of **der**: **Namen wie Nävius, Pacuvius, Attius usw. schießen weit über das Ziel des Gymnasiums hinaus und brauchen nicht in einem Lehrbuch desselben zu stehen** (*Zeitschrift für das Gymnasialwesen*, xi, p. 623). **Zwischen meiner letzten Heimkehr ins Vaterhaus und meinem endgültigen Verlassen desselben** (Raabe). In case of a reference to an amount or part we may also use an adverbial compound here: **Er hatte die von Anna ihm mitgegebenen Brotschnitte aus seiner Jagdtasche genommen; aber er aß nur einen kleinen Teil davon** (Storm's *Schweigen*). **Es blieb nichts übrig als den Bart abzuschneiden; dabei ging ein kleiner Teil desselben** (or **davon**) **verloren** (Märchen).

In the plural where the **ein** before the noun drops out and the reference becomes indefinite **solcher** (gen. pl.) or sometimes **von solchen** is usually employed instead of **derselben**: **Auf die Lexikographie angewendet, will das besagen, daß die Behandlung jeder einzelnen Terminologie oder doch einer beschränkten Anzahl solcher je einem anderen Philologen anzuvertrauen wäre, der in den betreffenden Fächern heimisch ist** (Dr. H. Tiktin in *Germanisch-Romanische Monatsschrift*, 1910, p. 247). **Die zweite Eigenschaft besteht in der Beschränkung der Aufmerksamkeit auf bestimmte Gegenstände und auf gewisse Teile von solchen** (Wundt's *Völkerpsychologie*, II, p. 80).

4. The simple dative forms of the personal pronouns are not freely used with reference to things, but occur with ever increasing frequency: **Die Unternehmungen meines Busens sind zu groß, als daß du ihnen im Wege stehen solltest** (Goethe's *Götz*, 4, 4). **Beide liebten das Zimmer und gaben ihm auf Kosten aller andern den Vorzug** (Fontane's *Schach von Wuthenow*, IV). The dat. forms **ihm, ihr, ihnen** are so thoroly identified with persons that with reference to things they are avoided by many who prefer here the dat. of **derselbe**: **Versuche, den Verein zu verfolgen, werden demselben nur neues Wachstum verleihen. Durch Höhe der Gebäude suchte man zu ersetzen, was denselben an Breite und Tiefe abging.**

The dat. **dem** is usually used with reference to the thought of a preceding clause or sentence: **Das Fräulein tat einen affektierten Schrei und wich zurück. Joachim schenkte dem keine Beachtung, sondern sagte bloß,** &c. (Marriot's *Der geistliche Tod*, chap. xviii).

5. A. *Personal Pronouns Replaced by Adverbial Compounds.* The dat. and acc. of the personal pronouns of all genders and numbers, when they represent things, are not usually used after prepositions, but are replaced by an adverbial compound formed by appending the prep. to the demon. adverb **da** (before consonants except in case of **darnach,** which occurs about as frequently as **danach**) or **dar** (before a vowel): **Hier ist ein Tisch, und drauf** or **da'rauf** (for **auf ihm**) **ist ein Buch. Er kam vor eine Tür und stieß da'gegen** (for **gegen sie**). A: **Er hatte mir versprochen, diese wichtigen Briefe auf die Post zu geben.** B: **Wenn Ihnen da'ran liegt, will ich da'mit** (with them) **hingehen. Seine Stühle waren uralt, aber er lud täglich jemanden ein, da'rauf zu sitzen** (Goethe).

In colloquial language these adverbial compounds *may* in a few cases be used with reference to **das Mädchen,** and hence in this one instance may refer to persons: **Nämlich der junge Mensch . . . in unserer Geschichtserzählung kriegt sein Mädchen ebenfalls, und wird so glücklich damit als möglich** (Raabe's *Gutmanns Reisen*, Intr.).

The one preposition **in** is changed to **ein** in these compounds to express the acc. relation (**223. I. 9. B. 4**): **Wer andern eine Grube gräbt, fällt selbst drein** or **da'rein,** but **Ist er im Hause? Nein, er ist nicht drin** or **da'rin.**

Sometimes another adverb can be used instead of **da: Endlich fanden wir das Zimmer und gingen hinein.**

In many cases the preposition has entered into such close relations with the verb that it forms a compound with it, in which case it is treated as a separable prefix, not as a preposition, altho it still retains its original prepositional force: **In diesem Zimmer liegen viele Bücher auf** In this room there are many books lying on the tables for reference, for use. The peculiar development of meaning in the compound differentiates this construction from the one described above. Where the differentiation of meaning is not so sharp fluctuation of usage follows: **Er sitzt am Tisch und stemmt die Ellbogen auf** (prefix) *or* **darauf** (adverbial compound). Compare **223. I. 9. B.**

In connection with the rule for the use of the adverbial compounds study carefully *e* and B below, where exceptions to the rule are given. The literary language of our time is not in general favorable to adverbial compounds as substitutes for pronouns, and the rule is not so broad and not so uniformly followed as the grammarians represent. See also **153. 2. A.**

a. This same construction is used when the reference is to persons, if they are taken collectively: **Viele Knaben waren da, aber Wilhelm war nicht da'runter** Many boys were there, but William was not among them, or in the crowd.

It is also used with reference to words representing persons where the reference is more to the abstract idea contained in the word than to an individual: **Hatten sie keinen Kaiser? Liebe Frau! Er ist nur der Schatten davon** (Goethe's *Götz*, 4, 4) He is only the shadow of one.

b. In the preceding compounds the accent rests upon the vowel of the preposition, and hence the vowel of the preceding adverb being slighted is often entirely suppressed. By shifting the accent from the preposition to the adverb **da** a new point of view is gained. In **da(r)**, which is of the same origin as the demonstrative **der**, the demonstrative force becomes strong with the aid of the accent, and the attention is called to the place or all the attendant circumstances: **nicht 'dadurch, 'hierdurch** not thru *that* entrance, but thru *this*. **'Daran erkenn(e) ich ihn** By that very thing I recognize him. **Was er einmal sagt, 'dabei bleibt er.** Often doubled, especially in popular language: **'Dadrin, nicht 'hierdrin.**

Note. In early N.H.G. the demonstrative adverb **da** was here not so closely united with the preposition as now, but could be separated from it by several words, and so occasionally even later in the classical period: **Da soll es bei bleiben** (Luther). **Da behüte mich Gott vor** (Goethe). In popular speech this usage is still common: **Da muß ein Loch in sein** (Jensen's *Schatzsucher*, p. 266). When thus separated the **da** has demonstrative force, and hence is strongly accented. Where, however, the demonstrative force is weak the **da** is often omitted altogether in easy colloquial and popular language: **Hängen Sie den ganzen Krempel an den Nagel! Kommt ja doch nichts bei** (= **dabei**) **'raus!** (Halbe's *Die Heimatlosen*, p. 52).

c. **Hier** + preposition usually has pure demonstrative force, being equal to **dieser** and preposition, and hence has the accent and cannot be contracted: **'Hierin haben Sie recht** In this respect you are right.

d. Thus we see in *b* and *c* that the demonstratives **der** and **dieser,** when they refer to things, are replaced after prepositions in the same way as the personal pronouns, differing from the latter only in accent.

e. The regular pronominal forms are, however, with ever increasing frequency preferred to the adverbial compounds in all grammatical and rhetorical uses, but especially in the plural (except in case of a collective idea) and where a thing or idea is personified, or is vividly pictured as having individual force or life: **Er nahm einen Bogen Schreibpapier, der vor ihm auf dem Pulte lag, und begann auf ihm mit dem Bleistift allerhand Schnörkel und Arabesken zu zeichnen** (Volkmann). **Unmittelbar hinter dem Pfarrhause steigt der Kirchhof lehnan, auf ihm so ziemlich in seiner Mitte die frühmittelalterliche Feldsteinkirche** (Fontane's *Stechlin*, I. p. 4). **Ihre blauen Augen waren vielleicht zu hell, aber es lag Seele in ihnen** (G. Ompteda). **In Straßburg bildete sich jenes Leben in und mit der Natur, jenes Gefühl der Verwandtschaft, des Einsseins mit ihr** (personifying nature) **bei Goethe zu der Kraft und Tiefe aus, die wir in seiner Dichtung der nächsten Jahre als einen bedeutenden Fortschritt zur modernen Auffassung der Natur bewundern. Die Dichtung ist kein photographischer Apparat, der Autor kommt in ihr doch stets zum Vorschein** (Richard Weißenfels). **Vom besten Stil und vom Wege zu ihm** (heading to chap. V in Eduard Engel's *Deutsche Stilkunst*). **Die genaue Auffassung der Bezugsart des Genitivs und des Grades seiner Abhängigkeit von einem andern Satzteil ist uns Deutschen einigermaßen erschwert durch unsere heutige Gewohnheit, den adnominalen Genitiv unmittelbar neben sein Nomen zu stellen und so engstens an es zu fesseln** (Brugmann's *Vergleichende Grammatik*, II. p. 615).

In the same manner we often find the adverbial compound **hier** + preposition replaced by a preposition followed by a case form of the neuter of **dies-**: **Nach diesem—es war wieder ein Sonnabend—gingen Lewin und Hirschfeldt in die Pfarre** (Fontane's *Vor dem Sturm*, IV. chap. xxvii). The adverbial construction, however, is quite uniformly used to refer to a verb, or to the thought contained in a preceding or following phrase or proposition, also to refer collectively to things already mentioned: **Wird er kommen? Ich zweifle daran. Aber sage mir doch, fragte die Weide den Dornstrauch, warum du nach den Kleidern der vorbeigehenden Menschen so begierig bist. Was willst du damit?**

f. In colloquial speech the pronoun is often omitted: **Das Haus ist nicht neben dem Berge, sondern auf** (Georg Edward). **Der Unfall ereignete sich nicht nach dem Balle, sondern vor** (id.).

B. Not all prepositions can, as in A, form compounds with the demonstrative **da**, but this construction is limited to **an, auf, aus, bei, durch, für, gegen, hinter, in, mit, nach, neben, ob, ohne** (only, however, in popular language), **über, unter, um, von, vor, wider, zu, zwischen.** In case of other prepositions, this construction is replaced by others:

a. The preps. **halb** and **wegen** are appended to the gen. of the demon. pronoun (see **129.** 2. A. *a*): **deshalb, deswegen** on account of it, therefore.

b. After all other preps. or prep. phrases with the force of a prep. the personal pronouns are usually replaced by **derselbe: Sie wollte sich durch das Geld Vorteile verschaffen, auf die sie ohne dasselbe nicht rechnen konnte. In meinem dritten Jahre befiel mich eine schwere Krankheit und ich blieb infolge derselben an allen Gliedern gelähmt.**

Note. We often find **derselbe** even after prepositions which can form with **da** the adverbial compounds described in A, as there is a desire for a more concrete expression of the idea of object than that afforded by an adverbial form: **Vnd segnete den siebenden Tag vnd heiliget jn | darumb | das er an dem selben geruget hatte von allen seinen Wercken** (Gen. ii. 3). **Vier Wochen später hatte er das alte Haus im gerichtlichen Aufgebot gekauft und hielt mit einem alten Gesellen und einer noch älteren Schwester seinen Einzug in dasselbe** (Storm's *Böljer Basch*).

The use of **derselbe** is especially common to represent a noun after one preposition in instances where two prepositions which take different cases govern one noun: **in der Kirche und um dieselbe** instead of the incorrect **in und um die Kirche.** In case of persons the personal pronoun should be used instead of **derselbe: mit dem Vater und ohne ihn.** Good authors, however, often disregard these rules of the grammarians and place both prepositions before the noun or pronoun, which is then governed by the second preposition: **um und neben dem Hochaltare** (Goethe). **Ihre Tochter wird meine Frau mit oder gegen Ihren Willen** (H. Seidel's *Lang, lang ist's her*). Sometimes the noun is repeated: **mit Gott und durch Gott** (Andresen's *Sprachgebrauch*, p. 193). Often in case of a pronominal object: **Was in ihm und um ihn und über ihm ist** (W. Wackernagel).

There is, in general, a feeling against the clumsy form **derselbe** and an evident tendency in choice language to replace it by a simple personal pronoun, as in A. *e*.: **Sie** (Frau von Olfers) **kannte ihre Grenze, aber innerhalb ihrer ihr Recht und ihre Befugnis** (Hermann Grimm's *Fragmente*, I. p. 379). **So sehen wir also, daß Raabe trotz seiner Vorliebe für die Fremdwörter doch statt ihrer oftmals schöne deutsche Wörter verwendet** (Otto Schütte in *Zeitschrift des Allgemeinen Deutschen Sprachvereins*, 1908, No. 2, p. 42).

Often in colloquial speech the pronoun is omitted: **Wie jammert mich Vaters Bärtchen: ich kenne ihn gar nicht mehr ohne** (Bismarck to his wife, Oct. 7, 1850).

Solch is usually employed instead of a personal pronoun when the reference is not to a definite individual but to a member of a class without a definite fixing of its identity: **U in du ist zweimal mit Längezeichen gedruckt, zweimal ohne solches** (Oscar Weise in *Zeitschrift für den deutschen Unterricht*, 1915, p. 430). Compare **131.** 3 (last par.).

6. Similar to the distinction between **sein, ihr** and **dessen, deren** (see **138.** 2. *d*) is the difference between **er, sie, es** and **derselbe, dieselbe, dasselbe. Er** refers to the subject of the preceding sentence, or in a complex sentence to the subject of the main clause, while **derselbe** (or **dieser**) refers to some oblique case in the preceding sentence, or in a complex sentence to some oblique case in the main proposition, or to some word in a preceding subordinate clause or infinitive phrase, be it a nom. or an oblique case: **Mein Bruder ist zu seinem Freunde gegangen. Derselbe** (or better **dieser**) **will ohne ihn den Kauf nicht abschließen** My brother has gone to his friend's. The latter will not close the bargain without him. **Tagtäglich ritt er (Graf Beust) aus auf seinem**

bekannten Schimmel, bis derselbe (i.e. **der Schimmel**) **in Paris an Altersschwäche starb. Der Knabe wollte nicht sagen, daß der Hund ihn gebissen hatte, damit man denselben** (i.e. **den Hund**) **nicht schlagen möchte.**

The personal pronoun should, however, always be used in all the above cases instead of **derselbe** or **dieser,** if no ambiguity would arise therefrom: **Die Diplomaten forderten die Völker auf, demütig Gott zu preisen und ihm Lob zu singen** (Raabe).

a. The oblique cases of either **er** or **derselbe** may refer to an oblique case in the preceding sentence: **Mein Bruder ist zu seinem Freunde gegangen. Er will dann mit ihm** (now more common than **demselben** or **diesem**) **in die Stadt gehen.** In case, however, the reference is to a thing, **derselbe** is quite common: **Durch Höhe der Gebäude suchte man zu ersetzen, was denselben an Breite und Tiefe abging. Die Pronomina demonstrativa bezeichnen einen Gegenstand dadurch, daß sie auf denselben hinweisen.** Always so in case of a gen. which points back to some definite thing and depends upon a noun modified by an article or pronominal adj.: **Die heutigen Mundarten haben die Geltung des Präteritums noch weiter eingeschränkt: weite Gebiete haben den Indikativ desselben auch als Form der einfachen Erzählung ganz oder teilweise eingebüßt** (Behaghel's *Die deutsche Sprache*, p. 324, 2nd ed.).

b. If there are two substantives in a sentence besides the subject, both of which are referred to in a following sentence or clause, it is often best to represent the one which in the following sentence or clause must be in the nom. by **dieser** and the other one by **derselbe: Der Herr nahm dem Bedienten das Geld wieder ab, als dieser ihm dasselbe gestohlen hatte,** or **als ihm dieses von demselben gestohlen worden war.** It is best to avoid such clumsy sentences wherever ambiguity would not arise, and use the simple personal pronoun for reference to persons: **Ich nehme meinen Kindern alle Bücher ab, sobald sie selbe nicht mehr brauchen** (Rosegger).

7. In general **derselbe** is used instead of a personal pronoun for sake of euphony or harmony. The following cases of this use occur not infrequently.

a. To prevent two **sie's,** or a **Sie** and a **sie** from coming together: **Ich bitte um die Zeitung, wenn Sie dieselbe gelesen haben.** Many good stylists, however, do not feel the repetition of **sie** as harsh: **Anna Elisabeth . . . faßte deswegen Onkel Harres Andeutungen einerseits ernster auf als Eva, anderseits beurteilte sie sie weniger streng als der Großvater** (R. Huch's *Ludolf Ursleu*, chap. xxi).

b. **Derselbe** is often used in a comprehensive sense to refer to some preceding word with all its modifiers, as it is felt as a more appropriate form than the light personal pronouns to represent a weighty expression or a heavy combination of words: **zum täglichen Umgang wackerer Leute sowohl als zur Briefwechslung zwischen denselben. Das Erscheinen der Wörterbücher von Kluge und Heyne konnte mich nicht von meinem Vorhaben** (intention to publish a dictionary) **abbringen, da dieselben** (i.e. **die Wörterbücher von Kluge und Heyne**) **in ihrer Anlage ganz verschieden von dem meinigen sind** (Paul's *Wörterbuch*, Preface).

Historical Note. In early N.H.G., **derselbe,** aside from its primary meaning *the same*, was often employed as a pure demonstrative or determinative = **der** or **derjenige.** See **132. 1. B.** *a.* The word gradually extended its boundaries so that it included the meanings of **der** and **er (sie, es).** The older use as a pure demonstrative or determinative has in large measure disappeared, but its use instead of the personal pronouns has increased so that it is often used without reason where a personal pronoun would be simpler and better: **Kleinigkeiten, die er von Mariannen erhalten oder derselben** (= **ihr**) **geraubt hatte** (Goethe). **Der Prinz Karl ist von seinem Unwohlsein so weit wieder hergestellt, daß derselbe** (= **er**) **nicht mehr das Bett zu hüten genötigt ist** (*Kölnische Zeitung*). At the present time grammarians quite generally censure this free use of **derselbe,** and urge that the simple forms **der** and **er** be used where it is possible. The best usage of our time has been given in the preceding articles.

8. The demonstrative **solch** is often used instead of the personal pronouns. See **1, 2, 3,** above, and also **131. 3.**

9. *Uses of* **es.** Except after prepositions the uninflected **es** has, differing from other personal pronouns, a wide field of usefulness:

a. Situation **Es.** Like **dies** (**128.** A. *a*) uninflected **es** is employed in the identification of persons and things, where **es** refers to an unidentified person or thing that becomes known thru the situation, or is identified by some person: **Es ist Hans** (uttered by someone who has just heard approaching steps). **Wer kommt die Treppe herunter? Es ist Hans,** or **Es ist mein Bruder. Wer ist an der Tür? Es ist eine arme Frau. Was liegt auf dem Tische? Es ist eine schöne Blume,** or in the plural **Es sind schöne Blumen. Sind es Ihre Kinder? Es sind die Kinder meines Bruders. Es** often points to something definite which is more or less clearly defined by the situation: **Es steht schlecht** Things are in bad condition. Compare **219.** 3 (last par).

b. As object in various constructions, especially referring to some fact or thing already mentioned or more or less understood, or to a condition of things: **Marie ist hier. Ich weiß es. Ich kann es nicht länger mit ansehen. Ich hielt es endlich nicht länger aus. Er bringt es weit** He is getting along in the world. **Machen Sie sich's bequem** Make yourself comfortable. **Er macht es zu arg** He carries things too far. **Er läßt es gehen, wie's Gott gefällt** He lets things go as it pleases God.

c. As a predicate, representing an idea already expressed. See **129. 2. C. (4).**

d. As a grammatical and anticipative subject. See **185.** A. I. 3; **251. I. 2.** A and B, and II. B.

e. As an anticipative object. See **185.** A. I. 3 and **272.** C. *a.*

f. As a mere formal subject in the various impersonal constructions described in **219.**

Reflexive Pronouns.

(Compare with **218.**)

142. 1. A personal pronoun can also show that the action which goes forth from the subject bends back upon that subject, and is then called a reflexive pronoun: **Ich lobe mich** I praise myself. Special pronominal forms to show this reflexive action are wanting except in the third person, where **sich** *himself, herself, itself, themselves* is used for all genders and both numbers and for both dat. and acc.: **er lobt sich; sie lobt sich; sie loben sich** they praise themselves; **er spricht immer nur von sich; sie spricht immer nur von sich,** &c. For the gen. of the third person and the gen., dat., and acc. of the first and second persons, the reflexives are identical in form with the personal pronouns: **du lobst dich; wir loben uns; ihr lobt euch,** &c. The reflexive by its very nature has no nom., as it is always an *object,* either of a verb or a prep., or dependent upon some adjective. Reflexive verbs in German usually take an acc. object, but certain verbs, contrary to the English idiom, take an object in the dat. or gen.: **Du lobst dich,** but **du spottest deiner, du schmeichelst dir.** To the gen. of the third person the indeclinable **selbst** is usually added, or otherwise it is ambiguous: **Er spottet seiner selbst.** Without **selbst** it would mean, He is ridiculing *him* (some one else), but with **selbst** *himself.*

a. In early N.H.G. there was except after prepositions no dative of the reflexive, its place being supplied by the dative of the personal pronoun, which usage occasionally occurs as late as the classical period, and in popular South German is still found: **Wer sich Knall und Fall, ihm (= sich) selbst zu leben, nicht entschließen kann, der lebet andrer Sklav auf immer** (Lessing's *Nathan,* 2, 9).

Note. The use of **sich** instead of the dative of a personal pronoun in the reflexive relation arose at the close of the O.H.G. period, at first however only found after prepositions. Luther much later still only uses dative **sich** after prepositions, elsewhere the dative of the personal pronoun, some writers of his time use the dative of the personal pronoun thruout. The present usage of employing dative **sich** thruout began to gain the ascendency about the beginning of the eighteenth century under Low German and Middle German influence. In Middle and Low Franconian dialect dative **sich** has in certain sections been modified to **sir** under the influence of **mir** and **dir.** On the other hand, in the South German dialects the old usage of employing the dative of the personal pronoun here is in general well preserved.

b. If the reflexive refers to subjects of different persons the first person usually has the preference over the second and third and the second person the preference over the third: **Ich und du (wir) retteten uns. Du und er (ihr) rettetet euch. Sich** is so frequently used with the verb in the third person plural that it has become so thoroly identified with this form that in loose colloquial speech and dialect it is also often used with the other person of the plural having the same form, namely the first person: **Bloß ich und ein paar Kameraden konnten sich** (instead of **uns**) **retten** (Hans Hoffmann's *Von Haff und Hafen,* p. 74). **Besonders in der Annaberger Gegend hört man selbst von Gebildeten oder liest man in der Lokalpresse: Wir müssen sich beeilen, Wir haben sich Mühe gegeben** (Göpfert's *Mundart des sächsischen Erzgebirges,* p. 75).

In S.G. this usage is, of course, confined to the accusative in the sections which according to *a* use **sich** only in the accusative: **Weil wir uns** (literary form instead of dialectic **sich**) **scheuen, das Red' zu haben, was wir uns** (literary form) **eigentlich zu sagen hätten und worüber wir sich** (dialectic form) **ausreden sollten** (Anzengruber's *Schandfleck*, chap. xviii).

2. A. The reflexive usually refers to the subject of the proposition in which it stands. The Germans also use a reflexive of the third person after prepositions if the reference is to the subject, while in English a personal pronoun is used here as a survival of older usage, where in general personal pronouns also served as the usual reflexive forms: **Er** (**sie**) **hat Geld bei sich** He (she) has money with him (her). In poetry older English usage survives also elsewhere: To their salute he bends *him* slightly (Byron).

a. In prepositional phrases modifying a noun a personal pronoun of the third person must be used according to C if the phrase is equivalent to a subordinate clause and the reference is to the subject of the principal proposition: **Diethelm traf die Brüder mitten im Gespräch über ihn** (Auerbach) [= **als sie über ihn sprachen**], but **Alle Unzufriedenheit des Menschen ist Frucht seines Widerspruchs mit sich selbst** (Thümmel) [= **Frucht des Widerspruchs, den er mit sich selbst empfindet**].

B. If there is a reference in the subordinate clause to the subject of the principal proposition, a personal pronoun should be used: **Er belobte die Soldaten, die sich gehorsam gegen ihn** (referring to the subject of the principal proposition) **bewiesen hatten.**

C. In participial, adjective, prepositional, and infinitive constructions which have the force of a subordinate clause, the reflexive refers to the subject of the contracted clause: **Wir erblickten einen Mann, der sich schnell entfernte. Wir erblickten einen sich schnell entfernenden Mann. Wir baten ihn, sich zu entfernen. Soll ich diese an sich verständliche Regel** (= **diese Regel, die an sich verständlich ist**) **wiederholen?** If there is a reference in the contracted clause to the subject of the principal proposition, a personal pronoun must of course be used: **Er bat uns, ihn zu besuchen. Sie trug ein ihr vollkommen ähnliches Kind auf dem Arme.**

a. Usage makes distinctions:

(1) If the infinitive has no subject expressed, or has passive force, the reflexive refers to the subject of the principal proposition: **Er hörte über sich schmähen** He heard someone talking abusively about him. **Er hörte sich** (acc.) **von seinem Freunde rufen** He heard his friend call him, lit. He heard himself called by his friend. **Dort ließ er sich** (dat.) **erzählen, wie alles gekommen** There he allowed himself to be told how all had come about.

(2) If the infinitive has an accusative subject and is active, it usually takes a personal pronoun as a reflexive object referring to the subject of the principal proposition: **Pentheus sieht die Furien ihm nahen** (Schiller). **Er ließ sie ihm zu Füßen fallen** (id.). **Er sah sein Luftschloß noch einmal ihm zuwinken** (Kurz). **Es fühlt der Mensch mit bleichem Beben den Tod ihm sitzen im Genick** (Lenau). Sometimes, however, we find a reflexive here instead of a personal pronoun, especially after **lassen**: **Da, als er aufblickte, sah er zwei Arbeiter mit ihren Feldgerätschaften sich entgegenkommen** (Storm's *Der Schimmelreiter*, Werke VII, p. 246). **Der Förster ließ sich den Wildschützen nicht nahe kommen** (Blatz's *Deutsche Grammatik*, II, p. 271). **Der Kanzler ließ sich das nicht anfechten** (id.). This is the survival of an old construction which required the reflexive in the infinitive clause when the reference was to the subject of the principal proposition: Ir gast si sich küssen bat (Parzival, 23. 30) = **Sie bat ihren Gast, sie** (referring to the subject of the sentence) **zu küssen.** This older usage is still lingering on, but its ambiguity is leading to the firmer establishment of the rule given above. It is, however, still the rule in (3).

(3) The old usage of employing a reflexive referring to the subject of a principal proposition is still the rule if the reflexive depends upon a preposition: **Er sah einen Fremden neben sich stehen.** A personal pronoun, however, is used if the reflexive would cause ambiguity: **Sie sieht ringsum im Waldesschlag die Wipfel ernst sich zu ihr neigen** (Redwitz).

(4) A reflexive verb is used as an infinitive where the reflexive refers to the subject of the infinitive: **Die Stadt sah den Hunger nebst seinem ganzen Gefolge mit schrecklichen Schritten sich nähern** (Goethe). **Er sah den Pithecus sich über ihn** (with reference to the subject of the sentence) **beugen** (Raabe's *Der Lar*, p. 220). **Ich hieß ihn sich setzen.**

(5) A reflexive often refers to an object of an infinitive when there is no ambiguity: **Beim Scheiden bat ich mir die Erlaubnis aus, ihn bei sich zu sehen** (Goethe's *Dicht. u. Wahr.*, Zweiter Teil, Zehntes Buch). **Wir wollen ihn sich selbst erhalten** (Gustaf E. Karsten). **Ich wollte ihn bei sich zu Hause sehen** (Georg Edward), but in **Er wollte ihn bei sich sehen** the **sich** is felt as belonging to **er,** the subject of the sentence. When the subject of the sentence is thus in the third person and it is desired to bring the reflexive in relation to an object of the infinitive in the third person we may often use the personal pronoun: **Er wollte ihn bei ihm zu Hause sehen** (Gustaf E. Karsten).

THE EMPHATIC ADJECTIVES Selbst AND Selber.

143. The indeclinable strongly stressed limiting adjective **selbst** or **selber** *self* is much used to emphasize personal and reflexive pronouns and also nouns, always following as an appositive the governing word but not always immediately as it was originally a predicate appositive and still often stands in the predicate referring to the subject: **ich selbst** or **selber, wir selbst** or **selber. Ich tat es selbst. Ich selbst habe ihren Brief gelesen,** or **Ich habe ihren Brief selbst gelesen,** the latter of which forms, however, may also mean: I have read her letter itself, not a copy of it. **Er kam selbst. Er ist die Ehrlichkeit selbst. Er lobt sich selbst** or **selber,** but not without the reflexive, as in **er lobt selbst. Selbst** may, however, be used alone after the prep. **von** and in a few other idiomatic expressions: **Die Mühle geht nicht von selbst. Selbst essen macht satt** If you want to get satiated you must do your own eating. **Selbst ist der Mann** If you want to have a thing done well, do it yourself. **Selbst eingebrockt, selbst ausgegessen** As you have brewed, so you must drink. **Selbstgebackenes Brot** home-made bread. Also in paying back an insult: **Er schalt ihn einen Betrüger. „Selbst Betrüger!" gab der Bescholtene zurück.**

Note 1. In M.H.G. the emphatic limiting adjective **selb** was inflected strong and weak. **Selbst** is the corrupted form of the old strong gen. **selbes** and **selber** is the old strong masc. nom. The frequent use of the old gen. and nom. led to their becoming established as set forms for all cases, genders, and numbers.

Note 2. As an adverb **selbst** (only rarely **selber**) may stand before or after a noun or pronoun, usually with the meaning *even*, always with weak accent: **Die Ermahnung selbst des Váters** (or **des Váters selbst**) **fruchtete nichts.**

THE RECIPROCAL PRONOUNS.

144. When the pronoun shows that the action of the verb is mutual between two or more persons, it is called a reciprocal pronoun. The following reciprocal forms are used:

a. The reciprocal pronoun for the dat. and acc. of all genders and persons is **ei'nander** *each other, one another*: **Wir loben einander; sie loben einander; sie sprechen voneinander.**

b. For the gen. **einer (eine) . . . des andern (der andern)** are used: **Sie gedenken einer des andern** They (lady and gentleman, or two gentlemen) are thinking of each other. **Sie gedenken eine der andern** They (two ladies) are thinking of each other.

c. For the dat. and acc. the reflexive pronouns are often used for the reciprocal when no ambiguity can arise: **Ihr seht euch oft** You see one another often. **Die Eheleute sind sich** (dat. = **einander**) **treu und lieben sich** (acc. = **einander**) **innig. Sie geben sich die Hände. Sie lieben sich** is ambiguous, as **sich** may mean *each other* or *themselves*, but by the addition of **selbst** or **selber** the reflexive idea is brought out, and **sich** may be changed to **einander,** or **einander** or more commonly **gegenseitig** may be added to **sich,** to make the reciprocal idea clear: **Sie lieben sich selbst** *They love themselves*, but **Sie lieben**

einander *They love one another.* **Sie halfen einander,** or **sich gegenseitig,** or sometimes **sich einander.**

Only when the reciprocal depends immediately upon a verb or an adjective, as in the first sentence, can it be replaced by a reflexive, hence after prepositions the reciprocal form is as a rule **einander: Sie saßen nebeneinander,** not **neben sich.** After the prepositions **unter** and **über,** however, either **einander** or a reflexive can be used: **Wir wollen das untereinander** (or **unter uns**) **abmachen. Sie machten das untereinander** (or **unter sich**) **ab. Sie fielen übereinander** (or **über sich**) **her.**

Several common intransitive verbs take **sich** as object: **Die zwei Jungen streiten sich, balgen sich, zanken sich,** or **Der eine streitet sich mit dem anderen usw.**

Note. In dialect **sich** is often used reciprocally instead of **uns** or **einander: Na, mir (wir) können sich net heiraten** (Anzengruber's *Jungferngift*, 4, 7).

Indefinite Pronouns.

145. The indefinites have been treated under adjectives, as most of them can be used as an ordinary adj., or used alone substantively. The following are more like real independent pronouns:

a. **jedermann** *everybody* has only the gen. sing. in **s,** the dat. and acc. being like the nom.

b. **jemand** *somebody,* declined: N. **jemand,** G. **jemandes,** D. **jemand,** or **jemandem** (a comparatively new str. form, but common), **jemanden** (see **106.** *Note* 3; like the preceding a new form, but not so common as earlier in the period), **jemande** (formerly in limited use, now obsolete), A. **jemand** or **jemanden** (new but common); very common in combination with **anders: jemand anders** or **anderer** somebody else, dat. **jemand(em) anders,** or **jemand(em) anderem,** acc. **jemand(en) anders** or **jemand(en) anderen.** In early N.H.G. the indeclinable form **jemands** is also found. See Numbers xvi. 40; Leviticus xxi. 17.

Note 1. In these cases **anders** is a dependent gen. and should as such remain unchanged, but according to common interpretation it is often construed as a neut. adjective-substantive in apposition with **jemand.** As there lies in the neuter gender a vague or general conception, it is often as here employed in German as the masc. is in English, to make a general reference, applying to either males or females. **Jemand anders** is often replaced by **jemand and(e)rer,** as the masc. is also as well as the neut. used to represent both genders. When any other adjective follows **jemand** it cannot now as **anders** stand in the genitive, but it may, like **anders,** be treated as an appositional adjective-substantive having either neuter or masculine form: **jemand Vertrautes** or **Vertrauter** someone who is an intimate acquaintance, (dat.) **jemand Vertrautem,** (acc.) **jemand Vertrautes** or **Vertrauten. Es mußte jemand Bedeutendes sein** (Anna Schieber's *Alle guten Geister*, p. 167). **Jemand Fremder ist angekommen** (Blatz's *Neuhochdeutsche Grammatik*, II, p. 380). **Beate duckte sich ein wenig im Kreuz, wie jemand Ertappter** (Hermann Bessemer's *Mondnacht in Amalfi*, p. 42). **Wenn sie mit jemand Erwachsenem sprach** (Rosegger). **Du siehst vorm Hause jemand Alten** (Kapper's *Christen und Türken*, 2, 121). **Als ob es sich um irgend jemand Gleichgiltigen dabei handelte** (Ertl's *Freiheit*, p. 182). **Ohne jemand anderen zu beachten** (Mewis's *Der große Pan*, p. 49).

In M.H.G. the adjective-substantive here was in the genitive, either singular or plural: ieman vremdes or ieman vremder = N.H.G. **jemand Fremdes** or **jemand Fremder.** Thus both forms still survive, but they are now felt as neuter and masculine nominatives, the genitive yielding to the appositional construction. The new construction, according to *c. Note* 1, began in M.H.G. Goethe is still acquainted with the old genitive form here: **Das ist ein Brief, er muß von jemand Hohes sein.**

Note 2. The str. and wk. forms of **jemand** (from **je** + **Mann**) show the influence of the adj. declension.

Note 3. The adverb **irgend** is often used in connection with **jemand** to increase the indefiniteness: **Wir werden wohl irgend jemanden antreffen, der uns Bescheid gibt.**

c. **niemand** *nobody,* inflected exactly like **jemand.**

Note 1. It has the same fluctuating construction of the following adjective-substantive: **Niemand anders** or **niemand anderer** no one else, **niemand Bestimmtes** (Carl Spitteler's *Imago*, p. 25), **niemand Fremdes** (Vogel's *Deutsches Nachschlagebuch*), **niemand andrer** (G. Keller's *Grüner Heinrich*, 4, 350), **niemand Rechtschaffener** (Moriz Heyne's *Wörterbuch*), **die niemand Lebenden betrifft** (Schiller an Goethe). **Solang man niemand Teuren hat sterben sehen, glaubt man nicht recht an den Tod** (Marriot).

The appositional construction was perhaps used here in M.H.G.: Darumbe ich *niemen vremden* füere in dize lant (*Nibelungenlied*, Aventiure 25). It is possible *vremden* here is a weak gen. singular or plural, but it seems more natural to assume that it is a strong accusative in apposition with *niemen*, for the adjective-substantive here is uniformly strong. The usual form here would be the genitive singular or plural, i.e. *vremdes* or *vremder*, but the adjective-substantive is here felt as an appositive and later this construction becomes general.

Note 2. In dialect various forms occur: **neamd, niemer, niemerd.** Compare *d. Note* 2.

d. **man** (in dialect often **me** or **ma**) or **einer** or sometimes **ein(e)s** *one* (as in *one says* = they say), *a fellow* (as in *What is a fellow to do?*), *a man, a person, a body.* The oblique cases of **man** are replaced by those of **einer:** N. **man,** G. **eines,** D. **einem,** A. **einen: So was erinnert einen an etwas, woran man nicht erinnert sein will; eines Haus und Hof** one's house and land. **Das wird einem sauer. Man ist erst ganz man selbst, wenn man wieder den**

eigenen, angestammten Boden unter sich hat (Frieda von Bülow). **Wenn man** (or **einer**) **Reisen gemacht hat, so kann man** (or **er** if the antecedent is **einer**) **etwas erzählen. Da soll eins nicht aufwachen, wenn 'n ganzes Ulanenregiment zum Felddienst ausrückt!** (Beyerlein's *Zapfenstreich*, 1, 5). The personal pronoun referring to **man,** as can be seen in the next to the last example and in the first, is **man,** but **er** if it refers to **einer,** and the corresponding possessive of both **man** and **einer** is **sein: Man** or **einer kann seinen eigenen Kopf nicht essen.**

Note 1. In popular or colloquial language **einer** or **ein(e)s** is often used with the force of **jemand.** It also frequently indicates that the person referred to excels in something, often in something bad: **Das soll einmal einer nachmachen** Let somebody imitate that if he can. **Er lügt wie einer** He lies equal to anybody, lies like a trooper. **Das ist einer!** He's a *fine* fellow! (ironical).

In colloquial language **man** or **einer** is often used with the force of a personal pronoun: **Wenn ich einmal deine Frau bin, tust du doch nichts mehr für einen** (= **mich**). **Wenn einem Mädchen ein Schurzband aufgeht, denkt der Verehrer an einen** (= **sie**).

Note 2. In dialect **man** is often reduced to the form of **me** or **ma,** or on the other hand assumes the form **mer, mar,** or **mr: Ma muaß sagen, was recht is** (Ludwig Thoma's *Die Medaille*, p. 94). **Es kann ja ein' Menschen recht sein, daß mer ihm merken laßt, mer weiß, was er für a Mensch is** (Anzengruber's *Das vierte Gebot*, **1, 12**).

e. **wer** (for declension see **147. 1**), which is used as an interrogative and also relative pronoun, is moreover not infrequently in colloquial language used as an indefinite = **jemand** or **einer: Ich glaube, wenn mein Bruder Alfred stirbt, oder vielleicht auch wer, der dir noch näher steht,** &c. (Fontane's *Unwiederbringlich*, chap. vi). **Ich habe auch keine Geheimnisse—wie wer anderer** (Schnitzler's *Liebelei*, p. 68). **Michael kümmerte sich wenig um mich—dem mußtest du erst klar machen kommen, daß ich auch wer bin** (Sudermann's *Es lebe das Leben*, p. 37). Also **sonstwer** *anybody else* is used: **Bezeichnend bei dieser Lage . . . daß weder von Correggio noch von sonstwem . . . die Probleme der Luftperspektive gefördert worden sind** (Lamprecht's *Deutsche Geschichte*).

Note 1. A following adjective-substantive has the same double construction as after **jemand** and **niemand** (*b, c,* above): **Schmidts haben Besuch; 's ist wer Fremdes da. Ich meine — wer Fremdes?** (Sudermann's *Blumenboot*, **4**, 10) I mean, was there any stranger there? **Wer Vornehmer hat dich empfohlen** (Blatz's *Neuhochdeutsche Grammatik*, II, p. 380). **Das Ding wird wer anderer gemacht haben** (Rosegger).

Note 2. From the indef. **wer** have come the interrogative and relative **wer,** in both of which the former indefinite force is still felt.

f. **etwas** (often in dialect in the assimilated forms **ettes, eppes, öppis,** &c.) or in colloquial speech often in its original simple form **was** *something, some, somewhat, what,* uninflected: **Er hat etwas getan. Soll ich Ihnen etwas von diesem Hammelbraten zukommen lassen? Er ist etwas** (somewhat) **von einem Gelehrten. Ich will dir was sagen** I'll tell you what. **Es mochte nun von Glaubenssachen . . . oder von was immer** (*anything whatever*) **die Rede sein** (Mörike's *Werke*, 6, 273). Note that the negative *not anything* is rendered, not by **nicht etwas,** but by **nichts: Haben Sie nichts von Ihrem Freunde gehört?**

Note 1. When a neut. adjective-substantive depends upon **etwas,** it was formerly in the partitive gen., but this usage has now given place to the appositional construction, the adjective-substantive agreeing with **etwas: etwas Gutes** something good, **von etwas Gutem. Es ist etwas Wahres** (once felt as a gen., but now felt as a neut. nom. in apposition with **etwas**) **daran. Ich kann vor etwas Schönem stundenlang stehen. Die Scham brennt Mascha auf den Wangen, nach rechts und links blickt sie scheu und ängstlich, etwas Schrecklichen** (old weak gen. to avoid the strong form in **-es,** which is not distinguished from the nom. and acc. in **-es**) **gewärtig** (Schubin's *Boris Lensky*, xi). **Ich muß dich noch wegen etwas anderen** (weak gen.) or **anderem** (as the prep. also governs the dat.) **fragen.** Only rarely is the partitive gen. of the adjective-substantive now found here, but the following example from Hauptmann's *Vor Sonnenaufgang*, p. 90, proves that it is not entirely extinct: **Du schwatzest von alter Freundschaft und so was Guts** (**106.** *Note* 2).

Note 2. In early N.H.G. corresponding to the neuter **etwas** was a masculine **etwer** (now replaced in literary speech by **jemand**) *somebody,* which is still widely used in the dialects in the assimilated forms **etter, epper, öpper,** &c.

g. **nichts** (in popular speech **nix**) *nothing,* uninflected: **Gott hat die Welt aus nichts erschaffen.** It is avoided in the gen.

Note 1. If a neut. adjective-substantive depends upon it, the same appositional construction is found as after **etwas** (see *f. Note* 1): **Wissen Sie nichts Neues? Kannst du dich mit nichts Besserem beschäftigen?**

Note 2. It was once inflected as a few set expressions still show. The old nom. and acc. form **nicht** (contracted from **ni wicht** = **nicht ein Wicht,** *not a thing, not a whit*) is used in a number of set expressions, preceded by the partitive gen.: **Hier ist meines Bleibens nicht** (nom.) *It's too warm* (fig.) *for me here,* or *I can't stay here.* **Wenn ich mit Menschen- und mit Engelzungen redete und hätte der Liebe nicht** (acc.) Tho I speak with the tongues of men and of angels and have not charity. The real gen. still survives in **nichtswürdig** *contemptible,* lit. worthy of nothing. In the expression **zu nichte machen** *to destroy,* it is dat. with the usual dat. case ending. The dat. form in **mit nichten** *not at all* has arisen from a contraction of M.H.G. **mit nihte en** (old negative; see close of this *Note*). The gen. **nichts** was formerly much used as a partitive gen. depending upon **nicht** (nom. or acc.), **nichtes nicht** *nothing at all,* lit. *nothing of nothing.* Later when **nicht** was felt as an adverb the gen. **nichts** remained as the regular nom. or acc. of the pronoun. This change of construction was facilitated by the fact that **nichts** remained as an old gen. in a number of set expressions where it was construed as a nom. or acc.: **Nichts** (old gen. felt as a nom. since **gebrechen** was often used with a nom. subject, as explained in **255.** II. 1. H. *c*) **gebricht** (formerly impers. verb with gen.) **uns** *Nothing is lacking to us.* **Er vergißt** (formerly with gen., now usually with acc.) **nichts** (an old gen. felt as an acc.). The old acc. **nicht** has now become the regular form for the adverbial negative *not.* This adverbial negative is in fact the adverbial acc. of degree (amount), and was in an earlier period only added to strengthen the negative **en** or **ne**: (M.H.G.) **er *enist niht* guot** He is not good, lit. He is not good, not in any respect or thing. After the close of the twelfth century **ne** or **en** was little used as an independent negative without the support of **niht** and gradually disappeared leaving to **nicht** the office of negative, or where there was no **nicht** disappearing without leaving any trace behind, as in case of **weder** (see **235.** A. *a*).

Interrogative Pronouns.

146. The interrogative pronouns are: **wer** who; **was** what; **welcher, welche, welches** which, what; **was für einer, was für eine, was für ein(e)s** what kind.

147. 1. **Wer** is declined:

	Masc. and Fem.	Neuter.
N.	**wēr** *who*	**wăs** *what*
G.	**wĕssen, wĕs** (poet.) *whose*	**wĕssen, wĕs** *of what*
D.	**wēm** (masc. and fem.), **wēr** (fem.; see B. *b*) *to whom*	**wēm** (B. *a*), **wō(r)** ⊤ prep. (see C. *b*); **wăs** (see C. *a*)
A.	**wēn** *whom*	**wăs** *what*

It is usual to say only **wer anders** *who else*, **wessen anders, wem anders,** &c., altho it is common to say either **jemand anders** or **jemand anderer, jemand(em) anders** or **jemand anderem,** &c. Compare **145.** *b. Note* 1.

A. *Genitive.* The neut. gen. **wes,** still common in early N.H.G., is now little used except in the adverbial compounds **weshalb** for what reason, **weswegen** on what account, why, also in attributive use, as explained in E below.

The corrupted form **wessent,** instead of the more correct **wessen,** is still quite common in composition with the prepositions **wegen** and **um — willen,** where the reference is to a person: **wessentwegen, um wessentwillen.** Ex.: **Um wessentwillen quälen wir uns denn überhaupt mit solchen Sachen?** (Fontane's *Stechlin,* XI. p. 145). As **wessen** is so often used with reference to a person, it is avoided with reference to a thing. The colloquial language employs here the acc. **was** instead of the more correct but ambiguous **wessen: Und wegen was denn?** (Wilhelm Fischer's *Die Freude am Licht,* p. 196). **Wegen was denn, hä?** (Hauptmann's *Fuhrmann Henschel,* 2). **Wegen was hast du dich so aufgeregt?** (Georg Edward). See also C. *a* below. The genitive **wessen,** however, is often used with a *verb* that governs the genitive: **Wessen hätt' es weiter bedurft!** (Jensen's *Pirol und Pirola*). But even here there is a strong tendency to avoid the ambiguous **wessen** and use the acc. **was,** even in careful writers who elsewhere use the genitive with these verbs: **Was bedurfte es mehr!** (Johanna Wolff's *Das Hanneken,* p. 241), but **Solange die Arbeitenden gesund waren, hatten sie ihr Auskommen und bedurften des Beistandes nicht weiter, als daß man ihnen die Kinder über Tag aufhob** (ib., p. 220).

a. In inquiring after an individual in a group of two or more we may use **welch-** or **wer: welches** (according to **148.** *a*), or **welcher,** or **wer von beiden ist Herr Schmid? Welcher** or **wer von Ihnen?,** but also the gen. after **welcher** if the definite article or a pronominal is used: **Welcher der beiden Brüder? Wer** in connection with **von** is also used where we employ attributive *what*: **Sie war gekommen, um den Schwestern die wichtige Nachricht zu überbringen, wer am morgigen Neujahrstage von jungen Mädchen** (*what young ladies*) **nun mit aller Bestimmtheit bei Hofe vorgestellt werden würde** (Ompteda's *Sylvester von Geyer,* XXXVII). Instead of **wer von jungen Mädchen** we could also say **welche jungen Mädchen.** In case of adjective-substantives the appositional construction is used: **Denn wer bin ich Großes, | daß ich zu fragen hätte?** (Sudermann's *Der Bettler von Syrakus,* 1, 1), in the plural: **Wer sind wir Großes, daß usw.** Compare E below.

b. Altho the gen. of **welch-** was common here in early N.H.G., it is now replaced by the gen. of **wer: Nu in der Aufferstehung | wenn sie aufferstehen | welchs** (in revised editions **wessen**) **weib wird sie sein vnter jnen?** (Mark xii. 23).

B. *a. Dative.* The masc. dat. **wem** usually refers only to living beings and is avoided when the reference is to things, but it *must* be used here with *verbs* that govern the dative: (Recha) **Allein — allein — das geht zu weit! Dem kann ich nichts entgegensetzen, nicht Geduld, nicht Überlegung, nichts!** (Sittah) **Was [geht zu weit]? Wem [kannst du nichts entgegensetzen]?** (Lessing's *Nathan,* 5, 6). **Wem anders aber als der vergleichenden Forschung verdanken wir eine sinngemäße Auffassung der Kasus mit richtiger Scheidung der in ihnen vielfach zusammengeronnenen Bestandteile?** (Hans Meltzer in *Anzeiger für indogermanische Sprach- und Altertumskunde,* 1903/1904, p. 234). Likewise with reference to the statement **Er sah den Schiffen nach** the question form must be **Wem sah er nach?** Compare A above.

b. The fem. dat. **wer,** tho not usually given by grammarians, is occasionally found in good authors: **Von Helios gezeugt? von wer geboren?** (Goethe) Begotten of Helios? Born by what mother? **Da du so eine Art Bruder von ihr bist — Von ihr? Von wer?** (Wilbrandt's *Die Maler,* 3, 3) Since you are a kind of brother to her — To her? To whom? Also other ways of making the gender clear occur: (Carl) **Er gibt Singstunde? Wem?** (Isolde) **Der.** (Carl) **Wem der?** (Ernst Rosmer's *Dämmerung,* Act 3). **Festgeregnet! . . . Wem und welcher steigt nicht bei diesem Worte eine gespenstische Erinnerung in der Seele auf?** (Raabe's *Keltische Knochen*).

c. W. Alexis has boldly used **wen** as a dative plural: **Mit wen? Mit den Bürgern?**

C. *With Prepositions.* The neuter dative is not used in connection with a preposition, in which case the form is either:

a. That of the acc., not infrequently in the classical authors and with ever increasing frequency in the language of our time, which is in general becoming averse to adverbial compounds (see *b*): **Zu was die Posse?** (Goethe). **Bestellt, gnädiger Kaiser? zu was?** (Wildenbruch's *Kaiser Heinrich*, 2, 18). **Zu was soll der eine was voraus haben?** (Halbe's *Haus Rosenhagen*, I. p. 43). Brigitta: **Sie liegt, weint, schwört: sie müsse ihn erlösen.** Gottfried: **Von was?** (Hauptmann's *Der arme Heinrich*, I. p. 33). Odysseus: **Herr, ich fürchte mich.** Eumaios: **Vor was?** (id., *Der Bogen des Odysseus*).

b. Or especially in choice language the adverbial compound **wo** (or **wor** before a vowel) + **a** preposition: **womit** with what, **wovon** of what, **worin** in what, &c. The prepositions governing the acc. also form compounds with **wo(r)** in the same way: **worüber** about what, **wofür** for what, **worein** (the one prep. **in** changes its form in these adverbial compounds to express the acc. relation, becoming **ein**) into what, **worum** (more commonly in this case **um was**) concerning what, &c. The accent fluctuates here. In questions direct and indirect the preposition is usually stressed, **wo'rauf,** &c., but in direct questions the accent for especial emphasis often rests upon **the wo.** These compounds cannot be freely formed, but occur only in case of the prepositions enumerated in **141.** 5. B. But also here there is a growing aversion to the adverbial forms: **„Rede, | damit wir uns verständigen." „Über was?"** (Wildenbruch's *König Laurin*, 3, 1).

D. *Plural.* The German like the English has no special form for the plural, but differs from the English in that the verb also remains sing., except in case of **wer** and **was** as predicate in connection with the verb *to be*: **Wer sind die Damen da? Ich weiß nicht, wer sie sind. Was sind die Dinge da? Das sind Blumen.** But as subject: **Wer war da?** *Who was* or *were there?* A general indef. pl. idea can be brought out by placing directly after **wer** (or **was**), or several words removed, the adverbial **alles: Wer kommt denn alles?** Who all are coming? **Ich weiß nicht, wen alles er eingeladen hat,** or **wem alles** (or **wem allem,** or sometimes to bring out the plural idea **wen allen** in colloquial speech and **welchen Leuten allen** in the literary language) **er eine Einladung geschickt hat. Was man doch nicht alles hört!** Well, I declare, what strange things one hears! **Es ist unglaublich, was uns hier jetzt alles als Schillerfest geboten wird** (*Hamburger Correspondent*, May 8, 1905). A plural may follow **wer anders** *who but, who else,* altho the verb is in the singular: **Wer anders wohnte denn zu jener Zeit vor den Toren der Städte als nur armes und geringes Volk, Gärtnersleute noch im besten Falle?** (S. Junghans's *Lore Fay*, I). In inquiries after definite persons or things, the sing. verb with **wer** or **was** alone is used, as usually the connection will show whether one is speaking of one person or thing, or of more than one. Some form of **welcher, e, es** should be used if some noun or pronoun can be understood: **Wer hat das gebracht? — Zwei Schüler. — Welche (Schüler)? Wer hat das gebracht? — Ein Schüler. — Welcher (Schüler)?** Thus in German **wer** usually introduces an inquiry of a more general and **welcher** of a more individual nature.

E. *Partitive Construction.* **Was** was formerly often followed by a dependent noun in the partitive gen.: **was Dancks habt jr dauon (davon)?** (Luke vi. 34). This construction is still occasionally found: **Aber was hast du nun Vorteils davon, Lieber?** (Lienhard's *Till Eulenspiegel*, 3). It is still the regular construction in case of adjective-substantives: **Was ist Gutes dabei?** What good is there in it? In case of these adjective-substantives all feeling for the genitive is lost, and the form is regarded as a nom. or acc. neut. in apposition with **was,** as in similar cases after **etwas** (see **145.** *f. Note* 1).

Except in case of adjective-substantives simple apposition is now little used, altho more common earlier in the period, and is usually replaced by the appositional construction introduced by **für** or by the construction with **welch: Was gibt es Vorzügliches im heutigen Konzert?,** but rarely **Mit was lieblichem Bezeigen | gab sie sich mir ganz zu eigen!** (Canitz), now **Mit was für einem lieblichen,** or **welch lieblichem,** &c. **Ach, was ist's ein Mann!** (Goethe's *Egmont*, 1), now **Was ist's für ein Mann! So weiß ich doch nun auch, auf was** [now **was für eine,** or **welche**] **Art sich die Teufel danken** (Schiller). **Was zahlt man Eintritt?** (Grillparzer's *Ein treuer Diener seines Herrn*, 2) (**Eintritt** here = **Eintrittsgeld,** now more commonly **Was zahlt man für Eintrittsgeld?**) **Was hast du hier** [now usually + **für**] **Geschäfte** [in apposition with **was** or possibly a pl. partitive gen.]? (Storm's *Ein Fest auf Haderslevhuus*, p. 258). **Zu was** [now **welchem**] **Zweck und Nutzen haben wir die weltliche Geschichte gelernt?** (Scheffel). In certain set expressions, however, the simple appositional construction has become established: **Was Wunder!** (the gen. here is also used: **Was Wunders, daß unser Dichter für diese in fast täglichem Verkehr vor ihm entfalteten Vorzüge nicht unempfindlich blieb** — Johannes Scherr's *Schiller*, II. chap. iii) *what wonder!* **was Teufel! Was der Teufel!** (Ebner-Eschenbach's *Verschollen*), but also with gen.: **Was Teufels einem doch plötzlich durch das Dach hereinschneien kann!** (Walther Siegfried's *Um der Heimat willen*, VIII). **Was Henker! Wes Geistes Kind ist er?** Of what mettle is he? **Wes Namens, Standes, Wohnorts seid ihr?** (H. v. Kleist). **Das preußische Kultusministerium hat in der Frage der marianischen Kongregationen gezeigt, wessen Geistes es ist** (*Hamburger Nachrichten*, Feb. 24, 1905). In some of these examples **was** or **wes** (recently also **wessen,** as in the preceding German sentence) is used almost or quite as an attributive adjective, and earlier in the period even assumed in the dat. of the fem. the form of a strong adjective: **Aus waser** (in revised editions **was für**) **macht thustu das?** (Matth. xxi. 23). In English, *what* has, indeed, become an attributive adjective in many cases, and can be used freely as such, while in German the appositional construction has in general been retained, and is usually, aside from certain groups described above, clearly marked as such by the **für** preceding the appositive. The construction with *for* is also found in older English:

What is he for a fool that betroths himself to unquietness? (Shakespeare's *Much Ado*, 1, 3). In dialect and colloquial language the development of usage here lies in the direction of the English, in that **was** is often used attributively: **Ne, was'n Jux, was'n Jux!** (Adalbert Meinhardt's *Allerleirauh*, p. 71) for the literary **was für ein Jux!** or **welch ein Jux!** Also separated: **Was gibst du mir denn gute Lehren, Mutter!** (Georg Hirschfeld's *Nebeneinander*, p. 35). For other examples see **134.** 2. *d.*

Wer was in M.H.G., like **was,** followed by a dependent partitive gen., as in wer herren, which is now replaced by a prep. construction, **wer von** or **unter den Herren.** Another stage of development, the appositional or attributive construction, as in case of **was,** is found in early N.H.G.: **Wer Künstler** (originally gen. pl.) **möcht's erdenken?** (Spee's *Trutznachtigal*, 91, 196). **Wen Schatz han [haben] wir gefunden?** (id.). This old attributive use of **wer** *what* survives, in case the following word is a pronoun: **„Er ist nicht da?"** **„Wer er?"** (Suttner's *Daniela Dormes*, III). (Carl) **Er gibt Singstunde?** **Wem?** (Isolde) **Der.** (Carl) **Wem der?** (Ernst Rosmer's *Dämmerung*, Act 3). Compare **Es ist kein Er; es ist eine Sie** (Raabe's *Frau Salome*, XI).

2. **Wer** and **was** are used in questions direct and indirect: **Wen meinen Sie? Ich weiß nicht, wen Sie meinen. Wer ist's?** (a biographical dictionary by H. A. Degener) Who is who?

a. **Wer** can be limited by a relative clause: **Wer, der es nicht mit Augen gesehen hat, vermag sich dies geheimnisvolle Gebiet auch nur vorzustellen?** (H. Hoffmann's *Rittmeister*, III. p. 133) *What person who*, &c.

b. **Was** is much used colloquially after the statement of an opinion or idea to ask for a confirmation of the same from the person addressed: **Hübsche Straße, was?** It's a fine street, isn't it? **Ich liebe schnelle Entschlüsse — Sie auch — was?**

c. Sometimes **was** is used adverbially in the meaning *why*: **Was lachst du?** Why do you laugh? It is also used sometimes like **wie** *how*: **Was sind Sie glücklich!** How happy you are!

148. Welcher, welche, welches *which, what,* used adjectively or substantively. For inflection see **134. 1.** Ex.: **Welches Buch ist das Ihrige und welches ist das seinige?**

a. **Welches** used with identifying force is treated like **dies** (see **128.** A. *a*): **Welches ist länger, der Bleistift oder die Feder? Welches ist der jüngste Sohn? Welches sind Ihre Brüder? Welches ist Ihre Hutnummer?** What is the size of your hat? **Welches sind die Ergebnisse dieses Sommersemesters?** (Wilbrandt's *Franz*, II). Also in indirect questions: **Welches die individuellen Ursachen von Raabes Wendung zum Pessimismus gewesen, läßt sich einstweilen nicht feststellen** (A. Bartels, *Deutsche Dichtung*, p. 56).

Was is also used here, but with a different shade of meaning. **Was** is more general, while **welcher** always points to an individual among individuals. Thus we say to a single gentleman in inquiring in a general way: **Was ist Ihre Erfahrung in bezug auf Seekrankheit?**, but in speaking to a number of gentlemen in turn we say: **Welches ist Ihre Erfahrung?** On account of the general meaning of **was** it is not used in inquiring after a definite individual: **Welches** (not **was**) **ist die Hauptstadt Rußlands?**

149. Was für einer, eine, ein(e)s *what kind.* For inflection see **134. 2.**

Relative Pronouns.

150. There are no independent forms for the relative pronouns, but as such are used: the demonstratives **der, die, das (151)** *who, which,* or the determinative (**130.** 3) **welcher, welche, welches (152)** *who, which*; the indefinites **wer** *who, whoever* (**155** and **156**), **was** *which, what, whatsoever* (**153.** 1; **157**); the adverbial compounds **worin, worunter,** &c. (**153.** 2. A), or **darin, darunter,** &c. (**153.** 2. B); the adverbs **wo, woher, wohin** (**153.** 3. A), **wie** or **als** (**153.** 3. B, D. (1)), **wie** (**153.** 3. E), **als, wenn, wann, wo, da, wie** (**153.** 3. C), **so viel** (**153.** 4); **so** (**153.** 5); **daß** (**153.** 3. C. *e*), **dergleichen** (**153.** 3. D. (3)), **derselbe** (**153.** 6), **was für ein** (**153.** 7), **wo** (**153.** 8), **als** (**153.** 8), **da denn** (**238.** 2. *c. Note* 2).

They have in course of time developed a different word-order from the original demonstratives and indefinites and now require the verb to stand at the end of the clause: **diejenigen Fürsten sind die besten, die mit Aufopferung ihrer selbst des Volkes Wohl befördern.**

The parent language did not contain relative pronouns. Hence they are comparatively modern formations that have developed independently in the different languages and consequently vary widely in structure, altho at points a number of languages employ materials that were originally common to them all. Glimpses into their development are given in **154.** *Note,* **153.** 5. *Note,* and **130.** 3.

151. *Inflection of the Relative* **Der.** 1. **Der, die, das** are inflected as the substantive forms of the demon. **der, die, das** (**129.** 1) except in the gen., where the forms **dessen** (masc. and neut. sing.), **deren** (fem. sing. and pl. for all genders) are used.

a. The forms of **der** are unaccented, thus differing from those of the demon. **der;** but the vowels except before **ss** are long and cannot be contracted, thus differing from those of the def. art. and resembling those of the demonstr.

b. In composition with the prepositions **wegen** *on account of*, **um — willen** *for the sake of*, **halb(en)** *on account of*, are the following corrupted gen. forms: **dessent,** gen. masc. and neut.; **derent** or **deret,** gen. fem. sing. and gen. pl. for all genders: **der Mann, um dessentwillen; die Frau, um derentwillen; die Absicht, um deretwillen das Buch geschrieben ist** (Dr. U. Zernial in *Anglia*, 1886, vol. IV, p. 27), &c. There is a pronounced tendency to restore the correct form: **Jenes Vorrecht, um dessenwillen sich einst Bayern unterworfen hatte** (Giesebrecht); **das Weib, um dessenwillen ich Jahre lang alles getan und gesprochen und geopfert habe** (H. Hoffmann's *Rittmeister*, II. p. 172). **Auf jenem schönen Turm habe ich der das Wiederkommen versprochen, um derenwillen ich jetzt diese weite Reise mache** (Storm's *St. Jürgen*). **Das also war die, für die sie drangegeben, um derenwillen sie um ihr Leben betrogen und bestohlen worden war** (Wildenbruch's *Vize-Mama*).

The short genitive **des** is often used here instead of **dessent** when the antecedent has a general or indefinite meaning or contains a collective idea: **Alles das, um deswillen er fünf Jahre gelebt und gelitten hatte** (Johannes Wilda's *Bei der Glockenboje*). Compare **153. 1. (1).** *a.*

The preceding forms refer to antecedents. When the reference is to the thought contained in a sentence, the short gen. forms **wes,** or now less commonly **des,** are used in composition with **wegen** and **halb(en): Vollkommenheit ist ein nie zu erreichendes Ziel, weshalb** (or now less commonly **deshalb**) **so wenige danach streben.** Also **wo'her** or **da'her** (**153.** 3. A) and **da denn** (**238.** 2. *c. Note* 2) are sometimes used here. Earlier in the period also **da'rum: Ich bin nicht werd | das du vnter mein Dach gehest | Darum ich auch mich selbs nicht wirdig geachtet hab | das ich zu dir keme** (Luke vii. 6-7).

If **wegen** precedes the relative, the regular uncorrupted long gen. forms are used: **Sie passen zu dem dreibeinigen Halunken, wegen dessen wir hier versammelt sind!** (Lienhard's *Till Eulenspiegel*, 1).

c. To give a clear formal expression to the idea of the dative relation the forms **dessen** and **deren** are sometimes still as occasionally also earlier in the period inflected like strong adjectives, when they stand before a masc. or a neut. noun in the dat. sing., altho they are in fact the gen. forms of the relative pronoun: **die letzten Reste ihrer** (i.e. **der Häuser**) **Fundamente, in derem Kalkgehalt sich eine kleine aparte Flora häuslich eingerichtet hat** (Fedor Sommer's *Ernst Reiland*, p. 197). See **129.** 2. A. *c.*

d. Instead of the gen. forms **dessen** and **deren** the older forms **des** (formerly written **deß**) and **der** still occur, the former often earlier in the period but now only in poetry, the latter, **der** (fem. gen. sing. and gen. pl. for all genders), now little used in the plural but still often used in the fem. gen. sing. even in plain prose when it is the object of a preposition, verb, or adjective, but never when it modifies a noun in the attributive relation: **Wo bist du, Faust, des Stimme mir erklang** (Goethe's *Faust*, erster Teil, Nacht). **Dann auf Wellen | fliegt der Mann, des Bild ich wirkte, in die Weite** (Wildenbruch's *Die Lieder des Euripides*, p. 26). **Fejervary hat die Regierung nach einer langen ministerlosen Zeit, während der** (= **deren**) **Graf Tisza die Geschäfte weitergeführt hatte, am 13. Juni übernommen** (*Hamburger Nachrichten*, Sept. 13, 1905). **Die Frau, der er so liebreich gedachte** (Eduard Engel's *Gutes Deutsch*, 152). Earlier in the period besides the short fem. gen. sing. and the gen. pl. form **der** there were the two longer forms **deren** and **derer.** Later **derer** became restricted to demonstrative use, but survivals of the older usage occur occasionally, especially after a preposition: **Das dauerte wohl eine Minute, während derer ich mich nicht zu regen, kaum zu atmen, wagte** (Spielhagen's *Was will das werden?*, I. chap. xi). **Einige bängliche Minuten, während derer Frau Curtis die Augen geschlossen hielt** (id., *Ein neuer Pharao*, p. 13).

e. The early N.H.G. occasional long form **deren** (fem. dat. sing.) has entirely given way to the short form **der,** as there seemed a desire, as in case of the demonstrative **der,** to distinguish, contrary to usage elsewhere in the inflection of fem. adjective forms, between the gen. and dat. sing: **O Fürstin, deren** (now **der**) **sich ein solcher Fürst verbunden** (Weckherlin). **The older** short form **den** (dat. pl.) is now entirely replaced by **denen.**

f. In the language of monarchical Germany the relative **der** is used in connection with **Allerhöchst, Höchst, Hoch** with reference to the antecedents **seine Majestät, seine Königl. Hoheit, seine Durchlaucht: Auf Anregung Ihrer Königl. Hoheit der Großherzogin von Baden und mit Genehmigung Sr. Majestät des Kaisers, Allerhöchstdenen für diese hochherzige Entschließung ehrfurchtsvoller Dank gebührt, erscheint zum hundertsten Geburtstage der Kaiserin Augusta der erste Teil einer Auswahl ihrer Aufzeichnungen und Briefe** (Paul Bailleu in *Deutsche Rundschau*, 1911, p. 161).

g. The relatives **das** and **welches** were earlier in the period employed like the identifying **das** (**129.** 2. C. (**1**)) as the subject of the clause, remaining unchanged for all genders and numbers: **Unter andern hat er eine Sündflut gemalt, das etwas Einziges ist** (Goethe). **Die Luftkanäle anzubringen, welches kleine Röhren von gebrannter Erde waren** (id.). **Dies Buch nannte man den Shakespeare, welches der Verfasser desselben war** (G. Keller). These relatives are now usually inflected and agree with the antecedent. The older usage is still sometimes found when the relative is used in a collective sense: **Ich kenne den Bruder und die Schwester, welches beides** (or more commonly **welche beide**) **sehr achtungswerte Personen sind** (D. Sanders). Different is the case where the relative is the predicate. See **153.** 1. (**3**), towards end of art.

2. *Where* **Der** *Is Not Used.* **Der** is not used adjectively at all, in which function it is replaced by forms of **welcher: Er sagte „guten Tag," welchen Gruß sie freundlich erwiderte.** Also in the expressions **welch ersterer** (or **welcher erstere**) *the former of which* and **welch letzterer** (or **welcher letztere**) *the latter of which*, where the substantive is understood: **Das Bild stellt Johannes den Täufer und den Christusknaben dar, welch letzterer von dem Täufer in die Welt eingeführt wird.**

3. *Uses of* **Der.** On the other hand, in the substantive relation **der** is more frequent than **welcher** both in the literary language and in common conversation. The leading points as to use are as follows:

A. **Der,** not **welcher,** is used in the gen. sing. and pl. if the gen. stands before the noun upon which it depends: **Das Haus in der Kaiserstraße, dessen Besitzer wir kennen, ist feil.** Elsewhere also the genitive of **welcher** is used with the limitation however that it is only employed in the plural and the feminine singular: **Die alte Mauer, innerhalb deren** or **welcher jetzt nur ein Teil der Stadt liegt, wird bald abgebrochen werden.**

It should be carefully noted that **dessen** and **deren,** differing from the English *of which, of whom,* must always precede the noun or pronoun upon which they depend, and that the definite article before the governing noun is then dropped: **das Gebäude, dessen Fenster geschlossen sind** *the building the windows of which are shut*; **Heldenlieder, bei deren jedem** (*in every one of which*) **sich eine reine Märchengestalt hinter einem geschichtlichen Namen verbirgt** (Wundt's *Völkerpsychologie*, II, p. 393). Sometimes apparent exceptions occur: **Die Statistik, auf Grund deren Prof. Lorenzi sein Werk aufbaute, erstreckte sich auf 419 Häuser** (*Hamburger Nachrichten*, Oct. 18, 1904). The relative **deren** does not here depend upon the substantive **Grund,** but upon the two words **auf Grund,** which together have the force of a preposition and hence precede.

a. In adjective use **welcher** must be used even if the gen. precedes the noun upon which it depends: **Denk' an Goethe, welches Dichters Werke dir oft empfohlen wurden.**

b. Earlier in the period also the gen. of **welch-** could stand before the governing noun: **Lieber | verderbe den nicht mit deiner Speise | vmb welches willen Christus gestorben ist** (Rom. xiv. 15). **Denn ein Weib hatte von jm gehört | welcher Töchterlin einen vnsaubern Geist hatte** (Mark vii. 25). **Eine so edle Tat . . . wie die ist, um welcher willen ich gefangen sitze** (Goethe's *Götz*, 4, 2).

B. **Der** is also usually employed when the relative refers to an interrogative, a personal or indefinite pronoun, or a noun in the vocative: **Wer, der es nicht mit Augen gesehen hat, vermag sich dies geheimnisvolle Gebiet auch nur vorzustellen?** (H. Hoffmann's *Rittmeister*, III. p. 133). **Er, der nur | gewohnt ist zu befehlen und zu tun, | kennt nicht die Kunst, von weitem ein Gespräch | nach seiner Absicht langsam fein zu lenken** (Goethe's *Iphigenie*, 1, 2). **Jeder, der ihn kennt. Niemand, der ihn kennt.** Especially after the indefinite

welch for sake of euphony: **Mit dieser Sorte von Spiritisten habe ich nichts zu tun. In den spiritistischen Klubsitzungen treiben sich immer welche herum, die da im Trüben fischen** (Blüthgen's *Die Spiritisten*, p. 275). After a vocative: **Ha, Herr Graf, der Sie nicht nach Massa wollten** (Lessing's *Emilia*, 3, 2). Much less commonly **welcher: O Du Lamm Gottes, welches Du hinwegnimmst die Sünden der Welt** (Lauff's *Pittje Pittjewitt*, p. 176).

a. If a personal pronoun referring to a vocative or repeating a personal pronoun of the first or second person already mentioned stands after the relative, which is very commonly the case when the relative is the subject of the verb, **der** is usually employed, and the verb must agree with the antecedent in person: **unser Vater, der du bist im Himmel** (Luther); **du, die du alle Wunden heilest** (Schiller) thou (friendship) who dost heal all wounds. The pronoun of the first or second person to which reference is made may be contained in a possessive: **Und tröste dich an meinem größern Jammer, | die ich getan, wo du nur unterlassen** (Grillparzer's *Medea*, 5.).

This construction originated in the fifteenth century and hence is younger than the two competing constructions described in *b*, but it is at present apparently the favorite.

Welcher, formerly little used here, is now beginning to compete here with **der.** For example see last sentence in B above.

Note. When such sentences are transferred to indirect discourse, the personal pronoun may be allowed to remain standing after the relative, altho it as well as its antecedent has become a third person in the indirect statement: **Wie kannst du, die du es selbst gesehen hast, das bezweifeln?** becomes **Er wunderte sich, wie sie, die sie es selbst gesehen habe, das bezweifeln könne.** The personal pronoun of the first or second person to which reference is made may be contained in a possessive: (independent form of indirect discourse; see **172.** *a*) **Sie hatte einmal gelesen: „Nichts ist ohne Zweck.“ Aber was war ihr Zweck? Ihr Zweck, die sie doch keine Blüte trieb. Sie war doch eine tote Frucht, sie war Tante** (G. Ompteda's *Cäcilie von Sarryn*, chap. xii).

b. Sometimes there is no personal pronoun after the relative as in the cases described in *a*, the verb, however, agreeing in the same manner with the antecedent in person: **Unselige, die** [du] **mir aus deinen Höhen, | ein Meteor, verderblich niederstreifst** (Goethe). This usage arose in O.H.G. under Latin models and in later times was favored by the example of French, which has the same construction, but it has never secured a firm foothold in German as in English. In the fifteenth century attempts were made to avoid the harsh clash here between the third person form of the relative **der** and the first or second person of the verb by inserting a personal pronoun of the first or second person after the relative and thus bringing the old historic foreign construction nearer to German feeling. This is the now common construction described in *a*. Much earlier a more simple way out of the difficulty was found, a pure German construction, in O.H.G. rare, later more common, and still quite frequent, but never as yet prevailing over the construction in *a*. The clash between the third person form **der** and the first and second person of the verb was avoided by placing the verb in the third person, thus bringing it into harmony with the relative: O.H.G. fater unser, der ist in himilom (*Freisinger Paternoster*, Emmeram MS.) = N.H.G. **Vater unser, der im Himmel ist. Ich bin Gabriel, der fur Gott stehet** (Luther; Luke I. 19). **Was kann ich tun, der selber hilflos ist?** (Schiller). **Wir, die Bergmann und Virchow** (professors) **hörten, haben den Eindruck usw.** (*Westermanns Monatshefte*, Feb. 1912, p. 897).

The verb cannot of course be controlled by the relative if some other word is subject: **O du, den ich suchte von meiner Kindheit an.**

The verb is in the third person if the pronoun to which the subject refers is in the third person: **Er, der es weiß.**

The relative **welcher** is sometimes used instead of **der: Du, welcher der Welt die Komödien des Plautus wiedergegeben hast** (K. F. Meyer).

Note. If the reference is to the polite form **Sie** referring to one individual, the relative and, provided the third person is employed, also its verb are in the sing., altho **Sie** is grammatically in the 3rd person pl.: **Das weiß eben niemand besser zu beurteilen, als eben Sie, der meine Mutter so gut kennt.**

c. The construction with the verb in the third person is still much used, but the newer form in *a* seems in general more common and in *one* case *must* be employed, as ambiguity might otherwise arise. If there are two pronouns in the principal clause, one in the first or second person, the other the uninflected **es,** the construction which repeats the personal pronoun after the relative should be chosen, if the **es** is predicate and the relative refers to the pronoun of the first or second person, which is itself the subject of the principal clause; but the construction which drops the personal pronoun and puts the dependent verb in the third person is of course used if the **es** is the grammatical subject and the following relative clause the real subject of the main verb: **Wer ist unglücklich? Ich** (subject) **bin es** (predicate), **der ich meine Eltern verloren habe** *Who is unhappy? I am, I who have lost my parents,* but **Ich** (predicate) **bin es** (subject; see **251.** II. B. *a. aa*), **der seine Eltern verloren hat** *It is I who has lost his parents.* In the second sentence the verb of the main clause is attracted into the person of the predicate **ich,** which stands before it, and hence it does not agree with its real subject. The relative here is usually **der** according to C.

C. In subject and object clauses where the relative is equal to **der(jenige) welcher,** we usually find **der:** Subject clause: **Selig sind, die Gottes Wort hören und bewahren.** Accusative clause: **Lehre, die dir folgen wollen, deine Wege.** Dative clause: **Ehre, dem Ehre gebührt.** Notice that in these clauses the partitive idea is expressed by the appositional construction, not by the genitive or the preposition **von: Die wir viel gelitten, wir scheuen uns davor, die dunkelsten, verborgensten Tiefen des eigenen Herzens zu durchleuchten** (Heyking's *Briefe, die ihn nicht erreichten,* p. 232) *Those of us who,* &c. Also when the provisional subject **es** precedes, the relative of subject clauses is usually **der: War ich's, der ihm sein Glück zerstörte?** See also B. *c.* Where the predicate is a noun or pronoun and *precedes* the subject, as in the last sentence, **welcher** is also often used: **Er selbst war es gewesen, welcher dem Freunde die letzten Liebesdienste erwiesen hatte** (Marriot's *Der geistliche Tod,* chap. xvii). **Welch-** is much rarer in object clauses: **Und sicherst deinen Kindern großes Gut: | sie dürfen nennen, welche sie gebar** (Grillparzer's *Medea,* 4). Earlier in the period **welch-** was used freely in subject and object clauses, but with a different shade. See *a* below.

Wer is also employed in subject and object clauses, but with a different meaning, namely, with generalizing or indefinite force. See **156.**

a. In early N.H.G. **welcher** was used in subject clauses with general or indefinite force just as **wer** (see **156**) is now employed: **Welcher isset | der isset dem HErrn** (Rom. xiv. 6). See also Rom. xiv. 2, 3. **Der** was also much used in subject clauses, but with a different shade of meaning, namely, with individualizing force. Compare **130.** 2. *b.* Later **wer** replaced **welcher** here for general or indefinite reference, and **welcher** assumed the definite force of **der** and often became interchangeable with it. **Welcher** is not, however, used here in subject and object clauses so much as **der,** and cannot be used so freely, as it is limited to the cases where the predicate is a noun or pronoun and precedes the subject. Compare **130.** 3.

D. **Der** is usually employed in predicate clauses (**270.** 1): **Du bist nicht, der du scheinst** (Fulda's *Talisman,* 1, 4). In early N.H.G. **welcher** was sometimes used here, but it has not become well established: **Welchen** (now usually **den**) **ich küssen werde | der ist's** (Mark xiv. 44). Compare **130.** 3. **Wer** is now used here if the relative has a general or indefinite meaning: **Ach Väterchen, wir** (in a broad general sense) **bleiben, wer wir sind** (Fulda's *Talisman,* 1, 10). In early N.H.G. **welcher** was quite common here. Compare C. *a* and **130.** 3.

General Note to B. C. D. In M.H.G. **welch** in its older form swelch was a general determinative like **solch** (**131.** 3), pointing not to definite individuals but employed for general or indefinite reference. The corresponding English forms *which* and *the which* once also had this same general or indefinite meaning, but they developed definite force much earlier than German **welch.** In the fifteenth and sixteenth centuries the general, indefinite meaning in **welch** was still stronger than the idea of definite reference. This older meaning is still in general keenly enough felt to prevent its use in B, usually also in C and regularly in D. On the other hand, in attributive relative clauses where there is a general, indefinite reference to a kind or class rather than to ind viduals there still often seems to be a preference for **welch: Aber lieber Papa, die Leute können sich doch Bücher verschaffen, welche sie wollen** (Frieda von Bülow's *Hüter der Schwelle,* p. 160). As illustrated in **130.** 3 **welch** had already in early N.H.G. begun to assume more definite force and since that time has been competing with **der.**

152. *Inflection and Uses of* **welcher.** 1. **Welcher (welche, welches)** *who, which* is inflected as a strong adjective except in the gen. masc. and neut. sing., where the strong ending **-es** is used instead of the weak **-en.** For those places where **welcher** is not usually found see **151.** 3. A, B, C, and D. In the construction mentioned in **151.** 2 **welcher** is used exclusively. Elsewhere there is a free choice between **der** and **welcher,** so far as these forms are used.

2. **Welcher** is much used in some parts of Germany, where it is preferred to **der,** and is, in general, very useful where a number of relatives occur in the sentence in relieving **der,** thus varying the construction, especially where one relative depends upon a word in another relative clause. Or, on the other hand, **der** may relieve **welcher;** and indeed it is more common in case there are two relatives to use first **welcher** and then **der: Es ist eine Reihe von Jahren her, als zu dem Artillerieregiment, welches hier in Garnison steht, ein Hauptmann versetzt wurde, der aus dem Westen Deutschlands kam** (Wildenbruch). Grammarians usually state that either **der** or **welcher** can be used in parallel clauses depending upon the same word, but that they should not relieve each other: **Worte, deren Sinn man einmal gefaßt, die man sich einmal ins Gedächtnis eingeprägt hat.** Even good authors do not always follow this rule, but sometimes prefer to change relatives for the sake of variety of expression, or as in the following sentence to heighten a contrast: **Ich beginne meine Geschichte mit unbegrenztem Wohlwollen sowohl gegen Mitwelt und Nachwelt, als auch gegen mich selber und alle mir im Lauf der Erzählung vorübergleitenden Schattenbilder des großen Entstehens, Seins und Vergehens—des unendlichen Werdens, welches man Weltentwickelung nennt, welches freilich ein wenig interessanter und reicher als dieses Buch ist, das aber auch nicht, wie dieses Buch, in drei Teilen zu einem befriedigenden Abschluß kommen muß** (Raabe's *Hungerpastor,* chap. i).

a. Some grammarians claim that **welch-,** not **der,** should be used if the relative is preceded by the demonstrative **der** and followed by the article **der,** to avoid an unpleasant repetition; but the colloquial language does not seem to be averse to this combination, as the words are so differently accented that they receive quite a different pronunciation: **Ach, das** (i.e. **die Schneider** *the daddy-long-legs*) **sind die, die die langen Beine haben** (Fontane's *Stechlin,* XXX). H. Seidel in his story *Die weißen Ratten* facetiously calls attention to a warning notice in a public park which shows a too liberal use of this repetition: **Die, die die, die die Anlagen beschädigen, zur Anzeige bringen, erhalten fünf Taler Belohnung.**

153. Der and **Welcher** Replaced by Other Words.

Both **der** and **welcher** are replaced by other words in the following cases:

1. **Was.** In the nom. and acc. relation **was** is usually employed under the following circumstances:

(1) If the antecedent is a word of general or indefinite meaning, or expresses a collective idea, such as **das, einiges, eins, das einzige, etwas** (or **was**), **solches, ein anderes, nichts, mehreres, manches, viel(es), allerhand, allerlei, das bißchen, wenig, genug,** an ordinal, as **das Erste, das Zweite,** with especial frequency **alles,** also a neuter abstract noun or adjective-substantive (**das Schöne** *the beautiful,* &c., especially a superlative, **das Beste** *that which is best*), also a neuter noun denoting a material or a collective idea, provided the reference is to an indefinite mass or amount: **Eins aber weiß ich, was ihr nicht mehr wißt: was Recht und Unrecht, Gut und Böse ist** (Hauptmann's *Versunkene Glocke,* p. 106). **Sie sprach wie von etwas, was sie gar nichts anging** (H. Böhlau's *Rangierbahnhof,* p. 43). **Infolge davon** (in consequence of grouping conjugational forms in accordance with their meaning) **hat sie** (i.e. **die traditionelle Grammatik**) **zum Teil solches, was formal zusammengehört, voneinander getrennt, und solches, was formal verschieden ist, vereinigt** (Brugmann's *Vergleichende Grammatik,* II, III. Teil, p. 42). **Sie sah aber nichts, was um sie vorging. Es gibt im Leben so manches, was uns rätselhaft erscheint. Freilich vieles, vielleicht sehr vieles, was dieser und jener noch wünschen würde, fehlt** (Fuchs's *Deutsches Wörterbuch,* Vorwort). **Und das Dritte, was der modernen Kunst als Schwäche anhaftet, ist ihr Streben, nur ästhetisch sein zu wollen** (Otto Lyon in *Zeitschrift für den deutschen Unterricht,* 1905, p. 5). **Er sprach mit ihm vertraulich von allem, was ihm nahestand. Er verzweifelt überhaupt an allem Heil, was der Menschheit durch die Gesellschaft zu teil werden kann** (Albert Geiger in *Die Nation,* 10th March, 1900). **Man kann das ja nicht im entferntesten ausdrücken: das Mysterium, was sich damals vollzog** (Hauptmann's *Michael Kramer,* Act 3). **Alles Weh, was**

er mir bereitet hat (Fontane's *Schach von Wuthenow,* chap. xxi). **Das Häßliche, was in seinem Gesichte lag, wurde durch sein gefälliges Benehmen zurückgedrängt. Er preiset das Höchste, das Beste, was das Herz sich wünscht** (Schiller). **Um ihn her war alles Getier lebendig, was auf der Heide die Junischwüle auszubrüten pflegt** (Storm's *Ein grünes Blatt*). **Das wenige Geld, was ich besaß, war in den nächsten Tagen vertan** (Raabe's *Die Leute aus dem Walde,* chap. x). **Wenn damals ein Säemann gekommen wäre, ein kluger, wahrhaft kluger, herzenskluger, und die Saat gestreut hätte, aus der Heil für die Menschen aufgeht, einzig und allein, Vergebung, Vergebung, Vergebung, statt des tauben, toten Zeugs, was so schöne Schulmeisternamen hat, Zucht und Ordnung, heilsame Strenge, und wie es heißt usw.** (Wildenbruch's *Neid,* p. 127).

Was often points to a definite person or thing, the speaker at first intentionally making the reference indefinite by the use of **was**, reserving the definite information for the last part of the statement: **Das erste, was ihnen hier begegnete, war die Krügersfrau** (Fontane's *Vor dem Sturme,* IV. 3).

Was is also used here contemptuously of a person: **Was ist das für ein ungebackenes Brötchen** (referring to Emil), **was da hinten sitzt und mitspricht** (H. Böhlau's *Rangierbahnhof,* p. 208).

The use of **was** as described above seems to be the outcome of a long process of differentiation. Earlier in the period **das** and **welches** were also used here. This older usage is still, especially in elevated diction, not infrequently found, as the process of differentiation is not yet completed: **Vieles, das diesem Volke gut hieß** (Nietzsche's *Zarathustra,* p. 80). It is possible that there is often here an intentional use of **das** or **welches** by way of differentiation, to refer to something definite, definite at least to the speaker: **Herr v. Körber erwiderte, er erachte die Schaffung einer provisorischen Fakultät als das einzig Richtige, das die Regierung vorläufig tun könnte** (*Hamburger Nachrichten,* Nov. 7, 1904). **Das Höchste und das Beste, das der Deutschlehrer in Schule und Universität leistet, kann immer nur Anregung sein** (Friedrich Kluge, in Marburg, 1913). We cannot, however, in many cases on account of the lack of clearness in the thought absolutely determine whether the **das** or **welches** is used merely as a survival of older usage to indicate a collective idea or something indefinite or general, or is employed intentionally in accordance with modern usage elsewhere, to refer to something definite. Thus **das** and **welches** are now as formerly still used with both of these two groups of meanings, with a tendency, however, toward the second group, while **was,** which also once fluctuated between both of them, is now established in the first group, as described above.

(*a*) In the genitive relation, **wessen** is sometimes used under the same circumstances which require **was** in the nom. or acc. relation: **Es handelt sich, Helmuth, nicht um das, wessen Du bedarfst, sondern es handelt sich um das, wessen die Kinder bedürfen** (Fontane's *Unwiederbringlich,* chap. vi). **Indessen beunruhigte ihn das, was ich ihm von dem Betragen seines Vaters in dieser Angelegenheit sagte, und alles, wessen er ohnehin von ihm gewärtig sein zu müssen glaubte** (R. Huch's *Ludolf Ursleu,* chap. xxvi). The older form **dessen** (or **dessent-**) is still the usual construction here, especially where as in the preceding paragraph the reference becomes a little more definite: **das Gleiche, dessen sie ihre Gegner anklagten** (Keller's *Seldwyla,* I. p. 194); **das unaussprechlich Innige aller Musik, vermöge dessen sie als ein ganz vertrautes Paradies an uns vorüberzieht** (Schopenhauer's *Die Welt als Wille und Vorstellung,* p. 347). **Der Nebensatz kleidet meist dasjenige in Worte, um dessentwillen die Periode ausgesprochen wird** (Armin Dittmar's *Syntaktische Grundfragen,* p. 8). Also **des** is used here. See **151.** *b* (2nd par.)

(*b*) In the dative relation **wem** is not used here. The old dative form **dem** is still uniformly employed: **Wir müssen das für recht halten, dem es der Verstand zuspricht** (Felix Stahl in *Preußische Jahrbücher,* 1915, vol. 159, p. 302).

(**2**) With reference to a thing, **was** is now usually used in substantive clauses. The student should remember this especially in case of clauses which are in apposition with **es**: **Nicht Furcht war es, was seine verstellte Hartnäckigkeit endlich besiegte** (Schiller). **Steht auf! sind's diese nicht und dieser Ort, | was euch zu Boden zieht** (Grillparzer's *Libussa*, 1). **Es ist nicht Furcht, was mich bewegt** (Hebbel's *Agnes Bernauer*). **Es war eine große Neigung, was sie zusammenführte** (Fontane's *Stechlin*, XIII. p. 164). **War es ein Traum, was sie erlebten?** (Wildenbruch's *Neid*, p. 61).

Thruout the entire present period **das** is more or less frequently found in substantive clauses instead of **was** as a survival of older usage: **Was ist's, das den Befehl des Königs hindert?** (Goethe's *Iphigenie*, 4, 2). **Was war es nur gewesen, das alle Menschen zu ihm hinzog?** (R. Huch's *Ludolf Ursleu*, chap. xxxvii).

When the predicate of the sentence precedes the relative clause, as in the preceding examples, the relative (either **der** or **welcher**) is very often attracted to the gender and number of the predicate: **Der Zweifel ist's, der Gutes böse macht** (Goethe's *Iphigenie*, 5, 3). **Denn eben diese kaiserliche Mild' und Gnade ist's, die sie bisher so ungeheuer mißbrauchten** (Goethe's *Götz*, 3, 1). **Diese Fragen und andere mehr waren es, welche die untern Räume des Hauses bewegten** (Raabe's *Frühling*, chap. xiii).

(**3**) In descriptive clauses where the reference is to the idea contained in a whole sentence: **Sie fürchtete wohl — was auch wirklich geschah — daß ich ihr auf alle mögliche Weise die Verbindung widerraten würde.** In the classics of the eighteenth century **welches** was still used here as in older German, indeed more commonly than **was**, and it even occurs sometimes in the language of to-day. For the sake of emphasis or a contrast both **was** and **welches** may be used here in the same sentence: **Davon sagte er zu niemandem etwas, was freilich ein Vergehen war, aber welches ihm vorzuwerfen mir, seinem Sohne, nicht ziemt** (R. Huch's *Ludolf Ursleu*, chap. xvi). The employment of **welch** here in early N.H.G. is explained by the general indefinite meaning that very commonly lay in **welch** in earlier usage. As it gradually acquired more definite force with definite reference to a particular person or thing it was gradually replaced here by the new general indefinite **was**. In M.H.G. and early N.H.G. **das** was used here, but as its force was felt as too definite it was gradually replaced by **welch**.

Welches should not be employed if ambiguity might arise from its use: **Er hat den Verkauf abgeschlossen, was** (or sometimes **welches**) **ich ihm widerraten hatte**, but **Mein Freund hat ein neues Haus gekauft, was** (referring to the fact of the purchase, but **welches** or **das** if the reference is to the house itself) **mir gefällt.**

A reference to the former or latter of two ideas is expressed by **was ersteres, was letzteres: Man baute eiserne Treppen, die von den Logengängen direkt ins Freie führten, was nutzt das aber? Sie sind zu steil und werden nie benutzt. Jetzt steckt man neuerdings ein Heidengeld hinein, um ein neues Gestühl und Gänge im Parkett anzubringen, was letzteres** (*the latter of which procedures*, i.e., putting in new seats and aisles) **allerdings sehr begrüßenswert ist** (Alfred Frhr. von Mensi in *Hamburger Nachrichten*, Oct. 27, 1905).

Both **was** and (less commonly) **welches** are used when the relative refers collectively to two or more things or ideas in the preceding proposition: **Sein Pelz hängt an der Wand zwischen einer Auswahl stark angerauchter Pfeifen, zwischen Bastbündeln, Hirschgeweihen, Leinwandsäckchen mit Sämereien, was alles im behaglichen Durcheinander sich darstellt** (H. Böhlau's *Rangierbahnhof*, p. 5). **So erkannte er, daß jenes Fenster nicht nach dem Flusse hinausging, vielmehr sich zwei Fuß hoch über der sichern Erde befand, welches** (more commonly **was**) **beides er bei etlicher Besonnenheit ohne große Geistesanstrengung genau hätte wissen können** (H. Hoffmann's *Rittmeister*, III. p. 41).

In another case **welches** is still not infrequent—when the relative is used as a predicate and the reference is not to individuals but to the idea contained in some adjective or noun: **Mein Bruder ist reich** or **ein Millionär, welches** (or perhaps more commonly **was**) **ich nicht bin.**

(4) **Was** is now avoided in choice language if the reference is to one object. See **157.** Earlier in the period, however, this usage was not infrequent even in the best authors, and still survives in loose colloquial speech: **Ottilie erinnerte sich jedes Wortes, was gesprochen ward** (Goethe). **Ihr wollt das Gut verkaufen, was über zweihundert Jahre in der Familie ist?** (Halbe's *Mutter Erde*, I. p. 52).

2. *Prepositional Relative Adverbs.* When the relative pronoun refers to a thing, it is very often replaced after prepositions by a compound adverb consisting of **wo** or **wor** (before a vowel) and the desired preposition: **die Feder, wo'mit ich dieses schreibe, ist sehr schlecht.** These compound adverbs cannot be freely formed, but occur only in case of the preps. enumerated in **141.** 5. B. This adverbial construction can even be used of persons if taken collectively: **Er bekam 30 gefangen, wo'von auf der Stelle 20 aufgehängt wurden.** These compounds are separable in popular speech: **Es war ein Loch, wo der Wind durch pfiff.** See also B below.

A. Besides these relative adverbs the appropriate forms of **der** and **welcher,** as **mit dem, mit welchem,** &c., are also employed here. Altho the relative adverbs are still common in popular and colloquial speech, as in older usage, there is in choice language, whether spoken or written, a decided preference for the inflected pronominal forms: **Es war eine Nacht, in der** or **welcher man nicht gern einen Hund hinausjagt. Lies nicht solche Bücher, aus denen du nichts lernen kannst. Einmal gibt es Situationen, in denen eine Regierung selbständig nach politischen Überzeugungen entscheiden muß** (*Hamburger Nachrichten*, April 29, 1921). The adverbial forms, however, are widely used in the three following categories, in the first and third of which it is the usual form of expression: (**1**) In descriptive clauses where the antecedent is a whole sentence: **Der Vater hatte nach dem Sohne geschickt, wovon dieser freilich nichts erfahren hatte.** In the cases given in 2 above, where the adverbial forms are not used, **der** must still be employed, even when the antecedent is a whole sentence: **Ich bin sehr gedrückt, infolge dessen ich nicht arbeiten kann.** With the prepositions **wegen** and **halb** the short gen. form of **was,** i.e. **wes,** is usually used. See **151.** 1. *b.* (**2**) When the antecedent is an expression of general or indefinite meaning, such as **alles, nichts,** &c.: **Er wußte alles, wovon ich mit Ihnen gesprochen hatte** He knew everything of which I had spoken to you. There is at present a strong tendency here to the use of **der, welcher,** or **was,** as described in *a.* (**2**), (**3**). (**3**) After names of places we find **wo,** compounded with **hin** or **her** according to the meaning: **Gumbinnen, wohin ich in Garnison kam** Gumbinnen, to which place I came to join the garrison.

a. After prepositions the relative pronoun is used: (**1**) If any ambiguity might arise from the use of the relative adverb: **Er hat ihm viele Vorwürfe gemacht, von denen** (with reference to **Vorwürfe; wovon** would refer to the statement of the main proposition) **aber nichts in die Öffentlichkeit gekommen ist.** (**2**) The relative pronoun **der** and **welcher** is also usually employed when it refers back to the general or indefinite determinatives **der, derjenige: Der liebe Gott gebe ihrer Seele das, zu dem** (or **wozu**) **er sie geschaffen, Freude.** As can be seen by the form in parentheses the relative adverb is also employed here in accordance with the once more general usage after indefinites, but the present tendency is toward the use of a pronominal form, **der** or **welcher,** as there is an aversion to the employment of an adverb in the function of a pronoun: **Bei den Sachen habe ich eine vielleicht willkürliche Auswahl getroffen, habe dasjenige verzeichnet, von dem ich glaubte, daß man es leichter und lieber hier nachschlagen würde als in der Inhaltsübersicht** (Behaghel's *Die deutsche Sprache*, Vorwort, 2nd ed.). In the accusative relation by the use of **was** we can give expression to the general indefinite idea here and at the same time avoid the adverbial form: **Die Kenntnisse dessen, um was man neidet** (Felix Stahl in *Preußische Jahrbücher*, 1915, p. 298). (**3**) After a neuter adjective-substantive present usage requires the relative **der** or **welcher: Viel Festes, an dem er nicht gerüttelt haben will; das Unmögliche, vor das er sie gestellt hatte.** (**4**) When there is a collective idea involved with reference back to two or more things already mentioned the relative **was** accompanied by the appositive **alles** is used: **Er tüftelte über diese Dinge, deren Zweckmäßigkeit und den Kostenpunkt, über die Jahreshoffnungen und den Stand der Feldfrüchte, von was allem er nicht den Teufel (223.** XI. B. *d*) **verstand** (Gottfried Keller's *Die drei gerechten Kammmacher*).

B. Instead of the relative adverb we still find sometimes the demonstrative adverb, a construction which was very common earlier in the period: **An dieser Stelle, einer Waldlichtung, lag das Haus, drin** (now more commonly **in dem** or **worin**) **Aloys und sein Bruder Stephan wohnten** (Fontane). These adverbial compounds are now little used with reference to the thought in a preceding sentence, but this usage was common earlier in the period: **Die Gesellschaft lachte, und er herzlich mit, bis er in einen Husten verfiel, der unsern Diskurs eine Zeit lang unterbrach, darauf denn der junge Mensch wieder das Wort nahm** (Goethe's *Werther*, am 1. Julius). See also **151.** 1. *b*, 3rd par. (last sentence).

Earlier in the period such adverbs also referred to persons, and were often separable: **ein Weib, da der Mann keine Freude an hat** (Luther), **den Berg, da du auf wohnest** (Luther).

C. This adverbial construction, except in the case mentioned in 2 above, must not be used of persons, as is often heard in the language of the common people: **Der Freund, mit dem or welchem** (not **womit**) **ich gereist bin.** Earlier in the period, however, these adverbs were also used with reference to persons even in the literary language: **der, womit man spricht** (Hagedorn); **das Mädchen, wovon du gestern das Lied sangst** (Goethe). **Ich dachte der lieben Brüder, der Westfalen, womit ich so oft in Göttingen getrunken** (Heine).

3. *Other Relative Adverbs.* Other adverbs and conjunctions can also take the place of the relatives after prepositions and sometimes elsewhere.

A. *Place.* **Wo, wo'her, wo'hin,** or in choice prose and poetry **da, da'her, da'hin,** for place: **Der Platz, wo** (= **an welchem**) **er stand; die Stadt, woher** (= **von welcher**) **er kam; die Stadt, wohin** (**nach welcher**) **er geht.** Also figuratively: **Fälle, wo** cases in which. The idea of place in **wo'her** (common form) and **da'her** (in choice language) often goes over into that of cause, *in consequence of which*: **Das war der Gewaltige, den das Land nur mit unterdrückter Empörung als das Geschöpf und Werkzeug der Despotenlaune nannte, der aber den Zauber einer bezwingenden persönlichen Liebenswürdigkeit besaß, daher er in der Familie ebenso geliebt wie anderwärts gehaßt und gefürchtet war** (Isolde Kurz in *Deutsche Rundschau*, Sept. 1905).

B. *Manner, Degree.* **Wie** for manner and **als** or now also **wie** for degree: **Die Art und Weise, wie** (= **in welcher**) **er auftrat. Seit jenem Tag verfolgt mich sein Vertrauen | in gleichem Maß, als ihn das meine flieht** (Schiller's *Piccolomini*, 1, 3). **Sie errichten Verschanzungen in dem Maße, wie sie vordringen** (*Hamb. Nachr.*, Oct. 25, 1905).

C. *Time*:

a. **Als** *when*, if actual occurrences or conditions are recorded: **im Jahre 1890, als ich in Berlin studierte.**

b. **Wenn** or **wann** (now rather infrequent, occurring only as a survival of earlier usage) *when*, if not a definite actual occurrence is before the mind, but something that is or was wont to happen, or a point in future time: **An schönen Abenden, wenn wir vor der Tür sitzen. Manchmal in tiefer Nacht, wenn alles rings umher ruhte, sang sie mir. O schöner Tag, wenn endlich der Soldat | ins Leben heimkehrt, in die Menschlichkeit** (Schiller's *Piccolomini*, 1, 4).

c. **Wo** *when*, the most common of the temporal particles used either of actual occurrences or conditions in the past or present, or of some point in the future, largely replacing **als** in case of present and often **wenn** in case of future time: **Und mit der Dämmerung kam ein Augenblick, wo jede Stimme verstummte** (Raabe). **Ich bin in einem Alter, wo mir die schönen Worte nichts mehr helfen** (Halbe's *Mutter Erde*, p. 75). **Ich war in den glücklichen Jahren, wo uns alles gefällt. Einst kommt der Morgen, wo ich . . . die Burg schon früh' verlasse** (Hebbel's *Nibelungen*, II. 1, 2).

d. **Da** is often used instead of **wo**, quite commonly earlier in the period and not infrequently still in choice prose: **Bis den Augenblick, da mich Ihr Billet aus dem Schlafe weckt** (Goethe). **Trotz des Zwischenfalls scheint die Zeit nicht mehr allzufern, da England findet, daß usw.** (*Hamburger Nachrichten*, Nov. 5, 1904).

e. Also the conjunction **daß** is used in a few expressions of time, especially after **Mal, Zeit,** where however it is now more commonly replaced in most cases by other words: **Das letzte Mal, daß** (or **als**) **ich ihn sah, war er wohl,** but still regularly: **Freunde, dies ist wohl das letzte Mal, daß ich den Krug euch führe zum Munde** (Goethe). **Die Zeit, daß** (or **während**) **du hier bist,** but **die Zeit als** (or **wo**, not **daß**) **du ankamst. Während der Zeit, daß** (or **in der**) **ich Don Karlos ausarbeitete, hat sich in mir vieles verändert** (Schiller). **Während der Viertelstunde, daß** (or **in der**) **ich diese kleine weiße Hand in der meinigen gehalten habe, hat das Herz des jungen Dinges fast zweitausend Schläge getan** (Raabe's *Frühling*, chap. xiii). **Die drei Monate — die kurze Zeit, daß** (or **während**) **ich hier bei euch futtere** (colloq. *eat, board*), **bin ich zwanzig Pfund schwerer geworden** (M. Dreyer's *Drei*, 1).

f. Sometimes **wie** is found instead of the more common **als** or **wo**: **Es fällt in die Zeiten, wie ich die von Miltenberg in der Wirtsstube fand** (Goethe).

D. *Such as.* The English *such as* is translated in various ways:

(1) By **wie** (earlier in the period **als**) followed usually by a personal pronoun of the third person or sometimes in the plural in case of indefinite reference **solche** referring to the antecedent (see **251.** II. A. *d*): **Es war eine Kälte, wie sie nur im Februar erlaubt ist. Das war ein Kampf, wie ihn keiner noch gesehen hat. Er zeigte eine Rührung, wie jener kleine Dienst sie gar nicht wert war.** A **solch, derartig, derlei, dergleichen, so** may precede the **wie (als): Solche (derartige, derlei, dergleichen, so große) Schiffe, wie (sie) hier gebaut werden, sieht man anderwärts selten. Grammatische Verstöße, wie solche die Umgangssprache der besseren Wiener Kreise verunstalten, kommen in der guten Berliner Gesellschaft nicht vor** (Suttner's *Die Waffen nieder!*, II, p. 170). **Dergleichen schlechte Übersetzer, als** (now **wie**) **ich Ihnen bekannt gemacht habe, sind unter der Kritik** (Lessing). **So ein armes Mädchen, als** (now **wie**) **ich bin** (Goethe).

Instead of the personal pronoun or **solch-** we also find **ein-** in the sing. and **welche, viele, wenige** in the pl.: **Auf der Stirn hat es ein Horn, aber nicht ein so krummes wie das Nashorn eins hat. . . . Von seinen vier Hufen ist der eine von Gold, . . . der vierte wie einer von den blauen Steinen, wie Mama welche um den Hals trägt** (Wildenbruch's *Neid*, p. 100). **So hat er** (Raimund) **sich hier als ein Volksdichter bewährt, ein Volksdichter im wahrsten, echtesten und schönsten Sinn des Wortes, wie Deutschland ihm nicht viele an die Seite zu stellen hat** (A. Sauer's *Ferdinand Raimund*). **Lehrhaft ohne Aufdringlichkeit ist es** (Grillparzer's *Der Traum, ein Leben*) **ein Volksstück der edelsten Art, wie die deutsche Literatur deren wenige besitzt** (id., *Festrede*).

To express the partitive idea the genitive **deren** or **ihrer** is sometimes used instead of the nominative or accusative of the pronoun: **Unweit wird die heilige Wiese sich befunden haben, wie deren in diesem Kulte oft vorkommen** (Wilamowitz-Moellendorff's *Griechische Tragödien*, I. p. 105). **Briefe, wie ich deren häufig erhielt.** See also **255.** II. 1. H. *c*.

The pronoun is sometimes omitted, the **wie** or **als** serving as a relative as in English the conjunction *as*: **Denn selten steht neben dem Perfektum des Nebensatzes dasselbe Tempus im Hauptsatz, außer in solchen Fällen, wie oben besprochen sind** (H. Blase in *Historische Grammatik der lateinischen Sprache*, III, p. 169). In general some pronoun in connection with **wie** is more common than the employment of simple **wie,** while in English simple *as* is alone used. In older English, however, an accompanying pronoun is sometimes found: Such young knyghtes as he is one ben neuer abydynge in no place (Caxton's *Blanchardyn and Eglantine*).

(2) After **solch-** also by the usual relatives: **solche Bücher, die dazu beitragen, das Herz zu beruhigen.**

(3) By **dergleichen** (uninflected): **Es überfiel ihn ein Unbehagen, dergleichen er in seinem Leben noch nicht empfunden hatte.** See also **161.** 2.

E. English *as* = *a thing* or *fact which* is translated by **wie** or **was: Er war Engländer, wie** (or **was**) **sie an seinem Akzent bemerkten.**

4. **Soviel.** Soviel is used relatively: **Die Fremden, soviele ihrer anwesend waren, unterhielten sich gut.**

5. **So.** In the nom. and acc. of all genders and numbers the uninflected form **so** was much used for **der** or **welcher** in early N.H.G., and is still occasionally found in poetry and in colloquial language in some sections: **Bittet fur die | so euch beleidigen** (Matth. v. 44). **Das Haupt, so er ihm abgehauen** (Uhland). **Kopf hoch! Lohnt sich ja nicht, daß man sich über den ganzen Rummel aufregt, so man Leben nennt** (Halbe's *Das Tausendjährige Reich*, p. 45).

Note. This **so** was originally a demonstrative adverb, i.e. a determinative (**154.** *Note*) pointing to the following asyndetic (**154.** *Note*) relative clause, just as the determinative **der** and **so** described in **154.** *Note.* Later this **so,** just as **der,** developed into a relative.

6. **Derselbe.** Earlier in the period **derselbe** was used occasionally as a relative, but this usage is now quite rare: **So hielten sie mich acht Tage im Gefängnis, nach Verlauf derselben** (now **nach deren Verlauf**) **sie mich zum Verhör holen ließen** (Goethe). **Die Kreise zu überschauen, innerhalb derselben** (now **deren**) **sich jene hohen Geister bewegten** (Heine).

7. **Was Für Ein.** In concessive clauses **was für ein** is used relatively: **Was er für Handelsgeschäfte beginnt, er gewinnt bei allen.**

8. *Popular Relative Forms.* The relatives **der** and **welcher** are not popular with the common people, and are often here replaced by the demonstrative **der**, the relative adverbs **wo** and **als**, the adverbial compounds **womit** (see 2. C above), &c., and the uninflected **was**: **Ach Vater, sagte Hänsel, ich sehe nach meinem weißen Kätzchen, das sitzt oben auf dem Dach** (Grimm's *Märchen*). **Das schlechte Messer, wo** (= **das**) **er hat** (Hebel). **Ist doch all manche zu Rang und Stand gekommen, wo** (= **der**, fem. dat. sing.) **man's nicht an der Wiege gesungen hat, daß die mal wird gnädige Frau heißen und vierlang fahren** (Halbe's *Das tausendjährige Reich*, p. 43). **Wer sind die, wo** (= **welche**) **eben gekommen sind?** (ib., p. 63). **Das Quecksilber in der Röhre ist demjenigen, als in dem Kölblein steht, gleich** (Hebel). **Der Knecht, was mit'm Wagen war, hat so was dergleichen g'redt** (Anzengruber). Compare **als** in the next to the last sentence with the cognate relative *as* that is used in older English and is still found in popular English: Those as sleep and think not on their sins (Shakespeare's *Merry Wives of Windsor*, 5, 5). Compare **was** in the sentence from Anzengruber with English *what* as used in popular speech: If I had a donkey what wouldn't go.

9. For the use of **da denn** as a relative see **238.** 2. *c. Note* 2.

154. Relative not Omitted in German.

Neither **der** nor **welcher** can be omitted as so often the relative in English: **Das Buch, das (or welches) ich gestern gelesen habe, ist interessant** The book I read, &c.

Note. In older periods the relative was often lacking in German: **In droume sie in zelitun den weg sie faran scoltun** (Otfrid's *Evangelienbuch*, I. 17. 74) In a dream they (the angels) told them the way *they should go*, In this primitive construction the relative clause *sie faran scoltun* is, as so often in English, merely placed alongside of the principal proposition without a relative pronoun, i.e. without a connective to indicate its subordination to the principal proposition, but the weakened demonstrative (i.e. the article) *den* before *weg* in fact points graphically as with an index finger to the following modifying asyndetic clause, i.e. a clause not introduced by a connective. When a demonstrative thus points to a following clause which determines or modifies the thought we often call it a determinative. Often in oldest German the determinative for clearness' sake was repeated after the noun and stressed: **Bigan tho druhtin redinon den selben zuelif theganon, | then thar umbi inan saȥun** (ib. IV. 10. 1) Then the Lord began to speak to the twelve disciples *who sat there about Him*, lit. *to those [they] sat there about Him*. The *then* is a dative plural as it is governed by the verb of the principal proposition. Often in Otfrid's language under Latin influence the repeated determinative assumes the case form required by the verb of the subordinate clause and thus passes from the principal proposition to the subordinate clause, i.e. the determinative becomes a relative pointing backward and asyndetic hypotaxis is replaced by formal hypotaxis (**267.** 4), the inwardly or logically subordinate clause receiving in the relative pronoun an outward sign of subordination.

The primitive asyndetic relative construction disappeared in German for the most part in the seventeenth century. The form without the repeated demonstrative is sometimes preserved after the determinative **der** when it refers to persons: **Der mich liebt** (asyndetic relative clause), **ist in der Weite** *He who loves me is far away.* **Du bist nicht, der du scheinst** *You are not the one* or *the man you seem to be.* **Die ich meine, heißt Frau Findeklee** (Hauptmann's *Versunkene Glocke*, l. 1047) *The woman I mean is called Mrs. F.* It is used here in German where the omitted pronoun is in the subject, predicate, or object relation, while in English it is only freely used where the omitted pronoun is predicate or object. On the other hand, it is used in English after nouns as well as the determinative *the one* and is used with reference to things as well as persons. Moreover, it is much more common in English, for in German the **der** is usually repeated, i.e. the asyndetic construction is replaced by formal hypotaxis with the relative pronoun: **Die, die ich meine, heißt Frau Findeklee.** In early N.H.G. the asyndetic construction was also used with reference to things: **Vnd wer nicht hat | von dem wird man nemen auch das** (now **was**) **er hat** (Mark iv. 25).

Just as the determinative **der** used to stand before and after a noun pointing to a following modifying asyndetic relative clause so the determinative **so** used to stand before and after the indefinite pronouns **wer** (**145.** *e*) and **was** (**145.** *f*) pointing to a following asyndetic relative clause, originally in the form "so wer (or waȥ) so", later "swer" "swaȥ", now **wer** *anybody*, **was** *anything*: **So will ich mich verlieben in wen ihr vorschlagt** (J. Paul's *Hesp.*, 118) *I'll fall in love with anybody you propose.* **Ich mach' ihn zu was** (acc. for dat.; see **147.** 1. C. *a*) **ich will** (Laube, 1, 124) *I'll develop him into anything I wish.* The original asyndetic construction with **wer** and **was** in the principal proposition is here preserved, but usually **wer** and **was** are now felt as relatives with the force of *whoso-ever, who-ever, what(so)-ever* and stand in the subordinate clause: **Wer einmal lügt, dem glaubt man nicht. Was Hänschen nicht lernt, lernt Hans nimmermehr.** In English the older form with *so, whoso-ever*, etc., is preserved but no longer understood, hence is now felt as a relative. The asyndetic construction is also found in German after the indefinite and general determinative **welcher** (**130.** 3).

Somewhat different from asyndetic hypotaxis is parataxis (**267.** 4), where the two propositions lie side by side without any outward or marked inward sign of subordination: **Gegen Frankfurt liegt ein Ding über, [es] heißt Sachsenhausen** (Goethe's *Götz*, 1, 4). **Ein Herr — [er] sieht aus wie ein Fürst — und ein Fräulein wie eine Prinzessin. Das sind ihre Bedienten** (Sudermann's *Heimat*, 3, 1). This construction is also found in English: There is a man at the door [, *he*] *wants to see you.* In both English and German it lingers on in colloquial speech, while in more formal language it is replaced by the hypotactic relative construction.

155. General and Indefinite Relatives: Wer, Was.

1. **Wer** *who, whoever, somebody who* and **was** *what, which, whatever, that which* are inflected exactly as the interrogatives **wer** and **was**. See **147.** 1.

a. The old gen. **wes** is sometimes still used instead of **wessen** in poetry and biblical language: **Wes das Hertz vol ist | des gehet der Mund vber** (Matth. xii. 34). The neut. gen. **wes** is still common also in prose in the compounds **weshalb, weswegen.** See **151.** 1. *b*. The masc. and neut. gen. **wes** is also still occasionally found in concessive clauses, where it is used seemingly as an adjective modifying a following gen.: **Einem Mädchen, wes Standes** (*of whatever rank*) **es sei, ist die Frage über ihre Wohlgestalt ein wichtiges Problem.** This attributive use of **was** has taken the place of an older partitive gen. construction, as explained in **147.** 1. E. The original partitive gen. is now only rarely found: **Dem Bischof gönnen wir willig, was Ehren er auch hat** (Freiligrath, 2, 174). It is still quite common in case of adjective-substantives, but is felt rather as a nom. or acc. in apposition with the **was: Es schien, als wollte jeder sich von allem entblößen, was er nur Bewegliches besaß** (Goethe's *Dichtung und Wahrheit*, I, 3). It is elsewhere usually replaced by the prepositional construction with **von** or now more commonly with **an: So stürzte ich alles, was ich von (or an) Geschirr erschleppen konnte, in gleiches Verderben** (ib., I. 1). The prep. phrase often precedes the **was: Marinja hatte, um sich mög-**

lichst rasch an Technik anzueignen, was ihr nach dieser Richtung fehlte, in ihrem Übereifer die rechte Hand übermäßig angestrengt (Schubin's *Refugium peccatorum*, VIII).

2. Both **wer** and **was** can be used in a general sense without an antecedent, but **was** has a wider range of usefulness, as it can also have an antecedent. See **157.**

For the development of these general indefinite relatives out of the indefinites **wer** (**145.** *e*) and **was** (**145.** *f*) see **154.** *Note.*

156. Wer is always used in an indefinite sense and may thus refer to one or more, but never has an antecedent and never refers to a definite person: **Nur wer die Sehnsucht kennt, weiß, was ich leide** *Only he who knows what yearning is knows what I suffer*—a statement in the singular, but with an indefinite reference to many. **Wer etwas gelernt, dēr** (**269.** 1. *a*) **gilt etwas. Wem nicht zu raten ist, dēm** (**269.** 1. *a*) **ist nicht zu helfen. Wer das gesagt hat, ist ein Lügner** Whoever (somebody, but I don't know who) said that is a liar. **Wer aber hereinkam, das war der Wilhelm** The one who came in—but I know you don't know who it was—just think, it was William. **Es tut doch wohl, wen** (*somebody whom*) **man lieb hat, einmal wieder mit Augen zu sehen.** In these sentences the relative **wer** still contains something of its original indefinite nature. See **145.** *e. Note* 2.

For more definite reference or for indefinite reference with individualizing force, i.e. to emphasize the idea of an individual with individual responsibility for his actions, with individual characteristics, experiences or to point to a group of fairly definite individuals **derjenige** or **der,** followed by **der** or **welcher,** is employed: **Derjenige, der dort unter dem Baume steht, ist mein Bruder. Derjenige, der sich mit Einsicht für beschränkt hält, ist der Vollkommenheit am nächsten** (Goethe). **Ich lege dies Drama in die Hände derjenigen, die es gelebt haben** (Hauptmann's *Einsame Menschen*). In accordance with older usage simple **der** is still often used here instead of **derjenige der.** See **130.** 2. *b.* **Solch** is also often used with the same general meaning as often found in **derjenige** or **der,** but it always seems to be a little more indefinite and hence is largely confined to the plural: **Es gibt immer solche, die nur an sich selbst denken.** Compare **131.** 3.

a. The double construction is employed after **wer** as found after **jemand** described in **145.** *b. Note* 1: **Grüßen Sie Lavatern . . . und wem Sie etwa Gutes** (or now usually **Gutem**) **begegnen** (Goethe an Karl August, I, 38).

b. Earlier in the period **wer** could have for an antecedent **der, jeder,** or **niemand: Glückselig der, wer Liebe rein genießt** (Goethe, Weimar, I. 9. 274, 2032). **Das mag nun jeder beurteilen, wer ohne Leidenschaft die Sache betrachtet** (id. I. 43. 228. 7). **Daß es niemand, wer es falsch auslegen könnte, zu sehen kriegte** (id., IV. 1. 169. 23). **Weh dem, wer sich der Welt verdungen** (Lenau's *Werke*, Nat. Lit., 2, 246, 945). Now **der** or **welcher** is used here instead of **wer.**

157. Was refers in a general or indefinite way to a thing or a thought, or indicates a collective idea, which may be definite or indefinite: **Was du heute tun kannst, das** (**272.** C. *a*) **verschiebe nicht auf morgen. Was du für recht hältst, dessen** (**272.** A, 3rd par.) **brauchst du dich nicht zu schämen. Was mir unrecht scheint, dem** (**272.** B. *a*) **versage ich meine Beistimmung. Was** (referring to a definite group of words, i.e. a definite statement) **du da behauptet hast, ist unrichtig. Was** (indefinite collective idea) **die Geschichte reicht, das Leben gibt, sein Busen nimmt es gleich und willig auf** (Goethe). **Was** (definite statement) **ich gesagt habe, dabei** (**272.** D. *a*) **bleibt's.**

Was can have an antecedent, if that antecedent be a word expressing an indefinite general idea, such as an indefinite pronoun, a neuter adjective used substantively, or a thought contained in a whole sentence, but it should never have for an antecedent the name of a definite object, tho some good authors do thus use it instead of the more correct **welcher** or **der** (see **153.** 1. (4)): **Alles, was er sagt, ist gut. Das war das Schlimmste, was ich befürchtete. Mein Bruder ist reich, was** (here also **welches** but not now **das**; for fuller explanation see **153.** 1. (3)) **ich nicht bin. Das Gut, was** (instead of **das** or **welches**) **der Vater hinterlassen hat** (Freytag). For fuller treatment of the use of **was** with an antecedent see **153.** 1 and the various articles thereunder.

After prepositions a prepositional relative adverb is usually employed instead of a form of **was: Wovon das Herz voll ist, (davon) läuft der Mund über. Wonach man eifrigst strebt, (das) bleibt oft unerreicht.**

a. In early N.H.G. **das** could also be used in plain substantive clauses in the sense *that which,* where it is now usually replaced by **was: Vnd wer nicht hat | von dem wird man nemen | auch das er hat** (Mark iv. 25). **Das** is most common in such substantive clauses as are in apposition with an **es.** See **153.** 1. (**2**).

b. **Was** is also used of persons in a collective sense: **Was von Offizieren im Lager war, wurde zusammengetrommelt** (Ompteda's *Sylvester von Geyer,* XLIX). **Was hier gemeinsames Los jedes Tages und jeder Stunde teilte, geht nun die verschiedensten Wege** (Stilgebauer's *Götz Krafft,* I, p. 5) *All those* (i.e. members of the graduating class) *who* &c. Especially in a broad sense to include little and big, or often males and females: **Was noch die Beine gebrauchen kann, das geht an Feiertagen aus.** Sometimes with the force of **wer** in a general indefinite sense: **Früh übt sich, was ein Meister werden will** (Schiller's *Tell,* 3, 1). **Was** in this meaning is often employed contemptuously: **Was so herumbummelt, bringt es zu nichts.**

c. When **was** denotes a collective idea the predicate appositive may be in the singular in accordance with the form of **was** or in the plural in accordance with the meaning: **So viel als möglich werde ich im folgenden nach diesem Beurteilungsgrunde das, was sich als bloßer Gräzismus verdächtig macht, von dem zu sondern versuchen, was wir als echt deutsche Eigentümlichkeit der alten Sprache mögen gelten lassen** (Ribbeck's *Syntax des Ulfila*). **Manches, was als Gräzismen in der Übersetzung erscheinen könnte, ist doch im Geiste der Sprache gewesen** (W. Krafft's *Die Kirchengeschichte der germanischen Völker,* I. p. 260).

158. Adverbs in Connection with Relatives.

1. The adverbs **immer, auch,** or combined **auch immer,** also **auch nur, nur immer** standing after **wer** and **was,** or several words removed, give generalizing force to the relative, and are much like our *ever, soever* in whoever, whatever, &c.: **Wer immer es gesagt hat, er hat gelogen. Von wem er es auch immer gehört haben mag, es ist gelogen.**

2. The adverb **da** which often earlier in the period followed **was, wer,** or **der** once had a concrete meaning, as described in the *Note* below, but now as we feel **was, wer,** and **der** as relative pronouns it has become meaningless and hence is usually suppressed: **Komme was da will. Vnd wer da suchet | der findet | Vnd wer da anklopfft | dem wird auffgethan** (Matth. vii. 8). **Wie nämlich jedes Ding sich putzt, | vor's andern Auge pfauisch stutzt, | dran da sich zeigt eines jeden Gab'** (Goethe, Weimar, I. 4. 206, 21). This use of **da** is still occasionally found. **Sie harrten der Dinge, die da kommen sollten** (Keller). **Sie schritten vor dem Vater und der Mutter her, mit einer gewissen Feierlichkeit, wie Menschen, die da wissen, daß ihnen eine große und bedeutsame Aufgabe zu teil geworden ist** (Wildenbruch).

Note. The **da** here was originally a determinative (**154.** *Note*) strengthening the preceding determinative **der** (**154.** *Note*) and explaining the preceding indefinite wer *anybody* or was *anything* by pointing forward to the following explanatory asyndetic (**154.** *Note*) clause.

3. Earlier in the period an **als** often preceded the relative pronoun or adverb, originally for the purpose of introducing the following descriptive clause as an appositive, i.e. as a loose explanatory clause bearing upon a preceding noun or the preceding statement as a whole: **Er wollte von den hohen, hohlgeschliffenen Schrittschuhen nichts wissen, sondern empfahl die niedrigen, flachgeschliffenen, friesländischen, als welche zum Schnellaufen die dienlichsten seien** (Goethe). This **als** has become rare in our time: **[Er] sagte laut und feierlich-grimmig: „Es lebe Alexius der Dreizehnte" — als worauf sich etwas Kurioses ereignete** (Raabe's *Eulenpfingsten,* chap. XVI). We feel the simple relative now as sufficient.

4. The demonstrative adv. **so** is placed after **was** to denote the general idea of quality, so that both words together convey the idea of *such things as*: **Was mag wohl darin sein? Allerhand Krimskrams: Kleider, Schürzen, Bänder, Flittertand, was so Frauenzimmer brauchen.**

Conditional Relative.

159. Wer *for anybody who, if any one* has the same declension as the relative and interrogative **wer.** It has the force of **wenn man, wenn einer,** and the clause in which it is found is treated as if it were a conditional clause, the verb standing at the end of the clause: **Freiheit? Ein schönes Wort, wer's recht verstände** (Goethe's *Egmont,* Act 4). **Fragen ist keine Schande, wer ein Ding nicht weiß** (Grimm). **Das (Selbstbeherrschung) ist eine schöne Errungenschaft,**

wer etwas davon hat (Bismarck to his betrothed, Feb. 23, 1847). **Wer's könnte, wie er!** (Boßhart's *Barettlitochter*, p. 136) *If one* (or here *if I*) *could only do as he did!* In early N.H.G. and as late as Goethe's day, **der** was also used in the same way.

Correlative Pronouns.

160. 1. A. Referring to a def. person or object: *He* (*she*, *that one* (of a thing), *the man*, *the woman*, *those*, *who* (*which*), are represented in German by the following correlatives:

a. **Der (die, das) jenige, welcher (welche, welches)** or **der (die, das).**

b. **Der (die, das), welcher (welche, welches).**

c. **Der (die, das), der,** &c.

d. **Er (sie), der (die)**; see 2. *a* below.

e. Without antecedent (see **130.** 2. *b* and **154.** *Note*): **Der** (not **welcher**) **mich liebt, ist in der Weite**; or **der, er** (see 2. *c* below).

f. **Solcher, der (welcher)** one which, of such a nature that, such as: **solche, die würdig sind** such as are worthy. We often find **wie** or **als** instead of **der** or **welcher,** and **derartig, derlei, so, ein** instead of **solch.** See **153.** 3. D.

g. **Derselbe, der** the same one who: **Er ist eben derselbe, den wir gestern sahen.**

h. **Der, so** (early N.H.G.; see **153.** 5) = **der, welcher.**

i. The first member in all the above cases can also, except in *d* and *e*, be used adjectively.

B. Referring indefinitely or in a general way to persons or to some thing:

a. **Wer, der: Wer das sagt, der lügt.** See **156,** and 2. *b* below.

b. **Das** (or **dasjenige, eins, etwas, nichts, alles, manches, vieles, das Beste,** or any adjective-substantive), **was** (not now usually **das** or **welches**) as in the earlier part of the period): **Das(jenige), was er sagt, ist wahr. Es gibt im Leben so manches, was uns rätselhaft erscheint.** See also **153.** 1. **(1)**.

2. *a.* The form **er, der** (1. A. *d* above) is different from the other forms in A. The determinative **derjenige** or **der** in *a*, *b*, *c* is of itself indefinite, and its meaning is only determined by the clause that always follows it. Hence the determinative forms *a*, *b*, *c* are used when the identity of the person in question is yet to be established. When the subject is a person already mentioned and thus known and some particular statement with regard to him follows in the relative clause, **er, der** are used: **Er** (Arneth, the Austrian historian, who is the subject of the sketch from which this sentence is taken and who has just been presented to the attention of the reader), **der im ganzen eines der glücklichsten Menschenleben hinter sich hat, genoß auch das große Glück, eine Mutter zu haben, die zu den herrlichsten deutschen Frauen gerechnet werden muß.**

Note. Occasionally **er** is used determinatively with the force of **der(jenige)** in accordance with an older usage, once quite common: **Für mich steht sie** (i.e. **die Musik**) **auf der untersten Stufe: gut für Kinder und Träumer, aber nicht für sie, die sich zu handelnden Menschen ausgewachsen haben** (Spielhagen's *Freigeboren*, p. 176).

In English the development is in the same direction. We still say in a determinative sense *he who*, but more commonly in the plural *those who* instead of the older and once common *they who*. On the other hand, we still use *they who* corresponding to German **sie die** when the reference is to persons who have just been mentioned, so that the differentiation of form that has resulted in German is also found in English in the plural. There is also a strong tendency to differentiate in the singular by using *he who* for pointing to a person already mentioned and *the man who*, or *the one who* in a determinative sense. *He who*, however, is also much used in a general indefinite sense = **wer,** so that differentiation here is not so close as in German.

b. The **der** in 1. B. *a* is not an antecedent of **wer,** but only the repetition of the subject **wer,** and not being necessary can be dropped. However, if **wer** and its seeming antecedent do not stand in the same case, it is not usually omitted: **Wer einmal lügt, dem glaubt man nicht und wenn er auch die Wahrheit spricht.**

c. The definite subject **der** can be repeated by a following **er** in the same manner as indefinite **wer** is repeated by **der**, as described in *b:* **Der meinen alten Gliedern Mut verlieh, | in eure Höhle mich hinauf zu wagen, | er steht mir bei, ich fühl's** (Hauptmann's *Versunkene Glocke*, Act 3, ll. 1382-4).

Stereotyped Pronominal Forms.

161. There are a number of compound pronominal forms which are now treated as indeclinables and are written with a small letter, altho some of them are in fact substantives.

1. **'meines** (**'deines, 'seines, 'ihres, 'unseres,** &c.) **'gleichen** *one of my* (*your, his, her, our*) *stamp, one who is my* (*your, his, her, our*) *equal*, fossilized genitives (see *a*) used substantively without change of form for any case sing, or pl.: **Seinesgleichen** (nom. sing.) **läßt sich kaum wieder finden. Seinesgleichen** (nom. pl.) **lassen sich kaum wieder finden. Er erkannte ihn für seinesgleichen** (acc. sing.). **Ich habe nie ihresgleichen** (acc. sing. or pl.) **gesehen** I have never seen the like of her (them). **Leute ihresgleichen** (gen. pl.) **finden sich selten. Er geht mit ihnen wie mit seinesgleichen** (dat. pl.) **um.** For stress see **47.** 3. A. *b. cc.*

a. Such forms as **meinesgleichen,** tho used with unchanged forms for all cases, are in fact fossilized genitives of the wk. masc. adjective-substantive **Gleiche** *equal, one who is like.* This gen. was once a real partitive genitive. It became fossilized in negative sentences: **Er findet nicht seinesgleichen** (partitive gen. depending upon **nicht**; see **145.** *g. Note* 2), literally *He will find nothing of one equal to himself.* Later this original construction was forgotten and the gen. was used for any case, sing. or pl., masc. or fem. The fossilized acc. sing. masc. is also used in **ohnegleichen, sondergleichen** *without a parallel*: **Sie erlauben sich Kühnheiten ohnegleichen** (in form a masc. acc. sing., but refers here to an abstract fem. noun in the pl.). The fossilized acc. form is also still found in **dessen Gleichen** and **deren Gleichen.** See 2.

In Luther's time **gleich** was still felt as a wk. masc. noun: **Denn er ist nicht mein Gleiche** (Job ix. 32). Compare **Ich bin's, bin Faust, bin deinesgleichen!** (Goethe's *Faust*, Nacht).

2. **Des'gleichen** (for the sing.) and much more commonly **dĕr'gleichen** (for sing. or pl., masc., fem., or neut.) *of such a nature, such, the like, of the* (*that*) *kind, of the same kind, such as*, used adjectively and substantively, demonstratively or relatively. Demonstratively: **Vnd dis gleichen Reuchwerg solt jr euch nicht machen** (Ex. xxx. 37). **Sie scheinen sich auf dergleichen Handel zu verstehen** They seem to understand trade of such a nature. **Eine dergleichen** (now more commonly **derartige,** as **dergleichen** does not now usually tolerate an indefinite article before it) **Lobrede** (Lessing), **dergleichen Scherze, dergleichen Leute. Bei dergleichen ist aber das Weib dem Mann über** (Rosegger) In such things a woman is ahead of a man. **Ja, ganz unverhofft; vor acht Tagen haben wir uns nichts dergleichen träumen lassen. Auf einem Tische hatte er die Gewinne ausgelegt: lauter Kleinigkeiten, Bonbons, Bildchen, Bleistifte und dergleichen. Der neugebackene Sextaner stand wie ein armer Sünder da und erwartete einen tüchtigen Rüffel; doch nichts dergleichen** (Ompteda's *Sylvester von Geyer*, XIII) *but nothing of the kind happened.*

Relatively: **wil wunder thun | der gleichen nicht geschaffen sind** (Ex. xxxiv. 10). **Und hat solche grosse straffe vber vns gehen lassen | Des gleichen vnter allem Himel nicht geschehen ist** (Baruch ii. 2). **Einen überlegenden Schurken, dergleichen Franz ist** (Schiller). **Er ging im Sonnenschein auf der Wiese, wo allerlei merkwürdige und unbekannte Blumen blühten, umflogen von Schmetterlingen, dergleichen er nie gesehen hatte** (H. Seidel's *Der Schatz*, III).

The above forms are fossilized genitives (see 1. *a*), but also the acc. is similarly used in connection with a gen. of a relative: **dessen Gleichen** with reference to a masc. or neut. sing. and **deren Gleichen** with reference to a fem. sing. or any noun in the pl. Exs.: **Den merkwürdigsten Platz, dessen Gleichen in der Welt vielleicht nicht wieder zu sehen ist** (Goethe). **Immer war ihr Antlitz von leuchtender Heiterkeit und all ihr Gebaren von einer leichten Anmut übergossen, deren Gleichen er noch nicht gesehen hatte** (H. Hoffmann's *Die Totenhochzeit*, p. 159).

a. **Dergleichen** is also used adverbially: **Die Hofrätin wußte, wo das hinaus wollte, tat aber nicht dergleichen** (Berlepsch's *Fortunats Roman,* p. 16) *but she didn't let on,* i.e. pretended not to know. Also **nichts** instead of **nicht: Und die Bewegung, die kurze, stolze, mit der sie die Blume zum Fenster hinauswarf, weil Edith sie welk gefunden — und ich nichts dergleichen getan hatte** (Schubin's *Refugium peccatorum,* II, 6) *because I had pretended not to notice* (that she wore the flower to show her love for me). Sometimes **desgleichen: Es schien unmöglich, daß Frau Uelzen nichts bemerkt haben sollte, wenn diese auch keineswegs desgleichen tat** (Spielhagen's *Das Skelett im Hause,* II).

3. **'Der'lei** (= **der'gleichen**) *of such a nature,* used as a demonstrative, both adjectively and substantively: **aus allen derlei Betrachtungen. Derlei waren damals die Ideale junger Leute** Such things were at that time the ideals of young people. Thus also a number of compounds with **lei: allerlei** all kinds of, **beiderlei** both, both kinds of, **einerlei** of one kind, all the same (**Das ist mir einerlei**), **mancherlei** many kinds of, **solcherlei** such kinds of, &c. See **126.** 1. *a.* For stress see **47.** 3. A. *b. cc.*

4. **'Aller'hand** (= **allerlei**) *all kinds of,* used adjectively and substantively: **allerhand Blumen** all kinds of flowers. **Es ist die Rede gewesen von allerhand** The conversation was about all sorts of things. **Allerhand Gutes** all sorts of good things. See **139.** 1. *a. Note.* For stress see **47.** 3. A. *b. cc.*

5. **Unsereins** (= **unsereiner** *one of our stamp*), tho usually inflected like a strong neuter adjective with contraction to **-eins** in the nom. and acc., is sometimes invariable thruout: **Mit unsereins** (instead of **unsereinem**) **machen sie nicht viel Umstände.** These modern compounds are formed by writing together two distinct words **unser** (gen. pl. of the personal pronoun) and **einer** or **eins,** substantive forms of the numeral **ein.** For the double gender here see **263.** I. 6. *b.* See also **263.** II. 4. *f.*

Unsereiner is now also often used with the force of **ich: Unsereiner hat's nicht so gut.**

THE VERB.

162. A verb is a word that predicates action or being.

Classification.

163. Verbs are divided into two classes: *transitive* and *intransitive.*

1. A *transitive* verb is one that requires a complement in the acc. case: **Ich liebe den Vater.**

2. An *intransitive* verb is one that either requires no complement, as **ich knie,** or takes a complement in the gen., dat., or in some case governed by a preposition: **Ich bedarf des Trostes. Ich begegne einem Freunde. Er trachtet nach dem Gelde.**

a. The following verbs can be used transitively or intransitively, sometimes however with a little different meaning in the two functions, in a few cases also with different principal parts according to the function: **anfangen, anheben, beginnen, backen, baden, biegen, braten, brechen, brennen, enden, flüchten, gleichen, hängen, heilen, irren, kleben, lehnen, kochen, quellen, rauchen, reifen, reißen, schlagen, schießen, schließen, schmelzen, speisen, spritzen, sprühen, stecken, stoßen, stürzen, treiben, trocknen, verderben, weiden.** Exs.: **Er hat das Glas gebrochen** and **Das Glas ist gebrochen. Er hängte den Hut an den Nagel** and **Der Hut hing an dem Nagel.** Compare **257.** 1. *a, b.* Germans very often employ a reflexive verb where in English an intransitive is used. See **218.** 3. B.

3. Under the above classes are distinguished:

a. Reflexive verbs which take an object designating the same person or thing as their subject: **Er lobt sich** (acc.). **Er schadet sich** (dat.). For the use of reflexive verbs see **218.**

b. Impersonal verbs used only in the 3rd person sing. with the formal subject **es,** expressed or understood: **Es schneit. Mir graut davor,** or **Es graut mir davor.** For the use of impersonal verbs see **219.**

GRAMMATICAL FORMS OF THE VERB.

ASPECT.

164. The verb distinguishes by its forms person, number, tense, mood, voice, and aspect. The terms persons, number, voice need no especial explanation here as they are in general used as in English. Tense and mood are treated at considerable length below.

At this point it is desired to say a few words about aspect: Aspect indicates the aspect, the type of the action. It often shows: (1) that the activity continues for some time in unbroken course, the durative aspect, as in **essen, schlafen, wachen** and in English *to eat, to sleep, to be awake,* or with an especial form to emphasize the idea of continuation, *to be eating, to be sleeping.* (2) That the activity represents only *one point* of time, the point-action or perfective aspect, as in **einschlafen, aufwachen, erscheinen** and in English *to fall asleep, to awake, to arise,* the ingressive perfective aspect calling attention to the first point, the beginning of the action or state, the moment when one enters into sleep, or comes into the waking state, or the moment when the sun appears; or on the other hand, as in **abblühen** *to cease blooming,* **verblühen** *to lose one's beauty,* lit. *to cease blossoming,* **aufessen** *to eat up,* the effective perfective aspect, calling attention to the final point in the activity, the moment when the blooming, blossoming ceases and the apple disappears in the throat. The durative aspect is usually expressed by the simple verb, the point-action or perfective aspect often by a verb with a dependent infinitive: **Es fängt an zu regnen. Es hört auf zu regnen.** In case of many very common verbs the ingressive perfective idea is expressed by giving a transitive verb reflexive form: (durative) **Er sitzt auf dem Stuhl,** but with ingressive force: **Er setzt sich auf den Stuhl.** Similarly **Er liegt auf dem Bette,** but **Er legt sich auf das Bett. Er steht auf den eigenen Füßen,** but **Er stellt sich auf die eigenen Füße.** Perfective force is in most cases expressed by the use of a prefix or particle. The particle or prefix originally had in every verb a concrete meaning, but it is often not felt to-day, as in **erscheinen** and English *arise,* and yet it usually has an appreciable meaning, for altho it has lost its concrete sense it has frequently developed point-action or perfective force. In **aufessen** and in *to eat up* it is quite evident that **auf** and *up* do not now have the original meaning of *upward,* for the apple in fact goes down. The particle here has become a mere grammatical form to indicate the final point in the activity. Sometimes a simple verb has by virtue of its meaning alone perfective force, as in **kommen** and in English *to come.* As the usual German way to indicate point-action or perfectivity is by the use of prefixes this question is treated under prefixes in **246.** II. 3. *b,* 4. *a,* 5. D. *a, b, c.*; **223.** I. 7. E. *b, c,* G. *d*; **191.** I. 4. In older German **werden** with the present participle of the verb to be conjugated was much used with ingressive perfective force, which has left traces behind in the literary language and the dialects, as described in **190. 1. C.** *a. Note* **1.** The different forms of the durative aspect are discussed in **175.** *Note.* Besides these formal characteristics of aspect there is an other which plays an important rôle in the spoken language—accent. Both transitive and intransitive duratives, when spoken somewhat more forcibly and rapidly than usual in connection with a strong rising intonation of the voice, become ingressive perfectives indicating the moment of a sudden change in the situation. This form of the ingressive aspect is most commonly found in joyful exclamations expressing satisfaction over the attainment of some end or over a pleasant discovery: **Ich hab's!** or **Ich seh's!** (Pollak in Paul and Braune's *Beiträge,* 1920, p. 414), an exclamation uttered upon finding a point in the landscape after a long search. Likewise in **Ich kann's!,** an exclamation spoken upon discovering that one can do something that one has been trying to do. It is also common in lively narrative to indicate a sudden turn in the development of the events: **Da wallt dem Deutschen auch sein Blut** (Uhland's *Schwäbische Kunde,* l. 29) *Then also the blood of the German begins to boil.*

There are also other aspects. The iterative aspect expresses the idea of the frequent occurrence and repetition of an activity, as in **streicheln** *to stroke.* For fuller discussion see **245.** III. 2 and 3. The diminutive aspect indicates an activity of diminutive proportions, as in **lächeln** *to smile.* See **245.** III. 2. *b.* The intensive aspect indicates intensification of the activity: **hören** *to hear,* but **horchen** (intensive) *to listen.* See **245.** III. 5. The desiderative aspect represents an activity as threatening, indicating that there is a strong and persistent impulse present to perform it: **Mich schläfert** I feel sleepy. See **245.** III. 3. *b.* For the terminate aspect see **175.** *Note,* last par.

TENSE (for formation see **177.** I, II, III and **190**).

165. There are three absolute tenses (present, pres. perfect, and future), which express time from the standpoint of the moment in which the speaker is speaking without reference to some other act; and three relative tenses (past, past perfect, and future perfect), which express time relatively to the preceding absolute tenses. The following articles on tense apply principally to the tenses of the indicative. The tenses of the subjunctive are treated under the head of the subjunctive mood.

1. *Present Tense.* The present tense represents an action as now taking place, or a state as now existing: **Der Baum blüht. Er ist sehr krank.** It often represents the act as something habitual, customary, characteristic: **Er wohnt im Winter in der Stadt. Er schreibt schön.**

It is also used:

a. To express a general truth: **Zweimal zwei ist vier.**

b. In narration, especially in lively style, to make more vivid past events and bring them nearer the hearer. This usage of the present, common also in English, is called the historical present. In German it frequently in narration relieves the past tense and thus furnishes a means to vary the style. Some authors are very fond of it, while others use it little or not at all. In Goethe's *Hermann und Dorothea* it is conspicuously absent, and is in general uncommon in epic poetry, where there is a calm and dignified movement.

Note. The historical present is most frequent in the language of the common people and familiar language generally, alternating often with the present perfect. See 2. *b.* It is, however, not only thus common in vivid, lively colloquial and popular speech but is also very common in the dry, learned style of annalists, historical grammarians, etc., who from time to time enter into their record items of historical importance: Zürnen **regiert im Mittelhochdeutschen den Akkusativ, wofür im Neuhochdeutschen der Dativ eingetreten ist** (Paul's *Deutsche Syntax,* p. 385, where there are other examples). Altho this form has always been characteristic of popular and colloquial speech and occurs a few times even in oldest German, it is not found in extended passages in the literary language before the fourteenth century. In both English and German it came into the literary language late along with a freer and wider sway of imagination and feeling which made it possible.

c. As the English present perfect to express that an action or state that was begun in the past is still continuing at the present time, usually accompanied by the adverbs **bereits, schon** *already,* **erst** *only,* **lange** *long,* or the prep. **seit** *since*: **Wie lange lernen Sie schon deutsch? Ich lerne es erst seit sechs Monaten** How long have you been studying German? I have been studying it for only six months. **Wir warten bereits seit einer Stunde auf ihn. Wie lange sind Sie hier?** How long have you been here?

Note. Thus also the perfect infinitive after modal auxiliaries must be rendered into German by the present infinitive, to show that something might have taken place and might now be continuing in existence: **Wenn du vernünftig gewesen wärest, du könntest, so jung du bist, längst Hüttenmeister sein** If you had been reasonable, you might, as young as you are, have been serving now for a long while as superintendent of the foundry.

d. Usually instead of the future in the subordinate clauses of purpose and condition and often elsewhere in both principal and subordinate propositions where an adverb of time or the context makes clear the thought, for this the oldest future form, long deeply rooted in German feeling, is still a favorite where there is no ambiguity: **Ich wünsche, daß du zu ihm gehst. Laß uns eilen, daß wir ihn noch erreichen. Wenn du dich beeilst,** or **beeilst du dich, so wirst du ihn noch einholen. Morgen kommt er. Wann kommt er? Ich weiß nicht, wann er kommt.** As in English the present is used after a future when both actions are contemporaneous: **Ich werde ihn gut empfangen, wenn er kommt.** The present by reason of its pithy terseness is felt as more forceful than the longer and more accurate but weaker future, hence is much used to express something confidently expected: **Kommt er? Er kómmt** Will he come? He surely will.

e. Instead of the imperative (see **177.** I. B. *b*).

f. The present is often used where the reference is to a past act and a present perfect might be used. The speaker uses the present tense as tho the words had just been spoken as he feels the matter as one of present interest: **Ich höre,** or **Man sagt mir, daß er noch sehr krank ist.** The present is also used in quoting from a book still read and studied even tho the author belongs to the past: **Goethe meint, daß usw.**

2. *Present Perfect.* The present perfect is used to represent that something is finished at the time of speaking, or that the results of a past act still continue in the present (see also 3, A. *a* below): **Ich habe den Brief schon geschrieben. Ich bin eben von der Stadt gekommen. Kolumbus hat Amerika entdeckt. Die Kirche ist im 14ten Jahrhundert erbaut worden.**

The present perfect is also used:

a. Instead of the future perfect: **Wenn du angekommen bist, werde ich dich besuchen** (instead of **Wenn du angekommen sein wirst,** &c).

b. Often in dialect and colloquial speech instead of the past tense in narrative: **„Wir haben gezittert am ganzen Leib,“ fuhr der braune Schmied fort, „wir haben ein Vaterunser beten wollen, aber die Zunge ist wie gelähmt gewesen vor Schreck“** (Rosegger). **Ja, wie wir nu in seinem Zelt gekommen sind, da ist er erst eine janze Weile so uf und abjegangen und hat nischt nich geredt** (Finke in Wildenbruch's *Die Quitzows*, 1, 8). **Darauf hat Tante Ida mich angesehen und gefragt, ‚na also — wer war's?‘ Weil ich aber doch gewußt habe, daß du's nicht haben wolltest, habe ich nichts gesagt. Da hat Tante Ida rote Flecke auf den Backen bekommen und gemeint,** &c. (Young Georg von Drebkau in Wildenbruch's *Vize-Mama*). The use of the present perfect here seems to result from the desire of the speaker to attach importance to each individual utterance by representing it as an independent fact worthy of attention, as explained in 3. A. *a* and *c* below. The common people are very fond of this form of exaggeration. This usage first appeared in the fourteenth century. In the dialects of the South from this time on the present perfect gradually within two centuries supplanted the simple past indicative, not only on account of a natural fondness there for the present perfect but also largely because of a mere formal factor, namely certain forms of the past indic. had by the suppression of final **e** become identical with those of the present tense, as in **er spielt** (3rd pers. present or past indic.). Thus the Swabian writer Berthold Auerbach in his beautiful story „Brigitta“ in keeping with the dialectic setting lets the heroine use thruout the entire book the present perfect in narrative instead of the literary past tense.

3. A. *Past Tense.* The past tense usually represents a past act or condition not in its completeness, but as being performed or continuing at the same time as some other act or condition, or it represents the act as completed in past time in connection with some other event. Hence the past tense has for its leading idea that of the simultaneity of two or more related past acts or conditions. It accordingly represents single acts or facts as links in a chain of facts, and for this reason it is the usual tense for the description and narration of all related events and conditions in the past, and is therefore the prevailing tense of narrative, history, and the novel. The past tense, however, is not confined to lengthy description, but is used even in a single sentence if it describes something as it once was without relation to the present: **Die deutschen Kaiser wurden in Frankfurt gekrönt.** Thus the past tense cuts us off from the present entirely, and leads us into the midst of past events and conditions which are developing at the same time with close relations to each other, but with no relations whatever to the present, and thus this tense differs rather sharply from the present perfect, which represents the act as now completed, the occurrence as now an accomplished fact. The past tense does not, however,

imply necessarily time very remote, but is used for time past, whether it refers to remote acts or to those of a few moments ago, if it turns the mind from the present to two past acts or events, or to a series of past events in their relations to each other: **Als die Bäume in vollster Blüte standen, trat heftiger Frost ein. Ich sang, indem er Klavier spielte. Ich sang beim Ankleiden.** See **246.** II. 4. *a* for the force which brought about the differentiation between the past and the present perfect.

a. Past Tense Compared with the Present Perfect. The past tense is often confounded with the present perfect. The latter is used when the results of a past act still exist in the present, or to represent a past event as an independent fact, not as a link in a chain of related events, and emphasizes the bearing of this past event upon the present. Thus the present perfect looks at the past from the standpoint of the present or of stern fact, while the past tense takes us into the past and enlists our interest in the events then taking place. Hence in the midst of a narrative where the past tense or past perfect has been uniformly used, the speaker changes to the pres. perf. at once, when he desires (**1**) to represent a past act not as a link in the chain of events, but according to his judgment as an important independent fact, or (**2**) to represent that the result of a past act still exists at the time of the narrative: (**1**) **Luther tat zu Worms einen Gang, dergleichen mancher Kriegsoberst in der schwersten Schlacht nicht getan hat.** (**2**) **In dem seiner Wohnung gegenüber liegenden Hause, wo sein Freund Wilhelm wohnte, war das Scharlachfieber ausgebrochen und, da Fritz allen Warnungen zuwider doch noch zu seinem dort wohnenden Freunde ging, so ist er ebenfalls erkrankt und liegt nun schwer danieder.**

b. Past Tense Used by Eye-witness. Thus also an eye-witness of events naturally uses the past tense in narrating these events as he has seen them take place in their relations to each other, and may use this tense even in giving a single sentence, as there is in his mind a complete picture of the whole occurrence: **Gestern ertrank ein Kind. Sie waren gestern in der Oper.** On the other hand, when these things are communicated to a third party by the one who has only *heard* them, he uses the pres. perf., because they are to the speaker only independent facts: **Gestern ist ein Kind ertrunken. Sie sind gestern in der Oper gewesen.**

c. English and German Past Compared. In both languages the past tense once performed the functions of four tenses, the past, present perfect, past perfect and future perfect. Examples of the use of the German past for the past perfect and the future perfect are given in C and 6 below. It is still often used where we should expect the present perfect, so that it seems to correspond to English usage: **Noch nie in der Geschichte war ein so gewaltiger Kampf** (König von Bayern, Aug. 19, 1915). While older usage thus often still appears, English and German now usually differ. In statements of independent facts conceived as having taken place recently English usually employs the past tense where there is reference to a definite time or place provided the time in question is now felt as absolutely past so that it cannot be considered as a part of the present moment, while German of course uses the present perfect as the reference is to an independent past act: *My brother bought two hats last year* or *this morning,* but *My brother has bought two hats this week,* as the speaker feels that the period in question is not yet closed, passed, while in German the present perfect must be used in both cases: **Mein Bruder hat voriges Jahr, heute Morgen, diese Woche zwei Hüte gekauft.** Wherever the idea of past time is not prominent, i.e. where the reference is general or indefinite the present perfect is used in English: My brother has often bought two hats at a time **Mein Bruder hat oft zwei Hüte auf einmal gekauft.** My brother has bought two new hats **Mein Bruder hat zwei neue Hüte gekauft.** When statements of independent facts refer to a time more remote English usually employs the past tense, while German inclines here to the use of the present perfect: **Das eigentliche Bayern ist etwa um 500 von den Deutschen besetzt worden. Romanen haben sich aber am Gebirge länger gehalten** (Behaghel's *Geschichte der deutschen Sprache,* p. 13) Bavaria proper was occupied by Germans about 500, but in the mountains the Romance population maintained itself somewhat longer. In German as a survival of older usage, however, the past tense is still often found here.

In German the present perfect always represents the act or state as absolutely completed, while in English it can be used of an act or state begun in the past but still continuing, where in German the present tense must be used as illustrated in 1. *c* above.

Thus it is perfectly clear that altho originally in both English and German the present perfect tense form was in reality a present tense, as explained in **191.** I. 1 and 4, it has in German acquired power to point to the past, even the remote past, while in English it still always has close relations with the present.

B. The past is also used as the past perfect in English (just as the present in German is used for the present perf. in English, as described in 1. *c* above) to describe an action as begun at some previous time, but as still continuing up to the time spoken of in the past: **Ich wartete schon zwei Stunden auf ihn, als er kam** I had been waiting two hours for him when he came.

C. In accordance with usage in older periods when there was no past perfect tense the past is often used for the past perfect: **Wir waren mit Uechtritz auf**

der Richards-Höhe, die meine Frau noch nicht sah (Hebbel's *Tagebücher*, Aug. 3, 1854). See also 4 *a* below and A. *c* above.

D. The past is also used for the future perfect. See 6 below.

4. *Past Perfect.* The past perfect tense represents a past action or event as completed at or before a certain past time: **Als er das gehört hatte, erschrak er** When he had heard that, he became frightened.

a. The past perf. is often replaced by the past: **Als er das hörte, erschrak er.** See also 3. A. *c*.

5. *Future Tense.* The future tense represents an action or event as yet to take place: **Mein Herz wird sich freuen, wenn ich dich wiedersehe.**

The future is also used of an action or event in past time that was yet to take place: **Die Dirne ging mit bloßem Kopfe, sie wird also den Holzschnitzer nur eine Strecke und nicht allzuweit begleiten** (Anzengruber's *Sternsteinhof*, p. 69).

The present tense often takes the place of the future. See 1. *d* above.

a. The future is also used instead of the imperative (**177.** I. B. *c*).

b. It is often, especially in colloquial speech, used to express a probability or supposition, often accompanied by **wohl,** usually with the force of a present tense: **Karl wird [wohl] krank sein = Karl ist wohl krank. Der Hund wird [wohl] sechs Jahre alt sein = Der Hund ist wohl sechs Jahre alt.** The **wohl** is not necessary with **werden** but must be used with the simple present. The **werden** here contains strong modal force and can often be replaced by a modal auxiliary: **Der Hund kann sechs Jahre alt sein.**

Often in interrogative form, especially to question someone on some well-known fact or truth in such a way as to encourage him to essay an answer: **Hans, wie wird der Mann heißen, der Amerika entdeckt hat?** Johnny, you can tell me, can't you, the name of the man who discovered America? **Hans, wie wirst du den Zinsfuß aus Kapital und Zeit und Zins berechnen?** Now, Johnny, you can tell me, can't you, how to ascertain the rate of interest, &c.? The question form is also often employed to indicate surprise at a preceding question which inquires after something that ought to be self-evident: A. **Bist du zufrieden?** B. **Wo werde ich denn zufrieden sein? = Wie kann ich denn zufrieden sein?**

On the other hand, in connection with **schon** it is used with a peculiar modal force to indicate emphatically a certainty of a certain *condition* of things at the present time: A. **Ich habe es nicht.** B. **Sie werden es schon haben** A. I haven't it. B. But I know you do have it. Bäcker. **'s Bluttgericht meenen Se (meinen Sie) woll?** Dreißiger. **Er wird (for Sie werden) schon wissen, welches ich meine** (Hauptmann's *Die Weber*, Act 1). This peculiar construction must not be confounded with another having the same form, which however points with emphasis to a future *act*: **Ich werde es schon tun** I'll do it, you can count on it.

Note. Scholars generally regard this form as the usual future tense, the thought being that the future will in the case at issue show that the assumption is true. As this form is common with this meaning in dialects where it is not used as a future proper it seems more probable to the author that it is the old periphrastic present tense described in **190.** 1. C. *a. Note* 1. For centuries it had the same force as the simple present tense but finally differentiated itself from the terse forceful simple form by becoming less positive, so that **werden** came to be felt more as a *modal* than a *tense* auxiliary, and after the analogy of modal auxiliaries forms its present perfect tense in the same peculiar way that modal auxiliaries do when used in this sense, as explained in **212.** 2. *e*: **Damals wird der Hund sechs Jahre alt gewesen sein** after the analogy of **Damals kann** or **muß der Hund sechs Jahre alt gewesen sein.** Both the present and the present perfect tenses of the periphrasis are already common in Luther's language: **Da werden on zweyffel die heiligen Engel gewest sein | Denn wo der Vatter, Son, unnd heiliger Geist sich lassen sehen | da wirdt das gantze himlische heer müssen sein** (Luther's *Werke*, LII, p. 101) See 6. *a. Note* below. The old periphrastic present with **schon** naturally developed a different force in accordance with the meaning of **schon.**

c. In North German popular and colloquial language there is often used in lively narrative a form which is exactly like the future but seems in fact to rest upon the dialectic periphrasis for the present tense described in **190.** 1. C. *a. Note* 1, usually alternating with a simple historical present or some other tense that points to the past. As this form uniformly refers to the past it is evidently a historical present, if it is in fact a present: **Der Herr Schmidt hatte ja wohl so ein zwanzig oder dreißig letzten Donnerstag weggeschickt, weil sie Sozialisten waren, und das werden sich ja die andern zu Nutzen machen und von dem Herrn Schmidt einen ganz erschrecklichen Lohn fordern. Na, gnädige Fräuleins, der Herr Schmidt wird ja wohl die Rädelsführer zur Tür hinauswerfen, und die werden mit den andern in hellen Haufen wiederkommen, um den Herrn Schmidt totzuschlagen, als der Herr Kapitän in der Tür steht und**

ein paar Pistolen herauszieht; und da werden sie ja wohl Fersengeld geben! Auf dem ganzen Hof ist seit gestern keine Katze nicht mehr (Spielhagen's *Sturmflut*, p. 239). Sometimes even in choice prose in lively narrative: **Dann greift er den Kleinen am Halse und nun werden die beiden anfangen, sich mitten in der Stunde regelrecht zu hauen** (Wildenbruch's *Das edle Blut, Sämtliche Werke*, VI, p. 100).

6. *Future Perfect.* The future perfect tense represents that an action or event will be completed at or before a certain time yet future. This clumsy form has not yet become thoroly established in common usage, where, as in older periods, the present perfect is still much used: **Wenn er diese Bedingung nicht vor Morgen erfüllt haben wird** (or more commonly **erfüllt hat**), **so ist der Vertrag nichtig.** We also find the past tense instead of the future perfect, as the past is here as often elsewhere used instead of the present perfect: Hildebrant: **Wie lange soll der Jammer denn noch dauern?** Dietrich: **So lange, fürcht' ich, bis der letzte fiel** (Hebbel's *Nibelungen*, III, 5. 1). **Es ist nicht das letzte Mal, daß ich mich hier befand** (Raabe's *Frau Salome*, chap. vii). **Das Trudchen war da ganz gut aufgehoben, bis wir es abholen** (id., *Meister Autor*, chap. vii). **Viel gibt es nicht; doch nimm damit vorlieb; | wir hauen ein, bis nichts mehr übrig blieb** (Fulda's *Talisman*, 1, 5). **Wenn der Nebel verzog und die Hörner der Sachsen zum Kampf laden, so ruft mich** (Lienhard's *König Arthur*, 5). **Du wirst glücklicher sein, als du es seit Jahren warst** (Hermann Hesse's *Roßhalde*).

When the idea of completion is not prominent the future perfect can be replaced, as in oldest German, by the present, which here as in older periods still often has future force, or it may be replaced by the modern future tense: **Sobald du etwas erfährst** or **erfahren wirst, telegraphiere.**

a. Future Perfect for Reference to the Past. Tho not common in the sense of a future perfect, the future perfect form is often, on the other hand, used to express probability or supposition, to represent an action as probably finished, or to state a supposition concerning some past act, often accompanied by **wohl: Er wird jetzt wohl geschrieben haben** He has probably written by this time. **Er wird wohl der Täter gewesen sein** He was probably the perpetrator. Often in interrogative form, especially to question someone on some well-known past event in such a way as to encourage him to essay an answer: **Jakob sah, daß Getreide in Ägypten feil war. Was wird er da zu seinen Söhnen gesagt haben? Hans, in welchem Fluß wird Friedrich Rotbart den Tod gefunden haben?** In the interrogative form it also expresses wonder: **Wo wird er die Nacht zugebracht haben?** (Lessing's *Minna*, 1, 1) **I** wonder where he has passed the night. Often to indicate surprise at a preceding question which inquires about something that ought to be self-evident: **„Wo bist du gestern auf einmal hingekommen?“ „Wo werde ich hingekommen sein? Nach Haus gegangen bin ich, ausschlafen.“** (Ertl's *Freiheit*, p. 324).

Note on the Origin of the Future Perfect. Grammarians generally regard the tense form employed in these suppositions as the future perfect, but to the author this theory seems untenable, as the form is much used in dialects where the future perfect is unknown. Moreover, the oldest examples of the form, which first appear in the sixteenth century, almost uniformly point to the past, not to the future, just as in colloquial speech of to-day. Luther, whose expression was close to the language of the common people, is very fond of this colloquial form: **Es ist blut | die Könige haben sich mit dem Schwert verderbet | vnd einer wird den andern geschlagen haben** (2 Kings, III. 23). Thus the form seems to be the present perfect tense corresponding to the periphrastic present tense used in suppositions, as explained in 5. *b. Note* above. Just as in colloquial speech of to-day Luther sometimes used the same form with exactly the same force with reference to the future, which, however, is not the future perfective tense of our grammars: **Wenn du es da hyn wilt sparen und solchen glawben so unversehens und schwind uberkommen, so wirstu zu lang geharret haben** (*Werke*, XIV, p. 24) If you desire to put it (i.e. acquiring of faith) off until then (i.e. until death) and then all at once assume such (i.e. a little bit of) faith, you have probably waited too long, *not* you will have waited too long. Just as in the colloquial language of our time Luther uses the regular present perfect to express the usual future perfect idea: **Und [ich] bitt' euch gar freundlich, wenn ihr mich getödtet habt, das yhr mich ya nicht widder auff wecket** (ib. XV, p. 254). Grammarians usually regard the future perfect form with **werden** as a real future perfect with the literal value of each word of the compound as used to-day in the literary language: **In einer halben Stunde werde ich die Arbeit getan haben** In half an hour I shall have completed the work, lit. shall have the work completed. In M.H.G. in the few cases where a real future perfect occurs we find **sollen** instead of **werden. Sollen** may have been replaced here by **werden** just as in the future tense, as explained in **190.** 1. C. *a. Note* 2. Such examples as the last one are probably real future perfects, but they rarely occur except in learned speech and have nothing in common with expressions of the same form so common in colloquial and popular speech.

Mood.

166. Mood is a grammatical form denoting the style or manner of predication. There are three moods in German, the *indicative*, *subjunctive*, and *im-*

perative. These moods are used much as they are in English. In German as in English the indicative represents something as a fact or as in close relations to reality: A fact: **Die Sonne geht jeden Morgen auf** *The sun rises every morning*. In close relations to reality: **Ich gehe nicht, wenn es regnet** *I shall not go if it rains.* The indicative here in both English and German does not state that it *is* raining but indicates that the idea of rain is not a mere conception but something close to reality, for the speaker feels it as an actual problem in his day's program with which he must reckon and is reckoning. In English we sometimes use the present subjunctive here, *if it rain,* which however marks the idea of rain as a mere conception, as something not felt as close to us. In both English and German we can by the use of the past subjunctive indicate that the idea of rain seems far off and quite unreal, so that we are not reckoning with it at all: **Ich ginge nicht, wenn es regnete** *I shouldn't go if it rained.* Compare **169.** 2. E. *Note* 2 and **171.** 2. B. *f.* Grammarians are wont to talk about the sloven use of the indicative and the slighting of the subjunctive in current English and German, while in fact the increasing use of the indicative doesn't indicate carelessness but rather a change in our way of thinking. To-day we decidedly prefer to look at many things not as mere conceptions but as things near to us, as actual problems with which we must deal. The indicative is never a substitute for the subjunctive but is always felt as an indicative. Even when used as an imperative (**177.** I. B. *c*) it does not lose its old indicative character, for it represents the command as executed, the desired act as an actuality.

The imperative is discussed in **177.** I. A and B, the subjunctive in the following articles.

Subjunctive.

167. The original idea of the Germanic subjunctive may have been optative, as explained in **169.** 2. E. *Note* 5. The basal idea of the German subjunctive as employed in the historic period is to represent something as not actually belonging to the domain of fact or reality but as merely existent in the mind of the speaker as a desire, wish, volition, plan, conception, thought, statement of another, sometimes with more or less hope of realization or in case of a statement with more or less belief, sometimes with little or no hope or faith. The different uses of the subjunctive may for practical reasons be classified under two general heads, which are here only briefly outlined, but which will be treated at considerable length in the following articles: (**1**) the *optative* subjunctive, which represents the utterance as something which is desired or planned, a present tense form indicating hope of fulfilment, a past tense form indicating little or no hope of fulfilment. By using a past tense form of the subjunctive and thus indicating that one does not count upon the fulfilment of one's wish one can avoid a blunt expression of will, so that the past tense subjunctive forms often lose in large measure the element of unreality and are used to express modestly an earnest wish or appeal, where it may be called the *subjunctive of modest wish.* (**2**) The *potential* subjunctive, which represents the statement not as an actual fact but only as a conception of the mind, a present tense form indicating that the speaker or writer feels the conception as probably conforming to fact or reality, or regards the occurrence of the act in question as probable, sometimes however indicating doubt as to the matter of fact or the occurrence of the act, a past tense form indicating decided doubt as to the matter of fact and pronounced improbability as to the occurrence of the act. By clothing one's thoughts in the language of doubt and uncertainty one can avoid a blunt expression of one's opinion, so that the past tense forms of the potential subjunctive often lose in large measure the element of doubt and uncertainty and are much used to state an opinion or seek information modestly, politely, or cautiously in a less positive and abrupt way than in the indicative. This is the *polite subjunctive* or the *subjunctive of modest* or *cautious statement.* Out of the potential subjunctive there has also developed more or less clearly the subjunctive of *indirect statement*, which is employed not to represent the statement as merely conceived, but to indicate *indirectness* of statement. For illustrative examples see **168.** II. F. *c.* (**2**) and G. *a.* (**2**), 2nd par. and *b*; **169.** 2. G. *a.* (**2**), 3rd par.; **171.** 1, 2nd and 3rd par. In the following discussion this subjunctive is treated under the head of the potential with which it is closely connected. This subjunctive of indirect statement should not be confounded with the subjunctive of *indirect discourse* treated in **170** and **171,** which is a broader category including also the optative and potential ideas.

The tense employed is often a point of vital importance to the meaning, and hence instead of grouping the different uses of the subjunctive under these two leading heads the different heads are treated under the different tenses. The two following groups stand out in general quite distinctly from each other: 1. Present tense forms, namely *the present*, *present perfect*, *future perfect*, i.e. the simple present subjunctive or a compound form containing an auxiliary in the present subjunctive. 2. Past tense forms, namely the *past*, *past perfect*, *past periphrastic* (**würde loben**), and *past perfect periphrastic* (**würde gelobt haben**), i.e. the simple past subjunctive or a compound form containing an auxiliary in the past subjunctive. The different tenses within each group mark different distinctions of time, but the tenses of one group as compared with those of the other group do not mark different distinctions of *time* but differ only in the *manner* in which they represent the statement. Thus the present and the past subjunctive both denote *present* time, but they usually differ in the *manner* of the statement. Likewise the present perfect and the past perfect subjunctive both denote past time but differ in the manner of the statement. The distinctions of manner are indicated briefly above and are explained at considerable length in the following articles.

The Subjunctive of Present Tense Forms.

168. The subjunctive of present tense forms (see **167.** 2nd par.) represents the statement not as an actual fact, but yet as a desire so reasonable that it is entertained with hopes of realization, or it represents the statement as a mere conception of the mind but yet indicating that the speaker or writer feels it as probably conforming to fact or reality or regards the occurrence of the act in question as probable. The special cases under these general heads are the following:

I. *Optative Subjunctive.* A present tense form of the subjunctive is used in the following expressions of will:

1. In principal propositions:

A. *Volitive Subjunctive.* The present subjunctive is much used in decided expressions of will—the volitive subjunctive. In principal propositions it is often employed to complete the wanting forms of the imperative. See **177.** I. A.

B. *Sanguine Subjunctive of Wish.* A present subjunctive is often used to express a wish which in all probability may be realized: **Lange lebe der König** Long may the king live. **Gebe Gott** may God grant. **So sei es** Let it be thus. **Das walte Gott** May God see to it. **Geh' es Ihnen gut!** (Wilbrandt's *Die Tochter des Fabricius*, 1, 10). This wish, however, is more commonly, except in a few set expressions as the foregoing, expressed by the subjunctive of **mögen** or more modestly **wollen** with a dependent infinitive: **Möge es mir nun vergönnt sein, das Begonnene zu Ende zu führen** (Wilmanns's *Deutsche Grammatik*, Vorrede). **O teure Herrin, eher mög' ich sterben, eh' sich in meinen Busen | solch ein Gedanke dränge** (Wilamowitz-Moellendorff's *Griechische Tragödien*, I. p. 144). **Gottes Gnade wolle mit Euch sein** (Bismarck to his wife, Oct. 1, 1850). **Wollen** is often used to one's readers or listeners as a polite admonition to pay especial attention to some particular point: **Auch wolle man nicht übersehen, daß usw.** I also beg that you may not overlook the fact that, &c. Earlier in the period **müssen** was used where **mögen** is now employed and in a narrower sense it is still found in wishes as described in **213.** 4. *c*.

a. In A and B normal, or more commonly question or inverted order may stand: **Er lebe hoch!** (used in toasts and cries of approval). **Hol' ihn der Teufel!** May the devil take him! **Es lebe die Freiheit! Er möge** or **möge er vollkommen glücklich werden!** Of course the sentence has inverted order if it begins with an adverb: **Lange lebe der König!** When the force of the utterance becomes a little more vigorous and approaches a polite request with volitive force the normal order is usually employed: **Das möge nicht dahin mißverstanden werden, als sei eine bloße Hypothese von Haeckel** (name) **in unwissenschaftlicher Weise als richtig angenommen worden** (Adolf Koelsch in *Frankfurt. Zeit.*, Feb. 15, 1914).

b. Sometimes, tho much more rarely than the pres. tense, the present perfect is used in wishes. It is employed to express the wish that some desired result may be accomplished in the future: **Doch er habe | umsonst sich der Verdammnis übergeben!** (Schiller's *Jungfrau*, 2, 2) May he in vain have given himself over to perdition! **Was hier geschehn, es sei in Traum zerfallen!** (Grillparzer's *Libussa*, Act 1) May that which has happened here soon have become nothing but a dream!

C. *The Subjunctive of Logical Reasoning*. The present subjunctive is much used in logical reasoning in laying down one or more desired propositions, from which conclusions are to be drawn: **Die Figur** a b c **sei ein gleichschenkliges Dreieck;** b d **sei ein Lot auf der Grundlinie** Let the figure a b c be an isosceles triangle and b d a perpendicular line on the base, &c.

2. In subordinate clauses:

A. *Concessive Subjunctive*. The present subjunctive is used in subordinate clauses with the force of a weakened volitive to concede, grant, admit that something may be true, but the indicative in the main clause, on the other hand affirms that the assertion of the main clause is, in spite of this admission, to be maintained and defended: **Der Berg sei auch noch so hoch,** or **Sei der Berg auch noch so hoch** (or quite commonly **Ist der Berg auch noch so hoch,** or **Mag der Berg auch noch so hoch sein,** or **Der Berg mag auch noch so hoch sein), ich ersteige ihn** Be the mountain (or Altho the mountain be, or Let the mountain be) ever so high, I will climb it. **Nein, es gibt kein Wiederfinden, heiße es Himmel oder Hölle** (Wiesner's *Die schwarze Dame*). **Wo der Berg auch liege** (or quite commonly **liegen mag,** or **liegt), ich ersteige ihn. Man kann es ihm nicht recht machen, was man auch tue, tun mag,** or **tut. Welche Entscheidung auch hier gefaßt werde** (also **gefaßt werden mag,** or **gefaßt wird), sie wird niemals eine Schande sein für die Versammlung** (v. Gagern, *Frankfurter Nationalversammlung*). **Was immer du seist, ich glaube, wir werden heut nicht spielen** (Schnitzler's *Der grüne Kakadu*, p. 118). **Er komme oder komme nicht, mir ist es** (or **es ist mir**) **gleichgültig,** or **Komme er nun oder komme er nicht, mir ist es** (or **es ist mir**) **gleichgültig** Whether he comes or not, it's all the same to me. The auxiliary **können** is also used, but is not so common as **mögen: Das mag** or (here and in similar expressions, but not freely) **kann wohl wahr sein, es ändert doch nichts an der Sache.** The imperative of **lassen** is sometimes used here: **Es hat's niemand gesagt, aber laß es jemand gesagt haben,** or **laß es gesagt [worden] sein, was kümmert's mich?**

a. Note that the word-order in the concessive clause is either normal or question order, if not introduced by a conjunction, relative pronoun, or relative adverb, in which cases the transposed order is of course used. However, if the auxiliary **können** is used instead of **mögen,** normal or inverted order is usually employed. The use of the normal or question order indicates clearly that the clause was originally an independent proposition. It has retained its original form, altho it has become logically subordinate.

After a conjunction, as **obgleich,** &c., the mood is usually indicative: **Obgleich ich ihn seit langem nicht gesehen hatte, erkannte ich ihn doch augenblicklich.** Occasionally the subjunctive appears here in accordance with older usage: **Und ob die Wolke sie verhülle, die Sonne bleibt am Himmelszelt** (Weber's *Freischütz*, III, 2). In rather choice language the subjunctive of **mögen** is found instead of the indicative when the normal or question order is used: **Er will unter allen Umständen die Wahrheit wissen, möge sie lauten wie sie wolle** (Bellermann's *Schillers Dramen*, p. 226).

B. *Sanguine Subjunctive of Purpose*. This subjunctive of purpose represents the statement only as desired or planned, but implies the expectation that the desire or plan will be realized. It expresses various shades of the volitive subjunctive and the sanguine subjunctive of wish described in **1.** A and B. **It is found:**

(**1**) In object clauses after verbs of advising, beseeching, warning, wishing, willing, demanding, taking care, seeing to, &c., which of themselves indicate a purpose or design: **Sie verlangt, daß er komme** (or more commonly **kommt**), or **kommen solle** (or more commonly **soll**), but **Sie verlangte, daß er käme** or **kommen sollte. Sie bittet, daß er kommen möge,** but **Sie bat, daß er kommen möchte. Ich wünsche, daß ich in diesem ernsten Streben zur Förderung dieser Aufgabe nach meinem Teile etwas beigetragen haben möge** (Bornhak's *Grammatik der deutschen Sprache*, Vorwort). For use of tenses and auxiliaries here see **171.** 4. *a.* Compare *b* below. The idea of *willing*, &c. is often not expressed at all, but implied in the governing verb: **Und außerdem schreibst du ihm, daß er mir seine Photographie und die deiner Schwestern schicke** (Raabe's *Horn von Wanza*, chap. viii). Often in subject and attributive substantive clauses, especially where the idea of *willing*, &c. is contained in a noun: **Es ist mein Wunsch, daß er gleich komme. Meister Richwin hatte zu Hause den strengsten Befehl gegeben, daß man den Hund wohl eingesperrt halte** (Riehl's *Der stumme Ratsherr*, II).

(**2**) In adverbial clauses after other verbs, if the subordinate clause itself expresses the purpose of the action of the principal verb: **Er bindet den Baum an, damit er gerade wachse** (in choice language), or more commonly **wächst,** but **Er band den Baum an, damit er gerade wüchse.** Compare *b* below.

(**3**) In choice language also in relative clauses expressing a purpose, and in early N.H.G. after the temporal conjunctions **bis** and **ehe: Schickt einen sichern Boten ihm entgegen, der auf geheimem Weg ihn zu mir führe** (Schiller). **Und nun male einen Pfeil, der hinüberweise nach der andern Seite** (H. Hoffmann's *Wider den Kurfürsten*, chap. xxxvi) And now draw an arrow which will point to the other side. **Vmb Zion willen so will ich nicht schweigen | vnd vmb Jerusalem willen so will ich nicht inne halten | Bis das jre Gerechtigkeit aufgehe wie ein glantz | vnd jr Heil entbrenne wie eine Fackel** (Isa. lxii. 1). For **ehe** see Psalm xxxix. 14. Sometimes still in choice language after **bis,** provided the verb of the principal proposition is in a past tense, or the principal proposition is in negative or interrogative form: **Das junge Brautpaar machte heut' gewissermaßen die Honneurs des Hauses und stand wartend, bis alles Platz genommen habe** (Jensen's *Jenseits des Wassers*, V). **O Gott! Du willst nicht warten, bis die Zeit mich schuldlos spreche?** (Wilamowitz-Moellendorff's *Griechische Tragödien*, I, p. 170). Sometimes also after **ehe,** if it follows a proposition containing another optative: **O teure Herrin, eher mög' ich sterben, eh' sich in meinen Busen | solch ein Gedanke dränge** (ib. I, p. 144). Sometimes when dependent upon an imperative: **Teile ihm deinen Wunsch mit, ehe er ihn durchs Gerücht erfahre** (K. G. Andresen's *Sprachgebrauch*, p. 127). **Eh' sich dies Land dem Sieger unterwerfe** (in rime with **Schärfe**), | **stehet uns Rede, wer ihr seid!** (Sudermann's *Die drei Reiherfedern*, 2, 11).

a. This subjunctive is much used in indirect discourse after the verbs in (**1**), but it must be noticed that after a past tense it is itself often attracted into a past tense (see **169.** 1. C. *a*). Thus like the subjunctive in indirect discourse in general its form fluctuates after a past tense between that of a present tense and that of a past tense, but without any difference in meaning.

b. After the verbs and nouns in (**1**) the indicative is now in lively language, especially in the North, often employed after a present tense to indicate that the expression of will is not felt as a mere wish or intention, but as an actual factor in the situation on which the subject is counting, or the indicative is used because a wish or intention is so vividly conceived that it is felt more as an actuality, as realized, than as a mere idea: **Ich muß denn durchaus darauf bestehen, daß nichts dergleichen geschieht** (O. Ernst's *Die Kunstreise nach Hümpeldorf*, p. 25). **Ich wünsche allen von Herzen, daß jeder mit den ihm zu Gebote stehenden Mitteln geistiger und materieller Art sein Ziel erreicht** (Stilgebauer's *Götz Krafft*, I. 1). If the principal verb refers to past time, the dependent verb which has a force that is future to the subject of the main verb often in the tone of lively narrative assumes the form of the past tense: **Und diese Furcht vor den Menschen erschien ihr so natürlich, so notwendig—so zugehörig zu ihrem Schicksal. Wie konnte er verlangen, daß sie frei davon war** (H. Böhlau). **Aber dein Vater und deine Großmutter wollten nun doch einmal nicht, daß Darnekow verkauft wurde** (Enking's *Die Darnekower*, p. 52). **Nachdem wir einmal auf die mitteleuropäische Karte den Krieg gewagt hatten, hätte es unsere vornehmste Sorge sein müssen, daß das Problem „Österreich" gelöst wurde** (Dr. W.

Schotte in *Preußische Jahrbücher*, 1921, p. 1). Instead of war and wurde we more commonly find the subjunctive here, which is well preserved after a past tense, usually a past tense form according to the old sequence (**171.** 2. A), i.e. wäre in the first example and würde in the second and third examples, but often also a present tense form according to the new sequence (**171.** 2. *B*), i.e. here **sei** and **werde.** Compare **171.** 4. *a* and **169** 1. C. *a*.

The subjunctive in (**2**) has been gradually declining. At present the indicative is very often used instead of the subjunctive, especially colloquially in the North after a present tense, as the present tendency is to look forward and imagine the design as accomplished rather than to regard the statement as merely planned: **Soll ich den Gemeinen Heiderieter** (name) **zurückschicken, daß er die Alarmkanone löst?** (Frenssen's *Die drei Getreuen*, chap. i). **Sie möchte etwas recht Hübsches sagen, damit man freundlich mit ihr ist** (H. Böhlau). **Es wär' doch gut, wenn er es bald erfährt, damit ihm der Mund gestopft ist** (Hirschfeld's *Agnes Jordan*, 5). If the principal verb refers to past time, the dependent verb which has a force that is future to the subject of the main verb often in the tone of lively narrative assumes the form of the past tense: **Da begannen die Menschen des Ackers zu warten, damit er ihnen im Herbst ihre Nahrung und Notdurft gab** (Enking's *Die Darnekower*, p. 162) (instead of gäbe). **Die Rambergs, deine lieben Vettern und Vormünder, haben die Traute an Grobitzsch verkuppelt. Einfach verkuppelt — nach allen Regeln der Kunst — jawohl! — damit du frei wurdest und dich verloben konntest** (Hartleben's *Rosenmontag*, 2, 7). Instead of **wurdest** and **konntest** we more commonly find the subjunctive here, which is well preserved after a past tense, usually a past tense form according to the old sequence (**171.** 2. A), i.e. here **würdest** and **könntest,** but often also a present tense form according to the new sequence (**171.** 2. B), i.e. here **werdest** and **könnest.** Compare **169.** 1. C. *a*.

The subjunctive in (**3**) is now largely replaced by the indicative in colloquial language, as the things in question are now not felt as mere conceptions of the mind but as actual factors in the situation which must be considered and dealt with.

C. *Optative in Conditions.* The optative subjunctive occurs here in two forms:

a. Instead of a subordinate clause with **wenn** we may use a clause with a volitive subjunctive, which has normal order and was originally independent, but has become logically subordinate: **Einer trage des andern Last | so werdet jr das gesetz Christi erfüllen** (Gal. vi. 2). **Bald, es kenne nur jeder den eigenen, gönne dem andern | seinen Vorteil, so ist ewiger Friede gemacht** (Goethe's *Vier Jahreszeiten*, 74).

b. A volitive subjunctive often stands in a proviso after **nur daß** *but let it be, on condition that*: **Ich seh' es gern, das steht dir frei, nur daß die Kunst gefällig sei** (Goethe's *Faust*, Studierzimmer).

D. *Optative in Relative Clauses.* This subjunctive is found in the following groups:

a. *Volitive Subjunctive.* A relative clause often contains a volitive subjunctive, which is translated into English by *we wish, it is desired,* &c. **Von dem Erbeschen Heftchen: „Verdeutschung der Kunstausdrücke in der Schule" ist ein Neudruck notwendig geworden und wird demnächst ausgegeben, worauf alle Mitglieder und Freunde des Allgemeinen deutschen Sprachvereins aufmerksam gemacht seien** *to which we especially desire to call the attention of all the members,* &c.

b. A sanguine subjunctive of wish is also used here to express a wish: **unser König, den Gott erhalte** *our king, whom, we pray, God may keep.* Also in clauses with reference to the thought in another clause: **Was würden wir tun, wenn — was Gott verhüte** (or **verhüten möge**) **— ein Unglück geschehen sollte?** If some misfortune should occur—which, however, I hope God may prevent—what should we do? More modestly with **wollen: So vertrauen wir der ewigen Allmacht, die unsere Abwehr stärken und zu gutem Ende lenken wolle** (Emperor William II to the Reichstag Aug. 4, 1914).

c. For a subjunctive of purpose in relative clauses see B. (**3**) above.

E. *Optative in Substantive Clauses*:

a. The volitive subjunctive not infrequently occurs in substantive clauses as already described in part in B. (**1**) above:

(**1**) In subject clauses: **Es ist billig, daß man ihn unterstütze** (= **man unterstütze ihn** *let the people help him*) *It is fair that the people help him.* **Es geziemt dem Manne, daß er auch das Schwerste willig tue** (= **er tue auch das Schwerste willig**). **Das Geringste ist, daß der Rechtsunterricht von dieser Fessel befreit werde** (*Hamburger Nachrichten*, Jan. 19, 1905) The least that should be done is that, &c. The indicative to emphasize the necessity of fulfilment: **Das Wichtigste ist, daß das Vertrauen zu uns wieder hergestellt wird** (Kurt Eisner, speech Nov. 30, 1918).

(2) In object clauses: **Er verdient es, daß man ihn unterstütze,** but to express a simple fact: **daß man ihn unterstützt.**

b. Sanguine Subjunctive of wish:

(1) In subject clauses: **Daß du an unserer Freude teilnehmest, ist unser inniger Wunsch. Mein letzter Wunsch aber ist: möge das ungemein reiche Buch recht eifrig benutzt werden!** (Otto Weidenmüller in *Die Neueren Sprachen,* 1916, p. 186).

(2) In object clauses: **Seine Persönlichkeit und seine Vergangenheit verdienen es, daß sein Gedächtnis lebendig bleibe** (*Hamb. Nachr.,* Nov. 10, 1904).

F. *Optative in Adverbial Clauses.* This subjunctive is occasionally used here in categories other than those previously described, especially after **so wahr** and **so** (= **wenn**): **In meinen Armen will ich dich durch das Leben tragen, so wahr Gott mir helfe** (Raabe's *Die Leute aus dem Walde,* chap. x). **Nein, nein, so Gott mir helfe** (Storm's *Chronik von Grieshuus,* p. 110).

II. *Potential Subjunctive.*

The potential subjunctive of present tense forms represents the statement as a mere conception, but yet as something which is quite probable, plausible, supposable, or as credible, but yet as only resting upon the testimony of others, or upon the subjective view of the speaker. This potential must not be confounded with the *unreal potential* (see **169.** 2) of past tense forms, which represents on the other hand the statement as barely possible, quite doubtful, or even as in conflict with fact or impossible. In the present period of the language the tendency is to observe this distinction between the subjunctive of present tense forms and that of past tense forms; but, as will be seen below, there are still many survivals of an earlier usage, which always, irrespective of the meaning, required, as at present in English, a past tense form of the subordinate verb, whenever it depended upon a past tense form: **Er sagte, er sei krank,** or often placing the tense of the subordinate clause in accord with that of the principal clause: **Er sagte, er wäre krank.** The thought in both of these sentences is exactly the same, but in other sentences a sharp distinction is often made between present and past of the subjunctive, the former expressing a probability, the latter an improbability of the truth of the statement. The tendency to distinguish between present and past tense forms of the subjunctive is stronger than the tendency to place the tense of the subordinate verb in accord with the tense of the principal verb, but as this growing tendency has not yet gained a complete victory, there is some confusion.

The potential subjunctive of present tense forms is now only employed in subordinate clauses, but it has nevertheless a wide field of usefulness, as will be seen in the following detailed statement of its uses:

A. *Subjunctive in Indirect Discourse.* The potential subjunctive of present tense forms is used in indirect discourse after verbs of *saying, thinking, feeling,* &c., to represent the indirect statement in the subordinate clause not as an actual fact, but only as a conception, as something conceived as probable or plausible by the speaker or writer, thus sometimes indicating his own individual opinion or feeling, sometimes, however, suggesting a doubt in his mind: **Titus pflegte zu sagen, der Tag, an welchem er nichts Gutes tue, sei für ihn verloren. Ich zweifle noch, ob er der rechte Mann hierfür sei.**

This subjunctive often differs markedly from other forms of the potential, as it is frequently no longer a potential pure and simple, but is often merely a grammatical form to express *indirectness* of statement. See G. *a.* (**2**), 2nd par., and *b* below. The subjunctive in this use has a broad field, not being confined to one grammatical category, and hence may reappear in a number of the following groups. It should, however, be carefully noticed that this subjunctive may not only differ in each category from the other potential in the same category in its lack of real potential character, but also in its much greater frequency of use, as it has become very productive in its employment as a formal indication of indirect statement.

This use of the subjunctive and the similar use in indirect questions are the most common in the language, and are treated at considerable length in **171–173.**

B. *Clauses of Manner.* The potential subjunctive is very much used in these clauses to indicate that the comparison rests upon plausible grounds, or is the subjective view of the speaker: **Es scheint mir, als ob er früher nicht fleißig gewesen sei, als ob er jetzt aber recht fleißig sei. Es war ihm, als höre er noch einmal durch den Regen und Wind den Nachtwächter von Wanza in der Ferne die Stunde rufen** (Raabe's *Horn von Wanza*, chap. xi). **Mir war zuweilen, als sei ich von unserm lieben Gott geschieden** (Freytag's *Rittmeister*, chap. ix) It seemed to me sometimes as if I were separated from God and his goodness. As according to **276.** A (2nd par.) such clauses are now felt as indirect discourse the conjunction **als** here is often omitted after the analogy of dropping **daß** in indirect discourse: **Ihm war, er höre einen zarten Engel weinen** (E. von Handel-Mazzetti's *Stephana Schwertner*, II, chap. IV).

a. This use of the subjunctive must not be confounded with the unreal potential of a past tense form, which implies that the comparison is unreal and contrary to fact. See **169.** 2. B.

b. As in indirect discourse, as explained in **171.** 2. B. *a*, a past tense form of the subjunctive is usually employed here if the present tense form is not distinguished from the indicative. Thus if the subjunctive in the sentence from Raabe were in the first person we should have to say: **Es war mir, als hörte ich usw.** Writers from the Southwest, however, employ also here present tense forms: **Er sah mich verwundert an, als ob ich irre rede und Fabeln erzähle** (K. F. Meyer's Novellen, I. p. 199). Compare **171.** 2. B. *a. Note.*

C. *Plausible Subjunctive of Result in Attributive Relative Clauses.* The indicative denotes an actual result, represents an act as actually taking place. The subjunctive of result represents the result or act as conceived by the speaker or writer rather than as actually taking place. In the attributive relative clause there are two categories:

a. The present subjunctive indicates a result that naturally follows from the character of a person or thing, so that the relative pronoun may be replaced by **von der Art daß er** (**sie, es**), but it represents this result not as actually taking place, but as only conceived, i.e. as something which *may* or *can* take place, in English usually rendered by *may* or *can*: **Nichts ist, das die Gewaltigen hemme** (Schiller). **Nimmer findet er den Heil'gen, der an ihm ein Wunder tu'** (Uhland). The subjunctive here is most common after a negative but it also occurs after a positive statement: **Ich will Auskunft erteilen, wie man ein Deutsch reden und schreiben soll, das vor dem Urteil der Sprachkundigen als richtig und gut bestehe** (E. Engel's *Gutes Deutsch*, p. 10, 1918). The present subjunctive here, tho a little earlier in the period quite common and still found in choice prose, is now usually replaced, on the one hand, by the indicative to represent the result confidently as taking place, or, on the other hand, by a past tense form of the subjunctive to indicate modestly that the result *might* possibly take place, implying that it does take place. Compare **169. 2. C.**

b. The present subjunctive indicates a result that follows from a free act or a combination of circumstances, but represents it not as actually taking place but as only conceived: **Keiner ist, der noch aufrecht stehe, als ich ganz allein** (Hans Hoffmann's *Rittmeister*, II, p. 203). **Mir ist kein Volk bekannt, das die Sprachreinigung so entschieden und entschlossen verteidige, das dem Fremdworttaumel so unentwegt und mit so großem Erfolge zu Leibe gehe, wie das dänische** (E. Mogk in *Sprachentwickelung und Sprachbewegung bei den nordgermanischen Völkern*, 1897). **So denkt der junge Mann und im Überschwang des Glücks suchte er jemand, der ihm helfe seine Gedanken tragen** (Heer's *Der König der Bernina*, VII). **Und alles, was kommen mag, nehm' ich auf mich — alles, was daraus erwachse, Segen oder Unsegen!** (Frida Schanz's *Letzte Botschaft*). The present subjunctive here, tho still used in choice language, is now largely replaced, as in *a*, by the present indicative or a past tense form of the subjunctive.

D. *Plausible Subjunctive of Result in Adverbial Clauses.* The usual mood in clauses of result is the indicative as the statement is felt as a fact, but in choice language a present tense form of the subjunctive is often chosen to indicate that the result is in an accurate sense conceived rather than actually attained: **Und will meine Erfahrungen so stellen, daß meine Arbeit andern nicht ganz unnütz bleibe** (Goethe's *Briefe*, 13, 18, 6). The most common categories in which this subjunctive occurs are here briefly described:

a. After **als daß** preceded by **zu** + the positive of an adjective or adverb: **Die Erklärung ist viel zu weitläuftig, als daß sie bei Entscheidung der vorhabenden Streitsache im geringsten zu brauchen sei** (Lessing). The present subjunctive is now usually replaced here by the indicative or a past tense form of the subjunctive: **Er ist zu reich, als daß er Sold nimmt** or **nähme** (Wilmanns). **Er war zu reich, als daß er Sold nahm** or **genommen hätte,** or **Er ist** or **war zu reich, um Sold zu nehmen.**

b. After **als daß** preceded by the comparative of an adjective or adverb: **Der ungeduldige Genius unsres Zeitalters bricht lieber herbe Früchte, als daß er ihre Reife abwarte** (Herder). **Wir alle wissen, daß in gegebener Lage der Offizier, der Soldat lieber blindlings kühn den ersten Schritt tun soll und muß, als daß er hin und her erwäge: soll ich oder soll ich nicht?** (Liliencron's *Krieg und Frieden*). In general, the indicative or a past tense form of the subjunctive is more common here.

c. After **daß nicht, ohne daß** (subjunctive more common after a negative than after an affirmative statement), earlier in the period also **geschweige daß** (**238.** 3. C. *d*): **Er kehret nie | von einer Reise wieder, daß ihm nicht | ein Dritteil seiner Sachen fehle** (Goethe's *Tasso*, 3, 4). **Die Alte hatte, um sich nach dem Tode des Mannes, ohne daß sie dem Dorf zur Last falle, durchzubringen, einen kleinen Kramhandel angelegt** (Wilhelm Jensen's *Auf Fanö und Manö*, I). **Aber eine Kultur von solcher Größe bricht nicht zusammen, ohne daß aus ihren Trümmern neues Leben erblühe** (Eduard Norden's *Die lateinische Literatur im Übergang zum Mittelalter*, Einleitung). **Er sagt weder, wie es heißt, noch wer der Verfasser desselben sei, geschweige daß er es für das rührendste von allen Stücken des Euripides erkläre** (Lessing). The present indicative or a past tense form of the subjunctive is now more common here.

d. After verbs modified by **so.** The sentence from Goethe in D above is a good example. The present indicative is now more common here, but a past tense form of the subjunctive is also used.

e. After **so** or **solch** + adjective or adverb: **Ich bitte Ew. Gnaden, es auf eine so behutsame Art zu tun, daß er nicht merken könne, daß ich ihn verraten habe** (Wieland). **Hältst du mich für so schwach, daß solch ein Fall mich gleich zerrütten könne?** (Goethe). The present indicative or a past tense form of the subjunctive is now more common here.

f. Earlier in the period a present subjunctive could be used in a clause of pure result (**276.** D): **So wird mirs gehen | das mich todschlage wer mich findet** (Gen. IV. 14).

E. *Probable Conditions.* In most conditions that are represented as probable the indicative is now used as in English, as the conceptions that are busying the mind of the speaker or writer, tho mere conceptions, are nevertheless felt by him as real factors in life with which he must reckon: **Ich gehe nicht, wenn es regnet** I shall not go if it rains.

The subjunctive is used in probable conditions in the following categories:

a. Subjunctive in Exceptions after a Negative Proposition. In early N.H.G. a present subjunctive was much used in clauses introducing an exception to a preceding or following negative statement: **Vnd so jemand auch kempffet | wird er doch nicht gekrönet | er kempffe denn recht** (2 Tim. II. 5). The subjunctive is usually accompanied by the adverb **denn,** which in earlier periods when the clause was negative in form was not absolutely necessary but which now is the distinctive mark of this old construction, altho it need not be rendered into English. The clause is now positive in form in German but is negative in English, where it is introduced by *if not, unless.* This clause of exception with positive form was not infrequent in the classical period and still occasionally occurs in poetry or choice prose: **Und kommt man hin, um etwas zu erhalten, | erhält man nichts, man bringe denn was hin** (Goethe's *Tasso,* 1, 4). **Wohin er (i.e. Gott) uns stellt, da müssen wir ausharren, er rufe uns denn selber ab** (Spielhagen's *Freigeboren,* p. 176). **Einmütig erklärte man von seiten der Städte, keine Reichssteuern bewilligen zu wollen, es sei denn die Aachener Beschwerde vorher erledigt** (Lamprecht's *Deutsche Geschichte,* V, p. 661). **Es ist, als trügen sie tief im Herzen eine goldene Saite, die nicht klingen kann, es rühre sie denn der Finger der Schwesterseele** (H. von Krause's *Sein Geheimnis* in *Westermanns Monatshefte,* March 1905, p. 804). The present subjunctive is replaced here by the past to convey the idea of unreality, improbability: **Die Nürenberger henken** (in the North **hängen**) **keinen, | sie hätten ihn denn vor** (Schiller's *Räuber,* 2, 3).

This old construction is not now common in plain prose except in **es sei denn** or **es wäre denn** *unless* and in case of **müssen** with a dependent infinitive. The two expressions **es sei denn** and **es wäre denn** differ from each other just as in general the present subjunctive differs from the past subjunctive. The former expresses more assurance: **Ich werde es nicht tun, es sei denn, daß er mich darum bitte** (or **bittet**) I shall not do it unless he begs me to [do it], but **Ich werde es nicht tun, es wäre denn, daß er mich darum bitten sollte** I shall not do it unless he should beg me to [do it]. The expression **es wäre denn daß** is often replaced by the subjunctive of **müssen** with a dependent infinitive, the past subjunctive of **müssen** for present or future time and the past perfect for past time: **Das werde ich nie von ihm glauben, er müßte es mir denn selbst sagen. Sie hing süßen Fragen und Vorstellungen nach, denn Elimar hatte beim Blindekuh, als er sie haschte, Worte fallen lassen, die nicht mißdeutet werden konnten, er hätte denn ein schändlicher und zweizüngiger Lügner sein müssen** (Fontane's *L'Adultera,* chap. VIII). The construction **es sei** (or **wäre**) **denn daß** arose in this category but it now belongs to *c* below. The forms are now little more than a subordinating conjunction like English *unless.* The original construction was an independent proposition and hence was paratactic (**267.** 4), while the new form introduces a subordinate clause. The new construction is now more common, as the **sei** and **wäre** are always clear subjunctives, while the old construction often does not have distinctive forms: **Ich werde es nicht tun, es sei denn daß sie mich darum bitten,** not **Ich werde es nicht tun, sie bitten mich denn darum.** The construction with **müssen** is the old paratactic construction, but it is still widely used when there is need of a past tense form as its form is distinctive, but it can't be used at all in the present tense.

The subjunctive of the simple verb as found in the first examples given above represents the utterance not as an actuality, but as a mere conception of the mind, but the positive form and meaning of the clause sometimes leads to the use of the indicative instead of the subjunctive, especially in lively language where the action is represented as having actually taken place: **Ich laß nicht ab, ihr gebt den Gefangenen denn heraus** (Grillparzer). **„Ich lasse dich nicht fort, Ansas," rief sie, „du sagst mir denn, was du im Sinn hast"** (Wichert's *Ansas und Grita*). Even in case of the verb **sein** we find the indicative for the expression of reality: **Der Arzt hatte nie in ihrem Hause zu schaffen, es war denn, daß er bei der Ankunft eines neuen Weltbürgers zugegen war** (Telmann). The positive form here is explained in *Note* below.

Note. In O.H.G. and usually in the classical period of M.H.G. the clause here has negative form: **Des sint ir iemer** ungenesen | got enwelle der arzat wesen (*Armer Heinrich,* Heidelberg manuscript) You cannot be cured unless God be the physician. The second proposition here is an independent utterance joined to the preceding independent statement to add a qualification to it. As it is not a statement of fact but a mere conception of the mind the subjunctive is used. As the two negative statements indicate a positive issue, the actual performance of the act mentioned in the second proposition, the old negative en or ne began in the classical period of M.H.G. to drop out and later entirely disappeared. Sometimes the subjunctive is in lively style replaced by the indicative to indicate actual realization, as illustrated above. Exactly the same development has taken place in negative clauses of result following a negative proposition, both in clauses of degree expressing a result (**277.** 2) and those of manner (**276.** D, 4th par.): Nieman lebt so starker, ern (= er en) müeze ligen tot (*Nibelungenlied*) **Niemand ist so stark, daß er nicht sterben muß.** The result here is represented as a mere conception of the mind, hence the subjunctive is used. The clause of result is an independent proposition added to the preceding negative statement to explain it more definitely: No one is *so* strong, i.e. he doesn't die. To-day such clauses of result are usually dependent clauses introduced by a subordinating conjunction with negative force, **daß nicht, ohne daß,** etc., but in lively poetic style the old paratactic (**267.** 4) construction without a conjunction still lives on in somewhat modified form. The subjunctive has been replaced by the indicative and the negative has disappeared as the result is felt as positive and as realized: **Es ist kein Mensch so arg, Er hat etwas gutts an sich** (Luther's *Vom Krieg wider die Türken*, vol. XXX, Section II, p. 127, Weimar ed.). **Kein Becher ward geleert, du hattest ihn | gefüllt, kein Brot gebrochen und verteilt, | es kam aus deinem Korb** (Hebbel's *Nibelungen*, III, 5, 9). The dropping of the negative in exceptions after a negative spread to unreal conditions in the peculiar expression **täte er,** or **wenn er täte = wenn er nicht wäre,** which was once widely used in Low German and for a time established itself in the literary language: **Was were fur ein Königreich in Israel wenn du thetest?** (1. Kings, XXI. 7) = **wenn du nicht wärest.** The conditions in this category, however, are quite different from those described above, hence the feeling for the negative idea present here revived the use of the negative, **wenn er nicht täte,** which maintained itself until it disappeared in the eighteenth century.

b. Subjunctive in Exceptions after a Positive Proposition. This usage, once common, is now restricted to the form **sei** in **es sei denn daß** *unless*: **Meine Untersuchung hat dargetan, daß . . . die Stämme, die derselben Mundart zugetan sind, auch seit uralter Zeit unmittelbar nebeneinander wohnen, es sei denn, daß besondere Anlässe einen Strahl des Volkes voraussprengten** (Grimm's *Geschichte der deutschen Sprache*, II. 609). The form is here positive, but it is negative in force as the form has retained the meaning of its older negative form. It is now a mere set expression, a conjunction with negative force. The positive form has arisen under the influence of the **sei** in *a.*

c. Hypotactic Form of a. The old paratactic construction in *a* is now usually, also not infrequently in M.H.G., replaced by a hypotactic (**267.** 4) form of expression, i.e. by a present subjunctive in a subordinate clause introduced by **es sei denn daß** *unless*: **ODer | wie kan jemand in eines starcken haus gehen | vnd jm seinen Hausrat rauben | Es sey denn | das er zuuor den Starcken binde** (Matth. XII. 29). **Direkt einzugreifen hat es kaum eine Veranlassung, es sei denn, daß es sich darum handle, die mit Bezug auf Korea vorhandenen Handelsrechte zu wahren** (*Deutsche Rundschau*, 1894, p. 273). The indicative might be used here but it would suggest a greater probability of realization. See also *a* (2nd par.). Instead of a subordinate clause here we often find a principal proposition, i.e. paratactic form: **es sei denn, es handle** (or **handelt**) **sich darum, die usw.**

d. Present subjunctive after **außer** *unless, except that,* **als daß** *except that* in clauses following a negative proposition: **Ich tue es nicht, außer er bitte** (act only conceived) **mich darum,** or **außer er bittet** (actual performance) **mich darum. So bleibt wohl nichts übrig, als daß man seine Kräfte zusammennehme** (Goethe), or now more commonly **zusammennimmt** or **zusammennähme.**

F. *Plausible Subjunctive in Relative and Interrogative Clauses*:

a. In attributive relative and interrogative clauses. Usage in attributive relative clauses is described in C. *a, b.* A present tense of the subjunctive, tho quite common here a little earlier in the period, is now rare and only found in choice language. It is, however, still the rule, if the relative clause is part of an indirect statement, even tho the governing substantive itself does not stand in a subjunctive clause with the outward form of indirect discourse: **Die Regierung der Vereinigten Staaten beschwerte sich über die Landung sovieler Armen, welche manche europäische Regierung fortschicke.**

Interrogative clauses are introduced by **ob** *whether*, or some interrogative adjective or adverb: **Die Frage, wie er zu dieser Auffassung komme, verblüffte ihn.** The subjunctive here, i.e. in indirect questions, is quite common.

b. In substantive relative clauses:

(1) As subject or predicate. As subject: **Komme, wer wolle, ich bin nicht zu Hause.** As predicate: **Und wer der Dichtkunst Stimme nicht vernimmt, | ist ein Barbar, er sei auch, wer er sei.** This subjunctive is only found in a few set expressions where the governing verb is in the optative (especially the concessive) subjunctive.

(2) As object: in a few set expressions after a concessive subjunctive: **er sage, was er wolle. Es koste, was es wolle.** Also occasionally elsewhere: **der aufkeimende Trieb der Liebe findet, was er ergreife** (Schiller's *Menschenfeind*, scene 8) love springing up like a shoot finds something to which it may cling. Except after the concessive subjunctive the past subjunctive is more common here.

c. In substantive interrogative clauses. This subjunctive is very common in clauses introduced by **ob** *whether*, or some interrogative pronoun or adverb:

(**1**) As subject: **Wer den Brief abgesandt habe, ist noch nicht ermittelt worden.**

(**2**) As object of a verb or a preposition: **Ich habe gezweifelt, ob man dem Herrn Cramer ein poetisches Genie zugestehen könne** (Lessing).

The subjunctive in (**1**) and (**2**) is often not the pure potential, but a mere grammatical form for the expression of an indirect question, and hence may stand after such words as **sehen** *to see*, **vernehmen** *to learn*, **wissen** *to know*, &c., the meanings of which naturally preclude the idea of doubt: **Du siehst, wie ungeschickt in diesem Augenblick ich sei** (Goethe). **Wenigstens würden sie dort wissen, wohin er sich gewendet habe** (P. Heyse). **Als er in wenigen vorläufigen Worten vernahm, worum es sich handle** (*what the business was about*, a matter of fact, but subjunctive on account of the indirectness of the form), **ordnete er an, daß**, &c. (G. Keller's *Kleider machen Leute*). See also G. *a.* (**2**), 2nd par.

G. *Plausible Subjunctive in Substantive* **Daß-** *Clauses.* This subjunctive is not infrequently used, especially in choice language, to represent something as a mere conception of the mind but yet as something which is probably true, or to indicate that the event or result in question is not altogether unlikely. The **daß** here may sometimes be suppressed. This subjunctive is often replaced by the past as described in **169.** 2. G. *a.* (**1**), (**2**). Of course the indicative is used if it is desired to represent the statement as a fact. This subjunctive is used in the following relations:

a. In subject and object clauses:

(**1**) As subject: **Denn es ist vnmüglich | das Gott liege (199,** 2. Division, 4) (Heb. vi. 18). **Denn es geschieht, daß vor Gott ein Ackersmann besser tue mit seinem Pflügen, denn eine Nonne mit ihrer Keuschheit** (Luther). **Es ist fast unmöglich, daß er die Abgeschmacktheit ganzer Seiten und Bogen nicht einsehe** (G. Keller). **Unter solchen Umständen war es ausgeschlossen, daß Friedrich den Dienst verlasse** (Suttner's *Die Waffen nieder!*, III). **Aber daß ein siegreiches Japan den Spruch „Asien den Asiaten" auf die Fahnen schreiben werde, das ist sicherlich zu gewärtigen** (*Neue Zürcher Zeit.*, Dec. 13, 1904). **Eine seiner fixen Ideen war, daß sein Sohn ihn unterdrücke** (Sudermann's *Frau Sorge*, chap. XIX). A subjective view is often introduced by **als** or **als ob: Leicht könnte der Schlußeindruck der sein, als bestehe die vielverbreitete Meinung von Nietzsches lediglich negativem Wirken zu recht** (Richard M. Meyer in *Zeitschrift für deutsche Wortforschung*, XV, p. 144). The subjunctive is common where it is felt as logically dependent upon some verb of believing. expecting, &c. as in the example from the "Neue Zürcher Zeit.", or wherever the subject clause explains a preceding noun, as in case of **fixe Ideen** in the next to the last sentence and **Schlußeindruck** in the last example, for the statement is felt as a form of indirect discourse. Elsewhere the present subjunctive, tho not infrequent in choice language, is now usually replaced in colloquial speech by the indicative, as the statement is felt as a fact, or if not as a fact at least a general truth, or where the act is not even certain is felt as a practical factor in daily life with which one must reckon rather than as a mere conception, as in **Es ist möglich, daß es morgen regnet,** or **Besser [ist] du läßt es.** On the other hand, a past tense form of the subjunctive is quite common here to indicate modestly or cautiously that the statement is at least conceivable and is probably true. See **169.** 2. G. *a.* (**1**).

(**2**) Object clauses. As object of a verb or a preposition: **Wenige Menschen können leiden, daß man sie auf ihre Fehler aufmerksam mache** (not a definite case but merely a general conception). **Er billigt es nicht, daß Marie allein geht** (a fact, a fixed plan), but **Er billigt es nicht, daß Marie allein gehe** (a mere conception which has not crystalized into a fixed plan). Where a prepositional object clause explains a preceding anticipative prepositional adverb the subjunctive is often used, as the statement is in a certain sense felt as a kind of indirect discourse, the clause explaining a preceding word as in the very common type of indirect discourse in *b* below: **Mein Glück hängt davon ab, daß dein Unternehmen gut vonstatten gehe** (or **geht** to indicate that the speaker is actually reckoning with this issue as a factor in his life rather than regarding it as a mere conception). Similarly in an adverbial clause of degree that explains a preceding anticipative demonstrative adverb: **Zunächst einigte man sich wenigstens so weit, daß an der vierjährigen Dauer der Grundschule unbedingt festgehalten werden solle** (*Berliner Tageblatt*, June 14, 1921). Sometimes as the object of an adjective: **Es ist wert, daß man einige Bemerkungen darüber mache** (Goethe, to whom the statement was a conception), or now more commonly **macht**, as the statement is felt as a fact.

The subjunctive in (**1**) and (**2**) is often not the pure potential, but a mere grammatical form for the expression of indirect statement, and hence may stand after such verbs as **beweisen** *to prove*, **melden, verkündigen** *to announce*, **sehen, ansehen** *to see*, **überzeugen** *to convince*, **versichern** *to assure*, **wissen** *to know*, **zeigen** *to show*, &c., likewise after such adjectives as **sicher**, &c., the meanings of which naturally preclude the idea of doubt: **Also hab ich mit unsern alten Liedern bewiesen, daß allein der Glaub' an Jesum Christum selig mach'** (Alberus, 1539). **Verkündet ihr, daß ich gerettet sei** (Schiller's *Wilhelm Tell*, 4, 3). **Die junge Frau war überzeugt, daß alles den Krebsgang gehe, solange sie hier liege und sich pflege** (Anna Schieber's *Alle guten Geister*, p. 28). **Er wußte wohl, daß sein Werk getan sei** (ib., p. 272). **Man ist sicher, daß Rußland infolge der überaus großen Schärfe der österreichischen Note einem bewaffneten Eingreifen Österreichs nicht untätig zusehen werde** (*Vorwärts*, July 25, 1914). **Ich war zugleich erheitert und entzückt, zumal der Vogel nach kurzer Pause zeigte, daß sein Reichtum noch lange nicht erschöpft sei** (H. Seidel's *Der Neuntöter*).

b. In attributive clauses: **Meine Herren, wir müssen uns den Fall vergegenwärtigen, daß die eine oder die andere Regierung nicht auf alle Bedingungen eingehe** (*Vorparlament*, p. 63). In one form of this clause this subjunctive is now very common—in indirect discourse: **ein eigenes Gefühl: er müsse den Ort kennen lernen** (Hirschfeld's *Dämon Kleist*). **Sie glaubten mich mit der Nachricht zu überraschen, daß ich schwindsüchtig sei** (ib.). Similarly in attributive clauses explaining a preceding prepositional adverb: **Sein Verzicht darauf, daß er zuerst rede, hat allgemein befriedigt.** The potential idea often disappears, the subjunctive not implying uncertainty, but merely indicating indirectness of statement: **Mein ganzer Feldzugsplan . . . fiel in sich zusammen vor der süßen Gewißheit, daß sie mich liebe** (Paul Keller's *Waldwinter*, XIV).

To express the idea of mere subjectivity or plausibility **als** (with question order) or **als ob** or **als wenn** (with transposed order) is often used instead of **daß**: **Die (die Rede) macht ganz den Eindruck, als ob es sich um ein abgekartetes Spiel handle** (*Hamburgischer Correspondent*, April 23, 1905). Compare **169.** 2. G. *b* (2nd par.) Where the comparison is made in quite a positive tone the indicative is also used here: **Trotzdem gewinnt es den Anschein, als ob die auswärtige Politik Englands auch nach dem Rücktritte Lord Salisburys von Fehlschlägen heimgesucht wird** (*Deutsche Rundschau*). See also **238.** 2. *d. Note*.

Note. Sometimes **falls** *if, in case that* is used with a present subjunctive in a conditional clause: **Ordnen Sie an — falls jemand komme — daß er nicht vorgelassen werde** (Suttner's *Im Berghause*, p. 47). The conjunction **falls** is derived from the noun **Fall** *case* and can be replaced by **im Falle daß** or **für den Fall daß**. The subjunctive here is thus the subjunctive of indirect discourse, as it originated in attributive substantive clauses after **Fall**.

The Subjunctive of Past Tense Forms.

169. The subjunctive of past tense forms (see **167,** 2nd par.) is used to represent that which is wished for without much hope of realization, also that which is conceived as quite doubtful, contrary to fact, or that which merely exists in the imagination, or rests upon appearances without foundation in facts. This subjunctive is used both in principal and subordinate clauses. It has only two tenses—the past to express present time, the past perf. to express past time: (pres. time) **Er sieht aus, als ob er krank wäre** He looks as if he were sick; (past time) **Er sieht aus, als ob er krank gewesen wäre** He looks as if he had been sick. The past subjunctive often points also to the future, as is usually made clear by the context: **Wenn ich so einen Mann haben sollte, der sich immer Gefahren aussetzte, ich stürbe im ersten Jahr** (Goethe's *Götz*, 1, 3). In conditional sentences (see 2. E below) in principal propositions, the simple past subjunctive can be replaced by the periphrastic past (**würde loben**), and the past perf. by the periphrastic past perfect (**würde gelobt haben**). In S.G. and with increasing frequency elsewhere the simple past subjunctive is thus also in subordinate clauses replaced by the periphrastic form, altho the practice is frequently condemned by grammarians. The case mentioned in 2. E. *Note* 3 below will serve in general as an illustration and partial justification of this forbidden construction, which is now often found not only in conditional, but also in optative and concessive clauses and clauses of manner and elsewhere, as indicated below. See 1. A. *a*; 1. B. *a*; 1. C. *b*; 2. B. *a* and D. *a* below, and **190.** 1. E. *a*.

This subjunctive often loses the element of unreality and is used merely to make a statement in a less positive tone than is expressed by the indicative, and hence is often called the subjunctive of modest or cautious statement. The especial cases are mentioned below under the different categories.

The following are the principal groups of this subjunctive:

1. The Unreal Optative:

A. The *unreal subjunctive of wish* is used in principal propositions to express a wish of the heart but one which under the circumstances the speaker scarcely hopes to see realized. In these wishes the question order is the rule, and the subjunctive is often accompanied by the adverb **doch**: **Käme er doch!** If he would only come! Past time: **Wäre er doch gekommen!** If he had only come! It is also common to put such optative sentences in the transposed order in the form of a subordinate clause introduced by **daß, wenn,** and the conditional relative **wer** (**159**), as explained in **284.** I. 3. *a*: **O daß ich das Glück hätte, einen von euch bei mir zu haben! Wenn er doch noch lebte! Eilende Wolken! Segler der Lüfte! Wer mit euch wanderte, mit euch schiffte!** (Schiller's *Maria*, 2098).

The subjunctive of the simple verb is often replaced by the subjunctive of **wollen, mögen,** or **können** with a dependent infinitive: **Möchte er doch endlich zur Besinnung kommen! Ach, könnte ich euch doch nur einmal besuchen!**

By using a past tense of the subjunctive and thus indicating that one does not count upon the fulfilment of one's wish one can avoid a blunt expression of will, so that the past tense subjunctive forms often lose in large measure the element of unreality, and are employed to express modestly an earnest wish or appeal, where it may be called the subjunctive of *modest wish*: **Wollte** (modest wish) **Gott sich deiner erbarmen, mein armes Herz, daß du nicht immer Schmerzen ausstehen dürftest** (modest wish)! (Bismarck an seine Frau, March 3, 1851). **Möchte diese kurze Charakteristik zu weiteren Forschungen Anlaß geben!** (Richard M. Meyer in *Zeitschrift für deutsche Wortforschung*, II, p. 291). In subject clause: **Daß du an unserer Freude teilnehmen möchtest, ist unser inniger Wunsch.** In clause of exception: **Es fehlt nichts, als daß du da wärst. Dem Weine fehlt nichts, als daß er völlig geklärt wäre.** Likewise the *modest* or *polite* volitive: **Herr Flemming möchte kommen!** (Otto Ernst's *Flachsmann als Erzieher*, 3, 10) Bid Mr. Flemming kindly step in.

a. The past periphrastic subjunctive is frequently, especially thruout the South, used here instead of the simple subjunctive of the verb, altho this usage is quite generally condemned by grammarians: **Justinus Kerner schreibt: Würdest du ihn nur auch kennen!** (K. Mayer über Uhland, 2, 183). **O, wenn doch der Herr Assessor mal kommen würde!** (Raabe's *Akten des Vogelsangs*, p. 184). **Wenn sie [die Rosen] doch nicht welken würden!** (H. Böhlau's *Adam und Eva*, chap. vi). The clumsy periphrasis here has justly incurred the disfavor of grammarians, but their censure is often indiscriminate. The use of the periphrasis in the sentence from H. Böhlau is beautiful and is in harmony with a tendency that also appears elsewhere. See **190.** 1. E. *a*.

b. In the colloquial and popular language of the North the indicative often replaces the subjunctive here as elsewhere: **Wenn wir man (= nur) erst draußen waren!** (Halbe's *Das tausendjährige Reich*, p. 73). With reference to past time the past indicative is sometimes found also in the literary language, as the wish originally was the subordinate clause of the conditional sentence described in E. *Note* 2: **O, betrat ich doch nie sein Haus!** (Wagner's *Meisters.*, 1, 1), originally **Betrat ich nie sein Haus, es kam nicht dahin.**

B. The *unreal concessive* subjunctive which stands in the subordinate clause implies that the conceded proposition upon which the conclusion is based is not a very probable one. Sentences in which this subjunctive thus stands in the subordinate clause are in respect to mood and tense in both principal and subordinate clause exactly like unreal conditional sentences (see 2. E below): **Und wenn Sie mir goldene Berge gäben, das würde ich nicht tun** Even if you should give me mountains of gold I should not do it.

a. The past periphrastic subjunctive is frequently used here in the subordinate clause, altho this usage is quite generally condemned by grammarians. Thus a prominent German educator writes: **Wenn wir nun auch in Deutschland jene Einrichtung nachahmenswerter finden würden** (instead of **fänden**), **so würden uns doch alle übrigen Bedingungen fehlen.** See also 2. E. *Note* 3 below, also **190.** 1. E. *a*.

C. Unreal subjunctive of purpose. In the three categories enumerated in **168.** I. 2. B, the unreal subjunctive of purpose is used to represent the thing desired or planned as a mere conception of the mind not resting upon any expectation of realization, or on the other hand by thus using here a past tense form of the subjunctive and thus indicating that one is not counting upon a realization of one's expectations one can often modestly express earnest wishes and plans which one inwardly hopes to see realized: (**1**) **Ich wollte, er wäre nicht gestorben. Ich wünschte, er käme.** The subjunctive here often loses the element of unreality and is used to express modestly a wish that may be fulfilled: **Darum bet' ich zu unserm Herrgott, er möcht' mir meine höchste Freud' geben** (Anzengruber's *Schandfleck*, chap. xii). **Und das hat damals einen so großen Eindruck auf mich gemacht, daß ich dich bitten möchte, du machtest es auch so und ließest auch zwei Kuppen aufsteigen und auf der zweiten Kuppe stände die Kirche von Adamsdorf** (Fontane's *Poggenpuhls*, chap. xii). (**2**) **Könnt' ich als Leiche vor dir niedersinken, damit du blühend stündest und verjüngt** (Uhland). **Es ist nur zur Nachfrage, wenn mir einmal der Einfall käme, daß ich gleich vor die rechte Schmiede ginge** (Goethe's *Götz*, 2, 4). (**3**) **So beschloß man, einen patriotisch-dramatischen Abend zu veranstalten, der zugleich Gelegenheit böte, die fünf Schauspieler der höheren Gesellschaft Frankenfelds vorzuführen** (Riehl). **Ich wartete, bis das Haus verkauft wäre** (Wilmanns). **Ich habe gewartet, bis ich Sie 'mal allein träfe** (Frenssen's *Jörn Uhl*, chap. vii). **Es blieb ihm nichts übrig als abzuwarten, bis diese wehevolle Orgie sich erschöpft hätte** (Ertl's *Die Stadt der Heiligen*). **Und ehe denn die Abendmette von den fernen Klostertürmen klänge, sollte aufgepackt werden** (Alexis's *Die Hosen des Herrn von Bredow*, I). **Papa hat nicht wieder aufbauen lassen wollen, ehe du nicht deine Anordnungen getroffen hättest** (Sudermann's *Frau Sorge*, chap. XXIII). Thus the subjunctive in (**3**) is not at all infrequent, while the sanguine subjunctive of purpose is here almost confined to relative clauses in choice language, being elsewhere usually replaced by the indicative.

a. After a past tense this subjunctive cannot be distinguished in form from the *sanguine* subjunctive of purpose (**168.** I. 2. B), as the latter subjunctive is often attracted into a past tense following the model of the principal verb: **Er befahl, daß es geschähe** (also **geschehe**). Here **geschähe** is evidently the sanguine *subjunctive of purpose*, attracted into this tense by the past form **befahl.** This, the old sequence (**171.** 2. A), is fairly well preserved in (**1**), as in this example, and even still better in (**2**), as in **Er band den Baum an, damit er grade wüchse**, but **Er bindet den Baum an, damit er grade wachse** or more commonly **wächst.** The present subjunctive, however, is often found here also after a past tense as the new sequence (**171.** 2. B) asserts itself here as elsewhere: **Allabendlich begoß sie den Kaiserbaum, daß er stattlich heranwachse** (Hillern's *Höher als die Kirche*, III). Compare **171.** 4. *a* and **168.** I. 2. B. *b*.

b. The periphrastic subjunctive is sometimes found here instead of the older simpler forms: **Röhrings und Benneckes** (names) **harrten in ihrer Loge aus, bis der Strom sich einigermaßen**

verlaufen haben würde (Wildenbruch's *Schwester-Seele*, II, chap. XI) instead of **bis der Strom sich verlaufen hätte.**

2. The Unreal Potential Subjunctive is used:

A. In statements and questions direct and indirect:

(1) *In direct statements and questions.* In earlier periods the unreal potential subjunctive was established most firmly in indirect discourse and in other subordinate clauses. It is forcing its way more and more into independent propositions. Its use in subordinate clauses is treated at length in the different categories described below. It is employed in the principal proposition in the following cases:

a. In the principal clause of unreal conditional sentences. This use is discussed in E below.

b. In questions to express that some claim that has just been made is contrary to fact: **Wann hätten wir Euch je gehuldigt?** (Wildenbruch's *Die Quitzows*, 3, 12) When, pray, did we ever do homage to you? In doubting inquiries or exclamations of surprise: **Sollte Karl das getan haben?** Can it be that Charles has done that? **Wär's möglich? Könnt' ich nicht mehr, wie ich wollte?** (Schiller's *Wallensteins Tod*, 1, 4). **Er hätte jedes Hindernis besiegt, | und in dem eignen Willen seiner Tochter | sollt'** (past subj.) **ihm der neue Streit entstehn?** (id., *Die Piccolomini*, 3, 8) Can it be that he has overcome every obstacle only to find in the wilfulness of his own daughter a new source of opposition? **Du wärst | so falsch gewesen?** (ib., 5, 1) Can it be that you were so false? **Dies wäre Ihre Schwester!** Well! this is your sister, is it? **Das wäre!** or **Ei! das wäre!** Indeed!, or You don't say so! **Wo wäre der?** Where in the world can he be? **Wäre diese Sprache keine Täuschung?** Is it really true or not that these utterances are no delusion? **Noch eins. — Das wäre?** I have another thing to say yet.—What is it? It is in a similar manner often used to express joy, satisfaction over the attainment of some end whose successful issue has seemed doubtful or over a final resolution after an inner debate or struggle, or to express surprise or regret over some unexpected result: **Gottlob, wir wären am Ziel!** God be praised we are there at last! **So hätte ich denn alles getan, was mir zu tun obliegt!** And so I have actually done all that is incumbent upon me to do! **Das wäre nun in Ordnung!** That's in good shape now, I hope! **Nun machte sie als energische Frau einen Strich unter die ganze Episode und sagte sich: Damit wären wir fertig!** Now, as an energetic woman, she inwardly decided to put an end to the whole (love) affair, and said to herself: 'Well! I guess that's ended!' **Und so wär' ich für dies Jahr Meister** (Goethe's *Egmont*, 1, 1) And so I'm master-marksman for this year. **So hätten wir doch wenigstens etwas zu stande gebracht. Bis dahin ist blutwenig geschehen** (*Frankfurter Nationalvers.*, p. 841). **So wären wir am Ende, Herr Professor** (Freytag's *Journalisten*, 2, 1) So I suppose, Professor, we are thru with each other (i.e. all friendship between us is past).

c. By clothing one's thoughts in the language of doubt and uncertainty one can avoid a blunt expression of one's opinion or desire, so that the past subjunctive often loses in large measure the element of doubt and unreality, and is much used to state an opinion or seek information modestly, politely, or cautiously, in a less positive and abrupt way than in the indicative: **Sie dürften sich geirrt haben** You may possibly have made a mistake. **Das dürfte das Richtige sein** That is probably correct. **Ich wüßte wohl, was zu tun wäre** I think I know what would be best to do. **Nicht gut! Ich dächte doch!** (Lessing's *Nathan*, 2, 1) You think I am not playing well? I rather think I am! **Ich müßte nun gehen** I think I must go now. **Es wäre Zeit, daß du gingest** I think it is about time for you to go. **Ausstellungen im einzelnen hätte ich kaum zu machen** I scarce think I have, &c. **Das Verhältnis dieser flexivischen Verschiedenheit zu der Wortstellungsentwicklung in beiden Sprachen wäre zu untersuchen** (G. Hübener in Paul and Braune's *Beiträge*, 1920, p. 95) The relation . . . ought, I think, to be investigated. **Möchtest du in den großen**

Ferien an die Nordsee gehen? (R. Blümel in *Germanisch-Romanische Monatsschrift*, 1914, p. 386), indicating that the father has not yet formed a definite plan, hence is only cautiously seeking the desire of his daughter, not extending to her a definite promise, while the present indicative **magst du?** here indicates a definite plan and amounts to a definite promise. A modest inquiry often amounts to a polite request: **Dürfte ich bitten, mir Bescheid sagen zu lassen?** Might I ask you to send me word? **Möchten Sie die Güte haben, mir zu folgen?** Would you be so kind as to follow me? **Wie wäre es mit einer Partie Billard?** How should you like a game of billiards? **Könnten Sie mir sagen, ob ich auf dem Weg nach K. bin?** politely indicates that the speaker desires but is not demanding a reply, but the indicative **können Sie** here implies that the speaker is expecting an answer. **Wollten Sie mir erlauben — ich hätte ein Wort mit Ihnen —** (Wildenbruch's *Schwester-Seele*, chap. XII) Would you be so kind — I should like to speak a few words with you. Similarly the declarative form is very common in introducing a wish: **Ich wünschte** (the present indic. **ich wünsche** has more of the bluntness of a command), **Sie schenkten mir Gehör** I wish you would be so kind as to grant me a hearing.

(2) *In indirect discourse*, to indicate that the statement in the subordinate clause is contrary to fact: **Was? [Sagen Sie,] Räuber wären es gewesen, die uns anfielen? — Mörder waren es, erkaufte Mörder!** (Lessing's *Emilia*, 3, 8). **Unterworfen hätt' ich mich | dem Richterspruch der Zweiundvierzig, sagt ihr? | Ich habe keineswegs mich unterworfen** (Schiller's *Maria Stuart*, 1, 7). **Die Leute lügen, die da unten schreien, | Ihr wärt ein andrer als Ihr waret** (Hauptmann's *Die versunkene Glocke*, 3, p. 96). **Wenn freilich ein italienischer Abgeordneter behauptet hat, es bestünde eine permanente Gefahr für das Leben und das Eigentum seiner Landsleute, so ist das, gelinde gesprochen, eine Übertreibung** (*Hamburger Nachrichten*, Nov. 9, 1904). **Leider können wir nicht sagen, daß sie** (i.e. **die Anklagen**) **unbegründet wären** (ib., March 23, 1906). **Deshalb bildet sich der gute Deutsche in einer gewissen Entfernung von den Tälern der Warta allen Ernstes ein, es gäbe keine polnische Nation mehr, weil man sie auf deutschen Kathedern für Staatsrecht und Geschichte theoretisch und wissenschaftlich totgemacht hat** (W. von Massow in *Deutsche Monatsschrift*, Dec. 1906, p. 402).

This subjunctive is also used to indicate that the statement is a mere fancy, not an actual fact: **Dann machte er Experimente in der Chemie, daß ich manchmal heimlich die größte Angst ausgestanden habe, das Haus flöge auf mit uns allen** (S. Junghans).

It is often used as in (**1**) *c* above to state an opinion modestly or cautiously: **Auf die Lexikographie angewendet, will das besagen, daß die Behandlung jeder einzelnen Terminologie oder einer beschränkten Anzahl solcher je einem anderen Philologen anzuvertrauen wäre, der in den betreffenden Fächern heimisch ist** (Dr. H. Tiktin in *Germanisch-Romanische Monatsschrift*, 1910, p. 247).

We cannot always distinguish the unreal subjunctive from the plausible subjunctive which has been attracted into a past tense after a past tense. Even after a present tense we are not absolutely sure that the past tense forms denote unreality, as they often, under the influence of dialect or to get a clear subjunctive form, are used to report indirectly simple statements made by others. See **171.** 2. A. *b. Note* and B. *a* (near end of 1st par). Thus a past tense of the subjunctive in indirect discourse is often not a genuine unreal potential at all. See also G. *a.* (**2**), 3rd par., below.

The past tense forms of the subjunctive are not now so widely used in indirect discourse as the present tense forms, but they nevertheless have a broad field of usefulness here, both as a pure potential and with less reason also as a grammatical form, to express merely indirectness of statement. This subjunctive of indirect discourse not being confined to one grammatical category, but assuming different grammatical forms, will reappear in a number of the following groups. It is discussed still more fully in **171–173.**

B. *Clauses of Manner.* The unreal potential is used to indicate that there is little foundation of fact for the comparisons made, or to suggest a vague semblance or mere surmise: **Ich halte Egmont hier, als ob ich ihm noch was zu sagen hätte** (Goethe's *Egmont*, Act 4). **Nettchen lehnte sich so zufrieden an ihn, als ob er eine Kirchensäule wäre** (G. Keller's *Kleider machen Leute*). **Der Braune griff so tapfer aus, als wäre er stolz auf seinen sichern Herrscher** The bay struck a brisk pace as if he were proud of his firm master. A present tense form of the subjunctive here has another meaning. See **168.** II. B.

The past tense forms of the subjunctive are also often used here as elsewhere to make a statement cautiously: **Ich bin nur eine alte Frau und kann mich also täuschen; aber — Kind, Kind, scheinen tut es mir doch so, als ob die Welt schriller würde** (*were becoming, might be becoming*, subj. of cautious statement) (Raabe's *Horn von Wanza*, chap. xiv).

a. The past periphrastic subjunctive is frequently, especially thruout the South, used here instead of the simple past subjunctive, altho this usage is quite generally condemned by grammarians: **Sie ließen sich gar nicht bei uns sehen, wie wenn sie das Elternhaus geflissentlich fliehen würden** (for flöhen) (G. Keller). **Jetzt fängt er verdrießlich wieder an zu graben; aber es war, als wenn er in einen Steinboden einhauen würde, alles umsonst** (Wilhelm Fischer's *Die Freude am Licht*, II. p. 75). See **190.** 1. E. *a.*

b. We often find the ideas of unreality, vague semblance, expressed by a past indicative both in poetry and common prose, most frequently in the language of the North, where there is a general trend toward the indicative: **Du hast genannt mich einen Vogelsteller, | als ob du selber keine Garne zogst** (Freiligrath). **Es war, als ob sich unter der Haut pulsierende Strähne hinzogen** (Auerbach's *Waldfried*). **Mir war, als ob er mich plötzlich anders ansah als sonst, als ob er mir nicht mehr frei die Hand geben konnte** (Hirschfeld's *Agnes Jordan*, 1, p. 42). **Es war alles wie verhext und verwunschen. Als wenn das nicht wirkliche Häuser waren** (Frenssen's *Jörn Uhl*, chap. v, p. 83). **Sieh', mir ist, | als waren lauter Puppen sonst um mich | die Menschen alle** (Schnitzler's *Der Schleier der Beatrice*, 1, p. 31). This use of the past indicative indicates that the statement is vividly felt as narrative, a tale of things once *felt* as actual facts.

Also the present indicative is frequently used here, when the reference is to present time as the speaker feels the utterance as an actual fact, of course with the opposite meaning when spoken in a sarcastic tone: **Dummes Zeug! Als wenn du überhaupt 'n Liebsten hast!** (Halbe's *Das tausendjährige Reich*, p. 41), in sarcastic tone = **Du hast keinen Liebsten! Wie kommen Sie hierher?** Answer: **Als ob man im Examen ist!** (Carl Busse), in sarcastic tone = **Ich bin nicht im Examen! Als ob ich nie allein fertig werd'!** (C. Busse's *Kleinstadtliebe*), in sarcastic tone = **Ich werde immer allein fertig!** Felt as an actual fact: **Ich weiß nicht, was das ist, daß ich nicht ordentlich lachen kann. Es ist, als wenn mein Gesicht gefroren ist** (Frenssen's *Jörn Uhl*, chap. xi). **Er ist den ganzen Tag in Unruh und kann doch nachts nicht schlafen . . . als wenn . . . ich weiß nicht . . . als wenn er ein schweres Gewissen hat** (id., *Das Heimatsfest*, 2, 3). **Es scheint, als wenn die Richter seiner Sache ziemlich günstig sind** (Otto Ernst's *Die Kunstreise nach Hümpeldorf*, p. 60). Aside from narrative as in the preceding paragraph the corresponding tense here for past time is the present perfect: **Die Mutter sieht ein bißchen gedrückt aus, als wenn sie früher mal was Nobleres vorgestellt hat** (ib., p. 55). **Sie haben so etwas Finsteres im Blick, als ob nie die Sonne in ihr Herz geschienen hat** (Halbe).

C. *Unreal Subjunctive of Result in Attributive Relative Clauses.* Altho the present tense forms of the subjunctive are not so common as formerly in attributive relative clauses, as described in **168.** II. C, the past tense forms are still quite common here. The present tense forms of the subjunctive are now usually replaced here, on the one hand, by the indicative as in English in order to represent the statement confidently as a fact, or, on the other hand, often by a past tense form of the subjunctive to indicate modestly or cautiously that the statement is at least conceivable and is probably true. Thus the idea of unreality which usually attaches to a past tense form of the subjunctive is in most cases overshadowed here by the derived meaning of modest or cautious statement: **Haben Sie nicht stärkeres Papier?** Answer: **Ich habe etwas, das stärker ist, aber nichts in der gewünschten Farbe, das stärker wäre. Die Geschichte kennt keinen Staatsmann, der sich größere Verdienste um Österreich erworben hätte als Prinz Eugen. Ich kenne niemand, der genauere Kenntnis der Sache besäße. Doch wie es selten nur eine unerfreuliche Sache gibt, die nicht auch wenigstens eine gute Seite hätte, so war es auch hier** (*Hamburger Nachrichten*, March 23, 1905). **Noch nie ist eine Unwahrheit gesprochen worden, die nicht früher oder später nachteilige Folgen gehabt hätte. Wo ist ein Berg im ganzen Lande, den er nicht bestiegen hätte?**

The old idea of unreality, doubt is also found here: **Aber wo ist einer, der das tun könnte, wollte?**

D. *Unreal Subjunctive of Result in Adverbial Clauses.* In all the categories of result described in **168.** II. D the present tense forms of the subjunctive are now usually replaced, on the one hand, by the indicative in order to represent the statement confidently as a fact, or, on the other hand, often by a past tense form of the subjunctive to indicate modestly or cautiously that the statement is at least conceivable and is probably true. A few examples will suffice: **Er denkt zu edel, als daß er nicht die Wahrheit sagte. Sie ist viel zu gescheit, als daß sie hineinfiele** or **hineinfällt** (Burckhard's *Theater*, p. 22). **Ariostens Lob aus seinem Munde hat mich mehr ergetzt, | als daß es mich beleidigt hätte** (Goethe's *Tasso*, 2, 1). **Ich bin nie in London, daß ich nicht das Museum besuchte** I never go to London without visiting the museum. **Er sprach nie, ohne daß er gefragt worden wäre,** or **gefragt wurde. Serlo** (name) **hatte sie nicht ein'mal zu Gastrollen gelassen, geschweige daß er ihnen Hoffnung zum Engagement gemacht hätte** (Goethe). **Und die Mutter schaffte ihnen noch braunlederne feine Halbschuhe an, statt daß sie sich selbst ein Sommermäntelchen gekauft hätte** (H. Böhlau's *Adam und Eva*, chap. II). **Jetzt ging alles wieder seinen alten Weg, kaum daß einer mehr des Abwesenden gedacht hätte. Weit entfernt, daß man den Feldherrn unterstützt hätte, ward sogar der Sold der Truppen verschwendet. Er ist nicht so weise, daß er alles wüßte.** Other examples in H. *c*.

a. The periphrastic past perfect subjunctive is frequently used here in the subordinate clause instead of the regular past perfect subjunctive: **Ihm hätte es häufig, selbst durch den ärgsten giftigsten Schnupfen hindurch, dreist nach moderigem Stroh riechen können, ohne daß er sich darob gewundert haben würde** (Raabe's *Wunnigel*, chap. VII). See also **190.** 1. E. *a*.

E. *Unreal Conditions.* The unreal potential is also used in conditional sentences in which the conclusion rests upon a condition that is not likely to be fulfilled, or upon one which is contrary to the facts in the case. The principal clause has the periphrasis or the regular subjunctive, the subordinate clause the regular subjunctive only, as illustrated in the following sentences:

Present Time.

a. **Ich würde den Brief schreiben, wenn ich Zeit hätte** *I should write the letter if I had time*, or

b. **Ich schriebe den Brief, wenn ich Zeit hätte** (about equal in meaning to *a*; see *Note* 1).

Past Time.

c. **Ich würde den Brief geschrieben haben, wenn ich Zeit gehabt hätte** *I should have written the letter if I had had time*, or

d. **Ich hätte den Brief geschrieben, wenn ich Zeit gehabt hätte** (equal in meaning to *c*).

Note 1. In the principal proposition the regular subjunctive is much more common than the periphrastic form in case of modal auxiliaries and the passive of all verbs in both present and past time. Elsewhere, however, the two forms may be considered as equally good and common with the exception that the periphrastic is more common in the principal proposition than the simple past, at least so in ordinary prose. See *Note* 3.

Note 2. In the description of a crisis or a stirring event in our past life or the life of another the past indic. sometimes takes the place of the past perf. subjunctive, either in the main or the subordinate clause, as the past acts described do not seem to us mere conceptions but things so close to us that we feel them as realities which we relate: **Mit diesem zweiten Pfeil durchschoß ich Euch, | wenn ich mein liebes Kind getroffen hätte** (Schiller's *Tell*, 3, 3). **Warf er** (i.e. Cæsar) **das Schwert von sich, er war verloren** (id., *Wallensteins Tod*, 2, 2). **Und kamst du nicht, ich tat es** (Grillparzer's *Ein treuer Diener seines Herrn*, 2). **Mit einer einzigen mühelosen Bewegung hätte ich, frei zugreifend, Liebe, Reichtum, Glanz, Ehre, alles zugleich gewinnen können, wenn ich das furchtsam grübelnde Gewissensbedenken nur eine Sekunde lang fahren ließ; allein dann war auch mein innerstes Wesen verwandelt, dann war ich nicht mehr ich, ich war tot, ich war nicht mehr eins mit dem Schicksal, nicht mehr der lenkende Gott auf dem rollenden Lebenswagen, sondern ich war der willenlose Sklave eines Glückes, das von außen zwingend wie ein goldenes Netz über mich geworfen war. War ich dann glücklich?** (Hans Hoffmann's *Iwan der Schreckliche*, chap. V).

Note 3. From Luther's day up to the present, especially thruout the South, the periphrasis is found with increasing frequency even in good authors also in the subordinate clause as well as in the principal, usually without difference of meaning from the regular subjunctive: **Wo aber jemand würde zu euch sagen** (1 Cor. x. 28). **Mit Vergnügen, wenn es etwas helfen würde** (Raabe's *Horacker*, chap. vi). **Wenn nun der Pastor von Gansewinckel, Herr Christian Winckler, alles dies und zwar in einem ähnlichen Tone wie sein Eheweib vorgetragen haben würde, so würden wir uns ganz gehorsamst dafür bedanken, irgend eine Bürgschaft für den Erfolg der Rede zu übernehmen** (ib., chap. viii). **Würde der Donnersberg so hoch unmittelbar von der Rheinebene aus sich erheben, so würde jedermann erstaunen** (K. Mayer über Uhland, I, 104). **Wenn man die Werke nach der Weltanschauung, die ihre Künstler aussprechen, bestimmen würde, so würde keiner der österreichischen Sezessionisten in die Gruppe von Zorn kommen können** (Hermann Bahr's *Gesammelte Aufsätze über die Sezession*, p. 96). **Ich würde mich nicht wundern,**

wenn ich in einer Zeitung lesen würde, daß usw. (Eb. Nestle from Maulbronn in *Zeitschrift für den deutschen Unterricht*, 1902, p. 132). Grammarians, however, quite generally condemn the use of the periphrasis here in the subordinate clause and insist upon the usage given above. The evident explanation of this opposition is that the clumsy periphrasis robs the statement of its terseness of expression. The periphrasis, however, has an inner strength of its own, for it is gradually supplanting the regular subjunctive in the principal proposition without meeting with any opposition from the grammarians. The reason seems to be that it has more future force than the regular subjunctive and hence is felt as more appropriate for use in the principal proposition, which usually has stronger future force than the subordinate clause. This distinct future force which lies in the periphrasis often leads to its use also in the subordinate clause to bring out more clearly the idea of futurity which is often found there. Thus there seems to be a tendency to differentiate the two forms in the subordinate clause, as illustrated in **190.** 1. E. *a*. Usage at present, however, is very unsettled at this point, especially in the South, where the periphrasis is often used without any justification whatever.

Note 4. Many sentences containing a subjunctive will upon study reveal themselves as a conditional sentence with a prepositional phrase instead of a conditional clause: **Unter anderen Umständen hätte ich zugestimmt.** A part of the sentence is often suppressed: **Ja wenn wir nicht wären, sagte die Laterne zum Mond. Da ging sie aus** (What would the world do) If we were not, said the street-lamp to the moon. Thereupon it went out. **Wer ein Narr wäre und redete mit fremden Leuten! [der würde das tun]** If one were a fool he might do it!, or Only a fool would do that! **Daß ich ein Narr wäre! = Wenn ich das täte, was mir zugemutet wird, so wäre das Ergebnis, daß ich ein Narr wäre.** Sometimes there is a mingling of two constructions: **Ich wäre beinahe gefallen** *I came very near falling* is a blending of **Es ist beinahe so weit gekommen, daß ich gefallen bin** and **Ich wäre gefallen, wenn ich mich nicht an das Geländer gehalten hätte.** Compare 1 below.

Note 5. The unreal conditional sentence is now usually felt as a potential category, but it was originally optative in character in both the principal proposition and the subordinate clause, as can still be seen in occasional sentences: **Kämest du** (originally **Kämest du!** *O that you would come!*), **ich gäbe dir gern etwas** (= **ich möchte dir etwas geben**) (Sommer's *Vergleichende Syntax*, p. 87). It is possible that the potential idea in general has developed out of the optative.

1. The subjunctive of *modest* or *cautious statement*, which is a weakened potential with a suppressed conditional clause, is used quite frequently to make the statement of a truth *modestly* or *cautiously*, in a less positive and definite way than in the indicative: **Ich könnte noch manches sagen (wenn ich wollte,** or **wenn es verstattet wäre).** See also A. (**1**). *c* above.

2. We have other unreal conditional sentences than the ones described in the preceding articles. The conditional conjunctions given in **238.** 3. F are often used with the past tense forms of the subjunctive to represent the statement as a mere conception of the mind, with various shades of meaning. See examples in **279.** See also **168.** II. E. *a*, *d*.

3. In conditions the indicative competes with the subjunctive, as explained in **166.**

F. *Unreal Subjunctive in Relative and Interrogative Clauses*. This subjunctive is much used to represent the statement as a mere conception of the mind without a basis in reality, on the other hand, however, often indicating that the speaker or writer regards the occurrence or performance of the act in question as *possible* or feels the conception as *possibly* conforming to fact or reality, hence often employed to state an opinion modestly or cautiously.

a. Attributive relative or interrogative clauses. Relative clauses: **Ich möchte gern einen Geldbeutel haben, der nie leer würde** (Grimm's *Märchen*). **Da ist der Kahn, der mich hinübertrüge** (Schiller's *Tell*, 1, 1). **Die Welt kann dir nichts darbieten, was sie von dir nicht empfinge** (Schiller's *Menschenfeind*, Act 8) *which it does not receive from you*, subj. of cautious statement. Other examples in C above.

The subjunctive in relative clauses also occurs in unreal conditional sentences: **Er wäre der letzte, den ich um Rat fragte [, wenn ich in Verlegenheit kommen sollte].**

Interrogative clauses are introduced by **ob** *whether*, or some interrogative adjective or adverb: **Jetzt warf man die Frage auf, ob man das Werk zu Ende führen könnte.**

b. In substantive relative clauses. It is very common in the following relations:

(**1**) As subject or predicate. As subject: **Wer sie nicht kennte, | die Elemente, | ihre Kraft | und Eigenschaft, | wäre kein Meister | über die Geister** (Goethe's *Faust*, *Studierzimmer*). **Wer mir vorausgesagt hätte, daß die Arme meines Geistes so bald zerschmettert werden sollten, mit denen ich ins Unendliche griff, und mit denen ich doch gewiß ein Großes zu umfassen hoffte, wer mir das vorausgesagt hätte, würde mich zur Verzweiflung gebracht haben** (id.). As predicate: **Die Menschen sind nicht immer, was sie sein könnten.**

(**2**) As object: **Kaufe dir, was du gern hättest** (Lessing's *Minna*, 2, 3).

c. In substantive interrogative clauses. This subjunctive is common in clauses introduced by **ob** *whether*, or some interrogative pronoun or adverb.

(**1**) As subject: **Es fiel ihm nicht ein, wieviel davon sich sagen ließe.**
(**2**) As object: **Ich brütete, wie ich dich retten könnte** (A. Hausrath).
The subjunctive in (**1**) and (**2**) is often not a pure unreal potential, but, as in **168.** II. F. *c.* (**2**), 3rd line, only a grammatical form for the expression of an indirect question, the tense having been attracted into the form of a historical tense after a historical tense: **Was mit dem Andree geschehen würde** [or **werde**], **kümmerte ihn nicht im geringsten** (P. Heyse). In such indirect questions a past tense form is not now in choice language so common as a present tense form.

G. *Unreal Potential Subjunctive in Substantive* **Daß**-*Clauses.* This subjunctive is very common to indicate a possibility, or to express a statement modestly or cautiously. The **daß** may be suppressed. This subjunctive is often used instead of the plausible subjunctive described in **168.** II. G. Of course the indicative is used if it is desired to represent the statement as a fact.

This subjunctive is used in the following relations:

a. In subject and object clauses:

(**1**) As subject. The subjunctive of modest or cautious statement is very common here: **Es scheint uns, daß mit einer solchen Zusage nicht viel gewonnen wäre. Es fehlte nur wenig** or **nicht viel, daß es ihm ebenso ergangen wäre** or **erging. Es konnte nicht fehlen** or **ausbleiben, daß sie sich nicht zuweilen getroffen hätten,** or **daß sie sich (nicht) zuweilen trafen** (Wilmanns's *Deutsche Grammatik*, III, p. 284). **Es täte not, ich ginge selbst hin.** See also Matth. xviii. 6.

(**2**) As object. Here there is a strong tendency to use the past subjunctive of an auxiliary with a dependent infinitive rather than the past subjunctive of the simple verb: **Ich rechnete darauf, daß er ausbleiben könnte** (instead of **ausbliebe**). **Ich fürchtete, daß mir die ganze Ernte verderben würde** (instead of **verdürbe**). The subjunctive of modest statement is very common in this category: **Ich glaube, meine Herren, damit wäre in starken großen Umrissen genug von unserem Aufenthalt in Wien gesagt** (*Frankfurter Nationalvers.*, p. 841). **Ich finde, der Verfasser müßte diese** (i.e. **die Ergebnisse**) **doch noch gesondert, in Zusammenfassungen, Tabellen, Karten oder wie sonst darbieten** (Baesecke's *Deutsche Philologie*, p. 41) I think the author ought by all means to present his results separately in the form of summaries, tables, &c.

There are also numerous traces of a tendency to give the subjunctive here the idea of unreality, especially to indicate a conflict with reality: **Da behaupten die Leute, Freunde in der Not wären selten** And now people say that friends in time of need are scarce (which is not my experience). **Ja, Knoten—, das sind sie, die Menschen, alle, wie sie gebacken sind, Beamtenknoten, Geldknoten, Berufsknoten! Und am knotigsten, wenn sie sich Lackstiefel anziehen, einen Frack darüber hängen und womöglich ein paar Orden dran stecken und sich einbilden, jetzt wären sie fein** (Wildenbruch's *Neid*, p. 80). See also A. (**2**) above, and **171.** 2. B. *c.* The speaker often, however, employs a past tense form of the subjunctive, not to call attention to a conflict with reality but to withdraw the question *entirely* from the domain of reality and present it as a mere conception, as a supposed or imaginary case: **Ich will mir einbilden, meine Pferde dort unten wären Schafe usw.** (Kleist's *Käthchen*, 2, 1).

The subjunctive in (**1**) and (**2**) is often not a pure potential, but, as in **168.** II. G. *a.* (**2**), 2nd par., a mere grammatical form for the expression of indirect statement or discourse, the tense having been attracted into a past tense form after a past tense: **Er faßte es nicht, daß diese Lippen erkaltet wären** (here of a fact), **die so oft, noch gestern mit ihm über alle Fragen der Menschen geredet** (Ompteda's *Eysen*, chap. viii). **Ich wußte wohl, daß es ohne Lärm nicht abgehen würde** (instead of **werde**) (P. Heyse). **Als er vernommen, daß es Deutsche wären** (here of a fact), **sagte er zu seiner Begleitung usw.** (Curt Gebauer in *Archiv für Kulturgeschichte*, vol. V, p. 462). In such indirect discourse past tense forms are in general not now in choice language so common as present tense forms. It would be a gain for the language if they should disappear entirely except in the cases mentioned in **171.** 2. B. *a.* This would leave room for the clearer development of the idea of possibility, unreality, and caution here. See also **171.** 2. B. *c.*

b. In attributive clauses. To express possibility: **Das hat ihn so furchtbar gequält, Marie. Die Angst, er könnte nie etwas erreichen** (Hirschfeld's *Mütter*, Act 4), or **die Angst, daß er nie etwas erreichen könnte.** The subjunctive of modest or cautious statement is common here: **Es wäre höchste Zeit, daß du gingest. Es ist Zeit, daß ich ginge.**

To express the idea of unreality **als** (with question order) or **als ob** or **als wenn** (with transposed order) may be used instead of **daß: Ebenso habe ich mich bemüht, meinen Urteilen über mundartliche Färbungen der Schriftsprache eine Form zu geben, durch die ich dem Mißverständnisse, dem sie früher ausgesetzt gewesen sind, vorbeugen möchte, dem Mißverständnisse, als beurteilte ich das Verhältnis usw.** (Matthias's *Sprachleben und Sprachschäden*, Vorwort). The past subjunctive here is often the subjunctive of modest or cautious statement: **Auch bei Wassermann** (name) **wird man das Gefühl nicht los, als ob doch manche Stoffe wenig zu novellistischer Behandlung geeignet wären** (Richard Dohse in *Die schöne Literatur*, Dec. 1, 1906, p. 490).

Sometimes as in 2. B. *b* above the present indicative is used here instead of the past subjunctive as the person in question *feels* the utterance as an actual fact: **Wenn man mit der Eisenbahn von Weltevreden nach Buitenzorg reist, so hat man zunächst den Eindruck, als ob man fast ununterbrochen im Walde fährt . . . in Wirklichkeit ist es ausnahmslos Kulturgelände, welches den Schienenstrang begleitet** (K. Giesenhagen's *Auf Java und Sumatra*, p. 23). **Gegenüber all den Darstellungen, als ob es sich dort um eine wild gewordene Soldateska handelt, ist die Armee tadellos hervorgegangen** (Graf Westarp in the Reichstag, Jan. 24, 1914). See also **238.** 2. *d. Note.*

H. *Unreal Subjunctive in Clauses of Degree* (see **238.** 3. D):

a. In clauses expressing a comparison (see **238.** 3. D. 1. A. *a*). This subjunctive is common here to express a possibility, or to make a statement modestly or cautiously: **Er ist so bescheiden, wie ein Mann sein könnte.**

b. In clauses expressing a restriction (**238.** 3. D. 1. A. *c*). This subjunctive is used here to express a possibility: **Ich bin nicht abergläubisch, versetzte Charlotte, und gebe nichts auf diese dunklen Anregungen, insofern sie nur solche wären** (Goethe's *Wahlverwandtschaften*, chap. i). **Angesichts der Gefahr, die von neuen Erfindungen und um sich greifenden Beschäftigungen und Vergnügen droht, ist es daher erfreulich, daß auch in unserer Zeit Vereine das Sprachgewissen schärfen und Behörden für die überflüssigen fremden Ausdrücke vernünftige deutsche einführen, soweit also nicht Verarmung des Sprachinhalts oder Mangel an Deutlichkeit zu befürchten wäre** (Sütterlin and Waag's *Deutsche Sprachlehre*, p. 15).

c. In clauses expressing a result (see **238.** 3. D. 2). This subjunctive is common here to express a possibility, or to make a statement modestly or cautiously: **Die Luft ist so still, daß wir sie kommen hören könnten. Es** (Frenssen's *Jörn Uhl*) **ist, von seinem Kunstwert ganz abgesehen, dabei so deutsch, daß keine andere Nation der Erde es hätte hervorbringen können. Es ist speziell so norddeutsch, daß kein Süddeutscher an seine innerste Kraft herankönnte** (Carl Busse im *Tag*, Nr. 11 vom 8. Januar 1902). **Sie war so ergriffen, daß sie fast einen Weinkrampf bekommen hätte** (Ompteda's *Eysen*, chap. xxviii) *that she almost fell into hysterics.* Of course the indicative is used here to state an actual result. A more detailed statement of the uses of the subjunctive here is given in D.

I. *Unreal Subjunctive in Clauses of Time and Place.* The past tense forms of the subjunctive are used in adverbial clauses of time and place to denote possibility: **Die Totengräber hatten über dem Sarge eine Art Gewölbe aus Brettern hergestellt, um ihn später wieder leichter ausgraben zu können, wenn die Gruft fertig gemauert wäre** (Ompteda's *Eysen*, chap. ix). **Von**

meinen Schülern aber werde ich niemals weichen, wo eine Gefahr sie bedrohen könnte (H. Hoffmann's *Wider den Kurfürsten*, chap. xlii). See also **274.** *b*; **275.** *b*.

J. *Unreal Subjunctive in Clauses of Cause.* The past tense forms of the subjunctive are used here to denote possibility: **Ich tue es gleich, weil es heute noch regnen könnte.** A past tense form of the subjunctive is often used after **weil** preceded by a negative or a word with negative force to indicate modestly that a suggested explanation is not the right one: **Zum ersten Male, solange ich denken konnte, griff der Urgroßvater diese Herausforderung nicht auf, weniger wohl, weil er durchaus nichts zu entgegnen gewußt hätte, als aus allgemeiner Betrübnis und Müdigkeit** (R. Huch's *Ludolf Ursleu*, chap. XXIII).

Indirect Discourse.

170. Indirect discourse is the indirect statement of the substance of the words, thoughts, suppositions, wishes, &c., of another, or is the speaker's report of the substance of his own words, thoughts, suppositions, wishes, &c. In German such indirect communications assume two general forms—the Indirect Form and the Independent Form.

Indirect Form of Indirect Discourse.

171. 1. *Mood.* In reporting the thought of another the speaker uses the indicative if he positively wishes to endorse the report, or represent it as evidently supported by facts; but if he desires to represent the report as doubtful, or wishes simply to submit to the judgment of the hearer the subjective views of himself or others, or to state his or their wishes, hopes, fears, intentions, &c., which are by their very nature not entirely certain of realization, he usually employs the subjunctive: **Der Arzt glaubt, daß ich krank bin** *The doctor believes me to be sick* (and I agree with him), but **Der Arzt glaubt, daß ich krank sei** *The doctor believes me to be sick* (but I don't agree with him). **Er sagt, daß er schon zwei Kapitel gelesen hat** *He says that he has already read two chapters* (and of course his word is good), but **Da sage einer, daß ich kein feiner Diplomat sei** *Now let someone say that I am not a shrewd diplomat!* (Who could now hold such a view, as I have already shown that I am one?). **Ludwig Salomon meint, man dürfe Wilbrandts „Maler“ neben Freytags „Journalisten“ stellen** Louis Salomon believes that Wilbrandt's play 'Die Maler' compares favorably with Freytag's 'Die Journalisten' (the subjective view of Salomon). **Mein Vater glaubt, es sei** (the subjunctive here contains nothing doubtful or disrespectful to the father, but simply indicates that the view expressed is his) **besser, diesen Weg einzuschlagen** My father thinks it is better to pursue this course. **Er wünscht nicht, daß sie es höre** He does not want her to hear it.

There is considerable fluctuation in the use of the subjunctive here according to the standpoint and feeling of the speaker or writer, but in general it is at present true that it is much more common after the second or third person than after the first, and more common after a past than a present tense, hence least frequent after the first person present: **Ich fürchte, daß es schon zu spät ist** *I fear it is already too late*, but **Er fürchtet, daß es schon zu spät sei. Ich zweifle, daß er lesen wird** (O. Weise) *I doubt whether he will read*, but **Ich zweifelte, daß er lesen werde** (id.). The subjunctive after a first person present, however, is common in case of verbs expressing *will, command*: **Ich will nicht, daß auch nur ein einziger schlaff werde durch Weibertränen und Weibergeschrei** (Sudermann's *Teja*, 1, 5) I do not desire that a single man should become enervated thru the tears and cries of women. The subjunctive after the first person is necessary to indicate that something is merely conceived or represented as true without however an actual basis in fact: **Ich kann doch nicht sagen, daß ich krank bin** *I hesitate to announce the fact of my sickness*, but **Ich kann doch nicht sagen, daß ich krank sei** (Hermann Auer's *Schulgrammatik*, p. 145) *I hesitate to* *pretend to be sick.* The subjunctive is also common after the first person when it is not a question of the truth or falseness of the utterance, but rather of the indirectness of the statement: **Ich erzählte ihm, daß ich am heiligen Abend immer ein wenig betrübt sei, denn so schön wie im Kloster könne für mich Weihnachten nie wieder werden** (Hermine Villinger's *Simplicitas*, 34). Likewise after the first person of the present tense: **Ich weiß nicht, ob die Frage damals weiter erörtert worden ist, und meine, es sei unter allen Umständen der Mühe wert zu untersuchen, ob wirklich der Dativ** (in the expression **Da kannst du dir am besten Rats erholen**) **bei jedermann Anstoß erregt** (J. Ernst Wülfing in *Zeitschrift für den deutschen Unterricht*, 1903, p. 730). **So glaube ich, daß auch mein Auge durch die lange Beschäftigung mit dem Gegenstand nicht verblendet, sondern dank der damit zusammenhängenden reichen Erfahrung vielmehr eigentümlich geschärft sei** (Günther Jacoby in *Journal of English and Germanic Philology*, 1914, p. 379). **Ich vermute stark, es handele sich um usw.** (F. Krüger in *Literaturblatt für germanische und romanische Philologie*, XXXIX. Jahrg., p. 126). All three writers are here quite sure of their statements, but they use the subjunctive because they feel that they are stating their views indirectly. Indirectness here in connection with a present tense form of the subjunctive expresses quiet confidence in the truth of the statement. If these writers had employed the indicative here instead of the subjunctive the statement would have been more personal and subjective, not at all, however, more suggestive of certainty. The frequent use of the indicative after the first person of the present tense results from the circumstance that we usually feel the words **ich glaube, ich weiß,** &c. as not so essential a part of the utterance as what follows and hence feel the utterance as a whole more as a declaration of fact than as an indirect statement: **Ich weiß, daß sie morgen kommen.** After a past tense the subjunctive is in general more common than after the present for the simple reason that when we speak of past events that have been told us we involuntarily fall into a narrative mood and hence feel all that we say as a report, an indirect statement and employ the subjunctive. Here the feeling of indirectness is more prominent than the desire to represent the utterance as a declaration of fact. We feel that we are narrating, not declaring. After a past tense, however, the subjunctive is naturally more common with reference to the future than to the past as we may report past events in the indicative as facts: **Es war gewiß, daß er log, gelogen hatte, lügen werde** (or **würde**).

As can be seen from the preceding sentences, the subjunctive employed in indirect discourse has not one distinct meaning, but is either optative or potential or both, as the statement may be represented as the will of someone, or as something that is possible, or it may be represented as both at the same time. Moreover, the subjunctive is often used merely because of the element of indirectness which lies in the statement, even tho the optative and potential ideas may be entirely absent: **Ich wußte wohl, daß der Hund von edler Art sei** (Riehl's *Der stumme Ratsherr*, III). See also **168. II. G.** *a* (**2**), 2nd par.; **169. 2. G.** *a.* (**2**), 3rd par; 3 (next to the last par.) below.

a. The indirect statement often depends upon a noun: **Den Vorwurf, daß er dich habe täuschen wollen, hat er nicht verdient. Die Behauptung, daß die Erde sich drehe, setzte Galilei mannigfachen Verfolgungen aus.**

b. The report of the speaker in the subjunctive may be interrupted by explanatory remarks of his own in the indic., but all remarks, explanatory or otherwise, which are a part of the original direct statement are put in the subjunctive when transposed into the indirect: **Karl erzählte, daß er das Haus, welches er von seinem Vater geerbt hat, verkaufen wolle. Seit Jahren** (sagte sie) **sei sie mit einem Standesgenossen verlobt gewesen, der gleich ihr arm gewesen sei.**

c. Often a subordinate clause is in the subjunctive in indirect statement, altho it has not the outward form of an indirect statement, which is easily explained by supplying some omission: **Die Athener** (Athenians) **verurteilten**

Sokrates zum Tode, weil [sie sagten, daß] er die Jugend verderbe. Mendel (name) **sollte dabei behülflich sein, wich aber aus. [Er sagte,] Er habe drei Wochen zu Bett gelegen, fühle sich noch sehr matt und sollte nach des Arztes Anweisung jede Aufregung vermeiden.**

In long continued indirect discourse it is not necessary in German to be continually intercalating such clauses as 'she said,' 'he continued,' &c., for the subjunctive, as in the preceding examples, indicates clearly that the speech is indirectly reported.

d. The unreal optative and potential subjunctives of the direct change in the indirect their person but not their mood and tense: **Er sagt** (or **sagte**), **er möchte Sie sprechen.** Direct: **Ich möchte ihn sprechen. Er sagt** (or **sagte**), **er würde gehen, wenn er Zeit hätte.** Direct: **Ich würde gehen, wenn ich Zeit hätte. Er sagt** (or **sagte**), **das könnten Sie am besten wissen.** Direct: **Das könnte er am besten wissen.** Past time: **Er sagt** (or **sagte**), **er hätte Sie sprechen mögen.** Direct: **Ich hätte ihn sprechen mögen.**

e. In N.G. dialect and colloquial language the subjunctive of indirect discourse is very largely replaced by the indicative: **So, also das sagst du und meinst, ich bin solch ein Mensch?** (Halbe's *Jugend*, p. 87). For other examples see 2. B. *f* below. The indicative is here used also in case of unreality, as the person in question is represented as feeling the statement as true: **Die Krüppel glaubten, nu haben sie mich** (E. von Keyserling's *Ein Frühlingsopfer*, p. 120). In South German the subjunctive is better preserved here: **Und sie hat mir g'sagt, sie hätt' mich nie mög'n, 'zwungen wär' s' worden** (Anzengruber's *Das vierte Gebot*, 2, 11). The indicative, however, is not infrequent in the South: **Alle sagen, daß du mich verlassen wirst! Nicht wahr, du tust es nicht . . .** (Schnitzler's *Liebelei*, p. 100). Mizi: **Er spielt ja nicht Baßgeigen, Violin spielt er.** Theodor: **Ach so, ich hab' gemeint, er spielt Baßgeige** (ib., p. 23).

2. *Tense*. The tense required in indirect discourse may as in English depend upon the tense of the principal verb. Thus a present, present perfect, future, or future perfect follows a present, as illustrated in A. *a* below, while a simple past, past perfect, periphrastic past subjunctive (**würde loben**), or periphrastic past perfect subjunctive (**würde gelobt haben**) follows a past, as illustrated in A. *b* below. Differing from English, the German may also, without regard to the tense of the verb in the principal proposition, use the same tense in the indirect as stood in the direct, so that the present, present perfect, future, and future perfect usually stand in the subordinate clause, as explained in B below. The former construction is the older, but the latter is steadily gaining upon it in the literary language. In the dialects, which often influence the literary language, the old historic usage has been entirely abandoned and new and different constructions have arisen. In the South, especially however in the Southwest, the present, present perfect, future, future perfect in the subordinate clause are the rule, whether they follow a present or a past, as illustrated in B below, while in the Southeast and the North the simple past, past perfect, periphrastic past subjunctive (**würde loben**), and periphrastic past perfect subjunctive (**würde gelobt haben**) prevail under the same conditions, as illustrated in A. *b*. *Note* below. Thus it appears that the new literary sequence has developed under the influence of Southwest dialect, but it differs from it in one essential feature — it abandons the new sequence and retains the old historic construction, if in any case the subjunctive of the present, present perfect, future, and future perfect would not be clearly distinguished in form from the corresponding indicative tenses, as explained in B. *a* below. For a history of the younger construction and present literary usage see 5 below.

The following points may serve to illustrate the form and use of these constructions:

A. *The old law of sequence*:

a. A present, present perfect, future, or future perfect follows a present: **Er sagt, er sei krank, er habe es schon getan, er werde morgen kommen, er werde es innerhalb einer Woche getan haben.**

b. A simple past, past perfect, periphrastic past subjunctive, or periphrastic past perfect subjunctive follows a past or past perfect: **Er sagte, er wäre krank, er hätte es schon getan, er würde** (would) **morgen kommen, er würde es innerhalb einer Woche getan haben.**

Note. Sometimes a past or past perfect subjunctive seemingly depends upon a present tense. Such constructions are elliptical, some verb in a past tense form being understood: **Und sag' Er** (**140.** *a. Note*) **ihr [, daß ich sagte], sie sollte sich in Acht nehmen, der Laharpe** (name) — **das wäre ein Spitzbube** (Gutzkow's *Zopf und Schwert*, I, 7). **Bringe Wendelin meine Grüße und [sage ihm, ich sagte,] es wäre hübsch von ihm gewesen, daß er dir diese Reise gegönnt** (Fontane's *Poggenpuhls*, chap. viii). Likewise in indirect questions: **Ein Kompliment an den Konrektor Eckerbusch, und [sagen Sie ihm, ich ließ fragen,] ob es morgen regnete** (Raabe's *Horacker*, chap. I). The past tense forms of the subjunctive are nowhere in indirect discourse so generally used as in these elliptical constructions. We often, however, find in the Southeast and the North a past tense form after a real present tense, as the speaker or writer desires to give a dialectic coloring to the language, or is unconsciously influenced by dialect: **Sie dürfen nicht Theater spielen und keine Bälle abhalten; der Hofer** (name) **sagt, für so etwas wäre jetzt kein Wetter** (Rosegger). This is especially common in naturalistic authors: **Sie sagt, du wärst krank. Das hab' ich doch immer jesagt, Robert** (G. Hirschfeld's *Mütter*, Act 4). **Dein Onkel Gottfried sagt, das wären die Folgen der Kadettenhauserziehung. Ob er recht hat, weiß ich nicht** (Ompteda's *Sylvester von Geyer*, LIX). See 2 above.

c. The unreal optative and potential subjunctives of the direct discourse do not change their tenses when transposed into the indirect statement, present time being always expressed by a past tense form, and past time by the past perfect tense, a preceding present or past tense not influencing the construction. For examples see 1. *d* above. Thus after a past tense the *unreal* optative and potential subjunctives cannot be distinguished by their form from the sanguine optative and the plausible potential which have been attracted into a past tense under the influence of a preceding past tense. For examples see **169.** 1. C. *a*, **169.** 2. A. (2), 4th par., **171.** 4. *a* (2nd par.). It will therefore be a real gain for the language if the old sequence be still further restricted in its use.

B. *The new law of sequence.* The same tense may stand in the indirect discourse as stood in the direct with the exception of the past and past perfect. The past and past perfect of the direct discourse are both rendered by the present perfect in the indirect, or the past perfect *may* be rendered by the special form described and illustrated in *e* below. The past and past perfect subjunctive are avoided in indirect discourse, as they can easily be misunderstood. The past subjunctive is used so much after a past tense to express present time that it is now no longer as in former periods felt as having a past force. The past perfect subjunctive might be mistaken for an unreal potential as found in unreal conditions for past time. The tenses of the subjunctive employed in indirect discourse according to the new law are therefore the present, present perfect, future, and future perfect, and the special forms described in *e* below, a preceding present or past tense having no influence whatever upon the following tenses:

	Direct.	Indirect.
(1)	**Ich bin krank**	**Er sagt** or **sagte, er sei krank**
(2)	(*a*) **Ich tat es** (*b*) **Ich habe es getan** (*c*) **Ich hatte es getan**	" " " **er habe es getan**
(2)	(*c*) **Nachdem ich gelesen hatte, schrieb ich einen Brief** (an additional illustration of the preceding point)	" " " **nachdem er gelesen [habe], habe er einen Brief geschrieben** (another indirect form for (2) (*c*) is given in *e* below).
(3)	**Ich werde kommen**	" " " **er werde kommen**
(4)	**Ich werde es innerhalb einer Woche getan haben**	" " " **er werde es innerhalb einer Woche getan haben.**

a. Modified new law. Altho the new sequence may be followed as stated above, it is more common to employ it only where its subjunctive forms are clearly distinguished from the corresponding indicative forms, and elsewhere to use the old historic sequence. Thus as the past tense distinguishes the subjunctive more clearly than the present tense a present tense form (a present, a present perfect, a future) is regularly replaced after a past tense by a past tense form (a past, a past perfect, a periphrastic past subjunctive) wherever the present is not a clear subjunctive: **Sokrates erklärte, alles, was er wisse, sei, daß er nichts wisse; viele wüßten** (the present subjunctive would be like the indicative) **aber auch dieses nicht. Sie sagten, sie hätten** (a past tense form instead of the present tense form **haben**) **es nicht getan. Sie sagten, sie würden** (a past tense form instead of the present tense form **werden**) **morgen kommen.** So strong is the feeling that a clear subjunctive form should be used that a past tense form is used instead of a present tense form even after a present tense, if a clear subjunctive form is thus secured: **Sie sagen, sie hätten es nicht gesehen, &c. Sagen Sie ihm, ich käme schon.**

In case of unclear forms the past tense forms are preferred even tho they themselves are not clear subjunctive forms: **Die Bildhauerei, sagen sie, könne keine Stoffe nachmachen; dicke Falten machten eine üble Wirkung** (Lessing). The very fact of choosing a past tense form here is felt as indicating a desire to express the subjunctive.

Thus the tense form used to-day in the subordinate clause does not depend upon the tense employed in the principal proposition, but results from a desire to secure a clear subjunctive form.

Note. Opposed to this change from a present to a past tense is the usage in the Southwest which employs present tense forms thruout in order that the tenses of indirect discourse may be conformed to those used in the direct: **Der äußerste [, sagte mir mein Führer,]. . . sei der Saturnus; der mit dem roten Schein . . . sei der Mars, und beide bringen** (instead of **brächten**) **wenig Glück den Menschen** (Schiller's *Piccolomini*, 3, 4). **,,Als ich damals mit dem Messer nach Ihrer Sohle stach,"** sagte sie, **,,dachte ich nicht, daß ich einst so Ihnen gegenüber sitzen werde"** (for **würde**) (G. Keller). **Ich merkte bald, daß ich einem Gegner gegenüberstehe** (K. F. Meyer). **Ich ließ merken, daß ich zur Not sie alle miteinander zu zwingen denke** (Hermann Hesse's *Peter Camenzind*, p. 59). This uniform use of the present tense forms often leaves us in doubt whether the forms are subjunctive or, as in *f* below, indicative, but the Germans in this section are not guided by the mere formal principle of always seeking a clear subjunctive form without regard to the tense, as they still have a lively feeling for the original principle employed in the new sequence, i.e. the retention in indirect discourse of the tenses of the direct, as explained in 5 below. See 2 above, also **168.** II. B. *b.*

b. Sometimes both constructions, the old and the new, alternate in the same sentence without any shade of difference or without any necessity at hand of resorting to the old rule as mentioned in *a* above: **Er sagte, Marie wäre wohl verschlossen, aber sie sei tief von Gemüt.** This is quite natural. The old and the new construction are both felt and will continue to exist side by side until the new construction has gained a complete victory. In the Southeast and North there is a natural tendency to use past tense forms more than is necessary, as these tenses are alone used in indirect discourse in the dialects of these sections. For examples of this usage see A. *b. Note* above, towards end.

c. The existence of the present and past tense forms of the subjunctive side by side in indirect discourse without a shade of meaning is contrary to the development of these groups elsewhere, where there is a marked tendency to use the present tense forms to express something as desired, probable, or as a subjective view, and to employ the past tense forms to express unreality or possibility. There are numerous traces of the idea of unreality also in indirect discourse: **Und wenn die alten Gelehrten da noch immer behaupten, Sie wären urgriechisch, wir beide wissen es viel besser** (Meinhardt's *Allerleirauh*, p. 177). **Es ist das Testament, von dem wir glaubten, daß es vernichtet worden wäre** It is the will which we erroneously believed to be destroyed. For additional examples see **169.** 2. A. (**2**) and G. *a.* (**2**), 2nd par. For the idea of possibility or cautious statement see *d* below and the reference there given. These ideas of unreality and cautious statement cannot develop strongly in the past tense forms in indirect discourse until the old sequence disappears, and even then will be limited by the cases where the new sequence cannot well be used, where the old sequence will consequently remain.

d. For the use of the cautious or modest subjunctive in indirect discourse see **169.** 2. G. *a* (**2**). See also *c* above.

e. Past Perfect of the Direct Sometimes Represented by a Special Form in the Indirect. The present perfect of the indirect discourse stands for the past, present perfect, and past perfect of the direct, and hence there is a lack of clearness sometimes in the indirect. There is a tendency to represent the past perfect of the direct in the indirect by a special form made by adding **gehabt** in case of transitives and **gewesen** in case of intransitives to the regular present perfect: **Er sagt** (or **sagte**), **er habe die Straße verlassen gehabt und sei schon in das Haus getreten gewesen, als der Schuß fiel** He says (or said) that he had left the street and had already entered the house when the shot was fired. This form is borrowed from dialect where it is the usual form for the past perfect. See **190.** 1. B. *a.* Likewise in the passive there is a tendency to represent the past perfect of the direct discourse in the indirect by a special form. The regular present perfect tense of the actional passive (**194.** 4) is here replaced by the regular present perfect of the statal passive (**194.** 4), which as explained in **194.** 4. *Note* 2 (2nd par.) often has the force of an actional past perfect and is so used where there is a desire of avoiding the past tense forms as here in the new sequence: **Er sei als wie von einem bösen Geist verfolgt gewesen, bis er eines Tages, als er sie in einer obern Kammer gewußt, ihr nachgegangen, ja vielmehr ihr nachgezogen worden sei** (Goethe's *Werther*, Am 4. September). **Die Ansicht, daß in Helsingland die göthische Herrschaft sich erhalten habe, nachdem sie im eigentlichen Schwedenlande bereits gebrochen gewesen sei** (Konrad Maurer in *Ger*. 18, 23). **Sie gingen auf eine Droschke zu, als Renard sich erinnerte, daß Lori ihm mitgeteilt habe: ihr Vater sei heute zum Reichskanzler geladen gewesen** (Wolzogen's *Die kühle Blonde*, I, 45).

f. The Indicative in Indirect Discourse. The use of the subjunctive in indirect discourse is one of the finest means of expression that the Germans have developed, for in exact thinking and in lively feeling it is often very desirable to represent things thought or spoken as mere subjective expression, or as the thoughts and words of others which we present with reserve, or to reinforce our own views, or which we brand as false. Moreover, one often uses the subjunctive here to clothe one's own thought and feeling in modest form. In every-day life, however, the subjunctive here is often replaced by the indicative, as the things thought and spoken are felt, not as mere conceptions, but as actualities with which one must deal, be they true or false. After a long struggle this practical way of looking at all that is thought and spoken as actuality has in English driven the subjunctive entirely out of indirect discourse. Between the English and the every-day German use of the indicative in indirect discourse there is, however, one important difference—in German the new sequence is often used, i.e. the same tense may be used as would stand in the direct statement: **Ich dachte, er arbeitet immer** (Hirschfeld's *Mütter*, Act 4). **Da tastete ich an den Riegeln und schlich hierher, denn ich wußte, du bist** (present time to the subject of the main verb) **hier, Meister!** (Sudermann's *Johannes*, 2, 8). **Wußte ja nicht, ob ich erwünscht bin** (Halbe's *Die Heimatlosen*, p. 77). **Ich erfuhr, daß meine Schwester schon seit Beginn des Krieges als freiwillige Pflegerin in einem Rotenkreuz-Spital in Kiew tätig ist** (aus einem Feldpostbrief eines Wiener Gymnasiallehrers, 1914) (in the direct discourse: **Sie ist seit Beginn des Krieges . . . in Kiew tätig**). **Haben die Leut' nicht erzählt, der Deichhauptmann ist vorbeigeritten auf'n Schimmel, Mama?** (Halbe's *Eisgang*, p. 80). **Ich fühlte mich glücklich, daß mir nichts geschehen ist** (Aus dem Feldpostbrief eines Steirers in *Grazer Arbeiterwille*, 1914). **Ich schaute schon, ob du den Schirm nicht vergessen hast** (Adele Gerhard's *Die Geschichte der Antonie van Heese*, I). **Ich hab' schon gewußt, es wird** (future time to the subject of the main verb) **dir recht sein** (Halbe's *Mutter Erde*, p. 89). **Ich hab' nicht gewußt, daß der Herr Olten kommt** (Hermine Villinger's *Das letzte Wort*) (the form **kommt** a present tense with the force of the future; future to the subject of the main verb at the moment in question, but past at the time of utterance); **'s ist gut, aber ich hätt' nicht geglaubt, daß du dies Jahr noch fertig wirst** (Hermann Hesse's *Peter Camenzind*, p. 254) (**wirst** used with the same temporal force as **kommt** in preceding sentence). **Sie wissen doch — er hatte mir doch geschrieben** (Hirschfeld's *Mütter*, Act 4).

If the principal verb refers to the past, the dependent verb which has a force that is future to the subject of the main verb often in the tone of lively narrative assumes the form of the past tense instead of the present or future: **Und diese Furcht vor den Menschen erschien ihr so natürlich, so notwendig, so zugehörig zu ihrem Schicksal. Wie konnte er verlangen, daß sie frei davon war** (H. Böhlau) (instead of **ist** or much more commonly **wäre**). **Man hätte befürchten müssen, daß man sich Nase und Gesicht an den metallenen Zacken zerriß** (Wildenbruch's *Vize-Mama*) (instead of **zerreißen wird** or **werde**). **Sie wissen, daß Frankreich, so oft es die russische Geldnot befriedigte, sich ausbedang, daß immer der größte Teil der Anleihe zum Zwecke der Kriegsausrüstung verwendet wurde** (Reichskanzler Bethmann Hollweg an den Reichstag, Aug. 19, 1915) (instead of **verwendet werde**).

A very common feature of indirect statement in the indicative mood is the use of the past tense instead of the present perfect, which would usually be employed. This shows that the speaker or writer is inclined to be influenced in his indirect statements by the form of lively narrative: **Sie telegraphierten über die neuesten Ereignisse, daß am 30. Oktober einige junge Armenier in das Regierungsgebäude drangen und dort auf den Kommandanten der Gendarmerie schossen** (*Kölnische Zeitung*). **Man sagt, er war früher katholischer Theolog** (Wilbrandt). **Ich erfuhr von dem Gastwirt, die Herrschaften kamen grade aus hiesigem Ort** (Hoffmann's *Rittmeister*, p. 97). This usage is especially frequent in a clause subordinate to a subordinate clause: **Er erzählte, schon in der Jugend, da sie noch auf derselben Schulbank saßen, seien sie gute Kameraden gewesen.**

3. *Mood and Tense in Indirect Questions.* Indirect questions (see *Note* below), which are a form of indirect discourse, have the same rules for mood and tense as are described above with the limitation that the subjunctive in the subordinate clause is now less common after a present tense in the main proposition: **Erzähle mir, was geschehen ist. Kein Mensch vermag zu sagen, ob er nicht | des Helmes braucht** (Schiller's *Jungfrau*, Prolog, 3). The subjunctive after a present tense *can* still be used if the attention is not called to a known fact or result so much as to the condition of doubt, inquiry, or anxiety in the mind of the person or persons in question as to the result or proper course to pursue: **Wie es bei der Medizin zu halten sei, weiß ich nicht** (Hermann Grimm's *Fragmente*, I, p. 363) What the procedure may be in case of (admitting women to) the study of medicine, &c. **Überlegen wir verständig und mit Bedacht, was zu tun sei** (Raabe's *Horacker*, chap. iv). **Im Vordergrunde steht die Frage nach der inneren Eignung, d. h., welche Sprache dem Zwecke der Mitteilung am besten und einfachsten diene, welche also zugleich für die Fremden am leichtesten zu erlernen sei** (H. Schuchardt in *Beilage zur Allgemeinen Zeitung*, No. 230, 1901). **Und wenn du die junge Dame kommen siehst, gehst du auf sie zu, nimmst deinen Deckel ab und fragst sie höflich, ob sie vielleicht zu Herrn Leutnant Rudorff wolle** (Hartleben's *Rosenmontag*, 3, 1).

After a past tense form the subjunctive here is the rule: **Ich wartete, ob er käme. Er erzählte mir, was er gesehen habe, wie es in der belagerten Stadt aussehe. Auch sah er sich nicht ein einzig Mal danach um, ob man ihm folge.**

The subjunctive may be used here as elsewhere in indirect discourse merely to give expression to the idea of indirectness of statement, even tho there is no doubt implied: **Der Vorsitzende Rev. J. L. Weldon,** headmaster **von Harrow, kein Neuphilologe von Fach, betonte in seiner Ansprache, ein wie großes Interesse er dem neusprachlichen Unterricht entgegenbringe** (W. Vietor in *Die Neueren Sprachen*, 1898, p. 572).

In the dialect of the Southeast and the North a past tense form of the subjunctive is here as in 2. A. *b. Note* above quite commonly used even after a present: **Der Strobel-Hies hat seinem Weib im Jähzorn einmal einen Streich gegeben, seitdem hat er die Höll' auf Erden, und seine bessere Hälfte schreit's um, was er für ein Büffel wär'** (Rosegger) The individual known as Strobel-Hies once gave his wife a blow in anger, since that time he has had in his home a hell on earth, and his better half is noising it about what kind of rude fellow he is.

Note. An indirect question is one that forms a subordinate clause and thus differs from the direct question, which always forms a principal proposition: **Wann kommst du?** (direct). **Sage mir, wann du kommst** (indirect). Indirect questions are introduced by the conjunction **ob** *whether*, an interrogative pronoun or adjective, as **wer, was, ein wie** (example given above), or by interrogative adverbs, simple or compound, as **wann** *when*, **wo** *where*, **wie** *how*, **womit** *with what*, **woher** *whence*, **wohin** *whither*, &c.

4. *Indirect Commands.* Imperative sentences when put into indirect discourse are in general governed by the same rules for mood and tense as declarative and interrogative sentences. The subjunctive of the simple forms of the verb is not usually employed here as elsewhere in indirect discourse. Instead of the subjunctive of the simple verb the following constructions occur:

a. The subjunctive of the auxiliaries **sollen** and **mögen**, the former with stronger imperative force: Direct: **Gehe schnell!** Indirect: **Sage dem Jungen, er solle schnell gehen.** Direct: **Kommen Sie morgen wieder.** Indirect: **Bitten Sie ihn, er möge morgen wieder kommen.** Father to son: **Hole deinen Freund!** In approaching his friend the boy says: **Der Vater schickt mich, daß ich dich holen möge.** After a verb denoting a strong expression of will we sometimes have here a subjunctive of a simple form of the verb as elsewhere in indirect discourse: **Sie verlangte, daß die Kerle schwiegen,** or **schweigen sollten.** After all other verbs the simple subjunctive is avoided here as the form may be taken for an indirect statement instead of an indirect command or request: **Sie läßt ihm sagen, daß er kommen solle** or **möge,** or in the former case more commonly **soll,** but in **Sie läßt ihm sagen, daß sie komme** or **kommt** the clause is an indirect statement. **Sie ließ ihm sagen, daß er kommen sollte** or **möchte** (indirect command or request), but **Sie ließ ihm sagen, daß sie komme** (indirect statement).

As in older German, the past subjunctive is still usually found after a past tense, i.e. the old sequence (2. A above) is still fairly well preserved here: **Sie bat, er möchte nichts sagen.** The old sequence is better preserved here after verbs of commanding, requesting, &c., than after verbs of saying, reporting, &c., as the time relations are much simpler, the verb of the dependent clause always representing a present tense of the direct statement, while after verbs of saying, &c., the complicated time relations—the verb of the dependent clause representing a present, past, present perfect, past perfect, future, or future perfect of the direct statement—have gradually led to the use of the new sequence (2. B above) with its clearer expression of the time relations and its fine differentiation (**167, 169. 1.** A) of meaning between the present and past tense forms of the subjunctive. As a natural result of its advantages the new sequence is now also often used here after verbs indicating an expression of will: **Der Furchenbauer** (name) **befahl jetzt, daß alles wieder aufgeladen werde** (Auerbach's *Dorfgeschichten*, p. 48). **Käpt'n (Kapitän) Krautsch schrieb nach zweijähriger Fahrt an der indischen Küste, daß er Fracht nach Amsterdam habe** (indirect statement). **Mutter Krautsch solle** (indirect command) **sich auf die Bahn setzen usw.** (Gustav Falke's *Die Kinder aus Ohlsens Gang*, p. 25). **Vom Reichsfinanzminister forderte er, daß er so rasch wie möglich die Fehlbeträge in den Betriebsverwaltungen des Reiches beseitige** (*Frankfurter Zeit.*, Nov. 10, 1920). **Er wollte, es ginge** (unreal subjunctive of wish) **immer so fort. Sie ließ ihm sagen, er möge** (request) **kommen. Sie ließ ihm sagen, er möchte** (modest or polite request) **kommen.** Compare 2. A. *c* above, also **168.** I. 2. B. *b* and **169.** 1. C. *a.* The new sequence has long been in use in the Southwest. See 5 below.

b. In case of complex sentences the verb of the subordinate proposition may in the indirect discourse be put into the subjunctive, while the principal clause is abridged to the infinitive construction, provided its subject is identical with the subject or object of the governing verb: **Anton befahl dem Führer, im Hause Wache zu halten** (= **daß er im Hause Wache halte**), **bis er zurückkehre.**

c. The indicative of the simple verb or the auxiliary **sollen**, to express confidence that a command will be complied with: **Ich gebiete dir aber, daß du pünktlich zurück bist. Es ist verboten, daß dieser Weg von fremdem Fuhrwerk befahren wird. Sage ihm, er soll gleich kommen.**

The indicative, however, especially in the North, is often used without such emphasis but yet with the implication that the speaker is counting on the performance of the act: **Bitte, Kniehase, sagen Sie dem Rittmeister, daß er mich draußen auf der Chaussee erwartet** (Fontane's *Vor dem Sturm*, iv. 17). **Sag' ihr, daß sie ihn verbrennt** (id., *Effi*, chap. xxiv). **Sagen Sie dem Zimmermädchen, daß sie meine Tasche und mein Plaid wieder hereinbringt** (Stern's *Der Pate des Todes*, I). The indicative of the simple verb is here quite common after the imperative of **sagen,** as the imperative of itself makes it clear that the following clause is an indirect command, but elsewhere after such verbs as **sagen** an auxiliary must usually be employed to indicate that the clause is an indirect command, as otherwise this clause would be taken for an indirect statement, as illustrated in *a.* Sometimes, however, the simple indicative is used also here if the context renders it clear that the clause is an indirect command: **Ich sag's dir, daß du den Schimmel nimmst** (Spielhagen's *Hans und Grete*, p. 63).

5. *Historical Development of the New Sequence.* In older German a thought, feeling, or command was much more commonly than now reported directly instead of indirectly. The person, tense, mood of the direct statement placed the whole situation vividly before the mind as if it were just taking place. The indirect form was used in the more objective, matter-of-fact reports. Here the first and second persons became third person, the mood became subjunctive, the tense after a past tense in accordance with the rigid Germanic sequence became past. Even in oldest German, however, attempts were made to break thru this fixed sequence. The present tense, which brought so vividly the whole situation before the mind began to be used in indirect discourse after a past tense. This present tense arose from the analogy of the present tense so commonly used in direct discourse, which in older German frequently alternated with the indirect form, just as in modern German it is sometimes possible to use the one form or the other: **Ganz unerwartet kam uns die Kunde: Gustav Falke ist nicht mehr!** (Richard Dohse in *Die schöne Literatur*, March 4, 1916), or indirectly **Gustav Falke sei nicht mehr. Er antwortete: Ich weiß es schon lange!**, or indirectly **er wisse es schon lange.** The influence of the direct discourse explains the occasional use of the present tense after a past tense in indirect discourse in the O.H.G. period, altho in general the old sequence was rigidly observed: Quadun . . . . , | zele ouh in giwissi, thaȥ er selbo krist si (Otfrid IV. 20. 18-19) **Sie sagten, er behaupte sogar, daß er der Gesalbte sei.** This is the beginning of the new sequence. Otfrid employed it repeatedly and even tho he was usually influenced by the consideration of rime it seems quite clear that the form was suggested to him by its use in colloquial speech. It did not, of course, occur in the learned literature of the period or in the M.H.G. court epics, but we find it again in the plain simple sermons of the thirteenth and fourteenth centuries: Do er horte, daȥ er so groȥeu zeichen bege (Predigtstücke in *Zeitschrift für das deutsche Altertum*, XIX, p. 183) **Als er (Johannes) hörte, daß er (Jesus) so große Wunder tue.** [Er] bat, daȥ er sich erbarme uber den armen mennisch (**Menschen**) (ib., p. 193). . . . er daȥ lerte, daȥ man elliv dinch laȥe vñ ime uñ sinen gebottin nah sol uolgen allaine (*Der sogenannte St. Georgener Prediger*, p. 296, G, about 1300 A. D.) **Er lehrte, daß man alles verlassen und ihm und seinen Geboten allein nachfolgen solle.** In the language of this period the use of a present subjunctive after a past tense has spread to pure purpose clauses introduced by **daß:** Die spise die hieȥ im unser herre ze sæmene cluben, daȥ diu iht verloren werde (Schönbach's *Altdeutsche Predigten*, III, p. 61, thirteenth century) **Der Herr hieß die Brocken sammeln, daß nichts umkomme.** Earlier examples are found in Otfrid. As the Southwest is at present the stronghold of the new sequence and as all the old manuscripts mentioned above as containing old examples show traces of the language of the Southwest it seems quite probable that this construction originated in this section. In early N.H.G. the new sequence became more and more common in the literary language supported in large measure by the dialects of the Southwest. As the dialects of the North and the Southeast do not show this development the literary language of these sections has more traces of the old sequence.

Independent Form of Indirect Discourse.

172. In a lively style the author or speaker often strips off all formal signs of subordination, and reproduces the thoughts, feelings, dreams, impressions, fears, &c., of another in grammatically independent form. The words are not represented as a free report of the author or speaker, but as a close tho indirect reproduction of the thoughts musings, reveries, &c., of another. The following two groups occur:

a. The tenses used are, just as in English, those usually employed in narrative: the past indicative to correspond to the present indicative of the direct discourse, whether used as a present or a future; the past perfect indicative to correspond to the present perfect or past indicative of the direct; the past perfect subjunctive to correspond to the past subjunctive of the direct; the periphrastic past subjunctive, i.e. **würde** with the infinitive, to correspond to the future indicative of the direct. The last form, i.e. **würde** with the infinitive, deserves especial attention. There is no tense in narrative corresponding to the future tense of the direct discourse. Narrative proper can only relate past events and hence can only use past tense forms. If in a narrative of past events there is a reference to the future it must be the thoughts and plans of someone, not actual events. We may report these thoughts and plans for the future in the subjunctive, thus indicating that we are reporting thoughts and plans not actual facts. The words *he thought, she thought* are never expressed here as the subjunctive alone indicates that the words do not relate events but merely report someone's thoughts, hence are indirect discourse. We may use here **würde** with dependent infinitive, but never **werde** with a dependent infinitive, hence employ a past tense form of the subjunctive, i.e. the old sequence in accordance with the general rule of using the old sequence in elliptical language, as described in **171.** 2. A. *b. Note.* In English we similarly use *would* or *should* with a dependent infinitive. In German, on the other hand, the past indicative is much used here instead of **würde** with a dependent infinitive, for in direct discourse the German often uses instead of the future the present tense in speaking of his plans for the future, thus vividly conceiving them as actual events. Thus we can relate these thoughts and plans for the future in the past indicative as if we were relating actual events. The question form of direct discourse is uniformly retained in this independent form of indirect discourse, but the tenses here follow the general rules stated above. The present infinitive used as an imperative (**177.** I. B. *e*) in direct discourse in admonitions to one's self is here retained without change of form, as illustrated in the last German example below. Examples: **Sie hörte plötzlich auf (zu weinen), ließ die Hände in den Schoß sinken und starrte ins Leere. Ja, warum denn eigentlich? Es war doch nichts Unrechtes geschehen. Das konnte ihr Marianne und jedermann bezeugen. Und ganz gewiß, sie hatte nicht mit einer Miene, nicht mit einem Wort Herrn Bodmann Gründe gegeben, sich in sie zu verlieben. War er denn überhaupt in sie verliebt? Nein, er empfand nur eine schöne, warme selbstlose Freundschaft für sie. Günther würde sich darüber freuen, daß ein so ausgezeichneter Mann sie einer edlen Freundschaft würdige** She suddenly ceased crying, allowed her hands to fall into her lap, and then stared blankly before her. Why, indeed, should she cry? Surely nothing wrong had happened. Marianna and everybody else could testify as to that. And surely she had never by a glance or a word given Mr. Bodmann reason to fall in love with her. Was he after all in love with her? No, he only had a beautiful, warm, unselfish friendship for her. Günther (her husband) would surely be glad that such an excellent man deemed her worthy of a noble friendship. **„Vielleicht kommt der Vater," sagte sie hinausgehend. Er schien es aber nicht zu sein, denn sie zog nachher die Stubentür zu und sprach geraume Weile draußen. Eine männliche Stimme war zu vernehmen. Fortunat spitzte die Ohren, während er zerstreut sein [von Leni gemachtes] Marterl betrachtete, den Jäger im Schnee, den winzigen Christus am Kreuz, kaum so groß wie ein Fingerglied, und das Stückchen Strauchwerk und Hecke, alles einfach mit kindlicher Phantasie und doch geschickt gemacht. Aus dieser Leni hätte etwas werden können! Wann kam sie nur wieder herein?** (Berlepsch's *Fortunats Roman*, pp. 80-81). **Allerhand Gedanken gingen ihm durch den Kopf. Sein Ämtlein freilich verlor er, wenn die Zensur abgeschafft wurde — was tat es? Dann würde er eine Zeitung gründen** (Ertl's *Freiheit*, p. 191). **Er freute sich auf den Tag. Die Stunde war sein. In dieser Stunde würde er sie alle, die Verwandten und Bekannten, die Lehrer und Schüler, das ganze Gymnasium und viele Fremde . . . in seinen Händen halten** (Stilgebauer's *Götz Krafft*, I, 3, p. 93). **Ewald Wiskotten las den hohen Gesamtbetrag. Wie kam der zusammen? Aber jetzt nur nicht fragen, nur nicht feilschen! Er unterschrieb.** (Rud. Herzog's *Die Wiskottens*, II, chap. 2). In the quotations from Berlepsch and Ertl the past tenses **kam, verlor, wurde abgeschafft, tat,** correspond to a present tense of the direct used as a future. English cannot usually thus employ a past tense pointing to the future. We can only use here the past of the auxiliary *to be going* with a dependent infinitive and even that in only a limited way: We might translate the simple past in the last sentence of the quotation from Berlepsch by the past of *to be going* with a dependent infinitive: *When was she going to come in again?* In all these cases the simple past tense might have been replaced by the past subjunctive **würde** with a dependent infinitive. In German the too frequent use of this clumsy form would be felt as inappropriate in this lively narrative form. The simple past tense here adds much to the liveliness of the style.

In the quotation from Berlepsch **hätte etwas werden können** corresponds to **könnte etwas werden** of direct discourse.

This independent form of indirect discourse has become very common in the novels of our time.

b. Instead of the tenses employed in *a* we also find the same tenses and moods as used in the direct discourse: **Und wie der Friedl nun so mit sich allein war, da versank er in ein Träumen, wie sonst noch nie. — Aus der Hosentasche zog er eine kleine goldene Uhr und schaute sie an und hob schon die Hand, um sie ins Gestein zu schleudern, tat's aber nicht. — Ob nicht die Rosel so was möchte? Ei natürlich, die soll sich's nur selber kaufen. Er wird überhaupt nicht mehr viel reden mit dem Geiß-Mädl, er hat ganz andere Aussichten, wenn er will. Manchmal einen Gefallen, wenn's drauf ankommt, kann man einer ja wohl erweisen. Aber ungut wird ihm schier, wenn er an diese — diese Stadtleute denkt. Es ist halt doch wahr, was man von ihnen sagt. So dachte er und schüttelte den Kopf** (Rosegger's *Durch!* p. 67).

Conjugation.

173. *The infinitive.* The form of the verb usually given in the dictionary is the infinitive, which ends in **en** except after **-el** and **-er,** where the **e** of the **en** is dropped, as also in the two isolated verbs **tun** to do, **sein** to be: **loben** to praise, **wandern** to wander, **wandeln** to saunter.

174. *The stem.* By cutting off **en** from the infinitive, or **n** after **-el** and **-er,** the simple stem of the verb is found, out of which grow all the varied forms of conjugation.

175. *Forms of conjugation.* Like the English, the German verb has a *common* and an *interrogative* form, and has besides in the second person a form for familiar language and another for polite intercourse, but lacks the *emphatic* and *progressive* forms of the English, the common form serving usually for the English common, emphatic, and progressive. The German has an emphatic form that corresponds in part to the English. See **185. B. I. 2. *e.* (2).** See *Note* below for the German methods of expressing the idea of progression or duration. The *polite* form is the same as the third person pl., and is distinguished from it by writing its subject, the pronoun **sie,** with a capital: **sie loben** they praise, **Sie loben** you praise. This polite form is the same in the sing. and pl. The familiar form, which is also used in solemn style, has **du** for its subject in the sing. and **ihr** in the pl. The personal endings of the verb are added to the stem:

Present Tense Declarative.	Present Tense Interrogative.
Singular.	
ich lobe I praise, am praising, do praise	**lobe ich?** do I praise?
(familiar form) **du lobst** you praise, are praising, do praise	**lobst du?** do you praise?
(polite form) **Sie loben**	**loben Sie?** do you praise?
er, sie, es lobt he, she, it praises, is praising, does praise	**lobt er, sie, es?** does he, she, it praise?
Plural.	
wir loben we praise, &c.	**loben wir?** do we praise?
(familiar form) **ihr lobt** you praise, &c.	**lobt ihr?** do you praise?
(polite form) **Sie loben** you praise, &c.	**loben Sie?** do you praise?
sie loben they praise, &c.	**loben sie?** do they praise?

Hereafter the polite form will be omitted in the conjugation, as it is exactly the same as the third person pl., except that its subject **Sie** is written with a capital letter.

Note. Different Forms of the Durative Aspect. The durative aspect (see **164**) is in both German and English usually expressed by the simple verb: **Er schreibt oft den ganzen Tag** He often writes the whole day. To emphasize the idea of duration indicating that the activity is progressing at a given time we have in English an especial durative form called the progressive form: He is now writing a letter **Er schreibt jetzt einen Brief.** Thus the English progressive form often corresponds to the simple verb in German. To emphasize especially the idea of progression, the German employs in connection with the verb the adverb **gerade** or **eben** or instead of the adverb a prepositional object, usually **an** + dative of the substantive, or these constructions may be replaced by a prepositional phrase consisting usually of the preposition **bei, in,** or **an** and the infinitive substantive of the verb: **Ich schréibe gerade** (or **eben,** both adverbs unstressed) I am writing. **Sie tánzten gerade, als ich eintrat** They were dancing when I entered. **Er schrieb an einem Briefe** He was writing a letter. **Sie ist beim Anziehen** She is dressing. **Die Kurse sind im Steigen, im Fallen** The value of stocks is rising, falling. **Sie hatte es grade mit einem Kinde zu tun, das am Kartoffelschälen war** She was just then occupied with a child who was peeling potatoes. It should be noticed that in this progressive form the object must assume the form of a prepositional object after the preposition **an,** as in the third from the last example, or it must form a compound with the infinitive-substantive as in the last example. Instead of the infinitive-substantive it is quite common to employ the prepositional infinitive in connection with **dabei: Ich bin dabei** or **gerade dabei, einen Brief an meinen Vater zu schreiben.** This form is especially common, as here, where there are objects and adverbial modifiers which would be difficult to unite with the infinitive-substantive. The progressive idea is also expressed by means of the participles **begriffen** and **beschäftigt** in connection with a prep. phrase: **Die Truppen sind im Anmarsch begriffen** The troops are advancing. **Ich bin gerade mit Schreiben beschäftigt. Die japanischen Matrosen sind beim Aufräumen der Minen im Hafen beschäftigt** (*Hamburger Nachrichten,* Jan. 7, 1905). As in the last sentence the object often assumes the form of an attributive objective genitive dependent upon an infinitive-substantive. The infinitive-substantive is often replaced here by the prepositional infinitive in connection with **damit,** especially where there are objects and adverbial modifiers which would be difficult to unite with an infinitive-substantive: **Ich bin (gerade) damit beschäftigt, einen langen Brief an meinen Vater zu schreiben.**

To indicate that an activity is sustained thruout a period we use in English *keep* or *keep on* in connection with the present participle, while in German the verb is compounded with the separable prefix **fort** and is often modified by the prepositional phrase **in einem:** He kept on laughing **Er lachte in einem fort. Das regnet ja heut in einem fort! Der Regen dauert fort. Er arbeitet unermüdlich fort.** To indicate a continuation of a condition of things *remain* with the present participle is used in English, **bleiben** with the infinitive in German: He remained standing, sitting **Er blieb stehen, sitzen. Etwas blieb hängen, an der Pfanne kleben. Die Uhr fiel hin, aber sie blieb gehen. Die Zigarre blieb brennen.**

Terminates, i. e. verbs in which the duration of the action is short, the action beginning and ending within a limited period, are closely related to duratives and, like them, have the simple form of the verb and are also often otherwise treated like them, as illustrated in **191.** I. 3, but they differ from them in that they indicate an action *as a whole* rather than as continuing: **Er winkte mir. Er hat mit keiner Wimper gezuckt. Er schoß ihn tot. Sie wiegte ihr Kind in den Schlaf. Er lachte sich halb zu Tode.** In many terminates the *final point,* as in the last example, or the *beginning,* as in the next to the last example, is quite prominent, so that the terminate aspect is often closely related to the point-action aspect (**164**), often merging into it, as indeed the point-action aspect has itself largely developed out of it. The point-action idea is present when the conception of a point becomes more prominent than that of the action. See **246.** II. 3. *b.*

Regular Conjugation.

176. There are two regular conjugations, the weak and the strong.

1. The weak forms its past tense by adding **te** to the stem, and its perf. participle by prefixing **ge** and adding **t** to the stem: **loben** to praise, past **lobte** praised, perf. participle **gelobt** praised. This is by far the largest class of verbs and is growing at the expense of the strong as from time to time a few strong verbs have left their old class and joined this class. Moreover new formations, such as **radeln** *to ride on a bicycle,* **telephonieren** *to telephone,* are almost invariably weak.

2. The strong forms its past tense by a change of vowel within the stem of the verb, and its perf. participle by prefixing **ge,** usually changing the vowel of the stem, and by adding **en** to the stem: **singen** to sing, past **sang** sang, perf. participle **gesungen** sung. This class is not so large as formerly. Altho a few words have from time to time joined it, there has in general been a steady decrease. Altho it is comparatively small it subdivides into classes and divisions. The full description of these classes and divisions and the lists of verbs belonging to each are given in **198–205.**

The Simple Forms of the Verb.

177. The simple forms of the verb are all active except the perf. part. and the modal verbals (**180**), which are passive. In the following paradigms all the simple forms of the verb are given, and besides a few common compound forms which supply the place of the wanting simple forms. The words inclosed in parentheses are under certain circumstances a regular part of the verbal form, while under other circumstances they are omitted. The accompanying reference will usually explain in full this point.

I. *The simple forms of the weak verb:*

Present. I praise, &c.		Past. I praised, &c.	Present.	
Indic.	Subj.	Indic. & Subj.	Imperative	
ich lobe	**lobe**	**lobte**	**lobe ich**	
			(familiar)	(polite)
du lobst	**lobest**	**lobtest**	**lobe,**	**loben Sie** praise
er lobt	**lobe**	**lobte**	**er lobe** let him praise, *or* **er soll loben**	
wir loben	**loben**	**lobten**	**loben wir** let us praise	
			(familiar)	(polite)
ihr lobt	**lobet**	**lobtet**	**lob(e)t,**	**loben Sie** praise
sie loben	**loben**	**lobten**	**sie sollen loben** let them praise	

Infinitive. Pres. (**zu**) **loben** to praise (**185.** A and B)

Participle. Pres. **lobend** praising; Perf. Passive **ge'lobt** praised

The Modal Verbals.

Predicate Form: **zu loben** (**180.** A).
Attributive Form: **der** (**, die, das**) **zu lobende** (**180.** B)

A. Imperative Forms.

The *imperative* of both strong and weak verbs has forms only for the 2nd person sing. and pl. of the familiar form: **Reiche mir das Buch! Vergeßt es ja nicht! Kommt doch mit!** (spoken entreatingly) *Do come along!* **Kómm** (see **50.** A. 2. *b*) **doch endlich einmal!** (spoken in a threatening, impatient tone) *Come this very minute!* These imperative forms spoken in an ironical tone in connection with the adverb **doch** or **doch nur** do not have the force of a command at all but are prohibitions: **Kommt doch nur mit!** *Don't you dare to come!*

The other simple forms given above are subjunctive forms used to replace the wanting imperative forms. The subjunctive imperative of the 1st pers. sing. is only rarely found: **Denn, gesteh' ich es nur, nicht ruft die nahe Gefahr mich | aus dem Hause des Vaters** (Goethe's *H. und D.*, iv. 137). **Ich sei, gewährt mir die Bitte, | in eurem Bunde der Dritte!** (Schiller's *Die Bürgschaft*). **Allein zu Lieb' und Ehe braucht es zwei; | und sag' ich's nur, mein Vater, euer Fürst, | war mir des Mannes ein so würdig Bild, | daß ich vergebens seinesgleichen suche** (Grillparzer's *Libussa*, 2). For the 3rd pers. sing. the subjunctive imperative has either normal or question order: **er lobe,** or **lobe er.** In the 1st pers. pl. and in the polite form of the 2nd pers. sing. and pl. the question order is alone used: **Doch, laß ruhen die Toten, sehen wir in die Zukunft** (Bismarck to his betrothed, June 13, 1847). If the imperative is preceded by a subordinate clause the first person plural subjunctive form with its question order cannot be used, as it would be felt as an indicative with inverted order. It must here be replaced by an auxiliary with a dependent infinitive: **Beten wir für einander, solange wir hier auf Erden sind,** but **Solange wir hier auf Erden sind, wollen wir für einander beten! Loben Sie** (polite form, sing. and pl.). The 3rd pers. sing. and pl. of the simple verb is usually replaced in colloquial speech by an auxiliary with a dependent infinitive. See B. *a* below. It is, however, still quite common in commands which have the indefinite **man, einer, keiner, niemand,** or **jeder, ein jeder** for a subject: **Man beachte folgendes** Let everybody note the following points. On the other hand, it is in general not infrequent in poetry and choice prose: **Dann zerbreche dies Britannien, wenn es zu ehrenhaftem Leben zu morsch ist** (Lienhard's *König Arthur*, 1). Less common in the plural, as the form is the same as for the indicative, but not entirely infrequent even here in commands or directions to a definite group of persons: **Alle stehen auf!** (Georg Edward). **Alle setzen sich!** (id.) **Alle gleichen Nummern treten hervor!** (military command).

Very common in a few formal expressions in polite language: **Erlauben mir die Herren, Sie mit einander bekannt zu machen: Herr von Leslie-Gordon, Herr Hofprediger Dr. Dörffel** (Fontane's *Cécile*, chap. 18). **Gestatten die Herren, daß ich Ihnen Herrn Lothar Brandt vorstelle** (Sudermann's *Die Ehre*, 2, 6). **Die Herrschaften verzeihen, aber,** &c., (ib.).

a. The pronoun in the familiar form is only expressed for especial emphasis or contrast: **Wartet ihr, indem wir voranlaufen.** The pronoun may not only follow the verb as in the example just given, but it may also precede: **Ihr da! seid aufmerksam! Du da! sei aufmerksam!** Instead of a pronoun, a noun can of course be used: **Karl, sei aufmerksam!** If, however, **du** and **ihr** accompany a noun in direct address they are not usually stressed: **Gehe hin zur Ameise, du Fauler; siehe ihre Weise an und lerne** (Prov. VI. 6, rev. ed.).

The **Sie** of the polite form is usually expressed in the literary language, but colloquially it is sometimes omitted, especially if it has been once expressed: **Na, das überlegen** (usually **überlegen Sie**) **sich man** (= **nur**)! (Halbe's *Mutter Erde*, p. 152). **Reiten Sie zur Fabrik und bringen** (usually **bringen Sie**) **mir — ich bitte flotte Gangart — Bericht** (Liliencron's *Kriegsnovellen*).

b. For the pres. perfect imperative see **190.** 1. A.

B. Substitutes for the Imperative of Strong and Weak Verbs.

The imperative is a formal expression of will, but it is not the only form of expression here, for different circumstances require different procedure, so that the will must formulate its demands in many ways, which in course of time have found a formal expression in the language. The simple imperative, the oldest of these forms, is still much used in commands, requests, admonitions, entreaties, supplications. The one form with its many meanings represents the simplicity of primitive speech. The meaning is indicated not alone by the form but as in primitive speech in general also by the situation, the accent, the tone of the voice. In course of time, however, other forms of expression have arisen. Of the different forms which are here gathered together under the general heading of substitutes for the imperative some are mere formal variants without a real difference of signification, while others have meanings more or less differentiated. These different forms of expressions are further differentiated by the modulation of the voice, which here as in the simple imperative plays an important rôle. The following groups appear:

a. The modal auxiliaries, which in connection with the infinitive of the verb to be conjugated are much used to replace the simple imperative and the wanting forms of the imperative. First person singular: **Möge ich ihn nie wiedersehen!** First person plural: **laß** (sing. familiar form), **laßt** (pl. familiar form), **lassen Sie** (polite) **uns loben!** The imperative with **lassen** arose early in the North and spread southward in large measure displacing the older simple form (**loben wir**). Even before Luther's day it had become well established in the Midland and was widely used in the literary language of the South, but later under S.G. influence the older simple form came into wide use again as it had remained firmly rooted in S.G. feeling. **Wollen,** like **lassen** a N.G. form that spread southward, competed earlier in the period with **lassen** for the mastery as over against the older simple form. It is still widely used: **Wollen wir einen Wagen nehmen? Nein, wir wollen** (indicative) **lieber zu Fuße gehen!** The question order is also used with **wollen,** altho not so commonly as the normal order: **Wollen** (subjunctive) **wir das annehmen!** (Storm's *Es waren zwei Königskinder*, p. 2). **Wollen** (subjunctive) **wir ihn** (Dr. Georg W. A. Kahlbaum) **in unserem Gedächtnis bewahren!** (Privatdozent Franz Strunz in *Beilage zur Allgemeinen Zeit.*, Aug. 31, 1905, p. 415). Of course the inverted order must be employed if some modifier of the verb is for emphasis placed at the beginning of the sentence: **Nun wollen** (indic.) **wir loswandern!** (Hauptmann's *Und Pippa tanzt*, p. 54). Second person: **Sechs Tage sollst du arbeiten; am siebenten Tage sollst du feiern** (revised edition, Ex. xxxiv. 21). The past subjunctive softens the force and imparts to the utterance the idea of advice offered modestly: **Neulich fragte sie noch nach dir. Die solltest du wählen** (Goethe's *H. und D.*, 2, 241). **Wollen** has much milder force here: **Traute, minnigliche Frau, wollest** (subj.) **nimmer fliehen** (Hölty). Imperative of **wollen: Wollet mir, geliebte Brüder im Herrn, Aufmerksamkeit schenken, daß ich euch ein Gleichnis erzähle** (Ertl's *Die Stadt der Heiligen*). **Bitte, wollen Sie Platz nehmen!** (Sudermann's *Fritzchen*). Past subj. of **mögen** is very common in polite language: **Möchten Sie die Güte haben, mir zu folgen?** The auxiliary **dürfen** is much used here in prohibitions: **Ihr dürft nicht laut schreien!** Children, you must not scream out loud! **Müssen** is much used here in the positive form of statement, to express the idea of compulsion: **„Geh!" „Ich will nicht." „Du mußt gehen!"** Third person: **Er soll** (indic.) **loben!** Let him praise! (command), or more mildly **er möge** (or still more mildly **wolle**; both subj.) **loben,** or **möge** (or **wolle**) **er loben!** May he praise! (wish). Plural: **sie sollen loben,** or **mögen sie loben. Wollen sich die Herren nur heraufbemühen!** (R. H. Bartsch's *Schwammerl*, p. 14). When the force becomes a little more vigorous and approaches a polite request the normal order is used with **mögen: Das möge nicht dahin mißverstanden werden, als sei eine bloße Hypothese von Haeckel** (name) **in unwissenschaftlicher Weise als richtig angenommen worden** (Adolf Koelsch in *Frankfurter Zeit.*, Feb. 15, 1914). Sometimes also the indic. of **mögen** is used: **Ist er gesonnen, ein Mörike-Album zu unternehmen, so mag er es sagen** (Schwind an Mörike, May 22, 1868). Often the indicative of **können: Du kannst gehen.** See also **213.** 2. D.

Of these auxiliaries **sollen** with its dependent infinitive in connection with the adverb **nur, doch,** or **doch nur** is not, when spoken in ironical tone, an imperative at all but a strong prohibition: **Wollen sie meutern? Rebellion machen? Sie sollen nur!** (E. von Handel-Mazzetti's *Stephana Schwertner*, II, chap. II) *Just let them dare to try it!*

b. The second person of the present indicative to express in a stern tone that the command must be obeyed: Kuhnert (trotzig): **Ich laß mir nicht'n Mund verbieten!** Die alte Kuhnert: **Still bist!** (Halbe's *Das tausendjährige Reich*, p. 66). In mild hopeful tone this form indicates confidence that a request will be complied with: **Du kommst mit!** Of course, you will come along! In deferential language the third person is employed, usually with question order: **Regt sich dannoch (dennoch) der Herr Pfarrer nit aso auf!** (E. von Handel-Mazzetti's *Jesse und Maria*, p. 15).

The first person of the plural is often used here instead of the second person singular when spoken in a stern tone: **Hans, du hast deine Aufgabe für heute nicht ins Reine geschrieben. Wir tun so etwas nicht wieder!** (Georg Edward).

A mild request is often expressed by the second person singular with the interrogative form of statement: **Kommst du nicht mit?** When spoken in stern tone this form often has the force of a threat indicating considerable impatience: **Kómmst du wohl bald?!** The stress is here uniformly on the first word. See **50.** A. 2. *b*. If the second person is used in connection with **wenn,** the transposed word-order, and rising intonation, it indicates a threat of future punishment: **Wenn du das noch einmal tust·!** In shopping the first person sing. present indic. or past subjunc. is a polite imperative: **Ich wünsche, bitte um, hätte gern,** or **möchte gern Stahlfedern.**

In dialect and colloquial language the impersonal passive (**219.** 5. B) is often used as an imperative expressing assurance and expectation that the command will be obeyed: **Jetzt wird mal aufgepaßt! Jetzt wird sich** (**219.** 5. B. *c*) **gewaschen!** Words of a physician to the mother of a sick child: **Gut, Sie werden der Tagespflegerin zur Hand gehen, aber nachts wird geschlafen und der Schwester** (i.e. the nurse) **wird hübsch gefolgt!** (Victor von Kohlenegg's *Eckerlein*).

c. The second person of the future indicative to express an admonition or give advice: **Du wirst hier bleiben!** You certainly will stay here. **Du wirst es tun!** You will do it if you follow my advice. Often in a more positive tone: **Du wirst den Apfel schießen von dem Kopf | des Knaben — ich begehr's und will's** (Schiller's *Tell*, 3, 3). Three lines further on the present indicative is used in still more positive tone. Often in the second person of the future in the interrogative form, spoken in positive tone: **Wirst du still sein?! Wirscht du glei' folgen, oder soll ich a Priegel** (= **Prügel**) **nehmen?!** (Hauptmann's *Die Weber*, act 5).

d. The perfect participle in short, sharp commands or warnings, or in brusquely urging a course: **Aufgestanden!** Stand up! **Den Wagen angespannt! Schnell Hilfe geholt! Vorgesehen!** Look out! **Nur nicht zu früh gefreut, Lenchen!** (Halbe's *Das tausendjährige Reich*, p. 48). **Nicht geplaudert!** No talking! **Aber reinen Mund gehalten!** But don't you tell a word of it. **Keinen verschont!** Spare nobody! **Aufgehört mit dem Spielen!**

Note. This form is usually interpreted by grammarians as a perfect participle, but to the author it seems to be the perfect tense of the infinitive with suppressed auxiliary of tense, as in **185.** B. II. *b*. As described in *e* the infinitive is widely used as an imperative. The perfect tense of the infinitive is employed as the speaker desires to emphasize the idea of the completion, the immediate and thoro execution of the act. All the meanings given above can easily be derived from this one. Here as in the present tense form the reflexive pronoun is often omitted, as explained in *e. Note* 1. (**3**): **Vorgesehen! Nur nicht zu früh gefreut, Lenchen!**

e. The present infinitive, to express a command or warning to children and informal commands in general, such as entreaties, requests, kind admonitions, directions, especially those directed to the public: **Maul halten!** Hold your tongue! **Schweigen!** Be still! **Aber dich nie wieder so dicht am Wasser auf die Erde legen und einschlafen! Verstanden?** (Wildenbruch) But don't ever lie down again so near the water and go to sleep! Do you understand? **Ruhig, ruhig! Nur ja nicht ärgern** (Hauptmann's *Einsame Menschen*, 1) (see (**3**) in *Note* below). **Nein, nein, bitte, setzen!** (Sudermann) No, no, please be seated. **Bitte, mich auch fliegen lassen!** Please throw me up into the air too! **Ich bitte, bitte: essen! nur einen Bissen davon, aber essen! „Nur nicht aufregen,“ warnte der Arzt, „dämpfen! Zerstreuung braucht er jetzt nicht, langweilen soll er sich“** (Ebner-Eschenbach's *Rittmeister Brand*, XVII). **Dann rief ich dem Kutscher zu: „umkehren.“ Briefe postlagernd Konstanz adressieren** (in an advertisement) Address letters to Constance, to be called for. **Einsteigen!** All aboard! (to passengers). **Umsteigen nach Hannover!** Change cars for Hanover! Often in telegrams: **Vater schwer krank. Kommen! Gottfried** (Ompteda's *Sylvester von Geyer*, LXIII). The infinitive is especially common in admonitions to one's self as found in the novels of our time where the author reports in lively narrative style the musings of his characters. The last German example in **172.** *a* is an apt illustration of this common usage. The infinitive here, however, is no longer felt with its original imperative force but is a narrative form which *relates* the admonitions of someone to himself.

Note 1. Observe in the above examples (**1**) that in a negative command the negative must precede the infinitive, (**2**) that the separable prefix is not separated, (**3**) that reflexive verbs in this imperative form sometimes take the reflexive pronoun and sometimes are without it, especially so in certain set expressions, as in the fourth and fifth examples. The omission of the reflexive pronoun is explained by the older substantive nature of the infinitive. Compare **185**. A. I. 6. *Note* 3.

Note 2. Compare carefully the meaning of *d* and *e*. They are both essentially N.H.G. developments and aptly illustrate the modern tendency to differentiate. They are both fine contributions of colloquial speech to the literary language. They have added to German new shades of meaning not contained in the older simple imperative.

Note 3. *Origin of the Infinitive Imperative.* The infinitive here was probably dependent originally upon some auxiliary understood: **[Du sollst dein] Maul halten!**

f. A substantive or adverb: **Achtung!** Attention! **Vorwärts!** Forward!

g. A subordinate clause: **Daß du so fortfährst und deinen lieben Eltern viel Freude machst!** Keep right on in this way, and thus bring your dear parents much joy! **Eduard! daß die Briefe noch vor 8 auf der Post sind** Edward! see to it that the letters are at the Post Office by eight. **Ób** (for strong accent here see **50**. A. 2. *b*) **du hergehst!**

C. Dialectic Variations of the Personal Endings.

The personal endings of the plural pres. indic. vary in different dialects from the above models. There is in some dialects a tendency to use uniformly the same personal ending thruout the plural, one form leveling the others. This is also true of strong verbs, as they have exactly the same personal endings as the weak. Thus in most editions of Goethe's *Götz*, 1, 1 (not, however, in the Weimar edition) we find in the dialectic language there employed **-en**, the ending of the 1st and 3rd pers. pl., also in the 2nd pl.: **Wollen ihr Ruh haben?**

The old ending **ent** for the 3rd pers. pl. is preserved in parts of the Southwest, especially in the Swabian and the eastern Swiss dialects, in many sections, however, in the reduced form **et**, and from the 3rd pers. has spread to the 1st pers. and in many sections also to the 2nd person, so that the whole plural ends in **ent** or **et**. This old 3rd pers. pl. ending in the form of **nd** is also preserved in the literary language in the one word **sind**, which form has also spread to the 1st pers. pl. In dialect the older 1st pers. pl. form **sein** often occurs and has spread to the 3rd pers.: **wir sein, sie sein.**

In some of the western Swiss dialects the ending for the 1st and 3rd pers. pl. is **e** (older form **en**) and **et** for the 2nd pers. In other western dialects the whole plural may end in **e** (older **en**), or the ending for the 1st pers. pl. is **e(n)**, for the 2nd pers. **et**, for the 3rd **ent**.

In Bavarian and Austrian dialects complete leveling does not take place in the pl. The ending for the 1st and 3rd pers. pl. is **e(n)** and for the 2nd pers. pl. **et** or **ts** (regular 2nd pers. pl. ending **t** + **s**, the latter element of which is the contracted form of the old dual **es**; see **140**. *g*).

In the literary language the 1st pers. pl. in **en** has leveled the old 3rd pers. pl. in **ent**. This development was greatly facilitated by the fact that the 1st and 3rd pers. pl. of the present subjunctive and the past indicative and subjunctive ended in **en**. This leveling began in M.G. and later spread to Bavarian and the literary language.

II. *The simple forms of the strong verb*:

A. **singen** to sing. B. **fallen** to fall. C. **helfen** to help.

Present.

Indic.	Subj.	Indic.	Subj.	Indic.	Subj.
ich singe	**singe**	**falle**	**falle**	**helfe**	**helfe**
du singst	**singest**	**fällst**	**fallest**	**hilfst**	**helfest**
er singt	**singe**	**fällt**	**falle**	**hilft**	**helfe**
wir singen	**singen**	**fallen**	**fallen**	**helfen**	**helfen**
ihr singt	**singet**	**fallt**	**fallet**	**helft**	**helfet**
sie singen	**singen**	**fallen**	**fallen**	**helfen**	**helfen**

Past.

Indic.	Subj.	Indic.	Subj.	Indic.	Subj.
ich sang	**sänge**	**fiel**	**fiele**	**half**	**hülfe**
du sangst	**säng(e)st**	**fielst**	**fielest**	**halfst**	**hülf(e)st**
er sang	**sänge**	**fiel**	**fiele**	**half**	**hülfe**
wir sangen	**sängen**	**fielen**	**fielen**	**halfen**	**hülfen**
ihr sangt	**säng(e)t**	**fielt**	**fielet**	**halft**	**hülf(e)t**
sie sangen	**sängen**	**fielen**	**fielen**	**halfen**	**hülfen**

Present Imperative

Singular.

1st	**singe ich**		**falle ich**		**helfe ich**
	(familiar) (polite)		(familiar) (polite)		(familiar) (polite)
2nd	**sing(e), singen Sie**		**fall(e), fallen Sie**		**hilf, helfen Sie**
3rd	**er singe**		**er falle**		**er helfe**

Plural.

singen wir	**fallen wir**	**helfen wir**
sing(e)t, singen Sie	**fall(e)t, fallen Sie**	**helf(e)t, helfen Sie**
sie sollen singen	**sie sollen fallen**	**sie sollen helfen**

Infinitive.	Participle.	The Modal Verbals. (**180**)
Pres. (zu) **singen** (**185.** A & B)	Pres. **singend** Perf. **ge'sungen**	**zu singen** (predicate form) **der** (&c.) **zu singende** (attributive form; see **180.** B)
Pres. (zu) **fallen**	Pres. **fallend** Perf. **ge'fallen**	lacking with intransitive verbs except those in **185.** A. 1. *b*. (**2**).
Pres. (zu) **helfen**	Pres. **helfend** Perf. **ge'holfen**	**zu helfen** (the attributive form is lacking; see **180** B. *b*)

D. The three models given above represent the three different forms of inflection in the simple mood and tense forms of strong verbs, concerning which the following particulars are given:

a. Those that have an **a** in the stem modify as a rule that vowel in 2nd and 3rd person sing. of the present indic., as in B above. **Laufen** and **saufen** are the only verbs in **au** that mutate here. **Kommen** *to come* sometimes mutates. For cause of mutation see **197.** C. *a*.

Note. In S.G. mutation is often suppressed here: **du schlafst, er schlaft for du schläfst, er schläft.**

b. Those that have an **e** in the stem change it in the 2nd and 3rd person sing. of the present indic. to **i**, if it stands before two or more consonants, and to **ie**, if it stands before one consonant or silent **h**: **ich treffe** *I hit*, **du triffst, er trifft,** but **ich lese** *I read*, **du liesest, er liest,** and **ich befehle** *I command*, **du befiehlst, er befiehlt.** Where the stem vowel is short, as in the first example, there are few exceptions, but where it is long, as in the second and third examples, the exceptions are more numerous than the verbs that conform to the rule. All exceptions are given in *d* below. For explanation of the change of vowel here in the sing. see **26.** C, **197.** C. *b*, **201.** *f*.

Erlöschen *to become extinguished, go out* changes **ö** to **i**: **du erlischest, er erlischt.** **Gebären** *to give birth to* changes **ä** to **ie**: **du gebierst, sie gebiert.**

Note. In earlier periods **i** was also found in the first person sing., and this old form survives in S.G. dialect: **Ich vergiß' ihr alles — sie vergißt mir nix** (Ebner-Eschenbach's *Glaubenslos*, chap. i).

c. The imperative of the class that changes **e** to **i** or **ie** in the 2nd and 3rd pers. sing. of the present indic. also has in the 2nd pers. (never in the 3rd pers. as it is in fact a subjunctive form) sing., except in case of **werden** *to become*, the same change of vowel, but does not have a personal ending: **triff, gib, befiehl,** but **werde.** The exclamatory imperative **siehe!** behold! look! (from **sehen**) deviates often from the rule, in that it not only has change of vowel but also after the analogy of the wk. imperative may take the personal ending **e.**

The imperative of all strong verbs not having an interchange of **e** to **i** or **ie** in the 2nd person either remains without an ending in the 2nd sing. according to long established usage, or takes an e after the analogy of wk. verbs: **fahr** or **fahre** drive, **sing** or **singe.**

The imperative is often replaced by other forms just as in the wk. verb. See I. B above.

d. The following exceptions occur to the rules given in *b* and *c* above: (**1**) In the 2nd and 3rd sing. pres. indic. and the sing. imper. **geben** *to give* changes long **e** to long or short **i**, **nehmen** *to take* and **treten** *to step* change long **e** to short **i** and also double the final consonant of the stem: **ich gēbe, du gĭ̄bst, er gĭ̄bt, gĭ̄b; ich nehme, du nimmst, er nimmt, nimm; ich trete, du trittst, er tritt, tritt.** (**2**) **Bewegen, gehen, genesen, heben, pflegen, stecken, stehen, weben,** and usually **melken** and **scheren,** do not suffer an interchange of vowel at all in the present tense of either the indic. or imper. Now and then in loose colloquial speech other verbs show no interchange in the present: **ich schelte, du schiltst** or **scheltest,** imper. **schilt** or **schelt(e).** **„Jetzt komm," lächelte sie, schon wieder zuversichtlich ihn an der Hand fortziehend,—„und schelt**

halt noch einmal, wenn ich es nicht recht gemacht hab'" (Berlepsch's *Fortunats Roman*, p. 18). In the language of the common people this tendency to level out the irregularities of form and become regular is much stronger than in the literary language.

e. The subjunctive never shows interchange of vowel in the present tense but in the *past* tense regularly suffers mutation where the vowel is capable of it and sometimes as in case of **hülfe** has a vowel different from that of the indicative, as explained in **200**, 2. Division. *a.* and 3. Division, also in **201.** *b.*

f. All strong verbs not described in *a* and *b* follow the inflection of **singen** in pres. tense indic.

g. Mixed Past Tense. In early N.H.G. the past tense indic. of strong verbs often added an **e** in the 1st and 3rd person sing., after the analogy of weak verbs: **Dct. Faustus name** (for **nahm**) **jm** (for **ihm** = **sich**) **wiederumb ein Gespräch für** (for **vor**) **mit seinem Geist zu halten** (*Historia* **von D. Johann Fausten, 1587**). The oldest examples of this usage go back to the eleventh century. It reached its widest boundaries in the third quarter of the seventeenth century. We find these forms only rarely in the classical period: **ich litte** (Lessing's *Nathan*, 3, 8, 14th line). **Es flohe Freund und Feind** (Goethe's *Götz*, 3, 13). To-day **wurde** (for older **ward**) is the only surviving form of this mixed past tense.

III. *The simple forms of the irregular verbs* **haben, sein, werden:**

a. **haben** to have. *b.* **sein** to be.

Present. Indic.	Subj.	Past. Indic.	Subj.	Present. Indic.	Subj.	Past. Indic.	Subj.
ich hābe	**hābe**	**hătte**	**hắtte**	**bĭn**	**sei**	**war**	**wäre**
du hăst	**hābest**	**hăttest**	**hắtt(e)st**	**bĭst**	**sei(e)st**	**warst**	**wär(e)st**
er hăt	**hābe**	**hătte**	**hắtte**	**ĭst**	**sei**	**war**	**wäre**
wir hāben	**hāben**	**hătten**	**hắtten**	**sind**	**seien**	**waren**	**wären**
ihr hābt	**hābet**	**hăttet**	**hắttet**	**seid**	**seiet**	**wart**	**wär(e)t**
sie hāben	**hāben**	**hătten**	**hắtten**	**sind**	**seien**	**waren**	**wären**

Imperative.	Infinitive.	Imperative.	Infinitive.
Sing.		Sing.	
1st **hābe ich**	Pres. (**zu**) **hāben**	1st **sei ich**	Pres. (**zu**) **sein**
2nd **hābe, hāben Sie**	(**185.** A & B)	2nd **sei, seien Sie**	(**185.** A & B)
3rd **er hābe**		3rd **er sei**	
	Participles.		Participles.
Plur.		Plur.	
1st **hāben wir**		1st **seien wir**	
2nd **hābt, hāben Sie**	Pres. **hābend**	2nd **seid, seien Sie**	Pres. **seiend**
3rd **sie sollen hāben**	Perf. **ge'hābt**	3rd **sie sollen sein**	Perf. **ge'wesen**

The Modal Verbals.

zu haben (predicate form) **der (, die, das) zu habende** (attributive)

Note. Instead of the usual subjunctive present singular of **sein,** we occasionally find the forms **ich seie, du seiest, er seie: Da meint er, es seie die Burg schon genommen** (Uhland's *Graf Eberstein*).

Earlier in the period the perfect participle **gewest** was often used instead of **gewesen** by Middle German writers, as Luther, &c. and it still survives in popular speech.

Instead of the 2nd pers. sing. imperative **sei** the old form **bis** (from the same stem as **bist**) is still found in many dialects, especially in the Midland and Switzerland.

In early N.H.G. instead of the past indic. sing. **war** the older form **was** was used. Luther employed it in his earlier writings.

c. **wērden** to become.

Present. Indic.	Subj.	Past. Indic.	Subj.	Imperative
ich wērde	**wērde**	**wărd** or **wŭrde**	**wǘrde**	**wērde ich**
du wĭrst	**wērdest**	**wărdst** or **wŭrdest**	**wǘrdest**	**wērde**
er wĭrd	**wērde**	**wărd** or **wŭrde**	**wǘrde**	**er wērde**
wir wērden	**wērden**	**wŭrden**	**wǘrden**	**wērden wir**
ihr wērdet	**wērdet**	**wŭrdet**	**wǘrdet**	**wērdet, wērden Sie**
sie wērden	**wērden**	**wŭrden**	**wǘrden**	**sie sollen wērden**

Infinitive.	Participles.
Pres. (**zu**) **wērden** (**185.** A and B)	Pres. **wērdend**
	Perf. (**ge**)'**wŏrden** (**178.** 2. C.)

Note. **Wurde** is the more common form in ordinary prose, **ward** is a favorite in poetry and choice prose. The plural forms **worden** and **warden** occur earlier in the period: **sie worden** (Luther). **Die Länder . . . warden Euch durch Margaretens Hand** (Grillparzer's *König Ottokar*, 1).

178. General Remarks respecting the Simple Forms of the Verb.

1. Sometimes in adding the various endings to the stem, sounds are brought together that are difficult to pronounce, in which case an **e** is placed between stem and ending to facilitate the pronunciation: **zeichnen** to sketch, draw, **du zeichnest** not **zeichnst; es regnet** (not **regnt**) it is raining, &c. This **e,** once a vital part of the word, has so lost its original force that it can thus be used to facilitate the pronunciation and dropped when it is not needed. It is also sometimes retained to distinguish the different inflectional forms more clearly from each other, as for instance the subjunctive from the indic. It is thus to-day sometimes a mere *connecting*, sometimes an *inflectional* vowel, and hence is used or dropped according to the requirements of euphony or grammatical clearness. A brief outline of its present use is as follows:

A. The connecting vowel is usually retained in the following cases:

a. If the stem ends in single **m** or **n** preceded by a consonant other than **l** or **r,** the connecting vowel **e** always stands between stem and ending: **atmen** to breathe, **du atmest; begegnen** to meet, **du begegnest, er begegnete,** &c., but **hemmen** to retain, check, **du hemmst; qualmen, du qualmst; lernen, du lernst,** &c.

Note. These stems ending in single **m** or **n** preceded by a consonant other than **l** or **r** are derived from nouns or other parts of speech in **-em** or **-en.** In the conjugation of the verb the **e** of the suffixes **-em** and **-en** is suppressed in harmony with the contraction of adjectives ending in **-en** (see **110**): **der Atem, des Atems,** but **atmen; der Regen, des Regens,** but **regnen.** In colloquial speech, however, the connecting vowel **e** is often suppressed in the verbal forms: **segent** or **segnt, ebent** or **ebnt.** Traces of this usage occur in the written language: **Meine Liebe tat zu viel für dich; rechen's ihr nicht zum Fehler an** (Goethe's *Götz*, 1771, Adelheidens Vorzimmer). **Nun kommt das Schlimmste noch; es regent** (Heine). In early N.H.G. this usage is quite common: **Das es regent auffs Land** (Job xxxviii. 26). In careless pronunciation the **n** is also often assimilated to the preceding consonant: **ebmt** instead of **ebnt.** See **41. 4.**

b. When stems ending in **d** or **t** would stand before the ending **t** (and often before **st**), the connecting vowel is usually placed between stem and ending, except in the 2nd and 3rd person sing. present tense of those verbs having a modification of vowel or interchange from **e** to **i** or **ie,** which latter classes never take the connecting vowel but the regular endings **st, t,** or in case of combinations difficult to pronounce suffer contraction: **beten** to pray, **er betet, du bet(e)st, du betetest, gebetet,** &c.; but **laden** to load, **du lädst, er lädt** (lɛ:t); **halten** to hold, **du hältst, er hält; treten** to step, **du trittst, er tritt; fechten** to fence, **du fichtst, er ficht,** but in the pl. according to rule: **ihr ladet, haltet, tretet, fechtet.**

Note. In early N.H.G., and still in the language of the youthful Goethe, contraction was here common, not only in the 2nd and 3rd person sing. of the strong verbs above mentioned, but in all verbs in any place where a **d** or **t** would be followed by a **t** in the inflectional ending: (Goethe's *Urfaust*) **angemäst** for **angemästet, geknät** for **geknetet, zugericht** for **zugerichtet.** A few adjective participles still remain as survivals of this former usage: (**der**) **Beamte** (for **Beamtete**), **beredt, durchlaucht, erlaucht, getrost** (for **getröstet**; see **208. 1.** *a*). On the other hand, in early N.H.G. verbs which have a modification of vowel or interchange in the 2nd and 3rd pers. sing. present tense indicative may sometimes have there either an uncontracted or a contracted form, as **hältet** (written in early N.H.G. **heltet**) and **hält, flichtet** and **flicht,** while to-day only the contracted form is here used in prose, the older usage continuing only in poetry.

c. When stems ending in a sibilant, as **s, sp, ss, ß, sch, z, x,** would stand before **st** the connecting vowel is inserted between stem and ending except in the 2nd pers. sing. present tense of verbs having a modification of vowel or interchange from **e** to **i** or **ie,** which latter classes may take the connecting vowel in choice language, but in ordinary conversation add only the regular ending **st,** or in case of combinations difficult to pronounce suffer contraction: **fischen** to fish, **du fischest;** but **waschen** to wash, **du wäschest** or **wäschst; wachsen** to grow, **du wächsest** or **wächst; essen** to eat, **du issest** or **ißt; lesen** to read, **du liesest** or **liest.** In familiar conversation contraction is also quite common here even when there is no interchange of vowel: **du paßt, ließt** instead of **passest, ließest.** The choice language of our time, however, is becoming ever more unfavorable to contracted forms.

d. *Use of* **e** *to mark the Subjunctive.* The connecting vowel **e** besides serving to facilitate pronunciation distinguishes the subjunctive from the indicative in the present and also in the past of the strong conjugation, but the indicative and subjunctive weak are identical in form in the past tense, and in the strong conjugation the **e** may drop out of the past subjunctive where the modification of the vowel already distinguishes the subjunctive: **du tust** (indic.), but **du tuest** (subj.); **du gingst** (past indic. of **gehen** to go), but **du gingest** (subj.); **du gabst** (past indic. of **geben** to give), but **du gäb(e)st** (subj.).

Verbs the stems of which end in single **m** or **n** preceded by a consonant other than **l** or **r** cannot distinguish between indicative and subjunctive except in the 3rd pers. sing.: **ich atme** (indic.), **ich atme** (subj.); **du atmest** (indic.), **du atmest** (subj.); **er atmet** (indic.), **er atme** (subj.).

e. In early N.H.G. the connecting vowel was much more used than at present, being found in many cases where it is not found at all to-day: **Der Weisen zunge machet die Lere lieblich | Der Narren mund speiet eitel narrheit** (Prov. xv. 2). The poet still often uses these old forms, either because old forms are in general well suited to a poetic style, or because they here and there suit his measure: **Ich bin der dunkle Edelstein, | aus tiefem Schacht gewühlet: | du aber bist der Sonnenschein, | darin er Farben spielet** (Geibel).

f. In the Bavarian dialects (including those in Austria) the past subjunctive usually retains the connecting vowel **e** and suppresses the personal ending, thus terminating in **et** or **at** (representing O.H.G. **ōti, ēti**) in weak and often in strong verbs, as the latter have come under the influence of the former: **Ich mag ihn ja nicht, wenn er mir gefallet** (= **gefiele**), **so saget** (= **sagte**) **ich nichts** (Raimund's *Der Verschwender*, 2, 1). **I möcht' bitt'n, daß i dös Beschwerdebuch allamal über'n Sonntag g'liehn kriegat'!** (Karl Ettlinger's *Das Beschwerdebuch*, p. 35). Also with vowel-gradation: **Wo nahmet denn unser Herrgott d' Finger her, wann er auf jeden einschichtigen Bauern deuten wollt'** (Anzengruber's *Die Kreuzelschreiber*, 2, 3). These dialects have no past indic. See **165.** 2. *b.*

In Alemannic dialect we find the same use of the weak ending in the past subjunctive of strong verbs but with the suppression of the connecting vowel **e**: **ich kämt** (Gotthelf) = **ich käme.**

B. On the other hand, instead of inserting an **e** between stem and inflectional ending we often in loose colloquial speech drop an **e** of the latter: **ich seh** for **ich sehe; dreh** (imper. 2nd pers. sing.) for **drehe,** &c. The dropping of **-e** in indicative forms is most common here before an enclitic pronoun, where it is often suppressed to avoid a hiatus: **Da hör' ich, da hört' ich,** &c. In general, however, there is elsewhere little disposition in German to avoid a hiatus. Compare **62.** F. *a.* Mutilations of any kind are avoided in choice language.

a. Verbs the stem of which ends in **-el** and **-er** in accordance with the old law described in **62.** C. *Note* always drop the **e** of the inflectional ending before **n** in the indicative and infinitive: **wir wandeln,** &c. When **e** constitutes of itself the inflectional ending, it can never be dropped, but the **e** of the suffix may then be suppressed in its stead: (indic.) **ich hand(e)le;** (imper.) **hand(e)le (du);** (subj.) **ich hand(e)le.** The full form is now more common: (indic. and subj.) **ich handele.** In dialect and loose colloquial speech the ending is sometimes dropped: **ich handel,** &c.

b. The infinitives **tun** and **sein** are regularly without **e,** and **tun** also in the plural of the pres. indic., and **sein** in the 1st and 3rd pers. sing. pres. subj.: **wir tun,** &c.; **ich sei, du sei(e)st, er sei.** All verbs, both str. and wk., may drop the **e** of the inflectional ending **en,** when the stem ends in a vowel or a vowel followed by **h: schreien** or **schrein; gesehen** or **gesehn.** This dropping of **e** is very common in ordinary conversation, but is not usually indicated in the written language, the full ending **-en** being there preferred. The poet marks clearly the full or contracted form in the orthography, so as to make plain the metrical scheme. Even tho the **e** drops out, the number of syllables in the word is not in natural prose diminished, as the **n** assumes full syllabic function: **blühen = bly:n̥.**

c. The imperative of the 2nd pers. sing. of the weak conjugation has regularly an **e,** and the strong in imitation of the weak often takes an **e,** except those that have a change of vowel from **e** to **i** or **ie** in the 2nd and 3rd sing., which never take it with the one exception **siehe: beiße** *bite* for **beiß; wasche** *wash* for **wasch; singe** *sing* for **sing;** but always, **nimm** take, **hilf** help, **gib** give, &c. On the other hand, the wk. imperative often drops its **e** in the 2nd sing., but those in **-el, -en,** and **-er,** usually retain it: **reich** *reach* for **reiche,** but usually **läch(e)le, öffne, stolp(e)re.** Those in **-el** and **-er** drop sometimes in colloquial language the **e** of the ending and retain the **e** of the suffix: **lächel, stolper.** Those in **-en** always suppress the **e** of the suffix and retain the **e** of the ending: **öffne.**

2. **Ge-** does not stand in the perf. participle of:—

A. Those verbs that have no accent upon the first syllable. For the reason of the absence of **ge-** here see **246.** II. 4. *a.* Such verbs are:

a. Those that have the following prefixes: **be, ent** (**emp** before **f: empfehlen**), **er, ge, miß** (usually; see **246.** II. 8. B), **ver, wider, zer;** and the following when unaccented: **durch, hinter, über, um, unter, voll, wieder: ver'letzt** injured, **be'schädigt** damaged, **über'setzt** translated, but **'übergesetzt** transported across, &c. Also when such verbs enter into other compounds: **'aner`kannt, 'ab-ver`dient.**

Note. Exceptions occur in words where the prefix has been contracted and blended with the verb so that its force as a prefix is not felt: **gefressen** part. of **fressen** *to eat* (of animals), from **v(e)ressen,** &c.

b. Many foreign verbs and a few German ones:

(**1**) Those ending in **'ieren: stu'diert** studied, **buchsta'biert** spelled, &c. Children and uneducated people, earlier in the period also good authors, often prefix **ge** here: **gestu'diert.**

(**2**) Those in **'eien: prophe'zeit** prophesied, **kas'teit** chastised, mortified, &c. Earlier in the period **ge** is often prefixed here, and sometimes still in case of **bene'deien** to bless: **Sie gebenedeite unter den Frauen** (Spielhagen's *Faustulus,* p. 19).

(**3**) A number of other verbs which cannot be designated by an outward sign: **a'launen** to alum, **cham'pagnern** to drink champagne, **fran'zöseln** to mix French words into one's speech, **hu'rraen** (also **'hurraen**) to hurrah, **ka'paunen** to capon, **kal'fatern** to calk, **kar'nüffeln** to pommel, **kra'keelen** to kick up a row, **kre'denzen** to hand (a cup of wine to someone to drink), **ku'ranzen** to drub, **mi'auen** to mew, **po'saunen** to trumpet, sound forth, **ro'boten** to do compulsory service for a lord, **ru'moren** to make a noise, rumble, **sal'badern** to twaddle, **schar'mützeln** to skirmish, **schar'wenzeln** or **scher'wenzeln** to bow and scrape, be officious, **schlam'pampen** to feast, live high, **schma'rotzen** to sponge on others, **spek'takeln** to make an uproar, **sti'bitzen** to pilfer, **trom'peten** to trumpet, **zi'geunern** to rove about like gypsies, and usually **offen'baren** to manifest, reveal, but it is also accented on the first syllable and hence takes **ge-** in the participle and usually so in its special sense of *divine revelation*: **ein offen'bartes Geheimnis,** but **Wer an keinen persönlichen Gott glaubt, kann sich zu keiner ge'offenbarten Religion bekennen** (Spielhagen's *Herrin,* p. 142). Earlier in the period usage fluctuated, so that **offen'baren** could also be used in the sense of *divine revelation*: **Da ward Daniel solch verborgen Ding durch ein Gesicht des nachts offen'bart** (Dan. ii. 19). Usage is even to-day not entirely fixed.

In the case of the following compounds **frohlocken** *to rejoice,* **liebkosen** *to caress,* **willfahren** *to humor a person,* usage fluctuates (with preference perhaps for first mentioned form) between **ge'frohlockt** and **froh'lockt, ge'liebkost** and **'liebgekost,** and sometimes **lieb'kost, ge'willfahrt** and **will'fahrt.** Thus the compound may be treated as a simple verb taking accent on the first syllable and prefixing **ge** in the participle, or the first component element of the compound may be treated as an inseparable prefix taking no accent and hence no **ge-** in the participle. See also **217.** *b.*

For explanation of the accent in German words that take the accent upon the second element see **47.** 2. A. *b. Note.*

In spite of its accent the adj. participle **gena'turt** (earlier in the period common, now little used except in popular language) *-natured* prefixes **ge,** after the analogy of **geartet: feiner gena'turt als die aus fettem Ton geformte Menschheit** (Musäus).

B. *Perfect Participle with the Form of an Infinitive.* The perfect participle has the form of an infinitive in case of certain auxiliaries or auxiliary-like verbs, when in a compound tense they have an infinitive depending upon them.

a. When there is a dependent infinitive the participle has the form of the infinitive (for historical explanation see *Note* 1): **Er hat es gemußt** *He has been compelled to,* but **Er hat es tun müssen** *He has been compelled to do it.* These auxiliaries comprise the following: **dürfen, können, mögen, müssen, sollen,** and **wollen;** and more or less frequently the auxiliary-like verbs **heißen** *to bid,* **helfen** *to help,* **hören** *to hear,* **lassen** *to let* or *cause,* **machen** *to make,* **sehen** *to see,* **brauchen** *to need* (to do something), sometimes **fühlen** *to feel,* **lernen** *to learn,* and rarely **lehren** *to teach,* **vermögen** *to be able,* and **wissen** *to know,* all eighteen of which except **brauchen** (**185.** B. I. 2. *a*), **vermögen** (see example below), and **wissen** (**212.** 2. *c*) take an infinitive depending upon them without **zu: Ich habe es gekonnt** *I have been able,* but **Ich habe es tun können** *I have been able to do it.* **Wie viel traute Stunden hatte mir der alte Bursche bereiten helfen!** (Paul Keller's *Waldwinter,* xxi). **Man fühlte aus den Redewendungen heraus, daß die Zeit doch ihr Werk getan, daß neue Eindrücke die alten verwischt, neue Gesichter die Erinnerung an die alten hatten verblassen machen** (G. Ompteda's *Eysen,* chap. ii). **Ich hätte mich bloß nicht einzumischen brauchen** (or **einmischen brauchen,** or less commonly, but more correctly **einzumischen gebraucht**) *I simply had no need of mixing myself up in the matter.* **Wir hätten diese Schuld auch dann noch auf uns lasten fühlen** (Wustmann's *Sprachdummheiten,* p. 60, 3rd ed.)—now more commonly **lasten gefühlt. Hier tritt die Judith wieder ein . . . die den Teufel hat zähmen lernen** (G. Keller an T. Storm, June 25, 1878)—now more commonly **zähmen gelernt [hat]. Sie hat die Verhältnisse vorher nicht zu übersehen vermögen** (Ida Boy-Ed's *Fast ein Adler,* VII)—usually **zu übersehen vermocht.**

Note 1. *Historical Development and Present Tendencies.* This construction originated in the thirteenth century in such sentences as **Ich habe ihn lassen kommen.** Here **lassen** is an old perfect participle, which at this time was regularly without **ge-**, hence was identical in form with the infinitive, so that the group seemed to consist of two infinitives. As the relation between the two members of this infinitive group is as close as between the components of a compound the two members of the group were early felt as a compound verbal element and became fixed and rigid in this form—the form of two infinitives, altho the governing word was in fact a perfect participle. The two-infinitive form was also common elsewhere, as in **Er will ihn lassen kommen,** and helped fix this form here. Thus it early became usual in all close groups consisting of an infinitive and a governing verbal to give the governing word the form of an infinitive whether it performed the function of an infinitive or participle. This usage spread early to **tun, hören, heißen, helfen,** later to the modal auxiliaries **müssen,** &c., **anfangen, bitten, brauchen, fühlen, machen, lehren, lernen, pflegen, suchen, türren** or **thüren** (**212.** 2. *f.* (**2**)), **vermögen,** and **wissen,** whenever they had a simple infinitive dependent upon them: Von einem han (= **habe**) ich hoeren sagen (Biterolf, 7746, thirteenth century). Of these verbs **anfangen, bitten, pflegen, suchen,** and **tun** have abandoned the construction entirely. There is at present a growing tendency for other of these verbs to discard this peculiar participial form and use the form they have when there is no dependent infinitive, usually so in case of **fühlen, lehren, lernen, wissen,** and for the most part **vermögen,** quite often in case of **brauchen, helfen, lassen** (*Note* 3), **machen,** and with great frequency in case of **hören** and **sehen.** The modal auxiliaries hold most tenaciously to the old construction, but the true participial form seems also here to be gaining ground. Two forces are at present active and have long been active in spreading the true form. Firstly, the strong ever growing general tendency to place the personal part of the verb at the end of the subordinate clause asserts itself also here, often in colloquial speech, less frequently in the literary language, which of course makes it necessary to use the true participle, as the auxiliary **haben** cannot stand after a simple infinitive: **Überdies ist jener Beruf** (i.e. photography) **ein Sammler und rettender Einfänger von vielen Geistern, die einstmals höher fliegen gewollt hätten** (R. H. Bartsch's *Die Haindlkinder,* p. 128). The auxiliary here as elsewhere is sometimes suppressed: **Wenn er doch sterben gedurft!** (G. Ompteda). Secondly, in the principal proposition the dependent infinitive is often for emphasis placed at the beginning of the sentence, so that the participle at the end, no longer felt as standing as a fixed element in a group formation, often assumes its true form: **Essen hab' ich nicht viel gemocht** (Schulze-Smidt). From these two categories the true participial form spreads to others: **Wir hatten es ja nicht besser haben gewollt** (Raabe).

The infinitive is usually employed when the dependent infinitive has passive form, but the true participle is sometimes found here: **Es ist überraschend, mit welchem Erfolg der Grundsatz hat durchgeführt werden können** (*Hamb. Nachr.,* June 3, 1905). **Den S-gefügen, die Beiheft I, Seite 5 als in Westfalen üblich aufgeführt worden sind, hätten noch Werksführer, Werksbesitzer usw. zugeführt werden gekonnt** (Professor M. Trautmann in *Wissenschaftliche Beihefte,* No. 3, p. 133).

Note 2. **Lehren, lernen, helfen,** and **heißen** may also require a **zu** before the dependent infinitive, as described in **185.** B. I. 2. *c, Note.* In this case their participles usually take the regular participial form with **ge-** instead of that of the infinitive: **Früh schon hatten sie sich kennen lernen** (or more commonly **gelernt**), but **Er hat sich zu beherrschen gelernt** and **Du hast gelernt, den Mund verschlossen zu halten. Brauchen,** however, quite commonly takes the infinitive form instead of the participial, whether the dependent infinitive has a **zu** or is without it. See example in *a.* Sometimes **heißen: Jesus hat die Armut und das Elend nie und nirgends konservieren wollen, sondern er hat sie bekämpft und zu bekämpfen heißen** (Harnack's *Das Wesen des Christentums,* Sechste Vorlesung).

Note 3. The participle of **lassen** *may* assume participial form but only in the meanings *to let go, slip, to allow,* never in its other meanings *to cause, to have done,* &c.: **Die Mutter hat das Kind fallen lassen** (or **gelassen**), but **Die Mutter hat das Kind taufen lassen.**

b. Either Participle or Infinitive. If the verb is understood, both constructions are found: **Wir haben nicht weiter [gehen] gekonnt,** or less commonly **können.** The use of the infinitive here is strictly confined to the modal auxiliaries.

c. Word-order. The participle which has the form of the infinitive, usually, as in **Er hat árbeiten mûssen,** stands at the end of the sentence, as this position has become functional and is employed without regard to its logical force, but it may sometimes in colloquial language in accordance with older usage stand before the dependent infinitive: **Er hat mûssen árbeiten.** The new word-order **Er hat árbeiten mûssen** has resulted from the natural tendency to conform to the peculiar stress usually found elsewhere at the end of the sentence, as described in **215.** II. 1. A (3rd par.) and **285.** II. B. *b aa, bb, cc.*

d. Form in the Passive. In the passive, however, the past participle of the auxiliary assumes its regular participial form: **Der Arzt wurde kommen gelassen. Es ist mir geheißen worden, dies zu tun.** The passive, however, is only used in case of **lassen, lehren, heißen,** and **machen,** and even with these verbs it cannot be used if the dependent infinitive has passive force: not **Die Brücke wurde bauen gelassen,** but **Man ließ die Brücke bauen.**

e. Infinitive instead of Participle in Perfect Infinitive. In the perfect infinitive made up of the perf. participle of the auxiliary and the infinitive of **haben** (as for example **gekonnt haben**), the participle of the auxiliary usually assumes the form of the infinitive, when an infinitive depends upon it, or may here sometimes remain in participial form: **Er muß es so haben tǘn wȍllen. Du wirst ihn so haben sắgen hȍren. Ich freue mich, ihn haben begrǘßen zu dȕrfen** (Wilmanns's *Deutsche Grammatik,* III, p. 163). Where the prepositional infinitive must be used as in the last example some prefer to use the participle in the perfect infinitive instead of the infinitive, feeling that **zu** ought not to stand before a form which is an infinitive in appearance only, in reality however a perfect participle: **Ich freue mich, ihn begrǘßen gedȕrft zu hắben.** The "incorrect" form, however, by reason of its familiar end stress is the more common one.

C. When an auxiliary and not an independent verb, **werden** drops the **ge-** of the past part.: **Er ist gelobt worden** *He has been praised,* but **Er ist krank geworden** *He has become sick.* See also E.

D. A few adj. participles without **ge,** survivals of a period when the part. had no **ge,** are still found: **rechtschaffen** *upright,* lit. created right; **trunken** drunk; **so'tan** (, i.e., **so getan**) *such,* lit. thus fashioned, now rare; the following participial compounds, which, however, also have a regular form with **ge:** **'altbacken** or **'altgebacken** stale, **'hausbacken** or **'hausgebacken** home-baked, home-made, **'neubacken** or **'neugebacken** new-baked, **'frischbacken** or **'frischgebacken** new-baked, **'halbwachsen** or **'halbgewachsen** half-grown, **'neuwaschen** or **'neugewaschen** newly-washed, **'hausgewebt** or **'hausweben** home-woven, and occasionally **'hausmachen** (for **'hausgemacht**) *home-made,* in analogy with those in **-backen.**

E. A few participles without **ge-** are found in early N.H.G. and less frequently still later in the classical period, and even to-day in S.G. dialect, especially **bringen** to bring, **finden** to find, **kommen** to come, **kriegen** to get, **werden** (even when an independent verb): **Ich habe das Geld erst den 19. Januar kriegt** (Goethe). Often still in case of **werden** in poetic or archaic style: **Der ist ein Welscher worden** (F. Dahn's *Ein Kampf um Rom,* I, 1). For further treatment and explanation see **246.** II. 4. *a.* (especially towards the end) and *c.* (**2**).

VERBALS.

179. Those simple verb-forms which partake of the nature of verbs and have in addition the function and inflection of adjectives or nouns are the *modal verbals, the participles,* and *the infinitives.*

THE MODAL VERBALS.

180. There are two modal verbals, one for the predicate and one for the attributive relation.

A. *Predicate Modal Verbal.* The infinitive with **zu** assumes a peculiar modal force in the predicate, here called the predicate modal verbal. Tho active in form, it here has passive force and expresses the necessity, possibility, or fitness of an action: **Es ist viel zu tun** There is much that must be done. **Luft ist überall zu haben** Air can be had everywhere. **Das steht nicht zu ändern** That cannot be changed. **Der Schmerz ist kaum zu ertragen** The pain can scarcely be borne. **Dieses Fleisch ist nicht zu essen** This meat is not fit to be eaten. **Er ist zu loben** He ought to be praised. **Er ist hoch zu verehren** He is to be (should be) highly respected. **Die Nachricht ist vorsichtig aufzunehmen** The news is to be (should be) received with caution.

This construction is found in the following common cases:

a. As predicate complement of the intransitives **bleiben** to remain, **gehen** to be possible, can, **harren** to remain, wait, **sein** to be, **stehen** (= **sein,** but not so common) to be, and sometimes **scheinen** to seem, **werden** to become: **Es bleibt abzuwarten** It remains to be seen. **Wie wunderlich, daß des einen Glück hienieden nur immer auf dem Unglück eines anderen aufzubauen geht!** (Hans Hopfen's *Stellvertreter*, II, 1). **Da war so vieles zu sehen** There was so much there to be seen. **Es war nicht zu ertragen** It was not to be endured. **Von diesem bin ich zu retten** I can be rescued by him. **Und leises Getön ward zu hören** (Wilhelm Fischer's *Sonnenopfer*, III). In English this passive construction survives in only a few expressions: The house is to let. He is to blame. Now usually passive form: He is to be censured. The older construction, however, is still quite common where the infinitive is used attributively: the man to blame, the thing to do. The passive form is also often used here: a question to be lightly touched upon. In German the attributive phrase must be rendered by a relative clause of which the modal verbal is the predicate, or the form in B may be employed: **der Mann, der zu tadeln wäre;** or **der zu tadelnde Mann.** Sometimes the infinitive form of the modal verbal is seemingly employed in German in the attributive relation, only, however, in the position *after* the noun as in English: **Er verübte sonst noch eine ganze Menge Schandtaten, gar nicht aufzuzählen** (Kröger's *Leute eigener Art*, p. 117). Such adjective elements like other adjectives that stand after a noun are not felt in German as attributive but rather as predicate adjectives that stand in elliptical relative clauses with the subject and the verb **sein** understood. Hence they are regular predicate modal verbals, only in a little different form.

Note 1. If the predicate verbal governs the gen. or dat., the subject of the sentence is always the impersonal **es,** expressed or understood: **Einem Einwurfe ist hier noch vorzukommen** (Lessing) There is here still one objection that must be met. Compare **219.** 5. A (2nd par.).

Note 2. Corresponding to the peculiar impersonal passive described in **219. 5.** B. *c*, which admits of an object, is the use of a reflexive object with the predicate modal verbal in colloquial language, a usage which is much censured by grammarians, tho occasionally used by good writers: **Doch ist sich darauf nicht zu verlassen,** instead of **Doch kann man sich darauf nicht verlassen.**

Note 3. After the verb **sein** this infinitive is used with intransitives and reflexives with the modal force of the modal verbal but with active meaning. See **185.** I. 1. *b*. (**2**).

Note 4. To bring out clearly the passive force and the idea of necessity we sometimes find the passive form of the infinitive dependent upon the prepositional infinitive of **müssen: Leider scheint diese Hoffnung endgültig aufgegeben werden zu müssen** (*Hamburger Nachrichten*, Sept. 27, 1907), instead of **Leider scheint diese Hoffnung endgültig aufzugeben.**

b. After **geben** in its impersonal forms, **es gibt** *there is*, **es gab** *there was*, &c.: **Es gibt noch viel zu tun** There is still much to be done. Also after the impersonal construction **es fehlt an: Dann fehlt's ja nicht an mancherlei zu tun** (Grillparzer's *Des Meeres und der Liebe Wellen*, 1).

c. As objective predicate, or object-complement, especially after **finden, haben,** and **sehen: Ich fand an ihr vieles auszusetzen** I found in her a good deal to criticise. See **185.** A. I. 6 for fuller list of such verbs.

B. *Attributive Modal Verbal.* This form is made up of the present participle with **zu** prefixed and like the participle has the declension of descriptive adjectives. It is a N.H.G. formation created in order to express attributively the same idea that had already proved so convenient in its predicate form (explained in A above). It has therefore the same force as the predicate modal verbal: **der zu tadelnde Schüler** the pupil who *is to be* censured: **die zu fällenden Bäume** the trees that are to be cut down; **ein von dir zu verbessernder Fehler** an error that must be corrected by you; **diese leicht zu lösende Aufgabe** this task that can easily be performed; **ein leicht zu erreichendes Ziel** a goal that can easily be reached; **allmählich zu leistende Zahlungen** payments that are to be gradually met; **ein nicht zu übersehender Umstand** a circumstance that ought not to be overlooked.

a. The attributive form is sometimes employed without modal force to indicate the simple idea of the future passive tense: **sein im Jahre 1873 zu vollendendes 70. Lebensjahr.** Grammarians usually demand that the idea of futurity here should be clearly expressed by a future form with simple future force, not by a form which usually has modal force: **sein 70. Lebensjahr, das er im Jahre 1873 vollenden wird.**

b. The attributive modal verbal is avoided in case of verbs which govern the gen. or dat.: instead of **der zu gedenkende Vorfall** *the incident that is to be mentioned* we can say: **Der Vorfall dessen man gedenken muß;** instead of **die zu gehorchenden Gesetze** *the laws which are to be obeyed* we can say: **Die Gesetze, denen man gehorchen muß.** Or if the short modal expression is preferred, the verb can be changed and a synonym selected which governs the acc. and thus admits of this construction: **Der zu erwähnende Vorfall** and **die zu befolgenden Gesetze.**

c. Origin of the Attributive Modal Verbal. This construction was originally a substitute for a relative clause containing a predicate modal verbal: **ein zu verbessernder Fehler** instead of **ein Fehler, der zu verbessern ist.** The frequent use of **zu** with modal force with the infinitive and the occasional use of the present participle with passive force, once more common than now as illustrated in **182.** 2. *a*, suggested combining the two forms in order to create a passive attributive form with modal force corresponding to the predicate modal form. It began to appear early in the seventeenth century in official style and by reason of its conciseness and preciseness gradually came into use there. Later it slowly became established in the literary language.

d. Since the attributive modal verbal is passive in force we should not naturally expect to find it formed in intransitive verbs, but it is sometimes used by good authors with active meaning and the peculiar modal force of the modal verbal: **Die voranzugehende Bedingung** (Hegel) the condition that must precede. This construction is quite limited in German, but the corresponding infinitive form is very common in English: He is the man to go = **Er ist der Mann, der gehen sollte** (or **müßte**).

This form is sometimes used in German without the modal idea of necessity, possibility, or fitness: **Daß man das Geschehene sich eher gefallen läßt, als daß man in ein noch zu Geschehendes** (*something that will happen*) **einwilligt** (Goethe), instead of **als daß man in etwas einwilligt, was erst geschehen soll. Heute verspätete sich der um 10 Uhr hier einzutreffende Zug** (*the train due here at 10 o'clock*) (*Süddeutsche Zeit.*), instead of **Heute verspätete sich der Zug, der um 10 Uhr hier eintreffen sollte.** Tho limited in German the attributive form is very common in English: The man to arrive first was John **Der Mann, der zuerst ankam, war Johann.** German grammarians oppose the attributive form in both these cases and demand that a full clause be used.

The Participles.

181. Participles are so called because they participate in the nature of both the verb and of the adjective. They sometimes have the force and construction of verbs, sometimes a force approaching nearer that of the adj., but they always have the inflection of the adj., except in their adverbial use (see *a*), and also when the adj. force is stronger than the verbal they are compared like adjectives: **Die Gefahr ist drohend, die drohende Gefahr, eine treffendere Antwort** an answer more to the point, **mein geliebtester Freund.** For points concerning comparison see **115.** 4 and **114.** 4.

a. Both participles can be used as adverbs and then remain uninflected: **siedend heißes Wasser** boiling hot water, **ein ausgezeichnet gelehrter Mann** a very finely educated man, **annähernd** approximately, **umgehend** by return mail, **unverhofft** unexpectedly, &c. The present part. often expresses manner: **Er lernt spielend** He learns as easily as if it were play.

The Present Participle.

182. The leading points concerning the use of the present part. are:

1. The present participle can be used:

A. As an adjective: **das singende Kind, die untergehende Sonne. Man fand ihn schlafend** (objective predicate). **Du liegst hier träumend** (predicate appositive).

a. The present participle is not only inflected as an adjective, but also governs the same case, or takes the same construction as the verb from which it is formed. If the part. has thus a complement or adverbial modifiers, they must stand before it: **der die Festung überraschende Feind** the enemy taking the fortress by storm, **die dem Fremden gehörenden Sachen** the things belonging to the stranger, **ein am Flusse stehendes Haus. Nun war Margarete ganz fremd im Vaterhause, allen ein Stein des Anstoßes, alle hassend, von allen gehaßt.** While the reflexive **sich** is usually dropped with the perfect participle it is now more commonly retained with the present participle, altho its omission here was quite frequent a little earlier in the period: **alle sich einschleichenden Irrtümer.** It is now most commonly omitted when used as a predicate appositive, especially as it can often here be interpreted as an adverb: **Vor diesem Hause hielt er wundernd an** (Schiller's *Tell*, l. 221). In the attributive relation it is now usually only suppressed in a few instances where the adjective force of the participle is very pronounced: **ein herablassender Herr, eine hingebende Freundschaft,** &c. Notice also that in the attributive relation, as in the first three examples, the participle stands immediately before the noun, not after it as in English. The position of the participle after the noun is rare in the attributive relation except in the cases described for the adjective in **104.** 2. B. *a.* The predicate appositive, however, as **hassend** in the fourth example, is usually separated from the noun.

b. The pres. part. is not used predicatively, if the verbal element becomes prominent. Thus we do not as in English say **Der Lehrer ist lobend,** but **Der Lehrer lobt** The teacher is praising. But when it is felt as an adj. it can like any adj. stand in the predicate: **Dieses Bild ist reizend** This picture is charming. **Die Frage ist brennend** The question is one that is exciting interest. **Der Beweis ist schlagend** The proof is a striking one. **Er ist noch immer leidend** He is still sickly. For the earlier use of the present participle in the predicate with verbal force see **190.** 1. G.

c. The English present participle is here often replaced by other constructions in German: The fog came pouring in at the window **Der Nebel kam zum Fenster hereingeströmt.** He came running **Er kam gelaufen.** I cannot go on doing nothing **Ich kann nicht fortfahren, nichts zu tun.**

B. *Present Participle as Noun.* As a noun to denote persons engaged at the time in question in an action, duty, or occupation, or in case of neuter substantives to denote the characteristic feature of an act, or to represent something as continuing or acting: **der Redende** the speaker, **ein Geschäftsreisender** a commercial traveler, **der Vorsitzende** the chairman, **die Umstehenden** the bystanders, **das Demütigende dieses Auftritts** the humiliating nature of this scene, **das Überraschende dieses Ereignisses** the surprising character of this event, **alles Seiende** all that exists. **Die Sprache ist kein fertiges, ruhendes Ding, sondern etwas in jedem Augenblicke Werdendes und Vergehendes.**

a. English Gerund and the Corresponding German Constructions. Corresponding to the English participle in *-ing*, the adjective-verbal, is a noun-verbal in *-ing*, the gerund. There is no such correspondence in German. The English gerund, which is often a parallel of the prepositional infinitive, often however employed where the infinitive cannot be used, is treated in detail in **268.** 4, **269.** 3, **270.** 3, **271.** I. *c*, **272.** C. *g*, **272.** D. *c*, **275.** *c*, **276.** D. *b*, **278.** *b*, **279.** *d*, **280.** *d*, **282.** *a.* It corresponds to quite different constructions in German, as can be seen below where it is treated in general outline according to its syntactical function: (**1**) Subject: Seeing is believing **Sehen ist glauben.** The least that should be done is the freeing of the teaching of law from this fetter **Das Geringste ist, daß der Rechtsunterricht von dieser Fessel befreit werde.** (**2**) Predicate: Seeing is believing **Sehen ist glauben.** (**3**) Non-prepositional object: She stopped writing **Sie hörte auf zu schreiben.** She finished writing **Sie kam mit dem Schreiben zu Ende.** I like getting up early **Ich stehe gern früh auf.** I don't like his coming here so often **Ich habe es nicht gern, daß er so oft herkommt.** I don't like being treated with pity and indulgence **Ich will nicht geschont sein.** Object of an adjective: I am tired of dancing **Ich bin des Tanzens müde.** I am afraid of their seeing it **Ich fürchte, daß sie es sehen.** It is worth considering, worthy of consideration: **Es ist dies wert, erwogen zu werden.** I am against (= opposed to) your going to his house **Ich bin dagegen, daß du zu ihm gehst.** (**4**) Prepositional object: This led to my getting transferred to another regiment **Dies führte dazu, daß ich zu einem anderen Regiment versetzt wurde.** A dandy prides himself upon being well-dressed **Ein Geck bildet sich etwas darauf ein, daß er wohl gekleidet ist.** We got to talking **Wir kamen ins Gespräch.** Who told you of your wife's being there? **Wer sagte Ihnen, daß Ihre Frau da war?** You may depend upon my doing it **Sie können sich darauf verlassen, daß ich es tue.** He prefers starving to working **Er verhungert lieber, als daß er arbeitet.** (**5**) Attributive phrase: The idea of his son's wanting to become a business man pleased him **Die Idee, daß sein Sohn Geschäftsmann werden wollte, gefiel ihm.** I see no reason for your leaving us so soon **Ich sehe keinen Grund dazu** (or **dafür**), **daß du uns so bald schon verlassen willst.** I make a point of going myself **Ich lege besonderen Wert darauf, selbst zu gehen.** She adorned her room with things of her own making **Sie schmückte ihr Zimmer mit Sachen, die sie selber gemacht hatte.** (**6**) An adverbial element. Time: After saying this he went away **Nachdem er dies gesagt hatte, ging er fort.** You must show me the letter before your uncle's seeing it **Du mußt mir den Brief zeigen, bevor ihn dein Onkel sieht.** Manner: I put my money into my pocket without looking at it

Ich steckte das Geld, ohne es zu besehen, in die Tasche. Instead of helping us he abandoned us **Anstatt uns zu helfen, verließ er uns.** Cause: I praise them for being diligent **Ich lobe sie dafür** (or **darum**), **daß sie fleißig sind,** or **Ich lobe sie, weil sie fleißig sind.** Condition: I praise them in case of their being diligent **Ich lobe sie, wenn** (or **im Falle daß**) **sie fleißig sind.** Concession: Notwithstanding his being unwell he will accompany her **Trotzdem er unwohl ist, will er sie begleiten.** Means: By practising daily upon the piano he became a good player **Dadurch, daß er sich täglich auf dem Klavier übte, wurde er zuletzt ein guter Spieler.** By working too much you will hurt your health **Indem Sie zu viel arbeiten, werden Sie Ihrer Gesundheit schaden.**

One of the marked differences between German and English appears here. In German there is a strong tendency to express modifying elements by the use of a full subordinate clause with a nominative subject and a finite verb as predicate, while in English there is a tendency to avoid the use of a finite verb by employing a verbal noun, especially the gerund or the prepositional infinitive, i.e. English is very fond of the old attributive or appositional thing type of sentence structure described in **250.** *a* (2nd par.) and **268.** 4. Compare **252.** 2. B. *a. Note* 1.

C. As an adverb. See **181.** *a*.

D. As a prep. in case of **während** (w. gen.) *during*.

E. As an appositive to a noun or pronoun where it with its modifiers is equivalent to a subordinate clause: **Dies hörend** (= **Als er dies hörte**), **brach er in Tränen aus.** It is also used absolutely. See **265.** B.

Note. The use of such participial clauses instead of complete subordinate clauses is more common in poetry than in prose, but in both prose and poetry is much less common than in English. In German the participial construction in its adverbial use can generally only be used, as in the example given above, where the subject of the participle is also the subject of the principal verb, but also there only sparingly. Only in one case is the adverbial participial construction quite common, namely, in place of a clause of manner to express manner proper or an attendant circumstance: **Den ganzen Tag arbeitet er mit einem alten Diener im Garten, schneidend, begießend, pflanzend, und hegend** (H. Seidel's *Eine Sperlingsgeschichte*). **„Der Winter war zu lang und streng für dich," sagte ihr Gatte, besorgt auf ihre bleichen Wangen blickend.** A participle may also sometimes denote a cause, usually, however, only when the cause of the act is represented as lying in the state of the mind of the subject of the leading verb, otherwise a complete subordinate clause must usually be used: **Einen Sturm fürchtend, kehrten wir nach dem Lande** (*shore*) **zurück,** but **Da ich keine Antwort erhielt, wußte ich nicht, wie ich handeln sollte.** The present participle sometimes denotes means: **Mich an dem Stricke festhaltend, rettete ich mich ans Ufer.** Sometimes also condition: **Wissend nur kann ich dir raten.** Sometimes also concession: **Selbst des Trostes ermangelnd, will ich versuchen, dir Trost zu bringen.** The participle in the last three sentences may also be interpreted as denoting manner or attendant circumstance and there is in general a lack of definiteness in this construction, as the idea of manner, means, cause, &c., is never formally expressed, but is only gathered from the context. Tho this indefinite construction was once quite common in German the present tendency is to avoid it in accord with the modern trend to give a clearer expression to the grammatical relations of the subordinate clause. Hence the student would do better to render English participial clauses used adverbially by complete subordinate clauses, as in many instances the participial construction cannot be used at all: **Als ich in Paris wohnte, brachte ich viele Zeit im Louvre zu** *While living in Paris I spent much time in the Louvre.* **Bevor wir die Stelle erreichten,** &c. *Before reaching the spot, we,* &c. It should be especially noted that participial clauses of cause formed with *being* or *having* should be rendered by complete subordinate clauses: **Da er noch nicht ausgehen konnte, mußte er zu Hause bleiben** *Not being yet able to walk out, he had to stay at home.* **Da ich nichts zu tun hatte, ging ich ins Theater** *Having nothing else to do, I went to the theatre.* The adverbial expressions *generally speaking, speaking in mild terms,* &c. (see **265.** B. *a*, 2nd par.) are translated by the perfect participle: **Mein Vater hatte sich, allgemein gesprochen, unter voller Selbstbeherrschung.** See **268.** 4. Adjective clauses, however, are very often rendered by present participles, but then the participle must usually be inflected and stand before the noun, and not after it as in English: **Die auf meinem Pulte stehende Flasche enthält Gift** The bottle *standing* or *which stands* upon my desk contains poison. It may also sometimes stand after the noun. See **104.** 2. B. *a*.

2. The pres. part. has as a rule active force. When it limits a noun, its relation thereto is such that the noun is conceived of as the subject of the action contained in the part.: **der blühende Baum** the blooming tree = **der Baum blüht.**

a. The pres. part., however, has also passive force, as seen in a few set expressions, which in our own time are reduced in number in comparison with former periods and in general are censured by grammarians: **die melkende Kuh** the cow that is milked, milch cow; **sein in Mythikon habendes Amt** (K. F. Meyer) the (pastoral) charge in Mythikon filled by him; **kraft seines tragenden Amtes** (Storm's *Söhne des Senators*, p. 301) by virtue of the office held by him; **für die Bedürfnisse und etwaigen Eventualitäten Ihres vorhabenden Ausfluges** (Spielhagen's *Was will das werden?*, II, 10), &c. We do not commonly say to-day as formerly **seine dabei hegende Absicht** the intention that is cherished by him, **die in der Hand habende kleine Orgel** (Goethe), the little organ that is being held in his hand, &c. Such common expressions, as **der betreffende Umstand** (i.e. **der diese Sache betreffende Umstand**) *the circumstance in question, referred to,* lit. *the circumstance relating to this matter*, do not belong here as the participle is active and transitive.

b. The noun in connection with the pres. part. is not always its subject, but is sometimes associated with it in a much freer way, to express a close relationship between the idea contained in the noun and the activity contained in the participle: **eine schwindelnde Höhe** a height at which one becomes dizzy; **eine wohlschlafende Nacht** a night favorable to sleep; **eine lächelnde Antwort; es ist jetzt zehn, also nachtschlafende Zeit** (Fontane's *Frau Jenny*, chap. xii) time for everybody to be asleep; **eine sitzende Lebensweise** a sedentary life; **mit spielender Leichtigkeit, ein reißender Absatz, eine stillschweigende Bedingung,** &c. This is a productive construction according to which from time to time new and felicitous expressions have been created, but the list is limited, and we cannot at will form kindred expressions, such as **eine zitternde Kälte** a temperature at which one trembles with cold, &c.

3. There is a decided paucity of participles in German, there being in the active only one form—the present. Hence the pres. part. is often used for the past and future active as well as for the present: **die vor kurzem noch blühenden Blumen = die Blumen, welche vor kurzem blühten; die jetzt oder früher oder künftig lebenden Menschen = die Menschen, welche jetzt leben, oder welche gelebt haben, oder leben werden; ein demnächst erscheinendes Werk.**

In a relative sense the present participle expresses time contemporaneous with that of some other action, and hence it should express the same time as that of the principal verb, but the real lack of different participles leads many to use the present participle also for time preceding or following that of the main proposition: contemporaneous action: **Siegend starb der Held.** Antecedent action: **Den 26. Oktober von Zürich abreisend, langten wir den 6. November in Nürnberg an** (Goethe). **Neben Marie tretend, sang Ada** (Spielhagen). Subsequent action: **Ada war in die Gesellschaft zurückgetreten, den Dank derselben entgegennehmend** (id.).

The Perfect Participle.

183. The leading points concerning the use of this participle are:

1. *Grammatical Function.* The perfect participle can be used:

A. Adjectively: **der gebrochene Stab. Der Stab ist gebrochen** (predicate). **Man fand ihn eingeschlafen** (objective predicate). **Er focht mit Wunden bedeckt** (predicate appositive with passive force). **Karl mußte ungegessen** (predicate appositive with active force; see 2. C. *c* below) **zu Bette gehen.** In the conjugation of verbs: **Er ist gekommen** (predicate). **Er wird geschlagen** (predicate). **Ich habe den Brief geschrieben** (objective predicate).

Note. The perf. part. is much more used in German in the predicate and appositive relation than it is in English: **Ich weiß wohl, was ihr mögt, ihr alten Böhmen! | gekauert sitzen in verjährtem Wust** (Grillparzer's *König Ottokar* 1). **Es klang ohne irgendwelchen Spott gefragt** (Jensen's *Die Kinder vom Oedacker*, I) There was no trace of sarcasm in the tone of the question. **Allgemein schießen die Leute (stehend oder knieend) freihändig besser als aufgelegt.** For other examples see 2. C. *c* below. We often translate the perfect participle by our present participle: **Das Beil war an den Block gelehnt** The axe was leaning against the block.

B. Substantively:

a. To denote persons or things in a state or condition produced by the action expressed in the verb (see 2 below): **der Getötete** the man who was killed, **der Gelehrte** the scholar, **die Angeklagte** the accused woman, defendant, **das Übertriebene dieser Behauptung** the exaggerated character of this statement, **das Geschehene** that which has happened, **Althergebrachtes** time-honored customs.

b. As subject, always without inflection, to indicate in a general way without definite reference a thing or a person briefly characterized by the participle: **Unversucht schmeckt nicht. Jung geheiratet lebt lang = Was jung geheiratet hat, lebt lang.** For fuller discussion see **111. 7. *h.* (2)**. This use of the participle differs from the preceding in that the participle here may have active force, while in *a* it has passive force in words formed from transitives and active force in words formed from intransitives conjugated with **sein.** See 2. A below. As can be seen in the second example the tense auxiliary **haben** is suppressed here as in 2. C. *c* and *d* below. In older usage when such expressions were coined there was a natural reluctance to add to a substantive a tense form which belongs only to a verb. As illustrated in 2. B below the verbal force of the participle is now felt so vividly that a formal expression is often given to the idea of tense.

C. As adverbs. See **181. *a*.**

D. As a prep. in a few cases, as in **unbeschadet** (w. gen. & dat.) without detriment to, **ungeachtet** in spite of.

E. As an imperative. See **177. I. B. *d*.**

F. As an appositive to a following or preceding noun or pronoun where it with its modifiers is equivalent to a subordinate clause: **Allzustraff gespannt (= wenn er allzustraff gespannt wird), zerspringt der Bogen.** For other examples see **271.** II. 6; **275.** *c*; **276.** A. *a*; **276.** B. *a*; **278.** *b*; **279.** *d*; **280.** *d*. It is also used absolutely. See **265.** B.

G. Participles are often used in lively narrative almost with the force of independent verbs indicating past time, as in animated speech the auxiliaries, the more formal elements of language, are crowded out by the perfect participles and their modifiers containing the important thought, which presses forward for immediate expression: **Ich bitt euch, schreibt nieder: Als Soldat die Pflicht getan. Im Tirolerland gefallen auf dem Felde. Im Frieden gestorben. Und das, das schreibt ihnen auch: Einen guten Menschen zur Seite gehabt** (Rosegger in *Wirt an der Mahr*).

2. *Grammatical Force.* A. The perf. participle used adjectively and substantively expresses usually a condition or state of things resulting from previous action but at the time in question finished and completed, and hence with the exception of the case in 1. B. *b* above can only be used (**1**) with transitive verbs with passive force, and (**2**) with active force with intransitive verbs that are conjugated with **sein** and represent a state or condition resulting from previous action. According to the very nature of this part., which expresses a condition, it cannot be used with intransitive verbs which are conjugated with **haben** and express action, or with reflexive verbs which express action of the subject exerted upon itself. Thus we can say: **Der gelähmte Fuß** the foot that has been lamed and is now in a lame condition; also **der umgefallene Baum** the tree which has fallen and is still prostrate, for we say **Der Baum ist umgefallen,** the auxiliary **sein** expressing state; also substantively **der Gesandte** the ambassador, i.e. the one who has been sent, **Erwachsene** grown people. But grammarians maintain we should not say (tho very many do) **die stattgehabte Unterredung** the interview which has taken place, for the participle does not represent a condition resulting from previous action, but expresses only simple action.

B. The lack of a perf. part. with active force for transitives and those intransitives that are conjugated with **haben** leads some to use the perf. part. (already described as limited to passive use with transitives and active use with such intransitives as are conjugated with **sein**) with active force, or more commonly to make a special form by adding **habend** to the perfect participle: **von seiner mit den Jahren zugenommenen Herzenskälte** (Gutzkow's *Söhne Pestalozzis*, 2, **394**), **der schon stark gefrühstückte Kantorssohn** (Fontane's *Unterm Birnbaum*, xi). **Wo es den Anschein hat, als wären solche** (i.e. **Zusammensetzungen**) **vorhanden, handelt es sich entweder um bloße Anlehnungen zweier früher lose nebeneinander gestandener Wörter wie teilnehmen usw.** (Dr. A. Jeitteles in Graz in *Zeitschrift für den deutschen Unterricht*, 1899, p. 205). **Er gab sowohl dem geprügelten Lord als auch dem geprügelt habenden Mitglied des Unterhauses den Laufpaß, womit der Friede wiederhergestellt war** (Baumbach's *Der Schwiegersohn*, I). **Das Wärterhäuschen trug überall die Spuren eines hier heftig getobt habenden Kampfes** (Liliencron's *Krieg und Frieden*, Das Wärterhäuschen). In case of reflexives and transitives the reflexive pronoun or substantive object is used in connection with these two participial formations: **an diesem nach und nach sich verbreiteten Geheimnis** (Goethe); **die zur rechten Zeit sich eingestellten Erfindungen** (Jacob Grimm); **das den Grafen befallene Unglück** (Goethe); quite commonly in case of **stattgehabt** and **stattgefunden: stattgehabte, stattgefundene Festlichkeiten. An die Stelle der sich überlebt habenden historisch-heroischen Tragödie** (Litzmann's *Das deutsche Drama in den literarischen Bewegungen der Gegenwart*, 3rd ed., p. 31), **ein sich seiner Selbständigkeit begeben habender Stamm** (S. Hoechstetter in *Beilage zur Allgemeinen Zeit.*, April 10, 1906).

These formations have resulted from two tendencies which at first operated with united strength—the desire to bring out clearly the force of the present perfect tense active and the general fondness for the attributive form of statement, noticeable also elsewhere. The short form, i.e. the one without **habend,** is the older one. See C. *c* below. In a large number of these short forms the attributive force has become more prominent than the verbal, so that they now have merely the force of adjectives, as in C. *a* and *b* below. Grammarians now generally recommend the use of only the words with adjective meaning, but the two original tendencies described above manifest themselves still and produce formations with the force of both an adjective and a verb, as in the examples given above. The longer form, which now seems to be more common, is probably due to the desire to give more emphasis to the *verbal* idea. This participle is a verbal adjective that has been formed from the present perfect tense of the verb. Compare C. *c* below.

C. There are, however, to the rule as stated in A above, the following exceptions which have been generally sanctioned by good usage:

a. A number of transitive verbs and intransitives which are conjugated with **haben** have a perfect participle with active force, which can be defended, as these participles are in reality felt as adjectives or adjective-substantives, since they denote a quality, fixed habit, or state: **abgesagt** professed, open (**ein abgesagter Feind**), **bewandert** versed, **gedient** (**ein gedienter Soldat, der nicht gediente Landsturm** the landsturm that has not seen service) veteran, **gelernt** by trade (**ein gelernter Schuhmacher**), **Geschworener** juryman, **studiert** well-read, educated, **trunken** drunk(en), **verlogen** mendacious, **verschwiegen** taciturn, &c.

b. The Perfect Participle of Reflexives Used Adjectively with Active Force. A large number of reflexives have in adjective function an active perfect participle, unaccompanied, however, by reflexive pronoun and tense auxiliary, as there is a reluctance to express a reflexive object or a verbal form in connection with an adjective: **altgedient** (**altgediente Soldaten, allerlei altgedientes Hausgerät**), **ausgesprochen** (**ein ausgesprochener Feind**), **erhitzt, erkältet, erklärt** (**ein erklärter Liebhaber**), **verirrt, verliebt,** &c. Thus we can say: **Das Kind hat sich erkältet** and **ein erkältetes Kind.** Also **Die Verhältnisse haben sich verändert, die veränderten Verhältnisse,** and **Die Verhältnisse sind verändert.** The reason that a perfect participle here can thus be used as an adjective is that the reflexive verb in German often has the force of an ingressive perfective (**164**) intransitive, so that its perfect participle has the force of an adjective indicating a new state as the result of the verbal activity. While we can often form an adjective participle from a reflexive verb used as an ingressive perfective intransitive, we should remember that by reason of its frequent ambiguity this usage is limited, so that often recourse must be taken to the much censured construction of placing the reflexive pronoun before the past part., or in choice language to the formation of a relative clause or some other construction: **Der sich zurückgezogene** or **sich zurückgezogen habende Seidenhändler,** or in choice language **Der Seidenhändler, der sich zurückgezogen hat,** or **Der in der Zurückgezogenheit lebende Seidenhändler.**

c. The Perfect Participle Used as Predicate Appositive with Active Force. A group of reflexive, transitive, and intransitive verbs form a perfect participle with active meaning when it is used as a predicate appositive. This perf. part. as a predicate appositive has relations with the principal verb, hence has adverbial force, i.e. the force of an abridged adverbial clause, but as a predicate appositive it also has relations with the subject, hence is also a predicate adjective and as an adjective in a few set expressions still takes the negative **un-** (246. I. 9. *a*, 2nd par.), altho it usually on account of its strong verbal force takes **nicht: Er ging unpräpariert** (lit. *not having prepared himself*) **zur Schule. Karl mußte ungegessen** (lit. *not having eaten*) **zu Bette gehen. Ich ritt ungewaschen und ungefrühstückt** (lit. *not having washed or breakfasted*) **gegen Sedan** (Bismarck). **Er zündete sich ungefragt** (lit. *not having asked permission*) **eine Zigarre an** (Riehl). **Er kommt gesprungen, geeilt, gegangen** (walking), **gefahren. Er kam mit dem Messer in der Hand herzugelaufen. Er kam mit einigen Freunden auf den Markt geritten. Heulend kam der Sturm geflogen.** The perfect participle here in accordance with its origin as a present perfect active tense indicates a single act or accompanying circumstance *as a whole* and hence differs markedly from the present participle which indicates an act as taking place at the same time as another act: **Er kam gelaufen** [**habend,** indicating an act as a whole, as in older usage where in this meaning **laufen** was used with **haben**] and **Er lebt eingezogen** [= **sich eingezogen habend**], but **Er kam in das Haus singend.** See also 1. A. *Note* above. The accusative in connection with the perfect participle of transitives indicates clearly that the participle was originally active: **Dies vorausgeschickt** [**habend**], **fahre ich in meiner Erzählung fort.** The reflexive object, however, is regularly omitted here: [**sich**] **zur Wirtin gewendet** [**habend**] **sagte sie usw.** (Auerbach's *Dorfgeschichten*, 8, p. 39). The use of the accusative object here, as in the next to the last example, has led to the accusative absolute construction described in **265.** B. *a*, *b*. (**1**).

As can be clearly seen by the last two of these examples **habend,** the auxiliary of tense, is suppressed in all these expressions. Originally the participle as an appositive was felt as an adjective so that there was a reluctance to express the auxiliary of tense, which properly belongs only to a verb. The participle, true to its name, participates in the nature of both an adjective and a verb. In the examples given above the verbal nature is much stronger than the adjective force and thus **habend** ought to be expressed. In English we regularly find the auxiliary here: Having finished this work I went to bed. In German as the feeling for the verbal force here became strong the participial construction was expanded into a full clause with subject and predicate: **Nachdem ich diese Arbeit vollendet hatte, ging ich zu Bette.** The retention of the old participial construction here in English along with the new feature of expressing the auxiliary is one of the marked syntactical peculiarities of the language as compared with German. In German, on the other hand, there is a curious bit of survival of the old participial construction in the expanded clause, as the auxiliary of tense is here still occasionally suppressed as in the original participial construction: **Nachdem ich diese Arbeit vollendet [hatte], ging ich zu Bette,** or still in older form: **Diese Arbeit vollendet [habend], ging ich zu Bette.** Tho the participial construction is still very common in English it is in general confined in German to use in the so-called absolute construction and the few set expressions given above. In M.H.G. the old participial construction is still used where modern German requires another expression: Her, mir tuot immer we, | sol er's genozzen [habende] scheiden hin (Parzival, 290. 9) Sir, it would pain me much if he should get away unpunished, lit. having enjoyed it. Likewise in early N.H.G.: **[mich] Dessen ungeschewet [habend], wage ich usw.** (Weckherlin, 1, 293, 31), now **Da ich mich nicht davor** (replacing older **dessen**) **scheue, wage ich usw.** Compare with *d* (last par.).

d. *Use of the Perfect Participle with Intransitives.* A perfect participle cannot be formed from all intransitive verbs that are conjugated with **sein,** but only from mutative perfectives (**191.** I. 4, 2nd par.), i.e. those in which a condition resulting from the action of the verb is expressed, or the final point or the beginning of an activity is indicated. Thus we can say **ein entlaufener Sklave** *an escaped slave,* because the slave has changed his condition by escaping from bondage, but we cannot say **ein gelaufener Sklave,** altho we say **Der Sklave ist gelaufen** *The slave has run,* because there is no change of state resulting from the action.

Thus also to indicate the final point or the beginning of an activity we can say: **die eben angekommenen Gäste, der vor einigen Minuten abgegangene Zug.** Usage, however, is capricious here and the student should be on his guard, as the participle cannot be freely used according to rule: **Die vorhergegangenen Ereignisse,** but not **die nachgefolgten Ereignisse; der ihm zugestoßene Unfall,** but not commonly **der ihm begegnete Unfall.** We must often use a full clause instead of the participle or employ another construction: **die Ereignisse, welche nachgefolgt sind,** or **die nachfolgenden Ereignisse; der Unfall, der ihm begegnet ist.** In general, however, the simple participle is much more freely used in German than in English; **ein auf den Baum gestiegener Knabe** a boy who had climbed up the tree. In English the participle can often not be used, as it would be construed as a past indicative: *the apples just fallen from the tree,* but not *the boys just jumped down from the tree,* where we mean *the boys who have just jumped down from the tree.*

The simple perfect participle of mutative perfectives is freely used in the predicate appositive relation, where the participle along with the words which accompany it has the force of an abridged adverbial clause: **Einer Gefahr kaum entronnen, stand er nun vor einer noch größeren** Having scarcely escaped one danger he now stood before a greater one = **Nachdem er einer Gefahr kaum entronnen war, stand er usw. Und nun sang Asmus, kühner geworden: „Horch auf den Klang der Zither"** (O. Ernst's *Semper der Jüngling,* p. 52) And now Asmus, having become bolder, sang &c. In modern German as in the oldest period of the language the perfect participle is here as in *c* treated as an adjective in accordance with its adjective function as predicate appositive altho it has strong verbal force. In English the feeling for the verbal force here has led to the use of the auxiliary *having* to give clear expression to the idea of tense. In German this idea can be clearly expressed only by expanding the words into a full clause with subject and predicate as illustrated above. A curious bit of survival of the old participial construction is sometimes still found in the full clause in that the tense auxiliary is sometimes suppressed as in the abridged participial construction: **Nachdem er einer Gefahr kaum entronnen [war], stand er usw.**

3. *Temporal Relations.* The past part. does not necessarily imply past time, but also often present or future time, as there is no other participial form with passive force. It refers to the past when the context points to the past, as in **Der am 15. ds.** (**dieses Monats**) **eröffnete Ausverkauf wird noch bis Ende des Monats fortgesetzt,** but it also refers very often to an action that continues in present time: **mein verehrter Freund, die geliebte Mutter,** &c. Thus also **Er ist bemüht, bestrebt,** &c. See also **184.** *e*. Future time: **Das Gericht wollte sich auch nicht so ohne weiteres mit einer vielleicht nachher getadelten Arbeit belasten** (Immermann's *Münchhausen,* 2, 321).

184. On account of the paucity of participles attempts are being made to form additional ones to supply the deficiency. The following will serve as examples of such, most of which are not yet generally accepted:

a. A present passive, formed with the perf. part. of the verb and the present part. of **werden: Der gehofft werdende Sprößling** the offspring that is being expected. **Es gibt solche Menschen in der Reihe der geboren wordenen und werdenden** (Rahel, 2, 6).

b. A future passive formed with the present passive infinitive of the verb and the pres. part. of **werden: die in acht Tagen begangen werden werdende Festfeier** the celebration that will be celebrated in a week. This construction is mentioned by Keller in his *Antibarbarus*, p. 66, but the author of the present work has not found it elsewhere.

c. A perf. part. with active force. See **183.** 2. B.

d. It is now common to use a perfect participle of the statal passive (**194.** 4), a participial expression made up of the perfect participle of the verb and **gewesen,** which latter form indicates that the *state* or *condition* expressed by the participle of the verb existed in past time: **der in jüngeren Jahren vielbegehrt gewesene Arzt** the physician who in younger years was much sought after.

e. Usually the perf. passive has but one participial form (**gelobt**), and cannot show here the shades expressed by the two forms (the actional and the statal passive; see **194.** 1. A. & 4) of the indicative. To emphasize, however, the idea of a *state* or *condition* of things in *past* time the statal passive form in *d* above is often used. Since the usual perfect participle is not only used for past time, but also for present time, as in **das von mir bewohnte Haus** (= **das Haus, das von mir bewohnt wird**), ambiguity may arise: **die von dem verstorbnen Rentier Sch. bewohnte Wohnung ist zu Ostern anderweit zu vermieten.** The writer of this advertisement intended the participial form as a perfect, but, as G. Wustmann in his *Allerhand Sprachdummheiten*, p. 162, 3rd ed., remarks with regard to it, the resultant impression is rather an uncanny one, since the form may be construed as a present passive. The ambiguity can in the present instance be removed by using the statal passive form which calls attention to a past *state* of things: **die von dem verstorbnen Rentier Sch. bewohnt gewesene Wohnung,** &c. In order to call attention to a past *act*, a perfect passive part. corresponding to the regular actional perf. passive indic. is occasionally formed by adding **worden** to the perfect participle of the verb: **die zwei verloren gegangenen oder vielmehr vergessen wordenen Väter** (Raabe's *Gutmanns Reisen*, chap. x).

f. Participles formed from the modal auxiliaries are now occasionally found, usually in connection with a dependent infin.: **der sein sollende Witz** the utterance that was intended to be witty, **das nicht enden wollende Gelächter** the laughter that did not seem to desire to come to an end.

The Infinitive.

185. The infinitive was in an earlier period inflected as a noun and at the same time preserved its verbal nature by admitting of a direct object. The remnant of this older usage of inflecting the infinitive is the so-called infinitive with **zu.** This form of the infinitive is in fact a noun in the dat. governed by the prep. **zu,** hence was originally an adverbial element modifying the verb. This **zu,** as can still be seen in many sentences, originally meant *towards* and pointed to that towards which the activity of the principal verb was directed: **Wir zwangen ihn zu dienen** (**zum Dienst**) We compelled him to serve. **Entschließe dich zu arbeiten** (**zur Arbeit**) Make up your mind to work. **Ich ging aus, einen Freund zu besuchen** I went out to call on a friend. This **zu,** however, is now often not felt as a prep. but rather as a part of the infinitive itself, and hence this prepositional infinitive is now no longer confined to the dat. relation, but may also indicate the nom. and acc. relations, where formerly the simple infinitive without **zu** could alone be used: **Nachzuahmen** (or still as in older German **nachahmen**) **erniedrigt einen Mann von Kopf. Sie fing an zu weinen,** but in M.H.G.: der helt (**Held**) dō (**dann**) trūren (**trauern**) began (Nibelungenlied). Thus the development of the prepositional infinitive is much like that of the simple infinitive, which was originally an accusative, used adverbially as an accusative of goal, as seen in B. I. 1. *b. Note* below, and as a direct object (B. I. 2. *a, b, c, d*) but already in oldest German had come into use in the subject relation. The first beginnings of the use of the prepositional infinitive as object go back to the O.H.G. period. It is even to-day often difficult to distinguish between a prepositional phrase as an adverbial element and as a prepositional object, as explained in **261** (3rd par.). The latter relation indicates a closer association with the verb. As the prepositional infinitive often stood in a close relation to the verb it gradually came to be felt as a prepositional object, as a necessary complement of the verb and hence sometimes after certain verbs took the place of the accusative object. The **zu** gradually lost its original prepositional force, so that the infinitive and **zu** were felt as one and in M.H.G. were sometimes used in the subject relation. The use of the infinitive with **zu** has greatly gained on that of the simple infinitive, and for centuries it along with its modifiers has been developing into a distinct subordinate clause and in this capacity has been crowding more and more out of common use the older **daß**-clause with a finite verb, so that it has acquired functions unknown to the simple infinitive, but as the latter is still in certain instances used in the nom. and acc. relation, it is necessary to note carefully the following detailed statements as to when the simple infinitive and when the infinitive with **zu** is used:

A. The Infinitive with **zu.**

I. The infinitive with **zu** is used:

1. In the following independent relations:

a. As the subject of a verb: **Zu überlegen ist nicht die Sache der Jugend. Sich mitzuteilen ist Natur** To communicate one's thought and feeling is the impulse of nature. **Seine Schuldigkeit getan zu haben ist ein Trost im Unglück.** The infinitive without **zu** is also used here. See B. I. 1. *a.* The form with **zu,** however, is always employed, when its object is a relative pronoun: **Sie** (**die bei Jena geschlagene Armee**) **erlag einem Verhängnis, das abzuwenden nicht in ihren Kräften stand** (C. Freiherr v. d. Goltz in *Deutsche Rundschau,* March 1906, p. 23). **Daß er** (W. Vietor) **ihnen** (i.e. **den Studenten**) **durch seine unbeirrbare Sachlichkeit, Treue und Wahrhaftigkeit ein Vorbild wurde, dem nachzueifern wahrlich lohnte** (F. Dörr in *Die Neueren Sprachen,* Band XXVI, p. 297).

b. In the predicate:

(**1**) After certain verbs (**180.** A. *a*) the prepositional infinitive of transitives is used as a modal verbal, i.e. contains the idea of the necessity, possibility, or fitness of an action, and has passive force: **Viel bleibt noch zu tun** Much remains to be done. More examples are given in **180.** A. *a.*

(**2**) After **sein** it often contains also in case of intransitives and reflexives the idea of necessity, possibility, or fitness, but of course has active force: **Es ist nichts zu danken, ein paar Rippen sind entzwei** (Goethe's *Götz,* 3, 9) There is nothing to be thankful for, i.e. that one can be thankful for, &c. **Was ist denn aber dabei zu lachen?** (Wildenbruch's *Der Astronom*). **War es zu verwundern, daß sich bei der wachsenden Spannung die Anstrengungen der Mächte, sich durch Flottenmacht zu schützen, steigerten?** (Albrecht Stauffer in *Beilage zur Allgemeinen Zeit.,* Jan. 23, 1906). The infinitive often preserves here in case of intransitives and reflexives a good deal of its older substantive nature and hence does not show the prepositions and reflexives which the verb always demands. Thus in the sentences from Goethe and Wildenbruch the prepositions **für** and **über** are omitted altho **danken** requires **für** and **lachen** takes **über.** In the sentence from Stauffer the reflexive is omitted. The English requires the prepositions and the reflexive where the verb requires them.

A few common impersonal verbs with passive form but active force, as described in **219.** 5. A (2nd par.), belong here: **Es ist nicht mit ihm zu leben,** or **Mit ihm ist nicht zu leben** *There* (formerly *it*) *is no living with him.* **Es ist ihm nicht zu trauen,** or **Ihm ist nicht zu trauen** *He cannot be trusted,* or *is not to be trusted,* lit. *There is no trusting him.*

(**3**) After the copulas **dünken** *to seem,* **scheinen** *to seem,* **ers einen** *to appear* the infinitive is used with active force and without the peculiar modal force found in (**1**) and (**2**): **Er dünkt sich ein großer Geist zu sein,** or without the infinitive: **Er dünkt sich ein großer Geist** or **einen großen Geist. Er scheint**

ein ehrlicher Mann zu sein, or **Er scheint ein ehrlicher Mann. Er scheint mir fleißig (zu sein). Er scheint mir, fleißig zu arbeiten. Er scheint, künftig noch fleißiger werden zu wollen. Er scheint, zu wollen aber nicht zu können. Er scheint, früher nicht fleißig studiert zu haben,** but the **sein** of the perfect infinitive is often omitted: **Seine Mutter scheint früh gestorben (zu sein). Die Leute erscheinen mir liebenswürdiger geworden (zu sein).** After **dünken** we find the infinitive of other verbs than **sein** only in older German: **Der dünkt mich in England nach Wölfen zu jagen** (Lessing). In M.H.G. **dünken** and **scheinen** could only be used as simple copulas with a predicate adjective or noun. In the fourteenth century **sein**—later replaced by **zu sein**—began to be added to **dünken,** a little later also to **scheinen.** Later also other infinitives than **sein** were used, but after **dünken** the infinitive except in case of **zu sein** has disappeared.

(4) The infinitive with **zu** is sometimes used in German as the progressive form or a participial predicate appositive in English: **Und als er wieder zu fischen war, | da ließ ich einen Schatz ihn finden** (Schiller's *Macbeth*, 1, 4) And when he was fishing, &c. **Er wußte, jetzt saß seine Großmutter zu sticken** (Enking's *Die Darnekower*, p. 130) He knew that his grandmother was sitting embroidering. **Sonst säß' ich jetzt bei ihm zu schustern** (id., *Wie Truges seine Mutter suchte*, IV). After *to be* this construction is sometimes found in older English: And I have been all this day to avoid him (*As You Like It*, 2, 5. 35). In older German also the simple infinitive was used here and in certain expressions is still common: **Er ist fischen. Er ist mit seiner Mama spazieren gewesen** (Wildenbruch's *Die Alten und die Jungen*. p. 55). **Er blieb sitzen.** Both constructions are old, originally infinitives of purpose. The simple infinitive, the original construction, is the infinitive of purpose described in B. I. 1. *b. Note* below. The original meaning is no longer felt, for the infinitive is now used as described above, often without a trace of the idea of purpose: **Spür' ich einen rechten Sturmwind wehn, | als wollt' das Schiff zu Grunde gehn, | da stehen meine Gedanken | zu wanken** (a popular song in Auerbach's *Dorfgeschichten*, I, p. 23). **Du warst damals erst sechs Jahre alt und standest am Sarg zu weinen** (Storm's *Werke*, II, p. 311). It is now little used in the literary language of the South, but in the North it still occasionally occurs in good literary style. After **stehen** and **sitzen** the present participle is now the common construction.

2. In the following dependent relations:

a. As the complement of a noun, pronoun, or adjective, performing:

(1) The function of the genitive of a substantive dependent upon an adjective: **Er ist müde länger zu leben** (= **Er ist des Lebens müde**). The passive force is sometimes expressed by acting form, but more commonly by the passive: **In solchen Ritzen | ist jedes Bröselein | wert zu besitzen** (Goethe). **Die ich höre, scheint mir wert zu krönen** (Schlegel's *Gedichte*, 1, 308). **Dieser Stein ist wert, in Gold gefaßt zu werden.**

(2) The function of an appositive genitive or a noun in apposition with a pronoun, substantive, or substantive clause: **Die Kunst zu schreiben** (= **des Schreibens**) **war den Ägyptern bekannt. Unter allen Rollen gibt es keine kläglichere als die, mehr zu gelten als zu sein. In dem rätselvollen Wirrsal von Leid und Scham gab es nur eines: schweigend den Schmerz zu ertragen** (Boy-Ed's *Die Ketten*, p. 223). **Nur ein einziges Laster beherrschte sie: zwischen bös und gut keinen Unterschied zu kennen** (Schiller). **Was die meisten Romantiker doch nicht konnten, brachte er fertig: das als notwendig Erkannte zu tun** (Ricarda Huch's *Ausbreitung und Verfall der Romantik*, p. 152). The simple infinitive is also quite common here. See B. I. 1. *c* below.

The appositional construction in 3 below might also be classed here.

(3) The function of a relative clause. The attributive use of the prepositional infinitive with the force of a relative clause, as illustrated also in **271. II.** 6, is quite common in English, but it is in general little employed here in German and must usually be rendered by a full subordinate clause, or where the force is passive, also often by a modal verbal (**180.** B): The king has no children to succeed him on the throne **Der König hat keine Kinder, die ihm auf dem Throne folgen könnten.** That is a circumstance not to be overlooked **Das ist ein Umstand, der nicht übersehen werden sollte,** or **Das ist ein nicht zu übersehender Umstand.** Other examples and the German renderings are given in **180.** B and *d* thereunder. When the relative clause contains the idea of purpose or result it is often replaced by the prepositional infinitive as in English: (purpose): **sein Bestreben, viel Gutes zu tun;** (result): **Erasmus war der Mann, den Glanz solcher Stellung zu genießen** (Paulsen's *Geschichte des gelehrten Unterrichts*, 2nd. ed., p. 145). Here the **zu** before the infinitive has its original force as a preposition, as in *b*. While English, starting from this same point, has developed the prepositional infinitive into the full force of a relative clause, German has scarcely passed beyond the first stage of development. As the **zu** with the infinitive has in general lost its original meaning, **um** is often prefixed to it to bring out clearly the idea of purpose or result: **Die Enden der Hirschgeweihe dienen als Haken, an welche man Hüte, Peitschen und Sporen hängt,** or **als Haken, um Hüte, Peitschen und Sporen daran zu hängen** The branches of the antlers serve as hooks on which to hang hats, whips and spurs, or as hooks to hang hats, whips and spurs on. This now common construction with **um zu** + infinitive—much censured by grammarians—is treated at considerable length in **255.** IV. 2. *a*. The use of **um** here indicates that German has developed a clearer expression for this idea than English.

b. In the dat. relation, as the object of the prep. **zu,** after verbs, nouns, and adjectives, to express, in accordance with the general meaning of **zu,** the aim, purpose, direction of the action or quality: **Da treibt's ihn, den köstlichen Preis zu erwerben. Er hatte den Hang, stets der Vollkommenheit seines eignen Wesens zuzustreben. Er ist geneigt zu übertreiben.**

Note. This is the original use of **zu** with the infinitive. Here the **zu** is not the mere sign of the infinitive as in **1.** *a*. and *b* above, but a real prep. used in its usual sense of *direction towards*.

c. In the acc. relation, as the direct object of the verb: **Das Kind beginnt zu reden, wie es anhebt zu denken. Warum versäumte man mich zu erinnern?** For exceptions see B. I. 2. *a*, *b*, *c*, *d*, *e*.

Note 1. The English-speaking student should be on his guard here as the infinitive is often used in German where in English a full clause or a gerund is necessary: (**1**) After verbs of believing or supposing (**glauben, meinen**), confessing or owning (**bekennen, einräumen, gestehen**), denying (**leugnen**), fancying or imagining (**wähnen, sich** [dat.] **einbilden**), maintaining, asserting, assuring, declaring (**behaupten, beteuern, versichern**), suggesting or proposing (**vorschlagen**), swearing (**schwören**), and the like: **Ich glaube, recht zu haben** I believe I'm right. **Er meint, recht zu haben** He believes, supposes he is right. **Er räumte ein, es getan zu haben** He confessed doing it, *or* that he did it. **Ich leugne, ihn gesehen zu haben** I deny having seen him, *or* that I saw him. **Die Zeit wähnte, sehr frei zu denken** (Treitschke, 5, 337) The period fancied or imagined that it was very liberal in its thought. **Er bildet sich ein, Philosophie zu verstehen** He fancies that he knows something about philosophy. **Er beteuerte, nichts davon gewußt zu haben** He maintained that he didn't know anything about it. **Er schlug vor, spazieren zu gehen** He suggested or proposed that they take a walk. **Ich schwöre, ihn in jener Nacht am Tatort gesehen zu haben** I swear that, &c. Compare II. 2. *e* below. (**2**) After verbs of commanding when the person to whom the command is directed is not mentioned: **Der General befahl, den Feind anzugreifen** The general ordered that the enemy be attacked, *or* He ordered the enemy to be attacked.

Note 2. The older usage of employing the simple infinitive as object of the verb lingers on as late as the seventeenth century: **Da gund** (for **begann**) **ich mich erholen** (Spee). Even in the sixteenth century, however, the new form with **zu** has gained the ascendency.

3. As explanatory of a preceding anticipative subject or object, which appears in the form of **es, dies, das** or a pronominal adverb. In apposition with a subject: **Es ziemt | dem edeln Mann, der Frauen Wort zu achten** (Goethe's *Iphigenie*, 5, 3). In the relation of subject the simple infinitive is also used here. See B. I. 1. *a* below. In apposition with the object of a verb: **Er wünscht es sehnlich, dich nur noch einmal wiederzusehen. Ich denke mir das aussichtslos, so etwas zu unternehmen.** In apposition with a pronoun which is the object of a prep., but which has in German only the form of an adverb: **Wir sind bereit dazu, dich zu unterstützen. Jeder muß danach trachten, seine Seele vom Bösen rein zu erhalten.** Occasionally we find here the simple infinitive preceded by a preposition, a construction similar to the English gerund in -ing: **Ihre einzige Sehnsucht ging jetzt nach Stille, nach nicht mehr hören und nicht mehr sehen** (Ernst Zahn's *Das Leben der Salome Zeller*, XVI). The simple infinitive, however, is often used instead of the form with **zu** when the infinitive for emphasis is placed at the beginning of the

proposition followed by the pronominal adverb: **Eine Sache anfangen und auf halber Tour hinwerfen — damit werden Sie nie im Leben zurechtkommen** (Anna Bemisch-Kappstein's *Das klingende Fließ* in *Deutsche Rundschau*, Sept. 1905, p. 325).

4. Certain complete substantive and adverbial clauses (see **269.** 3; **271.** I. *c*; **272.** A. *d*, C. *g*, D. *c*; **276.** A. *a* (2nd par.), D. *b*; **277.** 2. *b*; **279.** *d*, *e*; **281.** *b*) may be contracted to infinitive clauses with **zu, anstatt zu, ohne zu,** or **um zu.** For examples see the references just given. The infinitive clauses can usually without changing the meaning be expanded into complete subordinate clauses, and complete subordinate clauses can be contracted to the infinitive construction. It should be noted, however, that in case of the verb **wissen** there is a difference of meaning between the two constructions: **Er weiß, daß er seinen Willen durchsetzt** *He knows that he will get his own way*, but **Er weiß seinen Willen durchzusetzen** *He knows how to get his own way.*

5. The infinitive is often employed absolutely, as illustrated in II. 2. *c* below. It is thus much used with or without **zu** in exclamations and in general in excited or vivid language, where without precise grammatical relations it becomes the bearer of the thought: **Ich möcht' euch alle mit eigner Hand umbringen! Was, fortlaufen! Er hatte keine Handvoll Leute mehr! Fortzulaufen, vor einem Mann!** (Hauptmann in Lager scene in 3rd Act of Goethe's *Götz*). See also B. I. 4 below.

6. After **(an)treffen, bekommen, erhalten, finden, geben, gehen** (**180.** A. *a*) *to be possible,* **haben, kommen, lassen** (= **übrig lassen**), **machen** (see B. I. 2. *d*, toward end), **reichen** to reach, **schenken, schicken, schlagen, sehen, überlassen,** and the impersonals **es gibt, es gilt, es fehlt an** (**180.** A. *b*), where the infinitive with **zu** contains the idea of the necessity, possibility, or fitness of an action, in case of transitives usually passive in force and in this book in this meaning called a modal verbal (see also **180.** A), but active in force in case of intransitives and reflexives: **Wir trafen viele Unordnungen im Hause zu beseitigen an** We found on our arrival much disorder that had to be removed. **Er bekam oft Lügen zu hören (= er mußte hören). Es wird fortan nichts mehr zu lachen geben** (H. Hoffmann's *Rittmeister*, III, p. 210) From now on there will be nothing to laugh about, i.e. nothing that one can laugh about. **Da hat die Menge was zu gaffen** (Fulda's *Talisman*, 2, 12). **Hast de doch wieder was zu ärgern, Hans** (Hauptmann's *Einsame Menschen*, Act 1). **Er hat viel zu tun. Haben Sie mich noch wohin zu schicken? Ich komme noch auf ihn zu sprechen** I shall have occasion to speak about him later. **Sie kam neben ihm zu sitzen** Chance brought it about that she should sit near him. **Er kam unten zu liegen. Das läßt noch viel zu wünschen. Anna hat ihr wirklich nicht viel zu schaffen gemacht** (Hauptmann's *E. M.*, Act 3) (see also B. I. 2. *d*, toward end) Anna has really not caused her much trouble, work. **Weil die größeren Kostgänger des Pastors ihren Freund dabei mitunter überfielen und ihm den Kopf zu bluten schlugen** (Storm's *Hans und Heinz Kirch*, p. 12).

For the construction after **es gilt** see *Note* 2.

Note 1. Some of these words are used here in a certain measure as auxiliaries and not as independent verbs, and it should be remembered that they also can be used in the latter way: **Er hat** (has, possesses) **alte Röcke zu verkaufen.**

Note 2. The impersonal **es gilt** was originally construed only with the acc. of a noun: **Es gilt dein Glück, deinen Besitz** Your happiness, your possessions are at stake, lit. It will cost your happiness, your possessions. The simple infinitive has substantive force, and was used as an acc. here: **Hie gilt's im Finstern und blinzling gehen** (Luther, *v. Abendm.*, 1528). In early N.H.G. the genitive of measure could also be used here as elsewhere instead of the acc. of measure (see **223.** iv. 2. A. *a*): **Da gilt's Schweigens** (Luther, *v. Abendm.*, 1528). Formerly the construction with **um** was also used: **Und sollt's dem Teufel um ein Ohr gelten** (Schiller's *Räuber*, 2, 3). Sometimes still: **Es gilt um Tod oder Leben!** (Fritz Lienhard's *Wieland der Schmied*, p. 80). Later the gen. and in large measure also the prep. construction disappeared, and the infinitive with **zu** replaced in part the simple infinitive here as elsewhere, so that to-day both the infinitive with and without **zu** are used here: **Nur noch von Doktor Daun galt es Abschied zu nehmen** (Stilgebauer's *Götz Krafft*, **II. 14, p. 444**). **Doch es galt das zerrinnende Geld ersetzen** (Ompteda's *Eysen*, chap. xii).

Note 3. The infinitive often preserves in case of intransitives and reflexives a good deal of its older substantive nature, and hence does not show the prepositions and reflexives which the verb always demands. Thus in the sentence from Hoffmann given above the preposition **über** is omitted altho the verb requires it and English requires *about.* In the first sentence from Hauptmann the preposition **über** and the reflexive pronoun are omitted. The reflexive is also omitted in the substantive use of the infinitive described in **188.** *a.*

7. Quite rare is the construction of the accusative with the infinitive, as found in Latin and in part also in English, after verbs of reporting, thinking, knowing, supposing, wishing, &c. See B. I. 5 below.

II. 1. *Position and Repetition of* **zu.** The **zu** must stand immediately before the present infinitive, and if there are several, must be repeated before each one: **Der Lehrer gab uns ein Gedicht abzuschreiben und auswendig zu lernen.** If there are several perfect infinitives, the **zu** is used but once, and stands between the last participle and the auxiliary, which is also used but once, being found with the last participle and understood with the others: **Der Löwe, sagt Lichtenstein, greift einen Menschen oder ein Tier, das nicht vor ihm flieht, nie an, ohne sich vorher in einer Entfernung von zehn bis zwölf Schritten niedergelegt und seinen Sprung gemessen zu haben.**

a. In case there are a number of present infinitives there is a tendency to drop the **zu** after it has been used once or twice, as the simple infinitive here as in I. 5 naturally becomes the bearer of the thought, the exact grammatical relations having faded from the mind: **Wir sind nur da, über die Interessen unserer respektiven Staaten und Dynastien zu wachen, jeder drohenden Verringerung ihrer Machtstellung entgegenzuarbeiten und jede mögliche Suprematie zu erringen trachten, eifersüchtig die Ehre des Landes hüten, uns angetanen Schimpf rächen** (Suttner's *Die Waffen nieder!*, II, p. 183).

2. *Subject of the Infinitive.* The infinitive has for centuries been crowding more and more out of common use the full subordinate clause with a finite verb, but it is still less used in German than in English, especially since it is not much used in the construction of the acc. with the infinitive, which is so common in Latin and English. Thus the infinitive construction in English must often be rendered in German by a complete subordinate clause: *I wish him to come* **Ich wünsche, daß er komme.** See also I. 7 above and B. I. 5 below. Detailed information concerning the use of the infinitive in contracted clauses in German and English is given in **269.** 3; **271.** I. *c*; **271.** II. 6; **272.** A. *d*; **272.** C. *g*; **272.** D. *c*; **276.** A. *a*; **276.** D. *b*; **277.** 2. *b*; **279.** *d*, *e*; **281.** *b. Note.* The expression *contracted clause* as used in this book is explained in **268.** 4. The origin and development of the infinitive clause are sketched in **269.** 3 and **281.** *b. Note* (2nd par.).

In general we can say:

a. In German the infinitive can be freely used when the subject of the infinitive is identical with the subject of the principal proposition, often also when the subject of the infinitive is identical with an accusative or dative object in the principal proposition, provided however that it is perfectly clear from the connection that the subject of the principal proposition cannot be the subject of the infinitive: **Er verspricht, noch heute zu kommen. Dürfte ich Sie bitten, es zu tun? Er riet mir zu gehen.** Under similar conditions the infinitive can sometimes be used when its subject is identical with a genitive in the principal proposition or a genitive implied in a possessive adjective: **Ein Volk ist der Umschweif der Natur, um zu sechs, sieben, großen Männern zu kommen** (Nietzsche). **Erst standen wir alle von ferne, und wie unsere Neugierde größer ward, um zu sehen, was wohl Blinkendes und Rasselndes sich hinter der halbdurchsichtigen Hülle verbergen möchte, wies man jedem ein Stühlchen an** (Goethe). The subject of **zu sehen** is the **wir** implied in **unsere.** The infinitive can sometimes be used when its subject is not revealed by any word in the principal proposition but is suggested by the connection: **Statt aber von dem Ton und Inhalt dieser Blätter nur zu berichten, möge an dieser Stelle ein kurzer Auszug eingeschaltet werden** (Paul Heyse). The speaker here is evidently the subject of **zu berichten.**

Note 1. In a number of expressions the infinitive has a subject which is identical with the suppressed object of the principal verb: **Ich bitte zu bedenken** *I beg you to consider.* **Ich rate zu warten** *I advise you to wait.* **Ich wünsche wohl geruht zu haben** *I hope you have had a good night's rest.*

Note 2. Infinitive purpose clauses or clauses of result with **zu,** or **um zu** *in order to,* and infinitive clauses of manner with **ohne** *without* and **anstatt** *instead of* usually require their subject to be identical with the subject of the principal proposition. If such is not the case the subjects should be made to be identical by changing the subject in the principal proposition or in the infinitive clause, or the infinitive clause should be avoided and replaced by a complete subordinate clause, or, in case the verb in the purpose clause is not modified by too many objects or adverbial modifiers, be replaced by an infinitive substantive or a verbal noun: not **Die Unglücklichen sind hier untergebracht, ohne für ihre Pflege zu sorgen,** but **Man hat die Unglücklichen hier untergebracht, ohne für ihre Pflege zu sorgen;** or **Die Unglücklichen sind hier untergebracht, ohne daß für ihre Pflege gesorgt wäre. Er gab mir den Brief zum Abschreiben. Er schickte sein Buch einem Freund zur Durchsicht.** This rule requiring identical subjects in the principal proposition and the infinitive clause is not always strictly followed, good usage often admitting of violations where the thought is clear: **Die Mutter rief mich hinein, um ihr zu helfen.** Other violations of the general rule are given in *a* above. In general, however, the English-speaking student should keep rather close to the general rule.

b. The infinitive can be used in German when its subject is a general or indefinite one: **Gelegenheit, Gutes zu tun, findet sich immer. Er befahl zu öffnen** *He ordered somebody to open the door.* **Er ist kein Rothschild und die Hauptmannspension ist nicht, um sich einen Viererzug davon zu halten** (Ompteda's *Sylvester von Geyer*, LXI). The infinitive must here be replaced by a subordinate clause, if its subject can possibly be construed as identical with the subject or object of the principal verb: not **Er wünscht zu öffnen,** as the translation of *He wishes somebody to open the door*, but **Er wünscht, daß geöffnet werde,** or **daß man öffne,** for the infinitive construction might mean *He wishes to open the door.*

c. In German as in English, an absolute infinitive with **zu** is often used, the subject of which has no reference to the subject or object of the principal verb: **Die Wahrheit zu sagen, es sind schreckliche Leute, diese alten Cherusker** (Klopstock). **Ohne Ihnen meinen Rat aufzudrängen, so würden Sie viel besser tun, es zu lassen. Um es Ihnen geradeaus zu sagen, ich mag ihn nicht.** Even tho the infinitive precede the principal verb, there is no inversion except after **so.** See also **265.** B. *d* and **281.** *b.*

d. English, differing from German, often employs the infinitive construction when the subject of the infinitive is not identical with the subject or object of the verb in the principal proposition and when the subject of the verb in the subordinate clause is other than the indefinite *one*: Your plan for me to go at once does not please me **Ihr Plan, daß ich sogleich gehen sollte, gefällt mir nicht.** It should be observed that *for* must be used here in connection with the prepositional infinitive. For further details concerning this construction see **269.** 3, **271.** I. *c*, **271.** II. 6, **272.** C. *g* and D. *c*, **277.** 2. *b*, **279.** *d*, **281.** *b. Note* (2nd par.).

e. Even tho the subject of the subordinate clause is identical with the subject of the principal proposition a full clause with a nominative subject must be used in both English and German after verbs of saying and communicating, as **sagen, mitteilen, melden, berichten, erzählen, verkündigen, ankündigen,** &c., which impart facts and events, also after verbs of perceiving, noticing, picturing something to one's self, seeing (getting an insight into something), recognizing, comprehending, as **wahrnehmen, bemerken, sich etwas vorstellen, einsehen, erkennen, begreifen,** &c., which report events and facts that have been perceived by the senses or grasped by the mind: **Er sagte, er werde morgen kommen,** or **daß er morgen kommen werde,** not **Er sagte, morgen zu kommen.** After such verbs the real object is felt to be the following clause as a whole, not any word in it. As the prepositional infinitive is still often, as in the original construction, felt as a modifier of the principal verb it is here out of place where no one word has individual relations with the verb. English at one point preserves this old usage better than German as it usually requires a full clause with a nominative subject after the verbs in I. 2. *c. Note* 1, which have a meaning somewhat similar to those given above, while German can employ here either the prepositional construction or the full clause. German can use the prepositional infinitive construction as the prepositional infinitive with its modifiers is coming more and more to be felt as a grammatical unit, as the equivalent of a full clause with a nominative subject. At this one point the development has gone farther in German than in English, but at other points as can be seen in *d* the English development has outstripped the German. Thus altho in a very large number of cases the prepositional construction has about the same meaning as a full clause, as in **Ich hoffe, morgen gehen zu können,** or **daß ich morgen gehen kann,** it is only natural that in certain cases the old difference between the two constructions has become fixed, the infinitive serving as a modifier of the verb, the clause representing a thought as a whole: **Er vergaß, ihm zu danken,** but **Er vergaß, daß er ihm Dank schuldete. Er weiß, sich zu benehmen,** but **Er weiß, daß er sich heute gut benehmen muß.**

B. The Infinitive without zu.

I. The infinitive without **zu** is used in the following constructions:

1. In the following independent and dependent relations:

a. As subject of a verb, especially in short pithy sayings, also in general used here quite as correctly as the infinitive with **zu,** altho perhaps not so frequently: **Ungeliebt durchs Leben gehen, ist mehr als Mißgeschick, es ist Schuld** (Ebner-Eschenbach's *Unsühnbar,* V.). Also as explanatory of the preceding anticipative subject **es** or **das: Und herrlich deucht' es mich, die Fürstin sein | an eines Fürsten Seite** (Schnitzler's *Der Schleier der Beatrice,* p. 138). Also the perfect infin.: **Das wird mir ja unheimlich, sich dreißig Jahre — na, bis zum dreißigsten Jahre als** Commis voyageur **in der ganzen weiten Welt herumgetrieben haben und dann gar nichts mehr von ihr wissen wollen** (Raabe's *Gutmanns Reisen,* chap. ii). The infinitive without *to* is also found in older English: To know my deed, 't were best not *know* myself (Macbeth, 2, 2). Still common in old saws: Better (= it is better) bend than break. Better ask than go astray.

b. As a predicate, or to complete the meaning of the predicate after **bleiben** to remain, **fahren** to drive (intrans.), **gehen** to go, **heißen** to signify, **kommen** to come, **laufen** to run, **legen** to lay, **liegen** (rarely with infinitive, usually with pres. participle) to lie, **reiten** to ride, **sein** to be, **schicken** to send, **schleichen** to creep, **segeln** to sail, **sich setzen** to sit down, **springen** (see ex.) to spring, leap, **stehen** (rarely with infin., usually with pres. part.) to stand, **wandeln** to walk, stroll, and the auxiliary **werden** in the future, future perfect, and the periphrastic subjunctive: **Er bleibt sitzen. Wir gingen spazieren. Wir fuhren spazieren. Wir ritten spazieren. Wir segelten spazieren. Genua liegt schlafen** (Schiller's *Fiesko,* 2, 18). **Sich allein leben heißt gar nicht leben. Dem Himmel ist beten wollen auch beten. Die Mutter schickt das Kind schlafen. Unheilbares Siechtum bannte ihn ans Zimmer und gestattete ihm höchstens, bei schöner Witterung ein wenig in dem kleinen Garten spazieren zu schleichen** (H. Seidel's *Der Neuntöter*). **Die Alte hatte sich drinnen in ihren Lehnstuhl schlafen gesetzt. Der is** (for **ist**) **schon Klock** (for **Glock'**) **sieben spazieren gegangen. Das heißt: spazieren gesprungen, muß man eigentlich sagen** (Otto Ernst's *Die Gerechtigkeit,* 1, Verwandlung 1). **Was steht ihr horchen?** (Schiller's *Die Piccolomini,* 4, 5). **Und die Väter wandeln würdevoll in der nächsten Umgegend spazieren** (H. Seidel's *Die Geschichte eines Tales*). **Er wird loben. Er würde singen, wenn er nicht heiser wäre.**

The infinitive of certain verbs, as **sitzen, liegen, stehen, stecken, stocken, hangen, kleben, haften, leben, bestehen** is very common after **bleiben** and in poetic language the infinitive of **schweben** and **grünen** occurs, but this construction, tho sometimes found after other verbs, as in **Die Uhr fiel hin, aber sie blieb gehen** (Sanders's *Wörterbuch*) and **Die Zigarre blieb brennen** (ib.), cannot be freely used elsewhere, hence we cannot say: **Er blieb essen, trinken, schlafen,** &c.

Note. The simple infinitive cannot now be freely used after **fahren, gehen, kommen, laufen, legen, reiten, schicken, sich setzen,** and **springen,** but it still occurs in many set expressions: **Nach ein paar Wochen fuhr sie schon wieder eine andere Wohnung suchen. Er geht früh schlafen** *He retires early,* but **Er geht täglich eine Stunde, um besser zu schlafen** *He takes an hour's walk every day, so that he may sleep better.* **Er geht** (**kommt**) **Wasser holen. Er geht baden, essen, einkaufen. Ich gehe die Stimmung beobachten** (Freytag's *Die Journalisten,* 2, 2). **Komm frühstücken, Mama** (Berlepsch's *Fortunat's Roman,* p. 15.). **Der Wind läuft schulen** (L.G. *to hide*) There has fallen a dead calm. **Sie hat sich auf dem Sofa schlafen gelegt. Die Husaren sind furagieren geritten.** Altho in these and similar examples **zu** can sometimes be found the simple infinitive is still quite common. It must be remembered, however, that it has its limits. It is an old accusative of goal which in Old English and Old Saxon was in limited use also with common class nouns: (O.S.) he scolde gifaren is fader ođil (*Heliand,* 4495–7) *He was to go to His father's house.* The accusative of the infinitive denoted the goal, i.e. the purpose of the action. As even in oldest German this accusative had gone out of use with common class nouns and was only found with infinitives its original force had become dim and hence it gradually became more common to place before the infinitive the preposition **zu** or later also **um zu,** which brought out the idea of purpose more clearly. Compare: ni qam gatairan, ak usfulljan (Wulfila, Matth. v. 17) with Luther's translation of the same passage. The simple infinitive is also found here in older English: Go fetch me them (Gen. xxvii. 13). After **sein, stehen,** and **sitzen** the infinitive of purpose, now rather uncommon, has had a peculiar development. See A. I. 1. *b.* (**4**) above.

After **werden** the infinitive represents an older present participle which has been replaced by an infinitive, as explained in **190.** 1. G.

After **heißen** and **sein** the infinitive is usually a true infinitive used as a predicate noun. See examples above.

c. In apposition with the pronouns **ein(e)s, das eine, nichts anderes als, das,** a substantive, or a substantive clause: **Weil du nur eins kennst, mitmachen,**

dabei sein, dich vergnügen (G. Wasner's *Der rote Faden*). **Was mich quälte und ängstigte, mich stundenweise zur Verzweiflung brachte, war das eine: seiner selbst nicht sicher sein** (Ernst Heilborn's *Die Krone*). **Die Wahrheit zu sagen, hätte ihm nichts anderes bedeutet, als Vermutung auskramen und seinen besten Freund verleumden** (Hans Hoffmann's *Der Stellvertreter*, IV). **Ich denke mir das besonders trostlos, sich so mit malenden Damen herumschlagen** (Hauptmann's *Michael Kramer*, I.). **Wochen und Wochen vergingen, in denen es für Ernst** (name) **nur zwei Obliegenheiten gab: den Dienst versehen und die Mutter pflegen** (Fedor Sommer's *Ernst Reiland*, p. 230). **Der Arbeitgeber, der sein Interesse wahren will, muß unentwegt an der alten Losung festhalten: Herr im Hause bleiben!** (*Hamb. Nachr.*, Sept. 22, 1905). **Der Name dieser Veröffentlichung sagt schon zum Teil, was sie soll: Der Kunst, besonders der Dichtung und dem Schrifttum, dienen** (*Blätter für die Kunst*, Oct. 1892). The older simple infinitive is still quite as common here as the infinitive with **zu**. The use of the simple infinitive may often, as in the next to the last example, be ascribed to the fact that it not only contains the idea of apposition but also has the force of an imperative, as in *d*. Compare A. I. 2. *a*. (**2**) and **271.** I. *a*.

d. As an imperative. See **177.** I. B. *e*; **269.** 2. *c*; **271.** I. *a*; **272.** C. *d*.

2. The simple infinitive is used in a number of dependent and independent relations after certain very common auxiliaries and auxiliary-like verbs. The original construction is little felt or completely forgotten. This infinitive stands:

a. As object after the modal auxiliaries **dürfen, können, mögen, müssen, sollen, wollen,** and in colloquial speech quite frequently **brauchen** *to need to*, which has come under the influence of this group, as it has assumed one of the older meanings of **dürfen** and is in general by its new meaning related to these words: **Ich will gehen. Du brauchst bloß wollen** (in choice language more frequently **zu wollen**), **Hannes** (Hauptmann's *Einsame Menschen*, Act 2). We employ also in English the simple infinitive after *to need* when negatived, used in a question, and for the most part also when qualified: "He needs to hurry," but "He need not hurry," "Need he hurry?", and "He only need inquire of the porter."

Note 1. **Vermögen** differing from **mögen** requires **zu: Die betrübte Stadt vermag sich nicht zu trösten.** Earlier in the period the **zu** could be omitted: **Denn er vermag euch nicht erretten von meiner Hand** (2 Kings xviii. 29).

Note 2. **Brauchen** only rarely takes a genitive of the infinitive-substantive instead of the infinitive with or without **zu: Bin ich doch reich und brauche Stehlens nicht** (Grillparzer's *Die Jüdin von Toledo*, 2).

Note 3. The perfect infinitive is sometimes employed here instead of the correct present: **Was Huret über die Göttinger Studentensitten schreibt, hätte Emile Zola geschrieben haben können** (D. in *Deutsche Rundschau*, Sept. 1907, p. 464).

Note 4. The infinitive is often omitted as it can easily be inferred from a preceding finite verb: **Gehst du mit? Ich darf nicht [gehen].**

b. As objective predicate after **lassen** to cause (to be done), have (something done), lead to, let, allow: **Ich lasse ein Haus bauen** I am having a house built. **Ihr Benehmen läßt mich glauben, daß ich ihr nicht gleichgültig bin** Her conduct leads me to think that I am something to her. **Der Oberst ließ die Soldaten zwei Stunden ruhen** The colonel let the men rest two hours. **Er läßt sich betrügen** He allows himself to be deceived.

c. After **blasen** (see ex.) to command by means of the bugle, **heischen** to demand, require, **heißen** to bid, direct, tell (order), command, call, **helfen** to help, **lehren** to teach, **lernen** (but **verlernen** *to unlearn* with **zu**) to learn, **nennen** to call, name, and sometimes **vergessen** (usually with **zu**) to forget: **Ich wende mich zu meinem Hornisten: „Weber! Avancieren blasen!"** (Liliencron's *Kriegsnovellen*, Anno 1870, Unter flatternden Fahnen). **Die Pflicht heischt jetzt handeln, nicht trauern** (Kronprinz Rupprecht von Bayern, Aug. 29, 1914). **Er hieß ihn sich niedersetzen.** Sometimes, especially in older German, **Er hieß mich [mich] niedersetzen** to avoid the repetition of **mich,** but in current German the repetition is the more common usage as the grammatical conscience is more sensitive than formerly. **Er lehrte mich lesen. Das nenne ich schlafen** That is what I call a good sleep. **Vergiß nur nicht, der Adelheidchen guten Tag sagen, Kind** (Schulze-Smidt's *Denk' ich an Deutschland in der Nacht*, II).

Note. After **lehren** and **lernen,** and sometimes after **helfen** and **heißen, zu** *may* stand before the dependent infin., especially if the infinitive is modified by a clause or a number of words: **Er lehrte mich, den goldenen Mittelweg zu wählen. Ich will dir helfen zu lernen, daß es weder vornehm noch moralisch ist, mehr Geld auszugeben als man hat.** The **zu** stands regularly after the passive here. See **178.** 2. B. *d.* In German the passive is in general little used in connection with an infinitive, except as described in **178.** 2. B. *d.* Hence *He was directed to go* is usually translated by **Man hieß ihn gehen.** After the active or passive form of *to tell* (=*to order*) the infinitive with *to* may be employed in English, while in German the infinitive clause is replaced by a subordinate clause with a finite verb: *I told him* or *He was told to go* **Ich sagte ihm** or **Ihm wurde gesagt, daß er gehen müsse.**

d. As objective predicate after the following: verbs of perceiving, finding, meeting, and knowing, **ahnen** to forebode, **denken** or **sich denken** to imagine to one's self, **finden** (more commonly with pres. participle) to find, **fühlen** (and likewise **spüren** and **empfinden**) to feel, **glauben** to believe, **hören** (and likewise **vernehmen**) to hear, **sehen** (and likewise **bemerken, merken, erblicken, gewahren, entdecken,** and **schauen**) to see, **treffen** (also with present participle) to meet, **wähnen** to believe, fancy, imagine, **wissen** *to know*, but with **zu** in the sense *to be able to, know how to*; also after **führen** to lead, **haben** to have, **machen** to make, **tragen** to carry, **wiegen** to rock, **zeigen** to show: **Ich dachte es nicht so arg sein** (E. von Handel-Mazzetti's *Stephana Schwertner*, II, chap. VI), or much more commonly without **sein** in such cases where there is an objective predicate adjective: **Ich dachte es mir nicht so arg. Man denke sich** (dat.) **diese Herren in diesen Felsen hausen** (Gregorovius's *Korsika*, 1, 14). **Da fand ich sie eines Morgens mit kaum noch umflorten Augen auf ihren Kissen liegen** (Franzos's *Der Gott des alten Doktors*, p. 99). **Er saß noch lange, bis der Mond schon unter war und er alles schlafen glaubte** (Storm's *Ein Doppelgänger*, p. 213). **Er spürte seine Augen feucht werden** (Maria Janitschek's *Einer Mutter Sieg*, VII). **Der unten Stehende gewahrte nun endlich auch den Jungen wie eine große schwarze Raupe um den Baum herumhängen** (Storm's *Wann die Äpfel reif sind*). **Ich sehe sie tanzen** I see her dancing. **Ich traf ihn einmal in tiefe Betrachtungen versunken vor einem Obstladen stehen** (Dahn's *Erinnerungen*, IV, p. 135). **. . . losbrechen gegen den Einen, den sie schon mit abgehauenen Gliedern und aus Todeswunden blutend am Boden liegen wähnen** (Engel's *Ein Tagebuch*, I, p. viii). **Wenn ich euch da sitzen und frieren weiß** (P. Heyse's *Nov.*, 150) *When I know that you are sitting there freezing*, but **Er weiß solche Schwierigkeiten geschickt zu lösen** *He knows how to solve such difficulties adroitly*. **Er führte ihn am Arme spazieren** He took him out walking, holding him by the arm. **Er hat das Geld im Kasten liegen. Das machte mich laut auflachen. Er macht von sich reden. „Wo warst du denn?“ „Meine Sorgen etwas spazieren tragen“** (Maria Janitschek's *Einer Mutter Sieg*, IX). **Hab' ich doch schon manchmal ein großes Kind damit schlafen gewiegt** (Goethe's *Egmont*, Act 3). **Man zeigte uns das Schloß Chauvan blinken** (id.).

We sometimes find the infinitive with **zu** after **haben** and **machen** in accordance with the general trend from the simple to the prepositional infinitive: **Das macht mich zu lachen** (Goethe). **Er hat das Geld im Kasten zu liegen.** The infinitive with **zu** is no longer thus found in the literary language after **machen,** and after **haben** it has never been used here, altho it is common in dialect. In connection, however, with a dat. of the person interested, **machen** usually requires **zu** before the dependent infinitive according to A. I. 6: **Das macht mir zu schaffen** that gives me a good deal of work, keeps me busy. Also **haben** may be similarly used with **zu;** see (**2**) below.

Of course, a full clause must be used after all these verbs where the reference is to a thought as a whole: **Ich sah ihn kommen,** but **Ich sah, daß er zu spät kam.**

(**1**) The infinitive after the verbs in the above list is in many cases the mutilated form of the present participle, which once stood here, and which is still in case of **machen** preferred in certain expressions, and in case of **sehen** and **erblicken** is still occasionally used, and in case of (**sich**) **denken, finden, glauben, treffen, wähnen,** and **zeigen** is used quite freely: **Das macht ihn rasend. Er macht sein Recht an die Krone geltend** (formerly also **gelten,** as in Goethe's *Dichtung und Wahrheit*, II, 7) He urges the validity of his claims upon the throne. **Der hat zu Protokoll gegeben, daß er das Mädchen im Mondschein von ihres Vaters Dach kletternd und im Walde laufend gesehen habe** (Raabe's *Frau Salome*, chap. x).

In English there is a distinct shade of meaning between the participle and infinitive here. Compare *I saw him* COMING *up the road* and *I saw him* COME. The participle has descriptive force, while the infinitive calls attention to a statement of fact. In German no such distinction is regularly made between infinitive and participle, for in some cases the participle is rarely used or not employed at all. In some cases, however, this distinction seems to be observed: **Kaiser Otto III. fand den ersten deutschen Kaiser auf einem steinernen Stuhl sitzend, die Krone auf dem Haupt, den Reichsapfel in der Hand** (Moltke). **Im Kriege finden wir den König Opfer vollziehen** (Ranke). In earlier periods the infinitive and participle were both found with a number of these verbs. As a fixed differentiation did not develop, and the participle in careless pronunciation lost its final **d** and thus became identical in form with the infinitive, the latter construction in most cases became established and the possibility of making a beautiful shade of meaning was lost.

(2) **Haben** is used in a number of idiomatic expressions, of which some require no **zu** before the infin., while others require it: **Er hat gut reden** (construed as a substantive in the acc.) It is easy for him to talk. **Er hat zu reden** (modal verbal) He has to make a speech. **Er hat hier nichts zu befehlen** He has no right to give commands here. **Er hat mit mir zu tun** He has to do with me. See A. I. 6. In English the old objective form without *to* is still found in a few expressions: *I had* (past subjunctive = I should regard) *as lief* (= **lieb** = pleasant) *go as stay* **Ich möchte ebenso gern gehen als bleiben.** *You had better go at once* **Sie sollten lieber sogleich gehen.** *I had rather remain* **Ich möchte lieber bleiben.** In English the prepositional passive infinitive is freely used after *to have*, but in German this construction is usually replaced by others: *That has to be done* **Das muß getan werden,** or **Das hat man zu tun.** He will have to be told sooner or later **Man wird es ihm früher oder später sagen müssen.** The passive prepositional infinitive occasionally occurs in German, but it is usually censured by grammarians: **Beim Durchtrennen der Leber hatten drei starke Schlagadern unterbunden zu werden** (*Deutsche Zeit.*, Feb., 1902), instead of **mußten unterbunden werden.**

(3) This use of the infinitive after **wissen** should not be confounded with the case where an infin. in an elliptical clause apparently follows **wissen,** but in reality is dependent upon a modal auxiliary understood: **Sie wußte nicht, was [sie] aus der Sache machen [sollte]** She did not know what to make out of the affair.

(4) In English the simple infinitive is used after a number of these verbs in the active, while the infinitive with *to* is usually employed after the passive: *I heard him say, I made him come*; but *He was heard to say, He was made to come.* Such a passive construction is truly characteristic of English, which can transform any active construction into a passive one by putting the object into the nominative and the main verb into passive form, elsewhere preserving the construction as nearly as possible as in the active, as if the verb formed with its modifiers a compound. The passive is not used here at all in German. The transitives admitting of the present participle construction after them instead of the infinitive sometimes form a passive, where however the present participle is always employed: **Henning** (name) **wurde öfters schlafend auf Ausguck getroffen** (*Hamburger Nachrichten*, Dec. 10, 1904). English may also employ the present participle, sometimes exclusively, sometimes alongside of the more common infinitive. There is often differentiation of meaning as in the active: (descriptive) He was found sleeping; (statement of fact) He was found to be sleeping.

e. After **tun:**

(1) In the common expression **nichts tun: Er tut nichts als klagen** He does nothing but complain.

(2) For emphasis, when instead of the simple finite verb the infinitive of the desired verb is used dependent upon **tun.** Emphatic words are usually placed at the head of the clause or sentence, but a finite form of the verb rarely. If the verb is to be made emphatic, the infinitive, which alone contains the verbal *meaning* and hence the important part of the verb, now usually introduces the clause and is then followed by a finite form of the auxiliary **tun,** which merely marks the verbal *function*: **Loben tat sie nicht viel, sie hielt's vom Überfluß** She rarely praised anybody, as she thought it superfluous. **Kutscher will ich wohl sein und auf dem Bocke sitzen, aber selbst ziehen, das tue ich nicht.**

In dialect, also in the language of children and clumsy speakers in general, **tun** is often used with a dependent infinitive which is not restricted to the first place in the proposition. This construction, which first appeared about 1200, differs from the later development, the emphatic form described above, in that it is a mere periphrasis for the simple verb: **Da täten sie sich trennen = Da trennten sie sich.** In S.G. often in the passive: **Gelt, das wär' Euch so das Rechte, wenn für jeden einzelnen von Euch ein besonderes Kirchengesetz gemacht werden tät'!** (Karl Ettlinger's *Das Beschwerdebuch*, p. 32). For irregular past tense in this construction see **210.** *a.* In older English the *do*-form was thus used promiscuously with the simple form of the verb without a difference of meaning, but later a differentiation took place, so that the *do*-form become fixed in the emphatic, negative, and interrogative form of statement: It *does* matter. It doesn't matter. It *doesn't* matter. Does it matter? *Does* it matter? Doesn't it matter? *Doesn't* it matter? Notice that in English the *do*-form is always accented when the statement is emphatic, while in German the infinitive receives the stress and usually stands at the beginning of the proposition. The German emphatic form does not correspond closely to the English, for it is only used to emphasize the simple verb, not to emphasize the statement. German uses in the emphatic form of statement some adverb where English employs a stressed auxiliary or copula: **Ich árbeite ja** (unstressed)! I *dó* work, but the **ja** is strongly stressed to answer affirmatively in emphatic language an expressed doubt or negation: **Es ist já so** in answer to **Es ist nicht so. Wer in aller Welt schreibt solchen Únsinn?** Who *does* write such nonsense? **Was súchst du nur?** What *are* you looking for? **Was ist denn aber dabei zu láchen?** What *can* they find in it to laugh about? Compare **223.** XI. A. *a.* In German the word-order also plays an important rôle here. See **287.** B. (**7**).

Note 1. **Zu** stands with **tun** in the idiom **zu wissen tun** to announce, acquaint with, let somebody know, make known. Compare *we do you to wit* (2 Cor. viii. 1).

Note 2. After the analogy of repeating the verbal stem in such correct expressions as **Tun tue ich jetzt sehr wenig** we also find in colloquial speech an incorrect repetition of other verbal stems, as the infinitive, no longer being regarded as an object, is now felt to express only the verbal *meaning* and hence a finite form of the same verb is needed to mark the verbal *function*: **Haben hab' ich ihn** (Fontane's *Cécile*, chap. VI). **Reden red't er viel, aber tun tut er nichts.**

3. The infinitive without **zu** is used when it is employed to repeat an idea contained in a finite verb which has already been used, no matter what its construction in the sentence may be: **„Lehne dich an meine Brust und schlafe." Der Elsässer ermannte sich wieder: „Schlafen! dazu wird keine Zeit mehr sein!"** (Rosegger).

4. Where the situation makes clear the thought in questions direct or indirect introduced by some interrogative word the auxiliary is often suppressed as unimportant and the simple infinitive employed: **Ja, was da tun, Engelke?** (Fontane's *Stechlin*, chap. i) What in the world shall I do, Engelke? **Ich hätte nicht so beständig mit Ihnen Rücksprache genommen, wenn ich sonst gewußt hätte, an wen mich halten.** Sometimes the infinitive with **zu** is used: **Was nun zu tun?** (Grillparzer's *Die Argonauten*, 2). **Daß Liselotte nicht gewußt hätte, wie dagegen anzukämpfen** (Gabriele Reuter's *Liselotte von Reckling*, p. 26). Also other elliptical constructions occur: **[ich will] Auch ausfahren! Auch ausfahren mit der Mama!** As the original construction has often become indistinct, the simple infinitive is now used very freely, and in excited or vivid language without precise grammatical relations often becomes the bearer of the thought: **Aber wie Klarheit darüber gewinnen? Ihr schreiben? Wie den Brief in ihre Hände spielen? Und dann — qualvoll harren, bis die Antwort käme, vielleicht vergeblich harren!** (Franzos's *Der Gott des alten Doktors*, p. 135).

5. *Accusative with the Infinitive.* Under the influence of humanistic studies the accusative with the infinitive, as in Latin, was common in the fifteenth, sixteenth, and seventeenth centuries, and still occurs in the classics of the eighteenth century, but it has since disappeared. It is found after such verbs as **achten, denken, glauben, kennen, sagen, behaupten, urteilen, wissen, wünschen,** &c., more commonly without **zu** early in the period, and later with **zu**: **ich achte es billich sein** (2 Pet. i. 13), in revised editions **ich achte es billig zu sein,** but in such cases where there is an objective predicate adjective, participle, or prepositional phrase, it is now more common to drop the **sein**: **Ich achte es billig,** or more frequently **Ich achte es für billig;** now not **Ich glaubte ihn glücklich, im Recht zu sein,** but **Ich glaubte ihn glücklich, im Recht. Hier ruhet Martin Faulermann, wenn man den ruhen sagen kann, der seinen Lebtag nichts getan** (Weckherlin). In Lessing it is especially common in relative clauses: **Dieser Äschines, den er ein so elendes Leben zu führen glaubt.** The infinitive is now replaced by a subordinate clause with or without **daß**: **Dieser Äschines, von dem er glaubt, daß er ein so elendes Leben führe. Ich weiß, daß er wohl ist** *I know him to be well.* As can be seen by the English translation of this last sentence the infinitive, once in use in German, has been retained in English. Characteristic of modern English is the retention of the infinitive even in the passive form of statement in accordance with the general tendency in modern English to retain in the passive statement the active form with the exception that the object becomes nominative or in case of two objects the indirect object becomes nominative: (active) *He declared it to be true* **Er behauptete, es sei wahr,** or **daß es wahr sei,** in the passive: *It was declared to be true* **Es wurde behauptet, daß es wahr sei.** For a fuller discussion of English and German usage here see 272. C. *g.* Of course, the simple infinitive is used after **glauben** and **wissen** where it has the force of a present participle as described in 2. *d* above.

II. Form of the Infinitive to Denote a Past Act.

In the different constructions described in I, above, the infinitive stands uniformly only when it has present force. In case its force would be past,—

a. It assumes the form of the perf. infin. after the modal auxiliaries and the auxiliary **werden: Er will es gesehen haben** He pretends to have seen it. **Er wird jetzt wohl geschrieben haben** He has probably written by this time.

Note. The perf. infin. depending upon these modal auxiliaries should not be confounded with another construction having exactly the same form, but a quite different meaning—namely, **haben** in the infinitive depending upon a modal auxiliary, and having on the other hand a perf. part. with passive force depending upon itself: **Ich wollte alles historisch erklärt haben** I wanted to have everything explained from a historical standpoint. More frequent and forcible than **haben** is **wissen: Numa wollte keine Gottheit in menschlicher oder tierischer Gestalt vorgestellt wissen** Numa did not want to have any god represented in the form of man or beast. Also **sehen** is thus used: **Er wollte diese Frage mit heiterer Gelassenheit behandelt sehen** He wanted to have this question discussed with cheerful composedness.

b. Except often in the subject relation (see **1.** *a* above, under I), it assumes the form of the perf. part. in all the other constructions in I: in the subject relation: **Frisch gewagt [haben] ist halb gewonnen [haben].** In older German the auxiliaries **haben** and **sein** were often omitted here in the compound tense forms after the analogy of their absence in participial clauses as explained in **183.** 2. C. *c.* This older usage has in large measure passed away, but it persists tenaciously here in a very large number of pithy old sayings, preserved as it were by the charm of the terse apt expression: **Aufgeschoben** (subject) **ist nicht aufgehoben** (predicate) Having deferred a matter is not the same as having given up the idea altogether. **[Es ist] Besser schlecht gefahren, als zu Fuß gegangen.** Often also in the predicate relation: **Das heißt schlecht geworfen** That was a bad throw. **Das heißt gelogen** That was what people call lying. **Das heißt recht den Nagel auf den Kopf getroffen. Dies ist natürlich zu weit gegangen** *This is of course going too far*, or to bring out the force of the perf. part. *Here of course he went too far.* **Das war denn aber doch wohl etwas zu viel verlangt** But that was surely asking a little too much. **Das hieße den Bock zum Gärtner gesetzt** That would be making the goat the gardener. **Das heiße ich geschlafen** (objective predicate). There is little difference in any of these sentences between the perfect infinitive and the simple infinitive, so that instead of the last example we may say: **Das heiße ich schlafen.** As the perfect infinitive here often refers to a definite past act it may perhaps emphasize the idea of actuality. On the other hand, the perfect infinitive, altho common in a few set expressions, is not so widely used as the simple infinitive. In imperative function, however, the perfect infinitive has become a great favorite, maintaining itself here well as over against the simple infinitive and usually differentiating itself from it in meaning, as described in **177.** I. B. *d* and *Note* thereunder. In some cases, as after the verbs in I. 2. *d*, the perf. part. is the original construction, not an elliptical perf. infin.: **Er fühlte sich gekränkt** (objective predicate). **Ich will ihn bestraft sehen. Ein Wort macht alles ungeschehen** (objective pred.) One word will smooth over the unpleasant feeling (bring it about that all will be as if the unpleasantness had not happened).

186. Two Infinitives Connected by **als.**

When two infinitives connected by **als** depend upon one of the verbs mentioned above as not requiring **zu** with the dependent infinitive, they both are usually without the **zu,** but not infrequently the second infinitive takes **zu** contrary to rule: **Mit der Welt muß niemand leben, als wer sie brauchen will; ist er brauchbar und still, sollt' er sich lieber dem Teufel ergeben, als zu tun, was sie will** (Goethe). Compare: I had rather *be* a doorkeeper in the house of my God, than *to dwell* in the tents of wickedness (Psalm lxxxiv. 10). When two infinitives used as subjects are in the same manner connected by **als,** they usually both take **zu** or both are without it, but often contrary to rule the one takes **zu** while the other is without it: **Aber Brücken abzubrechen ist leichter als aufbauen** (Boy-Ed), instead of **sie aufzubauen.** The first infinitive may be without the **zu** while a later one takes it.

187. Passive Infinitive in Active Form.

The active infin. often assumes passive meaning in the following constructions:

1. After **heißen, hören** (sometimes also **zuhören**), **lassen, sehen,** and less commonly **fühlen: Ich höre ihn kommen. Ich habe müssen zuhören, Sie herabsetzen, erniedrigen, und konnte und durfte Sie nur halb verteidigen** (Goethe's *Die Leiden des jungen Werthers,* am 16. März). **Er ließ den Arzt holen** He had the doctor sent for. **Wir mußten die Tür vom Schlosser öffnen lassen** We had to have the door opened by a locksmith. **Ich lasse mir von dir nichts befehlen. Wir sahen den Stein emporwinden** We saw the stone being drawn up. We occasionally find the passive form instead of the active: **Wer hat je gesehen jemand also besprenget werden?** (Luther's *Werke,* vol. 49, p. 132). **Und da sitzest du nun und siehst ihn von dem braven germanistischen Pinsel von Vater und der lächerlichen Hexe seiner Mutter immer mehr verzogen werden** (Raabe's *Der Lar,* p. 158). The passive form is not infrequent after **lassen: Die Sage läßt Kronos von Zeus entthronen** or **entthront werden.** The passive form seems the rule in case of the verb **gebären: Den Bildhauer Thorwaldsen lassen einige auf der Überfahrt von Island, andere in Kopenhagen geboren werden** (August Gebhardt). Instead of a passive form of the infinitive we often find after **hören, fühlen, sehen** a perfect participle, which in case of transitives is here as elsewhere passive in force: **Alt, sich beim Vornamen gerufen hörend, hob schnell den Kopf** (Georg Wasner's *Der rote Faden,* II). **Er fühlte sich, sah sich von allen verlassen.** The employment of the perfect participle here with verbal force has developed out of its adjective use as objective predicate (**262.** III. 2. B): **Er fühlte sich gekränkt.** We can often replace the infinitive with passive force by a subordinate clause with a passive verb: **Ich hörte, wie er gerufen wurde** instead of **Ich hörte ihn rufen.** The infinitive was originally a noun, hence the reluctance to give it the passive form of a verb and the feeling that it should be replaced by other more expressive constructions in the passive rather than be treated as a verb. On the other hand, as it has in the course of time acquired considerable verbal force, there is a tendency after **lassen** and **sehen** to give it passive form in accordance with its present-day verbal force.

a. Sometimes it is doubtful whether this infin. is active or passive: **Ich hörte ihn rufen** means *I heard him calling,* or *heard him called by someone.* See 1 above for a clear passive form of this sentence.

b. Formerly also **machen** belonged to this list: **Man tat alles, um sich von dem König bemerken zu machen** (Goethe's *Dichtung und Wahrheit,* II, 7). Occasionally still: **Die „große Zeit" hob ihn selbst über schweren persönlichen Kummer, der ihn eben erst betroffen hatte, hinweg und machte diesen „leichter tragen"** (Caroline Vicker in *Westermanns Monatshefte,* June, 1905, p. 407).

2. After certain other verbs. See **180.** A. *a, b, c.*

The Infinitive-Substantive.

188. Different from the preceding infinitives, which can be used substantively either as subject or object, is the abstract neuter infinitive-substantive, which may take an article or other adj. modifiers before it and is declined as any noun in **-en** and is written with a capital letter: **Das unaufhörliche Weinen des Kindes** the constant weeping of the child. **Ich bin des Treibens müde. Der Erben Weinen ist ein heimlich Lachen** (proverb). **Auf Lachen folgt Weinen. Mit Warten wird nichts erreicht.** It is the presence of the article (or other modifying adj.) that distinguishes this substantive from the verbal infin. used as subject or object, and when these modifying words do not stand before the substantive it is sometimes difficult to distinguish between them: **Er lernt schreiben. Er lernt nicht nur Schreiben und Lesen, sondern auch Geographie und Geschichte.** In the first sentence, **schreiben** expresses *an activity,* hence is the verbal infinitive, in the second, **Schreiben** *a branch of study,* hence a noun.

Sometimes the compound tenses of the infinitive—the perfect active and the passive forms—are used as substantives: **jene dumpfe Angst des Versäumthabens** (C. Lara in *Westermanns Monatshefte,* Jan. 1905, p. 548), **das träge und knechtschaffene Sichgenügenlassen am Regiertwerden von oben herab** (*Der*

Türmer, Jahrgang VI, p. 352), **das Gefühl des Hinausgestoßenseins** (Boy-Ed). **Das Gefühl des Geprügeltwordenseins trieb ihm die Schamröte in die Wangen** (Georg Edward). **Eine solche Partei bietet keinen Schutz gegen das Überlaufenwerden des Deutschen Reiches von der roten Flutwelle** (*Hamburger Nachrichten*, Jan. 7, 1912).

In earlier periods the infinitive-substantive had in one respect more substantive force than now, for it could not show tense and voice as to-day. Thus in M.H.G. the form was active, altho the meaning was clearly passive, as in Welt ir uns tœtens machen vri, | so ritet daȥ i' u verre si (*Parzival* 259, 11-12) **Wollt Ihr uns von dem Schicksal des Getötetwerdens befreien, so entfernt Euch von uns.** Compare *b*. The old active form with passive force, however, is still often used: **Der Räuber fürchtet sich vor dem Hängen.**

a. In the case of the formation of substantives from reflexive verbs many now prefer, especially in case of the compound tense form, to retain the reflexive pronoun as it has become closely associated with the verbal stem: **Das immer tiefere Sichversenken in das Wort des Herrn** the penetrating ever deeper into God's Word, **das Bewußtsein des Sichfreigemachthabens. Ich will nicht einmal dagegen einwenden, daß diese unsere Schwäche ein freiwilliges Sichbegeben der Stärke sein dürfte** (Boy-Ed's *Die säende Hand*, p. 178). On the other hand in case of the simple infinitive many still prefer the older form without the reflexive pronoun: **Da war ein Freuen, wenn er wieder kam. Eine Hinneigung zur Natur, ein inniges Vertiefen in ihre Schönheiten** (H. R. Jockisch in *Westermanns Monatshefte*, Feb. 1907). The old form has become fixed in a few nouns, as **das Befinden** health, **das Betragen** conduct, **das Besinnen** reflection. See also **249.** II. 2. G.

b. Sometimes in early N.H.G., as quite commonly in earlier periods, the infinitive-substantive could, like the verbal infinitive, take an object in the acc.: **Wollen habe ich wol | Aber volbringen das gute** (now **Vollbringen des Guten**) **finde ich nicht** (Rom. vii. 18). The object in this construction partakes of the nature of the object of a verbal noun and also that of a verb. It stands *after* the infinitive-substantive just as the object of a verbal noun, and it is in the acc. just as the object of a verb. The object of the infinitive-substantive is now usually in the gen., which shows that the infin. is now felt as a true noun.

189. The infinitive-substantive, which has much the same force as the prepositional infinitive or the gerund in English (as, *To read* is profitable, or *Reading* is profitable), has an abstract meaning bordering upon the abstract verbal nouns ending in **-ung** and those formed from the past tense of strong verbs. The relation of this infinitive-substantive to the other verbal nouns is that the former is more abstract and hence cannot usually take a plural, while more of the concrete enters into the latter, as can be seen from the following instructive sentence: **Das Unterscheiden ist nicht leicht, denn der Unterschied zwischen zwei Dingen ist oft so versteckt, daß die Unterscheidung des einen von dem andern kaum möglich ist.** This close distinction cannot always be detected so clearly as in the preceding sentence, and hence they are often confounded, and we find the infinitive-substantive instead of one of the other more correct verbal nouns, especially as the infin. is a favorite construction: **das Aufgehen der Sonne** instead of **der Aufgang der Sonne** the rise of the sun; **das Anfertigen des Sarges** instead of **die Anfertigung des Sarges** the making of the coffin.

Formation of Compound Tenses.

190. 1. A. The *present perfect*, indicative and subjunctive, of transitive and most intransitive verbs is formed with the present indic. or subj. of **haben** and the perfect participle of the verb to be conjugated, but some intransitives (see **191**) form this tense with the present of **sein** and the perfect participle: (indic.) **ich habe gelobt,** but **ich bin gefallen;** (subj.) **ich habe gelobt,** but **ich sei gefallen.** For origin of this tense form see **191.** I. 1 and 4 (2nd par.).

The imperative in this tense has only two persons, the second and third. The second person is formed with the present imperative of **haben** or **sein** and the perfect participle, and the third person with the present subjunctive of **haben** or **sein** and the perfect participle: **Habe nie umsonst gelebt!** (Gutzkow). **Ins Grab! Die Schaufeln her! Er sei gewesen** (Kleist's *Käthchen*, 2, 8) Into the grave with him! Bring on the shovels! May he soon have ceased to be!

a. Another form of the pres. perf. indic. and subj. is now common even in good authors, however, with a shade of difference in meaning. To the regular pres. perf. form, **gehabt** is often added if the verb is trans., or **gewesen** if the verb is intrans., to indicate that a past *condition* or state of things is to be represented rather than a past *act*: **Nicht auf dir lastet die Schuld, du hast dein Herz der Liebe nicht verschlossen gehabt** (Jensen's *Das Bild im Wasser*, p. 433). **Wie ich erschrocken gewesen bin!** (Spielhagen's *Sturmflut*, 3, 30).

b. Omission of Tense Auxiliaries in the Present Perfect and Past Perfect. The auxiliaries **haben** and **sein** are sometimes omitted here:

(1) In the subordinate clause, only occasionally in plain prose, much more commonly in poetry: **Die alten Rechte, wie wir sie ererbt [haben] von unsern Vätern, wollen wir bewahren** (Schiller's *Tell*, 2, 2). **Er wußte auch ganz genau, wer dem Attentat die ausführende Hand geliehen [hatte]** (Hans Hoffmann's *Iwan der Schreckliche*, VI).

The most common case of omitting the auxiliary in plain prose is where the same form reoccurs in successive subordinate clauses which do not modify the same word. Even if the same form occurs here only twice it is felt as unpleasant and one of them is suppressed: **bis die Periode, für die der Reichstag gewählt worden [war], abgelaufen war.**

Altho present usage is not averse to an occasional omission of the auxiliary this freedom has almost disappeared in sentences containing a perfect participle with the form of the infinitive: **Wenn er diesen Brief selbst geschrieben [hat], so will ich ihn anstellen,** but **Wenn er diesen Brief selbst hat schreiben können, so will ich ihn anstellen.** In such sentences, however, as the last Lessing still frequently suppresses the auxiliary, and this omission occurs in rare instances later: **Seiner fast unbewußt, hatte er die Richtung eingeschlagen, die sein zürnender Brotherr ihn gehen heißen** (Helene Raff in *Deutsche Rundschau*, Aug. 1908, p. 172). At the beginning of the fifteenth century the omission of the auxiliaries began to be quite common and this remained so until the middle of the eighteenth century. From then on this freedom gradually disappeared. The causes for the rise and decline of this elliptical construction are given in **237.** 1. B. *a. Note*, **183.** 1. B. *b* and 2. C. *c*, *d*, and **185.** B. II. *b*.

(2) In the crisp style of telegrams and also in familiar style the auxiliaries often drop out in the principal proposition as they have weak stress and are not felt as necessary to the thought: **[ich habe] Eben telegraphisch die Angelegenheit gelöst** (from a telegram). **[hast du dich] Gut amüsiert, Kindchen?** Also in lively vivid style. See **183.** 1. G.

c. The participle is usually accented more strongly than the auxiliary of tense, but to emphasize the idea that an activity is all over the auxiliary receives the stress: **Er hât | gelebt — der Streich des Todes ist gefallen** (Schiller's *Turandot*, 1, 2). **Heinrich läuft heute nicht Schlittschuh; er íst gelaufen** (Georg Edward). The auxiliary is similarly stressed to emphasize the actuality or, on the other hand, the non-actuality of a past act or state: **Ich höre auf zu leben, aber ich hâbe gelebt** (Goethe's *Egmont*, 5, Gefängnis). **Ja, er hât gefühlt und gewählt, und ist männlich entschieden** (id., *Hermann und Dorothea*, V, 51). **Hätt' ich doch den Burschen aus dem Weg geräumt! Wär' ich doch dabei gewesen!** Often with omitted participle: **Lina, das is Handgeld und bringt uns Glück. Und hât auch** (Fontane).

On the other hand, to emphasize the idea that a *condition* of things is past the German stresses the participle, while the English accents also here the auxiliary of tense: **Er hat kein Geld mehr, aber er hat Geld gehâbt** (Georg Edward) He has little money, but he *hás* had money. See also **194.** 4. *Note* 2 for examples in passive form.

B. The *past perf.* of trans. and most intrans. verbs is formed with the past tense of **haben** and the perf. part. of the verb to be conjugated, but some intransitives (see **191**) form this tense with the past tense of **sein** and the perf. part.: (indic.) **ich hatte gelobt,** but **ich war gefallen;** (subj.) **ich hätte gelobt,** but **ich wäre gefallen.** Originally this form was a past tense just as the present perfect was originally a present tense, as explained in **191.** I. 1 and 4 (2nd par.)

a. As in certain dialects the pres. perf. replaces the past (see **165.** 2. *b*), the past perf. is replaced by a special form made by adding **gehabt** in case of transitives and **gewesen** in case of intransitives to the regular pres. perf: **Bin ich schuld, daß der Baron sich im Zimmer bei mir hat eingeschlichen** (perf. for past)?! **Ich hab' ihn nicht hinbestellt gehabt!** (instead of **hatte hinbestellt**) (Halbe's *Das tausendjährige Reich*, p. 31). **Dann hat sich's** (= **sie sich**) **über das Kind g'worfen** (perf. for past), **und hat's so lang niedergedrückt** (perf. for past) **in die Kissen mit ihrem ganzen Leib, bis das Dirnd'l** (= **Mädchen**) **erstickt ist g'wesen** (instead of **erstickt war**) **unter der Last** (Telmann). For the use of this form in indirect discourse see **171.** 2. B. *e*.

This formation is sometimes employed in the literary language in the infinitive with the force of the past perfect, altho grammarians have not generally recognized a past perfect infinitive: **Ludwig scheint sich entfernt zu haben** *It seems that L. has withdrawn*, or **L. scheint sich damals entfernt zu haben** *It seems that L. withdrew at that time*, but **L. scheint sich entfernt gehabt zu haben** (Wustmann's *Sprachdummheiten*, p. 110, 3rd ed.) *It seems that L. had withdrawn.*

b. A past perf. form, corresponding to the pres. perf. described in A. *a* above, is now common in good authors. The participles **gehabt** in case of transitives and **gewesen** in case of intransitives are added to the regular past perf. to form a past perf. with a slight difference of meaning. This past perf. differs from the regular one in that it expresses a *state* or *condition* of things instead of an *action*: **Ich hatte den Brief schon geschrieben gehabt, als ich deine Anfrage bekam. Der einige Monate verreist gewesen war** (P. Heyse's *Im Paradies*, 2, 347) *who had been away from town several months.* There is a tendency to use this past perfect tense form instead of the regular one, even where the reference is clearly to an act and not to a state or condition: **Das „Adieu" hatte sie genau in dem nämlichen Ton hervorgebracht, mit dem er es damals an der Gartenpforte gesprochen und sie drauf erwidert gehabt** (Jensen's *Das Bild im Wasser*, p. 307).

c. The auxiliaries **haben** and **sein** are often dropped in subordinate clauses as in the case of the pres. perf. See A. *b*. (**1**).

C. *a*. The *future*, indic. and subj., is formed with the pres. indic. and subj. of **werden** and the simple infin.: (indic.) **ich werde loben, ich werde fallen;** (subj.) **ich werde loben, ich werde fallen.**

Note 1. *The Historic Development of the Future Active and the Actional Passive.* The explanation of the infinitive form here is given in G below. It first appeared in the eleventh century but for a long time was little used, so that it did not become thoroly established until the fifteenth century. Thus thruout the M.H.G. period and in early N.H.G. we usually find not the infinitive but the present participle here, as in the following sentences from "Der sogenannte St. Georgener Prediger," completed July 24, 1387: Versůchent und merkent, wie süss Got ist, so werdent ir in minnende (p. 171) Try to see how lovely God is and you will love him. The present participle *minnende* here in connection with the auxiliary *werden* seems to be the modern future tense, but it is in fact a periphrastic present tense used as a future just as the simple present tense is often employed as a future. In many other places in this old book it is evident that this form is a periphrastic present tense: Recht als das wachs von der haissen sunnen smeltzent wirt und zerfliessent, also wirt du (= **die**) sele smeltzende von der waren sunnen, unserm herren Jhesu Christo (id., p. 37) **Wie das Wachs von der heißen Sonne schmilzt und zerfließt, so schmilzt die Seele von der wahren Sonne, unserem Herrn Jesu Christo.** In this old book as in general thruout M.H.G. and in earliest N.H.G. there is a regular periphrastic conjugation: er wirt smeltzent (used as a present tense or a future), er ward smeltzent (past tense), er ist smeltzent worden (present perfect), &c. These periphrastic tenses express the same time relations as the older simple tenses, but they have a different aspect (see **164**). Both **werden** and the present participle have here their original literal meaning, so that both taken together have ingressive perfective force (**164**), calling attention not to an activity or state as a whole but to one point, the moment of entrance into the state or activity: das wachs wirt smeltzent und zerfliessent the wax begins to melt and dissolve, lit. becomes melting and dissolving. At this time just as also to-day the perfective type was also expressed by means of prefixes, as explained in detail in **164**. Often later and sometimes in the old book quoted above the periphrastic forms lose their original meaning and assume a new force. The idea of entrance into an activity develops into the idea of an act as a whole, so that the periphrastic tenses have the same force as the older simple forms: Du (= **die**) werck du von tugenden gant, da mit werdent die tugend all gefůret und wachsend (p. 214) **Die Tugenden werden ernährt und wachsen von den Werken, die von den Tugenden kommen.** In this sentence we find this development not only in the active periphrastic forms but also in the passive, werdent gefůret, i.e. the perfect participle of a transitive verb in connection with *werden*. This development, i.e. the reference to the action as a whole, took place much earlier in the passive forms, indeed was firmly established in O.H.G. and thus facilitated the development in the active forms. This change of meaning in the active periphrastic forms does not represent a gain to the language, for the older simple tenses have the same meaning and are much handier, but in the passive forms this change resulted in the development of the actional passive (**194**. 4) and thus represents real progress, for there were no simple passive forms in existence and there was thus gained a clear passive form for the expression of action as over against the form with **sein** which denoted state: **Das Haus wird jedes Jahr angestrichen** (action), but **Das Haus ist angestrichen** (state).

Thus the forms in the active periphrastic system were on the one hand pure ingressive perfectives, as explained above, or on the other hand were a mere useless periphrasis for the older simpler tense forms and as useless gradually disappeared from the literary language with the exception of the present indic., now used in suppositions as explained in **165**. 5. *b*. *Note*, and the past subjunctive, which has become a useful form as described in E. *a* below. In dialect, however, the periphrasis has maintained itself better, as shown in E. *a* below. Also the ingressive perfectives have disappeared, not, however, by way of elimination but by the development of a new meaning. Even in the old book mentioned above there are evident signs that the ingressive present tense is differentiating itself from the simple present tense. It is the favorite where there is a reference to the future: Die sint sälig die rainnes hertzen sint, won sie sint Got sehent werdent (p. 259) **Selig sind, die reines Herzens sind, denn sie werden späterhin Gott sehen.** The idea of an entrance into an activity naturally suggests the idea of a future activity. This ingressive present gradually lost its original force and developed into a pure future tense. The establishment of the present ingressive as a pure future destroyed the whole ingressive tense-system as it no longer had a present tense to rest on. Its place has been taken by **anfangen** with a dependent infinitive, a construction that had from the start been competing with it, and also by other ingressive forms, as explained in **164**. The old ingressive system with **werden** and a dependent infinitive has been preserved in certain dialects. See G below.

Note 2. In M.H.G. and early N.H.G. the future was formed by means of the auxiliaries **wollen** and **sollen**, just as in English to-day. The Low German dialects also preserve this older usage. The literary form with **werden** developed in the South. It became fairly well established in the fifteenth century. It is a decided improvement, as it expresses the idea of futurity pure and simple, while **wollen** and **sollen**, and in English *will* and *shall*, contain a certain element of modality, implying in addition to the idea of futurity that of desire and authority. The use of **wollen** and **sollen** to express futurity still continues in the infin. See *b*.

Note 3. The stress in the future tense usually rests upon the infinitive form, but to emphasize the idea of actuality the tense auxiliary is stressed, often with the omission of the infinitive: **Wenn's mir nur gelingt! Es wird, es wird!** (Viebig).

b. The future infinitive is formed with the infin. of **wollen** and the infin. of the verb to be conjugated wherever the act is planned by the subject of the sentence: **Gordon gab übrigens die Versicherung, es gnädig machen zu wollen** (Fontane's *Cécile*, chap. vi) Gordon assured her, moreover, that he would not be too severe. **Man trennte sich früh, aber doch mit der Zusicherung, am andern Tage spätestens um sieben beim Frühstück sein zu wollen** (id., *Die Poggenpuhls*, chap. xiv). Figuratively: **Es scheint regnen zu wollen.**

Wherever the act is planned by someone else than the subject, or the outcome of events depends upon factors beyond the control of the subject **sollen** is employed here: **Das Gut scheint verkauft werden zu sollen. Was die politische Lage betrifft, so scheint das neue Regime keinem ernsten Widerstand begegnen zu sollen. Man durfte kaum erwarten, noch so viel Neues und Beachtens-**

wertes über Friedrich von Hagedorn erfahren zu sollen, wie diese Schrift enthält (Albert Köster in *Anzeiger für deutsches Altertum*, XXXVI, p. 159).

As yet there has appeared no tendency to use **werden** here as in the indic.

D. The *future perfect*, indic. and subj., is formed with the present indic. or subj. of **werden** and the perfect infinitive: (indic.) **ich werde gelobt haben, ich werde gefallen sein;** (subj.) **ich werde gelobt haben, ich werde gefallen sein.** For the origin of this form see **165.** 6. *a. Note.*

E. The *past periphrastic subjunctive* is formed with the past subj. of **werden** and the simple infinitive: **ich würde loben** I should praise, **ich würde fallen** I should fall.

a. The infinitive has replaced here the older present participle. See G below. The past periphrastic subjunctive is in fact the past subjunctive of the peculiar old past tense described in G below, consisting of the past tense of **werden** and the present participle or infinitive of the verb to be conjugated. The indicative of this past tense is now lost. Before it disappeared it had become a mere periphrasis for the usual simple past tense, having lost its original meaning: **Solon wart disen pilgram fragen, wie sein vatter genennet wer** (Hans Sachs, Goedeke ed., I, p. 132) = **Solon** (name) **fragte diesen Pilger,** &c. The present and past tense of this old periphrasis is widely preserved in the dialects: **ich werde gehen = ich gehe. Ich wurde gehen = ich ging.**

In the literary language this old periphrasis only survives in the past subjunctive (**ich würde loben, lieben,** &c.), which has become a very useful form. Grammarians would limit its use to the principal proposition of conditional sentences and to indirect discourse, but in accordance with its origin as a past subjunctive it is often used more widely, standing wherever the regular past subjunctive can stand, as described in **169.** 1. A. *a*; **169.** 1. B. *a*; **169.** 2. B. *a*; **169.** 2. *D. a*, and E. *Note* 3. On account of the lack of clear subjunctive forms here and the general dislike for the simple forms of this mood this usage is spreading, especially in the South. The best usage, however, instead of thus using interchangeably the periphrastic and the simple subjunctive, inclines, especially in clauses of manner and sometimes in conditional clauses, to differentiate them, so that the former expresses future time and the latter present time, or in subordinate clauses the same time as that of the principal verb: **Er spricht von meinen Besitzungen, als wenn ich so reich wie ein Herzog wäre** (present time), but **Die sehen nicht aus, als wenn sie so bald Brüderschaft mit uns trinken würden** (Goethe's *Egmont*, Act 4) (future time). **Wie sie laufen, als ob sie aus Zucker wären** (present time) **und die schweren, frischen Regentropfen an ihnen lecken und auflösen würden** (future time)! (H. Böhlau's *Adam und Eva*, chap. i). **Mir ist zu Mute, als ob ich geschlagen würde** (Hauptmann's *Einsame Menschen*, 4) (present time), but **Ich habe überhaupt manchmal ein Gefühl, als ob sich Hannes schon allein wieder 'rausarbeiten würde** (ib.) (future time). **Es hatte den Anschein, als würde** (*would*) **sich die Spekulation mehr der Peripherie der Stadt zuwenden** (future), but **Es hatte den Anschein, als wendete** (*were turning*) **sich die Spekulation mehr der Peripherie der Stadt zu** (contemporaneity). **Wenn er nur hier wäre!** (present time), but with reference to the future: **Wenn sie (i.e. die Rosen) doch nicht welken würden!** (H. Böhlau's *Adam und Eva*, chap. VI).

F. The *past perfect periphrastic subjunctive* is formed with the past subj. of **werden** and the perfect infinitive: **ich würde gelobt haben, ich würde gefallen sein.**

G. *Ingressive and Progressive Forms.* Rarely in O.H.G. but often later in M.H.G. and early N.H.G. compound tense forms consisting of the present, past, or present perfect tense of **werden** in connection with the pres. part. of the verb were used with ingressive force (**164**) to indicate the commencement of an action in the present or past: **Er wird laufend** He is beginning to run. **Er ward laufend** He began to run. See also C. *a. Note* 1 above. In the same way the present and past tense of **sein** were often in O.H.G., M.H.G., and early N.H.G. used with the present participle to indicate the continuance of an action, just as the *progressive form* of the verb in English: **Es waren aber Jüden zu Jerusalem wonend** (Acts ii. 5). The present participle in these constructions often goes over into the infinitive form: **Er ward laufen, er war wohnen.** The infinitive form here first appeared in the eleventh century after **werden** and after a slow development became established in the fifteenth century. In the fourteenth century it began to appear after **sein** after the analogy of usage after **werden.** This change of form was rendered easy and natural on one hand by the fact that the present participle had in careless speech become identical with the infinitive in form, on the other hand by the analogy of the infinitive after the auxiliary verbs **beginnen, sollen, wollen,** and **müssen.** In M.H.G. **beginnen** was commonly used with a simple dependent infinitive, not with the prepositional infinitive as to-day. As **werden with the present par-**

ticiple in M.H.G. usually had the same meaning as **beginnen** with a dependent infinitive there arose a tendency for **werden** likewise to take the infinitive. **Werden** also came under the influence of **sollen, wollen,** and **müssen,** as they were all often used as auxiliaries to indicate future time. Hence **werden** under the powerful influence of all these four verbs which took a dependent infinitive gradually became itself permanently associated with the infinitive. The participial and infinitive forms in connection with **sein** have lingered on even up to our own day in the case of the verb **vermuten: Ich war mir Sie in dem Vorzimmer nicht vermutend** (Lessing's *Emilia Galotti*, 2, 7). **Was gilt's, das warst du nicht vermuten** (id., *Nathan*, 2, 1). **So etwas war ich vermuten** (Müllner's *Die Schuld*, 4, 1). **Es gibt viele Redensarten für die Betäubung, die den Menschen überkommt, wenn ihm etwas begegnet, dessen er sich durchaus nicht vermutend war** (Raabe's *Hastenbeck*, chap. xiii). In certain dialects this old construction is better preserved and is found with other verbs: **Es ist, als wenn irgend etwas einen zwingen tät', im Gehen die Augen zuzumachen, wie wenn eins schlafend wär'** (Wilhelm Fischer's *Die Freude am Licht*, p. 54). As these compound forms, made up of **sein** and the present participle, were never deeply rooted in the language since the construction originated and flourished only under the influence of the Latin and as on the other hand these compound forms, as in the examples just given often had the same force as the simple tense, i.e. had become a mere periphrasis for the simple present or past tense and thus did not as in English develop a sharply differentiated meaning they gradually as useless forms disappeared from the language. The English progressive might possibly have met the same fate if the gerundial construction, as in "He is *fishing*" (from *a-fishing* from older *on fishing*), had not developed into the same form and given it more vigorous life. Also the German construction of **werden** with the infinitive has become obsolete except in two very common cases, where it has taken on a slightly different meaning, serving as the regular tense form of the future (see C. *a. Note* 1 above) and as a periphrasis for the past subjunctive (see E. *a*). In some dialects, however, as in Austria, the present participle survives here with its original force: **So oft die Red' auf'n Gelbhofbauer kommt, wird bei ihm's Radel laufend und da haspelt er die ganze alte Geschicht' aber** (Anzengruber's *Kreuzelschreiber*, **1, 1**). **Es sind etliche streitend worden** (Handel-Mazzetti's *Stephana Schwertner*, I). The infinitive form is preserved in N.G. dialect: **Dat ward (= wird) regen** (dialect of Glückstadt) = **Es fängt an zu regnen. Do wor (= wurde) he ween'n** (ib.) = **Da fing er an zu weinen.** In the North this old form has in some dialects developed into a mere periphrasis for the simple form of the verb, as described in E. *a*.

The present participle is still often found in connection with both **werden** and **sein,** but it now has here only the force of an adj.: **Er ist vermögend** He is rich. **Gebt jeden Zweifel auf, Euer Mann ist sterbend** (*in a dying condition*) (Ebner-Eschenbach's *Mašlans Frau*). **Ihre Stimme ist ersterbend, verhauchend** (Hauptmann's *Versunkene Glocke*, Act 5).

2. These compound tenses are often abbreviated by suppressing the non-personal part, i.e. participle and infinitive, when the suppressed words can easily be supplied from the context. Altho the auxiliary verbs are usually only lightly stressed they are here accented heavily in order to bring out clearly the idea of the actuality or non-actuality of a past act or the certainty of a future act. The abbreviation may assume two forms:

a. The personal part of the verb, i.e. the auxiliary, may alone remain, accompanied by one of the pronouns **das, es, was,** which represent the suppressed non-personal part of the preceding verb with all its modifiers, and thus stand for the whole thought expressed in the preceding sentence: **Du würdest sie ja nicht gezwungen haben? Nein, das hätte ich nicht,** or **Nein, das würde ich nicht** You, certainly, would not have forced her, would you? No, I would not. **Sie hat gebüßt, wahrlich sie hat es** She has atoned for it, indeed, she has. **Er hat studiert, was ich nicht habe.**

b. The personal part of the verb with its subject may alone remain, unaccompanied by the neuter pronoun, the suppressed words easily being supplied from the context: **Kann sein, ich habe sie auch wirklich geliebt. Aber — ich habe!** (Lessing's *Emilia Galotti*, 1, 1) It may be that I once really loved her, but that is now all past, lit. *I have* [loved her]. **Hättest du ihn nehmen mögen, Selma? Gewiß hätt' ich [ihn nehmen mögen]** Should you have wanted to accept him, Selma? Certainly, I should. **Wart! euch werd' ich [kuranzen]** Just wait, boys! I'll give you a good sound thrashing. **„Wenn's mir nur gelingt!" „Es wird, es wird!"** (Clara Viebig). Otto: **Wir hätten Straußberg auch ohne ihn bekommen!** Barbara: **Warum habt Ihr nicht?** (Wildenbruch's *Die Quitzows*, 2, 4).

THE USE OF **haben** AND **sein**.

191. The Germans have not yet developed in their language the idea of tense pure and simple as in modern English. In German, tense is closely associated with aspect (see **164**), so that each compound tense except the future has two different tense forms for the two different aspects, one with **haben,** one with **sein.** Hence the use of **haben** and **sein** as auxiliaries of tense presents peculiar difficulties to the English-speaking student, as the German has two auxiliaries for the one *to have* in English.

The following distinctions between the use of **haben** and **sein** are to be observed:

I. **Haben** is used:

1. With transitives: **Ich habe den Brief geschrieben** I have written the letter, originally a present tense: *I have the letter in a written condition.*

2. With durative intransitives, i.e. such as represent an act as continuing, in order to indicate the completion of the activity: **Ich habe gearbeitet, sie hat gesungen, wir haben gelacht. Sie hat lange gelitten. Er hat lange geirrt und geschwankt, ehe er den Boden fand, darin Wurzel zu fassen ihm beschieden war. Es hat geregnet.**

3. With terminate (**175.** *Note*, last par.) intransitives to denote the completion of *an act as a whole* without reference to the idea of duration, but with **sein** according to 4 (2nd par.) when the attention is directed to a change of place and to only one point of the activity, either to the beginning or to the end or result: **Der Schiffer hat** (to denote an act) or **ist** (to denote a change of place, the beginning of the voyage) **abgestoßen. Er hat** (to denote an act) or **ist** (to denote the end of the act and the resulting change of place) **gerückt. Der Habicht hat** (act) **auf Tauben gestoßen** *came upon by chance*, but **Das Schiff ist** (result) **auf den Grund gestoßen. Die Flotte hat** (act) or **ist** (result) **gelandet. Er hat** (act) or **ist** (result) **über den Bach gesetzt. Er hat** (act) **geeilt, zu seinen Eltern zu kommen,** but **Er ist** (goal) **nach Hause geeilt. Er hat** (to denote an act of only a moment's duration) **nicht gezuckt** *He* did *not wince.* **Er hat** (act) **der Schlange auf den Kopf getreten. In Zwölf Bobs hatten so innerhalb einer Stunde gestartet** (*Frankfurter Zeit.*, Feb. 1914) **hatten** represents the starting in each case as a momentary act, something complete in itself, not the beginning of a long ride, but of course **sein** is used in **Der französische Aviatiker Poulet, der vor einigen Tagen gestartet ist und die 25000 Kilometer lange Luftreise in 30 Tagen zurückzulegen gedenkt** (*Das Berliner Tageblatt*, Oct. 29, 1919).

4. With perfective intransitives—point-action intransitive verbs denoting not an act as a whole but only one point in the activity, either the beginning or the end—so far as they are non-mutative, i.e. do not indicate a change of place or condition: **Er hat laut aufgelacht** He broke out into a loud laugh. **Der Regen hat aufgehört. Der Sturm hat ausgetobt** The storm has spent its fury.

On the other hand, **sein** is used with mutative perfective intransitives, i.e. point-action intransitives denoting only one point in the activity, either the beginning or the end, in connection with a change of place or condition, expressed in an attained or contemplated goal or a resultant state. This goal or state is either (**1**) a final destination or condition: **Er ist eben angekommen, er ist nach Hause geritten, er ist heute gestorben, die Blumen sind abgeblüht** (*faded*, indicating a resultant state, but to indicate merely the end of an activity **der Weizen hat abgeblüht** *the wheat has ceased to blossom*); or (**2**) the beginning of a new state or activity: **er ist eingeschlafen, aufgewacht, errötet, abgefahren,** literally *he has gotten into sleeping, waking,* &c. The former class is called effective perfectives, the latter ingressive perfectives. Originally all these forms were present tenses, a present tense form of **sein** in connection with a perfect participle, which was originally felt as a predicate adjective expressing a resultant state. The full treatment of these perfectives is given in II below. The boundary lines of usage between **haben** and **sein** are not at every place clearly drawn. Earlier in the period **haben** was more widely used than to-day, especially in the North and Midland, as can be seen in II. B. *c*; C. 1. *a* and 2. *a*; D below. It has, however, under North German influence made small gains in the one group described in II. A. *Note.* Also in other groups the N.G. tendency toward **haben** occasionally manifests itself in the literary language, but in general S.G. usage, which favors a more liberal employment of **sein,** has prevailed. In English the development has been in the opposite direction, for *to be* has been entirely replaced here by *to have*, except in certain cases where *to be* may still be used to express the idea of a *state* or *result*: The melancholy days *are* come (Bryant). When he awoke, the boys of the village *were* gathered round him.

Note. The transitives **anfahren** to speak harshly to, rebuke, **angehen** to ask, solicit, concern, attack, **anlaufen** to touch (call) at (a port), **anwandeln** to come over, **durch′fahren** to drive thru, **durch′gehen** to go thru or over, **durch′laufen** to run thru or over, **durch′wandern** to walk thru, **durch′ziehen** to travel thru, **eingehen** to enter into (a contract, &c.), **passieren** to pass (as a verb of motion), **über′kommen** to come over, seize, are not only conjugated with **haben,** but also not infrequently with **sein,** as the force of the simple verb, which is primarily an intransitive conjugated with **sein,** asserts itself: **Bin ich ihn angefahren: Was er da beim Herd zu tun hätt'?** (Rosegger's *Martin der Mann*, p. 76). **Sie hatten schon immer allerhand im Halbschlaf gehört: Türen werfen, die laute Donnerstimme des Vaters; aber es war sie nichts angegangen** (concerned) (H. Böhlau's *Adam und Eva*, chap. ii). **Das ganze Dorf war ich schon durchwandert von einem Ende zum andern** (Paul Keller's *Waldwinter*, IV). **Der Bischof Wedekind bereute nicht selten gar sehr den Handel, welchen er mit dem Abt Heinrich zu Fulda eingegangen war** (Raabe's *Die Hämelschen Kinder*, chap. iii). **Hannover** (ship) **ist gestern Kap Henry passiert** (*Hamburgischer Correspondent*, May 30, 1901; five times with **sein** on one page). **Sie wußte selbst nicht, was sie überkommen war** (Storm's *Zur Wald- und Wasserfreude*, p. 188).

Ankommen to seize, come (hard, easy, &c.) for (one), and verbs of motion, as **gehen, kommen, laufen, reiten,** in composition with **vorüber** or **vorbei** (see also **259.** 36), are *usually* conjugated with **sein,** as the force of the simple verb asserts itself: **Denn es war jn ein schrecken ankommen** (Luke v. 9). **Sauer ist's mich genug angekommen** (Anzengruber's *Schandfleck*, chap. vii). **Kein Geschöpf bist du vorbeigegangen** (Herder). **Wir sind kein Wirtshaus vorübergegangen, ohne einzukehren** (Blatz).

The transitives **einschlagen** to take (a way, road), **über′gehen** to pass over, **um′fahren** to drive around, **um′gehen** or **um′wandeln** to walk around, are occasionally found with **sein** earlier in the period, but are now usually conjugated with **haben.**

Verbs that take a cognate accusative (see **257.** 2. A) are not real transitives, and hence usually take **sein** where the simple verb is conjugated with **sein: Ich bin so lange Eisenbahn gefahren, daß mich alle Kondukteure kannten. Haben** is, however, used here when the idea of motion disappears and that of an act or activity becomes prominent: **Ich hätte** (perhaps under the influence of *J'ai couru le risque*) **Gefahr gelaufen, mich zu verschnappen** (Lessing). **Die Soldaten haben zweimal Sturm gelaufen wider die Mauer** (Sanders's *Wörterbuch*). **Da aber hatte Brinckmann Attacke geritten** (Ernst Heilborn's *Zwei Kanzeln*, I). Present usage, however, inclines sometimes also here toward **sein** in accordance with the general trend of intransitives toward **sein: Ich bin** (**habe**) **große Gefahr gelaufen** (Blatz). In many other cases the acc. is an adverbial acc. and the verb is to be regarded as intransitive: **Ich bin diesen Weg noch nie geritten. Er ist die Zimmer alle durchgegangen.**

II. **Sein** is only used with intransitives:

1. When the verb is a mutative perfective with effective force, i.e. when the subject is thought of, not as acting, but as resting in a state or condition produced by the action, or as reposing at or moving toward some goal or destination that has been reached or will be reached by means of the activity indicated in the verb: **Das liebe Kind ist unter meinen eigenen Augen verkümmert** *wasted away*, &c. **Er ist seinen Leiden erlegen** *succumbed to*, &c. **Sein Leib ist in Staub zerfallen. Die Post ist soeben eingetroffen. Er ist nach der Stadt gegangen.** Other examples are given in I. 4 (2nd par.) above and B and C below.

Note. In M.H.G. we often even in the South find **haben** where there is a goal expressed: durch welhe schulde die helde her gevarn han (*Nibelungenlied*, Aventiure VII) *for what purpose the heroes have come here*. Here **haben** is used as the idea of action in *gevarn* is more prominent than that of goal. The mention of the goal here gradually brought these words into relations with pure mutative perfectives, as **kommen,** &c., which are used with a goal and are conjugated with **sein.** Hence **sein** is used here to-day. Compare **175.** *Note*, last par.

2. As the resultant condition and the attained goal are not only the outcome of an activity but also often the commencement of something new, **sein** often has ingressive force and points to the beginning of a state or activity:

Sein Herz ist zu ihr in Liebe entbrannt His heart has become inflamed with love for her. **Er ist abgereist** He has started on a journey. Other examples are given in I. 4 (2nd par.) above and in A, B, and C below. In the category explained in A and *Note* thereunder South Germans prefer **sein** to **haben** in order that they may give expression to the ingressive idea.

3. **Sein** is often used with certain verbs of motion pure and simple without mention of a goal or destination, for the reason that, being so often used with these words when a destination *is* expressed, it has become associated with them and remains even when there is no reference to a goal. Examples are given in C. 2. *a* and D.

These are the general principles which may serve as a general guide. The detailed treatment follows:

Sein is used as an auxiliary of tense:

A. With two verbs of rest, **sein** *to be* and **bleiben** *to remain*: **Er ist lange im Gefängnisse gewesen. Er ist den ganzen Abend zu Hause geblieben.** This little list only represents the literary usage of the North. In the literary language of the South the list is larger. See *Note* below.

Note. In M.H.G. a number of intransitives were used both as mutative perfectives and as duratives. Thus M.H.G. **sitzen** in the meaning *to sit down* was a mutative ingressive and was conjugated with **sein,** while in the meaning *to sit, remain sitting* it was a durative and was conjugated with **haben.** Gradually the durative idea overshadowed the perfective meaning, so that these verbs are now felt as duratives. In the South, however, **sein,** which was once so often used with these intransitives when they had perfective force, has become so thoroly associated with them that it is now regularly employed even tho these verbs are now usually felt as duratives. This development began in M.H.G. and became established in the South by the end of the thirteenth century. In the North, on the other hand, the strong durative force which these intransitives now usually have has gradually fixed the use of **haben** here except in case of **bleiben.** The following words belong to this group: **beharren** to insist upon, **beruhen** to rest upon, **bestehen** to insist upon, pass (a test, examination), **bleiben** to remain, **hangen** or **hängen** (intrans.) to hang, **hocken** to crouch, pore over, **kauern** to crouch, **kleben** to stick, **knien** to kneel, **liegen** to lie, **schweben** to hover, **sitzen** to sit, **stecken** to stick (intrans.), remain, **stehen** to stand, **verharren** to remain, continue. The following examples illustrate literary S.G. usage, where, however, the North usually employs **haben: Der junge Priester war auf der Entfernung der Bilder beharrt** (Marriot's *Der geistliche Tod*, chap. IV). **Du weißt, daß ich von jeher einem idealen Zuge nachgehangen bin** (G. Keller). **Neben dem Kutscher ist er gehockt, wie ein Häufele Elend** (Karl Schönherr's *Sonnwendtag*, p. 15). **Viele Monate war er im Spital gelegen** (Rosegger). **Ich finde dich anders, als du mir in der Erinnerung vorgeschwebt bist** (Marriot's *Seine Gottheit*, chap. XXVIII). **Er war halbe Tage lang an seinem Fensterchen gesessen** (Hermann Hesse's *Unterm Rad*, p. 216). **Ich bin nicht immer im Loden gesteckt, wie der Bär in seinem Fell** (Ebner-Eschenbach). **Nie ist das Deutsche Reich vor einer ernsteren Entscheidung gestanden als in dieser Stunde** (König Ludwig von Bayern, Aug. 1, 1914). In S.G. dialect there is a tendency to go beyond the boundaries mentioned above, as for instance in Basel, where **sein** is used in general with verbs denoting rest in a particular place: **I bi im Heu gschlofe = Ich habe im Heu geschlafen.** Earlier in the period **sein** is often found in the North where it is still used in literary S.G.: **Aus meinen eigenen Lippen hätt' ich den Verband gemacht, wenn ihr Vater nicht dabei gestanden wäre** (Hebbel's *Agnes Bernauer*, 1, 2). Occasionally in our own time: **Diese steinerne Bank war hier vorhin nicht gestanden** (Thomas Mann's *Königliche Hoheit*, p. 84). As the old mutative perfective force, i.e. the idea of a change of place or condition, is still occasionally felt **sein** of course sometimes appears with these verbs in the North: **Das Ding ist drin im Hahn gesessen** (Storm's *Im Brauer-Hause*, p. 103) The thing got fastened in the faucet. **Als er auf den Flur zurückgekehrt war, ist er vor der Treppe still gestanden** (stopped), **als müsse er auch hier die Stiegen noch hinauf** (id., *Eekenhof*, p. 72). **Dann sind zu den Enten die Gänse gestanden** (= **Dann haben sich — begeben**) **und alle haben die Hälse nach mir gereckt** (Raabe's *Schüdderump*, chap. xiv). **So etwas** (i.e. **das lange Kleid**) **hätte man bei uns im Busch nicht brauchen können, da wäre man bald auf der Nase gelegen** (Jensen's *Heimkunft*, VI). (**Er steht auf, reckt sich.**) **Ich bin wieder ganz steif gesessen** (Fulda's *Die wilde Jagd*, 3, 2) I have again become quite stiff from sitting. The one verb **bleiben** always takes **sein**, not only in its ingressive meaning, as in **Die Uhr ist stehen geblieben** *The watch has stopped* but also in its durative meanings, as in **Er ist stehen geblieben** *He remained standing.* The mutative perfective idea becomes most prominent in compounds, where **sein** is quite common even in the North: **Ihr ein Stützer zu sein in dem Schicksal, dem sie unterlegen war** (F. Lewald). Here, however, as often elsewhere, as for instance in C. 1. *a* below, the force of the simple verb asserts itself and conjugation with **haben** follows: **Die Republikanische Partei hatte im Vorparlament unterlegen** (Karl Biedermann's *Dreißig Jahre deutscher Geschichte*, I. p. 270). Of course **haben** should be used if the durative idea is prominent: **Bei den rein preußischen Zivildiplomaten, welche der Wirkung militärischer Disziplin gar nicht oder unzureichend unterlegen hatten, habe ich in der Regel eine zu starke Neigung zur Kritik gefunden** (Bismarck). In S.G. we often find **sein** in compounds even where we should naturally expect **haben**, as the force of the simple verb asserts itself: **Die Buchen waren doch dem Zerbrechen widerstanden** (Stifter's *Studien*, 2, 92).

Earlier in the period **sein** was also conjugated with **haben** in N.G. and M.G.: **Darumb hatt nie kein heylge ßo küne gewest** (Luther, Weim. Ausg., I, 220). Originally it did not belong here at all as it was from the start a durative. Hence in the North it was at first conjugated with **haben.** Since its meaning closely resembles that of the verbs in this group, such as **bleiben, stecken,** &c., it was in the South early after the rise of the present perfect tense attracted into this group, which in M.H.G. had already begun to take **sein** as auxiliary even when they were used with durative force. North German usage has at this point been gradually conformed to that of the South, likewise in case of **bleiben,** which tho now usually a durative is in the North conjugated with **sein** as in the South.

In a few cases **sein** is not the sign of the present perfect and past perfect tenses but an old present and past tense: **Das Dorf ist** (old present tense) **am Walde gelegen** (pred. adjective). **Jetzt ist er in Marburg angesessen** He is now a resident of M.

B. With verbs which represent the subject as resting in a new state or condition as the result of a change brought about by the action of the verb. The idea of rest is contained in the auxiliary, that of action is contained in the verb, and that of change *from* or *into* may lie:

a. In some prefix of the verb such as **ent** *away, from,* transition into, **er** *out of,* into a state of, **ver** to the end of, change into, **zer** dissolution, violent separation, a breaking to pieces, a scattering, **auf** *up,* **ein** *into,* &c.: **Das Mädchen ist errötet** The girl has blushed (literally, *has reddened out*). **Die Rose ist erblüht** The rose has come out into blossom. **Die Rose ist verblüht** The blooming of the rose has come to an end. **Er ist gestern abend entschlummert** He passed away in death quietly last evening. **Dadurch ist viel Streit entstanden** Thru that much strife has arisen. **Er ist verarmt** He has become poor. **Das Seil ist zerrissen** The rope has broken. **Hans ist aufgewacht. Hans ist eingeschlafen. Gestern abend ist einer im Fluß ertrunken.**

b. In some prepositional phrase or in a predicate adjective: **Der Wein ist** (to denote resultant state) **zu Essig gegoren,** but **Der Wein hat** (to denote an act) **gegoren. Der Wein ist klar gegoren. Er ist ganz blau gefroren.** The meaning has such a power over the form of conjugation that some verbs which usually take **haben** are conjugated with **sein** when they indicate a change of condition: **Eh, da müßte der Junge doch ganz aus der Art geschlagen sein!** (Raabe's *Finkenrode*, chap. xvi).

c. In the meaning of the verb itself in the following verbs when used intransitively: **altern** (also with **haben**) to grow old; **arten** (also with **haben**) **nach** to take after, resemble; **bersten** to burst; **bleichen** (also with **haben**) to turn pale, white; **brechen** to break; **frieren** to freeze; **gedeihen** to thrive; **gelingen** *to be successful*, and its opposite **mißlingen**; **genesen** to recover from sickness; **geraten** *to turn out* (to be so-and-so), *stray into*, and **mißraten** *to fail, turn out badly, prove a failure*; **gerinnen** to coagulate, congeal; **geschehen** to come to pass, happen; **glücken** *to prosper, succeed*, and its opposite **mißglücken; heilen** (also with **haben**) to heal; **keimen** to spring up, come up, bud out, germinate (in this meaning usually with **haben**); **krepieren** to burst, explode, die (of animals, and in coarse language also of men); **passieren** to happen, occur; **platzen** to explode; **quellen** to swell (of wood, &c.); **reißen** to break, tear; **rosten** (also with **haben**) to grow rusty; **scheitern** to be shipwrecked; **schleißen** to split (intrans.), wear out by use (intrans.); **schmelzen** to melt; **schwären** (also with **haben**) to fester, suppurate; **schweigen** or **geschweigen** to become silent, still in use in early N.H.G., as in Acts xv. 13, but now replaced by **verstummen; schwellen** to swell up; **spleißen** to split (intrans.); **sprießen** or **sprossen** to sprout up, to put forth buds or sprouts (in this meaning usually with **haben**); **springen** to break or burst (intrans.), spring (a leak); **sterben** to die; **wachsen** *to grow*; **welken** to wither, fade away; **werden** to become; **wurzeln** (sometimes w. **haben**) to take root: **Der Topf ist geborsten** The pot has burst. **Die Nadel ist gebrochen** The needle broke. **Getreide, welches angekeimt ist, kann den Nahrungswert nicht mehr haben, als wenn es noch nicht gekeimt hätte** (Bismarck's *Reden*, 10, 147). **Das Holz ist gequollen. Die Milch ist geronnen. Die Backen sind über Nacht geschwollen. Die Feder ist gesprungen** The spring broke. **Das Schiff war leck gesprungen und drohte zu sinken** (*Hamburger Nachrichten*, March 10, 1906).

Earlier in the period **haben** was used with a number of these verbs and is still found occasionally: **Die arabische Religion und Nationalkultur haßte diese Blumen (der Dichtung), vielleicht hätten sie in Europa der Zeiten auch noch nicht gedeihet** (now **gediehen**) (Herder). **Es hätt' ihm auch geglückt, wenn nicht,** &c. (Wieland). **Wie weit ihr's gelungen hat** (Schiller). **Die verborgenen Klippen, an denen die stolze Vernunft schon gescheitert hat** (id.). **Daß diese Pflanze des nationalen Russentums nur auf Moskauer Boden zu gedeihen vermag und auch nur gediehen hat** (*Gegenwart*, 1887, No. 34).

Altern, arten, bleichen, frieren, heilen, and **trocknen,** are still conjugated with **haben** when it is desired to emphasize the idea of an act rather than that of a resultant state: **Onkel Harre nämlich hatte in der letzten Zeit so merklich gealtert, daß es selbst für uns, die wir ihn fast täglich sahen, auffällig war** (R. Huch's *Ludolf Ursleu*, chap. xxi). But to call attention to a result: **Obgleich sie furchtbar gealtert war** (Gutzkow's *R.*, 9, 452). **Es hat** (act) **gefroren,** but **Das Wasser ist** (resultant state) **gefroren. Die Wunde hat** (act) **gut geheilt,** but **Die Wunde ist** (resultant state) **geheilt. Die Wäsche hat gut getrocknet,** but **Die Wäsche ist getrocknet.**

Note 1. In using the above words, care must be taken to distinguish between the idea of ***transitive*** and ***intransitive***, as only the latter use requires **sein** in the compound tenses. See **257. 1.** *b*.

Note 2. The meaning has such power over the form of conjugation that some verbs which usually take **haben** are often conjugated with **sein** in those meanings which are similar to those of the verbs in the above list. This is especially true of **einschlagen** (after the analogy of **geraten**) *to turn out* (to be so-and-so), succeed, and **fehlschlagen** (after the analogy of **mißlingen**) *to turn out unsuccessful*: **Eine politische Spekulation dem alten preußischen Fritz gegenüber ist auch nicht so eingeschlagen, wie man's wünschte und verhoffte** (Raabe's *A. T.*, chap. xiii). **Auch die Versuche, selbst die lateinischen Termini** (terms) **zu verdeutschen, sind immer wieder fehlgeschlagen** (H. Wunderlich). **Das Wagnis ist fehlgeschlagen** (*Frankfurter Zeit.*, Aug. 8, 1914). Here as elsewhere, however, the force of the simple verb or the idea of an act asserts itself, and hence we sometimes also find **haben: Alle seine Hoffnungen sind oder auch haben ihm fehlgeschlagen** (J. Grimm). **Alle ihre derartigen Versuche haben aber bis jetzt fehlgeschlagen** (*Neue Zürcher Zeit.*, Feb. 16, 1904).

C. With all intransitive verbs of motion from place to place, when the subject is thought of as resting at some goal, or as starting from some point of departure or towards some end or destination.

1. The idea of rest or the beginning of the activity is in **sein**, that of action is contained in the verb, and that of a destination, arrival, departure may lie:

a. In some prefix such as **er** *out of*, **ent** *away from*, or in those denoting away, arrival, up, out of, thither, hither, into, upward, forth, towards, down, &c. (**ab, an, auf, aus, hin** or **da'hin, her** or **da'her, ein, em'por, fort, zu, wieder,** &c.): **Auf meine Frage ist keine Antwort erfolgt** No answer has come to my question (lit. *has followed out of it*, i.e. the question). **Er ist dem Gefängnis entsprungen** He has escaped from prison. **Bei Schmidts ist ein Töchterchen angekommen** A wee daughter has arrived at Schmidt's. **Er ist die Treppe hinuntergegangen. Der Blitz ist herabgeflammt. Der Tag ist angebrochen. Dunkelheit ist eingebrochen,** but **Der Dieb hat** (act) **eingebrochen. Er ist durch Unglücksfälle ganz heruntergekommen** Misfortunes have ruined him (lit. He has come down on account of misfortunes). **Er ist abgefahren, abgedampft, ausgekniffen.**

Earlier in the period **haben** could also be used here: **Er hat nider gekniet | vnd sich gelagert wie ein Leve** (Gen. xlix. 9). Thus earlier in the period the idea of the act as a whole was felt more vividly than the local force of the prefix, while to-day attention is uniformly directed to the point of arrival or departure.

The intrans. **umschlagen** *to upset* (intrans.), *capsize, change suddenly* is usually conjugated **with sein** on account of the idea of change of location or state contained in the prefix, altho the simple verb is a trans. conjugated with **haben: Plötzlich tat nur ein lauter, naher Aufschrei kund, daß vermutlich das gefährdete Boot umgeschlagen sei** (Jensen's *Heimkunft*, II. 6). **Die wundervollen Illusionen waren schnell in ihr Gegenteil umgeschlagen** (Raabe's *A. T.*, chap. v). We often, however, find **haben** here, as the idea of an act as a whole is felt more vividly than the idea of change of place or state, or the force of the simple verb asserts itself: **Der Wagen hatte umgeschlagen** (Schiller). **In den Volksschichten hatte die Stimmung gründlich umgeschlagen** (Rosegger's *Martin der Mann*, p. 43). In the same manner other verbs fluctuate between haben and sein: **Auf dem Rückwege . . . bin ich bei meinem Bruder eingesprochen** (Lessing's *Gefang.*, 3, 2). **Ich habe bei ihm eingesprochen** (M. Heyne's *Wörterbuch*).

b. In a prepositional phrase or in an adverb: **Das leichte Gefährt war mit Vater und Tochter von dannen gerollt. Er ist über den Fluß geschwommen. Der Rasen war wild in die Höhe geschossen. Wir sind an den Rand des Waldes gelangt. Die polnischen Aspirationen wachsen ins Uferlose, sobald nur die Möglichkeit nahe gerückt ist, daß die Regierung sie erfüllen will. In Hessen ist besonders der Notstand zu Tage getreten. Es ist das erste Mal, daß ich auf ein derartiges Mißverstehen gestoßen bin. Er ist in's Zimmer geschlagen** *he fell head-foremost into the room* and **Es war mir ordentlich wie ein Schrecken in die Glieder geschlagen,** but to denote an act: **Der Blitz hat in die Eiche geschlagen.**

2. These same intransitive verbs of motion are conjugated with **haben,** and not **sein:**

a. When the idea of duration is prominent and no goal is designated by prefix, prepositional phrase, or otherwise, especially in the North: **Wir haben den ganzen Abend getanzt,** but **Wir sind aus einer Stube in die andere getanzt. So habe ich nie geritten, nie so toll gejagt** (Goethe). **In seiner Jugend hat er gut geritten,** but **Er ist fortgeritten. Die Fahnen, die auf dem Hinzuge so lustig im Winde geflogen hatten,** but **Der Vogel ist ins Nest geflogen. Der Wald hat gerauscht** *The forest has murmured,* but **Der Strom ist dahin gerauscht** *The river flowed on murmuring.* **Als wir drei Wochen marschiert hatten** (Frenssen's *Peter Moors Fahrt nach Südwest*, 172), but **Wir sind in drei Tagen hierher marschiert. Ihr Mann hatte als Kapitän gefahren** (Enking's *Wie Truges seine Mutter suchte*, III). Even if the goal is mentioned, **haben** is often in the North used, as the idea of duration or the idea of an act as a whole is felt more vividly than the idea of the goal: **So hat er lange Jahre neben seinem Hundefuhrwerk durch die Dörfer getrabt** (Frenssen's *Jörn Uhl*, chap. xi). **Er hatte nur einmal um den Brunnen getreten** (Ponten's *Jungfräulichkeit*, p. 463).

Usage has in part become unsettled here. Such verbs as **reiten, fahren, rasen** *to rush along,* **schwimmen,** &c., which are usually used in connection with a goal, and hence are often conjugated with **sein,** have become so thoroly associated with this auxiliary that they are often conjugated with it when no goal is mentioned, and even where the idea of duration is present: **Wir sind geritten ohne Unterlaß — denn die Verfolger waren schnell** (Wildenbruch's *Kaiser Heinrich*, 3, 9). **Seine überraschende Kenntnis seltener und kostspieliger Speisen erklärte sich daraus, daß er eine Zeit lang als Schiffsküchenjunge gefahren war** (Hoffmann's *Rohleders hohe Minne*). **Der ist gerast wie doll** (N.G. = toll) (Halbe's *Haus Rosenhagen*, 2, p. 94). **Heute sind wir tüchtig marschiert,** but also with **haben** as the idea of an act is still at times vividly felt: **Diese Truppe hat ununterbrochen marschiert und gekämpft** (*Frankfurter Zeit.*, Feb. 19, 1915). Perhaps the use of **marschieren** here with **kämpfen** helped suggest the employment of **haben. Sein** is also used even in figurative use: **Ich habe mich nie um den Morgen gekümmert und bin stets gut dabei gefahren** (Raabe's *Pechlin*, chap. x). Hence these words are gravitating towards the group D below. **Fahren** is often used with **haben,** not, however, as a verb denoting motion, but in the sense *to perform the duties of a coachman, be a coachman, have charge of the driving,* or with reference to the comfortableness of the vehicle: **Er hatte in Wien zehn Jahre gefahren** (Lessing's *Minna*, 3, 2). **Wir sind nach der Stadt gefahren. Wer hat gefahren?** *We rode to town. Who drove?* **Der Zug hat heute schlecht gefahren.**

Earlier in the period **haben** was common with pure verbs of motion: **Bin ich nicht dein Eselin | darauff du geritten hast zu deiner Zeit** (Num. xxii. 30).

b. In a few cases when the verbs are used figuratively, as the idea of an act is prominent: **Er hat fortgefahren zu lesen** *He continued to read,* but **Er ist fortgefahren** *He has driven away.* **Sein** is also used in figurative use, as the force of the simple verb asserts itself: **Er ist in der Erzählung fortgefahren** (M. Heyne). **Ich habe in ihn gedrungen** *I have urged him,* but with **sein** where the local idea is more distinct, as in **Er ist noch nicht in das Geheimnis gedrungen** He has not yet penetrated into the secret. We occasionally find **sein** in the former case, as the literal force of the verb asserts itself: [**Sie sagte,**] **Das seien nutzlose Beunruhigungen, weshalb sie denn auch in ihn gedrungen sei, von solchen Berechnungen Abstand zu nehmen** (Fontane's *Stechlin* VII. p. 107). **Er hat sich, ohne daß ich eigentlich in ihn gedrungen wäre, mit großer Offenheit über seine ökonomische Situation ausgesprochen** (Spielhagen's *Selbstgerecht* p. 75). We say **Der Kutscher ist** (change of place) or **hat** (act) **soeben in den Hof eingelenkt,** but in figurative use: **Er hat eingelenkt** (= **nachgegeben**). In **verfahren** *to proceed, deal with, treat, act,* the original idea of *going* is so little felt that the auxiliary **haben** is often used: **Man hat mit unerhörten Exekutionen verfahren** (Goethe's *Götz*, 5, 9). **Sie haben gegen mich wie gegen einen Spitzbuben verfahren** (Gutzkow). **Dora wußte dies, sonst würde sie eben anders verfahren haben** (Junghans). On the other hand, **sein** is also used here, and is now more frequent, as the force of the very common simple verb asserts itself: **Das Geschick ist nicht sanft mit mir verfahren** (Goethe). **Wir sind wohl alle nicht so ganz vollkommen ehrlich und aufrichtig gegen Sie verfahren, wie wir nach strengen Sittenlehren eigentlich sollten** (H. Hoffmann).

c. **Treten** is conjugated with **sein** to denote a change of position, but takes **haben** to denote an act: **Er ist auf den Hof getreten,** but **Er hat ihm auf die Hühneraugen getreten** (H. Paul) and **Er hat auf eine Raupe getreten** (id.). Instead of **haben,** however, we often find **sein** here: **Du bist mir auf mein Kleid getreten** (Fulda's *Jugendfreunde*, 2, 4).

D. With the following growing list of intransitives, in most part simple verbs of motion, **sein** is used even where the destination is not expressed, also where the idea of duration is present, **begegnen** (see a below) to meet, **bekommen** (sometimes with **haben**) to suit, agree with, turn out (well or bad) for one, **desertieren** to desert the army, **fallen** to fall, **fliegen** (except in the one case in C. 2. a) to fly, **fliehen** to flee, **fließen** (see a below) to flow, **folgen** (see a below) to follow, **gehen** to go, **gleiten** to glide, slip, **kentern** to upset (of a boat), **kommen** to come, **kriechen** (see a) to crawl, creep, **laufen** to run, **promenieren** to take a walk, **reisen** to travel, **retirieren** to retreat, **rinnen** to run, flow, **scheiden** to depart, separate, **schleichen** to sneak, **schreiten** to step, stride, **schwinden** to disappear, **segeln** to sail, **sinken** to sink, **sprengen** to ride at full speed, **steigen** to rise, **stranden** to run ashore, **straucheln** (see a) to stumble and fall, **stürzen** to fall, tumble, **wandeln** to walk, **wandern** to travel, journey, **weichen** to yield, **ziehen** to proceed, move (intrans.): **Er ist mir heute begegnet. Wie ist Ihnen das gestrige Fest bekommen** (agreed with)? **Wessen Uhr ist nun richtig gegangen?** (Raabe's *Gutmanns Reisen*, chap. viii). **Sie** (i.e. **die Uhr**) **ist nie ordentlich gegangen** (Heer's *Der König der Bernina*, III). **Ich bin den ganzen Tag gelaufen. Zwei Duelle . . . schienen ein rasches Sichnähern an sein Schneidigkeitsideal zu verbürgen und hätten ebensogut wie Wendelins Talente zu großen Hoffnungen berechtigen dürfen, wenn nicht das Gespenst der Entlassung wegen beständig anwachsender Schulden immer nebenher geschritten wäre** (Fontane's *Poggenpuhls*, chap. i). **Deine treue Liebe ist nicht geschwunden.**

It should be remembered that **haben** was much more common here earlier in the period: **DEnn wir haben nicht den klugen Fabeln gefolget** (2. Peter, I. 16). **Mein fus hat gestrauchelt** (Ps. xciv. 18). **Nur einem Traurigen hab' ich begegnet** (Schiller's *Jungfrau*, 3, 4). Survivals of this former usage can still be found: **Ich habe heute früh Doktor Mettner begegnet** (Schnitzler's *Das Vermächtnis*, p. 112), **haben** being most common with **begegnen,** as in this and the following example, in connection with an accusative object, altho the dative is also sometimes found here and in connection with **sein** is the usual construction. **Auf einem Waldgang nun habe ich den Riedel** (name) **begegnet** (Rosegger's *Sonnenschein*, p. 2). Also in case of other of these verbs do we sometimes find **haben** in accordance with older usage, especially in the North, where there is still a distinct feeling here for the idea of an act or activity: **Zwischen uns hat's schon manchmal auf Hieb und Stich gegangen** (Otto Ernst's *Jugend von heute*, 1, 15) = **Wir haben auf Hieb und Stich gefochten. Das tut sie immer, aus Spaß, wenn ich so toll gelaufen habe** (Frenssen's *Jörn Uhl*, XIV). **So flüsterte der See und die Bäume und der Wind in der Nacht in der Gegend, wo er noch vor vierzehn Tagen gewandelt hatte** (id., *Hilligenlei*, p. 571). **Et hat alles jot jejangen!** (Ponten's *Jungfräulichkeit*, p. 9) = **Alles ist gut gegangen. Uns hat es bisher noch nicht schlecht gegangen** (Feldpostbrief in *Magdeburger Generalanzeiger*, 1914). In colloquial speech also in the South: **Aber erzähl' doch, Fritz! Wie hat es gegangen?** (Ludwig Thoma's *Die Lokalbahn*, p. 25), but the "correct" Beringer on p. 53 of the same work says: **Nun, wie ist es gegangen?**

a. A few of the above list *may* take **haben** when the local idea disappears, and they become figurative, especially **begegnen,** in the sense *to meet with* (a difficulty), meet (an emergency), confront, coincide with, and often in the meaning *to treat* (friendly, &c.); **fließen, laufen, lecken,** and **triefen** in case of a metonymic subject; **folgen** in the sense *to obey, follow*; **kriechen** to crawl, cringe; **straucheln** to stumble (in a moral sense): **Gestern bin ich einem Bekannten begegnet,** but **Der Lehrer hat den Unarten der Schüler nachdrücklich begegnet** and **Und in einem andern Punkte hatten Hohenlohes und Bismarcks politische Gedanken sich schon früher harmonisch begegnet** (*Kölnische Zeitung*). **Er ist** or (laying the emphasis upon the idea of a conscious agent acting with intention) **hat mir hart begegnet** (met or treated). **Der Eiter ist aus der Wunde geflossen,** but **Die Augen haben geflossen. Der Wein ist aus dem Faß gelaufen,** but **Das Faß hatte schon einige Zeit gelaufen** (= **geleckt**), **ehe ich es bemerkte. Das Wasser ist aus dem Kessel geleckt,** but **Der Kessel hat geleckt. Der Schweiß ist von der Stirne getrieft,** but **Die Stirne hat von Schweiß getrieft. Der Sohn hat dem Vater** or **dem Rat des Vaters gefolgt. Hätt' ich nur gleich meinem Instinkt gefolgt! Er hat vor ihm gekrochen. Er ist gestrauchelt,** but **Er hat gestrauchelt** (morally). On the other hand, except in the case of a metonymic subject, we perhaps more frequently find **sein** with the above verbs also in figurative use, as the force of the verb in its literal meaning asserts itself: **Ferdinand VII. war vor der rauhen Macht Napoleons gekrochen** (v. Sybel). **Unter diesen Angehörigen war auch ein älterer Bruder von ihm, der ihm bis dahin ganz besonders unliebsam begegnet war** (Fontane's *Der Tunnel über der Spree*, V). **Ich bin seinem Rate gefolgt** (Vogel's *Deutsches Nachschlagebuch*), but Paul in his Wörterbuch says we *must* use **haben** when there is no object at all: **Warum hast du nicht gefolgt?**

General Note. Of course verbs that are usually intrans. and take **sein** are conjugated with **haben** when they become trans.: **Ich bin nach Hause gelaufen** *I have run home*, but **Ich habe mich außer Atem gelaufen** *I have run until I am out of breath*. **Er ist vom Dach gestürzt und hat dabei ein Kind tot gefallen.**

E. Intransitives that denote a beginning or cessation of activity pure and simple without reference to a change of place or condition are usually conjugated with **haben**: **Das Spiel hat eben angefangen. Der Regen hat aufgehört. Der Sturm hat ausgetobt.** The storm has spent its fury. **Drei Tage darauf hatte die alte Lisbeth ausgerungen** (Marriot's *Menschlichkeit*). **Meine Geschichte hat ausgeklungen** (Lauff's *Kärrekiek*, p. 392).

On account of the pronounced ingressive force or the idea of an end or result contained in some of these verbs there is a tendency to employ **sein** instead of **haben**: **Das Tier hat** (act) or **ist** (result) **verendet. Aber das Wort „Californien" klang doch wie Gold und Abenteuer, und**

es war zuerst vor seinem Ohr geklungen, da er aus jenem Briefe seines Vaters dessen drohende Verarmung herauszulesen meinte (Storm's *Bötjer Basch*, p. 30). **Ihm war es geklungen** (*had sounded*, i.e. *the impression had resulted*), **daß sie meine, seine Heiterkeit stamme von ihrem für ein Mädchen sonderbaren Anzug** (Jensen's *Heimkunft*, II, 4). **Der letzte Schlag war schon fünf Minuten ausgeklungen** (*Börne*). **Sein aschenfarbenes Gesicht — ein Granatstück hat die Brust zerrissen — ist, soll ich so sagen, ruhig ausgeklungen. Er hat keine Schmerzen gefühlt** (Liliencron's *Kriegsnovellen*, Anno 1870, Umzingelt). **Die Glocken aber waren verklungen** (Lauff's *Kärrekiek*, p. 374).

With such compounds as have a verb in D as a basal component **sein** must be used: **Die Maschine ist unter starker Belastung angelaufen** The machine started, &c.

a. In North German **anfangen** is not infrequently found with **sein: Bist du nicht angefangen?** (Gustav Falke's *Die Stadt mit den goldenen Türmen*, p. 81). **Du hast natürlich nicht daran gedacht, daß gestern die Pfingstferien angefangen sind** (Frenssen's *Die drei Getreuen*, II). **Ich bin von oben angefangen, von der hohen Uhl her, hoch von oben, und bin gesunken . . . gesunken. Von unten anfangen, das ist alles** (id., *Jörn Uhl*, XXVI). **Wie ich schon sagte, ist man erst in den letzten Jahren angefangen, von dem Kloster das zu erretten und zu erhalten, was noch zu erretten und zu erhalten ist** (O. E. Kiesel in *Hamburger Nachrichten*, Feb. 13, 1905). This is a common construction in Low German and literary Dutch. It was probably originally the common N.G. present perfect passive (see **194.** 1. B. *a*) and may possibly still perform this function in the first sentence from Frenssen, as the subject of the sentence is a thing, but in the other sentences it is now felt as an intransitive conjugated with **sein.**

192. Paradigm of the Compound Tenses of loben and fallen.

Present Perfect Tense.

I have praised, &c. — I have fallen (see **191.** II. D).

Indic.		Subj.		Indic.		Subj.	
ich habe	**gelobt**	**ich habe**	**gelobt**	**ich bin**	**gefallen**	**ich sei**	**gefallen**
du hast		**du habest**		**du bist**		**du sei(e)st**	
er hat		**er habe**		**er ist**		**er sei**	
wir haben		**wir haben**		**wir sind**		**wir seien**	
ihr habt		**ihr habet**		**ihr seid**		**ihr seiet**	
sie haben		**sie haben**		**sie sind**		**sie seien**	

Perfect Infinitive.

gelobt (zu) haben — **gefallen (zu) sein**

Perfect Imperative.

2nd per.	**habe gelobt, hab(e)t gelobt**	**sei gefallen, seid gefallen**
3rd per.	**er habe gelobt**	**er sei gefallen, sie seien gefallen**

Past Perfect Tense.

I had praised, &c. — I had fallen, &c.

Indic.		Subj.		Indic.		Subj.	
ich hatte	**gelobt**	**ich hätte**	**gelobt**	**ich war**	**gefallen**	**ich wäre**	**gefallen**
du hattest		**du hätt(e)st**		**du warst**		**du wär(e)st**	
er hatte		**er hätte**		**er war**		**er wäre**	
wir hatten		**wir hätten**		**wir waren**		**wir wären**	
ihr hattet		**ihr hättet**		**ihr wart**		**ihr wär(e)t**	
sie hatten		**sie hätten**		**sie waren**		**sie wären**	

Future Tense.

I shall praise, &c. — I shall fall, &c.

Indic.		Subj.		Indic.		Subj.	
ich werde	**loben**	**ich werde**	**loben**	**ich werde**	**fallen**	**ich werde**	**fallen**
du wirst		**du werdest**		**du wirst**		**du werdest**	
er wird		**er werde**		**er wird**		**er werde**	
wir werden		**wir werden**		**wir werden**		**wir werden**	
ihr werdet		**ihr werdet**		**ihr werdet**		**ihr werdet**	
sie werden		**sie werden**		**sie werden**		**sie werden**	

Future Infinitive.

loben zu wollen	fallen zu wollen

Future Perfect Tense.

I shall have praised, &c. — I shall have fallen, &c.

Indic.		Subj.		Indic.		Subj.	
ich werde	gelobt haben	ich werde	gelobt haben	ich werde	gefallen sein	ich werde	gefallen sein
du wirst		du werdest		du wirst		du werdest	
er wird		er werde		er wird		er werde	
wir werden		wir werden		wir werden		wir werden	
ihr werdet		ihr werdet		ihr werdet		ihr werdet	
sie werden		sie werden		sie werden		sie werden	

Periphrastic Subjunctive.

Past. I should (would) praise, fall, &c. — Past Perfect. I should (would) have praised, fallen, &c.

Past.		Past Perfect.		Past.		Past Perfect.	
ich würde	loben	ich würde	gelobt haben	ich würde	fallen	ich würde	gefallen sein
du würdest		du würdest		du würdest		du würdest	
er würde		er würde		er würde		er würde	
wir würden		wir würden		wir würden		wir würden	
ihr würdet		ihr würdet		ihr würdet		ihr würdet	
sie würden		sie würden		sie würden		sie würden	

193. Paradigm of the Compound Tenses of sein and werden.

Present Perfect Tense.

I have been, &c. — I have become, &c.

Indic.		Subj.		Indic.		Subj.	
ich bin	gewesen	ich sei	gewesen	ich bin	(ge)worden (178. 2. C)	ich sei	(ge)worden (178. 2. C)
du bist		du sei(e)st		du bist		du sei(e)st	
er ist		er sei		er ist		er sei	
wir sind		wir seien		wir sind		wir seien	
ihr seid		ihr seiet		ihr seid		ihr seiet	
sie sind		sie seien		sie sind		sie seien	

Perfect Infinitive.

gewesen (zu) sein	(ge)worden (zu) sein (178. 2. C)

Perfect Imperative.

2nd per.	sei gewesen, seid gewesen	sei (ge)worden, seid (ge)worden.
3rd per.	er sei gewesen, sie seien gewesen	er sei (ge)worden, sie seien (ge)worden (178. 2. C).

Past Perfect Tense.

I had been, &c. — I had become, &c.

Indic.		Subj.		Indic.		Subj.	
ich war	gewesen	ich wäre	gewesen	ich war	(ge)worden (178. 2. C)	ich wäre	(ge)worden (178. 2. C)
du warst		du wär(e)st		du warst		du wär(e)st	
er war		er wäre		er war		er wäre	
wir waren		wir wären		wir waren		wir wären	
ihr wart		ihr wär(e)t		ihr wart		ihr wär(e)t	
sie waren		sie wären		sie waren		sie wären	

Future Tense.

I shall be, &c. — I shall become, &c.

Indic.		Subj.		Indic.		Subj.	
ich werde	**sein**	**ich werde**	**sein**	**ich werde**	**werden**	**ich werde**	**werden**
du wirst		**du werdest**		**du wirst**		**du werdest**	
er wird		**er werde**		**er wird**		**er werde**	
wir werden		**wir werden**		**wir werden**		**wir werden**	
ihr werdet		**ihr werdet**		**ihr werdet**		**ihr werdet**	
sie werden		**sie werden**		**sie werden**		**sie werden**	

Future Infinitive.

werden zu wollen.

Future Perfect Tense.

I shall have been, &c. — I shall have become, &c.

Indic.		Subj.		Indic.		Subj.	
ich werde	**gewesen sein**	**ich werde**	**gewesen sein**	**ich werde**	**(ge)worden sein (178. 2. C)**	**ich werde**	**(ge)worden sein (178. 2. C)**
du wirst		**du werdest**		**du wirst**		**du werdest**	
er wird		**er werde**		**er wird**		**er werde**	
wir werden		**wir werden**		**wir werden**		**wir werden**	
ihr werdet		**ihr werdet**		**ihr werdet**		**ihr werdet**	
sie werden		**sie werden**		**sie werden**		**sie werden**	

Periphrastic Subjunctive.

Past. I should (would) be, become, &c. — Past Perfect. I should (would) have been, become, &c.

Past.		Past Perfect.		Past.		Past Perfect.	
ich würde	**sein**	**ich würde**	**gewesen sein**	**ich würde**	**werden**	**ich würde**	**(ge)worden sein (178. 2. C)**
du würdest		**du würdest**		**du würdest**		**du würdest**	
er würde		**er würde**		**er würde**		**er würde**	
wir würden		**wir würden**		**wir würden**		**wir würden**	
ihr würdet		**ihr würdet**		**ihr würdet**		**ihr würdet**	
sie würden		**sie würden**		**sie würden**		**sie würden**	

The Passive Voice.

194. The passive voice denotes that the subject receives the action. The passive in German has, as in English, no special tense or mood forms of its own, but is made up by combining the perfect participle with different auxiliary verbs. The following forms are used in German:

1. A. *Actional Passive Forms.* The usual passive form to express action, i.e. the actional (see 4 below) passive, is formed by combining the various moods and tenses of **werden** *to become* with the perfect participle of the verb to be conjugated, which remains uninflected thruout: (pres. indic.) **ich werde gelobt** *I am being praised*, **du wirst gelobt,** &c.; (past indic.) **ich wurde gelobt;** (pres. perf. indic.) **ich bin gelobt worden;** (past perf. indic.) **ich war gelobt worden;** (future indic.) **ich werde gelobt werden,** &c.; (pres. subjunctive) **ich werde gelobt, du werdest gelobt,** &c. The only irregularity in the conjugation is that the perf. part. of **werden** is here uniformly without the **ge: worden,** not **geworden.** No passive idea lies in **werden,** as it also, when combined with the present infinitive, forms the future active (**ich werde loben**), and the future perfect active when used with the perfect infinitive (**ich werde gelobt haben**). **Werden** retains in the passive its original meaning of *to become*, and thus denotes here a *passing into a state* which is indicated by the perfect participle: **ich werde gerettet** I am being rescued, lit. I am becoming or am going over into the state of being rescued.

B. However, **werden** is not the only auxiliary employed in the actional passive, but **sein** is still, according to a usage prevailing in earlier periods, frequently used, replacing **werden** often in the pres. perfect, past perfect, future perfect, past perfect periphrastic subjunctive, and even regularly replacing it in the imperative, and often in the present infinitive. See *a*, *b*, *c*.

a. In M.H.G. the pres. perfect was formed by combining the pres. of **sein** with the perfect participle of the verb to be conjugated: (indic.) ich bin gelobet. The past perfect was formed by combining the past of **sein** and the participle: ich was gelobet. Thus the present perfect and the past perfect of the old actional passive were formed by the aid of the auxiliary **sein** and were exactly the same in form as the present and the past of the modern statal (see 4 below) passive. This former usage still lingers on, especially in the North, tho no longer recognized by grammarians: **Über den Begriff der Philologie ist viel herumgestritten** (H. Paul, Paul's *Grundriß*, p. 1, 2nd ed.). **Im übrigen gibt der Staatsanwalt selbst zu, daß in der Nähe des Postens zweimal scharf geschossen ist** (*Hamburger Nachrichten*, Jan. 7, 1914). This form often occurs in the official reports of the Great War: **Der Brückenkopf von Friedrichstadt ist gestern erstürmt** (Sept. 4, 1915). This older usage is quite common with **gebären: Ich bin am 23. Mai 1844 geboren** (Wustmann's *Sprachdummheiten*, p. 107, 3rd ed.). The present regular passive forms with the auxiliary **werden** in the present perfect and the past perfect first appear in the thirteenth century, at first, however, very rarely. By the end of the sixteenth century they are fairly well established in the South.

b. The regular future perfect and the past perfect periphrastic subjunctive are still avoided on account of their clumsiness and nonconformity to the usual rules for end-stress (**215.** II. 1. A.), their place being often supplied by combining the future or the past periphrastic subjunctive of **sein** with the perfect part.: **ich werde gelóbt sèin** instead of **ich werde gelőbt wòrden séin; ich würde gelóbt sèin** instead of **ich würde gelőbt wòrden séin.**

c. In an earlier period of the language, **sein** was the more common passive auxiliary in the infinitive and imperative, and it has tenaciously defended these positions against **werden,** as it is still frequently found in the infinitive where we might naturally expect **werden,** and is used as a rule in the imperative, both in the 2nd and 3rd person, altho in the latter also **werden** is found. In the infinitive, **sein** seems to be especially common after the modal auxiliaries, particularly **wollen: Wenn er im Lager einherging, wollte er nicht gegrüßt sein** (Ranke). **Nur von dir möchte ich gut genannt sein, was die Welt von mir spricht, ist mir eins** (Heer's *Der König der Bernina*, XVIII). **Diese [Entschuldigung] beruht auf der Befürchtung, daß ich beleidigt sein müsse, an mein Alter erinnert zu werden** (Suttner's *Im Berghause*, p. 93). **Damit soll nicht gesagt sein, daß man nicht auch andere lieben kann** (Bartel's *Geschichte der deutschen Literatur*, II, p. 424). These examples can easily be multiplied, as the construction is still quite frequent, but the use of **werden** here is perhaps more common: **Es muß ja einmal gesagt werden** (Sudermann's *Die Ehre*, 2, 11). In the perfect infinitive, however, the older construction with **sein** may possibly be the preferred one: **Dann erzählte er, daß der junge Mensch seiner Gesundheit sowie seinem Beutel wohl zu viel zugemutet haben und von den Seinen in die Verbannung geschickt sein mochte** (Schubin's *Refugium peccatorum*, V), instead of the clumsy **geschickt worden sein mochte.**

The grammarians often give **werden** as the auxiliary with the passive imperative; usage, however, seems almost wholly upon the side of **sein** in the 2nd person and usually also in the 3rd person, which, however, is in fact the 3rd person of the pres. subjunctive. Second person: **Küsse Lieschen und die Kinder und sei geküßt von Deinem Theodor** (Fontane an seine Frau, March 10, 1857). **Seien Sie gesegnet für alles** (Sudermann's *Die Ehre*, 4, 12). Only rarely here with **werden:** oder wirt (older form, now **werde**) alhie erslagen (*Parzival*, 267. 20). **Komm — neue Erde will dich umgrünen, | will mit dir sich, der Blume, schmücken, | werde geboren!** (Wildenbruch's *Die Lieder des*

Euripides, p. 67). Third person: **Hier sei es bemerkt** Here may it be permitted me to remark. **Gott sei es gedankt!** Thank God for it! **Gesegnet sei dein Eingang, liebes Kind!** (Raabe's *Die Leute aus dem Walde*, III, chap. xi). **Auf einen wichtigen Punkt sei hier noch die Aufmerksamkeit gelenkt** (Brugmann's *Kurze vergleichende Grammatik*, p. 289). **Sein** is also used in a subordinate clause after a verb expressing *will, command*: **Herrin, ein alter Brauch | will, daß wenn Ostern kam ins Land, | wenn leise grünt der Dornenstrauch | .... daß dann die erste Vollmondnacht | fliegend und wiegend s e i durchwacht** (Sudermann's *Die drei Reiherfedern*, 3, 2.)

In the following rather rare examples **werden** is used as auxiliary in the 3rd person: **Geheiligt werde dein Name** (Luther). **Ihr seid von mir geschieden — werd' auch mir, | von euch zu scheiden, Kraft und Mut verliehen!** (Goethe's *Tasso*, 4, 2). **Ewig werde dein gedacht** (Schiller's *Siegesfest*). **Die Welt will betrogen werden, so werde sie denn betrogen** (*Über Land und Meer*).

The 2nd pers. imperative may be replaced by the imperative of **lassen** and a dependent infinitive: **laß dich überreden** (familiar form) *be persuaded*, or *allow yourself to be persuaded*; **laßt euch überreden** (pl. of familiar form); **lassen Sie Sich überreden** (polite form).

2. *Passive with* **bekommen, kriegen,** *or* **erhalten,** *instead of* **werden.** A peculiar passive construction is often found, which deserves attention. It is formed by placing the noun which denotes the objective point of the activity in the acc. as the object of the verb **bekommen, erhalten,** or **kriegen** (in popular language), and then making the real verb of the sentence an objective predicate in the form of a perfect participle: **Er hat es gesagt bekommen = Es ist ihm gesagt worden. Bekamen Sie das Geld drahtlich angewiesen?** Was the money wired to you? **Jedermann erhielt 15 Patronen zugezählt** Fifteen cartridges were dealt out to each man. **Ich kriege meine Mühe redlich bezahlt** I am well paid for my trouble. The passive idea here lies in the perf. part. The object may be suppressed, and the verb **bekommen** or **erhalten** remains almost with the force of the passive auxiliary **werden: Aber nicht doch — dafür bekomme ich ja von Fräulein Philippi bezahlt** (Wildenbruch's *Die Waidfrau*) Don't pay me—I shall be paid by Miss P.

A similar construction is found after **führen, bringen,** and **nehmen: Man führte ihn an einem Arm gefaßt** He was led along held by one arm. **Mädchen bringen den Hut auf einer Stange getragen** (Schiller's *Tell*, l. 2915). **Die Dienstboten brachten kleine Wälder in die Öfen geschleppt** (Maria Janitscheck's *Einer Mutter Sieg*, IX). **Man nahm ihn gefangen.**

3. *Passive with* **gehören.** Another passive construction is not infrequently found which is worthy of attention by reason of its pithy terseness. Instead of **müssen** *ought* (a necessity which lies in the nature of things) with a dependent passive infinitive a simple tense of **gehören** *to belong, be fit* is used followed by the perfect participle of the verb to be conjugated, which serves as a predicate complement: **Ein entlaufen Schaf gehört in seinen Stall geliefert** (Scheffel's *Ekkehard*, chap. xxi) A runaway sheep ought to be brought back to its fold. **Sauber gehalten gehört ein Kind und wohl verpflegt** (Hermine Villinger's *'s Romans-Hütt'*). **Dem gehört das Handwerk gelegt** (Karrillon's *O Domina Mea*, p. 123).

4. *Actional and Statal Passive.* Different from the above passive forms denoting an *action* is a statal passive which does not denote an *action* at all, but only a *state*. It is formed by combining the perfect participle of the verb to be conjugated with the different moods and tenses of the auxiliary **sein.** The difference between this statal passive and the actional passive is indicated by the difference in the meaning of the two auxiliaries employed. The forms with **werden** denote an *action* going on or an act conceived as a whole, while the forms with **sein** denote a *state* that has resulted from previous action: **Das Haus wird angestrichen** The house is being painted *and* **Das Haus wird oft angestrichen** The house is often painted, *but* **Das Haus ist angestrichen** The house is painted. **Die Tür wird jeden Abend um sechs Uhr geschlossen** *The*

door is shut (i.e. *some one shuts the door*) *every evening at six*, but **Die Tür ist geschlossen** *The door is shut.* **Die Schiffbrüchigen sind mit großer Gefahr der Brandung entrissen worden, jetzt sind sie gerettet.** Where we might upon the first thought expect to find a statal passive form with **sein** we often find an actional form with **werden,** as not the idea of a *physical state* is before the mind but that of a *mental operation* which the mind itself performs over and over again, or performs each time anew when the subject presents itself: **Jeder Kreis wird durch jeden Durchmesser in zwei gleiche Teile geteilt** Every circle is divided by each of its diameters into two equal parts. **Europa wird von Asien durch das Uralgebirge getrennt.** For the origin of the actional passive see **190.** 1. C. *a. Note* 1.

The statal passive forms a complete conjugation in all the moods and tenses: (pres. indic.) **ich bin erschöpft** I am exhausted; (past indic.) **ich war erschöpft** I was exhausted; (pres. perf.) **ich bin erschöpft gewesen** I have been in an exhausted condition; (past. perf.) **ich war erschöpft gewesen** I had been in an exhausted condition (at a time before a certain event in the past); (future) **ich werde erschöpft sein** There will be a time when I shall be exhausted; (pres. subjunctive) **ich sei erschöpft;** (past subj.) **ich wäre erschöpft;** &c.

Note 1. *Characteristic Differences between German and English.* Altho literary English is lacking in accurate passive forms colloquial speech has even fuller forms than German: (actional passive) The house often gets painted; (progressive actional passive) The house is getting painted; (statal passive) The house is painted. In German there is no progressive form, but this idea is sometimes expressed by combining a prepositional phrase with the perfect participle **begriffen: Das Haus ist im Bau begriffen** The house is being built. **Andere Pläne zur Erledigung der Frage sind in der Ausarbeitung begriffen.**

Note 2. *Characteristic Differences between the Actional and the Statal Passive.* The characteristic difference of nature between these two forms often becomes marked in the Present perfect. This tense represents the act as completed and the state as past at the present time, but in case of the actional form the results of the completed activity often remain intact at the present time, while in case of the statal form the state once obtaining is represented as having passed entirely away: **Die Wände sind eben tapeziert worden** The walls have just been papered and are now of course in fine condition, *but* Der Wirt: **Das Zimmer ist doch sonst galant (= elegant) und tapeziert** — Just: **Gewésen!** (Lessing's *Minna von Barnhelm*, 1, 2) Landlord: The room is elegant and papered — Just: It *hás* been. Notice that to *emphasize* the idea that the condition has passed away the perfect participle **gewesen** is strongly accented in German, while in English the personal part of the verb is stressed. In normal German speech, however, the perfect participle of the verb to be conjugated is stressed here as elsewhere, for the mere use of **gewesen** usually indicates that the state has passed away: **Diese Zeitschrift ist sehr verbréitet gewesen** This periodical *hás* heen widely read. In English the personal part of the verb must also in normal speech be accented as otherwise the statal form could not be distinguished from the actional. On the other hand, the present perfect of the actional passive often points to a past activity that has left behind no results which remain intact at the present time, but also here the actional form differs distinctly from the statal. The former merely points to a past act or activity, while the latter indicates that the past state continued for a while before it passed away: **Er ist viel geliebt und viel gehaßt, hoch bewundert und tief verachtet worden** (Kippenberg's *Handbuch der deutschen Literatur*, p. 385), but **Gottfried ist nicht nur von den Vertretern der Literatur auf lange Zeit gekannt und geschätzt gewesen, sondern er wirkte auch lebendig ein auf die Dichterwelt** (Bechstein's *Einleitung zu Tristan*, p. xxv).

What has just been said of the force of the present perfect tense in the passive does not apply at all to indirect discourse, for here the present perfect represents often the past tense of the direct, so that the present perfect of the statal passive merely points in indirect discourse to a state of things in the past without reference to the present: **Es ist die herrschende Ansicht, daß während der Blütezeit der mittelhochdeutschen Literatur eine von den Mundarten verschiedene Gemeinsprache bestanden habe, die allerdings nicht so fest geregelt gewesen sei wie die neuhochdeutsche Schriftsprache** (Paul's *Mittelhochdeutsche Grammatik*, p. 4). As a state of things in the past implies that the action which has produced the state has already taken place, the present perfect of the statal passive is in indirect discourse in the new sequence (**171.** 2. B), which avoids past tense forms, much used to represent an actional past perfect of the direct. Examples are given in **171.** 2. B. *e.* This same present perfect of the statal passive is of course regularly used as an actional past perfect tense also in direct discourse in dialects which use the present perfect for the past in narrative, for their present perfect statal passive always points to a past state and hence often indicates that the action which has produced the state has already taken place: **Die ist aber nicht ausgestiegen, sondern hat immerzu nach den Fenstern von unsere Wohnung raufgesehen, wo eben Licht angesteckt gewesen ist** (Therese in Sudermann's *Heimat*, 1, 10).

5. *Passive with Verbs governing the Genitive or Dative.* In case of verbs which govern a case other than the acc. the construction must be impersonal, the gen. or dat. being retained in the passive: **Meine Mutter hat oft gesagt, sie wolle in das Wasser gehen, da sei ihr allein geholfen. Weshalb habt ihr sie denn in die Erde gegraben, wenn ihr im Wasser geholfen war?** (Raabe's *Schüdderump*, chap. xiv). See also **219.** 5. A (last par.).

195. Synopsis of loben in the Actional Passive.

Indicative.	Subjunctive.
Pres. I am praised, am being praised, &c.	
ich werde gelobt	**ich werde gelobt**
Past. I was praised, was being praised, &c.	
ich wurde (or **ward**) **gelobt**	**ich würde gelobt**

Pres. Perfect. I have been praised &c.

ich bin gelobt worden **ich sei gelobt worden**

Past Perfect. I had been praised, &c.

ich war gelobt worden **ich wäre gelobt worden**

Future. I shall be praised, &c.

ich werde gelobt werden **ich werde gelobt werden**

Future Perfect. I shall have been praised, &c.

ich werde gelobt worden sein **ich werde gelobt worden sein**

Past Periphrastic Subjunctive. **ich würde gelobt werden** I should (would) be praised.

Past Perfect Periphrastic Subjunctive. **ich würde gelobt worden sein** I should (would) have been praised.

Imperative.

2nd sg. **sei gelobt** (see **194.** 1. B. *c*) be praised.
3rd sg. **er sei gelobt, or er werde gelobt** let him be praised.
1st pl. **seien wir gelobt** let us be praised.
2nd pl. **seid gelobt, seien Sie gelobt** be praised.
3rd pl. **sie sollen gelobt werden** (or **sein**) they shall be praised.

Infinitive.

Pres. **gelobt** (**zu**) **werden** (or **sein**; see **194.** 1. B. *c*) to be praised.
Perf. **gelobt worden** (**zu**) **sein** to have been praised.

Participles.

Used as a Verb, Adjective, or Substantive.

Pres. wanting, but often supplied by the perfect **gelobt** (see **183.** 3).
Perf. **gelobt,** or more rarely **gelobt worden** (see **184.** *e*).

SUBSTITUTES FOR THE PASSIVE.

196. I. In German more strictly than in English we are confined to the rule that *the passive is only used when it is desired to especially represent the subject as the objective point of an activity.* Often where in English the passive form is common or required, some other construction is used in German. The most common substitutes for the passive are the following:

1. Very frequently **man** with an active verb: **Bei uns schließt man die Türen um 10 Uhr** With us the doors are shut at 10 o'clock.

a. This construction is always used in German where in English an infinitive follows the passive of verbs of hearing, perceiving, knowing, thinking, believing, finding, or where the passive form of these verbs is introduced by anticipatory *it,* pointing forward to a following subject clause: **Man hörte ihn sagen** *He was heard to say.* **Man fand ihn schlafen** *He was found to be sleeping.* **Man sah, daß es zu spät war** *It was seen that it was too late.*

2. The simple reflexive construction described in **218.** 3. A and B.

3. The use of **lassen** reflexively with a dependent infinitive. See **218.** 3. A. *a.*

Note. There is a difference of meaning between these various passive constructions. The passive proper represents the subject as the objective point of an activity. **Der Garten wird von dem jetzigen Besitzer erweitert** The garden is being enlarged by its present owner. The construction with **man** (see 1 above) and the active represents an indefinite agent at work upon something: **Man erweitert den Garten.** The construction with **lassen** used reflexively with a dependent infinitive (see 3 above) indicates the possibility of a successful action: **Der Garten läßt sich erweitern** The garden can be enlarged. The simple reflexive construction (see 2 above) represents the subject as self-acting, either under the impulse of natural forces or some hidden force, so that it seems to act of itself: **Mein Herz erweitert sich** My heart is being enlarged (under the natural influence of sympathy). **Da öffnet sich behend ein zweites Tor** Then a second door is quickly thrown open (it seemed to open of itself). **Das ändert sich bald** That will soon be changed, circumstances will soon alter this condition of things. Very often this reflexive construction can be translated by an intrans. as in the first two sentences: My heart is growing broader, larger. Then a second door quickly flies open. Compare **218.** 3. B.

4. Also in a number of other cases active forms in the German are rendered by passives in English:

a. The auxiliary **sollen** is often rendered by *is said to, is expected to, is supposed to*: **Er soll sehr reich sein** He is said to be very rich. **Die Königin soll heute kommen** The queen is expected to arrive to-day. **Dieses Gemälde soll** (is supposed) **von Rubens sein.**

b. The auxiliary **dürfen** is often rendered by *to be allowed*: **Er darf nicht gehen** He is not allowed to go.

c. The active infinitive very often has passive force. See **187.** 1.

d. The modal verbals (see **180.** A. *a, b, c* and B), tho active in form, are passive in force.

e. An impersonal idiom is sometimes rendered by a passive: **Es bedarf keiner Hilfe** No help is needed.

f. The German intrans. **ertrinken** (of human beings) and **ersaufen** (of animals) are translated by *to be drowned*: **Der Knabe ertrank. Die Katze ersoff.**

g. In its intransitive use **heißen** is usually rendered passively in English *to be called*: **Herodot heißt der Vater der Geschichte** Herodotus is called the father of history. **Wie heißt das Kind?** What is the child called, or what is the child's name?

h. The intrans. **erschrecken** is translated by *to be frightened*: **Erschrick nur nicht!** Don't be frightened!

i. In German the passive is in general very little used in connection with an infinitive: He was known to be honest **Man wußte, daß er ehrlich war.** For fuller statement see 1. *a* above and **185.** B. I. 2. *d.* (**4**). With **lehren** and **heißen,** however, the passive may be used here. See **178.** 2. B. *d.* See also **185.** B. I. 2. *c. Note.*

5. The English passive construction with verbs which take a prepositional object must be rendered in some other way: *He is often spoken of* may be translated by **Man spricht oft von ihm.** The German construction, however, may correspond closely to the English where the preposition has entered into a compound with the verb: *The skiff was run into by a sailboat* **Der Nachen wurde von einem Segelboot angerannt.**

II. *Impersonal Passive.* On the other hand, in its impersonal form, the passive is often used where there is no person or thing represented as being acted on. See **219.** 5. B.

GRADATION (ABLAUT) CLASSES OF THE STRONG VERB.

VOWEL AND CONSONANT CHANGES.

197. A. *Gradation.* The conjugation of the weak verb is very uniform, and all can in general be conjugated after the model of **loben,** but the strong verb forms its simple tenses and perf. participle by a change of vowel in the stem instead of adding suffixes to the stem. This change of vowel in the different tenses is the result of a different accent which obtained in an earlier period, but is now used to make more clear certain grammatical distinctions such as tense and number. Strong verbs do not all show the same changes of vowel, but subdivide into classes and groups. Each class usually observes within itself a uniform change of vowel in the past tense. The pres. and past tenses cannot have the same vowel. The vowel of the perf. part. is in some groups the same as in the present, in others the same as in the past, or again it may have a different vowel from both. This change of the stem-vowel in the simple tenses and the perf. part. is called gradation. Each *class* usually has *subdivisions,* differing from each other in the quantity of the vowel or otherwise.

a. The nouns and adjectives made from strong verbs have also a relation to this gradation. Many masculine monosyllabics and feminine dissyllabics, also masculine derivatives **in -er** denoting agents, and neuter verbal nouns in **-en** and feminine verbal nouns in **-ung,** often corresponding to our nouns in -ing, have the same vowel as the present tense of the verb from which they are formed; other nouns have the same vowel as the past, which are usually masculine if monosyllabic and feminine if dissyllabic, and still other nouns are made upon the vowel of the perfect participle: **steigen** to mount, ascend, past **stieg,** perf. part. **gestiegen; der Steig** path, **die Steige** path, staircase, **der Steiger** climber, **der Steigende** the one who is now ascending, **das Steigen** ascending, **die Besteigung des Berges** the ascending of the mountain; **der Stieg** ascent, die Stege (see **198,** 2. Division, *d*) staircase; **der Hinaufgestiegene** the one who has ascended. Nouns denoting agents verbal and participial nouns, are made, as those given above, quite regularly upon the appropriate gradation form; but many other nouns, as **die Stege** (see reference given above), are seemingly irregularly formed, as they have retained in many cases the gradation form of the verb as found in earlier periods, or have undergone peculiar phonetic changes. On account of these irregularities these nouns are especially treated under the different classes, while those regularly formed will not require especial treatment.

Adjectives are not always so easily brought into relation with the present gradation classes as nouns, since they often have retained old gradation forms which the verb has exchanged for newer formations: **zahm** *tame*, from the past tense of the M.H.G. zëmen (now **ziemen, wk.)** *to be becoming*, past zam (pl. zâmen), part. gezomen, &c.

Note. The exact relation of nouns, adjectives, &c. to the gradation of the verb cannot always be definitely determined. Some nouns are taken directly from a gradation form of the verb and share its verbal force: (**der**) **Bäcker** *baker = one who bakes*, thus pres. and active in force. Other nouns, especially those showing the vowel of the past tense, altho they have the same vowel as a gradation form of the verb, do not have the same verbal force: **das Band** *tie, fetter = that which ties, fetters*, thus pres. in force, altho the word shows the vowel of the past tense of the verb. It is probable that this class of nouns were not formed from verbs, but that each noun was made directly from the stem from which also the verb was made. Similar phonetic conditions developed the same vowel in verb and noun. As the original stem of such words does not now appear anywhere in the language, it is profitable to associate every noun and adj., where it is possible, with the same gradation form of the verb, as this is the oldest related form to which it can be traced and from which light can be obtained as to its real meaning. Thus when (**der**) **Fluß** *river* is brought into relation to **flussen** (earlier form of the pl. of the past tense of **fließen** *to flow*) its real meaning becomes apparent. Altho originally such nouns and adjectives were not formed directly from the gradation forms of the verb, but developed a similar form under the force of similar conditions, they nevertheless, from long association with the verbal gradation forms, have come to be felt as directly derived from them. This is especially seen in a number of abstract nouns, such as **Kniff, Pfiff, Wuchs, Hieb,** &c., which have been formed within the present period directly from the gradation forms of the verb after the analogy of other nouns which seemed to be derived directly from the verb. It has become especially common to form such abstract nouns directly from the present tense of both strong and weak derivative and compound verbs: **Verderb, Beweis, Beleg, Nachweis,** &c.

b. The gradation classes are very old, and in course of centuries changes of gradation in individual words within a group or thruout a group, and shifting of words from one group to another, have taken place, and traces of these former gradation conditions can still be clearly seen, and will be noted under the individual groups. Verbs that are followed by Roman numbers used to belong to the classes indicated by the Roman characters. In dialect the groups do not always correspond to those of the written language, as many words have abandoned their group for a more popular one.

c. In several groups the Middle High German form is given below the New High German. In this case two vowels are given in the past tense, as the past tense had a different vowel in the sing. and the pl., as can still be seen in old sayings, where sometimes a rime has preserved the older form of the pl.: **Wie die Alten sungen** (now elsewhere **sangen**), **so zwitschern die Jungen.** In Luther's language this difference of vowel is still very common, but to-day it has disappeared except in *past present* verbs (see **212.** 1) and in the past tense of **werden: ich ward** (or **wurde**), **wir wurden.** Wherever the vowel of the past tense was different in the sing. and pl. the subjunctive had thruout the sing. and pl. the mutated vowel of the indic. pl., as can still be seen in past present verbs, the past of **werden** (past indic. **ich ward,** pl. **wir wurden,** subj. **ich würde,** pl. **wir würden**), and other cases mentioned under the different classes.

Also nouns often show even to this day the plural vowel of the old past tense. Thus (**der**) **Schuß** still shows the vowel of the plural of the old past tense of **schießen.**

d. Factitive verbs (which show that the subject *makes* something do or become something, as *the woodman fells*, i.e. makes fall, *the tree*) are formed from strong verbs by mutating the vowel of the past tense, the consonants remaining unchanged except that final **ß** and **ch** of the stem usually appear as **z** and **ck,** and **d** and **s** as **t** and **r** in **leiten** (factitive of **leiden;** see **198.** 1. Division, *c*) and **nähren** (factitive of **nesen,** now only found in the form of **genesen;** see **202.** 2. *General Note*). The mutation of **a** is usually written **e,** but in some verbs **ä.** Mutation does not always appear in M.H.G., especially before labials, but later thru the influence of Luther and M.G. writers became more general: (M.H.G.) ersoufen, **ersäufen.** These factitive verbs being derivatives are of course weak. Ex.: **erschrecken** to be afraid, to start with fright, **erschrak, erschrocken,** but **erschrecken,** new infin. from the mutated stem of the past, *to make start with fright, to frighten*, past **erschreckte,** perf. part. **erschreckt; liegen** to lie, **lag, gelegen,** but **legen** to lay (to make lie), **legte, gelegt; sitzen** to sit, **saß, gesessen,** but **setzen** to set, **setzte, gesetzt; stechen** to pierce, **stach, gestochen,** but **stecken** to stick (literally to make pierce), **steckte, gesteckt.** In older periods when the past tense had a different vowel in sing. and pl. the factitive had the same vowel as the singular. The factitives have retained the original singular vowel, while this vowel has in a number of cases disappeared in the past tense of the corresponding strong verbs, as the singular in this tense has often been leveled by the plural. In this way and also thru mutation and the change of the form of the final consonant in the stem the factitives have become disconnected from the parent verbs and are often not felt as related forms. Thus feeling for this formation is waning and a number have disappeared entirely. The change of **d** to **t** and that of **s** to **r** mentioned above clearly indicate according to **40.** 2. *a* that the accent of factitives was formerly upon the verbal suffix, not upon the stem as at present. The change of **ß** and **ch** to **z** and **ck** in the factitive arose from the fact that in prehistoric West Germanic the **j** that was then in the factitival suffix caused the doubling of the final **t** and **k** of the stem, as it later also caused the mutation of the stem vowel. In the O.H.G. period the **t** and **k** shifted to **ß** and **ch**, but double **t** and **k** to **z** and **ck** according to rule. In prehistoric West Germanic the **j** of the factitival suffix did not always double the preceding **t** after a long vowel or diphthong, so that here we find **ß** in some verbs and **z** in others: **flößen** (or less commonly **flözen**; see **199**, General Remarks on the 1. Division, *c*), but **beizen** (**198.** 1. Division, *c*).

B. *A-Mutation.* This is a partial assimilation of the stem vowel to the vowel in the following syllable. The stem vowel *u* was in an earlier period changed to *o*, when an *a*, *e*, or *o* followed in the next syllable, except before a nasal + consonant or before *j*. Thus the perf. participle **geholfen** (O.H.G. giholfan) has the mutated *o*, while in **gebunden**, perf. part. of **binden**, a verb belonging to the same gradation class, mutation did not take place, as it was hindered by the **nd** following the stem-vowel. This force of *a*-mutation can be seen only in its effects. It can be better studied in O.H.G. by reason of its preservation of the vowels of the unaccented syllable. See **26.** B. One result of this force has been that the third gradation class has been split into different sub-divisions.

Similarly an *i* became in this same older period *e* before *a*, *e*, *o* in the next syllable. For examples see **198.** 1. Division, *d*, 2. Division, *d*. See also **26.** B.

C. *I-, U-, and Nd-Mutation:—*

a. I-Mutation of the back vowels. In the 2nd and 3rd person sing. of the present indic. and thruout the subj. of the past tense mutation is the rule wherever the stem vowel is capable of it. See **26.** A. The **i** of earlier periods which has often here been the cause of the mutation has either entirely disappeared or has been reduced to the form of **e**: (2nd pers. sing. of **fahren**) O.H.G. du ferist, N.H.G. **du fährst**; (1st pers. sing. of the past subj. of **nehmen**) O.H.G. nāmi, N.H.G. **nähme.** In early S.G., mutation in the 2nd and 3rd pers. sing. indic. was not an absolute requirement even in the literary language. In some cases the vowel remained here unchanged, especially **au** before a labial, in other cases usage fluctuated. In S.G. dialect and colloquial language of our time non-mutation here is still quite common: **Du fahrst fort?** (Schönherr's *Sonnwendtag*, p. 45). See also **201.** *f*.

b. I-, U-, and Nd-Mutation of **e** *to* **i**. This change of **e** to **i** (see **26.** C) brought about in several classes a difference of vowel between the singular and plural of the pres. indic., and also was the cause of splitting the third gradation class into different subdivisions: (pres. tense indic. of **helfen** in O.H.G.) hilfu, hilfis, hilfit, pl. hëlfamēs, hëlfet, hëlfant; but **binden** in the same class takes in O.H.G. (also in N.H.G.) **i** thruout, as it always stands before n + t or d: bintu, bintis, bintit, pl. bintamēs, bintet, bintant. The 1st person sing. of **helfen** is now **ich helfe,** as explained in **201.** *f*.

D. *Leveling.* Another force at work among str. verbs is leveling. This is the natural tendency to level out the little irregularities in the conjugation and make it regular. This force has long been at work and is still continuing, as is illustrated below in **200**, 2. Division, *a*.

E. *Verner's Law* (see **40.** 2. *a*). The effects of a force which was at work in an earlier period upon the consonants of str. verbs—the so-called Verner's Law—can still here and there be seen. Owing to a difference in accent in different conjugational forms of the same word, there arose a difference in the consonants: **ziehen, zog, gezogen; leiden, litt, gelitten; war, gewesen.** Thus in the following classes there is occasionally a change in the same word or in related words of **d** to **t, h** (now a silent letter) to **g,** and **s** to **r,** as is indicated in each case below.

F. *Differentiation of Forms.* There is a tendency toward the wk. conjugation, and a number of str. verbs have wk. forms alongside of the regular str. ones. Sometimes the wk. and str. forms have the same meaning, sometimes an economic instinct has led to a differentiation of meaning. The wk. forms may be used more in familiar conversation, the str. ones may be choicer or have a slightly different application. Thus in familiar conversation **er scheltet** can be heard, while in choice language the form is **er schilt.** In the literal meaning **gären** *to ferment* is str., while in figurative language it is wk.: **Der Wein hat gegoren,** but **Es gärte in ihm.** There are also double str. forms. Here the older form is often used in old saws, poetry or elevated prose, while in common conversation the newer form is used. Thus **hub** is often used in poetry, while in prose it is usually replaced by **hob.**

198. I. Class. Gradation:

Pres. **ei**	Past **ĭ and ie**	Perf. Part. **ĭ and ie.**
M.H.G. ī	ei *or* ē-ĭ (**197.** A. *c*)	ĭ.

This class falls into two divisions strictly on the basis of the closing consonant of the stem. If the stem terminates in **ch, f, ß, t** (which includes **leiden** and **schneiden** by virtue of their past **litt, schnitt** and perf. part. **gelitten, geschnitten**), the vowel of its past tense and perf. part. is short i, while it is in all other cases long i (written ie).

Historical Note. The explanation of this division lies in an earlier condition of things. Formerly the vowel of the perf. part. and the plural of the past tense was uniformly short i. At the beginning of the modern German period all short vowels became long in open syllables; hence, as **ch, ff, ss, t** after a short root vowel according to **4.** 1. *b. Note* formed a closed syllable, words in which **ch, ff, ss, t** followed a short root vowel could not participate in that movement which made the short root vowel of words long in open syllables. Thus verbs of this class fell into two groups in the perf. part. and the plural of the past tense, one with the new vowel gradation ī (written **ie**), the other with the old short **i.** Formerly the singular of the past tense of verbs in this class had a double vowel gradation, *ei* in some cases, ē in others. These gradations have disappeared in the verbal conjugation, as the vowel form, **i** or **ie,** which each verb had in the plural has spread to the singular in accordance with the modern tendency to make the vowel uniform thruout the same inflectional system. This development began in the South at the close of the fifteenth century and gradually spread northward. The derivatives, however, still preserve in a number of cases the old singular vowel of the past tense. See *c* under 1. Division and *b, c, d* under 2. Division.

In English the singular vowel here in most words spread to the plural, while in a few others the singular was leveled by the plural, which has thus split this class into two divisions along a different line from that observed in German: *to drive, drove* (the sing. vowel, thus corresponding to M.H.G. treib), *driven*; *to bite, bit* (the plural vowel, which thus also, as in modern German, has entered the singular), *bitten.*

1. Division. Gradation:

Pres. **ei**	Past **ĭ**	Perf. Part. **ĭ.**
M.H.G. ī	ei-ĭ (**197.** A. *c*)	ĭ.

Examples: **beißen, biß, gebissen; schleifen, schliff, geschliffen; leiden, litt, gelitten; reiten, ritt, geritten.**

The following belong here: **beißen** to bite; **sich befleißen** *to apply oneself to,* but **sich befleißigen** with the same meaning is wk.; **bleichen** (modern representative of the two M.H.G. verbs blīchen, str., and bleichen [from adj. **bleich**], wk.) *to turn pale, white, bleach* (intrans.), *grow wan, fade,* sometimes str., usually wk. in the first three meanings, but str. in the last two, especially in compounds; **erbleichen** (modern representative of the two M.H.G. verbs erblīchen, str., and erbleichen, wk.) *to turn pale, turn, fade, die,* wk. in the first meaning, str. in the last, str. or wk. in the others, wk. especially in the past tense and str. in the perf. part.; **verbleichen** (modern representative of the two M.H.G. verbs verblīchen, str., and verbleichen, wk.) *to turn pale* (now little used in this meaning), *to grow wan, fade, die,* str. in the last meaning and str. or less commonly wk. in the others; the transitive factitive **bleichen** (from adj. **bleich**) *to bleach, turn white* is always wk., either in simple form or in compounds; **gleichen** *to resemble, smooth, level, make equal,* intrans. with dat. in the first meaning, trans. with the acc. in the other meanings and in all compounds, in early N.H.G. wk., and still so in all the meanings except the first, where it is now always str., also usually str. in compounds; **gleiten** *to glide, slide,* sometimes wk., and always so in **begleiten** (from **begeleiten,** and thus not related to **gleiten**) *to accompany,* but rarely so in the compound **ausgleiten** *to slip*; **greifen** to seize; **keifen** (rather coarse word) *to chide, 'jaw,'* str. in the language of Goethe and some other writers, but now commonly wk. as originally; **kneifen** (rarely wk.) to pinch; **leiden** *to suffer,* but the factitive **verleiden** (from adj. **leid**) *to render unpleasant, spoil, set against,* wk.; **pfeifen** to whistle; **reißen** to tear, pull, break away from; **reiten** to ride on horseback; **schleichen** to sneak; **schleifen** in M.H.G. *to slide, glide,* and still with this meaning in Austria, as in **Als der Schlitten vorüberschliff** (Rosegger's *Der Adlerwirt,* p. 37), and also elsewhere in the narrowed meanings *to shuffle with the feet* and *to slide on the ice* (in these two meanings also wk.), and from the idea of sliding back and forth on a surface come the common meanings *to polish, grind*; **schleißen** (now rare; see factitive in *c*) to split (intrans.), *wear out* by use (intrans.); **schmeißen** to fling, slam; **schneiden** to cut; **schreiten** to stride; **spleißen** to split (trans. or intrans.), sometimes wk.; **streichen** to stroke, cross out; **streiten** to contend; **weichen** *to yield,* but the factitive **weichen** *to soften, soak,* from the adj. **weich** *soft,* is always wk.; also other verbs belong here, but only rarely, and hence are not given; see **205.**

a. As the past tense and perf. part. contain a short vowel, a single final consonant must in these forms be doubled to show that the vowel is short and a final **d** is changed to **t** (**197.** E) and then doubled: **reiten, ritt, geritten; schneiden, schnitt, geschnitten.** For change from **ß** to ss see **4.** 2. D, p. 17.

b. Luther still used a different vowel in the sing. and pl. of the past tense as in M.H.G.: **ich reit, wir ritten.** See *Historical Note,* above. This old usage is still preserved in the old past tense **ich weiß** *I know,* **wir wissen,** but the form is now felt as an irregular present. See **212.** 1.

c. The factitives (**197.** A. *d*) in this division have still the vowels of the M.H.G. period when the past sing. contained an ei: **beizen** *to make bite into,* said of liquids in the mechanical arts, as *to stain* (wood), *soak* (wood), *corrode,* &c.; **leiten** *to lead,* lit. *to make go,* thus preserving an older meaning of **leiden** (formerly *to go, pass thru,* now only used in the derived meanings *to experience, suffer*); **reizen** *to provoke,* lit. to cause to break away from one's self-control; **schleifen** lit. *to make slide,* hence *to drag, trail, raze* (a fortress); **schleißen** *to split, to cause to wear out, wear* *out* (trans.), often confounded with the intrans. str. **schleißen** *to split, wear out*, hence the trans. is wk. or more commonly str.

d. A number of monosyllabic and dissyllabic nouns show the vowel of the past tense: **der Biß** bite, **der Schnitt** cut, **der Pfiff** whistle (sound); **die Schnitte** slice, &c.

Das Blech (from **bleichen** in its older meaning *to shine, glitter*) *sheet-metal* shows the mutated (*a*-mutation; see **26.** B) form of this vowel.

Some nouns have the vowel of the present tense: **der Streit** contention, **die Schneide** edge (of a knife, sword), &c.

2. Division. Gradation:

Pres. **ei**		Past **ie**	Perf. Part. **ie**
M.H.G. ī		ei *or* ē-ĭ (**197.** A. *c*)	ĭ.

Examples: **bleiben, blieb, geblieben; reiben, rieb, gerieben.**

Here belong: **bekleiben** (simple **kleiben** now entirely lost) *to take root, stand firmly rooted*, now rare and confined to poetry; **bleiben** to remain; **gedeihen** (see *e*) *to thrive*, earlier in the period occasionally wk.; **fleihen** (N.G., sometimes wk.) to put in order, arrange, fold; **leihen** to borrow, lend; **meiden** to avoid; **preisen** *to praise*, earlier in the period wk., now str., but the compound **lobpreisen** *to praise in song*, str. or wk., **lobpries** or **lobpreis(e)te, gelobpriesen, lobgepriesen,** or **gelobpreist; reiben** to rub; **scheiden** VII *to separate*, as a verb now always str. according to its present class, but in early N.H.G. (see Gen. xiii. 14) still in class VII, 1. Division, which former inflection still survives in the adjective participle **bescheiden** (see **204.** 1. Division, *a*), or in transitive use sometimes wk., as in Gen. i. 4; **scheinen** to shine, seem; **schreiben** to write; **schreien** to scream, in early N.H.G. also wk.; **schweigen** to be silent; **speien** *to spew, vomit* (fire, &c.), *spit* (formerly common in this meaning, now restricted to **Blut speien, Feuer und Flammen speien,** &c.), earlier in the period also wk., and still wk. in biblical and popular language; **steigen** to mount; **treiben** to drive, impel; **weisen** *to point out, show*, in early N.H.G. also wk. now str.; **zeihen** *to accuse*, sometimes wk.

a. Luther still used a different vowel in the sing. and pl. of the past tense, as in M.H.G.: **ich schreib, wir schrieben.**

b. The factitives (**197.** A. *d*) are: **kleiben** *to make stick, paste*, now little used, largely replaced by **kleben** (see *c*); **geschweigen** or **schweigen** (early N.H.G. and later, now only in limited use in the literary language) *to silence, hush*: **Du weißt, die Mutter hing oft ein Tuch über, um ihn** (i.e. **den Hänfling**) **zu geschweigen, wenn er so recht aus Kräften sang** (Storm's *Immensee*). **Er, der mit seinem Überlegenheitslächeln jede Unterhaltung zu Boden schweigte** (Carl Spitteler's *Imago*, p. 167).

c. The vowel i of the old plural of the past tense still appears in derivatives: O.H.G. klīban to stick (intrans.), which formerly belonged to this class and is still represented here by the poetic compound **bekleiben** given in the list above, is the source of two derivatives: **klimmen** (O.H.G. klimban III) II *to climb* (lit. *to stick*), which shows the gradation i of the old plural of the past tense of klīban and an insertion of a nasal (m) between the stem vowel and the consonantal termination, which, however, later became assimilated to the nasal; the wk. **kleben** (O.H.G. klebēn) *to stick*, at first intrans., later also trans., replacing largely in the latter function the factitive **kleiben** (see *b*). **Kleben** shows the gradation i of the old plural of the past tense of klīban changed to **e** under the influence of *a*-mutation (see **26.** B). The wk. **zeigen** *to show*, from **zeihen** *to accuse* (lit. *to show something against*), has preserved the vowel of the old sing. of the past tense. The g instead of **h** is the result of the operation of Verner's Law (**197.** E).

d. **Der Steig** *path*, **die Steige** *path, staircase*, show the vowel of the present tense; **der Unterschied** *difference*, **der Stieg** *ascent*, show the new vowel of the past tense, while in **die Stege** (S.G. from O.H.G. stega) *staircase*, **der Steg** *path*, we see the mutated (*a*-mutation; see **26.** B) form of the plural vowel of the old past. **Die Trift** (from **treiben**, hence *a place where cattle are driven*) *pasture* and **die Schrift** *writing* show the vowel ĭ of the old perfect participle and the old plural of the past tense. **Zeichen** *sign, mark*, related to **zeihen** *to accuse* (lit. *to show, point out something against*), has preserved the vowel of the old sing. of the past.

e. The old perf. part. of **gedeihen**, according to Verner's Law (**197.** E), was **gediegen.** This form still exists, but is now felt as an adjective with the meanings *solid, genuine, sterling*, meanings which are easily brought into relation to the primary signification of the verb. In the present period the older participle has been replaced by the leveled form **gediehen**, which has resulted from the tendency to level out little inequalities and to extend the same consonant thruout the same inflectional system.

199. II. Class. Gradation:

Pres. **ie, e, au, ü, i, ä, ö**	Past **ŏ**	Perf. Part. **ŏ.**
M.H.G. ie (iu in sing., ie in pl.)	ou *or* ō-ŭ (**197.** A. *c*)	ŏ.

This class falls into two divisions strictly on the basis of the closing consonant of the stem. If the stem terminates in **ch, f, ß, sch, t** (which includes **sieden** by virtue of its perf. part. **gesotten**), a double consonant or a combination of consonants, the vowel of the past tense and perfect part. is short **o,** while it is in all other cases long **o.** For some reason, however, **bieten** does not follow this law.

Historical Note. The explanation of this division lies in an earlier condition of things. Formerly the vowel of the perfect part. was uniformly short **o.** At the beginning of the modern German period all short vowels became long in open syllables; hence as **ch, f, ß, t,** double consonants or a combination of consonants at the close of a stem formed a closed syllable, words containing such final consonants in their stems could not participate in that movement which made the stem-vowel of words long in all open syllables. Thus verbs of this class fell into two groups in the perfect participle, one with the new vowel gradation ō, the other with the old ŏ. Later in the course of the fifteenth and sixteenth centuries the vowel of the perfect participle spread by force of analogy to the past tense, so that each verb had the same vowel in the past tense and perfect participle, and there thus arose two divisions of these verbs, each with the same vowel in the past tense and perfect participle.

The old past tense, which had been leveled away in the manner just described, contained in early N.H.G. two vowel gradations in the singular, **ou** before labials and velars (except **ch**) and ō before **ch** and dentals, while all alike had the same gradation in the plural, namely, short **u.** When later the vowel of the perfect participle replaced the old vowels of the past tense, the derivatives remained unaffected, and thus still show the old gradations of the past tense. See 1. Division, *c, d,* and 2. Division, *c, d* below.

This class was greatly enlarged by accessions from the other classes, as can be seen by glancing at the lists below. Words in other classes which contained a long or a short **o** in their perfect participle joined those verbs in this class which had there the same vowel, and along with them extended the vowel of their perfect participle to their past tense and became identified with them as members of one class. Their derivatives, however, did not make this change, and still show the older vowels.

Also in English words of this class the past tense was leveled by the perf. part.: *freeze, froze, frozen,* &c. Almost all of the words in class IV joined this group as they also had leveled their past tense by their perf. part., which likewise contained the stem vowel *o*: *bear, bore* (sometimes *bare* according to its original class), *born(e).*

1. Division. Gradation:

Pres.	**ie, ĕ, ĭ, au, ŏ**	Past **ŏ**	Perf. Part. **ŏ.**
M.H.G.	ie (iu in sing., ie in pl.)	ou *or* ō-ŭ (**197.** A. *c*)	ŏ.

Examples: **fließen, floß** (pl. **wir flossen**), **geflossen; sieden, sott, gesotten.**

Here belong: 1. In **ie: verdrießen** to vex; **fließen** to flow; **gießen** to pour; **kriechen** to crawl, creep; **genießen** to enjoy; **riechen** to smell; **schießen** to shoot; **schliefen** (S.G.) to slip; **schließen** to shut, close; **sieden** (choicer and less common than **kochen** *to boil, cook* and with a narrower range of meanings as it only means *to boil*) *to boil,* str. only when transitive and used of eggs and the like, which, when 'done,' are said to be **gesotten,** as in **gesottene Krebse, weich, hart gesottene Eier, Das Fleisch ist gar gesotten,** but elsewhere weak, as in **Das Wasser hat gesiedet, Mein Blut hat gesiedet, Ich siedete Wasser** (but **Ich sott Eier**); **sprießen** *to sprout,* sometimes wk., now largely confined to choice language, elsewhere usually replaced by the wk. **sprossen; triefen** to drip, **troff, getroffen,** now just as commonly wk. in the past and usually wk. in the perf. part., so that the form may be distinguished from **getroffen,** perf. part. of **treffen.**

2. In **e: dreschen** (**du drischest** or **drischst, er drischt**) III (O.H.G.), IV (M.H.G.) *to thrash,* perhaps more commonly in Class III, 3. Division, rarely wk.; **fechten** (**du fichtst, er ficht**) III (O.H.G. in the South and the Midland and M.H.G. in the Midland), IV (M.H.G. in the South) to fight; **flechten** (**du flichtst, er flicht**) III (O.H.G. in the South and the Midland and M.H.G. in the Midland), IV (M.H.G. in the South) *to braid, plat, plait,* rarely wk.; **melken** (**du milkst, er milkt,** or more commonly **du melkst, er melkt**) III *to milk,* str. and wk. forms in past tense and perfect participle both so common that it is difficult to decide which inflection present usage prefers here except that the strong form has become fixed in the adj. part. (**frisch gemolkene Milch** *milk just from the cow*); **quellen** (**du quillst, er quillt**) III to swell up, gush; **schellen** III *to sound* (intrans.), now replaced in the pres. by the wk. **schallen,** past **schallte,** in poetic or choice language **scholl,** in early N.H.G. **schall** (Mark i. 28) according to former class, perf. part. **geschallt,** str. only in poetic or choice language in certain compound words as **erschollen** *resounded,* and always in **verschollen** *forgotten,* lit. *sound* or *report* (*of him, her, it*) *died away*; **schmelzen** (**du schmilzest** or **schmilzt, er schmilzt**) III *to melt* (intrans.); **schwellen** (**du schwillst, er schwillt**) III to swell up, out (intrans.), sometimes wk.

3. In **ĭ: glimmen** III *to glimmer, smoulder,* str. or perhaps more frequently wk.; **klimmen** III *to climb,* str. or wk.; also the adjective participle **beklom-**

men *breathing with difficulty, anxious, oppressed in one's feelings, oppressive,* adjective and participle from the lost **beklimmen,** only rarely, however, as a real participle with verbal force: **Hat dir je den Busen Liebesschmerz beklommen?** (Platen).

4. In **au,** (ä), or **ö: saufen (du säufst, er säuft,** sometimes **du saufst, er sauft)** to drink (of animals, *or* as animals), **soff, gesoffen,** sometimes **wk.; erlöschen (du erlischest** or **erlischst, er erlischt)** III (O.H.G.), IV (M.H.G.) *to go out* (of a light, &c.), intrans., sometimes wk. Here also belongs the poetic part. **gerochen** from **rächen** IV *to avenge,* now usually entirely wk., in early N.H.G. **ich reche, du richst, er richt,** past **rach,** later **roch,** now entirely replaced by the wk. **rächte.** The strong part. is still occasionally found in prose: **Das soll sieben Mal gerochen werden** (Frenssen's *Heimatsfest,* 1, 1).

General Remarks on the 1. Division:

a. For the change of vowel in the 2nd and 3rd person sing. pres. tense, see **177.** II. D. *a, b, c, d, e, f.*

b. The 2nd and 3rd person sing. pres. still occasionally show in poetry old forms in **eu,** which were the rule in Luther's works: **fleußt, kreucht,** &c. for **fließt, kriecht,** &c. For the development of **eu** out of M.H.G. iu see (**2**), p. 2. The **ie** of the plural had in the Midland even before Luther's day largely supplanted the M.H.G. iu (N.H.G. **eu**) in the 1st pers. sing., but had not yet driven it out of the 2nd and 3rd pers. sing. Later the **ie** under S.G. influence leveled the entire sing. See also **201.** *f.*

c. The factitives (**197.** A. *d*) are: **ersäufen** *to drown,* from M.H.G. ersoufen; **flößen** to administer wine, medicine, &c., instil (courage, &c.), float or raft logs, as in **Holz flößen,** in this last meaning sometimes in the form of **flözen** (see **197.** A. *d,* toward end); **träufen** *to make fall in drops upon,* from M.H.G. tröufen; **löschen** to extinguish, quench, slack (lime), lay (dust); **quellen** to soak (peas, &c.); **schellen** to cause to sound, ring (bell for servant, &c.); **schmelzen** to cause to melt, melt (trans.), also strong, as it is under the influence of the strong intransitive, as in **Sie schmolzen Schnee und Eis** (Ludwig's *Zwischen Himmel und Erde,* XX), and, perhaps, more commonly so in the perf. part.; **schwellen** to cause to swell up. For the change of M.H.G. ou to N.H.G. **au** see (**4**), p. 3. Hence M.H.G. öu became N.H.G. **äu.** The last five verbs in the above list were formed when they were in their former class (III), hence the vowel **e** in their stem, but **leschen** was later corrupted to **löschen,** which form was also extended to the str. verb. The strong verb **löschen** is often confounded with the wk., hence the wk. forms which are frequently found instead of the more correct str. in the intrans. use: **Dann war es, als löschten alle diese Lichter aus** (Fontane's *Vor dem Sturm,* I. chap. i).

d. Most nouns made from the past tense of the original verbs of this class show the old vowel of the pl.: **der Verdruß** vexation, **der Guß** downpour (of rain), casting (of a bell, &c.), **der Genuß** enjoyment, &c.; **die Schluft** or more commonly **Schlucht** (from Low German) ravine. In other cases the **u** has changed to ŏ under the influence of *a*-mutation (**26.** B): **der Fluß** *river,* with old **u,** but **die Flosse** (O.H.G. flozza) *fin,* with **u** mutated to ŏ. In **Flöß** *raft* we have the old gradation ō of the past singular, and in **Schleife** (for the correct early N.H.G. **Schläufe**) *noose* the mutated form of the old gradation **au** (M.H.G. ou). For the explanation of the forms **Schall, Schmalz, Schwall** see **200.** 3. Division, *c.*

2. Division. Gradation:

Pres.	**ie, e, au, ü, ä, ö**	Past **ō**	Perf. Part. **ō.**
M.H.G.	ie (iu in sing., ie in pl.)	ou *or* ō-ŭ (**197.** A. *c*)	ŏ.

Examples: **biegen, bog, gebogen; wiegen, wog, gewogen.**

Here belong: 1. In **ie: biegen** to bend; **bieten** to offer; **fliegen** to fly; **fliehen** to flee; **frieren** to freeze; **kiesen,** see **küren** in 4 below; **schieben** to shove; **stieben** to fly away (in the form of mist, dust, or other small particles), to scatter (intrans.), sometimes wk.; **verlieren** to lose; **wiegen** and **wägen (du wägst;** see *Note*) V, the former *to weigh on the scales,* used transitively or intransitively, not only literally but also figuratively, as in **Das Fleisch wiegt** (past **wog**) **4 Pfund** and **Meyer wiegt hundert Schmidts auf** *Meyer outweighs,* &c., trans. **Er wiegt das Fleisch,** also *to weigh in the mind, have value, be important,* when used intransitively, as in **Seine Gründe wiegen schwer** and **Ein Freund wiegt in der Not,** on the other hand, **wägen** *to weigh with the mind, consider,* is usually only employed transitively and only in this figurative meaning, as in **Er wägt seine Worte nicht, Erst wäge, dann wage** (with object understood), **Ich erwäge, ob ich mich darauf einlassen soll,** often, however, especially in the South, **wägen (du wägst, er wägt, wog** or **wägte, gewogen** or **gewägt)** is uniformly used in transitive function, without regard to meaning, while **wiegen** (wog, gewogen) is employed only intransitively: **Der Metzger wägt das Fleisch und findet, daß es 4 Pfund wiegt;** (**wiegen** *to rock*, always wk. as it is a denominative from **Wiege** *cradle*, lit. *that which is moved*); **ziehen** to draw, pull, go, move (intrans.), **zog, gezogen.**

Note. The parts of **wiegen** and **wägen** *to weigh* (as in **Das Fleisch wiegt 4 Pfund,** lit. *moves, sets in motion the four-pound weight on the scales*), *move* (intrans., a meaning now in general obsolete in the original verb, but surviving in the factitive **bewegen** *to move* [trans.] and other derivatives) were in early N.H.G. according to V: **wegen** (**du wiegst, er wiegt**), past **wag** (sometimes **wug**), pl. **wōgen** (developed from M.H.G. wāgen; sometimes **wugen**), perf. part. **gewegen.** Later the present was split into two forms **wiegen** and **wägen** (corrupted from **wegen** under the impression that it was a derivative of **Wage** *pair of scales*), the former of which resulted from the leveling of the forms by the vowel of the 2nd and 3rd person sing., the latter from leveling by the 1st person sing. The plural form of the past **wogen** leveled the sing. to **wog,** and later the vowel o spread also to the perf. part. except in case of **verwegen** (see 2 below). The vowel of the old present survives in lengthened form in **Weg** *way* (lit. *that over which something moves*) and **sich verwegen** (see 2 below). The vowel of the old sing. of the past survives in lengthened form in **Wagen** *wagon* (lit. *that which is moved*) and in mutated form also in the weak factitive **bewegen** *to move* in *c* below and the strong factitive **bewegen** *to induce* (lit. *to make the will move*) in 2 below, which, however, ought to be weak. The vowel of the old M.H.G. plural of the past survives in **Wage** (*pair of scales*, lit. *that which moves up and down*). The modern vowel of the past is found in **Woge** *billow* (lit. *that which is moved*).

2. In **e: heben (hebst)** VI to lift, see also **heben** in **203**; **pflegen (pflegst)** V *to keep up* (friendship, &c.), *maintain* (relations), *carry on* (negotiations, &c.), past tense in poetical language sometimes **pflag** (according to its former class), now wk. thruout in the meanings *to be accustomed to*, *take care of*, *cherish*, altho earlier in the period strong forms occur; **scheren** (**du scherst,** or in poetic style also **schierst** *you cut* or *shear*, **scher'** or **schier dich fort** *get out of here*, **du scherst** or **schierst** *you bother*, **das schert** or **schiert dich nicht** *that doesn't concern you*) IV *to cut*, *shear*, *be off*, *bother*, *concern*, perf. part. usually str., past tense str. in the first and second meanings, wk. or less commonly str. in the fourth and fifth, and rare in the third, the word in this use being largely confined to the imperative; (**bescheren** *to give*, *present*, always wk.); **weben (webst)** V *to weave*, *be astir*, *float* (of clouds, mist, etc.), usually wk. in the second and third meanings, in the first meaning also usually wk., but often str., especially in poetic language and figurative use, sometimes with an adjective participle made according to its former class, as in **die festen hauswebenen** (for **hausgewebten**) **Stoffe** *the strong home-woven fabrics*; **bewegen** (**du bewegst**; see 1. *Note* above) to move the will, *induce*, but wk. in the other applications of the meaning *move*, as *to move the feelings*, *move objects*, &c.; **sich verwegen** or sometimes **verwägen** (**du verwegst** or **verwägst**; for construction see **262.** II. A. *b*) V *to dare*, *venture upon*, now only used in the perf. part. as adj. or adv. The adj. or adv. perf. part. **verwegen** *bold*, *daring* is formed according to the former class of **verwegen.** The adj. or adv. perf. part. **verwogen,** according to its present class, is also found, but now more commonly with differentiated meaning, *jaunty*: **Er hat einen alten Jägerhut ziemlich verwogen auf den schon stark angegrauten Kopf gesetzt** (Hauptmann's *Hannele*, 1, p. 12). **Ich seh' dich schon als verwogene Schloßherrin** (Halbe's *Haus Rosenhagen*, 2, p. 80).

3. In **au: saugen** (**du saugst,** in early N.H.G. also **du seugst** or **säugst**) *to suck*, elsewhere usually str., sometimes wk. thruout; **schnauben** (**du schnaubst,** in early N.H.G. also **du schneubst** or **schnäubst**) *to snort*, elsewhere usually wk., but in poetry and choice prose also str., **sich schnauben** (N.G.) *to blow the nose*, regularly wk.; **schrauben** (**du schraubst**) to screw, usually wk. as originally, sometimes str., especially in the adjective perf. participle **verschroben** *distorted*, *crazy*, *cranky*.

4. In **ü: küren** (from **die Kur** *choice*, and hence in a strict sense more properly wk.) or **kiesen** (more properly str.), both confined largely to a choice style with the meaning *to choose*, **kor** (rarely **kieste**) or **kürte, gekoren** (rarely **gekiest**) or **gekürt; lügen** (in early N.H.G. **liegen;** the present spelling has come from association with the derivative **die Lüge** *lie*) *to lie* (*falsify*), sometimes wk.; **trügen** (older form **triegen** still common in eighteenth century; the present spelling has come from association with its derivative **der Trug** *deception* and analogy with **lügen**) *to deceive*, occasionally wk.

5. In **ä** and **ö: gären** (earlier in the period **giert** in 3rd pers. sing., now **gärt**) V *to ferment*, *work*, *effervesce*, str. in the literal meaning, wk. when used figuratively, as illustrated by an example in **197.** F; see *Note* below; **schwären,** (**schwärt,** now rarely **schwiert**) IV *to fester*, *suppurate*, colloquially sometimes

wk. thruout to distinguish the forms from those of **schwören; schwören** VI to swear, **schwor** or perhaps more commonly **schwur** (according to its original class), **geschworen,** only rarely wk. thruout, see also **schwören** in **203**; **wägen** (M.H.G. wëgen), see **wiegen** under 1 above.

Note. **Gären** comes from M.H.G. jesen (ich gise, du gisest), jas (pl. jâren), gejeren. In N.H.G. the long *a* in the past developed here as often elsewhere into ō and spread to the singular of the same tense and then to the perf. part. Medial *s* has been leveled to *r* thruout. The initial *g* of the present tense sing. spread later to all the other forms. This development and the change of vowel from *e* to ä in the plural of the present tense and in the infinitive were probably furthered by the earlier grammarians, who derived the verb from gar.

General Remarks on 2. Division:

a. For interchange in 2nd and 3rd person sing. see **177.** II. D. *a, b, c, d, e, f.*

b. Old forms in **eu** occur in poetry in the 2nd and 3rd pers. sing.: **fleucht** &c. for **flieht,** &c. For explanation of the forms in **eu** see 1. Division, General Remarks, *b* and more at length in **201.** *f.*

c. The factitives (**197.** A. *d*) in this division are **beugen** *to make bend, bend* (the will, spirit, knee, head, &c.), from M.H.G. böugen; **bewegen** *to move,* made when **wegen** (see 1. *Note* above) was in class V; in Switzerland **entwegen** *to swerve,* from which comes the new but common literary perf. part. **unentwegt** *unswerving*: **an diesen Absichten unentwegt . . . festzuhalten** (Bismarck); **säugen** *to suckle,* from M.H.G. söugen; **stäuben** (sometimes replaced by wk. **stieben,** which is properly str. and intrans.) *to throw off fine particles* (*as dust, spray, mist*), *to scatter* (trans.), *strew,* from M.H.G. stöuben. Notice that in the original factitives of this class the stem vowel is **äu** (in **beugen** written **eu**), as according to (**4**), p. 3, M.H.G. *ou* has developed into N.H.G. **au,** and consequently M.H.G. öu is represented by N.H.G. **äu.**

d. The nouns made from the gradation of the past tense show the vowels of the old singular and plural: **der Staub** (from M.H.G. stoup, which, according to (**4**), p. 3, has become N.H.G. **Staub**) dust, **der Flōh** flea, **der Flug** flight, **die Lüge** (O.H.G. lugī) falsehood, **Frost** (*a*-mutation from old stem frosta; see **26.** B) frost, &c. The old **u** and **o** (*a*-mutation) were short, but at the beginning of the present period they became long before one consonant: **Lūg, Flūg, Gebōt,** but **Flŭcht (fliehen), Verlŭst, Frŏst.**

200. III. Class. Gradation:

Pres. **i, e**	Past **a**	Perf. Part. **u, o.**

1. Division. Gradation:

Pres. **ĭ**	Past **ă**	Perf. Part. **ŭ.**
M.H.G. ĭ	ă-ŭ (**197.** A. *c*)	ŭ.

Examples: **binden, band, gebunden; dringen, drang, gedrungen.**

Here belong: **binden** to bind; **dingen** to hire, **dang (dung)** or **dingte,** subjunctive **dänge, dingte, gedungen, gedingt,** originally wk.; **bedingen,** str. or now less commonly wk. in the sense *to reserve in a contract something for oneself,* but wk. in the adjective participle in the meaning *conditional* (**ein bedingtes Versprechen** *a conditional promise,* but **Das habe ich mir bedungen** *That I have reserved to myself*), always wk. in the meanings *to cause, bring about, require* (as a necessary condition of success), *constitute*; **dringen,** now usually intrans. *to penetrate, crowd, rush, press into,* earlier in the period also trans. *to press, crowd, push, force,* and still so in **abdringen** *to extort from,* **einem etwas aufdringen** (or **aufdrängen**) *to force something upon one,* and also in certain participial expressions, as **dringende Gefahr, eine gedrungene Gestalt, notgedrungen, ich fühle mich gedrungen,** also in **dringlich** *pressing,* **aufdringlich** *obtrusive, obtruding,* elsewhere now usually replaced in the transitive use by the wk. **drängen; finden** to find; **gelingen** to succeed; **klingen** *to sound,* either wk. or str. in the meaning *to clink glasses*; **ringen** to wrestle, wring; **schinden** to flay, skin (one's limb), **schund** or **schindete, geschunden,** originally wk.; **schlingen** to twine, swallow (in this meaning earlier with the form **schlinden,** from which **Schlund** *esophagus, abyss* survives; see **40.** 1. *b. Note* 6); **schrinden** to burst, chap (intrans.), **schrund** or **schrand, geschrunden,** now little used; **schwinden** to disappear; **schwingen** *to swing, wave, whirl,* but **beschwingen** *to wing,* derivative from **Schwinge** *wing,* always wk.; **singen** to sing; **sinken** to sink; **springen** to spring, leap; **stinken** to stink; **trinken** to drink; **winden** to wind; **wringen** *to wring (out),* N.G. form of **ringen,** but also in use in the South; **zwingen** to force.

a. Here belongs the adj. part. **gedunsen** (usually **aufgedunsen**) *bloated,* of the now otherwise obsolete **dinsen;** also the adj. part. **verwunschen** (also **verwünscht**) in the one meaning *enchanted,* from the otherwise wk. verb **verwünschen** *to curse, enchant.* In dialect also the perfect participle **gewunschen** (for **gewünscht**) occurs: **alles, was sich das Herz gewunschen hat** (Wilhelm Fischer's *Sonnenopfer*, I). In careless, colloquial language the weak **schimpfen** *to rail against, abuse,* often forms a perf. part. according to this class: **Hast doch sonst immer so flämsch auf das alte Nest geschumpfen** (M. Dreyer's *In Behandlung*, 1).

b. Luther still used a different vowel in the sing. and pl. of the past tense, as in M.H.G.: **ich band, wir bunden.** In archaic style we find the old pl. even in the nineteenth century: **Durch die das Paradies wir wieder funden** (Tieck's *Oct.*, 155). In the course of the seventeenth century the past tense was 'leveled,' the vowel of the sing. spreading to the pl. In two words, however, the pl. vowel has entered the sing.: **ich schund, wir schunden; schrund, schrunden.** Earlier in the period we find also other words that were leveled according to the pl.: **Der junge Graf, voll Löwengrimm, | schwung seinen Heldenstab** (Schiller's *Graf Eberhard*).

In English the past tense is in some words leveled by the singular vowel, in others by the plural: drank, rang, sang, sank or sunk, sprang or sprung, &c., but clung, stung, swung, wrung, &c.

c. The factitives (**197.** A. *d*) of this division are: **verschwenden** to squander; **senden** *to send*, lit. *to make go* from the lost str. intrans. **sinden** *to go*, from which there survives **Gesinde** (derivative of the lost **Sind** *journey*) *servants*, formerly *troops*, lit. those who journey with their prince in his military expeditions; **sengen** *to singe*, lit. *to cause to sing*, referring to the crackling noise of flames; **senken** to sink (trans.); **sprengen** to blow up, blast, to ride at full speed (originally trans., **ein Pferd sprengen** *to make a horse jump*, later construed as intrans. with **sein,** as the object was usually understood and finally not felt at all); **tränken** to give to drink, to cause to drink in (used of animals, persons, and materials: **Man tränkt das Vieh, ein Kind, die dürre Erde, Pflanzen, die Seele mit großen Empfindungen**); **wenden** to turn.

d. The nouns of this division made from the gradation of the past tense now show the vowel of the sing. and now the pl. vowel of the old past: **der Band** volume; **der Bund** alliance; **der Schwund** disappearance, &c.

2. Division. Gradation:

	Pres. (**177.** II. C, D. *b*, *c*)	Past	Perf. Part.
	ĭ, ĕ (**ĭ** in 2nd & 3rd sing.)	**ă** (subj. **ä̆** or **ö̆**)	**ŏ.**
M.H.G.	ĭ, ĕ (ĭ in sing. and ĕ in pl.)	ă-ŭ (**197.** A. *c*)	ŏ.

For an explanation of the change of vowel in the sing. of the present tense see **201.** *f.*

Examples: **spinnen, spann,** subj. **spänne** or **spönne, gesponnen; gelten (du giltst, er gilt), galt,** subj. **gölte** or **gälte, gegolten.**

Here belong: **beginnen** *to begin*, past **begann,** in early N.H.G. usually **begunde** (sometimes **begunte, begonste, beginnte, began, begun**), later **begunte, begon(n)te, begonn, begann,** perf. part. **begonnen,** in early N.H.G. **begunnen, begönt, begunt, begonnen; bersten (du birst** in choice language, in colloquial speech, perhaps, more commonly **berstest)** to burst, **barst,** sometimes **borst** and **berstete,** subj. **börste, bärste,** or **berstete,** perf. part. **geborsten; gelten (du giltst)** to be worth, pass for; **rinnen** to flow, run (of liquids); **schelten (du schiltst** or colloq. sometimes **scheltest)** to scold; **schwimmen** to swim; **sinnen** *to meditate*, in older German often with the meaning *to turn in thought toward*, from which survives **gesonnen** *turned in thought toward*, to be distinguished from **gesinnt** *disposed, minded*, derived directly from **Sinn** *bent of mind*: **Er ist übel gesinnt** *evil-minded*, but **Er ist gesonnen, es zu tun** *is willing, inclined*, or *intends to do it*; **spinnen** to spin; **gewinnen** to win.

a. In the earlier part of the N.H.G. period the M.H.G. *u* in the plural of the past indicative became *o* before *nn* and *mm* in accordance with a general phonetic law (see (**6**), p. 3), **sunnen, sünnen** (subjunctive) becoming **sonnen, sönnen.** In the other words of this group the plural vowel sometimes became **o** after the analogy of these words and under the influence of the **o** of their own perfect participle: **wir bursten** or **borsten.** This **o** then spread to the subjunctive (as in **börste**), which formerly had the same vowel as the plural of the indicative. The **u** and the **o** of the past indicative which were still used by Luther dropped out later entirely from the plural, or, speaking technically, the plural was "leveled" by the singular: **ich barst, wir barsten.** Occasionally, however, the plural vowel leveled the singular: **das Grundeis borst** (Bürger's *Lied v. br. Mann*). The **a** spread also to the subjunctive, so that there are now two forms, the older one in **ö** and the newer one in **ä: ich gölte** or **gälte.** The **ö** of the subjunctive tho warmly defended by the grammarians is slowly dying. This **ö** of the past subj. is most common in verbs with the stem vowel **e** in the present, as the new past subj. with the stem vowel **ä** is in these verbs identical in sound with the present: **gölte** better than **gälte,** as the latter form is the same in sound as the present **gelte.**

b. The factitives (**197.** A. *d*) are: **brennen (brannte, gebrannt)** *to burn* (trans. and intrans.), from the str. intrans. **brinnen** *to burn*, which earlier in the period belonged here, but is now replaced by **brennen,** which thus assumed the intrans. force of the parent word in addition to its own trans. meaning; **rennen (rannte, gerannt)** *to run* (dagger, &c.) *into* (trans.), *run* or *race* (intrans. with **sein,** originally trans., **ein Pferd rennen** *to make a horse run, race it,* later construed as intrans. as the object was usually understood and finally not felt at all), in the meanings *to curdle* (milk), *melt* (iron), *raft* (logs) always trans., usually with the principal parts **rennen, rennte, gerennt; schwemmen** *to wash away,* lit. *to make swim.*

3. Division. Gradation:

	Pres. (see **177.** II. C, D. *b, c*)	Past	Perf. Part.
	ĕ (ĭ in 2nd & 3rd sing.)	**ă**	**ŏ.**
M.H.G.	ĕ (ĭ in sing. and ĕ in pl.)	ă-ŭ (**197.** A. *c*)	ŏ.

For an explanation of the change of vowel in the sing. of the present tense see **201.** *f.*

Examples: **helfen (du hilfst, er hilft), half,** subj. **hülfe** or **hälfe, geholfen.** Except in case of **dreschen** the old past subj. with the stem vowel **ü** is still often, perhaps prevailingly, used, as the new form with the stem vowel **ä** is identical in sound with the form for the present tense.

Here belong: **bergen (du birgst)** to save; **dreschen (du drischest)** *to thrash,* past **dräsch** or almost or quite as commonly **drŏsch,** subj. usually **drŏsche,** past indic. sometimes **dräsch** and in that case to be placed in class IV; **helfen (du hilfst)** to help; **sterben (du stirbst)** to die; **verderben (du verdirbst)** to spoil (trans. and intrans.); **werben (du wirbst)** to enlist, woo; **werden** (see **177.** III. *c*) to become; **werfen (du wirfst)** to throw; the adjective **verworren** *in a state of disorder, confusion,* perf. part. of the lost **verwerren.** The related **verwirren** *to confuse* is entirely weak. Compare the adjective **verworren** with the wk. part. **verwirrt: Weil er ganz verwirrt war, war auch seine Rede verworren** *Because he was confused, his thoughts were in a state of disorder.* **Er ist verwirrt** *He is* (temporarily) *confused* (by something), but **Er ist verworren** *His thoughts are in a chronic state of disorder.*

a. Luther still used a different vowel in the sing. and pl. of the past tense as in M.H.G.: **ich starb, wir sturben** (sometimes **storben**).

b. The one factitive (**197.** A. *d*) is **verderben** *to cause to spoil, to spoil* (trans.), but usually now limited to spoil in a moral or a phonetical sense, that is, *to corrupt,* and in other senses now replaced by the str. **verderben: ein verderbtes Herz; ein verdorbener Magen.** But even in the moral sense the str. forms are common.

c. Notice the noun **der Wurf,** which still shows the pl. vowel of the old past tense of **werfen.** The nouns **Schall** *sound,* **Schmalz** *lard,* **Schwall** *swell* still show the old past tense sing. vowel **a** of the verbs **schellen** (now obsolete in pres. tense) to sound, **schmelzen** to melt, **schwellen** to swell, all of which have left this class for Class II.

201. IV. Class. Gradation:

	Pres. (see **177.** II. C, D. *b, c*)	Past	Perf. Part.
	ā, ĕ, ē,(**ĭ, ie** in 2nd & 3rd sing.), **ŏ**	**ā**	**ŏ, ō**
M.H.G.	ĕ (ĭ in sing. and ĕ in pl.)	ă-ā (**197.** A. *c*)	ŏ

For an explanation of the change of vowel in the sing. of the present tense see *f* below.

Examples: **brĕchen (du brĭchst, er brĭcht), brāch, gebrŏchen; erschrĕcken (du erschrickst, er erschrickt), erschrāk, erschrŏcken; trĕffen (du triffst, er trifft), trāf, getrŏffen; stēhlen, (du stiehlst, er stiehlt), stāhl, gestōhlen.** The *quantity* of the vowel is the same in the infinitive and perf. part. except in **nehmen.** The vowel of the past is always long. See also *a* below.

Here belong: **brĕchen (du brĭchst)** to break; **gebären (du gebierst,** often **gebärst)** to bear, bring forth, past sometimes wk.; **befehlen (du befiehlst)** III to command; **empfehlen (du empfiehlst)** III to recommend; **nehmen (du nimmst, er nimmt)** to take, **nahm, genommen; schrecken (du schrickst)** or more commonly **erschrecken** to be frightened, usually str. used intransitively or reflexively, but sometimes also wk. in both uses, often wk. instead of the more correct str. in compounds, as **aufschrecken** *to start up with fright,* **zurückschrecken** *to start back with fright,* and **zusammenschrecken** *to be overcome with fright;* **sprĕchen (du sprĭchst)** to speak; **stĕchen (du stĭchst)** to stick with a pointed instrument, sting, stab; **stecken (du stickst, er stickt,** common in the classical period but now usually replaced by the wk. forms **du steckst, er steckt)** *to remain sticking in*, intrans., past **stak** or perhaps more commonly **steckte**, perf. part. rarely **gestocken**, usually **gesteckt; stehlen (du stiehlst)** to steal; **treffen (du triffst)** to hit, **traf, getroffen; kommen (du kommst, kömmst,** the latter form common in the classics but now less frequent, especially in choice language) to come, **kam, gekommen.**

a. Those words that have double consonants or **ck** in the infin. and part. must drop one consonant or the **c** in **ck** in the past as the vowel is long. See examples.

b. **Befehlen, empfehlen, stehlen** have either **ö** or **ä** in the past subjunctive, preferably **ö** as it can be more easily distinguished from the **e** of the present subjunctive: **beföhle** or **befähle, empföhle** or **empfähle, stöhle** or **stähle.** Earlier in the period the past indicative often had the vowel **ō** after the analogy of the perfect participle. In English the perfect participle has thus leveled the past tense in almost all the words originally belonging to this class. See **199**, *Historical Note* (last par.). **Befehlen** and **empfehlen** were in earliest N.H.G. still in class III. Under the influence of the vowel of their perfect participle they then trended toward class II, as indicated above, and finally under the influence of **stehlen** became established for the most part here in class IV.

c. Here belongs **unverhohlen** *open, unconcealed*, adj. part. of the late M.H.G. verhëln, now replaced by the wk. **verhehlen** to conceal.

d. The factitives (**197.** A. *d*) are **erschrecken** *to frighten*, usually wk., but sometimes (as in case of the factitive **verderben** and others) is str. in colloquial language, as it is influenced by the str. intrans., as in **Du erschrickst ein'n aber auch** (Hauptmann's *Friedensfest*, 1); **quälen** *to torment*, from the lost **quelen** *to suffer pain* with the stem vowel **ä** instead of **e** as the verb is now felt as a derivative from the substantive **Qual** (see *e*); **stecken** (from **stechen;** see **197.** A. *d*) to make stick, stick (trans.)

e. Nouns are made from the gradation of the present tense: **der Befehl, der Schreck, der Stich,** &c. A number have the gradation of the past tense: **Die Sprāche, die Ausnahme, die Quāl** (from the lost **quelen** *to suffer pain*), &c. **Stachel** and its derivatives **stachelig, stacheln** have short **a**, the vowel of the old sing. In verbs this old gradation has disappeared, as the sing. was leveled by the pl. It remains, however, in mutated form in the factitives; see *d* above. Other nouns have **u**, which was once also the stem vowel of perf. part.: **der Bruch, die Geburt, die Ankunft,** &c. The old stem vowel of the part. suffered *a*-mutation (**197.** B), which was caused in an earlier period by the presence of an **a** (now **e**) in the participial suffix. The nouns originally belonged to the mutated **e**-plural class, and thus had **i** as the final vowel of their stems and were preserved from *a*-mutation. The effect of the original i in the stem can be still seen in the pl. in the *i*-mutation (see **26.** A) of most of these words: **der Bruch,** pl. **die Brüche.** The noun **der Brocken** *crumb* and the weak verb **brocken** *to crumb*, both from **brechen,** have, like the perfect participle, the vowel **ŏ.** The **k** was not shifted to **ch**, as it was doubled.

f. Change of Vowel in the Singular. Corresponding to M.H.G. short **i** of the first pers. sing. pres. indic. we find in N.G. and M.G. of the same period a long **e**, as in the Midland and North short **i** developed into long **e** in an open syllable, while in the closed syllables of the 2nd and 3rd pers. we find the old historic short **i: ich nēhme, du nĭmmst, er nĭmmt.** This change from **e** in the 1st pers. to **i** in the 2nd and 3rd pers. gradually became a fixed usage in the literary language. This type of inflection was facilitated by the similar change from unmutated vowel in the 1st pers. to mutated form in the 2nd and 3rd pers. in classes VI and VII. It was further supported by the N.G. and M.G. change from long **i** in open syllables to short **i** in closed syllables, as can still be heard in colloquial N.G.: **ich kriege, du krichst, er kricht** (see 4. *a. Note* (**1**) and **209**). In all these cases the vowel of the 1st pers. sing. was the same as the vowel of the plural and there was a change of vowel sound in the 2nd and 3rd pers. sing. This type influenced class II, so that the **ie** of the plural entered the 1st pers. sing.: **ich krieche, du kreuchst, er kreucht** (Luther). The type **ich kriege, du krichst** has never taken a deep root in the literary language. The type **ich krieche, du kreuchst** was once under M.G. influence widely used but later even in the Midland began to be replaced by the leveled type **ich krieche, du kriechst, er kriecht,** so that in the eighteenth century it was felt as poetic. The types **ich nehme, du nimmst; ich rate, du rätst** under M.G. influence have gradually become established in the literary language, not, however, without vigorous opposition in the South, where the former was in older German unknown and the latter never thoroly fixed. The older type without a change of vowel is still common in S.G. colloquial speech: **ich nimm, du nimmst, er nimmt; ich rat, du ratst,** &c.

Altho the literary language here rests upon N.G. and M.G., it has in matter of *quantity* gradually developed its own law. Instead of the N.G. change from a long vowel in the 1st pers. to a short sound in the 2nd and 3rd pers. the quantity usually remains thruout the inflection the same as in the plural: **ich lēse, du liest, er liest, wir lēsen; ich brĕche, du brĭchst, er brĭcht, wir brĕchen.** Where the vowel of the plural is now long the old short vowel of the 2nd and 3rd pers. sing. survives in only four verbs: **du nĭmmst, trĭttst, wĭrst, gĭbst** (in colloquial speech but in the choice language of the North and on the stage **gībst**), from **nēhmen, trēten, wērden, gēben.**

202. V. Class. Gradation:

Present (**177.** II. C, D. *b*, *c*)	Past	Perf. Part.
ĕ, ē, (ĭ, ie in 2nd and 3rd per. sing.), **ĭ, ie**	**ā**	**ĕ, ē**
M.H.G. ĕ (ĭ in sing. and ĕ in pl.), ĭ	ă-ā (**197.** A. *c*)	ĕ

1. Division. Gradation:
Pres. **ĕ, ē** (**ĭ, ie** in 2nd and 3rd sing.) Past **ā** Perf. Part. **ĕ, ē**

For an explanation of the change of vowel in the sing. of the present tense see **201.** *f.*

Examples: **ĕssen (du ĭssest** or **ĭßt, er ĭßt), āß** (pl. **wir āßen), gegĕssen; lēsen (du liesest** or **liest, er liest), lās, gelēsen.** The *quantity* of the vowel is the same in the infinitive and perf. part. The vowel of the past is always long.

Here belong: 1. In **e: essen (du issest** or **ißt, er ißt**; see also *a*) to eat; **fressen (du frissest, er frißt)** to eat (of animals or as animals); **geben (du gĭbst, er gĭbt)** to give; **genesen (du genesest,** earlier in the period **du geniesest)** to recover from sickness, earlier in the period occasionally wk. in the past tense and perf. part.; **geschehen (es geschieht,** in early N.H.G. **es geschicht)** to happen; **lesen (du liesest** or **liest, er liest)** to read; **messen (du missest** or **mißt, er mißt)** to measure; **sehen (du siehst, er sieht,** in early N.H.G. **du sĭchst, er sĭcht)** to see; **treten (du trittst, er tritt)** IV to step, tread; **vergessen (du vergissest** or **vergißt, er vergißt)** to forget; **sein** (which has replaced the regular **wesen** except in nouns, as **das Schulwesen** *the educational system,* and in part. adjectives, as **abwesend** *absent,* &c.) *to be,* **war, gewesen.**

a. The perfect participle of **essen** was in early N.H.G. **geessen,** and in contracted form **gessen.** Later the contracted form prevailed, but still later another **ge** was prefixed to it, as the first **ge** was no longer felt, the form thus becoming **gegessen.**

2. Those in **i, ie,** which do not show an interchange in 2nd and 3rd sing.: **bitten** to ask, beg, **bat, gebeten; liegen** to lie, **lag, gelegen; sitzen** to sit, **saß, gesessen.**:

General Note. **(1)** The factitives (**197.** A. *d*) are: **atzen** to feed (birds, animals, prisoners), **ätzen** to etch, feed (birds, &c.); **ergötzen** (corruption of **ergetzen**) *to amuse,* lit. *to cause to forget,* factitive of M.H.G. ergeȥȥen *to forget;* **legen** to lay; **nähren** (factitive of **nesen,** now only found in the form **genesen**; see **197.** A. *d*) to nourish, lit. to cause to recover or remain strong; **setzen** to set.

(2) **Atzung** and **Satz** have short **a,** the vowel of the old sing. of the past tense. Except in case of **atzen** verbs no longer show this old gradation, as the sing. vowel was leveled by the pl. It remains, however, in mutated form in the factitives **ätzen, setzen,** and in rounded form also **ergötzen.** In the other factitives it has become long, as it stands in an open syllable. See art. 4. *b. Note,* p. 13.

203. VI. Class. Gradation:

Present (**177.** II. B, D. *a*)	Past	Perf. Part.
ă, ā, (**ǟ, ä̆** in 2nd and 3rd sing.), **ē, ō̄**	**ū**	**ă, ā**

Example: **schlāgen (du schlǟgst, er schlǟgt), schlūg, geschlāgen; schăffen (du schăffst, er schăfft), schūf, geschăffen.** The perf. part. always has the same vowel as the infinitive except in case of **heben, schwören,** and **stehen.** The vowel of the past is always long.

Here belong: **bachen** (in early N.H.G. the literary word of the South and still used there) or **backen** (used by Luther and now the common literary word; **du bäckst** and now also not infrequently **backst, er bäckt, backt)** *to bake,* past tense **būch** (early N.H.G.), now **būk** or perhaps more commonly **backte,** perf. part. **gebachen** (early N.H.G.), now uniformly **gebacken** in this meaning, but in the North where there is a pronounced trend toward the weak forms there is also a weak perf. part. in the derived meaning *to cake, form a rigid mass,* as in **Eis und Schnee, die in der rauhen Rinde festgebackt waren; fahren (du fährst, er fährt)** to drive; **fragen (du fragst,** also **frägst** but less common than a little earlier in the period, **er fragt, frägt)** to ask, **fragte,** less commonly **frug,** perf. part. always **gefragt; graben (du gräbst, er gräbt)** to dig; **heben (du hebst, er hebt)** to raise, in early N.H.G. past **hub,** perf. part. **gehaben** (1 Cor. xv. 26), also sometimes wk. thruout, now usually in class II except in the past tense where we still not infrequently find the older **hub** alongside of the more common **hob,** which arose under the influence of **weben, wob** and since the 17th century has been gradually gaining ground; **jagen**[1] **(du jagst,** rarely **jägst, er jagt,** rarely **jägt)** to chase, hunt, **jagte,** rarely **jug, gejagt,** rarely **gejagen; laden (du lädst** or less commonly **ladest)** to invite (in this meaning properly

[1] The str. forms of **jagen** are earlier in the period sometimes employed in the literary language and still occur provincially, now usually with a different shade of meaning, being used in the derived meanings *to drive rapidly, dart, chase after, drive something before one*: **Ehe der Polizist die Nummer (des Wagens) merken konnte, jug** (shot, drove quickly) **der Bengel um die Ecke.**

wk. and still often so in the present, but usually found str. in the past and now always so in the perf. part.), to load (in this meaning str. except in the present tense, where the wk. unmutated forms are sometimes found); **mahlen** to grind, now entirely wk. except in part. **gemahlen,** in early N.H.G. str., **du mählst, er mählt,** past **muhl; schaffen** (**du schaffst, er schafft**), str. in the meaning *to create, produce,* wk. in the meaning *cause, bring about,* as this meaning is only the figurative application of the following meanings, which are always found with wk. form, but the str. form is also found as this meaning is quite similar to the preceding meaning, as in **Hier muß Wandel geschaffen werden** (Prof. Martin Havenstein in *Zeitschrift für Deutschkunde,* 1920, p. 46), always wk. in the meanings *to procure, bring to the spot, work, command* (in Bavarian dialect); **schlagen** (**du schlägst, er schlägt**) to strike; **schwören** (up to the 18th century usually **schweren**) to swear, past **schwur** or since the 17th century also but perhaps less commonly **schwor,** perf. part. **geschworen; stehen** (**du stehst, er steht**) to stand, in early N.H.G. there were also other forms in use, which still survive in certain S.G. dialects, the old indic. present **stā(h)** (**du stā(h)st**), the imperative **stand** and the subjunctive present **stande,** the last two forms representing the survivals of a longer stem in use in O.H.G. and still surviving in the literary language in the past tense forms **stund** (quite common earlier in the period) and the now usual form **stand,** past subjunctive **stände** and still quite frequently the older form **stünde,** and the perf. part. **gestanden,** which forms now serve as the past tense and the perf. part. of **stehen; tragen** (**du trägst, er trägt**) to carry; **wăchsen** (**du wăchsest or wăchst, er wăchst**) to grow; past **wŭchs,** perf. part. **gewăchsen; waschen** (**du wăschest** or **wăschst, er wăscht**), past **wŭsch,** perf. part. **gewăschen.**

a. The adj. **erhaben** *lofty,* lit. *lifted up,* is the old perf. part. of **erheben,** which has left this group for class II.

b. The one factitive (**197.** A. *d*) is **führen** (from **fahren**) to lead, guide.

204. VII. Class. Ablaut:

	Present (**177.** II. B, D. *a*)	Past	Perf. Part.
	ă, ā, au, ei, ō, ū	**ie, ĭ**	**ă, ā, au, ei, ō, ū**

1. Division. Gradation:	Pres.	Past	Perf. Part.
	ă, ā, aū, ei, ō, ū	**ie**	**ă, ā, au, ei, ō, ū**

Example: **halten (du hältst, er hält), hielt, gehalten.** The perf. part. always has the same vowel as the infin.

Here belong: **blasen** (**du bläst, er bläst,** rarely **du blasest, er blast**) to blow; **braten** (**du brätst, er brät,** sometimes **du bratst, er bratet**) to fry, roast, bake, past sometimes wk.; **fallen** (**du fällst**) to fall, **fiel, gefallen; halten** (**du hältst**) to hold; **hauen** (early N.H.G. **du heuest,** now **haust**) to hew, strike with a sword, switch, whip, to flog, chop, chisel in stone, &c., **hieb, gehauen** in choice language, in colloquial speech however the past tense is usually **haute** in certain expressions, as **Er haute seinen Bruder, Er haute mich an den Kopf, Er haute Holz, hieb** in others, as in **Er hieb mit dem Stock auf mich, Du hiebst mit ihm in dieselbe Kerbe, Er hieb dem Hunde die Ohren ab,** the perf. part. is **gehauen** in the North and the Southwest and **gehaut** in Bavaria and Austria; **heißen** (**du heißest** or **heißt, er heißt**) to bid, command, to be called, signify; **lassen** (in S.G. dialect and poetry still found contracted to **lan** as in earlier periods; **du lässest** or **läßt, er läßt**) to let, cause to, to have (something done); **laufen** (**du läufst**) *to run,* occasionally earlier in the period in the literary language and still often in popular speech with the past **loff** and perf. part. **geloffen** after the analogy of **saufen; raten** (**du rätst,** sometimes **ratst**) *to advise,* w. dat. of person and acc. of thing; **rufen** (**du rufst**) *to call* (somebody in), with acc., *to call out to some one,* with dat., earlier in the period also wk.; **schlafen** (**du schläfst**) to sleep; **stoßen** (**du stößest** or **stößt, er stößt;** in early N.H.G. also **du stoßest, er stoßt**) to thrust, push, kick. **Salzen** *to salt,* **spalten** *to split,* **schroten** *to grind coarse* have still a str. part. alongside of a wk. one, but are otherwise entirely wk.: **gesalzen** or now rarely **gesalzt, gespalten** or less commonly **gespaltet, geschroten**

or geschrotet. Entirely wk. is **schroten** to roll (casks, &c.). The strong past forms **spielt** and **schriet** occur in early N.H.G.

a. Here also belong: the adj. part. **bescheiden,** once part. of **bescheiden** *to instruct,* which has left this class for class I, 2nd division, now felt as an adj. with the general meaning *instructed,* hence *wise, sensible,* or more commonly *modest,* as it is felt as belonging to **sich bescheiden** *to be contented with*; the adj. part. **gefalten** *folded,* still found instead of the more common wk. form **gefaltet;** sometimes **geschmalzen** *greased, cooked in lard* (perf. part. of the otherwise wk. verb **schmalzen**) after the analogy of **gesalzen,** especially in the expression **weder gesalzen noch geschmalzen;** in popular language the past tense **kief** from **kaufen** *to buy* and the perf. part. **gemalen** from **malen** *to paint,* both of which in choice language are always wk.

b. The factitive is **fällen** *to fell.* Notice that the one factitive of this class, differing from those of the other classes, has the same vowel as the present tense.

c. Nouns: **der Fall** fall, **der Rat** advice, **der Ruf** call, **der Hieb** blow. &c.

2. Division. Gradation: Pres. **ă, ē** Past **ĭ** Perf. Part. **ă**

Example: **hangen (du hängst, er hängt), hing, gehangen.**

Here belong: **fangen (du fängst, er fängt;** in early N.H.G. also in the form of **fahen, du fehest, er fehet,** which still survive in poetry in the forms **fahen, du fähst, er fäht)** *to catch,* formerly also intrans. *to grasp after* and still occasionally so: **Unseliger, der nur die Angel ist, | mit der der Heide fäht nach deinem Volk** (Ludwig's *Makkabäer,* 2); **gehen (du gehst, er geht)** *to go,* in early N.H.G. there were also other forms in use, which still survive in certain S.G. dialects, the old indic. present **gā(h) (du gā(h)st),** the imperative **gang** (as in **Gangen's [gangen Sie] nur ruhig schlafen!** — Marriot's *Der geistliche Tod,* chap. I) and the subjunctive present **gange,** the last two forms representing survivals of a longer stem in use in O.H.G. and still surviving in the literary language in the past tense form **ging** and the perfect participle **gegangen,** which now serve as the past tense and the perfect participle of **gehen; hangen (du hängst, er hängt;** in early N.H.G. also **du hangst, er hangt)** or more commonly, but less correctly, **hängen (du hängst, er hängt)** *to hang* (intrans.), as it has become confounded with the trans. **hängen** (see *a*).

a. **Hängen** *to hang* is usually a weak transitive: **hängen, hängte, gehängt.** It has besides its wk. past **hängte** also the strong form **hing,** and besides its usual wk. perf. part. **gehängt** sometimes a strong perf. part. **gehangen,** a form once common. The str. trans. participle is becoming rare but it still occurs occasionally in good literature: **Glauben Sie, daß Sie dann nicht ebenso gut aufgehangen werden wie einer** (H. Hoffmann's *Rittmeister,* III, p. 105).

b. Nouns: **Der Hang** inclination, **der Fang** catch, **der Gang** walk.

c. The vowel of the past tense of this division was originally long, and the spelling **i** has only in comparatively recent years been generally recognized, the older spelling **ie** continuing long after the sound had become short. This shortening of the sound has split this class into two divisions. See also **4. 2. A.** *d.* **(2)** *Note.*

205. *Verbs formerly Strong.* Earlier in the period also the following verbs were strong which have since become weak or have disappeared: **bannen** (VII); **bauen** (VII), sometimes with strong participle (**gebauen**), now weak; **bellen** (III, II), now weak; **brauen** (II), sometimes with strong participle (**gebrauen**), now weak; **brinnen** (III), intransitive, now replaced by the irregular weak trans. **brennen,** now trans. and intrans.; **entbehren** (IV); **gellen** (III), the vowel of the old past tense still surviving in **Nachtigall; gleißen** (I); **greinen** (I), sometimes with a str. part., now usually wk.; **heischen** (VII), earlier in the period str. or wk., now wk. with the exception that a str. participle is sometimes found; **hinken** (III), str. part. sometimes still found in S.G.; **jäten** (V); **kneten** (V); **klieben** (II) to split; **kreischen** (I); **kriegen** (I; in early N.H.G. often in M.G. form: **kriegen,** past **kreig,** part. **(ge)kriegen,** later replaced by the wk. **kriegen)** to get; **nagen** (VI), the part. **genagen** still preserved in pop. language; **reuen** (II), in early N.H.G. still with a strong perf. part. **gerewen** or **gerawen; schaben** (VI), still with str. part. in S.G.; **schalten** (VII) to shove; **scherren** (III; Josh. vii. 21), now replaced by the wk. **scharren; schmiegen** (II); **schneien** (I); **schrimpfen** (III; Job vii. 5), now replaced by the wk. **schrumpfen; schweifen** (VII); **verseigen, versieg, versiegen** [Ps. cvii. 33], from the last form of which the wk. **versiegen** developed in the sixteenth century, later entirely supplanting the older **verseigen)** *to dry up*; **spannen** (VII); **walzen** (VII); **waten** (VI). Strong forms of these verbs have also appeared more or less frequently within the present period, but have now disappeared, or survive only in dialect or in an occasional participial form. Altho a few weak verbs have assumed strong forms as recorded under the different classes of strong verbs, the general tendency is toward the weak conjugation.

Note. In college slang just the opposite tendency is found, namely, for comical effect weak verbs are given strong forms: **bla'moren** for **bla'miert, eingebrungen** for **eingebracht, gedocken** for **gedeckt, gemorken** for **gemerkt, geschonken** for **geschenkt, geschumpfen** for **geschimpft, gewunken** for **gewinkt, überzogen** for **überzeugt.** Sometimes, however, an author or speaker conjugates a weak verb strong in all seriousness, as he has in this point been influenced by his native dialect, either following older usage or coining a new form after the analogy of a strong verb of similar form: **Die kleine Glocke auf der Kirche (wenige Schritte vor mir) ist eingeschnieen** (I; Swabian for **eingeschneit) und hat einen Klang wie Blei** (Mörike in a letter to Friedrich Kauffmann, dated Novem. 1827). **So spiesen** (a modern strong form according to class I following the analogy of similar forms, such as **weisen,** mostly confined to S.G. dialect) **wir denn vertraulich** (G. Keller, Werke, iii. 86).

206. *Conjugation of Strong Verbs in Compounds.* Strong verbs when compounded directly with some other word or prefix are conjugated as simple verbs: **erschlagen (du erschlägst)** to strike dead, **erschlug, erschlagen.** However, if the verb is compounded indirectly (see **217**), that is, when it is made from a compound noun the last component element of which is made from a str. verb, it is conjugated wk.: **ratschlagen** *to take counsel with,* made not from **rat** and the str. verb **schlagen,** but from the noun **der Ratschlag** *counsel,* past **ratschlagte,** perf. part. **geratschlagt;** thus also **radebrechen** *to break on the wheel,* derived from the noun **die Radebreche: Er radebrecht** (not **radebricht,** altho occasionally found in good authors) **das Deutsche** He speaks bad (lit. breaks on the wheel) German. See also **217.** *Note* 2.

Irregular Conjugation.

207. haben (in popular language contracted to **han**) *to have* is irregular in the pres. and past indic. and also in the past subj., which tho a wk. verb suffers mutation. For conjugation see **177.** III. *a.*

a. The obsolete reflexive **sich gehaben** *to behave one's self, find one's self* is entirely regular: **Er gehabt sich wohl** He is well. **Er gehabte sich besser.** Also **handhaben** *to handle* is entirely regular, as it is formed not from **haben,** but from the substantive **Handhabe** *handle.*

208. *Irregular Weak Verbs.* The so-called *irregular weak* verbs have a vowel in the past indic. and perf. part. differing from the vowel in the present, but are otherwise formed regularly according to the weak conjugation. They fall into two groups:—

1. Infinitive	Past Indic.	Past Subj.	Perf. Part.
brennen to burn	**brannte**	**brennte**	**gebrannt**

Here belong: **brennen; kennen** to be acquainted with; **nennen** to name, call; **rennen** *to run* (dagger, &c.) *into, run* (intrans.), *race,* sometimes in past tense and perf. part. **rennte, gerennt** instead of **rannte, gerannt,** and regularly so in certain other meanings, see **200.** 2. *b*; **senden** *to send,* past indic. **sandte** or **sendete,** perf. part. **gesandt** or **gesendet** (see *b*); **wenden** *to turn,* past indic. **wandte** or **wendete,** perf. part. **gewandt** or **gewendet** (see *b*).

a. *Unmutation.* These verbs had originally an **a** in the pres. tense, which according to **26.** A was mutated to **e** by a *j* or *i* that once stood between the stem and the inflectional ending of the present: N.H.G. **legen,** Gothic lagjan; N.H.G. **brennen,** Gothic brannjan. This *j* is the rule in most wk. verbs in Gothic. It disappeared early in O.H.G., but its effects can still be seen as in the preceding examples in the mutated vowel of the stem. The connecting vowel *i* that once stood between the stem and the inflectional ending in the past indic. and perfect participle of wk. verbs was in O.H.G. in certain verbs syncopated, which resulted in *unmutation,* i.e. a return to the original vowel as the stem was no longer affected by the *i*: (*a*) leggen, legita, gilegit, but (*b*) brennen, branta, gibrant, also gibrennit. Most wk. verbs formerly belonging to *b* now retain, as the result of leveling from the infinitive and the second form of the perfect participle, the mutated vowel thruout, only the few words in the above list now following *b.* In early N.H.G., however, the number in the latter class was greater, especially in Luther's language and in M.G. in general: **setzen, satzte, gesatzt,** also **gesetzet,** now **setzen, setzte, gesetzt.** This leveling has largely resulted from Bavarian and Austrian influence, where the mutated form of the perfect participle in *b* had begun already in the thirteenth century to supplant the unmutated form. In the fourteenth and fifteenth centuries the mutated vowel gradually gained the ascendency and spread to the past tense. The unmutated forms, **brannte, rannte,** &c. indicate the influence of Middle German, which here retained the older form. The mutated vowel, however, under the influence of the weak group in 2 below, found favor in the subjunctive: **brennte,** &c. This M.G. feature of distinguishing indicative and subjunctive in the past tense of this weak group in contrast to the general usage of not distinguishing them in the weak past has become established in the literary language. Unmutation here in the perfect participle is also due to M.G. influence. A few fossilized adjective participles still show the old unmutated form of the perfect participle, which was once preferred in adjective function: **durchlaucht** and **erlaucht** from **leuchten; gedackt** from **decken; gelahrt** (now only used in archaic, solemn, or comic style) from **lehren,** which after the analogy of the verbs in (*b*) once, especially in M.G. and L.G., had the parts **lehren, lahrte, gelahrt; getrost** from **trösten; mißgestalt, ungestalt,** and **wohlgestalt** from **stellen,** &c.

b. Earlier the forms **sandte, wandte** and **gesandt, gewandt** were more common than the mutated forms **sendete, wendete,** and **gesendet, gewendet.** At present, however, both forms can be quite freely used except in certain expressions where the newer mutated or the older unmutated forms have become fixed. Thus we say **ein gewendeter** (renovated, lit. turned) [not now **gewandter**] **Rock.** The old forms are especially firm in the words **Gesandter** *ambassador,* **gewandt** *skilful, clever,* **bewandt** *such,* **verwandt** *related.*

2. Infinitive	Past Indic.	Past Subj.	Perf. Part.
bringen to bring	**brachte**	**brächte**	**gebracht**
denken to think	**dachte**	**dächte**	**gedacht**
dünken to seem	{ **dünkte** / **deuchte (däuchte)**	{ **dünkte** / **deuchte (däuchte)**	{ **gedünkt** / **gedeucht**

Note. In early N.H.G. we find the forms **dünken, dunken** (now obsolete), **es daucht** (after the analogy of the past **dauchte;** now obs.), past **dauchte** (now obs.), subj. **deuchte,** perf. part. **gedaucht** (now obs.). The present tense forms **dünken** and **dunken** spread to the past and perf. part.: **dünkte** (now very common) or **dunkte** (now obs.), **gedünkt** (now very common) or **gedunkt** (now obs.). The form of the very common past subj. **deuchte** spread to the present tense: **es deucht** (a little earlier in the period very common and still not infrequent) or **deuchtet** (now rare) with the infinitive **deuchten** (now rare). This new infinitive produced the new past **deuchtete** (now rare). The new present tense form **deucht** transformed the original past indic. **dauchte** and perf. part. **gedaucht** into **deuchte, gedeucht.** The grammarians usually recommend the forms given in 2 above. The tendency to-day is to level: **dünken, dünkte, gedünkt.**

209. The verb **kriegen** *to get* is inflected regularly in choice language, but usually in the loose colloquial language of the North and Midland under the influence of dialect **ie** becomes **i** in a closed syllable, hence in the 2nd and 3rd pers. sing. of the present tense and thruout the past tense and also in the perf. part: **ich kriege, du kriegst** (pro. **krĭchst**), **er kriegt** (pro. **krĭcht**), **ich kriegte** (pro. **krĭchte**), **gekriegt** (pro. **gekrĭcht**). See **4. 1.** *a. Note,* **205,** and **201.** *f.*

210. The verb **tun** *to do* is very irregular: present **ich tue, du tust, er tut, wir tun, ihr tut, sie tun.** The subjunctive present is regular: **ich tue, du tuest, er tue, wir tuen, ihr tuet, sie tuen.** The past indicative is **tat,** subjunctive **täte,** perfect participle **getan.**

a. In early N.H.G. and still in poetic or humorous language the past tense forms **tät** (same as M.H.G. *tēt* and hence at present misspelled), pl. **täten,** are often used instead of the usual **tat,** pl. **taten,** at present, however, only when employed in connection with a following infinitive as a mere periphrasis for a simple form of the verb (see **185.** B. I. 2. *e.* (**2**)): **Vnd die Kinder Israel theten alles wie der Herr Mose geboten hatte** (Exodus xxxix. 32). **Er tät nur spöttisch um sich blicken** (Uhland) = **Er blickte nur spöttisch um sich.**

Note. In M.H.G. the past tense was *tët(e)* in the sing. and *tāten* in the plural. Later in the literary language the plural vowel passed over into the singular. Alongside of these forms we find, as described above, the forms **tät,** pl. **täten,** which have resulted from the leveling of the plural by the singular.

211. For the irregular **werden** see **177.** III. *c;* other irregularities in str. verbs under the gradating groups, **198–206.**

Past-Present Verbs.

212. 1. Among the most irregular verbs are the Past-Present verbs. Their present tense tho present in meaning has the form of the past tense of str. verbs and even to-day preserves the peculiarities of the medieval past tense better than any other word except **werden.** These evident marks of the past tense are: *a.* The 1st and 3rd pers. sing. are alike. *b.* The sing. and pl. vowels are different as was once the rule for the past tense, and still show in part the gradation classes to which they once belonged. *c.* The vowel of the subj. is the mutated vowel of the pl. indic. which was once the rule for the past subj., as can still be seen in the past subj. of **werden** (past subjunctive **ich würde,** past indicative **ich ward,** pl. **wir wurden**). The mutated forms of the present indicative plural, as **wir müssen, dürfen,** &c., are in fact subjunctive forms, as the latter mood has leveled here the former. These mutated forms have become established in the infinitive wherever they are found in the indicative: **dürfen** (infin.), **wir dürfen,** &c. After the old past had come to be used as a present the weak past was employed to express past time.

2. These verbs are: **wissen** *to know, know how to, be able to,* and the six auxiliaries of mood: **dürfen** *to be allowed*; **können** *to be able* (*can*); **mögen** *to like, to desire to* (also often expressing a possibility or a concession = *may*); **müssen** *to be compelled, to have to* (*must*); **sollen** expressed in English by *shall, ought to, am* (*is*) *to, is said to,* &c.; **wollen** (see *g*) *to be willing to, to be about to, to desire to,* &c. They are inflected as follows:

Present Indicative.

ich weiß	**darf**	**kann**	**mag**	**muß**	**soll**	**will**
du weißt	**darfst**	**kannst**	**magst**	**mußt**	**sollst**	**willst**
er weiß	**darf**	**kann**	**mag**	**muß**	**soll**	**will**
wir wissen	**dürfen**	**können**	**mögen**	**müssen**	**sollen**	**wollen**
ihr wißt	**dürft**	**könnt**	**mögt**	**müßt**	**sollt**	**wollt**
sie wissen	**dürfen**	**können**	**mögen**	**müssen**	**sollen**	**wollen**

Present Subjunctive.

ich wisse	**dürfe**	**könne**	**möge**	**müsse**	**solle**	**wolle**
du wissest	**dürfest**	**könnest**	**mögest**	**müssest**	**sollest**	**wollest**
er wisse	**dürfe**	**könne**	**möge**	**müsse**	**solle**	**wolle**
wir wissen	**dürfen**	**können**	**mögen**	**müssen**	**sollen**	**wollen**
ihr wisset	**dürfet**	**könnet**	**möget**	**müsset**	**sollet**	**wollet**
sie wissen	**dürfen**	**können**	**mögen**	**müssen**	**sollen**	**wollen**

Past Indicative.

ich wußte, durfte, konnte, mochte, mußte, sollte, wollte.

Past Subjunctive.

ich wüßte, dürfte, könnte, möchte, müßte, sollte, wollte.

Perfect Participle.

gewußt, gedurft, gekonnt, gemocht, gemußt, gesollt, gewollt.

The participle of **mögen** and **müssen** is only rarely **gemöcht** and **gemüßt: Wir hatten viele (Offiziere) nacheinander; doch habe ich nie einen gemöcht** (*Tagebücher des Grafen August von Platen,* p. 14). **Und wer von der Liebsten scheiden gemüßt** (Scheffel's *Trompeter,* Werners Lieder aus Welschland, XII).

The compound tenses are formed regularly (see also *e*):

Pres. Perfect.	**ich habe gewußt, gedurft, gekonnt, gemocht,** &c.
	ich habe (kommen) dürfen, können, &c. (but not **wissen;** see *b*).
Past Perfect.	**ich hatte gewußt, gedurft, gekonnt, gemocht,** &c.
	ich hatte (kommen) dürfen, können, mögen, &c.
Future.	**ich werde wissen, dürfen, können, mögen,** &c.
Future Perfect.	**ich werde gewußt haben, gedurft haben,** &c.
	ich werde haben (kommen) dürfen, können, &c.
Past Periphrastic Subjunctive.	**ich würde wissen, dürfen, können, mögen,** &c.
Past Perfect Periphrastic Subjunctive.	**ich würde gewußt haben, gedurft haben,** &c.
	ich würde haben (kommen) dürfen, können, &c., or
	ich hätte (kommen) dürfen, können, &c.

a. The imperatives and present participles are either deficient or rarely used. **Wissen** and **wollen** alone have an imperative: **wisse,** &c., **wolle,** &c. In popular language the imperative **will** (instead of **wolle**) is heard and is sometimes also found in literature (in Auerbach, Grillparzer).

The present participle is formed regularly: **wissend, könnend,** &c. With the exception of the participle of **wissen,** however, these forms are rarely found. The present participles of the modal auxiliaries are only used in connection with a dependent infinitive, as illustrated in **184.** *f*, and in the case of a few derivatives and compounds, in the most part adjectives, as **bedürfend** *requiring, in need of*, **vermögend** *wealthy*, **wohlwollend** *well-wishing*. Also the participial substantive **der Wollende** *the one that wills* is used.

b. The modal auxiliaries (not including **wissen**) do not use the weak perf. participle given above when an infinitive depends upon them in a compound tense, but a form exactly like the infinitive, for which construction see **178.** 2. B. *a* and *Note* 1 thereunder. Thus the construction of **wissen** differs from that of the other past-present verbs: **Er hat zu antworten gewußt** *He knew how to answer*, but **Er hat antworten können** *He was able to answer*.

c. Note that **wissen** and **vermögen** (see **185.** B. I. 2. *a. Note* 1) are the only past-present verbs that require **zu** before the dependent infin.: **Er weiß sich nicht zu halten** *He is not able to contain himself*, but **Er muß arbeiten** *He has to work*. However, the infinitive without **zu** is also used after **wissen,** but with a different meaning. See **185.** B. I. 2. *d*.

d. Earlier in the period in the Southwest the third person of the present tense of **wissen** sometimes assumed **t, weiß** becoming **weißt** after the analogy of words in the regular present tense: **Der seine Burg zu schirmen weißt** (in rime with **Geist**) (Wieland's *Gedichte*, p. 98). In early N.H.G. and as late as the classical period the forms **du sollt** and **willt** are found, now always **du sollst, willst.** Cf. Eng. shalt, wilt. In early N.H.G. also other forms occur, which have since disappeared in the literary language: **durfen** and **dorfen** for **dürfen, dorfte** and **dörfte** for **durfte** and **dürfte; künnen** for **können, kunde, kunte,** or **kunt** for **konnte; mügen** for **mögen; wellen** and **wöllen** for **wollen.**

e. In an earlier period of the language the German, like the English of the present day, could not form a perf. participle from the modal auxiliaries. The older German had to express the pres. perfect by putting the dependent infinitive into the perfect tense, and the past perfect by placing the past indic. of the auxiliary before the perfect infinitive of the dependent verb: ich kan getragen haben, now **ich habe tragen können;** ich kunde getragen haben, now **ich hatte tragen können;** ich künde getragen haben, now **ich hätte tragen können.** When the new forms were introduced the old forms did not drop out, but remained, often, however, with a new shade of meaning: **Er kann gesprochen haben** *He may have spoken*, but **Er hat sprechen können** *He has been able to speak.* **Er konnte schon gesprochen haben** *It was possible that* (at that time) *he had already spoken*, but **Er hatte schon sprechen können** *He had already been able to speak.* **Er könnte gesprochen haben** *He might possibly have spoken*, but **Er hätte sprechen können** *He would have been able to speak.* The English-speaking student must be cautious here, as there are pitfalls for him at almost every step. We must not translate *He should have done it* literally by **Er sollte es getan haben,** as the German *may* mean: *He was said to have done it.* The German form should be **Er hätte es tun sollen. Er könnte gekommen sein** corresponds to the English *He could have come* only in the sense that *it is a possibility that he has come.* If we mean that *it would have lain in his power to come* we must say **Er hätte kommen können.** Occasionally the old and new constructions are used without differentiation: **Ich sollte vorsichtiger gewesen sein,** or more commonly **Ich hätte vorsichtiger sein sollen.**

f. In early N.H.G. there were two other past-present verbs:

(1) Tügen (now **taugen,** entirely wk.) with the following principal parts: (pres.) **ich taug, er taug, wir tügen;** past **ich tuchte,** (subj.) **tüchte,** (ge)**tucht.** Ex.: **Moses sprach | Das taug nicht | das wir also thun** (Exodus viii. 26). Derivatives are **tüchtig** and **Tugend.**

(2) Thüren (now obs.) *to dare* (same word as Eng. dare) with the following principal parts: **ich thar, er thar, wir thüren,** past **ich thurste.** Later it was replaced by **dürfen,** which in turn has been replaced in this meaning by **wagen** and **sich unterstehen.**

g. From the standpoint of historical grammar **wollen** is not a past-present verb. It is, however, now justly classed here upon the basis of its present forms, which are those of past-present verbs. The present indicative was originally a past subjunctive, which formerly had the force of the past subjunctive of cautious statement (see **169.** 2. A. (**1**). *c*) as used to-day. Thus this original past subjunctive had the meaning of **ich wünschte wohl.** Later it took on the force of a present indic. and the forms of past-present verbs, as it was on account of its meanings under the influence of the past-present verbs.

Special Uses of the Modal Auxiliaries.

213. 1. Dürfen. *a.* A permission from someone to do something, or a right, cause, or liberty to so do, in so far as there is nothing in the dictate of circumstances or moral obligation or any authority to restrain or forbid: **Du darfst nicht hingehen** You are not allowed to go there. **Gefangene dürfen mit niemand verkehren** Prisoners are not allowed to associate with anybody. **Jedermann darf Waffen tragen** Everybody is permitted to carry arms. **Darf ich darauf rechnen, Sie morgen bei mir zu sehen? Er darf sich darüber nicht wundern** He must not (has no right, cause to) wonder at it. **Wir dürfen unsere Pflichten nicht vergessen** We should not forget our duties. **Wir dürfen es schon unseres Rufes wegen nicht tun** We cannot do this out of consideration for our reputation, *to say nothing about other things* (all in **schon**). This leads to the very frequent use of **dürfen** in negative sentences corresponding to **müssen** in positive form: **Ihr dürft nicht laut schreien!** Children, you must not scream out loud. **Müssen** here has a milder force. See 4. *c* below. The past subjunctive softens the force of **dürfen: Bald dürfte ich nicht!** (Lessing's *Minna*, 1, 2) I almost ought not to!

b. Need only to, need but: **Er darf nur winken, so sind wir da** He need but make a sign and we shall be there. **Sie dürfen nur klingeln** You need only to ring. **Sie dürfen nur befehlen** You need only to speak, to command.

c. The past subj. (potential; see **169.** 2. A. (**1**). *c*) is much used to state **in a modest way** something that one is pretty sure is or will be true: **Jetzt dürfte es zu spät sein** Now it is probably too late. **Es dürfte ein Leichtes sein** It would probably be an easy matter.

Note. Synonymous with **dürfen** in this connection are **können** and **mögen** with distinct shades of difference. **Können** denotes a mere possibility, **mögen** a probability or likelihood, **dürfen** a rather positive assertion, but stated politely: **Man könnte Sie fragen** One might question you. **Man möchte Sie fragen** You will likely be questioned. **Man dürfte Sie fragen** I warn you, you will be questioned.

d. Rarer meanings occur: (**1**) In early N.H.G. *to need*, now replaced by **bedürfen: Die Gesunden dürffen des Artztes nicht** (Luke v. 31). This is the original meaning, and still survives in **dürftig** *needy*, **bedürfen** *to need*, **Bedürfnis** *need.* (**2**) In early N.H.G. and still in the classical period and even later in negative sentences and questions *to need, have occasion for*, now replaced by **brauchen: Vor mir dürfen Sie sich Ihres Unglücks nicht schämen** (Lessing's *Minna*, 1, 6). **Wollte Gott sich deiner erbarmen, mein armes Herz, daß du nicht immer Schmerzen ausstehen dürftest!** (Bismarck an seine Frau, March 3, 1851). (**3**) In early N.H.G it replaced in part the obsolescent **thüren** (see **212.** 2. *f.* [2]) *to dare*: **Wie habt jr das thun dürffen** (Gen. xliv. 15). Luther retained **thüren** in a large number of cases, but the later revisions substituted **dürfen.** Compare Luther's translation of Matth. xxii. 46 with a revised edition. In our own day **dürfen** rarely occurs in this meaning, but is replaced here by **wagen** and **sich unterstehen.**

2. **Können. A. Ability or power: Er kann gut reiten** He can ride well. **Der Kranke kann nicht gehen.**

Note. In this sense alone is **vermögen** synonymous with **können**, only differing from it in being stronger and in requiring **zu** with the infin.: **Er war zu schwach, er vermochte nicht die Mitteilung zu Ende zu hören,** or **er konnte die Mitteilung nicht zu Ende hören.** In early N.H.G. the infin. depending upon **vermögen** is also without **zu.**

a. Often, *cannot bear to*: **Sie kann kein Blut sehen.**

b. Notice the idiomatic use of **nicht umhin können = müssen,** requiring **zu before the dependent** infin.: **Er konnte nicht umhin zu lächeln** He could not help smiling.

B. *Possibility* in the broad sense, that which is contingent upon circumstances, and often *probability* and in this sense synonymous with **mögen** in A, but more common than the latter in the pres. tense and not so common in the past: **Der Brief kann vor Dienstag nicht dort sein. Er kann jeden Augenblick da sein. Ich glaub', es kann wohl heute noch schneien. Verdamme ihn nicht, er kann** (may) **noch unschuldig sein. Sie können** (may) **mich morgen erwarten.**

Note. Observe the difference in meaning between the pres. of **können** with the perf. infin. and the pres. perf. of **können: Er kann den Brief geschrieben haben** He may have written the letter. **Er hat den Brief schreiben können** He has been able to write the letter. Notice also the difference between **Er könnte es getan haben** *He might have done it* (i.e. it is possible that he has done it) and **Er hätte es tun können** *He would have been able to do it.*

C. *Permission*, arising from the idea that something can be done, as there are no hindrances in the way: **Meinetwegen kann er kommen** As far as I am concerned he may come. **Von acht bis neun Uhr können wir noch in dem Garten ein wenig spazieren gehen. Sie können jetzt gehen.**

D. It often contains in polite form *instructions, directions, a request*, or even a *mild command*: **Ich habe jetzt nicht Zeit für euch, ihr könnt aber morgen wieder einmal nachfragen** I have not time for you to-day, but you might inquire again to-morrow. **Du könntest** (or in still stronger language **kannst**) **mir eigentlich das lästige Geschäft abnehmen** I think you might take this troublesome piece of business off my hands. A mild command: **Du kannst gehen** You may go. **Er kann gehen** Let him go. It sometimes contains a reproach: **Du kannst** (or **könntest**) **immer auch einmal mit angreifen!** I think you might take a hold and help us a little bit! **Das kannst du selber machen!** I think you might do that yourself!

E. Good grounds or reasons or good opportunity for an action: **Darauf können Sie stolz sein** You can well be proud of that. **Kann** (or **darf**) **ich nun anfangen?** Should I begin now? (Are things favorable for action?)

F. Also used as an independent transitive verb with noun or pronoun as object in the sense of *to know* or *understand thoroly, to be at home in*, which is the original meaning: **Er kann das Lied auswendig** He knows the song by heart. **Der kann etwas** That fellow understands his business. **Können sie Deutsch?** Can you speak German? **Der Schüler kann seine Vokabeln** The pupil knows his vocabulary. **Können Sie Klavier?** Can you play upon the piano? **Er kann sehr gut Französisch.**

Note 1. Here belongs the expression **Was kann ich dafür?** How can I help it, how can I be blamed for it? It has here changed the original idea of *being able to do something for* to that of *blame for not doing something.* Thus also: **Er kann nicht dafür** It is not his fault. **Was kann sie für ihre Mutter?!** (Franzos's *Der Gott des alten Doktors*, p. 142) How can she be held responsible for her mother being what she is?!

Note 2. Distinguish carefully between **können** to know something thoroly, to know by heart, to have a fair degree of skill or proficiency in something, **wissen** to know facts, **kennen** to know or be acquainted with persons or also those things which like persons can be recognized by certain characteristics: **Sie können Deutsch** They can speak German. **Die können ihre Sache** They understand thoroly the matter they have in hand. **Er kann das Einmaleins** He knows by heart the multiplication table. **Ich weiß, wo er wohnt** I know where he lives. **Ich weiß sein Haus** I know where his house is. **Ich kenne ihn gut** I know him well. **Ich kenne sein Haus** I am acquainted with the outside or inside or both outside and inside arrangements of his house. **Das Kind kennt die Buchstaben noch nicht** The child cannot distinguish the letters yet. **Ich kenne diese Melodie** This tune is familiar to me. **Das kennt man schon!** We know all about that, i.e. we have had experience in that matter.

G. Also as an intransitive verb in the sense of *to have the power, skill*: **„Du willst also?" „Mach' mich können, so will ich"** (Goethe). **Um zu können, mußt du in jedem Fall tun, um zu wissen, darfst du dich in vielen Fällen nur leidend verhalten** (Pestalozzi).

3. **Mögen.** A. Probability, plausibility, that which rests with more or less probability on facts, but which is after all only supposition, conjecture (see **können**, B): **Es ist unrecht, daß er nicht geantwortet hat, aber er mag krank sein** It is not right that he has not answered, but it may be that he is sick. **Er hat es keinem gesagt, er mag's wohl geheim halten wollen** He has told no one, he may probably desire to keep it a secret. **Das mag wohl sein** That may be. **Es mag wahr sein. Es mag jetzt zwölf sein** It may be 12 o'clock. **Sie mochte fühlen, daß sie mir unrecht getan** She probably felt that she had done me injustice. **Es mochte wohl Mitternacht sein** It might have been about midnight. **Er mag das gesagt haben** He may possibly have said that. Usage is here confined to the positive statement. In negative form **können** is used here: **Es kann nicht wahr sein. Kann das wahr sein?** (with negative force).

a. It is much used in the past subjunctive (potential) to state modestly something as probable, plausible (see also **dürfen**, *c. Note*): **Es möchte wohl besser sein, wenn wir es unterließen** It would probably be better if we did not do it. **Das möchte schwer zu beweisen sein** That might be hard to prove. **Daraus möchte wohl nichts werden** That is likely enough to fail.

B. To indicate that something is granted, allowed, at least that no objection will be raised on the part of the speaker, and from this arises the idea of concession in general, which is much used in subordinate concessive clauses: **Das mag er immerhin tun, was kümmert's mich?** Let him do it, what matters it to me? **Mögen die Leute reden, was sie wollen** Let people say what they will. In subordinate clause: **Was ich auch tun mag, so ist es dir nicht recht** No matter what I do, I can't satisfy you.

C. Akin to the preceding is the idea of *inclination, liking*, in this meaning also used as an independent transitive verb with a noun or pronoun as object: **Ich mag ihn jetzt nicht sehen** I do not care to see him now. As a transitive verb: **Ich mag diese Radieschen nicht. Vielleicht mögen Sie lieber Gurken** I do not like these radishes. Perhaps you like cucumbers better. **Mögen** is often strengthened by the adverb **gern: Ich habe nie gern tanzen mögen** I never liked to dance.

a. The subjunctive is much used in wishes in independent clauses with different meaning according as present or past tense is employed (**168.** I. 1. B, and **169.** 1. A). The present subjunctive is also used in mild commands direct and indirect. See **177.** I. B. *a*; **171.** 4. *a.* The present indicative and subjunctive are used in warnings and menaces: **Er mag nur aufpassen, sonst passiert ein Unglück** He should be on the look-out or some misfortune will happen. **Er möge sich hüten, mich zu reizen** Let him beware of provoking me.

b. The subjunctive of **mögen** is in indirect discourse often used instead of the subjunctive of the simple verb, especially after verbs of wishing, fearing, doubting: **Wir wünschten, daß er komme** or **kommen möge.**

c. The past and past perfect subjunctive (potential), the former with *present*, the latter with *past* force, differ from the indicative in meaning in that not the mere record of a strongly pronounced desire or a habitual inclination is made, but especial attention is called to that which at the time and under the circumstances the subject *feels inclined* or *would like* to do: **Fast möchte ich weinen** I almost feel like crying. **Ich möchte spazieren gehen** I should like to go out walking. **Ich hätte es ihm nicht sagen mögen** I should not have liked to tell it to him. **Da hätte er in den Boden sinken mögen** Then he felt as tho he would like to sink thru the floor.

The subjunctive of modest statement (**169.** 1. A, 3rd par.) is much used to state a wish modestly: **Ich möchte Sie um ein Stückchen Hammelschlegel bitten, nur zum Versuchen** I will thank you for a small piece of the leg of mutton, just to try it.

D. Its oldest meaning, that of *power* and *ability*, it has given over to **vermögen** in ordinary prose, but this meaning can still be found in elevated diction: **O lieb', so lang du lieben kannst** (can find an opportunity)! **O lieb', so lang du lieben magst** (are able)! (Freiligrath). This meaning occurs frequently still in the noun **(die) Macht** *might* and the adj. **möglich** *possible*, which have been derived from it.

a. After the analogy of **vermögen** (see 2. *Note* above) the infinitive with **zu** is in a few rather rare instances used here with **mögen** instead of the simple infinitive, especially when the infinitive precedes the auxiliary: **Die Gefahr von ihr zu wenden magst du ganz allein** (Goethe's *Die natürliche Tochter*, 2, 1).

4. **Müssen.** *a. Necessity* in the broad sense, either physical compulsion or that constraint which is imposed by the stress of circumstances, or lies in the very nature of things, or that which appears to the mind as necessary, appropriate, or belonging to the natural order of things, hence corresponding to the English words *must, have to, obliged to, ought to, need to*: **Das Kind mußte zu Bette gehen** The child had to go to bed. **Er handelt, wie er muß** He acts as he ought to do under the circumstances. **Du kommst nicht mit, denn du hast keine Kleider und kannst nicht tanzen; wir müßten uns deiner schämen** (we should indeed under the circumstances have to feel ashamed of you). **Kinder müssen bescheiden sein** In the natural order of things children ought to be modest. **Effi** (name), **eigentlich hättest du doch wohl Kunstreiterin werden müssen** (ought). **Mußt du denn alles wissen?** Do you need to know everything? Also translated in various other ways: **Wir mußten uns freuen** We could not but rejoice. **Ich mußte lachen** I could not help laughing. It is much used in commands. See **177.** I. B. *a.*

It often denotes a logical or inferred necessity: **Ihr Gesicht war regelmäßig und der Ausdruck desselben verständig; sie mußte in ihrer Jugend schön gewesen sein** She must have been, &c. **(Besieht ihn [i.e. den Brief]) Wahrhaftig, er ist erbrochen. Wer muß ihn denn**

erbrochen haben? (Lessing's *Minna*, 3, 10) Somebody must have broken it open, who could it be?

Note. Observe the difference of meaning between the pres. of **müssen** with the perf. infin. and the perf. tense of **müssen**: **Er muß vorbeigegangen sein** *He must have passed by*, but **Er hat vorbeigehen müssen** He was compelled to pass by. The simple past subjunctive and the periphrastic past subjunctive have in most auxiliaries about the same meaning where both forms can be used, but in **müssen** the meaning is often differentiated: **Du müßtest ihm helfen** *You ought to help him*, but **Du würdest ihm helfen müssen** *You would be obliged to help him*.

b. It often conveys the idea that the circumstance or happening in question is untoward, unfortunate, resulting in discomfiture to the person in question, translated by *unfortunately to happen to, to have of course to, it must needs be*: **Gerade ihn mußte ich treffen!** Whom should I unfortunately happen to meet but him!, or more idiomatically: Of course I had to run across him. **Und ich mußte so fern sein!** And bad luck would have it that I just happened to be so far away! **Mein Hund war ohne Maulkorb hinausgelaufen. Nun mußte auch gerade ein Polizist daher kommen** Now as bad luck would have it a policeman happened to come along just at that time, or Of course a policeman had to come along just then. **Es mus ja ergernis komen | doch weh dem Menschen | durch welchen ergernis kompt** (Matth. xviii. 7).

c. Just as in English the meaning *to be permitted, ought* is found in negative sentences, as in case of **dürfen** in 1. *a* above but with milder force: **Ich muß nicht vergessen, den Bettel zu vernichten** (Lessing's *Minna von Barnhelm* 1, 7) I must not forget to destroy the trifle. **„Ach," sagte Elisabeth, „das weiß ich ja auswendig; du mußt auch nicht immer dasselbe erzählen"** (Storm's *Immensee*, Die Kinder).

This old meaning of **müssen** comes close to the original one, *to find one's self in a situation to, have opportunity to, be free to, have occasion to.* Also the use in *b* approaches this sense with the additional idea that the result is unpleasant to the party in question. Later, as in *a*, the idea arose that the situation in which the subject finds himself is forced upon him, and that he has to act, not in accordance with his wishes, but under the stress of circumstances. The original meaning of **müssen** occurs not infrequently in early N.H.G. in different stages of development. In optative sentences the original force is still found in the classical period: **So müsse** (now **möge**) **mir Gott helfen** (Schiller). It is also still quite commonly found here in accordance with *a* above, where the wisher expresses the desire that somebody may be forced to suffer something: **Müsse der elend umkommen, dem je besser von dir begegnet würde als mir** (P. Heyse's *L'Arrabbiata*). **Wären wir Bettler! Müßten wir barfuß durch die Frühlingsnacht wandern!** (R. Huch's *Vita somnium breve*, I, p. 7).

The related noun **Muße** *leisure* has retained more of the original meaning than the verb, and has developed in quite a different direction.

d. It is also used as an intransitive verb in the sense of *to suffer compulsion*: **Kein Mensch muß** (according to *c*) **müssen** (Lessing's *Nathan*, 1, 3) No one should suffer compulsion. **Alle andere Dinge müssen, der Mensch ist das Wesen, welches will** (Schiller, 10, 214).

5. Sollen expresses thruout all its varied meanings a moral constraint, indicating that that which is to be done does not proceed from the will of the person represented as the subject of the verb, but from some other person, or some other source. The chief uses are:

a. The will of a certain definite person is to be carried out: **Du sollst nicht stehlen** Thou shalt not steal (God's will). The father says to John: **Du sollst fleißig sein** I want you to be diligent. In the 3rd person the expression of will is an indirect one to be transmitted by a third party: **Er soll gleich kommen** Tell him that he is to come at once. Hence its use in the imperative. See **177. I. B. *a*.** Also in toasts: Gugler (**sie stoßen an**): **Die Bauernstudenten sollen leben! Prosit!** (Schönherr's *Sonnwendtag*, p. 21).

Note. In this meaning the past and past perfect tenses of the subjunctive (potential) are used, the former with *present* force, the latter with *past* force, to state that something *ought* to be done or ought to have been done if the will or judgment of the speaker were consulted: **Die Gesellschaft sollte die Kunst fördern** Society ought to promote art. **Er hätte sich verteidigen sollen** He ought to have defended himself.

b. In a figurative sense it often means the will or dictate of circumstances or fate, *to be destined to, to have to, to turn out that, will* (expressing not mere futurity, but indicating that something *will* come about because it *must* according to the nature of the case and the probabilities), *to be apt to, to be likely to*: **Darin sollte er sich täuschen** In that he was destined to be disappointed. **Der Mann, der das kann, soll erst noch geboren werden** The man who does that has yet to be born. **So laß uns überlegen, wie du den Irrtum ungeschehen machen sollst** how you should *or* will have to (dictate of circumstances), &c. **Ich hoffe noch immer, die Nachricht soll sich nicht bestätigen** I am still hoping that it will turn out that the news will not be confirmed. **Ich denke, das soll noch kommen** I think that will yet come about. **Versuchen Sie diesen Kohl, er soll** (is apt to) **Ihnen schmecken. Ich will dir zeigen, wie du dieses Ziel erreichen sollst** (are likely to).

Note. In this use the potential subjunctive is much employed (**1**) to represent something as possible but as contingent upon the caprice of circumstances, especially in conditional clauses where it is translated by our *should, were to*: **Wenn es regnen sollte, würde ich nicht kommen** If it should rain I shouldn't come; (**2**) interrogatively to express a doubting or deliberative conjecture: **Sollte Karl das getan haben?** Can it be that Carl has done that? **Sollte das wahr sein?** Can that be true?

c. Used in threats indicating that the speaker is willing for some one to do something if he dares: **Sie sollen sich nur regen, wenn sie's wagen!** Just let them budge if they dare!

d. It may denote the will of the public, hence in general the constraint of custom, law, &c.: **Die Kinder sollen ihren Eltern gehorchen** Children ought to obey their parents. Here **sollen** can often be translated by *it is to be expected that*: **Wie sollte er sich rühren, wo vielleicht nur der Galgen zu gewinnen stand!** How was it to be expected that he should bestir himself there where perhaps only the gallows could be gained? Here **sollen** can also be translated by ***is it to*** *be tolerated*: **„Ein Fremdling," sprachen sie untereinander, „soll hierher kommen nach Bagdad, uns Ruhm, Ehre und Sieg zu entreißen?"**

e. The idea of willing a thing leads to planning its accomplishment, *to be intended to*: **Worte waren es nur, die ich sprach; sie sollten vor euch nur meine Gefühle verstecken** It was only empty words that I spoke; they were intended to conceal my feelings from you. **Soll das ein Scherz sein?** Is that intended as a joke? **Was soll das?** What is that for?

f. The idea of willing a thing or determining that it shall be done leads to that of promising, assuring it, *shall*: **Sie sollen es morgen haben** You shall have it to-morrow. **Der ehrliche Finder soll belohnt werden** The honest finder shall be rewarded. **Es soll geschehen** It shall be done. **In Berlin soll man lange suchen, bis man unter den hiesigen Gelehrten einen Mann von solcher Bildung findet** I assure you that you will hunt a long time in Berlin before you will find among the scholars of the city a man of such culture.

g. It often denotes the will of different parties, hence in general an agreement or arrangement, or the decision of some proper authority: **Ich soll zehn tausend Mark das Jahr erhalten** I am to receive ten thousand marks a year. **Sie sollen warten** The arrangement is that you are to wait. **Die Brücke soll neu gebaut werden** The bridge is to be rebuilt. **Er soll den Gesandten begleiten** He is appointed to accompany the ambassador.

Note. In this meaning, if **noch** is added, it is implied that a promise or arrangement has been broken and probably will not be fulfilled: **Er soll noch wiederkommen** He has never turned up.

h. Much used in questions to ascertain the will, idea, or thought of the person addressed: **Sollen wir jetzt nach Hause gehen?** Shall we go home now? **Was soll ich Ihnen vorlegen?** What shall I help you to? (at the table). A: **Ach, du hast keinen Geschmack! Die soll schön sein?** B: **Natürlich ist sie das.**

i. That which report will have something to be, *it is said*: **Dr. Faust soll in Erfurt gelebt haben** Dr. Faust is said to have lived in Erfurt. **Sieben Sträflinge sollen entkommen sein. Ich werde es wieder getan haben sollen** It will be said again that I did it.

j. Used to suppose a case for sake of argument: **Alfred der Große soll London erbaut haben. Wie erklären Sie dann, daß die Römer die Stadt schon vor Christi Geburt kannten?** Well! We'll say that Alfred the Great built, &c.

k. Used earlier in the period as a trans. verb with the force of **schulden** *to owe*: **Wer mir fünfzig Gülden soll** (Logau). This old meaning survives in **Soll und Haben** *credit and debit.*

6. **Wollen** differs from **sollen** in that it expresses *the will* or *desire of the subject*, while **sollen** even tho in the first person expresses *the will of another*: **Ich will gehen** *I desire, want to go*, but **Ich soll gehen** *I am ordered to go*. **Ich will mich gern geirrt haben** I wish (or hope) I may be mistaken. **Ich will nichts gesagt haben** Let it be as if I had not spoken.

It is used in many idiomatic expressions:

a. Figuratively: **Blumen wollen gepflegt sein** Flowers ought (lit. want) to be tended. **Auch das wollte beachtet sein** Also that needed to be considered. Notice the idiomatic expressions: **das will sagen** *that is to say, that means*, **das will nicht viel sagen** *that doesn't mean much, doesn't amount to much.*

b. Often, *to intend to, to mean to*: **Sie will den Kindern ein Fest geben** She intends to give a party for the children. **Er wollte es heute bringen** He meant to bring it to-day.

Note. Sometimes used to question the ability to carry out an intention or plan: **Wie wollen Sie das heut noch vollenden?** How do you expect to accomplish that yet to-day?

c. A claim that some one makes: **Der Zeuge will den Angeklagten gesehen haben** The witness claims to have seen the defendant. **Ich will es nicht gesehen haben** I will claim, pretend that I did not see it. **Er wird es wieder nicht gehört haben wollen** He will claim again that he didn't hear it. Figuratively: **Das Werk will mehr sein als eine Kompilation** The work professes to be more than a compilation.

Note. Observe the difference of meaning between the present of **wollen** with the perf. infin. and the pres. perf. of **wollen**: **Er will ihn gesehen haben** *He claims to have seen him*, but **Er hat ihn sehen wollen** He wanted to see him.

d. Often, *on the point of, to be about to*: **Es will regnen** It is on the point of raining. **Ich will es Ihnen sogleich geben** I am going to give it to you directly. **Ich wollte eben zu ihm gehen, als er hereintrat** I was just going to see him when he entered the room.

e. **Wollen** with the infinitive of the verb to be conjugated is also used to replace the wanting imperative forms. See **177.** I. B. *a.* It is also used in wishes. See **168.** I. 1. B and **169.** 1. A.

f. Sometimes with the idea of confidence, assurance: **Ich will es noch erleben, daß Klotz sich . . . zurückzieht** (Lessing, *Brief*, 1786) *I shall yet live to see*, &c. **Und wenn's nicht wär' durch falsche Leut' verraten worden, wollt' er ihm das Bad gesegnet und ihn ausgerieben haben** (Goethe's *Götz*, 1, 1). **Gehen Sie hinten zum Garten hinaus und auf der Wiese hin, bis es Mittag schlägt; dann kehren Sie zurück, und ich will den Spaß schon eingeleitet haben** (id., *Dichtung und Wahrheit*, II. 10) *then return, and I shall surely have made all preparations for the practical joke.* **Wart' nur ein Weilchen, bis der Mond aufgegangen ist, dann wollen wir den Weg schon finden** (Grimm's *Hänsel und Gretel*).

g. **Wollen** is often used more or less pleonastically, and must be variously rendered or not rendered at all. In these cases it represents the statement not so much as an actual fact as that it is the opinion or seeming intention of somebody, or is seemingly a fact or the probable outcome of the matter, or the natural result of the given circumstances: **Als er immer und immer nicht kommen wollte** (almost = **kam**), **wurde ein Postbedienter abgeschickt, ihn zu suchen** (Hebel) When after a long while he did not put in an appearance (or when it seemed sure that he did not intend to come), a postal clerk was sent to hunt him up. **Nun irrte er bereits seit zwei Stunden durch die Kiefern, und der Wald wollte kein Ende nehmen** (Baumbach)

Now he had been straying about among the fir trees for two hours already, and the forest seemed to have no end. **Verlegen, daß keine Nachrichten von dem Arzt kommen wollten** (Goethe) Puzzled, because it seemed that no news would come from the doctor.

h. Also used as a trans. verb with a noun or pronoun as object, in the sense of *to desire, to will*: **Wollen Sie Erbsen oder Blumenkohl?** Will you take peas or cauliflower? **Er will dein Glück. Gott will es** God wills it thus. **Das wolle Gott nicht!** May God forbid! Compare: *What wouldst thou of us?* (Shakespeare).

i. Also used as an intransitive verb in the sense of *to have the desire*: **„Willst du das?" „Wenn du willst." „Nein, du mußt wollen. — Mit freudigem Herzen. Sonst ist kein Segen dabei"** (Sudermann's *Die Ehre*, 3, 4).

214. *Omission of the Verb Depending upon the Auxiliary.* This omission is very common, and perhaps the following cases are the most frequent.

1. *a.* If the dependent verb is **gehen** to go, **reisen** to travel, **fahren** to drive, and verbs of motion in general: **Wohin wollen Sie (gehen)?** Where do you intend to go? **Ich muß nach Koblenz (gehen)** I must go to Coblentz. Compare the English of Shakespeare: *You may away by night, she must with me, thou shalt to prison.* In parts of Great Britain and America it is common to say: *I want in, I want out.* Quite general is the similar usage after *let*: *Let me in,* (to a conductor of a street-car) *Let me off at 12th Street.*

b. In case the dependent verb is **tun** to do, **heißen** to signify, and various other words: **Was soll ich (tun)?** What am I to do? **Was soll das (heißen)?** What does that mean? **Der Kranke darf kein Fleisch (essen)** *the patient must not eat meat.*

2. In case the verb depending upon a modal auxiliary is dropped, difference of usage occurs according as the verb is trans. or intrans. With intransitives nothing shows the omission of the verb, but with transitives the pronoun **es** or **das** *may* stand after the auxiliary as the object of the verb which is to be supplied: **Sprich lauter! Ich kann nicht** Speak louder! I cannot. **Kannst du das beweisen? Jawohl; ich kann es,** or **das kann ich** Can you prove that? Yes, indeed I can. Often the **es** or **das** thus used does not point to a definite object, but to an *idea* suggested by or contained in the previous proposition: **Schaffet und bestellet Klageweiber, daß sie kommen; und schicket nach denen, die es** (referring to the idea of **klagen,** suggested by the word **Klageweiber**) **wohl können** (Jer. ix. 17, revised edition). **Wollen Sie mir diesen Gefallen tun? Ich kann es** (referring to the general idea of *doing the favor,* not to **Gefallen,** which is of a different gender) **nicht** Will you do me this favor? I cannot. **O hätte ich mich gefreut, als ich es (= mich freuen) noch konnte!** O, had I enjoyed myself when I was still able to do so! **Er hat es getan, ob er es gemußt hat, weiß ich nicht.** With such transitives this object, however, is often omitted, especially in common conversational style: **Ich mache es so gut ich kann.**

Note. Distinguish between the cases where the auxiliary stands alone, the dependent verb being understood, and the cases where these words are not auxiliaries but independent verbs. The latter case occurs in **können, 213.** 2. F, G, in **mögen, 213.** 3. C, in **müssen, 213.** 4. *d,* in **sollen, 213.** 5. *k,* in **wollen, 213.** 6. *h, i.*

CONJUGATION OF COMPOUND VERBS.

I. General Statement.

215. 1. *Separable Compounds.* All accented prefixes (see II. 1. B) in compound verbs are separated in the following cases from the simple verb: (1) In the simple tenses (pres. and past) of principal propositions and such subordinate clauses as do not have the transposed word-order, the prefix is separated from the verb and placed at the end of the clause or sentence: (pres.) **ich fange meine Arbeit an;** (pres. imper.) **fang deine Arbeit an;** (past) **ich fing meine Arbeit an. Er sagt, er fange seine Arbeit an;** but **Er sagt, daß er seine Arbeit anfange.** (2) In the perf. part. the **ge** and in the infin. and the modal verbals (**180**) the **zu** is inserted between the prefix and the verb, but in these cases the prefix is not really felt as separated and hence is written as one with the verb: **ich habe meine Arbeit angefangen; ich habe versprochen, meine Arbeit morgen anzufangen;** (attributive modal verbal) **die morgen anzufangende Arbeit** the work that must be begun to-morrow. Elsewhere the separable prefix is not separated from the verb: (future) **ich werde meine Arbeit anfangen;** (pres. part.) **ein anfangender Rechtsanwalt** a young lawyer who is just beginning to practise his profession.

2. *Inseparable Compounds.* The prefixes (for list see II. 2) which are always unaccented are never separated from the verb. Such inseparable compounds do not differ in conjugation from simple verbs except that they never take **ge** in the perf. part.: **Er erreicht seinen Zweck. Er erreichte seinen Zweck. Er hat seinen Zweck erreicht. Er versucht** (is trying), **seinen Zweck zu erreichen.**

3. *Compounds Separable or Inseparable.* Certain prefixes (see II. 3. A) are separable or inseparable according as they are accented. If unaccented they are inseparable, if accented they are separable: **Er über'setzt das Gedicht** He is translating the poem. **Er hat das Gedicht über'setzt. Er versucht, das Gedicht zu über'setzen.** But **Die Truppen setzen über** The troops are crossing the river. **Der Fährmann setzt sie über** The ferryman is taking them across the river. **,Sie beabsichtigen** (intend) **'überzusetzen.** In the separable compounds each element usually has its full literal meaning, while the inseparable compounds have an altered or figurative meaning.

Historical Note. Originally adverbs preceded the verb in accordance with the old principle that a grammatically dependent element preceded the governing word. At the beginning of the historical period there was already in both German and English a strong tendency to place stressed adverbs and objects after the verb. This indicates the development of a new word-order, namely the removal of heavily stressed, logically important words to the end of the sentence in order by thus withholding them for a time to render them more conspicuous. Gradually almost all adverbs were removed to a place after the verb and this position has become functional for adverbs. Hence it became unusual to form new firm verbal compounds with a stressed adverb before the verbal element, as in **'ausging in er 'ausging,** for this stood in conflict with the new law that required the stressed adverb to stand after the verb. A new compound, or group-word as it is often called in this book, is always formed from a group of words that stand in a grammatical relation to each other, and hence the new compound usually has the word-order and stress of the group from which it was formed, as explained more fully in **47.** 2. B. *c* and **247.** 1 and 2. Thus the new group with the stressed modifier after the verb prevented the formation of new firm verbal compounds. The firm verbal compounds that had come down from the prehistoric period, such as **'ausging** (ein after andaremo 'uzgiengun—Tatian, **120.** 6 = **einer nach dem anderen ging hinaus**), **'abfuhr** (her 'abfuor—id., **228.** 4 = **er ging fort**), **'einging** (er tho sar thara 'ingiang—Otfrid, II. 11. 5 = **er ging dann sogleich hinein**) from the ninth century, did not long remain firm under the new conditions, in fact were even in oldest German more commonly treated as separables and later became regularly separable, **ging áus, ging éin,** &c. under the strong tendency to place the stressed modifiers of the verb after the verb. They have survived as inseparable compounds only in the subordinate clause, where the stressed modifiers of the verb still precede the verb as in the prehistoric period and sometimes in oldest historic Germanic. It is usually stated by scholars that there were in the Germanic languages no firm verbal compounds in the prehistoric period and in oldest Germanic, but the rather frequent use of firm compounds in Otfrid and in O.H.G. translations from the Latin as in Tatian and in old glosses rendering Latin words as 'uzgat (= **er geht aus**) for Latin exit, &c. makes it seem quite sure that, on the one hand, Otfrid's poetry faithfully preserves older German usage and that, on the other hand, the old translators felt the firm Latin compounds as closely related to the similar forms still in use in poetical style in their own language. The two languages were at that time not so far apart at this point as later, for at one time in prehistoric Latin as in prehistoric German the adverb standing before the verb in verbal compounds was usually stressed as still indicated by the reduced vowels of many Latin compounds: exigo (from ex+ago), incido (from in+cado), &c. The word-order and in many forms the accent survived in later Latin, so that in the O.H.G. period the Latin compounds were quite similar to those found in poetic German. In prehistoric Latin these compounds had become rigidly fixed in form and thus later remained intact, while in German they were dissolved by the forces that had formed them. Just as in the prehistoric period the old laws of Germanic word-order had brought the components together and formed them into syntactical units the new laws of word-order, as described above, dissolved them, except in the subordinate clause, where the new laws have never become established.

A few weakly stressed adverbs did not follow the general tendency to assume the new emphatic position after the verb as they were naturally unfit for this position by reason of their weak accent. Thus verbs that form compounds with adverbs fall into two classes—*inseparables*, in which the weakly stressed adverb still stands in its old historic position before the verb, and *separables*, in which the strongly stressed adverb stands in the important end position. The reason of the weak stress of the first component in inseparables is in a large number of cases perfectly clear. The adverbial force is very faint as the form has acquired almost pure prepositional force. See II. 3. A. *a* (2nd par.). In case of the prefixes **be, emp, ent, er, ge, ver, zer** the force is still fainter as the prefixes have lost almost every trace of their former concrete meaning and are now used only with perfective force (**246.** II. 3. *b*). See also **47.** 2. B. *c*.

In recent literature certain separables are manifesting a tendency to become firm compounds. The components are so often united in the infinitive and the subordinate clause that they are beginning to be felt as firm compounds: **'anerkennen, 'anerkannte,** &c. More examples are given in II. 2. *c* and *Note* thereunder. These beginnings are as yet very small. It remains to be seen whether the new development will spread. The firmness of form in these recent compounds does not indicate that they are felt more distinctly as units, for the older separables on account of their peculiar form and stress are just as vividly felt as units. Firmness of form here simply means that the origin of the form has been forgotten. If such forms become established they will join the great throng of units which in spite of their obscure origin are performing their parts in the language creditably.

II. Detailed Statement.

1. Separable Compounds.

A. *End-stress Now and Formerly.* The question of separation or non-separation is one of accent, and the accent is a question of the meaning and importance of the prefix. A clear understanding of the question of separable prefixes will result from a study of their origin and the position that the German gives to the important words in the sentence.

The word in a sentence that is logically the most important receives the strongest accent. Any word that for one reason or another seems especially important to the speaker is distinguished by stronger stress, tho it may ordinarily be quite unimportant. Logical accent is thus often a matter of subjective view and feeling, but on the other hand certain *grammatical* elements of a sentence are quite regularly more important than others, and are consequently distinguished by stronger accent. Usually the most important grammatical element is the predicate, and consequently it receives *grammatical* accent even tho some other word may for some especial reason receive a still stronger *logical* accent. The favorite position of the logically most important word is at the beginning of the sentence, while the favorite position of the grammatically most important element is the very last word in the clause or sentence. This position of the grammatically important element at the end of the sentence has in the literary language become fixed and stereotyped, and hence is retained even when the grammatically important word is immediately preceded by some modifier which is relatively more important, and in fact is more forcibly stressed: **Er hat eine Óhrfeige gekriegt.** Such grammatical elements are a predicate noun in the nom., an uninflected adjective standing as a predicate complement, a noun in the acc. or an uninflected adjective used as an objective predicate (see **262.** III. 2 and **104.** 2. A. *c*), a perf. part., an infin., and lastly a separable prefix, all of which are absolutely necessary to complete the meaning of the verb, and naturally as due to their grammatical importance stand at the end and receive accent: Predicate noun: **Er war stets in allen Kämpfen ein Mann.** Predicate complement: **Er war in allen Kämpfen tapfer.** Objective predicate: **Er hielt die Fahne in allen Kämpfen hoch** He held high the flag in every battle. Participle: **Er ist nach Hause gegangen.** Infinitive: **Er wird morgen kommen. Er wünscht mich kennen zu lernen.** Separable prefix: **Das Schiff ging mit Mann und Maus unter.**

The perfect participle and the present infinitive often have less stress than the other words that stand at the end of the sentence, for they are now felt as only a part of the verb and like the simple verb usually take less stress than the more important words that modify them. Their present position is the survival of older usage when they had more independent force and hence stood at the end by virtue of their importance. They were then not a part of the verb but an important complement of it: **Er hat einen Brief geschrieben** (originally a verbal adjective used as an objective predicate, lit. *written, in a written state*, still with its full original force when stressed: **Er hat den Brìef schon geschríeben**). **Er wird einen Brief schreiben** (originally **schreibend,** a predicate verbal adjective). **Er will einen Brief schreiben** (originally as now the object of **will**). The establishment of the infinitive in the last place preceded by its modifiers as in the last example, was greatly facilitated by the strong resemblance of this construction to that of old group-words (**247.** 2. *a*), as **Kópfverlètzung, Blútvergìeßen,** &c., where the verbal component is always preceded by its modifier. In course of time the old historic position of participle and infinitive at the end has become permanent, but it is now held as a grammatical or functional duty rather than as an indication of their logical importance. The common position of a participle or infinitive with secondary stress at the *end* of the sentence preceded by a more strongly stressed predicate, object, adverb, or prepositional phrase has brought about in sentences containing a compound tense form a new descriptive group-stress with the chief stress upon the first member, in this treatise called end-stress: **Er ist gesúnd gewòrden. Er hat Féuer gemàcht. Er will gesúnd wèrden. Er will Féuer màchen. Er ist nach Háuse gegàngen. Das Haus ist von Báumen umgèben.** See also **285.** II. B. *b. aa. bb. cc*; **50.** A. 6. This type of end-stress has become productive within the present period in that it has influenced other end-groups to assume the same word-order and stress. Luther's **Er hat es kònnen tún** has become **Er hat es tún kònnen.** Older **Er muß sèin gekómmen** and **Er kann den Brief hàben geschríeben** have become **Er muß gekómmen sèin** and **Er kann den Brief geschríeben hàben.** The future perfect shows the same word-order and stress: **Er wìrd den Brief geschríeben hàben.** In the subordinate clause with a compound tense form we often find the same stress, the result however of quite a different grammatical force, namely the law that requires the personal part of the verb in the subordinate clause to be placed at the end often causes an auxiliary to stand after a more strongly accented participle or infinitive: **ein Mann, der das ságen kànn; der Mann, der morgen kómmen wìrd; der Mann, der es geságt hàt.** For a fuller description of this development in the subordinate clause see **237.** 1. B. *a. Note.* Thus end-stress is now characteristic of principal propositions and subordinate clauses that have a compound tense form.

The predicate nominative, the predicate adjective, and the separable prefix of the principal proposition were originally, like the infinitive and participle, placed at the end on account of their stress and logical importance. In course of time this position has become functional. Of course, however, the predicate noun and adjective and the separable prefix are still often logically important and are consequently heavily stressed. Thus they have not only kept their old historic position but also their old stress.

a. Separable Prefix and Participle or Infinitive Come Together at the End. In the pres. perf. and past perf. tenses of a separable verb the principle of placing the most important grammatical element in the predicate at the end of the clause would require both the prefix and part. and in the future and fut. perf. both the prefix and infin. to stand last, which of course is impossible, as only one word can be last. The verb (part. or infin.) here as elsewhere has precedence and takes the favorite position at the end, but the prefix stands immediately before it, and, as both together form one idea, they are written usually as one word. However, a separable prefix differs markedly from an inseparable one, altho not separated from the verb, for it still retains its accent, since it is the important element of the verbal compound: **Das Schiff ist** or (past. perf.) **war mit Mann und Maus 'untergegangen. Das Schiff wird mit Mann und Maus 'untergehen,** or (fut. perf.) **wird 'untergegangen sein.**

Note. The poet often does violence here to the prose construction and separates the prefix from the verb: **Denn sie kann's nur vorhersehen, | ab es wenden kann sie nicht** (Grillparzer). Especially in the German spoken by certain foreigners (see **285.** II B. *b. ff.*) deviations from the usual rules occur. They often separate the separable prefix from the infin. and place it after the infin.: **Er ist eingezogen, zu spionieren. Wir wollen ihm kommen zuvor, daß uns nicht kann begegnen ein Unglück** (words from a Jewish character in Ebner-Eschenbach's *Der Kreisphysikus*).

b. Position of the Separable Prefix in a Subordinate Clause. The position of the separable prefix in the subordinate clause depends upon whether the conjunction introducing the clause is expressed or omitted.

aa. If the subordinate conjunction is expressed, the verb of the clause is required according to the German idiom to stand at the end, and, as the prefix on account of its grammatical importance must also stand at the end, this brings verb and prefix together. As both together form one idea, they are written as one word: **Wenn das Schiff vor Morgen nicht mit Mann und Maus untergeht, werden alle gerettet.** If the verb is in a compound tense the auxiliary goes to the end and the verb compounded with the prefix stands next to it: **Ich glaube, daß das Schiff mit Mann und Maus untergegangen ist.**

bb. If the conjunction **daß** is omitted, the prefix is treated just as if the clause were a main clause: **Ich glaube, das Schiff geht mit Mann und Maus unter. Ich glaube, das Schiff ist mit Mann und Maus untergegangen.**

cc. If the conjunction **wenn** is omitted, the verb stands the first word in the clause and the prefix the last in simple tenses, but in compound tenses the auxiliary stands first in the clause, and the prefix compounded with the verb stands last: **Geht das Schiff vor Morgen nicht mit Mann und Maus unter, so werden alle gerettet. Ist das Schiff morgen früh nicht untergegangen, so werden alle gerettet.**

c. Position of **ge-** *and* **zu.** The **ge** of the part. and the **zu** of the infin. and modal verbals stand between prefix and verb: **Er hat die Tür aufgemacht. Ich bitte, die Tür aufzumachen** Please open the door. **Die aufzumachende Tür** The door that is to be opened.

d. Non-separation in Pres. Part. Separation does not take place in the pres. part.: **Sind alle diese Kinder Ihre Enkel? fragte die junge Frau, sich teilnehmend im Zimmer umsehend.**

e. All separable prefixes remain unseparated in simple tenses in one particular case. If the separable prefix is placed at the head of the sentence for logical emphasis, as can be done with any word, inversion takes place according to the usual rule, and this throws prefix and verb together: **'Niederjagt die Front der Major** (Schiller's *Die Schlacht*) The major dashes down the space in front of the troops. The components are here more commonly, but certainly not more correctly, written apart: **Auf steigt der Mond, und nieder sinkt die Sonne** (Raabe's *Nach dem großen Kriege*, p. 2).

f. If there are two accented, separable prefixes, which is a rare case, the first prefix takes the accent. Such compounds, however, are only used in the cases where complete separation never occurs: **Zünfte, welche sich wieder nach ihren verschiedenen Gewerken 'unterabteilen.** In the part. the **ge** stands after the second prefix: **'unterabgeteilt, 'rückumgelautet** (Blatz's *Neuhochdeutsche Grammatik*, I, p. 535, 3rd ed.).

B. *Form and List of Separable Prefixes.* The separable prefix of the verb may be:

a. An adverb or preposition (**225.** 1. *a* and *b*): **ab** denoting a movement downward or off, away, often with the additional idea of deterioration; the taking back of a former order or announcement; separation or deviation from something or someone, often pure and simple, often with the additional idea of contrast, disapproval, disparagement, aversion, or deficiency; often losing every trace of its original concrete meaning and assuming perfective force expressing the end or result of an act, often with the additional idea of thoroness, on the one hand, and the idea of excess and injury on the other hand, as illustrated in **223.** I. 7. G. *d*; **an** at, upon, on, on to, to, expressing a rest at a permanent goal, arrival at a goal (**223.** I. 9. B. 1), motion toward, a general forward movement, or a steady continuation (**223.** I. 7. E. *a*), sometimes an upward movement, often the beginning of an activity or the idea of affecting an object only a little (**223.** 7. E. *b*. (**2**)); **auf** up, open, an arousing, a restoration to a previous condition, often losing every trace of its original concrete meaning and assuming perfective force expressing the beginning of an act or state or the end of an action, often with the additional idea of consuming, exhausting, as illustrated in **223.** I. 7. E. *c*; often rest upon or direction toward an object as illustrated in **223.** I. 9. B. 2.; **aus** out, out of, the finishing or cessation of an activity or a state, the pushing of an activity to a befitting end; **bei** by, at the side of, aside, expressing the idea of nearness, close association, coöperation, accompaniment, addition to, direction toward, hostility to; **be'vor** ahead of (of time); **da** (**dar** before vowels) *there* + preposition, as in **da'von, da'ran,** &c.; **dar** *to, before* (of place), early in the period used with the force of **da'hin** with reference to a definite place, now = **hin** without reference to a definite place, confined in its use to a few verbs; **ein** (**223.** I. 9. B. 4) into; **em'por** up; **fort** onward, away; **ent'gegen** *toward, against,* expressing a friendly movement toward, or a hostile resistance to, or movement against; **ent'zwei** (corrupted form of **in zwei**) in two, apart; **heim** home; **her** motion toward the speaker; **hin** motion from the speaker; compounds with **her** and **hin,** as **he'rab, hi'nab, da'hin,** *to that place, to it,* denoting motion toward a definite place, **da'her** or **ein'her** along, &c.; **hint'an** behind, in a secondary position, after; **los** loose, free from, off, a sudden and lively breaking forth of an activity that is conceived of as held in check, as **losschießen** to fire away, **losschlagen** to begin battle; **mit** with; **nach** after, a succession in order of time or place; **nieder** down; **ob** above, on top, upon, fig. of duties that rest or devolve upon us, or of work upon which we must bestow time and labor; **vor** (earlier in period sometimes **für;** see **für,** *b* in **230**) before, forward, also in compounds (**voraus,** &c.); **weg** away; **da'von** up and away; **weiter** continuation: **weitergehen** *to continue,* but **weiter gehen** *to go on further;* **zu** to, toward, lively unceasing exertion (**223.** I. 4. A), addition, shutting; **zu'rück** back; **zu'sammen** together; **zu'vor** before, ahead of (of time), &c.

b. An adjective, usually used as an objective predicate (see **104.** 2. A. *c*): **totschlagen** or **tot schlagen** to strike dead, **bloßstellen** to expose, lit. place bare, **'gutmachen** or **gut machen** to make good. This is a very large group of words, but there is no uniform way of writing them. The closer adjective and verb blend together by taking on a distinct meaning not contained in the words taken separately, the more liable they are to be written together.

c. A noun (see **249.** II. 1. D. (**1**)): **achtgeben** to give attention, **haushalten** to keep house, **Folge leisten** to obey, **teilnehmen** to take part in.

d. A prepositional phrase (see **249.** II. 1. C): **zu Schiffe gehen** to go on board, **zuteil werden** to be allotted, **zustande kommen** to be accomplished, **imstande sein, instand setzen, zugrunde gehen,** &c.

2. Inseparable Compounds.

The inseparable prefixes are: **be, ent** (written **emp** before **f: empfinden), er, ge, ver, wider** (except in **widerhallen,** &c.; see 3. A. *e* below, 3rd par.), **zer,** and usually **miß** (see *b* below). As they do not now as formerly have separate existence outside of compounds, verbs compounded with them are in reality not compounds, but only derivative verbs. These prefixes have, however, a distinct meaning, and often influence both the meaning and construction of the verb. Their meanings are treated in **246.** II at length, as their importance deserves. These prefixes are ordinarily without accent, but to make a contrast, they may receive stress: **In zu feuchten Gegenden muß man die Felder nicht 'be- sondern 'entwässern** In very moist regions, it is necessary to drain instead of irrigating. As they are usually unaccented they have in course of time changed considerably their original form, and have lost their identity as independent words which they once were, and are now so closely compounded with the verb that they are felt as one with it, and can never be separated from it.

a. In the perf. part. these prefixes never take a **ge** before them, but in the infin. and the modal verbals (**180**) the **zu** stands before them; **Er hat die Tür verschlossen. Ich bitte, die Tür zu verschließen** Please lock the door. **Die zu verschließende Tür** the door that is to be locked.

b. Among these prefixes **miß** occupies an exceptional position, as fully explained in **246.** II. 8.

c. When a separable prefix stands before an inseparable one, separation usually takes place, but there is in individual cases evidently a tendency to disregard this rule: **Ich erkenne die Verdienste des Mannes an,** but also **Ich anerkenne den Widerstreit der Meinungen** (Fontane's *Vor dem Sturm*, III, chap. ii). **Jukundus anerbot sich, die Mission zu übernehmen** (G. Keller's *Die Leute von Seldwyla*, 2, p. 317). **Die Waschfrauen zunächst einverleibten sie ihrem Verbande und verschafften ihr genügende Arbeit** (ib., p. 337). **Niemandem auf der Welt anvertraute er das Schicksal seines einzigen Kindes mit größerer Beruhigung als gerade ihm** (Ertl's *Mistral*, v). **Mein Vater vorenthält mir nicht seine lobenden Worte** (Gustav Falke's *Die Stadt mit den goldenen Türmen*, p. 18).

Note. There is also, especially in certain words, a trend toward non-separation even in case of separable prefixes which are not thus used in connection with an inseparable prefix: **Da weideten und wiederkäuten nebeneinander die verschiedenartigsten pflanzenfressenden Großtiere** (Dr. L. Heck in *Velhagen und Klasings Monatshefte*, Oct. 1905, p. 217). **Mir war, als obläge mir die Sorge über eine ganze Welt** (Rosegger's *Waldheim*, I, 186). **Sein Wille erlahmt an dem Widerstand seines leichtbeweglichen Herzens, dieses obsiegt über jenen** (Gustav Plähn in *Mitteilungen für die Gesellschaft der Freunde Wilhelm Raabes*, 1919, p. 10). Compare I. 3. *Historical Note* (3rd par.)

d. When an inseparable prefix stands before a separable one, the compound is inseparable: **An der Tür wird [Bettlern] nichts ver'abreicht.** Compare 3. B below.

3. Compounds Separable or Inseparable.

A. A few prefixes have double accent, accented or unaccented according to their meaning, and as a consequence are treated as separable or inseparable according to their accent and meaning. These prefixes are: **durch** thru, **hinter** behind, **über** over, above, **um** around, **unter** under, beneath, **voll** full, completion, **wider** (see *e*, 3rd par.) back, **wieder** again.

Verbs compounded with these prefixes are separable when the prefix receives the principal accent and is distinctly felt as the more important element of the compound. These verbs become inseparable when the accent is placed upon the verb. This shifting of the accent upon the verb may result in intensifying the verbal force of the new compound or the weakening of the distinctly local force of the prefix by the weakening of its accent, which latter result often facilitates the use of the compound in a figurative sense. These inseparable verbs take on figurative meaning if the simple verb is trans., and if the simple verb is intrans. the compound verb becomes trans. with figurative or literal meaning. In the latter case the inseparable verb takes on intensive force, and only in this respect and grammatical construction does it differ from the intrans. separable verb. Few inseparable verbs are intrans. **Hinter** is rarely accented in these compounds, and hence is usually employed in a figurative application. It is accented, and has its literal meaning only in popular and colloquial language: **Die Studentenmutter stieg mit ihrem neuen Mieter ins zweite Stockwerk hinauf und führte ihn einen halbdunkeln Gang hinter** (Sperl's *Burschen heraus!*, p. 291). The more detailed treatment is as follows:

a. The separable verb is trans. or intrans. with literal meaning: **Der Fährmann setzte die Truppen über** The ferryman transported the troops over the river, or intrans.: **Die Truppen setzten über** The troops went over the river on the ferry. The same verb is trans. and inseparable in figurative or altered meaning: **Der Schüler über'setzte das Buch** The student translated the book. **Er holt das Buch bald wíeder** *He will soon go to get the book*, but **Er wieder'holt seine Aufgabe** *He is reviewing his exercise*. Compare *hòld úp* and *ùphóld*, *sèt úp* and *ùpsét*, *rùn óut* and *òutrún*.

In this group of inseparables the prefix has, except in case of **voll-**, *adverbial* force, but on account of its figurative meaning it is little felt and hence is weakly stressed. The separable prefix **voll-** was originally a predicate adjective, an objective predicate, and as a predicate had a strong stress, and in concrete expression still has: **Hans hat sich tüchtig vóllgepfropft,** but in a figurative sense: **Ich habe die Tat vollbrácht.** In the inseparables in *b* and *c* the prefix has in most cases prepositional force and like prepositions in general has weak stress. In all separable verbs the prefix has strong *adverbial* force or in case of **voll-** is an objective *predicate* and hence has strong stress, for adverb and predicate are usually more strongly stressed than the verb. Altho in the separable prefixes the adverbial force predominates they have, as other separable prefixes that are related to prepositions, also considerable prepositional force, as illustrated in **223.** I. 9. B.

b. The separable verb is intrans. with literal meaning: **Er hielt nirgends an, er fuhr dúrch, ist 'durchgefahren** He stopped nowhere, he drove thru. **Die Milch ist 'übergelaufen** The milk has run over, overflowed. Also metonymically **Der Krug ist 'übergelaufen.** The inseparable verb is trans. with figurative meaning: **Der gellende Ruf durch'fuhr meine Glieder, hat meine Glieder durch'fahren** The piercing cry went thru my very limbs. **Ich habe die Rechnung nur über'laufen** I have only cast a glance over the bill. **Es über'lief mich kalt** My blood ran cold. **Seine Gläubiger über'laufen ihn** His creditors are annoying him. Also according to *c* with different shades of meaning: **Ich habe mich über'laufen** I have exhausted myself with running. **Tränen über'liefen sein Antlitz** Tears flowed fast down his cheeks.

c. The separable verb is intrans. with literal or figurative meaning: **Er reiste dúrch** He traveled right thru. **Er geht mit diesem Plane úm** He entertains this project. The inseparable verb is trans. with literal meaning and often has intensive force: **Ich um'ging die Stadt in einer Stunde** I walked around the town in an hour. **Er durch'reiste die Gegend** He traveled all over that part of the country. **Er ist durch das Dickicht 'durchgedrungen,** but **Das Öl hat das Holz durch'drungen.**

d. Few inseparable verbs are intransitive: **Sie mußten im Walde übernachten. Kurzum, er konnte sich nicht halten und übersiedelte** (also separable) **. . . nach England** (Fontane's *Cécile,* chap. x). **Vier Söhne sind hinterblieben** Four sons survive (the deceased).

e. There is often only a slight shade of difference between separable and inseparable verbs. The trans. inseparable may have perfective (denoting the outcome or result of an action) force, while the trans. separable compound has both durative (denoting duration) and perfective force: **Der Soldat durch'bohrt den Feind** *The soldier is despatching the enemy,* but **Der Tischler bohrt das Brett dúrch** *The joiner is boring a hole thru the board.* The first sentence represents only the final point in the action, while the second shows the action as continuing, at the same time, however, intimating that the hoped-for result will be attained. Sometimes there is little or no difference between the trans. inseparable and trans. separable.

There is often no difference between the inseparable trans. verb and the separable intrans., except that they require after them a different grammatical construction: **Das Pferd hat den Graben über'sprungen. Das Pferd ist hin'übergesprungen** The horse has jumped over (the ditch).

There is often no difference at all between separable and inseparable formations, especially in case of **wider: Die Töne haben in den Räumen 'widergehallt** or **wider'hallt. Die Räume haben die Töne 'widergehallt,** or **wider'hallt. Die Sonnenstrahlen leuchteten von dem oberen Teil der harzigen Stämme wíder** (*Daheim,* 15, 785a). **Die offenen Fenster wider'leuchteten im Winde winkend** (R. H. Bartsch's *Zwölf aus der Steiermark,* p. 46). **„Faust" klingt von diesen Eindrücken wíder** (Guhrauer, 1, 75). **In Ruprechts Herzen wider'klangen des Bruders bitter gemeinte Worte mit der Freudigkeit einer Offenbarung** (R. H. Bartsch's *Die Haindlkinder,* p. 146). **Dann wider'klang das Dorment von saftigen Lufthieben** (Hermann Hesse's *Unterm Rad,* p. 112). Likewise **widerschallen, widerspiegeln** (more commonly sep.), and **widerstrahlen,** but **wider'fahren, wider'legen, wider'raten, wider'reden, wider'rufen, wider'setzen, wider'sprechen, wider'stehen, wider'streben,** and **wider'streiten** are always inseparable. Compare **258.** 1. B. *a* (near end).

Über in **überfahren** *to drive over, run over* or *down* (with a carriage), **überreiten** *to ride over with a horse* is usually felt as a preposition and hence these compounds are usually inseparable, but the **über** is sometimes felt as an adverb and is stressed, when of course the compound becomes separable: **Er hat das Kind über'ritten,** but sometimes separable: **Wiebke Wiese** (name), **geh weg da; sonst wenn mein Vater kommt, reitet er dich über!** (Otto Ernst's *Asmus Sempers Jugendland,* p. 29). In a number of other compounds the **über,** tho felt as an adverb with literal meaning, has lost so much of its original concrete force that it is often unstressed, so that the compound becomes inseparable: **Als Kathi Fröhlich starb, überführte man seine** (i.e. Grillparzer's) **sterblichen Reste in ein Grab neben ihr** (Ehrhard-Necker's *Franz Grillparzer,* p. 35), but also often separable: **Die ersten großen Transporte Verwundeter, die dank der ausgezeichneten Vorbereitung in voller Ordnung und Schnelligkeit nach den Lazaretten übergeführt werden konnten** (*Frankfurter Zeit.,* Aug. 24, 1914). In some of these compounds the force of the **über** is so faint that it is never stressed, so that the compounds are always inseparable: **Er hat mir den Brief über'bracht.** Likewise **über'geben, über'tragen,** and **über'lassen,** which earlier in the period were also separable.

f. Sometimes the separable verb takes on figurative meaning, and yet remains separable where the force of the prefix is more vividly felt than that of the verb, and hence is too prominent to be united with the verb and lose its identity: **Das Wetter schlägt um** There is a sudden change in the weather. **Die Krankheit schlägt um. Er schlägt um** He changes his whole nature. **Er setzte seinen Plan durch** He carried his plan thru.

g. Sometimes the separable verb that is usually intrans. may become trans. with different meanings according as it is used literally or figuratively: **Das Pferd ist 'durchgegangen** The horse has run away. **Die Sohlen waren so dünn, daß ich sie gleich 'durchgegangen habe** The soles of the shoes were so thin that I soon wore them thru. **Ich habe die Arbeiten meiner Schüler oft 'durchgegangen** I have often gone over or looked over the exercises of my pupils.

B. When one of these prefixes stands unaccented before an accented prefix, usage varies. According to the analogy of the prefixes which are always inseparable, as described in 2. *d* above, such compounds ought to be inseparable, and they are generally so, but they often take a **ge** or **zu** after the accented prefix: **Er über'anstrengt sich. Er hat sich über'anstrengt** or **über'angestrengt. Sie sind über'anstrengt** (Anselm Heine's *Eine Gabe*, Am 13. Juni). **Ich war immer ein über'angestrengter, geplagter Mann** (Fulda's *Die wilde Jagd*, 4, 5). **Ich fürchte, mich zu über'anstrengen,** or sometimes **über'anzustrengen** (Frenssen's *Die drei Getreuen*, **III, 10**).

Nouns made from Compound Verbs.

216. Nouns made from verbs of course retain the accent of the verb: **'ausgehen, der 'Ausgang** outcome; **be'fehlen, der Be'fehl** command; **'übersetzen, die 'Übersetzung** transportation; **über'setzen, die Über'setzung** translation. For notable exception see art. **47.** 3. B. *a.*

Verbs Indirectly Compounded.

217. There is a class of verbs (see **206**) that seem to be compounded by prefixing a noun or adjective to a simple verb, but they are in reality made from compound substantives or adjectives. Verbs that have received their compound form in this indirect way have noun accent, i.e., accent on the first syllable, and are treated as simple verbs: **das 'Frühstück** breakfast, **'frühstücken** to take breakfast, **'frühstückte, ge'frühstückt; der 'Ratschlag** counsel, **'ratschlagen** to take counsel with, **'ratschlagte, ge'ratschlagt; die 'Handhabe** handle, **'handhaben** to handle, **'handhabte, ge'handhabt,** &c.

a. In some cases the noun or adj. from which the verb was made has gone out of use: **'wetterleuchten** *to sheet-lighten* from M.H.G. wëterleich. Thus also **'rechtfertigen to justify, 'brandschatzen** to lay under contribution, **'weissagen** to prophesy, &c.

b. This class of words has been productive in that other words have been formed after analogy with these, by simply welding two words which together form one idea into one word, and treating them then as a simple verb: **liebäugeln** to ogle, **'lobpreisen** to praise in song, **'lobsingen** (w. dat.) to sing praises to, **'willfahren** (w. dat.) to humor a person or gratify his wishes, **'liebkosen** to caress, &c. The last two, however, and also **frohlocken** may also be accented on the second syllable, and hence may be treated as inseparable verbs and drop **ge-** in the perf. part. See **178.** 2. A. *b.* (**3**). On the other hand, **lobsingen** and **lobpreisen** are sometimes in the infinitive and perf. part. treated as separable verbs: **lobzupreisen, lobgepriesen.**

Note 1. The verb **ehebrechen** is only used in the pres. part. and the simple infinitive form without **zu,** elsewhere being replaced by the verb **brechen** and the noun **die Ehe: eine ehebrechende Frau. Du sollst nicht ehebrechen.** But **Gott verbietet, die Ehe zu brechen.**

Note 2. Present usage fluctuates with regard to the inflection of the basal component of some of these verbs, the strong or the weak form or both occurring. The strong form asserts itself sometimes contrary to the rule of the grammarian, as the compound noun is not now in use while the force of the simple strong verb is distinctly felt: **der sie** (i.e. **die Sprache**) **. . . radebricht** (P Heyse, iii. 226). In early N.H.G. we find strong forms even where the compound noun is in common use: **Von dem tage an ratschlugen sie | wie sie jn tödten** (John xi. 53).

Fluctuation also prevails with regard to the firmness of some of these compounds, inseparable and separable forms occurring. The separable forms are in most part confined to the perf. participle and the infinitive with **zu,** the accent upon the first element suggesting the insertion of **ge** or **zu** after analogy of separable compounds, which are likewise accented upon the first element: **Ich habe erbgeschlichen** (Hillern's *Arzt*, 1, 186); **um erbzuschleichen; wettgelaufen, wettgerannt,** but **gewetteifert.** Usually: **Es ist schon fürgesorgt, daß dieser Fall nicht eintreten kann.** Sometimes complete separation: **Er wandelt nacht, also weck ihn nicht!** (Hauptmann's *Und Pippa tanzt*, p. 78).

REFLEXIVE VERBS

218. 1. The verb may be connected with the reflexive pronouns (see 142) in much the same way as in English. Most reflexive verbs govern the acc., but a few govern the dat. and a still smaller number the gen.:

Present Tense Indicative.

sich irren (w. acc.), to be mistaken.	**schmeicheln** (w. dat.), to flatter.	**spotten** (w. gen.), to ridicule.
ich irre mich	**ich schmeichele mir**	**ich spotte meiner**
{ **du irrst dich**	{ **du schmeichelst dir**	{ **du spottest deiner**
{ **Sie irren sich**	{ **Sie schmeicheln sich**	{ **Sie spotten Ihrer selbst**
er irrt sich	**er schmeichelt sich**	**er spottet seiner selbst**
wir irren uns	**wir schmeicheln uns**	**wir spotten unser(er)**
{ **ihr irrt euch**	{ **ihr schmeichelt euch**	{ **ihr spottet euer(er)**
{ **Sie irren sich**	{ **Sie schmeicheln sich**	{ **Sie spotten Ihrer selbst**
sie irren sich	**sie schmeicheln sich**	**sie spotten ihrer selbst**

a. In all tenses, the reflexive usually stands first in order of words among the modifiers of the predicate, preferring especially the place next to the verb, and in compound tenses next to the auxiliary: **Das Kind hat sich vor der Strafe gefürchtet,** or in the question order: **Hat sich das Kind vor der Strafe gefürchtet?** However, in the question order the reflexive must follow the *subject* if the subject be a pronoun: **Wie befinden Sie sich?** How do you do?

b. As indicated by its position the reflexive pronoun is entirely without accent. If it is to be made prominent, the word **selbst** must be added, which bears the accent: **Der leidenschaftlich erregte Jüngling tötete sich selbst, nicht seinen Beleidiger.**

2. There is a difference in reflexive verbs. Some are usually reflexive, pronoun and verb together forming one idea: **sich schämen** to be ashamed, **sich sehnen** to long (for), **sich freuen** to rejoice, **sich wundern** to be surprised, **sich erkälten** (N.G. and in parts of the South), **sich verkälten** (S.G.), or **sich verkühlen** (Austrian) to catch a cold, **sich schnauben** (N.G.) or **sich schneuzen** (S.G.) to blow the nose, **sich ausschnauben** (N.G.) to blow the nose thoroly, **sich ausschweigen** to keep perfectly still, i.e. refrain from making the slightest expression of opinion (as in **Hierüber schweigt Ludendorff sich aus**—Hans Delbrück in *Preußische Jahrbücher*, Oct. 1919, p. 92), &c. Some trans. and intrans. verbs are also used reflexively: **baden** to bathe, **ich bade mich; gehen** to walk, **ich gehe mich müde** I walk myself tired.

a. The reflexive pronoun in genuine reflexive verbs is not felt as an object in the strict sense of the term and hence is not treated as an independent element in the sentence, but merely as a part of the verb, and consequently the predicate complement does not agree with it in case, but refers back to the subject with which it agrees: **Er wundert sich als unerfahrener** (not **unerfahrenen**) **Neuling über alles.**

b. The predicate complement of verbs not really reflexive but used reflexively agrees sometimes with the subject and sometimes with the reflexive object, as usage has not yet become fixed at this point: **Ich fühle mich als der Apostel eines verfeinerten, veredelten Menschenvolks** (Ebner-Eschenbach's *Glaubenslos*, chap. viii). **Der Westwind stürzte sich vom Meer her über den Winter im Land und fing an, sich als den Stärkeren zu fühlen** (Frenssen's *Die drei Getreuen*, III, 8). **Briest gab sich als zärtlicher Großvater** (Fontane's *Effi*, chap. xxiv). **Es ist anstrengend, einem Gefühlsschwärmer, als welchen Paderewski sich ausschließlich gab, einen langen Abend hindurch zu folgen** (*Tägliche Rundschau*). **Du nennst dich einen Teil, und stehst doch ganz vor mir** (Goethe's *Faust*, 1). **Ich denk', er nennt mein guter Freund sich noch** (Kleist's *Der zerbrochene Krug*, 10). **Der sich wähnte den Herrscher der Welt** (Freiligrath, *Volksztg.*, 18, 191). **Es ist nichts Geringes, an der goldenen Tafel der Olympier zu sitzen, sich wohl gar einer ihrer zu wähnen** (Spielhagen's *Selbstgerecht*, p. 64).

Note. There is a tendency to make a distinction here between nom. and acc. The former is an objective statement of the outcome of an act or activity, often also a simple predication of a fact known and acknowledged, the latter indicates a desire or intention on the part of the speaker or someone else to show himself in the capacity mentioned in the predicate complement, and in general calls attention to a fact not before known to the person in question: **Herr B. erwies sich als fertiger Pianist, aber als ziemlich gewöhnlicher Komiker,** but **Die Folge ist weiter, daß sobald sich der deutsche Arbeiter oder Handwerker** (who in Paris for sake of personal security does not desire to be known as a German) **aklimatisiert hat, er sich als Franzosen entdeckt** (Franz Wugk in *Hamburger Nachrichten*, Feb. 25, 1905) and **Er** (Dr. Voß of Cologne) **bekennt sich als grundsätzlichen Anhänger der konfessionellen Schule** (*Die Frankfurter Zeit.*, June 16, 1920). **Er zeigt sich als ein gebildeter, unterrichteter Mann,** but **Traue nicht jedem, der sich dir als deinen Freund zeigen will. Man kann sich empfehlen als jemandes aufrichtigen Verehrer, ergebensten Diener** (He desires to show himself in these capacities), **aber nur als sein dankbarer Schüler** (He is already known as a student and hence need not make known his desire to appear in this capacity, but simply states it as a fact by using the nom.).

c. Because the reflexive is not felt as object, it cannot in the passive voice become subject. Hence reflexive verbs should not form a passive, but the people insist nevertheless on forming one, however an impersonal (never a personal) passive (see **219.** 5. B): **Da wird sich gerudert** (Halbe's *Mutter Erde*, ii, p. 24). The reflexive is also omitted in this construction: **Hier wird hingesetzt! 's ist Platz genug für 'n lustiges Kleeblatt** (Halbe's *Das tausendjährige Reich*, p. 133).

3. The reflexive verb in German has a wider field of usefulness than in English. It occurs in the following groups:—

A. *With Passive Force.* In a large number of cases where things come about of themselves Germans hesitate to use a passive, hence they employ reflexive form, which is so often, as in B, associated with intransitive meaning. But as this apparent intransitive force here always represents something as developing into a new state, consequently as affected, it usually develops into passive meaning, as often also in B. In English the strong passive idea here usually calls forth passive form, but sometimes, as in B, intransitive form. Examples: **Zwischen den Augen hatte sich eine tiefe Falte gegraben** A deep wrinkle had been formed or had formed (as the result of care) between his eyes. **Der Mut verlernt sich nicht, wie er sich nicht lernt** Courage is a natural gift that cannot be acquired or lost. **Der Wiesengrund ist schon so bunt und malt sich täglich bunter** The meadow is already resplendent with many colors and is daily adorned with still brighter ones. **Der Saal füllte sich allmählich** The great room was gradually filled with people. **So etwas spricht sich schnell herum** Such a thing *is* soon *spread* about, or soon *spreads*. **Der Schlüssel wird sich finden** The key *will be found*, or *will turn up*. **Das begreift sich leicht** That is easily understood.

a. Especially frequent is the reflexive use of **lassen** with a dependent infinitive which has passive force: **Das läßt sich leicht machen** That is easily done. **Das läßt sich leicht sagen** That is easily said. **Er läßt Holz auf sich hacken** He is easily imposed upon, He'll stand anything, lit. He allows wood to be chopped upon himself. **Er läßt sich leicht abschrecken** He is easily deterred.

B. *With Intransitive or Passive Force.* In German, reflexive form often corresponds to intransitive in English. In one large group the reflexive verb represents a person or, by way of personification, a thing as acting on himself or itself: **Sie kleidet sich einfach** She dresses plainly. **Die Erde dreht sich um ihre Achse** The earth turns on its axis. **Der Wind hat sich gedreht** The wind has turned. **Das Volk sammelt sich auf dem Rathaus** The people are assembling at the city hall. In another group reflexive form has a force closely related to intransitive use, so that the subject is not thought of as acting upon himself: **Die Ohnmächtige erholt sich** is coming to (herself again). **Der Kranke soll sich erheblich gebessert haben** is said to have improved. **Er hat sich nicht gezeigt** He didn't show up. **Das kleine Mädchen hat sich zu einem Fräulein ausgewachsen** has developed into. In another group of reflexive verbs passive develops out of intransitive force: **Der Dampf verflüssigt sich** The steam is becoming a liquid, hence is passing into a new state, which clearly indicates that it is being acted on. Similarly with passive force: **Solche Häuser vermieten sich leicht** Such houses rent or are rented easily. **Salz löst sich auf** Salt dissolves, or can be dissolved. English in a few cases clings here to intransitive form where in German the passive form is so clearly felt that passive form is used: **Die erste Sendung wurde in einer Woche ausverkauft** The first consignment *sold out* or *was sold out* in a week. **Sein Hut wurde in den Fluß geweht** His hat blew into the river.

The line of development here is clear. Reflexive force often develops into intransitive and intransitive into passive. When intransitive force develops, English often discards the old reflexive pronoun: I met a fool, who laid him down and *basked him* (now simply *basked*) in the sun (*As You Like It*, 2, 7, 15). As can be seen by the examples given above, English still often retains intransitive form after it has acquired passive force. It sometimes even retains the original reflexive form after the development of active and, still later, passive force: The fire *communicated itself* to the next house. German is usually tenacious of reflexive form even after its meaning has changed.

a. A few verbs are used intransitively or reflexively: **eilen** or less commonly **sich eilen** to hasten, **endigen** (or less commonly **enden**) or less commonly **sich endigen** (or **enden**) to end, **flüchten** or perhaps more commonly **sich flüchten** to flee, **gebaren** or more commonly **sich gebaren** to act, behave, **irren** or **sich irren** to err, make a mistake, **nahen** or more commonly **sich nähern** (or less commonly **sich nahen**; **258.** 1. A. *d*) to approach, **verbluten** or perhaps more commonly **sich verbluten** to bleed to death. &c.

There is sometimes a differentiation of meaning: **ausruhen** *to rest*, as in **Er ruht auf seinen Lorbeeren aus**, but to indicate purpose **sich ausruhen**, as in **Ich habe mich ausgeruht** and **Er setzte sich, um sich auszuruhen; erübrigen** *to remain*, as in **Es erübrigt noch, auf den letzten Punkt der Tagesordnung, einzugehen**, but **sich erübrigen** *to be superfluous, unnecessary*, as in **Es erübrigt sich, auf diese Frage einzugehen.**

b. Corresponding to the German reflexive verb we often have in English a transitive with an object of the thing: **Er bessert sich** He is mending his ways. **Er hat sich erkältet** He has caught a cold. **Er räusperte sich** He cleared his throat. **Lowell versuchte sich einmal an einem Roman** Lowell once tried his hand at a novel. **Er schlägt sich mit ihm** He is having a fight with him. **Er schreibt sich mit ihm** He is carrying on a correspondence with him. **Er küßte sich mit ihr** He exchanged kisses with her.

c. In many common cases the use of a transitive verb reflexively gives the verb intransive ingressive force. See **164**.

C. With intransitives (or transitives used like intransitives without an object) in the impersonal construction, to show that the action is proceeding, or is able to proceed in a certain manner, which is represented as the natural result of the given circumstances: **Es tanzt sich gut in diesem Saal** This room is good for dancing. **Es fährt sich bequem in diesem Wagen** It is pleasant riding in this carriage. **Wie ritt es sich lustig durch die gebirgigen Wege!** What jolly riding that was over the mountain roads! **Es schreibt sich schlecht auf diesem Papier** This paper is bad for writing on. **Mit der Eisenbahn fährt es sich rasch. Von eurer Fahrt kehrt sich's nicht immer wieder** From journeys like yours it is in the nature of things that one does not always return.

a. Sometimes a trans. verb and its object are conceived of as forming together an intrans. verb, and can thus form this impersonal reflexive construction: **Wie hübsch spielt sich's den Vater, wenn man so allerliebste Geständnisse zu hören bekommt** (Schiller) How nice it is to play the father when one gets to hear such charming confessions.

D. Frequent is the use of a reflexive in connexion with a prep. phrase or an objective predicate to denote a change of place or condition, or the result of an action, often corresponding in English to a transitive verb with an object of the thing: **Ich lief mich in Schweiß** I began to perspire from running. **Ich fiel mich wund** I became sore from a fall. **Er drängte sich herein** He pushed his way in. **Er schlug sich durch den Feind durch** He fought his way thru the enemy. **Er tastete sich zum Fenster** He groped his way to the window. **Er hat sich um vier Mark verrechnet** He made a mistake of four marks in counting.

E. **Haben** is often used reflexively as a strong negative reply to a preceding statement, but is in fact an affirmative assertion, uttered in an ironical tone: **Und das Geschäft blüht? Jawohl, blüht! Hat sich da was zu blühen!** (Eckstein) Is your business flourishing? Oh yes, it is flourishing finely (ironically).

IMPERSONAL VERBS

219. Impersonal verbs are conjugated like other verbs thruout the different moods and tenses, but are defective in having only a third person sing. and no passive at all (for exception see 5 below). The impersonal construction in German is a favorite one and has been very productive, and many verbs are now used impersonally which with other meanings are also personal. The **es** is not absolutely necessary here as the activity or state represented by the verb is not felt as standing in a relation to a subject, as explained in **250.** *a* (2nd par.): **Mich hungert.** The **es** was first inserted in such forms of the sentence where the verb stood in the first place: **Es hungert mich.** The **es** was thus first employed here to distinguish the declarative from the interrogative form of sentence. Another influence helped establish **es** as subject in these impersonal constructions. Even early in O.H.G. there was already a strong tendency to conform German expression here to the normal type of sentence structure with a subject and a predicate, hence to use a mere formal subject without meaning rather than to leave the sentence entirely without a subject. This is clearly indicated by the frequent use of es where it was not needed to distinguish the declarative from the interrogative form: Thar was fiur thuruh daȥ, wanta iȥ filu kalt was (Otfrid, IV. 18. 11) **Es brannte nun ein Feuer dort,**

weil es sehr kalt war. The employment of the formal subject **es** here was suggested by the use of anticipative **es** (**251. I.** 2. B) which, tho it had a little concrete meaning in that it pointed forward to a following clause, the real subject of the sentence, was nevertheless a mere formal element and as such could be omitted and can sometimes even still be omitted, as illustrated in **251. I.** 2. B. *Note.* Present usage with regard to the use or omission of impersonal **es** is defined in detail below.

The following groups are very common:

1. Verbs which alone or in connection with a predicate noun or adjective express phenomena of nature, the time of day, seasons of the year, divisions of the month, week, &c., distances in space and time, &c., where the situation makes the thought clear without the aid of a definite subject: **es regnet** it rains; **es schneit** it snows; **es hagelt** it hails; **es friert** it freezes; **es dämmert** it is twilight; **es düstert** it is growing dusky; **es tagt** it is dawning; **es taut auf** it thaws; **es donnert** it thunders; **es blitzt** it lightens, **es blitzte schelmisch in ihren Augen** there was a sly look in her eyes; **es wird Nacht** it is getting quite dark; **es ist gutes, schlechtes Wetter; es ist zu spät; es ist kalt, warm, heiß,** and sometimes after the manner of the French **macht's heiß?** (Grillparzer's *Libussa,* 2), **es macht kalt; wieviel Uhr ist es?** what time is it?; **es ist elf** it is eleven o'clock; **es geht auf elf; es schlägt elf; es ist dunkel, es ist Sommer, es lenzt** spring is coming, has come, **es herbstet. Es ist heute Feiertag** It's a holiday to-day. **Es ist Montag** It is Monday. **Es ist der erste Juni** It is the first of June.

Often in German and sometimes in English there is still as in oldest German no **es** here in case of a predicate noun, adjective, or adverb where some other word than **es** introduces the sentence, or where the predicate noun stands in a subordinate clause: **Heute ist der erste Juni** To-day is the first of June. **Morgen ist Feiertag** To-morrow is a holiday. **Morgen ist bei uns frei, auf der Mädchenschule nicht** To-morrow is a holiday with us, but not at the girls' school. **Heute morgen hat es gefroren, jetzt ist Tauwetter. Er trug immer eine braune Kutte mit einer Kapuze daran, die er über den Kopf stülpte, wenn schlecht Wetter war** (V. Blüthgen's *Das Peterle von Nürnberg,* chap. II). **Der wievielte ist heute?** What day of the month is to-day, *or* is it to-day? Compare **219** and also 4. B. *a. Note* and 5. B. *a* below. In English the preservation of the old impersonal form without a subject has been rendered easy by the now common simple device of placing the expletive *there* at the beginning of the sentence: *There* was a heavy frost last night. Also in German there is a tendency in *lively* modern as well as older colloquial speech to omit **es**, as there is still a distinct feeling that the activity or state expressed by the verb does not stand in relation to a subject: **Ist kalt heute!** Compare **250.** *a.*

The impersonal **es** here and elsewhere should not be confounded with the **es** which points to something definite which is more or less clearly defined by the situation: **Kommst du heute zu mir? Es** (i.e. the way, distance) **ist mir zu weit,** or **Es ist mir zu weit zu dir. Warten Sie bis nächste Woche. Es** (i.e. this period of waiting) **ist mir zu lange bis dahin.** This situation **es,** provided it does not stand in the first place in sentence or clause, is still often omitted in certain set expressions where the situation makes the thought clear: **Zu dir ist** (or **ist es**) **mir zu weit. Bis dahin ist** (or **ist es**) **mir zu lange.** Compare 3 (last par.) below. In *lively* colloquial speech also the **es** which stands in the first place may still drop out: **Ist mir zu weit!**

2. Many reflexive verbs or verbs used reflexively: **Es klärt sich auf** It is clearing up. **Es geht sich** (**218.** 3. C) **sehr gut** The walking is very good. **Es tritt sich auf dem Pflaster der Straße unangenehm. Auf diesem Wege fährt es sich gut. Es tanzt sich gut in diesem Saale. Es liest sich in der Dämmerung schlecht** *It's bad reading in the twilight,* but the **es** does not belong here at all where the reference is to something definite: **Es** (referring to a book under consideration) **liest sich angenehm** *It is pleasant reading,* or **Es liest sich, als wäre es wahr** *It reads like truth.*

Es is not omitted in this modern category which has developed under the domination of formal grammar, which requires a subject for every sentence.

3. Within the present period in both English and German the impersonal construction has come into much wider use than formerly as it seemed ever more desirable not to bring the activity or state into relation to a definite subject but to direct the attention solely to the activity. In German an impersonal transitive or intransitive verb with its formal subject **es** is employed, while in English the older form without a formal subject is preferred, introduced here as so often elsewhere by the expletive *there*, usually in connection with a predicate in the form of a verbal noun: **Es klopft** *There is a knock at the door.* In the English sentence *knock* is not a subject, so that the idea is not "A knock is at the door," but *knock* is a predicate, i.e. a knocking is predicated, and *is* is the formal sign of predication, just as the **t** in the German verb **klopft.** The German and English sentences are exactly alike in form and meaning. In both the attention is merely called to an activity without any desire of bringing it into relation to a definite subject. Altho the impersonal construction is very common in English the personal construction with the name of a person or thing in the nominative is sometimes found where the German construction is impersonal, so that in the following examples the two languages do not always coincide: **Es brennt!** Fire! Fire! **Es zuckte um seinen Mund** There was a twitching about his mouth. **Es reißt mir in allen Gliedern** I feel racking pains in all my limbs. **Es kocht in ihm** He is boiling with rage. **Da wallte es in ihm auf** Then his blood began to boil. **Manchmal lief es ihm kalt den Rücken herab** Many a time a cold thrill ran down his back. **Es setzt Schläge** It has come to blows. **Es wogte und tobte** There was a heaving and raging, i.e. their minds were in violent commotion. **Es zieht hier** There is a draught here. **Es schallt sehr in diesem Saale** There is a strong resonance in this hall. **Es riecht hier nach Talg. Es geht bergab mit seiner Gesundheit. Es braucht keines weiteren Wortes. Es bedarf nur eines Wortes. Es hapert irgendwo** There is a hitch somewhere.

Sometimes the **es** seems to indicate an indefinite, indescribable something and sometimes it imparts a weird, ghostly impression: **Es läßt mir keine Ruhe** A queer undefinable feeling of unrest disquiets me. **Oft ergriff es ihn mit dämonischer Gewalt** (Raabe's *Ein Frühling*, chap. vi). **Es geht im Hause um** The house is haunted. **Und als er im willigen Schlummer lag, bewegt es sich unter dem Bette** And when he was about to go to sleep something stirred under the bed. The verbs used here are such as usually have a personal subject. The vague, indefinite impression so often conveyed here by this construction seems to come from the fact that no definite person is mentioned with verbs that are usually associated with definite reference. The idea of indefiniteness thus attaches here to **es,** which altho subject does not reveal anything about the person or persons engaged in the activity.

The **es** is regularly expressed in this large modern category which has developed under the domination of formal grammar, which requires a subject for every sentence. Moreover the **es** is here often absolutely necessary to distinguish the declarative from the interrogative form of statement, for the verb here is usually important and naturally comes to the front by reason of its emphasis, or its prominence in the narrative style which markedly characterizes many of these sentences naturally brings it forward, as described in **251.** II. B. *a. bb.* Compare **219** and **250.** *a* (2nd par.).

The impersonal **es** here and elsewhere should not be confounded with the **es** or **das** which points to something definite which is more or less clearly defined by the situation: **Wird's bald?** Are you ever going to get thru?, lit. Will it (the work in hand) soon come into being? **Es geht nicht** It can't be done. **Es** (or **das**) **ist mir recht. Es ist mir einerlei. Es steht schlecht** Things are in bad condition. **Das regnet ja heut in einem fort! Das gibt ein Unglück. Es ist Hans** (uttered by someone who has just heard approaching steps). **Es** (i.e. the waiting) **dauerte lange, ehe er kam. Es brennt** (spoken in the house with reference to the fire in the stove), but **es** is impersonal in **Es brennt!** (a cry upon the street). This situation **es,** provided it does not stand in the first place in sentence or clause, is still often omitted in certain set expressions where the situation makes the thought clear: **Er kommt so bald als möglich** = **so bald als es** (i.e. **das Kommen**) **möglich ist. Er benahm sich nicht, wie sich schickte,** or **wie es sich schickte.** Compare **251.** II. A. *d.* See also 1 and 2 above.

a. The impersonal **es gibt** *there is, there are* from its unusual frequency demands a careful study. It simply calls attention to a giving, causing, producing without any attempt to bring the activity into relations to a definite subject, hence it closely resembles in construction **es regnet,** differing from it only in verbal meaning and of course also in grammatical function in that it is a transitive and takes an accusative object indicating the result of the verbal activity: **Es gibt viel Elend im Lande** *There is much misery in the land.* In the English form of this impersonal construction *misery* is not an object as in German but a predicate nominative, so that *misery* is simply predicated without being represented as a result of active forces as in German. When the idea of active natural forces disappears we find also in German the English form, but with **es** instead of *there*: **Es gibt Löwen in Afrika, aber nicht in Europa** *There are lions in Africa but not in Europe,* which is a natural result of the different state of civilization, but **Es sind weiße Elefanten in dieser Menagerie** *There are white elephants in this menagerie,* where the reference is merely to a state of things, not to active natural forces producing results. Notice that the **es** of the **es ist (sind)** construction drops out if it is not the first word, while *there* in English always remains: **In dieser Menagerie sind weiße Elefanten** *In this menagerie there are white elephants,* but **In Afrika gibt es Löwen** *In Africa there are lions.* The German is very fond of the **es gibt** form: **Es gibt eine Vergeltung im Leben** There is such a thing in life as retribution. **Es gab keinen größeren Meister in der Kunst des Halbdunkels als den Doktor Theophile Stein** (Raabe's *Hungerpastor,* chap. xx). **Es gibt solche Menschen** There are such people. **Es gibt nichts Dümmres als ihn** There is nothing more stupid than he is. **Was gibt's Neues? Es gibt nichts Neues.** What's the news? There is no news. **Es gibt Streit und Lärm** There is contention and noise going on.

After the analogy of a number of the above sentences where **es gibt** is used in a broad general statement it is sometimes employed to avoid particular mention, and to state something in a vague, general way: **Es gibt hier einen jungen Menschen, der seine Äußerungen ein wenig mehr bewachen könnte** There is here a young fellow (I do not desire to point him out) who might be a little more guarded in his remarks.

In English we sometimes find a personal construction where in German the impersonal form of statement is used: **Was gibt's heute? Es gibt heute noch Schnee** What shall we get to-day? We shall get some snow yet to-day. **Gestern zu Mittag gab es Kohl** Yesterday we had cabbage for dinner.

Note. The real nature of this construction is sometimes little felt, as in dialect the object of **geben** sometimes becomes the subject and this incorrect usage appears occasionally in the literary language: **Es ist ein Kauz, wie's mehr noch geben** (Goethe's *Urfaust,* l. 1175). **Es müssen auch solche Käuze geben** (*Kölnische Zeitung*).

4. A. Some verbs expressing states of the mind or body. There is here still, as in earlier periods, considerable fluctuation of usage as there often prevails the desire to call attention merely to an activity as going on in the body or mind without bringing it into a relation to a definite subject, when of course the impersonal construction is employed, or, on the other hand, it is often desired to call attention to a definite person or thing as the subject and thus indicate that the person is felt as passing thru an experience, or a definite person or thing is conceived as affecting the person: **Es erbarmt mich deiner** *I pity you,* **Mich erbarmt deiner, Du erbarmst mich, Dein Unglück erbarmt mich,** or more commonly **Ich erbarme mich über dich.** The impersonal idea which has proved useful in modern as well as older life and hence is well preserved in the other groups and has there even been spreading has in this group in general since O.H.G. been slowly yielding to the personal idea. In this group as in others impersonal **es** must be carefully distinguished from situation **es** (see 3, last par.), which points to something definite which is more or less clearly defined by the situation: **Es** (referring to a misfortune at hand) **betrübt mich tief. Es** (life) **gefällt mir in Berlin. Es** or **das verschlägt mir nichts** *It* or *that* (the issue, matter at hand) *is quite immaterial to me.*

On the basis of grammatical form this impersonal group falls into three classes:

a. Those that take an acc. of the person: **es dünkt** (rare form **dünkelt**) or **bedünkt (bedünkelt) mich** or **mir** it seems to me; **es brennt mich** it smarts; **es durstet** or **dürstet mich,** or **ich bin durstig** I am thirsty, **ich dürste nach; es friert mich** I am cold, **es friert mich an** (w. dat. of the part affected, as **den**

Füßen, sometimes also w. acc. **die Füße**), or with a little different meaning **in** with acc. (: **es friert mich bis in die Fingerspitzen**), or **ich friere an** (**den Füßen**), or **mir frieren die Füße; es fröstelt mich** or sometimes **mir,** also **ich fröstele** I feel chilly; **es hungert mich,** or **ich bin hungrig** I am hungry; **es juckt mich** I itch, **es juckt mich auf dem ganzen Körper, im Ohr, in den Zehen, die Zehen jucken mir,** or **meine Zehen jucken; es kitzelt mich** (or sometimes **mir**), **es kitzelt mich am Leibe, am ganzen Leibe; es kratzt** or **kitzelt mich im Halse; es schläfert mich** I am sleepy; **es schmerzt mich** it pains me; **es schüttelt mich** it sends a shiver thru me, I'm shivering; **es schwitzt mich,** or more commonly **ich schwitze** I am perspiring; **es würgt mich** I'm choking, I have a choking sensation; **es wurmt mich** (or now less commonly **mir**) it vexes me inwardly.

b. Those that take a dative of the person: **es ist mir bekehrt,** common in colloquial language in the expression **Ich weiß selber nicht recht, wie mir bekehrt ist** (Telmann's *Wahrheit,* XIII), or **Ich weiß nicht, wie ich bekehrt bin** I am sorely puzzled; **es beliebt** *it pleases* in certain set expressions, as **wie es Ihnen beliebt** *as you please,* also **es geliebt** *it pleases* in a few expressions, as **geliebt es Gott** *if God wills,* **geliebt's den Göttern** (Grillparzer's *Libussa,* 2); **es dämmert mir** it dawns upon my mind, as in **Es dämmerte mir in der Seele wunderbar bei seiner Rede,** but often also with a nom. subject of the thing, as in **Mir dämmert ein Strahl von Hoffnung; es eilt mir** I am in a hurry, **es eilt Ihnen ja auf einmal ganz gewaltig, Herr, mir gute Nacht zu wünschen** (Wilbrandt's *Vater Robinson,* II. chap. ii), also **ich habe Eile** and **es pressiert mir: Aber es ist doch besser, als daß Sie bis morgen warten müssen, wenn es Ihnen schon so pressiert** (Spielhagen's *Faustulus,* p. 60), or **ich bin pressiert; es fehlt mir an** (w. dat.) I lack; **es geht mir gut** I'm well; **es gelingt mir** I succeed, still sometimes used impersonally, as in **Es ist ihm damit gelungen,** but more commonly with a nom. subject of a thing, as in **Es, alles, nichts, der Versuch ist ihm gelungen,** or with an infinitive as logical subject, as in **Es ist mir gelungen, ihn zu besänftigen; es graut, grauelt, grauselt, graust, gruselt mir** or **mich** (**vor** w. dat.), or **ich graue, grau[e]le,** &c. **mich** (**vor**) I shudder (at), **es ist, wird mir angst, bange,** or sometimes **ich bin angst** (originally a substantive, now sometimes construed as a predicate adjective) and more commonly **ich bin bange** (originally an adverb, now quite commonly felt as an adjective), **bist du bange?** (Otto Ernst's *Jugend von heute,* 4, 6), or **es bangt mir** or **mich** I am, am getting anxious, afraid, **es bangt mir** or **mich für** (**um**) **mein Leben, meinen Freund, vor dem Tode,** or **ich bange mich** or **ich bange für etwas** (or **einen**) or **vor etwas, es fürchtet mir** (Swiss = **ich fürchte mich**); **es liegt mir daran** it is of importance to me; **es rappelt ihm** or more commonly **bei ihm** something is wrong with him in his upper story; **es schaudert mir** or **mich** I shudder, **mir schaudert** (**vor** + dat.), or **ich schaudere** (**vor** + dat.); **es schwindelt mir** (sometimes **mich**) I am giddy, dizzy; **sein** in connection with certain adjectives and adverbs, as **es ist mir kalt, warm** I am cold, warm, or sometimes after the manner of the French: **Hast du kalt?** (Wildenbruch's *König Heinrich,* 2, 4); **es ist mir schwach** I feel faint, **es ist mir übel** I feel sick at the stomach; **es ist mir wohl zu Mut** I am in good humor; **es träumt mir** (only rarely **mich**), or **ich träume** I dream; **es widert mir vor etwas,** or **etwas zu tun** I loathe something, or to do something, also with acc.; **mir zweifelt nicht daran** I have no doubt about it, now usually **ich zweifle nicht daran.**

c. There is a group of impersonal verbs with an acc. or dat. and a gen.: **Es erbarmt mich seiner** or **Mich erbarmt seiner** *I pity him.* These verbs are given in **262.** II. A. *c.* In early N.H.G. they formed a flourishing group, but since that time they have entirely or in part abandoned the impersonal construction and where it is retained the original form of expression has been considerably changed, as described in detail in **262.** II. B. *d.*

B. *a.* The constructions *a, b, c* under A may be varied by changing the order, either placing the dat. or acc. object before and the **es** after the verb, or by thus inverting the object but suppressing the **es: es graut mir,** or **mir**

graut es, or **mir graut.** Some verbs only take the **es** in the inverted word-order, when no other modifiers follow: **Ihn jammert es** It causes him pity, but **Ihn jammert des Volkes** He pities the people. After a number of the verbs describing a state of mind or body the **es** can usually only stand as the first word in this construction in the principal proposition and in the subordinate clause is usually omitted altogether: **Mich dünkt, er wird alt. Mich hungerte. Selig sind die da hungert vnd dürstet nach der Gerechtigkeit** (Matth. v. 6). **Es ist, als ob jemand anders das Wasser trinkt, nach dem mich dürstet** (Spielhagen's *Sonntagskind,* II, 5). **Es ist nicht kalt, wie mich dünkt** (M. Heyne, *Wörterbuch*). **Wie mir ekelt . . . wie mir ekelt!** (delle Grazie's *Vineta*). Notice also the sentence from Telmann in A. *b* above. More and more, however, the formal subject **es** is gradually forcing its way into these positions: **Mir, mich ekelt** (es) (Daniel Sanders).

Note. Originally such verbs did not take a formal subject, as the activity or state expressed by the verb was not felt as standing in a relation to a subject. Thus the omission of the **es** in the inverted and the transposed order is the survival of a once general usage. Compare **219** and also **250.** *a.*

b. Observe that, tho the impersonal construction may sometimes be replaced by the personal, as in **Es friert ihn,** or **er friert** *He is freezing,* sometimes there is a sharp distinction between them. The impersonal construction indicates that the force exerted comes from without, while the personal subject indicates that the act comes from the subject: **Er friert und hungert aus Geiz** He freezes and goes hungry from pure stinginess. Here the impersonal construction could not be used.

5. An impersonal construction with **es** either expressed or understood is found in the passive of verbs that govern the gen. or dat., and with many other intransitives, an idiom that is quite foreign to our language. Note the following points:

A. In transferring a sentence from the active to the passive, the acc. as in English becomes nom., but the gen., dat., and a prep. phrase remain unchanged and the subject becomes **es** expressed or understood: (active) **er spottet meiner;** (passive) **es wird meiner gespottet,** or **meiner wird gespottet; er schmeichelt mir, es wird mir von ihm geschmeichelt,** or **mir wird von ihm geschmeichelt. Er schickte mich nach dem Arzt** He sent me for the physician. **Es ist nach dem Arzt geschickt worden** The physician has been sent for. **Ich habe an ihn geschrieben** I have written to him. **Es ist an ihn geschrieben worden** He has been written to. When the agent is not expressed as in the last sentence, this impersonal passive, as in B below, represents an activity only in a general way without reference to a definite agent. For fuller description of this construction, see **258. 1.**

This construction is not only found with the regular passive forms but also with predicate modal verbals (**180.** A) which take a dative or a prepositional phrase, as this construction, i.e. a prepositional infinitive after the copula **sein,** is now felt as a passive form, since with transitive verbs it has passive force: **Es ist ihm** (or **Ihm ist**) **nicht zu trauen** *He is not to be trusted.* **Es ist ihm** (or **Ihm ist**) **nicht beizukommen** *There* (formerly *it*) *is no getting at him.* **Es ist nicht mit ihm auszukommen,** or **Mit ihm ist nicht auszukommen.**

As actional passive (**194.** 4) forms are used in all the examples given above the reference is to an act. The statal passive (**194.** 4) must be used here when the reference is to a state: **Ihr ist** (or **Es ist ihr**) **geholfen** She is cared for. Here the participle is always the predicate, but there is no actual subject, at most only a formal subject, **es,** which can only be expressed when it stands in the first place. In the objective predicate construction the object of the principal verb is the subject of the clause and the participle is the predicate: **Ich glaubte ihn geheilt** I believed him to be cured. In the impersonal objective predicate construction there can be no accusative object as there is no subject in the clause. The dative or prepositional object of the active is simply retained in the passive: **Ich glaubte ihr geholfen** I believed her to be cared for. **Ich fühle mir** (often **mich**) **durch Ihren Brief geschmeichelt.** Compare **262.** III. 2. B (last par.).

B. The impersonal passive of such intransitives as have no object at all and such transitives as are used like intransitives without an object does not represent the subject (see *a* below) as acted on, but denotes in quite a general way an activity or a state in and of itself without reference to a definite subject, and with no reference whatever to a direct object: **Es wird gelaufen** There (compare 3 above, 1st par.) is running going on; **Es wurde immer viel geplaudert, gescherzt und gelacht** There was always a good deal of chatting, joking and laughing. **Oben wird getanzt** There is dancing going on upstairs. **Es wird noch geschlafen** Some people are still asleep. **Für den lieben König und Herrn wird** [personal passive] **alles getan, wird** [impersonal passive] **treulich gekämpft, wird** [impers.] **willig geblutet, wird** [impers.] **freudig in den Tod gegangen, für ihn wird** [impers.] **mehr als gestorben: für ihn werden** [pers.] **starken Herzens auch die Kinder geopfert** (Vilmar's *Literaturgeschichte*). **Man muß Soldat sein für sein Land oder aus Liebe zu der Sache, für die gefochten wird.**

a. In principal propositions in both A and B **es** must, according to **219,** be used when the verb is not preceded by a modifier, for it is then needed at the head of the sentence to distinguish the declarative from the interrogative form of sentence, but drops out when some other word takes the first place. It is also omitted as a rule in subordinate clauses with transposed word-order.

b. This construction can only be used with intransitives which express an activity or condition that stands in a relation to a free moral agent: **Es wird gegessen, geschlafen** They (indefinite) are eating, sleeping, but not **Es wird gefunkelt, geblitzt, gerauscht** There is a sparkling, it is lightening, there is a rushing of water.

Note. This construction arose with transitives that can be used in the active without an expressed object and hence in the passive without an expressed subject: **Bittet | so wird euch gegeben | Suchet so werdet jr finden | Klopfet an | so wird euch aufgethan** (Luke xi. 9). The original passive force can here still be felt, but as there is in the active no object and in the passive no subject the transitive idea is overshadowed by the conception of an activity pure and simple, an activity that is conceived as proceeding without reference to any agent at work or to any definite subject as acted upon, so that the force is usually felt as intransitive and the construction is extended to intransitives. **Heute wird gelacht.** This passive construction, already in use in Gothic and O.H.G., became common in M.H.G.

c. In certain set expressions a trans. verb and its object are conceived of as together forming the idea of an activity, and hence the verb with its object, both together being treated as a simple intrans., may form this impersonal passive: **Es wurde Kegel** (acc. pl.) **geschoben** There was playing at ninepins going on. **Rastlos wurde fortgewirkt, gewaffnet, geübt, gekleidet und Verwundete** (acc. pl.) **geheilt** (Kohlrausch). **Unter diesen wurde fleißig Karten gespielt, gemäßigte Parkpromenaden gemacht, den Tafelfreuden gehuldigt und unabsehbar viel „kannegegossen"** (Suttner's *Die Waffen nieder!*, III). In the same manner a verb and its reflexive object is sometimes treated as a simple intransitive: **Da wurde geknufft und geprügelt, in zitternder Angst sich verkrochen und mit lautem Hallo losgestürmt** (C. Viebig's *Die Wacht am Rhein*, p. 48). Compare **177.** I. B. *b* (last par.). The reflexive construction has not found favor with grammarians, altho it is widely used in dialect and colloquial speech and for hundreds of years has from time to time occasionally appeared in the literary language.

PARTICLES.

220. A particle is a word that cannot be inflected at all. Particles are divided into adverbs, prepositons, conjunctions, and interjections, but these classes cannot always be sharply defined, as many prepositions and conjunctions are also reckoned among adverbs.

ADVERBS.

221. Definition. The adverb (i.e. belonging to a verb) is true to its name, a particle principally used to modify the meaning of a verb, but it may also modify an adjective or another adverb: **Der Sturm tobt sehr; ein sehr heftiger Sturm; ein sehr heftig tobender Sturm.**

a. The adverb is often used alone without reference to a verb, adjective, or other adverb: **herein!** come in! **vorwärts!** forward! **auf, auf, Kameraden!**

The Function and Form of Adverbs, Adjectives, and Prepositions Compared.

222. 1. The adverb borders very closely in its nature upon the adjective. It modifies a verb, adjective, or other adverb in the same manner as an adjective modifies a noun. Thus in general out of any adjective an adverb can be formed and there results a large number of parallel forms—an inflected one modifying a noun and an uninflected one modifying a verb, adjective, or other adverb.

2. The adverb has usually exactly the same form as the uninflected form of the adjective. Only in earlier periods of the language were they distinguished in form. Thus as the adverb has to-day usually the same form as the predicate adjective, and as both often approach each other closely in nature, the boundary between their respective functions is not always sharply defined, as illustrated in E below. Hence an adverb is often used for an adjective, where there is no corresponding adjective. Many adverbs which are now used adjectively were originally used as true adverbs, modifiers of a verb, and did not take on adjective function until after the verb (i.e. participle) had been dropped and they themselves stood alone in the predicate, and were felt as the real predicate complement: **Die Tür ist zu(gemacht).** It will be noticed in the articles below that these adverbs assumed adjective function first in the predicate. That they later were also used attributively and have taken on adjective inflection is only a natural development. The following cases of interchange of function, or form, or of both between adjectives and adverbs occur:

A. An adverb or adverbial phrase often takes on adjective function when there is no corresponding adjective:

a. In the predicate to express rest in a place or a condition, often with the verb **sein,** and sometimes as objective predicate after the verbs **lassen** and **wissen,** and sometimes when no verb is expressed: **Er ist da. Die Tür ist zu. Ich weiß ihn dort, laß ihn dort** I know that he is there, leave him there. **Hier** [**ist**] **der ergrimmte Feldherr, dort** [**ist**] **die Fürchterliche** (Schiller's *Jungfrau von Orleans*, 2, 6). **Er ist zu'frieden** (lit. *in peace*).

b. In the predicate to express motion to or from a place, lit. or figuratively, usually with the verb **sein: Sie sind fort** They are gone. **Die Wintersaat ist zwar** (**he**)**rein** (in). **Er ist von dort** He is from that place. **Er ist aus** (from) **Frankreich. Es ist aus mit ihm** It is all over with him.

c. In the predicate to express time: **Es war im März. Das Konzert ist aus. Das ist nun vorbei.**

d. Attributively, following the noun that it limits, in the case of those classes of adverbs described in *a, b, c.*: **der Mann da** the man yonder; **der da oben** He on high; **der Berg dort** the mountain yonder; **die Fahrt hierher** the journey to this place; **die Aussicht auf den Fluß; ein Wort fürs Herz; der Baum drüben; die Kämpfe in den Jahren 1813–15,** &c.

e. Sometimes in the predicate, in case of adverbs of manner after **sein** and sometimes **werden: Es ist so, anders** It is thus, different. **Es ist umsonst, or vergebens** It is in vain. **Er ist rechts, links** He is right-handed, left-handed. **Er wird mir zuwider** He is becoming disagreeable to me.

f. In dialect or popular language in case of an adverb of manner, when it stands before a noun in the attributive relation: **Es gibt so Gänschen** (i.e. girls), **die hübsch weiche Schnäbel haben** (H. Hoffmann's *Wider den Kurfürsten*, chap. i).

g. In the superlative (**112.** 3. B) in the predicate, instead of a superlative adjective: **Der Sturm war am heftigsten gegen Abend.**

B. As a number of adverbs (as those in A. *a, b, c, e*) could stand as an adjective in the predicate, it was only a natural development for them to assume adjective function also in the attributive relation. Thus **nahe, fern, selten, zu'frieden, vor'handen, be'hende, einzeln, täglich, ungefähr, teilweise, anderweit,** &c., have developed into full adjectives with adjective inflection. Other adverbs which have not proceeded so far in this development are thus used in colloquial speech and dialect and occasionally appear in the literary language: **Ich mußte also den ganzen Tag Einladungen an allerhand uninteressante und zuwidere** (see A. *e*) **Menschen verfassen** (Hermann Bahr in *Theater*, chap. ix). Dialect goes much farther, and uses other adverbs adjectively: **ein zues or zuenes Fenster** a closed window, **der entzweie Topf** the broken pot; **der hinene Stuhl** the broken chair, &c. Notice here that the adverbs **zu** and **hin** usually become **zuen** and **hinen** in adj. function. Quite a number of other adverbs can also in the literary language take on adjective function and inflection when they add the suffix **ig.** See **245.** II. 9. 2. B.

C. In the case of verbal nouns in **-ung** and nouns denoting agents in **-er** the adjective in fact fills the office of the adverb, as these nouns have in reality the meaning and force of verbs. Thus in **eine gute Erzählung** *a good story* and **ein guter Erzähler** *a good story-teller* the adjective marks the effectiveness of an action and not the quality of an object. In some cases such expressions may be ambiguous, as the adjective may also refer to the author of the action, and not the action. Hence such expressions cannot be freely formed. We may say **ein schwacher** (or **kein starker**) **Esser, ein starker Trinker, ein langjähriger Mitarbeiter, ein guter Beobachter, Redner, Reiter, Schachspieler, Schwimmer,** &c., but not **ein schöner Schreiber, ein guter, schlechter Schläfer,** &c. In such cases in German we must usually take recourse to compounds or group-words: **ein Lebemann** a fast liver, **der Frühaufsteher** or **Frühauf** early riser, **Schönschreiber** good penman, **Feinschmecker** one with a fine sense of taste, **Langschläfer** late sleeper, &c. It is often necessary in German to use a substantive-participle or a pure verbal form here: **Der richtig Ratende** the right guesser; **der Höchstbesteuerte** the highest taxpayer; **einer, der spät kommt** a late comer, &c.

D. In dialect the adverb standing before an adjective is often erroneously taken for an adjective, and hence assumes adjective inflection: **ein ganzer** (instead of **ganz**) **guter Mann.**

E. On account of the dimness of the line dividing adverb and predicate adjective the adverb has in N.H.G. given up in the positive and comparative the special form which it had in earlier periods, and assumed the exact form of the predicate adjective. However in poetry, elevated diction, and in case of a few isolated adverbs even in prose we still find occasionally the old adverbial form. See *Note.* In the superlative the adverb has in N.H.G. developed new special forms (see **114.** 2. 3), one of which is, however, also used adjectively in the predicate (see **112.** 3. B).

Note. In M.H.G. the positive of the adverb was often distinguished from the adjective by the ending **-e** or **-liche** (cognate with English *-ly*), and even to-day some adverbs have alongside of their short form also the M.H.G. form in **-e,** especially **lange, ferne, gerne, stille,** and in poetry and elevated diction also others as **balde,** &c. For survivals of the older adverbial form in **-lich** see **245.** IV. 2. *b.* In M.H.G. some adverbs were distinguished from the uninflected form of mutated adjectives by taking no mutation, and this usage is still found in the classics, and even to-day in poetry: **Wir haben keine Magd; muß kochen, fegen, stricken | und nähen, und laufen früh und spat** (now **spät**).—Goethe's *Faust,* 3111-2. **Was beginnt ihr morgen fruh?** (for **früh**) (Geibel). All feeling for this differentiation of form has in general disappeared, so that in the few cases in prose where double forms, one for the adverb, one for the adjective, still exist, each form has taken on a different meaning: **schon** *already,* but **schön** *beautiful;* **fast** *almost,* but **fest** *firm.* **Schön** and **fest** are now also used adverbially and then take the meaning of the adjectives **schön** and **fest**—*beautifully, firmly.* As here in case of **schon** and **schön, fast** and **fest,** so also, in general, related forms which have become separated from each other in speech-feeling may soon drift apart in meaning. For cases of the survival of the older meaning of **schon** see **223.** II. 3. *a* and XI. A. *e* and *j.* In M.H.G. the comparative of the adverb differed from the uninflected comparative form of the adjective in that it lacked mutation. For a survival of this older usage see **117.** 1. *d.*

3. Many adverbs approach close to the nature of prepositions. Their form and function are explained at length in **223.** I. 9 and the articles there referred to.

Classification of Adverbs.

223. Adverbs and adverbial constructions may be divided according to their meaning into the following classes:

I. Adverbs of Place which fall into the following subdivisions, indicating:

1. Rest in a place near the speaker: **hier** here, in early N.H.G. **hie,** still used in poetry, also in prose, in the set expression **hie und da** here and there; **hier** accompanied by other adverbs which mark some place near the speaker more accurately, as **hier oben** here above, **hier unten** here below, **hier außen** outside here, here in a foreign land, **hier üben** (always contracted; see below) here on this side (of the ocean, river, question, &c.), **hier vorne** here in front, written together in **hie'nieden** here below, on earth, &c.; contractions of the preceding, as **hoben** for **hie oben, haußen** for **hie außen,** were formerly in use, but are now common only in dialect except **hüben** for **hie üben: Wackere Männer standen hüben und drüben** Brave men stood on this side (of the question) and on the other side.

2. Rest or motion near the speaker according to the verb used, in adverbs compounded of **hier** and some prep. (see **141.** 5. A. *b* and *c* for the accent): **hieran** near this, **hierbei** by this, **hierauf** upon this, **hierunter** under this, **hieraus** out of this, **hierin** in this, **hierüber** over this, concerning this, **hierum** around this, **hierzu** to this, to this end, **hierneben** beside this; with preposition preceding and written apart: **von hier** or (in elevated diction) **von hinnen** from here, &c.

3. Motion *toward* the speaker either in a general way expressed by **her** or in a specific way expressed by a preposition in composition with **her,** very frequently with contraction, as **(he)'runter, (he)'raus, (he)'rein** (the one prep. **in** changes its form to **ein** in these adverbial compounds), **(he)'rüber, her'vor, (he)'rum, her'zu, her'nieder, (he)'ran, her'bei, (he)'rauf, (he)'rab;** with preceding prep. and adverb, as **von oben her, von oben herunter;** the indefinite **irgend woher** from somewhere, &c.: **Komm her** Come here. **Er steigt von der Anhöhe herunter** He is descending from the height (towards the speaker).

In oldest German the adverbial compounds **heraus,** &c., were quite rare. Just as in modern English, the mere preposition or rather adverb **aus,** &c., was sufficient: Lazarus, cum uȥ (Tatian, 135, 26), now **komm heraus,** but in English as in older German, *come forth* or *out.* In German the adverb **aus,** &c., has in large part lost its older concrete meaning and thus **her** is usually needed to bring out the concrete idea. Compare 7. G. *d* below.

a. In many cases the idea of motion towards the speaker contained in **her** disappears, and then this particle simply means *motion or rest with reference to some other person or thing* which is represented as the point of departure, centre of attraction, or as itself being in motion, sometimes implying in case of motion that the person preceding or following the person in question keeps step with him or goes at the same rate of speed, sometimes implying that the one party is in pursuit of the other: **Er ist von Berlin her** He is from Berlin. **Sie standen alle neugierig um ihn her. Der Heiduck läuft neben dem Wagen her. Die Musik geht vor, der Troß hinter dem Zuge her. Sie waren schnell hinter** (in hot pursuit of) **dem Ausreißer her. Er ist sehr hinter dem Gelde her** He is after money.

It sometimes represents an action merely as proceeding in a given way without reference to direction toward a definite object: **Es geht lustig her** They are having a gay time. **Der Zug ritt still und ernst ein'her** (*along*) or **da'her.** In N.G. colloquial language the force of **her** has become so faint that its original meaning is now no longer felt, and hence it is even used instead of **hin** to denote motion from the speaker: **Gehen Sie rüber** (for **herüber** instead of the literary **hinüber**) **und fordern Sie ihn auf, er soll den Wiesenweg sofort freigeben** (Halbe's *Haus Rosenhagen,* iii, p. 124).

b. **He'ran** denotes near approach to or movement toward the speaker on a plane surface or with upward movement, while **he'rauf** implies direction toward the speaker, but only with upward movement: **Ich winkte ihn zu mir heran. Er kletterte zu mir heran. Kommen Sie herauf** Come upstairs.

4. Motion *from* the speaker either in a general way expressed by **dar** (see D below) or more commonly **hin** or in a specific way expressed by a prep. in composition with **hin**, very frequently with contraction, as **(hi)'nan, (hi)'nauf, (hi)'nab, (hi)'nunter, (hi)'naus, (hi)'nein** (the one prep. **in** changes its form in these adverbial compounds to **ein**), **(hi)'nüber**; with preceding adverb, as **oben hin** superficially, touching upon a topic lightly in passing, **oben hi'naus** (see example below), **irgend wo'hin** somewhere: **Gehe rechts hin** Turn to the right. **Er polterte einen Stein in die Tiefe hinab. Ich weiß nicht, worauf er hinaus will** I do not know what he is driving at. **Er hat sich nur so obenhin darüber geäußert** He did not express himself fully concerning the matter. **Er will oben hinaus** He is haughty, gives himself airs.

Here as in 3 above the adverbial compounds **hinaus,** &c., were rare in oldest German: **inti** vvurpfun in uz (Tatian, 132, 20), now **und warfen** or **stießen ihn hinaus,** but in English as in older German *and threw him out.*

A. Besides **hin** also **los** and **zu** can be used with reference to movement towards a goal, but with different shades. **Hin** simply points to the goal, while **zu** implies a lively unceasing exertion to reach the desired end, and **los** emphasizes the beginning of the action and often implies that up to this time something has prevented action tho all was in readiness, and hence often denotes a *sudden, violent breaking forth*: **Nun schießt nur hin, daß es alle wird** Now fire away at the mark that the matter (as to who would turn out to be the best marksman) may have an end! **Schießt zu!** Shoot away with all your skill, and don't stop till you hit it! **Immer zu!** Go right ahead with all your might! **Schießt los!** Don't wait longer, fire away! **Er hat Jahre lang bedächtig und stetig auf dies Ziel hingearbeitet; wähnst du, wenn du nun ohne Bedacht darauf los arbeitest, es ihm gleich tun zu können? Der Zorn des Generals brach los.**

B. **Hin** may not only denote motion *from,* on a level surface, but may also denote movement *downward* towards a point at some distance away from the speaker. In this sense it is synonymous with **unter, nieder,** and **he'rab** or **hi'nab, he'runter** or **hi'nunter,** according to the relation to the speaker.

a. **Hin** simply denotes direction downward toward a point at some distance from the speaker, **ab** and **nieder** without any suggestion of distance, indicating only a relative direction with reference to the speaker, emphasizes the idea that the direction is from above downward, **unter** often adds to the idea of **nieder** that in the course of the downward motion the object disappears below something: **Der Apfel fiel auf die Erde hin** or **nieder. Der Reiter sitzt ab. Ein ins Wasser geworfener Stein sinkt nieder** or (to express out of sight, below the surface) **unter.**

b. Moreover, **nieder** seems more suitable for elevated diction where the idea of slow and gradual motion enters into it: **[Der Schiffende] sieht die Berge schon blau, die scheidenden, sieht in das Meer sie niedersinken** (Goethe).

c. **(Hi)'nab** or **(he)'rab** simply denote motion downward, while **hi'nunter** or **he'runter** add to this conception that the whole distance in question is passed over: **Er glitt einige Stufen herab, kam dann ins Stürzen und fiel so die ganze Treppe herunter. Er läßt sich herab** He condescends (lets himself down a little), but **Er ist in seinen Vermögensverhältnissen ganz heruntergekommen** He is in very straitened circumstances (dropped clear down from wealth to poverty).

C. **(Hi)'nan** with a prep. denotes a general movement forward on a plane surface with the intention of approaching something, with an adverbial acc. it may also add to the idea of pushing forward, the conception of an upward movement, and can refer to the whole distance in question or a part, while **hi'nauf** denotes only movement upward, and implies usually that the whole distance in question is passed over: **Wir ritten an den Feind hinan. Er fuhr den Strom hinan** (up stream). **Ich stieg die Quaderntreppe hinan und trat in eine Vorhalle. Er geht den Berg hinan** (is ascending). **Er geht manchmal den Berg hinauf** (to the top). **Er ist auf das Dach hinaufgestiegen.**

D. In early N.H.G. **dar** (O.H.G. dara) was used with the force of **dahin,** i.e. with reference to a definite place: **Die Diener aber kamen dar** (Acts v. 22). To-day it is employed less definitely with the force of **hin,** but is used only in a few compounds: **darbieten, darbringen, dargeben, darlegen, darreichen, darstellen, dartun.**

5. Motion, action, or change in a figurative or moral sense, without expression of a definite direction to or from the speaker, or at least with no conscious feeling of such on the part of the speaker, is always expressed by **her** simple and in compounds: **Er blickt auf uns herab** He looks down on us. **Er hat den Preis herabgesetzt** He has lowered the price. **Er ist (he)reingefallen** He has been taken in (lit. fallen in). Thus also many other figurative expressions: **ein Buch herausgeben** to edit a book, **jemand von oben herab behandeln** to treat somebody as an inferior, **einen herunter machen** to take somebody down (from his high horse).

6. Rest or motion with the idea of distance from the speaker:

a. Rest in a place at some distance from the speaker, as **dorten** (poetic) or **dort** yonder; in connection with other adverbs, as **dort oben** up yonder, **dort unten** down yonder. &c.

b. Motion from the speaker to some point distant: **Dorthin** yonder, to that place, with accent upon the first syllable to emphasize the place and on the second syllable to emphasize motion: **dort (hi)nauf** up yonder, **dort (hi)nunter,** &c. Exs.: **'Dorthin zu sieht man noch Türme von Madrid. Da wird dort'hin das Ohr lieblich gezogen** The ear is charmed and attracted in that direction. **Dort hinunter müssen wir.**

c. Motion toward the speaker from some point distant: **Dorther** (accented as **dorthin;** see *b* above), or **von dorther,** or **von dorten** (poetic) from yonder, &c. **Ich komme 'dorther.—Kommst du wirklich dort'her?**

7. Rest or motion without expressing definitely nearness to the speaker or distance.

A. **Da** there, **da'selbst** (demon. and rel.) at that place, at which place, **da'her, ein'her** along, **von da** from there, **da'her** (accented upon the last syllable except to emphasize especially the place), or **von da'her,** or (in elevated diction) **von dannen** from that place, **dahin** (accented in the same manner as **daher**) or in early N.H.G. **dar** (see 4. D above) to that place: **Er ist schon da. Er eilt da'her** He is speeding along. **Ich komme eben da'her,** or **Da komme ich eben her! Von Weißenfels? 'Daher bin ich** Are you from Weissenfels? That is the place I come from. **'Daher kommt die ganze Verwirrung.**

B. **Da** accompanied by adverbs: **da oben** up there, in heaven, **da unten** down there, **da außen** out there, out of doors, **da innen** inside there, **darüben** (usually contracted; see below) over on that side, on the other side of the ocean, in the other world, &c.; the preceding very frequently contracted as **droben, drunten, draußen, drinnen, drüben,** &c.; also with a double **da,** as **da d(a)roben, da drunten,** &c.

C. **Da** (**dar** before a vowel) in composition with prepositions, with accent usually upon the prep., except to especially emphasize the place, hence usually contracted (see **141.** 5. A): **d(a)'ran, da'bei, d(a)'rauf, d(a)'runter, d(a)'raus, d(a)'rein, d(a)'rin, d(a)'rüber, da'vor, da'hinter, da'zwischen, d(a)'rum,** &c. **Er trug eine Kette; da'ran war eine alte Münze. Ich fahre 'hieran und du fährst 'daran** I'll drive up here and you drive up there.

a. Earlier in the period and still in colloquial and popular language these compounds are separated, and often the **da** is lacking altogether. See **141.** 5. A. *b. Note.*

b. The O.H.G. had two forms corresponding to N.H.G. **da,** namely dara (now **dar,** still preserved in the group in 4. D above) and dār, the latter of which now takes the place of both in this construction, usually in the reduced form **da,** but in its former full form in compounds the second element of which begins with a vowel: **darin,** &c. The vowel, however, becomes short when the accent is shifted upon the second element: **'dārin,** but **dă'rin.**

D. The relative and interrogative **wo** where, the indefinite **irgendwoher** from somewhere, **irgendwo** somewhere, **anderswo** somewhere else, &c.; the relative and interrogative **wo** (**wor** before a vowel) in compounds, as **wo'bei** near which, **wo'runter** among which, **wo'hin** whither, **wo'her** whence, &c., or sometimes demonstrative compounds in their stead: **da'bei, da'runter,** &c. See **153.** 2. B.

Earlier in the period and still in colloquial speech these compounds are separable. See **153.** 2. and B thereunder.

a. Corresponding to N.H.G. **wo** we find in older German two forms **wo** (O.H.G. hwār) and **war** (O.H.G. hwara), the latter of which survives in only one word **wa'rum** alongside of **wo'rum.** The older language often makes no distinction between **worum** and **warum,** using both forms relatively and interrogatively in the sense of *for* or *on account of which, what*: **Erhabner Geist, du gabst mir, gabst mir alles,** | **warum** (now **worum**) **ich bat** (Goethe's *Faust*, Wald und Höhle). **Warum** (now **worum**) **soll ich bitten?** (Herder). These forms still occur occasionally in elevated diction without differentiation, but present prose usage distinguishes sharply between the two forms, employing **worum** in the meaning *for* or *on account of which, what,* **warum** as an adverb in the meaning *why.*

E. The adverbs denoting a relative position or direction in space with reference to the speaker: **oben** above, **unten** below, **außen** outside, &c.; **aufwärts** upward, **abwärts** downward, to one side, **heimwärts** homeward, **auf** up, **unter** (see 4. B. *a* above) down, **ab** (see 4. B. *a* above) down, **an** (see *a* below).

a. **An** denotes a general forward movement or a steady continuation: **Das Heer rückt gegen den Feind an. Der Lehrer spornt den Schüler an. Die Kälte hält an.** Where the goal is more prominent than the idea of a forward movement **he'ran** and **hi'nan** must be used: **Das Heer rückt heran. Ihr Jungen, kommt 'mal heran. Er reift zum Manne heran.** As motion forward on an inclined plane leads to the idea of motion upward **an** now in some words has assumed the idea of upward: **Der Pfad steigt an. Der Fluß schwillt an.** Where the idea of a goal becomes more important than that of an upward movement **heran** and **hinan** must be used: **Das Wasser steigt jedes Jahr bis zu einer beträchtlichen Höhe heran. Der Pfad steigt steil bis zu dem hoch aufragenden Felsen hinan.**

b. **An** often loses its concrete meaning, which fades away into mere abstract perfective (see **246.** II. 3. *b*) force, indicating: (**1**) the beginning of an activity: (**Das Brot**) **anschneiden** to make the first cut into, cut into, (**ein Lied**) **anstimmen** to strike up. **Lassen Sie die Maschine anlaufen** Start the machine. **Die Schraube zieht an** The screw begins to take hold. **Das Dienstmädchen wird morgen antreten** The maid will enter service to-morrow. **Einen Dienst, ein Amt, eine Reise, sein Erbe, den Beweis der Wahrheit, sein zehntes Jahr antreten;** (**2**) the affecting of the object only a little: (**einen Apfel**) **anbeißen** to take a bite of, eat some of, etc.

c. **Auf** often loses its concrete meaning, which fades away into mere abstract perfective (see **246.** II. 3. *b*) force, indicating: (**1**) the beginning of an action or state: **aufblühen** to come out into bloom, **aufmuntern** to cheer up (trans.), **aufwachen** to wake up (intrans.), **aufwecken** to wake up (trans.); (**2**) the end of an action: **aufbrauchen** to use up, **aufessen** to eat up, &c.

F. **Weg** *away*, disappearance in any direction, used only of objects in space, **fort** *on, forth*, movement forward in time or space, in one continuous direction; **Der Bruder sagt zur Schwester: setze deine Malerei jetzt weg** (aside), **wir wollen Klavier spielen. Nach einer Stunde aber sagt er: Es ist genug, setze deine Malerei fort** (Go on with your painting). However, this distinction is very often disregarded: **Er ist fort** (better **weg**).

G. Movement from a place is expressed by **ab** and **aus** with different shades.

a. **Ab** expresses the opposite of **an** and **auf,** hence movement *from a surface,* while **aus,** which is the opposite of **in,** expresses movement *out from within* something: **Wer auf dem Pferde sitzt, steigt ab,** but **Wer im Wagen sitzt, steigt aus.**

b. What moves from the surface of a thing leaves it altogether, but what comes out from within a thing may depart from it as from a base and thus may still remain in close connection with it; hence **ab** and **aus** may sometimes differ materially: **Er bog links vom Wege ab** (left the road entirely), but **Er bog aus** (turned to one side, out), **um nachher wieder in den Weg einzubiegen. Wer von einem Grundsatz ausgeht** (Whoever is guided by a certain principle), **hält an demselben fest, bei allem, was daraus folgt,** but **Wer von dem Grundsatz abgeht, verläßt ihn.**

c. As **ab** and **aus** (see *a* above) express motion *from,* they also may naturally express *separation,* to which, however, a third adverb or inseparable verbal prefix must be added, namely, **ent. Ab** denotes surface separation, **aus** separation from a position within something, and **ent** a separating something from that which entirely envelops it and is closely attached or intimately related to it. One says: **Ich balge das Tier ab,** when he is thinking of taking *off* the pelt, **Ich balge es aus,** when he is thinking of taking the animal *out* of its pelt, **Ich entbalge es** when he is thinking of the rather difficult task of stripping off the tightly fitting pelt. **Ich entgehe einer drohenden Gefahr, die mich fast schon gepackt hielt. Ent** represents also a more complete separation than **aus: Wer sich aus dem Staats- in den Hausrock geworfen, hat sich ausgekleidet, ohne doch entkleidet zu sein, wie der, der ins Bad steigen will.**

The difference between **aus** and **ent** is sometimes only a grammatical one. **Aus** is used in an adverbial phrase, and **ent** is compounded with the verb: **Und unsre Reisenden entstiegen ihrem Waggon** (Fontane's *Cécile,* chap. vii), **or stiegen aus dem Waggon.** Sometimes **aus** is used where there is only one simple case object, and **ent** where there are two simple case objects, a dative and an accusative: **Der Kooperator zog die Lade heraus und entnahm ihr einen großen, halb beschriebenen Bogen** (Ebner-Eschenbach's *Glaubenslos,* chap. ix).

d. Both **ab** and **aus** often lose their concrete meaning, which fades away into mere abstract perfective (see **246.** II. 3. *b*) force, indicating the end of an action: **Die Sache ist gut abgelaufen** or with the same meaning **ausgelaufen. Der Sturm hat abgetobt** or more commonly **ausgetobt.** There is a tendency to differentiate the two particles. The former indicates merely the end of an action, while the latter implies that the end is an appropriate conclusion of a development: **Die vom Wurm zernagte Rose blüht ab, ohne daß sie ausblüht. Ab** often contains the idea of excess or injury, while **aus** denotes an appropriate completeness: **Er arbeitete sich ab,** but **Er arbeitete seine Pläne sorgfältig aus. Er hat seine Wäsche abgenutzt,** but **Er hat seinen Vorteil ausgenutzt.**

H. The word *together* is represented in German by three words with different shades of meaning. **Bei'sammen** is only used with verbs expressing rest or an activity which is confined to a given place, and never with verbs of motion to or from, and hence it merely denotes that a number of objects are found in the same enclosed space, or in a merely local sense near together. **Mit'sammen** adds to this idea that of common participation in an activity with mutual relations, and **zu'sammen,** much more commonly used than either, may contain the meaning of either or of both: **In den Spinnstuben arbeiten viele Mädchen beisammen** (working in one room, but entirely independently at different wheels). **Es fließen wohl die Wellen mitsammen in das Meer, | es fliegen wohl mitsammen die Vögel drüber her** (Geibel's *Die junge Nonne*). **Die Menschen sind nicht nur zusammen, wenn sie beisammen sind; auch der Entfernte, der Abgeschiedene lebt uns** (Goethe's *Egmont,* 5, Gefängnis). **Man hat sie in ein Grab zusammen gelegt** (here **beisammen** could not be used). **Zwei Schriftsteller arbeiten zusammen an einem Buch.**

8. General diffusion thruout, or extension thru or around a given space: **über'all** everywhere, **durch'weg** or **'durchweg** *thruout,* hence usually as an adverb of degree *entirely,* **rings** round about, **um'her** around, **nirgends** nowhere.

9. *Adverbial forms with prepositional force:*—

A. A number of prepositions enter into compounds with **da, hier** and **wo** to form prepositional adverbs with the force of a preposition and a pronoun, as illustrated at length in **141.** 5. A and B, **147.** 1. C. *b,* **153.** 2 above, also in 2 and 7. C. D of this article.

B. A number of adverbs, all verbal prefixes, have also prepositional force. The more difficult idiomatic constructions are here treated briefly. Compare these articles with **225, 258.** 1. B, and **262.** I. *b.*

1. The prefix **an** is used:

a. With intrans. verbs to indicate rest at a permanent goal, where it takes a dat. obj. when the reference is to persons; with reference to things it is replaced by the prepositional construction, but may be retained if there is no object at all: **Ein Makel klebt ihm an. Das Pflaster klebt an dem Finger,** but **Das Pflaster klebt an.** A prep. obj. is used when **an** indicates arrival at a goal: **Er kam in der Stadt an.**

b. To express rest with trans. verbs **an** takes the prep. **an** with the dat. in case of things, but with reference to persons it takes the simple dat., expressed with reference to a person other than the subject, unexpressed with reference to the subject: **Er bringt einen Haken an der Wand an. Man sieht ihm Armut an. Man fühlt ihm seine Erregung an. Man hört ihm den Ausländer an. Sie hatte gestern ihr neues Kleid an.** Often with a prep. obj. in case of persons: **Ich will eine Bitte bei ihm anbringen.**

c. With intrans. verbs of motion it denotes motion *toward,* which is usually expressed again by a preposition, as **gegen,** &c.: **gegen jemanden, gegen etwas anlaufen.**

d. With trans. verbs of motion it denotes motion *toward* a person or goal and governs a dat. in case of a living object, while in case of the object of a thing the idea of direction *toward* is expressed again by the prep. **an** (with acc.): **dem Gefangenen Fesseln anlegen, dem Pferde den Zaum anlegen,** but **den Hund an die Kette anlegen.** The object of **an** is not expressed when it refers to the subject: **Er legte das Gewehr an.** Likewise other prepositional adverbs: **Er warf einen Mantel über.**

e. With many trans. and intrans. verbs the acc. obj. is the object of **an,** not the object of the verb: **den Feind angreifen, jemanden anflehen, jemanden anbetteln.** Likewise **über, be-** (**246.** II. 1), **ver-** (**246.** II. 5. B. *b* and *Note*): **jemanden über'fahren,** &c.

2. The prefix **auf** often has the force of a preposition, expressing rest upon or direction toward an object, which must often be supplied in thought: **Hier liegen Bücher auf** Books are lying on the tables here for reference. **Das Schiff sitzt auf** The ship is aground. **Er horchte auf** He listened intently (in the direction of the object in question). **Man setzt das Essen auf** (i.e. **auf den Tisch). Er setzt sich auf** (i.e. **auf das Pferd),** but also with adverbial force: **Er setzt sich** [**im Bette**] **auf.** A living object is usually in the dat.: **Er drängte ihm seine Ansichten auf.** The object of **auf** is not expressed when it refers to the subject: **Er setzte** [**sich**] **den Hut auf.** Compare **141.** 5. A (next to last par.).

3. For examples illustrating the use of the prefixes **durch, ent, entgegen, nach, unter, vor, wider** see **215.** II. 3. A. *b*. *c* and **258.** 1. B (and *a* thereunder).

4. One prepositional adverb and prefix has a different form according as it expresses rest or motion. Rest or motion *within* a given space is expressed by **in,** and motion into a place is expressed by **ein,** both of which words are only found in compounds, especially with adverbs belonging to the preceding classes, verbs, and sometimes with substantives: **Ich habe mich da'rin geirrt** *I have been mistaken in that,* but **Mische dich nicht da'rein** *Do not mix yourself up in the affair.* **Wo'rin hat er sich geirrt? Wo'rein hat er sich gemischt? Der 'inliegende Brief** *the inclosed letter,* but **Er legte den Brief ein** *He inclosed the letter.* **Feld'ein** into the fields, **wald'ein** into the woods, **'hafenein** (accent shifting forward in dissyllabics) into the harbor, **jahr'aus jahr'ein** year in year out; **Inhaber** *bearer,* **Inhalt** *contents,* but **Eintritt** *entrance,* **Einfuhr** *importation,* &c. **Ein** is much used figuratively to form compound verbs which are employed reflexively to indicate a practising of some activity for the purpose of attaining to (literally *entering into*) proficiency: **sich einschießen, sich einüben, sich einfliegen** to practise flying in an aeroplane, &c. It is similarly used in transitive compounds: **ein Pferd einreiten, einen einüben,** &c.

a. In M.G. and N.G. dialects and often in colloquial speech **in** is used for both **in** and **ein. Schlagen Sie in** (instead of **ein**) (Rauchhaupt in Hauptmann's *Der rote Hahn,* Act 4). Even in the literary language **inbegriffen** is often used instead of **einbegriffen.** From this failure on the part of dialect and colloquial speech to distinguish different forms for the different meanings there have also arisen in the literary language several cases where the two forms have been confounded, **ein** being used for **in: eingedenk** *mindful of,* **Eingeweide** *entrails,* and earlier in the period still others.

In some dialects we find the opposite usage—**ein** for **in: Jenseits der Alpen steht ein Grab, | gegraben am grünen Rheine, | drei wilde Rosen blühen drauf, | seine Liebe liegt dareine** (Scheffel's *Trompeter,* Werner's Lieder aus Welschland, v). **'s wird dir schier drein zu naß sein** (Anzengruber's *Wolken und Sonn'schein,* p. 238).

b. Instead of N.H.G. **in** for the preposition and adverb, M.H.G. had a differentiation of forms, **in** for the preposition, and **inne** or **innen** for the adverb. These adverbial forms are still sometimes found, **inne** especially in compounds, and **innen** both in compounds and uncompounded: **innehalten, innehaben, innewohnen,** &c.; **d(a)rinnen, von innen,** &c. In other instances, however, the adverbial forms have been contracted to **in,** in which case preposition and adverb cannot be distinguished in form: **in** (prep.) **dem Buch; darin** (adv.), common N.H.G. form for M.H.G. **darinne** or **darinnen.** In M.H.G. **in** had already begun to replace **inne** and **innen.** Later the long forms gradually kept yielding to the contracted one. The form **-inne,** as in **darinne,** is now restricted to poetry and popular language, and **-innen,** as in **d(a)rinnen,** is only in limited use, tho more commonly employed than **-inne.** In one meaning, *in the room, in the house,* with reference to some inclosed space, **drinnen** is quite common: **Struppmann (nach hinten weisend): Er ist drinnen** (Otto Ernst's *Die Gerechtigkeit,* 2, 4).

c. The words **offen** and **auf** have about the same relation to each other as **in** and **ein: Die Tür war offen** *The door was open,* but **Hans machte die Tür auf** *John opened the door.*

10. Place with its varied relations is also expressed by the case of a noun or by a preposition with its dependent noun as follows:

a. Place where or position are expressed, in certain adverbial expressions, by the gen. of a noun (fem. words often ending in **s** after the analogy of masc.) or by some expression formed after the model of such: **gehörigen Orts** before the proper authority, **höhern Orts** before a higher authority, **linker** (or **zu linker**) **Hand** to the left hand, **'aller'orts** (see **249.** II. 2. A. *a*) everywhere, **seines Orts** in the proper place, **'jeden'orts** everywhere, **hierlands** (or more commonly **hierzulande**) in the country, **unter'wegs** (an incorrect gen. formed after the analogy of the preceding, now, however, replacing the older correct dat. **unter'wege** or in pl. form **unter'wegen**) on the way or road, **'halbwegs** (**245.** iv. 2. *e*), **seinerseits** upon his part, **mütterlicherseits** upon the mother's side, **'anderseits** on the other side, **'beiderseits** on both sides, **seitens** (now used as a prep. with gen.) upon the part of. **Ich bekam ein Zimmer in der Buchstraße, nächster Tür mit Kings** (next door to King's). **Halben Weges** (or **auf halbem Wege**) **zwischen Brückenberg und der Obermühle trat er von dem tiefergelegenen Wolfshau her auf den eine lange Schräglinie bildenden Fahrweg**

(Fontane's *Quitt*, chap. xiii). **Inoslawski** (name) **ließ sich als Reiter erträglich an und hatte den „alten" Fahrern bald die Kniffe abgesehen, mit denen man beim Stalldienst die Vorgesetzten hintergeht, aber im Fußexerzieren fehlte es aller Enden** (in every direction, every respect) (Beyerlein's *Jena oder Sedan?*, iv). In a few set expressions after **woher: Woher des Weges und wohin?** (Rudolf Herzog's *Der Graf von Gleichen*, p. 7), lit. Where on your way did you come from and whither are you going? **Woher der Fahrt?** (Lienhard's *Till Eulenspiegel*, Der Fremde).

b. Separation is expressed by the gen. with certain verbs. For full treatment see **262.** II.

c. The use of the simple dative, or rather locative (**258.** 1), to express place, once more frequent, is now rare except in a few common adverbs whose origin is not felt: **allent'halben** (dat. pl. of the M.H.G. halb *side*, preceded by the modifying adjective **all,** which here has an excrescent **t** appended to its regular case ending) *on all sides, everywhere.* For other examples see **140.** *d. Note.*

d. In earlier periods and in part still the acc. **heim** *home* is used with verbs of motion to express the goal. The dat., or rather locative (**258.** 1), **heime** *at home* was formerly and in dialect is sometimes still used to denote the place of rest or the place where an activity is going on. The modern literary form of the older **heime is heim,** and thus dat. and acc. are not now formally distinguished. This has led to the use of **daheim** in the sense of the older **heime. Heim** (acc.) and **daheim** (= older **heime**) are in common use in S.G., but are in N.G. more commonly replaced by **nach Hause** and **zu Hause.** The dat. **heim** still lingers on in poetry.

e. In addresses and in references to books, magazines, &c. the place where is often expressed in colloquial speech and often even in the literary language by the uninflected form of a noun: **Ecke der Schadowstraße ist der Eingang zum Aquarium. Wo wohnst Du? Halbdorfstraße fünfzehn. Das Gedicht findet sich Bd. (Band) VI, S. (Seite) 4.** For the origin of such expressions see **228.** 1. *b.* The nominative is often used here to preserve the exact form of the name: **Er wohnt Grüner Markt. Beitr. 41, 74** (i.e. Beiträge zur Geschichte der deutschen Sprache und Literatur, vol. 41, p. 74) **wurde festgestellt usw. Vergl.** (vergleiche) **Graff** (author), **Altdeutscher Sprachschatz 2, 203.**

f. The place where and the goal or destination are more commonly expressed by means of some prep. with its dependent noun: **Er sitzt am Tische. Die Kinder gehen zu Bette.**

11. One of the marked features of German is the use of an adverbial element indicating the direction of an activity in connection with a verb that in its simple unmodified form does not express motion from one place to another: **Sie schrak auf** She started up with fright. **Sie schrak vor ihm zurück. Sie zitterte einen Schritt zurück. Eben hörte sie jemand von weitem heranschluchzen. Er zitterte in das Wirtshaus hinein.**

II. ADVERBS OF TIME fall into the following subdivisions, indicating:

1. *Definite time*, expressed by an adverb, the acc. or the uninflected form of a noun, a prep. phrase, or the gen. in case of **'dĕrzeit** *at present* (with a present tense), *at that time* (with a past tense): **heute** to-day, **jetzt** now, **nun** (see A below) now, **noch** *yet* and a number of derived meanings (see B below); **morgen** (originally a dat., but now felt as an acc.) to-morrow, **diesen Morgen** or **heute morgen** this morning, **diesen Abend** or **heute abend** this evening, **diese Woche** this week, **vorige Woche** last week, **Montag abend** Monday evening, **Montag, Donnerstag, Montag den 9. September. Schließlich verabredete ich Ostern 1899 mit A. Socin, der mich Herbst 1893 zu einer erneuten Besprechung über Rotwelsch hier besucht hatte, gemeinsame Arbeit, aber der Tod entriß den schon damals schwer leidenden Gelehrten Pfingsten 1899** (Kluge's *Rotwelsch*, Vorw.). **Der wird wohl die Ostern Quintaner?** (Stilgebauer's *Götz Krafft*, I. 1, p. 35). **Herbst, Ostern, Pfingsten** are now felt as accusatives, but they in fact represent the older prepositional expressions given below, which are still much more frequently used. Sometimes as in older usage the genitive is still used for definite time: **Wenn er den ersten Zug erreichte, könnte er mittags (= um Mittag) am Walchensee sein** (Fulda's *Lebensfragmente*, p. 82).

To mark time exactly, the hour is often accompanied by uninflected **Schlag** or **Punkt: Schlag** (or **Punkt**) **sieben** seven o'clock sharp.

With prepositions: **'übermorgen** (with the accent shifted upon the first element, as the word often stands in contrast to simple **morgen**) day after to-morrow, **gegen Abend** towards evening, **heute über acht Tage** a week from to-day, **in vierzehn Tagen** in two weeks, **im Herbst des nächsten Jahres, zu** (at) **Ostern, zu Pfingsten.**

The gen. may be used to denote the definite period *within which* in answer to the question *how often* or *how much.* See IV. 2. B. *d* below.

A. **Nun** represents the present in the light of its relation to the past and its complications in the present, but **jetzt** calls attention only to the present: **Ich habe mein Versprechen erfüllt, nun erfüllen Sie das Ihrige, und tun Sie es jetzt** I have fulfilled my promise, now (since I have done this) fulfil yours, and do so now.

B. *a.* **Noch** (or negatively **noch nicht**) means primarily *just now*, now, however, usually indicates a continuation at the present time of an action or a state of things, or in connection with a past or future tense a point in the past or future at which some act or condition was or will be continuing, or was or will be yet possible. It is translated by *yet, as yet, still, up till now, only* or *but* (with a past tense): **Das alte Haus steht heute noch** (still). **Damals lebte mein Vater noch** (still). **Er befand sich noch nicht wohl** (not well yet), **als ich ihn zuletzt sah. Das wird in Europa auch noch Mode werden** That will even yet become a fashion in Europe. **Noch vor einem Jahre** (only a year ago, or but a year ago), **da er sich doch gar nicht um das Gemeinwohl kümmerte, war es das süßeste Traumbild seines Ehrgeizes, einmal Ratsherr zu werden.**

We often, especially in the Southeast, find **nur mehr** instead of **nur noch** *only, merely, but*: **Wir sahen den Park nur mehr als einen dunklen Fleck in der Ferne liegen** (Stifter). **Bis zum Anbruch des Morgens hatten die Flammen gelodert, nun lag nur mehr ein Haufen von rauchendem Schutt** (Jensen's *Das Bild im Wasser*, p. 410).

b. From the idea of continuation it has developed the idea of intensity, multiplication, addition, repetition, survival, contrast to a former situation: **noch einmal so schön** twice as beautiful, **noch einmal so viel** as much again, **noch größer** larger still, **noch zwei Jahre** two years more, **noch mehr** still more, **noch einmal** once more. **Haben Sie nicht noch Mittel?** Have you no means left? **Der Hund knurrt nur noch ganz leise, er bellt nicht mehr im Kaufladen und denkt nicht von weitem ans Beißen.**

c. From the idea of continuing to a certain point of time comes the idea of reaching a certain limit in a scale or a certain goal: **Das geht noch an** That will work all right up to this point. **Du unterstehst dich noch, ihn zu entschuldigen?** You even dare to excuse him?

d. **Noch** is much used in concessive clauses: **Sei es auch noch so wenig** be it ever so little; **sei er noch so vorsichtig** be he ever so cautious.

e. It is often translated by *very*: **noch diese Woche** this very week. **Noch am Abend nach der Schlacht** (on the very evening after the battle) **ließ Graf Otto die gefangenen Ritter . . . enthaupten.**

2. *Indefinite time*, expressed by an adverb, the gen. or in a few cases the dat. of a noun, or a prep. phrase: **dann und wann** now and then, **immer** always, **nie** never, **nimmer** in poetry with the force of **nie,** or in S.G. = **nicht mehr** no more, no longer; **heutigestags** in these times, **jederzeit** at any time, always, **dieser Tage** recently (with a past tense), within a few days (with future tense), **letzterzeit, letzterer Zeit, letztens, letzthin,** or **letztlich** of late, **nächster Tage** some time soon, **eines Tages** one day, **eines schönen Tages** one fine day, **eines Mittwochs** on a certain Wednesday; **in einer dunkeln Nacht** on a dark night, **an einem herrlichen Sommermorgen.**

In the classical period we still find the following participial gen. construction: **Aber so lebten die Herren währendes Krieges** (*while the war was going on*), **als ob ewig Krieg bleiben würde** (Lessing's *Minna*, 2, 2). See **während, 228.** 4.

a. This genitive is often used in a general indefinite way to designate the time of day in which something happens: **Kommst du nachmittags** (sometime in the afternoon) **zurück? Nein, ich komme erst abends** (sometime in the evening) **zurück.** This general designation is often accompanied by a precise date, day, or hour: **am 16. Oktober abends** on October the 16th in the evening, **um acht Uhr morgens** at about eight in the morning. **Ich kam Dienstag nachts** (old gen.; also the acc.: **Dienstag nacht**) **an.**

b. In elevated discourse the dat. is occasionally found in accordance with older usage instead of the gen. or a prep. phrase: **Nächt** (old dat., *last night, in the night*) **ist in unsern Trieb | der gleißend' Wolf gefallen** (Uhland's *Graf Eberhard*, 4). **Nächten** (dat. pl. = **nächt**) **sah ich ihn im Traume** (Weber's *Dreizehnlinden*). The gen. ending **s** is also added to the dat. pl.: **So sind wir nächtens in dies Land gekommen** (Sudermann's *Die drei Reiherfedern*, 2, 2). The dative plural of **Weile** is regularly used in a few adverbs: **bis'weilen** sometimes, **einst'weilen** for the present, **je'weilen** from time to time, and the corrupted form **'weiland** once, formerly.

3. *Relative time*, expressed by an adverb, a gen. in earlier periods, and still in a few expressions, or more commonly by an acc., or a prep. phrase: **vor'her** before, before that (with reference to another act or time), before hand, **vor'hin** a few minutes ago, a short time ago, **hier'auf** hereupon, **nach'her** (also colloquially **her'nach**) afterwards, **seit'dem** from that point on, **seit'her** from that point to the present, **bis'her** up to the present, **schon** (see *a* below); **Vnd des nehesten tages kamen wir gen Mileto** (Acts xx. 15); **anderen Tags** on the next day, **tags drauf** the day after this, **tags vor'her** or **tags zu'vor** the day before this, **mittler'weile,** or less commonly **der'weile,** in the meantime; **den nächsten Morgen, den Tag drauf, den Tag vorher; am nächsten Morgen, am Tage vorher, am andern Tag, unter'dessen** in the meantime, **in'dessen** *in the meantime*, but now more commonly with adversative force, *however, yet*; **im Anfang** or **anfangs** at (or in) the beginning, at the outset, **am Ende** or **letzten Endes** in the end, after all, in fact, in reality, if you go to the bottom of it, if you come down to facts.

a. The adverb **schon** as explained in **222.** 2. E. *Note* was originally the adverb corresponding to the adjective **schön,** and hence meant *beautifully.* This idea led to that of completeness, which was once common, and is still not infrequent. The original idea, however, is now somewhat faded or indistinct. We often translate it by *quite, of itself, sufficient, without going farther*: **Das war schon** (quite) **ein ander Ding. Der von Folterqualen gebrochene Körper eines solchen Opfers würde schon** (of itself) **euer Mitleid erregen. Das ist schon gut** That will do (enough as it is without going farther). The older meaning is also perceptible in the uses described in XI. A. *e* and *j* below.

The older idea of completeness applied to time led to the newer, now more common meanings *already, yet, even, the very, as early as, first*, often difficult to translate by any word. In all these meanings it should be noticed that **schon** often only strengthens some other more important word, and hence is then unaccented: **Ist der Brief schon fértig?** Is the letter ready yet? but **Ist der Brief schón fertig?** Is the letter ready so soon? **Hatte sich der Meister vorher schon** (strengthening **vorher**; translate by *even*) **wenig um Haus und Beruf bekümmert, so tat er es jetzt noch viel weniger. Mit furchtbarem Schelten wurden sie hinauf zur Mutter geschickt und die beiden Knaben schon anderen Tages** (the very next day) **dem Schulmeister zur schärferen Zucht übergeben. In Versailles haben nicht nur die Prinzessinnen schon von zehn Jahren** (as early as the tenth year of their age), **sondern sogar die Puppen ihren Hofstaat. Da**

muß man schon mit vieren fahren, in Gold und Seide gekleidet sein, wenn sie es der Mühe wert finden, einen tot zu schlagen You must first be rich enough to ride in a coach and four, &c. **Heda! schon wieder?** Hollo! at it again?

4. *Customary time* or *repeated occurrence*, indicating the time at which something takes place according to custom or habit, or when something is repeated, is usually expressed by the gen. or by a prep. phrase in the singular and by an acc. or a prep. phrase in the plural: **Ich esse mittags zu Hause, abends pflege ich auswärts zu essen. Mittwoch und Sonnabend nachmittags** (every Wednesday and Saturday afternoon) **ist kein Unterricht. Des Tags** or **tags** in the daytime, **vormittags** or **des Vormittags** in the forenoon, **Montags** Mondays, **nachts** (old gen.) or **des Nachts** (after the analogy of masc. nouns) in the night. **Und aller** (more commonly acc. here; see IV. 2. B. *a* below) **Augenblicke muß sie sich jetzt schon hinlegen** (Hauptmann's *Einsame Menschen*, Act 4) Her health has reached such a state that she must lie down every few minutes. Also prepositional constructions are common: **am Tage** in the daytime, **in der Nacht.** The prepositional construction is the usual one in **im Herbst, im Frühling** (but quite commonly **winters** or **des Winters, sommers** or **des Sommers**), and in the more accurate designations, as **um zehn Uhr, um Mitternacht. Sie wußte nicht, weshalb ihr solche Erinnerungen gerade am Sonntag Vormittag kamen.**

III. ADVERBS OF MANNER (manner, specification, conformity, fitness): **so** (or earlier in the period **also** or in contracted form **als**) so, **leicht** easily, **schnell** fast, &c.

Manner is also expressed by:

a. A noun or adjective in the gen.: **derart** or **dergestalt** (see IV. 2. A. *c* below) *in such a manner, to such a degree.* **Er ist eines gewaltsamen Todes gestorben.** The genitive in this sentence is the old genitive described in **260.** In such a sentence as **Er kam schweren Herzens zurück** the genitive is a genitival predicate appositive, which, tho known in M.H.G., has for the most part developed in the present period under the influence of the predicate genitive described in **252.** 2. A. *c.* From these two starting points the genitive has spread and has come into wide use as a genitive of manner: **So leichten Kaufs kommst du nicht fort** You will not get off so easily. **Wir fahren dritter Klasse** (Storm) We travel third class. **Sie kamen unverrichteter Sache zurück** They came back without accomplishing anything. **Indem ich nach besten Kräften das Fräulein unterhielt, horchte ich doch stets halben Ohrs auf diesen schwarzen Mohren** (Raabe's *Meister Autor*, chap. xxii). **Er beugte sich halben Leibes über die Reling vor** (Schulze-Smidt's *O Tannebaum*, I). **Trocknen Fußes** dry-shod, **begreiflicherweise** as may easily be conceived, **glücklicherweise** fortunately, **notwendigerweise** necessarily, **törichterweise** foolishly, and many similar formations in **weise; anerkanntermaßen** as generally acknowledged, **besagtermaßen** as mentioned before, and many similar formations in **-maßen** (wk. gen. of **Maße;** see also IV. 2. A. *c* below); **kurzer Hand** or **kurzerhand** without any formalities, abruptly. **Er ließ sich des weiteren darüber aus** He explained himself at some length. **Ich danke bestens** I thank you heartily.

To this general head belongs the gen. of specification, once a common construction, but now reduced to a few expressions: **Seines Zeichens** (with respect to or by trade, profession) **ist er Schneider, Jurist.** Compare M.H.G.: Der war des libes schœne with **So war sie schon seit zehn Jahren, schlank von Leib und hoch von Brust und blank von Augen** (Frenssen's *Jörn Uhl*, chap. viii). This gen. was more freely used in early N.H.G.: **(Paulus) fand einen Jüden mit namen Aquila | der Geburt (= der Geburt nach) aus Ponto** (Acts xviii. 2). This old gen. is still found after certain verbs, adjectives, and participles, altho its force is no longer felt. See **260** and 3 thereunder and **262.** II. A. In compounds it is still quite common: **segensreich, handelsklug, geisteskrank,** &c. Compare with M.H.G. ein ellens (= **Muts**) richer man (*Nibelungenlied*, I. 7).

b. A noun or adjective after a preposition: **Er sprach mit Gelassenheit. Er hörte mit gespanntem Ohre zu. Die Vögel singen des Morgens am schönsten (114. 2). Pestalozzi war aufs eifrigste (114. 3) bemüht, seinen armen Mitmenschen zu helfen. Er ist seinem Handwerke nach ein Schneider. Es ist sechs nach meiner Uhr.**

c. A dative of reference indicating the thing with regard to which some statement is made survives in a few set expressions after the verb **sein,** now limited to pronouns, but in M.H.G. of broader application: **Wenn dem so ist** If it is thus with respect to that. **Ist dem nun so** If it is now thus with respect to that. **Wie dem auch sei** However that may be. **Dem sei, wie ihm wolle** Let that be as it may. **Die Geschichte ist gut; wenn ihr nur so wäre** (Raabe's *Höxter und Corvey*, chap. ix). In M.H.G. Wie ist disem mære? What is the state of things with regard to this story? In all these sentences **es** understood is the subject. Usually this dat. must be replaced by a preposition except in case of the few survivals of older usage mentioned above: **Wie ist es mit dieser Geschichte?** (modern expression for the above M.H.G. sentence). There is another somewhat similar dative of reference which is still quite common. See **258.** 3. A.

IV. 1. ADVERBS OF DEGREE (degree, order, measure, extent, price): **sehr, arg** (S.G.), **überaus** very, **höchst, äußerst** extremely, **zu** too, **ziemlich** tolerably, **fast** almost, **schier** (see *a*) well-nigh, entirely, **etwa** or **ungefähr** (in the South also **beiläufig,** which in the North has the meaning of *by the way, in passing*) about, **erst** (see *b*), **nur** (replaced often in the North colloquially by **man;** see (*b.* (**2**). *Note*) only, **zu'erst** first, **viel** much, **wenig** little, **über'haupt** (see *c*) in general, &c.

a. **Schier.** This word is of double origin, and hence has two different groups of meanings: (**1**) **Schier** (M.H.G. schiere *fast, soon*) in early N.H.G. *soon*, now *almost*, confined largely to poetic language.

(**2**) **Schier** (Old Saxon skīri *clean, pure*) common in N.G. and M.G., as an adverb, *entirely, thoroly*, as an adjective, *pure, clean, nothing but, sheer*: **Das leicht Errungene | das widert mir, | nur das Erzwungene | ergetzt mich schier** (Goethe's *Faust*, II, ll. 5169–73). **Gerd blickte ihn verdutzt und schier ohne Verständnis an** (H. Hoffmann's *Wider den Kurfürsten*, chap. xi). **Nun findet man dich und freut sich schier, | da schimpfst du uns Pack und Diebsgelichter** (Sudermann's *Die drei Reiherfedern*, 1, 6). **Da ist alles so klar und schier wie . . . in Ihrer jungen siebzehnjährigen Seele** (Spielhagen's *Herrin*, p. 34). **Schieres Fleisch** pure meat (i.e. without bones and fat), **eine schiere Unmöglichkeit** a sheer impossibility.

b. The adverb **erst** *first* has a number of derived meanings:

(**1**) *Not until, not before, no farther back than, only, but, once*: **Er (der Hund) schlich erst** (*not until*) **spät nach Hause zurück. Ein stattlicher Holzbau, erst** (*only* or *but*) **vor zehn Jahren von Grund aus neu aufgeführt. Und hat er uns erst** (*once* or *only*) **am kleinen Finger, so hat er uns auch ganz.** Often *still more, much more*: **Er ist sehr stolz und erst seine Frau! Er ist schon erbittert, wie wird er erst toben, wenn er das erfährt!** Especially frequent with **recht** in the meaning *all the more*: **Ich rief ihm zu, er solle zurückkommen, aber da lief er erst recht.**

(**2**) The adverb **erst** *only* should be distinguished from **nur** *only*. The former marks a point just reached in a supposed progress, while the latter represents the limit as fixed or final: **Ich hatte erst wenige Seiten gelesen, als er zurückkam. Ich bin erst an der dritten Seite** I am only at the third page. **Warte nur bis Morgen. Es kostet nur einen Taler.** Thus **erst** often implies that there is more to follow, while **nur** suggests that the progress is a limited one: **Er ist erst** (only as yet) **Hauptmann,** but **Er ist nur** (only, which is not much) **Hauptmann. Ich habe erst** (more to follow) **drei Briefe gelesen,** but **Ich habe nur** (not many) **drei Briefe erhalten. Nur** and **erst** may be combined: **Wie klein, wie armselig ist diese große Welt! Sie kennen sie nur erst** (*as yet*) **von ihrer Flitterseite** (Lessing's *Minna*, 5, 9).

Note. **Nur** is a contraction of O.H.G. *ni* (= **nicht**) *wāri* (= N.H.G. **wäre,** past subj.) and thus means *unless it were*. Its original use can still be found: **Er sieht nich', er hört nich'. Nur diese Person** (Hauptmann's *Einsame Menschen*, 4) He sees nothing, he hears nothing unless it be this person. From this original use has sprung up the general idea of limitation, as described above, and also the common use of limiting a preceding proposition: **Er mag zuhören, nur soll er schweigen** He may listen if he desires, but he must keep still. The adverb **bloß** is also used with the force of **nur** and sometimes both are combined: **Kennst du mehr als nur den Namen bloß von meinem Hause?** (Schiller). In N.G. dialect and colloquial language **man bloß** are often combined: **Es is ja man bloß von Fritze Belkow wegen, daß ich gefragt gehabt habe** (Wildenbruch's *Die Quitzows*, 1, 2).

c. **Überhaupt** expresses, as its parts signify (*passing over without counting the heads*, used in buying cattle by the lot without counting the heads), a statement in general without taking into consideration the limitations and conditions of a particular case. It may in part be translated by *in general, generally, as a rule, anyhow, really, after all, in any event, altogether, absolutely*, with negatives, after **wenn,** and in questions translated by *at all* and often difficult to render into English: **Gutes Wetter wäre nicht nur unserer Reise halber, sondern überhaupt** (in general) **zu wünschen. Wie kann man überhaupt** (anyhow) **umtobt von so wilden Kindern einen jungen Hund erziehen?** (Loth) **Es sind die ersten Austern, die ich esse** — (Frau Kruse) **In dar (der) Seisong (Saison) mein'n (meinen) Se (Sie) woll (wohl)?** — (Loth) **Ich meine überhaupt** (absolutely) — Hauptmann's *Vor Sonnenaufgang*, **1. Ich habe überhaupt** (at all) **kein Vergnügen an der Musik.**

2. Instead of an adverb of degree, the acc. of a noun or pronoun, less commonly a gen., may be used to express:

A. Extent or degree: **Das Dorf liegt eine Stunde** (an hour's *walk* or *ride*, according to the connection) **von der Stadt. Gehen wir einen Schritt weiter** Let us go one step farther. **Der See ist ein Kilometer lang und ein halbes breit. Er stand nur einen Fuß von mir entfernt. So geht das vier enggeschriebene Seiten fort** (Spielhagen's *Frei geboren*, p. 138) And so it (i.e. the letter) goes on for four closely written pages. **Das kümmert mich kein Haar** That doesn't worry me in the least. **Du glaubst nicht, was** (to what extent) **dies Tier mein Freund geworden ist** (Mörike). **Das Thermometer ist einen Grad gefallen.** In early N.H.G. the gen. was common here: **nicht eines fusses breit** (Acts vii. 5). Sometimes in our own day: **eines Strohhalmes breit** (P. Heyse's *Gesammelte Werke*, 5, 108).

a. The simple acc. or the acc. after the prep. **um** may stand after a comparative to express the measure of difference: **Friedrich ist einen halben Kopf** or **um einen halben Kopf größer als Wilhelm.**

In early N.H.G. the gen. was here quite common: **Da er vnter das Volck trat | war er eins heubts lenger denn alles Volck** (1 Sam. x. 23). It is still occasionally used: **Damit ist gesagt, daß er eines Hauptes länger als alle vorigen Heiderieter** (name) **ist** (Frenssen's *Die drei Getreuen*, III. 10).

b. The gen. is now often used to denote that something takes place at fixed intervals of space: **Und namentlich in Zeitungen ist aller paar Zeilen Ähnliches zu finden** (Theodor Matthias's *Sprachleben und Sprachschäden*, p. 334, 1st ed.). The older acc. is still more common here. Compare II. 4 above and B. *a* below.

c. The gen. of extent or degree is found in a number of idiomatic expressions: **dermaßen** (**maßen,** an old wk. gen. sing. of **Maße**) *to such an extent*, also *in such a manner*, **diesermaßen** *to such an extent*, sometimes *in this manner*, **einigermaßen** *to some extent*, **solchermaßen** *to such an extent*, sometimes *in such a manner*; **derart, dergestalt, solchergestalt** = **dermaßen, solchermaßen.** The gen. is used here under the influence of the gen. of manner which is employed with these words when they denote the manner of the activity. In most of these words the idea of *manner* is not now so common as formerly and in some cases, perhaps, not found any more at all, having been displaced by that of *degree*. Earlier in the period a prepositional construction was also in use: **ein Vorwurf, der in gewisser Maßen** (in 2nd edition of 1801 with simple gen.: **gewissermaßen) allen andern Sekten gilt** (Wieland's *Horaz*, 1, 37).

B. Duration or measure of time answering the questions *how long, how often*, &c.: **Er liest den lieben langen Tag** He reads the whole livelong day. **Er ist zwanzig Jahre alt. Ich bin schon drei Tage hier. Ziehen Sie auf uns 2 Monate dato** (from date) **für die Hälfte des Betrags. Alle Tage** every day, **alle zwei Tage** every other day, **alle acht Tage** every week, **alle zwei Stunden, einmal, zweimal,** &c.

a. We not infrequently find also, especially in the Midland, the gen. in sentences answering the question *how often?*: **Bleib doch nicht aller** (in both N.G. and S.G. usually **alle) zehn Schritte stehen** (a Leipzig mother to her child). See II. 4 above.

b. In a number of expressions containing numerals the gen. is only seemingly a gen. of measure, while in fact it is a partitive gen. dependent upon the numeral: **zwei ganzer Stunden lang** (Schiller) or now more commonly with the numeral after **ganz,** as in **wie er denn noch ganzer drei Monate da gewesen ist** (Lessing). The words **zwei** and **drei** are here in reality in the acc. of the measurement of time, but are now felt as attributive adjectives modifying the genitives **Stunden** and **Monate.** Also in such expressions the acc. of the noun is now more common: **ganze vier Jahre lang.**

c. The gen. is also used in a few set expressions denoting duration, as in **den Tag über** or **tagsüber** all day long: **Hunderte hatten tagsüber den Platz umlagert** (H. Böhlau's *Adam und Eva*, chap. i). **Wer das mal gesehen hat, vergißt's seiner** [or perhaps more commonly **seine**] **Lebtag' nicht** (Halbe's *Der Strom*, p. 14), also **seine(r) Lebtage** or **sein Lebtag** (a mutilated or contracted acc. sing. or pl.).

d. In answer to the question *how often*, or *how much within a given time*, the gen., or perhaps more commonly acc., of the noun expressing the given time within may be used in case of masculines and neuters, with feminines, however, only the acc., or both constructions may with all genders be replaced by a prep. phrase: **Das Schiff fährt zweimal des Tags,** or **zweimal den Tag,** or **jeden Tag zweimal,** or **an jedem Tage zweimal. Einigemal des Jahres zog die ganze Familie nach Tivoli** (R. Voss's *Psyche*, chap. xviii). **Dreißig Reichstaler des Jahres ließen sie ihm** (Raabe's *Odfeld*, chap. ii). Not **zweimal der Woche,** but **jede Woche zweimal,** or **zweimal die Woche,** or **zweimal in der Woche. Der Kutscher muß wenigstens 160** m. **(Meter) in der Minute zurücklegen.**

C. Weight, amount, price: **Es ist einen Zentner schwer. Die Rechnung beträgt einen Taler** The bill amounts to one taler. **Es kostet mir** or **mich viel Geld. Wie viel gilt es? Es gilt meinen Kopf** How much is at stake? My head. **Ich bin ihm 10 Taler schuldig** I owe him 10 talers. **Mit diesen Kirschen habe ich drei Mark den Korb verdient. Diese Kirschen kosten drei Mark den Korb. Hast du mir nicht immer den lateinischen Aufsatz gemacht, einen Silbergroschen das Stück?** (J. Rodenberg's *Klostermanns Grundstück*, p. 54). Notice that in the last two examples we have the accusative of price and also that of amount in the same sentence. Instead of the acc. of amount we perhaps more commonly find the nom. when the noun denoting the material in question is in the nom.: **Diese Kirschen kosten drei Mark der Korb. Das Bier gilt 14 Pfennig der Becher** (*Neue Zürcher Zeit.*, July 27, 1916). The two nominatives are in apposition with each other, the nom. replacing the older partitive gen. The construction becomes clear by changing the word-order: **der Korb Kirschen kostet drei Mark.**

Instead of an accusative of a noun we often find the acc. of a pronoun: **Er lief, was er laufen konnte. Sie** (i.e. **zwei reitende Batterien) rasen zu mir her, was das Riemzeug hält** (Liliencron's *Kriegsnovellen*). **Aber was kann das helfen!** (R. Huch's *Aus der Triumphgasse*, I).

a. Instead of the acc. the gen. is still used in a few expressions denoting a part of a whole: **teils** in part, **größtenteils** in most part. **Geh ihm gefällig halben Wegs entgegen** (Goethe). **Halbwegs entschlossen** half-way determined. See also **245.** IV. 2. *e.*

Earlier in the period we find the gen. of the amount or price also elsewhere: **Da gilt's Schweigens** (Luther). **Wie es so unsäglicher Mühsal gekostet** (Scheffel's *Ekkehard* [1855] 84). With **gelten** also a prepositional construction was used: **und sollt's dem Teufel um ein Ohr gelten** (Schiller's *Räuber*, 2, 3). Sometimes still: **Es gilt um Tod oder Leben!** (Fritz Lienhard's *Wieland der Schmied*, p. 80). Compare **185.** A. I. 6. *Note* 2.

3. Degree can also be expressed by a prepositional phrase: **teils** or **zum Teil** in part. **Das Schiff wäre auf ein Haar gekentert** The ship came within a hair's breadth of upsetting.

V. Adverbs of Cause or Reason, usually expressed by an adverb or a prep. phrase: **Man kann davon krank werden** One can get sick from that. **Er ist zornig darüber** He is mad about it. **Das Kind zittert vor Frost. Er starb an der Schwindsucht.**

The following five classes may also be considered as subclasses under the general class of *cause*.

a. A gen. of cause was once common in the language, and still survives in a number of expressions. For full treatment see **260** and **262**. II.

VI. Adverbs of Condition, usually introduced by a gen. or a prep. phrase: **nötigenfalls** if it is necessary, **günstigenfalls** if a favorable opportunity offers itself, **schlimmstenfalls** if worst comes to worst. **Nur bei großem Fleiße kannst du Fortschritte machen** You can make progress only on condition that you are very diligent.

VII. Adverbs of Concession, expressed rarely by a gen., usually by a prep. phrase: **jedenfalls** in any event, in any case whatever, **auf alle Fälle** at all events, by all means. **Trotz mancher Widerwärtigkeiten ist das Leben doch reich an Freuden.**

VIII. Adverbs of Purpose or End, usually expressed by an adv. or prep. phrase: **Dazu** (for that purpose) **kam ich nicht her. Man bestimmte ihn schon in der Jugend dafür (für den Soldatenstand). Er strebt nach Ehre.**

IX. Adverbs of Means, usually expressed by an adverb or a prep. phrase: **Man sprengt damit (mit Pulver) die stärksten Felsen. Durch falsches Zeugnis glaubt er sich zu retten.**

X. Adverbs of Material, usually expressed by an adverb or prep. phrase: **Schönes Tuch, wir wollen einen Rock davon machen lassen.**

XI. Modal or Sentence Adverbs, which denote in what manner a thought is conceived by the speaker. They are thus adverbs of manner, and, like them, are sometimes expressed by the gen. of a noun instead of a simple adverb, but they differ from them and all other adverbs in that they modify the thought in the sentence as a whole rather than any one word in it: **keineswegs** by no means, **meinesteils** as regards me, as for me, **meines Wissens** as far as I know, **meines Erachtens** in my judgment, **unseres Bedünkens** as we look at it, in our opinion, **(un)glücklicherweise, vielleicht,** &c. Of these adverbs only those most idiomatic and difficult of comprehension are treated below, which should be carefully studied, as each gives a distinct complexion to the sentence in which it stands:

A. Expressing an affirmation:

a. **Ja** indeed, truly, why, don't you see, you know: **Das ist ja nun alles vorbei** But that is now, you know, all past. **Was ist vorgefallen? Sie sehen ja ganz bleich aus** What has happened? You look very pale indeed. See also *g.* The German also uses this adverb in the emphatic form of statement where English employs a stressed auxiliary. See **185**. B. I. 2. *e.* **(2)**, toward end. These **ja**'s are all unaccented, but **ja** is strongly stressed: **(1)** to answer affirmatively in emphatic language an expressed doubt or negation: **Das werden wir aber ja tun** But we most certainly *will* do that. **(2)** To add force to a command: **Sie müssen ja eilen!** You just *must* hurry! **(3)** In purpose clauses to express certainty of realization: **Wie rückten da die Mädchen knapp zusammen, um ja kein Korn des Goldes zu verlieren!** (Grillparzer's *Sappho*, 1, 3) so as to be sure not to miss a grain of the gold. **Er kehrt um, damit er uns nur ja nicht zu grüßen braucht. (4)** In conditional clauses to indicate that the fulfilment is contrary to expectation, or with reference to the future will be contrary to expectation, i.e. unlikely: **Hast du es ja getan, so gestehe es ein. Wir wollen nicht mehr auf ihn warten; wenn er ja noch kommen sollte, mag er nachessen.**

b. **Ein'mal** or colloquially **mal** used to give emphasis to a statement: **Das ist einmal ein Bild!** That is a picture *for* you! or, I tell you that's a fine picture! **Tyrannisieren lasse ich mich einmal nicht** I want you to know that I cannot be tyrannized over. **Nun einmal** *cannot be helped*: **Das ist nun einmal hin** That is lost and can't now be helped. **Nicht einmal** often occurs in the meaning *not even*, making some particular word in the sentence emphatic: **Er regierte selber, und nicht einmal sein Kammerdiener konnte sich persönlicher Einflüsse rühmen.**

c. **Doch** has a different force according to the word-order and stress used: **(1)** In normal or inverted order it has the meaning of *after all, tho, just, truly, surely, in any event, any way.* It is used to strengthen a statement, but is employed adversatively to state something in contrast or opposition to what precedes, or it may be used in elliptical sentences, the **doch** expressing a contrast to something implied or understood: **Sie ist nicht wie die andern Mädchen, aber sie ist doch nur ein Mädchen** She is not like the other girls (afraid), but she is after all only a girl. **Setz' dich, Robert; ich muß dir doch etwas erzählen** Be seated, Robert; I have something which I just must tell you (altho you may not want to hear it). **Ich will doch sehen, ob man auch mich hinauswirft** (The last man I sent, they put out of the house) I want to see tho if they will go so far as to put me out too. **Wo die (Büchse) herumstehen muß? Die hat doch der Andres mit** I wonder where that gun can be! Andrew has it with him (didn't you know that?) More about this use in *g* below. **(2)** It is also used in sentences with question order to make in form of an exclamation some statement more impressive: **Habe ich doch oft**

schon Undank erfahren! I have indeed and in truth met with unthankfulness often enough already. **Hab' ich den Markt und die Straßen doch nie so einsam gesehen!** I declare I never before saw the public square and the streets so deserted! Compare **287.** B. (**7**). (**3**) In the preceding cases **doch** is unstressed. It is, on the other hand, stressed to contradict a statement firmly: **„Das ist nicht wahr." „Doch!"** In politer expressions, however, it is not stressed here at all: **„Die Musik ist schrecklich." „Na, das weiß ich doch nicht."**

d. **Denn** *evidently, as is well known, as the facts indicate, as it is evident from the preceding, as I learn, perceive*, and with various other translations of similar meaning: **Es war des Grafen Taaffe Wille, das Deutschtum in Österreich niederzuhalten, und das hat er denn** (as is well known) **auch, soweit es in seiner Macht lag, gründlich besorgt. Er ist denn** (as I now perceive) **doch** (after all) **ein Narr! Er sagt es, und so muß ich es denn** (seeing that he says it) **wohl glauben. Das ist denn** (as is very evident) **doch** (and it is contrary to my expectation) **zu arg** (bad).

e. **Schon** *never fear, no doubt, surely, as a matter of course*, used to express great assurance or emphasis: **Es wird ihm schon gelingen. Sie werden sich schon dort treffen** They will no doubt meet there. **Er wird schon kommen** He will doubtless come. **Ihr Herrn vom Handwerk kommt in allen Ländern herum und könnt schon** (as a matter of course) **erzählen.** Often united with **noch** to express assurance of a future event: **Ich werde ihn schon noch** (or **doch noch**) **kriegen** I'll get him yet. In all these sentences we have the original idea of **schon,** only somewhat faded. See II. 3. *a* above. Compare *j*.

f. **Ja wohl** a stronger affirmative than **ja,** but often used without any difference of meaning from it, merely to avoid the too laconic **ja.** Sometimes used after a question expressing doubt as to a matter or expecting a negative answer, when it answers strongly in the affirmative with adversative force as **doch: Du kommst wohl nicht? Ja wohl** You are not coming, are you? Yes, indeed, I am.

g. As **doch** is nearly synonymous with **wohl** (see *h* and D. *h*), so it often has the same general force as **ja** in *a*, but **doch** here, as elsewhere, asserts its adversative nature, and thus distinguishes itself from **ja: Mit Rat dürfen Sie mich doch unterstützen** You might certainly (even if your power be so limited as not to help me more directly) support me with advice. The substitution of **ja** for **doch** here would not in English change the translation, but in the German implies that nothing stands in the way.

h. **Wohl** strengthens a statement much as **doch,** but lacks its adversative force, *indeed, certainly*: **Der ist wohl dumm. Wohl war es eine lange, kalte Nacht** (Uhland's *Ernst*, **1, 1**). In popular ballads this **wohl** loses much of its force, so that its meaning becomes so faint that it can scarcely be rendered: **Es zogen drei Bursche wohl über den Rhein** (Uhland's *Der Wirtin Töchterlein*). **Nur** strengthens a statement in that it emphasizes the idea of urgency: **Ich muß nur bald meinen armen Herrn aufsuchen** (Lessing's *Minna*, **1, 1**).

i. An uncertain affirmation may be expressed by an adverb or a noun in the gen. such as **wahrscheinlich** probably, **vielleicht** perhaps, **etwa** possibly, perhaps, perchance, **wohl** used to modify the direct categorical tone of a statement, *likely, probably, I think*, **möglicherweise** (gen.) possibly: **Er kommt wohl** (I think) **noch heute. Er war es wohl nicht** It is not likely that it was he. Compare the use of **wohl** in *h*.

j. The following adverbs are often used with concessive force: **schon** I admit, **wohl** may be, **freilich** or **zwar** to be sure, **'aller'dings** it must be admitted. Exs.: **Das ist schon richtig, aber . . .** That is correct, I admit, but . . . **„Fragst du deinen Mann nie nach seinen Geschäften?" „Ich frage schon, aber er antwortet nicht."** Here we have the original idea of **schon,** only somewhat faded. See II. 3. *a*. **Er ist wohl ein geschickter Mann, doch traue ich ihm nicht** He may be a very clever man, but I don't trust him. **Er ist allerdings reich, allein er ist nicht glücklich.**

B. *Expressing a Negation.* This is usually expressed by an adverb, a noun in the gen., or a prep. phrase: **nein** no, **nicht** (in careless colloquial language often **nit** in S.G. and **nich** in N.G.) not, **'keines'wegs** by no means, **auf keinen Fall** in no event, **nicht etwa** not as you might be inclined to think, by no manner of means; the adversatives **doch** and **ja doch** (after a preceding negative proposition or a question implying a negative answer to affirm the contrary); **doch nicht** (affirming the contrary of that which is expected and already expressed or inferred by the preceding speaker or questioner); **nicht doch** (after a preceding affirmative sentence or a question expecting an affirmative answer, for the purpose of correcting, denying, disavowing its contents, or disapproving of the thought therein advanced); **Gott bewahre!, behüte Gott!,** or simply **bewahre!** or **behüte!,** and colloquially **i wo!** (all strong negatives); **ich dächte gar!, (ei** or **ach) warum nicht gar!, lieber gar!** *nonsense! what an idea!*, **hat sich was** (see **218.** 3. E), all used ironically in fact branding some statement as false: **Glauben Sie nicht etwa, daß ich morgen wieder komme** Don't think (as you might be inclined to do) that I shall come again to-morrow. **O bitte, es eilt nicht! Doch; es eilt** Oh please don't hurry off, there is no need for it. *But* there is need of haste. **Du gehst nicht ohne mich, Vater, du kannst nicht ohne mich leben; Vater, das fühl' ich jetzt an mir.** (**Der Vater, abwehrend**) **Ja doch** But I can tho. **Sie haben wohl keine Eile? Doch** You are not in a hurry, are you? Yes, I am tho. **„Ja, Sie denken auf Herrn Radegast!" „Doch nicht, Herr Ribezahl!" „Doch nicht? Warum doch nicht? Ist an dem Mann was auszusetzen?" — „Es wird wohl regnen." „Nicht doch, das Barometer ist sehr gestiegen." Meinst du, solchen Burschen sei es daran gelegen? Bewahre! Die wollen nur Zeit gewinnen. Aber hier handelt es sich um eine freche Beschmutzung meiner Ehre. Ach, warum nicht gar!** (Otto Ernst's *Die Gerechtigkeit*, 1, Verwandlung, 3).

a. Double and Pleonastic Negation. The Latin rule that two negatives make an affirmative has gained the ascendency in the literary language, but in the language of the common people two negatives make still, as in the literary language of the older periods, a strong negative: **Er war nirgends nicht zu finden** He was nowhere to be found. Compare popular English: I haven't got none. In German there are sometimes even three negatives: **Hat keiner kein Geld nicht?** The double negative was still common in Luther's language, even the threefold negative occurs. The old Germanic feeling was that two or three negatives, like two or three nails, are stronger than one. This old Germanic usage has under foreign influence entirely disappeared in the literary language in both German and English.

In the literary language of the classical period and the early part of the nineteenth century a *pleonastic* negative is often to be found, especially in those cases where the clause or infin. phrase is logically negative without a formal sign of negation. **Klotilde schien gegen alle zurückhaltend außer gegen ihren Vater nicht** (J. Paul's *Hesp.*, 63). Here **nicht** gives a clear formal expression to the negative idea that is contained in the statement and is indicated logically by **außer,** which however is not felt as a formal negative. Similarly in **Wir mußten ihn mit Gewalt hindern, daß er sich nicht ein Leids zufügte** We had to keep him by force from laying hands on himself. Here the verb **hindern** has negative force, but the speaker is conscious of the strong desire, which he had that his friend might *not* lay hand upon himself, and hence uses **nicht** to bring out this idea, tho it is not required on strictly logical grounds. Thus also in infin. phrases: **Sorgfältig hüteten wir uns, nicht . . . uns umzusehen** (Goethe).

The pleonastic negative is found: (**1**) Very commonly earlier in the period and sometimes still after verbs or expressions containing a negative idea, such as **abhalten, abraten, sich in acht nehmen, ausbleiben, sich enthalten, sich verwehren, fehlen, es fehlt wenig** or **nicht viel, fürchten, sich hüten, leugnen, verbieten, verhindern, verhüten, warnen,** the negative conjunction **ohne daß,** provided usually that it is preceded by a negative or a question—in all these cases not only as in M.H.G. when the verb of the principal proposition has positive form with negative meaning and the subordinate clause is negative in meaning and hence in a certain sense entitled to negative form, especially originally when it was felt as an independent proposition with negative force, as in the first two examples below, but in the present period also when the subordinate clause has positive force because of the fact that the principal verb with negative meaning stands in a question, as in the sentence from Goethe, or is accompanied by a negative, as in the quotation from Wilmanns and also the one from Muncker, or because the subordinate conjunction **ohne daß,** which of itself has negative force, follows a negative or a question: **Es fehlte nicht viel** or **nur wenig, daß es ihm nicht ebenso erging** or **ergangen wäre. Wir werden verhüten, daß kein Schaden geschehe** (Freytag's *Der Rittmeister von Altrosen,* II). **Was hindert mich, daß ich nicht eine der grünen Schnüre ergreife** (Goethe). **Christs** (name) **Einwürfe konnten ihn nicht abhalten, daß er nicht, nachdem er 1746 den ersten Gesang in Hexameter umgesetzt hatte, während des folgenden Jahres die zwei nächsten Gesänge in gleicher Weise umarbeitete** (Muncker's *Gottlieb Klopstock,* p. 67). **Es konnte nicht ausbleiben** (or **unterbleiben,** or **fehlen**), **daß sie sich nicht zuweilen getroffen hätten** (Wilmanns's *Deutsche Grammatik,* III, p. 284), or where the idea of actual fact is prominent **daß sie sich** (**nicht**) **zuweilen trafen** (id.). **Nun verging kaum eine Woche, ohne daß die beiden nicht zusammen in lustiger Gesellschaft einen vergnügten Abend verbracht hätten** (Paul Lindau's *Spitzen,* p. 326). Pleonastic **nicht** is least common after **fürchten** and in general most common in connection with an unreal potential subjunctive where the subordinate clause has positive force, as in the example from Wilmanns. It is worthy of note that after **hüten** and words of similar meaning the negative is still quite common in **daß** clauses, while it is dropped in the contracted infinitive clause: **Hüte dich, daß du nicht fällst,** but **Hüte dich, zu fallen.** It will be a distinct gain to the language if this pleonastic negative entirely disappears, for **nicht** is sometimes needed in the subordinate clause to make the statement affirmative: **In Ehrmanns Hause war es verboten, nicht zu rauchen** (Simrock an Düntzer) = **Jeder war gezwungen zu rauchen.** Of course, **nicht** must be used when it is not pleonastic, i.e. when the subordinate clause is a distinct grammatical unit and needs an independent negative for the expression of the thought which it contains: **Es fehlt nichts, als daß du nicht da bist,** or with an entirely different construction: **Es fehlt nichts, als daß du da wärst** (subjunctive of modest wish; see **169.** 1. A (3rd par.). (**2**) In clauses of degree after a comparative: **Es ging besser, als wir nicht dachten** (Goethe). This negative, now rare, but common a little earlier in the period, is illogical, but it once found favor in German and is still found in other languages, as it gives formal expression to the feeling often present that the state of things in question is *not* in harmony with the statement in the principal proposition. See also **277.** 1. B. *a.* (**3**) The pleonastic negative has become very common in the literature of our time in clauses introduced by **bis** or **ehe, bevor,** when they depend upon a negative clause: **Ich werde keine andere Arbeit beginnen, bis ich nicht diese beendet habe. Ehe nicht seine Verhältnisse geordnet sind, kommt er nicht zur Ruhe** (Fontane's *Poggenpuhls,* chap. xii). **Herr Sasonoff und Herr Viviani und jetzt Herr Briand haben übereinstimmend erklärt, sie würden das Schwert nicht in die Scheide stecken, bevor nicht der preußische oder der deutsche Militarismus niedergekämpft sei** (Reichskanzler Bethmann Hollweg an den Reichstag, Dec. 9, 1915). (**4**) Sometimes after **es ist lange her: Es ist lange her, daß wir nicht Regen gehabt haben.** (**5**) Sometimes in clauses introduced by **seit** or **seitdem: Du hast dich recht verändert, liebes Mädchen, | seit ich dich nicht gesehen** (Hauptmann's *Versunkene Glocke,* ll. 1069–1070). (**6**) Sometimes in connection with an adjective with the negative prefix **un-: Der Kundige wird in der Detailuntersuchung manche selbständige Ansicht des Verfassers nicht unschwer erkennen** (Heinemann's *Heinrich von Braunschweig,* Vorrede). Compare **246.** I. 9. *d.*

b. The negative **nicht** is often, especially earlier in the period, used in exclamations with the force of a strong affirmative: **Was du nicht alles weißt!** I declare if you don't know everything!

= You surely know everything. The negative in such exclamations has arisen from a mingling of two constructions. From **Wie viel tut die Einbildung?** and **Tut die Einbildung nicht viel?** (see D. *b* below) has come **Wie viel die Einbildung nicht tut!** The positive form of statement is now more common here.

c. For the force of **nicht** in questions see D. *b* below.

d. The acc. of certain words, such as **Henker, Teufel,** is often in rather coarse language used as a strong negative: **Er weiß den Henker davon. Da schert man sich den Teufel um die Ideen der Zeit** (Sudermann's *Heimat*, 1, 5). Sometimes the negative **nicht** is used in connection with **Teufel** with the same force as simple **Teufel: Er tüftelte über diese Dinge . . ., von was allem er nicht den Teufel verstand** (Gottfried Keller's *Die drei gerechten Kammmacher*).

C. An imperative may be strengthened by the adverbs **ein'mal** (often contracted to **mal),** **nur** (colloquially in N.G. **man**), and **doch. Einmal** emphasizes a request or command, but often has a force so slight that it cannot be translated. It can sometimes be rendered by *just*, sometimes it merely serves to give to the style a more lively conversational tone: **Denke dir einmal!** Just think! **Komm einmal her!** Come here a minute! **Hör' mal! Die Nachtigall singt. Nur** and **doch** are used to urge an action or course of action, the former rather persuasively, and the latter rather more firmly, or beseechingly even, in spite of evident opposition or reluctance, as there is always here, as elsewhere, adversative force in **doch: Fange nur an! Es ist ja nicht schwer** Do make a beginning; it is indeed not difficult. **Schonen Sie nur den Vater! Seien Sie recht aufmerksam auf seine kleinen Liebhabereien! Gut! Nur zu!** Good! Keep right on! **Nur nicht hitzig, mein Herr!** I hope you will not lose your temper. **Treten Sie man** (instead of **nur**) **ein! Ei! laß ihn doch!** Let him alone, I say. **Starren Sie mir doch nicht so polizeilich ins Gesicht, wie wenn ich gestohlen hätte! Setz dich doch!** O do be seated!

Tho **doch** and **nur** are both used in commands and entreaties there is a marked difference in their several meanings. **Doch** implies reluctance on the part of the person addressed, while **nur** implies that the speaker *desires* this course and urges the other to adopt it. Thus as this desire (**nur**) on the part of the speaker and the reluctance (**doch**) on the part of the person addressed may both enter as factors into the case, both words may appear in the same sentence: **Ach, so komm doch nur, bebte es noch einmal von Käthes Lippen.** Sometimes **doch** and **einmal** are combined in one sentence: **Erklären Sie doch einmal!** Come, do explain! **Klettere doch mal auf den Baum!** Don't you dare to climb that tree! Sometimes in lively conversational tone all three adverbs may be combined in one sentence: **Hören Sie doch nur einmal!** I beg of you, do listen a moment!

A strongly stressed **ja** is often used in emphatic language to imply a threat: **Tu mir das ja nicht wieder!** It is also employed in an urgent request: **Kommen Sie doch ja!**

a. Admonitions or commands are also often strengthened by **wohl,** especially such as have the form of a question, the speaker in all cases assuming compliance upon the part of the person addressed: **Überlege wohl, was du sagst. Willst du wohl machen, daß du fortkommst?**

b. In mild commands, direct and indirect, also in granting permission, **immer** is used to indicate that the speaker has no objection to the matter in question and sometimes to give encouragement: **Die Leute mögen es immer wissen, daß ich nichts mehr habe** (Lessing's *Minna*, 3, 7) Let the people know for all I care that, &c. **Laß sie nur immer toben! Du darfst den Apfel immer nehmen. Sage ihm, er möge immer reisen** Tell him he should go by all means.

D. A question.

a. **Denn** used to put a question in an interested, eager manner, inquiring after the cause or reason of some fact that is already known, or often only to ask a question in a tone of lively interest or of impatience: **Warum hast du's denn verkauft? Was ist denn passiert? Wie heißt sie denn? Siehst du es denn nicht?** Why, don't you see it?

b. **Nicht** expecting an affirmative answer: **Kommt er nicht?** He is coming, is he not?

c. **Etwa nicht** suggests a doubt in the mind of the questioner as to something which he once had thought settled in the affirmative and concerning which he now asks definite information, and in inverted order, **nicht etwa,** is often used politely to hint that the person addressed is in the wrong: **Kommt er etwa nicht?** Is there doubt about his coming? **Haben Sie mir etwa diese Blumen nicht geschickt?** (Sudermann's *Heimat*, 1, 2) Can it be that you have not sent me these flowers? **Irren Sie sich nicht etwa?** Don't you think you are mistaken?

d. **Etwa** or **vielleicht** in questions direct or indirect marking the matter in question as one of possible occurrence: **Gibt's etwa heute Regen?** Can it be that it will rain to-day? **Komme ich etwa ungelegen?** Can it be that I come at an inopportune time? **Zweifelt etwa** (or **vielleicht**) **jemand daran?** Can it be that any one doubts it? **Haben Sie etwa Geld bei sich?** Do you happen to have any money with you?

e. **Wohl** is used in questions in the following constructions: **(1)** In rhetorical questions (i.e. in such questions as need no express response, as the answer is self-evident) to which the speaker would give a negative answer, it is used in order to indicate that the speaker confidently expects a confirmation from the hearer of his own negative position: **Ist wohl der ein würdiger Mann, der im Glück und im Unglück sich nur allein bedenkt?** Is he indeed a worthy man who in fortune and misfortune only thinks of himself? **Nun glaubt Ihr wohl, Gott werde es zugeben, daß ein einziger Mann in seiner Welt wie ein Wütrich hause und das Oberste zu unterst kehre?** (Schiller). This use is similar to *h*, described below. **(2)** It is also very frequently used to ask after the opinion of the person addressed as to some doubtful point, and also often without reference to any person addressed, giving to the question the character of a mere inquiring conjecture: **Wer ist wohl der schlanke Bursche?** Who do you think that slender fellow is?

Kommt er wohl heute noch? Do you think he will come yet to-day? Very frequent in indirect questions: **Ob wohl die Vergoldungen echt sind?** I wonder if the gildings are genuine.

f. **Nur** in questions or exclamations with the force of questions, *I should like to know*, much used in questions, prompted by the desire to know and understand, and very often mingled with surprise: **Was ich nur anfange?** I should like to know what I ought to do in this case. **Aber was haben Sie nur vor?** What in the world are you planning to do? **Was suchst du nur?** What *are* you looking for? **Wer es nur gesagt hat?** I wonder who told it!

g. **Doch** with its usual adversative force expressing something to the surprise of or contrary to the wishes, expectation, &c. of the speaker: **Wo hab' ich's doch?** Where is it, any way? (I can't find it, but it *must* be on my person). **Sah euch doch niemand? Kein Mensch** But did not somebody see you? Not a soul. It is often used in questions put to one's self for the purpose of trying to recall something forgotten: **Was wollte ich doch eigentlich?** What was I just about to do, any way?

h. In questions having the form of declarative sentences **doch** and **wohl** are used to state the opinion or idea of the speaker, and ask for a confirmation of it; **nicht wahr** or often simply **nicht** and in the South **gelt** expect an affirmative reply to a simple question: **Du hast's ihm doch gesagt?** I suppose you told him? **Sie haben doch Bekannte hier?** I suppose you have acquaintances here? **Sie haben jetzt wohl viel zu tun?** You have now, I suppose, much to do? **Sie werden mitkommen, nicht wahr?** You will come along, won't you? **Sie waren im Theater, nicht?** You were at the theater, were you not? **Aber gelt, er steckte dir gewiß Geld in deinen Beutel?** He surely put money into your pocket, did he not?

In the above sentences **doch** and **wohl** have the same general meaning, but **doch** with its usual adversative force implies (often politely) that something to the contrary may possibly be urged against it, while **wohl** assumes that this will probably not be the case. Both particles can be combined with the combined force of them both: **Sie müssen doch wohl antworten?** You will probably have to answer, will you not?

Nicht added to **doch** or **wohl** in such sentences expects confidently a negative answer: **Du wirst doch nicht Fräulein Helene mit ihrer Schwester vergleichen wollen?** You certainly will not desire to compare Miss Helen with her sister?

Nicht etwa added to **doch** in such sentences express the hope that a fear or suspicion may not be realized, or may be without foundation: **Aber (er sieht sich um, leiser) sie wird's doch nicht etwa hören?** But (he looks around him, and speaks more softly) I hope she will not hear it; you certainly don't think she will? **Ihr verhaut den Hund doch nicht etwa? Nein, er haut uns.** A: **Ich gab das Geld Ihrem Kommis.** B: **Doch nicht etwa Schmidt?** Not to Schmidt, I hope.

E. An exclamation may express different shades according to the adverb used. Here **doch** expresses a surprise on the part of the speaker, often strong praise mingled with the feeling of surprise or the idea that it is contrary to expectation; **nur** (colloquially in N.G. **man**) an urgent wish that the person addressed may comply with some desire of the speaker, or look at something from his standpoint, sometimes more sharply in the sense of a rebuke, admonition, or threat; **denn** impatience; **nicht** (as in D. *b* and B. *b*) expressing that the person addressed will agree to the sentiment uttered: **Ich hatte doch Streichhölzer bei mir!** I thought I had matches about me. **Das nenne ich doch noch Humor!** I must say that's really humorous. **Das ist doch was!** That is something like it, something fine. **Es ist doch schön hier!** I must say it's really beautiful here. **Sie sollten ihn nur hören und sehen!** You ought (I do hope you will) to hear him and see him. **Sehen Sie nur, was Sie gemacht haben!** Just see what you have done! **Laß mich nur machen!** Let me alone! Let me do it myself! **Warte nur, ich werde dich lehren!** Just wait, I'll teach you. **Sitzt denn still!** Sit still then! **Wie glücklich waren wir nicht!** How happy we were! **Was ist er nicht für ein frecher Bursche!** What a bold fellow he is! Compare B. *b*.

F. A wish may express different shades by using different adverbs, such as **doch** or **nur** (colloquially **man**) only, **wenn doch** or **wenn nur** if only; much less frequently **erst** *only*, alone or with **nur**; **man nur** used very often colloquially in N.G. for **nur**. **Doch** is adversative, and shows that the wishes of the speaker do not harmonize with the facts, and cannot probably be made to do so. **Nur,** as in the preceding articles, expresses a wish that can be or could have been realized, but it often implies the fear that it may possibly not find realization. **Wenn er doch käme!** If he only would come (I fear he will not)! **Wenn ich nur nicht zu spät komme!** Oh that I may not arrive too late! **Wenn es nur so gewesen wäre! Wäre ich erst ein alter Mann! Wenn ich nur erst hundert Taler hätte!** Here, as often elsewhere, **erst** calls attention to what would follow (**223.** IV. 1. *b*. (**2**)).

Comparison of Adverbs.

224. Few genuine adverbs, from their very meaning, admit of comparison, but the many adverbs made from adjectives, like the latter, can be compared. The comparison of such adverbs does not differ at all in the positive and comparative from adjectives except that the adverbial forms are not inflected, and hence their comparison along with that of genuine adverbs is treated under adjectives. See **114–118.** In N.H.G. the adverb has developed new forms in the superlative which are given in **114.**

PREPOSITIONS.

NATURE.

225. Very closely allied in nature to adverbs are prepositions, which, like adverbs, limit the force of the verb as to some circumstance of place, time, manner, cause or reason, purpose or end, means, material, modal expression—in short the same circumstances as are expressed by the adverb *minus* degree; hence the preposition, unlike the adverb, cannot admit of comparison. Thus a preposition in connection with its dependent substantive is exactly equal in force to an adverb, but a preposition and an adverb differ in this that the latter limits the force of the verb in and of itself, while the former requires the assistance of a dependent noun or some other word: Mary was *in* (adverb), but Mary was *in* (prep.) *the house.* A preposition does not only serve to link thus its object to a verb, but also to an adjective, a noun or a sentence. As this connective particle usually stands *before* the dependent word, it is called a preposition (Latin prae *before* and positio *position*).

1. *a.* Sometimes a few prepositions and adverbs touch each other so closely that the prep. can only be distinguished by its dependent substantive, and if that be dropped the same word, which was only a moment before a prep., becomes an adverb: **Das Haus liegt abwärts** (prep.) **des Flusses** The house lies back from the river. **Das Haus liegt abwärts** The house lies to one side.

b. As described in **226** a number of adverbs have become common prepositions. The adverb, however, in entering into close relations to a noun and thus becoming a preposition did not always sever its relations to the verb, so that in compounds a prefix often has both the force of a preposition and an adverb, while the same form outside of a compound has only the force of a preposition. Examples are given **229.** 2 under **nach,** *f,* also under **entgegen.** While **nach** is both an adverb and a preposition in **Er lief dem Diebe nach,** it is only an adverb in **Ich will dir das Geheimnis mitteilen, du darfst es aber nicht nachreden.** In general, the prefixes of many verbs, tho used adverbially, have more or less prepositional force. See **223.** 1. 9. B, **258.** 1. B. *a,* and **262.** I. *b.*

c. Sometimes when there is a dependent noun, there is actual fluctuation of conception, usually the particle being construed as an adverb, but sometimes as a prep. This is true of **an** or **gegen** *about,* **über** *more than,* **unter** *less than*: **Es ist an** (adv.) or **gegen** (adv.) **ein Taler** or **an** (prep.) or **gegen** (prep.) **einen Taler Verlust dabei** There is a loss of about a thaler in the transaction. **Es ist über** (adv.) **ein Taler** or **über** (prep.) **einen Taler Verlust dabei. Es ist unter** (adv.) **ein Taler** or **unter** (prep.) **einem Taler Verlust dabei.** In this idiom, notice that the prep. **über** according to its idea of *going beyond* and **an** from the idea of *approaching* take the acc., but the prep. **unter** the dat., while all three used as adverbs remain without influence over the case. Compare **251.** I. 1. A. *b.*

2. Prepositions approach in some cases the nature of conjunctions, and lose their influence over the case of the following word. This is true of **anstatt** or **statt, außer,** and earlier in the period, and even occasionally later, also **ohne** *except,* which is now replaced here by **außer** and **ausgenommen: Er hat es mir anstatt meinem Bruder gegeben. Eine Maschine, die das Feuer treibt, anstatt der Fuhrmann** (Rosegger). **Ich will mit Stahl und Stein das Reisig zünden | und diesmal dir, statt Herr, ein Diener sein** (Hauptmann's *Der arme Heinrich,* 3). **Ja, niemand kann mir helfen — außer ich selbst** (Fulda's *Die Sklavin,* 2, 8). **Ich bin euch allen böse außer ihm. Sie fanden alles außer den Dolch,** or **außer** (prep.) **dem Dolch. Sie war es längst nicht mehr gewöhnt, was sie dachte und fühlte, gegen irgend einen Menschen, außer gegen Justus, frei zu äußern** (Spielhagen's *Sonntagskind,* I. 4). **Daß ich nicht nachdenken kann ohne mit der Feder in der Hand** (Lessing). **Nimmer mehr von Alfheim zu kehren aus dem Streit, | ohne mit Alfsonnen** (Geibel's *Juniuslieder,* 339).

a. The preceding prepositions connect as conjunctions only words, but **seit, bis, während** also connect sentences, as may also others when followed by some other conjunction, as **außer daß, außer wenn, anstatt daß,** &c.: **Persönliche Tapferkeit entscheidet weniger, seit sich die Heere der Schießgewehre bedienen. Wir gehen täglich, außer wenn es regnet.** Instead of **außer daß** we also find the simple connective: **Das hübsche Berghaus hat sicher ein Gastzimmer, und darin will ich mich — außer Sie jagen mich gewaltsam hinaus — volle drei Tage festsetzen** (Suttner's *Im Berghause,* p. 26). Formerly **ungeachtet daß** was common, but the simple connective is now preferred. Instead of the connective **seit** the form **seitdem** is also used. The preps. **anstatt** *instead of,* **ohne** *without,* and **um** *in order,* lit. *for, for the purpose of,* are very commonly found as conjunctions in connection with the infin. with **zu** in contracted clauses: **Anstatt weg zu laufen, kam der Bär heran. Ohne sich umzusehen, lief der Dieb davon. Wir leben nicht, um zu essen, sondern wir essen, um zu leben.**

b. In the case of **anstatt, statt,** and **außer** when they connect grammatical elements of like rank in the nom. or acc., the words can usually be used as preps. or conjunctions without difference of meaning: **Der Bauer brachte das Kalb anstatt der Kuh,** or **statt die Kuh. Niemand kommt mir entgegen außer ein Unverschämter** (Lessing's *Emilia*, 4, 3), or **außer einem Unverschämten.** But in case of **statt, anstatt** when there is only an indirect object after the verb, either in the simple dat. or a case after a prep., there is a sharp distinction between the prepositional and conjunctional construction. In the former construction, the noun following **anstatt, statt** is felt as the subject or author of an action, while a noun after these particles in the conjunctional construction is felt as the indirect object: **Sie dankte mir anstatt deiner** (instead of your doing so), but **Sie dankte mir statt dir** She thanked me instead of thanking you. **Er hat statt deiner** (instead of your doing it) **an mich geschrieben,** but **Er hat an mich statt an dich geschrieben** He wrote to me instead of writing to you.

3. A prep. often seems to show a relation of meaning between two nouns where in fact the relation is between a noun and a verb. Thus **Geld zur Reise** *money for the journey* is an elliptical expression = **Das Geld, das zur Reise bestimmt ist.** Thus also **Herr über Tod und Leben = Der Herr, der über Tod und Leben gesetzt ist.** In other cases the preposition may link together two nouns, the prep. phrase being a real adjunct to a noun representing an older simple case form: **ein Mäntelchen von Scharlach** = M.H.G. ein scharlaches mentelin. To-day, however, all these prepositional phrases are alike felt as attributive adjuncts.

4. Sometimes the same relations are expressed by a prep. and case as by a case alone, and sometimes by changing the prep. the idea may receive a new shade: **Man freut sich einer Sache,** or **an einer Sache** *One takes pleasure in a thing* (which one has), but **Man freut sich auf eine Sache** One takes pleasure in something that one is expecting for the future. Perhaps the prepositional construction is never entirely equal to the case construction, as the prep. often brings out more prominently some circumstance as cause, reason, &c.: **Ich bin müde vom** (*from*, on account of) **Arbeiten,** but **Ich bin des Arbeitens müde** I am tired of work, do not care to work longer.

5. Sometimes the prep. is followed by an adverb or a prep. phrase instead of a noun or pronoun: **von früh bis spät** from early till late; **von heute auf morgen verschieben** to put off from to-day till to-morrow. **Er dachte an zu Haus** (Ompteda's *Sylvester von Geyer*, XXV).

Government of Prepositions.

226. Originally the nouns which followed prepositions were not governed at all by the latter, but received their case directly from their relations to the verb, the preposition likewise limiting the verb by adding some especial explanatory circumstance of place, time, &c. Thus most of the oldest and most common prepositions were in fact adverbs, and the same prep. could be followed by two or even three different cases according to the relation of the noun to the verb, and hence possessed no governing power over the noun. But in course of time a closer relation developed between the prep. and the noun, and the former gained governing power over the latter, certain prepositions habitually requiring certain cases after them. As the prepositions before the dative, locative, ablative, and instrumental were more concrete expressions for the ideas already expressed by the endings of these cases the case endings themselves became more and more slighted and finally lost their distinctive form, all merging into one—the dative—the preceding preposition indicating the relation between the verb and the noun. See **258.** 1 (near end). The language thus lost three cases, but it gained in simplicity without losing any of its power of accurate expression. In this new period of development the prepositions not only assumed the functions of the case forms but they often retained and still retain the functions of the old adverbs out of which they had developed, as illustrated in **229.** 2 under **nach,** *f* and **entgegen.** See also **225, 223.** I. 9. B, **258.** 1. B. *a*, and **262.** I. *b*. A group of prepositions, discussed below, still allow two different cases to stand after them according to the relation of the noun to the verb, which fact shows that these prepositions are in fact still adverbs, for the verb has not lost its influence over the nouns following these prepositions.

As explained in **245.** V a large number of prepositions have come from other sources than from adverbs and still retain in good measure the power of governing the same case with which they were associated in their former capacity ere they became prepositions, but also from the crossing of different conceptions may take another case without any difference of meaning, as is discussed in detail below.

For the construction employed when several prepositions governing different cases stand before one noun see **141.** 5. B. *b*. *Note*.

Prepositions with their Dependent Cases.

227. The following lists contain the German prepositions. Those marked with a † usually govern some other case, but those with a * less commonly take another case. Those marked with ** govern different cases according as they precede or follow the dependent noun. Several of the prepositions have several forms, the more uncommon being inclosed in parentheses.

In articles **261** and **262.** IV, V, VI in connection with the government of verbs, adjectives, and participles these prepositions are treated at considerable length from another point of view, which throws additional light upon their use.

Prepositions with the Genitive.

abgerechnet	**diesseits***	**inhalts**	**östlich**	**unterwärts**
abschläglich	**eingangs**	**inklusive***	**ostwärts**	**unweit***
abseits	**einschließlich**	**inmitten**	**punkto**	**vermittels**
(abseiten)	**entlang†**	**inner(t)†**	**rechts**	**vermittelst**
(abseitig)	**(entlängst)**	**innerhalb***	**rings, ringsum**	**vermöge**
abwärts	**exklusive***	**inwärts**	**rittlings**	**von seiten**
abzüglich	**gegenwarts**	**jenseits***	**rücksichtlich**	**von wegen**
anbetreffs	**gelegentlich**	**kraft**	**rückwärts**	**vorbehaltlich**
anfangs	**gemäß†**	**längs***	**seitab**	**vorwärts**
angesichts	**halb**	**(längst)**	**seitens**	**während***
anläßlich	**halben**	**längsseit(s)**	**seitlich**	**wegen***
anstatt	**halber**	**laut**	**seitwärts**	**westlich**
antwortlich	**halbwegs**	**links**	**statt**	**westwärts**
aufwärts	**herseits**	**macht**	**südlich**	**zeit**
ausgangs	**herwärts**	**mangels**	**südwärts**	**zufolge****
ausschließlich	**hinseits**	**mittels**	**trotz***	**zugunsten****
außerhalb*	**hinsichtlich**	**mittelst**	**überhin**	**zunächst†**
ausweislich	**hinsichts**	**namens**	**um — willen**	**zusätzlich**
behufs	**hinterhalb***	**niederwärts**	**unangesehen**	**zuschläglich**
beiderseits	**hinterrücks**	**nördlich**	**unbeschadet**	**zu seiten**
besage	**hinterwärts**	**nordwärts**	**unerachtet**	**zuungunsten**
betreffs	**hinwärts**	**ob†**	**unfern***	**zuzüglich**
bezüglich	**hüben und drüben**	**oberhalb***	**ungeachtet**	**zwecks**
binnen	**infolge**	**oberwärts**	**ungerechnet**	
dank†	**inhaltlich**	**osten***	**unterhalb***	

With the Dative.

ab	**entgegen**	**mitsamt**	**samt**	**zufolge****
aus	**fernab**	**nach**	**seit**	**zunächst***
bei	**gegenüber**	**nächst**	**trotz†**	**zusamt**
benebst	**gemäß***	**nebst**	**von**	**zusamt mit**
binnen	**längs (längst)**	**nid**	**vorgängig**	**zuwider**
dank*	**mit**	**ob***	**zu**	

With the Acc.

auf und ab	**entlang***	**gen**	**per, pro, via, à**	**wider**
bis	**für**	**hindurch**	**sonder**	
durch	**gegen**	**ohne**	**um**	

With Dat. and Acc.

an	**hinter**	**neben**	**über**	**vor**
auf	**in**	**ober (S.G.)**	**unter**	**zwischen**
außer	**inner(t)**			

Note. For contractions of these prepositions with the article see **57.** B.

Origin, Meaning, and Use of Prepositions with the Genitive.

228. 1. The use of the genitive after most prepositions in modern times is easily explained by the substantive nature of a large part of them, for when one noun depends upon another the dependent noun is in the gen. The prepositions governing the gen. are in fact:

a. Nouns in the adverbial gen., or expressions formed after the model of such, often presenting in this form an abbreviated construction for an adverbial phrase. Thus instead of **Von Berlin aus liegt Magdeburg auf jener Seite der Elbe** we say more briefly **jenseits der Elbe.** This adverbial gen. in such prepositions usually ends in **s,** also in fem. words after the analogy of masculines: **diesseits, seitens,** &c. Many such prepositional forms are still written with a capital, as the original relation to the parent substantive is still vividly felt: **Ausgangs dieser**

oder Anfangs der nächsten Woche, Eingangs der sächsischen Schweiz, or perhaps more commonly **ausgangs, anfangs, eingangs.** There is here much caprice as to the use of capitals.

b. Nouns in an oblique case after a preposition expressed or understood: **in Kraft allein des Rings** (Lessing's *Nathan*, 3, 7), more commonly without the **in,** as in **kraft meines Amtes** by virtue of my office; **statt** or **anstatt meines Bruders** for **an meines Bruders Statt; um des Freundes willen** (acc. after **um**) for the sake of my friend; **von** (now usually omitted) **wegen** (dat. pl.) **des vergossenen Blutes; in Betracht seiner Jugend. Anfang** *in the beginning of*, **Mitte** *in the middle of*, **Ende** *the last of, toward the close of*, **Ecke** *on the corner of*, are now frequently used as prepositions dropping the preceding preposition and article, or both preposition and article may be retained: **Die Trippelli, Anfang** (or **im Anfang**) **der Dreißig, stark, männlich und von ausgesprochen humoristischem Typus, hatte den Sofaehrenplatz innegehabt. Ich werde Mitte** (or **in der Mitte**) **nächster Woche verreisen. Er war ein athletisch gebauter Mann Ende** (or **am Ende**) **der Zwanziger. Ecke** (or **an der Ecke**) **der Schadowstraße, aufgrund** (or more commonly **auf Grund**) **seiner Untersuchungen, anstelle** (or **an Stelle**) **des verstorbenen Vorsitzenden.** These prepositions are in different stages of evolution, and hence do not all stand in the same relation to the nouns from which they come. Some have thrown off the preposition before them, some retain it occasionally, some always, some drop it, but can be replaced by nouns with both preposition and article. In general, however, these prepositions differ from pure nouns in dropping the article, and in the more or less set form and position they assume in the sentence, usually admitting of no adj. modifiers, and standing always before the dependent genitive, thus having no freedom of position. For an interesting example where the word-order clearly distinguishes these prepositions from pure nouns see **151.** 3. A (toward end).

c. Adverbs and participles, the former in some cases also, like the adverbial nouns in *a*, ending in **s: links des Zuschauers** to the left of the spectator; **nordwärts** to the north of, **einschließlich** inclusive of, &c.; **während** (pres. part.; see **während** in 4 below) during, **ungeachtet** (past part.; see **ungeachtet** in 4 below) notwithstanding, **abgerechnet** aside from, not counting, **ungerechnet** not counting.

2. The double construction, gen. or dat., after some of these prepositions is explained by the crossing of two or more conceptions. On the one hand, when one noun depends upon the other, the dependent one must be in the gen. Thus, as can be seen from 1. *a* and *b* above, a number of these prepositions, being in fact nouns, require the dependent noun to stand in the gen. On the other hand, the idea that is contained in some nouns suggests the use of the dative after the analogy of other similar constructions. Thus we say **Jenseits des Flusses steht eine alte Kapelle,** but we also find sometimes **jenseits dem Flusse,** as the idea of rest is so often associated with the dative. On the other hand a few prepositions governing the dative are also found with a genitive, as their originally substantive nature is felt, or they are influenced by prepositions which were once substantives. Thus we say **trotz den Befehlen des Königs** in analogy with **man bietet den Befehlen des Königs Trotz,** but we also, and now more commonly, say **trotz der Befehle des Königs.** Similarly we usually say **dank dir** after the analogy of **Dir sei Dank,** but in recent literature we often find the gen. here after the analogy of the gen. with other prepositions derived from nouns. See **dank** in 4 below. The form **gemäß** is in fact an adjective governing the dat. and can still be inflected and compared, but it has become associated in meaning with the prepositional formations **in Gemäßheit** and **zufolge,** so that it likewise sometimes governs the gen.: **dem Befehl gemäß,** or **gemäß dem Befehl** or **des Befehls.**

a. We sometimes find non-inflection or the dat. after prepositions governing the gen. on purely formal grounds: (**1**) We not infrequently find an unmodified substantive in the singular uninflected after these prepositions: **Gambetta folgte ihnen ebenfalls dorthin, indem er Paris mittelst Luftballon** (instead of the more correct and in choice language now more common gen.) **verließ** (*Deutsche Rundschau*). Thus also in a number of expressions, especially in popular language, such as **wegen Todesfall** on account of death, **wegen Abbruch** on account of the tearing down of the building, &c., instead of the more correct and in choice language more common **wegen Todesfalls, Abbruchs,** &c. After **aufwärts, diesseits, jenseits, oberhalb, unterhalb, außerhalb, innerhalb, unweit, unfern, nördlich, südlich, östlich, westlich** we usually find non-inflection before names of places, altho these words elsewhere more commonly govern some case: **nördlich Iwangorod** (*Großes Hauptquartier*, Oct. 27, 1914), but **nördlich der belgischen Maas** (river) (ib. Sept. 6, 1914). The uninflected form is in fact a dative after a suppressed **von,** which as it is unstressed easily drops out. The **von,** however, is often expressed: **nördlich von Metz.** The genitive with articleless names, tho still not so common as elsewhere, is nevertheless slowly gaining ground: **innerhalb Breslaus** (*Breslauer Morgen-Zeit.*, Jan. 19, 1915).

(**2**) The use of the dat. instead of the gen. is especially frequent where the latter is not clearly marked in form: **während fünf Tagen** (instead of **Tage**) which is not clearly marked as a gen.). Also the correct gen., however, is often used in case of such nouns, prompted by the feeling that the proper case of the noun should be used here as so frequently elsewhere where the form is not distinctive. The dat. is quite common in case of the masc. and neut. sing. of the relative and interrogative pronoun **welcher,** which has a gen. sing. exactly like the nom. and acc. neut. See **während** under 4 below. The dat. is likewise common in case of other pronouns which cannot distinguish a gen. from the nom. and acc.: **wegen manchem** (R. Schweichel's *Verloren*). See also **anstatt, während, wegen,** below.

3. These prepositions are constantly increasing in number, much more so than all other classes. It can be seen from the above that it is impossible to include in the list all such prepositional particles which govern the gen., for many nouns, as in 1. *a* and *b* above, and others are occasionally pressed into service as preps., tho they still retain their initial capital. **In most**

cases only such are given in the list as are usually written with a small letter and pass generally for prepositions.

4. The treatment of prepositions governing the genitive as to their meaning and use follows, the prepositions being arranged alphabetically. In some cases the mere definition will suffice, as these prepositions do not enter into so many idiomatic combinations as prepositions governing other cases.

ABGERECHNET aside from, not counting: **abgerechnet einiger Städte** (*Ausld.*, 38, 821 *a*). The absolute construction in connection with an absolute acc. is more common here: **Narcissa, ihren Stolz abgerechnet, war ein liebenswürdiges Wesen.**

ABSCHLÄGLICH in part payment of: **abschläglich meines Honorars = auf Abschlag meines Honorars.**

AB'SEITEN, see **seitens.**

ABSEITS, less commonly **ABWÄRTS**, and the now rarer forms **ABSEIT, ABSEITEN, ABSEITIG** off to one side, aside from: **Abseits des Weges liegt das Haus. Abwärts des Eingangs. Vergebens hatte der letztere gegen den jungen Senator hervorgehoben, daß „kraft seines tragenden Amtes, abseiten des Ansehens der Familie," die Augen der ganzen Stadt auf ihn gerichtet seien** (Storm's *Söhne des Senators*, p. 301.) They sometimes occur with the dat.: **Etwas abseits dem Flecken und darüber erhöht lag ein einzelnes Schlößchen** (Hans Hoffmann's *Die Totenhochzeit*). **Abwärts** is also used in the meaning of *below, downward, down, down stream from*, usually with the gen., but often with non-inflection before names of places: **abwärts der Brust, abwärts Hamburg** below Hamburg (on the Elbe).

ABZÜGLICH deducting: **abzüglich der Transportkosten.**

ANBETREFFS, BE'TREFFS, IN BE'TREFF, IN ANBETREFF concerning, as regards: **Mein Plan betreffs einer Reise.** These prepositions are very closely related in meaning to **hinsichtlich, hinsichts, bezüglich: Seine Erzählung bedarf in Betreff,** or **in Anbetreff,** or **betreffs,** or **hinsichts,** or **hinsichtlich,** or **bezüglich mancher Punkte der Berichtigung.**

ANFANGS at or in the beginning of, often with non-inflection in case of articleless nouns: **anfangs** (or **Anfang**) **der fünfziger Jahre, anfangs September** (Carl Spitteler's *Imago*, p. 1).

ANGESICHTS in the face of, in view of, considering: **angesichts der Feinde, des Todes, der Gefahr.**

ANLÄSZLICH, auf or **aus Anlaß** spurred on, impelled by the occasion of, upon the occasion of: **anläßlich des 90. Geburtstages des berühmten Gelehrten erschien eine Festschrift.**

AN'STATT or **STATT** instead of: **Anstatt** (or **statt**) **des Vaters erschien die Mutter.** Sometimes, especially in popular language, with the dat.: **Anstatt dem Vater erschien die Mutter.** Also sometimes in the literary form of speech: **Statt Fluchen, Gähnen und dem schlürfenden Schritte der Trägheit hörte man auf diesem Hofe wieder den raschen, freudigen Tritt des Fleißes** (H. Seidel's *Der Schatz*, VI). Especially when the gen. form has not an ending which clearly marks it as a gen.: **Daß statt Bösem** (the gen. **Bösen** would not be a clear gen.) **Gutes daraus gewonnen wird** (Rudolf Hildebrand's *Vom deutschen Sprachunterricht*, p. 117). **Doch wie staunten sie, | als sie statt jenem, den sie hier gesucht, | nun einen Ritter sahen im schlichten Kleide** (M. Greif's *Heinrich der Löwe*. 2. 1).

For the conjunction **anstatt** or **statt** see **225.** 2 and *a* and *b* thereunder.

ANTWORTLICH, in Beantwortung, in Erwiderung in reply to: **Antwortlich Ihres geehrten Letzten (Briefes) teile ich Ihnen mit, &c.**

AUFWÄRTS up, above (on a river, &c.), with gen., and often non-inflection in case of names of places: **aufwärts des Stromes. Aufwärts Itschang** (place) **findet man Stellen, wo das Hochwasser Häuser . . . hinweggeschwemmt hat** (*Beilage zur Allgemeinen Zeitung*, Oct. 2, 1902).

AUSGANGS at the close of, often with non-inflection in case of articleless nouns: **ausgangs dieser oder anfangs der nächsten Woche.**

AUSSCHLIESZLICH exclusive of, **EINSCHLIESZLICH** inclusive of, usually with the gen., in case of unmodified nouns or nouns with uninflected modifiers usually with non-inflection in the sing., but the gen., less commonly the dat., in the pl.; instead of **ausschließlich, einschließlich** often the foreign forms **exklu'sive, inklu'sive,** with the same use of the cases: **einschließlich der Kosten, einschließlich Wartung und Risiko** (*Die Landwirtschaft*, Aug. 15, 1905). **Der Bierverbrauch stellte sich 1903 im deutschen Zollgebiet einschließlich Luxemburg auf rund 69 Millionen Hektoliter** (*Nordd. Allg. Zeit.*, 1905). **Wir waren alle da einschließlich vier Fremde(n).**

AUSZERHALB outside, **HINTERHALB** back of, behind, **INNERHALB** inside, **OBERHALB** above, **UNTERHALB** below, also sometimes with the dat., often with non-inflection in case of articleless nouns, especially names of places: **außerhalb der Stadt, unterhalb des Dorfs, innerhalb eines Jahrtausends, innerhalb vierzig Tage** (Martin's *Wolframs von Eschenbach Parzifal*, II. p. xxiv), **innerhalb zehn Tagen, innerhalb einem Tage** (Lessing; more commonly **eines Tages**), **außerhalb Bayerns** (*Hamburger Correspondent*, Feb. 27, 1903), **innerhalb Breslaus** (*Breslauer Morgen-Zeit.*, Sept. 19, 1914), **außerhalb Ricks** (name) **Welt und Verständnis** (Marie Diers's *Zum Bilde Gottes schuf er ihn*, chap. III), **an der Weichsel ober- und unterhalb Iwangorod** (*Frankfurter Zeit.*, Jan. 19, 1915). Instead of the preceding constructions we sometimes find the preposition followed by **von** w. dat., especially when there is no word which can clearly mark the case: **innerhalb von vier Wänden** (Raabe's *Pfitzers Mühle*, XIX). Often with names of places: **unterhalb von Luck** (*Großes Hauptquartier*, Sept. 28, 1915). The prep. construction is the rule with pronouns: **Wär' der Durchbruch 'ne halbe Meile unterhalb von uns passiert, dann könnten wir noch heut' auf unserm Hof sitzen** (Halbe's *Der Strom*, p. 15). **See also 2. *a*. (1) above.**

AUSWEISLICH, nach Ausweis, besage (rare) as shown by the documentary evidence of: **Dazu sind Sie ausweislich** (or **besage**) **des Vertrags verpflichtet.**

(*a*) Synonymous with these words in so far as the reference is to documentary or written evidence are: **gemäß** in accordance with, **inhalts** or **inhaltlich** (in official style), **laut, zufolge** (with the dat. when it follows the noun), and the very frequent form **nach** (with the dat.) according to; see also each of these words.

BE'HUFS, ZUM BE'HUF, ZWECKS for the furtherance of, with a view to, for the purpose of, much used instead of the more simple but not so explicit **zu** (w. dat.): **behufs Wahrung des Prestiges der italienischen Flagge** for the purpose of maintaining the prestige of the Italian flag. **Am 2. ds. (dieses Monats) brach die Kolbenstange zum zweiten Male, und das Schiff mußte infolgedessen behufs der Ausbesserung 41 Stunden still liegen. Er ist der Polizeibehörde zur,** or **behufs,** or **zwecks Einsperrung überwiesen worden.**

BEIDERSEITS on both sides of, with the same construction as **diesseits.**

BE'SAGE (from older **nach Besage**) see **ausweislich.**

BE'TREFFS, see **anbetreffs.**

BE'ZÜGLICH or **in Bezug auf** (w. acc.) with reference to; see **anbetreffs.** Sometimes instead of the gen. after **bezüglich** we find the prep. **auf** (w. acc.): **seine Bemerkungen bezüglich auf Farben organischer Körper** (Goethe).

BINNEN *within, inside of,* of space and time, more commonly the latter, often with dat. like in and also often, perhaps more frequently, with the gen. like **innerhalb: binnen Landes gemacht** (Möser), **binnen ihren notwendigen Grenzen** (Immermann); **binnen hier und einem Jahr** (Lessing), **binnen den nächsten drei Stunden** (Raabe), **binnen kurzem** (Marriot) *within a short time*; **binnen eines halben Jahres** (*Hamburger Correspondent,* April 20, 1905), **binnen knapper zwei Wochen** (Mann's *Buddenbrooks,* vol. III, p. 91), **binnen eines Monats** (Artikel 73 *der Verfassung des Deutschen Reichs*), **binnen zwei weiteren Wochen** (ib., Artikel 74).

DANK thanks to, often with gen., more commonly with dat.: **dank des für die Jahreszeit besonders schönen Wetters** (Schubin), **dank seiner fünfunddreißig Jahre** (Fedor Sommer's *Ernst Reiland,* p. 185), and many other examples from recent literature.

DIESSEIT or now more commonly **DIESSEITS** on this side of, **JENSEIT** or now more commonly **JENSEITS** on that side of, **HÜBEN UND DRÜBEN** on both sides of, lit. on this side and that: **diesseits des Flusses, jenseits des Grabes, hüben und drüben der Grenze.** Sometimes **von** is used in connection with the regular form: **Jenseit von des Oxus Wogen** (Rückert's *Morg.,* 1, 251). Earlier in the period the dative sometimes occurs instead of the gen.: **Diesseit den Alpen** (Lessing). In case of names of places non-inflection of the noun is not infrequent: **jenseits Bar.** See also 2. *a.* (**1**) above.

EINGANGS at the beginning of, at the entrance to: **Die eingangs dieser Zeilen wiedergegebene Zeitungsnotiz, in mittlerer und eingangs neuerer Zeit** (T. Frings in *Paul und Braunes Beiträge,* 1917, p. 248). **Er stand eingangs der Untersekunda. Eingangs der sächsischen Schweiz.**

EINSCHLIESZLICH, see **ausschließlich.**

ENT'LANG, see **längs.**

EXKLU'SIVE, see **ausschließlich.**

GEGENWARTS in the presence of, or more commonly **in Gegenwart: gegenwarts der Herren.**

GE'LEGENTLICH or **BEI GE'LEGENHEIT** as to the topic of, apropos of, embracing the favorable opportunity of, upon the occasion of: **gelegentlich dieser Gedichte will ich bemerken usw. Gelegentlich seiner Anwesenheit in der Stadt machte er einige Besuche. Gelegentlich** (upon the occasion of) **meines letzten Besuches auf Krasnawoda** (the name of a village) **lenkte sich das Gespräch auf einige neuerschienene Bücher.**

GE'MÄSZ (see **ausweislich**) in accordance with, sometimes w. gen. or more commonly w. dat. when standing before the noun, always w. dat. when following the noun: **gemäß Ihres Befehls** or more commonly **Ihrem Befehle gemäß. An die Sprache schließt sich aufs engste der Gesang an, dem fast alle Stämme gemäß ihres lebhaften und heiteren Wesens leidenschaftlich ergeben sind** (Prof. Dr. Keller's *Die ostafrikanischen Inseln,* p. 59). For explanation of the gen. see 2 above, toward end. **Gemäß** was originally an adjective governing the dative which regularly preceded it. In most cases it is still an adjective whether used as an independent word or as the basal element in a compound. It is only distinctly felt as a preposition when it precedes the substantive. The **s** found in compounds such as **standesgemäß** *in accordance with one's station in life,* **wahrheitsgemäß** *in accordance with the facts,* &c., is not the gen. ending, but the connecting **s** so often found in compounds after the analogy of gen. compounds, as in **standeswidrig, wahrheitsgetreu,** &c. Compare **gemäß** in **229.** 2.

HALB, HALBEN, HALBER, WEGEN express:

1. *a.* A motive, cause, reason, with the general translation *on account of,* sometimes with the dat. in case of **wegen: Ich bleibe des schlechten Wetters wegen** (or **halber, halben**) **zu Hause. Der Strauß kann wegen seiner zu kurzen Flügel nicht fliegen.** Of these words **wegen** is the most common in this meaning. The older form **von wegen** (dat. pl. of Weg) is still quite common in popular speech, and not infrequent in colloquial language: **Lieber packe ich dir noch ein paar wollene Strümpfe, 'ne warme Unterhose und eine Reservenachtmütze zu, von wegen möglicher Erkältung bei dieser Erhitzung fürs allgemeine deutsche Vaterland** (Raabe's *Gutmanns Reisen,* chap. i). For the dat. see **wegen,** below in the alphabetical arrangement.

b. A concern for a thing or that in regard to which some action is to be taken, or a regard for the interests of someone, translated by *for the sake of, on account of, with regard to, concerning, as far as it concerns* (me, you, him, &c.): **Wegen** (with regard to) **vergessener Sachen wende man sich an das „Büro für gefundene Sachen."** **Zwischen dem Vollbauer** (possessor of a hide of land) **Friedrich Schmidt von hier und dessen Kindern ist folgender Kontrakt wegen** (in regard to) **Überlassung des hier belegenen Bauerngutes abgeschlossen worden. Des Scheines halber** for the sake of appearances, **der Ehre halber, des Beispiels halber.** This meaning is also quite common in compounds (see **140.** *d* and *Note* 1) which these preps. form with the possessives: **Seien Sie meinetwegen** (on my account) **unbesorgt. Meinetwegen** (as far as I am concerned, for aught I care) **kann er gehen. Er hat es meinethalben** or **meinethalb** (out of regard for me) **getan. Meinethalben** (as far as I am concerned, for aught I care) **kannst du es tun.** The form **halben** is more common in these compounds than **halb.** Feminine nouns often take the gen. ending **s** after the analogy of the masculines, and are then written as compounds: **höflichkeitswegen** or **-halber, gesundheitswegen** or **-halber.**

This meaning in case of **wegen** is especially frequent in the language of the common people, where the original form **von — wegen** (see *a* above) is still much used: **Es ist man** (= **nur**) **von wegen das Vieh** (acc. instead of gen. in popular speech), **daß ich fragen wollte** (Wildenbruch's *Die Quitzows*, 1, 2). Earlier in the period this form was also used in the literary language: **Gebt Rechenschaft . . . von wegen des vergoßnen Blutes** (Schiller's *Jungfrau*, 1, 11).

c. The source or direction from which something comes, or the instance or occasion which calls forth some act, *by*, *on the part of*, *in pursuance of*, *on the authority of*, *by the order of*. In the literary language this meaning, once so common, only survives in the form **von — wegen** in a limited number of expressions: **von Rechts wegen** by rights, **von Amts wegen** officially, **von Staats wegen** by the State, **von Obrigkeits wegen, von Regierungs wegen, von Berufs wegen** professionally, **von Polizei wegen** by order of the police authorities. **Ohne mir einen Vorwurf zu erlauben — ich meine, Durchlaucht sollten die Fundamente des Staates, zu dessen Hüter Sie von Geburt und Partei wegen berufen sind, ein wenig höher einschätzen** (Sudermann's *Es lebe das Leben*, p. 21). **In irgend einer Weise werden wir von Fraktions wegen** (*as a party*) **wohl Stellung dazu nehmen müssen** (ib., p. 52). **Ich hatte zwei oder drei entfernte Verwandte von Vaters wegen** (*upon my father's side*) (Frenssen's *Die drei Getreuen*, III, 2). Notice in the preceding examples that the fem. gen. sometimes takes the ending **s** after the analogy of the masculines.

Colloquially, and especially in popular speech, this usage is not confined to the group of expressions given above: **Sag' ihm von meinetwegen, daß,** &c. (Goethe) Tell him "for me" (as coming from me) that, &c. **Es ist ja man** (= **nur**) **bloß von Fritze Belkow** (acc. in popular speech instead of the gen.) **wegen, daß ich gefragt gehabt habe** (Wildenbruch's *Die Quitzows*, 1, 2) It is only at the instance of Fritz Belkow that I asked.

2. **Halb, halben, halber** always follow the noun or pronoun, while **wegen** may precede or follow: **wegen seines Fleißes** or **seines Fleißes wegen, unserer Freundschaft halben** or **halber.**

Halb is now only found in composition with **des** and **wes,** and the possessives (see **140.** *d. Note* 1): **deshalb** on account of that, **weshalb** why, **meinethalb** for my sake, &c.

halben (but never **halber**) like **halb** enters into compounds with the possessives, and both **halben** and **halber** (now evidently the favorite, altho **halben** is common earlier in the period) follow substantives, the latter often entering into a compound with them: **meinethalben, eines kleinen Zwistes mit Schneider Busch halben** (Raabe's *Pfisters Mühle*, IX), **des lieben Friedens halber, ordnungshalber** (even fem. nouns taking **s** after the analogy of masc. in set expressions) for the sake of order, **krankheitshalber. Der Unruhen und der Unsicherheit halber wanderten viele Einwohner aus.**

HALBWEGS, sometimes **HALBWEG** or **HALBWEGE,** *halfway to, up, thru, between,* with gen. except before names of places, where non-inflection is the rule: **Man muß das Trinkwasser halbwegs des Berges holen** (Auerbach's *Joseph*, chap. 1) One must go halfway to the mountain for water. **Die Flüchtlinge erfuhren jetzo erst vom Waldrande aus, daß sie wohl halbwegs** (halfway up) **der Höhe der Vorhügel des Voglers sich befanden** (Raabe's *Odfeld*, chap. xv). **Halbwegs des Gedankens fällt ihm ein,** &c. (Hebel, 3, 101) When he is halfway thru the thought it occurs to him, &c. **Der Verwalter von meinem Vorwerk halbwegs Padua** (Fulda's *Zwillingsschwester*, 2, 8) halfway to Padua. **Der Vater und der Herr Behrend sind schon halbwege Blumeck** (Eckstein's *Familie Hartwig*). **Halbwegs Braunschweig und Hamburg** halfway between B. and H. **Halbwegs Ailly-Apremont wurde unsererseits angegriffen** (*Großes Hauptquartier*, July 7, 1915).

HERSEITS on his (her, their) side of, indicating the side towards the person in question, **hinseits** on the other side of: **Mit umständlicher Freundlichkeit leitete sie das Mädchen, herseits** (on her side of) **des Ladentisches schreitend, tiefer in den von Mehlduft erfüllten Raum hinein** (Ernst Zahn's *Verena Stadler*, I).

HERWÄRTS = **diesseits, hinwärts** = **jenseits,** with gen., dat., or non-inflection as in case of **diesseits.**

HINSEITS, see **herseits.**

HINSICHTLICH, HINSICHTS, IN HINSICHT with regard or reference to, in consideration of (see **anbetreffs** and **rücksichtlich**): **Hinsichtlich seines Fleißes kann ich nicht über ihn klagen.** Synonymous with these preps. are **rücksichtlich** and **bezüglich.** Sometimes **hinsichtlich** takes after it **auf** (w. acc.) instead of the gen. as in case of **bezüglich.**

HINTERHALB, see **außerhalb.**

HINTERRÜCKS behind the back of: **hinterrücks der Mutter.**

HINTERWÄRTS back of: **hinterwärts dieses Bauwerks.**

HINWÄRTS, see **herwärts.**

HÜBEN UND DRÜBEN, see **diesseits.**

IN'FOLGE and less frequently **ZU'FOLGE** in consequence of: **infolge or zufolge besonderer Umstände. Infolge (or zufolge) einer abermaligen schlechten Ernte und arger Unterlassungssünden der Ortsbehörden herrscht in Schardrinsk (in Rußland) Hungersnot.** Compare this use of **zufolge** with that in **229.** 2.

INHALTLICH or **INHALTS,** see **ausweislich** and **laut.**

INKLU'SIVE, see **ausschließlich.**

IN'MITTEN in the midst of, between, sometimes also w. dat. and w. **von** and dat.: **Inmitten des Waldes stand ein altes Forsthaus. O Vaterland** (Austria)! **Inmitten | dem Kind Italien und dem Manne Deutschland | liegst du, der wangenrote Jüngling, da** (Grillparzer's *König Ottokars Glück und Ende,* 3). **Inmitten von Kummer und Elend.**

INNER(T), see **inner**(t) under **231.** II.

INNERHALB, see **außerhalb.**

INWÄRTS = **innerhalb** or **in.**

JENSEITS, see **diesseits.**

KRAFT by virtue of, by dint of: **kraft meines Amtes.** For synonyms see **vermöge,** *Note.*

LÄNGS (only rarely **längst**) *along,* with the gen., less frequently the dat., preferring the position before the noun, rarely with the acc.; **ent'lang** (rarely **ent'längst**), a Low German form with the force of H.G. **längs** and of the same origin as English *along,* now also common in literary German, often with the gen., usually with the acc. but also frequently with the dat., either preceding or following the noun but with a decided preference for the position after the noun when the acc. is used: **längs des Ufers or dem Ufer; das Tal entlang, or dem Tal entlang,** or **entlang des Tales or dem Tal.** Originally **entlang** was an adverb. This accounts for its common position after the acc., which in fact is a cognate acc., the object of the verb: **Er kam den Weg entlang.** It is still often used as an adverb without an object: **Felix, die Hände in den Taschen seines kurzen Hausrockes, kam entlang** (Junghans). **Er kam am Bach entlang.**

LÄNGSSEITS or **LÄNGSSEIT** *alongside of:* **Das Boot glitt mit niedergeworfenen Segeln längsseits des Landungsstegs.** Also with dat.: **Unser Boot legte sich langseit dem englischen Dampfer** (Gerstäcker).

LAUT (in early N.H.G. **nach Laut,** thus in fact a dative of the noun **Laut** in a former meaning which is preserved in **Wortlaut**) according to (the contents, tenor of a letter, command, law, agreement, &c.), usually w. gen., often also the dat., especially when the noun is without an article or other modifying word: **Laut unserer Verabredung, laut seines Briefes. Laut alter Verträge war früher Ungarn mit Österreich unter einem Herrscher vereinigt. Laut ärztlichem Gutachten** (*Hamburger Nachrichten,* Oct. 9, 1904), **laut einem Privattelegramm** (ib. Aug. 7, 1905), **laut Berichten des Reuterschen Bureaus** (*Kölnische Zeit.,* Nov. 5, 1914), **laut einem Beschluß des Kuratoriums** (*Neue Zürcher Zeit.,* Sept. 12, 1916).

(*a*) Synonyms of **laut** are **inhalts or inhaltlich** (in official style), **zufolge** (usually following the noun), **nach** (see **nach,** *e.* (**2**). *Note* in **229.** 2; usually before, but also after the noun): **Das bestätigt sich laut, or inhalts, or inhaltlich neuerer Nachrichten, or nach neueren Nachrichten or neueren Nachrichten nach or zufolge.**

LINKS to the left of, **RECHTS** to the right of, both with gen., also with **von** + dat., and always so in case of a pronominal object: **links, rechts der Tür, or von der Tür. Links von ihm sah man mehrere holsteinische Geschichtswerke aufgeschlagen übereinander** (Frenssen).

MACHT (rare) = **kraft.**

MANGELS out of lack of, for want of, in default of: **Er wurde mangels der Beweise freigesprochen. Mangels Zahlung** in default of payment.

MITTELS, VERMITTELS, or the corrupted forms with excrescent **t VERMITTELST, MITTELST** by, by means of: **Viele Dampfschiffe werden mittels einer Schraube bewegt. Mittels Nachtmarsches war morgens früh vier Uhr die 18. Division vom linken auf dem rechten Moselufer eingetroffen** (Moltke). We not infrequently find non-inflection of the noun here in the singular. See 2. *a* above. The dative plural is also sometimes found, especially in case of articleless nouns: **Verfolgung des Wildes zur Winterszeit mittels Skiern** (Erik Voigt in *Hamburger Nachrichten,* Oct. 17, 1905).

(*a*) Synonyms of **mittels, vermittels are von, durch, mit.** The *direct* source of an act is expressed by **von,** hence limited chiefly to a living, thinking agent. The *indirect* means by which the aim is attained is expressed by **durch.** The instrument which produced the *immediate* result is expressed by **mit: Er wurde von** (by — the agent and author of it all) **dem Richter verurteilt, durch** (as the indirect means) **den Henker mit** (the instrument which produced the immediate result) **dem Beil hingerichtet zu werden.** Of these **durch** approaches the nearest to **mittels,** but the latter has a much more narrow range of usefulness. **Mittels** is only used of some force as a means or a dead instrument that is purposely utilized, directed, employed to lead to a certain definite end, while **durch** is used of a force that in itself has in some degree self-acting, transforming power, which, however, need not necessarily act toward some definite end: **Mühlen werden mittels des Windes, des Wassers, der Dampfkraft bewegt. Das Schiff wird durch die Strömung abgetrieben.** In (ver)**mittels** there also lies something of the technical, which does not admit of its use in elevated language so much. See also **vermöge,** *Note.* **Mit** is also used to express means and differs from **durch** in that it does not necessarily point to a result: **Er will uns damit anlocken,** but **Er hat uns dadurch verlockt.** In some cases either **mit** or **durch** can be used, the former calling attention to the effort and the means employed, the latter emphasizing the effective means and the result: **einen mit Worten or durch Worte antreiben. Durch** also approaches sometimes **von** in meaning, and hence English *by* is used to translate both words.

For examples see **durch** (*b*), (*c*) in **230.** In most of these examples the usual difference in meaning between **von** and **durch** is observed. In connection with a verbal noun, however, **durch** is usually employed to denote the agent where we should expect **von,** as the use of the latter, so common in the attributive relation to express other ideas, might be misunderstood: **die Meldung von der Übernahme der Regentschaft durch den Grafen Leopold zur Lippe-Biesterfeld** (*Deutsche Rundschau*, Nov. 1904, p. 308).

NAMENS or **IM NAMEN** in the name of: **Das fordere ich namens des Königs.**

NIEDERWÄRTS below.

NÖRDLICH to the north of, most commonly with gen., also with **von** + dat., sometimes with the simple dat., usually with non-inflection in case of articleless names: **nördlich des Rheins** or **vom Rhein; nördlich dem Oldenhorn** (Hermann Suchier in *Gröbers Grundriß*, I, p. 722); **das kleine Gefecht bei Lundby nördlich Hobro.** In case of pronouns the adverbial construction with **von** is usually employed: **am Barrenkopf** (mountain peak) **und nördlich davon** (*Großes Hauptquartier*, Aug. 24, 1915).

NORDWÄRTS = **nördlich,** now most commonly with gen., also with **von** + dat., and sometimes with the simple dat.: **an einzelnen Orten nordwärts der Alpen** (*Zürcher Zeitung*, **11. Jan.** 1903), **nordwärts vom Rhein,** occasionally **nordwärts dem Rhein.**

ÖB, see **ob** under **229. 2.**

OBERHALB above, see **außerhalb.**

OBERWÄRTS = **oberhalb.**

OSTEN = **ostwärts** with the same construction, rare: **Wo einst osten dem Dorfe ein Hafen der gefürchteten Vitalienbrüder gewesen sein sollte, sah man jetzt,** &c. (T. Storm's *Renate*, p. 1).

ÖSTLICH to the east of, with the same construction as **nördlich.**

OSTWÄRTS = **östlich,** with the same construction as **nordwärts.**

PUNKTO or in puncto (ablative of Latin punctum) = **wegen** on account of, with reference to, especially a legal term: **„Du meinst, der General ist allen geistlichen Leuten aufsässig?" „Allen ohne Ausnahme, seit er punkto gottloser Reden prozessiert und um eine schwere Summe gebüßt wurde"** (K. F. Meyer). **So mögen Sie sich, liebster Freund, den Weihnachtstrubel vorstellen, dem ich und meine Frau Do zwar freudig, aber doch mit einer gewissen Sorge in** puncto **unserer alten Köpfe und sonstigen mit feinen Nerven gesegneten Glieder entgegensehen** (T. Storm an G. Keller, 23. Dezember 1880).

RECHTS, see **links.**

RINGS round about (rare): **rings ihres kleinen Grabhügels** (Ense's *Denk.*, 6, 558). **Da ruhen die Gäste rings der Waldeswüste** (Lenau). We usually find **rings um** (with acc.) here, but now sometimes also **rings'um** with the gen.: **ringsum des Marktes** (Wustmann's *Allerhand Sprachdummheiten*, p. 197, 7th ed.).

RITTLINGS astraddle of, across: **Die Infanterie entwickelte sich rittlings der Straße** (Moltke).

RÜCKSICHTLICH with respect to, in consideration of (see **hinsichtlich**): **Die Arbeit verdient Lob hinsichts des Inhalts, aber hinsichtlich,** or **rücksichtlich,** or **bezüglich des Ausdrucks ist manches zu tadeln.**

Note 1. The difference between **hinsichtlich** and **rücksichtlich** sometimes becomes more prominent when a motive enters as a factor into the case. Then the **rück** *back* in **rücksichtlich** requires this word to be used in case of circumstances that are already at hand, passed or finished, while the **hin** in **hinsichtlich** points to a future act or state of things: **Ich tat es in Rücksicht** or **rücksichtlich des Vorteils, der mir daraus erwüchse** I did it out of consideration of the advantage, gain that might come to me. **Ich tue es hinsichtlich** or **in Hinsicht der guten Folgen, die daraus entspringen werden.**

Note 2. Sometimes **rücksichtlich** takes after it the prep. **auf** (with acc.) instead of the gen., as in case of **hinsichtlich** and **bezüglich.**

RÜCKWÄRTS back of: **seine Stellung rückwärts des rechten Flügels** (of the army).

SEIT'AB to one side of: **Eine Dame hielt allein in der Einsamkeit, auch auf einem Maultier, seitab des Weges auf einem Felsenvorsprung** (Raabe's *Frau Salome*, chap. iii).

SEITENS, VON SEITEN, AB'SEITEN on the part of: **Es steht seitens,** or **von seiten,** or less commonly **abseiten des Magistrats nichts entgegen.** The first of these forms, altho a new formation, is now very common.

SEITLICH alongside of: **Nachdenklich gehe ich den langen Korridor hinunter, in dessen glänzend gebohnten Streifen, seitlich des grünen Läufers, sich die gelben Messinggriffe der Türen widerspiegeln wie goldene, schwimmende Blumen** (Anselm Heine's *Bis in das dritte und vierte Glied*).

SEITWÄRTS to the side of, most commonly with gen., also with **von** + dat., and usually so in case of a pronominal object, sometimes with simple dat.: **seitwärts des heiligen Bezirks** (*Beilage zur Allgemeinen Zeitung*, Dec. 5, 1901), **seitwärts von unserm Hofe** (Storm), **seitwärts von ihm** (Frenssen's *Die drei Getreuen*, chap. iv), **seitwärts diesem Platz** (Stifter's *Stud.*, 1, 290). Usually with non-inflection in case of articleless names: **einen Flußübergang seitwärts Liaoyang** (*Neue Zürcher Zeit.*, Aug. 30, 1904).

STATT, see **anstatt.**

SÜDLICH to the south of, with the same construction as **nördlich.**

SÜDWÄRTS = **südlich,** with the same construction as **nordwärts.**

TROTZ in spite of, originally with dat., now also with gen., and perhaps more commonly so, but in the sense of *as well as, almost excelling, beating* usually with dat., as also in the expressions **trotzdem** *in spite of that* and **trotz dem und alledem: trotz alles Widerstrebens** (Raabe's *Zum wilden Mann*, chap. ii), **trotz seiner schneeweißen Haare und seiner wohlgezählten sechzig Jahre** (ib.); **trotz ihrem Alter und ihrer Müdigkeit** (Raabe's *Höxter u. Corvey*, chap. i). **Gesund**

bin ich jetzt, trotz einem I am now as well as anybody. **Er lügt trotz** (almost excelling, beating) **einem Zeitungsblatt,** or **trotz einem Münchhausen** (the famous liar of fable). **Er muß einen Wahrsagergeist haben trotz** (equal to) **der Magd in der Apostelgeschichte.** See **unangesehen.**

Zum Trotz also governs the gen., but it may stand after the dependent noun, and governs then usually the dat.: **Ich will doch einen großen Musikus aus dir machen zum Trotz eines jeden, der mich daran hindern will,** but **allem Menschenverstand zum Trotz** (contrary to). Sometimes, however, the gen. is found when the dependent noun precedes: **allen Abredens seiner guten Freunde zum Trotz** (Raabe's *Deutscher Adel,* chap. vii).

ÜBER'HIN on the other side of, rare: **Überhin der March** (river) **beginnt's zu grauen** (Grillparzer's *Ottokar,* 5).

UM — WILLEN for the sake of, on account of: **um Gottes willen, um des lieben Friedens willen; nie um der Laterne, sondern um des Lichtes willen** (Konrad Falke), or sometimes **nie um der Laterne willen, sondern um des Lichtes** (Georg Edward). The younger form **willen,** as in **ihrer selbst willen** (Rosegger), is not yet so common as the older **um — willen,** while on the other hand the younger form **wegen** has supplanted in most cases the older **von — wegen;** see **halb,** above.

UN'ANGESEHEN setting aside, notwithstanding, heedless of, now rare, and usually replaced by **UNGE'ACHTET** or **UNER'ACHTET,** or the rarer forms of **ohngeachtet, ohnerachtet,** either preceding or less commonly following the noun, but often found after pronouns, usually with gen., but sometimes with dat., when the prep. stands after the pronoun or substantive: **ungeachtet des Wetters, des Wetters ungeachtet, dessenungeachtet,** or sometimes **demungeachtet** (Marriot's *Seine Gottheit,* chap. ii) *notwithstanding that,* **aller persönlichen Erlebnisse und Kümmernisse unerachtet** (Wildenbruch's *Vize-Mama*), **allen Unfällen ungeachtet** (Lessing), **allem Abmahnen Truds unerachtet** (Fontane's *Grete Minde,* chap. iii). Originally **unangesehen** was a perfect active participle used as a predicate appositive, just as **ungeachtet** in the example under **ungeachtet** below, but it of course governed the accusative instead of the genitive. Later as a preposition it took the gen. after the analogy of **ungeachtet** with which it was closely related in meaning and development.

Trotz is a synonym of **ungeachtet,** but is a much stronger word implying a more forcible resistance to obstacles: **Er geht ungeachtet** or **trotz des schlechten Wetters spazieren,** but only **Er läuft trotz seines Stelzfußes** (wooden leg).

UNBE'SCHADET without waiving, without detracting from, without detriment to, in spite of, with gen. usually, but sometimes with the dat., usually found before the noun, but sometimes after it: **unbeschadet meines Anspruchs, meiner Rechte; unbeschadet Berlichingen** (dat.) **und unserer Verbindung** (Goethe's *Götz,* 2, 7). **Diesen unbedeutenden Einwänden unbeschadet bleibt Thumbs Buch ein des hochverdienten Forschers würdiges Werk** (P. Wahrmann in *Anzeiger für indogermanische Sprach- und Altertumskunde,* 1913, p. 16).

UNER'ACHTET, see **unangesehen.**

UNFERN or **UNWEIT** not far from, usually with gen., not infrequently with dat., sometimes with **von** and dat., or in case of names of places with non-inflection of the noun: **unfern des Feuers** (Goethe), **unweit des Dorfes** (id.), **unfern dem Haff und dem Ostseegestade** (H. Hoffmann), **unfern von Douay** (Ranke), **unweit von meines Vaters Stube** (T. Storm), **unweit Pillau** (Moltke).

UNGE'ACHTET, originally a perfect active participle used as a predicate appositive as in **183.** 2. C. *c*: **Des schlechten Wetters ungeachtet [habend] ging er hinaus.** For present meaning see **unangesehen.**

UNGE'RECHNET not counting: **ungerechnet des Qualmes.** Sanders gives a number of references in his *Ergänzungswörterbuch,* p. 409. The absolute construction with an absolute acc. is more common here: **Das Buch kostet, den Einband ungerechnet, fünf Mark.**

UNTERHALB, see **außerhalb.**

UNTERWÄRTS down; **unterwärts des Stroms, unterwärts** (at the foot of) **des Berges.**

UNWEIT, see **unfern.**

VER'MITTELS and **VER'MITTELST,** see **mittels.**

VER'MÖGE, earlier in the period **nach Vermöge** (old noun, now obs.), in virtue of, thru, by means of, in consequence of, by reason of, only rarely with dat.: **vermöge** (thru) **seiner Redlichkeit. Alle Körper streben vermöge** (in consequence of) **ihrer Schwere nach dem Mittelpunkte der Erde. Die Lande Österreich und Steier fallen, vermög' dem Majestätsbrief Kaiser Friedrichs, wohl an des letzten Lehnbesitzers Töchter** (Grillparzer's *König Ottokar,* 2).

Note. Synonymous with **vermöge** are **kraft** and **mittels. Vermöge** and **kraft** have much the same range of meanings, and are often almost identical. The latter, however, often emphasizes the actual *exercise* or *employment* of power, be it a natural force or power invested in one from without, while **vermöge** denotes an inherent *natural* force or power which is inseparably connected with the nature of a person or thing, and is conceived of as self-acting, as all natural forces: **Er selbst, der nur mittelmäßig Begabte, hatte auf seinem Felde Rühmliches geleistet, aber kraft** (by dint of) **seiner sittlichen Eigenschaften, nicht durch eine geniale Anlage** (Meyer). **Kraft** (by virtue of) **der Gewalt, die mir geliehen ist, kraft** (by virtue of) **meines Amtes, unseres Vertrages. Ein Stein fällt vermöge seiner Schwere zu Boden. Vermöge des Verstandes bildet man Begriffe. Die Maschine wird vermöge** (or more commonly **vermittels**) **des Dampfes bewegt.** Here **vermöge** touches **vermittels,** but differs from it in that it represents the power as a natural force, while **vermittels** represents it as controlled and operated by someone. See *a* under **mittels.**

VON SEITEN, see **seitens.**

VON WEGEN doesn't usually have the full causal force of **wegen,** but only the original meanings, *by the way of, on the part of, concerning, at the instance of.* **Wegen** without **von** has developed causal force, and in this meaning is widely used, while **von wegen** is now only found in a few set expressions (see **halb,** 1. *c*) in the literary language, usually with its original force, but it is still often employed by the common people in both the old and the new meaning (see also **halb** 1. *a*, *b* and *c*).

VORBEHALTLICH, VORBEHÄLTLICH, UNTER VORBEHALT with reservation of, upon the condition of: **Sie** (**die Verträge**) **wurden von der preußischen Regierung vorbehaltlich der Zustimmung ihrer Zollverbündeten am 2. August 1862 unterzeichnet.**

VORWÄRTS in front of, usually with the gen., usually with non-inflection with articleless names.

WÄHREND (originally a participle in the adverbial gen. construction: **währendes Krieges** becoming **während des Krieges**; see **223.** II. 2) during, usually with the gen., but also occasionally the dat., especially when the gen. does not differ in form from the nom. and acc.: **Während des Krieges schweigen die Gesetze. Während fünf Tagen** (or better **Tage**), **währenddessen,** or quite frequently **währenddem. Während** usually takes the dat. in case of the masc. and neut. sing. of the relative and interrogative pronoun **welcher: Erinnerst du dich noch jenes Gewitters, während welchem** (or still better **dessen**) **ich dich dort traf ganz unter den Vorsprung gedrückt?** (Raabe's *Frühling*, chap. v). In S.G. colloquial speech the dative is in general quite common here and hence it appears sometimes in the literary language instead of the genitive.

WEGEN (in S.E. dialect often in the form **z'weg'n**), or in colloquial language also still in the older form **von wegen,** on account of, with reference to, concerning (for other meanings see **halb,** 1. *c* above), usually with gen., but colloquially not infrequently with dat.: **Ich schäme mich von wegen dem ewigen Lug und Trug** (Fontane's *Effi*, chap. xxiv). The dat. is most common in the literary language where the gen. form has not an ending which clearly marks it as a gen.: **Sie will mich wegen Sommerkostümen** (the gen. would not be different in form from nom. or acc.) **um Rat fragen** (Fulda's *Die wilde Jagd*, 3, 2). **Wegen etwas anderem** (also the wk. gen. **anderen,** but not **anderes,** as it would not be felt as a gen.) *on account of something else.* Sometimes before unmodified nouns: **Die Bücher liegen hier bloß wegen Friedeberg, den ich der beigegebenen Zeichnungen halber fragen will** (Fontane's *Frau Jenny*, chap. 6). **So ist dir vielleicht lieber, du läßt dich abends wegen Ausbleiben von deinem Vater und deiner Mutter durchprügeln** (Raabe). **„Hast du Kummer?" Sie nickte. „Kummer wegen Vater?"** (Ompteda's *Sylvester von Geyer*, LXII). Sometimes with non-inflection: **Wegen dies und das!** (Frenssen's *Die drei Getreuen*, III, 1). See also **halb** above.

WESTLICH west of, with the same construction as **nördlich.**

WESTWÄRTS = **westlich.**

WILLEN, see **um — willen.**

ZEIT for the period of: **zeit meines Lebens, zeit'lebens** for life, as long as I live (as he lives, &c.).

ZU'FOLGE, see **infolge** above.

ZU'GUNSTEN, ZU GUNSTEN in favor of, for the sake of, **ZU'UNGUNSTEN, ZU UNGUNSTEN** against, with gen., but with dat.. when the preposition follows the word: **Der Richter hat zugunsten des Verklagten und zuungunsten des Klägers entschieden. Der Ruhm einer Universität sollte nicht sowohl in der großen Zahl bunt durcheinander gewürfelter Hörer und inskribierter Studenten, als in der nachweisbaren Gediegenheit ihrer Lehrerfolge und diesen zugunsten in der vornehmen Ablehnung zweifelhafter Besucher ihres Auditoriums gesucht werden** (H. Keferstein, in *Beilage zur Allgemeinen Zeitung*, Oct. 28. 1901).

ZU'NÄCHST, see **nächst** under the dative in **229.** 2.

ZUSCHLÄGLICH or **ZUSÄTZLICH** together with, with the addition of: **Das ergäbe zuschläglich jener 7 bis 7½ Milliarden Mark Kapitalanlage 20 Milliarden Mark, von denen Deutschland die Zinsen vom Auslande bezieht** (Sombart's *Die deutsche Volkswirtschaft im neunzehnten Jahrhundert*, p. 446).

ZU SEITEN *along the sides of*: **die Bäume zu seiten des Weges.**

ZUZÜGLICH *with the addition of*, opposite of **abzüglich: zuzüglich der Fracht.** In case of articleless nouns non-inflection in the singular is the rule: **zuzüglich Porto.**

ZWECKS, see **behufs.**

Meaning and Use of Prepositions with the Dative.

229. 1. The prepositions that properly govern the dat. govern also other cases only in a few words, as they are in large part old, and usage has at last definitely fixed their construction. On the other hand, a goodly number of the preps. governing the gen. govern also, as can be seen by a study of the preceding article, the dative. The reason of this partly lies in various analogies in meaning, as **laut** *according to* in analogy with **nach** *according to*, **unweit** *not far from*, **jenseits** *on that side*, &c., expressing, in general, rest as in case of **bei** *by*, **neben** *near*, &c., may take the dat. instead of the more correct gen.

2. The following are the prepositions with the dat. with their leading meanings, the preps. standing in alphabetical order.

AB *from*, of time or place = **von,** now replaced by the latter except in S.W. dialect, where it is still frequently used, also in the literary language in the set expression **ab'handen** *misplaced.* It is used quite frequently and widely in business style before local adverbs, names of places, and before nouns or adverbs of time, where, however, it is the Latin preposition **ab** *from, at*, or *from — on* or *forward*: **Fracht ab hier kostet 10 Mark. Unfrankiert ab hier** charges of transportation from this point not paid (by the sender); **Heu ab Wiese verkauft** hay sold at the meadow or at the farm, further expenses of transportation to be borne by the purchaser, similarly: **Kohlen werden ab** (at) **Bahnhof geliefert, ich liefere den Weizen frei ab Berlin; ab Berlin, 7** the train leaves Berlin at 7 o'clock; **zu vermieten ab Ostern** for rent after Easter; **ab morgen** *from to-morrow on*; **ab 1.** (read **ersten**) **Mai** (adverbial acc.); **ab nächsten Montag.** This usage is fast becoming established in the literary language: **Der Handel auf dem Strome gewinnt doch erst ab Regensburg einige Bedeutung** (Berthold Riehl in *Beilage zur Allgemeinen Zeit.*, Oct. 18, 1906).

AUS (*a*) movement from the inside of, *out of*, *from*: **Er geht aus dem Hause, aus dem Lande.**

(*b*) Origin, source, *from* (see *Note* under **von,** *d*): **Er stammt aus guter Familie. Er ist aus der Schweiz** He comes from Switzerland. **Ein Weib aus dem Volk** (common people), **aus Versehen** by mistake. Origin of knowledge, feeling: **Ich weiß es aus Erfahrung. Aus dem Auge schließt man aufs Herz** From one's eye, we judge of the heart. **Er bewies es aus der Bibel.**

(*c*) Material, *out of*: **aus weichem Ton gebildet. Granit besteht aus Feldspat, Quarz und Glimmer.**

Note. With materials, **von** is used before nouns without an article, replacing the gen. case, and thus forms with its noun an adj. element, standing attributively, or as a predicate adj., while **aus** with nouns of material forms an adverbial element, representing the object as *being fashioned out of* the mentioned material: **ein Ring von Gold** a gold ring. **Der Ring ist von Gold,** but **Der Goldschmied verfertigt Ringe aus Gold.** Compare **von,** *f.*

(*d*) Motive, *from*: **Aus welchem Grunde tat er das? Er handelt aus Liebe, Haß, Trotz. Er tat es aus freien Stücken** (from his own free will).

(*e*) Figuratively in many ways corresponding to the above lit. meanings: **Er hat mich aus** (out of) **mancher Verlegenheit gerissen. Er lachte aus vollem Halse** He laughed heartily. **Was wird aus ihm werden?** What will become of him? **Ein Märchen aus alten Zeiten, das kommt mir nicht aus dem Sinn** (from a poem by Heine).

(*f*) Synonymous with **aus** is **von,** and sometimes **vor.** In **aus** lies the idea of movement *out of* or *from within* something, while **von** merely states that the movement begins *near* or *from* something: **Die Quellen kommen oft aus den Bergen,** but **Die Flüsse kommen von den Bergen. Er steigt aus dem Wasser,** but **Er bricht den Apfel vom Baume. Der Reiter steigt aus dem Sattel,** but **vom Pferde.** When we desire to express movement from something that threatens personal safety, then **vor** is the word: **Er errettete seinen Freund aus dem Gefängnis und damit vor** (from) **dem Henkerbeil.**

BEI. 1. Now usually with dat. expressing nearness to some object in a general and indefinite way, but neighborhood or conjunction without contact, thus differing in part from **neben,** which denotes *close* approach to the *side* of an object but without contact, and differing from **an** in that the latter denotes a closer approach and very often contact with the side of the object in question: **Er stand bei** or **neben dem Baume,** but **Der Apfel hängt am Baume.** Only rest can be expressed by **bei,** and for motion we use **an, neben, zu,** of which **an** expresses motion close up to an object, often till it touches it, **neben** direction toward the side of an object without contact, **zu** movement toward, much as **an,** but differing therefrom in that it expresses a close and intimate relation between the persons and things thus brought together: **Er setzte sich an** (at) **den Tisch,** or **neben** (near) **den Tisch,** but **zu** (by) **mir** (in order to chat). See *Note* under **zu.**

(*a*) Especially frequent is **bei** in the sense of *bordering upon, in the vicinity of*: **Sachsenhausen bei Frankfurt, Linden bei Hannover. Die Schlacht bei Leipzig** the battle of Leipsic.

(*b*) Nearness applied to things in its metaphorical use (**1**) expressing usually a condition of things: **Er ist noch bei Leben** He is still alive. **Er ist schon bei Jahren** He is already quite old. **Er ist nicht mehr bei Kräften** He is no longer strong. **Er ist nicht bei Sinnen,** or **nicht bei Verstande,** or **nicht bei sich** He has lost his senses, is beside himself. **Er ist nicht bei Gelde** He is out of money. **Es bleibt beim alten** The old order of things still remains. **Er ist bei gutem Mut, guter Gesundheit. Bei Gericht** at court. (**2**) *In, in connection with, in case of*: **Bei diesem Geschäft kommt nichts heraus** In this business there is no money made. **Dieses Präparat ist bereits von vielen Ärzten als ein spezifisches Heilmittel bei** (in case of) **gichtischen Leiden erkannt worden.** (**3**) A succession, *after*, now little used: **Pfeiler bei Pfeiler stürzte nieder.** (**4**) Occupation, *at, busied with, over, all wrapped up in*: **Er ist bei** (at) **der Arbeit. Er ist beim Anziehen** He is dressing. **Er sitzt immer bei den Büchern** He is always poring over his books. **Sie saßen plaudernd beim Bier. Sie war mit ganzer Seele bei der Sache** She was all wrapped up (deeply interested) in the affair. **Er bleibt bei der Sache** He sticks to the point. (**5**) *On*: **Er verweilte bei** (dwelt on) **dieser Episode allzulange.**

(*c*) Nearness to persons, *at the house of, place of business of, upon the person of*: **bei** (at the house of) **dem Herrn Schmidt, bei mir** at my house, **bei** (at the store of) **dem Buchhändler, bei einem Professor hören** to attend the lecture of a certain professor. **Bei Gottfried Hermann hörte** (heard lectures on) **er Äschylus. Das bekommen Sie bei Schmidt** You can buy that at Schmidt's (store). **Er hat ein Konto bei** (at) **der Bank. Ich sprach bei ihm vor** I called on him. **Ich habe keinen Pfennig, kein Schnupftuch bei mir** (upon my person).

(*d*) Nearness applied to persons in its metaphorical use, *with, in the case of, in, to, in the works of, under*: **Ich halte es bei ihm nicht aus** I can't get along with him. **Er gilt viel bei ihm** He passes for a good deal with him. **Echt weibliche Naturen sind jedoch in der Regel entschlossenen Geistes; so war es auch bei** (in the case of) **dem sanften, bescheidenen Fräulein. Bei dir** (in your case) **wird die Hälfte genügen. Bei euch Jungen muß man streng sein** *In case of* or *with* you boys one must be strict. **Bei uns zu Lande** in our country, **bei den Alten** in antiquity, with the people of antiquity. **Er beklagte sich bei mir** He complained to me. **Er kann nichts bei** (to) **sich behalten** (keep). **Das Wort kommt bei** (in the works of) **Goethe nicht vor. Man lernte bei** (under) **ihm etwas.**

(*e*) **Bei** often marks a conjunction or near association of two things or persons, of which the one denoted by the object of **bei:**

(**1**) Marks the time of the other, *at, on, upon the occasion of, at the time of, when, while, in, by*: **Bei einer Hochzeit lernte ich ihn kennen. Bei dieser Gelegenheit** on this occasion, **bei nächster Gelegenheit** at the next opportunity. **Nach näherer Feststellung sind bei den letzten Überschwemmungen 500 Tote aufgefunden worden. Er half beim Aussteigen** He helped us when we were getting off the train. **Er ertrank beim Baden** He was drowned while bathing. **Bei ziemlich jungen Jahren wurde er zum Kardinal befördert** When quite young he was promoted to be a cardinal. **Bei** (in) **der Unterhaltung ist er ein guter Gesellschafter. Noch bei Menschengedenken** within the memory of man, **bei Tag, bei Nacht** by day, by night.

(**2**) Marks the cause of the other: **Bei dér Teuerung kann ich nichts kaufen** I can buy nothing when or since everything is so dear. **Bei solchem Fleiß muß es ihm gelingen** With such industry he must succeed. **Bei günstigem Winde segelt man schnell. Er zittert bei einem Gewitter. Bei zwei gegen eins ist die Partie ungleich** Two against one is not fair.

(**3**) Marks a concession in spite of which, however, the other statement is true, *with, in spite of*, usually followed by **all-: Bei aller stillen Sanftmut ihres Wesens war sie doch äußerst scharfblickend** In spite of all the gentleness of her nature she was nevertheless keen of observation. **Bei allem Fleiß ist es ihm doch nicht gelungen.**

(**4**) Marks the means of accomplishing the other: **Er liest bei Licht.**

(**5**) Marks an accompanying circumstance of the other, *along with, together with, in*: **Eine Buchbinderei, welche ebensowohl die leichteren einfachen, als die schwierigen eleganten Einbände, in gediegener und geschmackvoller Ausstattung bei unübertroffener Haltbarkeit zu liefern im Stande ist. Und bei solchen Kameralverhältnissen reisen Sie in Europa herum?** And when you are in such a state of finance you travel about in Europe?

(**6**) Marks the condition on which the other can occur: **Meine Preise für das Präparat sind 85 Pfg. (Pfennig) per Gramm, bei** (on condition that the purchaser buys as much as) **10 Gramm 75 Pfg., bei 100 Gramm 70 Pfg. Bei 20 M. franko** delivered free, if purchased to the amount of 20 marks. **Sie sagen, bei ungelöster Schnur kommen die Erdmännchen und spinnen am Rocken** (Freytag's *Rittmeister*, 5) They say that if the band is not taken off the wheel, &c.

(**7**) Marks the manner: **Sie kommen bei** (or **zu** or **in**) **Paaren,** or **Paar und Paar. Man verkauft etwas bei** or **nach Hunderten.**

(*f*) In oaths and kindred strong statements, where **bei** originally meant *in the presence of*, usually translated by *by, upon*: **Ich schwöre bei Gott. Er versicherte es mir bei** (upon) **seiner Ehre. Beim Himmel, dieses Kind ist schön!**

(*g*) Fixes the penalty: **Es ist bei Leib und Leben verboten** It is forbidden under penalty of death. In threats: **Bei Leibe nicht!** Not if you value your life!

(*h*) With numerals to express approximately distance, quantity, &c.: **bei mehreren Schritten Entfernung** at a distance of several paces.

(*i*) The measure of difference: **Er ist bei weitem** (by far) **der fähigste.**

(*j*) **Bei** expresses sometimes a closer approach and even contact, especially in case of a part of the body with verbs of seizing, and a few set expressions: **Er faßte ihn beim** (by) **Kopf, bei der Hand, bei den Haaren, beim Rockzipfel. Ich nehme ihn beim Worte. Ich rufe, nenne ihn beim Namen, bei seinem Namen. Wir fangen beim ersten Kapitel des Buches an. Er hat alles bei Heller und Pfennig bezahlt** He has paid everything up to the last penny.

2. **Bei** now rarely takes the acc. except in a few set expressions: **beiseite gehen** to go to one side, **einen beiseite nehmen** to take somebody to one side, **etwas beiseite bringen** to take something secretly away. In the colloquial language and dialect of the North and Midland, however, the acc. after **bei** is still often heard not only here but also after other verbs of motion, after the analogy of usage with **an, auf,** &c.: **Herr, wen der heute abend zu seiner Suppe einlädt, dem wird er auch einen schlimmen Löffel bei den Napf legen** (Raabe's *Odfeld*, chap. iv). **Ick muß bei een Herrn uff'n Bahnhof jehn** (Fielitz, in Hauptmann's *Der rote Hahn*).

Earlier this analogical acc. was common in the Midland, especially with Luther: **Da aber Saulus gen Jerusalem kam | versuchte er sich bey die Jünger zu machen** (Acts ix. 26).

BE'NEBST, see **nebst.**

BINNEN within, sometimes with dat., sometimes with gen.; see **binnen** in **228.** 4.

DANK thanks to, usually with dat., often, however, with gen.: **Ich bin, dank Ihren Bemühungen, gerettet.** See also **dank** in **228.** 4.

ENT'GEGEN against, contrary to, either following or, perhaps, more commonly preceding the dependent word: **entgegen unserem Abkommen** or **unserem Abkommen entgegen. Ihre Haare waren ein wenig zottig, was ich aber, entgegen meiner sonstigen Geschmacksrichtung, sehr liebreizend fand** (R. Huch's *Erinnerungen von Ludolf Ursleu*, chap. iii). Sometimes it *must* stand before the noun, so that it can be distinguished from the separable prefix **entgegen,** which follows the noun and has sometimes quite a different meaning, for, as explained in **226,** it is not only a preposition but also an adverb: **Er kam, entgegen meinen Wünschen** He came contrary to my wishes, but **Er kam meinen Wünschen entgegen** He met my wishes (complied with them).

For full description of its use as a prep. and adv. see *a* under its synonym **zuwider** below.

ENT'LANG, see under **längs** in **228.** 4.

GEGEN'ÜBER over against, opposite, standing before the dependent noun, or following it, the latter usually in case of personal pronouns: **Gegenüber dem Sofa,** or **Dem Sofa gegenüber hing ein großes Bild. Gegenüber der Festung Ehrenbreitstein liegt die Stadt Koblenz. Er nahm ihm grad gegenüber Platz,** but sometimes with the preposition before the personal pronoun when the meaning is figurative: **Gegenüber** (in contrast to) **mir glaubt Erdmann usw.** (L. Tobler in *Zeitschrift für deutsche Philologie*, 1875, p. 244).

(*a*) **gegenüber** (see its synonym **gegen,** *d*) in its figurative use is translated by *with respect to, towards, in the face of, in contrast to*: **Diesem stillen Wühlen, Planschmieden und Vorbereiten seiner Zunftbrüder gegenüber** (with respect to) **verhielt sich Gerhard Richwin kalt und zweideutig. Er sah voraus, daß seine Stellung** (attitude) **dem Justizrat gegenüber** (toward) **recht ärgerlich war. Gegenüber** (in the face of) **diesen Tatsachen kann nichts mehr beschönigt werden. Gegenüber** (in contrast to) **dem seit Einführung des Christentums sinkenden Latein trieben auf anderer Schicht und Unterlage die Romansprachen** (Romance languages) **empor** (Grimm).

(*b*) Earlier **gegenüber** was separated into its two component elements: **Ich sah mich gegen dem hohen Wall über** (Goethe). Sometimes still in dialect: **Gegen mir über ist die Tür** (Wilhelm Fischer's *Sonnenopfer*, II). Also the poetical form **genüber** is used: **Wie oft war sie an Festen mir genüber** (Grillparzer).

(*c*) Sometimes under the influence of *vis-à-vis de* we find **gegenüber von** instead of **gegenüber,** usually however only in case of names of persons and places in defining accurately the situation of a house or a city: **Es gibt so hübsche Häuser am Bollwerk, eins zwischen Konsul Martens und Konsul Grützmacher und eins am Markt, gerade gegenüber von Gieshübler** (name) (Fontane's *Effi*, chap. x), instead of **dem Gieshübler gegenüber. Gegenüber von Mannheim,** or more commonly **Mannheim gegenüber.**

GE′MÄSZ *in accordance with* the nature of, *in accordance with* the command, instructions, &c. of, either preceding or following the noun; sometimes also with the gen. when standing before the noun, after the analogy of **in Gemäßheit** and **zufolge** (see **gemäß, 228.** 4): **Er lebte seiner Gesinnung und seinem Stande gemäß sehr einsam. Gemäß deinem Wunsche** or **deinem Wunsche gemäß. Jeder Staatsbürger soll den Gesetzen des Landes gemäß sich verhalten. Gemäß** or **in Gemäßheit,** or more commonly **zufolge des erhaltenen Auftrags,** or *very* commonly **Dem erhaltenen Auftrag gemäß** or **zufolge übersende ich Ihnen die verlangten Werke.**

LÄNGS and **LÄNGST,** see under **längs** in **228.** 4.

MIT corresponds to Eng. *with* very closely in its varied meanings, and hence is not treated here in detail: **Der Vater geht mit den Kindern aus. Sie sprechen miteinander. Sie arbeiten mit Fleiß.**

(*a*) When events or ideas stand in close relation *with* a person or thing, **mit** may mean *with reference to*: **Was gibt's mit dem Schmettwitz?** What is that matter with reference to (Mr.) Schmettwitz? **Nun sag', wie hast du's mit der Religion?** How do you stand with reference to religion? **Das mit dem Brief müssen wir uns noch überlegen** We must reflect over that plan we have concerning the letter.

(*b*) In many idiomatic expressions **mit** is used where in English other words are found, or it is not used where the English requires *with*: **Er ist mit meinem Bruder gleichen Alters** He is of the same age as my brother. **Ich wohnte mit ihr in demselben Hause** I lived in the same house that she did. **Meine Schwester wohnt zwar in demselben Hause, sogar auf ein und demselben Flur mit ihm** (Ertl's *Der Handschuh*). **Ich bin Geschwisterkind mit ihm (ihr)** We are cousins. **Der Gärtner reißt die Pflanze mit** (by) **der Wurzel aus. Die Dame mit** (in) **dem seidenen Kleide, ein Mann mit Namen Schmidt** a man by the name of Schmidt, **Kaffe mit** (and) **Milch. Versuchen Sie es mit kaltem Wasser** Try cold water. **Mit einmal** (all at once) **sprangen die Flügel auf. Er traf mit** (on) **dem letzten Zug ein. Das ist sein Fall** That is the case with him. **Er neckte mich mit** (about) **ihr. Ich war immer ein unheimlicher, garstiger, brummiger Kerl, mit dem man die kleinen Kinder fürchten machen konnte. Mit einem Schlage** at one blow, **mit Sturm** by assault, **mit Gewalt** by force, **mit Erlaubnis** by permission, **mit einer Mehrheit** by a majority, **mit einem Worte** in a word, **mit der ersten Gelegenheit** by (at) the first opportunity, **mit der Post** by mail, **mit der Eisenbahn** by rail, **verwandt mit** related to, **mit Vorsatz** or **Absicht** on purpose, **in solcher Nähe mit ihm** in such proximity to him, so close to him. **6 mit** (by) **3 multipliziert gibt 18. Er spricht mit** (*to* or *with*) **ihr darüber. Mit dem** (in his) **fünften Jahre lernte er lesen. Was meinen Sie mit** (by) **diesen Worten? Jobst Hermann war vermählt mit** (to) **Elisabeth Julianne, Gräfin Sayn-Witgenstein, mit** (by; more commonly **von**) **welcher er 20 Kinder hatte** (*Hamburger Nachrichten*, Oct. 13, 1904). **Er handelt mit Holz, Tuch usw.** He deals in, &c. **Die (französische) Kammer hat die Ratifikation des Friedensvertrages von Versailles mit 372 gegen 53 Stimmen angenommen** (*Neue Freie Presse*, Oct. 3, 1919) by a vote of 372 to 53. **Spart mit Licht und Kraft!** (placard in Munich in Oct. 1919) Be economical in the use of light and electric power! **Privatstunden, die mit 50 Pfennig bezahlt wurden.**

(*c*) For the relation of **mit** to its synonyms **mittels, von, durch, vermöge,** see **mittels,** (*a*) in **228.** 4.

(*d*) With verbs, in the function of an adverb, **mit** has a different meaning according as it is accented or unaccented. Under stress, **mit** implies a close union and cooperation in the activity expressed by the verb, while unaccented it relinquishes the accent to the verb, and hence expresses mere contemporaneity or indicates that the main stress lies in the activity: **Wir wollen mítarbeiten** We desire to work along with you. **Wir wollen mit árbeiten** We desire to work too (at the same time as you work). **Wer nicht mit árbeitet, soll auch nicht mit éssen** Who does not join with us in *working* shall also not join with us in *eating*. An accented **mit** is often used where we use the pronominal adj. *one*: **Er war mit dabei** He was one of the party. **Er war mit der beste Schüler in der Klasse** He was one of the best pupils in the class.

MIT′SAMT, see **samt.**

NĀCH (*a*) direction towards, without implying whether the goal is reached or not, *in the direction of*. In this use **nach** has the same general force as **gegen** (less common except in set expressions): **Die Mutter blickte nach den Kindern. Er lenkt seine Schritte nach** or **gegen Westen. Das Haus liegt nach** or **gegen Norden. Das Fenster geht nach dem Hofe** The window looks out upon the courtyard.

Sometimes with the adv. **zu** or **hin: Er reitet nach dem Walde zu. Der Fluß wird nach seiner Mündung hin schiffbar.**

Figuratively: **Die Mutter sieht nach den Kindern** Mother looks after the children. **Mir ist nicht nach Lachen zu Sinn** I don't feel in a laughing mood.

(*b*) A definite goal (for modification of this rule see *Note* under **zu**), *to*, only used of things: **Er geht nach der Stadt, nach Berlin. Wie komme ich nach der Friedrichstraße?** How can I get to Friedrich Street from here?

Note 1. When the definite goal is a person in the literal sense, **zu** must be used, for **nach** (see *c*) has quite a different meaning: **Er geht zu ihm** He goes to him, to his house to see him, but **Er geht nach ihm** He goes to fetch him.

Note 2. Notice the idiomatic distinction: **Er geht nach Hause** and **Er ist zu Hause.** A little earlier in the period, **zu** could also be used for motion toward: **als wir zu Hause gingen** (Hebbel's *Agnes Bernauer*, i, 5). Older usage survives in dialect: **Ich geh nicht zu Hause** (Hauptmann's *Hanneles Himmelfahrt*, p. 30).

(*c*) Motion towards a person or thing with the intention of obtaining it, bringing it back, using, enjoying, hitting, or injuring it, *after, for, at*: **Er reicht nach** (after) **dem Apfel. Er läuft nach** (for) **dem Arzt. Er geht nach** (after) **Wasser. Der Hund schnappte nach** (at) **mir. Er sehnt sich** (longs to be) **nach** (in) **Berlin, nach** (with) **der Braut hin. Er fragt nach** (after) **ihm, nach der Ursache. Nach mir fragt niemand** Nobody cares for me. **Ein Herr ist da nach dem Eckzimmer** A gentleman is here inquiring after (with a view to renting) the corner room.

(*d*) A following or succession in space or time, of persons or things, *after*: **Er ging nach mir** He went after I did. **Er zog es nach sich** He dragged it after him. **Nach Jahren** years afterward, **nach Tisch** after mealtime. **Nach getaner Arbeit ist gut ruhen. Einer nach dem anderen sagte sein Sprüchlein.** Expressing rank: **Er war nach dem Kaiser der erste Mann.**

Note. Synonymous with **nach** in this use is **hinter**, only, however, when the idea of place is quite prominent: **Die Minister kamen nach** or **hinter** (following from behind) **dem Könige.**

(*e*) **Nach** standing before and sometimes after the noun denotes a correspondence, accordance between things, signifying:—

(**1**) Likeness, *of*: **Es schmeckt nach Wein** It tastes of wine. **Es riecht nach Veilchen.**

(**2**) The model or pattern after which something is fashioned or done, the standard of judgment or authority cited, or that which has guided the action, also the common standard of weight or measurement employed: **ein Lustspiel nach dem Französischen** a comedy following freely the pattern of the French original. **Er malt ihn nach der Natur** He is painting him from nature. **Er nannte sich nicht nach** (after) **seinem Vater. Ich kenne ihn nur dem Namen nach** (by). **Sie singt nach** (by) **Noten. Sie tanzen nach dem Takte** They dance keeping good time. **Sein Standpunkt, nach mir** (judged by my standard), **ist nicht sehr hoch. Seinem Alter nach** (judging by) **könnte er klüger handeln. Nach** (according to the authority of) **Engelien tönt das auslautende ng wie nk. Die Menschen beurteilt man am sichersten nach** (by) **ihren Taten. Richtet euch nach meinen Worten und nicht nach meinen Taten** Be guided by my words and not by my actions. **Man empfängt den Mann nach** (according to) **seinem Kleide, aber entläßt ihn nach seiner Rede. Man rechnet nach** (by) **Fußen, Ellen, usw. Wir werden nach der Stunde bezahlt. Nach dem Alphabet** in alphabetical order.

Note. Synonymous with **nach** are **gemäß, zufolge, laut. Nach** differs from them all in that the action, judgment, idea, expressed, is usually conceived of as a free one, the aim being to struggle to reach the model, pattern, standard, authority that has been set up, while the other prepositions imply that the resulting action is actually in accord with or in pursuance of these things, acknowledging their force and authority: **Er kleidet sich seinem Stande gemäß** He dresses as is becoming his station, as is required by one in his station. **Die Schotten kleiden sich zum Teil nach alter Landessitte** The Scotch still dress according to the old customs of their country (following these older patterns voluntarily). **Er richtet sich nach den Gesetzen** He conforms voluntarily to the laws. **Ihrem Wunsche zufolge schicke ich Ihnen das Buch** In accordance with your request I send you the book. **Es ging nach Wunsch** It went off just as I desired it (but not necessarily because I desired it thus). **Laut früherer Verträge machte Friedrich der Große seine Ansprüche auf Schlesien geltend** Frederick the Great laid claim to Silesia upon the grounds of former treaties. Even where the idea of necessity enters into the case, **nach** implies more the *following of a model, standard,* or *wise course* than *obeying the instructions* (as **zufolge**) *of an order*: **Der Lehrer muß sich nach dem Fassungsvermögen seiner Schüler richten** The teacher must regulate himself according to the comprehension of his pupils.

These words sometimes approach one another very closely in the sense of *from the purport of*: **Laut** (according to) **seines Briefes wird er heut kommen. Einem Brief zufolge** (according to) **kommt unser Freund. Nach** (according to) **diesem Briefe muß unser Freund bald kommen.**

(*f*) **Nach** has as a separable prefix in general the same meanings as the prep., but sometimes shades of difference arise as a prep. shows the relation between a verb and a noun (or pronoun) which is supposed to represent an object at rest, while the prefix **nach** as an adverb must modify immediately the verb, and hence must have reference to verbal action, and can refer to objects in motion: **Er lief nach** (after) **dem Arzt,** but **Er lief dem Diebe nach** He ran after the (fleeing) thief. In the second example **nach,** as explained in **226,** is both a preposition and an adverb, while in the first example it is only a preposition.

NĀCHST and **ZU'NĀCHST** next to, the former used literally and figuratively, the latter only of the place where, are formed from the superlative of **nahe** *near*, and still preserve their original meaning *nearest to*: **ein Haus nächst der Brücke. Ihr Bruder saß nächst mir. Er ist nächst dir der älteste. Nächst Gott kann ein Mensch dem andern am meisten nutzen. Zunächst** may precede or follow the noun, and sometimes governs the gen. when it precedes the noun: **zunächst dem Bahnhof,** or **dem Bahnhof zunächst; zunächst des Meeres** (Goethe). With adverb: **Er wohnt hier zunächst** He lives next door. **Zunächst** is also used as an adverb, of time and place: **Was wirst du zunächst** (*next*) **tun? Er übersieht das zunächst** (in front of, *before, close by*) **Liegende. Ich denke zunächst** (*above all*) **an dich.**

NĔBST and the strengthened form **BE'NĔBST** (in the language of the common people) = **zugleich mit** together with: **Die Stadt sah den Hunger nebst seinem ganzen Gefolge mit schrecklichen Schritten sich nähern** (Goethe).

(*a*) Synonymous with **nebst** are **mit** and **samt** with its strengthened forms **mit'samt, zu'samt, zu'samt mit.** Of these **mit** has the broadest meaning, as can be seen by consulting this word above. It differs from the others in that it expresses a closer and more intimate relation between the objects or persons in question, but may also usually replace the other two even in their especial fields. **Nebst** and **samt** denote a connection (see *b*), a being together, an acting or being acted upon at the same time, with the distinction not always clearly marked that the former expresses a looser connection which can easily be severed, while the latter denotes that the connection is a usual and natural association, not however, a live mutual cooperation as with **mit: Zur Aussteuer erhält die verehelichte Karoline Schmidt 1 Kuh nebst 8 Schafen. Die Wirtschaft ist zu verkaufen nebst den anstoßenden Grundstücken. Das Schiff samt der ganzen Mannschaft und Ladung ward ein Raub der Wellen. Die Mutter nebst** or **samt ihren Kindern,** but **Er hat den Baum samt der Wurzel ausgerottet.**

(*b*) **Nebst, samt,** and **mit** often have the force of the conjunction **und,** connecting only nouns or pronouns, thus not showing the relation directly between a verb and a noun, and hence when so used they are treated as conjunctions taking the verb in the pl., especially earlier in the period: **Vnd Saul sampt allen mennern Israel freweten sich** (1 Sam. xi. 15). **Der Pfarrer mit dem Vater gingen bedenklich dem Gemeindehause zu** (Goethe). **Ein Bedienter nebst einem Postillion folgten mir** (id.). Present usage prefers the sing. in such cases in accordance with strict grammatical concordance: **Mechtilde mit ihren zwei Söhnen erscheint auf der Zinne** (M. Greif's *Heinrich der Löwe*, 5, 1). See also **253.** I. 1. *d.*

NĪD = **unter(halb)** in Swiss dialect, but now found even there rarely, except in names of places: **Auch der Alzeller soll uns nid dem Wald** (*below the Forest*, a section of the canton Unterwalden) | **Genossen werben** (Schiller's *Tell*, 1, 4).

ŎB above, over, during, on account of, usually with the dative, often also with gen. in the last meaning after the analogy of **wegen,** in all the meanings now little used in colloquial language, as in the first three meanings it has been gradually supplanted by **über,** but not infrequent in early N.H.G., and still in poetry and choice prose: **Ob** (above) **dem Altar hing eine Mutter Gottes** (Schiller). **Denn reiche Zukunft schwebt ob deinem Haupt** (Uhland's *Ernst, Herzog von Schwaben*, I, p. 1). **Ich will dich mir so lachend, strahlend wissen,** | **so himmelhoch ob jedem schwarzen Müssen** (Sudermann's *Die drei Reiherfedern*, 3, 10). **Österreich ob der Enns. Vnd namen jre waffen** | **vnd fielen ein zu Simon ob** (during) **dem Mahl** (1 Macc. xvi. 16). **Zürnen Sie mir nicht ob meinem kühnen Geständnis** (Benedix's *Doktor Wespe*, 5, 7). **Dabei erhoben sie sich und standen verwirrt, schwankend ob all dem Abenteuerlichen, das der Abend enthüllt und gebracht hatte** (Raabe's *Zum wilden Mann*, chap. ix).

With gen.: **Versteinert ob solches nie dagewesenen regellosen Einbruchs** (H. Hoffmann's *Wider den Kurfürsten*, chap. xx). **Felix lachte ob meiner Sorgen** (Meinhardt's *Heinz Kirchner*).

SAMT, see (*a*) under **nebst.**

SEIT since, for, representing the duration of some act or condition of things beginning at some point in the past and extending to some point later on: **Wir leben schon seit 7 Jahren in Berlin** We have been living in Berlin now for seven years. **Seit** (since) **seiner letzten Krankheit hört er schwer.**

(*a*) Synonymous with **seit** are **vor** and **nach.** The two latter differ from **seit** in that they do not express duration of time, but refer to a definite occurrence. **Vor** refers to a definite occurrence counting back from the present, while **nach** refers to something that took place *after* some other event or some fixed time: **Er ist vor einem Jahr gestorben** He died a year since. **Er ist am Tage nach Ostern gestorben** He died on the day after Easter. **Er ist seit einem Jahre tot** (not **gestorben**) He has been dead for a year.

VŎN (for synonyms **aus** and **vor,** see *f* under **aus**) denotes in various ways the *starting point*, used of:—

(*a*) Place (the opposite of **nach** and **zu**), *from*: **Er ist von Paris nach Berlin gereist. Der Apfel ist vom Baume gefallen. Er geht von Haus zu Haus.** Figuratively: **Er wälzt die Schuld von sich. Ich muß mir erst meine Gegner vom Halse schaffen** I must first get rid of my opponents.

(*b*) The starting point of some action or state of things, and hence often denoting the direct cause, means, *from, with, on account of, on, by*, and after passive verbs the agent, *by*: **Von Worten kam's zu Schlägen. Das kommt vom Sitzen her** That comes from sitting too much. **Er ist müde vom** (from) **vielen Laufen. Naß vom** (with) **Tau. Er ist von** (with) **Rheumatismus gelähmt. Die Hand ist von** (with) **Frost erstarrt. Die Wasser sind von** (on account of) **dem Regen ausgetreten. Von** (on) **der Luft kann man nicht leben. Diese Menschen leben von** (on) **Kartoffeln, vom** (by) **Betteln. Der Leichnam war von** (by) **Wunden entstellt. Der Schüler wird vom** (by) **Lehrer gelobt. Der Baum wurde vom** (by) **Winde umgerissen.** In older English the agent with the passive was indicated by *of*, which is related to **von** and has a similar meaning: They were baptized of him in Jordan (Matth. III. 6). After verbal nouns the agent is indicated in German by **durch.** See **durch** (*b*) in **230.**

(*c*) The starting point of thought or perceptions, denoting the point or especial topic that busies the attention, *of, about, concerning*: **Er denkt schlecht von** (of) **mir. Dies Buch handelt von** (of) **dem siebenjährigen Kriege. Berichte mir von dir. Wir sprachen, redeten von** (about)

Ihnen. Er weiß von (concerning) **der Sache nichts. Er erzählt oft von seinen Reisen. Über** with the acc. is also used with these verbs, presenting the same thought from a different point of view. See **231.** II. über 2. B. *b*. This same meaning is found after nouns: **die Lehre von der Dreieinigkeit, das Märchen von Rotkäppchen, eine falsche Vorstellung von etwas.**

(*d*) Source and origin of things, descent, place of nativity or residence, *from, of, in, for, by*: **Ich habe es von ihm. Ich habe es von Hörensagen. Ich weiß es von guter Hand. Von ihm hat er allerlei Schlechtes gelernt. Er stammt von rechtlichen Eltern ab. Das Wasser von** (from) **dem Himmel,** but **das Wasser aus** (from) **der Erde** and **eine Stelle aus** (from) **Homer. Was wünschen Sie von** (of) **mir? Es war sehr unhöflich von** (of, in) **ihm. Sagen Sie ihm Lebewohl von** (for) **mir. Drei Kinder von** (by) **seiner ersten Frau. Ein Kaufmann von Berlin.** Thus also **von,** which serves now simply as the badge of nobility, originally denoted the place from which: **Alexander von Humboldt.** See **92. 5.**

Note. **Von** differs from **aus** in that it expresses a directer, more intimate relation: **Ich höre von ihm, daß Karl krank ist. Ich hörte aus seiner Art zu reden sehr wohl, daß er ein edelmütiges Herz hatte. Er kommt aus Preußen,** but **von Berlin.** For a difference from another point of view see **aus,** *f*.

(*e*) Time, *from*: **von Ostern bis Pfingsten, von Tag zu Tag, von Jugend auf, von diesem Tage an.**

(*f*) Material or that of which something consists, instead of the gen., which is now rare in prose, *of* (see *Note* under **aus,** *c*): **Der Tisch ist von Holz, ein Strahl von Glück, ein unverständliches Gemisch von Spanisch und Italienisch.** Altho **von** is used chiefly in a phrase which serves as an adjunct to a noun, it is also sometimes employed in adverbial phrases instead of the more common **aus: Man macht Papier aus** or **von Lumpen.**

Similar is the use of **von** in phrases indicating the quantity or measure: **eine Stadt von 20,000 Einwohnern, ein Betrag von 100 Mark, ein Weg von drei Meilen.**

(*g*) Quality or rank, instead of a gen. of characteristic, which is in certain expressions now rare, *of*: **Ein Mann von Ehre, von Stande, von Geschmack; ein Mann von Fach** an expert; **eine Sache von Wichtigkeit; ein Greis von achtzig Jahren.** In the predicate: **Das ist von großem Nutzen.**

(*h*) A particular point or respect in which something is true, sometimes after adjectives and before a following noun, thus forming a phrase which is translated by a phrase, an adj., or in various other ways: **Er ist klein von Person** (of stature). **Er war untersetzt von** (of) **Gestalt und dunkel von** (of) **Haar und Augen. Ich kenne ihn von Ansehen** or **Person** (by sight), **von Hörensagen** (by reputation). **Er ist von** (by) **Geburt ein Engländer. Sie ist bleich von Gesicht** (pale-faced).

(*i*) In a phrase which stands as an appositive to a preceding noun, just as *of* in Eng.: **Schurke von einem Wirt** rascal of a landlord. **Das ist eine Pracht von einem Becher** That is a jewel of a cup.

(*j*) A separation, desired or forced, which comes from the original idea of movement from a point: **Er hat mich von Kummer befreit. Die Blätter fallen vom Baume ab. Geben Sie mir etwas vom Fleisch.**

Hence also the whole, from which a part is taken, has often **von** before it, instead of being in the partitive gen., especially after numerals, pronouns (see **141.** 2. *Note*), and superlatives: **Zwei von meinen Freunden, keiner von uns, der Gelehrteste von allen.** Euphony sometimes alone decides between the use of the gen. or the dat. with **von: Sie hörte es von einer ihrer Freundinnen** is to be preferred to **Sie hörte es von einer von ihren Freundinnen** because it avoids the use of **von** twice. Sometimes the prep. **unter** is also used here: **Der stärkste unter allen Tapfern.** See also **255.** II. 1. H. *a* and *c*.

Also the objective gen. is often replaced by **von.** See **255. II. 1. D.** *c*.

(*k*) Besides the cases mentioned in *f*, *g*, and *j*, above, which now usually prefer **von** with the dat. to the simple gen., the following cases also very frequently prefer **von** to a gen.:—

(1) The names of places, always in common prose when they end in a sibilant: **Der König Preußens** or **von Preußen,** but only **die Bevölkerung von Paris.** The gen., however, occurs here in poetry. See **86.** 2. *e*.

(2) Nouns without an article or modifying word to show the case: **Er ist der Verfasser von Gedichten, ein Geräusch von Wasser, Blätter von Blumen.**

(3) To denote authorship rather than ownership: **Ein Bildnis von Raphael** a portrait by Raphael, but **ein Bildnis Raphaels** a portrait that belongs to Raphael or one that represents him. **Ein Buch von** (composed by) **meinem Freund,** but **ein Buch meines** (belonging to my) **Freundes.**

(4) With numerals which have no declension, as also with those which may be inflected: **die Gefangennahme von 83,000 Mann, die Aussage zweier** or **von zwei Zeugen, in neun von zehn Fällen** in nine cases out of ten. Likewise with other words that lack inflection: **die Zeitung von gestern** yesterday's paper.

(5) To avoid the recurrence of too many genitives: **Der Genuß der Frucht vom Baume der Erkenntnis des Guten und Bösen.**

(6) The gen. must sometimes be replaced by **von** with the dat. when the dependent word is to be separated from its governing noun, which is especially the case when it is placed at the head of the sentence in order that its governing noun, the subject, may take a more emphatic position further on in the sentence: **Von seinen Freunden hielten ihn éinige für schuldig, ándere für unschuldig.**

(7) With the idea of mastery and in a number of other set phrases denoting possession, a belonging: **Die Frau vom Haus. Ein Freund vom Hause, der leibliche Bruder von ihm, ein**

Freund von mir, or **einer meiner Freunde. Das war ein Fehler von ihm** That was a fault of his. **Das ist eine Ausnahme von** (to) **der Regel. Das ist das Ende vom Lied** That is the upshot of it all, &c.

(8) If it is desired to call attention to the word itself, not to the thing represented by it the genitive of possession is replaced by **von** or **zu** followed by the case form to which the attention is directed, not by the case form required by the preposition: **Ungewöhnlich ist der Plural von** or **zu Haß** (the nom., the form usually given in the dictionary to represent the word, not **vom Hasse**). **Stuhl ist der Singular zu** or **von Stühle** (not **Stühlen**).

(9) The use of **von** instead of the gen. is characteristic of the common people and familiar conversation. Hence there is often a shade of difference between the simple gen. and the dat. with **von**, the former being more choice, the latter more peculiar to the language of loose conversation or the dialect of the common people: **Der Vater von diesem Kinde** instead of **dieses Kindes,** &c.

VORGÄNGIG prior to: **Vorgängig dem Kongresse deutscher Gas- und Wasserfachmänner hielt heute nachmittag der schweizerische Verein von Gas- und Wasserfachmännern in der Aula des Hirschengrabenschulhauses seine 30. Jahresversammlung ab** (*Neue Zürcher Zeitung*, June 23, 1903).

ZU. I. It is used of motion, direction, rest, and time, but these varied meanings lie rather in the verb or dependent noun than in the prep., which in all these meanings expresses a close approach and intimate relation which is often difficult to render fully into English, but which is usually translated by *to, at, in, on, by, for, with,* &c.

Note. Synonymous with **zu** are **an** and **nach. Nach** expresses a general direction toward or a destination in a broad general sense, as a city, state, or other place, while **an** and **zu** express a more specific or definite goal, as a person or object, but in the case of **zu** also a broader goal where a specific purpose is evident: **Er geht nach der Stadt zu seinem Bruder. Ich poche an die Tür. Ich schreibe an** (to) **meinen Freund. Man fährt Steine zur** (for building purposes, *to the*) **Stadt,** but **nach Berlin, zu** not being used at all before names of cities with verbs of motion. Both **an** and **zu** denote a near approach, but the latter expresses a much closer and more intimate relation between the objects and persons brought together. **Ich schrieb an** (to) **ihn,** but **Ich sprach zu ihm. Er trat an das Bett** He went up to the bed, but **Er ging zu Bett** He went to bed (to sleep). It is difficult to draw a line between the uses of **an** and **zu,** and in cases they blend together, but in general the difference is marked between them as above indicated. With **zu** the idea of a definite place or goal is often entirely lost sight of and in its stead arise the associations that cluster around the place, the efforts that were necessary to reach it, the ends and aims there to be realized, and often the prep. and noun lose their several individual functions and become together the complement of the verb after the manner of a separable prefix, thus taking on general or abstract meaning instead of a concrete local one (see Note under **245.** IV. 3. B): **Die Kinder gehn zur Schule, zu Tische, zur Kirche** (not with any definite reference to a particular *school, table, church,* but with the general idea of *to learn, to eat, to devotional services*). **Er ist zu Gelde, zu Ehren gekommen** He has attained wealth, honor. **Viel Unglück ist ihm zuteil** (here equal to a verbal prefix) **geworden** Much misfortune has been allotted to him. **Mit vieler Mühe brachten sie endlich ein Feuer zuwege** With much trouble they finally started a fire, lit. brought it on the road.

II. The varied meanings of **zu** may be arranged into the following groups:—

1. The *local* meanings fall into the general heads of *motion* or *direction toward* a goal or destination (with the idea of near approach) and *rest* in a place.

A. *Direction toward* (see I. *Note* above) in its literal sense, of persons and things: **Ich will Sie zu ihm führen. Ich gehe zu ihm, zu meinem Bruder** I am going to see him (or to his house), to my brother's (house). **Man gelangte über Felsen zur letzten Höhe. Viel Getreide wird zur Stadt geführt. Er hat die Feder zu den übrigen gelegt** He has put away the pen with the others. **Er steckte es zu sich** (in his pocket). **Er nimmt niemals irgendwelche Speise zwischen den Mahlzeiten zu sich** (into his mouth). **Er führte seine Braut zum Altare. Die Straße zur Stadt, die Türe zum Keller.**

Note. The adverb **zu** has much the same force as the prep.: **Das Schiff segelt dem Hafen zu.** From its employment in such adverbial relations, where it stands after the dat., it has developed into a preposition governing the dat. and following the noun with the meanings *in the direction of, looking towards, facing*: **Zwei Türen hat der Kursaal zu Cannstatt, einander gegenüber an den Langseiten des Gebäudes gelegen, die eine westlich** (on the west side) **der Stadt** (dat. depending upon **zu**) **und dem Neckar, die andere östlich der Säuerlingsquelle und dem Sulzrain zu** (Raabe's *Pechlin*, II, chap. xi).

B. *Direction toward* in a number of applied relations:

a. Toward in an abstract or figurative sense: **Er bringt seine Gedanken zu Papier** He writes down his thoughts. **Er nahm es zu Herzen. Er kommt zu Fall. Es kommt mir zu Ohren. Er geht zu Grunde** (ruin). **Ein fallender Apfel führte den großen Newton zur Entdeckung eines der wichtigsten Naturgesetze. Solche Erfahrung führt zum Menschenhaß. Das Volk griff zu den Waffen** The people took up arms.

Especially in the sense of attaining a goal or end: **Er kommt zu Ansehen, Vermögen. Der Plan gelangte nicht zur Ausführung. Er gelangte zu Amt und Würden. Er kommt zu Kräften** (gathers new strength). **Er brachte es zu Ende, zustande.**

b. Attitude toward or close relation or association: **Er schwieg zu der ganzen Sache** He assumed an attitude of silence with regard to the whole affair. **Er lachte dazu. Was sagen Sie dazu? Er hält zu unsrer Partei** (sides with our party). **Warum machen Sie da so 'ne Bude auf, wenn Sie so unhöflich sind zu den Gästen?** (Hauptmann's *Michael Kramer*, Act 3). **War er doch ein weitläufiger Vetter zu** [colloq. and pop.; in the literary language more commonly **von**] **ihr** (Rosegger's *Die Stadt im Walde*). **Der Stillständer ist ja ein Vetter zu mir** (Heer's *Der König der Bernina*, II). **Was essen Sie zu** (with) **Ihrem Ochsenfleisch? Die Insel gehört zu** (not possession, but with the idea of forming an integral part of) **England. Zu einem großen Manne gehört beides: Kleinigkeiten als Kleinigkeiten und wichtige Dinge als wichtige Dinge zu behandeln. Sein Benehmen paßt nicht zu seinen Verhältnissen. Sie sang schöne Weisen zu** (accompanied by) **meiner Flöte. In der Nacht zum** (or **auf den**) **23. Januar** or **vom 22. zum 23. Januar** in the night before Jan. 23, **während der Nacht von vorgestern zu** (or **auf**) **gestern.**

c. Proportion: **Der Montblanc verhält sich zu dem Brocken** (Mont Blanc has the same relation to the Brocken) **wie ein Riese zu einem Zwerge.**

d. A fixed price, amount in money or weight, rate of interest, or in general any fixed measurement: **ein Brot zu 60 Pfennigen** a loaf costing 60 pfennigs. **Das Haus samt dem dazu gehörigen Stallgebäude und Garten ist zu** (at) **20,000 Mark abgeschätzt. Zum Selbstkostenpreis** at cost; **80 Ballen Twist** (cotton twist), **zu** netto (with a net weight of) **1000 Pfund jeder; die jährlichen Zinsen von 7500 M.** (Mark) zu (at) **4½%; 1 Kiepe** (measurement used in the dried fish trade) = **4 Stiegen, die Stiege zu 20 Stück** 1 kiepe = 4 stieges, each stiege containing 20 pieces. **Das Deutsche Reich, Skandinavien, Rußland, die Schweiz rechnen jeden Monat zu 30 Tagen. das Jahr zu 360 Tagen.**

Note. This German preposition is often in commercial language replaced by the French prep. **à: Wie viel betragen die Zinsen von M.** (Mark) **753,80 à 6% in 155 Tagen?**

e. The direction of an activity, inclination, growth, thought, or feeling toward an object or end, especially frequent before an infin.: **Er spricht zu mir. Der Vater hält das Kind zur Schule, zur Arbeit, zum Fleiß, zum Gebet an. Themistokles wollte Athen** (Athens) **zu einer unbezwinglichen Seefeste machen. Man nimmt zu** (to make) **diesem Gebäck auf** (to) **ein Pfund des feinsten Weizenmehls ein halbes Pfund der besten Butter. Er hat Lust, Neigung, Liebe zu der Sache. Mir ist nicht zum Lachen** I don't feel in a laughing mood. **Wir alle haben einen Hang zur Sünde. Und sie ist immer so gut zu mir gewesen** (Spielhagen's *Herrin*, p. 238). **Freundlich bin ich zu ihr gewesen** (Fulda's *Die Sklavin*, 3, 3). **Der Knabe wird zum Jüngling. Es wird ihm zur Gewohnheit. Ich hoffe zu siegen. Ich bin bereit zu sterben. Ich bin begierig zu wissen.** Here belongs the common meaning *an essay or paper upon the subject of*, lit. directed toward, especially in titles of articles in periodicals: **Zur neuesten Wallenstein-Literatur** (Something upon the subject of) The Latest Literature on Wallenstein. **Zur Akzent- und Lautlehre der germanischen Sprachen.**

f. The direction toward in the sense of *purpose* or *intention*, or that for which something is most suitable or serviceable, or to which it is best adapted, or for which it has been set aside: **Es geschieht zu deinem Besten. Er reist zur** (for the purpose of) **Erholung, zum Vergnügen, zur Ausbildung. Steinkohlen dienen zum Brennen. Wozu nützt so etwas? Es nützt zu nichts. Sie sind der Mann zu** (for) **diesem Werk. Wasser zum Trinken, ein Gefäß zu** (for holding) **Milch, Tuch zu einem Kleid, zum Andenken an** (w. acc.) in memory of. **Ich stehe Ihnen zu Diensten** I am at your service. **Ich stehe (Ihnen) zu Befehl** I am at your command. **Zu Befehl, Herr Hauptmann!** Right (or yes), sir! Often with the infinitive to express purpose (compare **281.** *Note*): **Er kommt, mich zu warnen.**

g. The point which an activity or quality has reached, or is expected to reach, hence in general expressing the extent, or force, or the result, or effect of the quality or action contained or implied in the predicate: **Es ist zum Rasendwerden** It is enough to drive one mad. **Sie ist schön zum Entzücken** She is so beautiful that one is charmed. **Brav ist er und gut mit den Kindern nicht zum Glauben** He is good and kind to the children to such an extent that one can scarcely believe it. **Er spielte seine Rolle zu allgemeiner Zufriedenheit. Es gereicht ihm zur Ehre. Ich habe ihn zum Freunde. Er hat sie jetzt zur Frau. Sie krönten ihn zum Kaiser. Der Onkel hat ihn zum Erben eingesetzt. Wir wählten ihn zum Vorsitzenden. Es kam zu einer Prügelei. Der Schnee wurde zu Wasser. Er fiel mir zur Last** He became a burden to me. **Der Knabe wuchs zum Jüngling heran. Der Richter verurteilte ihn zum Schadenersatz, zu Gefängnis, zum Tode. Zur Not** when it comes to a case of necessity, **zur höchsten Not, zum Teil** in part, **zur Hälfte** *half* (as in **Sie kennen mich zur Hälfte nur**), **zum Glück für mich** fortunately for me. Often with the infinitive to express result (compare **281.** *Note*): **Er ist nicht mehr zu jung, dies zu begreifen.**

h. Addition: **Tun Sie Zucker zum Kaffee** Add sugar to your coffee. **Sie gießt Milch zum Kaffee. Seitdem haben sie (die Österreicher) selbst zu** (in addition to) **der richtigen Tapferkeit auch die Fixigkeit hinzugelernt** (Engel's *Ein Tagebuch*, I, p. 51). **Da'zu** or **zu'dem** *besides, moreover.*

C. Rest or motion in or at a place, and thus synonymous with **an, bei, in** (see each word), but differing from them in general in that it denotes a closer relation between the object and the place: **Der Dom zu** (*in*, not temporarily, but permanently) **Köln** (Cologne), **die Universität zu Berlin. Er sitzt zu** (for the purpose of eating) **Tische. Die Tür steht zur rechten, linken Hand.** Before names of places there is often no difference at all between **in** and **zu,** except that the former is more used colloquially, and the latter belongs to higher diction. If, however, a modifying word stands between the preposition and the name of the place, **in** not **zu** must be used: **in** or **zu Rom,** but **in dem alten Rom.**

Especially frequent of a place thru which something goes in or out: **Da kamen zum Fenster zwei Täubchen herein. Dann gehen sie zum Tore hinaus. Er wirft sein Geld zum Fenster hinaus** (squanders his money). It is also used in a number of applied relations:

a. Noteworthy is the use of **zu** on the signboards of hotels and drug stores, like the English "At the Red Lion": **Gasthof zum weißen Roß. Ap. (Apotheke) zum Löwen, zum Pelikan** (also **Löwen-Ap., Pelikan-Ap.**).

b. Distributively and collectively: **Sie kommen zu** (also **bei** and **in**) **Paaren. Nun ging der Zug zu fünfen** (in groups of five) **zum Dorf hinaus. Nun saßen sie zu dreien** (three in all) **um dasselbe Tischchen. Wir sind nur zu vier** (or **vieren**) There are only four of us.

c. Manner or condition in a few set expressions, *by, on*: **Er reist zu Fuß, zu Pferde, zu Wagen, zu Schiff, zu Lande, zu Wasser. Begleitscheine** (giving weight, value, &c.) **müssen solchen**

Warenballen beigegeben werden, die zur Post oder pr. (per) **Fracht über eine Zollgrenze gehen. Etwas besteht zu Recht** (has legal force). **Mir ist wohl zu Mut** I feel well, cheerful.

2. In a temporal sense, *in, at, for*: **zu Anfang, zu Ende des Jahres, zu** (at) **jeder Stunde, zu** (in) **meiner Zeit, zur** (at) **rechten Zeit. Er kommt zu Ostern, Weihnachten. Er ißt zu Mittag, zu Abend bei uns. Von Tag zu Tag, von Stunde zu Stunde, zum** (for) **ersten, letzten Male, zuerst** first, **zuletzt** last. **Willst du wenigstens meine Aufgaben zu** (for) **morgen machen: den Aufsatz und die dummen Exempel?** (Spielhagen's *Sonntagskind*, I, 2).

ZU'FOLGE in accordance with, according to, in consequence of; see **gemäß** and also **nach, e. (2)**, *Note*, above, and in **228.** 4 the words **gemäß, infolge, laut,** (*a*). In the first and second meaning it usually governs the gen. when it stands before the noun, and the dat. when it follows the noun (the favorite position): **zufolge des Gesetzes, Ihres Briefes,** sometimes **zufolge dem Gesetze, Ihrem Briefe; dem Gesetze, Ihrem Briefe zufolge.** In the meaning *in consequence of* it usually precedes the noun and takes the genitive: **Zufolge wiederholter schlechter Ernten ist in Indien Hungersnot eingetreten** (Georg Edward). See also under **infolge** in **228. 4.**

ZU'NÄCHST, see **nächst.**

ZU'SAMT, ZU'SAMT MIT, see **nebst,** (*a*).

ZU'WIDER *contrary to, against, averse to,* always following the dependent word. Like **entgegen,** it is not only a pure prep., but also an adverb, serving as a separable prefix of a verb, hence it has the position of a separable prefix in the sentence, except where it is a pure prep., in which case it always follows the noun: **Der Konstitution zuwider** (prep.) **führte er fremde Truppen in ihr Gebiet. Am Kap der guten Hoffnung ist den Schiffern der Wind nicht selten zuwider** (adverb). **Zu viel Süßigkeiten sind mir zuwider** (adverb). **Das läuft dem Gesetz zuwider** (adverb).

(*a*) The synonym of **zuwider** is **entgegen.** As prepositions they both have the same force, that of *contrary to,* with the exception that **zuwider** is perhaps the stronger word. As adverbs they both still govern the dat. with the same force they have as prepositions, but **zuwider** has not so broad a field of usefulness here as **entgegen.** The former can only be used figuratively with the opposite force of **nach, gemäß,** and **zufolge** *according to,* hence with the meanings *contrary to the nature, commands,* or *instructions of,* also in general with the idea of opposition, or hostility, *opposed, hostile to*: **Er hat dem Befehle entgegen-** or **zuwidergehandelt. Die Arznei ist mir zuwider** (contrary to my nature, hence *disagreeable to*). **Das Glück war uns entgegen** or **zuwider. Dem steht nichts entgegen** or **zuwider** There is no obstacle in the way of it. **Der Wind war ihnen entgegen** or **zuwider. Entgegen** has also, as can be seen from the preceding examples, a force opposite to that of **nach** or **zufolge,** hence with the meanings of *contrary to the instructions, commands of, opposed to, hostile to,* but also, in addition to these meanings which it has in common with **zuwider,** it is used literally with verbs of motion in the sense of a friendly or hostile movement towards: **Er kam uns entgegen** He came to meet us. **Österreich scheint seinem Zerfalle entgegenzugehen** (to be approaching). **Die Armee geht dem Feinde mutig entgegen** (against).

Prepositions with the Accusative.

230. The following are the prepositions with the acc., with their leading meanings, the preps. standing in alphabetical order.

AUF UND AB up and down, always after the noun: **Und doch war die Korridore auf und ab niemand zu sehen** (Ernst von Hesse-Wartegg in *Daheim,* July 8, 1905).

BIS denotes in general a limit or boundary, used of time and place, before nouns and adverbs, and often prepositional phrases, *till, until, as far as, to, up to, except.* Time: **Er bleibt bis** (until) **Weihnachten, bis Montag, bis morgen, bis zehn Uhr, bis mit** (or **bis und mit**) **den 1.** (read **ersten**) **Oktober** up to October the first inclusive, **bis einschließlich 9. d. Mts.** (read **neunten dieses Monats**), **bis nächste Woche. Er bleibt zwei bis drei Tage** He will remain from two to three days. **Bis wann** or **bis wie lange bleiben Sie?** How long will you stay? **Bis wohin** or **bis wieweit gehen Sie mit ihm?** How far are you going with him? **Bis Montag!** Good-by until Monday. Earlier in the period and still in the dialects and in colloquial speech it is widely used to indicate the latest point of time at which something will take place, *by, not later than*: **Bis Mittag bin ich wieder da.** Similarly in questions where **bis wann** corresponds to simple **wann** in the literary language: **Bis wann geht's denn nach Rußland?** (Auerbach's *Dorfgeschichten*, 8, p. 42) How long will it be before it will be shipped to Russia? Place: **Sie kamen bis** (as far as) **Berlin. Wir reisten zusammen bis Italien,** and likewise before the name of any place, but not usually before the names of objects. There is a tendency, however, to extend this construction, and hence in short fragmentary utterances **bis** is sometimes found before names of objects: (Conductor of a street-car) **Wie weit?** (Passenger) **Bis** (instead of **bis zur**) **Kirche.** Before prep. phrases: **Er hat alles bezahlt b i s a u f** (except) **einige Kleinigkeiten. Er hat alles b i s a u f** (*up to,* here inclusive of) **den letzten Heller bezahlt. Es währt b i s g e g e n** (until in the neighborhood of) **Abend. B i s v o r** (until just before) **Ostern währte die Kälte. Sie wachten bis nach Mitternacht.**

Bis is also used as a conjunction without influence over the case of the following word, to connect individual words or different propositions: **ausgewählte Texte des 4.** (read **vierten**) **bis 15.** (also gen.: read **fünfzehnten**) **Jahrhunderts. Ich blieb im Bett, bis er aufgestanden war.**

DURCH and its strengthened form **HIN'DURCH** (always after the noun).

(*a*) Extension or penetration from one point of time or space to another, *thru, thruout*: **Der Vogel fliegt durch die Luft. Er geht durchs Zimmer. Das schnitt mir durchs Herz. Mir**

fuhr ein Gedanke durch den Kopf. Gott hat seine Kirche durch alle Jahrhunderte erhalten. Viele wohnen den ganzen Sommer hindurch auf dem Lande.

Note. Noteworthy is the common use of **durch** as an adverb when it has the position of a separable or inseparable prefix. It has the same general force as the prep. **durch,** but as it modifies directly the verb, the idea of *thru* gives the verb sometimes intensive force, which cannot lie in the prep. itself: **Er geht durch den Garten** He goes thru the garden, in one direction. **Er durchsucht den Garten** He searches the garden thoroly in all directions. For further light upon the use of **durch** as a verbal prefix, study carefully the different articles under **215.** II. 3.

(*b*) Means or agent employed to reach an end, either of things or persons: **Die Niederländer schützen sich durch Dämme gegen den Ozean. Ich habe mich durch eitele List verleiten lassen. Dividiere diese Zahl durch** (by) **jene. Durch ihn habe ich meinen Zweck erreicht. Die Ermordung Rizzios durch Darnley, die tatsächliche Fortführung der Regierung durch den Grafen Leopold.** The idea of agent with verbal nouns, as in the last two examples, is regularly expressed by **durch,** while with passive verbs it is expressed by **von.**

Note. For its synonyms see in **228.** 4 the prep. **mittels** (*a*).

(*c*) Cause, of persons or things: **Durch ihn bin ich glücklich geworden** He is the author of all my happiness. **Durch angestrengte Arbeit ist er krank geworden. Lissabon wurde im 18ten Jahrhundert durch ein Erdbeben zerstört. Er ist durch** (by) **seinen Feind verdrängt worden. Sie ist elend durch** (caused by, not necessarily intended by) **mich.**

Note. This use of **durch** approaches very close to **von** (see **228.** 4, **mittels** (*a*), and **229.** 2, **von** (*b*)), but they differ in this that the latter emphasizes more the starting place or the thinking agent, working to a definite end, while the former makes more prominent the manner or means.

(*d*) In the sense *all mixed up,* especially in the compound **durchei'nander: Er spricht deutsch und englisch, bunt durcheinander. Er erzählte, was er nur wußte, bunt durcheinander wie Kraut und Rüben.**

ENT'LANG, see **längs** in **228. 4.**

FÜR (in early N.H.G., expecially with Luther, often **fur**) in all its varied meanings corresponds almost exactly to the Eng. *for,* and will not need detailed treatment.

(*a*) As could only be expected the German deviates from the Eng. in a number of expressions:

(1) Für is used with the verbs **achten** to consider, look at, **erkennen** pronounce, make known, **halten** regard, **erklären** pronounce, **finden** consider: **Er achtet das für** (as) **nichts. Sie erkannten** (recognized) **die von dem Finanzminister abgelegte Rechnung als** (as) **falsch, aber aus Mangel an Mut erkannten** (pronounced) **sie dieselbe trotzdem für richtig. Ich halte ihn für einen ehrlichen Menschen. Er erklärte das für eine Lüge. Er fand es für notwendig.**

(2) In case of diseases and poisons the German uses **für,** or perhaps more appropriately **gegen** or **wider,** where we use *for*: **ein Mittel für,** or **gegen,** or **wider Kopfschmerzen (das Fieber,** &c.) a remedy for headache (fever, &c.). **Dieses Gift ist gut für** (for the destruction of) **Mäuse.** This construction is a survival of older usage where **für** had the force of **gegen.** This older meaning still occurs occasionally elsewhere: **Durchweg waren das minder kräftige Leute, dürftige, blasse Burschen mit fahlen Gesichtern, die er für den Tod** (to save his very life) **nicht ausstehen konnte** (Beyerlein's *Jena oder Sedan?,* II).

(3) In naming a price, the German uses **für,** where in Eng. *for* is used, but he goes farther, and uses it for amount, price in general: **Er kaufte es für 10 Mark. Für 25 Pfennig Schokolade** 25 pfennigs' worth of chocolate, **für 6 Mark Übergewicht** overweight on a trunk to the amount of 6 marks. **Lenz** (name) **rief seine Frau herbei und erklärte, er werde es ihr nie vergeben, wenn sie für einen Heller Werts ungetreues Gut ins Haus aufnehme** (Auerbach's *Dorfgeschichten,* 8, p. 164). **Für zehn Mark Geschirr hat se [sie] fallen lassen** (Hauptmann's *Einsame Menschen,* 1). **Die blaue Tüte [Tabak] enthielt für zehn Pfennige dieses köstlichen Krautes** (Heinrich Seidel's *Leberecht Hühnchen*). Often with the force of *as much as*: **Dann sauf' ich für sieben Mann!** (G. Keller an Adolf Exner, Aug. 27, 1875).

(4) In a few idiomatic expressions English *for* is rendered by other means: **Es ist jetzt kein Schiff nach** (for) **Boston in Bremen. Ich habe einen Brief nach** (for) **Berlin auf die Post gegeben. Er ist auf** (for) **acht Tage verreist. Viele Deutsche geben ihre Verachtung der** (for the) **Juden immer zu erkennen. Sie hätte einen unangenehmen Eindruck gemacht, diese Nase, wenn die Augen nicht gewesen wären** if it had not been for her eyes. **Sie war berühmt gewesen wegen ihres Teints** (for her complexion; Ossip Schubin has here **für ihren Teint**). **Zum** (for) **Frühstück erhält jeder von euch zwei trockene Wecken.**

(5) In a few expressions **für** is rendered differently in English: **Diese Tür ist für** (to) **dich geschlossen. Er dient für** (instead of) **seinen Bruder. Es ist sehr hart für** (upon) **ehrliche Leute, daß usw. Er stand ganz allein für sich** He stood all by himself. **Für sich** (stage direction) aside. **Er ist blind für** (to) **seine Fehler. Sie meinen also, für gewöhnlich** (as a rule, as a usual thing) **lüge ich?** (Spielhagen's *Sonntagskind,* II, 5). **Er ißt wenig, aber er trinkt dafür** (to make up for it) **viel.**

(*b*) Originally the nearly related words **für** and **vor** were more closely related. Both were used of time or space, the former with the acc. to express motion toward, and the latter with the dat. to denote rest. Early in the present period these relations became confused, as in N.G. and M.G. the two forms had merged into one, namely **vor.** This state of things can still be seen in the dialect of these sections. In the literary language of early N.H.G. **vor** had already assumed in large measure the meaning of **für** besides its own original meaning, and consequently governed the dat. or acc. according to the sense. On the other hand, as the result of this confusion **für** sometimes assumed the meaning of **vor,** and hence we find it with either the dat. (as in **Bäume . . ., die sich für der Last der Früchte zur Erde beugen**—*Goethe an Frau von Stein,* 3,

178—instead of **vor der Last.** &c.) or acc. according to the sense. These fluctuations still occur not infrequently in the eighteenth century, and even to-day in a few words, as **für'lieb** or **vor'lieb, vornehm,** or more rarely **fürnehm.** Gradually, however, **vor** replaced **für** also in the literary language, except in many derivative or figurative applications where **für** is still used, now always with the acc. Only in a few set expressions can its former literal meaning be seen: **Schritt für Schritt** (also **Schritt vor Schritt**) step by step, lit. one step before the other, **Punkt für Punkt,** &c. Occasionally in the classics **für** can be found in its original meaning, where present usage requires **vor: Ich ging im Walde | so für mich hin** (Goethe's *Gefunden*).

GEGEN and **WIDER,** both with the idea of direction or movement towards, the former in the sense of friendliness, hostility, or resistance, the latter only in the sense of hostility or resistance, used of time or space, literally or figuratively, *toward, to, about.*

(*a*) In the sense of a general direction toward or a position facing toward: **Wir ritten gegen den Rhein. Gegen Ende August** about the end of August. **Er wird gegen** (about) **drei Uhr zurückkommen. Das Haus liegt gegen Morgen** (to the east). **Es ist schwer gegen** or **wider den Strom zu schwimmen. Die beiden Heere kämpfen gegen-** or **widereinander. Man hält mich hier gefangen wider alles Völkerrecht.**

Note. In a few set expressions, especially in the Bible and poetry, before nouns without an article the shortened form **gen** is found instead of **gegen: gen Himmel, gen Osten, gen Westen, gen Rom.**

(*b*) The direction of thought or feeling toward, in a friendly sense, after **gegen** (here often closely related to its synonyms **zu** and **für**), or in a hostile sense or one of opposition, after **gegen** or **wider: Er erweist sich gefällig gegen Freunde. Seine Liebe gegen seine Geschwister, die Pflichten gegen Gott, seine Zuneigung gegen** (also **für**) **ihn, die Liebe gegen Gott** (or **zu**) **Gott, Ehrfurcht gegen das Alter, Ekel gegen das Lesen,** but usually **zu** or **für** with things: **seine übermäßige Liebe zum Branntwein, zum Vaterland, zum Spiel, zum Gewinn, Gefühl für das Schöne, Sinn für Ehre. Er hat einen Haß gegen** or **wider mich gefaßt. Was hast du gegen** or **wider mich? Das geschah gegen** or **wider alle Erwartung. Das geht ihm wider die Natur. Er tut es wider Willen.**

(*c*) Approach toward for the purpose of comparison, *in comparison with,* synonymous with **im Vergleich mit, im Verhältnis zu: Reichtum ist nichts gegen Gesundheit. Alle Bücher sind nichts gegen die Bibel. Gegen früher** in comparison with a previous period. **Ich wette hundert gegen** (to) **eins.**

(*d*) Attitude towards, synonymous with **gegenüber** (see this, *a*), sometimes, however, indicating a more positive attitude, *in the face of, to, in the presence of*: **Alles . . . . war darüber einverstanden, daß das Gemeinwesen in diesem Falle eine Pflicht zu erfüllen habe und daß es derselben gegen jede, wenn auch noch so respektable Privatgegenmeinung nachkommen müsse** (Raabe's *Villa Schönow,* v). **Kaiser und Reich regten sich nicht gegen diesen unermeßlichen Verlust. Die Regierung war gegen das entfesselte Element ohnmächtig. Er ließ sich gegen ihn nichts merken** He pretended to him that he did not notice it. **Gegen** (in the presence of) **andere rühmt er sich seiner Taten.**

(*e*) *In exchange for, for,* closely related to **für** and **um: Kriegsgefangene werden gegeneinander ausgetauscht. Man tauscht ein Ding gegen** (or **für,** sometimes **um**) **ein anderes. Sie können Ihr Geld gegen Quittung** (on receipt) **bekommen. Man pflegt Geld nur gegen einen Schuldschein zu leihen. Er gibt diese Ware nur gegen bare Bezahlung.**

(*f*) In estimates, an approximate judgment as to weight, magnitude, cost and the like, used as a prep. or as an adverb (see **225.** 1. *c*), *about*: **Die Stadt hat gegen dreißigtausend Einwohner.**

(*g*) **Gegen** and **wider,** now exclusively with the acc., governed earlier in the period either the dat. or acc. without any difference of meaning between the two case forms.

(*h*) In Austrian and Bavarian dialects the gen. is found after **gegen,** especially with pronouns: **Stemm' dich an gegen meiner, was [du] kannst** (Ganghofer's *Der Dorfapostel,* II).

General Note. **Wider** is only used in (*a*) and (*b*) of the above articles.

GEN, see **gegen,** *a. Note.*

HIN'DURCH, see **durch,** above.

OHNE (*a*) is the opposite of **mit,** and hence denotes lack, *without, but for*: **So lange ich meinen Freund zärtlich liebte, ging ich nicht ohne ihn. Er ist ohne Freude. Es gibt keine Freundschaft ohne gegenseitige Achtung. Ich kann die Suppe nicht ohne einen Löffel essen. Ohne ihn wären wir gestorben** But for him we should have died.

(*b*) In an earlier period in the sense of **außer** *except, not counting, besides,* and still found in certain expressions: **Es waren zwanzig Personen da ohne die Kinder.** Especially in the adverbial expressions: **ohne'das, ohne'dies, ohne'hin** besides.

(*c*) In early N.H.G. **ohne** governed also the dat., as can still be seen in the one word **ohne'dem** (= **ohnedas;** see *b* above), which is still sometimes used: **Ohnedem aber war für ihn nicht mehr an einen Verkehr in Grafenwang zu denken** (Perfall's *Der schöne Wahn,* p. 86). The dat. still lingers in the classical period: **Bald mit, bald ohne dem Mitleid** (Lessing). It survives in the dialect of the Southeast alongside of the genitive (see *d*).

(*d*) After the verbs **sein** and **werden** in an earlier period, **ohne** governed a gen. which usually preceded it, in the sense of *void of, free from,* and is still commonly thus used in the word **zweifels'ohne** *doubtless.* In Austrian and Bavarian dialects **ohne** with the gen. is also used with other verbs, usually, however, preceding the dependent noun, or more commonly pronoun, like a preposition with the meaning *without*: **Ich kann ohne Ihrer** (perhaps a dat., which is also used here) **Tochter nicht leben** (Raimund's *Alpenkönig,* 3, 16). **Sie würden auch ohne seiner das Essen fertig bringen** (Anzengruber's *Schandfleck,* chap. xx).

PER is a Latin prep. much used in commercial language, both in foreign expressions, as *per diem*, and with many German words, especially those without an article or other inflected word, but it is also sometimes employed before words which can show inflection. It is found in certain set expressions, denoting:

(*a*) Means, *by, per, in*: **Ich schicke es per** (or **durch die** or **mit der**) **Post, per Fracht. Es geht billiger per Schiff als per Bahn** (or **Eisenbahn**). **Heutzutage geht alles per Dampf** (= **Geschwindigkeit**). **Ich meldete es ihm per Telegraph. Per Maria** per steamship Maria, **per ersten Segler** by the first sailing vessel. **Er zahlt per Kassa** (in cash). **Ein Brief p e r** (= **unter der**) **A d r e s s e** (in care) **des Herrn Karl Schmidt.**

(*b*) Distributively, *per, a, for*: **Etwas kostet so und soviel per Zentner, per Pfund, per Elle, per Dutzend, per Stück,** or **der Zentner, das Pfund, die Elle kostet so und soviel.**

(*c*) A definite time when something is to be done, *due payable*: **Hierbei übersenden wir Ihnen M. 1000,00 pr. 1.** (read **ersten**) **Januar** We send you inclosed a draft for 1000 marks, due 1st Jan.

Note. Three other foreign preps. are much used in commercial language, but they are usually found before nouns without modifying words which can show case, occasionally, however, also before a word which marks the acc.—via (= **über**) with the same force as in English, **pro** *for* (= **per**, *b* above), à *each* (costing, containing, weighing): **pr.** (per, see (*a*) above) **Henriette via Neu-Orleans; Preis pro Paar M. 0,60** (60 pfennigs); **Preis pro Band geheftet** (unbound) **1 Mark; Insertionspreis pro fünfgespaltene Nonpareille-Zeile 60 Pfennig; große eckige Stücke** (**Seife**) **von 125 Gramm** à (each costing) **M. 0,25.**

SONDER = **ohne,** now little used except in poetical style, usually before nouns without an article, only very rarely with an indefinite article, sometimes with the dat.: **Sonder Zweifel, sonder allen Zweifel** (Jensen's *Auf der Baar*, III), **sonder'gleichen** without an equal. **Alle Hoheit der Erde sonder herzliche Liebe ist Staub. Sonder einer solchen Flasche blieb bei den Griechen ein zu begrabender Leichnahm ebenso wenig als sonder Kranz** (Lessing).

UM. 1. It has in general the force of *around*, either of rest or motion, but has developed out of this meaning a rich store of related literal and figurative ones as follows:

A. *Around* in a literal sense: **Alle Planeten bewegen sich um die Sonne. Die Gäste saßen um den Tisch. Es fahren viele Schiffe um das Kap der guten Hoffnung.**

(*a*) From the idea of movement around some central point comes the figurative idea of the central, material cause which excites and attracts our interest and feeling, *over, on account of*: **Er trauert um den Tod des Bruders. Ich beneide Sie um diese Reise** I envy you this journey.

(*b*) It often points to the person or thing about which thought, feeling, or action is busied, *concerning, about, with respect to, of, with, for*: **Weiß die Königin um diese Neigung? Es handelt sich um die Erbschaft. Just um diesen Brief war mir's zu tun** It was just this letter that concerned me. **Ich bin so in Unruhe um den Vater** I am so worried about Father. **Ich komme um den Oheim** I come (to consult with you) about Uncle. **Wie steht es um ihn?** How are things with (respect to) him? **Es ist eine schöne Sache um die Freiheit** Freedom is a beautiful thing. **Darum** (with respect to that) **seien Sie unbesorgt. Das habe ich nicht um** (of) **ihn verdient. Bismarck hat sich um das Vaterland verdient gemacht** Bismarck has deserved well of his country. **Es ist um ihn geschehen** It is all over with him. **Schade wär's um ihre Haare** The loss of her hair would be a pity. **Es tut mir leid um ihn** I am sorry for him. Compare **von,** *c* in **229. 2.**

(*c*) Movement around in a circle leads back to a starting point, hence the idea of change, succession, alternation: **Das Fieber kommt einen Tag um den andern** The fever appears every other day. **Bote um** (after) **Bote wurde ausgesandt. Sie sangen einer um den andern** They sang alternately.

(*d*) Movement in a circle implies a desire to encompass, close in on, gain something, hence **um** points to the desired object, the reward, end or purpose in view, *for, after, in order* (to): **Er schickt, schreibt um** (for) **etwas. Er tut alles um Geld. Er arbeitet um die Ehre. Sie arbeiten um die Wette** They are trying to outdo one another in working. **Viele bemühen sich um die Gunst der Mächtigen. Er bewirbt sich um die Hand des schönen Mädchens. Er bittet um Verzeihung.** Especially with an infinitive to denote purpose: **Ich komme, um** (in order) **Sie zu sehen.** The ideas of purpose and result are closely related. This leads to the use of **um** with the infinitive to express end or result: **Du bist alt genug, um dies einzusehen.** See also **281.** *Note.* It also denotes price and exchange: **um jeden Preis** at any price; **um einen billigen Preis; um alles in der Welt nicht** not for all the world; **um nichts und wieder nichts** for absolutely nothing; **etwas um** (more commonly **gegen** or **für**) **etwas tauschen; Auge um Auge, Zahn um Zahn.**

(*e*) In moving around an object we pass it by, miss it, hence the general idea of *loss*: **Es brachte ihn um sein Vermögen, um seinen Verstand** It caused him to lose his property, reason. **Ich bin um meinen Schlummer. Er ist ums Leben gekommen.** In moving around a circle one must sooner or later encompass it, come to the end of it, hence the general idea of *end*, especially in adverbial use: **Das Jahr ist um** (up). This idea may also be contained in some of the preceding sentences.

(*f*) Out of the figurative application of *distance around* comes the idea of *measure of difference*, not translated at all or rendered by *the* (adv.), *by, within*: **Er ist um einen Kopf größer als sein Bruder** He is a head taller than his brother. **Er kam um zwei Tage zu spät. Je fleißiger er ist, u m s o** (the) **mehr lernt er. Dieser Umstand vermehrte sein Leiden um ein Großes** (by a good deal). **Ums Haar hättst du mir die Terrine da umgeworfen** You came within a hair's breadth of upsetting the tureen for me. It also denotes amount, extent: **Er strafte ihn um zehn Mark** He fined him ten marks. **Er hat sich um eine Mark verrechnet** He made a mistake of a mark.

B. *In the neighborhood of, near,* used of space, time or number, in a more or less indefinite sense:

(*a*) Of persons and things in space, *around*: **Er hat keinen Freund um sich. Ich bin den ganzen Tag um ihn. Um Berlin herum gibt es viele Sandgegenden.**

(*b*) Of time and number, synonymous with **gegen**, *about*: **Es geschah um Mitternacht, um Ostern. Um dreihundert Hörer** an audience of about three hundred. But with the hours of the day **um** expresses time more accurately, *at*: **Er geht pünktlich um zehn Uhr zu Bette.**

C. Less frequently the logical reason (A. *a* above) instead of its synonyms **um — willen, wegen** *on account of*: **Ich lobe dich um deinen Fleiß,** or more frequently **um deines Fleißes willen** or **wegen deines Fleißes.** But very commonly the words **wa'rum, da'rum** instead of **weswegen** wherefore, why, **deswegen** therefore.

We sometimes find **um** with the genitive in this meaning after the analogy of **um — willen: O Gott! Ich danke dir mein Leben nur | um dieser Kunde** (Kleist's *Schroffenstein*, 2, 1). **Den der Papa um seines Geldes erkor** (Heyse's *Im Paradiese*, 1, 178). **Nur um der Wahrhaftigkeit frag' ich dich** (Hauptmann's *Michael Kramer*, p. 71).

2. Quite rare is the use of the dative after **um,** when it denotes rest, after the analogy of other prepositions which denote rest: **Das Eis um meinem Herzen** (Börne), **in und um unseren Dörfern** (Hans Müller-Brauel in *Hamburger Nachrichten*, March 23, 1906).

WIDER, see **gegen.**

Prepositions with either Dative or Accusative

I. *General Remarks.*

231. 1. These prepositions (see list **227**) govern the dat. when the place *in which* is denoted, whether motion or rest in that place is expressed, but the acc. when the direction *towards* or *into* an object is expressed: **Das Buch liegt auf dem Tisch,** but **Hans legte das Buch auf den Tisch. Hans lief in dem Zimmer herum** *John ran around in the room*, but **Er lief in** (into) **das Zimmer.** It is rather uncommon that with a verb of motion both the dative and the accusative can be used, the former to indicate rest, the latter to express the idea of motion toward: **Er verschwand im Walde** (place), but **in den Wald** (motion into). The dative is more common here, as the prefix **ver-** of the verb is perfective (**246.** II. 3. *b*) and the action is felt as completed, so that we conceive the person as within the wood rather than as moving into it. Likewise we say **Er kehrte in dem Gasthofe ein** rather than **Er kehrte in den Gasthof ein** as we do not think so much of the mere entrance into the hotel as the staying, resting in the place. On the other hand we do not say **Die Statue kam auf der Brücke zu stehen** as often as **Die Statue kam auf die Brücke zu stehen,** altho the dative fits the meaning better inasmuch as the statue finds a permanent place upon the bridge. Recent usage inclines, as in this example, toward the accusative with simple verbs of motion, but favors the dative with compounds with a perfective prefix, as further illustrated by the following examples: **Er kam in die Stadt,** but **Er kam in der Stadt an. Er legte das Glas neben die Flasche,** but **Der Hund legte sich dicht neben den Körben nieder. Der Fluß mündet in den Rhein,** but **In seiner Jugend ein radikaler Idealist, mündete Hehn** (name) **in einem konservativen Idealismus aus.** With simple verbs, however, denoting motion *between* objects on both sides the dative *must* be used, as illustrated under **zwischen** in II below. On the other hand, it is important for the English-speaking student to note that in countless cases, often even in case of perfective verbs, the *act* is more important than the resultant *goal* or *state* so that the accusative is with many words much more common than the dative, altho there is considerable fluctuation of usage: **Er hat mich in das Zimmer eingeschlossen,** but with the perfect participle which of itself denotes a state: **Er ist im Zimmer eingeschlossen. Sie hat sich in grünen Samt gekleidet** and also **Sie ist in grünen Samt gekleidet,** for we do not think of a resultant state but the *act* of her choosing green. **Er hat sich in die Arbeit vertieft** and **Er ist in die Arbeit vertieft,** for we do not think of him as passive but as penetrating deeper into his work.

a. Often the two ideas are only figurative: **ein Buch über Goethe's „Faust"** a book on (spreading itself over the subject of) Goethe's *Faust*; **über allen Zweifel** beyond (lit. raised above) all doubt. **Wilhelm kam auf einen guten Einfall** William hit upon a happy thought.

2. In applying this rule to time the following rule will be of service: In answer to the question *when* they govern the dat., but in answer to the question

how long and *until when* the acc.: **Wann kamen Sie nach Hause? In der Nacht. Wie lange, bis wann bleiben Sie in der Stadt? Bis tief in die Nacht.**

3. In abstract or figurative expressions where the idea of place or motion toward does not appear, these rules cannot always be applied, but in these cases the following rule will be found useful: When manner, cause, or means are expressed, **an, in, unter, vor** take the dat., but **auf** and **über** the acc. Manner: **in dieser Weise,** but **auf diese Weise** in this manner. **Er schreibt am schönsten** (see **114.** 2), but **Er schreibt aufs schönste** (see **114.** 3). **Der König zog unter dem Jubel des Volks in die Stadt** *The king marched into the city amid the hurrahs of the people,* but **Es geht über alles Erwarten schön** *Things are going along well even beyond all expectation.* Cause: **Wir freuen uns an dem schönen Wetter,** or **über das schöne Wetter** We rejoice over the beautiful weather. **Lena erwachte an** (aroused by) **einem wilden, markdurchwühlenden** (piercing) **Schrei,** but **Mehrere Leute liefen nun auf** (alarmed by) **den Lärm gleichfalls aus dem Felde herbei.** Means: **Man erkennt den Baum an** (by) **seinen Früchten.** Means is rarely expressed by **auf** or **über.**

4. Sometimes fine distinctions may be made by using the dat. when it is desired to represent the person or thing as already at the place where something is to occur and by using the acc. when it is desired to emphasize the movement of the person or thing towards the place in question: **Er wurde in** (he is already there) **der Gesellschaft freundlich aufgenommen,** but **Er wurde in die Gesellschaft aufgenommen** (admitted by ballot). **Setzen Sie sich auf diese** (rarely **dieser** as in Schiller's *Tell*) **Bank von Stein,** but: **Sie lagerten sich bequem auf dem Rasen. Dieses Land ist die schönste Perle in der Krone dieses Fürsten** (it has long been in his possession), but **Das ist ein frisches Blatt in seinen Lorbeerkranz** (it has lately been added to his wreath and is here vividly imagined as just entering it) and **Ach, liebe Frau Justizrätin, Sie dürfen mir glauben, der Junge ist ein Nagel in meinen Sarg** (Isolde Kurz's *Nachbar Werner*).

II. *Treatment in Detail.*

These prepositions follow in alphabetical order:

AN is synonymous with **bei, nach, neben, zu,** but often with sharp distinctions, as are described in **229.** 2, under **bei, 1,** and in the *Note* under **zu, I.**

1. With the dative.

A. Close approach to or contact with the side of an object, also with various figurative applications, *at, by, on, against, to, near to, in, about*: **Er sitzt am** (at) **Fenster. Er sitzt am** (by) **Ofen. Das Bild hängt an** (on) **der Wand. Frankfurt liegt am** (on) **Main** (river). **Er sitzt am Hügel** (on the hillside). **Der Stock lehnt an** (against) **der Wand. Sie stehen Kopf an Kopf. Arm an Arm** (in English, *shoulder to shoulder*). **Es liegt mir am** (near to) **Herzen. Er ist am** (near unto) **Tode. Wir stehen auf** (sometimes **an**; see *Note* below) **dem Boden,** but in a figurative sense to indicate a prostrate position: **Der Mensch** (Napoleon) **ist am Boden** (Treitschke's *Deutsche Geschichte*, 1, 551). **Es ist nichts an** (in) **ihm. Es ist nichts Wahres an** (in) **dem Gerücht. Er hat keine Spur von Stolz an** (about) **sich. Die Reihe ist an mir** It is my turn. **Dinge, die an (und für) sich** (in themselves) **gräßlich sind, werden in dichterischer Nachahmung ergötzlich.**

Note. Do not confound **an** *on* with **auf** *on*. The former denotes contact only with the side of an object, the latter with the upper surface: **an** (on the slope of) **dem Berg, auf dem Gipfel** on the summit. Originally **an** denoted contact in general as still in English, and hence implied contact with either the side or upper surface of an object. This older usage is still found in early N.H.G.: **an** (now **auf**) **dem Grase sitzen,** &c. It still survives in a few expressions: **an unrechtem Ort, am rechten Platz,** &c.

(*a*) Applied to time, only, however, in certain set expressions, *at, on, in*: **am Mittag** at noon, **am Abend** in the evening. **Er starb am** (on) **Mittwoch. Wir arbeiteten am Tage** (in day time). **Die Leipziger Schlacht wurde am** (on) **18. Oktober 1813 geschlagen. Es ist an der Zeit, an der Stunde** The time, hour is at hand.

Note 1. We say **am Tage** *in day time*, but **in der Nacht,** because **an** denotes a surface, hence that which is visible, while **in** expresses here the idea of an enveloping darkness. Thus we say **Es liegt am Tage** It is as plain as day, but **Es ist in Dunkel gehüllt** It is shrouded in darkness. Thus also **im Sommer, im Winter** because we regard ourselves *within* a period of time.

Note 2. **An** refers to time back of us, and **auf** to time ahead of us: **Jch bin am Sonnabende** (last Saturday) **dort gewesen,** but **Er wird mich auf den Sonntag** (next Sunday) **besuchen.** This distinction is not made in early N.H.G.: **Auf** (now **am**) **Montag der ersten Woche nach Advent zog Heinrich durch das Stift** (Luther). **Vnd es begab sich auff der tage einen | das,** &c. (Luke viii, 22).

(*b*) The idea of *near approach to* which lies in **an** leads naturally to its use in the adverbial superlative (**112.** 3. B) of the adjective and the relative superlative (**114.** 2) of the adverb: **Der Sturm war am heftigsten** (lit. at that which is most violent, i.e. in the most violent stage) **gegen Morgen. Er schreibt am schönsten von allen.**

(*c*) Close approach on a certain side gives rise to the meaning *in respect to, in, about, as to, of, in the way of*: **Es fehlt ihm an Geld, an Fassung** He lacks (lit. in respect to) money, self-command. **Das Land ist reich an** (in) **Mineralien. In Italien gewinnt der Kampf der Parteien an Schärfe. Ich zweifele an** (have doubts about) **der Aufrichtigkeit dieses Mannes. An** (as to) **Fleiß geht Karl allen andern Knaben vor. Mangel an Wasser, an guter Luft** lack of water, good air; **schwach am Leibe** (but **im Kopfe**). **So hatte sie in unbefangenstem Plauderton ausgekramt, was sie in ihrem Kopf an** (in the way of) **Gedanken vorgefunden.**

(*d*) Close approach gives rise to the idea of rapid succession, *after*: **Pfeiler an Pfeiler zerbrach.**

(*e*) Close approach gives rise to the idea of *close application, busying one's self with, being in the act of*, and often **an** together with an infinitive-substantive is equal to the progressive form of the verb in English: **Ich will dich nicht zurückhalten — du bist am Ausgehen** I will not detain you, as I see you are going out (down town). **Sie hatte es gerade mit einem Kinde zu tun, das am Kartoffelschälen war** She was just then occupied with a child who was peeling potatoes. It should be noticed that the progressive form of the verb in Eng. may have an object, while in German the object must form a compound with the infinitive-substantive as in the second example. Note also that **an** is here always contracted with the article. See also **175.** *Note.*

B. Out of the idea of *approach to* and *contact with* comes the conception of varied relations which the persons and objects thus brought together sustain to each other: **Er ist Lehrer an** (in) **dieser Schule, Prediger an der Hofkirche. Dieser Gelehrte arbeitet an** (on) **einem großen Werke. Er hat sich an seinem Gegner tätlich vergriffen** He laid violent hands on his opponent. **Es liegt an ihm** (it is his fault), **daß er nicht vorwärts kommt. Er nimmt an den Freuden der Kinder teil. Er stieß sich an der Wand blutig. Er wird an dir zum Verräter** He will betray you. **Er hat eine Stütze an** (*in*) **seinem Sohn. Er wird sich an seinen Feinden rächen. Du hinderst mich am Arbeiten** You keep me from working.

(*a*) This relation may be that of cause, *of, from*, &c.: **Er starb an** (of) **der Schwindsucht. Er leidet an** (from) **der Brust. Ich labe mich an** (with) **den Früchten. Er ärgert sich an** (at) **allen Dingen. Das Eis schmilzt an** (in) **der Sonne.**

Note. In earlier periods (and occasionally still) the simple gen. was used here. See **223. V. *a*.**

(*b*) This relation may be that of means, *by*: **Ich höre am Geläute, daß heute Sonntag ist. Man erkennt den Vogel an den Federn. Ich weiß es an mir** (by my own experience). **Er erkannte mich an der Stimme. Er geht am Stock** He walks with the aid of a cane.

2. With the accusative.

(*a*) Direction toward, implying close approach to the side of a person or thing, or even contact therewith, literally and figuratively: **Hänge das Bild an die Wand, das Kleid an den Nagel. Er setzte sich an** (at) **meine Seite. Er schreibt an** (on) **das Fenster**, but **Er schreibt am** (at) **Fenster. Er steckte den Ring an** (on) **den Finger. Er zog den Strumpf ans Bein. Ich habe viel an ihn verloren** I have lost a good deal to him (in cards, &c.), but **Ich habe viel an ihm verloren** *I have lost much in him.* Often with **bis** to mark limit: **Das Wasser reichte bis an die Knie. Er begleitete mich bis an das Tor.** Figuratively: **Er geht an** (to) **die Arbeit. Ich denke an ihn. Ich schreibe oft an** (to) **ihn. Hier ist ein Brief an** (directed) **Sie. Die Reihe** (turn) **kommt an mich.**

(*b*) Temporally, used only with **bis** to mark a limit of time: **Sie tanzten bis an den Morgen.**

(*c*) An approximate number, used as an adverb or prep. (see **225. 1. *c***), *about*: **Wie lange habt ihr prozessiert? An die acht Jahre. Es waren an hundert Menschen versammelt.**

AUF. 1. With the dative.

A. Contact with the *upper* surface of (see **an, 1. A.** *Note*), *on, upon*: **Auf christlichen Kirchen steht gewöhnlich ein Kreuz. Das Buch liegt auf dem Tisch.** Also without contact, but as a necessary part of: **Der Punkt auf dem i.** Figuratively: **Ich habe eine Angst auf dem Herzen. Die Sache beruht auf Ihnen. Es hat nichts auf sich** It is of no consequence. **Was hat es damit auf sich?** What of that?

(*a*) In a number of cases **auf** is used because the present or original conception is that of a place at some height, altho the place may be an enclosed one. It is translated accordingly in Eng. by *in*: **Er wohnt auf einem Schlosse, auf Nummer zehn** (in hotel). **Er ist auf** (of an upper room) **seinem Zimmer, auf der Burg, auf der Kanzel, auf den Galerien.**

(*b*) Before the common noun **Insel** *island* **auf** is used but before the articleless names of islands both **auf** and **in** are employed, the latter especially with large bodies of land which are thus conceived of as countries: **auf der Insel** *on* or *in the island*, but **auf** or **in Kreta.**

B. The idea of an upper surface gives way in many cases to that of a surface in general, considered as a base of operations: **Er arbeitet auf** (in) **dem Felde. Im Sommer lebt man angenehm auf** (in) **dem Lande. Friedrich der Große war ein Meister auf der Flöte. Wir kegeln auf der Kegelbahn. Wilhelm liegt auf dem Rücken, auf der Seite. Er ist blind auf** (or **an** *in*) **beiden Augen, taub auf** (in) **einem Ohr. Auf diesem Wege wird er zu nichts gelangen** In this way he will not accomplish anything.

Note. Sometimes there is quite a difference of conception in German and English, as the former regards certain things as extended surfaces or open public places while the latter looks at them as bounded spaces, hence in the former case we find **auf**, in the latter *in, at*: **Man kauft etwas auf dem Markt**, but *at* the market. **Man fährt auf der Straße, wohnt aber in der Straße**, while in Eng. one drives *in* the street but lives *on* (in U. S., but in England *in*) the street. Thus also **auf** (in) **dem Friedrichsplatz, auf** (at) **dem Bahnhof, auf** (*in*) **dem Chor, auf dem Lager** in stock, **auf** (in) **der Station, auf** (in) **der Wiese.**

(*a*) Closely connected with the idea of a literal base of operations is its figurative application to political, educational, business, and social organizations and individual activities which proceed on a definite open basis: **auf** (in) **dem Reichstag, auf dem Parteitag** at the party convention, **auf** (at) **der demnächst stattfindenden Sitzung des Ausschusses, auf dem Wiener** (of Vienna) **Kongreß, auf** (*at*, of a pupil, but **an** of a teacher) **dem Gymnasium, auf** (*at*, of a student, but **an** of a professor) **der Universität** or **Schule** (but **in der Schule** of elementary schools), **auf dem Kriegsschauplatz, auf dem Rückmarsch, auf** (at) **seinem Bureau, auf der Börse, auf** (at) **der Post, auf** (at) **der Messe, auf** (at) **der Weltausstellung in Chicago, auf** (at) **dem Balle, auf** (at) **der Hochzeit, auf der Jagd, auf** (in) **der Flucht, auf der Reise, auf** (at) **seinem Posten. Man ertappte ihn auf** (in) **der Tat. Er steht auf meiner Seite. Er ist auf seiner Hut. Auf diesem Gebiet** in this line (of study, art, music, &c.). **Er hält mich auf dem Laufenden** He keeps me posted. **Auf** (at) **einigen Punkten haben die sozialdemokratischen Stimmen seit der letzten Wahl zugenommen.**

Note. In the above, it can be seen how often the German and English conception differs, but on the other hand where the idea of a close body or corporation or position or action *within* a body distinctly appears, **in** is used in both languages: **in dem preußischen Ministerium, Kabinett. Doch blieb Luxemburg im deutschen Zollverein.**

2. With the accusative, with the general idea of direction toward.

A. Direction or movement toward the upper surface of, implying ultimate contact, *on, upon*: **Er setzt sich auf den Stuhl. Er legt das Buch auf den Tisch. Er klettert auf den Baum.** Also with movement toward without actual contact, but so close as to form a necessary part of (see 1. A above): **Er setzt den Punkt auf das i.** Coincidence: **Das Fest fiel auf einen Sonntag. Er kam auf den Glockenschlag. Er bezahlt mich immer auf den Tag. Er kam pünktlich auf die Minute.**

(*a*) Movement toward an object which according to the present or original conception is situated at some height (see **1. A. *a*** above), *to*: **Er geht auf das Schloß, auf sein Zimmer, auf die Burg.**

B. As in 1. B above, the idea of an upper surface gives way to that of a surface in general, considered as a basis of future operations when reached, *to, into, on*: **Die Arbeiter gehen auf das Feld. Sie fahren aufs Land. Sie gehen aufs Eis** (to skate). **Er macht sich auf den Weg. Er legt sich auf die Seite, auf den Rücken.** In nautical language, *for* (the port of): **Warum fuhr er nun seit zehn Jahren als Schiffszimmermann auf einem großen Dampfer auf Kalkutta?** (*Hamburgischer Correspondent*, May, 17 1903).

Note. The same differences of idiom between English and German as described in Note under 1. B., above, appear also when direction toward is indicated: **Man geht auf** (to) **den Markt. Der Hausbesitzer setzte die arme Familie auf** (into) **die Straße. Er biegt in** (into) **die Friedrichstraße. Die Friedrichstraße, Wilhelmstraße und Lindenstraße münden** (terminate) **konvergierend auf** (in) **den kreisrunden, mit Gartenanlagen geschmückten Belleallianceplatz.**

(*a*) Corresponding to **1. B. *a*** above: **Man geht auf die Post, auf den Ball, auf die Jagd. Er läßt sich auf den Kampf ein** He engages in the battle. **Auf diese Bedingungen, Vorschläge kann ich nicht eingehen** I cannot assent to, &c. **Man ging auf den Scherz ein. Er stellte mich auf** (to) **die Probe.** Often, instead of naming such society or action, mentioning some article or object which is suggestive of it: **Er lud mich auf** (to) **eine Mahlzeit, auf eine Suppe, auf ein Butterbrot, auf ein Glas Wein, auf eine Tasse Tee. Er forderte mich auf Pistolen** He challenged me to a duel with pistols. **Er hatte zwei schwere Forderungen auf krumme Säbel.**

C. Direction of some activity of the mind or of some feeling toward an object, in various relations, representing it:

(*a*) As an object of attack, attention, or of some feeling either hostile or friendly: **Das ist auf mich abgesehen** That is meant for (aimed at) me. **Er schimpft auf mich. Das Mädchen heftete seine Augen auf den Tänzer. Er ist auf mich gut** (or **übel**) **zu sprechen** He speaks well (or ill) of me. **Er zürnt auf mich. Er ist auf seine Frau eifersüchtig, stolz. Mein Handwerk halte ich hoch und lasse nichts darauf kommen** I think a great deal of my trade, and allow no one to say anything against it.

(*b*) As the object or point toward which the mental activity or the nature of a person or thing is directed, usually with a view to furthering, acquiring, enjoying it: **Böse Leute merken nicht aufs Recht. Er hält auf Ordnung, auf Ehre** He attaches much value to, &c. **Seid Ihr 'ne Bäckersfrau, die ihren Altknecht freit auf ihr Gewerb?** Are you a baker woman who marries her head-servant with a view to using him in her business? **Sie ist bis vor kurzem in Berlin gewesen auf** (in order to acquire) **feine Erziehung. Ein Ringen auf Sein und Nichtsein** a struggle for life or death. **Ich bereite mich auf das Fest vor. Wer sich von einem Studium aufs andere wirft, wird in keinem soviel erreichen, als wer sich ausschließlich auf eins legt. Ich verzichte auf meinen Anteil. Er versteht sich aufs Raten** He is good at guessing. **Er ist auf das Mädchen erpicht. Ich besinne mich nicht auf ihn. Bestellungen, Vorbestellungen auf die Theaterplätze** orders, orders in advance for the seats in the theater. **Die Kirschen sind nicht eigen auf Boden, gedeihen in leichtem und schwerem Erdreich** Cherry trees are not particular with regard to the soil in which they grow, &c.

(*c*) As the end, purpose, design: **Der Gelehrte prüft das Erz auf** (to see whether it contains) **Silber. Er geht auf** (in search of) **Abenteuer aus. Ich trinke das auf** (to) **Ihre Gesundheit. Diese Ware ist auf den Kauf gemacht** This article is made to sell. **Er reist auf** (also **in** with dat.; see **in**) **Schuhe** He is on the road with shoes, i.e. travels for a shoe house. **Er reist auf Baukunst** He travels to get ideas on architecture. **Das Ganze ist auf eine Überraschung angelegt. Wir bestehen auf seine Absetzung. Mich deucht, du hast nicht gerade auf den Pastor studiert** (Jensen's *Heimkunft*, VII) It seems to me that you didn't exactly study for the ministry.

(*d*) As a basis, as that upon which the action or feeling rests, and from which the actor draws strength, courage, inspiration, or as the false basis upon which a misdoer stands in order to conceal the true one: **Er baut ein Haus auf dem Berg** (place), but **Er baut ein Haus auf den**

Berg (firm basis) and **Er baut auf ihn** *He is counting on, trusting in him.* **Auf seinen Beistand darf ich rechnen. Auf diese und andere Anklagen hin wurde er in den Tower gesperrt. Auf deine Gefahr** (at your risk) **wage ich es. Sie bildet sich was auf ihre Schönheit ein** She prides herself on, &c. **Es kommt auf dich an** It depends upon you. **Ich frage dich auf dein Gewissen. Er hat es auf eigene Faust getan. Er wagte es auf** (trusting to) **gut Glück. Er machte ein Gedicht auf Bismarck. Es ist gut auf** (in) **den Herrn** (Lord) **vertrauen und sich nicht verlassen auf Menschen. Ich kann auf** (to) **seine Unschuld schwören. Das Kind ist auf meinen Namen getauft** (named for me). **Einer dieser Pässe lautet auf einen Schweizer, den Furier Koch** One of these passes is made out in the Swiss quarter-master Koch's name. **Er war auf den Namen Wilhelm Schmidt eingeschrieben** (registered under the name of, &c.). **So wird dann freilich der Fürst für tausend Dinge verantwortlich gemacht, von denen er keine Silbe weiß, und die ganze Umgebung sündigt auf** (on the strength of, under the cover of) **seinen Namen.**

D. Movement toward leads to the idea of some point of time or of some event in future time, and in general to the idea of futurity and expectation in varied relations (see **an** 1. A. (*a*). *Note* 2): **Es geht auf neun** It is going on nine (o'clock). **Es ist drei Viertel auf fünf** It is a quarter to five. **In der Nacht von gestern auf heute, in der Nacht auf den** (or **zum**) **1. Oktober** in the night before Oct. 1. **Man hofft auf bessere Tage. Er bat mich auf den Abend zum Essen. Es wird Regen geben auf die Nacht. Die Verordnung über die Einberufung des Reichstags auf** (on) **den 16.** (of next) **November ist amtlich bekannt gemacht worden. Meine Frau Pathe** (godmother) **habe ich in meinem Leben nicht gesehen, und Sie können denken, wie ich mich auf sie freute** (how glad I was at the prospect of seeing her). **Ich beschäftigte mich mit den neuen Sommerkleidern, welche mir die lieben Eltern auf das** (in consideration of the approaching) **Fest hatten machen lassen. Das Geld nahm er zu sich auf den Fall, wo er es gebrauchen würde. Diese Wohnung ist auf Ostern zu vermieten** This house can be engaged now for occupancy at Easter. In early N.H.G. **auf** was also used with reference to some point of time in the past. See **an**, 1. A. (*a*). *Note* 2.

E. Movement toward a moving object gives rise to the idea of pursuit, and this leads to that of immediate or rapid succession, and hence a sequence or response in general: **Er folgt auf mich** He succeeds me. **Auf Regen folgt Sonnenschein. Auf** (after) **das Essen darf man keine heftige Bewegung machen. Tropfen auf Tropfen schlug an das Fenster. Blitz auf Blitz, Schlag auf Schlag folgte. Auf die Dauer** (in the long run) **wird die kleinste Last schwer. Er hört** (heeds) **nicht auf meine Worte. Er hört** (answers) **auf** (to) **beide Namen. Er antwortete auf meinen Brief. Er kam auf den ersten Ruf. Die Hausfrau . . . stach um so vorteilhafter von der Schwägerin ab, welche auf den lieblichen Ruf** (*by the title of*) **Fräulein ging** (Raabe's *Hungerpastor*, XIII).

(*a*) From this idea comes that of following the will or desire of another, closely related in meaning to **nach** and **gemäß**: **Ich habe es auf** (in accordance with) **Ihren Befehl, auf Ihren Wunsch getan. Auf** (upon) **seinen Antrag erfolgte Freisprechung.**

(*b*) As that which follows upon something is often that which is caused by it, **auf** with its dependent noun is often considered as a cause: **Mehrere Leute liefen nun auf** (alarmed by) **den Lärm gleichfalls aus dem Felde. Der Graf hatte mit Bedauern vernommen, daß sein Dienstmann einen Bürger auf** (provoked by) **so geringfügigen Anlaß geschlagen habe. Der Baum fällt nicht auf éinen Hieb.**

F. The limit *up to* which something may extend, sometimes taken inclusively, sometimes exclusively: **Er ist auf den Tod verwundet. Ich bin elend, auf mein ganzes Leben elend. Er quälte mich** (bis) **aufs Blut** (almost to death). **Er will nur auf** (for) **einen Tag fortgehen. Er verließ uns auf vierzehn Tage. Auf Wiedersehen!** good-by till we see one another again! **Bei dem ungewissen Schein des Neumonds konnte man kaum auf fünf Schritte vor sich sehen. Er weiß es aufs Haar** or **auf ein Haar** (accurately). **Es kostet auf** (as high as) **100 Taler. Man schätzt die Zahl sämtlicher Rumänen** (Rumanians) **auf** (at) **10 Millionen.** Sometimes after **bis**: **Er trank das Glas bis auf die Neige** (excluded) **aus. Alle seine Freunde verließen ihn bis auf** (except) **einen.**

G. A trend in a certain direction gives rise to the idea of manner: **Auf diese Art, auf diese Weise wird er sein Ziel erreichen. Er empfing mich aufs freundlichste. Sie fechten auf den Hieb** (with broad-swords). **Er bezahlt es auf Abschlag** (making payments from time to time). **Er sagte es auf** (in) **Deutsch. Wollen wir die Droschke auf Zeit** (**auf die Stunde**) **oder auf die Fahrt nehmen?** Shall we hire the cab by the hour or for the trip. **Aufs Geratewohl** at random, **auf jeden Fall** in any case, **auf keinen Fall.**

Note. With superlatives both **an** and **auf** denote manner, but as **an** with the dat. denotes arrival at the goal, while **auf** w. acc. indicates only a movement toward the goal itself, the latter is more general, and hence its use with the absolute superlative of the adverb, while the former is used with the relative superlative. See **114.** 2 and 3.

H. Used distributively to show that which is alotted to, falls to the share of: **Die Steuern verteilen sich folgendermaßen** (are distributed as follows among) **auf die einzelnen Provinzen. Eine Steigung von 1 Fuß auf jede 100. Die Pariser essen angeblich zu viel Fleisch, jährlich 93 Kilogramm auf den Kopf** (*Hamb. Nachr.*). **Er verteilte den Vorrat auf viermal** He divided the rations so as to make enough for four different times. **Er aß alles auf** (at) **einmal. Er wurde auf einmal wieder lustig.**

I. The idea of resting something on something else gives rise to the idea of an underlying *condition*: **Man nimmt einen Koch, Bedienten auf Probe** (on condition that he gives satisfaction). **Ein Kauf auf Besicht, auf Probe** (subject to examination).

AUSZER. 1. With the dative:

(*a*) Position on the outside of an object or place which has fixed limits, once frequent, but now usually replaced by **außerhalb** with gen., and in case of greater removal from the object **aus** with dat.: **Die öffentlichen Predigten sogar außer** (for **außerhalb**) **der Stadt zu verhindern** (Schiller). **Ich bin verschiedene Tage außer** (for **aus**) **Leipzig gewesen** (Lessing). **Sie gehen in dem Raume außer dem Zelte** (for **außerhalb des Zeltes**) **quer über die Bühne** (Grillparzer's *Der Traum, ein Leben*, 3).

Note. In a few set expressions **außer** is still used where the position is entirely indefinite and general, *out of doors*, *out*: **Sie arbeiten außer dem Hause** (out of doors). **Wir speisen heute außer dem Hause** We dine out to-day.

(*b*) The figurative application of the meaning *out of*, *outside of*, *beyond*, now very common, as **außerhalb** by reason of its accurate local meaning is not usually applicable here: **Sie ist darüber außer** (*beside*) **sich. Ich habe mich ganz in mich zurückgezogen und habe keine Wünsche außer mir** (Frenssen's *Die drei Getreuen*, II, 3). **Der Kranke ist außer** (*beyond*) **Gefahr. Seid außer** (*without*) **Furcht, ich bin zugegen. Es ist außer** (*beyond*) **allem Zweifel. Er ist außer stande,** (*not able*) **es zu tun. Außer Hörweite, außer Schußweite.**

Note. Also **außerhalb** is here used when a definite limit is to be expressed: **Das liegt außerhalb des Planes.**

(*c*) Exclusion, *except* (in this meaning also used as a conj.; see **225.** 2. and *a* thereunder): **Alle waren zugegen außer dir.**

(*d*) Excess, *besides*: **Er verlangt außer dem Lohne auch gute Behandlung. Er ist dumm und außerdem faul.**

2. With the acc. with verbs of motion. The grammarians often demand the dat. here in accordance with older usage, but the acc. is not infrequently found after the analogy of other prepositions, which take the acc. with verbs of motion: **Da ich sie mit solcher Wahrheit reden hörte, kam ich ganz außer mich** (Goethe). **Du bist nun außer unsere Gemeinschaft gestellt** (G. Keller). The older dat. is also still used: **Was mich so außer mir brachte, war,** &c. (Spielhagen's *Selbstgerecht*, p. 66). The acc. has become well established in certain expressions: **außer allen Zweifel** or **Streit setzen** or **stellen, außer den Stand setzen,** &c.

3. With the gen. formerly, and still found with the gen. of **Land** and **Haus** in a few set expressions: **Er ist, geht, reist außer Landes** (in a foreign country). **Wußten Sie, daß ich außer Hauses war?** (Marriot's *Der geistliche Tod*, chap. x). Sometimes elsewhere under the influence of **außerhalb: Da aber, außer des selig weinenden Kreises, sprach plötzlich eine Stimme, vor derem** (**151.** 1. *c*) **Schmerzensklange ich erbebte** (Anselm Heine's *Eine Gabe*, Brockendorf im Lehrer-Häuschen).

HINTER. 1. With the dative:

(*a*) Position, *behind*, *back of*, *beyond*, *from behind*: **Der Hund liegt hinter dem Ofen. Der Hof liegt hinter dem Hause. Wir ritten hinter ihm her** We rode along behind him. **Die Stadt liegt hinter** (beyond) **dem Gebirge. Sie drehte den Schlüssel hinter ihm zu** She turned the key on him. **Er zog die Tür hinter sich zu** He pulled the door to after him. **Der Sekretär zog die Feder hinter dem Ohr hervor.** Figuratively: **Er hat es hinter den Ohren** He is sly. **Er hält hinter dem Berge** He conceals his views. **Hinter der Sache ist etwas** Something is at the bottom of all this. **Er bleibt hinter seiner Zeit zurück. Hinter deinem Rücken wird viel Wahrheit über dich gesprochen. Er hat eine schwere Zeit hinter sich** He has passed thru hard times. **Ich möchte es hinter mir haben** I should like to have it over with. **Er hat mehr hinter sich, als man meint** There is more *in* (or *to*) him, &c.

(*b*) *Pursuit*, or when compounded with such adverbs as **drein** and **her**, also *time after*, and thus closely related to **nach: Der Hund fuhr wie besessen hinter** (after) **dem Tiere drein. Ging ein ehrsamer Bürger auffallend raschen Schrittes durch die Straße, flugs sprang Thasso** (name of a dog) **hinterdrein** (after him). **Er ist hinter dem Gelde her** He is after money. **Er hat es mir hinterdrein** (afterwards) **gesagt.**

(*c*) Succession (see in **229.** 2 the prep. **nach,** *d. Note*) *after*: **Er kam hinter mir.**

2. With the acc. after verbs denoting a direction toward:

(*a*) Movement toward a position behind or back of something: **Der Hund legte sich hinter den Ofen. Sie hetzten** (set) **Hunde hinter** (on) **ihn.** Figuratively: **Der Schüler geht hinter die Schule** (plays truant). **Er schreibt sich's hinter die Ohren** He marks it well. **Ich komme hinter das Geheimnis** I shall find out the secret. **Er spannt die Pferde hinter den Wagen** He puts the cart before the horses. **Er führt mich hinters Licht** He deceives me.

Note. Once more common than now was the combination **hinter sich** in the sense of *backwards*: **Er fiel hinter sich. Die Heirat ist hinter sich gegangen** The match has been broken off.

(*b*) Repetition: **fünfmal hintereinander** five times running.

3. In Austrian and Bavarian authors **hinter** is found also with the genitive, both with verbs of rest and motion, more commonly, however, with pronouns than nouns: **Setze dich hinter meiner** (M. Jokay, *Andere Zeiten*, 2, 45). **Und schimpfen s' net her hinter deiner?** (Ganghofer's *Der Dorfapostel*, v), but **Keiner sieht net, was hinterm Mäuerl is** (ib.).

IN. 1. With the dat. it denotes rest or motion within a given thing, or on a surface within the given limits which form its boundary, corresponding thus in general quite closely to the Eng. *in* or *within*, also in their figurative applications, hence not treated here in detail: **Er sitzt, arbeitet in dem Hause. Er steckt tief in Schulden. In acht Tagen reise ich ab. In** (within) **einem Monat wird alles fertig sein.** For certain idiomatic differences here between the two languages see **auf,** 1. B. *Note.*

German **in** often corresponds to both English *in* (containing the idea of a bounded space) or *at* (representing a space in general as only a point where something takes place): **seine Wohnung in Weimar** his residence in Weimar, **seine Ankunft in Weimar** his arrival at Weimar; **in einem Augenblick** in a moment, **in demselben Augenblick** at the same moment, &c. Of course there are many other idiomatic differences: **im Durchschnitt** on an average, **in Geschäften** on business, **in Eilmärschen** by forced marches, **in den letzten Jahren** of late years. **Er reist in** (also **auf** with acc.) **Petroleum und tausend anderen Sachen** He is on the road selling &c.

2. With the accusative:

(*a*) Expressing a motion toward a position *within* something, corresponding quite closely to English *into*, but sometimes translated by *in, to*: **Ich komme in das Haus. Er fiel ins Wasser. Er ging in den Garten.** Translated by *in*: **ins Fäustchen lachen** to laugh in one's sleeve. **Ich steckte es in die Tasche.** English *in* is often used, not only to express rest or motion in a bounded space, but also to denote the direction toward an object or thing: *The pen is in the ink* and *I dip the pen in ink*. The German uniformly employs **in** with the acc. to denote motion toward an object. Translated by *to*: **Ich gehe in die Stube meiner Schwester. Ich gehe in die Oper, Schule, Kirche, ins Theater, in die Schweiz** (Switzerland). In numerous figurative applications variously translated: **Ein famoser Junge ist glücklich da. Wiegt stark ins achte Pfund hinein, der kleine Kerl. Schicke dich in andere Leute** Adapt yourself to other people. **Er fiel mir in die Rede** He interrupted me. **Er willigt in alles** He consents to anything. **Er ist in diese Dame verliebt** He is in love with this lady. **Er ist mir in den Tod verhaßt** I have a mortal antipathy to him. **Die (i.e. Komplimente) kann ich in den Tod nicht leiden** (W. Hegeler's *Pastor Klinghammer*).

Note. Before names of places having no article **nach** is used to express direction toward, while before names of places that have an article and can thus by their accusative form indicate clearly direction toward **in** is still used: **nach Berlin** *to Berlin*, **nach Deutschland** *to Germany*, but **in die Türkei** *to Turkey*, **in das geliebte Deutschland.** In early N.H.G. **in** could also be used before articleless names of countries.

(*b*) Direction of measurement or of an activity in general: **Die Stube hat achtzehn Fuß in die Länge und vierzehn in die Breite. Zehn Fuß in die Höhe, ins Gevierte** (square), **bis in das Einzelne** to the minutest detail. **Er klettert in die Höhe** He is climbing up. In some expressions the dative is also used here with a slight shade of meaning, namely, expressing the idea of extent within a given direction: **Das Haus hat achtzig Fuß in der Höhe.**

(*c*) Applied to time usually preceded by **bis**, except in figurative expressions: **Er spielte bis spät in die Nacht. Er bleibt mir treu bis in den Tod. Er geht ins zehnte Jahr** He is going on ten.

(*d*) With reference to materials, *in*: **Er arbeitet in Gold, in Silber.**

(*e*) An approximate judgment as to weight, magnitude, &c., with a more general and indefinite meaning than **an** or **gegen**, and besides much less common, usually like **an** with the definite article, *about*: **Judas schlug die Gottlosen | vnd bracht jr in die dreissig tausent vmb** (II Maccabees xii. 23). Sometimes the dative is also used here with a slight shade of difference, namely, expressing the idea of an indefinite extent within certain limits: **Es ist in den zwanzig Tausenden, was er schuldig ist.**

INNER, and in Switzerland also in the form **innert,** *within, inside of*, a preposition now little used, governing sometimes the gen., sometimes the dat. or acc., according to circumstances: **inner der Grenzen der Wahrheit** (Grillparzer), **inner des Hoftores** (T. Storm's *Zur Chronik von Grieshuus*, p. 113), **innert einer Stunde** (Pestalozzi), **ruft inner dem Schloßtore** (Grillparzer's *Ottokar*, 4), **inner diesen Wänden** (Anzengruber's *Schandfleck*, chap. x), **innert vierzehn Tagen** (*Neue Zürcher Zeit.*, Aug. 20, 1904), **inner die Grenzen aufnehmen** (J. von Müller).

NEBEN (in early N.H.G. also **bei'neben** and **be'neben,** usually, however, only in the dative relation) with dat. or acc. standing before the noun, occasionally in the form **zu'neben** with the dat., also following the noun: **Vor dem Sarge geht der Kaplan in Barett und Mantel, ihm zuneben der Sigrist mit dem Weihwedel und dem heiligen Wasser** (Ernst Zahn's *Wie dem Kaplan Longinus die Welt aufging*).

1. With the dative:

(*a*) Expressing rest or motion *alongside* of something: **Er sitzt, geht neben mir. Er wohnt neben** (next door to) **meinem Bruder.**

(*b*) In its figurative application, *in addition to*: **Mancher Kaufmann hat neben einem Tabaksgeschäft auch noch ein Weingeschäft.**

(*c*) Passing alongside of without hitting, hence missing the mark: **Das geht neben der Wahrheit vorbei. Er ist daneben gekommen** He didn't get anything.

2. With the acc. to express motion toward the side of something: **Er setzte sich neben mich. Er hat sein Haus neben das meinige gebaut.**

3. Formerly also with gen., and still occasionally found with this case in Austrian and Bavarian dialects, especially before a pronoun: **Z'neb'n meiner Tag über | geht's vorbei z' Roß und z' Fuß** (Anzengruber's *Die Kreuzelschreiber*, 1, 5).

OBER, a S.G. form for **über,** originally only with the dat., but now sometimes also with the acc. like **über: Da schau' ich auf und ober mir fliegt ein Adler** (Byr). **Sein Schnurrbart war ober die Lippe hinaufgestrichen** (Silberstein's *Dorfschwalben*, 2, 87). **Ober uns gebreitet | dies blauende Gewölbe** (Schnitzler's *Der Schleier der Beatrice*, p. 141).

ÜBER (with Luther **vber**), in M.H.G. only with the acc., but in the present period also with the dat., as it in this function has gradually supplanted older **ob** and **ober.**

1. With the dative:

(*a*) Position above something without contact, *over, above*: **Der Vogel schwebt über dem Dache. Er liegt immer über den Büchern. Ich bin eben über** (occupied with) **der Verpackung.** Figuratively of social position: **Sie steht über ihm.**

Note. The idea of place often mingles with that of cause (see 2. E below) and hence the dat. or acc. is used according as the idea of position or that of cause is more prominent: **Und noch jetzt scheint sie (i.e. die Natur) mit derselben Sorgfalt über ihm** (now usually **ihn** as the idea of cause is now in general felt as more prominent in such cases) **zu wachen, mit der sein Auge sein kleines Gärtchen übersieht** (Ludwig's *Zwischen Himmel und Erde*). **Sollte ein Kommissar über die Ausführung . . . wachen** (Ranke's *Päpste*, 2, 56).

(*b*) Position that can be reached only by going over something = **jenseits,** *over, on the other side of*: **Er wohnt über der Elbe.**

(*c*) Contemporaneity, closely connected with **während, unter,** *during, at*: **Er sprach über der Mahlzeit, über Tische davon. Ich konnte über dem Geschrei** (while the noise was being made) **nichts hören.**

Note. In the last sentence the idea of cause seems to mingle with that of time. The usual rule in this case is that the dat. emphasizes the idea of contemporaneity, the acc. that of cause: **Ich erwachte über** (while the noise was going on) **dem Lärm,** or **über** (on account of) **den Lärm.** Except in the case of **aufstehen, sich erheben, erwachen, nichts hören, vergessen, vernachlässigen,** which, perhaps, more commonly prefer the dat. both in the temporal and causal meaning, the actual practice of good authors seems to take little note of this rule, as the acc. is usually found, the idea of cause being in general more prominent. In **Und über das Versäumnis haben euch die Spanier das Netz über die Ohren gezogen** (*Egmont*, 2) Goethe emphasizes the idea of cause, and uses the acc. where to-day the idea of contemporaneity seems more prominent and the employment of the dat. more common.

2. With the accusative:

A. Denoting motion toward a point above something: **Der Adler erhebt sich über die Wolken.**

(*a*) A heaping up of something over something else, hence repetition, *upon, after*: **Er häufte eine Sünde über die andere. Ich habe ihn einmal über das andere gewarnt.**

(*b*) Superiority: **Der Major geht über den Hauptmann** A major is higher than a captain. **Zufriedenheit geht über Reichtum.**

B. Diffusion or extension over a given surface, usually with contact: **Sie breitet den Teppich über den Fußboden. Das Wasser geht über die Wiesen. Der Schweiß floß über sein Gesicht. Er war über den ganzen Leib wund, naß.** Figuratively: **Unglück kommt über mich. Er fiel über mich her** He pitched into me (abused me).

(*a*) Power, authority, supervision over a given domain, field: **Cäsar herrschte über die Römer. Bei Leipzig siegten die Verbündeten über die Franzosen. Der König über das Land, der Aufseher über die Arbeiter.**

(*b*) Mental activity directed in such a manner as to cover the matter in question, *on, about*: Dr. **Hermann Baumgart hat ein Buch über Goethes „Faust" geschrieben. Professor Schmidt liest** (lectures) **über Elektrizität. Ich spreche über** (at some length, while **von** *may* imply mere mention) **etwas. Er weiß manches darüber** He knows a good deal about it. Compare **von,** *c* in **229.** 2.

C. A passing over and beyond a certain limit: **Der Vogel flog über das Haus.** Figuratively: **Das geht über meinen Verstand, meine Begriffe, meinen Horizont,** &c. **Ich kann es nicht übers Herz bringen. Er lebt über seine Verhältnisse** (beyond his means).

(*a*) A passing by or thru, and then beyond, *via*: **Er reist über Hamburg nach London.**

(*b*) Excess in amount, weight, measure, number, &c., *over, above, more than, upwards of*: **Er gab über sein Vermögen** (more than his wealth justified him in giving). **Sie ist über alle Beschreibung schön. Es waren über fünfzig Personen da. Die Rede dauerte über eine Stunde. Das ist über meine Kraft. Das geht über meine Kräfte. Über'dies** (in the eighteenth century sometimes **über'dem,** after the analogy of **zu'dem**) moreover.

D. Of time:

(*a*) Represents a future event as to take place after the close of a given period of time: **Heute über acht Tage** (a week from to-day) **werde ich wieder kommen.** Thus **heute übers Jahr,** or without **heute, übers Jahr, heute über drei Wochen, übermorgen** day after to-morrow, &c. Formerly also with reference to past time, *after*: **Darnach vber drey jar | kam ich gen Jerusalem** (Gal. i. 18).

(*b*) Excess of time: **über** (more than) **eine Woche, über ein Jahr,** &c.

(*c*) In a few expressions, *duration*, the prep. standing in case of **Nacht** before, with other words after the noun: **Er blieb über Nacht. Den ganzen Sommer über war ich auf dem Lande.**

E. Cause: **Man soll sich nie über das Unglück eines Menschen freuen. Ich erstaunte über** (at) **diese plötzliche Erscheinung.** Earlier in the period we find also the dative here: **Vnd er . . . war betrübet vber jrem verstockten Hertzen** (Mark iii. 5).

Note. Also **an** w. dat. denotes cause. The difference between **an** and **über** in this respect is in general that **an** denotes, in accordance with its meaning of a close approach or contact, a closer and more intimate relation than **über**: **Er starb an einer Nervenkrankheit. Man lacht über einen guten Witz.**

UNTER. 1. With the dative:

A. A position below, under something: **Der Hund liegt unter dem Ofen. Der Hund fuhr bellend unter** (*from under*) **der Bank hervor.** Figuratively: **In der Kenntnis des Lateinischen stehe ich unter ihm.**

(*a*) Dependence, subordination: **Der Lehrling steht unter der Leitung des Meisters.**

(*b*) Below a certain degree, number, value, &c.: **Unter fünfzig Mark kann ich die Ware nicht geben. An manchen Orten blieb die Teilnahme unter der Erwartung. Ein Kind unter zehn Jahren. Das ist unter** (beneath) **aller Kritik.**

(*c*) Contemporaneity: **Manche schlafen unter der Predigt ein. Unter Karls V. Regierung war Antwerpen die lebendigste und herrlichste Stadt in der Welt.**

Note. Synonymous with **unter** is **während.** The latter usually expresses duration, while **unter** may denote also only a point of time: **Der Sakristan schlief während der Predigt,** but **Er ging unter der Predigt hinaus.**

(*d*) Very commonly used to add some attendant circumstance: **Der Kranke verschied unter** (in) **heftigen Schmerzen. Ich wollte ihn unter vier Augen sprechen. Ich lieh ihm das Geld unter** (on) **dieser Bedingung. Er tat es unter meinem Namen.**

(*e*) Cause, *under*: **Sie seufzten unter dem Drucke der Herrschaft. Seine Gesundheit hat unter der fortwährenden Aufregung gelitten.**

(*f*) Classification, *under the head of*, *by*: **Unter „Arm" lesen wir usw.** We find (in the dictionary) under the head of "arm," &c. **Was verstehen Sie unter diesem Ausdruck?** What do you mean by this expression?

B. Position in the midst of, *among* (see *Note* 2 under **zwischen**): **Ich saß unter den Zuschauern. Es steht viel Unkraut unter dem Weizen. Unter zwei Übeln muß man das kleinere wählen.**

C. Often used instead of a partitive gen.: **Unter** (of) **allen Getränken ist Wasser das gesündeste.** See also **141.** 2. *Note.*

2. With the accusative:

A. Movement to a point below or under something: **Der Hund legte sich unter die Bank. Wir setzten uns unter den Baum. Er wurde in der Schule unter** (in rank) **seinen Bruder gesetzt.**

(*a*) Change to a condition of dependence, subordination: **Unter dieses Joch wird man euch beugen. Sie stellten den Verbrecher unter die Aufsicht der Polizei.**

B. Movement toward a position in the midst of something, *among*: **Ich setzte mich unter die Zuschauer.**

(*a*) A belonging to a group: **Der Krieg gehört unter die größten Übel. Ich zähle ihn unter meine Freunde.**

(*b*) Distribution: **Der Wohltätige verteilt Geld unter die Armen.**

C. An interruption of an act: **„Du," sagte Georg unters Essen hinein, „muß dir was sagen,"** &c. (Anna Schieber's *Alle guten Geister*, p. 53).

3. With the genitive in **unter'dessen** *in the meantime, while*, and sometimes in a few expressions of time: **unter Essens** (Adelung) during the meal. **In der Wohnung war auch viel Besuch unter Tags** (Hauptmann's *Michael Kramer*, Act iv).

VOR. 1. With the dative:

(*a*) Position in front of, *in front of, before, in the sight of, at the siege of*: **Der Hund liegt vor der Haustür. Der Verbrecher erschien vor dem Richter. Vor Gott und der Welt strafbar** guilty in the sight of God and the world. **Er fiel vor Richmond.** Activity or motion in front of: **Er redete vor einer großen Versammlung. Sie haben ihn vor unserm Haus vorbeigetragen.**

(*b*) Surpassing in degree, rank, value, hence also precedence: **Sie war vor allen die Schönste. Er hat mich vor** (more than) **allen anderen beleidigt. Vor allen Dichtern gebührt ihm der Preis. Er hat vieles vor seinem Bruder voraus** He has many advantages over his brother.

(*c*) Applied to time, *before, ago, since, back, prior, ahead of*: **Er kam vor seinem Herrn an. Er kam vor mir, vor meiner Ankunft. Der Braten kam vor dem Gemüse. Ein Viertel vor 6 Uhr, vor einiger Zeit** some time ago, **vor nun zehn Jahren** now ten years since, **vor einigen Jahren** a few years back, **vor** (prior) **der Einführung der Gaslaternen. Moses lebte vor Christus. Du kommst vor** (ahead of) **der Zeit.**

(*d*) Reference to something which stands before one in such a manner or condition as to cause fright, horror, aversion, or from which one must defend or protect one's self: **Das Kind fürchtet sich** (is afraid of) **vor dem Hunde. Manche haben Ekel vor halbrohem Fleisch. Dem Feigen ist bange vor dem Tode. Er flieht vor** (from) **dem Feinde. Ich habe kein Geheimnis vor Ihnen. Nimm dich vor ihm in acht. Warme Kleider schützen vor Kälte. Ich warnte ihn vor dem Menschen.** See also **aus,** *f* in **229.** 2. Also awe or respect: **Achtung vor einem or etwas haben.**

(*e*) Cause in a number of set expressions, *for, on account of, with*: **Man kann vor Schmerz und vor Freude weinen. Das Herz schlug mir vor banger Erwartung. Er konnte vor Schmerz nicht schlafen. Er kommt vor Geschäften nicht zu sich selbst. Er sieht den Wald vor lauter Bäumen nicht. Er ist rot vor** (with) **Zorn.**

2. With the accusative to express motion toward a point or position before something, literally and figuratively: **Der Hund legt sich vor die Haustür. Er spannt die Pferde vor den Wagen. Man bringt die Sache vor den Richter. Komm mir nicht wieder vors Gesicht, vor die Augen. Er wirft seine Perlen vor die Säue. Er tritt vor den Riß** (breach). **Er sprach vor sich hin** He talked to himself. For **Schritt vor Schritt** see **für,** *b* in **230.**

ZWISCHEN with the dat. or acc. according as rest or movement toward is expressed, corresponding in meaning to English *between*: **Sie saß zwischen mir und ihrem Bruder. Er ist zwischen 20 bis 30 Jahren alt. Sie setzte sich zwischen mich und ihren Bruder.** When it is a question of movement or motion between objects on both sides, **zwischen** with the dat. is used, often in connection with some adverb as **hin, durch,** &c.: **Zwischen den Kirchenstühlen hin schritten sie wieder auf den Ausgang zu** (Fontane's *Vor dem Sturm*, IV, chap. xxv). **Und schnell und machtlos fällt der König des Gebirges** (i.e. **der Adler**) **zwischen dem Weg und dem Wald auf die grüne Matte** (Heer's *Der König der Bernina, II*).

Note 1. Also **unter** can be used of two instead of **zwischen,** if the noun is found in the plural in a collective sense including both parties, but never if two nouns are taken separately: **Es entstand ein Streit zwischen dem Manne und der Frau,** or **zwischen beiden Eheleuten,** or **unter den Eheleuten.**

Note 2. **Zwischen** does not mean exclusively *between two objects*, but may also refer to more than two. In this case, it differs from **unter** in that the latter indicates a confused mingling, a mass, while the former infers that the different objects in the group are homogeneous, and hence the introduction of a foreign object into their midst gives rise to the idea of a twofold division: **Ein Schwarm Spatzen stob mit erbostem, endlosem Gezwitscher auseinander, wie sie zwischen sie fuhr** (Ilse Frapan's *Mamsell Biene*). **Sein Blick streifte den jungen Gelehrten, der so vergnügt zwischen der ehrsamen Schneiderfamilie saß.** Also as in English to express the idea of *individual* relations between more than two: **Verkehr zwischen Nationen.**

CONJUNCTIONS.

Definition and Classification.

232. 1. A conjunction is a particle used to connect sentences or the elements of a sentence. Conjunctions are divided, as in English, into co-ordinating and subordinating.

2. Classification, however, as to their influence upon word-order in the sentence is a better method of grouping conjunctions for practical reasons. The particular word-order required by certain classes of conjunctions is in part explained by their origin and development. Originally a number of conjunctions were demonstrative pronouns or prepositional phrases containing a demonstrative pronoun, as explained in **240.** *a.* Many other conjunctions were adverbs. Certain adverbs not only performed their function of adverb within their own sentence, but also served to connect in thought the proposition in which they stood with the preceding or following. Thus many conjunctions still show traces of their adverbial nature in that like adverbs they have great freedom of position, as is illustrated in **234,** and also cause inverted word-order when they introduce the proposition in which they stand: **Wir waren eben vom Tische aufgestanden, da trat er in das Zimmer** We had just arisen from the table when he entered the room. Some adverbial conjunctions with this same freedom of position may or may not influence the word-order in the proposition in which they stand, as illustrated in **236.** While the adverbial conjunctions thus retain the freedom of position which they possessed as adverbs, the subordinating conjunctions have developed in course of time quite differently, and at present can only occupy the first place in the dependent clause and require the verb to stand at the end of the clause: **Ich muß gehen, weil ich Eile habe.** In contradistinction to adverbial co-ordinating conjunctions with their different manner of influencing word-order are the pure co-ordinating connectives, which influence in no way word-order, such as **und** and, **oder** or, **aber** but, &c.

Thus the position of the verb at the end of a subordinate clause introduced by a subordinating conjunction is imperative, while on the other hand co-ordinating conjunctions with regard to their influence upon the word-order are divided into three classes: pure co-ordinating, adverbial co-ordinating, and such as admit of a double construction, either influencing like adverbs the word-order, or leaving it undisturbed after the manner of pure co-ordinating conjunctions.

Pure Co-ordinating Conjunctions.

233. The conjunctions which connect sentences or parts of sentences of like rank and do not disturb the word-order are:

A. The pure conjunctions **aber** but, however, **a'llein** but, **denn** for, **ja** yes indeed, **nämlich** as, since, **oder** or, **sondern** but, **und** and; the following groups of words, all of which differ from the preceding pure conjunctions in that they do not usually connect independent sentences, each containing a verb, but only parts of the sentence of like rank: **wie, so'wie, ebenso wie, ebenso, wie auch** (all in a general way = **und,** with which they often alternate in the same sentence) *and, and also, and likewise, as well as*; the following combinations containing **als** or **wie**, now very common, tho new as coordinating conjunctions: **so'wohl — als (auch),** or **so'wohl — wie (auch)** *both — and,* **ebenso — wie** *both — and,* **wie — so** *both — and,* **nicht sowohl — als** (or **als vielmehr**) *not so much — as*; **beide — und,** or **beides — und** *both — and,* the former combination very common in early N.H.G., the latter replacing it in the sixteenth century but now itself little used; **beziehungsweise (bezw.), beziehentlich, respek'tive (resp.)** *or as the case may be,* **außer** (**225.** 2) *except,* **anstatt** (**225.** 2) *instead of,* **ausgenommen** *except,* earlier in the period also **ohne** (**225.** 2) *except.* Of these **wie** and **sowie** are in fact subordinating conjunctions, originally also **sowohl — als.** See *e* below. **Außer** sometimes connects two complete propositions without influencing the word-order. See **225.** 2. *a.* Examples:

Das Bild der Toten wich nicht aus meiner Seele, ja es steht noch heute vor mir. Zwischen Bozen, das stets eine zweifelhaft deutsche Stadt war, und Trient liegt das Gebiet, wo deutsche und italienische Sprache wie Nationalität sich abgrenzen und mischen. Auf den südlichen Halbinseln sowie in Süd-Frankreich blüht die Zucht der Esel und Maultiere. Im allgemeinen

ist das Klima (Chinas) **ein binnenländisches, durch die östliche Lage des Landes stark beeinflußt: heiße Sommer und kalte Winter, ebenso in den nördlichsten wie in den südlichsten Gegenden des Reiches. Sowohl sein Vater als auch seine Mutter kamen. Hier war es ziemlich ruhig sowohl bei Tage wie bei Nacht** (Rodenberg). **Dadurch** (i.e. its position) **ist München wie der Hauptsitz für die Erzeugung des Nationalgetränks so der große Getreidemarkt Bayerns geworden. Nicht sowohl die schlechte Finanzverwaltung als vielmehr die zahlreichen Kriege haben das Land mit dieser Schuldenlast beschwert. Die Artillerie und Kavallerie muß mit ihren Kanonen bezw.** (beziehungsweise) **Pferden gut umzugehen wissen** The artillery and cavalry must know how to handle well their cannons or horses as the case may be. **Alle rauchten, ausgenommen du** (but with different word-order: **dich** [absolute acc.] **ausgenommen). Ich sage es keinem Menschen, ausgenommen dir.**

a. Usually **und** connects two words, or, if there are a number, is placed before the last one, just as in English. Sometimes it is omitted and replaced by -, when two names are to be associated with one work or undertaking, either as co-workers or to represent one as the original worker and the other as the one who has carried it on after the author's death: **kritische Ausgabe von Lachmann-Muncker, der Denkmalsentwurf von Schmitz-Geiger,** &c. In contrast to the suppression of **und** here is the liberal use often made of it for purposes of style, especially to call attention to different activities separately in order to describe the situation in detail, as in **Und es wallet und siedet und brauset und zischt** (Schiller's *Taucher*), just as on the other hand the **und** is omitted altogether to indicate rapidity of action: **Alles rennet, rettet, flüchtet usw.** (id., *Die Glocke*).

b. The three adversatives **aber, allein, sondern** differ from each other in meaning. **Sondern** is only used after a negative, and introduces a contradictory statement, while **aber,** which is used after either an affirmative or negative proposition, concedes the statement of the first proposition, and introduces a limitation or a contrast: **Er ist nicht reich, sondern arm** He is not rich, but poor. **Er war zwar nicht krank, aber doch nicht dazu aufgelegt** He was to be sure not sick, but still he did not feel like it. **Er ist arm, aber ehrlich** He is poor, but honest. **Aber** and **allein** have the same general meaning, but the latter is much less used, hence more forcible in making a contrasting statement: **Ich war bei ihm, allein ich traf ihn nicht an** I was at his house, but did not find him at home. **Aber** has also a broader meaning than **allein;** the latter always introduces a limitation or a sharp contrast to the preceding proposition, while the former may also introduce something different from the preceding proposition without limiting it: **Er war ein großer Feldherr, allein er besaß nicht die Gabe umfassender Berechnung** He was a great general, but yet he did not possess the gift of comprehensive calculation. **Ich vertraute so fest auf ihn, allein ich sah mich bitter getäuscht. Klein aber mein** It is small, but it is mine. **Abel war ein Hirt, Kain aber ein Ackermann** Abel was a shepherd, Cain was a husbandman. **Aber** is also often (especially in the Bible) used without expressing any especial emphasis or contrast, merely to take up in a new sentence the thread of the story: **Der Teuffel aber sprach zu jm (ihm)**—Luke iv. 3.

c. **Nämlich** does not always introduce the proposition, but stands even more frequently after the verb, and **aber** has a still greater freedom of position, as it may be introduced at almost any point without influencing the word-order: **Ich konnte ihn nicht sprechen, er war nämlich krank** I could not see him as he was sick. **Ich hoffte es; ich fand mich aber getäuscht** I had hope, but I found myself disappointed.

d. Word-order after **und.** The proposition following **und** usually has normal order, sometimes, however, we find the question order as a survival of an older construction which allowed a verb to introduce a proposition if it was to be emphasized, lay nearer in thought, or if the statement as a whole was to be put in a more lively manner, or if the verb came to the front by the removal of the subject towards the end of the proposition for the sake of emphasis. See **251.** II. B. *b*.

e. The conjunctions **wie, sowie, sowohl als** (sub. conjunc. in Psalms xlix. 11), now used so frequently to connect, like **und,** two parts of a sentence of like rank, are in fact subordinating conjunctions, as appears occasionally when they stand in a clause containing a verb, in which case, as after genuine subordinating conjunctions, the verb stands at the end of the clause: **Für geheiligt galt die Person des Königs, wie (= und) ihm auch priesterliche Rechte beiwohnten.** The verb may be understood, in which case the contracted phrase is still treated as a subordinate clause, and a following principal proposition has inverted order: **Sowie die Schweiz [einmal zum Deutschen Reiche gehörte] gehörten auch die Niederlande zum Deutschen Reiche.**

f. Often several conjunctions are used together with the combined force of them all in a way that is difficult to render exactly into English. Especially is this true of **oder aber,** or **oder aber vielmehr** *or on the other hand,* making more emphatic the second member of the disjunctive phrase: **Der Angeredete wußte eine Stunde lang nicht, ob diese wunderlichen, wenn auch sehr höflich vorgebrachten Worte wirklich eine Artigkeit oder aber vielmehr die spöttische Einleitung zu einer unzeitgemäßen Herausforderung sein sollten** (Hopfen).

g. The co-ordinating conjunction **denn** *for* must be carefully distinguished from the subordinating **da** or **weil** *as, because*: **Er schreibt nicht, denn er kann nicht** *He doesn't write, for he doesn't know how to write.* Here the first proposition is an independent statement given for its own sake. The second proposition is an additional independent statement given by way of explanation. On the other hand, in **Er schreibt nicht, da er mir zürnt** *He doesn't write as he is angry at me,* the first proposition is represented as the result of the causal clause introduced by **da. Nämlich** *as, for,* adding an explanation for the preceding act or fact, indicates a looser connection than **denn,** but closely resembles it in meaning tho it is much less common: **Meine**

Zeit wird mit allerhand in Anspruch genommen, ich mache mir nämlich fast alle meine Kleider und Sachen.

Instead of **denn** we often find **ja** and **doch** in the position after the verb, the former with the force of English *you know*, the latter to add adversative force indicating that the reason is given to meet in advance some possible objection: **Er konnte uns helfen, er hat ja die Mittel. Ich habe alles gestanden, ich konnte doch keinen Meineid schwören.** Also so before an adverb often has the same force as **denn: Alles hat geklatscht, so gut hat er gesungen.** Instead of **denn** we sometimes find a principal proposition with question order. See **287.** B. **(7)**.

B. A number of other conjunctions apparently like pure connectives introduce a proposition or connect parts of a sentence without disturbing the word-order:

a. When adverbial conjunctions connect different subjects of one and the same verb or different parts of the sentence of like rank they do not disturb the word-order, but when there is more than one verb, and they thus connect different propositions, they have the full force of adverbial conjunctions: **Weder er noch ich war da** *Neither he nor I was there*, but **Der Neidische ist weder froh, noch gönnt er andern eine Freude.**

b. Often even when there are two distinct propositions with different verbs, the adverbial conjunctions may introduce a proposition or follow the subject without causing inversion, if it is the subjects that are emphasized or contrasted, for here as elsewhere the emphatic word takes the first place in the proposition: **Er billigte dein Verfahren nicht; auch dein Vater billigte es nicht** *He did not approve of your proceeding; also your father did not approve of it*, but when the emphasis rests upon the predicate, inversion takes place: **Er billigte dein Verfahren nicht, auch wollte er dich warnen** *He did not approve of your proceeding, also he desired to warn you.* **Selbst** *even* always lays the emphasis upon the subject or a modifier of the subject when it precedes the verb, and hence in spite of its adverbial nature never causes inversion: **Selbst die Pflanze wendet sich zum Lichte.**

C. The following explanatory or intensifying conjunctions connecting parts of a sentence do not influence the word-order of the proposition: **als**, or more commonly **wie** *as, such as*, **namentlich** or also *particularly*, **nämlich** *namely, to wit*, **selbst** *even*, **und zwar** explaining a preceding utterance more definitely, specifically, **zum Beispiel (z. B.)** *for example*, **das heißt (d. h.)** or **das ist (d. i.)** *that is*, **geschweige** (first pers. sing. pres. tense, the subject **ich** being understood) **denn** or simply **geschweige** *to say nothing about*. Exs.: **Aus der Schweiz werden einzelne Produkte in bedeutender Menge ausgeführt, wie (or als) Vieh, Käse u(nd) s(o) w(eiter). Der Kuckuck legt andern Vögeln, namentlich kleineren, selbst dem Zaunkönig, sein Ei ins Nest. Eine großartig entwickelte Fabrikation in Lederwaren (also Schuhen, Handschuhen usw.) liefert für Frankreich einen Gewinnüberschuß, der den Wert der Einfuhr übersteigt. Schicken Sie mir 2 Paar Handschuhe, nämlich 1 Paar lederne und 1 Paar seidene. Sie haben nur ein Kind, und zwar einen Sohn. Die Medizin wirkte kaum lindernd, geschweige denn befriedigend. Das hält ein jüngerer Mann nicht aus, geschweige ein alter.**

a. Sometimes **als** is followed by the particularizing adv. **da** and also by a verb, all three together containing the meaning *such as*: **„Viktualien?" fragte Wally** (name) **verblüfft. „Nun ja, eßbare Gegenstände," erklärte Suse** (name) **lachend, „als da sind: Kaffee, Mehl, Reis, Grütze, Schmalz."**

Adverbial Co-ordinating Conjunctions.

234. Adverbial conjunctions (except those enumerated in **236**), like true adverbs, generally cause inversion when they introduce the proposition, and have also in large part the freedom of position of adverbs. Hence these conjunctions can occupy almost any position in the proposition except the place between the subject and the verb: **Er ist reich, daher braucht er** (or **er braucht daher**) **solche Ausgaben nicht zu scheuen.** If some other modifier of the verb is for emphasis placed at the beginning of the proposition in which the conjunction stands, the conjunction *must* stand in some position after the verb and subject: **Diesen Menschen, der ich in Wirklichkeit bin, kennst du weder, noch liebst du ihn** (R. Huch's *Vita somnium breve*, I, p. 8).

235. *Classification.* Many adverbs with quite different meanings serve to connect sentences, thus indicating a variety of relations. They can be roughly divided into eight classes:

A. Copulative:

a. Connecting propositions of equal value: **auch**, also, **'außerdēm** or **außer'dēm** moreover, besides, apart from this, independent of this, **davon abgesehen** apart from this, independent of this, **gleichfalls, ebenfalls, des'gleichen** likewise, **zu'dem** moreover, **über'dies** furthermore, **nicht — noch**, or more commonly **weder — noch** neither — nor, or in older German **weder — oder**, also earlier in the period **weder — weder** and even **noch — noch**, the oldest of the correlative forms: **Er hat eine reiche Frau; außerdem hat er selbst ein großes Vermögen.** In O.H.G. **weder** appears as ne weder *not either one of the two*, so that the old negative *ne* has dropped out here as explained in **145.** *g. Note* 2. For another case of the survival of the old form **weder** see **239. 7.**

Note. The conjunction **auch** does not only correspond to English *also*, but has developed quite a rich store of adverbial and conjunctional meanings, the more idiomatic of which are here given:—**(1)** It often has the force of *too*, and together with a negative the force of *nor*: **ich auch** *I too*, **ich auch nicht** *nor I*. **(2)** Often = *even:* **Auch ein Kind**

muß das einsehen. Er hat auch nicht (or **nicht ein'mal**) **ein Wort davon gesprochen.** Often in connection with **nur: Er hat es nicht auch nur** (or **nicht ein'mal**) **erwähnt.** (**3**) Often in concessive clauses: **Wenn er auch nicht reich ist, or ist er auch nicht reich, or mag er auch nicht reich sein, hat er doch zu leben.** (**4**) It adds generalizing force to pronouns and adverbs: **Wer er auch sei** *whoever he may be,* **wo es auch sei** wheresoever it may be. (**5**) It introduces or stands within a proposition to represent something as naturally following out of the given or implied circumstance: **Die Nachricht ist seltsam, auch glaubt niemand daran** The report is very strange, and indeed no one believes it. **Ich will dir verzeihen, nur mußt du es auch nicht wieder tun** I will forgive you this time, but mind you do not do it again. **Du bist auch ein guter Junge** There's a good boy, *or* If you do that you'll be a real good boy. **Ich schenke dir auch einen Zehnpfenniger** If you do that I'll give you ten pfennigs. **Jetzt weiß ich auch, wo du gestern warst** Now I know (since I've found this out) where you were yesterday. (**6**) It is often used to confirm a preceding statement or to indicate the realization of the thought or intention expressed therein: (A) **Er sieht sehr gutmütig aus.** (B) **Das ist er auch.** (A) He looks very good-natured. (B) And so he is.—(A) **Er ist gar nicht dumm.** (B) **Das habe ich auch nicht gesagt, nur daß er höchst nachlässig ist** (A) He is not at all stupid. (B) I did not at all mean to say that he is, only that he is very careless. **Endlich versuchte ich es, und es gelang mir auch.** Often used ironically where the aim has not been realized at all: **Das ist mir auch ein Lehrer!** He's a fine teacher! **Jetzt ist es auch gerade Zeit dazu!** This is a pretty time for such things! (**7**) It stands after the verb in a proposition giving the reason for a preceding proposition: **Dieser Ring ist sehr schön. Er kostet auch viel** *This ring is very beautiful. It ought to be, it cost a good round sum.* Hence it is often used in reproaches, as the reproach gives the reason for the discontent felt: **Du kannst** (**aber**) **auch nie den Mund halten** It's too provoking, you never can keep your mouth shut. (**8**) It is often used in questions to indicate doubt as to whether the actual reality is in harmony or will harmonize with somebody's conception of it: **Hast du auch wohl bedacht, was du mir rätst?** Are you sure you have considered well what you advise me? **Wirst du es auch tun?** Will you be sure to do it? **Haben Sie aber auch selbst genug?** Are you sure you have enough for yourself? I'm afraid I'm robbing you.

b. The second proposition more emphatic or intensive than the first: **namentlich** particularly, **besonders** especially.

c. Ordinal conjunctions: **erst** first, **erstens** or **erstlich** in the first place, **zweitens** secondly, &c. **so'dann** in the next place, **dann** then, **so** (after a negative) then, **ferner** furthermore, **da'rauf** thereupon, **zu'letzt** at last, **endlich** finally, **bald — bald** now — now: **Erst besinn's, dann beginn's. Es dauerte nicht lange, so kam er. Es wird kein Vierteljahr dauern, so ist die Marie seine Frau. Kaum warst du weg, so kam er zurück.**

The ordinal conjunctions formed from numerals, as **erstens** or **erstlich, zweitens,** &c., are sometimes followed by a pause, and in print are then cut off by a comma, in which case they do not cause inversion: **Erstlich, Jesus löste mit scharfem Schnitte die Verbindung der Ethik mit dem äußeren Kultus und den technisch-religiösen Übungen . . . Zweitens, er geht überall in den sittlichen Fragen auf die Wurzel, d. h. auf die Gesinnung zurück** (Harnack's *Das Wesen des Christentums,* vierte Vorlesung).

d. Partitive conjunctions: **teils — teils** partly — partly, **einesteils — andernteils,** or **einerseits — ander(er)seits** on the one hand — on the other hand: **Reisen ist immer nützlich; einerseits bereichert man dadurch seine Kenntnisse, anderseits stärkt es den Körper und erheitert das Gemüt.**

B. Adversative: (restricting or limiting the contents of the previous proposition) **hin'gegen, 'dagegen** or **da'gegen,** and **'dahingegen** or **dahin'gegen** on the contrary, **übrigens** moreover, **gleich'wohl** or **dennoch** yet, however, notwithstanding, nevertheless, **'trotzdem** or **trotz'dem** in spite of that, **dessenunge'achtet** notwithstanding, **nichtsdesto'weniger** nevertheless; (the second sentence excluding the contents of the first) **sonst, andernfalls** otherwise, **viel'mehr** but rather. Exs.: **Cäsar wurde gewarnt, trotzdem ging er in die Sitzung des Senats. Afrika ist nicht überall mit Wüsten bedeckt, vielmehr zeigt es in vielen Gegenden eine außerordentliche Fruchtbarkeit.**

C. Illative, introducing an inference, conclusion, consequence, result: **da'rum** or **'dārum** for that reason, **deshalb** or **deswegen** (and earlier in the period **derhalb, derhalben** [Romans xvi. 19], **derohalben, derwegen, derowegen**) on that account, **dann** then, **nun** now, consequently, **infolge'dessen** in consequence, consequently, **da'her** hence, **so** so, and the conjunctions introducing an inference or conclusion, with the general meaning of *therefore, consequently* such as **mit'hin, so'mit, folglich, dēm'nāch** or **'dēmnāch, so'nāch** or **'sōnāch: In dem Koffer sind Bücher, darum ist er so schwer. Er ist reich, daher braucht er solche Ausgaben nicht zu scheuen. Er will uns nicht begleiten, so gehen wir ohne ihn. Du bist ein Mensch, folglich bist du sterblich. Ich war krank, folglich konnte ich nicht selbst kommen.** Instead of **darum** or **daher** we sometimes find a principal proposition with question order. See **287.** B. (**7**).

D. Causal: **ja, doch, so** with the general force of **denn** *for,* as illustrated in **233.** A. *g.* The idea of cause or reason is also found in the **auch** described in A. *a. Note* (**7**) above.

E. Conjunctions of time and place: **da** just then, **unter'dessen** in the meantime, &c.; **da, dort, hier,** &c.: **Der Weg macht eine Biegung, da übersieht man die ganze Gegend.**

F. Manner: **so: Die Sonne siehst du nur durch Sonnenlicht, so schaust du Gott durch Gott.**

G. Degree: **so, um so** or **desto, in'sofern,** &c.: **Der Krieg wurde rasch entschieden, so rasch hatte man es gar nicht erwartet. Das Leben ist kurz, um so sorgfältiger muß man es nützen. Es kann uns mehr oder weniger Kampf kosten, tugendhaft zu sein; insofern gibt es Grade der Moralität.**

H. Conclusion of a conditional sentence: **dann, so: Er kommt vielleicht; dann gehe ich mit ihm. Willst du mitgehen, so komme rasch!**

Co-ordinating Conjunctions with a Double Construction.

236. The following adverbial conjunctions introduce a proposition like the pure co-ordinating class without influencing the word-order, or, more commonly, may influence the word-order like adverbial conjunctions, and also like adverbs either introduce the proposition or follow the verb: **also** therefore, so, then, well then; **nur** or **bloß** only; **im Gegenteil** on the contrary; **doch, jedoch, in'dessen** however, yet; **ent'weder** (from older eindeweder *either one of two*; compare **235.** A. *a*) either; **so'gar** (now usually after the verb) even; **nun** well; **zwar** I admit; **vollends** added to this, to crown all (introducing a climax): **Es regnet, also gehe ich nicht aus,** or **ich gehe also nicht aus. Also, 'dărauf geht's hinaus?** So, that's the game, is it? **Also Sie kommen?** So you'll come? **Es ist also keine Hoffnung?** There's no hope then? **Es bleibt also dabei!** That's settled then! **Der ist groß und stark, wie nur einer sein soll, bloß er hat was Feineres und ist nicht so'n Untier, wie sein Großvater Grobschmied** (H. Hoffmann's *Wider den Kurfürsten,* chap. 1); or more commonly **Der ist groß und stark, wie nur einer sein soll, bloß** (or **nur**) **hat er,** &c.; or **er hat bloß** (or **nur**), &c. **Er ist reich, doch** (or **jedoch,** or **indessen**) **ich möchte nicht mit ihm tauschen;** or more commonly **doch möchte ich nicht,** or **ich möchte doch nicht mit ihm tauschen;** but for the sake of having the emphatic word in the first place the inverted order is avoided: **Doch seinem Vater, nicht ihm, kommt die Entscheidung zu** rather than **Doch kommt seinem Vater usw. Entweder tust du es jetzt, oder ich rufe deinen Bruder;** or **Entweder du tust es jetzt, oder ich rufe deinen Bruder;** but always without inversion when the conjunction connects different subjects of one and the same verb, or when the subjects are emphasized: **Entweder er oder sein Bruder muß zahlen** and **Entweder er geht, oder ich gehe. Wir sehen uns nicht nur gelitten, sogar wir sehen uns hochgeehrt** (Goethe), now **wir sehen uns sogar hochgeehrt. Nun** (pause), **ich will mirs überlegen,** or **Nun will ich mirs überlegen. Zwar, ich weiß es nicht bestimmt,** or **Zwar weiß ich es nicht bestimmt.**

a. The conjunction **nur** (or **bloß**) also quite commonly takes the form **nur daß** (or **bloß daß**), and then of course requires the verb to stand at the end of the clause: **Und doch weiß man von eben diesem furchtsamen Knaben etliche Schelmenstreiche zu berichten, die Heldentaten überraschend ähnlich sahen: nur daß eine Heldentat Sinn haben soll, und Ihre Streiche hatten keinen** (H. Hoffmann's *Wider den Kurfürsten,* chap. x).

b. Aside from the question of the influence upon the word-order there is in most cases little difference in the use of the adversative co-ordinating conjunctions **aber** and **doch.** Of these **doch** has the widest use, as it has more adverbial nature, and in its capacity of adverb can be employed when **aber** is not used, as for instance to put a principal proposition in contrast to a subordinate clause: **Wiewohl ich ihn oft gewarnt habe, ist er doch** (or **dennoch** or **trotzdem,** but not **aber**) **wieder hingegangen.**

c. **Doch** follows, or more commonly precedes, the verb, but when it introduces a thought which *seemingly* stands in conflict with the preceding, it *must* follow it: (A) **Mein Vater ist schwer krank.** (B) **Er war doch gestern noch ganz munter.**

Subordinating Conjunctions.

237. The list of the subordinating conjunctions is given in **238.** Their origin is discussed in **240.** *a.*

1. *Order of Words.* The subordinating conjunctions, including the relative and interrogative pronouns and relative and interrogative adverbs, now require the verb or in a compound tense the personal part of the verb to stand at the end of the subordinate clause: **Er kann nicht gut sehen, weil er alt ist. Es lebte einmal ein König, der kein Kind hatte** (see F below and **154.** *Note*).

The following exceptions occur:

A. There are a number of common cases where subordinate clauses are not introduced by subordinating conjunctions, and consequently do not have the word-order of the subordinate clause:

a. In substantive clauses **daß** may be dropped, especially in colloquial language, in which case the word-order is *normal,* or, if some other word than the subject introduces the subordinate clause, *inverted:* **Ich glaube, daß Sie die Wahrheit sprechen,** or **Ich glaube, Sie sprechen die Wahrheit.**

There is a decided tendency to drop the conjunctions **daß** and **wie** after they have been used once and to return to the normal word-order: **Der Apotheker unterrichtete Frau Rat Kirsten, daß ein alter seltener Wein in so staubigen und schimmeligen Flaschen auf den Tisch kommen müsse; das sei für den Kenner das Feinste** (H. Böhlau's *Ratsmädelgeschichten,* p. 14).

b. In a conditional or a concessive clause that precedes the principal proposition **wenn** *if, tho,* may be dropped, in which case the word-order is that of a question: **Wenn er kommt, so**

sehe ich ihn, or **Kommt er, so sehe ich ihn. Wenn auch die alten Bücher nicht zur Hand sind,** or **Sind auch die alten Bücher nicht zur Hand, sie sind in unsere Herzen eingeschrieben.**

Note 1. If there are two or more subordinate clauses connected by **und** or **oder,** the first of which is introduced by **wenn,** or if **wenn** is dropped and the question order takes place, the clauses after the first one, instead of taking the regular subordinate or question order, often have the word-order of a principal proposition: **Wenn er dann nach Hause kam** or **Kam er dann nach Hause, und die Frau hatte das Mittagessen nicht fertig** (instead of **die Frau das Mittagessen nicht fertig hatte** or **hatte die Frau das Mittagessen nicht fertig**), **so schalt er sie.**

Note 2. Such subordinate clauses with the question order now have the same intonation as other subordinate clauses in the same position, but originally they were often independent questions, as can be seen in the following passage from Luther, who places an interrogation point where the revised editions have a comma: **Ist jemand gutes muts? der singe Psalmen. Ist jemand Kranck? der ruffe zu sich die Eltesten von der Gemeine** (James v. 13, 14). On the other hand, in many cases a conditional clause of this form was originally an independent sentence expressing a wish: **Kämest du** (originally **Kämest du!** O that you would come!), **ich würde mich freuen.** As conditional clauses have often developed into concessive we find this form also in concessive clauses: **Käme er nun nach so langer Vernachlässigung, es würde mich nicht freuen.**

c. In the combinations **als wenn** or **als ob** *as if,* **wenn** and **ob** may be dropped, in which case, as in a conditional clause, the question order results: **Er sieht aus, als wenn er reich wäre** or **als wäre er reich** He looks as if he were rich. See also **239.** 1. *e. Note.*

d. In concessive clauses if the volitive subjunctive (**168.** I. 2. A) of the verb can be used the conjunction can be dropped, in which case either the normal or the question-order is found: **Obschon es tausend Leben kostet, rette ich dich,** or **Es koste tausend Leben, ich rette dich,** or **Koste es tausend Leben, ich rette dich.** Instead of the volitive subjunctive we often find the indicative of **mögen** here with the same word-order and same force: **Er mag (auch** or **gleich) zürnen,** or more commonly **Mag er (auch** or **gleich) zürnen, ich frage nichts danach.**

e. To emphasize the point of time of an action the conjunctions **wenn** or **als** *when* may be dropped, and the adverbs **kaum** *scarcely,* **schon** *already,* or **noch** *still* substituted in their stead, followed by inverted order: **Als Sie fort waren,** or **Kaum waren Sie fort, so trat er ins Zimmer. Noch harrte im heimlichen Dämmerlicht die Welt dem Morgen entgegen; noch erwachte die Erde vom Schlummer nicht: da begann sich's im Tale zu regen. An dem Seile schon zieht man den Freund empor, | da zertrennt er gewaltig den dichten Chor** When they had begun to draw up the friend (Phintias) to crucify him, behold there he (Damon) came pushing his way with all his might thru the throng. See **275.** *a.*

f. In the set expressions **es sei** (or **wäre**) **denn** *unless,* lit. *if it be (were) not,* or kindred expressions, as **er (sie, es) müßte denn** *unless he (she, it) should,* each of which is seemingly a negative conditional clause in force, the clause is not introduced by a conjunction at all, and the normal word-order is used. For fuller explanation of the construction see **168.** II. E. *a. Note.*

B. *Personal Part of the Verb Still Often before Participle and Infinitive.* The personal part of the verb often, in accordance with the older freedom of withdrawing the verb somewhat from the end as described in *a. Note,* stands before an infinitive, or participle, or their modifiers, instead of standing at the end of the subordinate clause, especially in the following cases:

a. In clauses where the perf. part. assumes the form of the infin.: **Ich weiß, daß er es hat tun können.** This order is quite fixed as the incongruity of a finite form of **haben** standing here after an infinitive form is so great that no one would ever think of placing it there. Hence it has become quite common to make use of the older freedom of withdrawing the auxiliary somewhat from the end as described in the *Note* below. This older freedom has been best preserved in this category, but as it is gradually becoming less and less used elsewhere it is slowly losing its influence also here. When, however, one feels inclined to place the auxiliary at the end it becomes necessary for the participle to assume participial form: **Überdies ist jener Beruf** (i.e. photography) **ein Sammler und rettender Einfänger von vielen Geistern, die einstmals höher fliegen gewollt hatten** (R. H. Bartsch's *Die Haindlkinder,* p. 128). Compare **178.** 2. B. *a. Note* 1.

Note. In M.H.G. and early N.H.G. the auxiliary containing the personal part of the verb often stood before the perfect participle or the infinitive to which it belonged. This removal of the weakly stressed auxiliary from the end resulted from the desire to put into the emphatic end position a more important word. According to **50.** A. 3. *b* and **284.** I. 3. *a* a simple tense in a subordinate clause stands at the end and is always stressed, i.e. is never entirely without stress. This stress with accented verb at the end is thus characteristic of a subordinate clause with the verb in a simple tense: When in M.H.G. and early N.H.G. an auxiliary was used in connection with the verb it was usually placed at the end in accordance with general usage which required the personal part of the verb to stand in the final position in the subordinate clause. The weak stress of the auxiliary, however, was often felt as incongruous when emphasis was to be conveyed as emphasis was associated with the close of the subordinate clause. Hence the auxiliary was often given an earlier position in the sentence to make way for the more heavily stressed participle or infinitive, or the stressed participle or infinitive preceded by a still more heavily stressed predicate word: **SJe** (sie) **brachten auch junge Kindlin zu jm** (ihm), **das** (daß) **er sie solt ánrüren** (Luke xviii. 15). **Ich sage euch aber | das** (daß) **auch Salomon | in aller seiner Herrlichkeit nicht ist bekleidet gewèsen | als der eines** (Luke xii. 27). Similarly the weakly stressed copula **sein** was often withdrawn from the end to make way for a strongly stressed predicate: **Hütet euch fur** (= vor) **dem Sawerteig der Phariseer | welchs ist die Heucheléi** (Luke xii. 1).

Another way to prevent this conflict between form and stress was to omit the tense auxiliary, which on account of its weak stress and lack of logical importance easily dropped out without attracting much attention. The suppression of the tense auxiliary was greatly facilitated by the fact that in the abridged participial form the auxiliary was regularly omitted, as explained in **183.** 2. C. *c,* and *d.* See also **190.** 1. A. *b.* (**1**).

Both of these constructions have been almost destroyed by a mere formal principle. In the last two centuries the general tendency to place the personal part of the verb, i.e. here the auxiliary, at the end of the clause has become so strong that it now usually prevails without regard to the laws of stress. The result of this long conflict between form and stress is the development in the subordinate clause of a new end-stress (**215.** II. 1. A, 3rd par.), a strong stress followed by a weaker one: **Der Mann, der das tún kànn.**

b. To avoid two similar forms of **werden** from coming together: **Ich bezweifle, daß diese Früchte je werden bei uns reif werden.**

c. Often when two or more uninflected verbal forms (infin. and perf. part.) come together at the end of the clause, the personal part of the verb may precede the uninflected verbal forms in order to prevent the heaping up of unaccented words at the end of the clause, but it is becoming ever more common to disregard the stress and follow the formal rule for word-order which requires the personal part of the verb to stand at the end: **Kein Abgrund des Wehes, dem nicht ein Laut wäre gewídmet gewèsen** (Goethe) or more commonly **gewidmet gewesen wäre.** In this category the old freedom of withdrawing the personal part of the verb somewhat from the end is most common before two infinitive forms: **So unzweifelhaft es immer Kämpfe wird gében mûssen, so sicher ist es oft die Aufgabe der Politik, sie zu mildern.** The position of the personal part of the verb at the end is not so common here as elsewhere, but this usage will doubtless become established: **Daß er** (Anton Schönbach), **ehe er an die Untersuchung über die Entstehung und den Zusammenhang der älteren Predigtsammlungen geht, sogar erst noch einen dritten Band erscheinen lassen wird** (Fedor Bech in *Zeitschrift für deutsche Philologie,* 1890, vol. XXII, p. 115). **Einem friedlichen Zeitalter, in welchem es** (**Bulgarien**) **das, was es mit blutigen Opfern erworben hat, ausnützen und zur Entwickelung der bulgarischen Volkswirtschaft verwenden können wird** (*Neue Freie Presse,* Sept. 26, 1915).

C. In case the predicate or a word in the predicate is modified by a clause or an infin. with **zu,** the personal part of the verb usually stands before the clause, or the infin. and its modifiers, or predicate complement: **Ich bemerkte, daß sie nicht gleich wußten, was sie tun sollten. Als ich am nächsten Abend mich anschickte, zu ihr zu gehen, war das Wetter trüb und stürmisch geworden. Gute Kinder, die sich mit Planen** (now usually **Plänen**) **und Aussichten beschäftigten, dich habhaft zu werden** (Goethe). In short clauses, however, it is often better to place the personal part of the verb at the end of the clause in case the predicate verb is modified by a short infinitive phrase, especially wherever the verb and the dependent infinitive stand in a close idiomatic relation to each other: **neulich als ich im Keller zu tun gehabt habe; bevor sie weiter zu sprechen vermochte; da in letzter Zeit eine Häufung dieser Mißhandlungen zu verzeichnen war.** Likewise if there is in the dependent infinitive phrase a relative that must introduce the clause: **Als jetzt der Name genannt worden war, den zu hören er lange gefürchtet hatte.**

D. Earlier in the period there was more freedom in the word-order, so that we often find some important modifier of the verb at the end of the clause instead of the verb itself, as illustrated and explained in B. *a. Note.* Altho the position of the verb at the end of the clause has in general become stereotyped, the older freedom is preserved in poetry, and asserts itself not infrequently in vigorous prose for the sake of especial emphasis: **Als er's wog in freier Hand, | das Schwert er viel zu schwer erfand** (Uhland). **Ins Gesicht will ich's ihnen sagen, was ich denke von dir und euch und eurer ganzen bürgerlichen Gesittung** (Sudermann's *Heimat,* 3, 14). In colloquial language also unimportant modifiers sometimes follow the verb.

This irregular feature which is employed for the sake of meter or emphasis in literary or colloquial German is a regular feature in the German spoken by Jews who have not eradicated all traces of Hebrew influence from their language: **Ob ich bin der Mann, oder ob es ist ein anderer; es ist doch zu machen, daß man kauft von jedem Menschen, was er hat** (Veitel Itzig in Freytag's *Soll und Haben,* chap. i). This order is also found in the German of Poles, Frenchmen, Englishmen, and other foreigners: **Weil ich warnen will vor dem reißenden Wolf im Schafspelz, welcher umherzieht und unschuldige Herzen will verführen** (the Polish chaplain in Halbe's *Jugend,* p. 96). Compare also the German of Riccaut in Lessing's *Minna von Barnhelm,* 4, 2.

E. When two subordinate clauses have an auxiliary in common it usually stands in the second clause and is understood in the preceding one: **Seine Unruhe vermehrte sich, da seine Gefühle nicht mehr von den sanften Tönen genährt und gelindert wurden.** Sometimes in easy colloquial language the auxiliary is found with the first clause, and is understood with the following one: **Ich glaube, wenn wir uns heute mal wieder hinsetzen würden und den Faust zusammen lesen, wir würden wieder wie junge Studenten werden** (Hirschfeld's *Der junge Goldner,* p. 62).

F. The relative pronoun **der** has arisen from the demonstrative **der,** from which it at present differs little except in requiring the verb at the end of the clause, and in the familiar language of every day life the demon. is still used with normal order in a descriptive (**271.** II. 7) clause, where in the literary language we should expect the relative with the word-order of the dependent clause: **Es lebte einmal ein kleiner Knabe, der hieß Hänschen. Es war einmal ein Kaiser, der hatte ein großes Land.** For the origin of the relative construction see **154.** *Note.*

2. *Position.* Subordinating conjunctions always introduce the dependent clause with the one exception that a prep. may stand before a dependent relative or interrogative pronoun: **Das Mädchen ging an einen Spiegel, in dem es sich betrachtete.**

238. *Classification of Subordinating Conjunctions.* Subordinating conjunctions, which join subordinate to principal propositions, may be divided into classes as follows:

1. Those which introduce *substantive clauses.* They are made up of the following groups of words (for illustrative sentences, see **269. 270, 272**):

a. The relative and interrogative pronouns: **wer, was; der** (**130.** 2. *b*; **151.** 3. C, D), **die, das; welcher, -e, -es** (**151.** 3. C, D).

b. A prep. with its dependent relative or interrogative pronoun: **mit wem, mit welchem,** &c.

c. The relative and interrogative adverbs: **da** (early N.H.G.; Matthew viii. 20) where, **wo** where, **wann** when, **wie** how, **wa'rum** why, **wo'mit** wherewith, **wo'durch** whereby, **wo'zu** to which end, &c.

d. The conjunctions **daß** *that, since,* **wenn** *if, when,* **wie** (= **daß**), **seit** or **seit'dem** *since,* **als** or **als ob** (instead of older **daß**; **168.** II. G. *a.* (**1**), **269.** 2. *b,* **272.** A. *a,* C. *d,* D. *b*), **weil** (= **daß**; **272.** C), and **ob** *whether*: **Ich sehe, daß er da ist. Ich weiß nicht, ob er heute mitgeht.**

Note. For origin of conjunction **daß** see **240.** *a.*

2. Those which introduce *adjective clauses.* They are made up of the following groups of words (for illustrative sentences see **271**):

a. Relative or interrogative pronouns: **wer** (**156.** *b*), **was** (**153.** 1. (**1**), (**3**)); **der, die, das; welcher, -e, -es; so** (**153.** 5); **der'gleichen, des'gleichen** (**161.** 2).

b. A prep. with a dependent relative: **mit dem, mit welchem,** &c.

c. Relative or interrogative adverbs: **wo** (see **153.** 3. A, C. *c*) where, in which, when; **wo'selbst** or occasionally **da'selbst** in which place; **da** (**153.** 3. A, C. *d*) where, when; **weshalb,** or **weswegen** (**151.** 1. *b*), or less commonly **wo'her** or **da'her** (**153.** 3. A), **da'rum** (**151.** 1. *b*), and **da denn** (*Note* 2 below); **wenn** (see **153.** 3. C. *b*) or **wann** (in indirect questions) when; **wie** (**153.** 3. B, C. *f*) as, how, in which, **als** (**153.** 3. B, C. *a*); the compounds **wo'rin** in which, **wo'bei, wo'ran,** &c., or occasionally in their stead the demon. compounds **da'rin, da'bei,** &c.

Note 1. In familiar speech the compound relative adverbs are often separated. See **153.** 2 and B thereunder.
Note 2. Goethe is fond of using **da denn** in the meanings *in consequence of which, under which circumstances*: **Auch sang der Alte nicht übel, und meine Mutter mußte sich bequemen, ihn und sich selbst mit dem Klaviere täglich zu akkompagnieren; da ich denn das** Solitario bosco ombroso **bald kennen lernte** (Goethe's *Dichtung und Wahrheit,* I, 1). **Er saß fast niemals, als wenn er seine Harfe nahm und darauf spielte; da er sie denn meistens mit Gesang begleitete.**

d. **Daß** (**168.** II. G. *b,* **153.** 3. C. *e*), **als ob** or **als wenn** (instead of **daß**; **168.** II. G. *b,* 2nd par., **169.** 2. G. *b,* 2nd par.; see also *Note* below), **weil** (instead of **daß**; **271.** I), **ob** (**168.** II. F. *a,* 2nd par., and **169.** 2. F. *a,* 3rd par.), **wie** (**168.** II. F. *a,* 2nd par., **169.** 2. F. *a,* 3rd par., **153.** 3. D. (**1**)), sometimes **als** (**153.** 3. D. (**1**)): **Wallenstein schmeichelte sich noch immer mit der Hoffnung, daß viele zu ihm noch umkehren würden.**

Note. The adjective nature of the clause introduced by **als ob** here is perfectly clear, but the governing noun in all such cases is a verbal substantive and suggests the use of **als ob,** which is so common after verbs in clauses of manner (**168.** II. B and **169.** 2. B) and more or less frequent in substantive clauses (**269.** 2. *b,* **272.** C. *d,* D. *b*). This modern use of **als ob** instead of **daß** emphasizes the subjective view or the unreality of the statement.

3. Those which introduce *adverbial clauses.* They are made up of the following groups of adverbial conjunctions, indicating:

A. Place: **wo** where, **wo'hēr** whence, **wo'hin** whither; in early N.H.G. and still in elevated diction **von wannen** (= **woher**) and **da** (= **wo,** for example see John vii. 34). Compare with **274.**

B. Time: **als** *when, as,* used of an actual occurrence or a definite state of things in past or present (see *c* below) time, more commonly, however, the former; **kaum — als** (**275.** *a*) *hardly* or *scarcely — when*; **nicht sobald** (both taken together = **kaum**) — **als** (**275.** *a*) *hardly* or *scarcely — when*; **wenn** (see *b* and *c* below) or now rarely **wann** *when, whenever,* used with a present or past tense to indicate that something is or was *accustomed* to happen, and with a future tense to indicate a point of time in the future; **wo** (see *c* below) = **als; da** (see *c* below) corresponding to M.H.G. **dô** = **als,** but now more frequent in elevated discourse than in plain prose, tho very common in early N.H.G. and the classical period; **da** (M.H.G. **dâ**), earlier in the period used with the force of temporal **indem** *while* and adversative **während** *while, while on the other hand,* and in the latter meaning still found in the form of **da doch; wie** = **als,** common in colloquial language, especially with a present tense (see *c* below), sometimes also = **sobald, wenn, indem; in'dēm** (earlier in the period also **indem daß**) *as,* see *c*; **kaum daß** or **kaum** (see *d*) when — scarcely; **so'oft [als]** as often as; **so'bald [als], wie** or now more commonly **so'wie** *as soon as*; **in'zwischen, in'zwischen daß,** and less commonly **mittler'weile** *while* (*in the meantime*); **während, während daß** (not now so much used), **in'dēm** (earlier in the period **indem daß**), **in'des** (M.H.G. innen des) or more commonly **in'dessen** (**240**; earlier in the period **indes daß, indessen daß**), **unter'des** or **unter'dessen** (**240**; now little used here; earlier in the period **unterdes daß, unterdessen daß**), and the following forms common in early N.H.G.: **weil, der'weil, die'weil,** all fifteen forms with the meaning *while,* of which the first, i.e. **während,** is now the favorite; **seit daß** (or in early N.H.G. **sint daß**), **seit'dem daß,** now more commonly **seit** (in early N.H.G. also **sint**) and **seit'dem** *since*; **so'lange** *as long as,* or the separated forms **so lange** (in the principal proposition) — **so'lange** or **als** (in the subordinate clause); **bis daß, so lange bis** (in early N.H.G. **bis so lange daß**; Isaiah xxxii. 15), now more commonly **bis** *until,* in early N.H.G. also *while, as long as* (Matth. xxvi. 36), in colloquial language **bis** *by the time that* (see *e* below), also especially in Austria = **wenn** *when* (see *e*) referring to future time and = **als** *when* (see *e*) referring to time now past but future with reference to the person involved in the action; **kaum so lange — als bis** *scarcely until,* **nicht eher — bis,** or **bevor,** or more commonly **als bis** *not until*; **ehe** (earlier in the period also **ehe denn, ehe als,** and **ehe daß**) or **be'vor** *before,* or sometimes with emphatic form **ehe und bevor; nach'dem** *after.* Compare with **275.**

a. Adversatives. From the meaning of contemporaneity **in'zwischen** *while in the meantime,* **während** (now the most common form), **in'dessen, wohin'gegen** (descriptive relative adverb; see **271.** II. 7), earlier in the period also **unter'dessen, da,** and **wenn,** *while, while on the other hand, whereas* assume adversative or contrasting force: **Manche Menschen bleiben in gewisser Beziehung ewig Kinder, während andere vor der Zeit Greise werden.** In the classics we often find **anstatt daß** here instead of **während.** For other adversatives from another point of view see G.

b. The form **wann** *when* is rare only as a conjunction. As an interrogative adverb it is the common form both in direct and indirect questions: **Wann kommt er? Ich weiß nicht, wann**

er kommt. The form **wenn,** like the English *when* of to-day, once had a wider meaning, being used as an interrogative adverb = **wann,** and also as a conjunction with the force of **als** in addition to its present force, and sometimes in dialect or colloquial language this usage can still be heard: **HErr | Wenn** (= **wann**) **haben wir dich hungerig gesehen | vnd haben dich gespeiset** (Matth. xxv. 37). **Sicher, du überlegtest nicht wohl, o Mädchen des Auslands, | wenn** (= **als**) **du, bei Fremden zu dienen, dich allzu eilig entschlossest, | was es heiße, das Haus des gebietenden Herrn zu betreten** (Goethe's *Hermann*, IX, 113–115). **Wenn** (for **wann**) **geht der beste Zug?** (Hauptmann's *Einsame Menschen*, Act iii).

c. There is considerable fluctuation in the use of conjunctions which indicate a point of time. With reference to an actual state, or actual event or occurrence in past time in connection with a past (or historical present) or past perfect tense, the conjunction which is most widely used in the literary language is **als,** in poetry and choice prose not infrequently also **da.** After the conjunction **als** *than, as,* **da** is preferred to **als** *when,* to avoid the unpleasant repetition of **als: Wie eine elegante, junge Dame stand Lenes Tochter da; schlank, noch ein wenig mager, doch voller, als da sie kam** (Wilbrandt). **Lange hatte Feldwebel Rinke sich nicht so gefreut, als da die Infanterie ausrückte, die öffentlichen Plätze zu besetzen** (C. Viebig's *Die Wacht am Rhein*, p. 264). In colloquial and popular language **wie** is also in general quite frequently used instead of either **als** or **da.** Also **wo** is employed here, especially after a preceding adverb, as in **damals, wo.** Also **indem** *as* refers to the past, but it usually implies only a short span of time and indicates that an act takes place *within* the period of the duration of another act: **Indem er so sprach, traf ihn die Kugel. Indem er dies sagte, trat sein Freund herein.** With reference to present time usage is quite unsettled. **Als** is sometimes employed here, and still more frequently **da,** especially in poetry and choice prose: **Es ist spät in der Nacht, als ich dies schreibe** (Raabe's *Sperlingsgasse*, p. 238). **Du kommst nur eben, da ich reisen muß** (Goethe's *Tasso*, 1, 4). **Und willst du jetzt, da deinen Wahn besiegt | Wahrheit und Treue, schwesterlich verwoben, | da Falsch und Echt entschleiert vor dir liegt, | nicht einmal noch zu deines Volkes Glück | die Wunderkraft des Talismans erproben?** (Fulda's *Talisman*, 4. 8). The most common conjunction here in the literary language is **indem** *as* if the conjunction is not preceded by an adverb of time: **Das Vergnügen, das ich empfinde, indem ich dies schreibe. Wie** is often used here: **Ich will nicht dabei sein, wie Mutters Brautkleid verkauft wird** (Halbe's *Das tausendjährige Reich*, p. 52). **Ja, wie ich das jetzt schreibe, erfahre ich es erst, wie gut sie bei seiner Mutter Bescheid wußte** (Raabe's *Die Akten des Vogelsangs*, p. 95). **Wo** is also often used here, especially when preceded by an adverb of time: **Und jetzt, wo wir glücklich dastehen** (Halbe's *Mutter Erde*, 1). **Ich glaube dir nicht, was du Augustchen geschrieben hast: Daß du solltest dein deutsches Gefühl in Frankreich verloren haben. Es wird doch schon nicht so sein, wo unser Deutsches Reich in hohen Ehren dasteht** (Schulze-Smidt's *Denk' ich an Deutschland in der Nacht*, II). With reference to a point in the future, **wenn** is the most common conjunction: **Und wenn du dann geheizt hast, gehst du in die Kantine** (Hartleben's *Rosenmontag*, 2, 1). **Wo** is also used in colloquial language: **Ja, wo du wieder da bist, hab' ich mir gedacht, sollen auch die Lichter wieder brennen** (Halbe's *Mutter Erde*, 1).

d. The adverb **kaum,** usually in the form **kaum daß,** also sometimes simply **kaum,** has developed into a conjunction with the meaning *when — scarcely* or *barely*: **Kaum daß ich Bacchus den lustigen habe, kommt auch schon Amor** (Schiller). **Kaum diese Worte gesprochen waren, wandte sich die junge, schöne Frauengestalt um und verschwand hinter der Tür** (Rosegger's *Martin der Mann*, p. 14). See **269. 1.** *b* (last par.).

e. Note the use of **bis** in the meaning *by the time that*: **Bis du nach Rom zurückkommst, ist die längst Großmutter** (Sudermann's *Johannes*, 1, 1). In Austria **bis** is similarly used to denote a point in future time = **wenn** *when* referring to future time and = **als** *when* referring to time now past but future with reference to the person involved in the action: **Wir erkennen sie (die wichtigen Stunden unseres Lebens) erst, bis** (= **wenn**) **sie vorüber sind** (Hermann Bahr's *Der Klub der Erlöser* in *Die neue Rundschau*, April 1906, p. 481). **Sie sollte die Scheidende erst vermissen, bis** (= **als**) **sie allein war** (Alfred Meißner's *Schwarzgelb*, 5, 40).

C. Manner or Quality:

a. Expressing a *comparison* and *manner* proper (see **239**): **wie, so'wie,** or **gleich'wie** *as,* **wie auch** *as also,* **wie denn** (Ephesians i. 4) *even as, just as, according as,* **als wenn, als** (**237. 1. A.** *c*), or **als ob** *as if,* **ob** (earlier in the period = **als ob**), **wie wenn** *as when,* **daß** (**276.** A) *that,* **als ob** (= **daß**). Compare with **276.** A and **239.**

b. Expressing an *attendant circumstance*: **in'dem** *as,* **ohne daß** *without,* **außer'dēm daß** or **abgesehen davon daß** *besides, apart from, independently of.* Ex.: **Die Lerche singt ihr Lied, indem sie sich in die Lüfte schwingt.** Compare with **276.** B.

c. Expressing an *alternative agreement*: **da'nāch** (still in proverbs), **nāch'dēm** (a little earlier in the period), **je nāch'dēm** (common form) according as: Ex.: **Ich werde verfahren, je nachdem er sich mir gegenüber benimmt.** Compare **276.** C.

d. Expressing a *result*: **so — daß** *so — that*; **solch** (or **dērärtig** or simple **der, ein,** or **kein** before a substantive; see **271.** I) — **daß** such — that; **da'nach** (in the principal proposition) — **daß** of the kind that, in the manner that; with negative force: **an'statt daß** or **statt daß** *instead of,* **ohne daß** *without,* **daß nicht** *that — not, without,* common earlier in the period, where **ohne daß** is now used, **geschweige** (1st pers. sing. pres. tense, **ich** being understood) (**denn**) **daß** *to say nothing about, much less,* **weit ent'fernt daß** *far from,* **kaum daß** *scarcely.* A question may replace the words in the principal proposition: **Was ist der Tod, daß er mich schrecken sollte?** (= **der Tod ist nichts derartiges, daß,** &c.). Compare with **276.** D.

D. Degree or Intensity.

1. Expressing a *comparison*:

A. Signifying a degree equal to that of the principal proposition:

a. Expressing a comparison: **so, also** (rare), or **ebenso** (in the principal proposition) — **als** or **wie** (see **239.** 3) *as — as,* **so** (with corresponding **so** in the principal proposition: **so hoch er stand, so tief und schmählich war sein Fall**) so. Compare with **277.** 1. A. *a.*

b. Expressing a *proportionate agreement*: **je** (in the sub. clause) — **desto,** or **um so,** or **um desto,** or now more rarely **je the — the** (as in **Je höher er stieg, desto bescheidener wurde er**), formerly also **so — so = je — je, da'näch** (still in proverbs), **näch'dēm** (especially in early N.H.G.), **je näch'dēm** (common form) according as, in proportion as, **in dem Maße** (or **in dem Verhältnisse**) **wie** in degree or proportion as. Compare with **277.** 1. A. *b.*

c. Expressing the *extent* or a *restriction*: **in'sofern, in'soweit, sò wéit** (in the principal proposition) — **als** (or **inwie'fern** or **inwie'weit**) in so far as, **sò séhr — als** as hard as, **sò víel — als** as much as, **(in)so'fern, (in)so'weit,** or **(in)wie'fern** (now rare) so far as, **so'gut** as well as, **so'fest** as firmly as, **so'sehr** as hard as, **so'viel** (formerly **als viel**) as much as, **sò wéit — daß** to the extent that, **daß** (**277.** 1. A. *c*), **was** (**277.** 1. A. *c*). Compare with **277.** 1. A. *c.*

B. Following a *comparative* expressing a different degree from that of the principal clause: **weder** (early N.H.G.; Job xxxiii. 12; now obsolete, see **239.** 7) than, **denn** (early N.H.G.; now less common, see **239.** 1. *a. Note* 2 and 6) than, **als** (common form) than, **wie** (**239.** 1. *a. Note* 1) than, **als** (more rarely **denn**) **daß** or sometimes **als weil** than that, **als wenn** than when. Compare with **277.** 1. B.

2. Expressing a *result*: **so, der** (see **271.** I), **ein** (see **271.** I), or **solch — daß so** — that, such — that; **nicht so — daß nicht** not so — but that, or that not; **'dērärt** (or **'dērärtig**) **daß** so — that, **'dērärt — bis** so — that; **kaum daß** so that scarcely; (in the principal proposition **nicht genügend** modifying a following adjective, participle, or verb) — **als daß** not sufficiently — to; (in the principal proposition **zu** + positive, or less commonly a comparative instead of **zu** + positive) — **als daß** or less commonly **um daß** too — to (as in **Die Fixsterne sind zu weit von uns entfernt, als daß wir von ihrer Natur etwas Genaueres wissen könnten**). The clause of result may follow a **genug, hinreichend, hinlänglich** in the principal proposition: **Ich hatte mir das Bild ihrer Liebenswürdigkeit tief genug eingedrückt, daß** (less commonly **um daß**) **es so leicht auszulöschen nicht war** (Goethe). Compare with **277.** 2.

E. Cause:

Cause or reason: **da'rum** (early N.H.G.; **1.** Thess. iii. 5), **da'rum daß** (early N.H.G.; Luke viii. 6) or **um daß** (early N.H.G.) because; **weil** (in early N.H.G. also **'alldieweil, die'weil;** Gen. iii. 17) because (material cause and motive), since, as; **weil nun doch,** or **weil nun ein'mal** seeing (or considering) that; **nicht daß** (**269.** 1. *b,* near end), **nicht weil, nicht als ob,** or **nicht als wenn** not that, not because; **nicht als ob — sondern weil** not that — but because; **in'dēm** in that, as (the idea of cause mingled with that of attendant circumstances); **näch'dēm** often used where the ideas of time and cause blend, as in Gen. xlvi, 30, formerly also and sometimes still, especially in Austria, with the pure causal force of **da** or **weil** *because,* as the causal idea has overshadowed the original temporal force; **da** (and in popular language also **wo**) as, since (logical reason); **da doch, da ja,** or **da nun ein'mal** as (introducing an obvious reason), seeing (or considering) that; **anerwogen** (in official or archaic language) in consideration of the fact that, considering that, now more commonly replaced by **in Anbetracht daß; in'maßen** or **maßen** (dat. pl. of **Maße,** both forms now little used) seeing that, since; **seit** or **sint** (both in early N.H.G.; the corresponding English form *since* still in wide use; now **seit** has only temporal meaning and **sint** has disappeared), **sintemal** (early N.H.G.; Acts xvii. 24) seeing that, since; **daß** (see *c* below) that; **zu'mal** or more commonly **zu'mal da** especially as; **nun** now since, now that; **desto,** or **um desto,** or **um so** (before a comparative in the principal proposition) — **als** (or **da** or sometimes **weil**) all the more — as; **da'von** or **da'ran,** or **da'her,** &c. (in the principal proposition) — **daß** from this (cause or source), by (because of) this — that. The adverb of manner **wie** or **wie denn** sometimes assumes causal force: **Ich habe, wie** (as) **die Sachen jetzt stehen, an mich selbst zu denken** (Goethe). **Wir gingen auseinander, ohne einander verstanden zu haben, wie denn** (as indeed) **auf dieser Welt keiner leicht den andern versteht** (id.). Compare with **278.**

a. The most popular of these conjunctions is **weil,** and it often has a wider use than the one above indicated, encroaching upon the territory of **da.** Compare *c* below.

b. In the classical period **weil** is also still used in a temporal sense = **so lange als** or **während: Das Eisen muß | geschmiedet werden, weil es glüht** (Schiller's *Piccolomini,* 3, 1).

c. In causal clauses **daß** often seems to contain the idea of cause, but in older German this conception lay in a preceding genitive or prepositional adverb, which later usually disappeared: **Ich freue mich [dessen** or **darüber], daß du so gut davon gekommen bist. Schäme dich [dessen], daß du in der Prüfung nicht bestanden hast! Ich bin [dessen] froh, daß ich ihn los bin.** As the genitive and the prepositional phrase have for the most part disappeared and **daß** does not by its form clearly express the idea of cause it is becoming ever more common to replace **daß** by **weil** except as in the preceding examples after verbs and adjectives denoting emotion: **Der Herr lobte den ungerechten Haushalter, daß** (now more commonly **weil**) **er klüglich getan hätte** (Luther). Older **daß** is now regularly replaced by **weil** after the genitive expressions **deshalb, deswegen,** which are still often retained: **Ich habe es ihm nur deshalb in Erinnerung gebracht, weil er vergeßlich ist.** See **272.** A, D.

F. A condition or exception: **ob** (early N.H.G.) or **so** (early N.H.G.) if, the former now obsolete, the latter now rare in prose but still in use in poetic language; **wo** (common in early N.H.G., now usually replaced by **wenn, im Falle daß,** or **falls,** but still common in **wo möglich, wo nicht**) if (lit. where, in case that), **wo anders** (earlier in the period) if, **wenn** (common form)

if, wenn . . . überhaupt if at all; **anders** (preceded by question order), **wenn anders,** or **vorausgesetzt daß** provided that; **da** or **dafern** earlier in the period, now replaced by **wo'fern** in case that, if, provided that; **wenn** (or in a few set expressions **wo**) **nicht** if not, unless; **wo'fern nicht** if not, unless; **im Falle daß, falls** (**168.** II. G. *b. Note*), or sometimes **im Fall** in case that, provided that, **für den Fall daß** or falls for use (or to be ready, to be at hand) in case that; **doch daß** but only on condition that; in early N.H.G. **ohne daß,** now replaced by **außer daß** or **ausgenommen daß** except that, unless; **abgesehen davon daß** except that; **außer wenn** if not, unless; **nur daß** if it were not that, except that, only that, but that, **nur daß** (with volitive subjunctive; see **168.** I. 2. C. *b*) but let it be, on condition that; (**kein anderer, wer anders, nichts** and other negative forms, or instead of these forms a question) — **als** (usually in elliptical constructions; see **279.** *e* and **239. 1.** *b*) but, than, else than, unless, except, save; (**nichts anderes**) **als daß** (nothing else) but that; **nicht — als wenn** unless; **wie** (**239.** 1. *b. Note*) but; **denn** (**239.** 6. *a*) but; **ohne daß** (after a negative proposition) but that, unless; **denn** (after a negative proposition and preceded by the present or past subjunctive with normal word-order; see **168.** II. E. *a*) or **es sei denn daß** (with transposed word-order; see **168.** II. E. *a* and *c*) if not, unless, **müßte denn** (with infinitive; see **168.** II. E. *a*) unless; **höchstens daß** unless, at most, at best; **wer** (**159**) for anybody who. Compare with **279.**

Note. The explanation of the negative meaning of **denn** or **es sei denn daß** *unless* in spite of its seeming positive form is given in **168.** II. E. *a* and *Note.*

The conjunctions **außer** and **nur** also introduce independent propositions without changing the meaning. See **225.** 2. *a*, **233.** A, and **236.** *a*.

G. A concession: **so doch** (early N.H.G.; Jeremiah iv. 10) altho, whereas, **ob** (Luke xvi. 31), or **und ob** altho, **ob — ob** (or **oder** or **oder ob**) whether — or, **ob auch,** or **wie'wohl** altho, and the more common words having the same general meaning of *altho*: **ob'gleich, ob'wohl, ob'schon, ob'zwar, wenn'gleich** (sometimes separated, but not so frequently as formerly, now usually only when a personal pronoun can stand between the parts: **ob — gleich, ob — wohl,** &c.), and the separable forms **wenn schon, wenn auch; auch wenn, selbst wenn,** or **und wenn** even tho, even if; **so** (followed by an adverb or an adjective, or a noun with its preceding modifying adjectives) — **auch** however (e.g., **So groß er auch ist**); **wie — auch = so — auch; wie = so — auch; so = so — auch; welch** (followed by a noun) — **auch** however, whatever, **wer auch** whoever, **was auch** whatever, **wo — auch** in whatever place, **wo'hin — auch** to whatever place; **unge'achtet** or **uner'achtet** (or more rarely **'ohngeachtet**), or now less commonly **unge'achtet daß** notwithstanding that, **trotz'dēm** or **trotz'dēm daß** in spite of the fact that, **unbe'schadet dessen daß** without impairing the validity of the fact that. Also certain temporal conjunctions assume adversative, concessive force: **da** (earlier in the period), **da doch, indem doch, während, während doch, wo doch** (colloquial), formerly also **wenn** while, altho. Compare with **280.**

a. Of the many concessive conjunctions containing **ob** or **wenn** the forms **und wenn, selbst wenn, auch wenn** *even tho* are only used when the case is merely an assumed one, while **wennschon** and **wenngleich** *even tho, altho* may be used whether the statement is a mere assumption or is an actual fact. The other forms usually correspond to English *altho* and are used in case of actual facts. Examples are given in **280.**

H. Purpose or end: **um daß** (now little used), **daß** (the oldest form but still much used in colloquial speech), **da'rum daß, auf daß** (old forms once more common than at present, the latter a favorite with Luther), **da'mit** (not often employed by Luther, but now the most common form; see also **240.** *a*, 2nd par.) in order that. Compare **281.**

I. Means: **da'durch** (or **da'mit,** &c.) **daß,** or separated **da'durch — daß** by, **da'ran daß** by, **in'dem** by. Compare with **282.**

239. *The Subordinating Conjunctions* **als, wie, denn, weder, was, wann.** The following subordinating conjunctions, much used in making comparisons, and in introducing an exception or a qualification, are by reason of their importance treated at some length below: **als** than, from, but, except, as; **wie** as, like, than, but; **denn** than, but; **weder** than; **als wie** as, than, but, **was** *than, but*; **wenn** *than, but.* The following may serve as a fair outline of their proper usage:

1. **Als** is used:

a. After a comparative: **Hans ist größer als Wilhelm. Röter als Blut. Täte er nicht besser daran, zu bleiben, als daß er so spät geht, or als so spät zu gehen?** Compare: I rather like him as (= **als**) otherwise (Scott's *St. Ronan's Well*). In German this construction is recommended by grammarians quite generally, but it has never been thoroly established in actual usage to the exclusion of other forms. In English it has disappeared from the literary language.

Note 1. **Als** and the still older **denn** are now very often replaced here by **wie,** not only in colloquial language, but also in a serious literary style: **Einem schöneren Jüngling wie diesem Gottfried von Tessow bin ich in meinem ganzen Leben nicht begegnet** (Suttner's *Die Waffen nieder!*, II). **Das Aufgebot an Menschen und Geschützen dürfte schwerlich noch größer werden wie im September** (*Hamburger Nachrichten*, Jan. 7, 1916).

Note 2. In early N.H.G. **denn** was usually and **weder** (see 7 below) sometimes used after the comparative: **Vnd die Schlange war listiger denn alle Thier auff dem felde** (Gen. iii. 1). In the middle of the sixteenth century **als** begins to appear instead of **denn.** The old usage **rot als Blut, röter denn Blut** has become **rot wie Blut, röter als Blut.** See also Note 1.

b. After the pronominal **ander-,** negatives, questions with negative force, and sometimes after **all-** and **jed-: Mein Urteil ist ein ganz anderes als das Ihrige. Ich urteile darüber ganz anders als Sie. Niemand als Sie würde das gewagt haben** Nobody but you would have dared to do that. **Ich fühle mich nirgends glücklich als hier** I am happy nowhere except here. **Ich wünsche mir nichts als Ruhe. Was kann er mir [anders** or **sonst] vorwerfen, als einen gewissen Stolz?**, where, as in all such questions, it is now in contrast to the eighteenth century more common to insert one of the words given in brackets. **Gefühllos jedem Schmerz, als ungeliebt zu**

sein (Wieland). **An allem Mangel leidend, als an Schmerz** (Grillparzer's *Medea*, 1) *suffering a lack of everything but pain.*

While **als** is still freely used after **niemand, nichts,** it cannot now as in the eighteenth century be freely used after other negatives but is usually replaced there by **außer: Ich kann nicht einmal ein Stückchen Papier finden als** (now **außer**) **dieses blaue** (Goethe's *Briefe*, 1, 263, 16).

After **zu** + adjective or adverb we still usually find **als** when a full clause follows, in the eighteenth century also when an abridged infinitive clause follows, but in the latter case **als** is now supplanted by **um: Sie gehen zu langsam, als daß Sie Ihren Freund einholen könnten,** or **um Ihren Freund einzuholen. Weil er sein Mädchen zu feurig liebt, als** (now **um**) **sie verlassen zu können** (Schiller).

Note. **Wie** is often used here instead of **als**, especially in colloquial language: **Sie sind mir wert und lieb, aber ganz anders wie du** (Auerbach's *Dorfgeschichten*, 8, p. 104). **Sie werten anders, wie Ihre Eltern werten** (Hauptmann's *Einsame Menschen*, 4). **Du hast's ja selber zu tragen! Kein anderer wie du!** (Halbe's *Das tausendjährige Reich*, p. 45). Also even in the higher forms of literature: **An sich ist also der Sinn des Genitivs hier kein anderer wie in positiven Sätzen** (Brugmann's *Vergleichende Grammatik*, II, 2, p. 612). **Und da ich nun einmal nichts wie zu lieben weiß** (Sudermann's *Die drei Reiherfedern*, 3, 10).

c. After **so'bald, so'oft** (formerly also **als oft**), **so'lange, so'fern, so'viel** (formerly also **als viel**), &c., in which cases it is now usually suppressed: **Komm, sobald [als] du kannst, und bleib, solange [als] du darfst.** If **als** is used, **sobald, solange,** &c. are adverbs and belong to the principal proposition, but when it is suppressed, as is now usual, **sobald, solange** become subordinating conjunctions and belong of course to the subordinate clause.

d. In the combination **so'wohl — als** *as well — as, both — and*: **Sowohl dem gegenwärtigen als auch dem vergangenen Jahrhundert verdanken wir große Fortschritte in Kunst und Wissenschaft.** Here we also now find **sowohl . . . wie,** and indeed **wie** is more common than **als** if the identifying **als** described in 4 below follows: **sowohl in seiner Eigenschaft als Berliner wie als Mensch überhaupt** (Raabe's *Die Villa Schönow*, V).

e. In the combinations **als wenn** (or also **wie wenn**), **als ob** *as if, as tho*, in comparisons that are represented as resting not upon absolutely assured facts, but upon personal impressions, appearances, or even represented as unreal, contrary to fact: **Es scheint, als wenn,** or **als ob sie reich wären.**

Note. In early N.H.G. **als** could be used alone without **wenn** or **ob** and still be followed by the dependent word-order. See 1 Sam. xx. 20. If **als** be used alone, present usage requires the question order. See **237. 1. A. *c*.**

2. **Wie** is used:

a. After the positive of adjectives: **weiß wie Schnee** white as snow. **Karl ist ebenso fleißig wie du. Karl ist so alt wie Wilhelm.**

When the adjective which would stand in the second member has already been mentioned, it may be suppressed in colloquial speech: Richard: **Amtlich?** (Is the dispatch) official? Holtzmann: **So gut wie** (Sudermann's *Es lebe das Leben*, pp. 43–44).

Note. Formerly **als** (in M.H.G. with its full form *also*, or instead of it simple *so*, of the same origin as English *as*) stood after the positive, as is still occasionally found in early N.H.G. See Matth. xxviii. 3. A survival of this older usage is still preserved in certain constructions, especially after **so** and **solch**, where **als** can occasionally be found: **so geschwind als** (or **wie**) **möglich.** This accounts for its use in 1. *c* and *d* above.

b. Also in connection with verbs to indicate likeness, similarity: **Das Schiff flog dahin wie ein Pfeil. Karl spricht, wie er denkt,** but **Er sprach anders, als** (1. *b*) **er denkt. Er handelt immer so** (often used in German, but not in English), **wie es sein Vorteil erheischt.**

Note. In early N.H.G. **als** (in M.H.G. also or simple so) was here still frequently used, and even later in the classical period. See Matth. xxii. 39. A survival of this former usage is still preserved in the construction mentioned in 1. *e* above.

c. Often in the combination **wie wenn** *as when* (or also **als wenn** after **so** or a negative) in comparisons which are represented as real: **Es zischt, wie wenn Wasser sich mit Feuer mischt.**

d. After the comparative. See 6 below under **denn**, also 1. *a*. *Note* 1 above.

e. After negatives. See 1. *b*. *Note* above.

f. After **umgekehrt** *the opposite* or *reverse*: **Die Sache ist umgekehrt, wie man sie darstellt** (Saran's *Deutsche Verslehre*, p. 48). **Das logische Verhältnis zweier Sätze kann auch geradezu das umgekehrte werden wie das grammatische** (Paul's *Deutsche Grammatik*, IV, p. 325).

3. In one case usage fluctuates between **als** and **wie**, with, perhaps, the preponderance on the side of **wie**, namely, in comparing different objects or actions as to the degree or intensity of certain qualities or forces. The grammarians demand **als** when degree, intensity, is to be expressed, and **wie** to express manner, likeness, quality. Degree: **Er schreibt so schlecht als du.** Manner: **Er schreibt schlecht wie du.** This distinction is a nice one theoretically, but it is not supported by practice, as can be seen in the best modern authors: **Es gibt keinen anderen Menschen mehr auf Erden, der so allein ist wie ich** (Raabe's *Zum wilden Mann*, chap. 5). The form **als** is regularly replaced by **wie** when another **als** immediately follows: **Als Schriftsteller dagegen steht er** (i.e. **Cicero**) **vollkommen ebenso tief wie als Staatsmann** (Mommsen's *Römische Geschichte*, V, chap. 12).

4. In the predicate, however, a sharp distinction is now made in choice language between **wie** and **als.** Here **als** is used in all appositional constructions and hence denotes *identity, oneness with*, while **wie** expresses mere *similarity*: **Ich ehre ihn als meinen Vater** I honor him as my father (which he is). **Ich ehre ihn wie meinen Vater** I honor him just as I would my father, or like my father. **Sie sprachen miteinander als Freunde** They were speaking together as friends (which they were). **Sie sprachen miteinander wie Freunde** (like friends, but they were not). **Leonidas focht bei Thermopilä wie ein Löwe und fiel als ein Held. Friedrich Wilhelm der Vierte haßte die Revolution nicht bloß wie, sondern als die Sünde.** For that class of appositional

constructions which merely add an explanatory word or words to a previous noun see **233.** C.

a. The distinction between **als** and **wie** described above is quite commonly neglected in colloquial language, as **wie** here as elsewhere replaces **als: Ich wie dein Alter, Kerlchen, ich hätt' all meinen Rotspon selber getrunken vor meinem End'! !** (Halbe's *Mutter Erde,* 3, p. 157).

5. **Als wie** was frequently used in the classical period instead of **wie** after a positive and instead of **als** after a comparative, and is still so used in colloquial N.G.: **Wir finden wohl heute abend keine Stätte in Amelungsborn, wo er besser ruhte als wie hier** (Raabe's *Odfeld,* chap. xxiv). Sometimes even in the higher forms of literature: **Selbst die Abendröte | schaut anders aus als wie zuvor** (Sudermann's *Die drei Reiherfedern,* 5, 2).

6. **Denn,** like English *than* (older form of *then*), was originally a co-ordinating conjunction: **Mein Bruder ist älter, dann** (older form of **denn**) [**komme**] **ich.** Altho **denn** *than* was very common as a subordinating conjunction after comparatives in early N.H.G., it is now in general much less used there, but it is not so rare as grammarians often represent: **mehr denn ein Menschenalter durch** (Raabe's *Höxter und Corvey,* chap. 13), **blühender denn je** (H. Hoffmann). **Es ist ein großer Bau, der mehr in die Breite denn in die Höhe geht** (Ernst Zahn's *Menschen,* II). See also *Note* 2 under 1. *a* above.

It is, moreover, quite frequently employed after the comparative instead of **als,** when there is already an **als** (the identifying **als** described in 4 above, or the **als** in the conjunction **als ob**) in the sentence: **Das betrachten wir eher als eine Tugend denn als einen Fehler** (G. Keller). **Letzterer sah mir mehr danach aus, als ob er eines Arztes bedürfe, denn als ob er selber studieren wolle** (Adelbert Meinhardt). **Wie** is perhaps still more common here, especially in colloquial language: **Als sie wahrnahm, daß ihr Besuch mehr als Störung wie als Freude empfunden wurde** (Fontane's *Effi,* chap. 9). **Viel höher wie als Epiker steht Hebbel als Lyriker** (Adolf Bartels).

a. **Denn** was common in early N.H.G. after a negative or a question, or after **ander-,** and survives in poetic language and choice prose: **Bei dir gilt nichts denn Gnad allein** (Luther). **Der Wind hatte seine Stimme wiederum erhoben; doch nicht so laut denn zuvor** (Raabe's *Else von der Tanne*). **Der Hausherr neckte bei aller Zartheit seine Frau so lustig und unbefangen, als wäre niemand zugegen denn ein alter Freund!** (O. Ernst's *Semper der Jüngling,* p. 120). **Wem wohl, denn ihr** (i.e. **der Frau**), **verdankt er des Liedes Keim?** (Otto Brahm in *Die neue deutsche Rundschau,* Dec. 1906, p. 1420). **Noch jetzt erscheint der Sohn mir im Traume anders nie denn frisch und blühend** (Uhland).

7. After comparatives we sometimes in early N.H.G. find the form **weder** (**235.** A. *a*) *than,* lit. *not the one of the two*: **Denn ein Nachbar ist besser in der nehe | weder ein Bruder in der ferne** (Prov. xxvii. 10) *A neighbor at hand is better than a brother far off,* lit. *Of the two a neighbor at hand is better, not a brother far off.* It has entirely disappeared except in S.G. dialect: **Sie ist gewiß viel bräver weder er** (Auerbach's *Dorfgeschichten,* 7, p. 198). Compare dialectic English: He is taller nor I.

8. In Austrian and Bavarian dialects **was** is found after a comparative or a negative instead of **als: Er ist gresser was i = Er ist größer als ich. Nix was lauter Guats = nichts als lauter Gutes.**

9. In certain Swiss dialects **wann** (= M.H.G. niuwan *except*) is found after a comparative or a negative instead of **als: größer wann i, niemand wann i.** In older German this usage was not uncommon in the literary language.

Conjunctions Used as Co-ordinating or Subordinating.

240. The following conjunctions may introduce either co-ordinate or subordinate propositions: **da'rum,** earlier in the period used as a co-ordinating conjunction with the meaning *therefore* and as a subordinating conjunction with the meaning *since, as,* as in I Thess. iii. 5, now only employed in the former function and meaning; **denn,** earlier in the period much used as a co-ordinating conjunction with the meaning *for* and also quite common as a subordinating conjunction with the meaning *since, as,* now only employed in the former function and meaning; **da** then, when; **insoweit, insofern** thus far, so far as; **in'dessen, unter'dessen** a little earlier in the period used as co-ordinating conjunctions with the meanings *in the meantime, however, yet* and as subordinating conjunctions in the meaning *while, while on the other hand,* now in the latter function **indessen** is less common than formerly and **unterdessen** little used, while in the former function they are so differentiated that **indessen** is used in the meaning *however, yet* as illustrated in **236** and **unterdessen** in the meaning *in the meantime*; **in'zwischen** *in the meantime, while in the meantime;* **trotz'dēm** nevertheless, in spite of the fact that; **seit'dēm** since; **nun** now, now that; **so** so (which tho usually a co-ordinating adverbial conjunction is also a subordinating conjunction in concessive clauses (see **238.** 3. G); **widrigenfalls** otherwise, employed in this meaning both as a co-ordinating and a subordinating conjunction, more commonly the former with inverted word-order; **sonst** or **ansonst** (now little used), earlier in the period also **anders** (Matth. ix. 17) *else, otherwise,* usually with inverted word-order: **Er war krank; trotzdem ging er aus. Trotzdem er krank war, ging er aus. Du hast dir Mühe gegeben, in'sofern kann ich dich loben. Inso'fern du dir Mühe gegeben hast, kann ich dich loben. Du hast mir das versprochen; nun mußt du Wort halten. Nun du das versprochen hast, mußt du Wort halten. Bezahl' mich jetzt; widrigenfalls muß ich dich verklagen. Van der Straaten, der es hörte, verbat sich alle derartig intrikaten Wortspielereien, widrigenfalls er an die Braut telegraphieren werde** (Fontane's *L'Adultera,* chap. viii). **Nach einem Beschluß des Obersten Rates soll Deutschland zur Räumung Litauens aufgefordert werden, widrigenfalls mit Repressalien**

gedroht wird (*Die Woche*, Oct. 4, 1919). **Gib dem Kinde das Spielzeug, sonst fängt es an zu weinen. Die kleinen Leiden mit der aufdringlichen Krapüle und was damit zusammenhängt, gehen auch bei mir immer fort, allein es lohnt am Ende nicht der Mühe, lange davon zu sprechen, ansonst man ja doppelte Beschwernis hat** (G. Keller an T. Storm, 5. Juni 1882).

a. Origin of Subordinating Conjunctions. In the oldest period of language development a formal expression to indicate the subordination of one proposition to another—hypotaxis—was unknown. The mere placing of one proposition alongside another—parataxis—was and is even still often sufficient with the aid of the context to indicate the grammatic relations: **Beeile dich, es wird spät** Hurry up, it is getting late, in hypotactical form, **Beeile dich, da es spät wird** Hurry up, as it is getting late. Hypotaxis has had within historic times a rich development becoming an ever more accurate expression of thought by means of its finely differentiated subordinating conjunctions. Most subordinating conjunctions were originally modifiers of the principal proposition. Thus **Ich sehe, daß** (the same word as the demonstrative **das** nom. and acc., from which it is first distinguished in orthography in the middle of the 16th century) **er zufrieden ist** originated in **Ich sehe das: er ist zufrieden.** Thus also **Ich tue es nicht, ohne daß ich Ihre Erlaubnis habe** originated in **Ich tue es nicht ohne das: ich habe Ihre Erlaubnis.** In both examples **das** is acc. neut., but later when it passed over into the subordinate clause the distinct feeling of its case passed away, and it, in a number of conjunctions, passed as a connective without inflection, the form **das**, later **daß**, standing even after a prep. governing some other case than the acc., as in **außer daß** *except*, **während daß** *while*, **anstatt daß** *instead*, or after a verb which governs the gen.: **Ich erinnere mich nicht, daß ich dies gesagt habe.** In other conjunctions the proper case of the original demonstrative still stands, as in **nachdem** *after*, **seitdem** *since*, **indem** *while*. In the same manner the demonstratives **der, die, das** were removed from the principal to the subordinate proposition and thus became relative pronouns. Compare **154.**
Note. Similarly **ehe** and **bevor**, originally adverbs with the meaning *before* (i.e. *previously*) standing in the principal proposition, were removed to the subordinate clause and became subordinating conjunctions with the meaning *before*, so that **Ich war zufrieden ehe** or **bevor: er kam** became **Ich war zufrieden, ehe** or **bevor er kam.** Notice that in all these examples the subordinating conjunction is a word that stood originally in the principal proposition pointing to the following proposition into which it finally merged. On the other hand, the co-ordinating conjunctions in the above list stood originally where they still stand, i.e. in the second proposition pointing backward to the preceding proposition: **Er war krank; trotzdem ging er aus.** In this position **das** is still found in its original function and form: **Er ist zufrieden, das sehe ich,** but **Ich sehe, daß er zufrieden ist.** The two propositions connected by a co-ordinating conjunction or a demonstrative pointing backward to the first proposition are both independent, but they are somewhat differentiated from simple parataxis by the use in the second proposition of a connecting word which shows a relation between the two propositions and thus indicates an intermediate stage of development between parataxis and hypotaxis—co-ordination. Compare **267.** 4. The subordinating conjunction **denn** *than*, used after comparatives, was once co-ordinating. See **239.** 6.

On the other hand, a few subordinating conjunctions stood originally in the subordinate clause as they were once relative adverbs standing in descriptive relative clauses (**271.** II. 7): **Fliehet aus Babel, damit ein jglicher seine Seele errette** (Jer. li. 6) = **womit ein jeder seine Seele erretten möge.** The idea of purpose here was at first indicated by the subjunctive of the verb in the relative clause, but later this idea became associated with **damit,** which in the relative function had elsewhere been replaced by **womit** and hence had ceased to be felt as a relative and began to be construed as a subordinating conjunction of purpose. Also the subordinating conjunctions **da** *when*, **als** *when*, **so** *when*, *if*, have developed out of relative adverbs, which are themselves developments out of older demonstratives which once stood in the principal proposition.

INTERJECTIONS.

241. An interjection is a single particle, or some other part of speech used as such, or a combination of particles, or a fragment of a sentence used to give vent to some sudden outburst of feeling or passion, or to give expression to some intimation of will, or on the other hand to imitate some sound in nature. The simplest interjections, such as **o!, au!,** belong to the oldest forms of spoken language and represent the most primitive type of the sentence. Compare **250.** *a.* In order to facilitate an understanding of the more idiomatic interjections illustrative sentences are given under the several words. A few of the most common or most difficult here follow in alphabetical order, others must be looked for in the dictionary:

aber nein! expressing surprise.
ach! expressing pain, anger, regret, displeasure.
ach was! pooh! or bah!, expressing disdain.
ah! expressing joy, admiration, surprise.
also doch! Well, I never should have expected that!
ätsch or **eetsch!** teasing expression of joy at the loss or discomfiture of another.
au! or **autsch!** expression of physical pain.
bauz! imitating a falling body: **Bauz, da liegt er!**
bei'leibe nicht = um Gottes willen nicht! kein Bein! (colloq.) not at all! **be'wahre!** by no means! **nein, ich bitte Sie!** expressing surprise.
bravo! or **gut!** hear! hear!, sign of approval, often in contrast to **hört! hört!,** which indicates disapproval, or is employed by one party in an assembly to call attention to

something just said which they believe to be unfavorable to their opponents.
brrr! whoa! (to stop a horse).
bums, imitating a falling body: **Bums, da liegt er!**
dalli (colloq.) = **flink!** quick!
Gehen Sie mir doch mit solchem Zeug! rot!
gütiger Himmel! good heavens!
i du meine Güte! good gracious!
holterdipolter, a heavy, dull noise: **Das ging holterdipolter** (in great haste and noisily).
hoppla, or **hoppsa,** or **hoppsassa!** excl. when some one stumbles or lets something fall.
hu'rra! (or **'hurra**) hurrah! **hurra hoch!** hip, hip, hip, hurrah!
husch! expression of rapidity: **Husch! fort war der Vogel!**
keine Idee, or **kein Gedanke!** not at all!
i wo! by no means!
juch'he! or **juch'hei!** hurrah!
kladdera'datsch, imitating a falling body.
knacks, imitating the breaking of some brittle substance: **Knacks, sagte es, da war der Henkel an der Tasse abgebrochen.**
ja Kuchen! (colloq.) It's all imagination!
man ja nicht! in no case!
na! unusually frequent, expressing surprise, displeasure, an urgent admonition to do something desired by the speaker, or encouraging words to someone to proceed: **Wer kommt mit? Na** (surprise)? **Keiner?** (What, no one?) **Na, das fehlte noch!** Well! That caps the climax! **Na, vorwärts!** Often used when the speaker thinks that something confirms, or soon will confirm his ideas, words: **Na, das sagte ich Ihnen ja gleich!** Used when one forms unwillingly a resolution which he cannot well avoid: **Na, ich will denn nur weiter gehen.** To express doubt as to the outcome: **Na, na, wenn es nur gut ausläuft!** A warning: **Na, na, na, nicht so hitzig!** Sharp rebuke: **na, na!** Appeasingly: **Na, na, es war nicht bös gemeint!**
na'nu, strengthened **na,** expressing surprise, pity, indignation, disappointment, impatience: **Nanu, was bedeutet denn das?**
na ob or und ob! in responses = well, I should think so! rather!
nē, very frequent = **nein.**
o! oh! O! oh!
pfui! for shame! shame on you!
pst! or **scht!** sh! hush!
Quatsch! bosh!
schön! or **gut!** all right!, indicating assent.
schwups, expressing suddenness: **Schwups! hatte er eine Ohrfeige.**

Note. As **bitte!** short for **ich bitte** *I beg,* is usually used with some expression understood, the suppressed words being easy to supply from the connection and in the spoken language from the tone of voice or gesture, it often has varied meanings: **bitte!** please! **Bitte um Verzeihung!** Beg your pardon! **Bitte, bitte!** Please, do it! **Bitte!** Please let me pass. **Bitte!** Please enter this room! **Bitte, das bleibt mein Geheimnis** Please don't inquire, that's my secret. **Bitte!** What did you say? **Nein, ich bitte Sie!** Well, I declare! (expression of surprise). **Bitte!** Don't mention it (answer to one returning thanks for a favor). **Bitte sehr** *I beg your pardon,* used to introduce politely something contradicting that which has just been stated by the person addressed.

PART III

WORD-FORMATION.

242. Words are divided with reference to their formation into three classes: Primitives, Derivatives, and Compounds.

PRIMITIVES.

243. Words were in most cases once longer than now. Altho we know almost nothing about the subject we often speak of the first syllable of these older words as the root, of the part next to the root as the root suffix, of both root and root suffix as the stem, of the final element as the inflectional ending, and of them all together as a word. As our ancestors in time lost all feeling for the real meaning of the different elements of each word they slighted them, so that these words have come down to us much reduced in form, often worn away to a single syllable or even a single vowel. We to-day have only feeling for the word as a whole. From these old words new words may be formed by the addition of prefixes or suffixes. These new words thus formed may in turn become the stems from which by the addition of other suffixes still other words may be formed. Words which have sprung up directly from the root syllable and now have no other suffixes than the usual inflectional endings, and which are themselves the stems from which other words by the aid of suffixes spring, are called primitives. The strong verbs of the present and past periods of the language form the primitive stems fron. which a large number of German words have sprung. In these primitives it is the consonants that give consistency to the roots, for the root vowels themselves differ in the different tenses: **singen, sang, gesungen.** This difference of vowel, called gradation, is due to a difference of accent in an earlier period. See **26.** D and **197.** A. It is no longer possible to tell what the original root-vowel was. Thus the original root has thrown up different stems which have become remarkably fruitful. The different classes of the gradating verbs are treated in articles **198–205.** The numerous nouns and adjectives which have been formed from the same roots as these strong verbs are, like the verbal stems themselves, in direct association with the root and are also true primitives. Usually, however, such nouns and adjectives are associated directly with strong verbs, as the original roots cannot be ascertained, and the strong verbs are the oldest related forms which can shed light on their real meaning. For fuller explanation of this point see **197.** A. *a. Note.* As certain primitive nouns and adjectives have the same gradation as the related strong verbs, they have been treated in detail under the different gradation classes (beginning at art. **198**) rather than here. A number of primitive nouns and adjectives have no relation to any existing strong verb, but can be traced back to verbs found in earlier periods of German or some older related language. Some primitives, however, cannot thus be traced back to verbal forms. Also a number of weak verbs must be regarded as primitives.

a. Next in nature to these primitives are those derivatives with endings that have no appreciable meaning. Such are the substantives formed by adding **e, de, te, d, dt, ft, st, t,** or **tt** to a primitive stem, and adjectives in **el, er, en, t: Grube** ditch, **Stand** condition, **Stadt** city, **Gruft** tomb, **eitel** vain, **bitter** bitter, **eben** level, **dicht** close.

Note. Such words have a change of **b** to **f** and **g** or **h** to **ch** before the suffix **t: treiben** to drive—**Trift** pasture, **schlagen** to strike—**Schlacht** battle, **geschehen** to happen—**Geschichte** history. See also **40. 1.** *b. Note* **1.** After **-l** and **-n** we often find **st,** and after **-m** the ending **ft** instead of simple **t: Geschwulst** swelling, from **schwellen** to swell; **Gunst** from **gönnen, Kunst** from **können, Gespinst** (**spinnen**); **Ankunft** from **ankommen, Vernunft** from **vernehmen.**

DERIVATIVES.

244. Derivatives are formed by adding or prefixing to a simple word a syllable that has an appreciable force and thus influences the meaning of the word: **Mann** man, **männlich** manly. To such a derivative still other suffixes can be added: **Männlichkeit** manliness.

Prefixes and suffixes were originally independent words altho now often not recognizable as such by means of their present form. They originally served as a component of a compound. Later after the compound had undergone a change of meaning and the syntactical relations had become obscured they suffered a reduction of stress and a consequent change of form and finally lost their identity. A concrete illustration of this development is given in **245.** I. 13. *Note.* While the history of some prefixes can thus be clearly traced the origin of most of them is entirely unknown.

FORMATION OF WORDS BY MEANS OF SUFFIXES.

I. *Derivative Substantives.*

245. 1. A. **e** (from O.H.G. ī, hence producing mutation), **heit** (cognate with *hood*, as in *falsehood*), **keit** (corrupted form of O.H.G. ic[k]heit, hence another form of **heit**), which form abstract feminine substantives. Those in **-e** may be formed from adjectives, and those in **heit** from adjectives, perfect participles, present infinitives, and nouns: **Güte** kindness, **Härte** cruelty, **Liebe** love, **Freiheit** freedom, **Dummheit** stupidity, **Ergebenheit** devotion, **Allwissenheit** omniscience, **Kindheit** childhood. Grammarians who claim that **Bedeutendheit** (or also **Bedeutenheit**) is the only case where **heit** is added to a present participle are not in accord with the facts of the language: **Treffendheit des Ausdrucks** (Fontane's *Vor dem Sturm*, II, chap. 2). **Sie sind einer gewissen Unausreichendheit begegnet** (ib., *Stechlin*, chap. 4, p. 48). The **-heit** may be added to adjectives, and hence also to adjective participles.

Those in **-keit** are chiefly formed from derivative adjectives in **-bar, -el, -er, -ig, -lich, -sam: Heiligkeit,** &c. Nouns formed from adjectives in **-los** and **-haft,** and from certain monosyllabic adjectives, add the lengthened form **-igkeit: Ehrlosigkeit, Ehrenhaftigkeit, Seichtigkeit,** &c. See II. 7. 2.

a. The forms in **-e** and **(ig)keit** often take on concrete meaning: **Höhe** hill, height, **Tiefe** the deep, **Süßigkeit** something sweet.

b. Sometimes **-e** and **-heit,** or **-keit** and **-heit,** stand in contrast with each other, the former representing something concrete, the latter something abstract: **Ebene** level, plain, **Ebenheit** levelness; **Neuigkeit** something new, piece of news, **Neuheit** newness, but also concrete, **eine Neuheit** a novelty, pl. **Neuheiten.** These three suffixes have the same general force, but when they are affixed to the same stem a little different shade of meaning sometimes develops, as plainly as in the preceding examples or in finer shades of abstract meaning. Often, however, the differentiation is not yet complete: **Süßigkeit** on the one hand with concrete meaning *something sweet, candy,* on the other with abstract force *sweetness,* but in the latter meaning sometimes for the sake of a better differentiation replaced by **Süßheit** or quite commonly in figurative use by the once more common form **Süße** *sweetness of manner.* In earlier periods of the language **e** (O.H.G. ī) was used much more frequently than now. It has been in many cases replaced by **heit** and also by **ung** and **nis.** In early N.H.G. we still frequently find words in **e** which are now replaced by other suffixes: **Die Gleiche** (now **Gleichheit** or **Ähnlichkeit**), **Schöne** (now **Schönheit**), &c. These words in **e,** however, have found favor with poets: **Wir tragen | die Trümmern ins Nichts hinüber, | und klagen über die verlorne Schöne** (Goethe's *Faust,* ll. 1613–16).

c. The suffix **heit** and its corrupted form **keit,** both of the same origin as our *hood* and *head* (in manhood, Godhead), represent a once independent noun with the meaning of *condition, kind,* which accounts for the meaning of these suffixes to-day, and sometimes leads to the use of **heit** to express a collective idea: **Gesundheit** health, lit. healthy condition, **Menschheit** human race, mankind, **Christenheit** the Christian world. See also 14. 2 below.

d. Not all the feminine words in **-e** are of the same origin as those described above. These other words in **-e** distinguish themselves by their lack of mutation in many cases and also by their concrete meaning: **die Flosse** (O.H.G. flozza) fin, **Grube** (O.H.G. gruoba) pit, &c.

B. There is another **e** (Gothic a(n) and ja(n), the latter of which has left its imprint in the mutation of the preceding vowel), which forms weak masc.

nouns denoting persons or other living beings: **Bote** messenger, **Bürge** bondsman, **Erbe** heir, **Gefährte** companion, **Geselle** fellow, comrade, **Schütze** marksman, **Hase** hare, &c. Some have lost the distinguishing suffixal ending in the nom.: **Schultheiß** (gen. **des Schultheißen**), **Herr** (gen. **des Herrn**), &c. In many words **-e** has been replaced by the foreign suffix **-er** (see **5** below), which is a great favorite: (Gothic) fiskja, (O.H.G.) fiscari, (N.H.G.) **Fischer,** &c. Formerly **-e** was also found in many weak masc. nouns denoting lifeless things, of which a few traces are left: **Name,** &c. For the history of these nouns denoting things see **68,** 2nd paragraph.

In older periods three suffixes were much used to denote living beings, namely **-e, -el,** and **-er,** each of which was a live force in the language. Of these **-er** has been gradually replacing the other two. The suffix **-el** is now least common, and its former meaning is no longer vividly felt. The **-e** is best preserved in names of peoples, where it competes with **-er**: **Preuße, Russe,** &c., but **Engländer, Spanier,** &c. In Swiss dialect **-i** competes with these three suffixes. See 8. 1. *f* and *Note* 3 below.

2. Accented **ei, ie** (i:), and unaccented **ien** (ĭən), different forms of the same foreign suffix, from which are made abstract and concrete substantives. In **Abtei** the **ei** goes back to M.H.G. *eie,* but elsewhere it corresponds to M.H.G. *īe,* which in N.H.G. passed over into **ei.** Later, especially in foreign nouns, the French form was restored to some of the words: **Theorei** (Klopstock, Gellert), now **Theorie.** In a few cases both suffixes remain: **Melodie** or sometimes in poetry for sake of a rhyme **Melodei.** In one word differentiation of meaning has taken place: **Partei,** party, faction; **Partie** parcel, match (in matrimony), game, party, picnic.

The suffix **-ei** does not usually mutate the stem vowel. However, as a number of the derivatives to which it is added already have a mutated vowel, as in the case of **Färber, tändeln,** &c., mutation has in several instances spread by analogy: **Sämerei, Büberei, Andächtelei,** &c.

The following general points with regard to their use may be of service:

1. The form **ei** is found:

a. Affixed to derivatives in **-er,** which denote persons engaged in a certain business or occupation. Here the **ei** denotes the idea of a trade, business, art, profession, or an act or state of the class of people in question: **Färberei** the dyeing business, **Gerberei** the tanning business, **Verräterei** treachery, **Überläuferei** desertion. These words often take on concrete meaning, and then denote the building where the business is carried on: **Färberei** dyeing establishment, **Druckerei** printing-house, **Bäckerei** bakery, &c.

Note. The suffix **ei** is, after the analogy of the above words in **-er,** sometimes added to the plurals in **-er,** as **Kinderei** childishness, **Abgötterei** idolatry, &c. This frequent reoccurrence of **ei** after **-er** has led to the erroneous idea that the suffix is **-erei: Büberei** knavery, **Schurkerei** rascality, **Sklaverei** slavery, **Pfafferei** or **Pfäfferei,** &c. In a few cases only is **-ei** added here directly to the stem or to a noun not ending in **-er: Abtei** abbey, **Dechanei** deanery, **Pfarrei** parish, parsonage, **Propstei** provost's residence or office, **Vogtei** prefecture, **Narrei** (early N.H.G.) or now **Narretei** *tomfoolery,* which has resulted from the mingling of the older **Narrei** with **Narrenteiding** or **Narrenteidung** (*Faust,* l. 5798), **Armutei** (Walther Siegfried's *Um der Heimat willen,* IV; S.G. dialect, sometimes also in the literary language) cramped financial condition, poverty, **Auskunftei** intelligence bureau. However, in student slang **ei** is still (not so much tho as formerly) in some university towns added to the name of a family, to indicate a house where students live: **Schiller wohnte zu Jena in einer Schrammei und Hoffmann von Fallersleben in einer Knabei.** Also the beer-halls where the different academic societies meet take this suffix: **die Beckei, Oppelei,** &c.

b. Affixed to verbs, to denote the abstract idea of repetition or prolongation of the activity expressed by the verb: **eine große Graberei** (Frenssen's *Jörn Uhl,* chap. 26) extensive excavations, **Liebelei** love-affair, flirtation, **Plackerei** pestering, **Plauderei** chatting, chat, **Neckerei** teasing, **Tändelei** toying.

Note. Only **ei** is added to stems in **-el** and **-er,** but monosyllabic stems affix **-erei: Ziererei** *affectation* from **sich zieren.** The noun **Andächtelei** (see *d* below) *false devotion* affixes -elei after the analogy of the verbs in **-eln.**

c. Sometimes **-ei** has collective force: **Reiterei** cavalry, **Bücherei** library, **die ganze Treibelei** (Fontane) the whole family or tribe of the Treibels.

Sometimes we find in **-el** the combined force of *c* and *d*: **Diese Treibelei war ein Irrtum** (Fontane's *Frau Jenny,* XVI) This whole Treibel business (striving to get into the Treibel family by marriage) was a mistake.

If the stem of the word does not end in **-el** or **-er,** the suffix here is **-erei: die ganze Felgentreuerei** (Fontane) the whole Felgentreu family.

d. In the uses *a* and *b* and sometimes *c*, the **ei** very often has a disparaging force: **Juristerei** business of a pettifogger, **Lauferei** much unpleasant running about, **Leserei** indiscriminate reading, **Reimerei** poem without poetic merit containing jingling rhymes, **Ausländerei** predilection for everything foreign, affectation of foreign manners, **Engländerei** Anglomania, **Rückwärtserei** reactionary movement, retrogression, **Schieberei** profiteering by selling things clandestinely in disregard of governmental regulations and restrictions, **Preistreiberei** *forcing prices up for sordid purposes* in contrast to **Preisabbau** *bringing excessive prices down to a healthy level.* **Und daß das Mädel bei dieser ewigen Warterei vielleicht um die schönsten Partien kommt, das kümmert Sie wohl gar nicht?** (Beyerlein's *Dämon Othello*, **1**, 8). The **Ge — e** (see **83.** *b*) formations have a somewhat similar meaning, but more distinctly abstract and verbal force, and cannot be used in the plural, as can those in **-ei,** as in **Zu allem, was er sonst . . . auf sich genommen, nun auch noch die Komiteesitzungen wegen des Kirchenbasars und die Laufereien von einem zum andern, um eine allgemeine Beteiligung der gebildeten Kreise zuwege zu bringen** (Telmann's *Wahrheit,* XI).

e. In a few geographical terms; see 3 below.

2. The form **ie** is used mostly in foreign words, especially in a number of scientific and geographical terms: **Theologie, Geographie, Geologie, Picardie, Normandie,** &c. Also in the arts: **Stenographie, Lithographie, Photographie,** &c.

3. The form **ien** is found in a number of geographical terms: **Spanien** (pro. ʃpa:ˈnĭən), **I'talien, Si'zilien,** &c., but **Picar'die, Norman'die,** &c. These foreign names in **-ien** have been conformed to the German model **Preußen** Prussia, &c., the **ie** becoming **ien.** In a few geographical names the form is **ei: Türkei, Lombardei, Walachei, Mandschurei, Mongolei.**

3. el masc., less commonly fem. and neut., suffix with the general idea of a close association, which has developed different groups of meanings more or less distinct: (**1**) the idea of a thing in close association with an activity, i.e. an instrument: **Hebel** (from **heben** to lift) lever, **Meißel** (from older **meißen** to hew, cut, now no longer in use) chisel, **Stempel** (L.G. and M.G. form of H.G. **Stempfel** from a L.G. verb corresponding to H.G. **stampfen** to stamp) stamp, pestle, **Stachel** (from **stechen** to prick) prick, spine, goad; (**2**) a person or living being in close association with an activity: **Krüppel** (originally a L.G. form with **pp** instead of H.G. **pf** from an older L.G. verb corresponding to older H.G. **krüpfen** to bend) cripple, **Gimpel** (from older **gumpen** to hop, jump) bullfinch, fig. block-head, dunce; (**3**) a thing in close association with a thing: **Knöchel** (from **Knochen** bone) knuckle, ankle, **Ärmel** (from **Arm** arm) sleeve, **die Eichel** (from **Eiche** oak) acorn, **die** (formerly **der**) **Angel** (from older **Ange** sharp point) fish-hook; (**4**) a person in close relation with a thing: **Tölpel** (from older Dutch dorper, where dorp corresponds to H.G. **Dorf** village) lout, rustic, dunce, lit. villager; (**5**) a person in close association with a person, a large productive group illustrated in **8. 1.** *f. Note* 3 below. For important additional matter see 1. B. (2nd par.) above.

In late M.H.G. this suffix lost its productivity as a form to indicate instruments, as in (**1**). It was replaced in new formations by **-er.** See 5. *c* below. Much earlier than this, even in O.H.G. **-er** began to crowd out **-el** in its functions to denote persons in a close relation to an activity, as in (**2**).

Note. The **-el** of these words represents O.H.G. **il, al, ul, ilo,** &c., of which **il, ilo** have left their imprint in the mutated vowel of the stem. The **el** is frequently in case of strong verbs affixed to the stem of the past, in other cases to the present stem: **Flügel** wing, from **fliegen** to fly; **Schlüssel** key, from **schließen** to lock; **Sessel** easy-chair—**sitzen; Zügel** rein—**ziehen; Griffel** slate-pencil—**greifen; Schlegel** mallet—**schlagen; Löffel** (corrupted N.H.G. form of M.H.G. **Leffel**) spoon—O.H.G. **laffan** to lick, lap.

4. en or sometimes only **e** or even disappearing entirely, usually a masc. suffix, less commonly neut. It is of different origin in different words, and has to-day no appreciable meaning. It is used in words which denote:

a. An instrument: **Spaten** spade, **Bogen** bow, **Haken** hook, &c.

b. A place for storing or securing something: **Laden** store, **Schuppen** shed, **Hafen** harbor, &c.

c. A part of the body: **Magen** stomach, **Rücken** back, **Daumen** thumb, &c.

d. An abstract idea in a few cases: **Glaube (n)** faith, **Friede (n)** peace, **Schreck** or **Schrecken** fright.

e. Various other things: **Same** or **Samen** seed, **Ost** or **Osten** east, &c.

f. It forms the ending of many geographical names. See **88.** 1.

5. er (O.H.G. āri, from Latin ārius = English er or the latinized form ar, as in baker, scholar), masc. suffix, used to form appellations of male beings. Compare **1.** B. 2nd paragraph. Mutation of the stem vowel is the rule when the suffix is added directly to the stem-word, but there are some exceptions: **Bäcker,** &c.; **Dampfer, Frager, Maler,** &c.; both forms without differentiation in **der Schlächter** or **Schlachter** *butcher*; with differentiation in case of **der Schläger** *beater, swordsman, sword, kicker* (of a horse) and **der Schlager** *something that takes*, of a play or a book, as in **Das Buch ist ein Schlager.** When **-er** is preceded by another suffix mutation is not so common, perhaps, as non-mutation: **Stamm (e)ler,** &c., but also **Pförtner,** &c. When the **-er** is added to names of cities and places a few irregularities occur in the form of the stem, which are the same as for the proper adjectives described in **II. 10. 1.** *b.* *Note* 2. The leading points as to use are as follows:

a. Affixed to substantives it indicates that the person either manufactures the article or thing named in the stem of the substantive or is associated with it in a business or professional way: **Hafner** potter, **Gärtner** gardener, **Sänger** singer, **Schauspieler** actor (on the stage).

b. Affixed to verbal stems it indicates either that the person is temporarily engaged in the activity expressed in the verbal stem, or is engaged therein in a business or professional way: **der Leser** the reader, **Bettler** beggar, **Schneider** tailor, &c. It is also used of animals: **Weidenbohrer** caterpillar of the goat-moth, &c. The **-er** is added to verbal stems indicating an involuntary activity in order to denote a single manifestation of such involuntary activity: **Seufzer** sigh, **Schluchzer** sob, especially in colloquial speech, as in **Rülpser** belch, etc. From this starting point **-er** has developed into a productive suffix to indicate an activity that is conceived as a unit, i.e. not indefinitely prolonged but as an individual performance or act: **Jodler** yodling-song, **Hopser** hop-dance, **Walzer** waltz, **Spritzer** (**ein Regen, der nur ein wenig spritzt**) shower, **Abstecher** excursion, little trip (**einen Abstecher nach B. machen**), **Jauchzer** shout, cheer, **Treffer** lucky hit, **Fehler** mistake, **Schnitzer** blunder, **Puffer** thump, nudge, **Diener** bow (**einem einen Diener machen**), &c.

As in case of **-ig** in **II. 9. 1.** *b* below **-er** is sometimes employed to form derivatives from compounds made from a syntactical group of words: **Befehlshaber = den Befehl haben + er; Eckensteher = an der Ecke stehen + er; Langschläfer = lange schlafen + er.**

Note. After the analogy of the numerous derivatives from stems in **el** and **en** in *a* and *b* above, as **Bettler** beggar and **Hafner** potter, the suffix **er** is lengthened to **ler** and **ner** in a large number of words with stems not ending in **el, en: Dörfler** (now more common than the older form **Dörfer**) *villager* from **Dorf, Gegenfüßler** antipode, **Hinterwäldler** backwoodsman, **Kriegervereinler** (Raabe's *Villa Schönow*, v) member of a club of veteran soldiers, **Künstler** artist, **Neusprachler** one who devotes himself to the scientific study of modern languages, **Wissenschaftler** or **Wissenschafter** scientific investigator, man of science, **Altertumskundler** archeologist, **Kriegsgewinnler** one who has made money out of the war, **Radler** cyclist, **Sommerfrischler** visitor at a summer resort, **Tischler** joiner, &c.; **Glöckner** *bell-ringer* from **Glocke, Harfner** harpist, &c. **Lügner** *liar* does not belong here, as it is derived from the older form **Lügen** (still in use in early N.H.G.), now **Lüge.** There is usually no disparaging sense in **-ler,** as is sometimes claimed. If such force exists it lies in the meaning of the stem word, as in **Zuchthäusler** (*convict*)—**Zuchthaus** (*penitentiary*) + **ler.**

c. Figuratively **er** is often applied to names of lifeless objects: **Wecker** alarm clock, **Bohrer** gimlet, **Schraubenzieher** screw-driver, **Verflüssiger** condenser, **Trockner** drying apparatus, **Eindecker** monoplane, **Zweidecker** biplane, **Bagger** dredger, **Operngucker** opera-glass, &c. In a number of words it indicates an object that is affected by an action: **Ableger** or **Absenker** layer, runner, lit. a shoot that has been bent to one side and sunk in the ground for the purpose of rooting it, **Hinterlader** breech-loader, lit. a gun that is loaded behind, **Wälzer** heavy, unwieldy book, lit. a book that must be rolled when it is moved, &c.

d. It forms a few masculines corresponding to feminines in **e: Tauber** or **Täuber** male pigeon — **Taube** pigeon, **Witwer** widower — **Witwe** widow; **Puter** (N.G.) turkey-cock — **Pute** (N.G) turkey-hen.

e. Affixed to names of cities, countries, and continents, it indicates a resident or subject of the place in question: **Römer** Roman, **Irländer** Irishman, **Euro'päer** inhabitants of Europe. In a number of words the **-er** is usually added to a shorter stem than the one found in the name of the place: **Barmer** inhabitant of **Barmen, Binger** inhabitant of **Bingen, Bremer** inhabitant of **Bremen, Emder** inhabitant of **Emden,** &c. For explanation see II. **10.** 1. *b. Note* 2 below.

In the lengthened form **-i'aner** it is often added to a name of a person to indicate a follower, disciple of: **Kantianer, Goethianer, Wagnerianer, Ritschlianer,** &c.

Note 1. There is, however, much irregularity in forming such nouns from names of countries, and often there is no mutation. Foreign names in **ien** drop **n** and add **r,** as **Gallier** inhabitant of Gaul (**Gallien**), **Spanier** inhabitant of Spain (**Spanien**), but exceptionally **Italiener** (pro. ita·'lĭeːnəʀ). In some other foreign names the endings **'aner, 'iner, 'enser** are added to the stem in imitation of the Latin endings *anus, inus, ensis*: **Ameri'kaner** American, **Floren'tiner** Florentine, **Atheni'enser** Athenian. Under learned influence these foreign endings have also become attached to native German words: **Weima'raner, Ba'denser, Bre'menser, Anhal'tiner,** &c. inhabitants of Weimar, Baden, Bremen, Anhalt, &c. Under the influence of the strong modern trend toward native German forms many scholars now recommend the use of the forms in **-er** here: **Weimarer, Badener, Bremer, Anhalter,** &c. In many other names the words end in **e,** and are inflected weak: **Preuße** Prussian, **Pole** Pole, &c.

Note 2. In popular language **-er** and **-erin** are often replaced by **isch.** The **isch** is added to the stem, and the word is then inflected as an adjective: **der Spanische** instead of **der Spanier, die Spanische** instead of **die Spanierin, Weimarsche** instead of **Weimarer,** &c.

f. In a number of foreign and, in colloquial language, a few German words the French form of this suffix, accented **-ier** (iːʀ), is found instead of **-er: Offi'zier** officer, **Juwe'lier** jeweler. This same suffix is also found in English in the form of *eer*, as in pioneer. In a few words the German suffix has been added to the foreign **-ier: Ka'ssier** or less commonly **Ka'ssierer** cashier, **Tape'zier** or **Tape'zierer** paper-hanger. The **-er** indicates that the noun has been brought into relation to the corresponding German form of the verb: **kassieren, tapezieren.** In a few cases the French pronunciation of the suffix has been retained, as in **Portier** (pro. pɔʀ'tĭeː) door-keeper, **Ban'kier** banker. In a few instances the French suffix with French pronunciation is added to German stems: **Kneipier** toper, beer-house keeper, &c. In a large number of foreign words Latin -or (unaccented in the sing. and accented in the pl.) and its French form **eur** correspond to German **er: der Pro'fessŏr** *professor* (pl. **Profe'ssōren**), **Redak'teur** editor, &c.

6. 1. in (usually causing mutation), fem. suffix, used to form **fem.** from masc. appellations denoting a rank, dignity, occupation: **Gräfin** countess, **Graf** count; **Pfarrerin** pastor's wife. For use with titles see **92.** 6.

a. Words ending in **e** drop it before adding **in,** as in **Fran'zösin** French lady, from **Fran'zose.** Words ending in **erer** may drop one of the **er**'s before adding **in,** as in **Zauberin** sorceress, from **Zauberer.**

b. In popular language **-in** is often weakened to **-en** or **-n: die Buchholzen** Mrs. Buchholz, **die Frau Junkern** Mrs. Junker. See **92.** 6.

c. In North German dialect **-in** is often replaced by **-sche: Sündersche = Sünderin),** &c. It is most commonly found after masculine stems in **-er** as here. It is derived from Latin -issa (as in abbatissa *abbess*) thru the French, and is thus of the same origin as English -ess, which also came thru the French. For the use of **-sche** in names see **92.** 6 (2nd par.).

2. Most appellations of male persons have corresponding forms for female persons, only a few words as **Gast** *guest* and most nouns in **-ling** have the same form for both genders: **Kaiser** emperor, **Kaiserin** empress; **Lehrer** teacher, **Lehrerin** lady teacher. But **Sie ist unser Gast. Sie ist der Liebling aller.** In the use of the feminine form German goes very much farther than English. See, however, **253,** III. 2. *a* for other exceptions to the rule.

7. ing (related to **ung** in **15.** 1 below), now commonly written **ling** (cognate with Eng. *ling*, as in *sapling*), except in the cases mentioned in *a* and *b*, usually a masc. suffix whether it be applied to males or females, sometimes, however, in the form **lingin** with reference to the latter, as **die britische Jünglingin** (Raabe's *Pechlin*, II, chap. 11), usually causing mutation if affixed directly to the stem. It is affixed to nouns, verbs, adjectives, and in a few cases to other parts of speech, to form designations of persons or other living beings, less commonly of things, with the meaning of intimate relation or association: **Säugling** child at the breast (so called from its close association with sucking), **Säuerling** mineral water with a sour taste, **Ankömmling** new-comer, **Nädling** (Walther Siegfried's *Gritli Brunnenmeister*; S.G., sometimes used in the literary language) a piece of thread cut off from the spool and drawn thru the eye of the needle for use in sewing, **Häuptling** one who is associated with others in the relation of head, chieftain, **Günstling** one who receives favors, favorite, **Peinling** (H. Hoffmann's *Rittmeister*, p. 204) one who gives, causes pain, pedant, **Lüstling** one who seeks the gratification of his senses, sensualist, **Gründling**, groundling (a kind of fish that stays upon the bottom of a body of water), **Hänfling** a bird that feeds upon hemp-seed, linnet, **Häftling** prisoner; derivatives from verbs sometimes with active, sometimes with passive force, as **Eindringling** *intruder*, lit. *one who intrudes*, **Sträfling** *convict*, lit. *one who is being punished;* **Frühling** spring, **Neuling** novice, **Finsterling** a friend of darkness and ignorance, obscurant. From the idea of a close relation to something or in a close association with someone in the work of helping, teaching comes the idea of littleness, youth, dependency: **Sämling** seedling, **Setzling** small rooted plant for setting out, young fish to be put into a pond for the purpose of propagation, **Schößling** shoot, **Nestling** young bird, **Däumling** hop-o'-my-thumb, **Pflegling** ward, **Schützling** protégé, **Zögling** pupil, **Lehrling** apprentice, &c. In dialect this idea of littleness and that of the closely related conception of endearment are more distinctly and commonly associated with the older form **-ing.** These ideas developed in Mecklenburg and Hither Pomerania in the course of the last century out of the older idea of association as found in names of animals, as **Brüning** (= **Pferdchen**), originally from association with the color of the horse. The idea of endearment naturally became associated with **-ing** when it was applied to a pet animal and the idea of littleness as naturally arose when it was used with little pets. See **8.** 1. *f* below. Also in the literary language the diminutive force in **-ling** is so strongly felt that an additional diminutive suffix is rarely added. In Old Norse and in modern English this suffix also has in a number of cases pure diminutive force, and the same is true of the corresponding Latin and Greek k-suffix.

A number of words in **-ling** have a depreciatory meaning: **Mietling** hireling, **Eindringling** intruder, **Nachäffling** one who apes another's ways, dress, **Auswürfling** scum, one cast out from human society, **Schädling** one who is a menace, a source of harm to society, &c. This **-ling,** from association with such words as have in themselves a depreciatory meaning or from the general idea of dependency developed in the suffix, often assumes depreciatory force and has become productive especially in this sense: **Höfling** courtier, **Dichterling** poetaster, **Günstling** one supported by the favor of a king, lord, &c., **Witzling** would-be-wit, **Emporkömmling** upstart, parvenu, **Einseitling** (H. Seidel's *Lang, lang ist's her*) one-sided, narrow-minded person, &c. Sometimes in a milder, humorous sense: **Feistling** (Raabe's *Stopfkuchen*, p. 129) fat fellow, 'fatty.'

a. The idea of close association early led to the idea of origin and gave rise to many patronymics as seen in the names of old Germanic tribes and families: **Thüringer, Merowinger, Karolinger,** &c. There are many modern family names that end in **-ing,** as **Henning, Grüning.** Corresponding to these names in **-ing** are also names in **s** or **sen: Ebers** (gen.) = **Ebers Sohn, Jansen** = **Jahns Sohn, Schmitz** = **Schmidts Sohn.** The Latin genitive ending i often occurs here instead of German **-s: Eberti** = **Eberz.** Instead of the genitive here the diminutive **-lein** (or **-līn, -le,** &c.) or **-ke** (Low German = **-lein**) may be added, or the adjective **klein** prefixed: **Böcklīn, Gödecke, Kleinschmidt,** &c. Many names of places are derived from the family names in **-ing,** usually ending in **-ingen,** the **en** being the dat. pl. ending after the prep. **zu** understood (see also **88.** 1): **Tübingen** city of Tübingen, **Göttingen,** &c.; also in shortened form, **-ing,** especially in Bavaria: **Freising.** In some sections of the Midland, as in Thuringia and Hesse **-ungen** is also found here, usually added to a noun designating a thing, thus indicating a close association with the thing in question: **Salzungen,** &c. In case of certain ruling families **-er** is added to **-ing: Karolinger** descendant of **Karl der Große,** Carlovingian, &c. This is a survival of older usage, which employed here **linger** interchangeably with **-ing.** Luther still uses both **Fremdling** and **Fremdlinger** (Luke xvii. 18).

b. The earlier form of the suffix was **-ing.** As it very commonly stood after al, il, ul, the preceding l became associated with it, and finally the lengthened form **-ling** supplanted it in most words. The few existing forms in **-ing** are thus older, and the force of the suffix is not now vividly felt or is not felt at all: **Hering** herring, **Messing** brass (both words of uncertain origin), **Bücking** or **Bückling** bocking (fish), &c. **König** and **Pfennig** originally had an **n** before the final **g** and hence belonged here. The particular group in *a*, however, always take **-ing**.

As the form **-ling** is added to many words in **-er**, the suffix has from analogy assumed the form **-erling** in a few words: **Heiderling, Windling** or **Winderling,** &c. For the form **-linger** see *a* above.

8. 1. lein (O.H.G. ilīn) and **chen** (earlier ichin, cognate with Eng. *kin* as in *lambkin*), neuter diminutive suffixes, different developments of the older simple form **-in** (see *f. Note* 3 below), affixed to nouns, usually causing mutation when they follow an accented syllable. The former is the original H.G. suffix, which in different dialectic forms is still used everywhere in the South in familiar language (see *f* below). In the form of **lein** and **lin** (more common in his later writings) it was employed by Luther in his translation of the Bible and elsewhere as the more dignified form, in preference to the M.G. **-chen,** but it has only limited use to-day in the literary language and only in the form of **lein,** being largely confined to a beautiful style and a few common words with endings that are difficult to unite with **chen,** as **Büchlein, Fischlein,** &c. Modern authors, however, do not seem to regard a number of these combinations as harsch: **die Fischchen** (Spielhagen's *Frei geboren*, p. 15). After stems in **ch** and **g** it is common to employ a double diminutive formed by adding **chen** to **-el** (the shortened form of **-lein**): **Büchelchen** booklet, **Sächelchen** little matter, pretty little thing, gimcrack, **Wägelchen** little wagon.

In the eighteenth century **-chen,** the diminutive suffix of the middle portion of the Midland, replaced **-lein** in the language of the prose writers Lessing, Wieland, Herder, and others who had taken the Upper Saxon dialect as their standard. Gradually **-chen** became established in the literary language in general and the familiar language of the North in particular, while under the influence of the poets Goethe, Bürger, Voss, and others **-lein** secured a permanent place of honor in poetry.

a. If a word ends in **e, el,** or **en,** these endings are often dropped before adding the diminutive suffix: **Bübchen** from **Bube; Näglein** from **Nagel,** but **Nägelchen; Gärtchen** from **Garten,** &c.

b. The diminutive endings are usually added to the sing., but may in familiar language be affixed to plurals in **er,** and also to the plural form **Leute** *people*: **das Kindchen,** pl. **die Kindchen** or **Kinderchen** (see *f. Note* 2 below), **Leutchen** "*small fry,*" *good people*, people spoken of slightingly or in a tone of friendly familiarity.

c. The mutation is often dropped, especially when the suffix expresses irony, and in case of proper names where the suffix has more the force of endearment than littleness (see 2 below): **Ich habe dies Jahr einen Roggen und Weizen, überhaupt ein Kornchen** (= **ein prachtvolles Korn** *a splendid crop of grain*) **gebaut wie noch nie. Dann kam auch noch ein kleines Schlaganfallchen!** (Sudermann's *Heimat*, 1, 4) Then there came in addition a nice little (ironical) stroke of paralysis! By dropping mutation we may emphasize the idea of *largeness* or *efficacy*, while the use of mutation makes prominent the idea of *littleness*: **Der Physiolog spricht von Blutkügelchen, ein Jagdfreund aber spricht mit begeisterter Liebe von seinen nie fehlenden Kugelchen. Vorläufig friert's und schneit's noch lustig weiter. Das gibt wieder ein Wasserchen** (Halbe's *Der Strom*, p. 20) *a great flood*. In the literary language it is the rule that the suffix does not cause mutation if it follows an unaccented syllable: **Monatchen, Hoffnungchen,** &c. Most of the exceptions to this rule occur after words in **-el** and **-er: Vögelchen, Brüderchen,** &c.

We say **Hänsel** (also **Hansel** — Rosegger), **Hänschen, Ännchen,** (but also **Annchen** —Bismarck to Herr von Puttkamer, April 5, 1848), **Fränzchen, Röschen,** but usually proper names remain unmutated: **Tonnerl, Lottchen, Karlchen,** &c.

The use of mutation varies a good deal: **Frauchen,** but **Fräulein; Onkelchen,** but **Väterchen, Jüngchen** (also **Jungchen** — Sudermann's *Der Sturmgeselle Sokrates*, 3, 3) or **Jüngelchen; Tantchen,** but **Bäschen, Mütterchen** (also **Mutterchen** — Sudermann's *D. S. S.*, 1, 17; **Schwiegermuttelchen** — Hauptmann's *Friedensfest*, p. 59), &c.

d. Sometimes the diminutives are fem. according to the natural sex instead of neut. according to grammatical gender: **die** (or **das**) **Gretchen** little Margaret. See **263.** I. 1, 2, 3, 4.

e. These suffixes are usually affixed to nouns only, but in familiar language can be added on to the case ending or the stem of an adjective used as a noun, and also to other parts of speech: **Alterchen** or **Altchen** dear old fellow, **mein liebes Dickerchen** (Raabe) my dear fat friend, **Dummchen!** You foolish thing!, **Geduldchen!** (noun used as an imperative) Just have a little patience! **Wieder nach einer Weile sagte Hedwig: „Ahne!" „Wasele?"** (Auerbach's *Dorfgeschichten*, 2, p. 91) "Grandmother!" "What, my Dear?" **Ich will mich sachtchen in mein Bettchen stehlen** (Goethe). **Warting** (see *f*) **noch!** Wait a moment! **Die jungen Mädchens, die sind ja hier so**

feining gezogen (M. Dreyer's *In Behandlung*, 1). In verbs the form l is very common: **lächeln** to smile, from **lachen** to laugh, &c. See III. 2 below.

f. In dialect these suffixes have assumed a great variety of forms which can be indicated here in only the roughest outlines: in southern Bavaria and Austria **-el, -erl, -l** with a plural of the same form or one in **-eln, -erln,** &c.; **-le** with a plural of the same form; **-le** or **-l** with the plural **-lan** or **-len**; in Upper Bavaria in palatalized form, **-ei, -ai, -i, -ö,** &c. with a plural of the same form: **Bübel, jedes Aderl, Herzerl** (with lengthened form after the analogy of many words in **-er**, as **Ader**, dimin. **Aderl**), **bissei** = **bissel** (S.G. for **bißchen**); in Switzerland **-li** with the plural **-li** or **-lini**; also found in palatalized form **-ji** or **-ti**: **Retli (Rädlein)**, pl. **Retli** or **Retlini; Meitji (Mädlein), Vogulti (Vöglein); i** (older **-in**; see *Note* 3) with the plural **-ini**, used as a pure diminutive, also in pet-names and in words denoting a relationship, also found in other sections of the German-speaking territory in pet-names: **Hīschi (Häuslein)**, pl. **Hīschini, Ruodi** (ʀu:odi:, character in Schiller's *Tell*, now **Ruedi** or **Rüedi**, pet-name from **Rudolf**), **Ehni** grandfather; in Württemberg **-le** with the plural **-le** or the three reduced forms **-la, -li, -lich** (from older **-lach**; see 17. *a*. *Note* below): **Tischle**, pl. **Tischle, Tischla, Tischli, Tischlich**; in Franconia **-la** (from **-lein**) with the plural **-li** (from older **-lach**): **Kindla**, pl. **Kindli**; in the Midland **-chen** or **che**, pl. **-chen** or **-cher**; in the North **-ken** with the plural **-ken, -kens, kes**; often in palatalized form **-je, tje** with the plural **-jes, -tjes**; sometimes **-ke, -eke,** **-elken, -sken, -tjen** instead of **-ken**: **Mäken (Mädchen)**, pl. **Mäkens**, &c.; **Annatje** = **Ännchen.** In Mecklenburg and Hither Pomerania **-ing** (see 7 above) is used as a diminutive, especially, however, as a sign of endearment.

Note 1. The Austrian and Swiss dialects are especially inclined to the use of diminutive endings, which in consequence of their frequent use naturally lose somewhat of their original force. Hence some words, as **Hörnl** (= **Hörnlein**), &c., are often found with diminutive ending, whether the reference is to something small or large, beautiful or ugly. The Swiss often refer to some familiar mountain even tho it be a high one as **das Bergli.** Thus the diminutive often seems to be only a means of sharp individualization, a kind of personification. Similarly the North German refers to his native village as **mein Dörfchen.** In general, however, the North is more sparing with the use of the diminutive than the South. In the dialect of some parts of the North the diminutive occurs very little. This may be a survival of older general usage. In the oldest historical period the diminutive was little used. It first became common in M.H.G. and spread from the South northward.

Note 2. In M.H.G. diminutives did not have a distinctive plural ending. As can be seen by a glance at *f* above most of the dialects have since developed a distinctive plural form. On the other hand, in the middle portion of the Midland, upon which the literary language rests, there is no such distinctive plural as words with the ending **-chen** are inflected according to the **e**-less plural class. The impulse, however, to give some expression to the plural idea in diminutives is often so strong that the stem word, if an **er**-plural, is given its regular plural form if the diminutive is used in the plural: **Kinderchen** instead of the strict literary form **Kindchen.** In loose colloquial speech and sometimes even in the literary language the **er**-plural here is not felt as incongruous as it is closely associated with the neuter gender and hence does not seem improper in the plural of a neuter diminutive. Such formations, **Kinderchen, Kinderlein,** &c., tho not strictly correct, began to appear in the literary language in the fourteenth century and have not since entirely disappeared. Further to the west in the Midland the dialectic form of the diminutive, **-che,** made it easy to find a plural form. The neuter plural ending **-er** is added to the suffix and in some dialects also to the stem word: **Kindche**, pl. **Kindcher** or **Kindercher; Mädche**, pl. **Mädcher** or **Mädercher.** In the last example the plural of the stem word does not end in **-er**, but this ending here has in certain dialects become a fixed type. Under N.G. influence a plural in **-s** also occurs: **Mädchens, Fräuleins,** See **80.** 3.

Note 3. The oldest diminutive forms are -ilo (masc.) or -ila (fem.) of O.H.G., -iko of Old Saxon, and -īn (identical with the **-in** in II. 3 below), all with the meaning close association with, coming from, springing from, hence often with the idea of endearment, sometimes with the conception of littleness: **die Eichel**, from O.H.G. eihhila acorn, something coming from the oak tree, O.H.G. eih, N.H.G. **Eiche; der Ärmel**, from O.H.G. armilo sleeve, something closely associated with the arm; Uulfilo coming from Wolfhart, i.e. son of Wolfhart, in oldest German a type widely used for pet-names, sometimes also with diminutive force. The suffix -īn survives as a fossil in **Schwein (Sau + in,** M.H.G. su + in) pig, lit. young of a sow, also in Low German **Küken** (= **Küchlein**). It is still found as a living suffix in Swiss dialect as the diminutive **-i**, especially in pet-names: **Äugi** (= **Äuglein**), **Ruedi** (pet-name), &c. In names the suffixes -ilo, -iko often lost every vestige of their original force, so that the words containing the suffixes became family names: **Wölfel, Reineke** or **Reinecke**, &c. As these suffixes from the very start had more frequently the idea of endearment than that of littleness -īn, or in shortened form ī, was even in oldest German sometimes added to the l or k to bring out clearly the diminutive idea: O.H.G. Kindilīn or kindilī; M.H.G. kindelīn, kindel. These strengthened forms are the common S.G. **-lein, -le, -el** or **-l**, M.G. **-chen**, N.G. **-ken** of to-day as given in *f* above. Modern **-el** (or **-l**) represents both O.H.G. -ilo and -ilī. Out of the diminutive idea of the strengthened forms arose the conception of endearment, so that these forms now indicate both littleness and endearment. As the **-el** that came from O.H.G. -ilo is now identical in form with the **-el** that came from O.H.G. ilī it is no longer felt as a separate suffix. In names also the strengthened suffixes have often lost every vestige of their original meaning as in case of the simple suffixes described above, and the words containing them have become mere family names: **Wölflin, Beyerlein** (for **Bayerlein**), &c. Compare 7. *a* above.

On the other hand, we often find in sections of the Southwest the present diminutive suffix **-le** with the meaning of close association, either as a survival of older usage or as a modern development out of the diminutive idea, in either case indicating the close relation between the two ideas: **der Pfarrerle** the son, nephew, or servant of the pastor, i.e. someone closely associated with the pastor; **der Studentle** (Auerbach's *Dorfgeschichten*, II, p. 97), here used of one who had once been a student, lit. one of or belonging to the students; **Räuberles** (**260.** 2. A under **spielen**) **spielen** to play robbers, lit. to play belonging to the robbers. This idea of association is also found in these sections in nouns made from adjectives: **der Geschwindle** a slow worker, lit. ironically "the swift one," **der Gescheidtle** one who thinks himself bright, &c. In the Midland we find **-chen** similarly used: **Soldätches spielen** (G. Asmus's *Amerikanisches Skizzenbuch*, p. 59). The old idea of association is well preserved in Swiss **-i**: **Götti** godfather, **Lufti (Luft + i = Windbeutel), Schlīchi** (= **Schleicher**), **Choli (Kohle + i)** coal-black horse, **Pläri (plärren + i)** one who starts to cry, bawl for every little thing, &c. There always lies in **-i** a touch of feeling, a tone o. endearment, playfulness, and often censure, disapproval, or scorn.

2. These suffixes have not only diminutive force, but are also used to express the idea of endearment, tenderness, comeliness, neatness, something affording satisfaction and pleasure, as well as the idea of slyness, stealth, and lastly contempt. Here **lein** and **chen** often form somewhat different shades of meaning. In the literary language of the North **chen** has usually the idea of endearment, comeliness, sarcasm, contempt, slyness, pleasure, and even of largeness, as the diminutive is often used ironically, implying the opposite of what is actually asserted: **Frauchen** dear wife, **Pa'pachen** dear Papa, **Hütchen** a

pretty hat, **Kästchen** an ornamental little box or jewel casket, **die jungen Herrchen** the young gentlemen (sarcastic), **ein Poten'tätchen** an insignificant little potentate, **ein hübsches Sümmchen** a nice little (meaning a big) sum of money. **Lein,** besides its use in beautiful poetic style, is also found sometimes in common style, be it prose or poetry, where it has more strictly than **chen** the idea of littleness and more intensely the idea of contempt: **ein Hündlein** a little dog, but **ein Hündchen** a nice dog; **das arme geschlagene Kaiserlein** (a contemptuous reference to Napoleon in a poem appearing in 1813), **feiste Pfäfflein** (contempt.), **das Produktlein modernen Aufklärichts** (Spielhagen's *Was will das werden?*, I, chap. viii) the product of modern sham enlightenment, &c. As **lein** is so little used in the North in plain prose, the simple idea of littleness is best expressed by placing the adj. **klein** before the noun. In South German authors the very opposite use of **lein** and **chen** above mentioned may be found. **Lein** denotes something nice and large, and **chen** something spoken of in a sense of disparagement and littleness: **ein Siebenträuberl** (Rosegger) a nice large bunch of seven cherries. **Das letzte schäbige Knechtchen, das er gehabt, hatte ihn schon seit einigen Wochen verlassen** (G. Keller). **Ein paar schlechte Kämmerchen** (id.).

The two forms **chen** and **lein** are in certain cases differently distributed, the one being used in connection with certain words, the other employed with others: We say **Ohrläppchen, Zündhölzchen, Liebchen, ein bißchen, Bleib noch ein Stündchen bei mir,** but **Bäuerlein, Brünnlein, sein Scherflein beitragen, Sein Stündlein hat geschlagen.** Sometimes differentiation takes place: **Frauchen** *dear wife* and **Fräulein** Miss; **Männlein** and **Weiblein** of human beings, **Männchen** and **Weibchen** of animals.

In a number of words and expressions *only* the diminutive form of the noun is used: **Gänsefüßchen** quotation marks, **Fräulein** Miss, unmarried woman, **Grübchen** dimple, **Häutchen** membrane, **Scherflein** mite, **sein Schäfchen scheren** to feather one's own nest, **sein Mütchen an einem kühlen** to vent one's anger upon a person, **ins Fäustchen lachen** to laugh in one's sleeve, &c. In case of **Fräulein, chen** is in colloquial language added to **lein** to bring out the diminutive force or to give expression to the idea of endearment, &c., as the original meaning of the **lein** is no longer vividly felt: **Da auf dem Tisch, gnädiges Fräuleinchen** (Sudermann's *Fritzchen*, 1).

9. nis (cognate with *ness* as in *goodness*; see **15.** 2 below), earlier in the period also **nüß (nuß)** especially in S.G., a neut. and less commonly fem. (**99.** 2. *b* and 3. *c*) suffix, usually causing mutation, affixed to nouns, adjectives, perfect participles (as in **Geständnis** *confession* = **gestand[en] + nis**), and verbs (especially such as have prefixes) to denote:

a. An act, performance, activity, function or something concrete which is represented as having active force: **Gelöbnis** vow, **Wagnis** daring deed, **Besorgnis** fear, concern, **Ereignis** occurrence, **Begräbnis** funeral, also tomb (according to *b*), **Gedächtnis** memory, **Verständnis** understanding, comprehension, **Vermächtnis** testament, legacy, **Hindernis** hindrance, that which hinders, **Ärgernis** that which gives offense, **Verhängnis** evil fate that brings about evil things.

b. That which is the result or object of the activity implied in the verbal stem of the noun, or that which is at the same time the result of an action and yet is itself an active force: **Verzeichnis** catalogue, list, **Erzeugnis** product, **Ergebnis** result, **Bedürfnis** need, that which one needs, **Verhängnis** sad or evil fate, **Bündnis** alliance, that which is the result of union and at the same time has active binding force.

c. A condition or quality or something concrete which possesses the quality indicated by the stem of the word: **Finsternis** darkness, **Fäulnis** rottenness, **Wirrnis** chaotic condition, confusion, **Geheimnis** secret thing, a secret, **Bitternis** bitter thing.

d. The place where the condition implied in the stem of the word is found: **Gefängnis** prison, lit. a place where one is caught, **Wildnis** wilderness.

10. rich, see **17.** *b.*

11. 1. **sal** or its weakened form **sel** (O.H.G. isal), usually neut., but in a few cases fem. (**99.** 3. *c*), and formerly also in a few cases masc. (**99.** 3. *c*), sometimes causing mutation. They are usually found after verbal stems, and only in several instances are affixed to nouns. These suffixes have in part a force similar to that of **nis,** but differ often from it in that they have a more comprehensive and intensive force. They have usually an abstract meaning and contain a collective idea, implying that the activity expressed in the verbal stem is long continued, oft repeated, customary, or is extended over a considerable field, or is associated with a large number of objects. Sometimes they may take on concrete meaning, especially **sel.** Nouns having these suffixes denote:

a. A thing which is represented as the subject, or the object, or result of the activity implied in the verbal stem of the noun: **Das Schicksal** that which sends, or is sent, hence *good* or *evil fate, destiny,* **der Stöpsel** that which stops, a *stopper,* **das** (also **der**) **Häcksel** that which is chopped, chopped feed, **das Füllsel** that which is filled in, stuffing, **das Rinnsal** that which has resulted from flowing water, a channel, watercourse, **das Labsal** anything (as food, drink, encouragement, &c.) which refreshes body or mind.

b. A condition, state, or an action: **das Wirrsal** confusion, confused state, **die Trübsal** affliction, **die** and **das Mühsal** difficulty, misery, **das Irrsal** state of erring, erring course, erring, serious error (as in religious belief), which causes a train of errors. In these same words and others the meaning may sometimes become more concrete, indicating something that causes this condition or state, or the place where the condition is found or the action takes place: **das Mühsal** that which causes misery, **das Wehsal** that which causes serious trouble, sorrow, **das Scheusal** that which instils fear and aversion, a monster, **das Irrsal** a place where one can easily err, a labyrinth.

c. **Sel** often denotes something insignificant or contemptible: **das Überbleibsel** something left over, remnant, **das Geschreibsel** a miserably written production, **das Hervorbringsel** inferior production. **Erschachert, indem er für ein Mitbringsel** (insignificant acquisition) **unsre Ehre preisgab** (Fontane's *Schach von Wuthenow,* chap. 6).

2. In derivatives in **-ig** *possessing, full of,* formed from words in **-sal,** this suffix becomes **sel: Wehsal** *sorrow,* but **wehselig** sorrowful; **Mühsal** toil, misery, but **mühselig** toilsome, miserable, full of misery; **Trübsal,** but **trübselig; Saumsal,** but **saumselig.** Sometimes the original noun has gone out of use: **armselig** *miserable,* from M.H.G. armsal *misery.* As these old nouns in **-sal** have disappeared or are little used **-selig** is now felt as an independent suffix with the meaning *possessing* or *full of* the thing indicated by the stem-word, so that new derivatives in **-selig** have arisen: **feindselig** hostile, **holdselig** charming, **habselig** rich (now little used but common in the derivative **Habseligkeiten** *effects, traps*), &c. Derivatives in **-selig** have the same form as compounds with the adjective **selig** *happy in, blessed with*: **gottselig** pious, **glückselig** happy, blessed with happiness, **redselig** talkative, **friedselig** peaceable, &c. The two groups cannot always be distinguished.

12. schaft (from **schaffen** to shape, create; cognate with Eng. *ship* as in *friendship*), once an independent noun, now a fem. suffix, affixed to the sing. or pl. of nouns, also to adjectives, participles, and verbs, to denote:

a. An act, activity: **Wanderschaft** traveling, journeying, **Urheberschaft** act of originating, authorship, **Täterschaft** perpetration, **Rechenschaft** account, **Wirtschaft** management of a house, business, or government, **Wissenschaft** scientific study, **Herrschaft** rule, authority, **Kaufmannschaft** business of a merchant, **Gesandtschaft** duties and position of an ambassador, embassy.

This suffix often assumes concrete meaning, denoting some person carrying on the activity or something which is associated with it or resulting from it: **die Herrschaft** master or mistress or according to *c* both, **Wirtschaft** restaurant, **Gesandtschaft** dwelling or office of an ambassador, **Errungenschaft** something won, achievement, **Meisterschaft** mastery, masterly skill, **Wissenschaft** news, information.

b. Relationship, condition: **Bruderschaft,** or now more commonly **Brüderschaft** relationship of brothers, close friendship, **Freundschaft** friendship, **Feindschaft** enmity, **Meisterschaft** championship, **Bereitschaft** readiness, **Gefangenschaft** captivity, **Brautschaft** state of being betrothed, engagement, **Witwenschaft** widowhood.

c. A collective idea: **Wissenschaft** science, **Bruderschaft** or now less commonly **Brüderschaft** fraternity, **Studentenschaft** student body, **Arbeiterschaft** working class, **Ärzteschaft** medical society, men of the medical profession, **die bayrische Ärzteschaft, Bürgerschaft** all the citizens of a place, **meine Herrschaften!** (in direct address) ladies and gentlemen!, **Gegnerschaft** opponents, opposing party, or (according to *a*) opposition, **Verbraucherschaft** consumers, **Kaufmannschaft** all the merchants of a place, **Gesandtschaft** embassy, an ambassador with his corps of assistants, **Ortschaft** city, town, village, **Wirtschaft** family, household (**Es sind vier Wirtschaften im Hause**), doings, goings-on, especially of wild, noisy, disorderly doings (**eine lustige, tolle, schöne** [sarcastic] **Wirtschaft**), **Hinterlassenschaft** property left by a person at his death, **Briefschaften** papers, written documents.

13. tel, reduced form of **Teil** (formerly neut.) *part*, a neuter suffix added to the stem of ordinals to form fractions. The final **t** of the stem of the ordinal is dropped before the **t** of the suffix: **Drittel** *third*, **Sechstel** *sixth*, **Zwanzigstel.** See also **126. 2.** *a.*

Note. Both ordinal and suffix were formerly independent words: M.H.G. daȥ vǖnfte téil. Later both words entered into a compound as they had in their union developed a peculiar oneness of meaning somewhat different from that suggested by the literal meaning of the components. The change of meaning obscured the original syntactical relations of the components and brought about the shifting of the stress from the second component upon the first in accordance with the usual principle of accenting compounds upon the first element. Thus **das fǘnft(e) Téil** became **das Fǘnftèil.** As the oneness of meaning became fixed and the stress firmly established upon the first element the second component lost more and more of its accent and suffered a further reduction of form. Thus **Fǘnftèil** became **Fǘnftel.** These changes, which have taken place in the present period, fitly illustrate the process by which, in general, words used as components have gradually under the loss of accent changed their form and at last lost their identity and become mere prefixes.

14. 1. tum (cognate with Eng. *dom* as in *kingdom*), once an independent noun, now a neuter (except in the two masc. nouns **Reichtum** wealth, **Irrtum** error) suffix, added to nouns, adjectives, and verbs, to denote:

a. The dignity, rank, profession of the class of persons mentioned in the stem of the noun, with all the peculiar characteristics which attach to such a dignity, rank, or profession: **Kaisertum** office and power of an emperor, **Priestertum** priesthood, **Volkstum** nationality.

b. A condition, state, or an action: **Siechtum** a state of poor health, **Wachstum** a state of healthy growth, **Reichtum** wealthy state, **Irrtum** state of error, erring, error.

c. A collective idea: **Bürgertum** the citizens of a place, **Judentum** the Jewish people, **Reichtum** all that which is implied by the word 'rich,' *riches*, **Altertum** all that period of time which can be said to have age, *antiquity*, **Pfaffentum** or **Bonzentum** priests (collectively and in a disparaging sense), priesthood, priestcraft, the arts and doings of crafty clericals, **Schiebertum** throng of profiteers who prey upon society, especially in times of distress, arts and doings of sordid profiteers who sell things clandestinely in disregard of governmental regulations and restrictions. These words may also take on concrete meaning: **Heiligtum** sanctuary, **Kaisertum** empire, **Eigentum** property, lit. all that which is one's own, **Altertum** an object that has been preserved from a former age.

Note. If **tum** and **schaft** may both be affixed to the same stem to show the collective idea, there is a little shade of difference in their meaning. The latter marks more distinctly the collective idea, the former the dignity or the peculiar character or nature which attaches to the dignity, rank, or profession: **Priesterschaft** priests taken collectively, **Priestertum** peculiar character and nature of the priesthood.

2. The suffixes **heit, schaft, tum** had originally about the same force, and are still so used, but in cases where these suffixes are added to the same stem as in the *Note* above, differentiation of meaning usually takes place: **Christenheit** Christian world, **Christentum** Christianity, peculiar character and nature of the Christian faith and life; **Eigentum** property, **Eigenheit** peculiarity, **Eigen-**

schaft quality; **Bereitschaft** outward readiness, preparedness, **Bereitheit** inward readiness, willingness. Their use is sometimes subject to caprice, not to a fixed difference of meaning: **Heidenschaft** *heathenism, heathen world,* but **Christenheit** *Christianity, Christian world.*

15. 1. ung (cognate with Eng. *ing* as in *warning*), usually a fem. suffix, affixed in most cases to the stem of verbs, especially compounds and derivatives, rarely to the stem of nouns. It means *close association with, origin* and hence is related to **-ing** (see **7** above), as can still be seen in the few words where the suffix is masculine: **die Nibelungen** the children of the mist (**Nebel**), name usually given to the sons and vassals of **Nibelung,** a mythical king. The form **-ungen** is found in the Midland in some names of towns instead of the more common **-ingen.** See **7** *a* above. Altho the prefix **-ing, -ung** originally denoted the close association of a person or thing to some other person or thing the form -ing in English and **-ung** in German early became useful to denote a close association of a person or thing to an activity.

The feminine suffix has become exceedingly fruitful and is now used to denote: *a.* An activity: **Bewachung** guarding, **Bewaffnung** arming, **Erziehung** education. This suffix gives the noun sometimes almost pure verbal force, so that it can usually take a dependent object or a prepositional phrase which has almost the force of an adverb: objective gen.: **die Erzìehung der Knáben; Gótteslầsterung;** acc. object, found only in group-words (**247.** 2) and compounds: **Háushầltung.** In case there are two objects one is usually understood: (acc. object omitted, gen. object expressed) **Ámtsentsètzung** (**Man entsètzt ihn des Ámtes**). Adverbial modifier: **Die Befrèiung aus der Nót** deliverance from distress. The **-ung** is also added to intransitive stems: **Die Binden stillten die Blutung** The bandages stopped the bleeding. With intransitive stems it can take a predicate noun, which is written as one word with the verbal substantive: **die Menschwerdung** the incarnation, lit. the becoming a man. These derivatives cannot only have active force as in the preceding examples, but also sometimes passive and even reflexive and reciprocal force: **Seine Erhebung auf den Thron verdankte er seinen Siegen** He owed his being elevated to the throne to his victories. **In der Opferung für andere seiner Seele Glück zu finden, ist nur wenigen gegeben** Only a few find happiness of soul in sacrificing themselves for others. **Die Kaiserbegegnung in Björkö** (substantive form of **Die Kaiser begegnen sich in Björkö**). See **189.**

Notice that the corresponding English verbal noun in -ing, the so-called gerund, has developed still more verbal force, as it can take an accusative object outside of compounds and can assume compound active and passive forms: the thought of *having performed my duty.* Gloves prevent the hands from *being injured.* In oldest English and German these verbal nouns did not have very strong verbal force. English began to develop it much earlier than German and has gone much farther in this direction.

Note. A number of such formations which were common in the eighteenth century and even later are now replaced by shorter formations: **Abschließung, Anhauchung, Betrachtung, Genießung, Reizung, Verlegung, Versteckung, Wachsung, Zurücknehmung,** now replaced by **Abschluß, Anhauch, Betracht, Genuß, Reiz, Verlag, Versteck, Wuchs, Zurücknahme.** The shorter form usually has more concrete force than the longer one in **-ung** and thus indicates the development of a finer differentiation. On the other hand, where abstract verbal force is prominent the derivatives in **-ung** are becoming ever greater favorites and the construction is extending its boundaries. An interesting extension is the now common construction which prefers to clothe the chief idea of the predicate in the form of a noun rather than that of a verb: **Das Stück wird bald zur Aufführung gebracht** (instead of **aufgeführt**) **The piece will soon be played.** See **252. 1.** *a. Note* 2.

b. A condition, state: **Aufregung** excitement, **Beklemmung** anxiety.

c. Sometimes it denotes something concrete which is closely associatea with an activity in the relation of an active force, a result, product, means, place, &c.: **Erfrischung** refreshment, that which refreshes, **Schickung** the Divine Will, the one that decrees, sends, a decree of Heaven, bitter affliction *or* trial, lit. something sent, **Zeichnung** the product of drawing, a drawing, **Kleidung** that with which one is clothed, i.e. *clothes*, **Wohnung** a dwelling-house, **Biegung** a bend in the road, **Krümmung a turn in the river, Festung** fortress, **Niederung low ground.**

d. A collective idea, since a number of persons or things may be involved in the same activity: **Regierung** government, **Bedienung** body of servants in a house, **Bemannung** crew, **Besatzung** (**besetzen**) garrison, **Dickung** (Hermann Löns in *Hamburger Nachrichten*, Dec. 16, 1905; for the more common **Dickicht**), **Winterbereifung** tires for winter use, **Leitung** pipes, management, &c. This collective idea is also seen in derivatives from nouns: **Waldung** large forest (in its entirety), **Holzung** wood, grove.

2. The suffix **-nis** sometimes approaches near to the force of **-ung**: **Verlöbnis** or **Verlobung** betrothal, **Hindernis** and **Verhinderung** hindrance, &c. However, in most cases the verbal force is stronger in **-ung**, as can be seen in the objective gen. which may follow it. In other cases the meaning of the two suffixes drifts still farther apart: **Bildnis** picture, lit. that which has been formed, **Bildung** education, culture, lit. that which has been formed; **Ergebnis** result, **Ergebung** resignation, submission.

16. A few suffixes which were originally used in forming proper names are later, as also to-day, used in common class nouns:

a. **bold** (from M.H.G. balt) *bold*: **Leopold** (*the bold one among the people*). This suffix in common class nouns indicates an inclination to that which is indicated by the stem of the derivative: **Witzbold** wit, one fond of getting off witty things, **Raufbold** one fond of getting into a fight, **Trunkenbold** drunkard, &c.

b. **jan,** Low German form of **Johannes** *John*, added to adjectival and verbal stems to indicate a person endowed with the quality or inclined to the activity expressed in the stem of the derivative: **Dummerjan** *a stupid fellow*, lit. *stupid Jack*, **Liederjan** *dissolute fellow*, **Murrjan** *grumbling fellow*. Other forms of this name or other names are similarly used with the force of a suffix: **Faselhans** driveler, **Zigárrenfrìtze** cigar-dealer, **Ángstmèier** coward, &c. Sometimes with the parts written apart with the original descriptive group-stress: **dùmmer Péter, dùmme Líse,** &c.

The suffix **-jan** may be replaced by the foreign suffix **ian** of like meaning; hence there is sometimes a double form, as in **Dummerjan** or **Dummrian.** Some have more commonly the foreign form: **Grobian, Schlendrian, Blödian** (Voegtlin's *Das neue Gewissen*, p. 169), **Fadian** (Anzengruber's *Das vierte Gebot*, II), &c.

17. A few suffixes occur only in a few words and have a force that is not always felt distinctly:

a. **icht** (O.H.G. achi or ach, early N.H.G. ich), usually a neut., sometimes a masc. suffix, sometimes both, affixed to nouns, adjectives, verbs to denote a collective idea: **das Röhricht** reeds or a place where reeds grow, **das Dickicht** thicket, **das Dornicht** thornbrake, **das Tannicht** grove of fir-trees, **das Rühricht** hotchpotch, **der** or **das Kehricht** sweepings, **das** (**der**) **Spülicht** slops, &c.

Note. In dialect this suffix occurs in different forms: (1) In S.G. dialects a neuter suffix in the form of **-ach,** used formerly of plants and trees to denote a collective idea, now only found in names of places: **Birkach,** formerly = **Birkengehölz** grove of birch-trees, now the name of a place. (2) As a plural of diminutives in **-le,** formerly in different dialects in the form of **-ach,** still in use in Franconian in the form of **a, i,** or **ich,** as in **Tischle,** pl. **Tischla, Tischli,** or **Tischlich** = **Tischlein.**

b. **rich,** in Gothic an independent word reiks *ruler*, in M.H.G. an adjective rīch *mighty*, *rich*, surviving in the adjective **reich** *rich* and the suffix **rich,** which is affixed to names of persons and plants with its original meaning *ruler*, but weakened in force: **Friedrich** Frederick, lit. prince of peace, **Wegerich** plantain, lit. ruler of the road, &c. **Enterich** (M.H.G. antreche) is now felt as belonging here, meaning ruler of the ducks, as its older form *-reche* developed in N.H.G. phonetically into **-rich,** which suggested relationship with the **-rich** in names, but in fact it is of different origin. The last part of the word is of the same origin as Eng. *drake*. The first part is the German **Ente. Gänserich** and **Täuberich** have been formed after the analogy of **Enterich,** but the older simpler form **Tauber** is still more common.

c. **nd,** present participle ending, but not felt as such; hence all words with this suffix have the inflection of nouns and are true fossils: **Heiland** (**heilen** to heal) the Savior, lit. the healing one, **Wind** (**wehen** to blow) wind, **Feind** (Gothic fijan to hate) enemy, **Freund** (Gothic frijōn to love) friend, &c.

18. A few words are about to be degraded to mere suffixes:

a. **a(ch)** (= M.H.G. ahe *river*, cognate with Latin aqua), employed in the names of a number of rivers and small streams and places named from them: **Salzach** (river), **Werra** (river), **Fulda** (river and city). The names of rivers are fem. but the names of places are of course neuter according to the rule for such names. This form is not a genuine suffix as it is employed as an independent noun in the names of a number of streams: **die Ach** (tributary of the Danube), **die Aach** (in Baden), **die Ohe** (in Hesse), &c.

b. **kunft,** formed from a former gradation (**201.** *e*) of **kommen** *to come*, once an independent noun with the meaning *coming* and occasionally so used within the present period, especially in poetic language (as in **des Heilands Kunft**—Bürger's *St. Stephan*), but now usually found only as a suffix: **Ankunft** arrival, **Herkunft** origin, **Zukunft** future, &c.

c. **nahme,** formed from the vowel-gradation of the past tense of **nehmen** *to take*, once a noun with the meanings *a taking, robbing*, now found as a noun only in S.G. dialect in the second meaning, usually employed as a suffix in the first meaning: **Aufnahme** reception, **Ausnahme** exception, **Besitznahme** taking possession, **Stellungnahme** attitude, stand, &c.

19. **at,** an accented foreign suffix from the Latin -atus affixed to foreign stems to denote a rank, office, position, building where the office-holder resides, state. It is always neuter in a number of words, as **Rekto'rat** rectorship, **Konsu'lat** consulship, **Majo'rat** (right of) primogeniture, **Novizi'at** novitiate, **Pasto'rat** pastorate, parsonage, where the suffix has the force of the native suffix **tum** and is consequently influenced by its gender. In others under learned influences the masculine gender is also found as in Latin: **der** (especially in the 2nd meaning) and **das Episko'pat** episcopate, body of bishops collectively, **der** and **das Pri'mat** primateship, **der** and **das Zöli'bat** celibacy, &c. In **Magi'strat** city council, **Or'nat** official costume, **Trak'tat** treaty, treatise, it is usually masculine.

20. *Hybrids.* Certain suffixes are added, not only to foreign words, but also to native German stems and such foreign stems as have become thoroly established and are felt as German words in spite of their foreign form. A large number of these hybrids now belong to serious normal speech, but in many cases the suffix gives a facetious turn to the thought or contains depreciatory force. Besides the forms **-aner, -ei, -enser, -er, -ian, -ianer** (**5.** *e*), **-ie, -ier, -iner,** and **-sche** (under **-in** in **6.** **1.** *c*) treated above are the following suffixes:

a. **'āge** ('a:ʒə), a fem. ending indicating a disagreeable activity or a collective idea with depreciatory force: **Pa'ckage** packing, riff-raff (in this sense from **das Pack** riff-raff under the influence of **die Ba'gage** riff-raff), **Klei'dage** (or in Low German form **Klē'dage**) duds, traps, &c.

b. **'ālien,** a plural form indicating a collective idea with depreciatory force: **Schmie'ralien** gifts for the purpose of bribing, scrawl, &c.

c. **'ant** a masc. ending to form appellations of male beings: **Pau'kant** (in student language) duellist, &c.

d. **'ēum,** a neut. ending indicating a place consecrated to the worship, service, or study of: **Mozar'tēum** building devoted to the study and enjoyment of the music of Mozart, **Lauso'lēum** facetiously used for **Entlausungsanstalt,** place where soldiers are freed from the lice which they have acquired in the trenches, &c.

e. **i'āde,** a fem. ending indicating facetiously a discourse or epic: **Jeremi'ade** lamentation in the plaintive style of Jeremiah, **Jobsi'ade** (a humorous epic by Karl Arnold Kortum dealing with the life and doings of Hieronymus Jobs), &c.

f. **ikus,** a masc. ending to form facetious appellations of male beings: **Luftikus** wind-bag, **Pfiffikus** sly-boots, &c.

g. **'insky,** a masc. ending with pronounced disparaging force: **Bucke'linsky** hunchback, **Liede'rinsky** dissolute fellow, **die Herren Radika'linskys** the extreme radicals, &c.

h. **'ismus,** a masc. ending corresponding closely to English *-ism*: **Berli'nismus** Berlinism, &c.

i. **'ist,** a masc. ending corresponding to English *-ist*: **Hor'nist** hornist, horn-player, **Blu'mist** florist, **Gar'dist** soldier of the guards, &c.

j. **i'tät,** a fem. ending indicating a condition of things: **Schwuli'tät** (student slang) uneasiness, &c.

k. **'ūr** (Latin *-ura*), a fem. ending indicating an activity or the results of an activity: **Dre'ssur** breaking in, training, from the common foreign verb **dre'ssieren;** **Fri'sur** act of dressing or curling the hair, or hair-dress, from the common foreign word **fri'sieren.**

II. *Derivative Adjectives.*

1. artig (= **Art** *kind*, *manner* + **ig**), an independent adjective with the meaning *well-behaved*, and also added seemingly as a suffix to nouns and adjectives to indicate a kind, manner, resemblance: **aalartig** like an eel, eely, **bergartig** resembling a mountain, **turmartig** tower-like, &c.; **fremdartig** strange, **großartig** grand, magnificent, **gutartig** good-natured, &c.; **ein aalartiger Höfling; mit seiner affenartigen Geschwindigkeit. Artig** is now perhaps often felt here as a suffix, but the real suffix is **-ig,** which is added to a compound or a group: **affenartig = Affenart + ig; gutartig = gute Art + ig.** Hence **-artig** really belongs to **9. 1.** *b* below.

2. bar (from O.H.G. beran, to carry, bear), once an independent adj., bāri *bearing*, now a suffix, affixed to nouns and verbs, to denote:

a. That the stem-word in the derivative is the object of the verb that is implied in the suffix: **streitbar** bellicose, war-like, lit. bearing war, **fruchtbar** fertile, lit. bearing fruit, **dankbar** grateful, lit. bearing thanks.

b. The possibility or ability to perform, or more commonly to receive the activity implied in the stem of the derivative: **streitbar** able to fight, in fighting trim, **unfehlbar** infallible, **nahbar** approachable, **lesbar** legible, capable of being read, **schiffbar** navigable, **gangbar** passable, **sichtbar** visible. Compare **11.** 2. C. *b*, 3 below.

Note. In some words both active and passive force lie in **bar: haltbare Leinwand** strong linen, linen that will hold; **eine haltbare Behauptung** a tenable assertion, one that can be held.

c. Rarely with other parts of speech: **offenbar, sonderbar.**

3. en (M.H.G. în), **n** (after **er**), **ern,** a suffix sometimes causing mutation, affixed to a name of a material to indicate that the substantive which the adj. modifies represents an object made of that material: **golden** golden, **hänfen** or **hanfen** hempen, **silbern** silver, **hölzern** wooden.

This suffix is closely related to the diminutive endings **-chen** and **-lein.** The original idea is that of *close association*, *origin*, from which come the derived ideas of *material* (literally coming from, made of wood, &c.), *endearment*, *diminution*, as explained in I. **8.** 1. *f. Note* 3 above.

a. The form **-en** is usually added to the stem of the noun unless the latter ends in **-e** or **-er,** in which case only **-n** is added: **Wolle** wool, **wollen** woolen; **Kupfer** copper, **kupfern** copper (adj.). In a number of cases the suffix **-n** is added to the plural of such words as form a pl. in **-er: Holz** wood, **hölzern** wooden; **Glas** glass, **gläsern** glass, of glass. After the analogy of many adjectives thus ending in **-ern** a number have likewise mutated the stem vowel and added **-ern** to the stem as if this were the regular suffix, especially in cases of stems ending in **l, n, s: stählern** steel, **beinern** made of bone, **steinern** made of stone, **zinnern** tin, **tönern** earthen, **wächsern** waxen.

Note. As explained in **73.** *a*, the **er** of the plural of nouns was originally not a plural case ending, but a suffix which was also found in the singular. Thus in case of nouns ending in **-er** in the plural the adjective suffix **-n** is only seemingly added to the plural, as it was in fact originally added to the singular. The **-er** in the plural of nouns, however, has long been felt and construed as a plural case ending, as the **-er** of the singular was dropped and its existence forgotten. Thus the **-er** in the adjective suffix **-ern** is now felt as belonging to the plural of the noun in question, or as a formation made after the analogy of such words, while in fact it is a fossil remnant of the original stem suffix. In most cases, however, it is not really the old stem suffix, as words not entitled to it have only assumed it after the analogy of the original group.

b. This suffix denotes that the object in question is entirely made of the mentioned material: **hölzerne Bänke** *wooden benches*, but **holzige Rettige** *radishes of a woody fibre.*

c. This suffix is not much used in the predicate, being there replaced by the preposition **von** and a noun, and in the attributive relation is sometimes replaced by a compound noun: **Der Tisch ist von Holz. Marmorsäule** *marble pillar*, instead of **marmorne Säule.** But in elevated diction the suffix is also found in the predicate: **Der Stuhl ist elfenbeinern, darauf der Kaiser sitzt** (Rückert's *Barbarossa*). Rarely in plain prose, occasionally, however, in case of **eichen: Die Bücherschränke waren in Eiche geschnitzt, und eichen war auch der breite Arbeitstisch** (Fedor von Zobeltitz's *Die papierne Macht*, p. 9). In figurative use adjectives with this suffix are quite commonly found in the predicate: **Sein Gesicht war jetzt grau und steinern** (rigid) **wie das der Riesen am Tor** (Volkmann's *Die beiden Weiser*).

4. erlei, see **126.** 1. *a.*
5. fach, see **126.** 1. *b.*
6. fältig, see **126.** 1. *b.*

7. haft (related to **Haft** clasp), once an independent adjective perfect participle, now a mere suffix. It is usually added directly to the stem, but weak nouns take **en** between stem and suffix, which is probably felt as the weak genitive ending usually found in weak nouns forming the first component of compounds, altho corresponding strong genitive formations do not occur here: **bärenhaft, knabenhaft, heldenhaft, riesenhaft, frauenhaft, lehrerinnenhaft** schoolma'am-like, but **mannhaft, schülerhaft, meisterhaft,** &c. Neuter **er**-plurals usually have their plural form here, as **kinderhaft, weiberhaft,** and it is possible to construe all the derivative stems in **-en, -el, -er** as plurals: **frauen-, gimpel-, schülerhaft.**

The leading points as to use and form are as follows:

1. *a.* Added to abstract nouns, it represents something as infected with, marred by, or as possessing the qualities implied in the stem of the derivative: **sündhaft** sinful, **lasterhaft** vicious, **fehlerhaft** faulty, **tugendhaft** virtuous, **schamhaft** bashful, &c.

b. Added to concrete nouns it represents something as possessing or inclining towards the thing or the characteristics of the thing mentioned in the stem of the derivative: **teilhaft** having a part, share in, **seßhaft** having a dwelling, settled, **wohnhaft** residing, **schalkhaft** having the characteristics of a wag, waggish, **riesenhaft** gigantic, **schülerhaft** schoolboy-like.

Note. Here **-haft** touches close to **-isch** and **-lich**: **heldenhaft** and **heldisch** *heroic*, **göttlich** divine. See also **10.** 2. *a. Note* below.

c. In the adjectives **boshaft** *malicious*, **krankhaft** *morbid*, **wahrhaft** *truthful*, **leckerhaft** *loving nice things to eat*, &c., it represents persons as resembling in their manner and ways the attribute mentioned in the stem or as having a fondness for things possessing this attribute.

d. Added to verbal stems it implies an inclination towards the activity that is mentioned in the stem-word, or indicates that the person or thing to which reference is made performs the activity or incites it: **naschhaft** fond of eating tit-bits, **schwatzhaft** loquacious, **schmeichelhaft** containing something which flatters, hence *complimentary*, **glaubhaft** containing that which inspires belief, hence *worthy of belief*, *trustworthy*, **ekelhaft** containing that which nauseates. It touches here close to **-ig** and **-isch.** See **10.** 3. *Note* below. Sometimes **-haft** and **-sam** differ only in that the latter emphasizes the idea of possession of pleasant or praiseworthy attributes: **lehrhaft** *didactic*, *moralistic*, but **lehrsam** *instructive*, as in **Sie** (**die Geschichten**) **sind natürlich, volkstümlich und lehrsam** (Max Dreyer's *Ohm Peter*, XXV).

2. In some words the lengthened form **-haftig** is also used with the same general meaning as the shorter one: **wahrhaftig** truthful, or now more commonly an adverb, *truly*, while **wahrhaft** is usually employed as an adjective, *truthful;* **teilhaftig** having a part, share in, **leibhaftig** bodily, in person, &c. The **-ig** was once more common and as a survival of older usage is still always thus added before **-keit** to form abstract nouns: **tugendhaft** virtuous, **Tugendhaftigkeit** virtuousness.

8. icht, closely related in origin and meaning to **-ig** (see **9** below), so that in most cases it has been entirely supplanted by the latter, or survives only as a less common variant: **bergicht,** or more commonly **bergig,** &c. Only the forms **töricht** and **regnicht** (or **regnerisch**) are established.

a. In M.H.G. **-icht** appears as ëht, oht, aht, and hence there is no mutation in these words, except **töricht** foolish.

b. Formerly **-icht** was most common after the suffix **-el,** as in **kitzlicht** (now **kitzlig**) in Schiller's *Wallensteins Lager*, 9, and it is still occasionally found there in the form of **-ich** instead of the more common **ig: fünf von den weißmäntlichen Kürassieren** (Fontane's *Vor dem Sturm*, III, chap. 12); **kurzärmlich** (id., III, 4).

c. In S.G. dialect **icht** often appears as **et: flachshaaret** for **flachshaarig,** &c.

d. This suffix in one meaning has assumed the form of **-lich.** See **-lich** in **11.** 2. B. *b. Note* below.

9. ig (cognate with *y* in *hungry*), a very common suffix with the general meaning of *having, possessing.* The leading points as to form and meaning are as follows:

1. *a.* Its O.H.G. form was ag or ig; hence there have resulted two groups of words, one with mutation, the other without it: **frostig, durstig, &c., but flüchtig, sündig,** &c.

b. It is affixed to all parts of speech, also to compounds, as in **affenartig (Affenart + ig)** monkeylike, **aalartig (Aalart + ig)** like an eel, and in a number of cases it is even added to compounds which do not exist outside of this combination, as in **vielköpfig** *many-headed* (but not **Vielkopf**), **eigenhändig (eine eigenhändige Unterschrift)** with one's own hand, **zweischneidig** two-edged, **warmherzig** warm-hearted, &c. Notice that in English *-ed* is often similarly used. The basal element of such formations is a syntactical group of two words which have entered into such close relations to each other that they have formed a compound, and like many other compounds with an adjective as the first element have the adjective without an ending: **éigenhàndig = èigene Hánd + ig.** The basal element may be a compound formed from a genitive group: **vólksmàßig** *popular* = early N.H.G. **in des Vòlkes Máße** *in the manner of the common people* **+ ig.** The first component of the compound here sometimes takes **-s,** sometimes **-en,** sometimes assumes the form of the bare stem, just as in compounds in general: **gefühlsmäßig, bühnenmäßig, gewohnheitsmäßig, schulmäßig, gesetzmäßig,** &c. The basal component is often a verbal stem, while the modifying component is an adverb: **schwérhòrig (= er hórt schwèr +ig), schwérfàllig, etc.** Compare I. **5.** *b* (last par.) For the stress here see **249.** II. 2 and **247.** 2. *b*.

2. Affixed to some parts of speech, it has a definite meaning, while after others it is a mere mechanical form used to make an adj. out of some other part of speech. The following points may be a guide as to its use:

A. It denotes:

a. The possession or the presence of the thing implied in the stem of the noun: **sonnig** sunny, **buschig** bushy, **fleißig** diligent, **sandig** sandy, **löcherig** full of holes, porous, **ein vierjähriges Kind** a four-year-old child, **eine dreiwöchige Reise,** a three weeks' journey. Compare B, also **11.** 2. A. *e* below. This idea leads sometimes to a causative relation: **freudige Nachrichten** news that contains joy, hence news which makes us rejoice, **verdächtig** causing, arousing suspicion.

b. The presence of the quality implied in the adj. stem, usually, however, in a less degree or a different shade: **spitz** running to a *sharp* point, **spitzig** (possibly from the noun **Spitze**) pointed; **fett** fat, **fettig** greasy; **laß** wearied, **lässig** indolent, lacking energy.

c. An inclination toward or a quality naturally associated with the activity implied in the verbal stem: **bissig** inclined to bite (as of a dog), **brummig** inclined to grumble, **fähig (fahen = fangen)** capable, **gefällig** of a nature such as to please, agreeable, anxious to please, **ergiebig** productive, **freigebig** liberal, **fällig** due, lit. which should now fall or be paid, **harthörig** hard of hearing, **fein-**

fühlig of delicate feeling, **sich einem Vorschlage zustimmig erklären** to announce one's readiness to assent to a proposition; (with reflexive force) **wendig** so constructed as to turn or maneuver easily (of an aeroplane), &c.

d. It has much the same force as **haft.** Some stems regularly take the one suffix, some the other, and some have both. If both suffixes are added to the same stem, they sometimes have the same force, sometimes a differentiation of meaning: **klatschig** or **klatschhaft** *prone to gossip*; **herzig** *lovely*, but **herzhaft** *courageous*: **gläubig** *believing*, but **glaubhaft** *inspiring belief*, *worthy of belief*. Sometimes the meaning of **-ig** is also identical with that of **-isch** and **-lich.** See **10.** 3. *Note* and **11.** 3 below.

B. It is a mere formal suffix used to make an adj. out of other parts of speech, when added to the stem of pronouns, prepositions, and adverbs: **derjenige, der meinige, die übrigen** (**über** over, above) **Personen** the remaining persons, **die jetzige** (**jetzt** now) **Mode** the present fashion, **die heutige** (**heute** to-day) **Zeitung** to-day's newspaper, **der obige Satz** the above sentence, **die dortigen Gebräuche** the customs of that place. In a few words of more than one syllable the stem is shortened: **die morgige Feier, in der übermorgigen Sitzung** (Sudermann's *Der Sturmgeselle Sokrates*, 1, 15). In several cases an **s** is now, contrary to earlier usage, inserted between the adverbial stem and the suffix to prevent two vowels from coming together: **die hiesigen** (**hie** here) **Fabriken** the factories of this place, **dasig** (**da** there) of that place. Thus also any noun or expression denoting the *time* or *duration* of an act or state may take on adjective function by affixing **ig: das nächtige Wegschleppen der Angeklagten** the dragging away of the accused in the night, **diese vierzehnmonatige Haft** this fourteen months' imprisonment. Also **lich** can be affixed to such nouns and expressions, but it denotes the *repetition* or *manner* of the activity. See **11.** 2. A. *e*, *f*. All such formations in **-ig** and **-lich** are in fact true adverbs, as they denote some circumstance of time, place, or manner, and hence are adjectives only in form.

10. isch (cognate with Eng. *ish* as in *childish*) or **sch** (see 1. *a* below), a common suffix denoting a belonging to that mentioned in the stem of the derivative. This original meaning can still be seen in the following groups which illustrate its present use as to meaning and form:

1. Affixed to names of persons, countries, peoples, districts, and places, it usually has the force of an English noun in the possessive case, or the objective after the prep. *of*, and thus indicates a belonging to, or something concerning, or a coming or descent from the person, people, or place mentioned in the stem, or indicates a participation in their personal or local peculiarities and characteristics: **die Schirrmachersche Hypothek** the mortgage held (i.e. owned) by Mr. Schirrmacher, **das Schmidtsche Haus** the Smith residence, **die Treibelschen Diners** the dinners given by the Treibels, **der Kommerzienrat Treibelsche Kutscher** the coachman of Mr. Treibel, councilor of commerce, **ein Schmidtsches Lieblingsthema** a favorite theme of Mr. Schmidt, **das Schmidtsche** that which characterizes a true Schmidt, **ich persönlich bin mehr ins Gieshüblersche geschlagen** I myself have taken more after the Gieshüblers (the father's side of the speaker's family), **die Paul Heyseschen Novellen** Paul Heyse's novelettes, **das Hallische Waisenhaus** the Orphans' Home of Halle, **die straßburgische Universität** the University of Strassburg, **die darmstädtische Verwaltung** the government of the city of Darmstadt, **die römische Geschichte** the history of Rome, or Roman history. In Austria adjectives in **-isch** are often used substantively much as the plural of a name is used in North German and English: **Es g'freut mich recht aufrichtig, daß ich und die Meinigen jetzt mit so scharmanten Familien, wie die Leodolterischen und die Beywaldischen es sind, in ein verwandschaftliches Verhältnis treten sollen** (Ertl's *Freiheit*, p. 62).

Adjectives formed from names of persons do not suffer mutation, and likewise most adjectives from names of places, but a few, as **hannöverisch** (or more commonly **hannoverisch**), **römisch,** and those in **-stadt** (**friedrichstädtisch,** &c., after the analogy of **städtisch** formed from the common noun **Stadt**), are mutated. Those derived from names of peoples usually mutate: **fränkisch, französisch,**

jüdisch, sächsisch, &c. A number, however, especially foreign words and new formations, do not suffer mutation: **badisch, amerikanisch, arisch, gotisch, russisch, spanisch,** &c.

a. The original method of adding the suffix was to affix it directly to the simple stem, as in **bremisch,** (from **Bremen**), **sächsisch** (from **Sachsen**), **schwäbisch** (from **Schwaben**), **Goethisch,** but the modern trend is to shorten the suffix to **sch** (also **'sch**), and then add it to the full name: **bremensch, Goethesch.** In this way the name is not mutilated, and can always be inferred from the adjective form. Proper adjectives made from names of countries do not as yet usually follow this new trend except in case of **polnisch** (from **Polen**). The new trend has in general gained the ascendency in adjectives made from the name of a person. The full suffix **isch,** however, is still used in case of a few names from antiquity: **Ho'merisch, Ho'razisch,** &c. Differentiation of meaning between the two forms sometimes takes place. The form **sch** is employed where there is reference to one person, and **isch** where the meaning becomes general or abstract: **die 'Luthersche Sprache** *Luther's language,* but **die lu'therische** (see also **47.** 2. A. *d*) **Kirche** *the Lutheran church.* The form **isch** is most commonly employed thus in the predicate relation: **die Gottschedsche Orthographie** the orthography of Gottsched, but **Die Orthographie ist Gottschedisch. Die Rankische** or more commonly **Rankesche Weltgeschichte** *Ranke's History of the World,* but **Er versucht zwar Ranke nachzuahmen, aber seine Darstellung klingt gar nicht Rankisch.** However, we also now find the shortened form in the predicate: **Ihre Losung ist hier ja, wir sind konservativ, sehr, aber nicht Bismarcksch** (Bismarck to his wife, July 20, 1849). **Ja, Corinnchen, in diesem Belang bist du auch ganz Schmidtsch** (Fontane's *Frau Jenny,* chap. 11). **Emil, der Professor, Bruder des Majors, ein großer vielleicht von allen am wenigsten Eysensch aussehender Mann** (G. Ompteda) looking least of all like an Eysen (family).

b. Many names of cities form indeclinable adjectives in **-er** (see **111.** 7. *a*) instead of taking **isch,** and some admit of either suffix: **Limburger Käse** Limburg cheese, **der kölnische** or **Kölner Dom** the cathedral of Cologne; **Hamburgischer Correspondent,** but **Hamburger Nachrichten** (newspapers); **das Bremer Rathaus** *the town-hall of Bremen* in contrast to **der bremische Staat** *the state of Bremen.* It should be noticed, however, that only the form in (i)**sch** can be used in the substantive relation or predicatively in the adjective relation: **Das Berlinische** *the dialect of Berlin,* not **das Berliner. Das ist Berlinisch** (not **Berliner**) that is a Berlin trait. A few adjectives in **-er,** however, become substantives by simply dropping the following noun: **Rüdesheimer (Wein), ein Leonberger (Hund), der Rheinländer (Tanz).**

Note 1. Also some names of countries, sections of a country, islands, valleys, parks, cemeteries, buildings, and other localities sometimes take the suffix **-er** instead of **-isch,** especially **Schweizer** (or **schweizerisch**), **Holländer** (or **holländisch**), **Holsteiner** (or **holsteinisch**), **Schwarzwälder** (very common, as in **Schwarzwälder Uhren**), **Dalmatiner Wein, Kärnthner Lieder, Banater Grenzsoldat, Krainer Höhlen, Steyrer Wagen, Tiroler Landsturm, Helgoländer Mundart,** &c.

Note 2. The adjectives of this group which take **-isch** usually add the suffix directly to the name, but **schweizerisch** and **wienerisch** regularly suffix **-isch** to the lengthened form in **-er.** The -er in adjectives formed from names of cities is usually added directly to the name of the city, but in case of names in **-hausen** (originally dat. pl.; see **88.** 1), **-ingen** (dat. pl.), **-leben** (dat. pl.) the suffix is usually added to the orig nal stem, so that **-hausen, -ingen, -leben** become **-häuser** (in S.G. **-hauser**), **-inger, -leber: Nordhausen,** but **Nordhäuser; Neuhausen** (suburb of Munich), **but Neuhauser; Tübingen,** but **Tübinger; Aschersleben,** but **Ascherslebe**r. Short forms are also found in a few other words, as **Barmer, Binger, Bremer, Emder, Spicherer,** but the tendency elsewhere and sometimes in the above cases seems to be to give the full form, so as to avoid mutilating the name: **das Alvenslebener Hügelland** (*Mitteilungen des Vereins für Erdkunde zu Halle a. S.,* 1904, p. 54).

c. In a number of cases usage adopts here the Latin adjective suffixes anus, inus, and ensis, converting, however, the last syllable into **isch: ameri'kanisch,** American, **floren'tinisch** Florentine, **atheni'ensisch** or more commonly **a'thenisch** Athenian, &c. The foreign form should be avoided in case of German words: **ha'nnoverisch** or **ha'nnöverisch** rather than **hannove'ranisch; 'weimarisch** rather than **weima'ranisch;** &c. **'bremisch** rather than **bre'mensisch** (used, however, by Hauptmann in *Neue Rundschau,* Jan. 1908, p. 9).

2. Affixed to common nouns denoting persons or things, it denotes:

a. The peculiar manner and character of the class of persons or things mentioned in the stem word: **teuflisch** devilish, **dichterisch** poetic, **kriegerisch** warlike, **durchgängerisch** inclined to run away (of a horse), **verschwenderisch** extravagant, **erfinderisch** inventive, **tierisch** animal, brutal, **höfisch** courtly, fawning, **städtisch** after the manner of city people, **irdisch** earthly, **höllisch** infernal, **demokratisch** democratic, &c. It is added to a plural in **freigeisterisch** free-thinking. There are a few contracted forms: **deutsch** (O.H.G. diot *people* + **isch,** used of the popular language in contradistinction to the Latin of the learned class) *German;* **Mensch** (contracted form of **männisch,** hence originally an adjective) *human being* = Latin homo; **hübsch** (originally another form of **höfisch** *courtly,* but now with differentiated meaning) *pretty.*

The suffix usually causes mutation here. Those in **-erisch,** however, only mutate when the stem word is mutated: **träumerisch,** from **Träumer;** but **malerisch, from Maler.**

Note. Here **-isch** has the signification of **-lich** and **-haft**, but when they can be added to the same word their meanings often diverge, the first of the forms sometimes taking on a disparaging sense: **kindlich** child-like (in a good sense), **kindisch** childish; **weiblich** womanly, **weibisch** (in early N.H.G. still in good sense; see Peter iii. 7) womanish, **weiberhaft** after the manner or ways of women, as in **weiberhaftes Klagen, Plaudern**, an objective statement without a tinge of censure; **männlich** manly, **männisch** (see also *b*) *like a man*, when used in a derogatory sense of a woman, or *coarse*, when used of a man, referring to his lack of refinement; **höflich** polite, **höfisch** fawning, &c. Thus nouns meaning primarily something good, as **Recht** right, **Gott** God, **Jungfrau** virgin, do not usually take **-isch**, and those signifying something bad, as **Satan** Satan, **Abgott** idol, do not take **-lich**. On the other hand, **-isch** does in some words occur in a good sense: **Ich bin kein Held, und das Heldische läßt sich nicht lernen** (Fontane's *Frau Jenny*, chap. viii). **Er brauche ja nur ein Bauerngewand, denn herrisch** (dressed like a gentleman) **dürfe niemand kommen** (Berlepsch's *Fortunats Roman*, p. 183).

b. Somebody or something concerned or connected with, something affected by or restricted to that which is mentioned in the stem word, usually causing mutation only in native German words: **historisch** historical, **philologisch** philological, **seelisch** of the soul, **festländisch** continental, **städtisch** municipal, **eine telegraphische Antwort** an answer by telegraph, **überseeisch** transatlantic, transmarine, **völkisch** national, **eine zweimännische Kurbel** a windlass for two men, **ein zweimännisches** (provinc.; or more commonly **zweischläfiges**) **Bett** a bed for two persons. We usually find **männlich** *male*, **weiblich** *female*, on account of the disparaging sense often found in **-isch**, but **männisch** is quite commonly used in a good sense in compounds: **männliche Studenten,** but **in fachmännischen Kreisen** in professional circles, **kaufmännische Beziehungen,** &c.

Note. Tho **-isch,** here as in *a*, has the same general meaning as **-lich,** it is decidedly the favorite with words of foreign origin, as nicely illustrated by the following examples: **Und doch, lieber Pentz, ich möchte heute, wenn es geht, etwas anderes von Ihnen hören als Kulinarisches oder Frühstückliches** (Fontane's *Unwiederbringlich*, chap. 16). **Mündlicher, schriftlicher Verkehr,** but **telegraphischer Verkehr.** Compare 2. A. *c* under **lich,** below.

c. As in 1 above, it contains the possessive idea, but this idea is more commonly expressed in this category by **-lich** (see **11.** 2. A. *b* below): **tierische Gewebe** *tissues of animals, animal tissues*, **die gegnerische Auffassung** the view of the opposing party, &c., but **pflanzliche Gewebe, das königliche Schloß,** &c.

3. Affixed to stems of abstract nouns or verbs, it denotes an inclination toward the thing or quality denoted by the stem, usually causing mutation: **zänkisch** quarrelsome, **neckisch** inclined to tease, droll, **mürrisch** morose. This is a favorite formation with the people, who extend it beyond the literary limits: **Robinson ißt immer so wenig, wiewohl er den Streußel ungeheuer gern mag. Aber so sind die Engländer, sie sind nicht so zugreifsch** (Frau Imme in Fontane's *Stechlin*, chap. 14, p. 186).

Note. Here **-isch** has the same force as **-haft** and **-ig,** some stems preferring one suffix, some another. Also **-sam** has the same general force, but it differs from the other three in expressing usually only an inclination toward praiseworthy things: **folgsam** obedient; **arbeitsam** industrious. See also 7. 1. *d* above.

4. It is suffixed to an adj. in the one word **linkisch** awkward, lit. left-handed, to an adverb in **heimisch** home-like, to a pronoun in **selbstisch** selfish.

5. The frequent occurrence of **-isch** after stems in **-er,** as in 2 above, has given rise to the idea that the suffix is **-erisch,** as can be seen in **regnerisch** rainy.

General Note. As there is a fluctuation of usage in English between forms in *-ic* and *-ical*, as in *heroic* and *heroical*, there is also in German in the same group of foreign words a fluctuation between **-isch** and **-i'kalisch,** but only in a few cases, as in **gra'mmatisch** or sometimes **grammati'kalisch.** In English both forms are often used with differentiated meanings, as historic and historical, but in German such differentiation is only found in a few instances as **physisch** physical (with reference to the body or the possible in nature: **meine physischen Kräfte**) and **physikalisch** physical (with reference to physics: **physikalische Instrumente**). In most cases the short form alone survives in German: **biblisch** biblical, &c. Only in a few instances has the long form become established, as in **musi'kalisch.**

11. lich (cognate with Eng. *-ly* as in *friendly*), once an independent word, now a suffix with the general meaning of resembling or befitting that which is contained in the stem of the derivative. The following points may serve as a guide to its use:

1. It is affixed to nouns, adjectives, and verbs: **männlich** manly, **zärtlich** tender, loving, **verständlich** intelligible, **begreiflich** conceivable.

a. An excrescent **t** appears after the stem, when it is an infinitive or a noun or adjective ending in **-en: hoffentlich** as is to be hoped, **wissentlich** wilful, **wöchentlich** (M.H.G. wochenlich) weekly, **gelegentlich** occasional, &c. In case of **tunlich** the infinitive form is preserved. Earlier in the period **tulich** was also common.

b. In some words the lengthened form **-erlich** is found instead of **-lich: lächerlich, leserlich, fürchterlich,** &c.

c. If the stem-word is a monosyllable the vowel is mutated, except in **behaglich, faßlich, folglich, fraglich, gastlich, gedanklich, glaublich, sachlich,**

sanglich, sorglich, sportlich, sprachlich, staatlich, stattlich, tauglich, unerforschlich, verdaulich, vertraglich (2. A. *c*), **wahrlich, widerruflich.** If the stem-word is a dissyllabic, it is also sometimes mutated: **brüderlich, mütterlich, väterlich, jämmerlich, nebensächlich.** The same stem-word may be mutated or not with a difference of meaning: **sächlich** neuter, **sachlich** sticking to the question at hand, objective.

2. It differs somewhat in meaning according to the part of speech to which it is affixed:

A. Affixed to nouns it denotes:

a. An attribute which naturally belongs to the person or thing denoted by the stem: **ein väterlicher Rat** a piece of paternal advice, **männlicher Mut** manly courage; **festlich** festive, **herbstlich** autumn-like, autumnal, **sonntägliche Stimmung. Mir ist nur immer merkwürdig, daß du, neben Homer und sogar neben Schliemann, mit solcher Vorliebe Kochbuchliches** (matters which belong to a cook-book) **behandelst** (Fontane's *Frau Jenny*, chap. vii).

b. Possession or origin, often when expressing the possessive idea equivalent to an attributive possessive genitive: **kaiserliche Schlösser** castles of the emperor, **pflanzliche Gewebe** tissues of plants, plant tissues, **sprachliche Eigenheiten** peculiarities of speech, **sein mütterliches Vermögen** property inherited from his mother. Compare **10. 2.** *c* above.

c. Something concerning, or concerned or connected with, or effected by that which is mentioned in the stem-word: **nebensächlich** concerning a minor point, of secondary importance, **Frühstückliches** (Fontane's *Unwiederbringlich*, chap. 16) matters pertaining to breakfast, **friedlich** peaceful, **ängstlich** anxious, **ein mütterlicher Onkel** an uncle on the mother's side, **unter den günstigsten vertraglichen** (compare C. *a*) **Bedingungen** under the most favorable conditions securable by contract, **künstliche Zähne** artificial teeth. Compare **10. 2.** *b. Note* above, under **-isch.**

Note. Notice the difference here between **-ig** and **-lich: der fremdsprachliche Unterricht** instruction in foreign languages, but **Österreich war früher ein vielsprachiges Land und hatte zwei- und dreisprachige Schulen** Austria was a land in which many languages were spoken, and hence it had schools in which two or even three languages were used as mediums for imparting instruction.

d. Somebody afflicted or blessed with that which is mentioned in the stem-word: **gebrechlich** afflicted with infirmities, **glücklich** happy.

e. Repetition: **eine jährliche Reise** a journey taken every year, **ein täglicher Gast** a daily guest, **unser tägliches Brot** our daily bread, i.e. bread that we need each day, **tägliche Kleidung** every-day clothes, **eine halbjährliche Prüfung,** &c.

f. An attribute of an abstract noun, indicating the *manner* in which an activity proceeds, or the *means* by which it operates, or the *agents* which direct the force: **eine Wohnung mit halbjährlicher Kündigung** a rented dwelling to which attaches the obligation to give notice six months before one leaves, **eine tätliche Beleidigung** an insult offered in the way of blows, **briefliche Auskunft** information obtained by letter, **eine schriftliche Zusicherung** a written assurance, **drahtliche Nachricht** news by wire, **sinnliche Wahrnehmung** perception thru the senses, **polizeiliches Einschreiten** intervention by the police. The suffix is, with this meaning, also added to adjectives, as **ein gänzlicher Mangel** a complete lack. Such adjectives are really adverbs in the form of adjectives, and hence cannot be attributes of objects, as they only modify the activity implied in the noun. Even when such adjectives modify nouns representing persons, they refer more to the activity exercised than to the persons: **ein glücklicher Spieler** a lucky gambler.

B. Affixed to adjectives and participles it has:

a. Adverbial force, being used just as the derivatives from nouns described in A. *f* above, to denote an attribute of an abstract, verbal noun: **bitterlich** bitterly, **völlig** complete, **gänzlich** complete, **wissentlich** wilful (sin, lie), **gütlich** amicable, &c. Ex.: **die gütliche Beilegung des Streites** the amicable settlement of the quarrel. In a number of cases such formations are only used adverbially: **freilich** to be sure, surely, **kürzlich** lately, **bekanntlich as is well known,** &c. See also **IV. 2.** *b* below.

b. The idea of approach to, partaking somewhat of the quality of with reference to things and the idea of inclination toward when applied to persons: **schwärzlich** blackish, **bräunlich** brownish, **länglich** oblong, **rundlich** roundish, &c.; **kleinlich** inclined to be small, pedantic, mean-souled, **kränklich** sickly, **süßlich** sweetish, affected, soft, fulsome, **schwächlich** weakly, **ältlich** elderly, &c.

Note. Earlier in the period and in dialect still the form **-licht** is found in certain words: **Der Sonne rötlichter** (now **rötlicher**) **Untergang** (Schiller). The older form indicates clearly that this suffix in this word and a number of others is identical with **-icht** described in 8 above and thus originally had nothing to do with **-lich.** The **l** became connected with **-icht** in M.H.G. as the suffix was often attached to words in **-el,** as in M.H.G. buckelecht, later **buckelig.** Thus arose M.H.G. rœtelecht, later **rötlich.** In most words older **-echt** or **-icht** later became **-ig,** but in the group in *b* it remained with the form **-licht** as an independent suffix with the meaning *having* or *possessing a little of,* the latter of which ideas seems to have been suggested by the *l*, which in verbs and nouns so often has diminutive force. Later this group was confounded with the group in **-lich,** which on account of the signification of the suffix **-lich** *like unto* had a similar meaning.

c. In other cases where there is a simple adjective and a derivative **in -lich,** a differentiation of meaning takes place: **arm** *poor*, **ärmlich** having the outward signs of poverty; &c.

C. Affixed to verbs, sometimes with a lengthened form in **-er, lächerlich,** &c., it has:

a. Active force, representing the person or thing to which it refers as acting, or acting upon something: **erbaulich** edifying, **schädlich** injurious, **schmerzlich** painful, &c. Exs.: **etwas tief Betrübliches** (Fontane's *Unwiederbringlich*, chap. 22), **nichts geradezu Verstimmliches** (id., *Stechlin*, chap. viii).

It also expresses a willingness, a natural tendency to perform the activity, or indicates that something is of such a nature as to incite it: **empfänglich** willing to receive, open to (**für Eindrücke, Schmeicheleien, das Schöne empfänglich**), **unterhaltlich** inclined to entertain and interest (**eine unterhaltliche Dame**), **beweglich** (from **sich bewegen;** see next par.) inclined to move around, active, vivacious (**die beweglichen Wellen, bewegliche Augen, eine bewegliche Zunge, ein beweglicher Mann**), **lächerlich** inclined to laugh (**Mir ist nicht lächerlich zu Mute**), of such a nature as to incite laughter, laughable, **weinerlich** inclined to weep, **küsserlich** fond of kissing, of such a nature as to incite kissing, **fürchterlich** of such a nature as to instil fear, **leserlich** of such a nature as to be easily read, legible, hence with passive force as in *b*.

Also with reflexive force: **Die in seiner Bibliothek befindlichen Bücher; den damals in Leipzig aufhältlichen Lessing** (Proelß's *Geschichte d. dram. Lit. und Kunst*, I, p. 40); **ein verträglicher Mensch. Mir ist brechlich** (colloq., from **sich brechen**); **eine einläßliche Charakterisierung (eine Charakterisierung, die sich auf den Gegenstand einläßt).** The reflexive is regularly suppressed.

b. Passive force, representing the person or thing to which it refers as a possible or deserving (often in a reprehensible sense) recipient of an action: **bestechlich** capable of being bribed, bribable, **beweglich** movable, **faßlich** comprehensible, **erhältlich** to be had (**Formulare sind bei allen Reichsbankanstalten erhältlich**), **löblich** deserving of praise, **beachtlich** worthy of being considered (**ein sehr beachtlicher Vorschlag**), **bedauerlich** to be deplored, deplorable, **sträflich** deserving punishment, **verwerflich** deserving rejection, bad, abominable, &c. With the idea of the possibility of an action but with active force, as in **unabkömmlich** indispensable (lit. unable to get away: **Ich bin hier unabkömmlich**), **dienlich** serviceable, &c.

Lich here touches close to **-bar,** but is more common in composition with prefixes, and not so common with simple stems: **brechbar, brennbar,** &c., not usually **brechlich, brennlich,** &c., on the other hand more commonly **zerbrechlich, verbrennlich,** &c. The **-bar,** however, can also usually be employed here, as it has a little different shade of meaning: it has more verbal force and emphasizes the idea of possibility. **Lich,** however, is always used in **möglich, leidlich, unausstehlich, üblich, löblich,** &c. See also **12. 1.** *b*. *Note* below.

c. Either active or passive force, according as a relation is felt to the intrans. or the trans. use of a verb, which is used both intransitively and transitively: **zerbrechlich** breaking easily *or* easily broken. The positive form is sometimes active, while the negative form is passive: **vergeßlich** forgetful, but **unvergeßlich** never to be forgotten, &c.

3. The meanings of **-lich** often touch very close to those of **-haft** and **-bar.** When **-lich** and **-haft,** or **-lich** and **-bar,** may be added to the same stem or two stems of kindred meanings, the different words sometimes have about the same force: **tugendhaft** and **tugendlich** virtuous. **Es war bei allem Tantlichen etwas ausgesprochen Onkelhaftes in der Art und Weise, wie sie das junge ängstliche Mädchen an den Handgelenken ergriff** (Raabe's *Eulenpfingsten*, chap. 5). Sometimes a shade appears: **schadhaft** injured, broken, **schädlich** injurious; **schmerzhaft** accompanied with pain, as **eine schmerzhafte Krankheit, Wunde, Operation, schmerzlich** causing pain, as in **Des Freundes schmerzhafte Krankheit ist uns schmerzlich** (D. Sanders); **glaubhaft** worthy of belief, trustworthy, **glaublich** credible, probable, likely, as in **Glaubhaft ist der Zeuge, glaublich seine Aussage; sündhaft, sündig** or **sündlich** sinful, all three of persons or things, but more commonly the first two of persons and the last of things, acts, as in **sündhafte** or **sündige Menschen, sündliche Handlungen; kostbar** costly, **köstlich** precious; **lesbar** decipherable, also readable, interesting, **leserlich** legible, easy to read. The meaning of **-lich** is sometimes identical with that of **-ig: kußlich** kissable, made to be kissed, **küssig, küsserlich** kissable, fond of kissing. Of these suffixes **-bar** is not employed with simple verbal stems to denote an inclination to perform the activity or to indicate that something is of such a nature as to incite it, and hence does not compete with **-haft, -lich,** and **-ig** at this point: **schwatzhaft** or less commonly **schwätzig** loquacious, but not **schwatzbar; lächerlich** or less frequently **lachhaft** laughable, but not **lachbar.** On the other hand, **-haft** is not used with verbal stems with passive force and does not compete here with **-bar** and **-lich.** See **12.** 1. *b*. *Note* below.

12. sam, related to the Latin *similis* similar, Eng. same and -some (as in winsome), and German **samt** *together with*, denoting originally a close, intimate connection with or similarity, but this meaning cannot always easily be detected. It is now usually affixed:

1. To abstract nouns and verbs to denote:

a. An inclination toward a thing implied in the stem of the noun, or an attribute which naturally belongs to it: **sorgsam** careful, **furchtsam** (originally belonging here, but now felt as belonging to *b*) timid, **gewaltsam** violent, **wonnesam** delightful, **mühsam** requiring laborious toil, **wegsam** passable (of a road, &c.), **unwegsam.**

Note. Here **-sam** touches close to **-lich,** sometimes with no difference, sometimes with a greater or less variation of meaning, **-sam** referring more to the inclination of the mind and character, and **-lich** pointing more to the exterior nature of the thing in question: **ein friedsamer Mensch** a peaceful man, but **ein friedliches Tal** a peaceful valley; **sittsam** *inclined to keep within the bounds of proper conduct, modest*, but **sittlich** *moral, concerning* or *conforming to the established code of morals*. Of the last two words the former sometimes has the idea of an unnatural exaggerated moral tendency: **O Sittsamkeit, | noch sittlicher als Sitte!** (Grillparzer's *Die Jüdin von Toledo*, 1). Other shades appear: **wundersam** (poetic for **wunderbar**) wonderful, **wunderlich** queer; **ehrsam** honorable (used to-day in a half comical sense), **ehrlich** honest, upright.

b. In a passive sense a possibility that the activity implied in the verbal stem may be performed, or in an active sense a possibility of performing it, or a natural inclination to do so: **bildsam** capable of being moulded, fashioned, **biegsam** flexible, **wirksam** efficacious, capable of making an effect, **kleidsam** becoming, **folgsam** willing to follow, obedient, **schweigsam** taciturn, **sparsam** saving, economical, **störsam** disturbing, apt to disturb, **überlegsam** thoughtful, reflective.

Note. The suffixes **-bar, -lich,** and **-sam** here touch close to each other in their passive meaning, sometimes blending entirely together, sometimes diverging. In **-bar** lies often the general idea that something can be done, while **-lich** implies sometimes more particularly that it can be done with reasonable ease: **Hartes Fleisch ist vielleicht verdaubar, aber jedenfalls nicht verdaulich** Tough meat can perhaps be digested, but at any rate it cannot easily be done. Somewhat different from **-lich** is **-sam,** which not only implies that the activity can be performed with fair ease, but also indicates that the reason for the easy performance lies in the nature of the object in question: **Die Metalle sind dehnbar** Metals are capable of being drawn out (into a wire, &c.), but **Gold ist sehr dehnsam** Gold is very ductile. In **-sam** may lie the idea that the activity leads to desirable results: **reizsam** open to impressions and stirred to activity by them, incitive, as in **ein reizsamer Idealismus** an idealism open to impressions and stirred to activity by them, but **reizbar** irritable. Also when they have active force **-sam** and **-lich** have meanings more or less similar: **empfindlich** sensitive, **empfindsam** sentimental. Sometimes **-bar** has passive, while **-lich** and **-sam** have active force: **ausführbar** practicable, **ausführlich** giving the details, full, complete; **genießbar** eatable, palatable, **bekömmlich** agreeing with one (of food, &c.); **lehrbar** teachable, **lehrsam** instructive; **furchtbar** dreaded, dreadful, formidable (**ein furchtbares Kriegsheer, Gewitter,** also in weakened meaning: **eine furchtbare Hitze**), **furchtsam** fearing, timid, and, with a meaning differing somewhat from that of the former, **fürchterlich** instilling fear, horror as in **ein fürchterliches Geschrei,** also in weakened meaning: **ein fürchterlicher Geruch**). See also **11.** 3 above.

c. An inclination of a person to act upon himself: **enthaltsam** abstemious, corresponding to **Er enthält sich (aller geistigen Getränke)**; **regsam** active, corresponding to **Er regt sich.** The reflexive is here regularly suppressed.

2. Affixed to a few adjectives, it denotes an inclination toward the quality indicated by the stem of the adjective or some condition associated with it: **langsam** slow, **einsam** lonely, **gemeinsam** joint, common. Differentiation takes place also here between adjectives in **-lich** and **-sam**: **länglich** oblong, **langsam** slow: **(un)lieblich** (un)lovely, **liebsam** (now little used) affectionate, **unliebsam** (not infrequent) unpleasant, disagreeable (**unliebsames Aufsehen erregen, unliebsame Erfahrungen machen**).

13. selig, see **I. 11.** 2 above.

14. zig (in the form of **-ßig** in **dreißig**), formerly an independent noun with the meaning *decade*, related to **zehn,** now used to form numeral adjectives: **zwanzig,** &c. In the lengthened form **-ziger** it is also employed to form nouns and adjectives. See **121.** 2. *b* and 5.

15. *Hybrids.* In slang and colloquial speech the French -eux in the form of **-'ös** is added to German stems to give a facetious turn to the thought and at the same time convey emphasis: **pe'chös** unfortunate, **schaude'rös** frightful, **sta'tiös** elegant.

III. *Derivative Verbs.*

Derivative verbs, which are in most part weak, constitute by far the greatest number of German verbs. They cannot only be formed from simple words but also from compounds, as explained at length in **217.** *a, b.*

The following suffixes are used in the formation of derivative verbs:

1. en (representing older jan, ōn, ēn), sometimes lengthened to **igen** after the analogy of the many verbs that have an **ig** in the stem preceding **en,** as **heiligen** to hallow, from **heilig** holy. Sometimes both of these forms may be added to the same stem without a shade of meaning, sometimes the one form is more common and the other more choice, sometimes a slight shade of meaning has developed: **beenden** or **beendigen** to end; **sich erkunden,** or more commonly **erkundigen** to inquire; **kreuzen** to cross, **kreuzigen** to crucify; **reinen** to cleanse, now only used in poetic style, usually replaced by **reinigen** to clean, cleanse; **befehlen** to command, order (someone), **befehligen** to command (an army); **begnaden** to bless, favor, formerly also to pardon, amnesty, **begnadigen** to pardon, amnesty. In many cases the older simple form has been replaced by the form in **-igen**: **beschönen** (still used in the early part of the eighteenth century) now **beschönigen.** Derivatives with the prefix **be-** show a preference for the forms in **igen.** See **246.** II. 1. *d. Note.*

A large number of these words suffer mutation (**ä** often appearing in the form of **e**) of the stem-vowel, as they had a **j** in the suffix (-jan) in an earlier period of the language: **fällen** (falljan) to fell, **legen** (lagjan) to lay. In verbs derived from adjectives mutation is in general characteristic of transitives and the lack of it the mark of intransitives: **wärmen** to warm, make warm, but **erwarmen** to grow warm.

The following common groups illustrate the meaning and use of this suffix:

(1) Affixed to the past tense of intrans. str. verbs it makes a trans. factitive verb: **legen** *to lay* from **lag,** past tense of **liegen** *to lie.* See **197.** A. *d,* and under each class of str. verbs (beginning at art. **198**) for a full treatment of this interesting group of words.

Also other derivatives are formed from the gradation forms of strong verbs. For examples see **198.** 2. Division, *c.*

(2) Affixed to the positive or comparative of descriptive adjectives it is used:

(*a*) To make factitive verbs: **härten** to harden, **zähmen** to tame, **heizen** (from **heiß;** see **197.** A. *d*) to heat, **befreien (frei)** to free; **vergrößern (groß)** to make larger, **verschlechtern** to make worse.

(*b*) To make verbs which denote a passing over into a condition or the condition itself: **erwarmen** to grow warm; **faulen** to rot, **hungern** to be hungry.

(**3**) Affixed to sing. or pl. of nouns it denotes:

(*a*) An activity which is directed toward the object implied in the stem of the noun, or which is employed to produce or procure this object: **köpfen** to cut off the heads or tops, **er blättert** (from pl. of the noun) **im Buche** he is turning over the pages of the book, **lochen** (from the sing.) to punch, punch a hole or holes in (**eine Fahrkarte, ein Eisen lochen**), **durchlöchern** (from the pl.) to punch holes in, perforate, **buttern** to churn, **fischen** to fish.

(*b*) A working or busying oneself with the object implied **in the stem: pflügen** to plow, **eggen** to harrow, **meißeln** to chisel.

(*c*) In student slang verbs are made from nouns in the freest manner: **ochsen** or **büffeln** to study hard (especially for examination), 'cram,' 'bone,' **holzen** to cane, **bechern** to drink freely, &c.

(**4**) It is sometimes affixed to other parts of speech:

(*a*) To particles: **bejahen (ja)** to answer affirmatively, **verneinen** to answer in the negative.

(*b*) To numerals: **vereinigen** to unite, **entzweien** to set at variance.

(*c*) To interjections: **juch'heien** to call out **juch'hei** (hurrah).

2. eln (O.H.G. -ilōn and -alōn), a suffix usually causing mutation, added to the stem of verbs, adjectives, and nouns, to express:

a. The idea of iteration, i.e. the idea of the frequent occurrence and repetition of an activity: **betteln** to beg for a living, **winseln** to whine, **streicheln** to stroke, **häkeln** to crochet, lit. to keep hooking, **schütteln** to shake. Also the idea of rapidity often enters into the meaning: **prasseln** to clatter down, fall thick and fast, **zappeln** to wriggle, strike out in all directions (with hands or feet or both). The blending of the iterative with the diminutive idea is very common. See *b* below. The idea of iteration is often coupled with more or less depreciatory force: **schmeicheln** to flatter (lit. smooth over), **heucheln** to play the hypocrite (lit. keep bowing), **schmuggeln** to smuggle, **verzärteln.**

b. A diminutive idea: **lächeln (lachen** to laugh) to smile, **tröpfeln** to fall in little drops, drip, **kritteln** to cavil, make trifling criticisms, **sticheln** to make mean, little, stinging remarks, **nörgeln** to find fault with in little things, **gängeln** to teach a child to make its first little steps. **Er fluchte nie, er flüchelte höchstens** (Siegfried's *Ein Wohltäter*). **Ach ja, es „menschelte"** (a bit of human nature or weakness cropped out) **überall. Mit diesem schönen Wort pflegte Holder** (name) **die Schwäche der Gesellschaft nicht zu bemänteln, aber dem Verständnisse näher zu bringen** (Stilgebauer's *Götz Krafft*, I. 1, p. 12). The iterative idea described in *a* often blends with the idea of diminution: **hüsteln** to hack, emit a short dry cough and repeat it often, **kränkeln** to be sickly, have frequent but rather light attacks of sickness. The iterative idea can also be felt in a number of the examples given above. The idea of diminution is often coupled with more or less depreciatory force: **geistreicheln** to try to write in a bright sprightly style, **klügeln** to affect wisdom, **tüfteln** to draw over-nice distinctions. **Weil er nicht auf dem geraden Weg der Uhrmacherei geblieben war, immer Neues entdecken wollte und daher immer allerlei probierte oder pröbelte, daher hieß er der Pröbler** (Auerbach's *Dorfgeschichten*, 2, p. 7).

c. The idea of likeness, similarity, close association: **Es füchselt** It smells of foxes; **anheimeln** to remind one of home, **ein hündelnder Höfling** a fawning courtier, **frömmeln** to affect piety, **schwäbeln** to speak the Swabian dialect, **näseln** to talk thru the nose. The idea of likeness, similarity, close association is often coupled with depreciatory force as in a number of these examples.

d. This prefix sometimes has ingressive perfective (**164**) force: **Es herbstelt** It is getting autumn. Often in the southern dialects: **Es knuegelet** (i.e. **gnügelt) mir = Es wird mir genug** *I am beginning to get enough.*

e. In Swiss dialects it is much used to express the feeling of endearment: (to a child) **Chumele** (i.e. **kommele) zu mir.**

3. ern (developed in part out of the **ern** which arises from the addition of **n** to a comparative suffix or the pl. of a noun as mentioned in **1. (2). (***a***)** and **(3). (***a***)** above), a suffix usually affixed to the stem of verbs to express:

a. The frequent repetition or the continuation of an action which is often conceived of as proceeding by jerks or with unsteady motion: **schnattern** to cackle (like geese), **stottern** to stutter, **flackern** to flicker, **klettern** to climb, lit. to keep on sticking, **plätschern** to splash, dabble.

Note. Here **-eln** and **-ern** approach each other very closely, some stems preferring the one suffix, other stems the other suffix. Where both suffixes may be added to the same stem **-eln** expresses a weaker activity: **wandeln** to saunter along slowly, leisurely, **wandern** to go from one place to another, **auswandern** to emigrate; **schütteln** to shake (hands, &c.), **schüttern** to shake violently (as the earth in an earthquake, or the human frame under the influence of violent emotion).

b. The irresistible desire of doing that which is implied in the stem, a usage rare in older periods, at first confined largely to popular speech, but now gaining a foothold in the literary language, especially frequent in impersonal constructions: **mich schläfert, trinkert, durstert, tanzert** I feel like going to sleep, &c. **Es lächert mich noch** (Wilbrandt's *Ein Mecklenburger*, p. 30). Also with a noun as subject: **Dann begann ein peinliches Darben, durch kurze und kraftlose neue Anläufe unterbrochen, deren Hoffnungslosigkeit ihn schier selber lächerte** (Hermann Hesse's *Unterm Rad*, p. 189).

c. In a few cases it makes factitive verbs: **folgern** to draw a conclusion, to conclude, lit. to make follow out of, **steigern** to raise (the price), to increase, lit. to make ascend, &c.

4. sen, schen, zen with iterative and weak diminutive force, **'enzen** (or **eln**) denoting likeness or inclination: **mucksen** to mumble, mutter to one's self in complaint, **klatschen** to clap (with the hands), **ächzen** to groan, **grunzen** to grunt, **duzen** to address by **du** *thou*, **fi'schenzen** (or **fischeln**) to smell of fish, **wil'denzen** to smell or taste of game, **po'lenzen** to be fond of the Poles and their ways, **grie'chenzen** to imitate the Greeks, **'faulenzen** to idle away one's time. The suffix **-'enzen** is a Middle German form and earlier in the period when M.G. writers were prominent was much used. In general the literary language now prefers as iterative and diminutive suffix the S.G. **-eln** (see **2.** *a*, *b*, *c* above). The verb **'faulenzen,** however, is still quite common, but its stress on the first syllable might indicate that it doesn't belong here but comes from **Faulenz = fáuler Lènz,** i.e. lázy Làwrence.

5. chen, cken, pfen, suffixes which in reality are the strengthening of the final consonants of the stem to express a strengthening or intensification of the meaning of the stem: **horchen** (**hören** to hear) to listen, **bücken** (**biegen** to bend) to bow humbly, **rupfen** (**raufen** to pull) to pluck (a chicken).

6. 'ieren (from the Old French ending ier), a foreign suffix, hence the accent. It has no distinct meaning, but is only a formal sign of the infinitive, affixed not only to foreign stems but also to German: **re'gieren** to rule, **mar'schieren** to march; **buchsta'bieren** to spell, **hal'bieren** to divide into two equal parts, **stol'zieren** to strut, &c.

a. From the last half of the twelfth century on, foreign, especially French verbs with this suffix began to appear, and later fairly swarmed into the language, assuming quite a stylish, aristocratic tone under the existing literary, political, and social supremacy of the French, but now for some time the tide has turned, and they are disappearing, and a number have sunk to the level of mere slang, or imply contempt, or mark something as being of a light, frivolous, "Frenchy" nature, as can be seen in the following ironical sentence from Lessing's *Minna von Barnhelm*, 3, 2: **Es war ein ganzer Mensch! Er konnte frisieren und rasieren und parlieren** (palaver or here perhaps 'talk French,' 'parley voo') — **und charmieren** (flirt).

b. Notice that the German ending **en** is added to the foreign infinitive ending, so that there are in fact two endings in all these words. In O.H.G. the German infinitive ending was added to the stem of the foreign word: tihtōn (from Latin dictare) now **dichten.** Sometimes we have the older and newer formation side by side with differentiated meaning: **dichten** and **diktieren; doktern** and **doktorieren; fabeln** and **fabulieren; ordnen** (L. ordinare) and **ordinieren; opfern** (L. operari) and **operieren; proben** and **probieren; spenden** (L. spendere) and **spendieren,** &c. These two endings are also added to German stems for purposes of differentiation: **hausen** and **hausieren, schatten** and **schattieren,** &c.

7. i'sieren, a suffix corresponding in large part to the English ize: **modernisieren** to modernize, **tyrannisieren** to tyrannize, **homerisieren** to homerize, write in the style of Homer, **goethisieren** to write in the style of Goethe, &c.

8. 'eien, a suffix corresponding to the foreign ending **ei** in nouns and the

M.H.G. infinitive ending īgen, īen. It has no distinct meaning: **prophe'zeien** to prophesy, **ka'steien** to chastise, &c.

General Note. It should be noticed that all these verbal suffixes frequently appear in nouns, as the infin. of a verb is often used as a neut. abstract noun: **Das Gehen ermüdet. Sie konnte vor Schluchzen nicht sprechen.**

IV *Derivative or Compound Adverbs.*

Most adverbs are particles which are derived from adjectives, participles, nouns, pronouns, and a few from verbs. The commonest of the adverbs derived from other words may be divided into the following groups:

1. From adjectives and participles, by casting off the inflectional endings: **gut** well, **kühn** boldly, **trefflich** excellently, **gelehrt** learnedly, **ausgezeichnet** splendidly, **entzückend** charmingly, &c.

a. Instead of assuming the simple uninflected form of the adj. or participle the adverb sometimes takes the form of a case of the adjective or participle, especially the gen. in **-s**: **rechts** to the right, **links** to the left, **anders** otherwise, **bereits** *already*, but in southwest Germany *almost*, **zusehends** perceptibly, &c.

2. From adjectives, nouns, and sometimes other parts of speech by adding the suffixes **-e, -lich, -lings, -wärts,** and by forming compounds with **Weg** and **Weise**: **gerne** willingly, **endlich** finally, **meuchlings** treacherously, **südwärts** southward, **kurz'weg** abruptly, **paarweise** by twos, &c.

a. In a few instances there is still, as in M.H.G., a slight formal difference between the positive of adjectives and adverbs. The adverb adds **e** to the stem of the adjectives, or if the adjective has mutation the adverb is distinguished from it by taking no mutation. See **222.** 2. E. *Note.*

b. Some adverbs, especially those formed from adjectives in **-ig,** were formerly distinguished from the corresponding adjectives by suffixing **-lich**: **traurig** (adj.), **trauriglich** (adv.). Also to-day a few of these formations in **-lich** are *only* used as adverbs, as **bekanntlich, ewiglich, fälschlich, freilich, gewaltiglich, gewißlich, höchlich, kürzlich, schwerlich, sicherlich, wahrlich.** In English the similar development of adverbial -ly has gone much farther. A number of formations in **-lich** are adjectives only in form, and are in reality adverbs. See II. **11.** 2. A. *f* and B. *a* above.

c. The adverbial suffix **-lings** (related to the masc. substantive suffix **-ling**) is suffixed to nouns, adjectives, verbal stems, prepositions, and adverbs to denote manner or indicate position or direction toward: **bäuchlings** lying flat on one's belly, **rücklings** backward, **blindlings** blindly, **rittlings** astraddle, **vorlings** forward. This suffix was common earlier in the period, often in the form **lingen** or **ling,** but is now restricted to a few words.

d. The suffix **wärts** denotes direction toward: **ostwärts, westwärts, vorwärts, seewärts,** &c.

e. The compounds with **-weg** and **-weise** denote manner and have arisen from prepositional phrases: (M.H.G.) in manegen wec *in many a way*, in menschen (gen.) wise *according to the ways of men*. The group with **-weg** is not large: **frisch'wĕg** resolutely, briskly, **glatt'wĕg** roundly, flatly, plainly, &c. The word **'halbwēg** *half-way* does not belong here as it comes from M.H.G. halben wec (acc. of extent). This word also appears in the forms **'halbwege** (acc. pl.) and **'halbwegs** (gen.) in the same meaning.

The group in **-weise** is quite large. In M.H.G. we find a prepositional phrase here: in kriuzes wise *crosswise*, now **'kreuzweise** as *in* dropped out and the group was felt as a compound. Now as in other compounds we sometimes find the first component in the form of the sing. or pl. stem, sometimes with the ending **-s**: **faßweise** or **fässerweise** by the barrel, in barrels, **paarweise** by pairs, **schrittweise** step by step, **stufenweise** by degrees, **ausnahmsweise** by way of exception, &c. These compounds in **-weise** are now often also used as adjectives: **das stufenweise Steigen, die teilweise Erneuerung, die versuchsweise Einführung.**

3. **From nouns:**

A. *a*. From the cases of nouns, especially the gen.: **vormittags** in the fore-noon, **teils** partly, **rings** round about, **Donnerstags** on Thursdays, **rechter Hand** to the right hand, **unnötigerweise** unnecessarily; and often with an **s** in the gen. in case of fem. nouns after the analogy of masculines: **meinerseits** on my part, **unserseits** on our part; (in the acc.) **heim** home, **weg** (= M.H.G. enwec, i.e. **auf den Weg**) away, **ein bißchen** a little bit, **jeden Tag** every day, **ein Jahr** one year, &c.; (in the old instrumental) **heute,** from older hiu tagu *on this day*, corresponding to Latin *hodie*, from older *hoc die*. The genitive construction is treated more at length in **223.** I. 10. *a*, II. 1, 2, 3, 4, III. *a*, IV. 2. A. *a*, *b*, *c*, B. *a*, *c*, *d*, C. *a*, VI, VII, XI, **249.** II. 2. A. *a*; the dative in **223.** I. 10, *c*, II. 1, 2. *b*, III. *c*; the accusative in **223.** I. 10. *d*, II. 1, 3, IV. 2. A, B, C.

b. From nouns or adjective-substantives with a preceding governing prep. or a following particle: **übermorgen** day after to-morrow, **ab'handen** removed from its proper place, **auf gut Glück** at random; **berg'auf** uphill, **jahr'ein, jahr'aus** year in, year out; **bei weitem** by far, **vor allem** above all, &c.

c. From two nouns separated by **und** or a prep.: **Knall und Fall** suddenly, **Tag für Tag** day by day, **Arm in Arm** arm in arm.

B. Among the cases mentioned in A. *a* and *b* that are especially worthy of notice is a large group of adverbs formed from nouns which have lost their original meaning and force, and now form together with the verb a single idea. Such adverbial nouns in an oblique case after a preposition are now in force true compound adverbs, and can be distinguished from genuine nouns by the dropping of their article, and also by this that they no longer retain their original restricted literal meaning, but have taken on a much more general or a figurative one: **zu Bette gehen** to go to bed (not any especial bed, but in a general sense of *to sleep*), **zutage kommen** to come to light, **in See gehen** *to put to sea*, not any especial sea, but the broad ocean in contrast to land, **zugrunde gehen** to go to ruin, **zuleide tun** to hurt, **außer acht lassen,** or **außer aller Acht lassen** to pay no attention to, **zu Herzen nehmen** to take to heart, &c. These adverbs are sometimes written with capitals, especially when a preceding inflected modifier reminds us of their originally substantive nature, but in many cases they are written with a small letter when the originally substantive nature is not distinctly felt. These adverbs are in force separable prefixes, and should be written in one word with the verb, but as yet this practice is not always followed, and some fluctuation in usage in this respect occurs: **zu Grunde gehen,** or **zu grunde gehen,** or most commonly **zugrunde gehen** to go to wreck and ruin; **in Stand setzen, in stand setzen,** or most commonly **instand setzen** to put into working order, &c. Compare **59.** III. *j* (and also *bb* thereunder) and **62.** E. *Note.*

4. From pronominal stems: **wo** *where*, from the same stem as **wer; da** *there*, **dann** *then*, both from the same stem as the demon. **der.**

5. From other particles: **Die Sonne hellt den Himmel auf. Ich habe ausgeschlafen** I have had my sleep out.

6. In composition with other particles: **dagegen** on the contrary, **hierin** in this, &c.

7. From verbs: **gelt** (= **es gelte,** pres. subj.) in the popular language of South Germany, expecting the confirmation of the speaker's position, *isn't that true?*, expressing assurance, *I say, I'm sure, indeed*, also as an introduction to an entreaty or command; **bewahre,** or **ei behüte,** or **Gott bewahre,** or **behüte** no, not at all.

V. *Formation of Prepositions.*

The oldest and most common prepositions were originally adverbs, as described in **226.** Similarly other parts of speech have from time to time been pressed into service at first temporarily to show the relation between a verb and some other word. In course of time the feeling of their former function disappeared, and the temporary office became a permanent one. Thus new prepositions are constantly being formed. The following instances may serve to illustrate in brief the varied origin of the prepositions that have come from other sources than from adverbs. In an earlier period the comparative of the adj. was followed by the dat. (just as in the Latin by the ablative). Later this dat. construction after a comparative died out except in case of the two comparatives **ehe** *sooner than* and **seit** *farther on.* At present all feeling that they are comparatives is lost, but since they still as formerly govern the dat. they are construed as prepositions with the dat. The latter of these words, **seit,** is now the common prep. *since*, and the former, **ehe,** is also felt as a prep., tho only found written together with its dependent dat. in the one word **ehedem** *before that* in the literary language, but often heard thus as a prep. in the language of the common people in such expressions as **Ehe** (before) **Dienstag kann ich nicht kommen. Anstatt** or **statt** *instead of* are examples of recently formed prepositions, the word **Statt** still existing independently as a noun. When the two elements of **anstatt** are separated the latter element is distinctly felt as a noun, as also **Statt** when preceded by an article or other modifying word, and hence written with a capital letter: **an Kindes Statt** in place of a child (of one's own), **Gutes Wort findet eine gute Statt,** and **Ich bitte, es an meiner Statt zu tun.** When **an** and **statt** are found together the compound is felt rather as a prep., and is written with a small letter, and likewise **statt** when there is no article: **Und nun anstatt** or **statt des Vaters erschien die Mutter.** The prep. **neben** is compounded of the prep. **in** and **eben** *level,* and hence its meaning *on a level with, alongside of.* See also **228. 1.** *b* and 4 under **während** and **ungeachtet.**

246. Formation of Words by Means of Prefixes.

Only two classes of words—nouns and verbs—have especial prefixes. Adjectives and adverbs have their prefixes in common with verbs and nouns. Of course, very many nouns derived from derivative or compound verbs have the same prefixes as the corresponding verbs: **Ver'stand** *understanding,* **ver'stehen** *to understand,* &c. In one prefix, however, the form differs in nouns and verbs, **Rück-** *re-, back* in nouns, but **zurück-** in verbs: **Rückfall** *relapse,* but **zurückfallen** to fall back, relapse. Only those prefixes are discussed here which are peculiar to nouns, adjectives, and pronouns, or which present difficulties when used with these parts of speech. The prefixes in derivative words were once independent words, but have in course of time lost their identity as such, and have now no existence outside of compounds. In connection with the loss of their independence is the loss of accent. In nouns, however, all the prefixes except **ge-** usually have stress. For details concerning accent, see Art. **47.**

I. *Formation of Nouns, Adjectives, and Pronouns by means of Prefixes.*

1. ab has two meanings:

a. Away, off, down: **Abfahrt, Abweg, Abgrund,** &c.

b. The idea of falseness, worthlessness, negation: **Abgott** idol, **Abschaum, abhold,** and in an earlier period abholz (= **Abfallholz**), abewitze (= **Unverstand**), &c.

2. aber, originally a comparative of **ab** *off* with the meaning *farther off,* with regard to time *later,* has three meanings:

a. It is still in early N.H.G. an independent word, meaning *again,* which naturally developed out of the original meanings *farther off, later*: **Vnd der HERR rief Samuel aber zum dritten mal** (1 Sam. iii. 8). To-day **aber** is in this meaning rarely used as an independent word, and is now found only as a prefix in a few words, as **abermals** *once more, again,* **Abersaat** second sowing, lit. later sowing or sowing again, **Aberglaube** superstition, lit. belief farther off (from the proper belief), &c.

b. In the conjunction **aber** the original idea of *farther off* naturally leads to the idea of something different, a contrast, in English rendered by *but, however.*

c. In a few words **aber** is a corrupted form of **ober** *upper, higher*: **Aberacht,** now under the influence of **aber** *again* felt as meaning a ban which has been proclaimed again and made more severe, lit. a higher imperial ban resting upon the former one.

3. after (identical with Eng. *after*), which is prefixed to nouns, participles, and adjectives and has the meanings *behind, after* in their literal local or temporal sense, and also in their applied meanings *undeveloped, imperfect, approaching to, inferior, false*: **Afterbürge** *one who stands behind another as security*, **Aftermieter** one who sublets, **Afterrede** *talk behind one's back, calumny*, **Aftermutter** *hard-hearted mother*, **Afterklaue** dew-claw, **Afterblättchen** bot. stipule, **Afterkugel** spheroid, **Afterkritiker** *would-be critic*, **Aftergröße** *false greatness*, **aftergelehrt** *having a superficial knowledge*, **afterweise** *would-be wise*.

4. ant (the full form corresponding to the unaccented **ent-, emp-**; see **II. 2** below), prefixed now only to two nouns **Antwort** *answer* and **Antlitz** poetic word for *face*. Here the prefix denotes *toward* or *against*.

5. et, prefixed to a few pronouns in order to convey to them a general or indefinite meaning: **etwas** something, **etlich** some, several.

6. erz (= Eng. arch-, Gk. ἀρχι), prefixed to nouns (**1**) to denote the leader of a class: **Erzbischof** archbishop, **Erzengel** archangel, **Erzherzog** archduke, **Erzpriester** archpriest, **Erzvater** patriarch, &c.; (**2**) to convey intensifying force: **Erzdieb** arrant thief, **Erzdemokrat** radical democrat, **Erzdummkopf** regular blockhead, **Erzlügner** infernal liar, arch-liar, &c. It is also added to adjectives to convey intensifying force: **erzdumm** extremely stupid, **erzfaul** very lazy, **erzkatholisch** ultra-catholic, &c. For accent of these substantive and adjective derivatives see **47.** 3. A. *b. aa, c*.

7. ge (cognate with *i* in English handiwork and Latin **co-, con-, cum**; compare II. 4 below), prefixed to the stem of nouns and verbs to denote:

a. A collective idea: **Gebirge** mountain-system, **Gebüsch** thicket of bushes, **Gesinde** all the servants of a household, **Gebrüder** two or more brothers of a family. See also **67.** *Note*.

b. A person engaged with another in the activity mentioned in the stem, or a person sharing something with another: **Gefährte** a fellow-traveler, **Gespiele** play-mate, **Tischgenosse** table-companion, **Geselle** companion, literally one sharing the same room (**Saal**) with another.

c. The idea of a collection or association naturally passes over into that of repetition, duration, that which is connected in order of time: **Gezwitscher** chirping, **Geplauder** conversation. Here the idea of duration or repetition may be unpleasant, and hence **ge-** often takes on the meaning of disparagement, contempt. See **83.** *b*.

d. In verbal derivatives **Ge-** denotes an aggregate that has resulted from the activity indicated by the verbal stem: **Gewächs** plant, lit. all that has resulted from the process of growing, **Geschick** fate, lit. all that has been sent to someone, **Gebäude** that which has resulted from building, **Getreide** (O.H.G. gitregidi, from **tragen** *to bear*) grain, lit. all that has resulted from the process of bearing, **Gemälde,** &c.

e. In adjectives the force of **ge-** is in general scarcely appreciable, as the stem-word is in most cases lost: **genug** enough, **genehm** acceptable, **gesund** healthy, &c. In a few cases where the stem-word is also in use a shade of meaning develops between the stem-word and the derivative: **treu** true (as in **ein treuer Freund**), but **getreu** loyal (to a ruler), true (**dem Original getreu**), close (**eine getreue Übersetzung**), faithful (**eine getreue Nachbildung**); **streng** strict, severe, but **gestreng** in use earlier in the period to address persons of noble rank, especially such as have the power of life and death over subjects, as in **gestrenger Herr** your Worship.

8. miß (in M.H.G. misse, which still survives in **Missetat,** cognate with Eng. *mis*, as in *mistake*), prefixed in most part to stems having an abstract meaning to denote:

a. The opposite of that contained in the stem: **Mißgunst** disfavor, **Mißfallen** displeasure; **mißfällig** displeasing, unpleasant, &c.

b. Something wrong, erroneous, defective, unsuccessful, bad: **Mißstand** abuse, **Mißheirat** mésalliance, **Mißverständnis** misunderstanding, **Mißton** dissonance, **Mißernte** bad crop, **Missetat** misdeed; **mißgestaltet** misshapen, **mißtönend** ill-tuned, discordant.

9. un (cognate with English *un-*), prefixed to the stem of nouns, adjectives, participles, and adverbs, to denote:

a. The opposite of that mentioned in the stem or mere negation or lack: prefixed to the stem of nouns: **Undank** ingratitude, **Unart** naughtiness, **Unsinn** nonsense, **Unverstand** want of judgment, **Unding** nothingness, impossibility, more commonly according to *b* absurdity, foolish thing. In a few words **un-** or **miß-** can be used without difference of meaning: **Unbehagen** or **Mißbehagen** uncomfortable feeling, &c. **Un-** is also prefixed to adjectives, adjective participles, and adverbs with the same force: **undankbar,** &c. For accent in substantive and adjective derivatives see **47.** 2. B. *a.*

In younger group-words (**247.** 2. *b*), however, where the negative is not used to indicate the absence of an inherent quality or force but to state a fact negatively, **nicht,** not **un-,** is employed, just as **nicht** is usually employed in negative statements, but differing from usage in a normal sentence it is stressed, as it is the first component of a younger group-word and the stress of course is that of a younger group-word: **ein 'Nichtbürger** one who is not a citizen, an alien, **ein 'Nichtraucher** a car where there is no smoking, **'nichtadelig** not of noble birth, **das 'Nichthalten eines Versprechens, die 'Nichteinklagbarkeit von Zechschulden** the irrecoverableness of drinking debts (but **eine 'uneintreibbare Forderung** a claim that can't be collected under the law, i.e. a claim of a certain kind). Present participles usually have almost pure verbal force and indicate acts or facts, hence like verbs they usually take unaccented **nicht: die nicht tanzenden Herren** the gentlemen who are not dancing. Only when they approach the nature of pure adjectives do they take **un-,** as in **'unbedeutend, 'unwissend, 'unzutreffend,** &c. Perfect participles can of course only take **un-** when they are used adjectively. In adjective function they take **nicht** when they denote an act, **un-** when they denote a state: **Der noch nicht geȍffnete Bríef** the letter that hasn't been opened yet; **der úngeȍffnete Bríef** the únȍpened lȅtter; **der Brief ist noch nicht geȍffnet** [**worden**] The letter has not yet been opened; **der Brief ist ùngeȍffnet** The letter is ùnópened. For the stress here see **47.** 2. B. *a.* In **183.** 2. C. *c* a few traces are seen of an older order of things, where in the predicate appositive relation **un-** can be used even when the perfect participle denotes an act.

b. Something defective, bad, aside from the regular and usual, unnatural, hence sometimes repulsive, contemptible, also something worthless, unpleasant: **Untat** (usually **Untätchen**) spot, blemish, **Unsitte** bad custom, **Unkosten** *transportation charges*, that is, charges aside from the regular price of the goods, also *disagreeable expenses*, **Unmensch** a brutish person, **Unnatur** that which is contrary to nature, **Unland** land swampy and good for nothing, **Unkraut** weeds, **Ungeziefer** vermin, **Unwetter** bad, stormy weather, **Unmut** or **Mißmut** ill humor.

c. A strong intensification of the idea contained in the stem, however, with indefinite force so that the extent of the idea is not accurately defined: **eine 'Untat** an atrocious crime, **eine 'Un'menge** or **'Un'masse Menschen** a great crowd of people, **eine 'Unzahl Maikäfer** a great number of may-bugs, **ein 'Untier** a monster, **'Un'summen** vast sums of money, **'Untiefe** *a great depth, a deep place in a river*, or according to *a*, above, just the reverse, *a shoal.* For accent see **47.** 3. A. *b. aa, c.*

d. In dialect and a few expressions in the literary language **un-** is sometimes used pleonastically, somewhat as **nicht** (see **223.** XI. B. *a*): **unzweifellos = zweifellos,** &c. Compare **223.** XI. B. *a.* (6).

10. ur (full form corresponding to unaccented **er-**; see II. **3** below), a prefix originally meaning *out,* which can still be seen in its present signification, *the* *extreme*, in the direction of the beginning, source, from which or out of which a thing may come, or of the end of something, literally the coming out of some condition: **Urwald** primeval forest, **Urgroßvater** great-grandfather, **Urbewohner** aborigines, **Urheimat** original home, **Uranfang** first beginning; **Urenkel** great-grandson, **Urfehde** oath to put an end to a feud, lit. feud at an end.

a. In most words **ur-** is long, but in **Urteil** *judgment, sentence*, it is short.

b. The idea of *the extreme* has in adjectives given to **ur-** intensifying power: **'ur'alt** very old, **'ur'plötzlich** very sudden, all of a sudden, **'ur'kräftig** extremely powerful. For accent see **47.** 3. A. *b. aa.*

11. *Foreign prefixes.* Besides **erz-**, described in **6** above, the following foreign prefixes are placed before German or foreign words: **anti-, ex-, hyper-, super-, quasi-, pseudo-, vize-.** They have the same force as in English: **anti'deutsch, 'Exminister, hyperaristo'kratisch, 'superklug, 'Quasigelehrter** would-be scholar, **'Pseudofürst, 'Vizekönig,** &c.

II. *Formation of Verbs by means of Prefixes.*

The long list of separable prefixes are not discussed here, as they largely consist of words which have an independent existence outside of compounds. Verbs containing such prefixes are compounds, not derivatives. Some of these prefixes, however, are little used outside of compounds and are approaching the nature of the inseparable prefixes discussed below. They are treated under the other separable prefixes in **215.** II. 1. B and at greater length under adverbs in **223.** The following inseparable prefixes were once also independent words, but as they are now only used in derivatives and have lost their former concrete meaning they present many difficulties and are hence treated here in detail.

1. be (related to the prep. **bei**) has the meaning *around, on all sides of*. Originally **be** was also a preposition, as can still be seen in **be'hende** (= M.H.G. behende = **bei der Hand**) *quick, nimble.* Originally this preposition governed also the acc., and this former construction still occurs in composition with intransitive verbs, where the compound takes an object in the acc. which is in fact the object of the preposition **be.** See *a* below.

The original local meaning *around, on all sides of* can still be seen in a number of verbs: **bedenken** to study something from all sides, consider, **bedrängen** to press someone hard on all sides. The idea of *around, encircling* leads directly to *grasping, seizing*: **begreifen** to grasp mentally, comprehend, **benehmen** seize, take away (**Etwas benimmt einem den Atem**), **sich gut benehmen** to conduct oneself well, lit. to have a good grasp, hold on oneself. The idea of *around, encircling, shutting in* is seen in **befangen** (**in einem Wahn befangen** wrapped up in a delusion), **belagern** to besiege, lit. put a camp around, &c.

The original local meaning of **be** is no longer vividly felt, but out of it distinct groups of applied meanings have been developed. The idea of around, encircling often leads to the idea of a definite, limited sphere or plane, *upon* which the action plays or *over* which it extends, or *into* which it penetrates. Hence **be-** is often used:

a. To bring the action expressed in intransitive verbs to bear *upon* some object, and change thereby intransitive verbs into transitive: **Sie weint** *she weeps*, but **Sie beweint den Tod ihrer Mutter,** or **beweint ihre Mutter** *she is mourning over the death of her mother*, or *weeping over her mother*, lit. *around, in the sphere of, concerning, about.* **Furcht und Entsetzen befällt mich** *Fear and horror seize me*, lit. fall around me, in my sphere, near me. Thus also **besitzen** to possess, lit. sit upon, **betreten** to step upon, **bekommen** to get, lit. come upon, &c. Older **bekennen** *to know, know about* survives in the participles **bekannt** and **Bekannter** and in the factitive **bekennen** to cause another to know about: **seine Schuld bekennen** to confess his guilt, lit. cause another to know about his guilt. One of these verbs has a genitive instead of an accusative object: **Er bedarf des Trostes** He needs consolation, lit. is needy in the sphere of, with regard to consolation.

b. In composition with verbs already trans., to bring the action to bear *upon* some object or extend the force of the action entirely *over* or *about* something: **Sie begießt die Blumen** She is watering the flowers. **Der Landmann bebaut** (cultivates) **das Feld. Er stahl einen Rock** He stole a coat, but **Er bestahl seinen Herrn** He robbed, stole from his master.

Note. Observe that the object of the simple verb often becomes in the construction with the derivative a dative after the prep. **mit: Die Arbeiter laden Getreide auf das Schiff** *The workmen are loading grain on to the ship,* but **Die Arbeiter beladen das Schiff mit Getreide.**

c. To give intensifying force to the simple verb. The idea of *around, on all sides* leads to the idea of completion, doing something well, thoroly, accurately: **bekommen** to agree with (one's health, more lit. *to come along, go along well,* in early N.H.G. of plants *to do well, flourish*), **besehen** to examine carefully, lit. *look at on all sides,* **berechnen** to compute, calculate accurately, **bestehen** to stand firmly, pass thru a test successfully, insist upon, **beheben** (**Übel, Hindernisse, Widersprüche beheben,** growing ever more common instead of the simple form **heben**) to remove entirely, **befolgen** to follow closely (**Gesetze, Lehren, Regeln, Vorschriften befolgen**), &c.

d. In composition with adjectives, to indicate that the attribute in question is placed all around, is bestowed upon or put *in, on, over* something: **feucht** moist, **befeuchten** to moisten; **ruhig** calm, **beruhigen** to calm; **reicher** richer, **bereichern** to enrich. Thus **beschleunigen** to hasten, **betrüben** to grieve, **belustigen** to amuse, &c.

Note. Some verbs are formed after the analogy o those derived from adjectives in **-ig,** and thus end in **-igen,** altho there is no **ig** in the stem from which they are formed: **beeidigen (be + Eid), beerdigen (be + Erde), befriedigen, bekräftigen, benachrichtigen,** &c.

e. In composition with nouns to indicate that that which is implied by the noun is placed all around, is bestowed upon someone, or that something or somebody is supplied, furnished, endowed with what is contained in the noun: **Laub** foliage, **belauben** to furnish with foliage; **Saite** string (of an instrument), **besaiten** to furnish with strings; **Seele** soul, life, **beseelen** to put life into, animate.

f. There is also an ironical application of the idea *over, on* in some verbs formed from adjectives or nouns: **Ich bin elend! Ach was, ich will dich beelenden!** I feel miserable! What, I will give you something to make you feel miserable about. **Sie behauptet, sie sei die Frau Junkern (245. I. 6. 1.** *b*), **aber ich will sie bejunkern, daß sie an mich denken soll** She pretends to be Mrs. Junker, but I will 'junker' her so that she will remember me. **Was Latein?** (What! you want to study Latin?) **ich will dich Knirps belateinen** (Raabe's *Hungerpastor*, chap. 5).

g. Altho the decided tendency has been for these derivatives to become transitive, a few of them are nevertheless intransitive with the same general meanings: **beharren** (*c*) to stand firmly by (**Er beharrt auf seiner Meinung**), **bekommen** to agree with one's health (see example and explanation in *c*), **bestehen** (*c*) to insist upon, pass (come off well in a test), **beruhen** to rest upon, **behagen** to be agreeable to, afford comfort or pleasure to, lit. put protection around someone, **begegnen** to meet, lit. come into the sphere, neighborhood of, **bedürfen** (example and explanation in *a*).

2. ent (or **emp** before a few verbs in initial **f**), which is found in its original form **ant-** only in **Antwort** and **Antlitz,** is identical with Greek ἀντί and hence meant originally *toward, against.* This meaning can now only be found in a few words: **entbieten** to send to, **entgelten** to pay for, atone for, **enthalten** to contain, **entsprechen** to answer, correspond to, **empfangen** to receive, **empfehlen** to recommend, **empfinden** to feel, be sensible of.

The following derivative meanings are now more common:

a. From the original meaning of movement toward comes that of a beginning of an activity, a change, a passing into, a putting into a new state or condition: **entbrennen** to take fire, become inflamed, **entstehen** to arise, originate, **entzünden** to inflame, **entfachen,** to enkindle, **entschlummern** to fall asleep (in death), **entleeren** to empty, **entblößen** to lay bare, strip, **einem etwas ent-**

fremden to alienate something from someone, **sich entledigen** (**262.** II. A. *b*) to free one's self from, **sich entblöden** to become ashamed, most commonly used negatively (: **Du entblödest dich nicht, mir das ins Gesicht zu sagen?**), &c. As can be seen from the examples the basal part of such verbs is either a verb or an adjective.

Note 1. The prefix of a number of the verbs in this group whose basal element is a verb is in fact the modern corrupted form of O.H.G. in (identical with N.H.G. prep. in) *toward, into,* which was closely related in meaning to the original force of ent, and in certain verbs became confounded with it, as int (the O.H.G. form of ent) was itself often used in the corrupted form of in.

b. A change is not only a movement in the direction of that which is new, but is also a breaking away from the old, hence in general *separation, removal, withdrawal,* now the most common meaning: **entreißen** to snatch away from, **enttäuschen** to disappoint, lit. to tear away from a pleasant illusion, **entlassen** to turn off, dismiss, **entlohnen** (= **ablohnen**) to pay off, lit. to send someone off rejoicing with his pay, wages, **entkommen** to escape, **entsagen** to renounce, **entgleiten** to slip out of; **entblättern** to strip off the leaves, **enthaupten** to take off the head, decapitate, **entthronen** to dethrone, **entkräften** to enervate; **sich entblöden** to have the audacity, lit. to tear one's self away from being modest, shy, bashful, to make one's self bold, now little used in this meaning altho common in the meaning in *a.* As can be seen from the examples, the basal part of such verbs may be a verb, noun, or less commonly an adjective. Verbs of this class of meanings are called privatives. For comparison of this meaning of **ent-** with its synonyms see **223.** I. 7. G. *c.*

c. Intimately related to the preceding is the idea of *reversal,* denoting the opposite of the simple verb: **ehren** *to honor,* but **entehren** to dishonor; **laden** *to load,* but **entladen** *to unload*; **siegeln** *to seal,* but **entsiegeln** to unseal.

d. With the idea of separation there is often associated the idea of a careful, systematic or natural unfolding or division: **entwirren** to disentangle, **entwickeln** to unravel, develop, **entfalten** to unfold, develop, **entwerfen** to sketch, map out, lit. to throw or take apart, **entfallen** to fall to one's regular share, &c. This meaning stands in marked contrast to that in *b,* which usually contains the idea of violent or unnatural separation. The idea of care and system did not originally lie in **ent** but in the verb itself, as in the first examples. From these verbs the idea may have become attached to the prefix and then spread to other verbs.

3. er (in Austrian and Bavarian dialects **der**), which is found in its original form **ur** only in nouns and adjectives, originally meant *from within out, out of,* and building upon this has developed a rich store of shades, all of which can be brought into connection with the fundamental meaning.

a. In its original literal sense or much more frequently its figurative application, but only dimly felt if felt at all: **erpressen** to press out (wine out of grapes), extort, **erziehen** to educate, lit. *to draw out,* **erbauen** to edify, **erheben** to elevate the thought or feeling, **erschöpfen** to exhaust, **sein Inneres erschließen** to disclose one's feelings, &c.

b. The prefix gradually lost its original local meaning, which faded away into mere abstract perfective force, i.e. the idea of point-action, not calling attention to the act as a whole but to only one point in it, the beginning or the end, in ingressive perfectives calling attention to the beginning, in effective perfectives calling attention to the end, that is, the idea of motion *from within outward* passed, on the one hand, into that of *change* or *transition* into a state or condition, or, on the other hand, into the idea of the final *result* or *outcome* of an action: (ingressives) **erblühen** to come out into blossom, **erwachen** to wake up (intrans.), **erwecken** to wake (trans.), **ermüden** to become tired, to tire out (trans.), **erwärmen** to warm, make warm, **erwarmen** to grow warm, **erblinden** to grow blind, **erröten** to blush, **sich ermannen** to summon up courage; (effectives) **erleben** to live to see, **erliegen** to succumb (the action resulting in somebody's lying down, i.e. giving up), **erlöschen** to become extinguished, **ergeben** (**die Untersuchung hat seine Unschuld ergeben** has proved his innocence, lit. has given his innocence as a final result), &c. As can be seen from the examples, the basal part of such verbs may be a verb, adjective, or, less commonly, a noun. Also **ver-** in composition with verbs derived from nouns and adjectives has perfective force. See **5.** D. *a*, *b* (and *Note*), *c* below.

The derivatives with **er-** often stand in a more or less marked contrast to their simple verbal forms, the simple verb representing an action in its duration, the derivative form representing only a particular point in the course of the action, namely, the entrance into the state or condition, or the outcome or result of the action: **grünen** *to be* or *remain green*, but **ergrünen** *to become green*; **wachen** *to be awake, watch*, but **erwachen** *to wake up*; **wählen** *to choose* (i.e. the entire act, including the period of deliberation and the final act of settling upon a choice), but **erwählen** *to select, elect, choose* (referring only to the resulting choice, excluding the preceding period of deliberation); **steigen** *to climb*, but **einen Berg ersteigen** to attain the summit of a mountain by climbing. **Ich sterbe, sterbe, und kann nicht ersterben** (Goethe's *Götz*, 5, 10). The derivative form often has a figurative application, while the simple verb has its literal meaning: **sättigen** to satisfy (one's stomach, &c.), but **ersättigen** to satisfy (one's longings, &c.); **weichen** to soften (leather, &c.), but **erweichen** to soften (the heart, feelings, &c.). In a few verbs **er-** converts intransitives into transitives: **warten** to wait, **erwarten** to await, expect. In some cases the distinction of meaning between the simple verb and the derivative is very faint.

Note. In ingressives **er-** often represents the change as coming from within from *inner* causes: **Lackmuspapier in Säure getaucht wird rot** *Litmus-paper, dipped into an acid, becomes red*, but **Das Mädchen errötet vor Scham** *the girl blushes* (lit. turns red) *for shame.*

c. The original idea and the more common one of result can be clearly seen in such expressions as **etwas erfragen** *to get something out of one by questioning.* From such expressions comes the very common meaning of getting, obtaining something in the manner described by the simple verb: **erfahren** to experience (i.e. to get by going, passing thru), to learn (i.e. to get in driving along, to pick up, in contrast to the laborious process indicated by **lernen** to learn), **erflehen** to get by entreaty, **erstürmen** to get something by storm, as a city, &c., **erstreiten** to get by fighting, **ergaunern** to obtain by knavish tricks, **erreichen** to obtain by reaching, to reach (an object, a river, a town, &c.) Compare the force of the simple verb with that of the derivative in the following: **Das Kind reichte nach den Früchten, aber es konnte sie nicht erreichen.**

d. **Er** refers in so many cases where a result is expressed to the life within, as in **erbittert** embittered, **erfrischen** to refresh the inner man, **erlösen** to save the soul from sin, &c., that it is associated in general with the vital forces, and when placed before certain verbs it indicates that the person died or was killed in the manner described by the simple verb: **erdolchen** to stab to death, **erdrosseln** to throttle, **erschießen** to kill by shooting, **erschlagen** to kill by striking, **ertrinken** to drown, **erlegen** (huntsman's expression) to kill, lit. to lay out dead, **erdrücken** to press to death, &c

e. In accordance with the original meaning of *from within out* and the more common meaning of *a result*, there is a distinction made between **freuen** and **erfreuen.** The former is used of some *thing*, the existence of which merely *occasions* us joy, the latter of some *body* or *thing* that working from within outward, i.e. intentionally or by virtue of inherent qualities, *produces* joy: **Es freut mich, Sie zu sehen,** but **Erfreuen Sie mich doch mit einer Antwort, Ein weiser Sohn erfreut den Vater,** and **Der Wein erfreut das Herz.** The reflexive **sich erfreuen (an,** w. dat.) expresses a warmer, deeper interest than **sich freuen (über,** w. acc.) The participle **gefreut** is not used adjectively, because it is here the question of a result: **Er ist darüber erfreut,** not **gefreut.**

4. ge is cognate with *i* in English hand*i*work and Latin co-, con-, cum-, and hence denotes a collection or union (of persons, or things, or related parts). This meaning, so common in nouns, as in **Gebirge** *a chain* or *system of mountains*, **Geläut** a *chime of bells*, is now only rarely found in verbs: **gerinnen** to coagulate, lit. to run compactly together, **gefrieren** to freeze, **gefallen** to please, lit. to fall together with, coincide with (one's wishes). More common are the following derived meanings:

a. Like **er-** (see **3.** *b* above), tho now much less common, **ge-** is used to represent a particular point in the course of an action, namely, the entrance into a state or condition, or the outcome, or result of the action: **gebrechen** *to lack*, originally meaning in its impersonal form **es gebricht** *there arises a breakage, a loss*, hence *a lack*; M.H.G. bern (now no longer used) *to carry, bear*, **gebären** *to give birth to*, referring to the result.

From the idea of a result comes the idea of completeness: **horchen** to hearken, **gehorchen** to hearken to faithfully, hence to obey. The idea of completeness is most commonly found in the **ge-** of the perfect participle: **Er hat einen Brief geschrieben.** The use of **ge-** with this meaning in the present perfect has gradually differentiated this tense from the past tense, which represents an act as going on in past time at the same time as another past act. Originally **ge-** here had only perfective force, thus not expressing the completion of an act as a whole, an accomplished fact as now, but only calling attention to one point in the action, namely the beginning or the end or result. As a survival of older usage when **ge-** had pure perfective force it cannot even to-day stand in the perfect participle before the perfective prefixes **be-, emp-, ent-, er-, ge-, miß-, ver-, zer-: begangen,** not **gebegangen.** According to older feeling **ge-** was here superfluous as the perfective prefixes expressed the perfective idea. For the same reason **ge-** could not, a little earlier in the period, stand before a word that of itself had perfective force expressing the idea of entrance into a condition or that of end, result, such as **werden** *to become*, **kommen** *to come, arrive*, **kriegen** *to get.* This older usage still survives in the perfect participle **worden** when used as an auxiliary in the passive.

The perfect participle of these derivatives with an unstressed perfective prefix has influenced the form of all other verbs unaccented on the first syllable in that they too, contrary to older usage, now assume no **ge-** in the perfect participle: **stu'diert** (not now as formerly **gestu'diert**), &c. See also **178. 2.** A. *b* (**1**), (**2**), (**3**). Thus it is clear that the absence of **ge-** in the perfect participle before the unstressed prefixes **be-, emp-, ent-, er-, ge-, miß-, ver-, zer-** is no longer understood and hence is ascribed to their lack of accent, so that this usage has spread to other verbs unaccented on the first syllable. For further suppression of **ge-** in the participle in S.G. see *c.* (**2**) below.

b. The idea of coincidence and result naturally gave rise to the idea of succeeding or doing something satisfactorily: **gefallen** to please, lit. to fall together with, coincide with (one's wishes), **gedeihen** to prosper, **gelingen** to be successful, **genesen** to recover (from sickness), **geraten** to turn out well, **gewinnen** to win, **geziemen** to befit.

c. In a number of words all feeling of the meaning of the prefix has been lost, and in general it has in connection with verbs ceased to be productive and is frequently a mere fossil. This can be seen: (**1**) from the fact that in some cases the simple verb has been lost and now the compound alone exists: **genesen, geschehen,** &c. (**2**) In a number of words, especially those whose stem begins with **l, r,** or **n,** the vowel of the prefix is suppressed and is no longer felt: **glauben, gönnen,** &c. In S.G. the **e** of the prefix in the perfect participle is usually suppressed followed by the hardening of the **g** of the prefix to **k** and of a following **b, d, g** to **p, t, k** and the assimilation of the **k** of the prefix to a following **p, t, k,** so that the prefix is felt little or not at all: **k'wese, pote, tienet, tanzet, kange, kesse** for **gewesen, geboten, gedient, getanzt, gegangen, gegessen.** On the other hand, its force in the group in *b* must be dimly felt, for when **miß-,** which means the very opposite of **ge-,** is added the **ge-** is dropped: **gefallen,** but **mißfallen; gelingen,** but **mißlingen; geraten,** but **mißraten.** Notice also: **gebieten,** but **verbieten.**

5. ver is a very common prefix with meanings not always clearly defined and sometimes even contradictory. This is accounted for by the fact that it represents three older prefixes—Gothic fra, faur, fair, Latin pro-, por-, per-—with all their meanings. Thus **verzuckern** may mean *to spoil by sugaring too much* (A. *c*), *to cover with sugar* (C), *to turn to sugar* (D. *b*). On account of this ambiguity **ver-** has in the last centuries been gradually replaced in many cases by other prefixes or other expressions. On the other hand, in certain groups described below **ver-** has become productive. The development of meanings is here given with as much accuracy as possible, but at a number of points we are not able to attain to even a reasonable degree of certainty as the prehistoric growth is hidden from view.

A. Groups of meaning corresponding to those of Gothic fra:

a. The commonest meaning seems to be that of *away, forth*: **verlaufen** to pass away (of time, &c.), **verreisen** to go away on a journey, **verschenken** to give away, **verjagen** to chase away, **vergeben** to forgive, lit. give away, let (a fault) go by, **verkaufen** to give away in exchange for something, to sell, **verheiraten** to give away in marriage (**eine Tochter verheiraten**). This idea often leads to the conception of a change of place: **verlegen** to move (as in **Die Universität wurde von Ingolstadt nach München verlegt**), **versetzen** to transplant (**einen Baum versetzen**), promote (**einen Schüler in eine höhere Klasse versetzen**), put (**Versetzen Sie sich in meine Lage**), &c.

b. The idea of *away* may lead to that of the *end, exhaustion, entire consumption of*, even *waste*, and *reckless* and *lavish use of*: **verblühen** to come to an end of blooming, **etwas verschmerzen** to get over something (as sorrow, &c.), **verhallen** to die away (of a sound), **verbluten** to bleed to exhaustion or death, **verkümmern** to waste away, **verhungern** to die of starvation, **verbrennen** to burn (something) up, **verbrauchen** to use up, **versaufen** to squander away in drink, **verschlafen** to sleep (precious time, &c.) away, **vertändeln** to trifle away. This is a very productive group.

c. The idea of *away* may lead to that of loss, destruction, error, out of the proper place, wrong, improper doing, spoiling, and the reversal of the meaning of the simple verb: **verwirken** to forfeit, **verderben** to destroy, **verurteilen** to condemn, sentence, **verführen** to mislead, seduce, **verraten** to betray, originally to give advice or information that leads to the destruction of someone, now also used in the derived meanings to disclose, divulge, show (as in **Es verrät eine Meisterhand**), **verdrucken** to misprint, **sich verrechnen** to make a mistake in figures, **verschreiben** to write incorrectly, **sich verschreiben** (as in **Ich habe mich verschrieben** *It's a mere slip of the pen*) to make a mistake in writing, **sich versprechen** (as in **Ich habe mich versprochen** *It was a mere slip of my tongue*) to make a mistake in speaking, **sich verlaufen** to lose one's way, **verlegen** to misplace, **verkehrt** wrong, lit. turned wrong (as in **die verkehrte Seite, etwas verkehrt anfangen**), **verrenken** to dislocate (**den Arm verrenken**), **sich an jemandem vergreifen** to lay violent hands on someone, **versalzen** to spoil by oversalting, **verzuckern** to spoil by sugaring too much, **verzärteln** to spoil by too much coddling, **verachten** to despise, opposite of **achten, verkennen** to misjudge, **verlernen** unlearn, forget (little by little), &c.

B. Groups of meanings corresponding to Gothic faur:

On the basis of the few meager known facts we attempt to distinguish here three groups:

a. The general idea of **ver-** in this group is that of a general forward movement toward a goal, or a general outward movement: **verkündigen** to announce, make known to, **verbeugen** to bow to, lit. bend forward, **versehen (mit)** to look ahead, i.e. provide with, **sich versehen** to look forward, expect (as in **Ich hatte mich des Angriffs nicht versehen**), **verschlagen** to knock, push forward, i.e. to avail (as in **Es verschlägt nichts**), **versetzen** to deal (**jemandem einen Schlag versetzen**), to reply (lit. to put forward), **versprechen** to promise, **verlegen** to lay out or put up (the money) for, i.e. to publish (as in **ein Buch verlegen**).

b. The general idea of movement forward into a position before something as found in *a* leads to the idea of protecting, guarding, defending, concealing, hindering, refusing, obstructing: **verfechten** to fight for, lit. to go fighting before something to defend it, **verschließen** to lock up, lit. to put a lock before to protect, **verantworten** to answer for, be responsible for, **verwesen** to manage, conduct (as a substitute for another), **vertreten** to take the place of, represent,

versetzen to pawn, lit. to give as security for, **verschleiern** to veil, **verwehren** to hinder, prevent, **versagen** to refuse, (**jemandem den Weg**) **verlegen** to cut off, (**einem Hause die Aussicht**) **verbauen** to shut out, &c.

Note. Also **be-** has a similar meaning. It has, however, only the general idea of *over, upon*, while **ver-** implies that the covering is to protect or conceal: **bedecken** to cover (the earth, &c. with snow, &c.), **verdecken** to cover (one's face to remove it from the observation of others or to conceal one's feeling); **bekleiden** to clothe, **verkleiden** to disguise.

c. The idea of a general forward movement leads to the conception of going beyond the goal, indicating excess: (**eine Gelegenheit, den Zug**) **versäumen** to miss, (**den Zug**) **verschlafen** to miss the train by sleeping too long, **sich verschlafen** to oversleep one's self.

C. Meaning corresponding to Gothic fair:

The original meaning of the prefix represented by Gothic fair cannot be clearly gleaned from the few Gothic words that have come down to us. From these meager materials it might possibly be assumed that the original idea was *around, encircling, covering*, as seems to be suggested by a few words still in use: **verschütten** to cover over with earth, &c., fill up (a ditch, &c.), **vergolden** to cover over with or as with gold, to gild, **versilbern** to cover with silver plate, **verzuckern** to sugar over, **verhüllen** to wrap up, cover over, &c.

D. The more or less concrete meanings in A, B, C have in many words faded entirely away into mere abstract perfective (see **3.** *b* above) force. There are three groups more or less distinct:

a. We often find in **ver-** pure effective (**3.** *b* above) force, so that it indicates that the activity is sustained to the end, meets with successful issue, or is directed with energy to a certain goal or end: **verbleichen** to grow pale in death, **verbleiben** to remain until the end, **verlesen** to read (a roll of names, &c.) to the end, **verbüßen** to serve out (as in **seine Strafzeit verbüßen**), **vernehmen** to perceive, lit. to take a firm hold of (with the senses), **verfangen** to operate, take effect, avail, lit. to catch a good hold on, **verhelfen** to help someone to get something, lit. to help so effectually that the object is attained, **verstehen** to understand, lit. to stand firmly and thus have control of the situation, **verfolgen** to pursue (a course, design, &c.), **verhandeln** to negotiate, transact, **verkehren** to ply, go back and forth between definite points (as in **Die Züge verkehren stündlich zwischen diesen Orten**), to associate with, **versuchen** to try, test, lit. to seek thoroly, persistently, &c.

b. It often has pure ingressive (**3.** *b* above) force, so that it denotes a change, transformation into a state or thing indicated now usually by some adjective or noun which forms the stem of the verb: **verarmen** to grow poor, **verbilligen** to reduce the price, the expense of, render cheaper, **vereinfachen** to simplify, **verdeutschen** to translate into German, **veredeln** to ennoble, **verdicken** to thicken, **versumpfen** to become like a swamp, stagnant, **vergöttern** to deify, idolize, **verketzern** to brand as a heretic, **versilbern** to cash, **vertonen** to set to music, **einen Roman, ein Drama verfilmen** to film a novel, a drama so that it can be presented in the form of moving pictures, **vertrusten** to form into a trust, **verzuckern** to turn (intrans.) into sugar. This is a large productive group.

Note. Also **er-** has perfective force, indicating a change or transformation into a state or thing, some verbs preferring **er-**, others **ver-**: **erhöhen**, but **vertiefen**; **erweitern**, but **verengen**; **sich ermannen**, but **sich vernarren**. In a number of cases **ver-** has supplanted **er-** since early N.H.G.: in early N.H.G. **erarmen, erfaulen, ergrößern, erhungern**, &c., all now with **ver-**. In other cases **er-** has supplanted **ver-**, as in **erschrecken**. In dialect, however, the form may be preserved that has been rejected in the literary language: **Er ist ganz verschreckt** (Uschei in Marriot's *Der geistliche Tod*, chap. vi). Except in a few cases **ver-** is now used exclusively in case of verbs formed from nouns: **versteinern, verwässern**, &c. There is a slight shade of difference in meaning between verbs with **er-** and those with **ver-**, not always, however, can the difference be seen. Those with **er-** represent the transformation as a process of development, while those with **ver-** represent it as a final result: **ergrünen** to grow green (of the grass), but **verewigen** to immortalize, **versteinern** to petrify; **jemanden erbittern** to exasperate, irritate somebody (of a temporary condition), but **jemanden verbittern** or **jemandem das Leben verbittern** to embitter someone or someone's life (of a chronic condition).

c. It often has effective (**3.** *b* above) force, denoting a close fusion or union: **verschmelzen** to fuse, blend, **vermischen** to mix all up, confound, blend, **verwachsen** to grow together, **verbinden** to join, **verketten** to join together in close intimate relations, &c. This is a large productive group.

E. It sometimes converts intransitive verbs into transitives: **verlachen** to deride, from **lachen** to laugh; **verspotten** to ridicule, from **spotten** (**über** with acc.) to make fun of, make sarcastic remarks about; **verfluchen** to curse, damn, from **fluchen** to swear, &c. Also **be-** converts intransitive verbs into transitives, but there is usually a difference of meaning, resulting either from the former concrete meaning of the two prefixes or from gradual differentiation: **belachen** to laugh at (in mirth), **verlachen** to deride: **Die guten Witze wurden belacht, die schlechten verlacht. Man belacht den Sonderling,** but **Er verlachte mich mit meinen Träumereien.** Both **be-** and **ver-** indicate intensity, but **ver-** contains the additional idea of a desire to injure or a desire to attain to a definite end: **befolgen** to follow closely (**Regeln, Vorschriften befolgen**), **verfolgen** to pursue, persecute, give chase to (**Christen, Ketzer, ein Schiff verfolgen**), pursue, follow, hold (**einen Weg, einen Kurs verfolgen**).

6. wider *against* and *re-* or *back*: **wider'sprechen** (w. dat.) to contradict, **wider'legen** to refute, **wider'stehen** (w. dat.) to resist; **wider'rufen** (**258.** 1. B. *a*) to retract, repeal, lit. to call back; **widerhallen** (**215.** II. 3. A. *e*) re-echo, &c.

7. zer denotes separation, a breaking to pieces, dissolution, a scattering: **zerbrechen** to break to pieces, **zerschneiden** to carve, **zerfleischen** lacerate, **zerfließen** to melt away, **zerstreuen** to scatter.

8. miß. A. This is a very productive prefix, expressing failure, error, something false or the opposite of the simple verb: **mißlingen** to fail of success, **mißdeuten** to interpret falsely, **mißfallen** to displease, **mißbilligen** to disapprove of, **mißgönnen** to begrudge, the opposite of **gönnen** to be glad to see somebody have something.

B. The meaning of **miß-** causes no trouble, but its accent in composition with verbs has become uncertain. In some verbs the prefix is usually unaccented, in others it is either strongly accented or unaccented, and is hence treated as a separable or inseparable prefix. In the main, however, even tho accented, it is not separated from the verb in the literary language except by **zu** and **ge-** in the infinitive and participle, where sometimes three forms can be found for the one word: **zu miß'deuten, zu 'mißdeuten, 'mißzudeuten; miß'deutet, ge'mißdeutet, 'mißgedeutet.** Thus the infinitive and participle can in a number of verbs be treated as separable or inseparable verbs, and the participle may in addition be treated as if made from a compound noun (see **217**): **ge'mißbilligt** (also **miß'billigt**), &c. The prefix was originally unaccented, but its newer use of placing the derivative in contrast to the simple verb naturally resulted in shifting in such cases the accent upon the prefix in accordance with its logical importance. Such participial forms as **'mißgedeutet,** &c., are after the analogy of adjectives and adjective participles such as **'mißgelaunt** *ill-humored*, which (see **47.** 2. B. *c. bb*) uniformly accent the prefix. Moreover for rhythmical reasons the prefix is regularly stressed in all forms before an unaccented prefix: **míßzubehagen, míßzuverstehen, míßverstanden. O wie mißverstehen Sie mich!**

Tho the prefix is in general only separated in the above-mentioned cases, there is a slight tendency toward complete separation, as can be occasionally heard in facetious or sarcastic language: **O wie verstehen Sie, mein Vater, mich einmal wieder recht gründlich miß!** (Immermann's *M.*, 2. 5.) Vogel in his "Grammatisch-orthographisches Nachschlagebuch" even recommends separation in case of **mißstimmen: Du stimmst mich stets miß.**

COMPOUNDS AND GROUP-WORDS.

247. 1. *Compounds.* A compound is a word formed by the close union of two or more words whose meanings blend so thoroly as to produce one single idea. The natural tendency is to distinctly mark this oneness of meaning by a oneness in form, that is, by writing together the different words of a compound: **Abendmahl** *Lord's Supper*, not literally *evening meal.* Languages differ in the accuracy with which they distinctly mark compounds as such by writing the parts in one word. German, tho more careful than English in this respect, often fails to recognize the distinct unity in a group of words: **alt und jung** old and young = **jedermann** everybody, **die heilige Schrift** Holy Writ = **die Bibel** Bible, **kaltes Blut** sang-froid = **Kaltblütigkeit.**

A compound originates in a group of words which stand in close syntactical relations to one another and have a certain oneness of meaning. Such a group —here called a group-word—has two strong stresses, one a little stronger than the other. The origin and classes of group-words are discussed at considerable length below. A compound often develops out of a group-word as the different syntactical members of the group-word often lose their literal meaning, as in case of **Âbendmàhl** *Lord's Supper*, originally and historically *evening meal*, or their meaning and syntactical force, as in case of **Hérzòg** *duke*, lit. *leader of the army*, but now no longer felt as having this meaning or as indicating these syntactical relations, altho originally the literal meaning and the syntactical relations were distinctly felt. Sometimes the members of the group-word acquire a distinct oneness of meaning and a peculiar signification altho the literal meaning and the original syntactical relations are still felt, as in **das Drítteìl** *third*, from **das drìtte Téil** (formerly neut., now masc.) *the third part.* In proportion as the idea of the oneness of meaning grows the idea of group becomes obscured and the compound develops. If this development continues, the compound develops into a simple word with only one strong stress: **Schúlze** *village mayor*, from **Schúlthèiß** (i.e. **Schuldheiß**) *mayor*, lit. *one who commands the performance of duty*, a compound still in use; **Dríttel** *third*, from **Drítteìl.** When the same unaccented syllable occurs in a number of reduced compounds, as in **Drittel, Viertel, Fünftel,** &c., the syllable becomes a suffix. Thus out of compounds develop suffixes and simple words. On the other hand, where the idea of group remains intact as in a group-word, the vowels of the components have the same quality as in independent words, while the vowels of compounds are often different from those of independent words. Thus in the group-word **Heerführer** *commander*, lit. *leader of the army*, the first component has the same vowel as in the independent word **Heer** *army*, the vowel having become long in early N.H.G. in both component and independent word, while in the compound **Herzog** it is still short as in M.H.G. In the compound **élènd** *miserable*, lit. *in a foreign land* no one now feels that the second component has any relation to **Land.** The two stresses—somewhat reduced in strength however—alone indicate that the word is a compound. It stands on the boundary between a compound and a simple word.

2. *Group-words.* Group-words are old syntactical groups or modern formations after the analogy of old syntactical groups which have differentiated themselves more or less from modern groups, so that they are written as one word by way of distinction: **Kópfverlètzung** (group-word), but **Verlètzung des Kópfes** (modern group). In the group-word the first member is stressed, in the modern group the last member.

There are three classes of group-words and compounds, which represent different stages of development.

a. Old Group-words and Compounds. In old group-words the first member of the group has no case ending. It is a bare stem and represents the oldest stage of development when the language did not have inflectional forms for adjectives and nouns. With the help of a fixed word-order—the modifying element always being in the first place—the mere juxtaposition of the members suggests the syntactical relations and makes the idea clear: subject relation, with the force of a subjective genitive: **Érdbèben** earthquake, i.e. the earth quakes; the relation of a genitive of origin or cause: **Wásserschàden** damage from or caused by water; the relation of a possessive genitive: **Báumsaft** sap of the tree, **Fußgelenk** joint of the foot; the object relation: **Wéintrìnker, Schúhmàcher, Blútvergìeßen**; the prepositional relation: **blútbesprìtzt (mit Blút besprìtzt)**; the adjective relation: **Gástfrèund (ein Freund, der ein Gast ist), Stéinkrùg (ein Krug, der von Stein ist).** Notice that in this primitive type of expression subject, object, &c. precede the member containing the verbal idea or the governing noun, as they are felt as modifiers of it or as having grammatical relations to it. There is here, however, little danger of confusion as attested by the wide use of this construction in modern speech. Notice also that instead of **Blútvergìeßen,** &c. we say in English *shèdding of blôod,* as we have dissolved all such old descriptive group-words into modern groups, which require the stressed member to stand in the last place in the group. German more easily retained the old group-word form since it was supported elsewhere by old descriptive groups with the same word-order and stress, namely: (**1**) in *attributive adjective groups*: **der vom Régen trìefende Hut, das vom Méere umgèbene Land;** (**2**) in end-groups, in groups at the end of the sentence with end-stress (**215. II. 1.** A, 3rd par.): **Er will Blút vergìeßen. Er hat Blút vergòssen. Das Haus ist von Bâumen umgèben.** Old group-words are also well preserved in English and have attained even wider boundaries than in German where the *logical* force of the first member is distinctly felt: cótton cròp, pure fóod làws, ínfant clàss, tóothbrùsh, &c., as we feel the logical contrast to other kinds of crops, laws, classes, brushes. For fuller treatment of English usage see **255. I.** *b* (2nd par.). In *descriptive* groups, however, old group-words are much less used than in German, so that such old group-words must in English usually be dissolved into modern descriptive groups: **múskelschwàch** *wèak in múscle,* **méerumgèben** *surròunded by the séa,* **Stéinkrùg** *stòne jár,* &c. Notice that in the last example the old group is in English transformed into a modern group, not by changing the word-order but by merely transferring the stress from the first to the second member, as this simple procedure is sufficient to convert an old group into a modern group when the first member is construed as an adjective. See **215. I. 3.** *Historical Note* for the explanation of the fact that compound verbs do not assume the form of old group-words.

A large number of German group-words from this class have developed into compounds: **Ábendmàhl, Grôbschmìed** a smith who manufactures coarse iron articles, **Áugàpfel, Kőnigsèe** (city), **Sálzàch** (river), &c. Also Old English compounds have been well preserved, as the oneness of meaning and the loss of concrete literal force, i.e. the loss of feeling for the meaning of the parts, were factors that naturally tended to preserve the original form, for the forces that were elsewhere active for dissolution of the parts were here not felt at all: stárbòard, cówslìp, brídegròom, &c.

b. Younger Group-words and Compounds. In many later formations we find inflection in the modifying word to indicate the grammatical relation: (subjective genitive) **Sónnenàufgang, Hérzensergùß;** (objective gen.) **Lándesvertèidigung;** (dative) **érdenfèrn;** (adjective) **Rótkèhlchen, Áltenbùrg, Néuenbùrg, jédermànn (-mann** with its older meaning of **Mensch** as still preserved in English *man*); (preposition) **Únterseebòot, Űberseedàmpfer,** &c. We say **ein ròtes Kéhlchen, eine jùnge Fráu, ùber Sée,** but **ein Rótkèhlchen, eine Júngfràu, ein Űberseedàmpfer.** The clear development of the idea of a group-word or compound in a modern group thus often converts a modern group into a younger group-word or compound. Modern group-words and compounds, however, often preserve their original modern group-stress. See *c* below. The reason that all modern compounds and group-words do not thus assume younger group-word stress is that the accent of the younger compound or group-word stands in open conflict with the pronounced descriptive force of these groups. Compare **249. II. 1. A.**

Group-words and compounds with an endingless adjective as the first member may in some instances have been originally old group-words and compounds, but it is probable that most of them are younger group-words and compounds from the older periods when the adjective did not have distinctive forms for all its cases and genders, as explained in **249. II. 1.** In all cases, however, they have the stress of old group-words and compounds, indicating thus clearly that they have given up their modern stress under the influence of the old group-words of the same form. Also many group-words with an inflected adjective as the first member have followed the analogy of old group-words and take the stress upon the first member. Both of these classes of group-words are here designated younger group-words in contrast to the modern group-words in *c* which retain their original stress. They are younger formations than the old group-words, but they now have the stress of the old group-words.

A large number of *stressed* genitives that in oldest German and English stood before the governing word, now stand after it, while unstressed genitives, as in the oldest period, still stand before it: **Gòethes Lében** *Gòethe's lífe*, but **das Lèben Góethes** *the lìfe of Góethe*. The tendency to place the strongly stressed genitive after the governing noun is common in all the Germanic languages and stands in close relation to the tendency to place the strongly stressed modifier of the verb after the verb. Just as the strongly stressed modifier of the verb, however, often remains before the verb, so does a strongly stressed genitive often remain before the governing noun. Such a strongly stressed genitive did not follow the tendency to take a place after the governing noun because it was felt as having a different force. Thus the meaning became differentiated according to the position of the modifying word. When the stressed genitive stood before the governing noun, it had logical force, indicating a desire to *distinguish*, or *classify*, when it followed, it had descriptive force, indicating a desire to *describe*: with distinguishing force: **An meine Mútter schrieb ich, nicht an meinen Váter; Lúthers Gebùrtstag, nicht Góethes** *Lúther's bìrthday, not Góethe's*. With distinguishing or classifying force: **eine Fráuenhànd** *a wóman's hànd*, **ein Mánneswòrt** *a mán's wòrd*, **ein Wéspennèst** *a wásp's nèst*, **ein Horníssennèst** *a hórnet's nèst*, but with descriptive force: **die Belàgerung der Stádt** *the besìeging of the cíty*, **der Èinzug der siegreichen Trúppen** *the èntrance of the victorious tróops*, &c. As can be seen by the translation of the German examples the younger groupword is also in English a favorite. It is often employed where the old groupword form is used in German, but this construction has its limitations in English, as it is of necessity confined to words that may take an s in the genitive, i.e. designations of living beings and words denoting a unit of measurement: a bírd's nèst **ein Vógelnèst,** a bréwer's càrt **ein Bráuerwàgen,** báker's brèad **Bắckerbròt;** a bóat's lèngth **eine Schíffslànge,** a stóne's thròw **ein Stéinwùrf,** &c., but a whíp-stòck **ein Péitschenstìel,** a stréet-còrner **eine Stráßenècke,** &c., as the first member cannot take s in the genitive. Thus outside of these two groups English must employ the old group-word form, to convey distinguishing force. In English a modern group very often corresponds to an old or a younger groupword in German: brèach of prómise **Wórtbrùch,** lètter of thánks **Dánkbrìef,** cròwn of thórns **Dórnenkròne,** tòur of inspéction **Besíchtigungsrèise,** prèsence of mínd **Géistesgègenwart,** &c. The evident reason for English usage is that such groups have descriptive force. Here as elsewhere English observes much more carefully the characteristic differences in meaning between the old and the younger group-word form on the one hand and the modern group on the other—the former with distinguishing, the latter with descriptive force. Compare **255.** I. *b* (2nd par.). Altho this differentiation is not so sharp in German the tendency is in the same direction. Both old and younger group-words are freely used with distinguishing force but without any fixed rule for the use of the older or younger form, an old group-word being preferred in some instances, a younger group-word in others: **Ohrverletzung, Ohrenkrankheit; Kindtaufe, Kindesgefühl, Kleinkínderbewàhranstalt,** &c. There is sometimes a differentiation of meaning between old and younger group-words: **Herzkrankheit,** &c. with reference to the organ of the heart, but **Herzensangelegenheit,** &c. with reference to the heart as the seat of feeling, emotion. In general, however, there is a strong tendency to replace the old with the younger formation, as it expresses the grammatical relations more clearly. Many younger group-words now in use had the older form in early N.H.G. See **249.** II. 1. B. *b*.

A *stressed* modifying genitive that precedes its governing noun still not infrequently has descriptive force as in older usage, which did not recognize distinguishing or classifying force as the normal meaning of a stressed genitive that preceded its governing noun: **beim Kríegsàusbruch** = **beim Àusbruch des**

Kríeges, gegenseitige Fréundschaftsversìcherungen = gegenseitige Versìcherungen der Fréundschaft, das Fránkenrèich = das Rèich der Fránken, &c. Very often also in old group-words, altho the modifying form still as in the prehistoric period has no formal expression for the grammatical relations: **das schmale méerumgèbene** (= **das vom Méere umgèbene**) **Land.** As the stress here on the first member, as in a compound, gives the impression of oneness of meaning, it is often felt as desirable on mere formal grounds to employ the old or the younger group-word form: **Der Vertágungsàntrag Klotz** (name), where by its form the group **Vertagungsantrag** is brought as a whole, as a unit, into apposition with **Klotz.** The impression of oneness is imparted not only by the stress upon the first member, but also by the use of the article or other adjective modifiers that limit the second, i.e. the basal, component and hence the thought as a whole: **diese einzige, kleine Grénzüberschrèitung.** Of course, the old or younger group form cannot be used at all when for any reason it is desired to break up the idea of oneness and call attention to a detail concerning the first member. Thus in the last example we should have to use the modern group if we should desire to modify **Grenze: Die Überschreitung ihrer (unserer,** &c.) **Grenze.** Furthermore, the old or younger group form is often found useful to avoid ambiguity: **Die durch den Krieg notwendig gewordenen Gesétzentwȗrfe** rather than **die Entwȗrfe der Gesétze, die durch den Krieg notwendig geworden sind,** as the relative **die** might be construed as referring to **Gesetze** instead of **Entwürfe,** as here intended. Of course, the old or younger form has become absolutely fixed in compounds, as the oneness of the meaning and the loss of concrete literal force resist dissolution into a modern group: **Fránkrèich** *France,* formerly = **das Rèich der Fránken; Sígmȗnd** (name), originally = **der Schȗtz des Síeges,** &c. English development is somewhat different. Old English group-words with distinguishing force are well preserved, as in círicbèll *chúrch-bèll,* but those with descriptive force have been dissolved into modern groups, as in círicbrȳce *brèaking into a chúrch.* Compare **255. I.** *b.*

Younger group-words have in many cases developed into compounds: **Ménschensòhn** *Sòn of mán,* **Kṓnigsbèrg,** &c. As we say **Fȗrstenbèrg** but **Fȗrstenwálde** scholars have tried to establish the rule that the stress has been put upon the second element for rhythmical reasons wherever as in **Fȗrstenwálde** it has two syllables. The dative ending **e** here in **-walde,** however, seems rather to indicate that the name originated in a modern group—**an des Fȗrsten Wálde**—and hence naturally stresses the second member. Many other names have a monosyllabic form as the second component and nevertheless take the stress upon that member, which seems to indicate that they are felt as modern groups: **Frìedrichsrúh, Rìppoldsáu,** &c.

c. Modern Group-words and Compounds. A modern group becomes a modern group-word when a modern group acquires a distinct oneness of meaning, with especial frequency where by a change of function a group becomes a single word: **ein freiwilliges Sìchbegében** (from **sìch begében**) **der Stärke, ȃnstátt, ȋndém,** &c.

Out of modern group-words have arisen a large number of modern compounds, which have differentiated themselves from modern group-words by their peculiar signification: **zȗfríeden** (**zȗ Fríeden**) contented, **eine ȃlte Júngfer** an òld máid, **das gèlbe Fíeber** yèllow féver, **das Schwàrze Méer, der Wèiße Sáal** the Whíte Ròom (of the Imperial Palace of William II in Berlin), **unsere lìebe Fráu** the Holy Virgin, **Nèustettín, Jȗngdéutschland** (literary movement); **eine Mȗttergṓttes** a picture of the Holy Virgin, **der Sòhn Gṓttes** the Sòn of Gód, **die Kìnder Gṓttes,** &c. As modern group-words and compounds have no peculiar form differing from that of a modern group few of them have as yet found a formal expression in the written language. In a small number the parts are written together, in a few others the adjective component is begun with a capital.

The modifying adjective in such group-words and compounds is usually, as in a modern group, inflected, but as a survival of older usage it remains uninflected in many set expressions containing a neuter noun, as in **Nèujáhr** (see also **249.**

II. 2), **Grỏßberlín, Jùngdéutschland, auf gùt Glűck** *at random*, **bàr Géld** *cash*, &c., in poetry sometimes also with other genders in order to add a touch of endearment, as in **jùng Wérner** (better **Jung-Werner**) in Scheffel's *Trompeter*. In some names of places, as **Schỏnbrúnn,** the old uninflected masc. form is found in its literal meaning. See also **249.** II. 1.

3. *Abbreviated Compounds.* Compounds are often, especially in colloquial language, shortened by cutting off the final element: **der Korn,** short for **der Kornschnaps; der Ober,** short for **der Oberkellner; der Schnauz,** short for **Schnauzbart; das Vieruhr** for **das Vieruhressen; das** (under the influence of **das Theater**) or **der Kino** for **der Kinematograph; das Kilo** for **das Kilogramm; der Vize** for **der Vizefeldwebel;** &c. Similarly in decomposites the final element of the modifying component may be suppressed: **Ölzweig** instead of **Ölbaumzweig,** &c.

Parts of a Group-word or Compound.

248. A. Tho a group-word or compound may consist of two words or several, it can as a rule have only two component elements—the *basal component,* which contains the more general idea, and the *modifying component,* which contains the more special meaning, usually some *essential* modification of the meaning of the basal component, and hence, on account of its logical force, accented: **Zwéig-eisenbahn** a branch railroad, **Váterlands-liebe** love of native land. Each element can thus be either simple or compound. The exceptions to the rule that a compound has but two components are found in **249.** II. 2.

a. If several compound words have the same basal or modifying component, the element which they have in common need only be expressed once, but a hyphen must in the written word follow the modifying element, in the first-mentioned case, and precede the basal element, in the second case: **Würfel- und Schachspiel** the games of dice and chess; **Wortableitung und -zusammensetzung** formation of words by derivation and composition.

b. One of the components is often shortened by dropping a word, as the natural tendency is toward simpler forms: **Bahnhof** railroad depot, for **Eisenbahnhof.**

B. The basal component determines the part of speech to which the compound belongs except in such cases as in **249.** II. 2, where there are more than two components. Since every part of speech except the article can become the basal component, all parts of speech except the article can form group-words and compounds: **Mannesmut** courage of a man, **hilfsbedürftig** requiring help, **fünfzehn** fifteen, **dersélbe** the same, **bergáb** down hill, &c. In inflected words the basal component stands last and assumes the inflectional endings of the compound and in case of substantives also the gender: **frühstücken** to breakfast, **ich frühstücke; das Frühstück, des Frühstücks.** This rule, however, holds only in a broad general sense, the limitations being discussed in **249.** II. 2.

C. The accent usually rests upon the modifying element, as it is the special point to which the attention is called. There are, however, manifold exceptions, and the whole question of accent in compounds is treated at length under the head of Accent, **47.** 3. The general historical explanation has been given in **247.** 2, where also the accent is treated in considerable detail.

249. Form of Group-words and Compounds.

I. Old Group-words and Compounds.

The first member is a bare stem, which in words of more than one syllable ending in a vowel is often shortened: **Hausherr (Haus + Herr), ehescheu (Ehe + scheu), Birnbaum (Birne + Baum),** &c.

a. In an earlier period of the language the stem of a word was not always identical with its nom. sing. as to-day, but often ended in one of the vowels **a, i, u.** In compounds the first element always stood in its simple stem-form, the second element was inflected: (O.H.G.) N. taga-sterro or taga-stern *morning star,* G. taga-sterren or taga-sternes, &c. As a survival of this older usage are still found a few words with the final stem vowel **e** (which is the usual N.H.G. weakened form of O.H.G. **a, i, u**): **Tagereise** a day's journey, **Badehaus,** &c. In a few words this **e** is not a stem-ending but a contraction of the genitive ending **-es** before an s-sound, as in **Hundeschnauze, Pferdesattel,** &c. Other words have been formed after this model: **Pferdefuß,** &c. In a number of these cases the **e** is now felt as a pl. ending: **Tagebuch, Pferdestall,** &c. In most cases, however, the former final stem-vowel has disappeared: **Tagwache, tagtäglich,** &c. This vowel instead of disappearing has become productive in case of verbal stems, which now freely add **e,** especially if the stem ends in **b, d, g, s: Sterbezimmer, Ladestock, Zeigefinger, Lesebuch, Haltestelle,** &c.; many, however, without the **e,** as in case of nominal stems: **Schreibfeder, Kaufleute,** &c. In general the old stem-vowel **e** has not only disappeared in a large number of words, but this old formation of stem-composition is often replaced by composition with inflection in the modifying component, as described in II, especially in modern words: **Tagespresse,** &c. The same modifying component often shows all three formations, the forms differing in different compounds or even in the same compound: **Tagedieb** or **Tagdieb, Tagelohn** or **Taglohn, Tagewerk** or **Tagwerk, Tagereise, Tageslicht, Tagesordnung,** &c. In case of adjectives the modifying component may have different forms with the same basal element: **wortbrüchig,** but **vertragsbrüchig; gehaltreich,** but **verkehrsreich, inhalt(s)reich; gottfürchtig** (Luke ii. 25), now **gottesfürchtig,** &c.

b. In case of verbs whose stems end in **en** (now always contracted to **n**), as **rechnen** *to count, compute,* we find the full stem only in compounds and group-words: **Rechenlehrer** *arithmetic teacher.*

c. If the stem ends in a vowel it is usual in most cases to suppress the vowel, but in certain cases the vowel is retained, especially in proper names, where there is a growing aversion to mutilation: **Erdball, Saalbahn** Saale Railroad, but **Rachedurst, Saale-Zeitung** (newspaper published at Halle a. S.), &c.

II. Group-words and Compounds with Inflected Modifying Component.

There are here two classes:

1. *Younger Group-words and Compounds with Stressed Modifying Component.* These formations, such as **Dríttèil, Édelmànn,** &c., tho not so old as old group-words and compounds, often bear plainly the marks of an older structural system than found to-day in a normal modern group. As explained in **104.** 2. E. *a*, the modifying adjective, tho here never a bare stem and always a form that in the older periods could stand in a normal group of a sentence, often seems to us to be uninflected, as in the course of the natural *phonetic* development of the language the endings have disappeared. In oldest German descriptive adjective forms with the endings -er, -e, -aȥ (now **es**) after the analogy of the common demonstrative forms der, die, daȥ (now **das**) had already begun to replace the older seemingly uninflected forms. In our own day these new forms have in the ordinary normal modern group gained a complete victory over the older forms without an ending, but the latter survive in many younger compounds that have come down to us from the older order of things. The old forms survived because the groups in which they stood developed into compounds, which as *set* expressions naturally resisted further development. Many recent group-words and compounds have been coined after the analogy of these older formations.

The following groups appear:

A. *Group-words and Compounds with an Adjective as First Member.* When the idea of a group-word or compound develops in a modern group there is a tendency in many cases to convert the modern group into a younger group-word or compound by transferring the stress from the second to the first member. There are two classes of such younger group-words and compounds, one in which the adjective is seemingly without an ending as in older periods, as explained in 1 above, one in which there is a weak or strong ending: **Dríttèil** a third, **Kléingèld** change, **Rőtkèhlchen** robin rédbrèast, **Édelmànn, Hőchstprèis** (from **der hȍchste Préis**) *maximum price allowed by law,* a common word during the Great War, **Hóchkìrch** (city), **Déutschlànd** (formerly **das dèutsche Lánd**), **Kléinschmìdt** (family name); **Wéißenfèls** (from **zum wèißen Féls**), **jédermànn** (gen. **jédermànns,** from late M.H.G. ièder mán, gen. ièdes mánnes), &c. Compare **247.** 2. *b.*

a. The different compound elements of such compounds have in a number of cases become so contracted and corrupted in the course of time that they are no longer clearly distinguished:

Hoffart *pride, arrogance*, from older hochfart, from **hoch** *high* and **Fahrt** *riding, living*; **Jungfer** *maid, miss*, from **Jungfrau; Junker** *young nobleman*, from M.H.G. juncherre = **junger Herr**, &c.

B. *A Genitive of a Noun as First Member.* In some group-words and compounds the syntactical relation between the components is clearly that of a noun and its modifying genitive: (str. gen.) **Góttesdìenst** divine service, public worship of God, **Frúhlingsrègen** spring rain, **Wírtshàus** inn, tavern, **Hérzenslùst** desire of one's heart, **Gláubensfrèiheit;** (wk. gen.) **Hírtenstàb** shepherd's staff, **Gráfenstànd** dignity and rank of a count; (pl. gen.) **Stúndenplàn** time-table, program of studies or recitations, **Blúmenzùcht** floriculture, lit. culture of flowers, **Wírteverèin** association of tavern keepers, **Gásterècht** the rights of foreigners, **Stádtebùnd** confederation of cities, **Vólkerbùnd** league of nations, **Gótterlèhre** mythology, treatise on the ancient gods; also many proper names: **Kónigsbèrg,** &c.; (gen pl.) **Pharaónenrèich** realm of the Pharaohs, &c.

Such substantives are formed by placing the singular or the plural ending of the strong or weak genitive form of the modifying component before the basal component. In declining such compounds the genitive form of the modifying component remains constant thruout the different cases, only the basal component assuming the inflection.

Note. M.H.G. usage often placed the article which belonged to a governing noun before the preceding dependent genitive: der gotes segen. As many such old forms remained after this M.H.G. usage gave way to the N.H.G. rule that the preceding modifying genitive retains its article, while the governing noun is without one, as in **des lieben Gòttes Ségen,** it is evident that in case of these old forms the preceding genitive and the following governing noun were no longer felt as a modern group, but as a younger group-word or compound in which the genitive had strong distinguishing or classifying stress and force, often with the full meaning of a stressed classifying adjective, so that the words naturally did not develop into a modern descriptive group with unstressed genitive and the article in accordance with the general rule for group-words and compounds followed the gender and case of the last component: **der Góttessègen** the divíne blèssing, **die Kíndesùnschuld** the chíldlike ìnnocence, **das Schäfsgesìcht** the stúpid lòok, **das Díebsgesìcht** the fáce of a thìef, **der Fréundesdìenst** the fríendly sèrvice, **der Knábenhùt** the bóy's hàt, &c. Thus this N.H.G. change of construction has forced the recognition of such group-words or compounds in the common orthography. In German the form of the article reveals to us at once whether the words are considered as a group-word or a modern group, but in English we have no such formal evidence, as the article is uninflected: **dieser Hírtenstàb** *this* (pause) *shépherd's stàff*, **dieses Hìrten Stáb** *this shèpherd's* (pause) *stáff = the stàff of this shépherd.* The accent in both English and German is usually different in these two cases. As explained in **247.** 2. *b*, the accent is upon the first member in case of a group-word or compound. There is thus also in English a real difference between these two forms, but it has not found a formal expression in the orthography as in German.

a. In a number of words the old weak genitive still stands in such group-words and compounds, altho the same words have elsewhere long since become strong, or in case of feminines in the singular have lost inflection: **Greisenalter** (see **76.** I. 3. *b*) old age, **Schelmenstück** piece of roguery, **Herzogenbusch** (**70.** 1. *c*. (**2**)), **Spionenriecher** (**63.** 7. *c. General Note*) one who is always on the lookout for spies, **Epigrammendichter** (**63.** 7. *c. General Note*) epigrammatist, **Gelehrtenversammlung** (**111.** 10. *Note*); **Sonnenschein** sunshine, **Freudentag** day of joy, &c. In a number of words the old feminine genitive of the strong declension, which was exactly like the nominative, has been retained: **Rachegott** god of vengeance, **Mußestunde** hour of leisure, &c. In an earlier period some of these strong feminines added **e** in the genitive singular, and the vowel was mutated. See **70.** 2. *c*. This old genitive survives in a few compounds: **Gänsefeder, Bräutigam** (the first component being the genitive of **Braut** with an **i** corrupted from **e,** the second component an old noun, not now found elsewhere, the modern form of O.H.G. gomo *man*, related to Latin homo), &c.

b. The connecting of the two components by an **s** or **es** (**62.** D. (**1**)) has become very popular, probably to give formal expression to the feeling that the modifying component stands in a syntactical relation to the following basal component, hence the **s** has spread to a large number of words originally without it, often even to feminines, where Luther rarely has an **s.** Note especially the following cases where the **s** is now used:

aa. When a fem. modifying component ends in **-at, -ut, -heit, -schaft, -t** (in compounds and derivatives only), **ion, ung, tät: Freundschaftsdienst, Hochzeitstag** (but **Zeitpunkt;** see *dd* below), **Krönungstag,** &c.

bb. Usually after the modifying components **Acht, Geschichte, Hilfe, Liebe,** and often **Miete: Achtserklärung, Geschichtsforscher, Hilfstruppen, Liebesdienst, Miet(s)leute, Miet(s)wagen,** &c. Also in **Kindtaufskuchen** (see *dd* below), **Frauensperson, Frauensleute, Seelengüte** or **Seelensgüte** (after the analogy of **Herzensgüte**). In the last three cases the **s** is added to the weak gen. Colloquially the **ns** often occurs instead of **n** in **Menschenskind** fellow, lad, 'my boy': Jakob: **Ist es nicht so, Ohm Reinhold?** Ulrichs: **So ist es, Menschenskind!** (Halbe's *Der Strom*, p. 8).

cc. In a few feminines in **-d** and **-nahme: Geduldsfaden, Aufnahmsbedingung,** &c.

Note. The **s** in the cases in *aa, bb, cc* after feminine nouns has resulted from analogy, the feminines following the example of the masculines and neuters. It first appeared in the thirteenth century, but for a long time spread only slowly.

dd. Often when the modifying compound is itself a compound, except of course when the modifying component ends with a feminine other than those described in *aa, bb, cc*: **Weihnachtsabend,** but **Nachtfalter; Handwerkszeug,** but **Werkzeug; Reichsverkehrsminister,** &c., but **Reichswehrminister,** &c.

Note. The reason that the connecting **s** is thus often found in decomposites and not in simple compounds is that decomposites were little used in earlier periods, when the old group-word type was so common. They came into use late, when the younger group-word type had become the favorite formation, hence the **s**. There was, however, also a natural tendency to use **s** here as it served as a clear boundary line between a compound modifying and the basal component: **Tobsuchtsanfall,** &c.

ee. The connecting **s** now often stands where Luther has the old group-word form: **Aber der Vnterheubtman gleubet dem S c h i f f h e r r n vnd dem S c h i f f m a n mehr | denn dem das Paulus saget** (Acts xxvii. 11), in the revised edition **Schiffsherrn** and **Schiffsmann.**

Sometimes the same word has both the younger form with **s** and the older form without it, with differentiation of meaning: **Landmann** peasant, **Landsmann** fellow countryman; **Wassernot** lack of water, **Wassersnot** inundation.

ff. The connecting **s** now so common in group-words and compounds does not always have the force of a genitive singular ending. It may indicate: (**1**) that the modifying component is to be considered as an appositive to the basal component: **Jägersmann, Rittersmann, Lieblingsbuch,** &c., after the analogy of **Volksmann, Volksbuch,** where, however, the **s** represents a real genitive ending. (**2**) It may in fact contain a plural idea: **Diebesbande, Gastwirtsverein, Freundeskreis, Anwaltstag, Bischofsversammlung, Jünglingsverein** Young Men's Christian Association, **Kardinalskollegium** college of cardinals, **Heringsfang, Offizierskorps** (Beyerlein's *Jena oder Sedan?*, xiii), **das beste Offiziersmaterial** (ib.) the best material out of which officers can be made, **Schiffsverkehr, Zwillingspaar,** &c. Nouns with the plural ending **e** do not with absolute freedom enter compounds with their regular plural ending as do most other nouns, but they often take an **s**, as in the examples given above, or frequently have the form of an old group-word, or in the case of certain nouns (see *a* above) which were once weak, or which are now weak or strong, or after the analogy of such assume the weak plural ending **en: Offizierkorps** (preferred to the form in **s** by a number of grammarians), **Kopfzahl** number of persons present, &c.; **Sinnenaufregung, Spionenriecher, Dokumentenwurm, Inseratenteil,** &c. In S.G. strong nouns can readily enter into compounds with their regular plural, as the plural ending **-e,** which often seems to be avoided in group-words and compounds, is regularly dropped even in the simple form of the word, and thus the endingless plural easily enters the compound as a sort of mutated stem: **die Tannenästbahre** (Meinrad Lienert's *Der Strahler*, p. 191). The **e** in the formations described in I. *a* above, may in part be felt as a plural ending, but it was originally an old stem-suffix. (**3**) It may contain the idea of a comparison: **engelsgut, finger(s)lang, lebensgroß, kerzengerade,** &c. In a number of cases this **s** has resulted from the analogy of similar noun formations where the **s** represents a real genitive ending: **Engelsgüte, Fingerslänge,** &c. (**4**) It may have the force of an accusative: **das Ineinander von wirklichkeitsbejahendem Realismus und wirklichkeitsüberflügelndem Idealismus** (Otto Eißfeldt in *Preußische Jahrbücher*, 1919, p. 380), **geistestötend** (more commonly **geisttötend**), **verfassungsgebend** (more commonly **verfassunggebend**), **wahrheitsliebend,** &c. after the analogy of **Geistestod, Wahrheitsliebe,** &c. (**5**) The force of a predicate nominative: **weniger von jenem seligen Rausch der Jünglingswerdung** (R. H. Bartsch's *Die Haindlkinder*, p. 61). (**6**) The force of a dative: **gegenwartsnäher** (Prof. Karl Lamprecht in *Frankfurter Zeit.*, May 6,

1914) = **der Gegenwart näher; mittelstandsfeindlich** (Dr. Wirth in the "*Nationalversammlung*," April 26, 1920) = **dem Mittelstand feindlich, regierungsfreundlich, reichsfreundlich,** &c. after the analogy of **Reichsfreund,** &c., but real compounds, not derivatives from them, see **111.** 7. *c.* (**1**); **erfahrungsgemäß, wahrheitsgetreu.** (**7**) It is often equivalent to a prep. phrase: **eine Auflachensneigung ihrer Lippen** (Jensen's *Schatzsucher*, p. 288) = **eine Neigung ihrer Lippen zum Auflachen; Arbeitslosenfürsorge** = **Fürsorge für die Arbeitslosen; Auslandsaufenthalt** (*Die Neueren Sprachen*, Oct. 1914, p. 377) = **Aufenthalt im Ausland; in dem Kreuzestod Christi** (Adolf Metz in *Preußische Jahrbücher*, Nov. 1914, p. 214) = **in dem Tode Christi am Kreuze; Vom Gegenwartswert des griechischen Unterrichts auf dem Gymnasium** (ib., Dec. 1915, title of an article by Max Siebourg) = **vom Wert des griechischen Unterrichts auf dem Gymnasium in der Gegenwart,** but much clearer and hence better as it brings **Gegenwart** near the word (**Wert**) which it modifies.

The use of **-s** in such varied relations clearly shows that it is no longer felt as a genitive ending. It is a new formative indicating a syntactical relation between the two components, thus performing exactly the same grammatical function as in old group-words the simple stem, which in quite a different way, namely by the entire absence of inflection, also indicates a syntactical relation between the two components. Altho both the old form with the simple stem and the new form with the ending **-s** merely indicate a syntactical relation without specifying it definitely the connection usually makes the thought entirely clear, so that both constructions by reason of their pithy terseness have come into wide use.

c. The connecting of the two components by an **-en,** the weak genitive ending, tho not so popular as that of **-s,** has spread to a number of words originally without it. Especially those feminines now ending in **-e** which were originally strong take this **-en** in compounds after the analogy of weak feminines, which formerly ended regularly in **-en** in the genitive sing.: **Gnadenakt, Säulenknopf, Entenschnabel,** &c. Some words enter into compounds with their simple stem or the weak genitive ending with differentiated meaning: **Erdgeruch** *smell of fresh earth*, but in figurative sense **Erdengeschick** *lot of this earth* or *world, human fate*, &c.

Masculines do not usually take an **-en** when they are not entitled to it, but weak masculines often take an **-en,** especially in derivatives, altho corresponding strong nouns enter similar formations, not with the strong genitive ending **-s,** but with their simple stem: **bubenhaft,** but **schülerhaft; Fürstentum,** but **Kaisertum,** &c. See **245.** II. 7. The **-en,** as **-s** in *b. ff.* (**1**) above, not only denotes the genitive relation but may also indicate that the modifying component is to be considered as an appositive to the basal component: **Hirtenknabe, Botenfrau,** &c. Sometimes this weak genitive is used where in a strict sense a predicate nominative should be employed: **Die Zeit der Austrocknung, Versandung und Wüstenwerdung** (Dr. Max Eckert in *Westermanns Monatshefte*, Oct. 1906, p. 140). Thus **-en** is now sometimes used, just as **-s** in *b. ff* above, as a formative to indicate a grammatical relation between the two components.

C. *An Adverbial Element as First Member.* In many group-words the modifying component stands in the relation of a modifying adverb or prepositional phrase: **hochbegabt** highly endowed, **weitverbreitet, aufstehen, Aufstand, Wohltat, Anteil, Ausland, Inland, Hinterland, Mitbürger, Nebenfluß, übergroß, landesüblich, ortsangesessen, Inbe'triebsetzung,** &c. To this group of group-words belongs the large class of verbs with a separable prefix (**215.** II. 1. B. *a*) or prepositional phrase (**215.** II. 1. B. *d*). These are not fixed group-words, as the prefix is separable in simple tenses in principal propositions. Nouns made from such verbs are, however, fixed formations: **Ausgang, In'standsetzung,** &c. There is also in case of verbs a tendency toward the fixed form. See **215.** II. 2. *c.*

Instead of a younger group-word or an end-group (**247.** 2. *a*), or an attributive adjective group (**247.** 2. *a*) we still often find the old group-word form, where the preposition and sometimes the number of the noun and other grammatical relations must be gathered from the context: **régentrìefend = von Régen trìefend, wíndumràuscht = vom Wínde umràuscht, báum- und búschum-gèben** (Spielhagen's *In Reih' und Glied*, 3, 76) = **von Bâumen und Bûschen umgèben.** In many instances the plural idea here finds a formal expression by means of a plural ending, but it is the mere plural stem without expression of the idea of case: **von den Riesenstädten mit ihren schiffewimmelnden Häfen, der häuserumgebene Platz,** &c.

D. The modifying component may be:

(**1**) The object (**215.** II. 1. B. *c*) of the verbal stem contained in the basal component, as in **stattfinden** *to take place,* **freudebringend, menschenbeglückend,** or in case of adjectives it may be the objective predicate (**104.** 2. A. *c* and **215.** II. 1. B. *b*), as in **großziehen** *to bring up, rear.* Such compounds are in large part separable verbs, and hence are not fixed compounds. In case of verbal nouns the object is sometimes in the acc., sometimes in the gen.: (acc. sing.) **Máßhalten** or **Máßhaltung, Besítzergreifung, Áuskunftgeber,** acc. pl. **Hûte-schwenken;** (gen. sing.) **Gehórsamsverweigerung, Fríedensbrecher,** &c. The words in the accusative group, tho for the most part modern formations and now felt as accusatives, may also be classed as old group-words, for they have also the form of old group-words and the oldest members of the group had in Gothic a distinctive stem (**I.** *a*) ending, indicating clearly that they were old group-words.

(**2**) The modifying component may be the object of an adjective in the gen. or dat. according as it governs the gen. or dat. in the sentence: **lébensmüde** tired of life, **vórwurfsvoll** reproachful, **herzensfroh, seelenfroh** or **seelensfroh** (after the analogy of **herzensfroh**), **strahlenreich, problemenreich** (*Beilage zur Allg. Ztg.*, No. 203, 1904, p. 446; pl. here weak after the analogy of **strahlen-reich,** &c., as the pl. in **-e** is often avoided here as in B. *b. ff.* (**2**).); **mílchähnlich** milklike, **góttergeben** resigned to the will of God, devout. Altho the gen. form is always clearly marked here, the dat. form rarely takes a clear dat. ending except in case of weak nouns, and there it remains uncertain whether the number is sing. or pl.: **góttähnlich** (not **gotteähnlich**), but **ménschenähnlich.** In **erdenfern** *far from earth and its cares* we have a clear case of the old dative form.

Instead of a younger group-word the old group-word form is still very common here: **kampfmüde** tired of fighting, **denkgewohnte Männer** men accustomed to think (= **des Denkens gewohnte Männer**), &c.

E. The modifying element may be a predicate noun or adjective: **die Mensch-werdung** the incarnation, lit. the becoming a man, **das Flüssigwerden fester Körper, das Gefühl des Stärkerseins;** (objective predicate) **Bekanntmachung,** &c.

2. Modern Group-words and Compounds.

The development of modern group-words and compounds with stress upon the second member out of modern groups with stress upon the second member and their differentiation in meaning from old and younger group-words have been treated in **247.** *b* and *c.* While in general the two classes are clearly distinguished by the *logical* force of the modifying component in old and younger group-words and compounds and its *descriptive* force in modern groupwords and compounds, this distinction sometimes entirely disappears in compounds made from sentences or fragments of a sentence, where the desire is not to convey the sentence with the concrete force of the words *as a sentence* but to indicate a type of people, animals, or things by a short characterization. It here becomes necessary to distinguish the compound from the sentence by placing the stress upon the first member as in younger group-words and compounds (**247.** 2. *b*), altho it has no logical force whatever: **Páckàn** big watch dog, but with literal meaning in a sentence: **Pàck án!** Seize him! Likewise **Sáufàus, Lúgàus, Lúg-inslànd, Sprínginsfèld, Schlágetòt,** &c. A younger group-word with an adjective as second member can be used thus without a change of accent, as it already has this stress, but it differs from an ordinary younger group-word in having no inflection: **ein alter Schádenfròh.** These sentence compounds are common also in English: a gád-abòut, &c. On the other hand, such modern groups in German, even tho used as substantives, often have modern group-stress where the literal force of the components is distinctly felt, as in **ein warmes Lèbewóhl.** See also H below.

Likewise a number of proper names, where the literal force of the components is not felt at all, have given up their modern descriptive stress upon the last component and have assumed the stress of younger group-words and compounds: **Ámstèg, Ímhòf,** names of places; (**2**) certain Swiss family names: **Vón der Mùhl, Áuf der Màuer,** &c.

The development of a new or somewhat different meaning in modern descriptive groups in which the first member is an adjective or a preposition often results in development into younger group-words and compounds (**247.** 2. *b*): **Kúrzwàren** hard-ware, i.e. nails, screws, etc., but sometimes still with its modern endings and modern group-stress: **kùrze Wáren.** The trend toward younger group-words is especially strong in decomposites, and in derivatives it has become the fixed form: **Kúrzwarenhȁndler; mein wármhèrziger Freund,** but **Mein Freund hat ein wàrmes Hérz; ȕbersèeisch,** but **ȕber Sée; vórmȁrzlich,** but **vòr dem Mȁrz (des Revolutionsjahres 1848); wídernatȕrlich,** but **wìder die Natúr;** &c. See also **245.** II. **9.** 1. *b*. The memory of the original modern group-stress here, however, is often so strong that it is retained even where inflection has been dropped and the parts are written together: **Nèujáhr** *Néwyèar,* still perhaps more common than **Néujàhr; Míttàg** from older **der mìtte** (adjective) **Tág,** now the prevailing form, but the original modern group-stress is still found in poetry, as in **Nách Mittáge sáßen wir** (Goethe's *Stirbt der Fuchs, so gilt der Balg*), and in many modern dialects; **Àrmsȕnderglócke, das Àrmsȕndergesícht** or **Àrmesȕndergesícht, die Schwàrze-Mḗer-Flótte** or **Schwàrzmḗerflótte, das Zwèimȁrkstȕck,** &c. See also **94.** 6.

Of course, the desire to *distinguish* often leads to transferring the stress from the second member to the first: **Ich wohne nicht in Áltstrèlitz, sondern in Néustrèlitz,** but usually **Altstrélitz, Neustrélitz.** On the other hand, the opposite tendency is found. In a few names of places, as **Sàlzbrúnn, Sàlzschlírf** the desire to *describe* rather than to *distinguish* has removed the stress from the first to the second element. See also **47.** 3. A. *e* (**10**) and *g*. This tendency is marked in a large number of onomatopœic formations: **piffpáff,** &c. See also **47.** 3. A. *e* (**11**). In a number of names of places there is fluctuation of usage. The people who live in **Weißensee** say **Wèißensée** as descriptive stress seems natural and sufficient to them, but others pronounce **Wéißensèe** as they feel the first component as having distinguishing force. In Berlin the desire to describe leads to the common pronunciation **Vormíttag, Nachmíttag,** which of course become old groups again when there is a desire to distinguish: **Komm nicht vórmittags, sondern náchmittags!**

In general, however, compound nouns retain intact their original group form and stress: **Áufgàng, áufgèhen; Verstánd, verstéhen; das gèlbe Fíeber, das kàlte Fíeber** (ague), **das Ròte Méer,** &c., which retain their original group form and stress except that occasionally for logical reasons they assume logical stress, as in **káltes Fìeber, nicht gélbes Fìeber.** For exceptional development of **Dúrchstich** from **durchstéchen** see **47.** 3. B. *a*.

The following groups will illustrate the kinds of modern group-words and compounds:

A. The compound consists of a noun and its modifying adjective, which is inflected as well as the noun: **der Hòhepríester** high-priest, **ein Hòherpríester, des Hòhenpríesters; das Hòhelíed** Song of Solomon, **des Hòhenlíedes,** &c. Also many geographical names: **Nèuentéich** (= **zum nèuen Téich**), &c. Many of these compounds have a stress upon the first member as they have become younger compounds (1. A above), sometimes with the modern endings of the adjective, sometimes with the old seemingly endingless form: **Áltenbùrg,**

Hóhenstèin; ein Zwéitmädchen or **ein zwèites Mädchen; der Gehéimrat** or **der Gehèime Rát; aus Lángwèile** or **Làngerwéile.**

a. A number of adverbial compounds consist of a noun in the adverbial gen., modified by an adj. in the gen., often with logical stress upon the first component: **nötigenfälls** or **nötigenfälls** *in case of need*, **jédenfälls** *at all events*. In a number of pl. compounds, where all feeling for the original construction has been lost, the substantive element of the compound has dropped its gen. pl. ending, and after the analogy of the sing. compounds taken on the ending **s**, altho the modifying adjective still remains as originally in the gen. pl.: **aller Dínge** (seventeenth century), **allerdíngs** (present form) *to be sure, certainly*, **állerórts** *everywhere*, &c. In a number of such compounds the substantive element adds **s** even to fem. nouns, following here the analogy of masculines: **séinerseits** *upon his part*, **mütterlicherseits** *upon the mother's side*. For a similar formation see **unterwégs, 223.** I. 10. *a*.

B. The article forms a compound with a following adj. or noun: **dersélbe, desgléichen.**

C. A noun forms a group-word or compound with its modifying gen.: **Muttergóttes, zeitlébens.** For accent see **47.** 3. A. *e*. (**3**). Also many geographical names (**47.** 3. A. *g*): **Rippoldsáu,** &c.; sometimes also common class nouns as described in **47.** 3. A. *e*. (**3**): **Tagesánfang,** &c., very common in English in groups containing a genitive of measure: a day's jóurney, *a thirty years' wár*, &c. The words of this group resemble in form the younger compounds with distinguishing force, described in **1.** B above, but differ from them in having modern group-stress with descriptive force (see **50.** A. 6. *f*, **247.** 2. *b*., and **255.** II. 1).

D. The name of a material or something measurable forms a group-word with some word denoting a measure, quantity, or weight: **Viertelstúnde** *quarter of an hour*. See **126.** 2. *a*. *Note*.

E. A prep. forms a group-word or compound with its dependent noun: **abséiten. Du hattest doch hier 'n sichres, warmes Zuháuse** (Hauptmann's *Friedensfest*, 1). Also verbal derivatives are formed from such prepositional phrases: **übernáchten, überwíntern.**

a. In some of these words, all feeling for the nature of the compounds having disappeared, inflectional endings are added to the oblique case ending: **vorhánden** (dat. pl.) *on hand*, **die vorhándenen Vorräte** the provisions on hand.

F. In some group-words and compounds the syntactical relation between the parts is that of apposition, co-ordination, or addition: **Gòttménsch** God incarnate, **Fürstbíschof** a bishop who has also the dignity of a prince, **Prìnzregént** a prince temporarily filling the place of the ruler, **Hànswúrst** jack-pudding, **Hànsnárr** tom-fool; **Österreich-Úngarn** Austro-Hungary, **Mèyer-Brémen** *Meyer who lives in Bremen*, **das Ministèrium Bísmarck, die schwarzróte Fahne Württembergs** the flag of Württemberg consisting of black and red, **das schwarzrotgóldene Banner Deutschlands 1848** the banner of Germany in 1848 consisting of black, red, and gold; **Nordóst, Südwést; einundzwánzig; bimbambúm! piffpáff!**

a. Not all words indicating a co-ordination of parts are written together as one word. In a number of cases a pair of words connected by **und** or **oder** form a single idea, when the two words are synonyms, and thus represent the same thing from two different standpoints, or are opposites or complements, and thus show the whole range of the idea from the two extremes (see **94.** 5): **sein ganzes Hàb (die Habe) und Gút** *all he owns* or *all his property*, **der Verlust ihres Hàb und Gútes, sein Tùn und Lássen** *his actions*, **in die Krèuz und Quére fragen** to cross-examine, **in die Krèuz und Quére schwatzen** to talk, chat upon this subject and that, and the other similar examples in **94.** 5; **auf èin oder die ándere Weise** *in one way or another*, **schwàrz und wéiße Fahnen** *flags consisting of black and white*, and the other similar examples in **111.** 7. *b*. In the preceding examples the inflection of only the second of the two words, the heavier stress upon the second word, and the use of the article which belongs to the second word as the article for the combination, clearly stamp them as compounds, tho not written as such. In many other cases words are in fact compounds as indicated by the stress upon the last component, but the absence of an inflectional ending in the second part does not show it so clearly: **wèit und bréit, in Sàck und Ásche trauern** to repent in sackcloth and ashes, **durch dìck und dǘnn, über Lànd und Méer.**

G. In some modern group-words the syntactical relation between the parts is that of verb and object: **das immer erneute Sìchflǘchten zu dem Herrn** (Brückner), **Sìchüberhében, Sìchvergéssen.** In accordance with older usage the reflexive object is still often omitted here, especially in certain words, particularly in connection with **selbst: sìch befínden,** but **Befínden; sìch híngeben,** but **Híngàbe** or **Híngèben; sich sélbst behèrrschen,** but **Sélbstbehèrrschung,** &c. See also **188.** *a.* A dative object is sometimes found: **Sichsèlbstüberlássensèin,** &c. A dative of reference is also found: **Das Mènschenmǿgliche hab' ich getan** (Halbe's *Der Strom*, p. 109).

There may be a double object, an acc. object and an objective predicate: **Sobald ich am Menschen dieses unnötige Wesen und Sìch-máusig-màchen bemerke, so lasse ich ihn laufen** (G. Keller an T. Storm, 5. Juni 1882). Also a dative and a direct object in the form of a dependent infinitive: **das träge und knechtschaffene Sìch-genügen-làssen am Regiertwerden von oben herab** (*Der Türmer*, Jahrg. VI, p. 352).

The verbal stem may be modified by both an object and a prepositional phrase: **Dein seliger Vater würde darin kaum eine Ursache zum Sìchimgrǽbúmdrèhen finden** (Baumbach's *Der Schwiegersohn*, v).

H. A whole sentence, or the important part of it, may become a group-word or compound, especially in imperative sentences: **Lèbehóch, Lèbewóhl, Gòttlób (Gòtt sei Lób), Gòttseibéiuns, Grüßgótt, Vergíßmeinnìcht, unser Märchen vom Tìschleindéckdich, ein warmes Gùtenácht (Ich wünsche Ihnen eine gùte Nácht), Jelàngerjelíeber,** &c. Here we have modern group-stress, but many words have old group-stress, as explained in 2 above.

I. Some group-words and compounds consist of two components, of which the first is a modern group-word or compound and has the principal accent, which is placed according to the rules for a modern group: **Gùtenáchtgrùß, Drèikǿnigsfést, Àltwéibersómmer, Dùmmerjǘngenstréich, in dieser Dròschke-ersterKlásse-Geséllschaft** (Raabe's *Im alten Eisen*, XVII), **die Kaiser-Wilhelm-ÍÍ.-Reálschule** (read **Wilhelm der Zwéite**), **die Lòs-von-Rǿm-Bewégung.** The first element is sometimes inflected, and sometimes remains uninflected. See **94.** 6.

3. A large number of words which by their form belong to one or other of the above-described categories form with respect to accent and meaning a distinct group, namely compounds the first element of which does not contain an essential modification of the basal compound, but only an intensification of the idea or a concrete or specific illustration of it, and hence does not take the principal accent: **hundselend** very miserable, **stockfinster** very dark, **pechschwarz** jet-black, **kreuzfidel** as merry as a cricket, &c. For particulars as to accent see **47.** 3. A. *b. aa, bb, cc, c, d.*

PART IV

SYNTAX.

The Simple Sentence and its Parts and Kinds.

250. A sentence is an expression of a conception by means of a word or words used in such form and manner as to convey the meaning intended. The sentence may be: (1) exclamatory, uttering an outcry, or giving expression to a command, prohibition, warning, request, wish, or desire, closing with an exclamation point—perhaps the oldest form of the sentence; (2) declarative, stating a fact, closing with a period; (3) interrogative, asking a question, closing with an interrogation point.

It is usually considered that there are two essential elements in every sentence—the subject and the predicate: **Karl singt.** The subject is that which is spoken of. The predicate is that which is said of the subject. In a normal sentence both subject and predicate are present, but sometimes the one or the other or both may be absent and yet the sentence be a complete expression of thought. See *a* below.

The proper intonation employed in the different kinds of sentences is described in **53. 2.**

a. Sentences Lacking the One or the Other or Both of the Essential Elements. In accurate thinking we often need a large vocabulary and intricate grammatical form, but language also adapts itself readily to the simpler needs of practical life, where action and the situation are often more expressive than words and grammatical form. If we call out: **Fritz!**, to indicate that he should come we pronounce in loud prolonged tones **Fritz** as a dissyllabic, fRI-Its. If we scold him we pronounce **Fritz** as a monosyllabic, fRIts, and raise the tone of the voice. If we desire **Fritz** to hold his tongue we say to him in a stern tone: **Schweig!** If in the dead of the night we wake up and find the house in flames we cry out in loud excited tone: **Feuer!** Often an adverb suffices: **Herein!** Frequently a pronoun spoken in angry tone is sufficient to express a threat: **Du!** Still as in primitive speech an interjection often conveys our meaning: **Au! (241).** In answer to a question **ja** or **nein** is a complete thought, similarly **gleichfalls** in answer to a wish, as in **„Glückliche Reise!“ „Gleichfalls!“** *The same to you.* Short terse expression was not only characteristic of primitive speech when language was undeveloped but in passionate, excited, or lively language this older type has maintained itself thruout the ages and thrives even to-day in the inflectional period, indeed inflection suggests and facilitates its employment: Subject: (in distressed tone) **Mein Hut! = Mein Hut ist in Gefahr!** Predicate: (in tone of lively assent) **Stimmt = Es stimmt** That's true enough. Accusative: (in tone of a command) **Meinen Hut!** Dative: **„Wem soll ich den Apfel geben?“ „Mir, mir, mir!“** Non-inflection of the adjective, thus clearly indicating that it is a predicate: **Prächtig!** In all these cases the expression of the thought is perfect. The sentences, tho brief, are complete. In the setting in which they appear, not a word, not a syllable is lacking. A learned grammarian with mistaken enthusiasm might desire to expand these brief utterances into full sentences, but in spite of his grammatical skill the language would be bad, for it would violate good usage. We do not here usually employ full sentences and for a good reason. Fuller expression would be incomplete expression, for it would mar the thought, take something vital away from it. Thus such brief sentences are as complete as those of exact scientific language, where, however, the thinker removed from plain everyday life must express himself fully if he would describe accurately the hidden forces he is studying. In this book the brief constructions for the want of a better expression are called elliptical, but this word does not denote incomplete expression, it indicates that according to good usage certain parts of a normal sentence are under the given circumstances regularly lacking as they are not necessary to make the thought complete, or would mar the thought. Compare **219, 1, 4. B.** ***a.*** *Note*, 5. B. *a*; **251.** II. A. *d*; **252.** 1. *a. Note* 1. (2), *b. Note*; **177.** I. B. *e. Note* 3.

The oldest form of the sentence contained only one word, which, however, was a complete sentence, not a word in its modern sense, for a word is a later development in language growth than a sentence. This oldest type of sentence still survives in case of exclamations, as **au!**, and the simple imperative forms. In course of time successive sentences often stood in such close relation to each other that the different *sentences* developed into *words*: **Sieh! Da! Feuer!** becoming **Sieh da das Feuer!** In the oldest form of the sentence, the thing type, which in somewhat changed form is still widely used, the single word which constituted the sentence indicated a thing. This thing—an action, quality, place, person, or thing—in connection with the situation suggests the thought, as illustrated by a number of examples in the preceding paragraph. In a later stage of development the thought may be suggested by the association of two things by simply placing one word alongside of another word, which in reality is a predicate but in form an appositive noun, adjective, adverb, or prepositional phrase, as in the early period when this construction arose the idea of predication by means of a verb had not yet come into use: **Träume Schäume. Alles still. Wer da?** More examples of the appositional variety of the thing type are given in **252.** 1. *b. Note.* In this appositional type wherever the appositive was a verbal noun it became common in the prehistoric period to append to it personal endings in order to bring the action into relation to a personal subject. The verbal appositive thus became a verb and the old style of expressing thought by the association of two things was in large measure replaced by the new style of representing the subject as resting, acting, or being acted upon: **Der Junge schläft, arbeitet, arbeitete, wird geschlagen, wurde geschlagen, kleidet sich,** &c. With the new style came new possibilities of human expression. The new type—the predicating type—can represent the subject in a number of the different phases of its life, while the old appositional thing type can represent it in only one phase, that of the present moment. Moreover, the new predicating type possessed great possibilities of future development. Wherever in the old appositional type the appositive was a noun, adjective, adverb, or prepositional phrase a verb without a concrete meaning, now called a copula, was in the prehistoric period inserted before the appositive in order to conform the sentence to the new predicating type: **Der Fluß ist tief.** A fuller explanation is given in **252.** 1. *b. Note.* Altho the normal sentence has thus contained a verb from the earliest historic times the older verbless thing type has never been entirely displaced, as illustrated above and more fully in **252.** 1. *b. Note.* Moreover, even tho the copula is now usually found before a predicate noun, adjective, adverb, &c., the *spirit* of the old thing type of sentence survives, for we always feel the thought as suggested by a thing, not by the copula. Indeed the modern form of the old thing type of sentence with a copula is now such a favorite that it is one of the marked features of current speech not to put the main thought into the verb but to express it by means of the name of a thing, i.e. a noun, in connection with a copula-like verb, i.e. a verb that is chosen not to convey the desired meaning but merely to indicate predication: **Das Stück gelangt bald zur Aufführung** *The drama will soon be put upon the boards,* instead of **wird bald aufgeführt** *will soon be played.* For other examples see **252.** 1. *a. Note* 2. We should, however, not forget that the modern form of the old thing type is a great improvement upon the original form, for the copula brings with it the power to express the time and modal relations. The spirit of older speech is not only thus preserved in modern form in sentences containing a verb of incomplete predication, such as a copula or a copula-like verb, but sometimes also in sentences containing a verb of complete predication: **Es regnet** *It rains.* There was originally no **es** or *it* here, for there is no subject expressed or understood. Later in oldest German and English we usually find here a formal subject, **es** or *it,* which was inserted to conform such sentences in a mere formal way to the predicating type, which requires a subject for a verb, but the spirit of the older sentence remains, for the activity has not yet been brought into relation to a real subject. For fuller discussion see **219** and **219.** 1, 3 and *a* thereunder.

251. *The Subject.*

I. The Case and Forms of the Subject.

1. A. The subject of a finite verb is in the nominative: **Der Schüler lernt.** The genitive cannot stand in an elliptical subject without a governing word, as in English: **Von den drei Kraftwagen ist der Wilhelms der beste,** or in loose colloquial and popular language: **Von den drei Kraftwagen ist dem Wilhelm seiner der beste** *Of the three autos William's is the best.* **Goethes Leben war in fast jeder Beziehung ein glückliches** *Goethe's was in almost every respect a happy life,* which we say instead of *Goethe's life was in almost every respect a happy one,* as we desire to avoid the use of weak, meaningless *one.*

a. The subject can still as in older German be in the gen. or now more commonly in the dat. after **von.** See **255.** II. 1. H. *c.*

b. In a number of instances a noun in an oblique case after a prep. is considered the subject of the sentence, since the real origin of the construction is no longer felt: **Gegen hundert Mann sind gefallen** About a hundred men fell. **An die tausend Menschen waren versammelt. Aus Deutschland werden jährlich für mehr als 100 Millionen Mark, namentlich an Damenkonfektion, ausgeführt, aber für viel mehr bleibt im Inland** (Sombart's *Die deutsche Volkswirtschaft,* p. 339). In these sentences the prep. **an, für, gegen** are now usually felt as adverbs with the force of **ungefähr** and **etwa.** Compare **225.** 1. *c.*

B. The form of the subject may be that of:

a. A noun: **Die Sonne leuchtet.** Things are often personified: **Das Messer schneidet gut. Eine Brücke verbindet das rechte Ufer mit dem linken.** The subject is often metonymic, i.e. indicating not the real subject but a thing or a person in close association with it: **Das Faß fließt über. Die Bank sitzt voller Menschen.**

After certain words, **anscheinlich, angeblich, wahrscheinlich,** &c., the subject has the logical force of a predicate of a relative clause: **Der angebliche Chirurg ist eigentlich ein Barbier = Der, der als Chirurg angegeben wird, ist eigentlich ein Barbier.**

b. A pronoun: **Ich schreibe.**

c. An adjective or participle used substantively: **Der Fröhliche lacht. Zu grob ist unanständig, und die Rechnung wird das ausweisen** (Raabe's *Der Dräumling,* XXVI). **Der Trauernde weint. Der Besiegte trauert.**

d. An infinitive with or without **zu: Andern zu dienen macht ihr Freude. Mäßig leben macht stark.**

e. Any other part of speech used substantively: **Auf ist eine Präposition.**

f. A whole clause: **Wer nicht hören will, muß fühlen.**

2. A. *Grammatical* **Es.** Sometimes there are two subjects in a sentence—the *logical* and the *grammatical* subject: **Es** (grammatical subject) **war einmal ein König** (logical subject). The grammatical subject is usually the uninflected **es,** which as a provisional subject serves only as a formal introduction to the sentence, and points forward to the logical subject in the nom., which follows the verb: **Es sind viele hier gewesen** *There have been many here.* The logical subject is here the real subject, as it regulates the number of the verb. In inverted order the **es** drops out: **Hier sind viele gewesen.** It is also dropped when the real subject stands at the head of the sentence: **Viele sind hier gewesen.** For the use of the grammatical subject see II. B below.

It should be noted that this use of **es** as grammatical subject corresponds in part to the use of *there* in English, but the construction has in German a wider field of usefulness, as it is in English not used at all with transitives in the active and is not freely employed with intransitives and passives: **Es weiß ja niemand, wann er zuletzt zur Beichte gegangen ist** *Indeed, nobody knows when he confessed* (to the priest) *last.* In English, on the other hand, the expletive *there* is in one particular case more used than **es** is in German, namely, it can be used even when some other word introduces the sentence, while in German **es** is then uniformly dropped: *A few years ago there lived in this house a lonely old man* **Vor einigen Jahren wohnte in diesem Hause ein einsamer, alter Mann.** Are there many people here? **Sind viele Menschen hier?**

Note. In oldest German the grammatical subject was very little used. The position of the verb in the first place unaccompanied by the subject suggested that the subject would follow later: **Stuant tho thar umbiring filu managediling** (Otfrid, I. 9. 9, ninth century) **Es stand da in dem Kreise mancher Edelmann.** Later after the analogy of anticipative **es,** as in **Es freut mich, daß er morgen kommt, es** gradually became established as a formal grammatical subject wherever the subject did not introduce the sentence and the verb stood in the first place. Originally anticipative **es** had a little concrete force as it pointed to the following clause but even in oldest German it was felt as a mere formal element and later suggested the use of **es** as grammatical subject, as the feeling had arisen that the verb in the first place gave the impression of a question, as explained more fully in **219.** On the other hand, as anticipative **es** was in O.H.G., perhaps even originally, a mere formal element it was often omitted just as impersonal **es,** which had arisen under its influence, was often used or omitted. As, however, anticipative **es** was and still is often needed to make the thought clear it has persisted thruout the centuries and has become more firmly established than ever except in certain categories described below. In English the expletive *there* is not omitted when another word is placed at the beginning of the sentence as it is an adverb, not a grammatical subject, and hence like any other adverb can take a later position if not needed in the first place. Altho English uses the expletive *there* to point forward to a following emphatic simple subject it employs the anticipative subject *it* to point forward to a following infinitive or substantive clause which is used as subject, here corresponding in general to the German use of **es,** as illustrated in B below.

a. In poetical style a grammatical subject agreeing in gender, number, and case with a following logical subject is found: **Und eilig trocknet' er ab die Träne, der Jüngling edeln Gefühles** (Goethe's *H. u. D.*, IV, 65–6). **Ein unermüdlicher Arbeiter war er, dieser Novemberwind** (Hans Hoffmann).

b. Somewhat different from the above is the common case where the logical subject is placed for emphasis at the head of the sentence in the form of an exclamation and then is immediately or after an interval of several words again referred to by a personal pronoun or demon. which agrees with it: **Die Freiheit, sie ist kein leerer Wahn. Der arme Mensch! Nun ist er ganz verlassen. Das Pergament, ist das der heil'ge Bronnen?** (*Faust*, l. 566).

B. *Anticipative* **Es.** Similar to the *grammatical subject* in A is the *anticipative subject* **es,** which points forward to a following infinitive or substantive clause which explains the **es** more fully: **Es macht mir großes Vergnügen, Sie hier zu sehen. Es ist nicht gut, daß der Mensch allein sei.** This **es** differs from the grammatical subject **es** in having more independent force in that it is often needed to make the grammatical relations clear, for such sentences with an infinitive or substantive clause as subject are more involved than sentences with a simple subject. Hence it is usually retained even when some other word stands at the head of the sentence: **Heute macht es mir großes Vergnügen, Sie hier zu sehen.** It drops out, however, when the real subject stands at the head of the sentence: **Sie hier zu sehen macht mir großes Vergnügen.** For the origin of the anticipative subject see A. *Note* and **219.**

Note. The anticipative subject **es** is sometimes omitted in accordance with older usage where it had not yet become necessary to introduce thus formally the logical subject: **Mich freut** [es], **daß ich dich so besonnen finde** (Grillparzer's *Medea*, 4). The anticipative **es** is regularly omitted when an unemphatic predicate word, such as a predicate adjective, noun, or modal verbal (**180.** A), introduces the sentence, for the presence of the unemphatic predicate here and the rising intonation after the verb pointing forward indicate that the subject has been withheld for emphasis and must follow. An illustrative example is given in II. B. *a. aa. Note.* Similarly the anticipative **es** is not needed if an intransitive verb preceded by an unstressed modifying word introduces the sentence and there is a rising intonation—here indicated by a raised period—after the verb pointing forward to the following emphatic subject clause: **Hieraus folgt˙, daß usw. Zum Dichten gehört˙, daß dem Menschen Bilder vor Augen stehen, daß er den Drang fühle, sie darzustellen** (Hermann Grimm's *Fragmente*, I, p. 378).

The **es** is regularly dropped when the principal proposition is inserted in the subordinate clause: **Dies, wurde gesagt, sei falsch. Warum, ist nicht leicht zu sagen** It is not easy to say why.

3. *Situation* **Es. Es** is much used as subject to point to something definite which is more or less clearly defined by the situation. Examples are given in **219.** 1 and 3 (last par.), where this **es** is distinguished from impersonal **es.** Attention is here called to the peculiar word-order employed here when the predicate is a personal pronoun. In this case the predicate usually comes first in the sentence, and so influences the verb that the verb agrees with it instead of agreeing with the subject: **ich bin es** it is I, **du bist es** it is you, **er ist es** it is he, **wir sind es** it is we. In question order: **bist du es?, ist er es?** Only rarely as in English: **Herr, ich höre Pferde im Galopp! Zwei! Es sind sie gewiß** (Goethe's *Götz*, 1, 2). Quite commonly so in Swiss dialect and colloquial language: **Nein, es ist ihn** (**252.** 2. C. *a*) **nicht** (J. Gotthelf's *Geld und Geist*, 366). The predicate, however, stands at the end when the proposition is introduced by an adverb or a demonstrative pronoun: **Wenn jemand hier gelogen hat, dann bist es du. Hier ist das Bild, dies bin ich und das sind Sie.**

The form **ích** (emphatic predicate) **bin es** *it is I* should be distinguished from the **ich** (subject) **bín** (emphatic to emphasize the fact) **es** (**129.** 2. C. (**4**)) *I am*, which is given in answer to such a question as **bist du treu?** *are you faithful?* While English distinguishes these cases sharply by a difference in form, German cannot so do, except often, as in these examples, by the accent, emphasizing in case of the expression of identity the predicate and in the latter case the verb.

4. *Impersonal* **Es.** This construction is treated at considerable length in **219.**

II. Omission or Expression of the Subject.

In general every sentence must have a subject expressed, but usage admits of certain irregularities, which are here treated briefly:

A. The *logical subject* is omitted:

a. As a rule in imperative sentences in the familiar form (**177. I. A.** *a*): **Fliehe! Flieht!**

b. In the first person in a few set expressions: **Danke** I thank you, **bitte** I beg of you, please, **geschweige** (**233.** C). **Bedauere sehr, kann nicht dienen** I regret very much that I cannot serve you. Besides these and a number of other set expressions the subject is frequently omitted in business and crisp epistolary style in general, and also often in poetry and familiar language: **Ihr Schreiben vom 16. d. M.** (**dieses Monats**) **habe erhalten. Habe nun, ach! Philosophie, | Juristerei und Medizin, | und leider auch Theologie! | durchaus studiert, mit heißem Bemühn** (Goethe).

c. Often in the 2nd person in poetry and familiar language, and less frequently in the 3rd person: **Füllest** (speaking of the moon) **wieder Busch und Tal | still mit Nebelglanz, | lösest** (dost free from oppressive care) **endlich auch einmal | meine Seele ganz** (Goethe). **Warum hast denn bis jetzt kein Feuer angemacht?** (Auerbach). [**Sie** *you*, 2nd sing.] **Sehen ja frisch und blühend aus wie die Gesundheit selbst! Es** is especially dropped in familiar conversation: **Mag sein** *It may be.* **Kann nicht erlaubt werden** It can't be allowed. **Wird schon kommen** It will surely come.

d. As in English, a pronominal subject, predicate, or object is often omitted in clauses introduced by **wie** *as, how, such as*, **als** *as, than*, **so'weit** *as far as*. The subject is omitted especially in case of situation **es** (**219.** 3, last par.) or a pronoun which can easily be supplied from the context: **Er sprach, wie folgt. Er benahm sich nicht, wie sich schickte. Es läßt sich leicht denken,** but in the subordinate clause after **wie: wie sich denken läßt,** or in a question after **wie: Wie läßt sich da bessern? Bringen Sie mir soviele Bücher, als auf dem Tische liegen. Er hat schon mehr getrunken, als ihm bekommen dürfte. Denen ist geholfen und mehr, so scheint's, als ihnen gut ist** (Otto Erler's *Struensee*, p. 66). **Hm, hm, ich habe, bei Gott, wüstere Tanten in meinem Dasein gesehen, als da eben auf dem Balkon stand** (Raabe's *Eulenpfingsten*, chap. viii). **Bisher haben sich den Witbois** (dat. pl., tribe of Africans), **soweit bekannt ist, die Hottentotten angeschlossen** (*Hamburger Nachrichten*, Nov. 27, 1904). Omission of predicate: **Ich möchte dich nicht anders, als du bist.** Omission of object: **Das ist mehr, als ein Mensch ertragen kann. Ich traute Ihnen eine solche Niederträchtigkeit nicht zu, wie Sie begangen haben.** These expressions are the survivals of a much older period when speech had not yet become fixed in conventional forms, with expressed subject, object, &c. Parts of the sentence were not expressed when the situation made the reference clear without the use of words. Situation **es,** however, was early in the historic period placed at the beginning of the sentence in order to keep the verb from standing in the first place and thus creating the impression of a question which requires yes or no for an answer. Where, however, some conjunction or adverb like **wie,** &c., stands in the first place older usage without a formal subject or object here is in set expressions still quite common, as the conjunction or adverb clearly indicates that the sentence is not such a question. The **wie** or **als** in these old expressions is now often felt as a relative pronoun used as subject or object, regularly so in case of English *as* after *such*.

In German, however, in accordance with the demands of modern formal grammar subordinate clauses often have an expressed subject, predicate, or object where English does not admit of it: **Sie trat an den Tisch und, ihre Brieftasche öffnend, legte sie eine Banknote unter den brennenden** (illuminated Christmas) **Baum, größer als sie noch je in dieser armen Hütte gesehen worden. Die Gräfin bekümmerte sich mehr um ihre Kinder, als es in Wien der Fall war. Wir trinken eine Flasche besseren Weines, als man ihn uns im Kurhause vorsetzen würde.** When the reference is to a preceding predicate adjective, or predicate noun, or the thought contained in the preceding proposition, the pronominal predicate or object here is **es** or **dies: Du bist auch bescheidener als ich es bin. Ihre Überraschung war groß, aber nicht so freudig, wie er dies erwartet hatte.** After the word *such* in English adjectival clauses introduced by *as* we regularly suppress a pronominal subject or object since *as* is felt as subject or object, while in German the pronoun is regularly inserted: **Aus dem Krug floß kein Dünnbier, sondern ein Wein, wie der weitgereiste Schuster noch keinen getrunken hatte** Out of the jug came no small beer, but a wine such as even the shoemaker, who had traveled so much, had never drunk. For fuller information here see **153.** 3. D. (**1**).

e. If several verbs have the same subject, it may usually be expressed only once, but the subject *must* be expressed in each proposition where some modifier of the verb (such as an adverbial element or an object) or a predicate noun or adjective stands before the verb: **Er kam zu mir, ging aber sogleich weg,** but **aber sogleich ging er weg.** The word-order need not necessarily be the same in the different propositions: **Nach wie vor besuchte er wöchentlich mehrmals das kanzleirätliche Haus und hielt den Damen Vorträge über pompejanische Ausgrabungen im besonderen und über Altertum im allgemeinen** (Baumbach's *Der Schwiegersohn*, v). In this sentence an adverbial element is in fact understood before the second proposition, as the adverbial modifier of the preceding proposition belongs also to the following one. This point is usually not vividly felt, so that inversion does not follow. Sometimes, however, we find the inverted order and the subject repeated, as the presence of the preceding adverbial element, object, or predicate noun or adjective is felt: **Schön war sie (die Stadt Kiel) niemals, ist sie auch nicht geworden und wird sie nie werden** (Jensen); or also **Schön war sie niemals, ist es auch nicht geworden und wird es nie werden.** Sometimes the subject is expressed but once and follows the last verb: **Als Leser denke und wünsche ich mir vor allem Studenten, die usw.** (Brugmann's *Kurze vergleichende Grammatik*, p. iv).

B. *Omission or Expression of the Grammatical* (see I. 2. A) *and the Anticipative* (I. 2. B) *Subject.* The general rules for the omission of these subjects have already been given in the articles I. 2. A and B. Moreover, the retention or omission of the grammatical and anticipative subjects is a question of emphasis or style which deserves careful attention.

a. The **es** is retained in the following cases:

aa. To make emphatic a predicate noun, pronoun, adjective, or modal verbal (**180.** A). In this case the predicate is placed at the head of the sentence in accordance with the general law for sentence accent, and is then followed in the first place by the main verb, in the second place by the anticipative subject **es** spoken with falling intonation (**53.** 2)—here indicated by a period—and in the third place by the real subject, which assumes the form of a relative clause or a clause introduced by **daß: Déutsche** (predicate) **waren es.** (anticipative subject), **die das Pulver, die Buchdruckerei erfunden haben** (subject clause). **Ích bin es., der es getan hat. Síe waren es., der anfing. Dú bist's., dem Ruhm und Ehre gebührt. Ríchtig ist es., daß er morgen kommt. Zu lóben ist es., daß er dies getan hat.** Notice in these sentences that in case of a predicate noun or pronoun the verb does not agree with the grammatical subject **es** or with the real subject, but with the predicate, being attracted into its person and number. This emphatic form also has the following word-order in case of predicate nouns: **Es ist dein Brúder., den du damit kränkst. Es ist bloßer Néid., was aus ihm spricht.** This form with normal word-order cannot be used if the predicate is a personal pronoun. See **I. 3** above.

Note. Where the predicate word is brought forward to the beginning of the sentence, not for emphasis but in order that the subject clause may take the emphatic end position the anticipative **es** drops out and is replaced by the rising intonation after the verb—here indicated by a raised period—which points forward to the subject clause which is to follow: **Richtig ist˙, daß Ibsen seine gewohnten Tagesausfahrten zufolge des anhaltend winterlich rauhen Wetters bis auf weiteres hat einstellen müssen** (*Hamburger Nachrichten*, Nov. 28, 1904, where the passage in question is given to correct a false report that represented Ibsen as dangerously sick). See also **269. 1.** *b* (2nd par.).

bb. It is also used when it is desired for emphasis or some other reason to bring the verb forward from its usual position. As the verb cannot stand first in the sentence without giving it the impression of a question or of a conditional clause, it is necessary in simple tenses of a principal declarative proposition to introduce the sentence by **es**, if it is desired to bring the verb forward for emphasis: **Es írrt der Mensch, solang er strebt** Man errs as long as his aspirations last. The **es** is not used here in case of the pronominal subjects **er, sie, es, sie,** as they themselves can introduce the sentence as well as **es: Er múß es tun.** As all the personal pronouns are light unstressed forms the verb in all such cases is felt as practically standing at the head of the sentence altho technically it is in the second place.

This emphatic word-order is sometimes replaced by another construction. In this case the predicate verb may take the form of an infinitive depending upon **tun: Lóben tat sie nicht viel, sie hielt's vom Überfluß** She rarely *praised* anybody, as she thought it superfluous. This construction is also used when the subject is a noun, especially in colloquial and popular language.

There is no need of the construction with **es** in compound tenses where the emphasis is to be placed upon the participle or infinitive, as the participle and infinitive which contain the important part of the predicate can be placed at the head of the sentence: **Genómmen ist die Freiheit, nicht gegeben. Laß nur stehen! Éingießen wird sich jeder selbst.** Likewise with modal auxiliaries: **Aber éssen kannst du doch zu uns kommen** (Maria Janitschek's *Einer Mutter Sieg*, XVIII).

In ballads and epics the past or present tense is often brought forward in accordance with the importance that attaches to the verb in narrative. The sentence at the beginning of the poem is usually introduced by **es** followed immediately by the verb: **Es zogen drei Bursche wohl über den Rhein.** Further on in the narrative lightly stressed **da** takes the place of **es** at the head of the sentence, as in ll. 19, 29, and 41 of Uhland's "Schwäbische Kunde." In colloquial and popular speech as in older literary usage the verb itself in all these cases stands in the first place. See *b* below.

cc. The construction with **es** must be used if it is desired to emphasize especially the subject by placing it after the verb. In this case **es** becomes the grammatical (I. 2. A) subject: **Es wanken | schon ganze Regimenter, Garnisonen** (Schiller's *Die Piccolomini*, 5, 1). As this construction is used to emphasize either the verb or the subject, the accent and context sometimes alone make clear which in each particular case is to be made prominent. It is the subject that is to be emphasized when it is found removed from the verb standing near the end of the proposition, which is usually an emphatic position: **Es irren in Fällen von so mißlicher Natur selbst weisere Männer. Es haben in Fällen von so mißlicher Natur selbst weisere Männer geirrt. Es weiß ja níemand, wann er zuletzt zur Beichte gegangen ist.** Often also a personal pronoun: **Es irrte auch ér.**

In the same manner a subject clause can be removed to the end of the sentence for the sake of emphasis: **Es ist eine der hauptsächlichsten Eigentümlichkeiten, die ihn** (i.e. Cæsar) **von Alexander, Hannibal und Napoleon unterscheidet, daß in ihm nicht der Offizier, sondern der Demagog der Ausgangspunkt der politischen Tätigkeit war** (Mommsen). For important points under this head see *aa. Note* above and also I. 2. B. *Note*.

In colloquial speech the **es** is often suppressed. See *b*.

b. In popular language and in poetry the **es,** following older usage still common in early N.H.G., is often omitted, so that the verb introduces the sentence: **Sah ein Knab ein Röslein stehn** (Goethe's *Heidenröslein*).

Originally there was more freedom in the word-order than now, so that even a verb could introduce a declarative sentence, if it was to be emphasized, lay nearer in thought, or if the statement as a whole was to be put in a more lively manner, or if the verb came to the front by the removal of the subject to the end of the sentence for the sake of emphasis, as described in *a. cc* above. Later in order to prevent the possibility of interpreting such a sentence as a question which must be answered by yes or no **es** was often placed at the head of a sentence and immediately after it the verb, so that the declarative character of the sentence was thus made perfectly clear and at the same time, as indicated in *a. bb, cc,* prominence given to the verb or the subject. Thus by a simple expedient the old historic word-order can still be used. The common people and poets do not comply with the formal rules of grammar, but often cling to older historic forms, and thus use here the old freedom of putting a verb at the head of the sentence, especially to make a statement in a stronger, more lively manner: **Natürlich müssen wir hin. Gleich—bald. Bin ich neugierig, Mutti!** (Adele Gerhard's *Die Geschichte der Antonie van Heese*, IV). Other examples in **287.** B. (**7**). Sometimes in ballads and epics the verb as the essential element in lively narrative is placed at the head of the sentence as in older usage: **Wandte der König sein Antlitz ab, und wieder zum Fenster, | und versuchte Hilfe beim höchsten Herrn zu erlangen** (Frenssen's *Bismarck*, p. 198). This construction is common in colloquial German, tho it is in English found only in a choice literary style: **Kommt da plötzlich ein Kerl herein, hat einen Revolver in der Hand, schießt den N. nieder; glaubt doch alles, es handle sich um persönliche Feindschaft, aber usw.** (Heinrich Winkler in *Anzeiger für deutsches Altertum*, Jan. 1901, p. 297). In English we can approach the spirit of the old Germanic construction by beginning the sentence with *there* (or in older English *it*) followed immediately by the verb: *There* entered suddenly, &c. In German colloquial speech as in older literary German the subject may for the sake of emphasis be withheld until the end of the sentence, so that the verb often stands in the first place: **Ich mache die Tür auf—steht da vor der Tür ein baumlanger Mensch** (Rudolf Blümel in Paul and Braune's *Beiträge*, vol. XXXV, p. 525). In English we can again approach this old Germanic construction by beginning the proposition with *there* (or in older English *it*) followed immediately by the verb: *There stood there*, &c. Tho we can thus still approach this old Germanic construction we cannot now, except in a rather choice literary style, put the verb in the first place. In German the older freedom is also sometimes still found in the literary language within the body of the sentence after the conjunction **und: Ganz einfach wie ein Stückholz ist sie gewesen, und half da kein Zureden und kein Bitten** (Hans Hoffmann's *Von Haff und Hafen*, p. 114). Often in colloquial language and dialect: **Neue Lasten! Und drucken** (S.G. for **drücken**) **uns die alten schon zentnerschwar** (for **zentnerschwer**)**!** (Schönherr's *Sonnwendtag*, p. 91).

c. The grammatical subject **es** must not be confounded with the **es** described in **141.** 9. *a*, which is used in expressions of identity. In the former construction the noun following the verb is the real subject, while in the latter construction it is the predicate. **Es war ein König** *There was* (*once upon a time*) *a king*, **or** if it is the latter construction *It was a king*. The difference between the two constructions becomes apparent in the inverted order, as the grammatical subject **es** there according to rule (see I. 2. A above) drops out, while the **es** in the expression of identity remains: **Einmal war ein König in großer Not** *There was once a king in great need*, but **Ein König war es** *It was a king*.

C. The *impersonal subject* **es** is sometimes omitted. See **219** and **1, 4. B.** ***a***. *Note*, and 5. B. *a* thereunder.

The Predicate.

The Forms and Case of the Predicate.

252. 1. The predicate can be:

a. A finite verb of complete predication: **Reichtum vergeht. Die Vögel singen. Die Würmer kriechen. Marie schreibt schön. Marie schreibt schöne Briefe.** Verbs of complete predication are often not complete of themselves and need some other word or words, as in the last two examples, to make the meaning complete, but the term "verb of complete predication" is not without inner justification. Such verbs stand in contrast to copulas (*b* and 2. B. ***a*** below), which in a mere formal way perform the function of predication and do not in an actual sense predicate. Verbs of complete predication, on the other hand, predicate, say something of the subject, they present a general line of thought, which is basal, even if it has to be supplemented often by details.

Note 1. The verb often becomes quite an unimportant element in a sentence, and by reason of the overtowering importance of some other part of the predicate loses a part or all of its original force and significance, or may be entirely or in part omitted. With nouns or adverbs which express a goal, destination, direction, the idea of the destination becomes so prominent that the idea of the *manner* of reaching it, which is contained in the verb, remains in the background and receives little attention. Thus we say: **Ich gehe morgen nach Berlin** I am going to Berlin to-morrow, altho in fact we intend to go on the cars and not on foot, as would be naturally suggested by the real meaning of the verb **gehen.** We thus use **gehen** with any manner of locomotion, as we do not stop to think of its real meaning, but are thinking rather of the destination. Some form of the verb is often suppressed: (**1**) In compound tenses we may retain only the auxiliary and omit entirely the verb of motion, where there is a goal or destination mentioned: **Er ist nach Haus** [**gegangen**]. **Ich wollte nach Berlin** [**gehen**]. **Sie sind fort** [**gegangen**]. The auxiliary here performs the verbal *function*, and the adverb or prep. phrase contains the verbal *meaning*. Also in other cases the auxiliary is alone used when the omission can easily be supplied from the context: **Du wirst Papa unterrichten, nicht wahr? Natürlich werde ich** [**ihn unterrichten**]. (**2**) The verb often drops out even when there is no auxiliary to perform the verbal function, as the really important part of the predicate is contained in some modifier of the verb, and the verb itself can easily be supplied: **Das Fenster auf und die Frühjahrsluft** (**he**)**rein! Ratsch! riß er dem Hansjörg die Pfeife aus dem Mund, und dann im gestreckten Galopp auf und davon** (Auerbach). **Achtung! Vorsicht! Schönen Dank** (**sage ich**)**!** I thank you! **Guten Tag! Wohin** (**gehen Sie**) **des Weges?** Where are you going to? (To the ticket agent at the railway station) **Zwei dritter Berlin!** Two third class tickets for Berlin! **Mir auch einen Apfel! Alle Mann an Bord!** but with quite a different meaning spoken in a narrative tone in reporting a fact: **Alle Mann** [**sind**] **an Bord. Hinaus mit ihm! Hierher! Zurück! Herein!** (**3**) The auxiliary often drops out where it can easily be supplied: (**Hast du**) **Ausgeschlafen?** Have you had your sleep out? Likewise in the passive: **Arbeiter aufs Land** [**werden**] **dringend verlangt!** (notice posted in an employment bureau).

Note 2. A marked feature in both German and English is the frequency of the usage which prefers to clothe the chief idea of the predicate in the form of a noun rather than in that of a verb: **Es wird in Erwägung gezogen** *It is under consideration*, instead of **Es wird erwogen** *It is being considered*. **Es gelangt bald zum Druck** *It will soon be in print*. Similarly: **etwas zur Entscheidung bringen** to bring something to the push, **etwas zur Ausführung bringen** to put something into execution, &c. English has developed much farther in this direction than German: Shine, Sir? **Wollen Sie sich nicht die Stiefel putzen lassen, mein Herr?** I got a shave **Ich ließ mich rasieren.** I got a good shaking up **Ich wurde schön durchgeschüttelt.** Let me have a look at it **Laß mich mal sehen!** Give it a good rub **Reib's mal tüchtig!** After dinner we had a quiet smoke **Nach dem Essen rauchten wir eine gemütliche Zigarre.** Let me have a taste **Laß mich mal kosten!** All these cases indicate a reluctance in colloquial speech to predicate by means of a full verb as this method is felt as too formal, too scientific, precise. In colloquial language there is always a tendency to concreter forms of expression, hence a noun is nearer popular feeling than the abstracter verb. The verbs that are used here in colloquial speech, tho transitive, are all otherwise of the nature of the intransitive copulas described in *b* and in the *Note* thereunder. They merely serve to connect the predicate noun, the real predicate, with the subject.

b. A verb of incomplete predication in connection with a predicate complement, the verb assuming in a mere formal way the *function* of predication, the complement serving as the real predicate: **Die Walfische sind Säugetiere.** A verb of incomplete predication is called a copula. In other tenses than the present the copula acquires more predicating force as it, like a verb of complete predication, indicates also the time relations. The copulas **sein** and **werden** often enter into such close relations to a predicate participle or infinitive that the copula and predicate complement fuse into a new whole and become a verb of complete predication: **Er ist gekommen. Er ist gefangen worden. Er wird gehen.**

Altho the copula is usually weakly stressed and may often even be omitted it is strongly accented to express the idea of actuality: **Gut íst er doch! Ein Schurke íst er doch!**

Note. Origin of the Copula. Next to the introduction of the verb of complete predication into language the introduction of the copula is the greatest event in the prehistoric Indo-European period. Originally the predicate noun or adjective was an attributive element, an appositive added to or placed before the subject to explain it more fully. In this primitive time the mere placing of the noun or adjective alongside the subject suggested the thought. This older usage is preserved in old-saws and is still the favorite form of expression in excited language and in exclamations of all kinds, where the predicate in the form of a noun, adjective, adverb, or prepositional phrase is placed alongside the subject without any formal sign of predication: **Bescheidenheit [ist] das schönste Kleid. Ehestand Wehestand! Er mein Freund?!** (spoken with rising intonation and in indignant tone). **Unser der Sieg! Eingang links. Jedermann zufrieden? Niemand hier?! Alles in Ordnung.** Similarly in the subordinate clause: **Ich tue es so gut wie [es] möglich [ist].** It is still very common in expressing strong feeling to employ an attributive adjective instead of a predicate adjective in the modern form of the sentence: **Der gute Gregor!** (words uttered by the pastor in Halbe's "Jugend", as he looks after the receding chaplain.) **Úngeréimtes Zéug! Úndánkbares Kínd!** Similarly in terse vigorous expression in general: **Fréies Wórt jeder Partei** (on the title page of "Der Tag") *The columns of this newspaper are open to every party.* The old attributive appositional type of sentence with the predicate after the subject, as in the first examples given above, is still regularly used in the objective predicate construction in **262.** III. 2 and also B thereunder and in the objective genitive construction in 2. A. *c* (3rd par.) below. Compare **250.** *a* (2nd par.) and **269.** 1. *b* (last par.). We often find the old attributive type with the predicate in attributive form before the subject blended with the modern type with a finite verb: **Ein érnstes Spíel wird euch vorübergehen** ("Prolog" to Uhland's "Herzog Ernst"). In the deep feeling of the author the sentence had originally assumed the old attributive form: **Ein érnstes Spíel!** In relating this impression the author retained the original form of expression blending it with the modern type instead of using the pure modern form: **Ernst ist das Spiel, das euch vorübergehen wird.**

The copula **sein,** originally a word with concrete force but at the time of its introduction into language as a copula without concrete meaning, was introduced as a mere formal sign of predication in order to mark the predicate noun, adjective, &c. formally as the predicate and thus conform the expression to the normal type of sentence with a finite verb as predicate. Altho the copula did not bring any concrete meaning with it, it is a great improvement upon the older form of expression, for it is not only a clear formal expression of predication, but it also indicates the time and modal relations by virtue of its tense and mood forms. Moreover it distinguishes the predicate noun, adjective, &c. from an attributive appositive. The other verbs which now often similarly lose their originally concrete force and are used as copulas, such as **werden, heißen, bleiben, stehen,** &c., introduce like **sein** the important predicate word but by virtue of their differentiated meanings introduce it with a different shade of thought, thus greatly enriching the language.

c. *Predicate Appositive.* The predicate may be a verb of complete predication in connection with a predicate complement, usually called a predicate appositive: **Er kam krank an. Er bat mich weinend** or **in Tränen. Er kam schweren Herzens** (**223.** III. *a*) **zurück.** The predicate complement often not only adds a remark about the subject, but it often also has the force of an adverbial clause thus sustaining relations to both the subject and the principal verb: **Jung (=wenn man jung ist) ist man leichtsinnig. Damit stand er auf, den um den Tisch Sitzenden den Rücken zuwendend (= indem er den um den Tisch Sitzenden den Rücken zuwendete.)** Compare **104.** 2. A. *b*, C; **268.** 4; **273.** 1. *c*.

2. The predicate complement may be:

A. A noun:

a. In the nominative after verbs of incomplete predication, i.e. the intransitives **sein** to be, **werden** to become, **bleiben** to remain, **heißen** to be called, named, **dünken** to seem, **scheinen** to seem, **erscheinen** to appear, and the passive forms of the transitives (see **262.** III. 2. A. *a*) which take a predicate accusative in the active: **Sokrates war der Sohn eines Bildhauers. Ich wurde von ihm ein Feigling gescholten.**

Note. After such verbs as **lassen** *to let,* **heißen** *to bid, command,* **lehren** *to teach,* **sehen,** &c., the predicate complement of the dependent intrans. of incomplete or complete predication is often in the acc. attracted into this case by the preceding acc., which is the object of the principal verb: **Laß mich deinen Freund sein** (Wildenbruch's *König Heinrich*, 4, 5). **Lassen Sie mich Ihren Schüler werden** (Stilgebauer's *Götz Krafft*, II, 14, p. 438). **Laß deinen Vater nicht als ehrlosen Lumpen in die Grube sinken** (Boßhart's *Die Barettlitochter*, p. 134). **Er hieß ihn einen Tyrannen werden** (D. Sanders). In earlier periods of the language the acc. here was more common than the nom., and this is, perhaps, still the case, except after **lehren,** but at present the nom. seems to be gaining upon the acc.:

Lieber Gott, laß mich kein Liederdichter werden (Heer's *Joggeli*, p. 107). **Laß mich ein solcher Tor sein** (Boßhart's *Die Barettlitochter*, p. 68). **Laß den wüsten Kerl, den Grobitzsch, meinetwegen ihr Komplice sein — deshalb bleibt sie doch immer die Schuldige** (Hartleben's *Rosenmontag*, 3, 2). **Mich laß ein wilder Jäger durch den Nebel fahren** (Traeger). **Lassen Sie mich in Ihrem Tempel weilen als ein frommer Beter, als ein ergebener Verehrer** (Ring). **Laß mich als der letzte, ärmste Eurer Kinder mit bunten Kieseln spielen auf Euren Straßen** (Paul Keller's *Das letzte Märchen*, p. 44). **Lehre du ihn ein Mensch sein** (Meinhardt). If, however, the predicate complement has no modifiers, it is usually in the nom.: **Laß mich Herr sein.** When the object and the unmodified predicate are the same word, the latter usually stands in the acc., but the nom. also occurs in accordance with the general rule: **Laß den Narren Narren sein. Laß dir den Menschen Mensch sein** (Grillparzer's *Ein treuer Diener*, 5).

On the other hand, the predicate complement of a prepositional infinitive is uniformly in the nominative, as it is felt as the predicate of an abridged clause: **Er beauftragte mich, der Bote zu sein. Mich verdroß, der letzte zu sein.**

b. The predicate noun is in certain cases introduced by **als** or the prepositions **für** (w. acc.) and **zu** (w. dat):

(**1**) The predicate nom. after **erscheinen** *to appear*, **gehen** *to pass* (*for*), and the passive forms of **ansehen** *to look at*, **begrüßen** *to greet*, **betrachten** *to consider*, **behandeln** *to treat*, and all others (for list see **262. III. 2.** A. *b*) which in the active take a predicate acc. introduced by **als,** also predicate appositives after intransitives of complete predication and after passives, are introduced by **als,** which here denotes *identity*, *oneness with*: **Dies erschien uns als der einzige Ausweg. Er war viel zu schön für einen Mann und hätte gut als Frau gehen können** (Bernhard Kellermann's *Yester und Li*, chap. XVI, p. 249). **Er wird als ein Taugenichts betrachtet. Er wird als tapferer Held gepriesen. Kommst du zu uns als unser Feind oder unser Retter? Als Tyrann wurde er von allen gehaßt.**

In case of predicate appositives the **als** is frequently omitted in poetry: **Ein Feind kommst du zurück dem Orden** (Schiller). This is a survival of early N.H.G., which did not yet require here the **als,** which first appeared here in the present period and has gradually come into wide use, growing at the expense of the older simple nominative and the **für** construction. Compare **262. III. 2** (2nd par.). In certain set expressions the older simple nominative construction is still preserved in prose, and has even become productive, so that new expressions are formed after the analogy of the old ones: **Bote** (see also **257.** 2. A) **laufen** to go on an errand, **Gevatter stehen** to stand godfather, **bei einem Kinde Pate stehen** to become sponsor for a child at baptism, **Braut stehen** to stand as a bride before the altar, be married, **Modell sitzen** or **stehen** to serve as an artist's model: **Nein, es ist ein Kunstwerk, zu dem Sie einfach Modell gesessen haben!** (Fulda's *Die Wilde Jagd*, 3, 10). In case of **Wache stehen** *to stand guard* this construction has replaced an older prepositional one: ih sihe den videlære an der schiltwache stan (*Nibelungenlied*, 1778, 4). Similarly **Wache sitzen: Jetzo sitze ich hier Wache** (Raabe's *Meister Autor*, chap. xxiii). Some grammarians feel some of these articleless nouns as cognate accusatives (see **257.** 2. A), and in fact a clear acc. form is sometimes found: **„Sie waren verreist?" „Ja, bei einer Nichte in Oberschlesien Paten gestanden"** (Paul Keller's *Waldwinter*, IX). On the other hand, the nom. sing. is sometimes used with reference to more than one, which shows that the noun has lost its identity and has entered into relations with the verb to form a compound: **Pate stehen sollten Gottfried von Geyer und Major von Schirrmacher** (Ompteda's *Sylvester von Geyer*, II).

(**2**) After the passive forms of a few verbs the predicate is introduced by **für** (with acc.) which does not positively affirm complete and absolute identity as does **als,** but only equality, and hence denotes that something is considered or represented as able or worthy to pass for the thing expressed by the predicate: **Er wird für einen reichen Mann gehalten** He is regarded as a rich man. Sometimes after the active form **gelten** and certain passive forms **für** and **als** are both used with the same verb, either with the same or with a different shade of meaning: **Er gilt für einen** or **als ein Dichter** He passes for a poet. **Er wird als ein Narr** or **für einen Narren angesehen** He is looked upon as a fool. Instead of the acc. here after **für** we often find the gen. where the substantive is in fact a substitute for a predicate adjective (see **253.** IV): **Er gilt ärztlich nicht für ersten Ranges** (Fontane's *Effi*, chap. xxiii). Tho **für** is pretty well established after a few verbs, especially **halten** and **erklären, als** is in general the favorite. The passive and the intransitive active constructions with **für** and **als** are not so common as the transitive active one, and hence the use of **für** and **als** is more fully illustrated in the active construction described in **262.** III. 2. A. *c* and *Note* 1.

Note. In M.H.G. **für** was more widely used than now to introduce the predicate. It could stand where **als** is now used, as described in (**1**) above: Si komen alle dar für kint, | die nu da groȥe liute sint (*Parzival*, 471. 1–2). It was at first a preposition governing the accusative, but from such sentences as the one just given where kint can be construed as a nominative, a predicate appositive, as well as an accusative it became in part an adverb with the force of **als** used to introduce an appositive. This usage has become established in the common construction **was für ein.** See **134.** 2. *d*. Elsewhere it is in the literary language regarded as a preposition governing the accusative. Compare **262.** III. 2 (2nd par.).

(**3**) The predicate after **werden** to become, **heranblühen** to blossom into, develop into, (**heran**)**gedeihen** to grow up to become, ripen into, and with similar intransitive force the reflexive verbs **sich entwickeln, sich auswachsen** to develop into, is introduced by **zu** with the dat. if it is desired to show an actual or desired transformation or development into the state indicated by the predicate: **Diese schönen Hoffnungen wurden zu Wasser** These fine hopes ended in smoke. **Er wurde zum Bettler** He became a beggar. **Der Knabe wird zum Mann. Das Wasser ist durch den Frost zu Eis geworden. Mein Leben wird mir zur Last** My life is becoming a burden to me. **Die Ausnahme darf nicht zur Regel werden** The exception must not become a rule. **Dein Vater ist zum Schelm an mir geworden** (Schiller's *Wallensteins Tod*, 3, 18) Your father has become a scoundrel thru his treatment of me. **Sie war zu einer kräftigen Schönheit herangeblüht. Du bist zum Jüngling gediehen. Indem nun werden in allen diesen Sätzen zu einem bloßen Verbindungswort geworden ist, hat es sich zu einer Kopula entwickelt.** Notice here the common use of the generalizing (**59.** I. C) definite article in contracted form, **zum** and **zur,** where English usually requires the indefinite article. In earliest N.H.G. the indefinite article was the rule as in English and as can be seen by the above examples is still sometimes used, but it can usually be replaced by the definite article as the definite article is now more common in a generalizing sense. In case of a mass or a material the article is here dropped in German and English as illustrated in examples given above. Compare **262.** III. 2. A. *d*.

If it is the finished state or condition reached or to be reached rather than the process of development that is before the mind the **zu** drops out: **Sie wurde Schauspielerin. Er wird Kaufmann** He is going to be a merchant. **Ein Kronprinz wird König, wenn sein Vater stirbt. Dieser Mohammedaner wird Christ; wird er aber auch zum Christen?**

The use of **zu** here was already well established in oldest German. Compare **262.** III. 2 (2nd par.).

c. Predicate Genitive. After the verb **sein** *to be,* more rarely after **werden** *to become,* **scheinen** *to seem,* a predicate genitive is used to express several ideas also found in the attributive gen., namely, *quality, origin,* and in choice language *possession,* or the first two of these ideas, and also that of *material,* and sometimes the *partitive* idea may be expressed by a prep. phrase (see **253.** IV): **Darüber kann man verschiedener Ansicht sein. Der Gedankenaustausch mit Münchnern ist jetzt geradezu eine Freude, so weh es in solchen Augenblicken auch tut, daß wir mit ihnen nur eines Sinnes, nicht auch eines Staates sein können** (*Neue Freie Presse*, Oct. 8, 1919). **Wir sind gleichen Alters** We are of the same age. **Seien Sie guter Dinge** Be of good cheer. **Er ist andern Sinnes geworden** He has changed his mind. **Also du bist wirklich des Glaubens, Michael hätte keinen sehnlicheren Wunsch gehabt, als seinen Sitz im Reichstag loszuwerden?** (Sudermann's *Es lebe das Leben*, p. 40). **So konnte Mommsen glauben, daß ich mit Unrecht gegen ihn ankämpfe, während ich natürlich der Überzeugung war und noch heute bin, daß ich zum Widerspruch verpflichtet war** (Otto Seeck's *Zur Charakteristik Mommsens*, Deutsche Rundschau, Jan. 1904). **Zuweilen, wenn er schlechter Laune war, behandelte er ihn allerdings wie einen Lakaien** (Beyerlein's *Jena oder Sedan?*, viii). **Das Verhältnis war nicht derart, daß es Johanna große Verlegenheit verursacht hätte. Ich bin willens, es zu tun** I am disposed, intend to do it. **Das ist mir einerlei** (**126.** 1. *a*) That is all the same to me. **Das ist so Rechtens** That is according to law. **Sie waren deutschen Ursprungs. So gebet dem Keiser | was des Keisers ist | vnd Gotte|**

was Gottes ist (Matth. xxii. 21). **Ich tu', was ich muß, der Ausgang ist Gottes** (Hebbel's *Agnes Bernauer*, 4, 4). **Das ist meines Amtes** (Suttner's *Im Berghause*, p. 54) That is my duty, my work. **Dringt in die Häuser, was ihr darin findet, | Frauen und Kinder, Schätze, Hab' und Gut, | ist der Soldaten** (Wildenbruch's *König Laurin*, 5, 14). **Es ist nicht dieses Ortes** (it is not the province of the present treatise), **festzustellen usw.** (Jakob Wackernagel's *Die griechische Sprache*, p. 294). **Und wessen sind die schönen Blumen, die Euch gegenüber die Fenster schmücken?** (Herr's *Der König der Bernina*, V). **Wenn er uns damals überfallen hätte, so wären wir alle des Todes gewesen** If he had fallen upon us at that time we should all have been doomed. **Er ist von Adel** He is of noble birth. **Die Sache ist von großer Wichtigkeit. Seien Sie ohne Furcht. Er ist von schlechter Herkunft. Der Tisch ist von Holz. Er ist von denen** (one of these men), **die ihr Gelübde halten** (Freytag).

We often find this genitive in the predicate appositive relation: **Er kam schweren Herzens zurück.** Compare **223.** III. *a*.

An objective predicate genitive of quality is used after **machen** *to make*, **zeigen** *to show*, **sich dünken** to regard one's self, &c.: **Jedenfalls rechne nicht darauf, mich anderen Sinnes zu machen** (Fontane's *Frau Jenny*, xii). After some verbs the objective predicate genitive is introduced by **als** or **für**. For examples see **262.** III. 2. B. *a*. The objective predicate genitive here as the objective predicate accusative in **262.** III. 2. is joined to its subject, the object of the principal verb, without the aid of a copula as the statement is felt to be of the old appositional type of sentence described in 1. *b*. *Note* above, where the predicate is placed alongside the subject like an appositive without the aid of a finite verb.

The gen. is quite common in the categories mentioned above in such expressions as those given in the illustrative examples and other similar ones, but in general it cannot be freely used. In poetry, however, it is often employed where in plain prose it would be replaced by **von** with the dat.: **Elisabeth ist meines Stammes, meines Geschlechts und Rangs** (Schiller's *Maria Stuart*, 1. 2). The possessive gen. is, aside from certain set expressions, found only in rather choice language, and is replaced in colloquial speech by **gehören** with dat.: **Das Haus gehört meinem Freunde.**

B. The predicate complement may be an adjective or participle:

a. In the nominative after verbs of incomplete predication, i.e. intransitives which have lost their concrete meaning and are now felt as copulas, such as **sein, werden, scheinen** (**185.** A. I. 1. *b*. (**3**)), **erscheinen** (**185.** A. I. 1. *b*. (**3**)), **dünken** (**185.** A. I. 1. *b*. (**3**)), **vorkommen, bleiben, heißen**, and **gehen, kommen, laufen, stehen** in certain set expressions, also the passive forms of the transitives (**262.** III. 2. B) which in the active take a noun or a non-reflexive pronoun as direct object and an adjective or participle as objective predicate, now in all these cases usually without grammatical forms except in the superlative (see **112.** 1): **Sie ist schön. Sie scheint betrübt. Das ist rührend. Karl ist der jüngste. Sie wurde krank. Das kommt mir lächerlich vor. Man versuchte das ertrunkene Kind zu beleben, aber es blieb tot. Drei tausend blieben** (i.e. fell) **tot. Das heißt ehrlich. Er geht müßig** (is idle, does nothing). **Die Vorstellung geht los** (begins). **Das Wasser geht tot** (ceases to flow). **Das Sägeblatt geht tot** (ceases to cut). **Der Schlüssel geht verloren. Der Angeklagte ist frei- or losgekommen. Das Faß läuft leer** (becomes empty, runs dry). **Das Faß läuft voll. Die Wohnung steht leer. Ein Kranker ist gesund erklärt worden, ist totgeglaubt worden, ist totgesagt worden. Er ist nicht totzukriegen** Nothing can knock him out, lit. with passive force, he can't be knocked out. **Er wurde totgeschlagen.** Here also belongs the perfect participle in the compound tenses of intransitives that are conjugated with **sein: Er ist gekommen.** Compare 1. *b* above.

A noun is often used in the predicate with the force of an adjective, indicating a quality or characteristic of the person or thing which it represents: **Seine** (Fulda's) **letzten Stücke heißen „Jugendfreunde" und „Herostrat"; jenes ist**

trotz guter Erfindung durchweg Blumenthal-Kadelburg (Bartels's *Die deutsche Dichtung der Gegenwart*, p. 256). **Du bist doch die geborene alte Jungfer** (Fontane's *Effi*, chap. 1) You are a regular old maid.

Note 1. If it is desired not simply to predicate a certain quality of the subject, but to assign it to a definite class of objects or ideas, the predicate adj. is preceded by **ein** or negatively **kein,** and is inflected: **Diese Kirsche ist s a u e r** (sour), but **eine sauere** (a sour kind). **Das Exemplar, das ich bezogen** (procured) **habe, war ein gebundenes. Diese ganze Frage ist eine rein ästhetische. Der Genuß davon ist mehr ein sinnlicher, kein rein geistiger.** Usage, however, goes farther, and employs this construction also as a more emphatic form of predication than the simple uninflected adjective: **Die Aufregung war bedeutend,** or more emphatically **eine bedeutende. Die Stellung des neuen Direktors war eine außerordentlich schwierige.** In the pl. **ein** of course drops out: **Die Leistungen waren ganz hervorragende.** This favorite construction is a modern form of the old attributive type of sentence, a blending of the old attributive form with the modern form with a finite verb, as described in 1. *b. Note* above. Thus also in English we often prefer *He is a kind-hearted fellow* to *He is kind-hearted.* On the other hand, English is very fond of a predicate adjective in connection with a complementary prepositional phrase as a more concrete form of statement than a transitive verb with an accusative object: You are forgetful of the fact that, &c. **Sie vergessen die Tatsache, daß usw.** I was ignorant of these facts **Ich wußte diese Dinge nicht.** Here as in **182.** 1. B. *a* we see the strong tendency in English to avoid a finite verb of complete predication. To be sure there is here a finite verb, but it is always the copula, a word with the grammatical function of predication but entirely void of concrete meaning, so that the old appositional type of sentence described in 1. *b. Note* above is preserved in spirit.

Note 2. Some adjectives are principally used attributively and are not used predicatively at all, as the idea of condition or state which lies in the uninflected predicate adjective ill accords with the meaning of the subject, but they are often used in the predicate in attributive form, which, as we have seen in *Note* 1, is a favorite type of predication: **(1)** Derivatives in **-lich** when the subject contains a verbal stem and regularly adjectives in **-er:** not **Die Zusammenkunft war nächtlich,** but **eine nächtliche (Zusammenkunft** understood). **Berliner Porzellan,** but according to **245.** II. **10.** 1. *b* **Das ist Berlinisch. (2)** Adjectives in **-en, -ern** made from names of materials: **golden** golden, **hölzern** wooden. In elevated diction and in figurative language, however, these adjectives are also used in the predicate. See **245.** II. 3. *c*. **(3)** Adjectives in **-ig** derived from adverbs of time and place: **heutig** *of to-day*, from **heute; damalig** *of that time*, from **damals; dortig** *of that place*, from **dort.** Not **Diese Zeitung ist hiesig,** but **Dies ist die hiesige Zeitung** This is the newspaper of this place. **(4)** All relative superlatives and the comparatives in **117.** 2, all of which are used only attributively and require an article before them, the noun being expressed or understood: Not **Karl ist jüngst,** but **der jüngste. Die vordern Zimmer** the front rooms. **Dies sind die vordern Zimmer. (5)** When the subject is a verbal noun: **Die Verbreitung des Buches ist eine schnelle. (6)** A present participle can only be used in the predicate when it has the force of an adjective. See **182.** 1. A. *b*. It cannot now as formerly be used here with pure verbal force. It can, however, be freely used in the predicate as elsewhere in attributive form: **Das ganze Verfahren ist ein durchaus den Gesetzen widersprechendes.** The constructions **(5)** and **(6)** show clearly that the old attributive type of sentence described in 1. *b. Note* above is still a favorite and is always reappearing in somewhat altered modern form, even where, as here, the modern type with a finite verb of complete predication is in common use: **Das Buch hat sich schnell verbreitet. Das ganze Verfahren widerspricht durchaus den Gesetzen.**

Note 3. On the other hand, a number of adjectives can only be used as a predicate complement. See **111.** 7. *c*.

b. In the nom. as predicate appositive. See **1.** *c* above and **104.** 2. A. *b*, C, D.

c. Instead of the simple nom. construction the predicate is in certain instances, as in case of nouns, introduced by **als** and **für: Er gilt als der beste von allen. Er wurde für unwürdig erklärt** He was pronounced unworthy. **Er blieb für tot liegen** He was left for dead. **Er gilt für tot.** The predicate appositive is often introduced by **als: Mein Freund hat als enterbt keine Mittel mehr.**

C. The predicate complement may be a pronoun in the nom.: **Sein Glück ist meines. Er bleibt derselbe. Das Pferd ist ein Säugetier; der Walfisch ist es (129.** 2. C. **(4)) auch.**

a. In Swiss dialect the personal pronouns are frequently in the acc. when used as predicate: **Seid Ihr ihn etwa selbst?** (J. Gotthelf's *Uli der Pächter*, 76). **Seht, da ist es ihn ja selber** (Spitteler's *Conrad*, p. 52). Compare with popular English: *It is me, us.*

D. An infinitive:

a. Without **zu,** used as a predicate or to complete the meaning of the predicate after the verbs enumerated in **185.** B. **I.** 1. *b*: **Er bleibt stehen.**

b. With **zu,** used as predicate:

(1) With passive and modal force in case of transitives, as described in **180.** A.

(2) Also the infinitive of intransitives and reflexives is used in the predicate with this same modal meaning but with active force. See **185.** A. I. 1. *b* **(2).**

(3) After certain verbs the prepositional infinitive is used in the predicate without modal force. See **185.** A. I. 1. *b* (3) and (4).

E. An adverb or prepositional phrase: **Die Schule ist aus. Die Tür ist zu. Gott ist überall. Das Fest ist heute. Wann ist das Schauspiel? Die Mühe war umsonst. Wie ist das Bier? Er ist hier. Er ist zu Hause. Es ist alles in Ordnung.** In many cases the verb **sein** here has concrete force, as in **Das Fest ist heute = findet heute statt,** but this force is so faint that the form is felt as a mere copula and like the copula may often be suppressed: **Alles in Ordnung. Niemand hier?**

Also the predicate appositive often appears in the form of a prepositional phrase: **Die Feinde zogen sich in guter Ordnung zurück.**

F. A clause: **Du bist nicht mehr, der du warst. Nicht jeder scheint, was er ist.**

Agreement between Subject and Predicate.

253. The predicate agrees with the subject in number, and where it is possible in person, gender, and case.

I. Number.

1. If the subject is singular, the verb is also sing.: **Das kleinste Haar wirft seinen Schatten.**

a. Often in speaking *to* and sometimes also *of* persons of relatively higher social or official standing, the verb is in the pl., tho the subject is in the sing.: **General Manteuffel schreibt mir eben, daß Seine Majestät der König die Gnade gehabt haben, Dir diese Auszeichnung zu verleihen** (Moltke an den Neffen Henry, March 22, 1864). **Seine Majestät der Deutsche Kaiser, König von Preußen, haben das nachstehende Handschreiben vom 26. Juni dieses Jahres allergnädigst an mich zu richten geruht** (König Ludwig von Bayern, July 5, 1915). (zu Edith) **Gnädiges Fräulein hatten mir doch versprochen, mir das letzte Bild zu zeigen, das Sie gemalt haben** (Fulda's *Das verlorene Paradies,* 1, 5). **Wollen Herr Kommerzienrat wirklich diese Nacht noch zurückfahren?** (Hartleben's *Rosenmontag,* 2. 3, where a first lieutenant addresses respectfully a visiting 'Kommerzienrat'). **An Seine Exzellenz den preußischen Ministerpräsidenten Hirsch: Herr Ministerpräsident haben die Berliner Studenten, die Hindenburg huldigten, als unreife Burschen bezeichnet usw.** (telegram of Hamburg students to the Prussian minister in Nov. 1919). **Die gnädige Frau sind ausgefahren** (language of a servant) My mistress has gone out driving. It is difficult to define usage here accurately. Sturdy independent natures resist this servile style, while others, as on the one hand servants, and on the other hand persons that move in circles dominated by official or social formalities, employ it to show their respect and deference to superiors, or use it in general as a mere mark of esteem or politeness. It is sometimes used in mock-respectful tone: **Herr Doktor wurden da katechisiert** (Goethe's *Faust,* l. 3523).

b. If the **dies, das, jenes, es,** or **welches** used in expressions of identity is subject, the verb agrees with the predicate. See **128.** A. ***a*; 129.** 2. C. **(1)** and **251.** I. 3; **141.** 9. *a*; **148.** *a*.

c. The grammatical subject **es** has no influence over the number, the verb agreeing with the logical subject: **Es zogen drei Bursche(n) wohl über den Rhein.**

d. If a subject in the sing. is associated, by means of the preps. **mit** *with,* **samt** *together with,* **nebst** *along with,* **auf** *upon,* **nach** *after,* with other words which logically tho not formally constitute a part of the subject, the verb is in the sing.: **Das Schiff samt der Ladung und Mannschaft ging zu Grunde. Moses nebst seinem Bruder Aaron stieg auf den Berg Sinai. Schlag auf Schlag folgte. Ein Tag nach dem andern verstrich.** The pl. is also sometimes found after the first three of these prepositions in accordance with older usage as explained in **229.** 2, under **nebst,** (*b*).

e. German usage often differs markedly from the English where the predicate consists of the copula **sein** *to be* and a predicate noun. In German where the subject for the sake of emphasis stands at or near the end of the sentence the copula agrees with the subject in number: **Das einzige Düstere auf dem ganzen Gewässer waren die schwarzen Schwäne auf dem See. Der Hauptfluch sind Steuern.** In these examples the noun in the nominative that stands after the copula seems to be the subject, while the nominative before the copula seems to be the predicate, but in many similar sentences it is often difficult to distinguish subject and predicate, sometimes even so difficult that thoroly trained scholars differ in their decisions. If one of the nominatives is a plural it becomes necessary to decide this difficult question. In German the tendency here is to avoid a decision on this perplexing point by regulating the number of the copula by a mere formal principle, namely as the nominative after the copula is often the subject it has become the rule to place the copula in accord with the following plural nominative whether it be a subject or a predicate: **Der Hauptmangel sind Bücher** (subject) The chief want is books. **Alles, was du anbringst, sind nur leere Entschuldigungen** (predicate) All the things that you bring forward are mere empty excuses. As can be seen by the English translations the number of the English copula is also regulated by a mere formal rule, namely the nominative before the copula is construed as subject whether it be in fact the subject or the predicate, and the copula is accordingly made to agree with it. In German we often find the copula in the sing. where several nouns after it indicate a distinct collective idea or a single noun in the plural is felt as containing the idea of a fixed amount, extent, or mass: **Seine speise aber war Hewschrecken und wild** (now **wilder**) **Honig** (Matth. III. 4) His meat was locusts and wild honey. **Es ist** (viewed collectively) or **sind** (viewed individually) **sechs Jahre, daß ich hier wohne. Eine Krone ist** (or **sind**) **zehn Mark.**

If the nominative after the copula is in the singular, the copula more commonly agrees with the nominative before it: **Gerötete Augen sind ein Zeichen innerer Erregung.**

f. If the subject is sing. in form but has several adjective modifiers which do not qualify the one thing but each a different thing, the verb is in the pl.: **Die nördliche und südliche Hälfte scheinen unter gleichen Breitegraden ungefähr dieselbe Erdkrümmung darzubieten** The northern and southern hemispheres appear to have about the same curvature on the same parallels.

g. A collective noun or pronoun, or noun of multitude in the sing. now usually requires the verb in the sing: **Das Heer ist versammelt. Das kleine Volk lief voraus. Der Rat** (council) **ist in seinen Ansichten geteilt. Vieh grast auf den Dünen. Beides ist richtig** *Both* (i.e. *both points, both views*) *are correct,* but **Beide haben recht** *Both* (i.e. *both persons*) *are right.* **Am Sonnabend war es kaum sieben Uhr, als bereits das Ehepaar Bennecke erschien** (Wildenbruch's *Schwester-Seele,* chap. XV). The earlier part of the period was not so completely under the domination of grammatical rule as the present. Luther frequently uses the plural here, or places the first verb in the sing. and all following ones in the plural: **Aber das Volck | so (153.** 5) **jren Gott kennen | werden sich ermannen** (Dan. xi. 32). **Vnd alles Kriegsuolck das bey jm war zoch hinauff | vnd tratten [h]erzu | vnd kamen gegen die Stad** (Josh. viii. 11). The plural of a verb still occurs here in the classical period, but much more rarely: **Wie eine rasende Menge mit Stäben, Beilen, Hämmern, Leitern, Stricken versehen, von wenig Bewaffneten begleitet, erst Kapellen, Kirchen und Klöster anfallen, die Andächtigen verjagen** (Goethe's *Egmont,* 1, 2). In our time the plural here is quite rare in the literary language, and perhaps only found in a relative clause referring back to a collective noun, where it is also rare: **Endlich teilte sich das Volk in eine rauhere Partei, welche . . . gerne nunmehr nachgeholt hätten, was, wie sie meinten, bei der Eroberung des Landes versäumt worden und die Italier für ihren heimlichen Haß mit offener Gewalt zu strafen begehrten** (Felix Dahn's *Ein Kampf um Rom*). The older freedom of usage here is preserved in English: *The Council is* or *are of the opinion that,* &c.

If, however, a noun in the gen. pl., or a dat. pl. after **von,** or an appositive in the pl. follows the collective noun, the verb may be in the pl.: **Dort hatten sich eine Masse chinesischer Fruchtverkäufer angesammelt. Eine Menge Äpfel lagen unter dem Baume.** The plural is also found after a singular noun that follows the plural **deren: In einem Aufsatze bespricht Gustav A. Erdmann diese Frage zwar eingehend, aber doch nur von einem einzigen Gesichtspunkte aus, während deren eine ganze Reihe sind** (v. Duvernoy in *Deutsche Monatsschrift,* April, 1906, p. 105). Also the singular can be used here, and in general the rule can be laid down that the use of the sing. and pl. depends upon whether the subject presents itself to the mind in the form of a closed mass or group, or as individuals: **Ein Schwarm Bienen flog auf,** but **Eine Menge Hasen wurden geschossen** (one at a time).

If a plural predicate noun follows collective **was** the principal verb is in the plural. **Früh übt sich, was ein Meister werden will,** but **Was ehrliche Mörder sind, werden dich unter sich nicht dulden** (Lessing's *Emilia Galotti*, 3, 8).

Note 1. In the case of **ein Paar, ein Dutzend** there is a difference of meaning involved, the pl. verb denoting an indefinite number, the sing. an exact number—*two, twelve*: **Ein paar** (a few) **Häuser sind abgebrannt,** but **Draußen wartet ein Paar auf die Trauung. Es kamen uns ein Dutzend** (a number) **Husaren entgegen,** but **Das Dutzend Zigarren kostet 1 Mark.**

Note 2. The indefinite numerals **viel, wenig, mehr,** and **genug** were in early N.H.G. used as sing. neuter substantives, often with a dependent partitive gen., and accordingly when used as subject could have a sing. verb even tho the reference was to a number of persons or things, while later usage requires here quite uniformly a plural verb: **Wenn der gerechten viel ist | frewet sich das volck** (Proverbs xxix, 2), but **Aber diesem Rufe folgten heute nur wenig** [see **139.** 3. *i*, *Note*] (Fontane's *Quitt*, chap. 6). Luther also employed the plural here: **Sintemal sich's viel vnterwunden haben** (Luke i. 1). **Denn es sind viel falscher Propheten ausgegangen in die Welt** (1 John iv. 1).

Mehr als ein + a sing. subject may be used with a sing. or pl. verb: **Mehr als ein Fall ist bekannt,** or **Es sind mehr als ein Fall bekannt.** The sing. is more common.

The plural is employed after the subject **was** when modified by a plural partitive genitive and used in connection with the adverb **mehr** *besides, else*: **zwei Schultheißen, vier Venner** (formerly an official in Swiss cities) **und was der Würden mehr waren** (Boßhart's *Die Barettlitochter*, p. 32).

h. **Nichts als** before a pl. noun is always found with a pl. verb as it simply has the force of **nur: eine Fabrik, in welcher nichts als Nähnadeln gemacht werden.**

2. If the subject is pl., or if there are several subjects, the verb is pl.: **Die Kinder bedürfen der Aufsicht. Gut und Ehre vermögen viel über die Menschen. Der Pastor wie der Verwalter eilten zu ihren Berufsgeschäften.**

a. If there are several sing. subjects, the verb *may* agree with the nearest one, provided it does not thus stand after them all, in which case it is usually pl.: **Mein Bruder kommt heute und meine Schwester,** but **Mein Bruder und meine Schwester kommen heute. Nu aber bleibt Glaube | Hoffnung | Liebe | diese drey** (1 Cor. xiii. 13). There is now a strong tendency here to use the plural in accordance with strict formal principles: **Da lagen der Taufschein, der Paß und der Totenschein ihrer Mutter** (Schubin's *Refugium peccatorum*, III). The verb must, however, be in the sing., even when it follows the different subjects, if for any reason it is expressly desired to associate the activity implied in the verb with each subject separately, as, for instance, to denote consecutiveness, to indicate a contrast, or to present the subjects as individuals: **Da hebet sich's schwanenweiß, | und ein Arm und ein glänzender Nacken wird bloß** (Schiller's *Der Taucher*) There out of the water something white as a swan raises itself and an arm is seen and then a glittering neck. **Der Thron, zu dessen Rechten der Raja, ihm gegenüber meine Wenigkeit Platz nahm** The throne at the right of which the rajah seated himself and opposite to him my humble self. **„Woher aber dann die beiden Kinder?" „Ich weiß nur, daß es ein Knabe und ein Mädchen ist von etwa acht und zehn Jahren"** (Ertl's *Der Handschuh*).

b. If the subjects are in part sing., in part pl., the verb if pl. should be so placed that it will not follow a sing. subject, or if the sing. verb be preferred it should precede a sing. subject: **Das alte Theben** (Thebes) **und seine Trümmer sind tausendmal beschrieben worden. Er sagte ihnen zum Trost, daß er es ihnen überließe, unter sich auszumachen, welcher dableiben und welche** (pl.) **wandern sollten** (Gottfried Keller's *Die Leute von Seldwyla*, I, p. 239). **Wer weiß, ob nicht morgen schon dein innigstes Sehnen dahin geht, es möge Pech, Schwefel und Quadersteine auf die Teilnehmer, die Mitwirkenden an deiner großen Feier herabregnen** (Raabe's *Der Dräumling*, XIII).

c. In the case that several co-ordinate *singular* subjects are felt as forming a distinct collective idea, a close union or oneness of idea, the sing. verb may be used: **Haus und Hof ist verkauft. Lob und Dank sei dem Herrn. Freude und Jubel schallt uns entgegen. Arm und Reich ist** (or **sind**) **im Tode gleich,** but always **Die Armen und die Reichen sind im Tode gleich. Es kamen Tage, an denen die Arbeit, die Sorge zu viel und zu groß war** (R. Voss's *Psyche*, chap. 7). Two subjects can express a oneness of idea if they are opposites or complements of each other, and thus show one idea in all its range of meanings from the two extremes: **Weil ich weiß, was ein guter Wandel nicht bloß vor Gott, sondern auch vor den Menschen bedeutet und daß Glück und Unglück daran**

hängt (Fontane's *Quitt*, chap. 7). Of course the verb is in the pl. if such words are considered separately: **Denn hier sind Recht und Unrecht nah verwandt** (Goethe's *Tasso*, 2, 4). **Gut und böse streiten wunderlich in dir** (Frenssen's *Das Heimatsfest*, 3, 1).

Opposed to the usage described above is a formal principle which requires strict grammatical agreement: **Unauslöschlicher Groll und Gram erfüllten jeden Winkel ihrer Seele** (Isolde Kurz's *Das Vermächtnis der Tante Susanne*).

The sing. is also used in case of a general or indefinite reference: **Keiner und keine bleibe daheim** (Rosegger). **Diesen hier mußte wohl jeder und jede schön finden** (Spielhagen's *Freigeboren*, p. 148).

d. If a single pl. subject or several sing. or pl. subjects are felt as forming the idea of a firm mass or fixed amount, the verb is in the sing.: **Es wurde nur fünf Prozent (96. 4. 1) der Masse gerettet. 10 Pfennig (96. 4. 1) ist mehr als 5 Pfennig. Ein Kilo und 327 Gramm ist** (not **sind**) **genug. Zweimal zwei ist vier. Zwei Mark und noch 2 Mark sind** or **ist 4 Mark. Zwei Taler und 4 Groschen sind** or **ist genug. Drei Viertel des Buches ist der Insel Java gewidmet,** but **Drei Viertel der Schiffbrüchigen wurden gerettet.** Here the plural of the verb is used wherever instead of the conception of oneness the idea of two or more distinct units of the same order occur to the mind, but not if one unit of one order and a number of a lower order (as in the third example) are used and the reference is to a firm mass. There is, however, a distinct tendency here to use the plural on mere formal grounds: **Sechs Siebentel des Buches werden von einem Wörterverzeichnis eingenommen** (Jellinek's *Geschichte der neuhochdeutschen Grammatik*, I, p. 167). Contrary to English usage the German says: **Es waren zehn Grad Kälte** It was ten degrees below the freezing-point.

Of course, the verb is in the singular if the plural subject does not indicate a number of objects but is a mere grammatical form: **Stühle ist der Plural von Stuhl.**

e. In case several subjects are followed by a neut. pronoun which refers to the previously mentioned subjects collectively or distributively, the verb is in the sing.: **Die Öffnungen der Mauer, die soliden Stellen derselben, die Pfeiler, jedes hatte seinen besonderen Charakter. Seine fortgesetzte Aufmerksamkeit, ohne daß er zudringlich gewesen wäre; sein treuer Beistand bei verschiedenen unangenehmen Zufällen; sein gegen ihre Eltern zwar ausgesprochenes, doch ruhiges und nur hoffnungsvolles Werben, da sie freilich noch sehr jung war: das alles nahm sie für ihn ein.**

f. In connection with the conjunctions **oder** *or*, **entweder — oder** *either — or*, **weder — noch** *neither — nor*, **sowohl — als** *both — and, as well — as*, **nicht allein** (or **bloß** or **nur**) **— sondern auch** *not only — but also*, **nicht sowohl — als vielmehr** *not so much — as*, **desgleichen** *likewise*, **wie auch** *as also, and*, **teils — teils** *partly — partly*, &c., the different subjects are usually considered singly and hence the verb agrees with one of them—the next one to it—and is understood with the others: **Werden Ihr Bruder und Ihre Schwester kommen? Nein, beide können sie nicht kommen, aber jedenfalls wird mein Bruder oder meine Schwester kommen. Sowohl meine Schwestern wie auch mein Bruder wird kommen,** or more smoothly **Sowohl meine Schwestern werden kommen, wie auch mein Bruder. Nicht allein mein Bruder, sondern auch meine Schwester wird kommen. Nicht mein Bruder kommt, sondern meine Schwester. Nicht meine Brüder, sondern meine Schwester kommt. Nicht meine Schwester, sondern meine Brüder kommen. Nicht sowohl die alten Anschauungen der Römer in Stadt und Land als vielmehr das Wohlergehen der außeritalischen Provinzen war für die Politik der römischen Kaiser maßgebend. Zur Reise fehlte mir teils Zeit, teils Lust, teils Geld.**

After all these conjunctions except such as **oder, entweder — oder, nicht — sondern,** which positively exclude the statement in the one proposition or the other, the verb can also be in the pl., as that which is predicated of one subject applies to them all: **Sowohl meine Schwester als auch mein Bruder werden kommen. Weder meine Schwester noch mein Bruder werden kommen.**

Weder der Kaiser noch der Kanzler kann (neither of them alone) or **können** (both of them together) **das verhindern.** Even after **oder,** the pl. of the verb may be used, if the strict exclusive force of the conjunction disappears and it takes on the meaning of **und: Wolf oder Bär kommen selten davon, wenn ein Lappe ihnen aufs Blatt hält.**

g. If the subject of the sentence is the name of a book, play, newspaper, or boat, consisting of a pl. noun or several nouns, the verb is sometimes in the sing., more commonly in the pl., the former, however, regularly when the subject is a couple of proper names linked by **und** and not preceded by a pl. article, or when the predicate is a noun in the nom. sing., even tho the subject is preceded by a pl. article: **Heute wurden Schillers Räuber aufgeführt. „Die Hamburger Nachrichten" erscheinen täglich dreimal,** but the names of English newspapers are sometimes treated as singulars, as in English, as illustrated in **96. 1. Die „Zwei Gebrüder"** (name of boat) **hatten die Hohewegsbalje bereits erreicht** (Hermann Rückner's *Küstenfahrer,* I). But: **In der Klasse wird Hermann und Dorothea gelesen. Die Räuber ist der Titel von Schillers erstem Drama.**

h. If the subject is accompanied by explanatory words in the appositional construction, the verb may agree strictly with the grammatical subject or often agrees with the appositive, when this more vividly represents the idea contained in the subject than the subject itself: **Viel trägt dazu bei, daß alles, was zum Hause gehört, also Eheleute und Ehehalten** (servants), **nun für einige Monate zusammenbleiben kann** (v. Hörmann). **Meine Kinderjahre, die schöne, unvergeßliche Zeit, verfloß mir als Berliner Schusterjungen** — Rodenberg.

i. A plural subject or several subjects in the nominative absolute construction found in subject clauses do not influence the number of the verb, which is invariably in the sing., as the reference is to a single idea. See **265.** B. *b.* **(2),** 2nd paragraph.

j. A few originally pl. nouns are now often felt as singular, and hence the verb is often, perhaps more commonly, in the sing. when such words are used as subjects. See **96. 1.**

k. Notice the difference of conception between German and English in the following sentence: **Zwei Tage Aufenthalt genügten, ihn erkennen zu lassen, daß usw.** A two days' stay was sufficient, &c.

3. The predicate noun agrees with the subject in number: **Kleobis und Biton waren Brüder.**

a. The predicate noun does not agree with the subject in number if it is a name of a material, or a collective or abstract noun: **Ihr seid das Salz der Erde. Die Franzosen sind ein romanisches Volk. Gute Kinder sind die Freude ihrer Eltern.**

In a number of cases the predicate noun may be in the sing. or pl., according as it is desired to give expression to the abstract idea of quality or the concrete one of different individuals: **Beide Brüder sind Soldat** or **Soldaten.** Concrete nouns often assume abstract meaning in the predicate by uniting with the verb to form a single idea. For examples see **94.** 1. *e.*

b. Also the interrogative pronouns **wer** and **was** do not agree with the subject when they are used as predicate, but remain uniformly in the sing.: **Wer waren diese Leute? Was sind diese Männer?**

c. When the subject is the polite form of the personal pronoun, which is really 3rd pers. pl. in form, tho it is used as 2nd pers. sing., the predicate stands in the sing. if the reference is to a singular subject: **Sie, mein Herr, waren mein Retter.**

d. The predicate does not agree in number with the subjects **dies, das, jenes, es, welches** used in expressions of identity. See **128.** A. *a*; **129.** 2. C. **(1)**; **141.** 9. *a*; **148.** *a.*

II. Person.

The verb agrees with its subject in person. If there are several subjects of different persons the following rules are usually followed:

1. If the subjects are connected by **und,** or by conjunctions of kindred force as **sowohl — als** (or **wie**) *both — and, as well — as,* **wie auch,** or **sowie** *as also,* the first person has the preference over the second and third, and the second person the preference over the third, and often a pronoun comprehending the different subjects is added: **Ich und du haben gleiche Schicksale,** or **Ich und du, wir haben gleiche Schicksale. Du und dein Bruder seid meine Freunde,** or **Du und dein Bruder, ihr seid meine Freunde. Ich sowohl wie du sind das gewohnt. Sowohl ich als mein Freund, wir sind dafür verantwortlich. Ich fürchte, er wie ich sind zu lange fortgeblieben.** Occasionally the third person is preferred: **Ich weiß, daß du und mein Vater in Krieg verwickelt sind** (Börne).

a. If sing. subjects are connected by **sowohl — als** (or **wie**), **wie auch, sowie,** it is also common for the verb to agree with the first subject in the sing., even tho it stands after both, especially if the emphasis is upon the first subject: **Ich sowohl wie du bin** (or **sind** or **wir sind**) **es gewohnt. Du sowohl wie ich bist** (or **sind** or **wir sind**) **es gewohnt,** but usually **Du und ich** (**wir**) **sind es gewohnt.**

b. Sometimes in case of subjects connected by **und** the verb is in the sing., agreeing with the nearest subject: **In dieser Sache irrst du und ich. Ich und alle Welt erkennt das an.**

2. If different subjects of different persons are opposed, or in contrast to each other, or are considered separately, the verb agrees in person and number with the nearest subject: **Du bist es gewohnt, nicht ich,** or **Du, nicht ich bin es gewohnt. Weder du bist es gewohnt noch ich,** or **Weder du noch ich bin es gewohnt,** or **Weder du noch ich sind es gewohnt. Du oder ich müßte** (ought) **es gewohnt sein. Ich oder du müßtest es gewohnt sein. Nicht nur ich sondern auch du bist es gewohnt. Teils unser Freund, teils ich, teils du bist daran schuld. Teils unser Freund, teils du, teils ich bin daran schuld.** Sometimes the verb agrees with the first subject if the statement only holds good for it: **Ein alt Gesetz, nicht ich, gebietet dir** (Goethe's *Iphigenie,* 5, 3). It also agrees with the first subject if the following subjects are regarded as only explanatory: **Keiner von uns, weder du noch ich, ist es gewohnt** (D. Sanders).

3. If the subject is a noun or a pronoun and the predicate a personal pronoun, the verb agrees with the predicate in *person* and *number*: **Der Mann, von dem Sie sprechen, bin ich. Ich bin es** It is I. For further examples see **128.** A. *a*; **129.** 2. C. (**1**); **141.** 9. *a* and **251.** I. 3; **148.** *a*. See also **151.** 3. B. *c*, toward the close of the article.

4. The person and number of the verb in relative clauses present several idiomatic peculiarities that are considered at length in **151.** 3. B. *a*, *b*, *c*.

III. Gender.

1. The predicate noun does not in general agree with the subject in gender, as it has its own gender: **Sein Tun ist der Ausdruck seiner Liebe.**

2. The predicate noun can assume a grammatical form in accordance with the natural sex of the person represented by the subject in only one case—when the subject represents a person or something that is personified. Then the predicate noun may take a masc. form if the subject is represented as a male and a fem. form if the subject is represented as a female, provided, however, such forms are elsewhere in common use for persons (see **245.** I. 6. 2): **Gott ist mein Zeuge. Hunger ist der beste Koch. Das Unglück ist der beste Lehrmeister. Das Mädchen wird Erzieherin. Das ist unsere Freundin. Sie ist eine gemeine Diebin. Die Geschichte ist eine Lehrerin der Menschheit** (Herbart). **Die Natur war die erste Erzieherin des Menschen. Die Nationalbank ist Inhaberin des Wechsels.** In the fourth sentence the natural sex, not the grammatical gender of the subject, has influenced the gender of the predicate, while in the second sentence and the last three the grammatical gender of the subjects has suggested the form of the predicate, as things have no sex. In

the third sentence the subject is a neuter noun which cannot suggest sex at all, and thus the mind is free here to select a gender according to fancy.

a. The predicate noun does not assume a fem. form to agree with a fem. subject when it is the abstract idea pure and simple, devoid of all reference to sex and its attributes, that is before the mind: (Maria Stuart speaking to Queen Elizabeth) **Regierte Recht, so läget ihr vor mir | im Staube jetzt, denn ich bin Euer König** (Schiller). **O die, die könnt' General sein** (Auerbach's *Dorfgeschichten*, 7, p. 175). **Die Frau ist hier Herr und Meister im Hause. Meine Mutter konnte ihres Verdrusses nicht Herr und Meister werden. Die Bibel ist unser bester Führer auf unserm Lebenswege. Die Eile ist ein schlechter Berater.** But the force of the gender of the subject often asserts itself even here, especially when the predicate has inflected modifiers before it: **Sie wußte ihre Überraschung zu verbergen und war die unumschränkte Herrin ihrer Gebärden** (Raabe's *Im alten Eisen*, xiii). Some words, however, as **Gast, Kerl, Mensch,** have regularly the masc. form for reference to females as well as males, as the idea of sex is not felt: **Alles in allem, sie ist ein guter Kerl** (Spielhagen's *Frei geboren*, p. 378). **Agnes, mein' Tochter, hör' mal zu . . . Du bist ein vernünftiger Mensch** (Sudermann's *Fritzchen*, 2). **Professor, Arzt,** and **Doktor** may retain in the predicate relation the masculine form with reference to females, but the feminine form is also used: **Sie ist Doktor der Philosophie. Sie ist der beste weibliche Arzt** or **die beste Ärztin in der Stadt.**

If an adjective or pronoun is used in the predicate substantively referring to the abstract idea contained in some preceding adjective or noun, the neuter gender is used: **Mein Bruder ist reich, was ich nicht bin. Es ist wahr, Bräutigam und Deichhauptmann sind fast** incompatible; **aber wenn ich letzteres nicht wäre, wüßte ich doch gar nicht, wer es sein sollte** (Bismarck to his betrothed, Feb. 23, 1847). **Er** (i.e. **Cäsar**) **war ein großer Redner, Schriftsteller und Feldherr, aber jedes davon ist er nur geworden, weil er ein vollendeter Staatsmann war** (Mommsen's *Römische Geschichte*, V, chap. xi).

IV. Case.

The predicate word agrees with the subject in case, and thus both stand in the nominative: **Erst wenn ich auf die Berge komme, da werd' ich so recht ich selbst** (Wilbrandt's *Die gute Lorelei*, vi). For an exceptional usage in Switzerland see **252.** 2. C. *a*. The adjective here in general loses its inflection except in the superlative. In an earlier period the predicate adjective agreed with the subject in gender and case in all the degrees of comparison. Fossil remnants of this former usage still exist. See **111.** 8. Sometimes (see **252.** 2. A. *c*) a prep. phrase or a gen. stands in the relation of a predicate adjective, just as they often stand in the relation of an attributive adjective: **Der Ring ist von Gold** (instead of **golden**). **Er ist unsrer Gesinnung** (instead of **gesinnt wie wir**). **Er gilt ärztlich nicht für ersten Ranges** (Fontane's *Effi*, chap. xxiii).

Subordinate Elements of a Sentence.

254. The subordinate elements of a sentence are called modifiers. They are divided into the following general classes:

1. *Attributive adjective modifiers*, which modify a noun or pronoun.
2. Modifiers of the verb, adjective, and adverb, which fall into two classes—*objective* and *adverbial modifiers*.
3. *Independent elements*, which are not related grammatically to other parts of the sentence.

Attributive Adjective Modifiers.

255. Attributive adjective modifiers are treated as follows:

I. Attributive Adjective and Participle.

Attributive adjectives and participles modify nouns and pronouns and agree with them in *gender*, *number*, and *case*, except when used without an article or other limiting adjective in the appositive relation, in which case they remain uninflected: **Der fleißige Knabe lernt. Der blühende Rosenstrauch duftet. Der beleidigte Freund verzeiht. Ein gutes Buch ist eine nützliche Gesellschaft.** Appositive adjectives: **Durch ein Gebirge, w ü s t und l e e r, wie die Erde beim Beginn der Schöpfung,** but **Friedrich der Große.** As explained more fully in **104.** 2. B the appositive form is not so common in German as in English. In German the adjective or participle often stands before the noun where in English it *must* follow the noun: **diese mißlungene, weil überstürzte Arbeit.**

a. Repetition of Adjective and Article. When an adjective modifies two or more nouns having different genders or representing different persons or things, the strict grammatical rule requires the repetition of the adjective before each noun: **mit solchem Eifer und solcher Beständigkeit, Wörterbuch der deutschen und der französischen Sprache.** This rule would often require tiresome repetitions, and hence is in familiar conversation and even in serious discourse frequently disregarded when no ambiguity would arise: **großer Schmerz und Angst** instead of **großer Schmerz und große Angst; mit seiner gewöhnlichen Trockenheit und Ernst** (Goethe); **ein geweihtes Barett und Degen** (Becker); **den ersten besten Knüppel und Holzscheit** (Raabe); **mit einem verzerrten Lächeln, in dem geheimer Grimm und Scham sich deutlich genug ausprägten** (Marriot).

The simple article and limiting adjectives are not in such cases so easily suppressed as descriptive adjectives, and are more commonly repeated, even in familiar style: **Der König und die Kaiserin. Eigenes Haus und** [descriptive adjective not repeated] **Kindersegen erschien dem römischen Bürger als das Ziel und der** [article repeated] **Kern des Lebens** (Mommsen's *Römische Geschichte*, I, chap. v). Frequently, however, in case of the def. art. each noun may drop its article, and thus the awkward repetition may be avoided: **Eingang zu Garten und Kegelbahn** instead of **zu dem Garten und zu der Kegelbahn; zwischen Weichsel und Bug** (*Großes Hauptquartier*, Aug. 7, 1915) instead of **zwischen der Weichsel und dem Bug** (rivers); **zwischen oberer Weichsel und Bug** (ib., Aug. 1, 1915). This is especially the case, as in the preceding examples, when the nouns are connected by **und.** The article, however, cannot be suppressed here if its demonstrative force becomes prominent, as for instance where it points to a following restrictive relative clause: **Möchte das schöne Buch, das uns Grimm geschenkt, überall mit der Wärme und dem Ernst aufgenommen werden, mit denen es geschrieben ist** (Wilhelm Bölsche in *Deutsche Rundschau*, December 1895, p. 472). The simple indefinite article is rarely omitted: **Er kaufte eine Taube, eine Gans und einen Hasen.** If the different nouns each take a definite article or limiting adjective of the same form, it is usually felt as necessary to use it but once: **die Gnade, Weisheit und Liebe Gottes; die Dramen des Äschylus und Sophokles, des Shakespeare und Schiller; das Mündungsgebiet der Elbe, Weser, und Jade; ein wahres Musterbild des Friedens, der Ordnung und Sauberkeit; die Lehrer und Schüler.** While this usage is the rule where the persons and things represented by the different nouns stand in similar relations the repetition of the article or limiting adjective is usually felt as necessary when the persons or things stand in unlike or contrasting relations: **Die Griechen und Römer hatten besondere Formen für den Ruffall** (Eduard Engel's *Gutes Deutsch*, p. 91) *had especial case forms for direct address*, but **die Griechen und die Römer haben Kriege miteinander geführt** (ib.) and **der Fuchs und der Hase leben in Feindschaft miteinander** (ib.). If the nouns are in different numbers it is now usual to repeat the article or limiting adjective: **die Mutter und die Schwestern; die Gesellschaft seiner Mutter und seiner Schwestern; die Anordnung seiner Bibliothek und seiner Gesellschaftszimmer.**

If the article modifies two nouns both representing the same person or thing, or parts of a whole, it should only be used once, while, on the other hand, if the nouns represent different persons or things which it is desired to contrast or to mark especially as distinct and separate, the article should be repeated before each noun: **Die Schuld trifft allein den Pfarrer und Ortsschulinspektor N.** (one person), but **Leider muß der Deutsche Berlin und München einander noch als die politische und die künstlerische Hauptstadt des Reiches gegenüberstellen** and **Der Pfarrer und der Schultheiß** (two persons) **leben öfters miteinander in Uneinigkeit. Die deutsche und die englische Sprache,** but **der erste und zweite Vers des Gedichts.** For more detailed account of usage here see **96. 11.**

Where two adjectives modify the same noun, which is, however, in a different number in each instance, the noun need only be expressed once, as the modifying adjectives clearly indicate the number: **Dieser und ähnliche Aufrufe.**

b. Nouns not Used with Adjective Force in German. One of the marked features in English is the great freedom with which nouns, adverbs, phrases, and sentences can stand before a noun in adjective function. In German every attributive element that stands before a noun must assume adjective form if it has adjective meaning and function. Corresponding to many of the peculiar English adjectives that have adjective force but not adjective form there are in German adjectives with adjective form. In many other cases these peculiar English adjectives must be rendered by attributive elements that stand *after* the governing noun in the form of a prepositional phrase, a genitive, an adverb, a clause, or they must be translated by compounds or group-words (**247.** 2). The following examples will illustrate the characteristic differences between English and German expression here: a bàby bóy **ein männlicher Säugling,** a bòy lóver **ein jùgendlicher Líebhaber,** the pòet philósopher **der dìchtende Philosóph,** the Schmìdt résidence **die Schmidtsche Wóhnung,** the abòve remárks **die òbigen Bemérkungen,** a clòckwork tóy **ein Spìelzeug mit Úhrwerk,** an up-to-dàte díctionary **ein Wòrterbuch neuesten Dátums** or **ein Wörterbuch, das auf der Höhe der Zeit steht,** my nèxt-door néighbor **mein nàchster Háusnachbar** or **mein Nàchbar nebenán,** a quarter past sèven tráin, **ein Viertelàchtzùg,** the ùnderground ráilroad **die Úntergrundbàhn.**

In *all* the English groups in the preceding paragraph the chief stress rests upon the last member, i.e. descriptive stress (**50.** A. 6) prevails. Descriptive stress is also characteristic of the German groups except in case of the group-words, which have the principal stress upon the first member and hence have distinguishing or classifying stress (**50.** A. 6), altho they often have pronounced descriptive force as the corresponding English expressions. In these German group-words survives a bit of the older life of both English and German when group-words with the stress upon the first member often had descriptive force. See **247.** 2. *b*. To-day in both English and German, group-words with the stress upon the first member usually have distinguishing or classifying force, with the difference, however, that in English this is always true: wéll wàter **Brúnnenwàsser,** schóolboy fèrvor **Schúljungenèifer,** a thrée-day trìp **eine Dréi-Tage-Tòur.** Thus in English we to-day in contrast to oldest English and to oldest and modern German make a sharp difference between descriptive and classifying groups. In descriptive groups, as those in the preceding paragraph, we stress uniformly the second member, giving the first member less stress as we now regard it an adjective. In classifying groups we still as in oldest English stress the first member as we still regard it the first component of a compound or group-word.

c. Logical Relations of the Adjective to its Governing Substantive. The attributive adjective has the force of a predicate, i.e. it is something predicated of the governing noun: **der dumme Junge, der verwundete Soldat.** After certain words, **angeblich, anscheinend, scheinbar, wahrscheinlich, vermutlich,** &c., the governing noun itself is felt as predicate, as something predicated of a pronoun: **Der angebliche Chirurg ist eigentlich ein Barbier = Der, der als ein Chirurg angegeben wird, ist eigentlich ein Barbier.** Originally the adjective was an appositive, a word placed alongside another word to explain it. Thus when it was used as an appositive to the subject it was a predicate appositive. Hence the attributive adjective even to-day often has the force of a predicate appositive and like other predicate appositives, as illustrated in **252.** 1. *c*, is equal to an adverbial clause, thus sustaining relations to both the subject and the principal verb: **Der gráusame Mánn achtete nicht auf das Flehen des Unglücklichen = Der Mann achtete nicht auf das Flehen des Unglücklichen, weil er grausam war. Diese álte Fráu putzt sich noch gern = Diese Frau putzt sich noch gern, obgleich sie alt ist.**

II. Attributive Genitive.

1. A noun or pronoun in the genitive may modify a noun.

In the oldest period the genitive usually preceded the governing noun. Later in accordance with the general trend to place heavily stressed modifiers after the governing word the genitive gradually became established after the governing noun, just as the strongly stressed modifiers of the verb became established after the verb. Thus the old group **Féuers Màcht** became the modern group **die Màcht des Féuers.** Of course the genitive remained before the governing noun if it was not stressed: **Wilhelms Hút.** This is quite common in case of proper names but not so common in case of names of things, but it occasionally occurs as also the genitive of things is sometimes less important than the governing noun and consequently has less stress: **Nach Osten ergaben sich frühlichte Dachfenster für das Gesinde, und des Dàches andere Hälfte war Bodenraum** (R. H. Bartsch's *Die Haindlkinder*, p. 32). Many *stressed* genitives, however, even names of things, remained before the governing noun just as many stressed modifiers of the verb remained at the beginning of a sentence before the verb. These stressed genitives did not follow the other stressed genitives to their new position after the governing noun as they were felt as having a little different force. In time this differentiation became clearly defined. The stressed genitive before the governing noun *distinguishes one object from another* or *classifies it*; the stressed genitive after the noun *describes one object*: **Es ist Wílhelms Hùt, nicht méiner,** distinguishing one object from another, but with descriptive force: **Schlag auf Schlag wie die Bòtschaften Híobs waren die Antworten aus Sturzens** (name) **Munde gekommen** (Ertl's *Freiheit*, p. 552). **Féuersmàcht** classifies the power distinguishing it from other powers, but **die Màcht des Féuers** merely describes. The old uninflected genitive is still widely used, especially in classifying: **Wásserkràft, Dámpfkràft,** etc. Compare **247.** 2. *a* and *b* and **50.** A. 6. *f*.

If there are two genitive modifiers of a noun, one genitive should stand on each side of the noun, the genitive of origin preceding: **Schwabs Leben Schillers** Schwab's 'Life of Schiller,' **Rankes Geschichte der römischen Päpste.** The dependent gen. should not be cut off from the noun upon which it depends: **Die Anhänglichkeit sämtlicher Angestellten an mich** (not **die Anhänglichkeit an mich sämtlicher Angestellten**) the attachment of all the employees to me. A gen. dependent upon a gen. usually follows it, except that a dependent gen. of a noun denoting a person can precede a governing genitive: **die Geschichte**

der Erbauung der Stadt, trotz des Verbotes des Doktors, während der Krankheit meines Freundes, or **während meines Freundes Krankheit. So lang's daran nicht mangelt und an frischem Mut, lach' ich der Fürsten Herrschsucht und Ränke** (Goethe's *Götz* 1, 2). **Trotz Veltens naseweisen, unverschämten Einredens, trotz der Frau Amalie abwehrenden Kopfschüttelns und Lächelns** (Raabe's *Die Akten des Vogelsangs*, p. 41), **während Hainhofers** (name) **Aufenthaltes in Stettin** (A. Haas in *Archiv für Kulturgeschichte*, 1905, p. 46).

The governing noun is usually omitted in such expressions as **bei Müllers.** See **93.** 1. *a.*

The attributive genitive expresses different classes of ideas briefly described in the following articles. These categories are not all peculiar to the attributive use, but several of them are found in the genitive which is used in connection with verbs, adjectives, and participles, and probably originated in the use of the genitive with verbs. This seems quite clear in the categories described in D and H. *a* (2nd par.) below, and in **260.** The common genitive of origin and possession described in A and B and the genitive of quality and characteristic described in F. (**1**) are not only used as attributive forms but are also employed as the predicate complement of the verb **sein.** In a few cases the attributive genitive is evidently derived from the use of the genitive with verbs. In these instances the peculiar genitive which is employed in connection with certain verbs is also used with nouns derived from these verbs, as explained in I below. On the other hand, it seems quite probable that some of these categories have not sprung directly from the genitive used with verbs, but have developed out of other attributive categories, as indicated in the different categories discussed below.

A. *Genitive of Origin*, representing a person or thing as associated with another person or thing in the relation of source, cause, authorship: **Der Sohn des Fürsten, die Kinder dieser Frau, die Nachkommen Abrahams, die Taten des Herkules, die Verwüstungen zweier Kriegsjahre, Goethes Faust, Schillers Werke.** This same idea is found in the genitive used in the predicate with the verbs in **252.** 2. A. *c.*

a. This one use of this case form has given to it the name of *genitive* (from Latin genitivus *pertaining to generation or birth*), which has become a fixed name not only for this use, but also for all the following relations expressed by the same case form.

b. If two names connected by **und** represent persons that are joined together in authorship or business the second name alone assumes the gen. ending: **Die Deutsche Geschichte Gutsche und Schultzes** or **Gutsche-Schultzes,** or **Gutsche und Schultzes Deutsche Geschichte** or **Gutsche-Schultzes Deutsche Geschichte,** or **die Gutsche-Schultzesche Deutsche Geschichte.**

c. In case of proper names this genitive is often replaced by an attributive adjective in **-isch.** See **245.** II. 10. 1.

B. *Possessive Genitive*, denoting possession, inherence, a belonging to, association with, or relation to, ideas that may be developed out of the general idea of "sphere," as explained in **260: Das Hàus meines Brúders** the house in the sphere of my brother, i.e. owned by my brother, **die Wèisheit des Sókrates, der Mùt des Hélden, die Blätter des Báumes, die Sträßen der Stádt, die Kûhle des Ábends, der Schnèe der Álpen, die Kàmeraden des Soldáten, das Hàupt des Stámmes, der Hèrr des Húndes** the master of the dog, i.e. the master in the sphere of the dog, with reference to the dog, not *the master owned by the dog,* **der Bùrgermeister der Stádt, der Vàter des Kíndes.** This is a very productive category from which have probably sprung A, C, F, G. The same idea is found in the genitive used in the predicate with the group of verbs in **252. 2. A.** *c.*

The possessive genitive so common in both German and English in nouns denoting time has in English spread from here to adverbs of time, where, however, in German we must use an adjective in **-ig: Die Post dieser Woche** this week's mail; to-day's mail **die heutige Post.** See **245.** II. 9. 2. B.

In this category normal or descriptive group-stress (**50.** A. 6) with the accent upon the second member usually prevails, but to distinguish objects we often find distinguishing stress (**50.** A. 6): **Wilhelms Pfèrd ist das beste** William's hòrse is the best, or sometimes William's is the best horse.

a. In English we here sometimes use the dative after the prep. *to*, where in German the gen. should be employed: **Sie ist eine Schwester meiner ersten Frau** She is a sister to my first wife. Sometimes it is possible in German to use either gen. or dat. with a slight shade of difference: **ein Vater der Armen,** or more impressively **den Armen ein Vater** a father to the poor. Sometimes in both German and English there is a marked difference of meaning between the dat. and gen.: **dem Verfolgten ein Freund** *a friend to the persecuted man*, but **ein Freund des Verfolgten** a friend of the persecuted man. When the modifying word is a pronoun the gen. must in all these cases be replaced by the prepositional construction with **von** or **zu.** See **229.** 2, **zu,** II. 1. B. *b.*

b. The gen. must be replaced by the dat. with **von** in case of names of places ending in a sibilant. See **86.** 2. *e.* There is elsewhere sometimes a difference between the genitive and the construction with **von: der Kaiser von Deutschland** (a mere title), but in warm poetic language **Deutschlands alter Kaiser** (i.e., **Wilhelm I.,** indicating pride in ownership).

c. In case of proper names the genitive is often replaced in certain categories by other constructions: (**1**) by an appositive, as explained in **94.** 3. A. *c*; (**2**) by an attributive adjective in **-sch,** as illustrated in **245.** II. **10.** 1. Elsewhere it is often replaced by an adjective in **-lich,** as illustrated in **245.** II. **11.** 2. A. *b.*

d. If a dependent genitive which precedes its governing noun is itself modified by other attributive elements containing nouns, each element maintains its own syntactical force and its own proper inflection, while in English the different elements are considered as forming a compound, and hence the *s* is added at the end of the compound, even tho the last component to which the *s* is added is in fact in the objective case after the prep. *of*: **Dieser eine war Till Eulenspiegel, des Herzogs von Braunschweig Hofnarr** (Lienhard's *Till Eulenspiegel*, Der Fremde) This one was the Duke of Brunswick's court-fool.

e. Instead of a simple genitive we often find in colloquial language a genitive or a dative in connection with a possessive. See **138.** 2. *c.*

f. If two names connected by **und** represent persons that are joined together in possession the second name alone assumes the genitive ending: **Karl und Wilhelms Zimmer, Vater und Mutters Zimmer,** as the two common nouns are felt as names.

g. The word for house or place of business is often omitted after the name of a person: **Geh zu Schmidts** or **zum Schmidt** Go to Schmidt's (house or place of business according to the connection). **Ich kaufte es bei Schmidts** or **beim Schmidt.** We must use the second of these two constructions, i.e. the dative preceded by a preposition and article when the reference is to a person engaged in an occupation or trade and there is no mention of the name: **Geh zum Bäcker** Go to the baker's. As can be seen by the English translation of the last German example the elliptical genitive construction is more common in English than in German. In English also the words *church, hospital, park, castle, theater* can be suppressed after a name: St. Paul's [Cathedral], St. Bartholomew's [Hospital], &c. Except in case of English names of churches, &c., German requires here the expression of the common noun after the name: **die St. 'Michaëlskirche, das St. Hedwigs-Krankenhaus,** &c. On the other hand, German often omits **Tag** after names of church festivals, after the analogy of the Latin usage of dropping *dies* here, while in English Day is usually expressed: **Heute ist Allerheiligen** (gen. pl.), **Allerseelen** (gen. pl.) This is All Saints' Day (Nov. 1), All Souls' Day (Nov. 2). **'s ist heut' Simons und Judä** (Latin gen. of **Judas**) (Schiller's *Tell*, I. 146) This is St. Simon's and St. Jude's Day (Oct. 28). These forms, however, are not now felt as genitives but are used for any case: **Micha'ēlis** (Latin gen. felt as nom.) **fällt auf den Donnerstag. Ich komme zu Michaelis.** Compare **88.** 2.

C. *Subjective Genitive*, which represents a living being as associated with an action in the relation of author: **die Rüge des Lehrers** the reproof of the teacher, **die Liebe einer Mutter, der Gesang der Vögel.** A personal pronoun rarely stands in the subjective genitive: **Meine Mutter hatte meine Abwesenheit beim Tee durch ein frühzeitiges Ausgehen meiner zu beschönigen gesucht** (Goethe's *D. u. W.*, Erster Teil, Fünftes Buch).

D. *Objective Genitive*, which denotes the object toward which the activity is directed: **die Erziehung der Kinder** the education of the children, **die Erbauung des Hauses.** This genitive is a development out of the adverbial genitive of specification (**260.** 4th par.): **Johannes vollzog die Taufe Christi** (adverbial genitive of specification, i.e. *with reference to Christ.*)

As possessive adjectives are derived from the genitive of the personal pronouns they still often have various meanings of the genitive, hence also sometimes the force of an objective genitive: **mein** (= a gen. of origin) **Sohn, mein** (= a possessive gen.) **Buch, meine** (= a subject gen.) **Liebe zu Gott, meine** (= an objective gen.) **Verhaftung.**

a. This objective gen. is limited in general to those substantives that contain a verbal stem which has a pronounced transitive force: **die Erfüllung** (from **erfüllen** *to fulfil*) **der Pflicht.** Earlier in the period verbal nouns in general, even tho they did not have pronounced transitive force, could take an objective gen., while to-day in many cases a prepositional object is either required or is much more common, even in case of nouns formed from transitive verbs, except in poetry, where older usage still lingers: **Aber ich kenne euch | das jr nicht Gottes liebe** [now in prose **Liebe zu Gott**] **in euch habt** (John v. 42). **Und überall . . . . fand ich den gleichen Haß der** [in plain prose **gegen die**] **Tyrannei** (Schiller's *Tell*, 2, 2). **Ich stritt aus Haß der Städte und nicht um euren Dank** (Uhland's *Die Döffinger Schlacht*). We now usually say: **Die Furcht vor Gott, aus Haß gegen die Städte, der Angriff auf die Stadt,** &c. Older usage, however, is still the rule in group-words (**247.** 2. *b*) and compounds: **Menschenliebe, Menschenhaß, Gottesfurcht,** &c.

A verbal noun formed from a verb governing a gen. or dat. cannot take an objective gen., but where such verbs are also used with an acc. and hence are also felt as transitive verbs the objective gen. can of course be used: **der Genuß** (from **genießen** with gen. or acc.) **des Weines, der Mißbrauch amtlicher Stellung.**

Thruout the period attempts have been repeatedly made to extend this usage to verbal nouns made from verbs which govern the dative, which practice is quite generally condemned by grammarians: **Daß er mich mit Entsagung seiner eignen Glückseligkeit glücklich gemacht habe** (Lessing, 2, 40). **Von jener erstaunenswürdigen Entsagung der Krone** (Schiller, 4, 93). Very commonly in case of **Dienst: der Dienst Gottes** (Goethe), **Gottesdienst.** Also often in the language of our time: **zur Abhilfe der dringendsten Bedürfnisse, zur Steuerung des Unfugs, die Beiwohnung des Manövers, diesen** (i.e. **den gewohnheitsmäßigen Spielern**) **Unterkunft zur Fröhnung ihres Lasters zu gewähren** (leader in *Hamburger Nachrichten*, June 27, 1905), &c. Some of these expressions are difficult to avoid, but grammarians recommend a change of word or recourse to a prep. phrase: **zur Befriedigung der dringendsten Bedürfnisse** instead of **zur Abhilfe der usw. Er zürnt mir,** but **sein Zorn auf mich. Sie widerstanden den Römern,** but **ihr Widerstand gegen die Römer. Er entsagt dem Throne,** but **die Entsagung auf Ansprüche,** also in the form of an old group-word, as in **Thronentsagung.** The genitive after **Entsagung,** as in the example given above, may be explained in another way, namely, according to I below, as the reflexive construction is also sometimes used: **Entsagen Sie sich im guten aller Ansprüche** (Lessing's *Die glückliche Erbin*, 1, 2).

Verbal nouns made from verbs requiring a prep. object usually retain the same prep. construction: **Er spottet über den Armen** and **der Spott über den Armen.** See also IV. 1 below.

b. The use of a possessive before a governing noun instead of the subjective gen. or of some appropriate preposition instead of the objective genitive will usually distinguish the objective gen. from the subjective: **Seine Verachtung der Menschen** his contempt for men, **die Liebe zu Gott** love to God, **der Haß gegen den Tyrannen.** The subjective gen. can be distinguished by placing it before the noun that is to be modified, except in case of relative pronouns, which must always precede even when used as object: **Gottes Liebe** *love that comes from God*; but also **Dieses Vorurteil, dessen** (objective gen.) **Bekämpfung uns schon viel Mühe gekostet hat** *This prejudice, the combating of which has already cost us a good deal of trouble.* If there are two genitives, one a subjective, the other an objective gen., the latter is often replaced by a prep. phrase, or enters into a group-word with the governing noun: **Die Verachtung der Christen gegen den Tod,** or very frequently **die Todesverachtung der Christen** the contempt of the Christians for death. The thought can often be made clear by the use of the preposition **von seiten** or **durch** instead of a subjective genitive: **die Begnadigung von seiten des Königs** or **durch den König** the king's pardon, **die Eroberung des Landes durch den General, das Lob des Schülers von seiten des Lehrers.**

c. A personal pronoun rarely stands in the objective gen.: **Die unglückliche Nachricht der Arretierung Deiner** (Johann G. Reuter in a letter to his son Fritz, Nov. 4, 1833). The objective genitive as the second member of the group in which it stands takes the group-stress. Hence the natural unconscious feeling for the melody of the sentence leads one to avoid placing a light pronominal in this important position. A possessive adjective can often be used here and as it stands in the unimportant place before the governing noun its stress conforms to the sentence rhythm: **Die unglückliche Nachricht deiner Arretierung.** The objective genitive of a personal pronoun may stand after a governing noun if an accented word follows which can bring the expression into harmony with the sentence melody: **Behèrrschung deiner sèlbst,** &c. If there is no following accented word, as in this example, or if by reason of a lack of clearness the possessive adjective cannot be used, it sometimes becomes necessary to place the genitive of the personal pronoun after the governing noun, altho the stress does not conform to the usual rhythm of the sentence: **Doch entstand wohl nur aus einem Übersehen ihrer** (i.e. **der Verständniszusammenhänge**) **die prinzipielle Skepsis in den einzelnen klassischen und modernen Philologien gegenüber der sprachwissenschaftlichen Methode** (Gustav Hübner in *Anglia*, 1915, p. 278). The strong transitive force of the governing noun here demands an objective genitive, but elsewhere a prepositional object can often be used, which by reason of its heavier weight conforms more to the rhythm of the sentence: **die Liebe zu ihm** or **gegen ihn, die Verachtung gegen ihn,** &c.

Also nouns rarely stand in the objective gen. in those cases where they are without an article, such as abstract nouns denoting materials when used in an indefinite partitive sense, or plurals of concrete nouns, when the reference is to an indefinite number. The gen. is here replaced by **von** with dat.: **Menschenbedürfnis konnte zumeist ohne viel Bitten auf ein Vorsetzen von Speise und Trunk rechnen** (Jensen's *Das Bild im Wasser*, chap. i). **Auch die Japaner sind mit dem Aufwerfen von Verschanzungen beschäftigt** (*Hamb. Nachr.*, Oct. 25, 1904).

d. Nouns formed from verbs which take a dative of the reflexive pronoun and an accusative of the noun, as **sich** (dat.) **das Trinken abgewöhnen,** drop according to **249.** II. 2. G the reflexive pronoun. Corresponding to the accusative of the verbal construction is the genitive of the substantive form of expression: **Sie** (i.e. **diese große Leistung**) **verlangt Anpassung an fremdes**

Klima, Aufgabe vieler heimischer Gewohnheiten, Abgewöhnung des Alkohols (Kolonialdirektor Dernburg in *Hamburger Nachrichten*, Jan. 22, 1907).

E. *Genitive of Material or Composition* denoting that of which something consists: **ein Schmuck des feinsten Goldes, der Strom seiner Gedanken, ein Dach schattender Buchen** a roof of shady beeches, **der Zweige laubiges Gitter** the leafy trellis-work of the branches. **Ungern vermiss' ich ihn doch, den alten kattunenen Schlafrock | echt ostindischen Stoffs** (Goethe's *H. u. D.*, I, 33–4). **Eine Kette aufsteigender Rebhühner, eine Reihe blühender Kinder. Die Sonne versinkt hinter einer Wehr weißer Berge im Westen** (Ernst Zahn's *Wie dem Kaplan Longinus die Welt aufging*). This category is closely related to H.

a. The gen. here is not common in plain prose, and is now largely confined to figurative or poetic language. In prose the gen. is usually replaced by **von.** See in **229.** 2, the prep. **von,** *f.*

F. *Descriptive Genitive.* This genitive is closely related to the possessive genitive. There are two groups:

(1) *Genitive* of *Quality* or *Characteristic*: **Waren erster Güte** goods of the best quality, **Dìnge dieser Árt** things of this sort, **èiner seines Schlágs** one of his stamp, stripe, **eine Dròschke zweiter Klásse, ein Pfèrd arabischer Rásse, ein Gàsthof ersten Ránges, ein Mànn vórnehmen Stándes, der Gòtt der Líebe, der Gèist der Lúge, ein Mànn der Tát. Es handelt sich leider um Dìnge des bíttersten Érnstes. Gerüchte sind in Umlauf gesetzt worden des Inhalts, daß,** &c. Reports have been set in circulation to the effect that, &c. This same idea is found in the genitive used in the predicate with the verbs in **252.** 2. A. *c*.

If this group has classifying force we usually find it in group-word (**247.** 2) form: **Kínderspràche** a chíld's lànguage, **Kínderschùh** a chíld's shòe, **Hérrenstìefel** a géntleman's shòe, **Dámenstìefel** a lády's shòe, **Fráuenhànd** a wóman's hànd, **Wéspennèst** a wásp's nèst. **Er starb den Héldentòd** He died a héro's dèath.

a. The gen. is here often replaced by the dat. with **von: Waren von verschiedener Güte, ein Weib von schöner Gestalt, eine Mehrheit von sechs gegen eins** a six to one majority, **eine Untersuchung von Haus zu Haus** a house to house investigation, &c.

b. The simple genitive of a personal pronoun assumes the force of a genitive of quality when placed before a numeral: **unsereiner** one of our kind, class, **seiner vier** four of his kind, four like him.

(2) Quite similar is the *Genitive of Measure*: **Die Àrbeit eines ganzen Jáhres, auf die Dàuer eines Táges** (but **von zwei, drei Tágen**). This genitive is usually replaced by **von** with the dat. or an adjective in **-ig: ein Krìeg von dreißig Jáhren** or **ein drèißigjähriger Kríeg, eine Verzṓgerung von drei Stúnden** or **eine drèistündige Verzṓgerung.** English preserves the genitive better here as it has become fixed in modern group-words and compounds (**247.** 2. *c*): *a thirty yèars' wár, a three hòurs' deláy*. In both English and German these groups have descriptive stress (**50.** A. 6), i.e. accent upon the second member. A classifying genitive with classifying stress (**50.** A. 6) is used in units of measurement, but this form is a possessive or an objective genitive: **eine Schíffslänge** a bóat's length, more commonly in old group-word form (**247.** 2. *a*) in German: **eine Kópflànge** *a héad's lèngth*, **ein Stéinwùrf** *a stóne's thròw*, &c.

G. *Appositive Genitive,* explaining the preceding governing word: **der Fehler des Argwohns** the fault of always entertaining mistrust, **das Laster der Trunksucht** the vice of intemperance, **die Zeit der Kreuzzüge, die Strafe der Verbannung, die Gabe des Gesanges, der Beiname des Großen, der Titel eines Geheimrats,** &c. The possessive genitive was the starting point of this genitive construction, as can still be seen in such examples as **der Segen einer guten Erziehung,** &c., where the genitive can be construed either as a possessive or an appositive genitive.

When the appositive is not thus added to a noun to define its meaning more accurately but to indicate a class to which a thing or a person belongs who has just been characterized as an individual by the governing noun, **von** with the dative is used instead of the genitive construction: **Der Schurke von (einem)**

Wirt the rascal of a landlord. Other examples in **94.** 2 and **229.** 2 under **von** (*i*). This construction is not known in M.H.G. and oldest English. It has probably come into both languages from the French. Originally it came from the Latin appositive genitive, which is an outgrowth of the possessive genitive, as in scelus viri rascal of a man, i.e. the rascal is a man, belongs to the class represented by man, monstrum mulieris monster of a woman, i.e. the monster is a woman, belongs to womankind. All feeling for the origin of this construction has been lost, for the common class noun after **von** can now be replaced by a proper name: **Wo ist das Vieh von (einem) Fingal?** (Krüger's *Vermischte Beiträge zur Syntax*, p. 118) = **Wo ist das Vieh, der Fingal?** Where is that beast of a Fingal? = Where is that beast Fingal? Thus the word after **von** is now felt as an ordinary appositive to the preceding noun. In German, things cannot be personified here as in English: It was a perfect beast of a night **Es war eine reine Hundenacht.**

a. Also the appositional construction can be used in case of the category described in III. 1. B, the appositive agreeing with the preceding word in case or standing in the nom., cut off by quotation marks: **der Begriff Schön** or **der Begriff des Schönen. Er erhielt den Titel eines kaiserlichen Rates** or **den Titel „Kaiserlicher Rat."** Other examples of appositives in **94.** 1. *d* and in III. 1. B below. The appositional construction is the rule with proper names: **die Stadt Berlin** the city of Berlin, **die Universität Berlin** the University of Berlin, **die Bergfeste Ehrenbreitstein,** the rocky fortress of Ehrenbreitstein, **das Königreich England** the kingdom of England, **der Monat Mai,** or simply **der Mai** the month of May, or simply May, **die Insel Sardinien, das Kap Horn,** &c. In case of rivers, lakes, bays, straits, mountains, valleys, passes, tunnels, and waterfalls the appositive and governing noun are written together in the form of an old or younger group-word (**247.** 2. *a* and *b*), the modifying word, i.e. the appositive, preceding the governing noun in accordance with oldest Germanic usage, which required the modifying word to precede the governing noun: **der Rhéinstròm** the Rhine, **der Míchigansèe** Làke Míchigan, **die Béringstràße** Bèring Stráit, **das Ríesengebìrge, das Rhéintàl** the Rhìne válley, **der St. Gótthardtùnnel** the Saint Gòthard túnnel, **die Niágarafàlle** Nìagara Fálls, &c. The name sometimes assumes adjective form: **der Biskàyische Méerbusen** the Bày of Bíscay.

The appositive genitive and the appositive in the strict appositional construction often preceded the governing noun in oldest English and German. That the appositive now in contrast to oldest Germanic usually follows the governing word is explained by its stronger stress and its descriptive force: **Das Làster der Trúnksucht, die Stàdt Berlín.** The law for modern descriptive group-stress (**50.** A. 6) requires the more heavily stressed member of a group of two words to stand last. The words for rivers, lakes, &c., as **der Rheinstrom,** &c., resisted this development as they had become compounds and the form had thus become fixed. Under the influence of analogy other words have assumed this old form: **Húdsonbài,** &c. In many English words, as Hùdson Báy (older type Húdson Bày, corresponding to German **Húdsonbài**), &c., the old word-order so common in Old English has been retained, but the accent has been conformed to modern descriptive group-stress by simply transferring the chief stress to the second member, which is impossible in German but easy in English, as the first member is now construed as an adjective according to I. *b* above, something quite contrary to the spirit of German. In German according to I. *b* above adjective function requires adjective form with the suffix **-isch,** as in **der Biskàyische Méerbusen** given above, which of course conforms to modern group-stress.

b. This gen. is often replaced by an infin. with **zu: Die Kunst zu schreiben war den Ägyptern** (Egyptians) **bekannt.**

H. *Partitive Genitive,* denoting the whole, of which only a part is taken: **die Hälfte meines Vermögens, der erste Vers des Liedes, eine Flasche des besten Weins, einer meiner Kameraden. Unter der Pelzmütze zeigt sich ein kleiner Teil eines gutmütigen, gebräunten Gesichts.** The same idea is found in the genitive used with the verbs in **260.** See also *c* below.

Notice the following difference of idiom between German and English: **einer der Freunde meines Vaters** a friend of my father's, with a double expression of the gen., once with *of*, once with *-s;* **einer meiner Freunde** a friend of mine. The double English gen. is not always partitive: that wife of yours **Ihre Frau.**

The genitive of gradation is only a variety of the partitive genitive: **der König der Könige** the king of kings, **das Buch der Bücher, die Frau der Frauen.**

a. *Appositional Construction instead of the Partitive Genitive.* In case of common nouns after indefinite pronouns and nouns denoting weight, measure, extent, or quantity, also in case of certain proper names, this gen. has in the language of every day usually gone over into the appositional construction. This important construction is treated at length in **145** (read carefully the *Notes* there under *b. c, e, f, g*) and **94.** 3. A, and *b* thereunder.

Attention is called here to the peculiar word-order often found in this appositional construction when the word indicating the part is a noun denoting an indefinite amount, or more commonly an indefinite limiting adjective used substantively. The word denoting the whole may precede the word denoting the part, and often introduces the proposition: **Es ist Wein die Menge da. Solche Fehler können die Menge im Plinius sein** (Lessing). **Harmonisches Getön war wenig dabei** (Raabe's *Horn von Wanza*, xvi). **Das** (i.e. **Ach, du bist ja ein dummer Junge**) **sagt er auch immer, und Antwort ist's doch keine** (Maria Janitschek's *Einer Mutter Sieg*, xviii). **Gäste waren wenige da** (Ertl's *Walpurga*). **Gefahr ist nicht die Spur** (Paul Keller's *Waldwinter*, xiv). **Sorgen braucht er sich keine zu machen** (Ertl's *Auswanderer*). **Ähnliche Geschichten gibt es unzählige** (H. Seidel's *Hundegeschichten*). The word-order in a number of these sentences indicates clearly that the word denoting the whole is not now felt as belonging to the substantive in an attributive relation, but that it is felt as the subject or object of the verb. As the subject it regulates the number of the verb, as in the sentence from Lessing. As an emphatic object it may introduce the proposition causing inversion, as in the last two sentences. The freedom of position in case of the word denoting the whole in all these instances indicates that it was originally not an attributive genitive modifying the noun denoting the part or quantity but was an adverbial genitive of specification (**260**): **Des bearbeiteten Stoffs liegt eine große Menge bereit** (Goethe), lit. *With regard to the material already worked upon a good deal lies ready.* **Brots hat er die Fülle** (Luther), lit. *With regard to bread he has a plenty.* Early the gen. here was felt as a partitive gen. subject (see *c* below), as in the former example, or as a partitive gen. object (see *c* below), as in the latter example, and the word denoting the part or quantity was construed as a predicate appositive, adding an explanatory remark about the preceding subject or object. This appositional construction is still in wide use, but in its present modern form the partitive genitive subject is usually replaced by a nominative subject and the partitive genitive object by an accusative object, as in the examples given at the beginning of the paragraph. The old partitive gen. subject or object, however, is still often found when the reference is to a *number* of individuals, as in **Aber der wirklichen und scheinbaren Ausnahmen sind nicht wenige** (Krüger's *Schwierigkeiten des Englischen*, II, p. 683), but where the reference is to a *mass* it is now replaced by the modern partitive construction of **von** with the dative or by the modern appositional construction: **Von seinem Vermögen verlor er die Hälfte. Geld** (acc. object) **hat er genug** or **keins** (pred. appositive). The old gen. construction, however, has become fixed in a few expressions: **Er tut des Guten zu viel. Des Neuen wird hier wenig geboten** (W. Franz in *Germanisch-Romanische Monatsschrift*, 1910, p. 653). On the other hand, the original gen. of specification was often felt as an attributive gen. and this double conception of the gen. as a partitive subject or object or as an attributive element explains the twofold development found here. When felt as an attributive element the gen. here as elsewhere often followed the governing noun: **die Fülle Brots** instead of **Brots die Fülle.** Altho the attributive gen. was well established in O.H.G. and M.H.G. it has been largely replaced in the last centuries by the attributive appositional construction: **ein Glas Milch** (gen., but on account of the lack of an ending now felt as an attributive appositive); **ein Glas Wasser** (an attributive appositive after the analogy of **Milch** in the preceding example). Similarly in the old gen. appositional construction the lack of distinctive endings facilitated the change from a gen. subject or object to a nom. subject and an acc. object: **Worte** (originally a gen. pl. subject, now felt as a nom. subject) **sind genug** (pred. appos.) **gewechselt. Schmerz** (acc. object instead of the older gen. object **des Schmerzes**) **empfand ich keinen** (pred. appos.). But here the idea that the nom. is the proper form for the subject and the acc. for the object is a strong factor in the development.

A *pronoun* dependent upon these groups of words, however, less commonly takes the appositional construction. It is either placed in the dat. after **von** (see *b* below), or it may still follow the old usage and stand in the gen., especially when it precedes the governing word: **Es waren ihrer mehr als hundert** There were more than a hundred of them. **Ihrer sind mehr als unser** There are more of them than there are of us. **Wie viel sind unserer?** (Schiller's *Räuber*, 2, 3). But also the appositional construction occurs here: **Je mehr wir sind, desto besser** the more of us there are, the better. **Es wäre zu wünschen, daß es mehr Gieshübler** (name) **gäbe: es gibt aber mehr andere** (Fontane's *Effi*, XXIX). **Wir sind ja nur noch so wenige beisammen!** (Raabe's *Die Akten des Vogelsangs*, p. 119). **Wir sind zehn. Wie viele sind wir denn?** (Storm's *Der Herr Etatsrat*, p. 216). **Jeder meiner Freunde, jeder von uns** (the gen. not now used in case of personal pronouns), or with the appositional construction: **Wenn wir jeder uns geben, wie wir sind, und tun, was unser Gewissen uns vorschreibt, wird's ja wohl das Rechte sein** (Telmann's *Wahrheit*, XXIV). The genitive and appositional constructions are sometimes combined: **Sie waren ihrer elf Geschwister, zwischen vierundzwanzig und zwei Jahren** (*Kölnische Zeitung*). **So wären wir unser zehn** (Fontane's *Vor dem Sturm*, II, chap. 15). The possessive is often in colloquial language used in connection with the appositional construction: **Vor allen Dingen waren sie ihre zwanzig** (Sudermann's *Der Sturmgeselle Sokrates*, 1. 9).

In general after measures the gen. of nouns is much more common in the pl. than in the sing.: **eine Menge kleinerer Fahrzeuge.** The gen. sing. of a noun modified by an adjective is still in choice language not altogether infrequent here, in recent usage seems even to be on the increase again, but the gen. of an unmodified noun is now rather uncommon in prose: **Er aß fast nichts und trank zwei Gläser schweren Weins** (Maria Janitschek's *Liebeswunder*, viii), but now usually **ein Glas Wein, ein Schluck Bier,** occasionally, however, the genitive: **drei Stückchen Zuckers** (Julius von Ludassy in *Velhagen und Klasings Monatshefte*, Oct. 1906, p. 255), **drei Stunden Weges** (still common). **Bei den weiten Strecken Ackerlandes, über die der einzelne Mensch [in Norddeutschland] verfügt, hat er nicht nötig, den Boden zu parzellieren** (O. Weise's *Die deutschen Volksstämme*. p. 4).

In a choice style the gen. still occurs after limiting adjectives, expressing the idea of number, and used substantively, as described in **139.** 3. *i. Note*, but very rarely after indefinite pronouns expressing the idea of amount, which now usually require the appositional construction, altho the gen. was much used earlier in the period, and survives in a few set expressions. See **145.** *f. Note* 1 and *g. Note* 1.

If the noun dependent upon a limiting adjective, or any measure, or weight is modified by an article or pronominal adj., it must usually stand in the partitive gen. or in the dat. after the prep. **von** or **unter: Die obere Hälfte des Berges, viele dieser Bücher,** or **von diesen Büchern,** or **unter diesen Büchern; ein Pfund dieser Kirschen,** or **von diesen Kirschen.** For an exception see **94.** 3. A, last par. The partitive gen. is also still much used after comparatives, superlatives, and ordinals: **die bessern meiner Schüler, die besten meiner Schüler; der erste, der zweite, der letzte der Klasse.**

Note. Observe that in case of the relative pronoun, resembling the Latin and differing from the English, the partitive construction is replaced by the appositional, when *all* are embraced in the statement: qui omnes = **die** (or **welche**) **alle** = all of whom. For further examples see **139. 1.** *d, Notes* 1 and 2 (**1**) and *f* (last example in 1st par.).

b. The gen. is here often replaced by the prep. construction of **von** w. dat., which emphasizes more sharply the partitive idea. See last of *a* above, and also the prep. **von,** *j* in **229.** 2.

c. Genitive or Von + *Dative as Subject, Predicate, or Object.* A partitive gen. or much more frequently a dat. after the prep. **von** is sometimes used independently of a noun or pronoun as the apparent subject, predicate, or object of the verb, to indicate that the thing or things in question should be considered as a part of a whole, or as individuals of a species. The genitive construction was not infrequent in older periods. The dative construction after **von** in part replaces the older genitive construction, in part is of French origin. Under French influence it was quite common in the eighteenth century and is not infrequent in the colloquial speech of our own time, but it is now in general avoided in choice language.

As subject: **Aus Aristophanes lassen sich ihrer nachweisen** (J. Grimm) Some (monologues) can be found in Aristophanes. **Dort zeigte sich, selbst wo sie von Eichenholz war, die Belattung und Verschalung gänzlich morsch; und solcher Stellen waren überall** (Ludwig's *Zwischen Himmel und Erde*, III). **So viele Hände, als ihrer zur Stelle waren, griffen nach dem ausgeworfenen Tau** (H. E. Wallsee in *Ham. Nachr.*, June 11, 1905). The dative after **von** instead of the partitive genitive: **Gestern, denkt, gingen von seinen Leuten vorbei** (Goethe's *Egmont*, 1, 3) Just think, yesterday some of his men went by. **Es war von Luthers Geist und Mannheit auf ihn übergegangen** (Alexis). **Dann steht da wohl auch von** (something about) **den Ulrichs** (family) **drin** (i.e. **in dem Buch**)? (Halbe's *Der Strom*, p. 13). Notice that the verb is in the singular or plural according as the reference is to an indefinite *quantity* or an indefinite *number*. In Otfrid's "Brast in thar thes wines" (II. 8. 11) the genitive was often felt as an adverbial genitive of specification (**260**) and is now usually replaced by an adverbial phrase: **Es gebrach** or **fehlte ihnen an Wein,** but with these impersonal verbs it was also often construed as a partitive genitive subject and was later often replaced by a nominative subject: **Es gebrach** (once common here) or now more commonly **fehlte ihnen Wein** (nom.). With some verbs (**262.** II. A. *c*) the idea of a subject prevailed, so that later the old partitive genitive subject was replaced by a nominative subject: **Sein Benehmen** (nom.) **verdrießt mich,** where we now no longer feel that the genitive was once used here.

As predicate: Thu bist judiisger man, | inti ich bin thesses thietes (Otfrid, II. XIV. 17), now **Du bist Jude und ich bin aus** or **von diesem Volke hier. Das sind einmal wieder von euern Streichen** (Kotzebue).

As object. The gen. is not infrequent here in poetic language: **Weil ich deines Weins verschmähte** (Kleist's *Käthchen*, 1, 1) Also in prose in case of pronominal objects: **Aber es gab ihrer, und gar nicht wenige** (Raabe's *Horn von Wanza*, chap. 9) *But there were such people and*, &c. Sometimes in case of substantival objects: **Der Typen und Originale gab es überall** (Bernhardine Schulze-Smidt's *Mein Rückblick*). More common than the gen. is **von** + dat.: **Seiner dafür so dankbaren Witwe schreib' ich alle Jahre noch einmal, schicke ihr auch von meinen Sachen** (T. Storm an G. Keller, 3. Jan. 1882). **Der Pfarrer soll von unserm Wein probieren** (Hauptmann's *Versunkene Glocke*, Act 3).

The partitive gen. occurs frequently thruout the period as subject or as object in connection with the negative **nicht,** where originally **nicht** was a substantive and was the real subject or object and the gen. a partitive gen. depending upon it (see **145.** *g. Note* 2): **Wenn ich mit Menschen- und mit Engelzungen redete und hätte der Liebe nicht** (1 Cor. xiii. 1, revised ed.). Sometimes similarly after the negative **kaum: Schließlich ist vielleicht auch kaum des Nennenswerten an der ganzen Affäre** (Lauff's *Pittje Pittjewitt*, p. 20). As the original force of the negative is not now felt, the gen. is now retained as object or subject of the verb in the positive form of statement in a few expressions: **Jetzt, da ich der Liebe** (after the analogy of the language in 1 Cor. xiii. 1) **habe, ohne die wir ein tönendes Erz und eine klingende Schelle sind — es ist seltsam, wie ganz ich jetzt ein anderer geworden bin!** (Otto Ernst's *Aus verborgenen Tiefen*, p. 39). **Was wir wissen, ist allein, daß unsres Wandels** (after the analogy of the negative form of statement in **Hier ist meines Bleibens nicht;** see **145.** *g. Note* 2) **auf Erden ist** (Telmann's *Wahrheit*, XII). As explained in **139.** 3. *i. Note*, the partitive gen. after **kein** is in certain set expressions now construed as a nominative or an accusative, i.e. as the subject or the object of the verb: **Auch ist hier kein Besinnens** (Goethe) *There is also here no time for reflection*, but also: **Da gilt auch kein langes Besinnen** (id.). **Es war kein Haltens mehr** *There was no stopping them*, but also with the correct nom. form, **Es war eben kein Halten mehr** (P. Heyse, 8. 345). Also in questions with negative force: **Wie wäre da Haltens gewesen!** (**Immermann, 12, 53**). Also the partitive gen. **Federlesens,** which was originally dependent upon **viel,** and is still frequently so used, as in **ohne viel Federlesens** (Ertl's *Walpurga) without much ceremony, making short work of it,* is no longer vividly felt as a genitive, and can be used without **viel** as an accusative: **Kein Hufschmied brächte je sein Eisen rund, | macht' er mit solchen Bübchen Federlesens** (Hauptmann's *Die versunkene Glocke,* 4). Except in the cases mentioned above and the few exceptions given in **145.** *g. Note* 2 this gen. is now rare, aside from the words **Dings** and **Zeugs** (see **83**), which were originally in the gen. depending upon some word as **viel, nicht, was,** but are no longer felt as genitives.

Often **an** w. dat. is used as a partitive object: **Ein langer Vokal oder eine starke Konsonantenhäufung in der Nähe einer betonten Silbe erfordert zu ihrer Aussprache eine größere Kraft als eine ganz kurze Silbe; und sie entzieht daher dem Akzent der betonten Silbe an Kraft** (Minor's *Metrik,* p. 59, 1st ed.). **Allmählich verloren die Sterne an ihrem Glanz** (Jensen's *Heimkunft,* I).

I. *Attributive Genitive Corresponding to the Genitive with Reflexive Verbs.* Nouns formed from reflexive verbs which take a genitive object, as **sich einer Sache bemächtigen,** may also take a genitive object, but may drop, according to **249.** II. 2. G, the reflexive pronoun: **durch Bemächtigung eines Stromes** (Lohenstein's *Arminius,* 1, 3), corresponding to **Er bemächtigte sich eines Stromes; freiwillige Begebung aller Freuden und Bequemlichkeiten dieses Lebens** (John. Mart. Miller's *Siegwart,* 1, 30), corresponding to **Er begab sich aller Freuden dieses Lebens; diese fast gänzliche Entäußerung der Leidenschaft** (Goethe), corresponding to **Er entäußerte sich der Leidenschaft; diese Enthaltung aller geistigen Getränke,** corresponding to **Er enthielt sich aller geistigen Getränke,** in compounds often with the old uninflected gen.: **Der Reichstag nahm mit 230 gegen 132 Stimmen bei 9 Stimmenthaltungen** (=**9 enthielten sich der Abstimmung**) **den Antrag an** (*Berliner Tageblatt,* Oct. 27, 1921). **Diese Entschädigungen . . . . sind dürftige Entledigungen der Verbindlichkeit der Gesellschaft gegen sie** (Fichte, 6, 33). **Durch sein Hirn zuckte die Erinnerung der Zeit** (Spielhagen's *Faustulus,* p. 1), and likewise in compounds: **Das gleichfalls 1881 geschriebene Kapitel seiner** (i.e. **Auerbachs**) **Kindheitserinnerungen** (Anton Bettelheim in *Beilage zur Allg. Zeit.,* Sept. 20, 1905, p. 549). **Es kommt bei seiner Arbeit sehr auf eine Befleißigung größerer Kürze an** (Georg Edward), and likewise in compounds, as **Rechtsbeflissener.** There is a tendency to use a prep. construction with the verbs of this group instead of a gen., and this tendency is still more pronounced with the derivative nouns: **diese Enthaltung von allen geistigen Getränken; die Erinnerung an die Zeit; die Entwöhnung von der Gesellschaft, vom Wein,** &c.

Instead of dropping the reflexive as in the examples given in the preceding paragraph the reflexive is often retained, especially in case of infinitive substantives: **Ich will nicht einmal dagegen einwenden, daß diese unsere Schwäche ein freiwilliges Sichbegeben der Stärke sein dürfte** (Boy-Ed's *Die säende Hand,* p. 178).

Nouns formed from verbs which take an acc. of the person and a gen. of the thing now require the gen. of the person and a prep. construction with the thing: **die Entsetzung des Beamten von Amt und Stelle, die Entkleidung des Gedankens von allem Zierat.** The gen. here is in accordance with the general rule that the gen. object with nouns corresponds to the acc. object with verbs. The employment of the prep. construction with the thing is in accordance with the tendency among derivatives from the reflexive group described above. The gen. of the thing is found here earlier in the period: excommunicatio, **das heißet Entsetzung derselben Gemeinschaft** (Luther). Also still in a few expressions: **unter der Beschuldigung des Diebstahls, die Beraubung der Ehrenrechte;** also in a few compounds, as **Amtsentlassung, Amtsentsetzung, Eidesentbindung,** &c. The old gen. may survive in **diese Versicherung seiner Teilnahme,** but it may also be construed as the attributive gen. corresponding to the acc. object after the verb, for we can say **Er versicherte mir seine Teilnahme,** or **Er versicherte mich seiner Teilnahme.** The force of the verbal noun is sometimes passive and the genitive corresponds then to the genitive after a passive verb: **seine gegenwärtige gänzliche Geschäftsentlastung** (Raabe's *Kloster Lugau,* p. 4).

2. Instead of the genitive in all the above relations **von** with a dative is now often used, as discussed in **229.** 2, under the prep. **von,** *f, g, j, k,* except in certain cases mentioned in H. *c* and I.

III. Apposition.

1. A noun which explains or characterizes another noun is placed alongside of it, and from its position is accordingly called an *appositive* (placed alongside of): **mein Bruder, der Kaufmann; die Lerche, die muntere Sängerin; meine Vettern Rambergs** (Hartleben) my cousins the Rambergs; **die Massaï, ein kriegerisches Volk** (not able here to agree in gender or number with the noun it explains) **Ostafrikas; diese Bücher, mein Stolz und meine Freude** (agreeing neither in gender nor number); **diese Frau, ein Muster von Sanftmut; Friedrich der Zweite.** The relations of the gen. to its governing noun are, as unfolded above, varied, but the relation of an appositive to its noun is very simple, as it was originally equivalent to a loose explanatory clause or sentence, of which it is the predicate, and is still very often so used, as in **Kairo, [welches] die jetzige Hauptstadt Ägyptens [ist], ist zugleich auch die vornehmste arabische Stadt unsrer Zeit.** In a formal sense an appositive is an attributive element as it is attached to its governing noun in much the same way as an attributive adjective. Hence grammarians now demand that the appositive agree strictly according to the Latin rule with its governing noun, but in accordance with its real nature as a predicate noun we sometimes find, as noted in the following articles, the *nominative,* irrespective of the case of the governing noun. In **252.** 1. *b. Note* we have seen that the predicate noun and adjective after **sein** have actually developed from the attributive appositive construction. On the other hand, in many cases, as in B below, governing word and appositive have in course of time come into such close relations with each other that they now together form one group with one principal stress.

The idea of apposition is also expressed by the appositive genitive, so that here apposition and the genitive compete with each other, as illustrated in **II. 1. G.** *a* above. Another common appositional category is that of a sentence explaining a preceding word, now divided into two distinct groups called *substantive clause* and *adjective clause,* described in **271.** I and II. As these two clauses are not now vividly felt as appositives they are not discussed here. Adjectives and participles standing in the predicate but referring to the subject —predicate appositives—are now felt as also having relations to the principal verb and hence as performing the function of an adverb or rather an adverbial clause, as described in **252.** 1. *c* and **268.** 4. There is still another common appositional category, the prepositional infinitive, which competes with the appositional genitive, as in **die Kunst des Schreibens** or **die Kunst zu schreiben,** and also with the substantive clause, as described in **271. I.** *c.*

Attributive appositives form two groups:

A. The appositive follows the governing word in a loose grammatical relation with the force of an explanatory relative clause, as explained in 1 above, and is in the same case and if possible also gender and number: **Dido, die Gründerin Kar'thagos, soll um das Jahr 814 v. Chr. gelebt haben. Die Athener verurteilten den Sokrates, einen der berühmtesten Weisen Griechenlands. Friedrich den Großen hat teils sein Genie, teils die Eifersüchteleien seiner Gegner gerettet. O, ich Unglücklicher!** In some of these examples as in the last one the governing word and the appositive seem to come close together, but there is even here a slight pause between them.

If the appositive is not modified by an article or adjective, it is often uninflected, but perhaps more commonly inflected: **Das Werk des berühmten und hochgestellten Verfassers, Mitglied** (or more commonly **Mitgliedes,** or **eines Mitgliedes**) **der meisten gelehrten Gesellschaften; unter F. Piquets, Professors an der Universität Lille, sachkundiger Leitung** (*Zeitschrift für Deutschkunde,* 1920, p. 448). If the appositive is in the wk. declension it inclines here more readily to inflection: **Die Expedition des Gouverneurs von Deutsch-Ostafrika Obersten v. Schele.** If, however, the noun is an adjective substantive, or is modified by an adjective, it *must* be declined: **von Baron von W., Gesandtem des Deutschen Reichs,** or **deutschem Gesandten.**

For details concerning the inflection of adjectives and adjective-substantives used in the appositional relation see **111.** 4. *b*, 5. *a*, *b*.

a. A noun which is in apposition with a whole sentence stands in the nom.: **Er will aufbrechen, ein Entschluß, der ihm sehr schwer geworden ist.**

b. When the appositive stands in direct address it is in the nom.: **Dir möchte ich diese Lieder weihen, geliebtes deutsches Vaterland!**

c. Under the influence of lively or excited feeling an appositive in the nom. may often precede the pronoun which it explains or characterizes, altho the pronoun may be in some other case: **Der armselige Ehekrüppel** (feeble old man), **den soll ein frisches Mädchen heiraten!**

d. Remarks and explanations that are made in passing or parenthetically, and do not have as vital a connection with the word explained as a regular appositive, are usually placed in the nom.: **Das Grab war gut unterhalten, mit Reseda und Monatsrosen, die Lieblingsblumen der Verstorbenen.** There is a tendency in recent literature here as elsewhere toward strict grammatical concordance: **Mit Recht wurde der Kunsthalle die dreifache Darstellung der Frau Marie Zacharias von Kalckreuths Meisterhand einverleibt, einer Frau, die dabei durchaus hamburgisch in ihrem Wesen, doch in dieser Hinsicht eine Ausnahme darstellte** (Heinrich Spiero in *Velhagen und Klasings Monatshefte*, 1911, p. 44).

e. An appositive which refers collectively or distributively to two or more nouns, or to a noun in the plural, usually stands in the nom.: **Ich war mit weißen, weitfaltigen Beinkleidern und langem Kaftan, beides aus dem leichtesten Zeuge, bekleidet** (Junker). **Sie sahen zwei junge Herren mit hohen Hüten daherkommen, jeder mit einer hübschen, jungen Dame am Arme** (G. Keller). **Da war auch der Thronerbe mit drei seiner Vettern, sämtlich allerliebste Bürschlein von 7–9 Jahren.**

f. Explanatory appositives are often introduced by conjunctions as illustrated in **233.** C. Especially frequent is the use of **wie** and **als** with appositives, and it requires care to distinguish here the true appositive relation from other constructions which are associated with **wie** and **als**: **Bei manchen Tieren, wie dem Biber, der Spinne, zeigt sich ein hervorragender Kunstsinn,** but **in einem Augenblicke wie der gegenwärtige [ist].** In the first example **wie** connects an appositive with the noun it explains, and hence both words are in the same case. In the second example **wie** is a subordinate conjunction and introduces a clause, and hence the following word is in the nom., as it is the subject of the clause. There is, however, in recent literature a strong tendency here toward the appositional construction: **in einer Zeit wie der unsrigen,** instead of **wie die unsrige [ist].**

Care must be exercised to distinguish between the case where **als** joins to a noun another noun which explains it, and the case where **als** introduces a noun as the predicate complement of a verb which lies concealed in the form of some preceding noun: **Ich verrate es nur dir als meinem besten Freunde,** but **Der Rektor sprach über d a s W i r k e n S y b e l s a l s a k a d e m i s c h e r L e h r e r (= Sybel wirkte als akademischer Lehrer).** In the first sentence **als** connects two words in the same case, of which the second is a true appositive to the first. In the second sentence the noun following **als** is a predicate appositive after the verb, which lies concealed in the form of the noun **Wirken.** The verb that is concealed in the preceding noun is not always literally contained in the stem of the noun, but it is always naturally suggested by the idea that it is implied in the stem: **Man hatte ihm die Stelle als Legationsrat (= er sollte Legationsrat werden) angeboten.**

This distinction is not by any means always followed. At this point considerable confusion prevails, some mechanically conforming the noun after **als** in case to the preceding noun, some distinguishing between the constructions as above described.

g. If the appositive is a title of a work or the name of something, it usually remains in the nom., whatever be the case of the noun it explains: **Wir lesen einen Auftritt aus „Nathan der Weise"** We are reading a scene out of (Lessing's) "Nathan the Wise." **An Bord des „Kaiser Wilhelm der Große"** (Heyking's *Briefe, die ihn nicht erreichten*, p. 174). Grammatical feeling however, often prompts the writer or speaker to give the title a case form in accordance with the structure of the sentence: **Bei keinem früheren Werke ist mir diese visionäre Entstehungsweise so deutlich bewußt geworden wie bei „Wieland dem Schmied"** (Fritz Lienhard's *Wieland der Schmied*, p. vii).

h. A noun in apposition with a preceding possessive adjective is usually in the gen. in accordance with the natural conception that the idea of possession lies in the gen.: **Du wirst doch wenigstens meine, deines Freundes Hilfe annehmen!** In prose, as in the preceding sentence, the appositive stands between the possessive and the noun that it modifies, but in poetry the appositive may follow the noun, as in the following sentence from Schiller's *Piccolomini*, where Thekla speaks of herself and her father, the great Wallenstein: **Ich hatte keine Wünsche, kannte mich | als seine Tochter nur, des Mächtigen.**

The appositive usually follows the noun when introduced by **als**: **Sie** (i.e. **die Griechen**) **sind unsere geistigen Ureltern. Ihre Würde als s o l c h e r ist anerkannt** (Hermann Grimm in *Deutsche Rundschau*, Mai 1896, p. 244). After **als** the appositive is more commonly in the nom. construed as predicate as in *f* above: **Sein Beruf als Richter (= der Beruf, den e r a l s R i c h t e r hat) verpflichtete ihn zur strengsten Unparteilichkeit. Meine Pflichten als König**

von Preußen und als deutscher Fürst gestatten mir nicht, den Entwurf als die Grundlage einer neuen Bundesverfassung anzunehmen (Wilhelm I. in Frankfurt).

i. An exact date, which follows a more general one, usually stands in the acc. in accordance with the general rule for exact time (see **223.** II. 1), altho the noun it explains may be in some other case: **Die Wahl fand S a m s t a g** or **a m S a m s t a g d e n 28. A p r i l statt.** Here **den 28. April** is not a real appositive to **am Samstag,** but both expressions are adverbial modifiers of the same verb, and take the case required by their respective relations to the governing verb, **Samstag** dat. after the prep. **an, den 28. April** acc. of time. The appositional construction, however, is also used here: **am Samstag, dem 28. April.**

j. Learned men often allow the appositive to stand in the nom. in titles of their books, and hence cannot justly complain that people generally follow this practice in the titles they use in addressing letters to them: **Geschichte der holländischen Baukunst, v.** Dr. **G. Galland, Privatdozent** (instead of the more correct **Privatdocenten**); **An Herrn N., ordentlicher** (instead of the correct **ordentlichen**) **Professor** (address on a letter).

k. To complete the confusion that is so prevalent with respect to the proper case of the appositive noun the dat. is used by various authors, especially in Austria, uniformly without regard to the case of the preceding noun: **Wegen Hagens, diesem jungen Laster!** (Ebner-Eschenbach's *Bertram Vogelweid,* p. 203). See also **94.** 3. A. *a.* (2nd par.).

B. The appositive may be a proper name and enter into such close relations with the preceding governing word that it forms with it a group with the stress upon the last member, i.e. the appositive: **der Kàiser Wílhelm, das Gròßherzogtum Báden, die Universitȁt Berlín,** &c. For full rules for inflection see **92.** For an explanation of the stress and the position of the appositive see **II. 1. G.** *a* above.

In many cases the appositive is not a proper name but a noun with a similar force, namely a word or expression representing a thing as an individual, not as a member of a class: **der Schnìtter Tód, Kȍnig Erfólg, der Dȁmon Álkohol, das Gespènst Reaktión, das Wòrt vór, die Vòrsilbe gé-, der Begrìff Schȍn,** &c. The close relations here between the appositive and its governing word cannot always be indicated by the stress, as the appositive is often not a single word, but a thought as a whole which may expand into an entire clause or sentence: **Unter dem Namen „Allgemeine Forstgesellschaft" ist eine neue Gesellschaft gegründet worden. Auf ihrem Grabsteine stehen nur drei Worte: „Ehre dem Herrn." Eins weiß ich: es geschieht nie wieder.** For inflection see **94. 1.** *d,* also *a* below.

a. If the appositive is the title of a work, the name of something, or a technical phrase it usually remains in the nominative, whatever be the case of the noun it explains: **Wir lesen einen Teil des Gedichtes „die Glocke." Und gerade hier wurde immer die Fahrt schon verlangsamt wegen der Nähe des Bahnhofs „Zoologischer Garten." An Bord des „Kaiser Wilhelm der Große"** (Heyking's *Briefe, die ihn nicht erreichten,* p. 174). **Wir planten, mit meinem gegenwärtig im Bankhause Schmitt & Söhne liegenden Vermögen ein Gut zu kaufen. Von seiner Verwendung im Heldengedicht hat er (der Hexameter) den Namen „heroischer Vers."** See also II. 1. G. *a* above.

2. The employment of the appositional construction instead of the gen. of earlier periods is explained in II. 1. H. *a* above, and **94.** 3. A. (also *c* thereunder).

IV. A Prepositional Phrase as Modifier of a Noun.

A noun or pronoun may be modified by a prepositional phrase, which usually follows it. The following groups occur:

1. Nouns denoting an *action* or a *quality* can by virtue of their verbal or adjective nature be modified by a prep. phrase, which is usually identical in construction with the phrase that modifies the verb or adjective of the same origin: **Die Trauer um den Vater, die Freude über den Sieg,** for we say **Man trauert um den Vater** and **Man freut sich über den Sieg; Beliebtheit beim Volke, Zufriedenheit mit seiner Lage,** for we say **Er ist beim Volke beliebt** and **Er ist mit seiner Lage zufrieden.** The idea of agent, however, is regularly expressed here by **durch,** while with passive verbs it is regularly expressed by **von: Die Ermordung Rizzios durch Darnley.** The prepositional phrase after nouns not only corresponds to the similar use of the phrase after a verb, but it is often employed where the corresponding verb governs the accusative or dative. See II. 1. D. *a* (1st and 3rd par.).

Abstract verbal nouns, as in the preceding examples, often take such modifiers as they have almost pure verbal force, but verbal nouns which represent persons are not in German thus freely modified: **ein Streiter für Wahrheit und Recht** and many similar expressions, but in many others the construction is unusual, as in **die Verschwörer gegen meinen Frieden,** where it is usual to employ a pure verbal form, as in **diejenigen, die sich gegen meinen Frieden verschworen haben.** Only in such substantives as have a verbal form, as in case of participles, is this construction freely used: **ein an Schlaflosigkeit Leidender** a sufferer from insomnia, **ein zum Mormonismus Übergetretener** a convert to Mormonism, &c.

On the other hand, this construction is often used in German where there is no closely corresponding expression in English, namely with group-words (**247.** 2). There are two different cases. In the first one the phrase modifies the second component: **Luftangriffe auf Monastir** (*Frankfurter Zeit.*, Jan. 25, 1916). In the other case the phrase modifies the first component: **das schwedische Ausfuhrverbot von Zellstoff** (ib., Jan. 25, 1916), **die feindlichen Angriffsversuche auf Torbole** (*Hamburger Nachrichten*, Dec. 31, 1915). The context here alone determines whether the phrase modifies the first component or the second. Both constructions have been found very convenient and are widely used, altho frequently opposed by grammarians.

2. It is common to modify many other nouns by a prepositional phrase: **der Schreiber beim Rechtsanwalt** the copyist at the lawyer's. Sometimes in descriptive language the prepositional phrase precedes the governing noun: **Auf dem Sims zunächst bei mir eine kleine Katze hat auch die Augen zugedrückt** (Mörike's *Maler Nolten*, 150).

a. Attributive Prepositional Infinitive Clause of Purpose. To 2 above belongs the common prepositional construction with **zu** which expresses the ideas of a goal, end, purpose: **der Weg zur Kirche, zur Armut, ein Ofen zum Brotbacken, ein Zimmer zum Musizieren, ein Raum zum Holzspalten.** In the last example **Holz,** the object of the activity expressed in the verbal stem, is written as one word with the substantive infinitive. In more involved expressions it is necessary to replace the substantive infinitive by the prepositional infinitive: **eine Gelegenheit, viel Gutes zu tun.** When the governing noun is a verbal noun we often, perhaps more commonly, find **um zu** instead of simple **zu** after the analogy of usage with verbs in purpose clauses, just as in **238.** 2. *d. Note* we often find **als ob** in attributive clauses after a verbal noun after the analogy of usage with verbs in clauses of manner: **Dieser war mir ohnehin höchst günstig, weil ich mir seinen „Messias" so zu eigen gemacht hatte, daß ich ihm bei meinen öftern Besuchen, um Siegelabdrücke für meine Wappensammlung zu holen, große Stellen davon vortragen konnte** (Goethe's *D. u. W.*, Teil I, Buch IV). After the analogy of the use of **um zu** here to express purpose it has become quite common to employ **um zu** instead of older simple **zu** also after nouns denoting concrete things wherever the prepositional infinitive clause indicates the purpose for which the thing in question is designed: **Der Mensch braucht nur wenige Erdschollen, um drauf zu genießen, weniger, um drunter zu ruhen** (Goethe's *Werther*, am 9. Mai). **Es darf nicht sein, solange diese Heuchler | noch Öfen haben, um sich Brot zu backen, | und Brunnen, um zu trinken** (Hebbel's *Nibelungen*, II, IV, 2). **Gefütterte Steppdecke über das Bett, um darauf oder darunter zu liegen** (Lexer's *Mittelhochdeutsches Taschenwörterbuch*, explaining the M.H.G. word kulter). **Die Literatur also ist der mächtige Hebel, um jene Materialien empor zu schaffen, die usw.** (Friedrich Kluge's *Unser Deutsch*). **Eines von den Mitteln, um dahin zu gelangen, ist aber dieses usw.** (O. Weißenfels in *Zeitschrift für das Gymnasialwesen*, Feb.-March, 1906, p. 101). Grammarians are wont to censure this usage in both of the cases described above and recommend the employment of simple **zu**, but as literary writers and scholars alike feel the graphic force of this new attributive clause form with a distinctive conjunction which gives clear expression to the idea of purpose it has come into wide use just as the corresponding new adverbial clause of purpose described in **281.** *b. Note* (2nd par.). Compare **185.** A. I. 2. *a.* (**3**). The establishment of **um** with the prepositional infinitive to indicate purpose naturally led to its employment to express the closely related idea of result, at first in adverbial clauses, as illustrated in **276.** D. *b* and **277.** 2. *b* and then in the attributive relation: **Das war der Mann, um Freda zu verstehen; und Freda war das Weib, um diesen da zu würdigen** (Wildenbruch's *Schwester-Seele*, chap. XI).

V. An Infinitive as Modifier of a Noun.

A noun or pronoun may be modified by an infin. with **zu: Das Bestreben sich auszubilden ist lobenswert. Ich habe heute rechte Lust zu studieren** I feel like studying to-day. For fuller treatment of present usage see **185. A. I. 2.** ***a.*** (**2**), (**3**), ***b***; **271.** I. *c*, also IV. 2. *a* above.

VI. An Adverb as Modifier of a Noun.

An adverb may modify a noun in the same way as a phrase (see IV. 2 above) may do: **Der Mensch da, das Buch da, der Felsen dort.**

The adverb often in descriptive language precedes the governing noun: **Links das niedliche Gehöft gehört einem Schwaben** (Viebig's *Das schlafende Heer*, 30). **Drüben die Villen jenseits der Straße machten den Eindruck, als schlummerten sie** (Ompteda's *Maria du Caza*, 286).

VII. A Clause as Modifier of a Noun.

A clause may modify a noun: **die Hoffnung, daß wir ihm helfen werden, verleiht ihm Mut. Die Tat, welche der Verzeihung bedarf, ist nicht gut.**

a. Logical Relations of the Attributive Clause to its Governing Noun. An attributive clause, tho formally connected only with its governing noun, often has logical relations to the principal verb: **das Kind, das ja noch zu jung ist** (with the force of an adverbial clause of cause), **hat einen Vormund erhalten. Ein Bettler, der etwa kommt** (with the force of a conditional clause), **wird abgewiesen.**

A Noun and its Modifier replaced by a Group-word or Compound.

256. All the above kinds of adj. modifiers, except the last two, can sometimes be replaced by terser forms of expression by converting them into the modifying component of a group-word (**247.** 2) or compound: **(1) ein leichter Sinn = Leichtsinn, (2) ein Tropfen Wassers = ein Wassertropfen, (3) dieser Mann, ein Ritter = dieser Rittersmann, (4) ein Aufenthalt für den Sommer = ein Sommeraufenthalt, (5) die Begierde zu herrschen = die Herrschbegierde.**

Objective Modifiers.

Accusative Object.

257. The original concrete meaning of the accusative is unknown. Its Latin name accusativus, i.e. the accusing case, throws no light on its history, altho it in part aptly characterizes it by calling attention to one of its chief meanings, namely that of indicating a person or thing toward which an activity is directed. In Old Saxon the accusative was sometimes used with intransitive verbs of motion to indicate the concrete goal: He scolde gifaren his fader ođil (Heliand 4495–7) *He was to go to his father's house.* In an abstract sense it is still in modern German employed with a simple infinitive, originally the accusative of a verbal noun, to indicate the goal, i.e. the end, purpose of the action: **Er geht baden.** This old meaning explains the commoner one of indicating an object toward which an activity is directed, which within the historic period has quite overshadowed the older idea of a literal goal after verbs of motion: **einen Vogel im Fluge schießen, einen Wagen waschen, ein Haus** (the goal, i.e. the result of the activity) **bauen.** Certain prepositions, such as **auf, an, vor, hinter,** &c., have become associated with the accusative when they indicate movement toward a definite goal. The older idea of goal also explains the common use of the accusative to indicate an object as the goal, the passive recipient of an action in contrast to the nominative which indicates the author of the act: **Der Knabe schlägt den Hund.** The original idea of goal also explains the common use of the accusative to indicate the limit, extent of the action in space and time: **Er ging einen langen Weg. Er lebte viele Jahre.** Out of the idea of the accusative as an object has come the more abstract conception that the accusative is the proper case form of a noun employed to complete the meaning of the verb, a potent modern force which is deeply affecting the language, as illustrated in 2. A below and in **260.** The present abstract force of the accusative clearly shows that the older concrete meaning which we have here tried to trace theoretically has become very dim or has been lost altogether.

The use of the accusative as object appears in the following groups:

1. All transitive verbs require an accusative object to complete their meaning. This acc. represents a thing either as affected by an action, or as the result of it: **Der Knabe schlägt den Hund** (thing affected). **Er hat einen Brief** (result of the action) **geschrieben.** The accusative often represents somebody or something as in a new place or a new condition as the result of the action: **einen in eine Falle locken, sich** (dat.) **die Schwindsucht an den Hals ärgern, Butter aufs Brot streichen, einen tot schlagen, sich arm schenken** to make one's self poor by giving.

In changing such a sentence from the active to the passive, the acc., except the acc. of a reflexive pronoun, becomes nom. and the nom. is put into the dat. after the prep. **von: Der Hund wird von dem Knaben geschlagen** The dog is being beaten by the boy. The nom. subject of a passive verb denotes the same thing as the acc. object of a trans. verb, but from a different point of view. The acc. denotes the person or thing toward which another person or thing is directing an activity, and thus emphasizes the idea of an active agent at work. The nom. subject of a passive verb represents an object as receiving an activity and thus emphasizes the idea of a passive recipient.

a. Omission of Object. Many transitives which usually require an object are used without one when the activity they express is represented only in a general way without reference to an effect upon a particular object, a construction found also in English, but not so wide-spread as in German: **Der Mensch denkt, Gott lenkt** Man proposes, God disposes. **Er gibt gerne** He likes to give. **Ich habe ihn** (i.e. **den Ausdruck „es erübrigt sich"**) **kürzlich immer häufiger gelesen, und stehe jetzt nicht an—Gewöhnung versöhnt** [**einen**] **ja—die Wendung als Bereicherung unserer Sprache anzuerkennen** (J. Ernst Wülfing in *Zeit. für den deutschen Unterricht*, 1899, p. 139). **Die Kenntnis dessen, um was man** [**einen**] **neidet** (Felix Stahl in *Preußische Jahrbücher*, 1915, p. 298). Sometimes also with reference to a definite object, which is so clearly indicated by the context that it is not formally expressed: **Entschuldigen Sie** [**mich**]! Excuse me!, I beg your pardon. **Schlagen Sie** [**Ihre Hand in meine**] **ein!** Give me your hand on that! Compare **258.** 1 (third from the last par.).

b. A number of verbs (**163.** 2. *a.*) are trans. or intrans. according to the idea to be conveyed—trans. when the subject is represented as acting on an object, intrans. when the subject is represented as moving toward a certain goal or as passing over, of its own initiative, into the state caused by the action of the verb: **Das Pferd zieht** (trans.) **den Wagen,** but we also say intransitively **Er ist nach Berlin gezogen** He has moved to Berlin. **Ich habe das Ei gebrochen,** but we also say of the egg when it seems to break of itself without our intending or wishing it **Das Ei ist gebrochen** The egg broke. Thus also **Die Saite ist gerissen** The violin string broke. Here the German by means of the intrans. auxiliary **sein** shows more distinctly than the English that these verbs are considered intrans.

c. In transposing a sentence into the passive voice only the object of the principal verb of the active construction should in the passive be put into the nom., never properly the object of a dependent infinitive. However, in actual usage the object of an infinitive depending upon **anfangen, beginnen, suchen, versuchen, vergönnen, wünschen,** often appears in the nom. in the passive: **Man sucht einen Hühnerhund zu kaufen** becomes **Ein Hühnerhund wird zu kaufen gesucht.** A more correct passive form would be: **Es wird gesucht, einen Hühnerhund zu kaufen.**

d. The object is often expressed in German when it is omitted in English. See **251.** II. A. *d.*

e. In English the accusative is used in some groups of ideas where prepositional constructions are more commonly employed in German. It is usual to explain such differences by saying that the idiomatic structure of the two languages is different. While matters of idiom are often very subtle, some of these things can be explained. For instance, the German has in a number of cases preserved the old idea of instrument better than English. Originally there was a special case form for this idea. Later the dative assumed besides its own functions also those of the instrumental. Still later prepositional constructions replaced the simple dat. Thus to-day we say in English: *The dog is wagging his tail, He shook his head, He is winking his eyes, He threw stones at him,* while the German says: **Der Hund wedelt mit dem Schwanze, Er schüttelte mit dem Kopfe, Er winkt mit den Augen, Er warf ihn** (or **nach ihm**) **mit Steinen.** Compare also **mit den Augen blinzeln** to wink one's eyes, **mit der Peitsche knallen** to crack one's whip, **mit den Zähnen knirschen** to gnash one's teeth, **mit dem Kopfe nicken** to nod one's head, **mit den Flügeln schlagen** to flap its wings, **mit den Lippen schmatzen** to smack one's lips, **mit dem Fuße stampfen** to stamp one's feet, **mit den Händen winken** to wave one's hands, **mit den Schultern zucken** to shrug one's shoulders. While the accusative is also in German sometimes used here, the native German in speaking English often provokes a smile from English-speaking people by a too liberal use of the prepositional construction here.

f. The object may assume the form of the infinitive with or without **zu** (see **185.** A. I. 2. *c*, 3, B. I. 2. *a*, *b*, *c*, *d*) or the form of a clause (**272.** C).

2. *Intransitives Used Transitively with Objects.* The following classes of intransitives often take an object in the acc.:

A. *A cognate accusative,* that is, an object of a meaning cognate or similar to that of the verb, may repeat and also explain more fully the idea expressed by the verb: **Er schlief den Schlaf des Gerechten. Er starb den Tod fürs Vaterland. Er lebt ein elendes Leben. Die Sache geht ihren ruhigen Gang. Sie singt ein Lied.**

This construction has become very productive, so that now an acc. can be quite freely added to an intransitive to complete its meaning. This productive construction stands in close relations to the common tendency to form old group-words (**247.** 2), so often found elsewhere, i.e. to form a compound out of a group of words with a certain oneness of meaning, not however by expressing the grammatical relations between them as in a modern group of words but by merely putting the words side by side without a preposition or the case ending required to express the grammatical relations, as in the old group-words that have come down to us from the prehistoric period. Thus in case of many of these so-called cognate accusatives the form is in fact not an accusative at all but a prepositional construction in which the preposition is suppressed as in group-words (**249.** II. 1. C). Thus instead of saying **mit der Eisenbahn fahren** we can say **Eisenbahn fahren.** Thus in fact this is an adverbial construction. In a number of cases where the preposition is not now used we find the preposition in earlier usage. The dropping of the preposition usually leaves a case form of the noun that is identical with the accusative and often leads to the complete confounding of the prepositional construction with that of the cognate accusative, so that the accusative is used even where the prepositional idea is prominent: **Schon damals bin ich für mein Leben gern Elektrische gefahren** (*Frankfurter Zeit.*, Aug. 31, 1913). In the example quoted below from Hauptmann's "Der arme Heinrich" it can be seen that the accusative also sometimes replaces an older articleless nominative. The verb **spielen** formerly governed the genitive as is illustrated in **260.** 2. A. Even an imperative sentence may thus complete the meaning of the verb: **Die vier Schützen standen habacht** (E. von Handel-Mazzetti's *Stephana Schwertner*, II. chap. II) = **standen in strammer militärischer Positur.** The meaning of the verb is similarly completed by the two nouns **Knall und Fall,** which tersely represent the thought of the sentence **Der Knall des Gewehrs und der Fall des Erschossenen war eins: Er entließ ihn Knall und Fall** He dismissed him very suddenly, or He gave him the grand bounce. Thus this productive construction is growing at the expense of several constructions. It seems quite clear that all these formations are now felt as group-words in which the accusative or an uninflected form which can be construed as an accusative is felt as the proper form for the first component just as in substantive, adjective, and participial compounds and group-words the genitive is now often felt as the proper form of the first component, even tho the genitive does not fit the grammatical relations at all, as illustrated in **249.** II. 1. B. *b. ff* (last par.). Examples: **Er läuft Schlittschuh, Spießruten** *He is skating, is running the gauntlet.* **Er fährt Eisenbahn, Pferdebahn, Omnibus, Kahn, Rad, Nichtraucher, Karussell. Ich verstehe jetzt, warum wir dritte** (also gen.; see **223.** III. *a*) **Klasse fahren mußten** (Spielhagen's *Frei geboren*, p. 43). **Ich fahre nur Arbeiterzug** (Hauptmann's *Einsame Menschen*, 2). **Er reitet Galopp, Schritt, Trab, Karriere** (post haste), **Post** (post haste), **Patrouille, gestreckten Galopp** (at full speed). **Ein ausgezeichneter Reiter, der zum Leid meiner Mutter Rennen ritt** (Ompteda's *Frieden*, I). **Wobei japanische Husaren eine brillante Attacke ritten** (*Hamburger Nachrichten*, Oct. 17, 1904). **Eines Nachts, vor besetztem Dorfe, zögerte er, Erkundung zu gehen** (Fritz von Unruh's *Opfergang*, p. 12). **Er raucht Pfeife. Sie spielten Karten, Schach, Domino, Blindekuh, Haschen, Verstecken, Räuber usw. Er schläft Mittagsstunde. Dann redeten wir Bismarck, Kulturkampf, soziale Frage und was sonst dazu gehört, um einen Abschiedsabend unter guten Freunden hinzubringen, ohne zu sehr zu merken, wie die Zeit läuft** (Raabe's *Pfitzers Mühle*, xx). **Wenn ich nur den Verdacht los würde, daß Sie hier Pose stehen** (Sudermann's *Heimat*, 2, 9). **Ich soll nun für drei Batzen Boten gehen** (go on an errand) (Hauptmann's *Der arme Heinrich*, 3), or **Ich will euch** [als] **Bote laufen** (Freytag). **Sie sollen mir Rede** [earlier in the period **zur Rede**] **stehen** (id., *Soll*, 1. 118). **Über das, was die Jungmannschaft von St. Moritz in Gemeindeangelegenheiten getan, stehen wir gerne Rechenschaft** (Heer's *Der König der Bernina*, xv). **Gefahr laufen** *to run the risk*, but earlier in the period with or without **in: Der Witz läuft schon bei seinem Ursprunge in Gefahr zu witzeln** (Goethe). **Man müßte also diese Gefahr laufen** (Schiller). **Lauf Sturm wider die Ringmauer** (id., *Räuber*, 5, 1). **Auf Posten stehen,** now also **Von elf bis eins stand Vogt zum letzten Male an diesem Wachttage Posten** (Beyerlein's *Jena oder Sedan?*, iv). **Er steht Wache** (either nom. or acc.) or **auf Wache. Wir Bauern lassen doch unsere Jungens nicht Pastor studieren** (K. v. d. Eider's *Meerumschlungen*, I), also **auf** (see **auf,** 2. C. *c* under **231.** II) **den Pastor studieren.** Usually **am Pranger stehen,** but now also without the preposition: **Die Gottesbraut mußte gleich einer Metze Pranger stehen** (E. von Handel-Mazzetti's *Stephana Schwertner*, II, chap. IX). In case of an unmodified weak noun the acc. ending is not always expressed as in the sentence from Hauptmann, but in accordance with usage elsewhere the noun may remain uninflected: **Und wenn der Graf bei ihnen hier Herr spielen wolle — sie wollten es ihm schon verleiden** (Spielhagen's *Sturmflut*, vi, 15), but **Er will den großen Herrn spielen. Sie spielen Soldat** or with pl. form **Soldaten.** It would, perhaps, be more in accord with actual feeling here to regard **Soldat** in the last example or **Herr** in the sentence from Spielhagen as a simple stem, the modifying component of a compound or group-word, of which **spielen** is the basal element. Of course, a plural form can also be used here, as in case of **Soldaten** in the last example, for the plural is often used in group-words, as in **Völkerbund** *league of nations*.

a. Here also belongs the acc. after verbs of motion which denotes the ground over which the motion passes: **Er geht ruhig seinen Weg** He goes quietly on his way. **Der Wein läuft die Kehle hinunter. Er kommt die Treppe herauf.** See also **260.** 2. A. *a*.

b. Instead of a cognate acc. of a noun, the acc. neut. of a pronoun, such as **eins, es, etwas,** is much used: **Er hat wieder eins gelogen** He has lied again. **Sing eins, daß die Zeit vergeht! Laß uns eins plaudern** Let us have a little chat. **Ich wollte, du lachtest eins mit** I wish you would join us in laughing. **Der junge Bursche schob den Hut aus der Stirn, pfiff sich eins, und schritt weiter** (Beyerlein's *Jena oder Sedan?*, I). **Wir wollen uns eins gemütlich rauchen! Die Eifersucht über Spanien gewann es** (won the victory) **über diese politische Sympathie. Er hat mir oft etwas vorgesungen.**

c. The cognate acc. construction cannot usually be transferred to the passive, but like other intrans. constructions can form the impersonal passive (**219.** 5. B), where the cognate acc. remains acc. as in the active, as it has entered into such close relations with the verb that it has formed with it a compound and thus does not change its form: **Es wurde Karten** (acc. pl.) **gespielt** There was playing at cards going on. In some cases the cognate acc. approaches the usual force of the acc., and hence becomes nom. in the passive: **Er singt ein Lied** becomes in the passive **Ein Lied wird von ihm gesungen. Damit würde also derselbe Weg beschritten werden, der im Jahre 1897 gegangen wurde** (*Hamb. Nachr.*, Nov. 1, 1904).

B. Intransitives sometimes take on the trans. idea of *causing, producing, showing* that which results from or accompanies their action, or represent somebody or something as in a new place or a new condition as the result of the action: **Tränen weinen, Zorn blicken, Liebe lächeln, Wut schnauben** to breathe rage, that is, to show rage in breathing. **Er hat mich wach geschrien. Er hat mich halbtot geschwatzt. Er geht sich** (dat.) **Blasen unter die Füße** He walks until blisters form on the soles of his feet. **Er hat sich** (dat.) **ein Loch in den Kopf gefallen. Er hofft, sich in den Himmel zu beten. Er hat sich mit Liebesreden fest an ihr Herz gelogen. Er redete sich um den Kopf. Er räsonnierte sein Herz um jede gute Empfindung. Sie können dich doch nicht um dein Ansehen lachen. Er lachte sich krank, halb krank, tot, zu Tode, bucklig, froh.**

C. *Accusative after Compounds.* When simple verbs enter into compounds many intransitives become transitive, while transitives remain transitive, either with the same force of the verbal element as found in the simple verb or with a different kind of an object. The following groups are common:

a. The accusative after many compound verbs is in fact the object of the preposition compounded with the verb: **einen anreden** to address (lit. to speak *to*) someone. This construction is treated more at length in **215.** II. 3. A. *a, b, c*; **246.** II. 1. *a, b, d, e*; **223.** I. 9. B. 1. *e*, 2; **258.** 1. B. *a*; **262.** I. *b* (2nd par.). In many of these compounds the preposition has lost its old concrete force, so that, as in case of **ver-** (**246.** II. 5. B. *b*), the original construction is no longer distinctly felt: **die Wahrheit verfechten** to defend the truth, lit. to go fighting *before* the truth to defend it.

b. In a large number of compounds the acc. is the object of the verbal element of the compound: **einem einen Stein nachwerfen, dem Käufer Waren vorlegen,** &c.

c. In case of many compounds the accusative is not the object of either of the two components but the object of the compound or group-word (**247.** 2) as a whole. Here as after simple verbs the accusative often represents something as the result of the action, or represents somebody or something as in a new place or a new condition as the result of the action: **den Gipfel ersteigen** to reach the summit, lit. to climb until it results in reaching the summit, **seine Wohnung erfragen** to ascertain his residence, lit. to ask questions until it results in finding out his residence; **die Leute zusammentrommeln, sich durchkämpfen** to fight one's way thru, **einen hereinwinken, einem etwas abbetteln, sein Geld verspielen, sich** (dat.) **die Augen ausgucken, sich** (acc.) **in die Höhe arbeiten, sich** (acc.) **herausreden** to talk one's self out of a difficulty. The object is here often metonymic, i.e. indicating not the real object but something which stands in close association with it: **Er wischt den Staub** (real object) **vom Tische ab** and **Er wischt den Tisch** (metonymic object) **ab.** The prefixes **ab, auf,** &c., indicating a change of place are potent forces in the language. The simple verb **schmeicheln** governs the dative, but **abschmeicheln** *to coax by flattering* takes an accusative object: **Er hat seinem Vater Geld abgeschmeichelt.** In early N.H.G. **abdanken** *to discharge troops*, lit. *to send off with thanks* took a dative like simple **danken** but later under the influence of its prefix **ab-** required an accusative. For another apt illustration see **aufbieten** in **258.** 1. A. *e.* But we usually say **einem heraushelfen** and **einem zu einer guten Stellung verhelfen,** as the influence of the simple verb now in contrast to older usage is stronger than that of the prefix.

In case of many other compounds the accusative represents the person or thing affected: **sich überarbeiten, den Wagen überladen,** &c.

The prefix **ab-** is often used to indicate a goal, end: **eine Gelegenheit abwarten, eine Strafe absitzen, sich abarbeiten.**

The prefixes **er-** and **ver-** sometimes merely convert intransitives into transitives. See **246.** II. 3. *b* (2nd par.), 5. E.

3. *Accusative after Adjectives.* Some adjectives and adjective participles take an accusative object to complete their meaning. See **260.** 3.

Dative Object.

258. The connection of the dative with a verb or adjective is of every degree of closeness, from constituting their necessary complement to forming an almost or entirely independent element which expresses an emotional interest in the statement of fact as a whole: **Das Kind ähnelt der Mutter** The child resembles the mother. **Ich lobe mir mein Dörfchen hier** I for my part have always a word of praise for our village. In the first sentence the dat. is necessary to complete the thought contained in the verb, while in the second it is a lively rhetorical means to show the interest of the speaker in the statement, but it qualifies the thought as a whole rather than the verb alone.

1. Some intransitives take a dat. object to complete their meaning: **Der Spott galt mir** *The ridicule was aimed at me.* The dative seems originally to have denoted in a literal sense *direction toward*, which can still be often felt, as here, after certain verbs, also often after the preposition **zu** *to, toward.* Thus originally both the accusative and the dative indicated a goal or an object toward which an activity is directed. Even in oldest German, however, we find the two forms in general differentiated in meaning as we know them to-day, so that the accusative often indicates that a person or thing is affected in a literal, exterior sense, while the dative indicates that a person or thing is affected in an inner sense, or that a person is involved in an act or statement as his material or higher interests are connected with the act or statement: **Er kitzelt mich,** but **Er dankt, flucht, schmeichelt, hilft, antwortet mir. Er schlug mich** and **Das Feuer hat das Dach beschädigt,** but **Die Arznei schadet dem Kranken** and **Ein wenig Geiz schadet dem Weibe nichts, so übel sie die Verschwendung kleidet** (Goethe). **Ich habe mich an der Hand beschädigt,** but **Das Gerede schadet ihrem Rufe. Die Nachricht ist meinem Vater** (person interested in a statement) **wichtig.** This distinction, tho often observed, is in many verbs entirely disregarded as in the course of the development of the language this principle of clear discrimination has been steadily opposed by the simpler principle of placing, without regard to meaning, the object in the accusative, the case form most commonly employed for the object, so that with a number of verbs the dative has been replaced by an accusative. On the other hand, the idea of a person affected inwardly or interested or involved in an act has in many words proved so strong that an original accusative has been replaced by a dative. This difference in meaning between dative and accusative appears again in the passive, for in changing such active constructions into the passive the acc. becomes nom., but the dat. remains a *dative*, instead of becoming nom., and the sentence is thus without a subject, or in order to conform to the now prevailing grammatical pattern is introduced by **es,** which serves as a formal subject (**219.** 5. B. *a*): **Ich wurde geschlagen,** but **Mir wurde,** or **Es wurde mir von ihm nicht gedankt** I was not thanked by him. Likewise in case of the predicate modal verbal (**180.** A): not **Der ist nicht zu helfen,** but **Dem ist nicht zu helfen.** However, not all intransitives which take a dat. object can form this passive. This construction is limited to such verbs as represent an *activity* as proceeding from a *person*. Thus **Er gefällt mir** *He pleases me* cannot be transferred to the passive, as the verb **gefällt** indicates a *quality* of the person denoted by the subject and not an *activity* which proceeds from him. The main characteristic of this impersonal passive is that it emphasizes an *activity*, and hence the commonest form of the construction has no subject at all, or at least no definite subject, nor any reference to an agent, placing the sole stress upon the activity: **Mir wurde hart begegnet,** or **Es wurde mir hart begegnet** They treated me harshly. It is often desirable, however, to represent some person or thing as acted upon, even with these verbs which govern the dat., and hence under French and English influence and in still greater measure under the pressure of natural feeling this impersonal passive is often, even in good authors, tho severely condemned by grammarians, replaced by the personal passive: **Sei** (**du** understood) **dafür herzlich gedankt,** instead of **Dir sei dafür herzlich gedankt. Wenn vollends die hochtonige Stammsilbe von einer tieftonigen Nebensilbe gefolgt ist** (Bernhard Maydorn in *Wissenschaftliche Beihefte des Allgemeinen Deutschen Sprachvereins*, Fünfte Reihe, Heft 34, p. 128). This contested construction is especially common in the form of an appositional participle, where the noun or pronoun which is limited by the participle is the real subject of the verbal idea in the participle: **Er ging hinab, gefolgt von Peters** (Spielhagen's *Herrin*, p. 194). The passive is often used in the expression **Ich fühle mich geschmeichelt.** It is also common to say: **Er ist in dem Porträt geschmeichelt** and **Das Bild ist geschmeichelt.**

The dative is often omitted when the activity is represented only in a general way without reference to a definite object: **Scheiden tut [einem] weh. Höflichkeit schadet [einem] nie.** Sometimes also with reference to a definite object, which is so clearly indicated by the context that it is not formally expressed: **Verzeihen Sie [mir]!** Pardon me! I beg your pardon! Compare **257.** 1. *a*.

There is another dative of quite a different origin and force which is used with both transitives and intransitives. It gives expression to the ideas of place, position, separation, point of departure, source, association. For examples see B below. As explained in **226** the dative here represents the old locative, ablative, and instrumental (association and instrument) cases, which aside from a few traces of the instrumental had disappeared before the O.H.G. period. The dative after the prepositions **zu** (when it denotes rest in a place), **an, auf, bei, hinter,** &c., corresponds to the old locative, after **von** and **aus** to the old ablative, after **mit** to the old instrumental.

The dative object is found after the following groups of intransitives, some of which pass for transitives in English:

A. *Dative after Simple or Derivative Verbs.* Those which signify:

a. Inclination or *aversion*, a *pleasing* or *displeasing*, a *serving* or *resisting*: **behagen** to please, suit, afford comfort to, **mißbehagen** (opposite of **behagen**), **belieben** (used in a number of set expressions; see also **259.** 8) and **gelieben** (earlier in the period; see 2 Peter ii. 15) to please, **danken** (**abdanken** *to discharge troops*, &c. in early N.H.G. also with dat., but later with acc.; see **257.** 2. C. *c*) to thank, **dienen** to serve, **dominieren** (dat., with more force **über** with acc.; with the acc. in the second meaning) to domineer over, command (i.e. overlook, as from a superior position), **drohen** to threaten, **essen** (early N.H.G. and biblical; see Rom. xiv. 6) to eat unto, **fluchen** (but **verfluchen** with acc.) to curse, **fronen** to toil or slave for, **frönen** to be a slave to (passion, &c.), be addicted to, truckle to, indulge (passions, &c.), **gefallen** to please, **mißfallen** to displease, **gnaden** to have mercy upon, **gratulieren** to congratulate, **grollen** to bear ill-will against, **hofieren** to pay court to, **huldigen** to pay homage to, swear allegiance to, **einem jauchzen** or more commonly **zujauchzen** to hail someone with shouts of joy, **kondolieren** to condole with, **konvenieren** to suit, **lächeln** to smile upon (lit. as in **Lächle deinen Gästen**—Wildenbruch's *König Laurin*, 4, 2—or fig. **Das Glück lächelt mir**), **lachen** to smile upon (lit. and especially fig., as in **Das Glück lacht ihm**), favor (as in **Die Gelegenheit lacht ihm**), **leben** to live entirely given up to or devoted to, live up to, **leuchten** to light the way for (someone), **munden** to taste well to, **pochen** (rare) to defy, **schmecken** to taste (well, &c.) to, **schmeicheln** and **flattieren** (both occasionally with acc. earlier in the period) to flatter, **schmollen** to be sulky toward, **schwören** to swear (the oath of allegiance) to, **trotzen** to defy, **tun** to do unto, treat, **widern** (sometimes with the acc.) to be repugnant to, **willfahren** to gratify, indulge, grant, **zürnen** to be angry at (somebody), &c.: **Nehmen Sie, was Ihnen beliebt** Take your choice. **Was beliebt Ihnen?** What's your pleasure? What can I do for you? **Wie es Ihnen beliebt** as you like. **Nur die Vorstellung der Möglichkeit, es könnte ihr jemand über den Kopf wachsen, ihr dominieren . . . bringt sie außer sich** (Spielhagen's *Herrin*, p. 238), but **auf einer den Hafen dominierenden Höhe** (*Nat.-Z.*, 18, 413). **Und wer die Ruhe stört, Gott mög' ihm gnaden** (P. Heyse, 3, 149). **Wollte die Weisheit dem Herrgott gefallen, | dann gnad' er dir, Herrin, und gnad' uns allen** (Sudermann's *Die drei Reiherfedern*, 3, 4). **Bis dahin lebte er seinen einsamen Studien, seinen Schriften und der Gesellschaft. Diesem allem** (up to all this) **hatte Riekchen seitdem gelebt** (Fontane's *Stechlin*, chap. xii). **Bitte, leuchten Sie dem Herrn** (id., *Cécile*, chap. xxi). **Dann, wie mit Zauberinnen man verfährt, so wollten sie ihr tun** (Wildenbruch's *König Laurin*, 2, 3). **O, muß meine Seele immer | von dieser Speise essen, die ihr widert!** (H. von Hofmannsthal's *Elektra*, p. 20). **Man hat ihm in diesem Punkte gewillfahrt. Sie sah seine bittenden Augen auf sich gerichtet und willfahrte seinem Wunsche** (Ompteda's *Sylvester von Geyer*, XV).

Note. It must be remembered that the dat. object is found only when it is desired to indicate the person interested or involved in the action, or sometimes to indicate a *thing* which by way of personification is conceived as having interests like any person. When a person is not involved in the action, or if it is desired to indicate a result, an acc. or prep. phrase may sometimes be used to complete the meaning of the verb, even after verbs which usually govern the dat.: **Der Feind droht der Stadt mit einer Belagerung,** but **Die Verhandlungen mit Frankreich zogen sich lange hin, drohten mehrmals sogar den gänzlichen Abbruch. Er antwortete** (see *e*) **mir** *He answered me*, but **Er antwortete keine Silbe** *He answered not a syllable* and **Er antwortete auf meine Frage** *He answered my question.* **Er schmeichelte mir,** but **Er schmeichelte es aus mir heraus** and **Er schmeichelte sie beiseite** He coaxed her to one side. This is in general true of all verbs which govern the dat., and hence applies to the verbs in *b*, *c*, *d*, *e*, B, C, D below.

In order to denote that the activity of the verb is directed toward some *thing* **be-** is placed before several of these verbs, which then govern the acc.: **Er antwortete** (see *e*) **mir** and **Unsern Rufen** (personified) **antwortete niemand** (Raabe's *Finkenrode*, xi,), but **Er beantwortete den Brief. Er folgte** (see *d*) **mir, seinen Lüsten** (personified), but **Er befolgte meinen Rat** He followed (heeded) my advice. The prefix **be-** is also used before a few of these verbs to denote that an activity is directed against a *person*. In this case the derivative verb with **be-** governs the acc., and usually has a different shade of meaning from the simple verb, which governs the dat.: **einem dienen** *to serve, be of use to one*, **einen bedienen** *to wait upon* (at the table, &c.). In the same way a shade of meaning arises between these simple verbs, which govern the dat., and their derivatives with other prefixes which govern the acc.: **einem folgen** *to follow one*, **einen verfolgen** *to pursue, persecute one*; **einem schmeicheln** *to flatter one*, **einen um'schmeicheln** *to caress*; **nächtlichem Gesange lauschen** *to listen to nightly music*, **etwas** (acc.) **erlauschen** *to get* or *learn by listening*. In all these cases, as also elsewhere, the dat. brings to the front the idea of a person or a thing with personal attributes that is in one way or another interested or involved in the action, while the acc. emphasizes the idea of the *immediate* object of the activity, and implies that the object is thoroly affected, or (as in the last example) that the action results in the attainment of a definite goal or end.

The action may be directed not only *toward an object*, but also *for* or *against the interests of someone.* In this case the acc. of the thing expresses the first idea, and the dat. (see 3 below) of a noun or pronoun the second: **Er beschädigt mir den Baum.**

b. *Benefit* or *injury*, *fullness* or *lack*: **bekommen** to agree with, **bescheren** to give a present to, **entstehen** or **erwachsen** to accrue to, result, come to, **entstehen** (Lessing's *Minna*, 4, 8; now little used) to fail, be lacking to, **erstehen** to arise, **fehlen** to be lacking to, **frommen** to avail, benefit, profit, **fruchten** to avail, **gebrechen** to be lacking to, **gedeihen** to succeed, **gelten** to be of value to, be intended for, **genügen** to suffice, satisfy, **geschehen** or **passieren** to happen to, serve (see ex.), **glücken, geraten, gelingen** (**219.** 4. A. *b*.) to succeed, **mißglücken, mißraten, mißlingen, helfen** (**259.** 17) to help, **kümmern** (rarely with dat., see **262.** II. A. *c* and B. *d*) to concern, matter to, **mangeln** (see also **260.** 2. A) to be lacking to, **nutzen** or **nützen** (earlier in the period also with acc.; in the meaning *to make use of*, both are trans. with acc., either in the simple form or more commonly in the form **benutzen** or **benützen**) to be useful to, be of service to, aid, **remedieren** to remedy, **schaden** to injure, **sekundieren** (also trans. with acc.) to second, aid, **sein** to ail, **einem stimmen** (Swiss for **für einen stimmen**) to vote for, **streuen** to make a bed for (cattle), **stunden** to grant time to someone for payment, **taugen** (also **für** with acc.) to be good for, be useful to, be adapted to, **vergeben** (see **259.** 34), **versagen** to fail, **verzeihen** (**259.** 34), **wachen** (in the Southwest sometimes **einem Kranken wachen,** usually **bei einem Kranken wachen**) to watch by the bedside of, **zinsen** to pay tribute to: **Die Speise bekommt mir nicht. Unten an dem Christbaum bescherte ich meinen Leuten: den beiden Mägden, dem Kutscher, dem Forstläufer, dem Jägerburschen** (Spielhagen's *Selbstgerecht*, p. 158). **Was fehlt Ihnen?** What is the matter with you? **Alle Mühe fruchtet Ihnen nichts. Es gebricht dem Armen am Gelde. Alles gedeiht ihm. Das gilt mir gleich** It is all the same to me. **Der Spott**

galt mir the ridicule was intended for me. **Es geschieht dir recht** It serves you right. **Was kann's dem Monde kümmern, | wenn ihn der Hund anbellt** (Körner's *Zriny*, 3, 4). **Es nutzt dem Lügner nichts. Was würde es Ihnen nutzen? Es nützt seiner Verdauung** (H. von Hofmannsthal's *Elektra*, p. 14). **Der kann mir nicht schaden. Was ist Ihnen?** What ails you? **Er streut dem Vieh. Zwei Schülern habe ich stunden müssen** (Hauptmann's *Michael Kramer*). **Es taugt dir** (or **für dich**) **nicht. Die Füße versagten mir.** The verb may be understood, or may be unnecessary: **Drum rett' erst ihn, zum zweiten dieses Kind, | die dritte Fahrt der Schwester und der Mutter** (Grillparzer's *Ein treuer Diener*, 4).

c. Fitness, a *belonging to, believing, trusting, obeying, listening*: **anstehen** to look well on, become, be fitting, please, suit, **bleiben** to remain to, **eignen** to belong to, be characteristic of, **folgen** to follow, obey, **gebühren** to be due to, belong to, be becoming to, **gehören** (sometimes with a possessive instead of a dat.: **Das gehört mein**, a blending of **Das gehört mir** and **Das ist mein**) to belong to, **gehorchen**, or now less commonly **gehorsamen**, in colloquial language also **pa'rieren**, to obey, **glauben** (see **259.** 15), **haften** (poetic for **anhaften**) to adhere to, stick to, **horchen** (**259.** 18), **hören** (now no longer common with the dat. in the first three meanings, now usually here **auf einen, auf etwas hören**) to mind, pay attention to, answer to (a name), listen to (in this meaning still with dat. in elevated diction, but replaced in plain prose by **zuhören** with dat.), **lassen** to become, look pretty on, **lauschen** (perhaps more commonly **auf** with acc.) to listen to, **liegen** to be adapted to, **pa'rieren** (see **gehorchen**), **passen** to fit, suit, be agreeable to, **sein** (poet.) to be accorded to (see ex.), **sitzen** to fit, **stehen** to become, look well on, **trauen** to trust, **mißtrauen** to distrust, **vertrauen** to confide in, **werden** (in choice language) to come into one's possession, fall to one's lot, **ziemen** or **geziemen** (or **es ziemt** or **geziemt sich für**) to befit, be befitting for: **Das Haus eignet mir. Nur der Körper eignet jenen Mächten, die das dunkle Schicksal flechten. Den Löwen eignet es, einsam zu lagern. Und doch bin ich der einzige, dem er** (der Pudel) **hört** (Lessing's *Minna*, 1, 8). **Ich höre staunend Euren Worten** (Gutzkow's *Uriel Acosta*, 1, 1). **Selbst der Zorn läßt ihr schön. Gehen wir schließlich zu dem unseres Wissens ersten Versuch der auf belletristischem Gebiet beliebten Frau Ilse Frapan-Akunian über, so will mich bedünken, daß auch dieser talentvollen Dame das dramatische Genre nicht liegt** (Stöckhardt in *Die schöne Literatur, Beilage zum Literarischen Zentralblatt*, Nr. 24, 3. Jahrg.). **Der Rache sei ihr Recht, dem Recht sei Rache!** (Grillparzer's *Ein treuer Diener*, 4). **Dieser Rock sitzt Ihnen wie angegossen** This coat fits you to perfection. **Ehre ward euch und Sieg** (Schiller). **Ein grandioserer Anblick ist mir nie geworden** (Liliencron's *Kriegsnovellen*, Anno 1870). **Dergleichen ziemt mir nicht.**

The verb may be understood: **Der Wahrheit die Ehre!** May honor be accorded to truth. **Dem gemeinsamen Vaterlande alle Wünsche, alle Gedanken, alle Kräfte!** (Admiral von Knorr, Aug. 5, 1914).

Earlier in the period **sein** was used with a dative of possession: **Wem ist das Haus da drüben?** (Goethe's *Stella*, 1). Occasionally still: **Der Graben war uns!** (Generalleutnant z. D. Schott in *Kriegs-Chronik des Daheim*, Band III, p. 32). This construction probably rests upon Latin and French usage and has never taken deep root in German.

d. Approach, restraining, yielding, similarity, dissimilarity: **ähneln** or less commonly **ähnen** to bear some resemblance to, **ahnden** (earlier in the period), now entirely replaced by **ahnen** (now with non-personal subject when the dat. is employed, earlier in the period sometimes also when the acc. was used; also with a personal subject and an acc. object) to have a presentiment of, **begegnen** (earlier in the period, not infrequently with the acc., and still occasionally so) to meet, treat, **sich beugen** (with simple dat. or **vor** with dat.) to bow to, submit to, **erliegen** to succumb to, **erscheinen** to appear to, **folgen** to follow, **sich einem** or more commonly **zu einem gesellen** to join (go to) someone, **gleichen** to resemble, be like, **kommen** to come to (in a figurative sense), attack, treat, speak to, (**sich**) **nahen** or more commonly **sich nähern** to approach, to come very close to, i.e. to be almost equal to (in this sense always **sich nähern: Seine Aufregung nähert sich der Raserei**), earlier in the period both verbs also with **zu** with the dat. instead of the simple dat.), **pa'rieren** to parry one's thrust, meet one's arguments, **schwanen** to have a presentiment of, **steuern** to check, **träumen** (see also **219.** 4. A. *b*) to appear to in a dream, dream of, **verfallen** to meet with (a sad fate, &c.), become a prey to, **wehren** to hinder, restrain, check, **weichen** to yield to: **Der Sohn ähnelt oft dem Vater. Und ähn' ich so dem Tiere mehr — | wohlan! so häut' ich mich vielleicht einmal, | und es entpuppt, wie's ja zuweilen schon | geschehen ist, sich aus dem Tier der Heilige** (Hauptmann's *Der arme Heinrich*, 2, 6). **Es ahnt** (formerly also **ahndet**) **mir** (formerly also **mich**) **nichts Gutes. Ich ahnte nichts davon. Ich bin ihm auf der Straße begegnet. Da begegneten wir Wunderlich, den Assessor, auf der Treppe** (Bismarck to his wife, Sept. 26, 1850). **Er begegnete auf der Straße die Lehrer vom Gymnasium** (Ompteda's *Sylvester von Geyer*, xxii). **Nicht deine Jahre zählte das Volk, nur deine Taten . . . . Greise beugten sich willig deiner Jugend** (Sudermann's *Teja*, 3). **Beuge dich vor dem Alter! Sich diesen zu gesellen, fiel Opitz aber nicht ein** (Fontane's *Quitt*, chap. iii). **Er gleicht seinem Vater, wie ein Ei dem anderen. Diese Einsicht kommt Ihnen spät. Kommen Ihnen da keine Gedanken, Ohm Reinhold?** (Halbe's *Der Strom*, p. 11). **Wir kommen ihm eben, wie man so einem kommen muß. Langsam, vorsichtig, Schritt um Schritt!** (ib., p. 55) We shall attack it (the river, in attempting to regulate its course), &c. **Laß dir nicht so kommen!** Don't put up with such treatment! **Komm mir nicht so!** Don't speak to me in that way! **Wagte sie einmal, ihren Mann nach Heinz zu fragen, so blieb er entweder ganz die Antwort schuldig oder hieß sie ihm mit dem Jungen ein für alle Mal nicht mehr zu kommen** (Storm's *Hans und Heinz Kirch*). **Ich habe das Gefühl, daß alles halbwegs Gescheite, das ich im Hirn hatte, verausgabt ist, um Ihnen zu parieren** (Suttner's *Im Berghause*, p. 33), but

Ich parierte den Schlag mit einem Stock. Mir schwant nichts Gutes. Mir schwant nichts von Gefahr. Mir schwant, daß usw. Heute kommt er gewiß; es schwant mir so. Er steuert der Unordnung. Als sie endlich schlief, träumten ihr häßliche Dinge (H. Böhlau's *Adam und Eva*, chap. i). **Er verfiel einem traurigen Schicksal. Ich verfiel den Ideen, die du kennst** (Otto Ernst's *Jugend von heute*, 4, 7). **Man muß dem Bösen wehren mit harter Strafe.**

After transitive verbs of removal the dative is much used to indicate the person from whom the thing in the acc. is taken: **Er nahm mir meine Brieftasche weg** He took my pocket-book away from me. **Er stahl mir meine goldene Uhr. Der Wolf raubt dem Hirten Schafe.** This dat. is thus often rendered in English by *from*, but in German it does not in fact express separation, but is a *dative of interest* (see 3. B below) denoting the person that is benefited or injured by the action.

e. A declaration, response, announcement, signaling, advice, thus in general in accordance with the original meaning of the dative indicating the direction of an activity toward a goal, now usually a person: **antworten** (see *a, Note*) to answer, **aufbieten** (earlier in the period **einer Armee, allen seinen Kräften, allem aufbieten,** now with the acc., **alle seine Kräfte, alles aufbieten,** as the idea of a change of place here as in **257.** 2. C. *c* has suggested the use of the acc.) lit. *to send word to* (an army, one's physical or intellectual forces, &c.) *to rise*, now felt as meaning *to call out, summon*, often fig. *to do one's utmost*, **beten** (with dat. only in elevated style, usually with **zu** + dat.) to pray to, **blinken** or **blinzeln** to *wink at*, **bürgen (einem für etwas bürgen)** to answer, vouch, be responsible to someone for, guarantee, **entgegnen** to reply to, **erwidern** to reply to, **flehen** (dat. common in early N.H.G., now with **zu** + dat.) to pray to, implore, **klagen** to complain to (in this meaning usually in connection with an object: **einem sein Leid klagen),** mourn for (earlier in the period with dat., now with acc. in poetic style, and in plain prose replaced by **beklagen), klingeln, schellen,** or **läuten** to ring the bell for, **kündigen** to give notice to leave (a dwelling, position, &c.), **lügen** to tell a lie to (in early N.H.G.; see Judges xvi. 10; now replaced by **einen belügen),** lie to or deceive (still in poetic language), **pfeifen** (see **259.** 26), **predigen** to preach to, **raten** advise, **einem rufen** (see **259.** 26), **einem** or **an einen schreiben, telegraphieren, depeschieren, drahten, telephonieren** to write, telegraph, telephone, to someone, **schreien** (see **259.** 26), **winken (259.** 26): **Antworte mir auf die Frage! Er erwiderte mir nichts auf diesen Vorwurf. Der Herr klingelt dem Bedienten. Von fünf zu fünf Minuten hat er dem Kellner geläutet** (Franzos's *Der Gott des alten Doktors*, p. 270). **Mir ist gekündigt** I have received notice to leave (my position or dwelling, according to the connection). **Denn alles log mir, was ich hochgeachtet** (Schiller's *Wallensteins Tod*, 2, 7). **Wem nicht zu raten ist, dem ist auch nicht zu helfen. Er predigt tauben Ohren.**

f. Poetry prefers the dat. in a large number of cases where in prose some other construction, especially a prep. phrase, is used: **Seinen [= vor seinen] Blicken, seinem Winken | möcht' ich in die Knie sinken** (Goethe's *Faust*, l. 6630); **schmunzeln** (ib., l. 6100), **rümpfen** (l. 5272), &c. **Das macht mich dem Tod erblassen** (Grillparzer's *Ahnfrau*, 2). **Ich will lachen seinem Wüten** (ib.). **Nie hab' ich dem Tod gezittert** (ib.). **Dumpf ertönte die Gegend dem [= von dem] Sturze** (id., *Die Argonauten*, 2). Many other verbs might be added to these. Compare 3. A. *b* below.

g. In early N.H.G. other verbs not included in the above lists governed the dat., such as **bescheiden** (Matth. xxviii. 16), **lieben** (Ecclus. vii. 28; the dat. still surviving after the derivatives **belieben** and **gelieben**; see *a* above) in early N.H.G. *to be dear to*, **betten** (see **259.** 9), **schonen** or **verschonen** (1 Sam. xv. 15), **schweigen** (Job xi. 3; now **zu** with dat.), **seg(e)nen** (2 Sam. xxi. 3), **sorgen** (1 Cor. vii. 21), **verhindern,** &c. The fine shade expressed in the dat. is not felt so vividly as in earlier periods, and thus the dat. is gradually losing ground, yielding to the acc. Poetry still preserves here occasionally in case of **betten** and **schweigen** older usage.

B. *Dative after Verbs Compounded with Prefixes.* The dative object stands after the following prefixes: **ab, an, auf, aus, bei, be'vor, ein, ent-, ent'gegen, fern, gegen'über, gleich, inne, nach, nahe, ob, unter, vor, vo'rauf, vo'raus, vor'bei** (see **259.** 36), **vor'her, wider, zu, zu'vor,** and in a few cases **über** and **um.** Exs.: **Sein Betragen fiel mir auf** His conduct attracted my attention. **Der Name fällt mir nicht gleich wieder ein,** but in **Sie heizt ihm ein** *She is making it warm for him, is pitching into him* the dative is not governed by **ein** but belongs to the whole sentence and hence is a dative of interest (see 3. B below). **Der Jäger stellt dem Wilde nach** The hunter is on the watch for the game. **Es kam mir sonderbar vor. Er eilte mir voran** He hurried on ahead of me. **Mir ist großes Unrecht widerfahren. Mir ist viel Gutes von ihnen widerfahren. Wider'sprich mir nicht. Er setzte mir mit Bitten stark zu. Er kam mir zuvor.** For exceptions see **262.** I. *b*, 2nd par.

In M.H.G. **mit** belonged to this list, and survives in the transitive **mitteilen (einem etwas mitteilen)** *to communicate to*, lit. *to share with* and in the intransitive **mitspielen** *to treat* or *use ill* or *roughly, play a nasty trick on (someone)*, lit. *to tilt with*: **Wie kannst du mir so mitspielen?**

The idea of personal interest is prominent in many of these datives, but the ideas of a goal, place, position, separation, point of departure, source, are also common: **Er geht seinem Schicksale mit Ruhe entgegen. Das Schiff steuerte dem Lande zu. Er lebte seinem Vorbilde nach. Es ist merkwürdig, daß manchem Namen etwas wie eine mystische Macht innewohnt** (Fontane's *Poggenpuhls*, chap. xi). **Ein Makel klebt ihm an,** but where the object is a thing, the prepositional construction is used, or the object is suppressed: **Das Pflaster klebt an dem Finger** and **Das Pflaster klebt an. Mir liegt eine schwere Verpflichtung auf,** but **Die Zeitungen liegen auf dem Tische** and **Zeitungen liegen auf. Mir lag diese Pflicht ob** This duty devolved upon me, lit. lay *upon, over* me. Compare **223.** I. 9. B. 1. *a*. **Neuere Nachrichten lassen es als ziemlich sicher erscheinen, daß Hendrik Witboi der aufständischen Bewegung nicht fernsteht** (*Hamb.*

Nachr., Oct. 15, 1904). **Die Sprache steht den reichsten nahe, wenn nicht gleich oder über** (*Archiv für das Studium der neueren Sprachen*, 63, 197). **Im Neuhochdeutschen kann sich dieser mechanische Trieb dem logischen Bedürfnis überordnen** (Andreas Heusler in *Anzeiger für deutsches Altertum*, 1902, p. 328). **Er sagt ihm ab** (early N.H.G.) He sends him a challenge, breaks with him, lit. announces that he has separated himself *from* him. **Er schwört seinem Gott ab,** or **Er schwört dem Kaiser ab** He renounces his god, or the emperor, lit. swears that he has separated himself *from* his god, or from the emperor, but the acc. often occurs here indicating a different point of view: **seinen Gott, seinen Glauben, seine Farben abschwören** to swear that one has given up (lit. put away) his god, his former faith, his colors. **Ich habe allem Glück entsagt** I have renounced (lit. separated myself from) all happiness. **Er weicht mir, dem Wagen aus. Du bist meinem Einflusse entwachsen. Er ist der Gefahr entflohen. Das Wort ist meinem Munde nur im Zorn entfahren. Er entstammt einem alten patrizischen Geschlecht.**

a. Transitives having these prefixes take a direct object of the person or thing in the acc. and an object of the person or thing in the dat., denoting the individual to whose advantage or disadvantage the action accrues, or indicating a goal, place, association (see **262.** I. *b*, 3rd par.), separation, source: **Er sagte, schrieb, telegraphierte, telephonierte ihm den Besuch ab** He canceled his promised visit by spoken word, by letter, by wire, by phone, or often the acc. is suppressed: **Er sagte, schrieb usw. ihm ab. Er trocknete ihm den Schweiß ab.** In poetic language **Er trocknete der Stirne den Schweiß, das Blut ab,** but in plain prose **von** usually replaces the dative of the thing: **Er trocknete den Schweiß von der Stirne ab,** also the dat. of the person after **abwenden: Er wandte sich von mir ab. Er drängte ihm seine Ansichten auf,** or with the omission of the dat., where it refers to the subject: **Er setzte [sich] den Hut auf,** but where the prepositional object is a thing the prepositional construction is usually employed or the object is suppressed: **Man setzt das Essen auf den Tisch,** or **Man setzt das Essen auf. Er legt meinen Worten einen andern Sinn unter** He puts another meaning into my words. **Sie singt uns heute abend das Lied vor** She is going to sing the song to us this evening. **Er sagt mir Böses nach** He speaks ill of me. **Er bot mir seinen Beistand an. Er widersetzte sich der Obrigkeit. Du hast den Jüngling dem Verderben zugeführt. Er legt dem Pferde den Zaum an. Er setzte dem Pferde einen Sattel auf. Er setzte dem Buche eine Vorrede vor. Er legte dem Huhne Eier zum Brüten unter. Binde dir das Tuch um! Du hast mich allem Leiden entrückt. Er hat das Beste in seinen Werken (von) den Alten entlehnt.** In the passive the accusative becomes nominative, the dative remains: **Eier wurden dem Huhne zum Brüten untergelegt.**

At the first glance it might seem that the dative in many of these compounds depends upon the preposition contained in the compound. A closer inspection, however, will show conclusively that the dative is used with **an, auf, unter, vor** even with verbs of motion, where according to usage elsewhere the acc. should be used. Contrary to older usage (see **262.** I. *b*, 2nd par.) the dative is now used with these prefixes without regard to the idea of rest or motion. Different factors have brought about this uniformity. In many of the compounds the idea of reference (3. A below) or personal interest is stronger than the usual force of the preposition, and thus leads to the use of the dative. The words often have a figurative or altered meaning, so that the usual force of the preposition is not vividly felt. The use of the dative with the transitives here is made easy by the fact that the construction is thus conformed to one of the commonest types in the language, namely, the use of the dative in connection with an accusative. For additional treatment of this common type see **262.** I. *b*.

The employment of the dative with **wider** here while it elsewhere only governs the accusative is explained by older usage, according to which it took either dative or accusative. To-day we find the dative after **wider'fahren** to happen to, befall, **wider'stehen** to be repugnant to, **wider'streben** to strive or struggle against, be opposed to, **wider'sprechen** or **wider'reden** to contradict, **wider'streiten** to clash with, militate against, **sich wider'setzen** to resist: **Es widerstrebt meinem Gefühl. Das widerstreitet unseren Freiheitsbriefen. Er widersetzte sich dem Schutzmann.** The accusative is used with **wider'raten** to speak against, advise someone against, **wider'legen** to refute: **Das sind Erscheinungen, welche die Verordnung eines Heilmittels widerraten. Ich hatte es** (object of wider) **ihm widerraten.** A little earlier in the period also **wider'sprechen** was often used with an accusative. This older usage survives in **unwider'sprechlich** incontrovertible, which presupposes a transitive **wider'sprechen: wiewohl Notizen dieser Art gehen unwidersprochen in die Welt** (*Hamburger Nachrichten*, Jan. 1, 1907). Of course, such words as **wider'rufen** to retract, repeal, lit. to call back, **wider'hallen** (trans.; see **215.** II. 3. A. *e*), &c. take the acc. as the noun is the object of the verb, the prefix being an adverb.

b. Also a foreign prefix can take a dat. object if it has the force of a German prefix: **Wir meiden den Bezirk, welcher dem schwedischen Kriegsvolk kontribuiert** (= **beisteuert**) (Freytag's *Rittmeister*, chap. iv). **Wie können Sie mir dergleichen imputieren, was mir doch nicht einmal im Traume einfallen würde!** (Spielhagen's *Sturmflut*, I. 9). **Mit dem Adjektiv hat das Partizipium gemein, daß es einem Substantivum des Satzes attribuiert ist** (Brugmann's *Kurze Vergleichende Grammatik*, p. 606). **Wo ein Relativsatz einem einfachen Attribut koordiniert ist** (*Anzeiger für deutsches Altertum und deutsche Literatur*, xxix, 3. Januar 1904, p. 173). **Ja sehen Sie, wenn man den Frauen opponiert** (**entgegentritt**), **so nennen sie das immer Grobheit** (Otto Ernst's *Jugend von heute*, 1, 10). Thus also **adhärieren** to adhere to, **aggregieren** to attach (an officer) to, **akklamieren** to acclaim, applaud, **applaudieren** (sometimes also with acc.) to applaud, **ein Wort einem anderen apponieren** to place one word in apposition with another, **assentieren** to agree with, **assistieren** to help, be present at, **attachieren** to attach to the suite of (as in **Er ist der [or bei der] Gesandtschaft attachiert**), **einem seine Ankunft avisieren,** or **einen von seiner Ankunft avisieren** to notify someone of, &c., **imponieren** to impress forcibly, awe.

präsidieren (sometimes with acc.) to preside over, **einem etwas proponieren** to propose something to someone, **einer Sache eine andere substituieren** or **eine Sache statt der anderen substituieren** to substitute one thing for another, **suggerieren** to suggest to, **sukzedieren** to follow, succeed.

C. *Dative after Loosely Compounded Verbs.* The dative object also stands after a number of verbs loosely compounded with an adjective, noun, adverb, or prep. phrase: **sich Bahn brechen** to break a path for one's self, **anheimfallen** to fall to (one's lot), devolve upon, escheat to, fall a prey to, **es fällt mir leicht** it is, comes easy to me, **es geht mir gut** I am (doing) well, **mit Rat und Hilfe zur Hand gehen** to assist by word or deed, **zu Leibe gehen** to attack, **zum Ruhme gereichen** to redound to (one's) glory, **standhalten** to hold one's own against, **worthalten** to keep one's promise with, **zugute kommen** to be to one's benefit, **heimkommen** to come home to (in a fig. sense), **zu Hilfe kommen** to come to one's aid, **zustatten kommen** to come in handy to, be of use to, **zu stehen kommen** (see **259.** 29) to cost, come to, **einem** (or now often also incorrectly **einen**) **zur Ader** [Blut understood] **lassen** to bleed (draw blood from) someone, **heimleuchten** to make short work with (someone), give (someone) a piece of one's mind, turn (someone) off, **einem** or **einen** (the dat. to be construed as the indirect object of the verb and **angst** as a noun used as direct object; the acc. to be construed as the direct object of the verb and **angst** as an objective predicate adjective) **angst machen** to frighten, alarm one, **einem** or **einen bange** (to be construed as an adverb with dat., or as an objective predicate adj.) **machen** to make one afraid, **einem gruselig machen** to make one feel creepy, **einem** or **einen heiß machen** to make one angry, excited, **einem warm machen** to make it hot for someone, **einem mit alten Erinnerungen warm machen** to warm someone up or thaw him out by arousing old memories in him, **einer Dame den Hof machen** to court, pay one's addresses to a lady, **einem dreinreden** to put in words and thus interrupt someone, **das Wort reden** to defend, **einem für etwas gutsagen** to stand responsible to someone for something, **lobsingen** to sing praises to, **hohnsprechen** (sep.) to scoff at, **einem zur Vernunft sprechen** to urge one to come to reason, be reasonable, **Rede stehen** to answer one, account to someone for something, **zu Diensten stehen** to be at one's service, **einer Sache** (**den Umständen usw.**) **Rechnung tragen** to take into account, make allowance for, **genugtun** to satisfy, **guttun** to do good to, benefit, **leid tun** to fill one with pity (see ex.), **not sein** or **not tun** to be needed (by someone), be lacking to, be necessary for, **wehtun** to hurt, grieve, **sauer werden** to become troublesome to, cause difficulty to, **zuteil werden** to fall to (one's) lot., **einem Dank für etwas wissen** to be thankful to someone for something, **wohlwollen** to be kindly disposed toward, **heimzahlen** to pay (someone) back (fig.), and many others of like formation. Exs.: **Das gereicht ihm zum Ruhme** That redounds to his glory. **Das kommt ihm zugute** He gets the benefit of it. **Die Erfahrung kommt ihm zustatten** Experience stands him in good stead. **Das soll ihm teuer zu stehen kommen** He shall pay dearly for that. **Er hatte offenbar die löbliche Absicht gehabt, mir ein bißchen gruselig zu machen** (Paul Keller's *Waldwinter*, IV). **Das Kind sprach der Mutter zur Vernunft** (Wildenbruch's *Die Alten und die Jungen*). **Selbst mir, seinem besten Freunde, hat er nicht darüber Rede gestanden, was aus einer projektierten oder wirklich vollzogenen Heirat geworden ist, von der vor etwa sechs Jahren ein Gerücht erging** (Heyse's *Im Paradiese*, I, chap. vii). **Die Arznei wird Ihnen guttun.** **Sie tun mir leid** I feel quite sorry for you. **Mut ist uns not und ein gefaßter Geist** (Schiller). **Lenke deine Seele jetzt auf andere meinetwegen irdische Dinge, es tut dir not** (Hauptmann's *Der arme Heinrich*, 4). **Das ist, was uns not tut.**

We often find this favorite dative construction where in English we have a prepositional object. In German both of these constructions are used with a slight shade of meaning. The preposition points to a person toward whom the activity is directed, while the simple dative represents the person as involved in the action in an emotional way or thru personal interests: **Es war der erste bleibende Eindruck, den ein weibliches Wesen auf mich gemacht hatte** (Goethe's *Dichtung und Wahrheit*, I, 5). **Welchen Eindruck hat sie Ihnen gemacht?** (Suttner's *Im Berghause*, p. 42).

Such compounds occur often in connection with a dat. of the person or thing, and an acc. of the person or thing, or a clause: **Eines Tages stieg auch er langsam und gewichtig die drei Treppen zu Susannes Wohnung hinauf, um sich der Tante in Erinnerung zu bringen** (Isolde Kurz's *Das Vermächtnis der Tante Susanne*). **Ich führte ihm zu Gemüte, daß usw.** I impressed upon his mind that, &c. **Er gab seine Familie dem Elende preis.** **Ich hielt es seiner Unwissenheit zugute** I put it down to his ignorance. **Aber man wußte, daß der alte Herr seiner Zeit in Polchow nicht angenommen worden war, und hielt ihm deshalb seinen Zorn zugute** (Spielhagen's *Herrin*, p. 208) made allowance for his anger. **Man kann ihm nichts zu Dank machen** One can never please him. **Niemand kann es ihm recht machen** No one can satisfy, please him. **Mach' mir nichts weis** Tell me no fibs. **Er täte keiner Fliege was zuleide.**

D. A number of impersonal verbs take a dat. object. These verbs are enumerated in **219.** 4. A. *b.*

2. *Dative after Adjectives, Participles, Adverbs, Nouns.* Also adjectives, participles, adverbs, and nouns, take a dative object to denote that (usually a person) toward which the given quality or activity is directed, often preserving faithfully the original dative idea of *direction toward*, which in English must be expressed by a preposition: **Er ist mir, den Lügen feind** He is an enemy to me, to lies.

A. The following are the principal adjectives, participles, and adverbs which are used with the dative:

a. Those signifying inclination, attitude (harshness, kindness, favorableness, &c.), gratification, comfort, service, benefit, a sufficiency, a belonging to, being peculiar to, fidelity, obedience, fitness, nearness, association, similarity, conformity, superiority, and their opposites, all of which conform in general meaning to the verbs in 1. A above: **Er ist mir gram** He has conceived a dislike toward me. **Er ist mir böse** (angry at). **Sie ist mir, meinem Plane nicht hold. Ihr Besuch ist mir stets angenehm. Weil — — weil's nicht wahr ist; und weil mir nichts zuwiderer ist als die Unwahrheit** (Wildbrandt's *Die gute Lorelei*, vii). **Sein Vergehen ist ihm leid** He is sorry for his fault. **Laß dir das nicht leid sein!** Don't be uneasy about that! **Das Unternehmen wurde ihm leid** He began to repent of his enterprise. **Diese Speise ist dem Kranken nicht zuträglich** or **bekömmlich. Die Maikäfer sind den Bäumen schädlich. Die mir gehörigen Bücher** the books which belong to me. **Naschen ist den Kindern eigen. Das Mädchen ist ihm treu. Er ist seinen Idealen abtrünnig geworden. Er wohnt uns am nächsten. Meinem Hause benachbart liegt das Haus eines jüdischen Mannes** (Heyse's *Maria von Magdala*, 1, 5). **Der Knabe ist dem Vater sehr ähnlich. Die Kamele lagern Felsblöcken gleich im Sande. Die Richtung des Stromes, der Stromstrich, läuft hier dem Ufer nicht parallel. Er ist mir darin über** *He is superior to me in that*, but when the subject is a thing **über** has developed a meaning somewhat different in its application: **Das Leben, das sie jetzt führte, war ihr ohnehin über geworden** (Telmann's *Wahrheit*, IX) *She had besides become sick of the life*, &c.

Note. The dative after adjectives, participles, and verbs is often replaced by a prep. construction. Except in figurative language, or in case of personification where things are represented as having interests, as in the tenth sentence, the prep. construction is the rule for nouns representing things, and is also common for persons, as the various prepositions can express so many appropriate shades of meaning: **Er ist mir geneigt** *He is favorably inclined toward me*, but **Der Mensch ist zum Bösen geneigt** *Man is inclined to evil*. **Die Schuhe passen mir** *The shoes fit me*, but **Der Deckel paßt auf den Topf** The lid fits on the kettle. **Die beiden Leute passen recht zu einander** The two form a good match. **Das Haus gehört** (belongs) **mir. Er gehört in das Haus** The house is the place for him. **Er gehört unter meine besten Freunde** He is one of my best friends. **Er gehört zu unsrer Freundschaft** He belongs to our circle of friends. **Dieser Schuh gehört auf den linken Fuß. Die Anmerkung gehört nicht hierher, sondern an eine andere Stelle.**

b. The dat. also stands after adjectives in many set expressions in connection with a verb, especially an impersonal verb: **Mir ist wirr im Kopf** My head is confused. **Mir ist gar nicht lächerlich zu Mute** I am by no means in a laughing mood. **Mir wird von alledem so dumm, als ging' mir ein Mühlrad im Kopf herum. Mir ist übel** I feel sick at my stomach.

B. *Dative after Nouns*. The dative is sometimes found with nouns which have meanings and form corresponding to verbs in 1 and adjectives in A above: **Vergebens war es, daß der Bürgermeister Gehorsam dem Gesetze forderte** (Immermann's *Münchhausen*, 6, 11). **Diese Kunstwerke sind bloß seit 1816 nach ihrer Einverleibung dem britischen Museum in die allgemeine Kenntnis übergegangen** (Springer's *Kunsthistorische Briefe*, p. 197). **Ich schwöre Treue der Verfassung, Gehorsam den Gesetzen usw.** (official oath prescribed Aug. 14, 1919). Altho this dative has been attempted by different authors, it has not become established, and is usually replaced by a prep. construction: **Daß sich für die Jugend Gehorsam unter das Gesetz zieme** (Gutzkow). **Der Gehorsam der Untertanen gegen die Obrigkeit.** In many cases, however, the dative is seemingly connected with a noun, where in reality it belongs to the sentence as a whole, i.e. it is in fact a sentence dative as described in 3, A, B, C below: **Er war mir ein Vater. Er ist . . . ein Muster Bürgern und Bauern** (Goethe's *H. und D.*, III, 53). **Das war euch eine Freude** That was a joy, I can tell you.

3. *The Sentence Dative*. The dative in the preceding articles is more or less connected with a single verb, verbal expression, or an adjective whose meaning it completes, but the dative of the person (or far less commonly of the thing) interested in the statement is often used to qualify the whole sentence, and thus is not limited to a definite group of verbs or adjectives. This dative shows the following shades of use:

A. *The Dative of Reference*. The dative often denotes the person to whom the statement seems true, or with reference to whom it holds good: **Wir heißen ihm nur Kinder** We are to him only children. **Sie ist mir schön** To me she is pretty. **Das ist mir ein Rätsel** That is a riddle to me. **Das bleibt mir ein großer Trost. Das Kleid ist mir zu lang** The dress is too long for me. **Der Rock ist ihm nicht weit genug. Das ist mir nicht ganz klar. Es klang dem peinlich gespannten Ohr wie fernher rauschendes Wasser. Bin ich derselbe denn nicht mehr, dem hier sonst alle Türen sprangen?** Am I not any more the same man, to whom once all doors stood open? **Mir** (upon me, as far as I am concerned) **hinterließ seine Rede einen tiefen Eindruck. Das ist mir nicht erinnerlich** I do not remember that. **Er machte es mir leicht** He made it easy for me. **Er machte es mir möglich zu reisen. Dem Zornigen wallt das Blut,**

schwellen die Muskeln; dem Ärgerlichen läuft die Galle über. „Willst du sein Werben eine Drohung nennen?" „Es ist die schrecklichste von allen mir" (Goethe's *Iphigenie*, 1, 2). **Mir war zuweilen, als sei ich von unserm lieben Gott geschieden** (Freytag's *Rittmeister*, ix). **Ich möchte dir was sein können** (Hauptmann's *Einsame Menschen*, 2). **So** (because he was supposed to be unacquainted with the German language) **konnte er sich kleine Frechheiten erlauben, die einem anderen nicht durchgegangen wären** (Beyerlein's *Jena oder Sedan?*, iv). This dative is often found in the old verbless attributive type of sentence described in **252.** 1. *b. Note*: **Freies Wort jeder Partei** (on the title page of *Der Tag*) *The columns of this newspaper are open to every party.* The noun **Wort** is here the logical subject and the attributive adjective **freies** is the logical predicate. The dative is also often used here where the attributive adjective is the logical objective predicate: **Freie Bahn dem Tüchtigen!** *Let us keep the road* (to employment, promotion in public service, &c.) *open to able men.* **Freie** is here the logical objective predicate to **Bahn,** which is the object of some verb understood. Compare **262.** III. 2. B. Similarly the dative is found in verbless subordinate clauses of the old appositional type: **So sprich von Szylla, leiblich dir Geschwisterkind** (Goethe's *Faust*, l. 8813).

A preposition can often replace the dative here, usually, however, with a shade of meaning: **Die Nachricht war meinem Vater wichtig** *The news was important to my father*, i.e. he felt it as such, but **Die Nachricht war für meinen Vater wichtig** *The news was of importance for my father*, i.e. in and of itself, whether he was conscious of it or not. **Er ist den Armen ein Vater** *He is a father to the poor* (and they feel the results of this relation), but **Der nicht jung war mit unsern Jünglingen, | dem unsre Worte nicht zum Herzen tönen, | kann er ein Vater sein zu seinen Söhnen?** (Schiller's *Jungfrau*, Prolog, 3), because the poet calls attention to the attitude rather than its resultant effects upon the persons.

a. Dative of Agent. After the predicate modal verbal (**180.** A) and after verbal adjectives in **-bar, -lich,** and **-sam,** this dat. has the force of a *dative of agent*, as the natural inference is that the person in the dat., with reference to whom the statement of the necessity or possibility of performing the action holds good, is also the one who actually performs it: **Eine Last hab' ich getragen — [es ist] keinem Sterblichen zu fassen!** (Lienhard's *König Arthur*, 5, p. 103). In the expression **Das macht mir zu schaffen** (**185.** B. I. 2. *d*, toward end) the dative is the usual expression. In connection with the modal verbal, **von** is, in general, more common in plain prose and often necessary to make the thought clear: **Von diesem bin ich zu retten.** In connection with **-bar, -lich,** and **-sam,** the dat. is usual: **Das weimarische Theater war auf seinem höchsten ihm erreichbaren Punkt** (Goethe) The theater at Weimar was at the highest point of perfection that could be attained by it. **Alles dem Auge Erreichbare** (id.). **Steil ist der Fels, die Burg ganz unbezwinglich | und keinem, der nicht Flügel hat, erschwinglich** (Gries) The precipice is steep, the fortress is impregnable and cannot be reached by one who has not wings. **Wollt ihr nun mein als einer Frau gedenken, | lenksam dem Zaum, so daß kein Stachel not, will freudig ich usw.** (Grillparzer's *Libussa*, 1). The prepositional construction with **für** is often in plain prose more common here: **Er** (i.e. **dieser Versuch**) **macht jedoch keineswegs den Anspruch eine erschöpfende, grammatische Analyse der Sprache Shakespeares bieten zu wollen; eine solche ist für den Augenblick weder praktisch, noch war sie für mich zur Zeit ausführbar** (Franz's *Shakespeare-Grammatik*, Vorwort). The **für** here gives the statement more objective force, while the simple dative would impart a subjective meaning representing the thought as the personal view of the speaker. Also when **lassen** has a reflexive object and a dependent infinitive with passive force, the agent can be in the dat.: **Drauf läßt er sich dem** (or more commonly **von dem**) **Volke sehen** (Gellert). Other examples are given in **262.** III. 2. C. *c.* In poetic style this dative is also found with a passive perfect participle: **keinem Zeugen behorcht** (Klopstock) = **von keinem Zeugen behorcht.**

b. Poetic Dative of Cause. In poetic language the dative is very common to denote a person or thing involved in the action in the relation of a cause: **Sieh, ich bebte nicht dir** (in prose **vor dir**), **ich bebte der furchtbaren Göttin** (Bürger). **Dem** (in prose **von dem**) **Stoß des Widders bebt der morsche Stein** (Platen's *Treue*, 2). The list of verbs given in 1. A. *f* might also be classed here. In prose the dative is usually replaced by a prep. construction.

B. *The Dative of Interest.* The dat. often denotes the person to whose advantage or disadvantage the action results: **Sein Herz schlug der ganzen Menschheit** His heart beat for all humanity. **Dir** (for you) **blüht gewiß das schönste Glück der Erde. Irre ich | so jrre ich mir** (Job xix. 4). **Das Pferd lief ihm fort** The horse ran away from him, lit. ran away to his discomfiture.

This dative, tho not infrequent with intransitives, is much more common with transitives, where it is often used even when from an English standpoint there seems to be no need of it: **Schreiben Sie mir diese Aufgabe ab** Copy this exercise for me. **Komm' auch, sieh' dir's an** Come too and look at it for yourself. **Er kauft seinem Sohne ein Pferd.** Kämmerer: **Sie stirbt.** Ute: **Ich könnt' ihr** (for her sake) **wünschen, es wäre so!** (Hebbel's *Nibelungen*, II, vi, 5). **Keinem anderen wollte sie den Karren ziehen, aber ihm** (Carl Busse's *Die schöne Andrea*). **So nahm ich mir** (not translated into English) **zu Hause nur Zeit, mich anzuziehen** (dress) **und zu frühstücken, und fuhr sofort wieder nach Siebenschloß** (name of a castle).

This dative is much used in prose, but very much more so in poetry: **Wohl wittert jedes Wesen seinen Feind; | drum hegt auch dir** (in prose **gegen dich**) **der Kaiser wildern Haß | und unversöhnlicheren, als mir** (= **gegen mich**) **selbst** (Uhland).

a. This dat. is used with unusual frequency instead of a possessive or a genitive: **Der Kopf brummt mir** My head is just roaring. **Mir juckt der ganze Leib. Sie putzt sich die Zähne** She is brushing her teeth. **Mir** (or **Dem Wilhelm**) **scheint die Sonne ins Gesicht** The sun shines in my (or William's) face. Here, as in English, the possessive or gen. might also be used: **Die Sonne scheint in mein Gesicht** (or **in Wilhelms Gesicht**). These two constructions are not, however, exactly equivalent in force: **Dem Pferde sitzt eine Wespe auf dem Rücken,** but **Dies Bild zeigt ein schönes Pferd, auf dessen Rücken ein kleiner Knabe sitzt.** Compare with: "She looked me tenderly in the eyes" as contrasted with "The doctor looked in my eyes" (to examine them). The dat. makes more prominent the person to whose advantage or disadvantage the action accrues. Thus the possessive, not the dative, is used in **Da zerriß der Hohepriester seinen Rock** (Mark xiv. 63), as the high priest had no desire of injuring himself in tearing his coat, but the dative is in place where it is desired to show that an injury or loss ensues: **Der Junge zerriß sich beim Fallen den Rock.** Sometimes both dat. and possessive are used: **Es gibt böse Geister, | die in des Menschen unverwahrter Brust | sich augenblicklich ihren Wohnsitz nehmen** (Schiller). This double construction is in our own time a characteristic of popular speech: **Wenn ich an den Arend** (name) **jetzt denke und an Sie, Herr Kunemund, und an die Gertrud und die Hunde und das übrige Vieh und das ganze gute alte Leben, so könnte ich mir mein Hemde in meinen Tränen waschen** (Raabe's *Meister Autor*, chap. 17). See also **138. 3.**

In all these examples the dative can still be construed as a sentence modifier, a dative of interest, but there has long been a tendency here, as in the last example, to bring the dative into relation to some noun in the sentence with which it is associated in thought. This tendency often, as in **138.** 2. *c*, goes so far that the dative ceases to be a sentence modifier and becomes a modifier of the noun.

C. *Ethical Dative.* The dat. is not only, as in the preceding article, used to denote the person who has a *material* interest in the action, but is also often employed to denote the person who has or is expected to have an *emotional* interest in the statement, especially a dat. of a personal pronoun in the 1st or 2nd person which is frequently in conversation inserted here and there, in some particular proposition, to indicate that that particular point seems important to the speaker or should be noted by the person addressed: **Sieh mir nicht so finster aus** Pray, don't look so sullen. **Das war euch eine Freude** That was a joy, I can tell you. **Seid mir recht artig, ihr Kinder** Come, children, I do want you to be real good. **Daß mir keiner aufs Eis geht!** I don't want one of you to go upon the ice. **Rede mir doch nur!** Come, don't be bashful, speak right out, for I am anxious to hear it. **Sprich dem Vater** (not an indirect object here, but an ethical dat.) **lieber nicht erst von diesem Vorhaben** Don't say anything to father about this plan now, for you can expect from him no interest in it, but rather opposition. **Krümmt mir kein Haar auf dem Haupt eures Herrn!** (Ebner-Eschenbach's *Jakob Szela*, p. 117) I warn you, don't you harm a hair on the head of your master. **Immer wußte sie etwas Neues, und so giftig kam Ihnen bei ihr alles heraus** She always had something new to relate, and I tell you, she had a mean way of telling it. This dat. cannot easily be rendered into modern English, tho the same construction is common in Shakespeare: Whip me such honest knaves (*Othello*, **I**, 1. 47).

4. In the eighteenth century and even later a dat. is found with **fühlen, kennen, wissen,** and **wollen, begehren, fordern,** where a prep. phrase is now used: **Ich fühle mir** (now **in mir**) **Hoffnung, Mut und Kraft** (Goethe). **Ich hatte eine größere Heiterkeit des Geistes gewonnen, als ich mir** (**an mir**) **lange nicht gekannt** (Goethe). **Und hätt' ich dir** (**bei dir**) **ein so versöhnlich Herz gewußt** (Schiller). **Weiß ich, was Saladin mir** (**von mir**) **will?** (Lessing). **Was sie ihm**

wolle (Freytag's *Bild*, 1, 200). **Was mir (von mir) die Göttliche begehrt, das weiß ich** (H. v. Kleist). **Ein andrer Kaiser fordert Euch (von Euch) dasselbe** (Grillparzer's *Ottokar*, 3).

5. It is a marked peculiarity of the uneducated in the North that they use an accusative often where a dative is in place, and on the other hand a dative where an accusative should be employed: **Laß mir in Ruh! Ich hab' nichts mit dich zu schaffen!** (May in Halbe's *Das tausendjährige Reich*, p. 128). This is due to the fact that in Low German the personal pronouns do not have a different form for dat. and acc.: mī = H.G. **mir** and **mich**; dī = H.G. **dir** and **dich.**

Either Dative or Accusative according to Meaning or from Unsettled Usage.

259. Some verbs take the dat. or acc. according to the meaning involved, while others, on account of fluctuation of usage, admit of both cases without a difference of meaning. The difference of construction with the same verb usually results from analogy, the verb breaking away from its original construction to follow that of another verb of the same meaning.

1. **ANGEHEN** *to concern*, usually with acc., but occasionally also with dat. in accordance with the nature of the dat. to express a relation which concerns inner or material interests (see **258.** 1): **Was gehen dem Christen dieses Mannes Beweise an?** (Lessing, 10, 10). **Hier sieht's doch aus, als ob dem, der hier wohnt, die ganze Sache draußen gar nichts anging** (Otto Erler's *Struensee*, p. 2), but more commonly **Das geht mich nichts an.**

2. **ANKOMMEN:** (A) *to depend or hinge upon*, with dat. of interest: **Es kommt mir auf ein paar Taler nicht an** I do not mind giving a few talers more. (B) *To get at*, with dat.: **Man kann dem Verbrecher nicht ankommen.** (C) *To come* (hard, easy, &c.) *for*, with acc. early in the period, but later also with dat., the fluctuation continuing without a marked preponderance of either form, the dat., however, gaining ground: **Vnd es kam sie hart an vber der geburt** (Genesis xxxv. 17). **Es ist mir schwer angekommen** (Schiller). **Und das hinzunehmen, wäre mir hart angekommen** (Fontane's *Frau Jenny*, xvi). **Sauer ist's mich genug angekommen** (Anzengruber's *Schandfleck*, VII). **Es kam mich hart an, mich zu verstellen** (Marriot). **Sie fühlte, daß sie den größten Verlust erlitt, daß es für die anderen, so schwer es sie ankam, doch nicht das bedeutete, wie für sie** (G. Ompteda). (D) *To befall, come upon*, with acc. in early N.H.G., later also frequently with dat., now perhaps more commonly with acc.: **Furcht vnd zittern ist mich ankomen** (Psalm lv. 6). **Nicht einen Augenblick ist mir eine Furcht vor der Hölle angekommen** (Goethe). **Der verstorbene Schickedanz hatte, wie der Tod ihn ankam, ein Leben hinter sich, das sich in zwei sehr verschiedene Hälften teilte** (Fontane's *Stechlin*, xii). **Daneben hatten es ihre Briefe an sich, daß etwas wie leichte Bergluft daraus hervorzuquellen schien, so daß mir Neid und Weh ankam** (R. Huch's *Ludolf Ursleu*, XXV). **Mich kam ein gewaltiges Erschrecken an** (ib.). (E) *To appear* (to the senses, imagination), *seem*, with dat.: **Die Kaffeetassen klapperten so heimlich auf den Untersetzern, daß es ihr ankam, als habe sie schon jetzt einen Vorgeschmack der paradiesischen Freuden** (Lauff's *Frau Aleit*, p. 76).

3. **ANLIEGEN** *to entreat*, usually with dat., tho occasionally the acc. after the analogy of **angehen** *to entreat* is found: **Ich lag der Mutter an, und diese suchte den Vater zu bereden. Hier lag Antonio den König sehr an, ihm beizuspringen** (Lessing, 6, 163).

4. **ANWANDELN** *to befall, come over*, usually with acc., occasionally also intransitively with dat.: **Furcht wandelt mich nicht an. Was ist dir angewandelt?** (Tieck). **Und sollte es einem mal so anwandeln, daß man von einem anderen denkt usw.** (Boy-Ed's *Das A B C des Lebens*, p. 140).

5. **AUSBIETEN** *to give notice to leave the house, city*, &c., with dat. or acc., now replaced by **ausweisen** with acc.: **Ich biete dem Junker aus** (Schiller) I'll give the young gent notice to keep off the premises. **In Wien hat man alle Fremden ausgeboten** (Goethe) In Vienna all strangers have been given notice to leave.

6. **BEDEUTEN** *to instruct, inform, give a sign to somebody that* or *to* (with dependent clause or infin.), *to give somebody to understand, to order*, except in the first two meanings usually with dat. of the person and the acc. of the thing, or instead of the acc. a clause or infinitive: **Man bedeutet ihm zu schweigen** (Otto Ernst's *Flachsmann als Erzieher*, 3, 8). The acc. of the person is the rule for the first two meanings and is also not infrequently found in the other meanings: **Therese bedeutete den Verwalter in allem** (Goethe). **Da sie ziemlich laut sprach, kam der Pfarrer ans Fenster und fragte, was es gebe. Sie bedeutete ihn** (id., *Dichtung und Wahrheit*, II, 10). **Die Frau, die ihn stehend empfangen hatte, bedeutete ihn mit einem Winke der Hand, Platz zu nehmen** (Wildenbruch's *Vice-Mama*). **Mattes Ehrnreich . . . bedeutete sie durch Gebärden, daß er das Geld bei sich habe** (Schönherr's *Sonnwendtag*, p. 71). Earlier in the period sometimes with the acc. of the person and the gen. of the thing: **(er) bedeute ihn seiner Pflicht** (Goethe's *Briefe*, vol. 27, p. 187) *Let him instruct him as to his duty.* The acc. of the person in these constructions explains the frequent passive construction here: **Schnell werden wir bedeutet, hier sei von einer Mehrheit die Rede** (Goethe). **Er will sich nicht bedeuten lassen** He will not listen to reason. **Laß dich bedeuten.** Sometimes the dative here: **Laß dir bedeuten, Artur** (Kleist's *Homburg*, 2, 2).

7. **BEFEHLEN, BEFEHLIGEN, GEBIETEN:** (A) **befehlen** *to commend, commit*, with acc. of the thing, now limited to elevated diction: **Vater | Ich befelh meinen Geist in deine Hende** (Luke xxiii. 46). **Befelh dem HERRN deine wege** (Psalm xxxvii. 5). (B) **Befehlen** *to command*,

to give a command to, with dat. of person: **Er befahl mir hinzugehen.** (C) **Befehlen** *to order to appear at, summons, invite* (used in circles where the invitation is equal to a command as in case of an invitation or request from a prince, king), with acc. of the person: **Der Fürst befahl ihn zur Tafel** The prince invited him to dinner. In the meanings *to desire, order to bring* or *pass* (a thing) with acc.: **Befiehlst du deine Pfeife, Papa?** (Sudermann's *Heimat*, 1, 6). **Befehlen Sie noch etwas Suppe?** May I help you to some more soup? (D) **Befehligen** usually used in the sense of *to have command of* (in a military sense), with acc. of the thing: **Er befehligt das Heer, den linken Flügel des Heeres.** (E) **Gebieten** with a simple acc. of the thing, *to enjoin, impose, require*: **Er gebietet Stillschweigen. Die Freundschaft gebietet es.** With the simple dative of the person or personified thing, *to govern, rule, curb, bridle*: **So vielen gebietest du!** (Schiller's *Wallensteins Tod*, 2, 3). **Er gebietet seinen Leidenschaften.** With dat. of person and acc. of thing: **Er gebietet ihnen Stillschweigen.**

8. **BELIEBEN:** (A) *to choose, please, like*, with dat. when the subject is a thing, when it is a person, with acc.: **Es beliebte ihm nicht zu antworten** He did not choose to answer. **Nehmen Sie, was Ihnen beliebt** (pleases). **Belieben Sie** (would you like to have) **roten Wein?** (B) *To inspire love in somebody for something*, with dat. of person and acc. of thing, a Swiss idiom: **[Er] wandte sich an die Regierung, indem er ihr die Erhaltung einzelner schöner Bäume als einen allgemeinen Grundsatz belieben wollte** (Keller's *Seldw.*, 2, 262).

9. **BETTEN:** (A) *to make the bed(s)*, always intrans.: **Das Mädchen hat noch nicht gebettet.** Also a dat. of interest can be associated with the verb, *to prepare a couch for, to bed* (horses, &c.): **Wem** (for whom) **die Liebe bettet, ruhet gut** (Chamisso). **Er bettet dem Vieh.** (B) In the sense *to lay one's self* or *someone down to repose* **betten** was used earlier in the period intransitively with a dat. of interest, while present usage employs it transitively with a direct object after the analogy of **sich hinlegen,** or **einen ins Bett legen: Bettet ich mir in die Helle | Sihe | so bistu auch da** (Psalm cxxxix. 8). **Noch versuch' ich's, sie zu retten, | wo nicht, auf ihrem Sarge mir zu betten** (Schiller's *Maria*, 3, 8). **Ich bettete mich auf weiches Moos. Die Mutter bettete das Kind in die Kammer.** The dative still survives in poetic style.

10. **BEZAHLEN** *to pay*, with the dat. of the person and acc. of the thing when there are two objects, but with the acc. of the person if the thing stands after a prep. or is omitted altogether: **Ich habe dem Schneider die Rechnung bezahlt. Ich habe den Rock** or **für den Rock bezahlt. Ich habe die Rechnung bezahlt. Ich habe den Schneider für den Rock bezahlt. Ich habe den Schneider bezahlt.** Sometimes, however, the dat. in the latter case, especially in a figurative sense: **Das Mädchen selbst . . . . mit deren Hoffnung | er gern mir zu bezahlen schiene** (Lessing's *Nathan*, 4, 4). **Ich will ihnen** (more commonly **sie**) **mit ihrer Münze bezahlen** (Freytag's *Der Rittmeister von Alt-Rosen*, chap. VII).

11. **DÜNKEN** (and the rare form **dünkeln**) and the less common form **BEDÜNKEN** (and the rare form **bedünkeln**) *to seem* took in early N.H.G. the acc. almost regularly, but now, after the analogy of **vorkommen** and **scheinen** *to seem*, take also the dat.: **Es dünkt mich** or **mir, daß usw.** Compare **185.** A. I. 1. *b*. (**3**).

12. **GELTEN:** (A) *to be aimed at, be intended for*, with dat.: **Der Anschlag galt nicht seinem Leben, sondern seinem Geld. Wem gilt diese Bemerkung?** (B) *To concern, be valued at, be worth*, with adverbial acc., sometimes also with dat. of interest in addition to the acc.: **Es gilt sein Leben** It concerns his life, or His life is at stake. **Das Buch gilt einen Taler. Das Gemälde gilt mir zehnmal mehr** (acc.) **als es mir kostet.**

13. **GELÜSTEN** *to covet, long for, lust after*, with acc. of the person and gen. of the thing, or more commonly the thing is in the dat. after the prep. **nach: Las dich nicht gelüsten deines Nehesten Weibs** (Exodus xx. 17). **Es gelüstet das Kind nach dem Obst.** Also the dat. of the person is here sometimes used, after the analogy of the dat. with other verbs of kindred meaning as **belieben, gefallen: Es gelüstete ihnen nach einer Zyane** (blue-bottle) (von Hörmann). See also **262.** II. B. *d*, 2nd par.

14. **GETRAUEN, TRAUEN:** (A) The simple verb **trauen** in the meaning *to trust in, rely upon*, takes the dat. or a prep. phrase: **Ich traue ihm** or **auf** (**261.** A) **ihn. Ich traue ihm nicht über die Gasse** I would not trust him across the street. (B) **Trauen** or now more commonly **getrauen** *to dare, venture*, with acc., rarely with dat., if there is no dependent infinitive: **Ich (ge)traute mich nicht dorthin** I did not venture to go there. **Ich (ge)traue mich nicht zu ihm** (to go to this house). (C) **Trauen** or now more commonly **getrauen** *to trust one's self*, or *have confidence in one's self*, or *be bold enough to undertake something, to dare*, with acc. or dat., if there is a dependent infinitive: **Ich (ge)traue mich** or **mir, es zu tun.** If there are two inflected objects, one of the person and one of the thing, the person is in the dat. and the thing in the acc.: **Ich getraue mir den Sprung nicht** I haven't the courage to make the leap. Earlier in the period, the acc. of the person and the gen. of the thing was common here, and still occurs in poetic language: **Ich getraue mich dessen** I have the courage to attempt it. In such sentences as **Er (ge)traut sich's** we have the M.H.G. construction, altho it is not now felt. The **es,** which is in reality a gen. (see **140.** *c*), is now taken for an acc., and the **sich** is correctly construed as a dat., and thus arose the now common construction of the dative of the person and the acc. of the thing. This change of construction was quite easy, as the dative and accusative type is now a favorite construction. (D) **Trauen** *to unite in wedlock*, always with the acc.: **Der Prediger wird meine Schwester trauen.**

15. **GLAUBEN:** (A) *to believe* in the sense of having confidence in the veracity of somebody, or the reliability of something, with the dat.: **Ich glaube ihm. Ich glaubte meinen Augen kaum, als ich ihn sah.** (B) *To believe to be true*, with the acc.: **Diese Geschichte glaube ich nicht.** The dat. of the person represented as the authority for the statement can also accompany the

acc. of the thing: **Kein Mensch glaubte ihm das** No one believed him when he said that. Only rarely the genitive of the thing in accordance with older usage: **Meine erste Bestürzung . . . hatte mich des glauben gemacht** (Schiller's *Werke*, 4, 75). (c) To have a firm belief that something exists, or that the claims, teachings of somebody are worthy of implicit confidence, usually with the acc. after the prep. **an**, but sometimes with the simple acc.: **Er glaubt an Gott, an Christum, an Geister, an die Wahrheiten der Religion, an die Auferstehung der Toten.** Goethe: (Gretchen asks:) **Glaubst du an Gott?** (Faust replies:) **Wer darf ihn nennen? | Und wer bekennen: | ich glaub' ihn** (= **an ihn**)? **| Wer empfinden | und sich unterwinden | zu sagen: ich glaub' ihn** (= **an ihn**) **nicht? Schaff' ihnen Brot, damit sie Gott glauben** (Voegtlin's *Das neue Gewissen*, p. 32). **Mußte ich aber Gott damals leugnen, und muß ich Ihn heute glauben, so ist usw.** (Ernst Heilborn's *Die Krone* in *Deutsche Rundschau*, June 1905, p. 366).

16. **GRAUEN, GRAUSEN, GRAUSELN, GRUSELN,** &c. For fluctuations of usage among impersonal verbs, see **219. 4.**

17. **HELFEN:** (A) *to help*, now usually with the dat. Rarely with the acc.: **Lieber Pappe [Papa], ich helfe dich** (Goethe's *Des Künstlers Erdenwallen*, 1) (probably used here in imitation of the language of a child.) In the colloquial language of the North we sometimes find an acc. of the thing, a construction well known in English and Low German: Jan: **„Och, Kaptein,—ick kunn dat doch nich helpen!" — und die kleine Frau Doktorin lächelte den Gestrengen äußerst reizend an und meinte: „Wirklich — er konnte es nicht helfen** (usually **ändern**), **Herr Kapitän"** (Schulze-Smidt's *O Tannebaum*, III). This accusative also occurs in the Swiss writer Ernst Zahn: **Ohne daß sie es helfen konnte usw.** (*Das Leben der Salome Zeller*, near end). This **es**, earlier in the period more common, is now felt as an acc. but in fact it is a gen. of specification (**260**): **Ich kann es nicht helfen** I can't offer, suggest any help, remedy with regard to the matter. (B) *to avail* or *profit*, with dat., or earlier in the period also quite frequently the acc. of the person: **Was hülff's den Menschen** [acc. sing.] **| wenn er die gantze Welt gewünne | vnd neme an seiner Seelen schaden** (Mark viii. 36). **Was hilft dich's, der beste zu sein?** (Goethe's *Rein.*, *F.*, 8). **Es hilft ihn nichts** (Uhland). Occasionally still: **Was half ihn die wachsende Habe, wenn nirgends eine Ruhe und ein Behagen war?** (Anna Schieber's *Alle guten Geister*, p. 328).

18. **HORCHEN** *to hearken, listen*, usually w. dat. or more commonly a prep. phrase, sometimes w. acc. in elevated discourse: **Er horcht dem Gesange der Vögel. Du siehst, ich horche deinen Worten** (Goethe's *Iphigenie*, 5, 4). **Er horcht auf die Musik. Man darf vor dem Knaben nicht reden, er horcht auf jedes Wort. Horche auf meinen Wunsch. So sangen die Parzen; | es horcht der Verbannte | in nächtlichen Höhlen | der Alte [auf] die Lieder, | denkt [an] Kinder und Enkel** (Goethe's *Iphigenie*, 4, 5). The prep. inclosed in brackets would be required in prose.

19. **KLEIDEN** *to clothe*, always w. acc., but in the meaning *to become, look well upon*, w. either the acc. or dat. (not rare as stated by grammarians): **Die weiße Binde kleidet dich nicht** (Goethe). **Die Possen kleiden, wie üppige Kränze nur braune Locken** (C. F. Meyer's *Plautus*). **Manchem kleidet es zu sprechen, und manchem kleidet es zu schweigen** (Fontane's *Stechlin*, XV, p. 197).

20. **KOSEN** *to caress, make love to*, w. acc., rarely w. dat.: **Ist's möglich, daß ich, Liebchen, dich kose?** (Goethe's *Div.*, 8, 7). **Dir mit Wohlgeruch zu kosen** (ib., 7, 2). Now more commonly **mit einem kosen.**

21. **KOSTEN:** (A) *to taste*, always w. acc. when used transitively. (B) *To cost*, w. dat. or now perhaps less commonly acc.: **Diese Arbeit hat mir** or **mich viel Mühe gekostet.** The acc. here leads **kommen** *to cost* to take sometimes the acc. instead of the correct dat.: **Das käme Sie sehr kostspielig** (*Über Land und Meer*). See also 29 below.

22. **LIEBKOSEN** *to caress*, formerly with the dat., and in choice language still with that case: **Ich liebkoste dir** (Heyse's *Meleager*, I). Now quite commonly with the acc. after the analogy of **küssen** and **herzen: Die Mutter liebkost ihr Kind.**

23. **LOHNEN** *to reward*, w. dat. of the person and acc. of the thing when there are two objects: **Er lohnt mir meine Mühe** or **für meine Mühe** He pays me for my trouble. When there is only one object, and that is a thing, it is now occasionally in the genitive in accordance with older usage (as in Lessing's *Minna*, 5, 9), more commonly, however, in the accusative and sometimes in the dative: **Es** or **Der Gewinn lohnt der Mühe** (genitive now usually confined to this word) or less commonly **die Mühe nicht. Man sehe zu, daß ein Schritt geschehe, der der Mühe und Unannehmlichkeiten auf die Dauer lohnt** (Dr. August Schmits in *Zeitschrift des Allgemeinen Sprachvereins*, 1920, p. 71), but in case of other nouns than **Mühe** more commonly the acc.: **Der neue Fund lohnt die angestrengtesten Forschungen.** Sometimes the dat.: **Solchen gottseligen Taten kann nur Gott lohnen** (Goethe). **Lebhafter Beifall lohnte auch dieser Rede wie allen vorhergegangenen** (H. Hoffmann's *Wider den Kurfürsten*, chap. 27). If the single object is a person it may be in the dative or accusative, the dative emphasizing the idea of inner gratification, the accusative that of financial compensation: **Lebhafter Beifall lohnte dem Redner. Du hast ihm mit Undank gelohnt. Das Handwerk lohnt seinen Mann. Der Weinbau lohnt hierzulande nicht. Dort lohnt man die Arbeit besser. Er lohnt** (*is paying, paying off*, now often replaced here by **löhnen, ablohnen, ablöhnen, entlohnen**) **die Arbeiter.** This distinction is not strictly observed: **Rauschender Beifall und ein mächtiger Lorbeerkranz mit wallender Schleife lohnten den Künstler für seinen trefflichen Vortrag** (*Hamburger Nachrichten*, Oct. 29, 1904). **Ist es nicht wahr, daß es der Gesang ist, der den braven Mann lohnt?** (Hans Delbrück in *Preußische Jahrbücher*, Oct. 1919, p. 85).

24. **NACHAHMEN** *imitate*, **NACHAFFEN** *to ape, imitate*, **NACHMACHEN** *to copy, imitate*: (A) The person is in the dat. and the thing in the acc. if there are two objects: **Er macht**

mir das Kunststück nach He is copying this trick from me. **„Ich verachte dich serr," äffte ich ihr nach und betonte das „serr" noch schärfer als sie** (Carl Busse's *Digga*). (B) If there is only one object and that the name of a thing or a person whose name is used instead of his works, it is now usually in the acc.: **Er ahmt den Gang und die Gebärden seines Bruders nach. Wie ich als Knabe den Terenz nachzuahmen wagte** (Goethe). (C) If there is only one object and that a noun representing a person or a thing which is endowed with personal attributes, it is in the dat. when the verb has the meaning of striving in a laudable way to imitate somebody, but the acc. when the verb is used in the sense of mechanical copying: **Ahme deinem Vater in der Tugend nach. Der Schauspieler ahmt** (imitates in the role that he is playing all the external characteristics of) **einen Franzosen nach.**

25. **RATEN:** (A) *to advise*, w. dat. of the person, or if there are two objects w. the dat. of the person and acc. of the thing: **Sie rieten mir dazu** You advised me to do it. **Er riet mir Gutes** He gave me good advice. (B) *To guess*, w. acc. of the thing: **Man rät ein Rätsel.**

26. **RUFEN** *to call*, **SCHREIEN** *to cry out to*, **PFEIFEN** *to whistle for*, **LOCKEN, KÖRNEN, KÖDERN** *to decoy*, **KLINGELN, LÄUTEN, SCHELLEN** *to ring*, **WINKEN** *to make a sign to*, **FLEHEN** *to implore*, take a dat. to denote the person toward whom the action is directed, and with the exception of **schreien, schellen, läuten,** and **klingeln,** may with a slight shade of meaning take the acc. to represent the person as the direct object of the action: **Sie wird bei Susen sein; ruft ihr doch!** She is probably with Susan; call out to her! **Wer ruft mir?** (Otto Ernst's *Die Gerechtigkeit*, 2, 1), but **Rufe sie!** Call her! Altho the simple dative was not infrequent earlier in the period as a survival of the original dative meaning of *direction toward* (**258.** 1) and survives in part still, present usage inclines toward other constructions in case of some of these words. **Rufen, locken, körnen,** and **ködern** usually take the acc., **schreien** and **flehen** require **zu** + dat., while **winken** may still take a simple dat. and **klingeln, läuten,** and **schellen** either a simple dat. or a prepositional construction: **Als sie Berta Witt sah, winkte sie ihr** (Frenssen's *Die drei Getreuen*, II, 5), or more commonly **winkte sie ihr zu. Der Herr klingelt dem Bedienten** or **nach dem Bedienten. Klingeln, läuten,** and **schellen** may also take an accusative in connection with a prep. phrase: **Bald war ich auch am Doktorhause und klingelte den alten Doktor Snittger aus den Federn** (Storm's *John Riew'*). **Rufen, schreien,** and **winken** can still be used with a dat. of the person in connection with a direct object of the thing, an infinitive, or clause: **Bald rief mir meine Mutter** (or more commonly **Bald rief mir meine Mutter zu**): **„Komm,"** or **zu kommen,** or **daß ich kommen sollte. Man winkte ihm Aufmunterung (zu). Rufen** is used with the simple dat. in a few expressions and **pfeifen** quite commonly so, and **pfeifen, rufen,** and **winken** can also take the acc. of the person in connection with a prep. phrase: **Er rief seinem braunen Hühnerhund (zu), der in einem Winkel gelegen hatte** (T. Storm). **Dem Männchen rufen** or more commonly **zurufen** to call the male. **Er pfeift seinem Hunde** or sometimes **pfeift seinem Hunde zu. Er pfiff den Hund zu sich hin.** In Switzerland **rufen** with dat. is used in the sense of *to call for*: **Die Beschaffenheit der Schullokalitäten ruft dringend einer Reparatur** (Blümner's *Zum schweizerischen Schriftdeutsch*, p. 47). **Dies ruft einer neuen Definition des Urteils** (Bernhard Fehr in *Archiv für das Studium der neueren Sprachen*, 1919, p. 102).

27. **SAGEN** *to say, tell*, w. a dat. of the person and an acc. of the thing, when there are two objects: **Er sagte mir die Wahrheit.** However, the simple dat. is replaced by **zu** w. dat. when the exact words of direct discourse are reported: **Die Kinder sagen meist zu ihren Eltern Papa und Mama. Er sagte zu mir: „Ich komme morgen wieder,"** but indirectly: **Er sagte mir, er komme morgen wieder.** Dialectic and French influences often affect the construction here and cause the dropping of the **zu** in direct discourse: **„Ich habe," sagte sie ihm** (for **zu ihm**) **mit bewegter Stimme, „deine Gegenwart gewünscht."**

28. **SPRECHEN, REDEN:** (A) *to speak*, usually require some prep. as **mit, zu, an** before the case of the person: **Ich sprach einige Worte zu ihm. Ich sprach mit ihm. Ich rede mit ihm.** We sometimes find an acc. of the thing and the dat. of the person: **Solch ein vernünftiges Wort hast du mir selten gesprochen** (Goethe's *H. und D.*, II, 106). When a prep. phrase modifies the verb in connection with a personal object, we not infrequently find the simple dat. of the person instead of a prepositional construction: **Niemand spricht gern einem andern von seiner Liebe** (Zschokke). **O mein Bruder! sprich mir nicht von der Ehe!** (Ebers). The simple dat. here is usually a gallicism which is not especially to be recommended, but it is sometimes a good German *dative of interest* or an *ethical dative*, as in the last sentence. (B) **Sprechen** (not **reden**) *to talk* (consult) *with*, w. acc. of the person when there is no object of the thing: **Ich möchte Sie auf einige Augenblicke allein sprechen.**

29. **STEHEN:** (A) *To become, look well*, w. dat.: **Das blaue Kleid steht ihr ausgezeichnet.** (B) *To take one's stand against*, w. dat.: **Ich stehe selbst in meinen Jahren noch dem Feinde.** Also in the milder sense *to face*: **dem Sturm, seinem Schicksal stehen.** (C) *To be equal to, to be a match for*, w. acc.: **Er steht seinen Mann** He is a match for any fellow. **Der Mann steht** (*comes up to*) **seinen Ruhm** (Lessing). (D) **zu stehen kommen** *to cost*, usually with the dat.: **Etwas kommt einem teuer zu stehen.** After the analogy of **kosten** *to cost* the acc. is also used: **Das kommt dich billiger zu stehen** (Spitteler's *Conrad*, p. 158). Sometimes simple **kommen** is still used here. See 21 above.

30. **STEUERN:** (A) *to steer*, trans. w. acc.: **Der Schiffer steuert sein Schiff.** (B) *To check, prevent*, w. dat.: **Der Lehrer steuert dem Zuspätkommen der Schüler.**

31. **TRAUEN,** see **GETRAUEN,** above.

32. **ÜBER'KOMMEN:** (A) *to come over, seize*, usually with acc. but occasionally with dat.: **Eine tiefe [geistige] Lähmung überkam ihm** (Lewald). **Sie wandten der oben Nachschauenden den Rücken, und sonderbar, wie mit einer Augentäuschung überkam es dem Blick Sibylle**

Lundhorsts (Jensen's *Jenseits des Wassers*, ix). (B) Regularly w. the dat. in intrans. use with the meaning *to be transmitted to, be delivered to*: **Der Name ist mir überkommen und so kann es mir persönlich nur obliegen, ihm, nach dem bescheidenen Maße meiner Fähigkeiten, Ehre zu machen** (Fontane's *Cécile*, chap. 13). **Ein Brief ist mir überkommen.**

33. **ÜBER'WIEGEN** *to outweigh*, w. acc., rarely w. dat.: **Der Tadel überwog das Lob.**

34. **VERGEBEN** and **VERZEIHEN:** (A) **vergeben** *to forgive*, w. simple dat. of the person, or if there are two objects w. dat. of the person and acc. of the thing: **Vnd vergib vns unsere Schulde** (now **Schulden**) | **wie wir unsern Schüldigern vergeben** (Matth. vi. 12). **Ich vergebe dir die Beleidigung.** (B) **Vergeben** *to poison*, correctly with the dat., but after the analogy of **vergiften** also with the acc., now rather uncommon in this meaning. (C) **Verzeihen** *to pardon, condone*, with the same construction as **vergeben** in (A): **Verzeih mir. Verzeih mein Unrecht. Verzeih mir mein Unrecht.**

35. **VERSICHERN:** (A) *to assure*, w. dat. of the person and acc. of the thing, or the acc. of the person and gen. of the thing.: **Ich versichere Ihnen dies,** or now less commonly **Ich versichere Sie dessen** I assure you of this. The acc. of the person is often incorrectly used with acc. of the thing. See **262.** II. B. *b*. The thing is usually expressed by a clause and then either the dat. or now less commonly the acc. of the person is used: **Ich versichere Ihnen** (or **Sie**), **daß ich dies tun werde.** (B) *To insure* (one's house, &c.), always w. acc.: **Ich werde mein Haus gegen Feuersgefahr versichern lassen.**

36. **VOR'BEI, VO'RÜBER** *past*, in composition with verbs of motion take a prepositional phrase as a complement, or a little earlier in the period the accusative (the original construction) or the dative: **Er ging an mir vorbei, ohne mir guten Tag zu sagen. Bei einem einzeln stehenden Hause ziehen wir vorbei** (Liliencron's *Kriegsnovellen*). **Du gehst dein Schloß vorüber** (Uhland). **Kaum ein Wagen ging mir vorbei** (Wildenbruch's *Die heilige Frau*, p. 122).

The verb of motion is often omitted in these constructions: **Bald war der Oberst dieser Truppe, nur von einem Trompeter begleitet, bei mir vorüber [geritten]** (Liliencron's *Kriegsnovellen*).

37. *Accusative or Dative of the Person Affected.* Usage often makes a fine distinction between the dat. and acc. after such verbs as *to beat, strike, hit, bite, seize*, &c., when the activity of the verb is represented as affecting a person. If the person alone is mentioned without indication of the particular part of the body affected, the acc. is used: **Die Mutter schlägt das Kind mit der Rute.** If the part of the body affected is mentioned, the acc. of the person or personified thing is used, when the person is represented as the objective point of the activity in a literal, exterior sense, but the dat. is employed when he is represented as more or less interested or involved in the action, either as to his material interests, comfort, or his inner feelings, or as affected by an accident or the operations of a natural law: **Der Mörder hatte ihn mitten ins Herz gestochen,** but **Am Schaufenster stach mir ein schöner Brillant ins Auge** and **Deine Klagen schneiden mir ins Herz. Er hat mich auf den Kopf geschlagen,** but **Der herabfallende Ziegel schlug mir gerade auf den Kopf.**

Genitive Object.

260. The original *function* of the genitive is not known. In oldest German it is used with verbs, nouns, and a few adjectives. Its free use with verbs and a few verbal adjectives in the oldest period seems to suggest the possibility that it was originally employed with verbs in an adverbial relation or as an object and later with its acquired meanings was attached to nouns in attributive function and still later to a large number of adjectives. Altho we can trace step by step a theoretical development of the attributive genitive from the use of the genitive with verbs it seems more probable in a number of cases, as indicated in **255.** II. 1, that certain categories of the attributive genitive developed out of other attributive categories.

The original *meaning* of the genitive is also unknown, but a study of the older periods where the genitive was much more used than now seems to indicate that the central idea of this case is *in a sphere*: **Das ist meines Amtes** *That is in the sphere of my duty.* **Wer dis wassers trinket | Den wird wider dürsten** (John iv. 13) *Whoever drinks of this water*, &c., literally *within the sphere, extent of this water, something belonging to this water*, i.e. not all of it but only a part of it. **Nu aber mus ich dursts sterben** (Judges xv. 18) *But now I must die of thirst*, literally *in the sphere of thirst*, hence on account of thirst. To this idea of sphere can be traced theoretically either directly or indirectly the genitives found in the predicate, as described in **252.** 2. A. *c*, the possessive, partitive, and other attributive genitives described in **255.** II, and the adverbial genitives described in **223.** I. 10. *a, b*, II. 2, 3, 4, III. *a*, IV. 2. A, B. *a*, C. The many shades of meaning which were developed in older German resulted in much confusion, as it was often not clear which shade was intended. After the verb alone in its relation as object the genitive expressed nine ideas, sphere, a part, goal, specification, cause, means, deprivation, removal, separation, all of which survive, altho the genitive under the impulse for clearer expression has in large measure been replaced by other constructions.

There is now no strongly marked shade of meaning in the gen. object in contradistinction to the acc. object, and hence those verbs which have a force similar to that of transitives have in common prose become transitive, and now take an acc., while those that have pronounced intransitive nature take a prep. object. In the latter construction by the choice of an appropriate preposition the various meanings can be rendered with accuracy. In choice language, however, a number of verbs still prefer the gen. object to the acc. or prep. object, and in certain cases the old and new constructions are both used with the same verb with a fine and beautiful shade of meaning. The acc. here represents the object as thoroly affected by the action, while the gen. sometimes represents the activity as not affecting the whole object but only a part of it, i.e. as merely operating somewhere within the sphere of it: **Die Spitzbuben haben mir alles genommen,** but **Vnd der Priester sol des bluts nemen vom Schuldopffer** (Leviticus xiv. 14) *And the priest shall take some of the blood of the trespass offering.* The partitive gen. is treated more fully in 1 below. Similar to this partitive gen. is the gen. of the goal or sphere, which represents the activity as operating within the sphere of an object, i.e. as missing, desiring, coveting, forgetting within the sphere of or with regard to the object, in modern speech missing, desiring, coveting the object, as we to-day put the word that completes the meaning of the verb in the accusative: **Mit diesem zweiten Pfeil durchschoß ich — Euch, wenn ich mein liebes Kind getroffen hätte, | und E u r e r — wahrlich, hätt' ich nicht gefehlt** (Schiller's *Tell*, 3, 3). **Wer ein Weib ansihet jr (140.** *b*) **zu begeren** (Matth. v. 28). The gen. of goal is now usually replaced by the acc. in plain prose. Sometimes a prep. construction is now used instead of the gen. of the goal. See next paragraph. Sometimes the acc. expresses a material or superficial relation, while in choice language the gen. may denote a deep, inner relation, or be used in figurative or changed meaning: **Die Kugel verfehlte ihr Ziel,** but **Die Rede verfehlte der Wirkung. Das ist einen Taler wert,** but **Dein Vater ist eines Thrones wert** (worthy of). Other shades may arise. The gen. may be used with **vergessen** when the activity proceeds from an act of the will, while the acc. is employed when the act of forgetfulness is an unconscious and thoro one: **Und taten übel vor dem Herrn und vergaßen des Herrn, ihres Gottes, und dienten Baalim und den Hainen** (Judges iii, 7, rev. ed.). **Und vor dem Einschlafen . . . . faltete er die Hände und betete zu ihr, der Verklärten: daß sie in ihrer himmlischen Seligkeit ihres einzigen Sohnes auf Erden nicht vergessen und nicht zugeben möge, er tue etwas, das ihrer unwürdig sei** (Spielhagen's *Herrin*, p. 178). But **Ich habe das Wort vergessen.** When the forgetting is represented as only temporary, and consequently the act as only imperfect, the old partitive gen. is still quite frequent: **Lehnert aber, der all die Zeit über mit besonderem Fleiße gearbeitet hatte, hatte seines in die Hobelspäne gestellten Kaffees ganz vergessen** (Fontane's *Quitt*, chap. ix). [In spite of the word **ganz** here the forgetting was only temporary, for his mind soon returned to the thought of his coffee.] **Und wenn er eine Minute lang seiner Trauer vergaß, so war ihm das bei Gott nicht zu verdenken** (Ganghofer's *Der Dorfapostel*, I). With verbs denoting a lacking the genitive indicates the sphere where the lacking occurs, so that it is here a genitive of specification: **Es bedarf der Verbesserung** It needs improvement, lit. There is need, a lack in the sphere of, in the matter of improvement.

Instead of the genitive we now often find a prepositional object. The old genitive of sphere is still used, as in **Walte deines Amtes** *Attend to your duties*, but the prepositional construction is more common here: **Ein Gott waltet über dich.** The genitive of sphere is still found in a few set expressions after **leben: Der Gerechte wird seines Glaubens leben** (Rom. I. 17). **Wer das glaubt, der lebt des kindlichen Glaubens, daß die tief im Boden der eigenen Interessen wurzelnden Bedingungen und Notwendigkeiten des Völkerlebens durch höfi-**

sches Wollen einfach zur Seite geschoben und ausgelöscht werden können (*Hamburger Nachrichten*, June 6, 1906). **Ich lebe der** (or **in der**) **Hoffnung, daß usw.** *I live in hopes that* &c. From the idea of sphere arise other shades of meaning: Specification: **Es mangelt mir des nötigen Kleingeldes,** or with a preposition **an dem nötigen Kleingeld.** Cause: **Nu aber mus ich dursts sterben** (Judges xv. 18; compare the gen. and acc. with **sterben** in **223.** III. *a* and **257.** 2. A). **Er ist des Todes verblichen** *He died*, lit. *turned pale in death.* But usually with a preposition: **Er starb an der Schwindsucht.** Sphere or goal: **Er wartet nur eines Winkes, um loszubrechen** (Häusser's *Deutsche Geschichte*, 3, 187) *He is waiting in the sphere of a sign*, i.e. *waiting for a sign*, &c., but more commonly: **Er wartet auf einen Wink, um loszubrechen.** The preposition here often calls attention to the outward direction of the activity, while the genitive may emphasize an inner causal relation between the activity and the object: **Über wen lacht man? Über Wilhelm. Aber du HERR wirst jrer lachen | Vnd aller Heiden spotten** (Psalm lix. 9). **Er lacht der Gefahren** (Felix Hollaender's *Der Weg des Thomas Truck*, II, p. 412).

In case of several compound verbs the gen. is in fact an attributive objective gen., as it modifies the noun element in the compound: **Nimm der günstigen Gelegenheit wahr!** (M.H.G. war *observation, notice*), or now more commonly in plain prose: **Nimm die günstige Gelegenheit wahr!,** as the two elements of the compound enter into such close relations that the noun loses its identity, and the compound is felt as an old compound verb and takes an acc. object.

Sometimes in case of adjectives and some verbs the acc. has arisen from a misapprehension. The old gen. **es** (see **140.** *c*), which is still often used here, is mistaken for an acc. This leads to the use of the acc. in case of other pronouns, and even in case of nouns. For examples of this acc. see **walten (2)** in 2. A and also the last example in 3. *b* below.

The gen. object is now found in the following groups, which are fairly complete for the present period, but were still fuller in early N.H.G.

1. *Partitive Genitive Object.* This object is used in elevated diction with a few verbs of pronounced transitive nature, much as *of* is used in English with the corresponding group of words. The most common of these German verbs are **bringen** to bring, **essen** to eat, **geben** to give, **gießen** to pour, pour out, **haben** to have, **naschen** to nibble at, sip of, **nehmen** to take, **senden** to send, **schenken** to pour out, **spenden** to bestow, be lavish with, **trinken** to drink. Exs.: **Wer dis wassers trincket | Den wird wider dürsten. Wer aber des Wassers trincken wird | das ich jm gebe | den wird ewiglich nicht dürsten** (John iv. 13–14). **Sorgsam brachte die Mutter des klaren herrlichen Weines** (Goethe's *H. u. D.*, 1, 166). **Es schenkte der Böhme des perlenden Weins** (Schiller's *Graf v. Habsburg*). **Kaum mag ich des Weines naschen** (Scheffel's *Trompeter*, Werner's Lieder aus Welschland, xi). See also **255.** II. 1. H. *c*. Compare: She gave him of that fair enticing fruit (Milton).

Such verbs, except in a few expressions, now usually take in plain prose the acc. without the article, or, to make prominent the partitive idea, **von** with the dative becomes object, or the real object is placed in apposition with **etwas: Er nahm Brot,** or **von dem Brot,** or **etwas Brot.** The partitive gen. objects, **dessen, deren,** are, however, still quite common. See **255.** II. 1. H. *c*.

The partitive idea appears also in the gen. object of a number of the verbs enumerated in 2. A below.

2. A. *Genitive Object after Intransitives.* The gen. object is used with the following intransitives, or verbs originally intransitive, especially in elevated diction, but other constructions, as indicated after each verb, are also found, especially in certain meanings of the same word, and are often more common in ordinary prose:

abgehen *to desist from, give up*, with the gen. only in early N.H.G., now with **von** with the dat.: **Will er der Sach dann nit abgan** (15th century). **Er geht vom Gesagten nicht ab.**

abkommen *to get away from, escape*, now with **von** with the dat.: **Er wird nicht von der Strafe, vom Stricke** (rope, i.e. hanging) **abkommen.**

abstehen *to desist from, give up,* with the gen. in early N.H.G., now rarely so, usually with **von** with the dat.: **Der Morgenstern hat ihn mit Trost durchleuchtet, daß er noch seines ganzen verdorbenen Lebens wird abstehen können** (Wilhelm Fischer's *Sonnenopfer*, III). **Er steht von seiner Forderung ab.**

abwarten *to attend to, take good care of,* earlier in the period with the gen. or the dat., now with the acc.

achten (**1**) *to heed, pay attention to, care for,* still with the gen. in choice language, usually, however, with **auf** with the acc., sometimes with the simple acc.: **Drinnen aber in seinem Geschäfts- und Arbeitszimmer saß der Gestrenge selbst . . . nicht achtend des heiteren Glanzes, der durch die Fenster zu ihm hereinströmte** (Storm's *Waldwinkel*). **Achte nicht des Vorteils, der Ehre. Auch ihrer Gesundheit hatte man geachtet und ihr ein Ausruhen gewährt, wenn sie müde geworden** (Johanna Wolff's *Das Hanneken*, p. 236). **Ich achte nicht auf dich und deinen Zorn. Großmutter steht ihm bei; | die, weißt du, achtet nicht dein Zorngeschrei** (Hauptmann's *Versunkene Glocke*, 3). (**2**) *to take notice of,* in this meaning now usually in the form **beachten** with the acc. (**3**) *to respect,* with the acc.: **Ich achte ihn, aber ich kann ihn nicht lieben.**

achthaben *to heed, pay attention to,* or in negative form **gar keine Acht haben,** quite commonly with the gen. in a few expressions as **es** (see **140.** *c*) **achthaben,** also elsewhere, but more commonly with **auf** with the acc., sometimes with the simple acc.: **So, in mich hineinbrütend, hatte ich Jettchens Gegenwart und ihres Spiels gar keine Acht mehr gehabt** (Spielhagen's *Was will das werden?*, VII).

aufhören *to stop, cease,* now with **mit** with the dat.: **Aufgehört mit dem Spielen!**

aufkommen *to arise from, get up from, recover from (sickness),* now with **von** with the dat.: **Er wird vom Lager, von seinen Wunden nicht wieder aufkommen.**

bedürfen (or earlier in the period **dürfen**) *to need, require,* usually with the gen., sometimes with the acc., especially in case of the interrog. acc. **was,** as illustrated in **147.** 1. A: **Er bedarf des Trostes, des Arztes, der Schonung. Es bedarf nur eines Wortes von dir.**

begehren (**1**) *to desire, long for, covet,* with the gen. or more commonly the acc., or with **nach** with the dat.: **Begehre nicht des Reichtums** (or **den Reichtum,** or **nach dem Reichtum**). **Man sieht sie an, ohne ihrer zu begehren** (Herman Hesse's *Diesseits*, p. 284). (**2**) In the meaning *to demand* with the acc.: **Ich begehre die Arbeit fehlerfrei.**

benötigen *to have need of,* more commonly with the acc., sometimes with the gen., both constructions of recent date, employed instead of the older and still common **benötigt sein** (see 3 below): **Er war es, der dem Alpenbund die Geldmittel lieferte, deren dieser zur Insurgierung Tirols benötigte** (E. Wertheim in *Deutsche Rundschau*, July 1904, p. 92).

brauchen *to need, be in need of,* with the gen., especially in figurative language, more commonly with the acc.: **Das** or impersonally **es braucht keines Beweises mehr. Er braucht mich.**

danken *to thank for,* always with the dat. of the person, sometimes with the gen. or the acc. of the thing, or more commonly with **für** with the acc. except that the gen. is still common in a few expressions such as **Gott sei es** (old gen.; see **140.** *c*) **gedankt: [Ich] danke der gütigen Nachfrage** (Raabe's *Frühling*, VIII), or more commonly **Ich danke für die gütige Nachfrage. Ihr dank' es** (old gen. now felt as an acc.; see **140.** *c*) **. . . ihr danke Reich und Leben** (Fulda's *Talisman*, 4, 7).

darben *to be without,* also with the acc. or **an** with the dat., now only in choice language, freely used, however, where there is no object in the meaning *to suffer need;* where there is an object now usually replaced by **entbehren: die jedes Schmuckes darbenden armseligen Hütten** (Dahn's *Erinnerungen*, IV, p. 60).

denken *to remember,* now especially *to think of,* now more commonly with **an** with the acc., in poetic language also with the simple acc.: **Denke meiner** (or more commonly **an mich**). **Was kamst du her, nichts denkend als dich selbst?** (Grillparzer's *D. M. u. d. L. W.*, 3).

entbehren *to be without, dispense with, miss,* still often with the gen. in poetic style and in a few set expressions also in plain prose, now usually with the acc.: **Mein Haus entbehrt des Vaters. Diese Gerüchte entbehren jeder Unterlage. Ich kann ihn leicht entbehren.**

entgehen *to escape,* now with the dat.

entgelten *to pay (atone) for,* only in early N.H.G., now with the acc.: **Vnser Veter haben gesündigt . . . vnd wir müssen jrer missethat entgelten** (Lamentations, v. 7). **Laß mich seinen Fehler nicht entgelten.**

entraten *to get along without, dispense with,* sometimes also with the acc., little used except in the infinitive: **Ich kann deines Beistandes nicht entraten.**

entsagen *to renounce, give up,* now usually according to **258.** 1. B.: **Er hat sie auf dem Gewissen, daß er des Mets nicht entsagte, da es Zeit war** (Frenssen's *Die drei Getreuen*, II. 9.)

entwohnen *to become disaccustomed to,* earlier in the period with the gen. or acc., now except in the perfect participle (see **entwohnt** in 3 below) usually replaced by **sich entwöhnen** (**262.** II. A. *b*).

erharren *to await with patience,* now with the acc.

ermangeln see **mangeln** below.

ermüden *to become weary from,* usually with **von** with the dat.: **Zwei Ruderer ermüdeten der Fahrt** (Grillparzer's *D. M. u. d. L. W.*, 3).

erröten *to blush at,* now usually with **über** with the acc.: **Immer erröte ich dessen** (Börne, 2, 485). See also **261.** A.

erschrecken *to take fright at,* now with **über** with the acc. [formerly also the dat.], or **vor** with the dat.: **Ich war über den Mord, vor dem Räuber erschrocken.**

erstaunen *to be astonished at*, formerly with the gen., sometimes in poetic language with **ob** with the dat., sometimes with the simple dat. (**258.** I. A. *f*), usually with **über** with the acc.

erwähnen or **Erwähnung tun** *to mention, make mention of*, the former with gen. or acc., the latter usually with the gen., but often with **von** with the dat. when the statement is negative, or instead of both forms often **Erwähnung** (nom.) **geschieht** *mention is made of*, with the gen.: **Sie erwähnten gewisser Opfer, die Sie bringen mußten** (Baumbach's *Der Schwiegersohn*, X). **Sie tat dieses Falles, ihrer Freundin Erwähnung**, or **keine Erwähnung. Es geschah ihrer Erwähnung**, or **keine Erwähnung. Von der Gefährdung pekuniärer Interessen tat ich keine Erwähnung.**

erwarten, see **warten** below.

fehlen or more commonly **verfehlen** *to miss* (a mark, road, &c.), *fail of*, with the gen. in choice language, more commonly the acc.: **Der Schnee, der lag, gab gerade Licht genug, um des Weges nicht zu fehlen** (Fontane's *Vor dem Sturm*, IV, 19). **Ich hatte den richtigen Weg verfehlt.** See also **260**, 3rd par.

fluchen *to swear at*, earlier in the period sometimes with the gen. of the cause, now **über etwas, über einen fluchen.**

frohlocken *to exult at*, more commonly with **über** with the acc.

fürchten (**1**) *to fear*, now always with the acc. (**2**) *to fear for*, with the gen. in the biblical expression **unsers Lebens fürchten** (Josh. ix. 24), now usually **für unser Leben fürchten.**

gebrauchen *to use*, **mißbrauchen** *to misuse*, both now with the acc.

gedenken (**1**) *to mention*, earlier in the period also with **von** with the dat. in this meaning: **Er gedachte meiner mit keinem Worte. Noch einer anderen Unregelmäßigkeit in der Flexion ist hier zu gedenken** (H. Gürtler in Paul and Braune's *Beiträge*, 1911, p. 508). (**2**) *to think of*, earlier in the period also with **an** with the acc., in this meaning now usually replaced by **denken** with **an** with the acc. (**3**) *to remember*, usually with the gen. in this meaning, *to remember* (with the intention to avenge), with the dat. of the person and the acc. of the thing: **Gedenke deines Versprechens. Ich werde dir diese Beleidigung gedenken.**

gelten, see **185.** A. I. 6. *Note* 2.

genesen (**1**) *to recover from*, with the gen. or with **von** with the dat.: **Daß sie ihres Fiebers völlig genesen** (Niebuhr), more commonly **von dem Fieber genesen.** (**2**) *to be delivered of* (a child in child-birth), with the gen.: **Sie genas eines gesunden Knaben.**

genießen (in early N.H.G. also **nießen**) *to enjoy*, in choice language not infrequently with the gen., in colloquial language more commonly with the acc.: **Abend für Abend genoß ich so eines eigensten Schauspiels** (J. J. David in *Die neue Rundschau*, July 1906, p. 876). **Die einzelnen Tiere genossen bei den Kadetten eines besonderen Rufes, je nach ihren vermeintlich guten oder bösen Eigenschaften** (Ompteda's *Sylvester von Geyer*, XXXIX). **Er hat eine gute Erziehung genossen. Er genoß das Leben der Hauptstadt in vollen Zügen.** (**2**) *to partake of, eat*, formerly with the gen., now with the acc.: **Er hat das heilige Abendmahl genossen. Ich habe unterwegs nichts genossen.**

geschweigen, see **schweigen.**

gestehen (**1**) *to acknowledge the validity, force, legitimacy of*, now no longer in use here: **[Sie] wollten mir keines Texts gestehen** (Luther) = **Sie wollten sich durch keinen Text für überwunden bekennen.** (**2**) *to admit, acknowledge*, with the acc.: **Ich gestehe dir mein Unrecht.**

gesunden *to recover from*, now with **von** with the dat.

gewahren or **gewahr werden** *to perceive*, the former now usually with the acc., the latter either with the gen. or acc.: **Sie stirbt vor Ekel, wenn sie mein** (usually **mich**) **gewahrt** (Hauptmann's *Der arme Heinrich*, 2, 6). **Ich wurde meines Irrtums** (or **meinen Irrtum**) **bald gewahr.**

gewarten, see **warten** below.

gewärtigen *to expect*, sometimes with the gen., more commonly with the acc. of the reflexive and the genitive of the noun, or with the dative of the reflexive and the accusative of the noun: **Melanie gewärtigte keines Rigorismus** (Fontane's *L'Adultera*, XIX), or more commonly **M. gewärtigte sich keines Rigorismus**, or **gewärtigte sich** (dat.) **keinen Rigorismus.**

gewohnen or **gewöhnen** *to become accustomed to*, the former earlier in the period with the gen. or the acc., the latter still occasionally with the acc., now except in the perfect participle (see **gewohnt** in 3 below) usually replaced by **sich gewöhnen an** (with acc.): **bis sie (die Menschheit) hellern Wahrheitstag gewöhne** (Lessing's *Nathan*, 4, 4). **Und das sollte man gewöhnen!** (Hebbel's *Agnes Bernauer*, 1, 15). **„Man gewöhnt's!" — das ist eine ständige Redensart unter den Soldaten** (aus dem Feldpostbrief eines Wiener Kadetten, 1914). **Man gewöhnt sich an alles.**

glauben, see **259.** 15. B.

harren *to wait patiently for, await, be in store for*, with the gen. or **auf** with the acc., sometimes with the simple dat.: **Pfarrer Franz Krupnik hatte eine Fahrkarte nach Klaj gelöst, wo seiner ein Wagen harrte** (*Hamburger Nachrichten*, Oct. 29, 1904). **Gewaltige Aufgaben harren unser** (Dr. David at Weimar, Feb. 7, 1919). **Ich harre schon lange auf dich, auf eine Antwort. Wie so oft in Peking, war mir an jenem Tage, als sei die ganze Welt erstarrt in Angst, als harre sie atemlos Unbekanntem, Unheimlichem** (Heyking's *Briefe, die ihn nicht erreichten*, New York, Jan. 1901).

herrschen *to rule over*, usually with **über** with the acc., sometimes with the simple dat. or acc., with the simple gen. only in early N.H.G.

hoffen *to hope for, expect, trust*, usually with **auf** with the acc., with the simple gen. now only in case of **es**, which, however, is felt as an acc. and has led to the use of the acc. elsewhere:

Ich hoffe auf die Hilfe Gottes. Mein Gott, ich hoffe auff dich (Psalms, xxv. 2). The acc. is used in poetic style of something which one hopes to receive or realize: **Ich hoffe ein ewig Leben** (Gellert, 2, 191). It is also found in a few common expressions: **Er darf es** (old gen., now felt as an acc.) **kaum hoffen. Das will ich nicht hoffen** *I hope not.* **Ich hoffe das Beste von seinem Einflusse. Von Ihrem edlen Herzen hoffe ich Verschwiegenheit** (Benedix's *Vetter*, 1, 4). Hence the passive: **die bald zu hoffende Ankunft.**

höhnen *to scoff at*, also with the acc., or with **über** with the acc., only rarely with the dat.: **Er höhnte meiner,** or more commonly **mich** or **über mich.**

hohnlachen *to laugh at in scorn*, also with **über** with the acc.: **Denn jetzt hohnlach' ich deiner** (Wildenbruch's *Die Quitzows*, 3, 14). **Er hohnlachte über die Warnung.**

hören *to hear* formerly sometimes with the gen., usually with the acc., *listen to* (i.e. *lend ear to, heed*), sometimes with the dat. as illustrated in **258.** 1. A. *c*, usually with **auf** with the acc.

hüten *to guard, tend* (sheep, &c.), usually with the acc., only in early N.H.G. with the gen.: **Ich wil lieber der Thür hüten in meines Gottes hause | denn lange wonen in der Gottlosen Hütten** (Psalms lxxxiv. 11).

kosten *to taste (of)*, formerly with the gen., now with the acc., or sometimes with **von** with the dat.

lächeln *to smile at*, more commonly with **über** with the acc.

lachen (1) *to laugh at*, with **über** with the acc.: **Er lachte über meine Bemerkung.** (2) *to laugh scornfully at, make light of*, with the gen.: **Er höhnte mir mein Amulett, | hielt nichts von Mitteln, lachte aller Sprüche!** (Hauptmann's *Der arme Heinrich*, 3, 1). See also **260,** 4th par. The derivative **verlachen** *to deride* is transitive and takes the acc.

lauern *to lie in wait for*, more commonly with **auf** with the acc.: **Dort im Sommer, wenn der große | Meerlachs seine Rheinfahrt macht, | lauerte mit scharfem Spieße | sein der allemannische Fischer** (Scheffel's *Trompeter*, Drittes Stück).

lauschen *to listen to*, gen. rare, usually dat. or **auf** with the acc. (see **258.** 1. A. *c*): **Der Sturmwind fuhr ums Haus, ich lauschte sein, und wie ich lauschte, wurde sein Brausen zum Wiegenlied** (*Glauben und Wissen*, No. 1, p. 1).

leben, see **260,** 4th par.

leugnen *to deny*, usually with the acc., with the gen. in early N.H.G.

lohnen, see **259.** 23.

mangeln or **ermangeln** *to be without, lack*, the latter usually with the gen., the former with the gen. and in early N.H.G. also the acc., now more commonly impersonal with **an** with the dat., or with the thing lacking as subject: **Du ermangelst gänzlich des Fleißes. Es mangelt ihm der nötigen Energie** or more commonly **an der nötigen Energie,** or **Ihm mangelt die nötige Energie.**

mißbrauchen, earlier in the period with the gen., now with the acc.

missen *to miss* (goal, way; now obsolete in this meaning), *miss* (*notice* or *feel the absence of*; see 1 Kings xx. 39), *be without*, with the gen. in early N.H.G., now with the acc.

niederkommen, early N.H.G. **eines Kindes niederkommen** *to be delivered of a child*, now **mit einem Kinde niederkommen,** early N.H.G. **eines Fiebers niederkommen,** now **an einem Fieber erkranken.**

pflegen (1) *to attend to, take care of*, with the gen. or more commonly the acc.: **Du pflegtest deiner Wunden** (Kleist's *Penthesilea*, 9). **Nun pflegten sie seines schier erstarrten Leibes drinnen in der Stube nach Brauch, um das Leben in ihm wieder flüssig zu machen** (Wilhelm Fischer's *Sonnenopfer*, III). **Er pflegt seine Gesundheit, seine Hände.** (2) *to discharge the duties of*, usually with the gen.: **Auf dem Friedhof pflegt der Totengräber hastig seines Amtes** (Ernst Zahn's *Wie dem Kaplan Longinus die Welt aufging*). (3) *to carry on* (a conversation, &c.), with the gen. or more commonly the acc.: **Während er mit dem Schiffer dieser kleinen Heimlichkeit pflog** (H. Hoffmann's *Wider den Kurfürsten*, chap. 33). (4) *to give one's self up to, indulge in*, with the gen.: **Er pflegt der Wollust.** (5) *to take* (counsel, one's rest, &c.), with the gen. or acc.: **Er hat Rücksprache** or **Rat** or **Rates mit seinem Rechtsanwalt gepflogen. Er pflegt der Ruhe, seiner Bequemlichkeit.**

scherzen (1) *to make fun of, make sport of*, formerly with the acc., now with the gen. in Switzerland, elsewhere replaced by **spotten** with the gen. or **verspotten** with the acc.: **Geben Sie acht, daß die irdischen Weiber nicht Ihrer „scherzen"!** (Carl Spitteler's *Imago*, p. 49). (2) *to jest at, joke about*, with **über** with the acc.

schonen or **verschonen** *to spare, have regard for, use tenderly*, now usually with the acc., the former sometimes with the gen., both formerly also with the dat. (**258.** 1. A. *g*): **So triff mich, aber schone meines Volks!** (Grillparzer's *König Ottokar*, 5). **Schont seines Schmerzens!** Schiller's *Tell*, 1, 4). **Des Champagners hatte man nicht geschont** (Spielhagen's *Herrin*, p. 233).

schweigen (1) *to be silent about*, formerly with the gen., now usually with **von** with the dat., or **über** with the acc.: **Ich schweige der freuden** (Psalm xxxix. 3). (2) **schweigen** or more commonly **geschweigen** *to pass over in silence, to say nothing about*, usually with the gen., especially frequent in the infinitive with **zu: Ein breitschultriger und kurzhalsiger Mann von Mitte Dreißig, dessen Stutzhut und hechtgrauer Rock mit grünen Rabatten (des Hirschfängers ganz zu schweigen) über seinen Beruf keinen Zweifel lassen konnte** (Fontane's *Quitt*, chap. 1). **Der anderen Dinge zu geschweigen.**

sorgen *to worry, be anxious about*, now with **um,** sometimes **für,** with the acc.

sparen or **ersparen** *to spare*, now usually with the acc.

spielen *to play*, now usually with the acc. or according to **257.** 2. A **the simple stem of the noun,**

formerly with the gen. and still occasionally so in case of an infinitive-substantive and the diminutives, especially in dialect and in the language of children: **Versteckens, Räuberles, Soldätles, Indianerches** (G. Asmus's *Amerikanisches Skizzenbüchelche*, p. 59) **spielen**, now usually **Verstecken, Räuber, Soldat, Indianer, Pferd, Ball, Schach spielen.**

spotten *to scorn, mock, make sport of*, with the gen. in figurative language and also elsewhere, more commonly with **über** with the acc.: **Das spottet jeder Beschreibung.** Sometimes **spotten** takes the simple dat. and is also sometimes a transitive with an acc. object, hence the biblical expression **Gott läßt sich nicht spotten** God is not mocked. The transitive form is usually **verspotten.**

staunen *to be astonished at*, more commonly with **über** with the acc., sometimes with the simple dat. (**258.** I. A. *f*): **Sie staunten der Pracht nicht, mit der die Tante angetan war** (Felix Salten's *Die kleine Veronika*, p. 47).

sterben, *to die*, see **260,** 4th par.

tun *to discharge the duties of*: **Erst auf Grund der Drohung, die Sache bei dem deutschen Konsul Grafen Hardenberg anzuzeigen, veranlaßte er ihn seines Amtes zu tun** (*Hamburger Nachrichten*, Dec. 14, 1904).

verdienen *to be deserving of*, now with the acc.

verbleichen *to grow pale*, see **260,** 4th par.

verfehlen, see **fehlen,** above.

vergessen *to be forgetful of, forget*, more commonly the acc., in S. G. literary language and sometimes in the North **auf** (less commonly **an**) with the acc. after the analogy of **sich besinnen auf, sich erinnern auf,** and the popular **denken auf** (instead of literary **an**), usually with a little different meaning with the acc. *to forget, leave behind somewhere*, as in **einen Regenschirm vergessen,** but with **auf** in the sense *not to think of, not to turn one's attention, one's thoughts to*, as in **auf seinen Regenschirm vergessen** to forget to take one's umbrella along, i.e. not to think of it, **auf seine Pflicht, auf Gott vergessen: Der Herr hat mein noch nie vergessen, vergiß, mein Herz, auch seiner nicht** (Gellert). **Wenn sie also gekniet hätte aus Liebe zu ihm, während er fern von ihr weilte und allgemach ihrer vergaß** (Ertl's *Walpurga*). **Vergeßt nur nicht auf Eures Vaters Süpplein, Jungfer!** (Storm's *Zur Chronik von Grieshuus*, p. 109). **Dann vergaß ich auf die Sache** (Rosegger's *Geldtragen*). **Du vergißt ganz aufs Essen, Oltschi** (Berlepsch's *Vendetta*). **Herrgott, die Torte! Rein vergessen hätten wir jetzt auf die!** (delle Grazie's *Sphinx*). **Da hatte ich auf die Geschichte schon beinahe vergessen** (Ertl's *Nachdenkliches Bilderbuch*, p. 247). **Dann vergesse ich auf alles und dann spreche ich mit Martha schlesisch** (Paul Keller's *Waldwinter*, XVII). **Ich habe, glaub' ich, schon wieder an uns beide vergessen** (Hirschfeld's *Der junge Goldner*, p. 226). For further discussion see **260** (3rd par.).

verlangen *to long for*, with the gen. in poetic style, for prose construction see **262.** II. B. ***d***.

verleugnen *to deny, disown*, sometimes in early N.H.G. with the gen., now with the acc.

vermissen *to miss, feel the want, absence of*, now with the acc., in early N.H.G. also with the gen., as in I. Sam. xx. 18.

verzagen *to despair of, be in despair on account of*, with the gen. in poetic language, usually **um einen, seinetwegen, an einem, an seinem guten Willen, an seiner Gesundheit verzagen.**

wachen *to watch over*, formerly with gen. or dat., now with **über** with the acc. (formerly also dat.).

wahren (**1**) *to look out for*, with the gen.: **So dachte die Frau . . . | ihrer Ehre zu wahren und doppelt war sie verloren** (Goethe). **Wahr' deiner Haut** (Werner's *Ostsee*, I, 39). (**2**) *to keep*, with the gen.: **Der weise Talbot, der des Siegels wahret** (Schiller's *Maria*, 1, 7). (**3**) *to look after*, with the gen. in a few expressions: **Wahre deiner Pflicht, deines Amtes!** (**4**) *to defend, vindicate*, with the gen. in poetic language, usually with the acc.: **Ich geh' zum König, wahre meines Rechts** (Grillparzer's *Medea*, 1), but usually **Ich wahre mein Recht.** (**5**) *to guard, care for*, earlier in the period and still in poetic language with the gen.: **Hätten sie sich alle gehalten wie er und ein Knecht, es wäre mein und meines kleinen Häufchens übel gewahrt gewesen** (Goethe's *Götz*, 3, 6). **Und [der König] wahrte mein, wie eines teuern Sohns** (Grillparzer's *Medea*, 1). Usually with the acc.: **Sie wahrte ihn wie ihren Augapfel.** (**6**) *to observe, save*: **den Anstand wahren** *to observe the decorum*, **den Schein wahren** *to save appearances.*

wahrnehmen (**1**) *to take care of* (children, &c.), with the gen.: **Nehmt der Kinder . . . wahr** (Goethe's *Rein. Fuchs*, 3). (**2**) *to take advantage of* (an opportunity, &c.), with the gen. or more commonly the acc.: **Nimm der günstigen** or more commonly **die günstige Gelegenheit wahr.** (**3**) *to perceive*, now with the acc.: **Ich habe an ihm keine Veränderung wahrnehmen können.** (**4**) *to look after* (one's interests), now with the acc.: **Er nimmt mein Interesse wahr.** (**5**) *to reimburse one's self* (for his expenses), now with the acc.: **Er nimmt seine Auslagen wahr.**

walten (**1**) *to discharge the duties of, have charge of*, with the gen.: **Am nächsten Morgen waltete sie jedoch ihrer Pflichten am Frühlingstische** (Mewis's *Der große Pan*, p. 376). (**2**) *to bring to pass*, now also with the acc.: **Möge es** (**140.** *c*) **Mithras, der Allgütige, walten** (*Fam. Bl.*, 4, 459, *a*). **Das** (or **des**) **walte Gott!** (**3**) *to hold sway over*, with the simple gen., or more commonly the acc. or dat. after the prep. **über,** sometimes in poetic style with **ob** with the dat.: **Macht, die seines Schicksals waltete** (Freytag's *Bild.*, I. 406). **Ein Gott waltet über uns alle (allen).**

warten (**1**) *to await, expect, wait for*, in the first meaning with the gen. or more commonly **auf** with the acc., in the first meaning and its figurative application *to be in store for*, sometimes also the dat., in the second meaning once with the gen., but now replaced by **erwarten with**

the acc., in the third meaning now with **auf** with the acc. when the idea of duration is prominent and replaced by **erwarten** with the acc. when the attention is directed more to the end, result: **Er wartete des Erfolges seiner Fangvorrichtung** (H. Seidel's *Der Luftballon*). **Ich habe ein unbestimmtes Gefühl, als warte meiner irgendwo draußen ein stürmisches Meer** (Heyking's *Briefe, die ihn nicht erreichten*, p. 185). **Traurige Nachrichten warteten auf ihn. Es warteten mir noch heiße Tage** (Gotthelf, 5, 203). **Ich erwarte einen Freund. Ich erwarte nichts Gutes von ihm. Ich warte auf ihn. Erwarten Sie mich auf dem Bahnsteig. Ich kann die erste Rose kaum erwarten.** Earlier in the period **gewarten** (now little used) and **erwarten** were also used with the gen. in these meanings. (**2**) *to tend*, with the gen.: **Da saß ein Mann und wartete der Fähre** (Schiller's *Tell*, 2, 2). (**3**) *to care for, look after*, with the gen., or more commonly the acc., formerly also the dat.: **Warte des Leibes, der Pflicht, deines Amtes! Da begannen die Menschen des Ackers zu warten, damit er ihnen im Herbst ihre Nahrung und Notdurft gab** (Engking's *Die Darnekower*, p. 162). **Sie (die Kinderwärterin) wartet die Kinder. Man wartet die Pferde.**

zürnen *to be angry at* (something), in choice language sometimes still with the gen. of the thing, in Switzerland sometimes a transitive with the acc. as in M.H.G., now usually with **über** with the acc.: **Zürnt nicht der dreisten Frage, wie konntet Ihr dies einsame Leben unter dem wilden Volk vertragen?** (Freytag's *Rittmeister*, III). **Wie kann ein Mensch menschlicher Fehle zürnen?** (*Zeitschrift für den deutschen Unterricht*, 1919, p. 170). **Sie hätten mein Ausbleiben fast gezürnt** (Gotthelf, 6, 63). **Ich zürne dir es nicht** (K. F. Meyer's *Novellen*, 2, 146). **Er zürnt über jede Kleinigkeit,** but **Er zürnt mir, mit mir,** or **auf mich.**

a. The genitive object is also found after the following verbs, where, however, it may also be classed as an adverbial gen.: **fahren** to drive, **gehen** to go, **kommen** to come, **schleichen** to sneak, **schreiten** to step, go, proceed, **schwanken** or **torkeln** to stagger, **stolpern** to stumble, **wandern** to wander, **ziehen** to go. Exs.: **Ein wirtlich Dach | für alle Wanderer, die des Weges fahren** (Schiller's *Tell*, 1, 2). **Die Knaben gingen verhältnismäßig still ihrer Wege** (Ompteda's *Sylvester von Geyer*, VII). **Laß jeden seines Pfades gehen. Sachte schlich ich meiner Wege. Ganze Züge von Kamelen schwankten schwerbeladen des Weges** (Dominik's *Kamerun*, p. 4). The accusative is also used after these verbs, usually without difference of meaning, but sometimes with a shade of difference. The gen. represents the action as beginning, or as directed toward only a part of the object, while the acc. represents the action as a thoro one, or as extending entirely over the object: **Geh deinen Weg** *Go on your way, keeping to it till you reach the end of it*, but **Geh deines Weges** *Start out on your way.* The gen. was once widely used here, but is now a decaying construction confined largely to masc. words in a few set expressions. It is rare with fem. nouns, found mostly in poetry. The simple acc., tho more common than the gen., has its limitations. The usual mode of expression here is the acc. in connection with an adverb or preposition. **Er ging die Straße hinunter. Er kam die Treppe herauf. Er ging die Straße, den Fluß entlang.**

B. *Passive Form of Statement.* In changing sentences containing a genitive object into the passive construction the genitive does not become nominative, but remains genitive for the same reason that the dative object remains dative in changing from the active to the passive (**258.** 1). The subject of the passive sentence must then become the impersonal **es,** expressed or understood: **Man gedenkt meiner** *They are thinking of me* becoming in the passive **Meiner wird gedacht,** or **Es wird meiner gedacht.** Those verbs that also admit of the accusative object in the active may likewise be treated as regular transitives, in which case the accusative of the active becomes nominative in the passive: **Er erwähnte diesen Umstand** or **dieses Umstands** *He mentioned this circumstance* becoming in the passive: **Dieser Umstand wurde erwähnt,** or **Dieses Umstands wurde erwähnt.** In case of those verbs which prefer the prep. object in prose, the impersonal passive must be formed: **Er spottete über mich** *He scoffed at me* becoming in the passive: **Es wurde über mich gespottet,** or **Es wurde meiner gespottet.**

3. *Genitive after adjectives, adverbs, participles, and nouns in Connection with a Verb.* The genitive here denotes sphere (**260**), goal, specification, cause, deprivation, removal, separation, or it often has the force of an objective genitive. In earlier periods the genitive was much more common here in some of these categories than it is to-day. Former usage often survives in group-words (**247.** 2) and compounds: **sonnenverbrannt, schicksalsschwer, handelsklug, geistesabwesend, geisteskrank, segensreich,** &c. In old group-words (**247.** 2. *a*) the genitive is not marked by a formal ending, as this type originated in the period before the introduction of inflection: **zielbewußt,** &c.

The genitive now stands after the following words in elevated language and in large part also in common prose, but other constructions too are found with the same forms, as is indicated after each word: —

achtlos *heedless of, not paying attention to,* in choice prose with the gen., more commonly with **auf** with the acc.

ahnungslos *having no presentiment of*: **Unterdes ließ Ebba sich, ahnungslos solchen Übelwollens, die Verdienste der Fliederbüschen** (name) **erzählen** (Boy-Ed's *Die säende Hand*, p. 77).

ansichtig werden *to get sight of,* originally with the acc., now also with the gen. and perhaps more commonly so.

bar *void of, free from,* rarely with **von** or **an** with the dat.: **Ich bin alles Trostes, alles Rates bar. Bar jeden** (weak gen.; see **106.** *Note* 1) **Chauvinismus, frei von Überheblichkeit wollen wir . . . immer wieder zeigen, was die Größe und Kraft deutschen Geistes vermag** (R. Pechel in *Deutsche Rundschau,* March 1920, p. 463).

bedürftig *in need of.*

beflissen *given, devoted to, engaged in the study of*: **ein der Rechte Beflissener.**

begierig or **gierig** *desirous of, eager for,* with the gen. in choice language, more commonly with **nach** with the dat., or **auf** with the acc.: **Und zuletzt des Lichts begierig, bist du, Schmetterling, verbrannt. Er ist nach Geld begierig. Er ist auf den Ausgang begierig.**

beholfen in einem beholfen sein *to be of assistance to someone by means of,* with the gen. or **mit** with the dat., both constructions in use in early N.H.G., now obsolete.

benötigt sein *to be in want, in need of,* sometimes with the acc.

beraubt *deprived of, stripped of, robbed of.*

berechtigt *entitled to,* with the gen. now only in compounds, as in **vorkaufsberechtigt** *entitled to the refusal*; outside of compounds now with **zu** with the dat.

bereit *ready for,* earlier in the period occasionally with the gen., still quite commonly so in compounds, as **angriffsbereit, gefechtsbereit, befehlsbereit, verkaufsbereit,** &c.; outside of compounds now with **zu** with the dat.

berichtet (in early N.H.G. also contracted to **bericht**) *versed in,* still in use in the classical period: **Die Steuerleute . . . sind des Fahrens | nicht wohl berichtet** (Schiller's *Tell,* 4, 1). See also **262.** III. 1. *k.*

bewußt *conscious of,* sometimes with the acc.

bloß *not furnished with, wanting, free from,* usually with the gen., sometimes with **von** with the dat., *exposed to,* with the dat.

eingedenk or **gedenk** (poet.) *mindful of,* sometimes with the acc.: **Ich bin meines Versprechens stets eingedenk. Diese strapaziöseste Tour seines Lebens kam auch auf Konto der Franzosen, die wollte er ihnen eingedenk bleiben** (C. Viebig's *Die Wacht am Rhein,* p. 413).

eingeständig, see **geständig.**

einig or **eins** *agreed upon,* with the gen. in the expressions **des Preises, des Handels, des Kaufes einig** or **eins,** elsewhere **über etwas** (acc.) **einig.**

empfänglich, formerly with the gen., now according to **261.** B.

entraten (provinc.) *rid of*: **Eines Dieners mit Weisheitszähnen bin ich baß** (better) **entraten; d i e Dinger sind nur für uns gelehrte Leute** (Storm's *Pole Poppenspäler*).

entwohnt or more commonly **entwöhnt** *disaccustomed to,* the former with gen. or less often the acc., the latter with the gen, dat., or **von** with the dat.

erfahren *experienced in, skilled in, versed in,* with the gen. earlier in the period, now with **in** with the dat.

erfüllt, see **gefüllt.**

ersättigt *satiated with*: **Denn ich hatte nicht nur einen des Lebens ersättigten Greis mit dem weisen Willen der Natur übereinstimmend sich von der Erde weg einer unbekannten Ewigkeit zuwenden sehen,** &c. (R. Huch's *Ludolf Ursleu,* chap. XXXVII).

Erwähnung tun *to make mention of,* sometimes with **von** with the dat.

fähig *capable of.*

frei *free from,* with the gen. earlier in the period, now usually with **von** with the dat. The old gen. here is still common in compounds: **vorwurfsfrei, schuldenfrei.**

froh (**1**) *enjoying, rejoicing in* (the possession of), *happy in,* usually with the gen.: **Er wird seiner hohen Stellung, seines Geldes nicht froh. Sie werden ihrer Liebe nicht mehr froh.** (**2**) *glad of, rejoiced at, over,* usually with **über** with the acc.: **Ich bin froh über dich, über deine Leistung.** The older gen. or the uninflected stem is found in group-words (**247.** 2): **schadenfroh** *rejoicing over the misfortunes of others,* where **schaden** is an old weak gen., **sturmfrohe Möwen** sea-gulls rejoicing over the storm.

gefüllt and **erfüllt** *filled with,* the former with the gen. in poetic style, usually with **mit** with the dat., the latter with the gen. in a few expressions or more commonly with **von** or **mit** with the dat.: **Zweifelnd und doch aller Gewißheit erfüllt** (Raabe's *Gutmanns Reisen,* chap. XI).

geizig *eager after, coveting,* now usually with **nach** with the dat.

gereuig werden *to regret*: **Als er auf den Domplatz kam, wurde er seines Entschlusses fast gereuig** (Ruth Waldstetter's *Das Haus zum großen Kefig*).

gesättigt *satiated with, tired of,* with the gen. or perhaps more commonly **von** with the dat.: **Ich bin gesättigt des süßen Weins** (Halbe's *Lebenswende,* 1, p. 20).

geständig or **eingeständig sein** *to confess, plead guilty to* (an offense), sometimes with the acc.: **Er ist des Verbrechens geständig** or **eingeständig.**

gewahr werden *to perceive,* with the gen. or acc.: **Ich wurde meines Irrtums** or **meinen Irrtum bald gewahr.**

gewaltig sein or **werden** *to have control of* (one's senses, &c.), *get the mastery of,* in early N.H.G. with the gen., later **über** with the acc., now little used here.

gewärtig *expecting, on the look-out for,* sometimes with the acc.: **Ich war mir seines Angriffs**

gewärtig. Den sind die Lochstafelkinder gewärtig, ehe sie abziehen (Ernst Zahn's *Menschen*, I).

gewiß *certain of*, sometimes with the acc., earlier in the period with **von** with the dat.

gewohnt or **gewöhnt** *accustomed to*, both more commonly with the acc., or in case of **gewöhnt** still more commonly with **an** with the acc., **gewohnt** sometimes with **an** with the acc.: **Da sind viele, sonst des sanften Gehrocks gewohnte Gestalten kaum wiederzuerkennen in dem Gewande des Krieges** (*Tägliche Rundschau*, Oct. 22, 1914). **Wir sind des Furchtbaren so gewöhnt, daß es wenig Schrecken für uns mehr gibt** (Paul Block in *Berliner Tageblatt*, June 3, 1919).

habhaft werden *to get hold* or *possession of*, sometimes with the acc.: **Sie wurden des Verbrechers nicht habhaft.**

Herr sein or **werden** *to have* or *get the mastery of*, also with **über** with the acc.: **Er wurde nicht Herr seiner Leidenschaft.**

imstande sein *to be able to*: **Wenn es also entschlossen ist, den Krieg zu führen, bis es zu einem ihm günstigen Frieden gekommen ist, dann ist Japan dessen auch imstande** (*Neue Zürcher Zeitung*, March 13, 1905).

inne or less commonly **innen werden** *to become conscious of, perceive*, also with the acc.: **Sie werden ihres Wahnes inne werden** (Schiller's *Jungfrau*, 5, 4). **Wenn sie würden innen | hier mein seltsames Beginnen** (Grillparzer's *Ahnfrau*, 2).

klar *clear with regard to*, more commonly with **über** with the acc.: **Jedermann ist sich der Beweggründe klar, welche zu diesen Flottenvergleichen Anlaß boten** (*Neue Zürcher Zeitung*, March 2, 1905).

kündig (now rare) or more commonly **kundig** *well acquainted with* (a road, &c.), *versed in.*

laß (poet.) *tired of.*

ledig *free from*, with the gen. or **von** with the dat.: **Ich bin aller Schuld bar und ledig.**

leer *void of, free from*, now usually with **von** or **an** with the dat., common in old group-words (**247.** 2. *a*): (poetic) **aller Falschheit leer. Dies Gasthaus ist nie leer von Gästen. Sein Kopf ist leer an nützlichen Kenntnissen. Fischleere Teiche, eine baumleere Grasflur, inhaltleere Worte.**

los *rid of, free from*, with the gen. in poetic language, now usually with the acc.; earlier in the period with **von** with the dat. also after **sein** and **werden**, now with **von** with the dat. only after other verbs than **sein** and **werden: Ich bin ihn los,** but **Er ist vom Militär losgekommen. Er machte sich von mir los.** The older gen. is preserved in compounds: **anspruchslos,** &c.

mächtig *master of, in control of*: **Er ist des Englischen mächtig. Er war seiner Sinne nicht mächtig.**

Meister sein or **werden** *to be master of, get the mastery over, have, get the control of, get the better of*, also with **von** with the dat. or **über** with the acc.: **Der Zunge bin ich Meister, nicht des Auges** (Kotzebue).

müde *tired of*, also with the acc.

müßig used earlier in the period with **gehen,** less frequently **sein, stehen, bleiben,** in the meanings *to keep aloof from, avoid, abstain from, free one's self from.*

nötig or **von nöten haben** *to need*, with the gen. or now more commonly the acc., **nötig sein** (S.W.G.) *to need, require*, also with the acc., **not sein** *to be in need of*, with the gen. or now more commonly the nom., **not haben** *to have need of*, with the gen. or now usually the acc.: **Nun habt ihr keines Vormunds nötig** (Lessing's *Sinnged.*, I, 124), now usually **keinen Vormund. Ihr habt jetzt meiner** (usually **mich**) **weiter nicht von nöten** (Schiller's *Tell*, 1, 2). **Es war der Anstrengung nötig, um bei diesem Gedanken, der an der Seite Goethes meine Seele durchschauerte, eine gewisse Art Beklommenheit verbergen zu können** (Prof. J. Röckl in 1808 as quoted in *Beilage zur Allgemeinen Zeitung*, Aug. 27, 1905, p. 391). **Vieles Redens ist jetzt nicht not. Eins** (gen., but felt as a nom.) **ist not. Mut ist uns not und ein gefaßter Geist** (Schiller's *Wallenstein*). **Sie hat's** (the es a gen., but felt as an acc.) **nicht not** (R. Wagner's *Flieg. Holl.*).

quitt *free from, rid of, clear of*, sometimes with the acc., earlier in the period also **von** with the dat.: **Ich bin meines Versprechens quitt. Ich bin aller Sorgen quitt.**

satt *satiated with, tired of*, with the gen. in choice language, colloquially more commonly the acc.: **Ich bin des ewigen Gezänkes** (or **das ewige Gezänk**) **satt.**

schuldig *guilty of* with the gen., **unschuldig** *innocent of* with the gen. in poetic language, usually with **an** with the dat., **schuldig sein** *to owe, owe for* with the acc., **an etwas** (dat.) **schuldig** (usually **schuld**) **sein** *to be the cause of something*, in biblical language **an einem** or **etwas schuldig sein** in the general meaning *to sin against*, altho variously rendered into English, as in 1. Sam. xxii. 22, 1. Cor. xi. 27, **des Todes schuldig sein** *to deserve death, forfeit one's life*: **Er ist des Verbrechens schuldig. Er ist an diesem Verbrechen unschuldig. Ich bin ihm eine Antwort schuldig. Ich bleibe Ihnen 20 Mark schuldig. Ich bin** or **bleibe die Ware schuldig** *I owe for the goods, took the goods on credit.* **Wer mit seinem Bruder zürnet, der ist des Gerichts schuldig** (Matth. v. 22, revised ed.).

selig *happy in*, usually with **in** with the dat. or **durch** with the acc.

sicher *sure of*, only rarely with **von** with the dat.

teilhaft or **teilhaftig** *sharing in*: **Alle seid ihr teilhaft seiner Schuld** (Schiller's *Tell*, 3, 3).

überdrüssig *weary of*, with the gen. or acc., formerly also with **über** with the acc.

über'hoben *relieved from*, usually with the gen., sometimes with the dat.: **eine . . . seiner weltlichen Eingriffe überhobene, selbständige Stellung** (Ranke's *Päpste*, 1, 162).

unachtend *paying no attention to*: **Unachtend der braunen Löckchen, die von der Stirne ihm in die Augen hingen** (Storm's *Doppelgänger*).
unbe'kümmert *unconcerned about*, now with **um** with the acc. or **wegen** with the gen. See also **261.** B.
ungläubig *incredulous with regard to*, with the gen. in biblical language, as in Acts xxvi. 19.
unwissend, see **wissend**.
verdächtig *suspected of*: **Er ist der Tat verdächtig.**
vergessen *forgetful of*, still in use in poetic style.
verlustig *forfeiting, losing*: **Er ist der Ehre verlustig gegangen.**
verlustigt *deprived of*, now obsolete.
vermutend or **vermuten sein** *to be expecting*, more commonly with the acc.: **So wenig sich ein moderner Leser . . . dessen in einer attischen Tragödie vermutend ist, so weitverbreitet war in privaten Konventikeln diese Art von Selbstheiligung** (Wilamowitz-Moellendorff's *Griechische Tragödien*, p. 116).
versichert *assured of*.
verständig *versed in*, earlier in the period with the gen., now usually found in this meaning only in compounds: **rechtsverständig** versed in the law, **ein Sachverständiger** an expert, specialist, &c.
voll or sometimes, especially before an unmodified object, **voller** (see **111.** 8), with the gen. when the object is modified by the definite article or a descriptive adjective or by both, especially in case of the superlative, also before an unmodified plural object; with **von** (sometimes **mit**) with the dat. when the object is unmodified and precedes, also when the object is a personal pronoun, also when it stands before an object modified by a limiting adjective other than the definite article, often also before an object modified by a descriptive adjective, where in general the gen. is more common; usually with non-inflection of the object in the singular when there is no modifying word before it; sometimes with the simple dat. instead of the more common gen.: **voll der innigsten Teilnahme, voll des größten Lobes, voll treffender Bemerkungen, Briefe voll verräterischen Inhalts, ein Glas voll starken Weines** or **voll von starkem Weine. Der Baum hängt voll Früchte** (gen., sometimes dat. **Früchten**). **Ein Hafen, der von Schiffen voll ist; ein Spielplatz voll Kinder** but always **voll von ihnen; ein Herz voll von Ihnen. Er hat den Kopf voll von seinem Plan, voll von anderen Dingen. Er hat den Kopf so voll mit seinem Unglück** (Fulda's *Die Kameraden*, 2, 4). **Ein Glas voll Wasser** (earlier in the period **Wassers**), **das Herz voll schrecklichem Höhnen** (Frenssen's *Bismarck*, p. 337) or more commonly **schrecklichen Höhnens.**
wert *worth*, formerly with the gen. and still in certain expressions, now usually with the acc., *worthy*, with the gen.: **Das ist der Mühe, der Rede wert. Das ist keinen Schuß Pulver wert. Er ist der Ehre wert.**
wissend (in poetic language) *knowing of, informed concerning*, **unwissend: Dann mach' ich ihn wissend der Zaubermacht, | durch die er sie finden und binden kann** (Sudermann's *Die drei Reiherfedern*, 1, 2).
würdig *worthy of*.
zufrieden *satisfied with*, now usually with **mit** with the dat., in the eighteenth century also with **von** with the dat.: **Auch bin des Dienstes** (now **mit dem Dienste**) **ich wohl zufrieden, den sie mir geleistet** (Goethe). The older gen. is still sometimes used where the reference is to a thought as a whole: **Schon während der Mobilmachung waren Schnaps und selbst Bier auf Bahnhöfen verboten, und unsere wackeren Jungen waren dessen zufrieden** (Engel's *Ein Tagebuch*, I, p. 46). **Ich bin es** (old gen.; see **140.** *c*; still quite common) **zufrieden. Ich bin davon** (now **damit**) **zufrieden** (Goethe).

a. Instead of a gen. of a noun or pronoun an infinitive with **zu** (or more rarely **um zu**) or a clause is often found with these adjectives: **Ich bin froh, Sie zu sehen. Er ist nicht fähig, (um) es zu begreifen. Ich bin froh, daß Sie gekommen sind.**

b. The acc. after the above adjectives is more common in case of pronouns than nouns. Especially the neut. acc. **es** is common even after adjectives, which do not usually admit of the acc.: **Wenn ich es ganz und gar überhoben sein könnte!** If I could be relieved from it entirely! The **es** is here in reality the gen. (see **140.** *c*), but is now felt as an acc. The acc. now very commonly used after some of the above adjectives and participles has arisen from this misunderstood pronominal form **es**, and then spread to other pronouns, and also to nouns: Weislingen: **Seid Ihr mich schon müde?** Adelheid: **Euch nicht sowohl als Euern Umgang** (Goethe's *Götz*, 2, 9).

c. The gen. object usually precedes the governing adjective: **Sind Sie Ihrer Sache gewiß?**

Prepositional Object.

261. In the preceding articles the object of verbs or adjectives is in some simple case form, but it may also be in some case after a prep., usually, however, with a different shade of meaning or feeling, if the same verb also governs a simple case: **Ich denke dein** *I am thinking of you* is choicer and more expressive than the more common **Ich denke an dich.** Further shades of meaning can be introduced by using different prepositions: **Denke auf deine Rettung** Be thinking of some plan to bring about your rescue. **Ich habe lange über das Rätsel gedacht** I have long pondered over the riddle. Many verbs, adjectives, and participles have an object or objects in a simple case form in some expressions, but have prepositional objects in other expressions, other words have only prep. objects: **Eins bitte ich dich,** but **Ich bitte um Entschuldigung. Jeder war auf das Äußerste gefaßt.**

In the passive the prepositional object remains and the subject becomes **es** expressed or understood: (active) **Man bittet um Antwort;** (passive) **Es wird um Antwort gebeten,** or **Um Antwort wird gebeten.** See also **219.** 5. A and B. *a.*

For purposes of illustration a number of the most common verbs, adjectives and participles which need a prepositional object are listed below along with the prepositon or prepositons which each word requires. No attempt is made to distinguish here the prepositional phrase in the object relation from the prepositional phrase in the adverbial relation, as there is never a difference in form and no fundamental difference in function. In general we call the phrase an object when its relation to the verb, adjective, or participle is very close, so close that it is necessary to complete its meaning. The relation of the adverbial phrase to the verb, adjective, or participle is less close. It is, however, often impossible to discriminate between the two classes sharply.

By glancing at the preceding and following articles it will be seen that verbs which once took an object in a simple case form now often take a prepositional object. The prep. construction has become a marked favorite, and hence the study of the prepositions, their meaning and grammatical use, is a vital one. This subject is treated at considerable length in **225–232.**

A. Verbs with Prepositional Object:—

abhängen von to depend upon, be dependent upon: **Das hängt vom Glück ab. Ich hänge nicht von meinen Verwandten ab.**

abnehmen an (with dat.) to decrease in: **Er hat an Reichtum, Körperkräften abgenommen.**

abonnieren auf (with acc.) to subscribe for: **Ich habe** (or less commonly **ich habe mich**) **auf die Zeitung abonniert** (an act). **Ich bin auf die Zeitung abonniert** (a state). Now often trans. with acc.: **Eine Tageszeitung können sie aus finanziellen Gründen nicht abonnieren** (*Frankfurter Zeit.*, April 2, 1914).

abreisen nach to depart, set out for.

abstechen gegen (also **von** or **zu**) to contrast with.

abzielen auf (with acc.) to aim at, have in view.

achten auf or **achtgeben auf** (with acc.) to pay attention to: **Achte auf meine Worte,** or **Gib auf meine Worte acht.** See also **260.** 2. A.

afterreden von einem, über or **gegen einen,** or more commonly **einem Übles nachreden** to slander someone.

angrenzen to border on: **Seine Felder grenzen an die unsrigen,** but without prep. obj. **Deutschland und die angrenzenden Länder.**

anhalten bei to stop at: **unterwegs bei einem Wirtshause —; um ein Mädchen** — to propose to a girl.

anklopfen to knock on: **Man klopft an die Tür,** but without prep. obj. **Es ist zweimal angeklopft worden.**

anknüpfen an (with acc.) to begin a discourse, treatise by referring to something already said or known, to start from: **Er knüpfte an die letzten Worte der Erzählung an.**

anspielen auf (with acc.) to allude to.

auffahren bei to start at (a sudden sound).

aufhören: — **mit** to stop, cease: **Hör' endlich mit deinem ewigen Jammern auf!** Also with the infinitive: **Hör' auf, zu jammern.**

aufmerken to listen to, give ear to: **Merke auf meine Worte, auf meinen Wunsch,** but without prep. obj.: **Mit fremden Menschen nimmt man sich zusammen, da merkt man auf.**

auftauchen aus emerge from.

aussehen nach to have the appearance of, be a prospect of: **Es sieht nicht nach schönem Wetter aus.**

bauen auf (with dat. in 1st meaning, acc. in 2nd) to build upon, rely upon: **Er baut auf dem Sande. Ich baue auf ihn.**

beben vor (with dat.) to tremble, quiver, shiver with: **Mein Herz bebt vor Furcht. Die runden Schultern Josephines bebten von verhaltenem Lachen.**

beginnen mit + verbal noun, often used where in English a direct object is employed: **Zunächst habe ich mich durch den Wunsch des Herrn Verlegers bestimmen lassen, mit dem Druck zu beginnen** (Bülbring's *Altenglisches Elementarbuch,* Vorwort) to begin the printing.

beharren bei (also **auf** or **in** with dat.) to persist in, persevere in: **Er beharrt bei (auf, in) seinem Irrtum, seiner Meinung.**

bellen auf (with acc.) to bark at: **Der Karo bellt wohl auch mal auf seinen Herrn, wenn er schlecht gelaunt ist** (Halbe's *Haus Rosenhagen,* p. 65). Here used facetiously after the model of **auf einen schimpfen.** We usually say: **Der Hund bellt einen an.**

bestehen aus to consist of: **Messing besteht aus Zinn und Kupfer,** but **Charakterstärke besteht nicht im** (*in*) **Eigensinn;** to insist upon: **Er besteht auf seinem** (also **sein**) **Recht.**

bitten um to ask, beg for (a thing). See also **262.** III. 1. *a.*
blicken auf (with acc.) to look at, on: **Er blickt auf die Karte, auf den See, auf den Fleck im Rock,** but to indicate a more minute investigation **anblicken** is employed: **Er blickte die Karte an** He examined the map, looking at its general make-up. **Er blickte den Fleck im Rock an.** We also say: **Er blickte mich freundlich, zornig an.**
brennen vor to burn with: **Er brennt vor großer Ungeduld; brennen auf** (with acc.) to burn with a desire to: **Er brennt auf den Kampf** He burns with a desire to begin the battle. **Er brennt darauf, ins Leben einzugreifen.**
deklamieren über (with acc.) to declaim upon.
duften nach to smell of (roses, &c.), give forth the fragrance of.
eingehen auf (with acc.) to enter into, comply with: **ohne auf die einzelnen Umstände einzugehen, (auf) eine Wette eingehen, auf Bedingungen eingehen.**
einwilligen in (with acc.) to consent to, agree to.
enden, endigen to end: **Das Wort endigt (sich; 218.** 3. B. *a*) **auf einen Vokal. Der Weg endigt in einem** (or **einen**) **Wald. Die Pacht endigt mit dem 1. Mai.**
entfliehen (1) to flee: **Die Hasen entfliehen vor den Hunden. Er ist vor mir, vor der Krankheit entflohen.** (2) to escape, get away: **Er entfloh (aus) dem Gefängnis,** but only **Er entfloh mir.**
entspringen aus to escape from: **Er ist aus dem Zuchthaus entsprungen,** but **Er ist seinem Aufseher entsprungen.**
entstehen aus to arise from.
erhellen aus to become clear from: **Daraus erhellt, daß usw.**
erkennen auf (with acc.) to pass sentence of: **Das Gericht erkannte auf ein Jahr Zuchthaus.**
erkranken an (with dat.) to get an attack of (fever, &c.).
erröten über (with acc.) to blush at, for: **Ich erröte über die Unwahrheit, über dich; vor** (with dat.) to blush with: **Ich erröte vor großer Scham.** See also **260.** 2. A.
erschallen von to resound, ring with.
erwachen aus to awake from.
erwachsen aus to accrue from: **Es wird dir aus diesem Schritt manches Leid erwachsen.**
fahnden auf (with acc.) to be on the lookout for, to search for, try to seize: **Man fahndet bereits auf den Dieb.**
fallen an (with acc.) to fall to: **Die Erbschaft fällt an den Sohn.**
feilschen um to try to screw down the price, haggle over: **Er feilschte um eine Mark. Sie feilschten um den Preis.**
festhalten an (with dat.) to stick, cling to.
feuern auf (with acc.) to fire at.
fischen nach to fish for.
flehen um to entreat, beg for: **bei einem um Hilfe flehen.**
fliehen vor (with dat.) to flee from.
folgen auf (with acc.) to follow: **Auf Regen folgt Sonnenschein; — aus** to ensue, follow from.
forschen nach to search for, inquire after, investigate.
fragen nach to ask, inquire for, after; **nach dem Wege, Preise fragen** to ask after the way, ask the price, **nach jemandem fragen** to ask for, after someone.
fressen, nagen an (with dat.) to prey on: **Der Kummer nagt an seinem Herzen.**
funkeln vor to sparkle with: **Seine Augen funkeln vor Zorn.**
fußen auf (with acc., usually dat. in 3rd meaning) to rely upon, base one's hopes upon, stand upon: **Ich fuße auf den Vertrag, mein Recht. Man sieht es den Leuten ja an, daß sie nicht auf sicherem Boden der Heimat fußen.**
gehören to belong to: **Das gehört mir,** but **Das gehört an den Nagel, in den Schrank, unter den Tisch, vor das Gericht. Die Insel gehört zu** (see **229.** 2 under **zu** II. 1. B. *b*) **England. Er gehört diesem Vereine an.**
gewinnen an (with dat.) to be gaining in: **Er gewinnt an Macht.**
glühen vor (with dat.) to glow with: **Er glüht vor Begeisterung; — nach** to be burning for: **Er glüht nach grausamer Rache.**
graben nach to dig for.
greifen to grasp: **Er griff mir an den Puls** He felt my pulse. **Das greift an den Beutel** That runs into money. **Er griff dem Pferde in die Zügel** He seized the horse by the bridle. **Ein Ertrinkender greift nach einem Strohhalme. Das Feuer greift um sich** The fire is spreading. **Er griff mir unter die Arme** He came to my assistance. **Er griff zu strengen Maßregeln** He adopted severe measures. **Ich mußte zu diesem Mittel greifen** I had to resort to this expedient.
grenzen, see **angrenzen.**
grübeln über (with the acc. or sometimes dat.; see **231.** II under **über, 1.** *a. Note*) to ponder on, over.
gucken nach to peep at.
halten an (with dat.) to hold to: **An diesem Glauben halte ich fest; an sich** — to restrain one's anger, feelings; **— auf** (with acc., formerly also dat.) to attach value, importance to, insist upon, take care of: **Sie hält peinlich auf äußern Anstand. Er hält auf seine Ehre, seine Gesundheit.**
handeln: an einem gut, schlecht — to do well, ill by someone; **— mit** to deal, trade in; **— von** to treat, be about: **Dieses Buch handelt von der Freundschaft.**
hangen, hängen an (with dat.) to hang on: **Sein Rock hängt am Nagel. Sein Herz hängt an seinem Liebling, seiner Heimat.**
haschen nach to scramble for, aim at, strain for: **Er hascht nach Effekt.**
herablächeln auf (with acc.) to smile upon.
hereinbrechen über (with acc.) to burst upon: **Ein Gewitter bricht über uns herein. Ein Unglück ist über uns hereingebrochen.**
herfallen über (with acc.) to rush, fall upon (someone), attack (the dishes): **Sie fielen über mich mit Knütteln her. Sie fielen über das Essen her.**
hervorbrechen aus to break forth from.
hervorgehen aus to result from.
hervorschießen aus to dart from.
heulen hinter jemandem her to hoot after someone.

hinarbeiten auf (with the acc.) to work towards: **Er arbeitet auf seine Beförderung hin.**
hinausgehen über (with the acc.) to improve on: **Er ging über das, was zu seiner Zeit geleistet war, weit hinaus.**
hindeuten auf (with acc.) to hint at, point to.
hinweisen auf (with acc.) to refer to.
hören: Ich höre auf (mit) dem einen Ohr schlecht. Er hört stets auf mich, meinen Rat. Höre nicht auf ihn! Don't mind him. **Sie hört auf die Klingel** She answers the bell. **Er hört bei einem Professor** He attends a professor's lectures. **Ich habe von ihrer Schönheit gehört.**
hungern nach to hunger **for.**
hüpfen vor (with dat.) **to jump for, with** (joy, &c.).
kaufen to buy: **Ich kaufte es von** (of, from) **ihm. Ich kaufe bei ihm** (of him, at his store, deal with him). **Ich habe meinem Sohne** (or **für meinen Sohn**) **einen Anzug gekauft. Kaufe das Nachbargrundstück an dich!**
klagen über (with acc.) to complain of; **— um** to mourn for; **— gegen** to go to law against; **— gegen jemanden auf** (with acc.) to bring a suit against someone for: **Er klagt auf Schadenersatz.**
kleben an (with dat.) to stick to.
klettern auf einen Baum to climb (up) a tree.
knixen vor (with dat.) to curtsy to.
knurren über (with acc.) to snarl at.
kochen vor (with dat.) to boil with (rage, &c.).
kommen wegen to call for (something).
kriechen vor (with dat.) to cringe to.
laufen (schwimmen, singen, werfen, &c.) **um** (sometimes **in**) **die Wette** to run a race (vie in swimming, &c.).
leben to live: **Er lebt von seiner Hände Arbeit** by the work of his own hands. **Er lebt vom Spiel** by gambling. **Sie lebt von milden Gaben** on charity.
lehnen to lean: **Er lehnt an der Wand,** (in answer to the question **wohin**) **Er lehnt,** or more commonly **lehnt sich an die Wand.**
leiden to suffer: **Man leidet an einer Krankheit. Wir leiden unter der Hitze. Ich habe viel von ihm, von der Hitze zu leiden.**
losgehen auf (with acc.) to fly at someone.
loshacken auf (with acc.) to peck at.
merken auf (with acc.) to pay attention to, mark, mind.
mitwirken bei to co-operate in.
nachdenken über (with acc.) to meditate upon.
nachlassen to relax one's efforts, cease: **Laß nicht nach mit Beten und Bitten. Laß nach in deinem jähen Zorn.**
nachsinnen über (with acc.) to muse upon.
nachsuchen um to apply for, make application for.
prahlen mit to brag of.
präsidieren bei to preside at: **Er präsidierte (bei) dem Feste.** See **258.** 1. B. *b.*
raten auf (with acc.) to guess: **Auf dich, auf diesen Ausgang haben wir nicht geraten. Ich riet auf den Verfasser, bis ich ihn erriet; — zu** to counsel: **Ich rate zur Vorsicht.**
rauchen von to reek with: **Diese Hand hat von Menschenblut geraucht.**
reichen bis an (with acc.) to reach to: **das Wasser reicht bis an die Brust.**
reimen to rime: **Dieses Wort reimt auf** (with) **jenes. Dieser Vers reimt nicht zu dem folgenden.**
reisen nach to leave for, set out for.
riechen nach to smell of.
rühren to touch: **Rühre nicht an die Schüssel!,** or **Rühre die Schüssel nicht an! Er rührte mir das Herz. Berühre mich nicht mit deiner unsauberen Hand! Wir wollen diesen Punkt nicht berühren** (touch on). The steamer touches at this city **Der Dampfer läuft diese Stadt an.**
schäumen vor (with dat.) to foam with.
schelten über etwas, auf jemanden to scold about something, rail against someone.
scherzen über (with acc.) to jest at, over.
schicken nach or **um** to send for.
schielen auf (with acc.), **nach** to cast stolen (furtive) glances at.
schießen auf (with acc.), **nach** to shoot at; **— hinter jemandem her** to dart after someone.
schimpfen auf (with acc.) to rail at.
schmähen auf (with acc.) to inveigh against.
schreiben: einem or **an einen —** to write to someone; **— an etwas** (dat.) to be writing something: **Ich schreibe an einem Werk; — um** to write for (something to be sent); **— über** (with acc.) to write about.
schreien nach to cry for.
schwärmen von to swarm with: **Es schwärmt von Menschen auf der Straße.**
schwören to swear: **Ich kann auf** (to) **seine Unschuld, auf** (by) **seine Worte schwören. Man schwört auf** (on) **die Bibel, bei** (by) **Gott und den Heiligen.** But **Man wettert gegen ihn los,** or **Man flucht ihm, auf** (or **über) ihn** They are swearing at him. To swear, profess allegiance to: **Er schwört zur Fahne, zum Katholizismus, zu Moskau** (i.e. communism) **usw.**
segeln nach to sail for.
sprechen: Er ist schlecht auf Sie zu sprechen He is angry at you. **Ich sprach deinen** or **mit deinem Lehrer** I had a talk with your teacher. **Sprechen wir von etwas anderem** Let us speak about something else. **Er spricht schlecht über dich. Er spricht über Kunst. Er redete mich auf der Straße an** He spoke to me on the street.
starren: Es starrt von Spitzen It bristles with sharp points. **Du starrst von** (or **vor) Schmutz** You are wallowing in dirt, are covered with dirt. **Du starrst vor großer Kälte** You are benumbed with cold.
sterben: Er stirbt Hungers or **vor** (of, from, or with) **Hunger, vor Freude, aus** (from) **Erschöpfung, an** (of or with) **einer Krankheit, durch** (by) **jemandes Hand.**
sticheln auf einen to make little stinging remarks about someone.
strahlen: Etwas strahlt von Gold Something is radiant with gold. **Er strahlt vor großer Freude** His face is beaming with intense joy.
streben nach to strive for.
stutzen to be startled, be taken back: **bei** or **über** (with acc.) **etwas, über einen stutzen. Ich stutzte vor großer Verwunderung.**
subskribieren auf (with acc.) to subscribe for: **Ich habe auf das Werk, die Lieferung subskribiert.**
suchen nach to seek for.

taugen zu to be fit for.
teilhaben an (with dat.) to share in, take part in, participate in.
teilnehmen an (with dat.) to take part in, participate in.
trachten nach to strive for, aspire to.
trauen auf (with acc.) to trust in *or* to, rely upon: **Ich traue auf ihn. Ich traue darauf, daß er es tut.** Compare **259.** 14. A.
trauern um to mourn for.
träumen von to dream of.
treten in (**ein Zimmer**) to enter (a room).
triefen von (in the Bible **mit**) to drip with, overflow with.
trinken auf (with acc.) to drink to (someone's health, &c.): **Wir trinken auf sein Wohl;** — **aus** to drink from.
überströmen vor (cause) or **von** (means) to overflow with: **Sein Herz strömt über vor Freude,** but **Dieses Schriftstück strömt über von Redensarten der Ehrfurcht und des Gehorsams.**
umkommen vor (with dat.) to perish with: **Sie kommen vor Hunger um;** — **durch** to perish by (the hand of).
urteilen nach, über (with acc.) to judge by, of: **nach sich über andere urteilen,** or **von sich auf andere urteilen** to judge of others by one's self.
verweilen bei to dwell upon: **Er verweilt zu lange bei Nebendingen.**
verzichten auf (with acc.) to give up, renounce, waive: **Ich verzichte auf die Welt, auf einen Anspruch, auf dieses Vergnügen.**
vorsprechen bei to call on, visit.
weinen über etwas or **einen** to weep over, cry about; — **um** to mourn over; — **nach** to cry for (bread); — **vor** (with dat.) to weep with (joy, &c.).
weisen auf (with acc.) to point at, to: **Er wies mit dem Finger auf mich. Die Uhr weist auf 10.**
werden aus to become of: **Was wird aus ihm werden?; fett** — **von** to grow fat on; **ohnmächtig** — **vor** (with dat.) to faint with.
wetten auf (with acc.) to bet: **Ich wette auf** (on) **sein Pferd. Ich wette auf Kopf** I say heads. **Ich wette mit ihm um** (**auf**) **eine Mark** I bet him a mark.
widerhallen von to echo, resound with.
wissen um eine Sache, or **von einer Sache to** know of, about a matter.
zanken or **sich zanken über** (with acc.) to quarrel about.
zeigen auf (with acc.), **nach** to point to.
ziehen auf (with acc.) to draw (a draft) on someone: **Sie können auf mich ziehen.**
zielen auf (with acc.) to aim at.
zittern to tremble: **Er zittert am ganzen Leib. Er zittert aus** or **vor Furcht, vor Frost, für jemandes Leben. Das Espenlaub zittert bei jedem Hauch.**
zürnen über (with acc.), **auf** (with acc.), **mit,** or with the simple dat.: **Man zürnt über etwas,** but **Man zürnt einem, auf** (or **über**) **einen, mit einem.** Compare **260.** 2. A.
zurückkommen auf (with acc.) to return, revert to: **Darauf kommt er immer zurück** He is always harping on that string.
zurückschrecken vor (with dat.) to shrink from.
zutreten auf einen to step up to one, walk up to one.
zweifeln an (with dat.) to have one's doubts about, despair of: **Ich zweifle nicht daran. Man zweifelt an seinem Aufkommen.**

B. Adjectives and Participles with Prepositional Object:—

abgestorben für dead to.
abhängig von dependent upon.
achtlos auf (with acc.) heedless of, not paying attention to. See also **260.** 3.
achtsam auf (with acc.) careful, regardful of
angeekelt von disgusted with.
angesteckt von infected with.
angewiesen auf (with acc.) dependent, relying upon: **Er ist auf die Mildtätigkeit anderer angewiesen. Er ist auf sich selbst, auf sein Einkommen angewiesen** He has no other resources than himself, his income.
ängstlich wegen anxious about.
anstoßend an (with acc.) adjoining, contiguous to.
anstößig für (or with the simple dat.; see **258.** 3. A) giving offense to, offensive to.
anwendbar auf (with acc.) applicable to.
ärgerlich über (with acc.) vexed at.
argwöhnisch wegen suspicious with regard to; — **gegen einen** mistrustful of someone.
arm an (with dat.) poor in.
aufgeblasen von puffed up with.
aufgebracht über (with acc.) angry at (something); — **gegen** angry at (a person).
aufgelegt zu inclined, disposed to: **Ich bin nicht zum Schreiben aufgelegt.**
aufgeregt durch excited by.
aufmerksam auf (with acc.) watchful of, attentive to (some duty, task); — **gegen** attentive to (some person), full of attentions to.
ausgedörrt durch parched by.
ausgezeichnet durch eminent for.
bange vor (with dat.) fearful, afraid of: **Mir ist bange vor dem Mann;** — **für** or **um** uneasy about, solicitous with regard to: **Mir ist bange für** or **um sein Leben.**
banke'rott an (with dat.) bankrupt in: **an Saft und Kraft und Geld und Gewissen und gutem Namen bankerott** (Schiller).
barmherzig gegen merciful to.
bedacht auf (with acc.) thoughtful of, intent on: **Du bist nur auf dich, auf deinen Vorteil bedacht.**
bedrängt von pressed with, beset with: **von Not, Hunger, Sorgen bedrängt.**
befestigt an (with dat.) tied, attached to.
befriedigend für (or with the simple dat.; see **258.** 3. A) satisfactory to.
befriedigt von satisfied with: **von seiner Arbeit befriedigt,** but **mit ihm zufrieden** satisfied with him.
begierig nach eager for: **Er ist nach großem Reichtum, hoher Ehre begierig;** — **auf** (with acc.) eager or anxious to see, hear, get, learn what someone will say: **Ich bin begierig auf deinen neuen Freund, auf deine Nachricht; immer auf einen Fang begierig** (Keller's *Seldw.*, 2, 171). **Nun bin ich auf die Theaterdirektionen und die Kritiker begierig** (Hebbel's *Tagebücher*, 24. Dec. 1851) am anxious to learn what they

will say, how they will pass judgment. Instead of **nach** or **auf** we also find the gen., especially in poetic language.
bekannt mit acquainted with, versed in; — **unter** (with dat.) known by (the name); — **wegen** known on account of, famed for.
bekümmert über (with acc.), **wegen,** or **um** concerned about, solicitous with regard to, worried over.
beleidigt durch affronted at, offended by.
beliebt bei popular with.
belustigt durch amused at.
bemerkenswert wegen remarkable for.
berauscht von intoxicated with.
berechnet auf (with acc.) calculated for, aimed at, intended for: **auf den Effekt berechnet.**
bereit zu ready for, to: **Ich bin bereit zur Abfahrt. Er ist zu allem bereit. Ich bin bereit, es zu tun.** See also **260. 3.**
berühmt wegen famous for.
beschäftigt mit engaged in, occupied with.
beschämt über (with acc.) ashamed of.
besorgt für or **um** careful of, attentive to; — **für** or more commonly **um** or **wegen** anxious about.
bestanden covered: **mit** or **von Bäumen, Gesträuch bestanden.**
bestimmt für intended for: **Die Rüstungen sind für die Fortführung des Krieges bestimmt;** — **zu** intended to become; **zum Kaufmann bestimmt;** — **nach** bound for.
bestürzt über (with the acc.) dismayed at.
betäubt von stunned by.
beteiligt an or **bei** interested, concerned in, a party in or to.
betört von infatuated with.
betroffen von struck with: **von ihrer Schönheit betroffen.**
beunruhigt über (with the acc.) or **wegen** uneasy about, worried over: **Ich bin über die** (or **wegen der**) **Zukunft beunruhigt.**
bezaubert von enchanted with, charmed by: **von ihrer Liebenswürdigkeit bezaubert,** but **Sie hat mich mit ihrer** (or **durch ihre**) **Liebenswürdigkeit bezaubert.**
blaß or **bleich vor** (with dat.) pale with.
blind auf (with dat.) blind in (one eye); — **gegen** or **für** blind to: **Er ist blind gegen** or **für seine eigenen Fehler,** or sometimes with the simple dative: **Er ist seinen eigenen Fehlern blind;** — **vor** (with dat.) blind with (rage, &c.).
blutig von bloody with.
böse auf (with acc.) angry at (somebody), **über** (with acc.) or **wegen** angry about (something). **Ich bin bitterböse mit dir** I won't speak a word to you, won't have anything to do with you. **Der Zwerg war bös zu ihr!** (Fritz Lienhard's *Wieland der Schmied*, p. 36) The dwarf treated her badly, roughly!
dankbar gegen thankful to.
dicht an (with dat.) or **bei** close to.
dick von thick with.
dienlich serviceable: **Das ist mir** (or **für mich**) **nicht dienlich. Ein kleines, zur Wohnung nicht übel dienliches Haus.**
ehrgeizig nach ambitious for.
eifersüchtig auf (with acc.) jealous of.
eigen in (with dat.) particular in: **Er ist eigen im Essen, in seinen Sachen** He is particular in matters of diet, wants things just so; **eigen auf** (with acc.) particular with regard to: **Die Kirschen sind nicht eigen auf Boden, gedeihen in leichtem und schwerem Erdreich** Cherry trees are not particular with regard to soil, &c.
eingebildet auf (with acc.) conceited about.
eingenommen für partial to, prejudiced in one's favor; — **von** captivated with.
eitel auf (with acc.) vain of: **Sie ist eitel auf ihre Schönheit.**
empfänglich für willing to receive, open to: **Er ist für Trost, Schmeicheleien, Eindrücke, das Schöne empfänglich.**
empfindlich für or **gegen** sensitive to: **empfindlich für** or **gegen chemisch wirksame Strahlen. Ich bin empfindlich gegen die Kälte;** — **über** (with acc.) irritated at.
entbrannt von inflamed with: **von Zorn entbrannt.**
entrüstet über (with acc.) indignant at.
entschlossen zu bent upon: **Ich bin entschlossen zu gehen.**
entzückt delighted: **Ich bin über die** (or **von der**) **Sängerin entzückt,** but **Sie hat mich mit ihrem** (or **durch ihren**) **Gesang entzückt.**
erfahren in (with dat.) expert at.
ergriffen von struck with: **von Schrecken ergriffen.**
erhaben über (with acc., sometimes dat.) or also in poetic language **ob** (with dat.) superior to, above: **ein großer Mann, der über seine Leiden erhaben ist; über allen Zweifel erhaben; über jedem kleinlichen Sichverletztfühlen erhaben** (Stilgebauer's *Götz Krafft*, I, 3, p. 75).
erheitert durch cheered by.
ermüdet von fatigued by.
erpicht auf (with acc.) intent upon, eager for, after: **auf Ehre, Ruhm, Reichtum, Beute, aufs Heiraten erpicht.**
erschöpft durch worn out by, with.
ersichtlich aus apparent from.
erstaunt über (with acc.) astonished at.
erstickt von suffocated with.
falsch gegen false to.
feucht von moist with.
frech gegen insolent to.
freigebig gegen liberal to.
freundlich gegen friendly to.
fruchtbar an (with dat.) productive of.
furchtlos vor fearless of.
geblendet von dazzled by.
geboren von (see Matth. xi. 11; John i. 13) born of.
geduldig gegen patient with.
geeicht auf (with acc.) adjusted to (of weights and measurements which are adjusted to a standard), *fig.*: **Es gibt im Englischen einige Laute, auf die unsere Werkzeuge schlechterdings nicht geeicht zu sein scheinen** (Max Meyerfeld's *Von Sprach' und Art der Deutschen und Engländer*, p. 27).
geeignet zu suitable for, qualified for, cut out for.
gefaßt auf (with acc.) prepared (mentally) for (some trial, misfortune, &c.).
gefühllos gegen insensible to.
geizig mit (sometimes **auf** with acc.) sparing of, stingy with; — **nach** eager for, greedy after.
gekrönt: von Erfolg — crowned with success.
genau mit particular about: **Sie nimmt es mit**

allem, mit ihrem Rufe genau. Er nimmt es mit den Mitteln nicht genau.
gerecht gegen just to.
gereizt durch provoked by; — **über** (with acc.) irritated at.
gerührt von struck by, with, moved, touched by: **vom Blitz gerührt** struck by lightning, **vom Schlag gerührt** struck with apoplexy; **kalt und ungerührt | vom Jauchzen unsers Danks** (Lessing's *Nathan*); **von der Erzählung, von dem Elend gerührt.**
gesättigt von satiated with. See **260.** 3.
geschickt in (with dat.) skilful in or at, a good hand at.
gesund an (with dat.) healthy in: **Er ist gesund am Leib und an der Seele. Das ist mir** (or **für mich**) **nicht gesund.**
gewöhnlich bei usual with.
gierig nach greedy after.
gleich an (with dat.) equal in: **Er ist seinem Bruder an Größe gleich.**
gleichgültig gegen indifferent to.
gnädig gegen gracious to: **Er ist mir** or **gegen mich nicht gnädig.**
grau vor grey with.
grausam gegen cruel to.
greifbar für (or the simple dat.; see **258.** 3. A. *a*) palpable to: **Das ist für jedermann greifbar.**
grenzend an (with acc.) adjacent to.
großmütig gegen generous to.
gut gegen, zu, mit good to. The expression **mit einem gut sein** also means *to be on friendly terms with someone.*
gütig gegen kind to.
habgierig nach grasping after, greedy after.
hart mit hard, severe on: **Weil ich ein wenig hart mit Kriemhild** (name) **war** (Hebbel's *Nibelungen*, II, 5, 2), but also **hart gegen: Er ist hart gegen mich.**
hervorragend durch eminent for.
höflich gegen, zu, mit polite, civil to.
interessant für (or the simple dat.; see **258.** 3. A) interesting to.
interessiert interested: **Er ist bei diesem Geschäft** — He is interested in this business, owns a part of it; **kein in phonetischen Dingen Interessierter** (Vietor's *Elemente der Phonetik*, Vorwort, 5th ed.), but **Er interessiert sich für allerlei, für die Phonetik, für den Fortgang der Arbeiten, für ihn** He is interested in or takes an interest in everything, &c. Also **Die Geschichte interessiert mich** I am interested in the story or The story interests me. **Oldenburg ist durch seine Eisenbahnen stark daran interessiert, einen möglichst großen Teil des Unterweserverkehrs zu gewinnen** (*Hamburger Nachrichten*, Dec. 10, 1904) Oldenburg is greatly interested in getting, &c. **An dem, was er uns gibt, ist neben dem Iranisten auch der Indologe auf das ernstlichste interessiert** (*Deutsche Rundschau*, April 1905, p. 156).
klein: — **an Geist** of inconsiderable parts, weak intellectually; — **von Gestalt** small of stature.
lahm an or **auf** (with dat.) lame in: **Er ist an** (or **auf**) **beiden Beinen, an** (or **auf**) **dem einen Fuße lahm.**
langmütig gegen forbearing toward.
leutselig gegen affable to.
liebevoll gegen affectionate to.
lüstern nach lusting after.
mild gegen mild, gentle to, toward.
mißgestimmt auf or **über** (with acc.) out of humor with (someone or something).
mißtrauisch gegen mistrustful of (someone).
mitleidig gegen compassionate to.
mörderisch für fatal, death to.
müde von weary with: **von der Arbeit müde;** with gen. tired of: **der Arbeit müde.**
nachsichtig gegen indulgent to.
nachteilig für injurious, detrimental to.
naß von wet with.
neidisch auf (with acc.) envious of.
neugierig auf (with acc.) curious about, eager to know: **Ich bin neugierig darauf. Ich bin neugierig auf ihn** I am eager to learn what kind of man he may be.
offen für (or often with the simple dat.) open to: **ein für alle Eindrücke offenes Herz. Sein Ohr ist der Schmeichelei offen.**
rasend vor (with dat.) frantic with.
reich an (with dat.) rich in.
reif ripe: — **für** (representing a stage of development for which someone is ready) **reif für die Freiheit,** (sarcastically) **reif für das Tollhaus, für den Galgen;** — **zu** (representing a goal as a final stage of the previous development): **Ein Geschwür ist reif zum Aufbrechen. Die Sache ist noch nicht reif zur Ausführung.**
rot vor (with dat.) red with (anger, &c.), but **rot von Blut, Gold,** &c. red with blood, gold, &c.
ruhig bei calm at (the misfortune of others, &c.).
schimpflich für a disgrace to: **Das ist für mich, für die ganze Verwandtschaft schimpflich.**
schmerzlich für (or the simple dat.; see **258.** 3. A) painful to.
schüchtern gegen or **gegenüber** shy, timid to, in the presence of: **Er ist schüchtern gegen mich,** or **mir gegenüber.**
schuldlos an (with dat.) guiltless of.
schwach: Er ist schwach am Leibe, auf den Beinen, auf der Brust, im Kopfe, von Begriffen or **von Geist. Er ist schwach gegen die Kinder.**
schwarz von black with: **Binnen kurzem war das Ufer schwarz von Menschen.**
sparsam mit saving of.
steif vor (with dat.) stiff with.
stolz auf (with acc.) proud of.
streng gegen severe on, strict to.
taub auf (with dat.)deaf in (one ear); — **gegen** (also **für, zu,** and sometimes also with the simple dat.), deaf to: **Er war taub gegen** (or **für**) **unsere Bitte, taub zu unserer Bitte,** or **Er war unserer Bitte taub.**
tauglich zu apt for, good for.
toll vor (with dat.) mad with.
tot für dead to: **Er ist tot für die Welt;** — **vor** (with dat.) dead with: **Ich war fast tot vor großem Schreck.**
traurig über (with acc.), **wegen** sorry for, sad on account of.
treulos gegen disloyal to.
über'legen an (with dat.) superior in: **Er ist uns allen an praktischer Umsicht überlegen.**
über'rascht durch surprised at, by.

über'tragbar auf (with acc.) transferable to: **Wir wollen zum Schluß der Frage nicht ausweichen, wieweit diese Anschauungen übertragbar sind auf uns und unsre Tage** (*Deutsche Monatsschrift*, July 1906, p. 459).

über'wältigt von overwhelmed with.

um'geben von surrounded by: **von einem Fluß, von Eis umgeben, von Schwierigkeiten umgeben** beset with difficulties, but **mit** is used to denote the passive idea that something is the result of an act: **Die Stadt ist mit einer Mauer umgeben.**

um'wölkt von clouded with.

unbe'kümmert um careless of, about, indifferent to, unconcerned about; — **wegen, über** (with acc.), **vor** (with dat.; of a future evil or danger) unworried by. See also **260.** 3.

unbe'merkbar für (or the simple dat.; see **258.** 3. A. *a*) imperceptible to.

undurch'dringlich für (or the simple dat.; see **258.** 3. A. *a*) impenetrable to.

unempfänglich für insensible, dead to: **unempfänglich für Eindrücke, unempfänglich für jedes Schamgefühl.**

unempfindlich für, gegen insensible, indifferent to: **unempfindlich gegen den Tadel.**

unfreundlich gegen unfriendly to.

ungeduldig über (with acc.) displeased at.

ungehalten über (with acc.) displeased at.

ungewiß über (with acc.) doubtful of, concerning, uncertain with regard to.

un'sichtbar für (or the simple **dat.**; see **258.** 3. A. *a*) invisible to.

verderblich für ruinous to.

vergleichbar mit (or sometimes the simple dat.) comparable to.

verletzt von or **durch** offended at, aggrieved or hurt by: **Er fühlte sich von dieser Äußerung verletzt.**

verliebt in (with acc.) in love with.

verlobt mit engaged to.

verschieden von different from.

verwandt mit (or sometimes the simple dat.) related to: **Ich bin ihm** or more commonly **mit ihm verwandt.** In the meaning *of the same nature, congenial to* the simple dat. is the usual construction: **Ich fühle mich ihm innerlich verwandt. Sie ist ihm geistesverwandt.**

vorteilhaft für advantageous to.

wachsam auf (with acc.) watchful of.

wesentlich für essential, material to.

wohltätig für beneficial to: **Das Grün ist für die Augen wohltätig.**

zornig auf (with acc.) or **gegen** angry at (a person); — **über** (with acc.) angry at (a thing).

zusammengesetzt aus composed of, compounded from, made up of.

Double Object.

262. An acc., dat., gen., or prepositional object may not only each be used singly after a verb, but two objects may be employed, one in the acc. to denote the direct object of the verb and one in the simple dat., gen., acc., or in some case after a prep., to denote a second object, which stands in various relations to the verb or some other word or the sentence as a whole, as described below. Sometimes both objects are prepositional objects.

I. Dative of the Person and Accusative of the Thing.

This construction is found after a great many verbs, especially those with the general meaning of giving, devoting, dedicating, consecrating, adapting, pardoning (**einem etwas verzeihen**), concealing (**einem etwas verbergen**), taking, bringing, sending, saying, commanding, owing, selling, preventing, refusing (**einem etwas verweigern**), doing (**einem viel Gutes tun**), making or causing (**einem einen Rock, viel Freude, Sorgen machen, einem ein Haus bauen**), explaining, wishing, promising, swearing (**einem Treue schwören**), robbing, &c. The accusative denotes the direct object or thing affected or produced, and the dative the indirect object, the person or thing to whose advantage or disadvantage the action accrues, or the person to whom the statement seems true or with reference to whom it holds good, or the person who has or is expected to have an emotional or sympathetic interest in the statement, where, however, often in case of an indirect object, as in the first six of the following examples, beneath these the predominant meanings of the dative somewhat of the old original concrete idea of *direction toward* (**258.** 1) is still felt: **Ich schenke, gebe, schicke Ihnen dieses Buch. Er gibt sich diesem Gedanken hin. Er widmet sich der Kunst. Ich habe mich dem Studium geweiht. Ich füge mich deinem** (or **in deinen**) **Willen. Er bequemt sich den Umständen** or **nach den Umständen. Er entzieht mir seine Unterstützung** He withdraws his support from me. **Ich verschaffe mir einen Paß. Der Bube hat mir den Rock entwendet. Ich verdanke dir mein Glück. Man trägt ihm die Speisen auf. Er macht ihm ein Paar Schuhe. Er hat mir viel Verdruß verursacht. Sie verwehrten dem**

Feinde den Übergang They prevented the enemy from crossing. **Er hat mir viel Zeit geraubt. Er hat dem Mädchen einen Kuß geraubt. Der Schreck hat ihm das Bewußtsein, die Vernunft, die Sprache geraubt.** As in a number of these examples, the verb is often compounded with certain prefixes. See **258.** 1. B. *a.*

The idea of personal interest is prominent in many of these datives, but the ideas of a goal, place, position, association (see *b*, 3rd par.), separation, source are also common, especially after verbs compounded with a preposition: **Er führte uns bewohnteren Gegenden zu. Er führte die Frage einer neuen Entscheidung entgegen. Ich unterwerfe mich blindlings Ihrem Ausspruch. Ich unterziehe mich dem schwierigen Geschäft, der Operation. Warum entziehst du dich unserem Verkehr? Er hat das Gleichnis dem** or **von** (or **aus**) **dem Homer entlehnt. Ich entnehme** (**aus**) **Ihrem Briefe, daß usw.** I learn from your letter, that, &c. For fluctuation in usage here see *b* below.

In the passive the accusative becomes nominative and the dative remains dative: (active) **Mir hat er einen neuen Hut gegeben;** (passive) **Mir ist ein neuer Hut gegeben worden.** The same usage obtains in English, as in "A new hat has been given to me," but in colloquial language the dative may become nominative and the accusative remain accusative: "I have been given a new hat." Here the accusative with its modifying adjective enters into such close relations with the verb that it forms with it a kind of compound verb. This takes place regularly in the passive whenever the indirect object becomes subject. The subject is then represented as acted upon in the manner described by the compound verb, which is made up of the simple verb and the accusative. Compare III. 1. *f. Note.*

a. The acc. is often replaced by an infinitive with **zu** or by a clause: **Meine Geschäfte erlauben mir keinen langen Aufenthalt,** or **Meine Geschäfte erlauben mir nicht, mich lange aufzuhalten,** or **Meine Geschäfte erlauben** (**mir**) **nicht, daß ich mich lange aufhalte.**

b. A Productive Type. This double object construction is productive, and is growing at the expense of other double object constructions. Thus **gewähren,** which in early N.H.G. belonged to II (as in **Der HERR gewere dich aller deiner bitte** — Psalm xx. 6), now usually belongs here (as in **Der Herr gewähre dir alle deine Bitten**). In a number of cases this change of construction has resulted from a confusion of forms. Thus we sometimes find such expressions as **Untersteh dir's** (instead of **dich's = dich es**), **Mädel!** (Beyerlein's *Dämon Othello*, 2, 2). The dative and accusative in such cases originated, perhaps, in such expressions as **Er untersteht sich's,** where **sich** is in fact an accusative and **es** an old genitive (**140.** *c*), but **sich** is construed as a dative and **es** as an accusative in conformity with the familiar dative and accusative construction. Sometimes the thought influences the construction. As the idea of separation is associated with both the dative and the genitive, a number of verbs fluctuate between the dative and genitive: **Du mußt dich des Rauchens entwöhnen,** but also **Wie wir bemüht sind, allem zwecklos Schönen | . . . uns zu entwöhnen** (P. Heyse in *Nord S.*, 28, 65). As **von** also expresses the same idea it is likewise sometimes used alongside of the gen. or dat., or of both, or, as in the following sentence, is preferred in certain expressions: **Der Säugling ist jetzt von der Brust entwöhnt.** Fluctuations between dat. and gen. also occur in the expression of the idea of a goal, as both cases contain this meaning with certain compound verbs: **ein gutes Land, | wohl wert, daß sich ein Fürst sein unterwinde** (Grillparzer's *König Ottokars Glück und Ende*, 3). **Er weigerte nicht, daß auch er demselben Glauben sich unterwinden werde** (Freytag's *Bild.*, 1, 256). The dat. is the object of the preposition in the compound, while the gen. is an old *gen. of goal,* which was once more vividly felt than it is to-day.

This construction of dative and accusative has gained its most complete victory in connection with verbs compounded with a preposition. The dative is here almost exclusively used in connection with an accusative object, altho the force of the preposition requires the accusative: **Man legt dem Stiere das Joch auf.** For other examples see **258.** 1. B. *a.* In M.H.G. we find: Ir muoter bot ir dienest in güetlichen an (Nibelungenlied, IX) = **Ihre Mutter bot ihm ihre Dienste freundlich an.** In the M.H.G. version *dienest* is the object of the verb *bot* and *in* the object of the preposition *an.* For the reasons given in **258.** 1. B. *a*, wherever there is to-day more than one object the dative is almost invariably used as the object of the preposition, so that the construction is now conformed to the common dative and accusative type. We have a marked exception in case of **annehmen** wherever the object of **an** is a reflexive pronoun: **Er nimmt sich des Kindes an.** Here the accusative of the reflexive is retained and the M.H.G. accusative object of the verb becomes a genitive, as the construction has been conformed to a type still well-known, namely the accusative of a reflexive pronoun in connection with a genitive. Outside of the common dative and accusative type the dative has not secured so complete a victory. Thus with intransitives where there is no accusative as object of the verb the force of the preposition still asserts itself: **Bin ich ihn angefahren: Was er da beim Herd zu tun hätt?** (Rosegger's *Martin der Mann*, p. 76). **Sie wußte selbst nicht, was sie überkommen war** (Storm's

Zur Wald- und Wasserfreude, p. 188). **Er redete mich an.** The idea of an interested person, however, has in a measure weakened the influence of the preposition, and hence the dative is sometimes used here: **Wie meiner guten Mutter dieser traurige Zustand anflog, weiß ich nicht** (Gutzkow's *R.*, 2, 117), but also **Plötzlich flog ihn eine Freude an** (J. Paul's *Tit.*, 4, 44). A number of fluctuations here are given in **259.** 1, 2, 3, 4, 32. The force of the preposition was more vividly felt in early N.H.G., and hence the accusative could then be employed where to-day the dative is used: **welche nicht freiet | die sorget was den HErrn angehöret | das sie heilig sey | beide am Leibe vnd auch am Geist. Die aber freiet | die sorget was die Welt angehört** (1 Cor. vii. 34). Where the accusative has become established, as in case of **anfahren** and **überkommen** given above, the transitive idea has developed, which leads to the use of **haben** in the compound tenses. Thus instead of the form **bin** in the sentence from Rosegger we can also say **habe.** See also **191.** I. *Note.*

The common type of dative and accusative is not so common, sometimes even poetic, in one particular category, namely to give expression to the idea of association, where usually **mit** with the dative is used. Sometimes **mit** indicates a mere accidental association, while the dative suggests a close intimate association: **Man kann die verschiedensten Dinge miteinander, einen klugen Mann mit einem törichten, vergleichen, eben um ihre Verschiedenheit recht zu erkennen** (Sanders's *Wörterbuch*), but **Wer diese meine Rede höret vnd thut sie | den vergleiche ich einem klugen Mann | der sein Haus auff einen Felsen bawet** (Matth. vii, 24) and **In diesem Buch steckt soviel Beobachtung, ein so gründliches Erfassen alles Menschlichen paart sich technischem Können, daß man ihm viele Freunde wünscht** (E. A. Greeven in *Die schöne Literatur*, Oct. 7, 1905).

II. Accusative of the Person and Genitive of the Thing.

A. In this construction the accusative denotes the person or thing directly affected, and the genitive expresses the idea of cause, means, removal, separation, deprivation, a goal, specification, or indicates a person or thing related in various other ways to the activity implied in the verb: **Sie erfreut sich des Geschenks** She is rejoicing over (on account of) her present. **Sie schämt sich ihres Vaters. Deines Schwerts wirst du dich nähren** (Gen. xxvii, 40, revised ed.). **Man verwies ihn des Landes** They banished him from the land. **Der Fürst hat ihn des Amts entsetzt** The prince has put him out of office. **Er befleißigt sich der Kürze** He aims at brevity. **Ich werde mich des Erfolges** (gen. of specification; or **wegen des Erfolges,** or **über den Erfolg**) **vergewissern.** The genitive object can also be replaced by a clause or an infinitive phrase: **Es reut mich der Tat,** or **daß ich es getan habe,** or **es getan zu haben.**

In a few cases both objects represent things. See **haben** and **wissen** in *a*.

This construction is found after the following groups of verbs:

a. The Accusative and Genitive after Transitives other than Reflexives. The following decreasing list of verbs, which still usually take an accusative but now frequently also admit of or prefer a prepositional phrase instead of the genitive, or instead of the accusative and genitive now take another construction, as indicated after each verb:

abgewöhnen *to break someone of* (a habit, &c.), formerly with the gen. or **von** with the dat., now with the dat. of the person and the acc. of the thing, as in **einem das Trinken abgewöhnen.**

anklagen *to accuse*, with the gen., also **wegen** and **um — willen** with the gen. or **um** with the acc., sometimes with **über** with the acc. and in the Bible **über** with the dat. as in Acts xxvi. 6. The genitive simply calls attention to the specific charge brought against the offender, while the prepositional constructions indicate the grounds for the action: **Sie klagten ihn der Veruntreuung an** They accused him of embezzlement. **Sie klagten ihn wegen einer Veruntreuung an** They indicted him for embezzlement. **Ich werde angeklaget vmb der hoffnung und aufferstehung willen der todten** (Acts xxiii. 6).

anmuten *to expect of*, with the gen. in early N.H.G., later **einem etwas anmuten,** now **einem etwas zumuten,** but **dieses Mädchen mutet mich an** This girl pleases me.

anschuldigen *to accuse of*, formerly also sometimes with the dat. of the person and the acc. of the thing. Also with the same prepositional constructions as with **anklagen.**

beargwöhnen (beargwohnen), formerly also **verargwohnen** *to suspect of.*

bedeuten, see **259.** 6.

befreien *to free from*, now usually with **von** or **aus** with the dat.

beklagen *to accuse of*, now replaced by **anklagen.**

belehren *to instruct concerning*, now usually with **über** with the acc., earlier in the period also with **von** with the dat.: **Ich will dich eines Besseren belehren** I'll teach you better than that. **Ich belehrte die Zuhörer über diese sonderbare Erscheinung.**

benehmen (**246.** II. 1. *c*) *to free one entirely from*, with the gen., *to take something entirely away* *from someone*, with dat. and acc.: **Ein Liedchen, welches zwar doch nur von weltlicher Liebe und Torheit handelte, mich aber doch zugleich aller Furcht und Unruhe benahm** (R. Huch's *Teufelei*, p. 46). **Der Schreck benahm mir die Sprache.**

berauben (or earlier in the period simple **rauben**) *to rob, deprive of, take away from*: **einen seiner Ehre, aller seiner Freuden berauben.**

berechtigen *to entitle one to, warrant one in*, gen. now replaced by **zu** with the dat.: **Seine schnellen Fortschritte berechtigen uns zu den schönsten Hoffnungen.**

bereden, see III. 1. *h*. below.

berichten, see III. 1. *k* below.

bescheiden *to apprize one of, instruct concerning*, usually with **über** with the acc.: **Ich beschied ihn eines Besseren** I set him right on the point. **Ich beschied ihn über den Punkt.**

beschuldigen, *to accuse of*.

betrügen *to cheat out of*, formerly with the gen., now with **um** with the acc.

bezichtigen *to accuse of, charge with*, formerly also with **mit** with the dat.

bitten *to ask for*, with the gen. in early N.H.G., now with **um** with the acc. See also III. 1. *a* below.

entbinden *to release from*, with the gen. or **von** with the dat., *to be delivered of* (a boy, girl), with **von** with the dat.: **Entbinde mich meines Versprechens** or **von meinem Versprechen. Sie ist von einem Knaben entbunden.**

entblößen *to strip of, bare of*, usually with **von** with the dat.

enterben *to cut off from* (by disinheriting), deprive of, usually with **von** with the dat.

entheben *to relieve from, dismiss* or *remove from*, also with **von** with the dat., sometimes with the simple dat.: **Der Mensch des Südens ist so vieler Mühseligkeiten enthoben. Enthebe ihn doch seines Amtes** or **von seinem Amte. Das Kind an seiner Seite enthob ihn plötzlich weiteren Erwägungen** (A. Behrens-Litzmann's *Ein Sommerabend* in *Deutsche Monatsschrift*, Aug. 1904, p. 653).

entkleiden *to divest of*, sometimes with **von** with the dat.

entladen *to free from, relieve of a burden*, more commonly with **von** with the dat.: **von allem Wissensqualm entladen** (Faust, I).

entlassen *to discharge from, release from*, also **aus** or **von** with the dat.: **Er hat den Knecht des Dienstes** or **aus dem Dienste entlassen. Man entließ ihn aus** or **von der Haft.**

entlasten *to disburden someone of, free from*, also with **von** with the dat.: **einen der Geschäfte, der Sorgen, eines Verdachts entlasten.**

entledigen *to free from*, also with **von** with the dat.: **Entledige ihn seiner Pflichten.**

entleeren *to empty of*: **ein Faß seines Inhalts entleeren.**

entschließen *to free from* (chains, &c.), now obsolete.

entsetzen *to dispossess of, depose from*, occasionally with **von** with the dat.

entübrigen *to relieve from*, now little used and when employed usually found in the perfect participle with some form of **sein**, as in **einer Person, eines Dinges entübrigt sein** *to do without, dispense with*.

entwehren *to rob of*, with the gen. or more commonly **einem etwas entwehren,** both constructions early N.H.G., now obsolete.

entwöhnen *to disaccustom to, wean away from*, also with **von** with the dat., sometimes with the simple dat. (see I. *b* above): **Der General entwöhnt seine Truppen des Alkohols. Der Säugling ist jetzt von der Brust entwöhnt.**

erfreuen *to rejoice, delight* or *gladden with* or *by means of*, now usually with **mit** with the dat.

ergötzen (earlier in the period **ergetzen**) *to make up, compensate for, cause to forget*, now obsolete: early N.H.G. **einen seines Leides ergetzen,** now **einen sein Leid vergessen machen,** or **einen für sein Leid entschädigen.**

erinnern *to remind of*, now usually with **an** with the acc.: **einen an sein Versprechen erinnern. Das Bild erinnert lebhaft an Böcklin** (*reminds us of Böcklin's art*).

erlassen *to release from*, now **einem etwas erlassen: Ich habe Sie Ihrer Verbindlichkeit erlassen** (Lessing's *Minna*, 5, 5).

erledigen *to free from*, also with **von** with the dat., now in this meaning usually replaced by **entledigen.**

erleichtern *to relieve from*: **einen der Last** or usually **von der Last erleichtern.**

ermahnen *to exhort to* usually with **zu** with the dat., *remind of* with the gen. or **an** with the acc.

erretten *to save* or *rescue from*, with the gen. in early N.H.G., now with **von** or **aus** with the dat.

fragen *to inquire after, ask for*, with the gen. in early N.H.G., now with **nach** with the dat. or **um** with the acc. See also III. 1. *b* below.

freisprechen *to acquit of*, usually with **von** with the dat.

geben in the expression **es einem schuld geben** *to blame someone for it*: **Ihm allein habe ich es schuld gegeben, daß meine Sache so auf die lange Bank geschoben werde** (Lessing an E. König, 1773). The **es** is here an old gen. as explained in **140.** *c*. It is now usually construed as an acc. and hence in case of other words the gen. is now replaced by an acc.: **Am Ende gibt Mama dann auch das mir schuld** (Raabe's *Kloster Lugau*, p. 70).

gemahnen *to remind one of* (a promise, &c.), *to put one in mind of*, now more commonly with **an** with the acc. See also *c* and B. *d* below.

gewähren *to grant*, with the gen. in early N.H.G., as in Psalm xx. 6, and as late as Grillparzer, now with the dat. of the person and the acc. of the thing: **Schließ deinen Helm, dann sei des Kampfs gewährt** (Grillparzer's *König Ottokar*, 5). **Er gewährte mir die Bitte.**

haben in the expressions **es** (old gen. as explained in **140.** *c*, now usually construed as an acc.

and hence in case of other words the gen. is replaced by an acc.) **nicht Wort haben** *not to admit it*; **es nicht Hehl haben** *to make no secret of it*, now also **kein Hehl daraus machen; es Ursache haben** *to have good reasons to do* or *think so*, now more commonly **alle Ursache dazu haben** as in **Ich habe alle Ursache dazu; es** (old gen.) or **das** (acc.) **schuld haben** *to be to blame for it*, now more commonly **daran schuld sein** (or **haben**).

lösen or **erlösen** *to free from*, now with **von** or **aus** with the dat.

lossprechen *to acquit of, release from*, now usually with **von** with the dat.

mahnen *to remind of*, usually with **an** with the acc., *to dun for* with **um** with the acc. or **wegen** with the gen., *to urge to* with **zu** with the dat.

schelten *to scold someone for*, now with **wegen** with the gen.

sichern (Schiller's *Tell*, 3, 3) *to assure of*.

strafen still with the gen. in the set expression **jemanden Lügen strafen** *to give one the lie*, where Lügen tho gen. pl. is now usually felt as an acc. pl.

trösten *to console over*, now with **über** with the acc. (formerly also dat., as in John xi. 19) or **wegen** with the gen.

über'führen *to convict of*.

über'heben *to relieve from, spare one* (the trouble, &c.) *of*, sometimes with the dat.: **Über'heben Sie mich des Gegenbesuchs. An diesem Maßstabe gemessen, bleibt die Verfasserin unserer Aufzeichnungen solchem Vorwurfe überhoben** (Paul Hoffmann in *Euphorion*, 1903, Band X, p. 106).

über'weisen *to convict of* with the gen., *convince of* with the gen. or **von** with the dat., in the second meaning now replaced by **überzeugen**.

über'zeugen *to convince of*, usually with **von** with the dat.

unter'richten and **unter'weisen**, see III. **1.** *f* below.

verdächtigen *to suspect of*.

verdenken *to blame for, find fault with someone for*, earlier in the period: **Wer will sie des verdenken?** (Luther), or **Wer will sie darum verdenken?**, now **Wer will es ihnen verdenken** or **verargen?**

vergewissern *to assure of* (the truth of a statement, of the existence of some state of things, &c.), also with **über** with the acc., **von** with the dat., or **wegen** with the gen.

verjagen *to drive out of*, now with **von** or **aus** with the dat.

verklagen *to accuse of*, now replaced by **anklagen**.

versichern *to assure of* (one's friendship, &c.). See also B. *a* below and **259. 35.**

verwarnen *to caution against*, now with **vor** with the dat.

verweisen *to banish from*, also with **aus** with the dat.: **Er verwies den Verräter des Landes.**

warnen *to warn*, now with **vor** with the dat.: **Ich habe dich vor dem Schwindler gewarnt.**

weisen *to show*, now usually with the dat. of the person and the acc. of the thing: **Der wies ihn des Weges aufwärts durch wirres Strauchwerk** (Wilhelm Fischer's *Sonnenopfer*, II), or more commonly **Der wies ihm den Weg.** The former construction in part survives in such expressions as **Er läßt sich weisen** He can be guided.

wissen in the expression **es einem Dank wissen** *to be grateful to someone for something*. The **es** is here according to **140.** *c* an old gen., but it is now felt as an acc. and hence in case of other words the gen. is sometimes replaced by the acc.: **Ich weiß dir deine Freigebigkeit großen Dank** (Alex. König, 1001 *Nacht*, II, p. 15). **Das wußte er ihr Dank** (A. Behrens-Litzmann's *Ein Sommerabend* in *Deutsche Monatsschrift*, Aug. 1904, p. 648). Usually the gen. is replaced by **für** with the acc.: **Ich weiß dir für die Gabe Dank.**

würdigen *to deem worthy of*.

zeihen *to accuse of*.

b. The Accusative of the Reflexive Pronoun and a Genitive. The following list of verbs which usually take the accusative of the reflexive pronoun but sometimes admit of or prefer a prepositional phrase instead of the genitive, or instead of the accusative and genitive take another construction, as indicated after each verb:—

sich abgewöhnen *to disaccustom one's self to, leave off, give up*, formerly with the acc. of the reflexive and the gen. of the noun or **von** with the dat., now with the dat. of the reflexive and the acc. of the noun, as in **Ich gewöhne mir das Trinken ab.**

sich abtun *to free one's self from, renounce, give up*, now little used: **Wie wenn der falsche Mann . . . . sich seines Glaubens abgetan?** (Bürger's *Lenore*).

sich anmaßen *to arrogate to one's self*, now more commonly with the dat. of the reflexive pronoun and the acc. of the thing: **Wenn sie** (i.e. **die Rolle**) **von einem Komödianten gespielt wird, der sich dieses Titels in der Tat anmaßen könnte** (Lessing, 4, 182). **Du hast dir dieses Recht nur angemaßt.**

sich annehmen *to interest one's self in* or *for*: **Nimm dich doch meiner, meiner Sache an.** In S.G. we often find **um** with the acc. here instead of the gen.: **Er nimmt sich um gar keinen Menschen an** (Auerbach's *Dorfgeschichten*, 8, p. 36). See also **262.** I. *b*. (2nd par.).

sich ärgern (**1**) *to be vexed at, by, with*, sometimes still with the gen., usually with **über** with the acc. or earlier in the period **über** with the dat.: **Ich ärgerte mich der fatalen Rücksichtslosigkeit** (J. J. David in *Die Neue Rundschau*, July, 1906, p. 875). **Dann war ich fortgegangen, hatte ihn nach der Mutter Tod allein gelassen, mich oft seiner geärgert** (Hermann Hesse's *Peter Camenzind*, p. 168). (**2**) *to be worried by*, with **an** with the dat.: **An dem ungezogenen**

Schüler ärgere ich mich zu Tode The naughty pupil worries almost the life out of me. This construction with **an** *is* also used in biblical language with the meaning *to be offended because of*, as in Matth. xxvi. 31.

sich bedanken *to thank for*, now with **für** with the acc. or **wegen** with the gen.: **Ich bedanke mich bei ihm wegen des schönen Geschenks (or für das schöne Geschenk).**

sich bedenken *to bethink one's self of*: **Er hat sich eines Besseren bedacht** *He changed his mind.*

sich bedienen *to make use of.*

sich befahren *to fear*, now obsolete.

sich befleißen (or in early N.H.G. **fleißen**; see 2 Macc. xv. 12) or **sich befleißigen** (or in early N.H.G. **fleißigen**; see Rom. xii. 17) *to apply one's self to, aim at*: **Befleißige dich der Wahrheit. Er befleißigt sich** (*is studying*) **der Rechtswissenschaft. Er befleißigt sich der Kürze. Der Sparsamkeit beflissen** (*given to*).

sich befreien *to free one's self from*, now with **von** with the dat.

sich befürchten *to fear*, the reflexive verb now replaced by the transitive **befürchten** with an acc. object.

sich begeben *to renounce, waive, strip* or *deprive one's self of, refrain from*: **Ich begebe mich meines Rechtes. Ich begebe mich** (refrain from) **jedes Urteils.**

sich behelfen *to get along with*, now with **mit** with the dat.: **Ich behelfe mich mit einem geringen Gehalte.**

sich beklagen *to complain of*, now with **über** with the acc.

sich bemächtigen *to take possession of.*

sich bemeistern *to seize on, overcome, take possession of.*

sich bereden, see III. 1. *h* below.

sich berühmen (Fontane's *Quitt*, chap. 7), now usually replaced by **sich rühmen.**

sich bescheiden *to refrain from, reserve, acquiesce in* with the gen., *content one's self* with **mit** with the dat.: **Er bescheidet sich seines Urteils. Ich bescheide** (acquiesce) **mich dessen. Bescheide dich mit wenigem. Ich bescheide mich mit dem, was Sie sagen.**

sich beschweren *to complain of*, now with **über** with the acc.

sich besinnen with the gen. in **sich eines Besseren** (or **anderen**) **besinnen** *to think better* or *differently of something, to change one's mind*, with the gen. or more commonly with **auf** with the acc. in the meanings *to call to mind, recollect*: **Besinne dich auf deine Worte. Ich besinne mich fortwährend auf den Namen.**

sich besorgen *to fear, apprehend, be apprehensive of*, also with **vor** with the dat., both constructions now little used. **Besorgen** is now a transitive with an acc. object: **Ich besorgte nichts Böses.**

sich bessern *to improve* or *grow better by means of*, now with **durch: Nu hatte ich bereit den Katechismum geleret, des** (now **wodurch**) **sich viel Leute gebessert hatten** (Luther).

sich bestreben *to strive after*: **Ich bestrebe mich einer ebenso reinen und edlen Liebe als er** (Lessing's *Minna*, 5, 9).

sich entäußern (or earlier in the period simply **äußern**) *to rid one's self of, cast off, give up, sell, transfer, renounce.*

sich entblöden *to be so bold*, with the gen., sometimes with the acc., now little used in this meaning and these constructions: **Was? Dürft ihr solches Unfuges euch vor meinem Aug' entblöden?** (Schlegel's *Span.*, 2, 168). **Was könnte der Mann sich entblöden?** (Wieland). Compare **246.** II. 2. *a* and *b*.

sich entblößen *to strip one's self of*, now with **von** with the dat.

sich entbrechen *to refrain from*, now little used except in negative form with a dependent infin.: **Ich konnte mich nicht entbrechen, ihm die Wahrheit zu sagen.**

sich entgürten *to ungird*: **Des Schwerts entgürte dich** (Hebbel's *Genoveva*, 1, 2).

sich enthalten *to abstain from*, sometimes with **von** with the dat.

sich entkleiden *to divest one's self of.*

sich entladen *to ease one's self of*, sometimes also **von** with the dat.

sich entlasten *to free one's self from*, also with **von** with the dat.

sich entledigen (1) *to free one's self from, cast off*, usually with the gen., sometimes **von** with the dat.: **Ich habe mich meiner Fessel, meiner Sorgen entledigt.** (2) *to perform* (a duty, task), *execute, make good*, with the gen.: **Ich habe mich meines Auftrags, meines Versprechens entledigt.**

sich entleeren *to empty itself*: **Der Selbstentlader entleert sich seines Inhalts.**

sich entmemmen *to free one's self from the cowardice of* (one's dejected thoughts, feelings): **Entmemme dich deiner verzagten Gefühle!** (Heine).

sich entringen *to disengage one's self from, free one's self from*, usually with the dat.: **Sie haben an mir ein Beispiel, wie man sich selbst solcher Fesseln entringen kann** (Franzos's *Der Gott des alten Doktors*, p. 130).

sich entsagen *to renounce*, sometimes with **von** with the dat. The reflexive is now replaced by the intransitive **entsagen** with the dat. according to **258.** 1. B, or sometimes **auf** with the acc., earlier in the period and occasionally still with the simple gen. See **260.** 2. A.

sich entschlagen *to free one's self from, banish* (care, thoughts, &c.): **Entschlage dich dieser Sorgen, dieser Gedanken.** Sometimes according to I. *b* with dat. instead of gen.: **Das lastet nur, ich muß mich ihm entschlagen** (Goethe's *Elegie*, l. 112).

sich entschließen *to decide upon*, gen. now usually replaced by **zu** with the dat. except in case of gen. **es** (**140.** *c*) or acc. **das** or **was** instead of **es: Ich habe mich zur Reise, zu nichts, zur Tat entschlossen,** or with an infin. instead of a noun **Ich habe mich entschlossen zu gehen.**

Ich war es entschlossen (Fontane's *Irrungen*, 261), or **das** instead of **es**: **Das bin ich fest entschlossen** (Iffland's *Hausfrieden*, 55), or more commonly **dazu** instead of **es** or **das**.

sich entschuldigen *to excuse one's self on account of*, now usually with **wegen** with the gen.

sich entschütten *to get rid of, throw off*, much used earlier in the period.

sich entsetzen *to be terrified at*, usually with **vor** with the dat. or **über** with the acc.

sich entsinnen *to recollect, call to mind*, with the gen. or **auf** with the acc., rarely a transitive with an acc. object: **Ich entsinne mich nicht mehr dieses Mannes, or auf diesen Mann. Entsinnst du den Jeronimo?** (H. v. Hofmannsthal's *Das gerettete Venedig*, p. 33).

sich entwöhnen *to disaccustom one's self to*, also with **von** with the dat., sometimes with the simple dat.: **Du mußt dich des Rauchens** (or **von dem Rauchen**) **entwöhnen. Unter den Schachtelsätzen, deren wir uns seit Nietzsche mehr und mehr entwöhnt haben** (A. Heusler in *Anzeiger für deutsches Altertum*, 1902, p. 324). See also I. *b* above.

sich entziehen *to withdraw from*, usually with the dat., sometimes with **von** with the dat.: **Verschlossen in dem Innern der Gemächer, | entzieht er sich des Reiches** (Grillparzer's *Esther*, 1). **Warum entziehen Sie sich unserem Verkehr immer mehr?**

sich erbarmen *to take pity on*, more commonly with **über** with the acc. See also B. *d* below.

sich erdreisten *to be bold enough, have the cheek*, sometimes also with the acc.: **der sich jener Tat erdreistet** (Goethe); **was sich kein anderer erdreistet hatte** (J. Paul). Now usually with the infin.: **Erdreiste dich nicht, mir das zu sagen.**

sich erfrechen *to have the impudence to:* **Erfrechst du dich so gottverdammter Lügen mir ins Gesicht?** (P. Heyse, 20, 84).

sich erfreuen (**1**) *to take pleasure in* (doing something), *enjoy*, with the gen. or more commonly with **an** with the dat.: **Ich erfreue mich an einem schönen Spaziergang, an einer gut besetzten Tafel, an einem guten Glas Wein.** (**2**) *to have, possess*, usually with the gen.: **Ich erfreue mich einer guten Gesundheit.**

sich ergötzen (earlier in the period **ergetzen**) *to make up, compensate for, cause to forget*, now obsolete: **Da wil ich mich meiner mühe vnd meines hertzenleides ergetzen** (Jer. viii. 18), now **Da will ich mich für meine Mühe und mein Herzeleid entschädigen.**

sich erheben (Goethe's *Rein. F.*, 5) *to boast of, be haughty on account of*, now replaced by **sich überheben.**

sich erholen (**1**) *to seek* or *apply for* (advice, &c.), with the acc. of the reflexive pronoun and the gen. of the thing, or with the dat. of the reflexive pronoun and the gen. or acc. of the thing, as in **Ich erhole mich bei ihm Rats** or **Ich erhole mir bei ihm Rats** or **Rat.** (**2**) *to retrieve*, with the gen. or more commonly **von** with the dat., as in **Ich will mich meines Schadens** or usually **von meinem Schaden erholen** and **Er erholt sich von seinem Schaden an einem anderen.** (**3**) *to recover from*, with the gen. or more commonly **von** with the dat., as in **Erhole dich erst von dem Schreck, von der Arbeit, von den Strapazen, von der Krankheit.**

sich erinnern *to remember*, with the gen., often also with **an** with the acc., sometimes with **auf** with the acc. after the analogy of **sich auf etwas besinnen**, especially in the meaning *to recall*, sometimes with the acc. or dat. of the reflexive pronoun and the acc. instead of the gen., often, especially in the extreme North, as in English used as a transitive with a direct object in the acc., perhaps after the analogy of **vergessen** with the acc.: **Ich erinnere mich nicht mehr des Vorfalls, or an den Vorfall. Vergebens suchte er sich auf das Aussehen der anderen Frau zu erinnern** (G. Freytag). **Das erinnere ich mich wieder** (Goethe). **Das kann ich mir jetzt nicht deutlich erinnern** (Otto Frommel's *Grundlsee*). **Aber das müßte man doch erinnern** (Timm Kröger's *Das Wunderbare*, I). **Sieh mal, Jürgen, du erinnerst unser Zusammentreffen im Garten** (Frenssen's *Jörn Uhl*, chap. 24). The simple acc. is the rule in the meaning *to censure*: **Ich fand manches zu erinnern.**

sich erkühnen *to make bold*, sometimes with the acc.: **Nur Graf Lester durfte sich | an diesem Hofe solcher Tat erkühnen** (Schiller's *Maria*, 4, 6). **Sie darf sich was erkühnen** (Geibel, 1, 48).

sich erkundigen *to inquire after*, now usually **nach** with the dat.: **Ich erkundigte mich bei ihm nach Ihnen, nach der Ursache usw.**

sich erledigen, with the meanings and constructions of **entledigen**, but much less common: **wie man des Drucks sich möcht' erledigen** (Schiller's *Tell*, 1, 2). **Erledigen** is quite common, however, as a transitive with an acc. object in the related meanings to finish, settle, pay: **Er hat seine Korrespondenz, den Streit, die Schuld erledigt.**

sich erleichtern *to relieve one's self from*: **sich der Last** or usually **von der Last erleichtern.**

sich ernähren, see **nähren** below.

sich ersättigen *to become satiated with*, more commonly with **an** or **mit** with the dat.: **Endlich als er sich des ersten Schmerzes ersättigt, erhob er sich usw.** (L. Forster's *Die Flinte von San Marco*, XIII, *Deutsche Rundschau*, April 1896).

sich ersehen *to perceive, look out for, avail one's self of*, more commonly with the dat. of the reflexive pronoun and the acc. of the thing, or used as a transitive with an object in the acc.: **Ich habe mich meines Vorteils, des Augenblicks, der Gelegenheit ersehen,** or **Ich habe mir den Vorteil, den Augenblick, die Gelegenheit ersehen,** or **Ich habe meinen Vorteil, den Augenblick, die Gelegenheit ersehen.**

sich erwegen or **erwägen** (2 Cor. I. 8) *to give up, renounce, despair of*, now obsolete.

sich erwehren (or earlier in the period **entwehren**) *to ward off, refrain from, resist*: **Er konnte sich der Hunde, der Diebe nicht erwehren. Ich kann mich des Schlafes, des Lachens, der Tränen nicht erwehren.** Rarely with the dat. of the reflexive: **Geht die Sonne des Morgens auf . . . , erwehr' ich mir niemals auszurufen usw.** (Goethe's *Werther*, den 8. Februar).

sich freuen *to rejoice in, over, take a pleasure in* (a thing, the idea of, thought of), with the gen. and also with prepositions: **Freue dich deiner Gesundheit, deines Glückes,** or **an deiner Gesundheit, an deinem Glück,** or **über deine Gesundheit, über dein Glück. Man freut sich über das Geschehene, an dem Gegenwärtigen, auf das Künftige. Ich freue mich auf des Freundes Ankunft.** Formerly **über** governed the dat.: **Sie aber frewen sich vber meinem schaden** (Psalms xxxv. 15).

sich fürchten *to fear*, early in the period **ich fürchte mir eines Dinges,** later **ich fürchte mich eines Dinges,** now with the gen. only in the expression **sich der Sünde fürchten** *to be afraid of committing the sin of*, usually with **vor** with the dat.: **Ich fühlte mich so glücklich, daß ich mich der Sünde fürchtete, noch glücklicher werden zu wollen. Ich fürchte mich vor diesem Menschen.**

sich gebrauchen *to use* and **sich mißbrauchen** *to misuse*, now replaced by the transitives **gebrauchen** and **mißbrauchen** with acc. object.

sich getrauen, see **259.** 14.

sich getrösten (**1**) *to expect confidently*, with the gen.: **Ich kann mich der Hilfe sicher getrösten.** (**2**) *to comfort one's self with*, with the gen., or **an** or **mit** with the dat.: **In behaglicher, wunschloser Ruhe sehen wir Handewitter die schnatternden Völker der Wanderschwäne über die Baumgruppen unserer Höfe streben, indem wir uns derweilen unserer gefüllten Torfställe und Holzschuppen für den kommenden Winter getrösten** (Kröger's *Der Schulmeister von Handewitt*, p. 24). (**3**) *to console one's self over*, with the gen. or more commonly with **über** with the acc.: **Die Ehe blieb kinderlos, dessen sich jedoch beide in christlicher Ergebung getrösteten** (Fontane's *Vor dem Sturm*, I. 6).

sich gewärtigen *to expect*, with the gen., or with the dat. of the reflexive pronoun and the acc. of the thing: **Du mußt dich eines Verlustes gewärtigen. Was könnte ich mir für eine Antwort gewärtigen?** (Lessing). A clause instead of the acc. of the thing: **Du mußt dir gewärtigen, daß er kündigt.** Instead of the reflexive construction **gewärtigen** can be used as a transitive with an acc. object: **Ich gewärtige von dem Herrn . . . den Beweis** (Bismarck's *Reden*, 2, 125). See also **260.** 2. A.

sich härmen *to worry about, grieve about, be annoyed at, by*, more commonly with **wegen** with the gen. or **über** or **um** with the acc.: **Wer sich des Klanges härmet, | der mag ins Kloster gehen** (Scheffel's *Trompeter*, Lieder Jung Werners, VI).

sich kümmern or **bekümmern** *to concern one's self with*, usually with **um** with the acc.: **Er kümmert** or **bekümmert sich um seine Mutter. Kümmere** or **bekümmere dich nicht um Dinge, die dich nichts angehen.** Compare **kümmern,** *c*, B. *d* below, also **bekümmern,** IV below.

sich lohnen or **verlohnen** (**1**) *to reward, be worth*, with the gen. or instead of this construction a nom. employed as logical subject: **Es (ver)lohnt sich der** (also nom. **die**) **Mühe nicht. Es lohnt sich nicht, das zu tun.** (**2**) *to be rewarded by*, sometimes with gen., more commonly with **für** with the acc.: **Des bloßen Hinstarrens lohnte sich doch die Mühe des Weges aus deinem weichen Bett nicht** (Raabe's *Unruhige Gäste*, chap. 6).

sich mäßigen *to be temperate in*, now with **in** with the dat.

sich mißbrauchen, now a trans. with an acc. object. Compare **260.** 2. A.

sich nähren or **ernähren** *to feed, live upon, make one's livelihood by*, earlier in the period with the gen., but now with **mit** or **von** with the dat., or **durch** with the acc.: **Deines Schwertes wirst du dich nähren** (Gen. xxvii. 40, revised ed.). **Ich** (the wolf) **nähre mich bloß mit** (here more commonly **von**) **toten Schafen** (Lessing's *Fabeln*, 3, 20). **Die Massageten, ein von Fischen und Milch sich nährendes iranisches Volk** (Hommel's *Grundriß der Geographie*, p. 213). **Dieses Tier nährt sich von Fleisch** (Traut-Fritsch's *German Grammar*, p. 139). **Daher scheint es mir höchst unzeitgemäß, wenn man das von Jahrhunderten errichtete Gebäude der Kultur verlassen und sich wieder mit wildem Honig und Heuschrecken ernähren will** (Konrad Falke in *Deutsche Monatsschrift*, Sept. 6, 1906, p. 858). **Er ernährt sich von, mit, durch seiner Hände Arbeit. Sie ernährt sich durch Stundengeben, mit Weben.**

sich reinigen *to purify, cleanse one's self from*, now with **von** with the dat.

sich rühmen *to boast of*, with the gen. or **wegen** with the gen., sometimes with **mit** or **von** with the dat.: **Er rühmt sich seiner Stärke. Du rühmst dich noch (wegen) des Streiches?**

sich sättigen *to appease* (one's hunger, &c.) *with*, now with **an, mit,** or sometimes **von** with the dat.: **Ich habe mich am Kohl, an den Kartoffeln gesättigt.**

sich schämen *to be ashamed of*, also with **wegen** with the gen. and **über** with the acc.: **Schäme dich des Betrugs, über den Betrug,** or **wegen des Betrugs.** But **Ich schämte mich vor** (in the presence of) **ihm.**

sich scheuen *to be shy of, shrink from*, now only rarely with the gen., usually with **vor** with the dat.: **sich keiner Arbeit scheuen** (*Gartenlaube*, 19, 367 *b*). **Er scheut sich vor der Krankheit, vor der Verantwortung.** Often with the infinitive: **Ich scheue mich nicht, die Wahrheit zu sagen.**

sich schmeicheln *to flatter one's self with*, a little earlier in the period with the dat. or acc. of the reflexive pronoun and the gen. of the thing, or with the dat. of the reflexive pronoun and the acc. of the thing, now usually with the dat. of the reflexive pronoun and **mit** with the dat.: **Ich schmeichele mir** or **mich dessen,** or **Das schmeichele ich mir** I venture to hope so. **Ich schmeichele mir mit der Hoffnung, daß usw.** I flatter myself with or cherish the hope that, &c.

sich trösten (**1**) *to console one's self over*, more commonly with **über** with the acc. (formerly also the dat.) or **wegen** with the gen.: **Er konnte sich über seinen Verlust nicht trösten.** (**2**) *to find comfort in*, usually with **an** or **mit** with the dat. or **durch** with the acc. (**3**) *to rely on, rejoice in*, with the gen.: **Denn darauff wir vns verliessen | das ist vns jtzt eitel schande vnd des**

wir vns trösteten | des müssen wir vns jtzt schemen (Jer. III. 25). **Sondern er tröstet sich dieses guten lebens** (Psalm xlix. 19).
sich über'heben (**1**) *to elevate one's self above others on account of, be unduly proud of*, with the gen. or wegen with the gen.: **Überhebe dich nicht deiner Kleider, or wegen deiner Kleider.** (**2**) *to spare one's self* (*the trouble*, &c.) *of*, usually with the gen., sometimes with the dat.: **Dieser Mühe kann man sich überheben.**
sich über'reden, see III. 1. *i* below.
sich über'zeugen *to convince one's self of*, usually with **von** with the dat.
sich unter'fangen *to dare to undertake*, usually with the gen., sometimes with the acc.: **So ist es mit allem, dessen sich der Mensch unterfängt** (Goethe). **Du verzeihst . . ., was sich die Frechheit unterfangen** (Schiller).
sich unter'stehen *to be so bold as to, to dare to do*, usually with the gen., sometimes with the acc. sometimes also with the dat. of the pronoun and the acc. of the thing: **Wer untersteht sich dessen? Vergib, daß ich des Worts mich unterstanden** (Lenau). **Was vnterstehet sich der Arme | das er vnter den lebendigen wil sein?** (Eccl. vi. 8). Sometimes **Ich untersteh' mir das nicht.** See also I. *b* above and III. 1. *l* below.
sich unter'winden *to dare to undertake, assume the charge, care of, adopt*: **Wie kann ich solcher Tat mich unterwinden!** (Schiller's *Jungfrau*, 1, 10). See also I. *b* above.
sich unter'ziehen *to undertake, undergo* (an operation, &c.) with the gen. or more commonly the dat.: **Ich unterzog mich der großen Mühe, dem schwierigen Geschäft, einer Operation.**
sich verantworten *to justify one's self concerning, with reference to*, with the gen. (as in Acts xxv. 16) or more commonly with **wegen** with the gen.: **Du sollst dich wegen deines Verfahrens verantworten.**
sich vergewissern *to assure one's self of* (the truth of a statement, &c.), also with **wegen** with the gen., **über** with the acc., or **von** with the dat.: **Ich werde mich des Erfolges, über den Erfolg, or von dem Erfolg vergewissern.**
sich verleugnen *to deny, disown, renounce*, now replaced by the transitive **verleugnen** with an acc. object.
sich verlohnen, see **sich lohnen** above.
sich vermessen *to dare*: **Wessen vermessen (or unterstehen, unterfangen, erkühnen) sie sich? Sie vermaßen sich hoher Dinge** (Ranke's *Päpste*, 1, 108). Often with an acc. of an indefinite pronoun instead of a gen.: **Wenn die Bestien, die Franzosen sich nur etwas gegen mich vermessen sollten** (Goethe).
sich vermögen (Swiss) = **wofür können** (see **213**. 2. F. *Note* 1): **„Ist sie da?" „Nein, Herr Heideck! Aber was vermag ich mich dessen?"** (Boßhart's *Die Barettlitochter*, p. 100) = **Was kann ich dafür?**
sich vermuten *to suppose, expect*, earlier in the period **sich eines Dings vermuten**, now **ein Ding** (acc.) **vermuten: Ich habe deinen Besuch nicht vermutet. Das konnte ich (mir) nicht vermuten.**
sich versagen *to refuse to enter into relations with, withdraw from*, more commonly a dat. instead of a gen.: **Wenn die dänische Regierung in der Tat gesonnen sein sollte, sich amtlicher** (usually **amtlichen**) **Verhandlungen auf die Dauer zu versagen** (*Preußen im Bundestag*, 1851 *bis* 1859, 1, 30).
sich versehen *to expect something* (*confidently*) *of one*, **sich** (acc.) **eines Dinges zu** (or **von**) **einem versehen** or **sich** (dat.) **ein Ding von** (or **zu**) **einem versehen: Einer solchen Aufnahme hatte sich der arme Vetter zu der reichen Sippschaft seines Weibes nicht versehen. Ich hatte mich eines Besseren zu Ihnen versehen. Mit banger Sorge würde sich das deutsche Volk die Frage vorlegen, wer denn der Nachfolger werden und wessen man sich von ihm zu versehen haben würde** (*Hamburger Nachrichten*, Nov. 13, 1908). **Das hätte ich mir von** (or **zu**) **Ihnen nicht versehen.**
sich versichern *to make sure of, gain over, seize*: **Versichern Sie sich des Ministers** *Make sure of, gain over the minister*. **Man wird sich der Häupter versichern** (Goethe's *Egmont*) *will seize* &c.
sich verstehen *to understand*, formerly with the gen. as in Acts xxv. 20, now usually with **auf** with the acc.: **Ich verstehe mich auf solche Sachen nicht.**
sich vertrösten *to put reliance on, trust in* or *to*, with gen. as in 2 Chron. xxxii. 10, but now rare in this meaning, *to cheer one's self by looking forward and counting on*, with **auf** with the acc.: **Die Besten hatten sich auf diese letzte Instanz vertröstet.**
sich verwegen (sometimes **verwägen**) *to dare, venture upon, renounce, give up, do without*, now little used except in the adjective perfect participle (see **199**. 2nd Division, 2): **Solcher Gewalttat hätte der Tyrann wider die freie Edle sich verwogen?** (Schiller's *Tell*, 4, 2)
sich verweigern *to refuse*: earlier in the period **sich eines Dinges** or **einem Dinge verweigern**, now according to I above.
sich verwundern *to be surprised* or *astonished at*, with the gen., as in Luke ii. 47, or more commonly **über** with the acc.: **Ich habe mich über dich, über die Rede verwundert.**
sich verzeihen *to renounce, give up*, now obsolete in this meaning and construction.
sich wehren *to defend*, usually with **gegen: Ich wehre mich meiner Haut, meines Lebens. Ich wehrte mich gegen ihn, gegen seinen Spott**, but with different meaning **Ich wehrte** (prevented) **dem Bettler den Eintritt.**
sich weigern *to refuse*, sometimes with the dat.: **Er weigerte sich dessen. Der Alte bat um das Gewehr, dem aber weigerte sich der junge Mann** (Immermann's *Münchhausen*, 1, 151). Now little used except with an infin. instead of the gen., or without any object at all: **Er weigerte sich, es zu tun. Ich weigere mich nicht.** Compare **verweigern**, I above.

sich wundern *to be surprised at*, sometimes with the gen. as in Luke iv. 22, usually with **über** with the acc. The gen., according to III. 2. B (2nd par.), is common in the expression **Sie wunderte sich des Todes** (or **zu Tode,** or **sehr**) *She was greatly astonished.*

c. Accusative and Genitive, or Dative and Genitive after Impersonal Verbs. The impersonal subject **es** may be expressed or understood, as explained in **219.** This construction was once a favorite, so that it occasionally took the place of other constructions, but it did not permanently hold its gains and in recent literature has been largely replaced by other constructions, as is indicated after each verb. Here belong the following impersonal verbs:—

dauern *to pity*, in early N.H.G. and in archaic and poetic language still with the acc. and gen., now usually according to B. *d* below: **Mich dauerte der heimatlosen Kleinen** (Grillparzer's *Sappho*, 3, 5), now usually in plain prose: **Mich dauerte die heimatlose Kleine.**

denken or **gedenken** *to remember*, earlier in the period with the acc. (or dat.) and gen.: **Mich denkt des Ausdrucks noch recht wohl** (Lessing's *Nathan*, 2, 2). **Es gedenkt mir aus meinen Knabenjahren eines armen Manns** (Riehl's *Wanderbuch*). See also B. *d* below.

ekeln *to loathe, be disgusted at*, with the acc. and gen., or perhaps more commonly the dat. and gen.: **Mich ekelt meiner Kunst** (Fritz Lienhard's *Wieland der Schmied*, p. 56). **Es ekelte ihn des funkelnden Gaukelspiels** (Paul Keller's *Der Sohn der Hagar*, p. 261). **Wenn ihm beinahe des ganzen Lebens ekelt** (Lessing). The more common prose construction is given in B. *d* below.

erbarmen *to pity*, here with the acc. (or formerly also dat.) and gen., or more commonly according to A. *b* above: **Und doch erbarmt mich deiner** (Schiller's *Tell*, 5, 2).

freuen *to rejoice*, here with the acc. and gen., or more commonly according to *b* above: **Mich freut des verwegenen Entschlusses** (J. H. Voß).

gebrechen *to be lacking, wanting*, with the dat. and gen. only rarely even in early N.H.G., as the nom. had already supplanted the gen. according to B. *d* below: **Zenan den Schrifftgelerten vnd Apollon fertige ab mit vleis | auff das jnen nichts** (in fact a gen., but soon felt as a nom.) **gebreche** (Titus iii. 13).

gelüsten or **lüsten** *to covet, lust after*, earlier in the period with the acc. (or dat.) and gen.: **Las dich nicht gelüsten deines Nehesten Weibs** (Exod. xx. 17). Present usage is given in B. *d* below.

gemahnen *to put one in mind of, seem to one like, remind one of*, earlier in the period with the acc. (or dat.) and gen.: **Es gemanet mich** (sometimes **mir**) **der welt wie eines bawfelligen hauses** (Luther's *Tischreden*). Present usage is given in B. *d* below.

genügen *to suffice*, early N.H.G. **es genügt mich or mir eines Dinges.** Present usage is given in B. *d*. below.

jammern *to grieve, pity*, earlier in the period with the acc. (or sometimes dat.) and gen.: **Vnd da er das Volck sahe | jammert jn desselbigen** (Matth. ix. 36). Present usage is given in B. *d* below.

kümmern *to concern* now little used here: earlier in the period **Es kümmert mich dessen nicht.** Present usage is given in B. *d* below.

reuen or **gereuen** *to repent, rue*; earlier in the period with the acc. (or sometimes dat.) and gen.: **Denn er ist Gnedig | Barmhertzig | Gedültig | vnd von grosser Güte | vnd rewet jn bald der straffe** (Joel II. 13). Present usage is given in *B. d* below.

verdrießen *to vex*, earlier in the period with the acc. (or sometimes dat.) and gen.: **Der Müh' mich gleich verdrießen tut** (H. Sachs). **Verdroß ihm** (usually **ihn**) **der Schlacht und des Lebens** (J. Müller, 24, 177). Present usage is given in B. *d* below.

verlangen *to long for*, only rarely with the acc. and gen. The usual construction is given in B. *d* below.

wundern *to wonder at, be surprised at*; formerly with the acc. and gen., now usually according to *b* above or B. *d* below: **Des wundert ihn gar mächtiglich** (Wieland).

B. The different constructions in A are not so common now as in early N.H.G., and are in instances now confined to elevated discourse. In common prose they are often replaced by the following constructions, but sometimes the old and the new constructions exist side by side with or without a different shade of meaning.

a. In a number of cases the acc. of the person and the gen. of the thing can be replaced by the dat. of the person and the acc. of the thing: **Dessen versichere ich Sie** I assure you of that, or now more commonly **Das versichere ich Ihnen,** or with a clause: **Ich versichere Sie** or now more commonly **Ihnen, daß ich es gesehen habe.** See also I. *b* above, and **259.** 35.

b. The old gen. **es** (see **140.** *c*) still occurs in a number of idiomatic expressions, and, not being any longer understood, has been construed as a nom. or acc. neuter. This false conception has led to the use of the nom. and acc. of other words, where the gen. should stand, and has thus given rise to several common but in fact erroneous expressions: **Es** (gen., but felt as a nom.) or **das** (instead of **dessen**) **nimmt mich Wunder** (nom.) That surprises me, or literally according to the original genitive construction: Wonderment seizes me on account of it. **Das** (instead of **dessen**) **versichere ich Sie.**

c. In a number of cases, as can be seen in the many remarks after the verbs in A above, the gen. is usually in prose replaced by a prep. construction. Also the prep. construction can be used with verbs which usually take the gen., if it is desired to express some different shade of meaning. Thus **sich erfreuen** w. gen. denotes possession, while w. **an** it denotes a lively interest or pleasure in something: **Ich erfreue mich einer guten Gesundheit** I enjoy (have) good health. **Ich habe mich recht an ihm erfreut** I was delighted with him.

d. The gen. in the construction in A. *c* is not now common in prose. Instead of the gen. we now with some verbs find the nom., which becomes subject, as explained in **255.** II. 1. H. *c*: **Vnd ekelt mich jr nicht also | das mit jnen aus sein solt'** (Lev. xxvi. 44), but **Weil ihn das nackte Schauspiel ekelte** (K. F. Meyer's *Gustav Adolfs Page*). **Es erbarmt mich seiner,** or more commonly **Er erbarmt mich,** or still more frequently according to A. *b*: **Ich erbarme mich seiner** or **über ihn** I pity him. **Mich freut dessen,** or more commonly **Das freut mich,** or according to A. *b*: **Ich freue mich dessen** or **darüber. Da meiner Leuchte das Öl gebrach** (K. F. Meyer's *Nov.*, I, 253), or more commonly **Da es meiner Leuchte an Öl** (dat.) **gebrach.** The sentence from Luther's *Tischreden* given in A. *c* would now read: **Die Welt gemahnt mich** (also **mir**) **wie ein baufälliges Haus,** or more commonly **Die Welt gemahnt mich an ein baufälliges Haus,** or sometimes w. acc. of the person and gen. of the thing: **Daß, wenn dein Herz | der Stunde dich gemahnt, du sagen kannst, | ich weiß von ihr nichts** (Wildenbruch's *König Laurin*, p. 76). **Mich** (occasionally **mir**) **gereut die Tat, der getane Schritt. Es genügt mir an deinem Wohlwollen,** or **Dein Wohlwollen genügt mir. Mich jammert nur der Vater** (Schiller's *Tell*, 1, 4). **Das kümmert mich nicht, nicht im geringsten, wenig, nichts, gar nichts, kein Haar,** or often according to A. *b* above. **Sein Benehmen verdrießt mich. Das wundert mich,** or **Ich wundere mich darüber.**

The impersonal construction, however, is still quite common after **gelüsten** and **lüsten** (both sometimes w. dat. of the person instead of the acc.), **verlangen** (w. acc., sometimes dat.), and **ekeln,** but with a prepositional object instead of a gen.: **Es gelüstet die Frau nach dem Obst. Mag's der Mönch alleine tun, wenn ihm danach gelüstet** (von der Gabelentz's *Der Mönch*, last chap.). Also w. personal construction: **Ich gelüste nach dem Obst. Mich verlangt nach dir. Wenn du wüßtest, wie mir gerade danach verlangt!** (Fontane's *Effi*, chap. 10). **Tag und Nacht verlangt ihn, sie zu sehen** (E. von Handel-Mazzetti's *Stephana Schwertner*, II, chap. VI). **Verlangen** sometimes takes a gen. object. See **260.** 2. A. **Mir** (or also **mich**) **ekelt vor etwas** (dat.), **etwas ekelt mich,** or now also **ich ekele mich vor etwas** (dat.) or **an etwas** (dat.): **Mir ekelt vor der Speise,** or **Ich ekele mich vor der Speise,** or **Diese Speise ekelt mich. Er blickte sich wie ein Verirrter im großen Raume um mit all den Spuren des gestrigen Gelages und ekelte sich daran** (Schulze-Smidt's *Denk' ich an Deutschland in der Nacht*, I). An infinitive or a clause may replace the prep. object: **Es lüstete sie, einen Schmetterling zu fangen** (P. Heyse). **Es verlangt einem allmählich, daß Sie die Stille wieder unterbrechen** (T. Storm an G. Keller, 13. September 1883).

After **denken** and **gedenken** both the acc. and gen. construction and that with the nom. and acc. have, perhaps, disappeared, tho both are found earlier in the period. The dat. of the personal pronoun is now usually found instead of the acc., but also this construction is now rare: **Mir denkt's kaum, daß ich sie einmal sah** (Mörike). **Gedenkt dir's noch, wie uns nach Friedrichs Krönung | die Römer hart am Tiber überfallen?** (M. Greif's *Heinrich der Löwe*, 3, 2).

C. Of the constructions in A only *a* can be transferred to the passive. Then the acc. of the person becomes nom. and the gen. of the thing remains: **Er beraubte mich aller meiner Hoffnungen** becoming in the passive **Ich wurde**

aller meiner Hoffnungen beraubt. The nom. may become an acc. object: **Nur ein paar Mal meinte ich das scharfe S vor einem anderen Konsonanten zu vernehmen, dessen ich selbst freilich mich längst entwöhnt glaubte** (T. Storm).

III. Double Accusative.

A double accusative is found in the following constructions:

1. *Accusative of the Person and Accusative of the Thing.* This construction, as described in I. *b*, was once more common than now. It is at present limited to the following verbs: **bitten** to ask (a favor), **beschwören** to implore, **fragen** or **befragen** to ask (a question), **abhören, überhören,** or **verhören** to hear recite, **hören** (especially in the set expression **einen,** also **einem die Beichte hören**) to hear, **heißen** to bid, bid to do, **anweisen** to instruct, order (to do), **kosten** to cost, **lehren** and in early N.H.G. **unterrichten** to teach, **führen** and **leiten** to lead, **lenken** to guide, **bereden** to persuade, **überreden** to persuade, **zeihen** to accuse, **berichten** to inform, **sich unterstehen** (with acc. of the reflexive and the acc. of the thing) to be so bold, **verstehen** to understand, most of which admit of other constructions, hence are treated below separately.

a. **bitten** has two accusatives only when the thing is a neut. pronoun or a numeral, otherwise the *thing* is in the acc. after the prep. **um: Bitte mich alles in der Welt, nur das nicht. Eins bitte ich dich** One thing I ask of you. **Er bittet mich um eine Gefälligkeit.** In poetry the simple acc. of the thing is sometimes used instead of **um** with acc., when the acc. of the person is not expressed: **Ich bitte nicht Gnade** (Klopstock). Sometimes also in terse vigorous prose: **Reiten Sie zur Fabrik und bringen mir — ich bitte flotte Gangart — Bericht** (Liliencron's *Kriegsnovellen*, Anno 1870, Der Richtungspunkt). According to II. A. *a* above, **bitten** was in early N.H.G. used with an accusative of the person and the genitive of the thing. The old genitive construction survives in case of **alles** and **eins,** as found in the first two examples given above, but these forms are now felt as accusatives.

Beschwören has the same limited use of the double acc. as **bitten: Was ich dich jüngst so heiß beschworen, o mache den Propheten stumm!** (Lenau).

b. **fragen** and **befragen** have in a few set expressions, especially such as contain **a** neut. demon. or indef. pronoun, two accusatives, the acc. of the person and the acc. (in early N.H.G. also the gen., as in earlier periods) of the thing, but more commonly, aside from these set expressions, the thing is in the dat. after the prep. **nach** *after, concerning*, or in the acc. after the prep. **um** *for:* **Fragte er dich das? Er fragte mich wenig. Er fragte mich etwas. Ich habe Sie verschiedenes zu fragen** (Wildenbruch's *Der unsterbliche Felix*, 2, 19). **Lasse mich heimlich den Tapfersten sehen, den Otto von Bismarck, daß ich ihn alles befrage, was meine Seele belastet** (Frenssen's *Bismarck*, p. 109). **Ich fragte ihn nach seinem Namen** I asked him his name. **Ich fragte ihn nach der Ursache. Ich fragte ihn um Rat.** In early N.H.G. the prep. **von** was also used here: **Vnd wenn die Leute am selben ort fragten von seinem Weibe | so sprach er** (Genesis xxvi. 7). The simple acc. and the construction with **nach** are, however, sometimes used with a different shade of meaning. The acc. of the thing asks for a formal statement or explanation of some problem or task, not for information, but to ascertain whether the one questioned is informed, while the dat. after **nach** asks for information about something: **Der Lehrer fragt den Schüler die Vokabeln, die Regeln, die Jahreszahlen** The teacher is asking the pupil to give the vocabulary, rules, dates. **Ich fragte ihn nach dem Weg** I asked him the way. The passive of this construction is formed as in *c*.

c. The words **abhören, überhören, verhören** *to hear recite*, **prüfen** *to examine*, **hören** *to shrive*, have a double construction — the acc. of the thing and either the dat. or the acc. of the person: **Der Lehrer hat dem Schüler** (or sometimes also **den Schüler**) **die Aufgabe, die Vokabeln abgehört** (or **überhört,** or **verhört**) The teacher has heard the pupil recite the exercise, vocabulary. **Der Herr überhört die Kinder ein auswendig gelerntes artiges Gedicht** (Goethe's *Wan-*

derj., 3, 10). **Der Lehrer hat dem** (or **den**) **Schüler die Geschichte geprüft** examined the pupil in history, or **hat ihn in der Geschichte geprüft. Der Priester hört einen** (sometimes also **einem**) (**die**) **Beichte. Hören** is also sometimes used with a double accusative in its primary meaning: **Höre mich noch ein paar Worte** (Goethe). The acc. **Worte** is an adverbial acc. of extent (**223.** iv. 2. A).

Überhören, verhören, and **fragen** may form a passive in the following ways, which are without material difference of meaning. The acc. of the person becomes nom. and the acc. of the thing may either remain acc., or may form a prep. phrase with **nach** in case of **fragen,** and with **über** in case of all three words: **Diesen Abschnitt sind wir gar nicht gefragt, verhört worden,** or **Nach diesem Abschnitt sind wir gar nicht gefragt worden,** or **Über diesen Abschnitt sind wir gar nicht gefragt, überhört, verhört worden.** Instead of these different constructions the acc. of the thing of the active may become nom. in the passive, and the dat. of the person remain dat.: **Dieser Abschnitt ist uns gar nicht abgefragt, abgehört, überhört worden.**

d. **Heißen** cannot freely take an acc. of the person and also of the thing, but is limited to an acc. of the person and a neut. acc. of a pronoun, or to an acc. of the person and an infinitive: **daß du mir Gehorsam schuldig bist in allem, was ich dich heiße** (Schiller's *Räuber*, 4, 2). **Jeden Mord, den du mich begehen heißt** (id., 3, 2). **Liebe Laura! Du kannst mich das heißen? Ich heiß' ihn eilen.** The acc. of the person is now, perhaps, more commonly replaced by the dat., where the object of the thing is not an infinitive: **Was ein evangelischer Geistlicher einem andren heißen konnte, konnt' er auch selber tun** (Telmann's *Wahrheit*, VIII), but usually **Ich habe dich das tun heißen.** In the latter case the dat. of the person is also sometimes found: **Wann hieß ich dir die Schrift an Burleigh geben?** (Schiller's *M. Stuart*, 5, 14). The dative is more frequently used if the infinitive with **zu** is employed: **Nun erzählte der Mönch, wie er das Mädchen in den Armen des betrunkenen Soldaten angetroffen und daß er ihr geheißen habe, das lärmige tolle Fest zu verlassen** (G. von Gabelentz's *Der Mönch*). In the passive the person is usually in the dat. and the thing in the nom.: **Das ist dir geheißen worden. Es ist dir geheißen worden, das zu tun.**

Anweisen *to instruct, order* (*to do*), much like **heißen,** in meaning, may likewise take an accusative of the person and a neuter accusative of a pronoun: **So wurde es Georg auf einmal ganz klar, daß er ebenfalls ganz aus eigenem Antrieb Pfarrer werden wolle, und daß es ihn niemand anweisen dürfe** (Anna Schieber's *Alle guten Geister*, p. 123). More common than the acc. of a neuter pronoun is an infinitive with **zu: Ich habe ihn angewiesen, dir das Geld zu zahlen.**

e. **kosten** (see **259.** 21. B)

f. **lehren** (and sometimes incorrectly **lernen = lehren**) admits of the acc. of the thing and either acc. or dat. of the person, the latter (dat.) appearing about 1600 and later gradually spreading until it has come into wide use, but at present is generally opposed by grammarians: **Sie lehrte ihn** in choice language but in colloquial speech often **ihm kleine Lieder. Der kleine Sylvester, dem die Mutter selbst Lesen und Schreiben lehrte** (Ompteda's *Sylvester von Geyer*, vi). Altho the dative is often used here in connection with the accusative it is replaced by the accusative if it is the only object: **„Was kann ich dir lehren? Lehre du mich!" sagte Bruder Nathaniel** (Hauptmann's *Der Narr in Christo*, p. 43). Where there are two objects the simple infinitive or the infinitive with **zu** may replace the acc. of the thing. See **185.** B. I. 2. *c* and *Note* thereunder. Also a clause may replace the acc. of the thing: **Er lehrte ihm, daß jeder Gegenstand seinen genau vorgeschriebenen Platz hatte** (Ompteda's *Sylvester von Geyer*, xxvi). Compare in English: "He taught me" (acc.). "He taught me (acc. or dat.) that," but a clear modern dative in "He taught it to me" and "It was taught to me."

In the passive this construction assumes different forms: (**1**) The acc. of the person of the active construction becomes here nom., and the acc. of the thing remains acc.: **Ich werde das nicht gelehrt.** (**2**) The acc. of the thing becomes nom. and the acc. of the person remains acc.: **Das wird mich nicht gelehrt.** (**3**) The acc. of the thing becomes nom. and the dat. of the person remains dat.: **Das wird mir nicht gelehrt.** The last construction is now much more common than the others. A clause or an infinitive with **zu** may replace the nom.: **Mir ist gelehrt worden, daß dies meine Pflicht sei. Mir ist gelehrt worden, den Eltern zu gehorchen.**

In early N.H.G. **unterrichten** and **unterweisen** *to teach, instruct,* might take either a double acc. or an acc. (in passive a nom.) of the person and a gen. of the thing: **das er sie die Wort des Gesetzs vnterrichtet** (Neh. viii. 13). **Auff das du gewissen grund erfarest der Lere | welcher** (in revised ed. **in welcher**) **du vnterrichtet bist** (Luke i. 4). **Er wird jn vnterweisen den besten weg** (Psalm xxv. 12). Older usage is still occasionally found: **Gott habe den apostolischen Vater des rechten Weges unterwiesen** (*Rundsch.*, 2, 5, 220). The acc. or gen. of the thing is now usually replaced by a prepositional construction: **Er unterrichtet uns im Französischen. Ich wurde davon unterrichtet** I was informed with regard to it, It came to my knowledge. **Er hat seinen Enkel im Lesen unterwiesen.**

Note. Such accusatives as **das** in (**1**) and **mich** in (**2**) are to-day little used as there is a feeling that an object is out of place in connection with a passive. Formerly when the force of these accusatives was more vividly felt the accusative was freely used in both the active and passive, as it was the only form that could express the meaning here involved. Accusative and verb were so closely united as to form a kind of compound, and hence the accusative was just as appropriate in the passive as in the active. Later this feeling was blunted by the new conception that the action was carried on for the benefit of somebody, which led to the dative construction in (**3**). The older construction is better preserved in *c*: **Welchen Zeitraum bist du gefragt** (**geprüft**) **worden?** See also first example in the second par. in *c*. Compare in English: "I was taught that." "I was asked that." Compare I, last par.

g. **Führen, leiten,** and **lenken** take an acc. of the person and an acc. of the way: **Er führt mich diesen Weg. Janthe, komm und leite mich den Pfad** (Grillparzer's *Des Meeres und der Liebe Wellen*, 4). **Wollt ihr nun mein als einer Frau gedenken, | lenksam dem Zaum, so daß kein Stachel not, | will freudig ich die Ruhmesbahn euch lenken** (id., *Libussa*, 1). As in **260**. 2. A. *a* we also find here the genitive instead of the accusative: **Zwei von ihnen hielten den Mittleren an den Ohrläppchen gefangen und führten ihn so des Weges** (Wilhelm Fischer's *Die Freude am Licht*, p. 34).

In the passive the acc. of the person becomes nom. and the acc. of the way remains: **Ja, ja, wir werden eben unerforschliche Wege geführt** (Raabe's *Schüdderump*, chap. xxxvi).

h. **Bereden** *to make believe something false* often has a pronominal acc. of the person and the acc. of a thing instead of the older and more correct acc. of the person and gen. of the thing: **Mich wollt ihr das bereden?** (Schiller's *Don Carlos*, 3, 4). We sometimes find the dat. of the person here and the acc. of the thing: **Es (das Herz) läßt sich alles bereden, was Ihrer Einbildungskraft ihm zu bereden einfällt** (Lessing's *Samps.*, 2, 3). **Bereden** *to persuade* takes the acc. of the person and the prep. **zu: Er beredete ihn dazu.** Earlier in the period the gen. of the thing was used instead of both the acc. and the prep. construction: **Ich kann mich dessen schwerlich bereden** (Lessing). In the meaning *to talk over, discuss* **bereden** takes a simple accusative: **Ich habe den Plan mit ihm beredet.**

i. **Überreden** *to persuade* usually has the acc. of the person and the prep. **zu: Er hat mich zu der Sache überredet.** Earlier in the period we find the acc. of the person and the gen. of the thing: **Ich kann mich dessen nicht überreden** (Adelung). In Goethe the double acc. is also frequent: **Der Mensch ist gemacht, daß man ihn das Abenteuerlichste überreden kann** (*Werther*, Am 15. Aug., Ausgabe letzter Hand, 1828; in the earlier editions $E^{1\text{-}2}$ **ihm** instead of **ihn**). As in the earlier editions of Werther the dative was once also elsewhere common.

The object in all the above constructions may in case of the thing be replaced by an infinitive (Acts xviii. 13) or a clause (Acts xxvi. 28).

j. **Zeihen** *to accuse* has sometimes an acc. of a neut. pronoun instead of the correct gen.: **Was ich ihn zeihe, werd' ich selbst** (Schiller's *Don Carlos*, 4, 6).

k. In early N.H.G. **berichten** *to inform* took an acc. of the person and the gen. of the thing, which construction still survives in **jemanden eines Besseren berichten** to disabuse a person of an opinion. Early in the period the gen. is replaced by a prep. phrase or an acc.: **einen von** (or **über**) **etwas berichten,** or **einen etwas** (double acc.) **berichten.** The acc. of the person is now replaced by a dat.: **einem etwas** (or **über etwas**) **berichten.** The former acc. construction here still survives in such expressions as **Wenn ich recht berichtet bin,** or **Du bist falsch berichtet.** See **260.** 3.

l. The reflexive **sich unterstehen** belongs properly to II. *b* above, but as the gen. object **es** (**140.** *c*) which is so often used with it is construed as an acc., the real acc. is sometimes used: **Was vnterstehet sich der Arme | das er vnter den Lebendigen wil sein?** (Eccl. vi. 8). **Wie ich mich das unterstehen kann?** (Hopfen's *Die fünfzig Semmeln des Studiosus Taillefer*, p. 66) You wonder how I am so bold as to do that! This word is usually employed with the object **es** and an infinitive clause which stands in apposition with the **es,** or with the infinitive clause alone which takes the place of the **es: Aber die blasse, abgespannte Jadviga . . . fuhr auf wie ein wildes Tier, wenn er sich's unterstand, sie mit seinen Zärtlichkeiten belästigen zu wollen** (Schubin's *Refugium peccatorum*, vi). As the **sich** in such sentences is not a distinct acc. form, it is sometimes construed as a dat., and elsewhere a real dat. is employed: **Untersteh dir's, Mädel!** (Beyerlein's *Dämon Othello*, 2, 2). It is quite common to suppress the object of the thing in a few expressions: **Untersteh dich nicht!** In early N.H.G. **unterstehen** was also a transitive verb, taking as object an acc. or an infinitive clause: **Vmb des willen haben mich die Jüden im Tempel gegriffen | Vnd unterstunden mich zu tödten** (Acts xxvi. 21).

m. We sometimes find two accusatives with **verstehen** *to understand*: **Ich kann ihn nicht alles verstehen.** The dative of the person occurs here sometimes instead of the acc.

2. *Accusative of the Direct Object and an Objective Predicate.* This construction differs from the double acc. in 1 above, in that the two accusatives together form logically a sentence in which the first acc. performs the office of the subject and the second acc. the office of predicate: **Sie nannten i h n e i n e n V e r r ä t e r** (= **Er ist ein Verräter**). **Ich sehe i h n l a u f e n.** The simple infinitive here as in the last example is the accusative of an old type of verbal noun which still as in the prehistoric period has no article before it. The two accusatives in each of these examples as elsewhere are the direct objects of the verb. As the construction is very old there has sprung up in course of time a close association between the two accusatives, so that the second one is now felt as the predicate to the first one, the subject. The predicate is here joined to the subject without the aid of a copula, as the statement is felt to be of the old appositional type of sentence described in **252.** 1. *b. Note*, where the predicate is placed alongside the subject like an appositive without the use of a finite verb.

The objective predicate is now, except in the group in A. *a* below, usually introduced by **als, für,** or **zu,** with differentiated meanings. Earlier in the period the predicate noun is often a simple accusative where we to-day find **zu, für,** or **als** before the predicate. This indicates that the *literary* language of that time was under strong Latin influence, for even in oldest German **zu** and **für** were often used here. The literary language of our own day has a lively feeling for the strong concrete force of these old forms, which have always been in wide use among the people. The **zu** represents the new state as the result of a development or as the purpose of the action, while **für** represents the new state as entirely or seemingly identical with the conception held by the person in question. These old conceptions are still well established in the language, but the new form **als** (see A. *b* below), which has sprung up in the present period, is growing at the expense of **für,** which it is gradually displacing, and also at the expense of the simple forms. Compare **252.** 2. A. *b*. (**1**), (**2**). *Note,* (**3**).

The following groups occur: —

A. A noun or pronoun is used as an objective predicate:

a. After **erachten** (also according to *b* and *c*; see *c Note* 1) to deem, **ernennen** (now rare here, usually according to *d* below) to appoint, **glauben** to believe, **wähnen** to fancy, imagine, **grüßen** to greet with the title of, **heißen** to call, name, **nennen** to call, **rufen** to call, **spotten** to call in derision, **taufen** (also **auf einen Namen taufen**) to christen, **titulieren** to call, style, **schelten** (also according to *b*) to call unjustly, call (one a harsh name), **schimpfen** (stronger than **schelten**) to call (one a bad name), **fluchen** to call (one a terrible name), **machen** (now rare here, usually according to *d* below), **sagen** (poetic here, but common in B below) to claim to be, **träumen** (also according to *b* below) to dream, the objective predicate is a simple acc.: **Beliebige Fremdlinge, „Schriftsteller," „Dichter!" erachten es keinen Raub, ohne jeden Grund mir halbe Stunden zu stehlen** (Dahn's *Erinnerungen*, IV, p. 218). **Vielleicht wäre ich der, den du mich glaubst** (Lessing). **Der Vater wähnet Hippodamien | die Mörderin** (Goethe's *Iphigenie*, 1, 3). **Wir nennen Gott unseren Vater. Warum schiltst du mich einen Feigling? Ihr sollt mich Hundsfott fluchen, | findet ihr das Mausloch leer** (Sudermann's *Die drei Reiherfedern*, 1, 3). **Sie schalt ihn einen Narren. Er hat ihn einen Grobian geschimpft. Zittre du für dein Leben, weil du mich Herzog** (may be construed as acc. or nom.; see *Note*) **spottest** (Schiller's *Fiesko*, 5, 14). **Käthchen von Heilbronn, die dein Kind du sagst, | ist meines höchsten Kaisers dort** (Kleist's *Käthchen*, 5, 1). **Dann kommen mir wohl Momente, wo ich mich ihren Bruder träume** (Spielhagen's *Selbstgerecht*, II, p. 35).

Both of these accusatives become nom. in the passive: **Warum wurde ich von dir ein Feigling gescholten? Er wurde Karl** (or **auf den Namen Karl**) **getauft.**

Note. Instead of the predicate accusative we often find a nom.: (1) in order to preserve the exact form of direct address: **Er nannte sie mein lieber Schatz, mein Engelchen, mein Kind** (Hölty). **Und ich sage Euch, daß ich kein Bedenken trüge, ihn heiliger Ruffinus zu nennen** (Ertl's *Die Stadt der Heiligen*). The nominative with the definite article is often used to preserve the usual declarative form of statement: **Nicht ohne Grund habe ich ihn schon: Philipp, der Schweigsame, genannt** (Spielhagen's *Frei geboren*, p. 225). **Es war ein alter halbgelähmter Bettler da — er nennt sich der lange Hitz** (Heer's *Der König der Bernina*, xx). (2) In case of articleless weak masculine nouns. See **94.** 1. *c*. In case of articleless strong nouns and feminines it is not possible to distinguish here whether the form is nom. or acc.: **Ich könnte jetzt das arme Würmchen nicht Velten** (name) **rufen** (Raabe's *Die Akten des Vogelsangs*, p. 173). **Er schreibt sich Meyer, nicht Meier. Sie fühlt sich Mutter.** With a number of reflexive verbs there is a fluctuation of usage. See **218.** 2. *b* and *Note*.

After **rufen** we also find the dative instead of the first accusative: **Sie hieß Agnes, doch rief man ihr Agi** (Hermann Hesse's *Peter Camenzind*, p. 197). **Ich rief meiner Frau „Anna"** (*Fliegende Blätter*, Oct. 17, 1911).

b. After the verbs **anerkennen** to recognize, **anführen** to cite (as an example), **ansehen** to regard, **ansprechen** to claim, **anweisen** to assign, **sich aufspielen** to pose, **auslegen** to construe, **begrüßen** to greet, **behandeln** to treat, **beschreiben** to describe, **besingen** to celebrate, **betrachten** to consider, **bezeichnen** to designate, **darstellen** to represent, **dekla'rieren** to declare (to be), **sich** (dat.) **denken** to picture to one's self, imagine, **denun'zieren** to denounce, **einführen** to introduce, **empfehlen** to recommend, **erfinden** to find (someone) out (to be so and so), **erwähnen** to mention, **sich erweisen** or **sich herausstellen** to turn out to be, **geben** to give, **kennen** to know, **kennzeichnen** to characterize, **kleiden** to dress up as, make look like, **preisen** or **rühmen** to praise, **schätzen** to prize, **schildern** to depict, **sehen** to see, **verdingen** or **vermieten** to hire out as, **zeigen** to show to be, &c., the objective predicate is introduced by **als**, which here denotes *identity* or *oneness with*: **Er spielt sich als Schönredner auf. Ich betrachte ihn als einen Narren. Ich denunziere Sie hiermit dieser Gesellschaft als notorischen Atheisten!** (Lienhard's *Münchhausen*, 1).

For fluctuation of usage in case of reflexive verbs see **218.** 2. *b* and *Note* thereunder. For the inflection of an unmodified objective predicate after **als** see **94.** 1. *c*.

In the passive both of these accusatives become nom. See **252.** 2. A. *b*. (1).

Note. In early N.H.G. there was often no **als** here, and this older usage survives in poetry: **vnd hast sie Lügener erfunden** (Rev. ii. 2). **Als ich . . . | mich einen Fremdling sah in diesem Kreise** (Schiller's *Piccolomini*, 3, 4).

c. After a few verbs the objective predicate is introduced by **für** (with acc.), which here does not positively affirm complete and absolute identity as does

als, but only equality, and hence denotes that something is considered or represented as able or worthy to pass *for* the thing expressed by the predicate: **Man erklärte ihn für einen Betrüger** They pronounced him a fraud. **Er gibt sich für einen Gelehrten aus** He makes himself out to be a scholar. **Ich halte ihn für einen Schmeichler** I consider him a flatterer. **Ich achte es für eine große Ehre** I esteem it a great honor. **Ich erkenne ihn für einen Freund** I own him as my friend. For the passive construction see **252.** 2. A. *b.* (2).

Note 1. Several verbs, as **erachten, ansehen, (aus)deuten, auslegen, erkennen, ausschreien, ausrufen** (to proclaim as), are followed by either als or für according to the shade of meaning required: **Sie erkannten** (recognized) **die von dem Finanzminister abgelegte Rechnung als** (*as*, here expressing identity) **falsch, aber aus Mangel an Mut erkannten** (pronounced) **sie dieselbe für** (simply letting it pass as) **richtig.** Often there is a sharp distinction between **als** and **für; als,** however, is decidedly the favorite, and is even used when **für** would be more appropriate.

Note 2. In early N.H.G. there was often no **für** with those verbs, and this older usage survives in poetry: **Sölch unsinnige verfluchte Gojim halten sie uns** (Luther, *Erlanger Ausgabe*, 32, 226). **Du hältst es Recht** (Goethe's *Tasso*, 2, 4).

d. As after **werden** (**252.** 2. A. *b.* (**3**)), so also after the verbs **machen** *to make*, **aufwerfen** *to constitute* (*one's self*) *to be*, **einsetzen** *to appoint, designate*, **wählen** *to elect*, **ernennen** *to appoint*, **befördern** *to promote to be*, **erklären** *to pronounce to be*, **ausrufen** *to proclaim*, **sich fallen** *to make one's self by falling*, **schlagen** *to beat, strike*, **verkochen** *to convert into by boiling*, **verarbeiten** *to make* or *convert into*, **zerstoßen** *to pound*, **laden** *to invite to be*, and with similar meaning **haben** *to have as*, **nehmen** *to take as, make*, &c., the prep. **zu** (with the dat.) introduces the objective predicate to denote a transformation into a new condition: **Der Zwang der Zeiten machte mich zu ihrem Gegner. Er macht sie zu seiner Frau. Der Hund hat sich zum Beschützer des Kätzchens aufgeworfen. Der König ernannte ihn zum Offizier. Und** [**sie**] **erklärten den forschen Kundschafter zu ihrem Gefangenen** (*Hamburger Nachrichten*, Sept. 22, 1907). **Er hat sich zum Krüppel gefallen. Einen zum Krüppel schlagen, einen zu Brei schlagen** to beat someone into a jelly, **Fleisch zu Kraftbrühe verkochen** to make a strong broth out of meat by boiling, **Hanf zu Seilen verarbeiten, etwas zu Pulver zerstoßen, einen zu Gaste laden, einen zum Freunde haben, etwas zum Muster nehmen. Er nimmt sie zur Frau.** In the passive the acc. becomes nom., but the objective predicate remains as in the active: **Er wurde vom König zum Offizier ernannt.**

Notice here as in **252.** 2. A. *b.* (**3**) the common use of the generalizing definite article in contracted form, **zum** and **zur,** where English usually requires the indefinite article. In case of a mass or a material the article is here dropped in German, while in English the indefinite article is used, as illustrated in examples given above. Notice also that the article is lacking in a few old set expressions, as **einen zu Gaste laden.**

Note. In early N.H.G. the **zu**-construction was often displaced by the Latin construction of the simple accusative: **Darnach wollen wir all deutsche Bischoff Cardinel machenn** (Luther).

B. The objective predicate can be an adjective or a participle, now usually uninflected, unless preceded by an article or some other modifying word: **Er weinte sich die Augen rot. Er schlug ihn tot. Man sagt ihn tot. Ich glaubte ihn geheilt.** Here belongs the perf. participle in compound tenses: **Er hat einen Brief geschrieben.** Compare **104.** 2. A. *c.*

Instead of an adjective or participle we often find here a gen., an adverb, or a prep. phrase: **Jedenfalls rechne nicht darauf, mich anderen Sinnes zu machen** (Fontane's *Frau Jenny*, XII). **Er fiel sich tot** or **zu Tode. Ich komme, sobald ich ihn hier weiß. Ich ließ ihn in guten Händen.**

The predicate adjective, participle, genitive, adverb, or prepositional phrase predicates a quality or state of the object, but the copula **sein** which often formally announces the predication is here as in 2 above not expressed, as explained in 2 above and in **252.** 1. *b. Note.* In this old attributive or appositional type of sentence, as explained in **252.** 1. *b. Note*, the predicate adjective is not only found as an appositive with uninflected form but it is in exclamatory style often in attributive form: **Freie Bahn dem Tüchtigen!** *Let us keep the road* (to employment, promotion in public service, &c.) *open to able men.* **Freie** is here the logical objective predicate to **Bahn,** which is the object of some verb understood.

In all the preceding examples the accusative object of the principal verb is the subject of the clause and the adjective, participle, adverb, or prepositional phrase is the predicate. In the *impersonal* passive construction (**219.** 5. A), however, the participle is as usual the predicate but there can be no accusative object in the sentence as there is no subject in an impersonal construction. The dative, genitive, or prepositional object of the active is simply retained in the passive: **Ich fühle mir** (often **mich**) **durch Ihren Besuch geschmeichelt. Ich glaubte ihr geholfen. So findet man doch eines Alten erwähnet** (Lessing's *Sämtliche Schriften*, Lachmann-Muncker, 3rd ed., 8, 301, 21). **Ich will an Julianen nicht mehr gedacht wissen** (ib., 1, 346, 3). Compare **219.** 5. A (last par.).

a. Instead of the simple uninflected form this objective predicate is in certain instances, as in case of nouns (see A. *b* and *c*), introduced by the particles **als** or **für: Wir betrachten die Sache als abgemacht. Er hält mich für reich.** The objective predicate here can also be a genitive or a prepositional phrase: **Ibsen hat die vier Werke, die er so selbst als einen Geistes empfand, in Christiania geschrieben** (Otto Brahm in *Die neue Rundschau*, 1906, p. 1433). **Sie versäumte nichts, um sich als klug und trefflichen Gemütes zu zeigen** (Enking's *Die Darnekower*, p. 306). **Der offiziöse Berliner Telegraph hält es für seines Dienstes, der Welt mitzuteilen, daß usw.** (*Hamburger Nachrichten*, Dec. 23, 1904). **Das Schlimmste aber ist, daß die heranwachsenden Kinder die ganze lottrige Wirtschaft für in Ordnung halten** (Frenssen's *Jörn Uhl*, chap. v).

Note 1. **Als** and **für** are more extensively used in case of certain adjectives than of nouns, as the simple adjective objective predicate may be mistaken for an adverb: **Er schalt mich heftig** = He scolded me severely, or He called me passionate. The ambiguity is removed by using **als** or **für**, or by converting the adjective into a substantive: **Er schalt mich als heftig,** or **Er schalt mich einen Heftigen.** Thus also, unless the context makes the thought clear, it is better to say **Ich erkläre euch für Freie** than **Ich erkläre euch frei.** Usage in general with regard to these particles is not entirely fixed. Some verbs take **als,** others **für,** still others both **als** and **für,** either with about the same meaning or a different shade, as in the following: **Die Preisrichter erkannten ihn als vorzüglicher, aber sie wollten ihn aus Rücksicht auf den mächtigen Mitbewerber nicht dafür erkennen.**

Note 2. Earlier in the period there were often no **als** and **für** here: **Unsittlich wie du bist, hältst du dich gut?** (Goethe's *Tasso*, 2, 3), now usually **für gut. Siehst du den Ring? Wie teuer hältst du ihn?** (Hebbel's *Gyges und sein Ring*, 1), now usually **Für wie teuer usw.**

C. An objective predicate infinitive is found after: **ahnen** to have a presentiment of, **bemerken** or **merken** to notice, **sich denken** to imagine to one's self, **empfinden** to feel, **erblicken** to notice, **finden** to find, **fühlen** to feel, **führen** to lead, **gewahren** to perceive, **glauben** to believe, **haben** to have, **hören** to hear, **lassen** to let, order, cause, **machen** to make, **schauen** to see, **sehen** to see, **spüren** to feel, **tragen** to carry, **treffen** to meet, **vernehmen** to hear, **wähnen** to imagine, **wiegen** to rock, **wissen** to know, **zeigen** to show. Exs.: **Ich höre ihn kommen** I hear him coming. **Ich lasse ihn kommen** (with active force) I shall have him come. **Ich lasse mir von ihm einen neuen Rock machen** (with passive force) I am having a new coat made by him. For other examples see **185.** B. I. 2. *d.* In some cases the infinitive here has developed from a present participle, which is still more or less frequently used. See **185.** B. I, 2. *d.* (**1**).

The modal verbal is also used as objective predicate after certain verbs. See **180.** A. *c.*

a. If the infin. should have as an object a pronoun of the same form as the object of the principal verb, one of the forms is usually suppressed in older German, but modern usage employs both forms or avoids the construction: **Laß uns eignen Wertes [uns] freuen** (Grillparzer's *Ahnfrau*, 1), or in prose: **Freuen wir uns eigenen Wertes!**

b. After some of these verbs a prep. phrase is often found as a predicate instead of an infinitive: **Ich sah ihn weinen,** or **in Tränen.**

c. In the eighteenth century the dative of the person instead of the acc. is frequently found after **lassen** and **machen,** especially the former, and sometimes after **sehen: Ein Geschenk, das mir jeden neuern Verlust ertragen machte** (Goethe an Karl August, I, 113). This construction is in part due to the influence of the analogous French expressions, as *faire voir quelque chose à quelqu'un*, and in part to the general tendency toward the dative of a person in connection with the accusative of a thing. This usage still lingers on in the literature of our time: **Er ging aber vergeblich die Fremdenliste durch und war endlich froh, die Insel, der er seine Mißstimmung entgelten ließ, nach zweitägigem Aufenthalt wieder verlassen zu können** (Fontane's *Cécile*, chap. xvii). In general this incorrect construction is avoided now in choice language.

In the reflexive expression **sich etwas merken lassen** *to betray, show, "let on,"* the dat. of the person is now much more common than the older acc.: **Laß dir** (or **dich**) **nichts davon gegen ihn merken** Don't let on to him. **Ich fürchtete mich so sehr als die andern, ließ mich es aber**

nicht merken (Goethe). **Doch ließ ich mir nichts merken.** (id.). **Ich fürchte, ich habe mir merken lassen, wie widerwärtig mir das alles war** (Spielhagen's *Frei geboren*, p. 35). The **es** in such expressions as in the first sentence from Goethe is in reality not an accusative, but an old genitive (**140.** *c*) of specification, which was not infrequent in early N.H.G.: **Ich ließ mich dessen nicht merken, daß ich's verstünde** (*Buch der Liebe*, 194[d], Frankfurt, 1587), literally *I did not allow myself to be observed with regard to that.* The genitive form es is now construed as an accusative, and hence the original construction is no longer understood and the thought has become obscure, which naturally leads to the use of the dative of reference here: **Ich ließ mir es nicht merken,** literally *I did not allow it to be observed on me.* The acc. of the thing here is omitted after a comparative: **Diese Erkenntnis war denn auch meinem Onkel viel eher gekommen, als er sich merken ließ** (R. Huch's *Ludolf Ursleu*, chap. xxi).

In some expressions the acc. or dat. of the person may be used, but with quite different meaning: **Er ließ mich vorlesen** *He had me to read to him*, but **Er ließ mir vorlesen** *He had someone to read to me.*

Provincially the nom. often occurs here instead of the acc. of the person: **Jahne: Na, Indrik! Trembe fragt schon nach dir. Indrik: Laß er fragen** (Keyserling's *Ein Frühlingsopfer*, 2). This peculiar idiom is the result of the blending of two constructions: **Er mag fragen** and **Laß ihn fragen.**

IV. Accusative of the Person or Thing and a Prepositional Phrase.

This is a very common type: which is growing at the expense of the other types, as can be seen by a careful study of the preceding articles: **Er legte den Hut auf den Tisch.** In the passive the accusative becomes nominative and the prepositional phrase remains: **Der Hut wurde auf den Tisch gelegt.**

A number of the most common verbs which take an accusative and a prepositional object are listed below along with the preposition or prepositions which each word requires. The selection has been made with regard to idiomatic difficulties that beset English-speaking students of German.

abhärmen: sich — über (with acc.) to grieve at, about.

abhärten: sich or **einen — gegen** to inure one's self or someone to.

ablegen: Rechnung — von or **über** (with acc.) to give (or render) an account of.

abnehmen, see **ziehen.**

abrichten: einen Hund, Pferd — zu and sometimes **auf** (with acc.) to train a dog, horse for some particular performance: **Er richtet das Pferd zum Reiten, den Hund zur Jagd, aufs Apportieren ab.**

absehen: es — auf (with acc.) to aim at, have designs upon: **Er hat es auf meinen Geldbeutel abgesehen. Das Unglück hat es auf mich abgesehen.**

adressieren: einen Brief — an (with acc.) to address a letter to.

andrängen: einen — an (with acc.) to press, push one against.

anheften to fasten on (with tacks, nails, &c.): **man heftet ein Bild an die Wand,** but without prep. obj. **er hat das Bild schon angeheftet.**

anklagen: einen — bei to bring action against someone before; **einen — wegen** to charge one with: **einen wegen schweren Diebstahls anklagen.** See also II. A. *a.*

anklammern to cling to: **Das Kind klammert sich immer an die Mutter,** but without prep. obj. **Da hat es sich wieder angeklammert.**

anstellen: eine Untersuchung — über (with acc.) to examine, inquire into.

anwenden to apply, direct to a definite end: **Wende alle deine Kraft zur Ausbildung deines Geistes an;** *fig.* apply: **Die Theorie auf die Praxis —.**

ärgern: sich — über (with acc.) to be vexed at.

aufwenden to spend money, time, effort upon: **Geld für seinen Garten, seine Kräfte für eine große Aufgabe —.**

aufziehen: einen mit etwas or **jemandem —** to tease someone about something or someone.

ausdehnen: etwas — auf (with acc.) to extend to, apply to: **Wir dürfen die Regel auf jenen Fall nicht ausdehnen.**

ausgeben: etwas — für to expend something for.

ausgießen: etwas — über (with acc.) to pour something out upon.

ausschelten: einen — wegen to upbraid someone for.

aussprechen: sich — zu einem (or **gegen einen**) **über** (with acc.) to have a good talk with someone about; **ein Urteil — über einen** to pronounce a sentence upon someone.

austauschen: etwas — für (or **gegen** or **mit**) to exchange something for.

austeilen: etwas — an (with acc.) to distribute something among, portion out to.

balgen: sich — um to grapple, fight for.

befähigen: einen — zu to fit, qualify one for.

befestigen: einen, etwas — an (with acc.) to fasten someone, something to.

befragen: einen — über (with acc.) to question someone upon; **sich wegen** or **in einer Sache bei einem —** to inquire of someone about.

begegnen to coincide: **sich** (acc.) **mit einem in einem Wunsche, in einer Ansicht —. Ihre Wünsche, Ansichten begegnen sich** (dat.).

beglückwünschen: einen — zu to compliment someone upon.

begrüßen: sich mit einem — to exchange greetings with.

beklagen: sich bei einem über etwas (acc.) **—** to complain to someone of.

bekleiden: einen or **sich — mit** to put on: **Ich habe mich nur mit einem dünnen Rock bekleidet.**

bekümmern: sich — über (with acc.) or **wegen** to be concerned, worried about something or someone; **sich —** or **kümmern um** to concern one's self about, with: **Er bekümmert** or **kümmert sich um alles. Bekümmern** or **kümmern Sie sich um sich!** Mind your own business! **Er bekümmert** or **kümmert sich gar nicht um mich** He never comes to see me any more, doesn't seem to know that I am alive. **Er ist über mich, über den Verlust bekümmert** He is worried, &c. Compare **kümmern,** II. A. *b*, *c*, B. *d* above.

belästigen: einen — wegen, mit to trouble someone about, bother him with.

belaufen: sich — auf (with acc.) to amount to: **Die Kosten belaufen sich auf einen Taler.**

belustigen; sich — mit to amuse one's self with; **sich — über einen** to amuse one's self at the expense of someone, to make fun of someone.

bemühen: sich um jemandes Gunst — to court a person's favor; **sich um eine Stelle —** to try to obtain, secure a position; **sich für einen —** to interest one's self for someone; **sich zu einem —** to take the trouble to go to: **Es tut mir leid, daß Sie sich haben zu mir bemühen müssen.**

beneiden or **neiden** to envy: **Ich (be)neide dir dein Glück,** or more commonly **Ich beneide dich um dein Glück.**

benennen: einen — nach to name someone after; **einen mit einem Spitznamen —** to give one a nickname; **das Kind beim rechten Namen —** to give a thing its right name.

beordern: eine Maschine auf rückwärts — to order the engine to be reversed.

beraten: sich — mit einem über (with acc.) to take counsel with someone about.

berufen: sich — auf (with acc.) to appeal to.

beschirmen: einen — vor (with dat.) to shield one from.

beschränken: sich — auf (with acc.) to confine, limit one's self to.

beschützen: einen — vor (with dat.) to protect one from.

beschwatzen: einen — um to talk one out of.

besprechen: sich mit einem über etwas (acc.) — to confer with someone about.

betören: einen — um to fool one out of.

betrüben: sich — über (with acc.) to grieve at, over.

betrügen: einen — um to cheat one out of. See also II. A. *a* above.

beugen: sich — vor (with dat.) to bend, bow to.

bewahren: einen — vor (with dat.) to preserve one from.

bewerben: sich — um to apply for (a situation, &c.), compete for (a prize), woo, canvass for (votes).

bewundern: einen — wegen to admire one for.

beziehen: etwas or **sich — auf** (with acc.) to refer to: **Ich bezog diese Anspielung auf einen Vorfall der neuesten Zeit. Ich bezog mich auf dich. Diese Bemerkung bezieht sich wohl auf ihn.**

bilden: etwas — aus to fashion something out of; **etwas — nach** to model something after.

binden: etwas — an (with acc.) to bind something to.

bitten: einen — um to ask, beg someone for.

brauchen: etwas — zu to need something for.

bringen: etwas — über (with acc.) to bring something upon: **Du hast nur Unglück über mich gebracht; einen — um** to cause someone to lose: **Er hat mich um meinen guten Namen gebracht.**

bücken: sich — vor (with dat.) to bow down to.

drehen: sich — um to turn, hinge upon: **Alles dreht sich um diesen Punkt.**

duzen: sich — mit to be on such familiar terms with as to use the address **du.**

eindrängen: sich — bei, in (with acc.) to intrude upon, thrust one's self upon: **Du hast dich bei uns, in unseren Kreis eingedrängt.**

einführen: einen — bei, in (with acc.) to introduce to (someone's family), into: **Er hat mich bei ihr, bei Hofe eingeführt. Er will dich in unsere Gesellschaft einführen.**

einigen: sich — über (with acc.) to agree upon.

einlassen: sich auf eine Schlacht — to engage in battle. **Ich lasse mich darauf nicht ein** I shall have nothing to do with it.

einmengen: sich — in (with acc.) to meddle with.

einrichten nach to suit to, regulate by, conform to: **Er richtet seine Ausgaben nach seinem Einkommen ein. Er richtet sein Leben nach dem von ihm erwählten Muster ein.**

einschiffen: sich — nach to embark for.

einschwören: sich — auf (with acc.) to swear by, have implicit faith in: **Auch ist sie** (Helene Böhlau) **ein viel zu selbständiger Geist, um sich auf irgend ein metaphysisches Credo einzuschwören** (Max Krieg in *Nord und Süd*, May 1905, p. 335).

eintauschen: etwas — für (or **gegen** or **um**) to take something in exchange for.

empfinden: Ekel — vor (with dat.) to sicken at, be disgusted with.

entlassen: einen — aus to discharge one from (office, &c.). See also II. A. *a*.

entnehmen: etwas — aus to gather, learn something from: **Wir entnehmen (aus) Ihrem Briefe, daß usw.**

entscheiden: sich — für to decide, fix upon: **Wir entscheiden uns für einen anderen Plan; sich — für einen** to decide in favor of someone.

entschließen: sich — zu to resolve upon: **Ich entschloß mich endlich zur Reise;** to fix one's choice upon: **Ich habe mich für diese Wohnung entschlossen.** Compare II. A. *b*.

entschuldigen: sich — bei to make excuse, apologize to; **sich — wegen** to excuse one's self for.

ergreifen: Besitz — von to seize upon.

erheben: einen Anspruch — auf (with acc.) to lay claim to; **Steuern — von** to levy taxes upon.

erkennen: einen — an (with dat.) to recognize one by.

erkundigen: sich — bei einem nach to inquire of one for, about; **Ich hatte mich bei ihm nach der Ursache erkundigt.**

erraten: etwas — aus to guess, divine something from.

ertappen: einen auf (also **bei, in,** sometimes **über, ob) der Tat —** to catch a person in the very act.

erwähnen: einen mit Namen — to mention someone by name.
erwecken: einen aus dem Schlafe — to arouse one from sleep.
erzürnen: sich — mit einem to fall out with someone.
fesseln: einen — an (with acc.) to fetter to; also to confine to: **Die Gicht fesselt ihn ans Bett.**
finden: Vergnügen — an (with dat.) to find pleasure in; **sich — in** (with acc.) to reconcile one's self to: **Finde dich in deinen Beruf, in das Unglück.**
folgern: etwas — aus to infer something from.
fordern (emphasizing the idea of a right to demand) or **verlangen** (emphasizing the idea of a desire to demand) to demand: **Ich fordere Gerechtigkeit von Ihnen. Ich habe von ihm** (formerly and sometimes still also **an ihn**) **noch 100 Mark zu fordern. Fordere ihn doch vor die Pistole, vors Gericht! Ich verlange nichts Unbilliges von dir. Jene Mischung der geistigen Kräfte, die wir von dem** (formerly and sometimes still also **an den**) **humoristischen Schriftsteller verlangen.**
fragen: einen — nach einer Sache, or **über** or **um eine Sache,** or **wegen einer Sache** to ask someone about a matter, or sometimes **von einem etwas fragen; einen um Erlaubnis —** to ask someone for permission; **einen um Rat fragen** to ask someone's advice. Compare **bitten** *to ask,* which has a different meaning.
fügen: sich — in (with acc.) to fit one's self into, reconcile one's self to, yield, submit to: **Er fügt sich in die Umstände.**
fürchten: sich — vor (with dat.) to be afraid of.
gewöhnen: sich — an (with acc.) to accustom one's self to, get used to.
grämen: sich — über (with acc.) to grieve over, worry about, over.
gravieren: einen Namen — auf or **in** (with acc.) to engrave a name upon.
gründen: sich or **etwas — auf** (usually with acc., sometimes with dat.) to found one's self or something upon: **Das gründet sich auf einen Irrtum.**
haben: Anteil — an (with dat.) to have a share in; **Mangel — an** (with dat.) to be in want of; **die Oberhand — über** (with acc.) to hold sway over; **Überfluß — an** (with dat.) to have plenty of; **einen in Verdacht —** to suspect one.
halten: etwas an das Feuer — to hold something close to the fire; **etwas auf (dem) Lager —** to keep something in stock; **viel** or **große Stücke auf einen —,** or **viel von einem** or **einer Sache —** to think highly, much of someone or something; **etwas gegen das Licht —** to hold something up to the light; **wenig, nichts von einem, von einer Sache —** to think little, nothing of, despise someone or something; **sich an** (now with acc., formerly dat.) **die Wahrheit, die Tatsachen, seinen Glauben —** to keep, hold to, &c.; **einen bei dem Versprechen —.**
hängen: etwas — an (with acc.) to hang something on.
hassen: einen — wegen to hate one for.
herauswickeln: sich — aus to extricate one's self from.
herausziehen: etwas — aus to extract something from, take something out of: **einen Splitter aus dem Finger herausziehen; sich — aus** to get out of, extricate one's self from: **Ich habe mich aus der Schlinge herausgezogen.**
hindern: einen — an (with dat.) to hinder, keep from: **Du hinderst mich am Arbeiten.**
hinweisen: einen hinweisen auf (with acc.) to direct or refer a person to: **Ich habe ihn auf den rechten Weg, auf seine Fehler hingewiesen.**
hören: etwas — von or **über** (with acc.) to hear something of, about.
hüten: sich — vor (with dat.) to beware of, be on one's guard against.
interessieren: einen an einem Geschäft — to induce one to take an interest, share in a business; **einen für etwas (z. B. die Botanik) —** to interest one in something (as botany); **sich für etwas —** to take an interest in something (as botany, &c.).
ketten: etwas — an (with acc.) to chain something to.
kümmern, see **bekümmern** above.
küssen: sich — mit to exchange kisses with.
leimen: etwas — an (with acc.) to glue to.
loben: einen — wegen to praise one for.
machen: sich — an (with acc.): **Er macht sich an die Arbeit** He sets to work: **sich — auf** (with acc.): **Er macht sich auf den Weg** He sets out on his way; **Anspruch — auf** (with acc.) to lay claim to; **sich beliebt — bei** to ingratiate one's self with; **Einwendungen — gegen** to make, raise objections to; **einen unfähig — zu** to unfit one for; **sich verdient — um** to deserve well of: **Er hat sich um das Vaterland verdient gemacht.**
mengen or **mischen: sich — in** (with acc.) to meddle with.
mischen: sich — unter (with acc.) to mingle with.
nageln: etwas — an (with acc.) to nail to.
necken: einen mit jemandem — to tease one about someone; **sich mit jemandem —** to exchange good-natured railleries with someone.
nehmen: Anstoß — an (with dat.) to take offense at; **Interesse — an** (with dat.) to take an interest in someone or something; **Anteil — an** (with dat.) to take an interest in, sympathize with; **einen beim Worte nehmen.**
neiden, see **beneiden.**
neigen: sich — auf (with acc.) to be inclined in favor of: **Ich neigte mich auf seine Seite; (sich) — zu** to lean to: **Ich neige mich zu seiner Meinung. Er neigt zur Erkältung** he catches cold easily; **sich — vor** (with dat.) to bow to.
nennen to call: **Das Kind beim rechten Namen —** to call the thing by the right name; **einen mit Namen** or **bei seinem Namen —**
packen: etwas in eine Kiste packen.
prügeln: sich mit einem — to have a fight with.
rächen: sich — an (with dat.) to avenge one's self on.
reiben: sich — an (with dat., sometimes, especially earlier in the period, with acc.) to rub against: **Die Schweine reiben sich an den Bäumen** or **an die Bäume.**

richten: etwas — an (with acc.) to address (a letter, &c.) to; **eine Frage — an einen** to put a question to someone; **etwas — auf** (with acc.) to direct, point something at; **sich — nach** to conform to, regulate one's conduct by: **Er richtet sich nach dem Gesetz. Das Verbum richtet sich** (agrees) **nach** (with) **dem Subjekt. Ich richte mich ganz nach dir, nach meinem Gaste.**

rümpfen: Die Nase — über (with acc.) to turn up the nose at.

runzeln: die Stirne — über (with acc.) to frown at.

schätzen: etwas — auf (with acc.) to estimate something at: **Ich schätze das Alter des Kindes auf einen Monat.**

schelten: einen — wegen to scold someone for.

schicken: einen in einem Auftrag — to send someone on an errand; **einen in den April —** to april-fool someone; **sich in etwas —** to adapt one's self to: **Er schickt sich in alle Verhältnisse.**

schlagen: etwas ans schwarze Brett — to post, placard something; **sich mit einem auf Säbel, auf Pistolen —** to fight a duel with.

schließen: einen an die Brust schließen to clasp one to one's bosom. **Hieran schließen wir die Bemerkung, daß usw.** To this we would add that, &c.

schmiegen: sich — vor (with dat.) to cringe to.

schreiben: einen Brief — an (with acc.) to write to (a person); **einen Brief — nach** to write to (a place); **sich mit einem —** to correspond with.

schützen: einen — vor (with dat.) to protect someone from.

sehnen: sich — nach to long for.

stecken: etwas in Brand — to set something on fire.

stehen: sich mit einem gut — to be on good terms with someone. **Er steht sich gut dabei** He is not a loser by it, he has profited by the transaction.

stoßen: einen — an (with acc.) to push someone against.

stützen: sich — auf (with acc.) to lean upon, rely upon, be based upon.

suchen: Hast du was an mich zu suchen? (Hebbel's *H. und M.*, 4, 3), now usually **Hast du etwas von mir zu erbitten?**

tadeln: einen — wegen to censure someone for.

taxieren: etwas — auf (with acc.) to estimate something at: **Ich taxiere den Wert auf einen Taler.**

tragen to entertain (thoughts, &c.): **Er trägt sich mit Selbstmordgedanken. Er trägt sich mit der Absicht, sein Geschäft aufzugeben.**

trennen: sich von einem — to part with or from somebody; **sich von etwas —** to part with something: **Ich kann mich nur schwer davon trennen.**

tun: Eingriffe — in (with acc.) to encroach upon.

überschütten: einen — mit to pour, shower something upon: **Beide Gegner überschütten sich mit Schrapnells.**

unterhalten: sich — über (with acc.) to converse about.

verbergen: einen — vor (with dat.) to conceal someone from.

verbreiten: sich — über (with acc.) to expatiate upon: **Ich will mich des weiteren über diesen Fall nicht verbreiten.**

vergehen: sich an einem — to do someone a wrong; **sich tätlich an einem —** to offer violence to someone, inflict bodily injury upon someone.

verhaften: einen — wegen to arrest someone for; **einen auf frischer Tat —** to arrest someone in the very act (of stealing, &c.).

verhängen: eine Strafe — über (with acc.) to inflict a punishment upon.

verheiraten, vermählen to give in marriage, marry: **Ich habe mich, meinen Sohn mit unserer Nachbarin,** or **an unsere Nachbarin,** or in rather choice language with the simple dat. **unserer Nachbarin verheiratet, vermählt.**

verkaufen to sell: **Verkaufe dich niemals dem** (or **an den**) **Teufel für** (or **um**) **alles Geld. Er verkaufte es mit Verlust.**

verklagen: jemanden wegen Verleumdung — to prosecute someone for libel; **jemanden auf Schadenersatz —** to sue someone for damages.

verkleiden: sich in einen Bettler, or **sich als Bettler** or **als ein(en) Bettler —** to disguise one's self as a beggar.

verkuppeln to persuade to an ill-sorted marriage: **Er verkuppelte das Mädchen an den Wüstling,** or less commonly **er verkuppelte das Mädchen dem Wüstling.**

verladen: Waren — nach to ship goods to.

verlangen, see **fordern.**

verlassen: sich — auf (with acc.) to rely upon.

verlässigen: sich — über (with acc.) to make sure of, convince one's self of: **Es ist nicht zu bestreiten, daß der Staat das Recht hat, sich als Arbeitgeber über die Leistungen des Arbeitnehmers zu verlässigen** (W. A. Lay's *Experimentelle Didaktik*, p. 456).

verlieben: sich — in (with acc.) to fall in love with.

verlieren to lose: **viel an jemandem —** to lose much in a person, to lose a good friend in him; **viel an jemanden —** to lose much in dealing or playing with someone; **viel bei jemandem —** to lose much in someone's estimation.

verloben, versprechen: sich — mit to become engaged to.

vermählen, see **verheiraten.**

vermögen: es über sich (acc.) **—** to bring one's self to: **Darum vermochte sie es über sich, geduldig zuzuhören und auszuharren.**

verraten to betray: **Du hast mich an den Gegner verraten. Ich darf dir das Geheimnis nicht verraten.**

verschieben: etwas auf einen anderen Tag — to put something off until another day.

verstecken: einen — vor (with dat.) to hide one from.

verstehen to understand: **sich — auf** (with acc.) to understand, be a judge of: **Er versteht sich auf Pferde; etwas aus dem Zusammenhang —** to understand something by, from the connection.

vertagen: sich — auf (with acc.) to adjourn until; **die Sitzung — auf** (with acc.).

vertauschen: etwas — gegen (für, mit, um) to exchange something for.

verteilen: etwas — an or **unter** (with acc.) to distribute something among: **Geld an** or **unter die Armen verteilen; etwas — auf**

(with acc.) to divide something up among: **Leistungen und Lasten auf die Bürgerschaft verteilen.**
verweisen: einen — auf (with acc.) to refer one to: **Ich verweise den Leser auf das, was ich früher gesagt habe.**
verwenden to spend on (a thing): **Er hat viel Geld, viel Zeit auf die Erziehung der Kinder verwandt.**
vorbereiten: sich — auf (with acc.) to prepare for (a speech, examination, an approaching ordeal); **sich — zu** to get ready for, make preparations for: **Ich habe mich zur Reise vorbereitet.**
warnen: einen — vor (with dat.) to warn someone against.
wegwerfen: sich — an (with acc.) to throw one's self away on.
weisen: einen — an (with acc.) to refer a person to: **Er hat mich an Sie, an die richtige Quelle gewiesen; einen — auf** (with acc.) to point out to: **Er wies mich auf den rechten Weg; einen — aus** to expel one from (school, &c.); **etwas von der Hand** or **von sich —** to decline something.
wenden: sich — an (with acc.) to apply to, turn to: **Er wandte sich an mich; etwas — an** or **auf** (with acc.) to spend something on.
wissen to know: **etwas auf** (against) or **gegen einen —; etwas aus** (from) **guter Quelle —; etwas aus** (*by*) **Erfahrung —; etwas von einem** or **etwas über, um einen** or **etwas —** to know something of, about, concerning someone or something.
ziehen or **abnehmen: den Hut vor einem —** to take off one's hat to someone.

V. Dative of the Person and a Prepositional Phrase.

This group is much smaller than the preceding one. A few illustrations follow: **Es fehlt mir an Geld. Es gebricht mir am Gelde** or **an Geld. Es genügt mir an deiner Liebe, an deinem Wohlwollen. Las dir an meiner Gnade genügen** (2 Cor. xii. 9). **Er gratulierte mir zur Beförderung. Er half mir bei der Arbeit. Er half mir über den ersten Schmerz. Ich habe ihm beim Tode des Vaters kondoliert. Wozu raten Sie mir? Ich traue ihm nicht um die Ecke. Er hat mir zu einer guten Stellung verholfen. Ich rate dir zur Amanda** (Auerbach's *Dorfgeschichten*, 8, p. 62) I advise you to choose A. A number of peculiar or idiomatic combinations which in a formal sense belong here have been treated in **258.** 1. C from another point of view.

In a number of words the prepositional phrase here represents an older simple gen.: **einem der Gabe danken,** now **einem für die Gabe danken; einem eines Dinges bürgen,** now **einem für ein Ding bürgen;** &c. A gen. is now only found in **sich** (originally acc., but now also dat.) **bei einem Rats erholen** (II. A. *b* above). Thus this gen. has almost disappeared, while the gen. in connection with an acc., as described in II. A. *b*, is fairly well preserved.

VI. Double Prepositional Object.

A verb quite frequently has a double prepositional object: **Sie klagt gegen ihn auf Ehescheidung** She is suing him for divorce. **Er trug bei seinem Vorgesetzten auf Beförderung an** He applied to his superior for promotion.

Synesis.

263. Different parts of speech, especially pronouns, often assume a different *gender* or *number* from that required by the strict rules of grammatical concordance, following in these points the *meaning* of the word in the particular use in question rather than the usual grammatical gender or number of the antecedent or the word to which reference is made. This assignment of gender and number according to meaning is called Synesis (i.e. understanding, sense).

I. *Synesis of Gender.* Words may assume their gender according to meaning in the following cases:

1. A neuter diminutive, or any other neut. or masc. word representing a female, such as **Weib, Weibchen, Weiblein, Fräulein, Frauenzimmer, Mädchen, Mädel, Mägdlein, Töchterlein, Töchterchen, Kind, Geschöpf,** and **Mensch,** require usually the article and any other attributive adj. standing before them and also the relative pronoun referring to them to be neut. or masc., but the personal pronouns, possessive adjectives, and all other adjectives, on the other hand, which refer to them are much more commonly fem. according to the sex of the person represented: **Das Fräulein ist nicht zu Hause; sie ist spazieren**

gegangen. Du böses Tantchen! Du bist das leutseligste Komteßchen, das es nur auf der Welt geben kann. Dieses Weib hat ihrem Gatten Kummer gemacht. Du schönste der Weiber! (Heyse's *Maria von Magdala*, 3, 10). **Aber du bist eine von den wenigen glücklichen Frauenzimmern** (M. Dreyer's *Winterschlaf*, 1). **Mutterchen, goldene — es ist wohl nichts?** (Marianne Mewis's *Mettes Kinder* in *Velhagen und Klasings Monatshefte*, Sept. 1905, p. 89). Altho synesis of gender is more common in this category than any other, present usage is inclining more and more to stricter grammatical concordance: **Es war keine andere Obhut für Lili geblieben, als die alte Haushälterin des Verstorbenen, ein auf seine „Bildung" stolzes, aber ungebildetes Weibchen** (Wilbrandt's *Vater Robinson*, II, chap. 1). **Sophie ist das schönste** (also **die schönste**) **der Mädchen. Er rief der Pritzke** (name) **. . . zu, sie solle nebenan dem Mädchen sagen, es möge aufstehn, er habe nachher mit ihm zu reden** (Telmann's *Wahrheit*, IX). **Anna sah die Tante zögernd an; da diese aber nur ein wenig lächelte, so tat das Mädchen, was ihm geboten war** (H. Seidel's *Die Augen der Erinnerung*, II). **Seit jenem Tage hatte ich nichts anderes mehr im Kopf als das Prinzeßchen und seinen Garten** (Isolde Kurz's *Nachbar Werner*). **Kannst du nicht ein bißchen nachhelfen, Mutterchen, einzigstes?** (M. Mewis's *M. K.* in *V. und K. M.*, Sept. 1905, p. 90).

a. In the expression **Ihr(e) Fräulein Tochter** *your* (unmarried) *daughter*, **Ihr(e) Fräulein Schwester**, &c., the possessive or article is perhaps more commonly neut.: **von Ihrem Fräulein Braut** (Spielhagen's *Herrin*, p. 258), **ein Fräulein Nichte** (H. Hoffmann's *Rittmeister*, p. 115), **Ihr Fräulein Tochter** (Sudermann's *Heimat* (twice in 4, 8), **Ihres Fräulein** (not **Fräuleins**) **Tochter** (Jensen's *Unter der Tarnkappe*, VI). The fem., however, is not infrequent, especially earlier in the period: **mit Ihrer Fräulein Tochter** (Schiller), **gegen deine Fräulein Schwester** (Raabe), **Ihre Fräulein Schwester** (H. Hoffmann), **die Hand Ihrer Fräulein Tochter** (Sudermann's *Heimat*, 4, 8). In colloquial language we often find the fem. article or the feminine form of the adjective here before a name: **die** (instead of the choicer **das**) **Fräulein Ehrhard. Gute Fräulein Marie!** (G. Keller an Marie Exner, June 17, 1874). The simple word **Fräulein** was formerly treated as a fem., and is sometimes still so used in popular language: **Nein, das war eine alte Fräul'n, die schon immer bei ihnen gewohnt hat** (Mizi in Schnitzler's *Liebelei*, Act I).

b. The synesis of the relative here was not uncommon earlier in the period, and is still found in popular speech, and sometimes even in the literary language: **Jenes Mädchen ist's, das vertriebene, die du gewählt hast** (Goethe's *H. und D.*, 4, 210). **Bitte, grüßen Sie das gnädige Fräulein, die so gut ist** (Frau Hulen in Fontane's *Vor dem Sturm*, IV, chap. vii). **Dieses kleine Mädchen hier, die ihr eigenes Herz noch nicht kennt** (Agnes Harder's *Franzinens Geschichte* in *Velhagen und Klasings Monatshefte*, April 1907, Roman-Bibliothek, p. 177). Synesis is more common in case of a second relative, as the pronoun does not immediately follow the antecedent, and the speaker or writer has the natural sex in mind rather than the grammatical gender of the antecedent: **Denn der Alte hatte ein Enkeltöchterchen bei sich, zu dem sie Pate gestanden und deren sie sich auf allerlei Art anzunehmen pflegte** (Storm's *In St. Jürgen*). We now usually find strict grammatical concordance here in choice language: **Wir haben da ein sehr zartes Frauchen, das eine Weile gepflegt werden muß** (H. Böhlau).

2. Diminutives of masc. common nouns representing males usually require grammatical concordance. They take the neut. article: **das Männlein, das Söhnlein**, &c. Pronouns referring to such nouns are as a rule neut., altho synesis often occurs: **Ein kleines schwarzes Männlein, welches auf der Bank an der anderen Seite der Tür saß** (Raabe's *Schüdderump*, chap. 1). The synesis of the personal pronoun becomes more common, the further it is removed from the noun to which it refers. The synesis of the relative occurs only in older literature: **Ein Kerlchen, den Frau Fortuna zu ihrem Liebling gedrechselt zu haben schien** (Klinger).

In dialect and popular language synesis may occur: **Den Wurstl** (i.e. **den kleinen Hanswurst**) **meinst?** (Storm's *Pole Poppenspäler*).

3. If a feminine or a neuter other than a diminutive represents a male, the same rule is now followed as is given in 2 for diminutives: **Als Seine Majestät, | der Kaiser, Ihren** (*his*) **mutigen Armeen | ein ruhmgekröntes, kriegserfahrnes Haupt | geschenkt in der Person des Herzogs Friedland** (Schiller's *Piccolomini*, 2, 7). **Fast drehte sich im kaiserlichen Lager | . . . um Heinrichs Jäger, Arzt, Roß, Hund und Federspiel | mehr das Gespräch als um die Majestät | des Kaisers selbst, die nie zur Tafel ging, | Heinrich von Aue schritt ihr denn zur**

Seite (Hauptmann's *Der arme Heinrich*, 2, p. 57). **Draußen rief er eine Ordonnanz und schärfte ihr ein, Leutnant von Edelfleth zu benachrichtigen, daß er gegangen sei** (Ompteda's *Sylvester von Geyer*, lviii). **Nun ward es eine untersetzte, breitrückige Mannsperson, deren Kleidung sich nicht deutlich unterscheiden ließ** (Jensen' *Schatzsucher*, p. 164). **Das Mitglied des Kongresses, das, &c.; die Schildwache, die vor der Tür steht.** Except in the case of the relative, synesis sometimes occurs: **Exzellenz zauberten uns hier einen seiner schönen Gärten** (Gutzkow).

4. The article, or a limiting or descriptive adjective, before the diminutive form of a proper name which represents a person has often natural gender in certain dialects, while other dialects are not unfriendly to the neut. gender: **die Liesel** (Anzengruber's *Kreuzelschreiber*, 3, 3), **die Sepherl** (ib., 2, 11), **der Tonl** (ib., 1, 3), **arme Liesel** (Anzengruber's *Gänseliesel*), **das Bärbele** (Auerbach's *Tonele*, chap. 1), **das arme Hannele** (Hauptmann's *Hanneles Himmelfahrt*, p. 75). Likewise common nouns when used as names: **die Mutterchen muß ihren Tee haben** (Schulze-Smidt's *Denk' ich an Deutschland in der Nacht*, II). **Der Herrchen darf nicht schelten** (ib.). The masc. form of the article is often used in the Swabian dialects before the diminutive of a name or a common class noun referring to a male. See **245.** I. 8. 1. *f. Note* 3. The neuter form of the article or a limiting or descriptive adjective is preferred in the literary language: **Das kleine Hänschen, du gutes Hänschen, mein kleines Dortchen.** In the literary language as well as in dialect all pronouns and possessives referring to diminutive names are quite commonly selected according to the natural gender except relatives, which usually in choice language follow the gender of the antecedent: **„Mutter, so viel Geld hast du bekommen!“ rief Lieschen, als sie auf dem Fensterbrett eine Reihe Silbermünzen liegen sah. Lieschen und ihre Mutter.** Sometimes the pronoun or the possessive is selected according to the grammatical gender: **Schweigend verbeugte sich Elslein, wofür ihm ein hochmütiges Nicken wurde. Was aus dem Korderl** (**Kordula** + **lein**) **seiner** (*her*) **Mutter und dem Herrn Ingenieur geworden, hatte ich nicht erfahren können** (P. Heyse's *Ein Idealist*). If there is an inflected adjective before the diminutive, synesis of the relative is not now common in the literary language, altho it occasionally occurs in case of reference to females: **das kleine Hänschen, das unter dem Baume sitzt. Das hübsche Lisettchen von Amberg, der** (instead of the more common **dem**) **das Kostüm des vorigen Jahrhunderts allerliebst zu Gesichte steht** (National-Zeitung, 28, 47). Synesis of the relative is, however, quite common even in case of masculines, if there is no inflected adjective before the diminutive: **Röschen, die der Mutter Freude war; Hänschen, der ein sehr guter Knabe ist.** But also here we sometimes find grammatical concordance: **Vrenchen, welches nur das eine zu fühlen fähig war** (Keller's *Romeo und Julie*).

5. If the word **Frau** stands before the title of the husband, the article agrees with **Frau** instead of with the title: **Die geehrte Frau Professor.**

6. Aside from the above cases, a noun, pronoun, or adjective-substantive representing a person usually has natural gender, but where the sex is a matter of doubt or little concern, as in case of children or the young of animals, the substantive is often neut., as this gender gives grammatical expression to the idea of vagueness: **Der Freund** (male) friend, **die Freundin** lady friend, **der Kranke** or **die Kranke**, but **das Kleine** the young child, **sein Kleinstes** his smallest child, **das Junge eines Schafes.**

a. After the indefinite pronouns **jemand, niemand, wer,** the following adjective-substantive is in the neut. or masc., to indicate that it may represent either a male or female. See **145,** *Notes* under *b, c,* and *e.*

b. The masc., less frequently the neut., is used in general references, referring to either males or females, or both, and also in cases where it is desired to emphasize the abstract idea in the word without reference to sex: **Teuer ist mir der Freund, doch auch den Feind kann ich nützen; zeigt mir der Freund, was ich kann, lehrt mich der Feind, was ich soll** (Schiller). **Der Gerechte wird seines Glaubens leben** (Romans i. 17). **Die Hütte scheint mir etwas zu eng. Für uns beide doch geräumig genug, versetzte Charlotte. Nun freilich, sagte Eduard, für einen Dritten**

ist auch wohl noch Platz. Warum nicht? versetzte Charlotte, und auch für ein Viertes (Goethe's *Die Wahlverwandtschaften*, chap. i). **Es ist ja kein Fremdes, das danach fragt, ich bin ja doch dein Kind** (Anzengruber's *Schandfleck*, 11). For an example of the use of the masc. for an abstract idea see **253.** III. 2. *a.* The neuter is also used to denote an abstract idea, but its use differs from that of the masculine. See **253.** III. 2. *a*, 2nd par. General references applying to either males or females are especially common in case of pronouns and pronominal adjectives. Here the masc. form is now usually found, but the neut. forms **es, das, dies, jedes, alles, keins, ein**(e)s, **was**, &c., are also found, especially in the cases recorded in II. 4 below: **Es ist keiner vor dem Tode glücklich zu preisen, denn jeder ist dem Wechsel des Schicksals unterworfen. Vater und Mutter sind jedes ein Mensch für sich, und die Menschen sind verschieden** (Wildenbruch's *Neid*). **Knaben, Männer und Frauen, keins blieb unberührt** (Goethe). **Wenn ich nur eines meiner eigenen Angehörigen jetzt bei mir hätte!** (Auerbach). **Gesehen habe ich von meinen Großeltern keines** (Hermann Stehr's *Drei Nächte*, p. 48). **Früh übt sich, was ein Meister werden will** (Schiller). For fuller description of the use of **was** see **157.** *b.* There is sometimes a shade of difference between the neut. and masc. of some of these words, the former having collective, the latter individualizing force: **Und jedes** (each and all of the brothers and sisters) **quälte seine Phantasie, | mit einem neuen Reize dich zu schmücken. | Der gab dir Pallas' Aug', der Heres Arm, | der Aphroditens reizdurchwirkten Gürtel** (Grillparzer's *Sappho*, 1, 3). Instead of a masc. or neut. sometimes both masc. and fem. are used to emphasize especially the idea that both sexes are included: **Keiner und keine bleibe daheim** (Rosegger). **Diesen hier mußte wohl jeder und jede schön finden** (Spielhagen's *Frei geboren*, p. 148). **In dem Schlafrock mußt du dich photographieren lassen, dann widersteht dir niemand und keine!** (Wildenbruch's *Schwester-Seele*, chap. XV).

c. When a pronoun refers to no definite noun, but to a general or indefinite idea, the neuter is used: **Er meint es gut mit dir. Er hat es bequem. „Die Erfüllung ist an eine Bedingung geknüpft." „Welche Bedingung? sage mir's"** (Freytag). The **es** here cannot refer to the fem. **Bedingung**, but to the unknown purport of the condition.

d. A demonstrative pronoun used as the subject or object of a verb and referring to a preceding individual usually agrees in the literary form of speech with its antecedent in gender, but colloquially the neuter is often used without reference to the antecedent: **Ich kenne deinen Vater wohl: der** (colloquially **das**) **ist ein braver Mann. Sind sonst wackre Brüder. Aber das denkt wie ein Seifensieder.**

7. The relative is neuter if the reference is to a fem. noun denoting an indefinite quantity: **Fräulein Hermann wußte eine Menge** (= **viel**) **über Goethe zu sagen, das nicht ganz dem entsprach, was Professor von Rangenhofen vorgetragen hatte** (Ompteda's *Cäcilie von Sarryn*, chap. 18).

8. Sometimes the predicate noun does not assume a grammatical form in accordance with the natural sex of the person represented by the subject. See **253.** III. 2. *a.*

9. In the expression **seinerzeit** *in his* (or *her*, *their*, *my*, *our*) *time* the possessive may remain constant without reference to the gender of the antecedent. See **138.** 2. *a.*

II. *Synesis of Number.* The number of a word may be regulated by the sense instead of by the rules of grammatical concordance in the following categories:

1. The cases where the number of the verb is regulated by the sense are described in **253.** I. 1. *d*, *g* and 2. *c*, *d*.

2. In the earlier part of the period a personal pronoun (**er, sie, es, derselbe, solch-**) is not infrequently in the pl. if it refers to a sing. noun containing a collective idea: **Den Teufel spürt das Völkchen nie, | und wenn er sie beim Kragen hätte!** (Goethe's *Faust*, Auerbachs Keller). This usage continues in our own time, but the trend toward strict grammatical concordance has become very strong, so that the sing. here is now more common in the literary language. Synesis is, however, still quite common when the pronoun refers to a noun in the sing. representing not an individual but a whole class: **Ich hatte mir . . . eingebildet . . ., auf dem Bock säße der Tod in einem schwarzen, flatternden Mantel, auf seinem klappernden Schädel einen blanken, niedrigen Hut, wie ich solche an unseren Droschkenkutschern zu sehen gewohnt war** (R. Huch's *Ludolf Ursleu*, chap. 26).

Synesis of the possessive was common earlier in the period: **Da riß alles Volk seine goldenen Ohrringe von ihren Ohren** (Luther). **Ein echter deutscher Mann mag keinen Franzen leiden, | doch ihre Weine trinkt er gern** (Goethe's *Faust*, Auerbachs Keller). This usage still continues: **Wenn wir Deutsche nach Frankreich gehen, so lernen wir vorher die Sprache ihres Landes** (Riehl).

The trend to-day is decidedly toward strict grammatical concordance or toward the avoidance of a conflict by changing the construction: **Die Treue des Volkes zu seinem König.**

Synesis of the relative occurs earlier in the period: **Denn der HERR hat dis Geschlecht | vber die er zornig ist | verworffen vnd verstossen** (Jer. vii. 29). **Des Hauses Espinay —, die nicht in den Krieg zögen, um reich zu werden** (Schiller). To-day the synesis of the relative is in the strict sense almost unknown. For an instance see **253. I. 1.** *g.* It is usually only used when the relative stands in a loose relation to its antecedent, introducing a free and independent statement with reference to either a preceding collective idea contained in a sing. noun together with its modifying adjective, or with reference to a noun in the sing. representing not an individual but a whole class: **Manches aufstrebende Talent, deren einige nunmehr zu Ruf und Ruhm gelangt sind. Jeder Witz, an denen er es nicht fehlen ließ, wurde stürmisch belacht. Ist's nicht ein Mönch, deren du tausende sahst?**

3. Sometimes we find a plural pronoun referring to a noun which is sing. in form, but which in the passage in question by its synecdochical or metonymic use represents a plural idea: **Das edle Weib ist halb ein Mann, ja ganz, erst ihre Fehler machen sie zu Weibern** (Grillparzer's *Die Jüdin von Toledo*). **Rußland sucht sein Gebiet in Asien zu erweitern; sie sind abermals vorgerückt.** While this usage continues in our own day the trend is toward strict grammatical concordance or toward avoidance of a conflict by changing the construction.

On the other hand, a singular noun is often used distributively with reference to several individuals: **Die Herren zündeten sich eine Zigarre an** (Ompteda's *Eysen*, II, 29). Other examples in **96. 12.** It is necessary, however, to observe caution here as this usage is limited. Thus we say: **Die Kinder nehmen die Bücher** (not **das Buch**) **vor** and *may* say: **Die Herren zündeten sich Zigarren an.**

4. The neuter sing. of a pronoun or adjective-substantive is often used without reference to the sex or the number of the persons or things referred to:

a. **Alles** is used to give the general idea of universality, including males and females, young and old: **Alles freut sich der Frühlingszeit** Everybody rejoices in spring. **Alles** (everybody) **war entzückt. Alles rät ihm, ein milderes Klima zu suchen. Heute ist Familientag, und dazu muß alles da sein, was unseren Namen trägt** (Ompteda's *Eysen*).

b. **Jedes** is used to indicate that the statement applies to all the members of a certain group, both males and females: **Vater und Mutter sind jedes ein Mensch für sich und die Menschen sind verschieden** (Wildenbruch's *Neid*, Werke, VI, p. 161). **Der Pfarrer hat doch prächtig gepredigt. Da hat sich jedes was herausnehmen können, sei es ledig oder verheiratet** (Auerbach's *Edelweiß*, XVI). The masc. sing. is also often used here.

c. Also **das, dies,** and **es** are used collectively, embracing a number of things previously mentioned or pointed out by gesture: **Gold und Schätze, Macht und Hoheit, das begehre ich nicht. Schönheit, Ehre, Reichtum, dies alles ist vergänglich. Es** is used here quite often in subordinate clauses introduced by **als** (or **als wenn** or **als ob**): **Sie sprach mit ihren Steinen oft, als wären es belebte Wesen** (Wilhelm Fischer's *Die Freude am Licht*, II, p. 19).

d. **Das** is often used referring to individuals, not as such, but as members of *one class*: **Schon so große Töchter hast du? Wie das heranwächst!** Are your daughters so large already? Well, how girls do grow! See also **129. 2. C. (3).**

e. The neut. sing. **beides** is used in a collective sense, including both of two things: **Ich habe beides, Brief und Paket richtig erhalten. Sommer und Winter trug sie ein schmieriges, schwarzseidenes Fransentüchlein um den Kopf und einen verschossenen, türkischen Schal um die Schultern, beides sorgfältig nach hinten ins Dreieck gelegt** (Isolde Kurz's *Das Vermächtnis der Tante Susanne*).

f. The neut. indefinite **eins** (or the masc. form **einer**) often stands after the gen. pl. of a personal pronoun to indicate that the different persons of the class referred to in the personal pronoun, whether they be males or females, are included in the statement, and that not a mere reference to one is intended: **Wenn unsereins** (or very commonly **unsereiner) am Spinnen war, | . . . stand sie bei ihrem Buhlen süß** (Goethe's *Faust*, Am Brunnen) When we (here: hard-working girls like you and me) used to be, &c. Sometimes the fem. form is used to make a distinct reference to females: **Wahrscheinlich zu alt, zu erhaben über ein armes Ding wie ich, um vernünftig mal über eine Sache mit unsereiner . . . zu reden** (Raabe's *Gutmanns Reisen*, chap. 17).

g. An adjective-substantive is often used in the neut. sing. to indicate in a general way the idea of a collection or indefinite number of things: **Man hört viel Gutes und viel Dummes** We hear many good and foolish things. **Er hat mir viel Liebes und Gutes erwiesen.** See also **109.** *a.* (2). For the use of **das, was,** and **es** in a collective sense see **153. 1. (1); 157** and *b* thereunder; **141.** 9. *a.* For the number of the predicate appositive after **was** see **157.** *c.*

h. **Das, dies, es, jenes,** are often used as subjects referring to one or several, to a masc., fem., or neut., whenever they represent the thing or things pointed out by a gesture or the context as identical with the thing or things indicated by the predicate: **Das ist mein Buch. Das sind meine Bücher. Die unbekannte Wohltäterin, von der ihr sprachet, das ist diese Frau. Es sind meine Brüder** They are my brothers. Here the gesture or preceding words always make the reference so clear that close grammatical concordance does not seem necessary.

i. The neut. pronominal forms **es, das, was,** often stand as a predicate, referring to a masc., fem., or neut., a sing. or pl.: **Sie hält sich für eine große Künstlerin, ohne es zu sein** She thinks she is a great artist, although she is not. **Wir hofften willkommene Gäste zu sein, und wir waren es wirklich** We hoped to be welcome guests and we were indeed so. **Er ist ein Gelehrter; das ist sein Bruder nicht. Was ist seine Schwester? Eine Schauspielerin.** Here these pronouns do not refer to the sex of the persons denoted by their antecedents, but rather to the general abstract idea contained within these antecedents, hence the lack of literal grammatical concordance with the words to which they refer and the selection of the neuter form.

5. In the expression **seinerzeit** *in his* (or *her, their, my, our*) *time* the possessive may remain constant without reference to the number of the antecedent. See **138.** 2. *a.*

Adverbial Modifiers.

264. Adverbial modifiers assume the form of simple uninflected adverbs, nouns in an oblique case, a prepositional phrase, or a clause: **Große Seelen dulden still. Frohen Mutes trat er herein. Sie weinte vor Freude. Während wir schliefen, brach der Sturm los.** This subject is treated at considerable length under the head of Adverbs, beginning at **223.** The adverbial clause is treated in **273–282.**

The adverb, as indicated by its literal meaning *joined to a verb*, is an appositive to a verb, i.e. is placed before or after a verb to explain its meaning in the case at hand more clearly, much as an adjective as an appositive is placed before or after a noun to explain it: **Das Mädchen zürnt sehr.** This same form is similarly used as an appositive to an adjective or another adverb and here is also called an adverb altho of course it is here not true to its name: **Das Mädchen ist sehr schön. Das Mädchen singt sehr schön.** An adverbial element, tho usually different in meaning from a genitive, dative, accusative, or prepositional object, always performs the same function, i.e. serves as an appositive to a verb or adjective, and often, as explained in **261** (3rd par.), is closely related in meaning to the object, often even so closely that it is confounded with it, as illustrated in **185.**

Independent Elements.

265. Independent elements are words, phrases, or clauses, which are not related grammatically to other parts of the sentence, or which stand all alone without filling any grammatical office. In some cases these elements are in fact grammatically independent, while in others they are only seemingly so, as they in reality belong to some word understood. A historical study of these constructions shows clearly that most of them were originally dependent. The following are the most important classes of such elements:

A. *Direct Address.* The name of a person who is called is often spoken alone without other words. Like interjections (**241**) such names are independent sentences of a primitive type, which, tho a single word, can in connection with the situation and an appropriate accent convey a thought, as in **Fritz!** spoken in loud tone and prolonged vowel to call him into the house, or **Fritz!** spoken quickly with a short vowel and angry tone when we scold him. See **250.** *a.* They are also often inserted in a modern sentence without grammatical relations to the other words: **Kinder, ich habe euch allen etwas mitgebracht.** Such words now stand in the nom., in an earlier period, however, they stood in a distinct case, called the *vocative.*

B. *Absolute Construction.* Words are often used *absolutely,* that is, without a grammatical connection with any other word in the sentence. This construction may assume different forms:

a. An uninflected participle may be used absolutely, with the force of a subordinate adverbial clause which has a subject of a general meaning: **Diesen Mangel abgerechnet, ist die Wohnung gut** If one doesn't take note of this defect, the house is a good one. **Abgesehen [habend] von diesem Lärm, an den man sich bald gewöhnte, konnte man in Versailles glauben, im tiefen Frieden zu leben** (Moltke). The second example gives an insight into the origin of the construction. Originally, as still in this example, the perfect active participle was an appositive to some noun or pronoun, usually the subject as here. The **habend** of the perfect active participle was regularly suppressed in M.H.G., as explained in **183.** 2. C. *c*: Iuch möcht' des waldes han bevilt, | von erbuwenem lande her geritn [habende] (Parzival, 250. 20) The forest must have seemed very large to you having ridden hither from a cultivated country. Here *geritn* is in apposition with *iuch* and has with its modifiers the force of a conditional clause, just as the participle with its modifiers in this construction still often has. As an active perfect participle is not now employed to denote an act this old perfect participle construction is no longer understood, so that the perfect participle is now often used absolutely, i.e. without relations to any noun in the sentence, the reference becoming general or indefinite, as in the first example. The object, if it be a reflexive pronoun, is still regularly suppressed here, as in **183.** 2. C. *c*: **Beim Sonnenuntergang glaubt man immer, von der Stelle, wo man steht, bis nach Westen hin reicht das Abendrot, da ist noch Licht, [sich] rückwärts gekehrt erscheint alles dunkel** (Auerbach's *Dorfgeschichten*, 2, p. 77).

In recent literature this old perfect active participle is often felt as belonging to the impersonal passive (**219.** 5) construction, in which the form, tho passive, is active in force: **Gelinde gesprochen [= wenn gelinde gesprochen werden soll], ist das eine Übertreibung** Speaking in mild terms that is an exaggeration. Similarly **im Vertrauen gesagt** speaking confidentially, **offen gestanden** to tell the truth, &c.

Sometimes also the present participle is used absolutely: **Die Sache selbst betreffend, so ist zunächst zu bemerken** Concerning the point itself, it is necessary to remark. **Die alte Sprache anlangend . . . so denke ich ganz wie Sie usw.** (T. Storm an G. Keller). **In einer anderen Abteilung werden Schiffskanonen aller Kaliber und Arten zu sehen sein, mit denen des 15. Jahrhunderts beginnend.**

b. Absolute Accusative and Nominative.

(**1**) *Absolute Accusative.* An absolute acc., analogous to the ablative absolute in Latin, often forms, in connection with an uninflected adjective, a participle, an adverb, or prepositional phrase, a construction that is equivalent to a subordinate adverbial clause of which the acc. is the logical subject, and the adj., part., adverb, or phrase, the predicate. Attendant circumstance: **Wilhelm**

hatte, den Kopf in die Hand gestützt (= **indem der Kopf in die Hand gestützt war), nachdenklich zugehört. Der Mann näherte sich ihm langsam, die Arme herunterhängend, die Augen starr. Und so kehrte ich denn in die Heimat zurück, nichts mein als einen leeren Beutel. So stand er da, die Füße auswärts, den Kopf empor, die Arme übereinander. Friedrich ging, die Hände auf dem Rücken, im Zimmer auf und ab.** Time: **Dies getan, entfernte er sich** After this was done he withdrew. **Goethe ist der König seines Volks; ihn gestürzt und wie leicht dann mit dem Volke fertig werden** (Börne). **Dies geschehen, nahm der Student Konrad an der Hand und führte ihn usw.** (Hans Hopfen's *Verdorben zu Paris*, II, 155). Cause: **Diese** (i.e. **die Tür**) **zu, ging das Feuer auf dem Herd aus** (Hans Hopfen's *Verdorben zu Paris*, I, 265). Condition: **In der Hand den Lilienstengel, wäre er ein Heil'genbild.** Concession: **Den Tod schon im Herzen, kämpfte er tapfer weiter.** The accusative is sometimes omitted: **Da sagt' ich: kleine Hexlein, grüß' euch Gott! | Was braut und backt und kocht ihr hier im Dunklen? | Doch kaum gesagt — hui! stob der Schwarm davon** (Hauptmann's *Der arme Heinrich*, I, p. 19). This construction is most commonly used to give some attendant circumstance of an action. Sometimes it can be construed as having temporal, causal, conditional, or concessive force.

The accusative here and the accompanying adjective, participle, adverb, or prepositional phrase have the force of an adverbial clause. The relation of this clause to the verb of the principal proposition is not indicated by a conjunction, but by the accusative form of its subject. That the relation of this construction to the principal verb is that of an adverb to its governing word is plainly indicated by the fact that an adverbial genitive or prepositional phrase is often used instead of the absolute construction: **Wankenden Schrittes, mit Tränen in den Augen, erscheint der alte Mann auf der Schwelle** (Raabe). **So mit dem Felleisen auf dem Rücken und ein paar Groschen in der Tasche glaubte man Herr der Welt zu sein** (Baumbach's *Der Schwiegersohn*, VIII). In these prepositional clauses the predicate sometimes assumes the form of an *attributive* participle or adjective instead of a *predicate* participle or adjective: **Nach getaner Arbeit ist gut ruhen. Er geht mit bloßem Kopfe.** The attributive form is quite common in a few expressions: **nach geschlossenem Frieden, nach beendetem Kriege, nach aufgehobener Tafel, bei einbrechender Nacht, bei drohendem Regen,** &c. It is the common construction where the logical predicate is an adjective: **Er ist bei schönem Wetter abgereist.** The attributive form is also the rule in the adverbial genitive: **unverrichteter Sache** without having attained one's end, without accomplishing anything, **stehenden Fußes** immediately, **tränenden Auges** or **mit tränenden Augen,** &c.

Note. Historical Development of the Accusative Absolute. The attributive form, i.e. the old appositional thing type of sentence described in **250.** *a* (2nd par.), is in many cases the outgrowth of attempts to translate the Latin form of this type found in the ablative absolute, as in "Haud aliter *dissolutis nebulis* hausi coelum" *Just as the mist was scattered I saw the sky.* The O.H.G. writers in trying to approach the Latin original employed the dative instead of the ablative: also *gestobenemo nebele* sah ih ten himel (Notker, B. 17. 23). In fact neither the ablative nor the dative is used here absolutely as they stand in an adverbial relation to the verb in that the words in the dative and ablative form an adverbial clause in which the noun is subject, the adjective predicate, and the ablative or dative the sign of subordination to the principal verb. As the simple dative was not in natural German expression thus used to modify the verb it later became customary in this attributive type of adverbial clause to use in certain expressions the more natural adverbial genitive instead of the dative: **unverrichteter Dinge,** &c. In some other cases the prepositional construction was employed, which in general is much used in German in the adverbial relation: **Nach zerteiltem Nebel erblickte ich den Himmel.** Aside from a few set expressions given above the old attributive type with the adjective element *before* the noun has not taken deep root in German where the adjective element is a perfect participle, altho a descriptive adjective is quite common here. The old attributive type is very common, even in oldest German, where the adjective element is a prepositional phrase and stands *after* the noun: [Er] fand sia drurenta | mit salteru *in henti* (Otfrid, I. 5. 9) = **Er traf sie voller Trauer an mit dem Psalter in der Hand.** The weakly stressed preposition **mit** which stands here before the first noun of the adverbial clause has disappeared in a number of set expressions, as in **Komm zu mir und setz dich nieder, | wir kosen Hand in Hand.** The first noun in such expressions, as **Hand** in this example, is now felt as an absolute accusative as can be clearly seen when it is modified: **Sie ging fort, ihren ältesten Jungen an der Hand.** Thus there has arisen a real absolute accusative where in older German there was a prepositional phrase. The absolute accusative here arose under the influence of the absolute accusative in elliptical constructions: **Solche hindernis alle ungeachtet** [habend], **richtet gott diesen zug durch das rote meer gleichwol aus** (Luther, Weimar 16, 265, 19). Originally the perf. participle was felt here as having active force, often as here taking an object, and was not absolute but was an appositive to the subject, as in this example. As explained in *a* above and in **183.** 2. C. *c* such perfect active participles are found in M.H.G. and early N.H.G., but as they are no longer used the original force of this construction is not now understood. As the accusative here is not now felt as an object, it is construed as the logical subject of the adverbial clause and the participle is construed as the predicate of the clause. The construction has become productive, so that we now find as predicate of the clause not only a perfect participle of a transitive verb, but also the perfect participle of an intransitive verb, an adjective, adverb, or a prepositional phrase, as illustrated above.

(2) *Absolute Nominative.* The absolute nominative is not infrequent. It does not seem to be as closely related to the principal proposition as the accusative absolute. It limits the main verb by adding the time or some circumstance of the action, but it has the force of an additional contracted proposition of which the verb is **sein** understood rather than that of a subordinate clause. It is most common in descriptive style and usually adds some additional detail to render more complete the picture: **Endlich so kommt der Graf hergefahren, der Wagen schwer bepackt, voraus ein Reiter** (Schiller). **Ich geh ins Dorf hinaus, allein und nicht einmal mein Hund bei mir** (Auerbach). **Mein Freund! Am Tische sitzen wir zusammen, nichts zwischen uns als reiner, goldner Wein** (Freytag). **Ich kann mehr wie die Kerle alle, mein eigner Vater mit inbegriffen** (Hauptmann's *Michael Kramer*, 3). **Zu seinen Häupten der wolkenlose Himmel, zu seinen Füßen dieses Leben, dachte er der Tausend und Abertausend, die der Strudel der Weltstadt unbarmherzig in seine Tiefen reißen würde!** (Stilgebauer's *Götz Krafft*, II, 14, p. 446).

The absolute nominative is also used in subject clauses in connection with an appositive participle or adjective which serves as the logical predicate: **Diese sechs Punkte erfüllt war nichts Geringeres als der Sieg des Konstitutionalismus über die königliche Prärogative** (*Brachvogel*) *The carrying out of these six points meant nothing less than*, &c. **Einige Schurken weniger im Lande würde der Welt nichts schaden.**

c. Besides the quite common cases in *a* and *b* above other participles are sometimes used absolutely, referring to persons or things not mentioned at all in the principal proposition: **In die Stadt zurückgekehrt, beendigte ein Ball das Fest** Having returned to the city, they closed up the festival with a ball. Here the subject of the sentence is **Ball,** which would regularly be the subject of the participle, but the context implies that it was the people, not the ball, that returned to the city. This construction is generally condemned by grammarians. In spite of their frequent protests it is sometimes used by good authors: **Lustig davonfahrend, wurden die Eindrücke des Abends noch einmal ausgetauscht** (Riehl's *N. Nov.*, 154).

d. Absolute Infinitive. The infinitive with or without **zu** is often used absolutely; see **185.** A. I. 5, II. 2. *c*. Also the infinitive with **um zu** is used absolutely: **Wie viele interessante Entdeckungen haben in der neuesten Zeit allein Sweet und Jespersen gemacht, um nur zwei Namen zu nennen** (W. Franz in *Englische Studien*, 32. Band, p. 232). Compare **281.** *b* (2nd par.).

C. Interjections are often inserted in a proposition without having any grammatical connection with it, and exclamations often stand alone, filling no grammatical office. Such utterances assume the following forms:

a. They are uninflected words, or have the form of a sentence or a phrase. See **241.**

b. Exclamations may be nouns, the person or thing which causes the feeling being (**1**) very often in the nom.: **O ich Ungeheuer von einem Toren** O what a monstrous fool I am! **O mein verlornes Glück!** (**2**) In the gen. of cause: **Ach, der vielen, vielen Evatöchter, die, erwachend, innewerden, daß ihr Paradies nichts war als ein kurzer schöner Traum!** (Spielhagen's *Freigeboren*, p. 11). **O, des Glücks! O, der Wonne!** (id., *Was will das werden?*, IX, chap. xiii). **O, der sonnigen Tage, mit keiner Wolke, weder am Himmel noch in ihrem Gemüt** (Rodenberg's *Klostermanns Grundstück*, II). **O der Schlemmerei am frühen Morgen!** (H. Hoffmann's *Rittmeister*, II, p. 40). This construction was very common earlier in the period and even still frequent in the classics, and, as can be seen from the sentences quoted above, not yet entirely extinct. It is usually replaced to-day by the nom., as in (**1**), or the prepositional constructions in (**5**) below. The genitive is much more common than the nominative in exclamations as a word to strengthen the force of **leider** *alas*: **Freilich starb er leiderdessen** (Storm in *Westm.*, 259, 10 b). More frequently with **Gottes: Viel ist nicht geworden, leider Gott's** (Hauptmann's *Michael Kramer*, 2) (**3**) Sometimes in the dat.: **O mir!** (Schiller) Woe is me! **Pfui allem Tod!** |

Ei, ich will leben, ich (Grillparzer's *Ein treuer Diener*, 4). **Pfui dir,** or more commonly **Pfui über dich** Shame on you! We sometimes find the acc. after **pfui: Pfui dich!** (Lienhard's *Eulenspiegels Heimkehr*, 1). Sometimes with the genitive of cause described in (**2**) above: **Pfui, des Kupplers!** (Grillparzer's *Ottokar*, 1). The dative of **Seele** is quite common in the expression **meiner Seele,** or **meiner Seel'** (Fulda's *Die Zwillingsschwester*, 3, 11) *upon my soul*! Sometimes uninflected: **Mein Seel', sie hat so unrecht nicht, Ihr Herren** (Kleist's *Der zerbrochene Krug*, 7). These forms are short for **bei meiner Seele!** The preposition is also found: **bei meiner armen Seele** (Lessing's *Minna*, 3, 7). The dative, too, is common after **weh(e)** to denote the person affected: **wehe mir!** woe is me!, **wehe mir Armem!,** or **wehe über mich Armen!,** or **o weh! ich Armer!** The dative is also often used to denote the person threatened: **Wehe ihm, wenn er zu kommen wagt!** In early N.H.G. the genitive was used to denote the cause of the feeling: **O weh des tages | Denn der Tag des HERRN ist nahe | vnd kompt wie ein verderben vom Allmechtigen** (Joel i. 15). The dative is also common after **Heil, wohl,** and **Fluch: Heil dem König!** Long live the King! God save the King! **Wohl ihm, daß er das noch erlebt hat!** How fortunate for him that he has lived to see that! **Fluch dir, Fluch den falschen Freunden | und ihrer schändlichen Geschäftigkeit!** (Wilamowitz-Moellendorff's *Griechische Tragödien*, I, p. 156). (**4**) Only rarely in the acc.: **O mich Vergeßlichen** (Lessing) Plague on my forgetfulness, lit. on me forgetful one. (**5**) Very often in the dat. after the prep. **mit** or the acc. after **über: Mit dir feigem Kerl!** (Goethe's *Götz*, 5, 5) O, you cowardly fellow! **Mit diesem Menschen!** Plague on this fellow! Johannes: **Aber du wirst doch noch 'n Rest Pietät für 'ne Feier aufbringen, die noch vor . . .** Braun: **Du mit deiner Pietät** (Hauptmann's *Einsame Menschen*, 1). **O über sie! O! O, sie sind nicht gekommen.**

Classes of Sentences

266. Sentences are divided according to their structure into three classes—simple, compound, and complex. A simple sentence contains but one independent proposition. A compound sentence contains two or more independent propositions. A complex sentence contains one independent proposition and one or more subordinate clauses. As the simple sentence has already been discussed, there remain only the compound and complex sentences to be treated.

The Compound Sentence.

267. The compound sentence consists of different independent propositions or members. These members may be two or more simple sentences, or one member may be a simple sentence and the others complex sentences, or there may be any combination of simple and complex sentences. The members of a compound sentence need not necessarily be complete. When two or more members have in common an element which has the same construction in each member this element need only be expressed once: **Die Eintracht baut, die Zwietracht zerstört das Haus.** In such a sentence as **Er hat uns nie gefallen, also auch nie enttäuscht** the **uns** has the same form in both members, hence is by some suppressed as here in the second member, but it is a dative in the first member and an accusative in the second, hence with a different construction in the two members, which leads others to insert it also in the second member: **Er hat uns nie gefallen, uns also auch nie enttäuscht.** This is a choicer form of expression.

The members of a compound sentence are usually connected in the following ways:

1. The members are connected by co-ordinating conjunctions. This manner of joining sentences is treated at considerable length under the head of Conjunctions, articles **233–236.** It should be noticed in these articles that different conjunctions have different influence over the word-order in the members.

a. The most important case of contraction when two or more members have in common an element which has the same construction in each member is when several subjects have one verb in common. The question of the number and person of the verb in such cases is treated in articles **253.** I. 2 and II.

Note. Sometimes still, not however in choice language as earlier in the period, a pronoun, such as **das, dieses, was,** or a noun without an article, is expressed but once, even if it has a different construction in the two members, provided, however, that the pronoun or noun have the same form for the different cases: **Nur das** (eine) **hielt er mit seinem ganzen Herzen fest, und konnte ihm nie ausgeredet werden. Was heißt und zu welchem Ende studiert man Universalgeschichte?** (title of one of Schiller's productions). See also **271.** II. 3. *a*; **272.** C. *c*.

b. Sometimes two sentences have the form of two independent propositions connected by a co-ordinating conjunction, while in fact one of them is logically dependent: **Seien Sie so gut und kommen Sie** (with the logical force of a subordinate clause of result). An explanation is given in 4 (3rd par.) below.

2. The connection between the members may be made by means of demonstrative pronouns, or adverbs, which point to a preceding sentence, and thus bind the thought of the several propositions together: **Ans Vaterland, ans teure, schließ dich an; das halte fest mit deinem ganzen Herzen; hier sind die starken Wurzeln deiner Kraft.**

3. One member may have an adverb or conjunction which refers to a corresponding element in the other, and the several members may thus be bound firmly together: **Erst denke, dann rede! Bald** (now) **weint er, bald** (now) **lacht er.**

4. *Parataxis.* Sometimes there is no formal link binding the members together, the logical connection, however, forms a sufficient tie: **Kinder sind wie die Blumen, sie können nicht zu uns herauf, wir müssen uns zu ihnen niederbeugen, wenn wir sie erkennen wollen** (Wildenbruch's *Der Letzte*).

Upon close investigation it will become clear that such apparently independent propositions are not always absolutely independent. One of the propositions often stands in some grammatical relation to the other, such as that of subject, object, &c., or in an adverbial relation, such as that of result, cause, purpose, concession, condition: **Es ist besser, du gehst** (subject clause). **Den Brackenburg** (name) **solltest du in Ehren halten** (object clause), **sag' ich dir** (Goethe's *Egmont*, 3). **Sie kam ihm wie eine Fee vor** (result), **sie war so schön. Es ist dieses Jahr Mißwachs gewesen; alles ist teuer** (result). **Du mußt gleich gehen; es ist spät** (cause). **Man hatte ihm Geld angeboten; er sollte still sein** (purpose). **Der Berg sei auch noch so hoch,** or **Sei der Berg auch noch so hoch** (concession), **ich ersteige ihn. Er soll nur kommen** (condition), **ich werde ihm schon heimleuchten.** For other forms of condition here see **237.** 1. A. *b* (also *Note* 2 thereunder), **279.** *b.* (2).

Such sentences represent an older order of things, which was once more general than now. In the earliest stage of the parent tongue from which the various Indo-European languages have come there were no subordinating conjunctions as now, i.e. no formal expression had as yet been found for the idea of the subordination of one proposition to another. This placing of a subordinate proposition by the side of a principal proposition without a formal sign of subordination is called parataxis. The development of a distinctive formal sign of subordination in the form of conjunctions and relative pronouns—hypotaxis as it is called—is characteristic of a later stage of language growth and belongs to the individual life of the different languages after the migration of the different peoples from their original home. It has required many centuries to develop the present hypotactic forms, but actual subordination, altho without a formal expression, was present at a very early stage of language growth as can still be seen in the old verbless type of sentence preserved in old saws: **Ende gut, alles gut = Wenn das Ende gut ist, so ist alles gut.** An early stage of formal hypotaxis, asyndetic hypotaxis, i.e. hypotaxis clearly marked in thought and form but not yet indicated by a separate word such as a conjunction or a relative, is illustrated in **154.** *Note.* Here of the two originally independent sentences one of them, lying alongside of the other in close relation, often even embedded literally in it, is so markedly dependent logically and also formally dependent by reason of its peculiarly abridged and closely linked form that it is no longer felt as an independent sentence but as a relative clause. This primitive type of relative clause is still very common in English: The book *I hold* [*it*] *here in my hand* is a German grammar. An imperative sentence that lies alongside of another sentence often becomes dependent to it and develops into a subordinate conditional clause: **Geh hin, du wirst sehen,** or **so wirst du sehen. Einer trage des andern Last, so werdet ihr das Gesetz Christi erfüllen** (Gal. vi. 2, rev. orthog.). Likewise a question is often degraded to a subordinate conditional clause: **Ist jemand gutes muts? der singe Psalmen** (James v. 13). Luther used an interrogation point, but to-day a comma is used here and the tone is that of a subordinate conditional clause, not that of a question. In general the formal hypotactic stage was preceded by co-ordination, the connecting of sentences by the co-ordinating conjunctions, **dann, da, und, oder,** &c. mentioned in 1 above. Co-ordination frequently indicates a close relation between two propositions, the context often showing clearly that one of these is dependent upon the other: **Höre meinen Rat und es kann sich alles ändern** Just listen to my advice and the whole situation may change = **Wenn du meinen Rat hörst, kann sich alles ändern** If you listen to my advice the whole situation may change. The older construction of co-ordination cannot as accurately as hypotaxis give expression to many fine shades of meaning required in exact thinking, but it is by reason of its simple directness often more forceful than the younger exacter construction of hypotaxis and consequently is still widely used in certain styles. Examples of its use are given in **275.** *a*, **277.** 2 (last par.), **279.** *b.* (**3**), **280.** *b.* (**4**). Likewise the oldest construction here, parataxis, still has its distinct advantages in lively language, as illustrated in **277.** 2 (last par.), **278** (last par.).

The Complex Sentence.

Subordinate Clauses.

268. 1. *Grammatical Function.* A complex sentence consists of an independent proposition and one or more subordinate clauses. This is true, however, in only a general sense. In an exact sense there is often no principal proposition at all: **Wer wagt, gewinnt.** Here one of the essential elements of the sentence, the subject, has the form of a subordinate clause, a subject clause, but there is no principal proposition in the sentence distinct from the subordinate clause. The so-called principal proposition is merely a predicate. Not only an essential element but also any subordinate element can assume the form of a clause: **Ich weiß, daß er gekommen ist.** Here the object has the form of a clause, an object clause. The subordinate clause may also be merely a modifier of some word within one of the component elements: **Das Buch, das auf dem Tische liegt, ist eine deutsche Grammatik.** Here the clause is not the subject but only a modifier of it, i.e. an adjective clause. Thus according to their grammatical function subordinate clauses are divided into *subject, predicate, adjective, object, adverbial* clauses.

a. These clauses might be reduced to three if we divide them according to the part of speech they represent: (**1**) substantive clauses which represent a substantive, including *subject, predicate, object* clauses, and such adjective (**271.** I) clauses as represent an appositive noun, a gen., or a prep. phrase; (**2**) adjective clauses; (**3**) adverbial clauses. The former classification, however, is for practical reasons usually employed in the following articles, while for the same reasons the latter classification is also at times used.

2. *Word-order, Mood, Conjunctions.* These subordinate clauses differ in form from the principal proposition in that they often have the transposed word-order and often have also different moods and tenses from those of the principal sentence, and hence will be treated more or less at length according to the difficulties they present. The discussion of the subjunctive is given in articles **167–171.** The subordinate conjunctions are given in **238.**

a. Formal Words. Just as the pronoun es may anticipate the logical subject, so may an **es** or a demonstrative pronoun or adverb in the principal proposition anticipate a subordinate clause, or the pronoun or adverb may follow the subordinate clause, summing up in a word its contents: **Dessen erinnere ich mich nicht, daß Sie mir das gesagt haben. Dazu** (for that purpose) **hast du nicht das Geld, daß du es so verschwendest. Wer einmal lügt, dem glaubt man nicht, und wenn er auch die Wahrheit spricht. Denn wo das Strenge mit dem Zarten, | wo Starkes sich und Mildes paarten, | da gibt es einen guten Klang** (Schiller's *Glocke*). **Was ich nun tun soll, darüber bin ich im Unklaren. Wenn du lange wartest, dann versäumst du den Zug.** Especially frequent is the use of **so** to point back to a preceding subordinate conditional or concessive clause, altho now not absolutely required: **Wenn du dich nicht fügen willst, so wirst du im Leben nie durchkommen. Wenn es auch finster ist, so finde ich doch meinen Weg.** It is also found elsewhere and is still common in certain set expressions: **Wie man's treibt, so geht es. Was das betrifft, so meine ich, man hätte anders verfahren sollen.**

These inflected words and uninflected particles are all of more or less formal nature. Sometimes as in case of **darüber, dazu, dessen, dem,** &c. they serve to make the grammatical relations clearer, but in many cases **da, so,** &c. have lost every vestige of concrete meaning and are mere formal particles. Originally they were helpful in binding the two propositions more closely together, but to-day the proposition preceding **da, so,** &c., is often so distinctly felt as a subordinate adverbial clause by reason of its peculiar form and word-order that it is not now felt as necessary to indicate the subordination further by means of **da, so,** &c., pointing back to it.

3. *Position of the Subordinate Clause.* As each subordinate clause which is not merely a modifier of some word *within* one of the component elements has a definite function in the sentence as if it were a simple word, its position in the sentence is regulated by the same principles that determine the position of a simple word with the same function and logical force. For instance, just as an emphatic subject stands near the close of the sentence an emphatic subject clause assumes the end position, as illustrated in **251.** II. B. *a. cc.* A subordinate clause may often not only precede or follow the principal proposition but may also be embodied in it: **Während ich schlief, hat man mir meine Uhr gestohlen,** or **Man hat mir meine Uhr gestohlen, während ich schlief,** or **Man hat mir, während ich schlief, meine Uhr gestohlen.** In contrast to older usage, which allowed a much greater freedom of position, it is now in general a fixed rule that a subordinate clause which depends upon another subordinate clause must either follow it or be embodied in it: **Daß Karl sehr fleißig gewesen ist, während er in Rom war,** or **Daß Karl, während er in Rom war, sehr fleißig gewesen ist, habe ich schon von anderer Seite gehört.**

4. *Abridged Clauses.* These various clauses are the result of a long development and represent the active efforts of the German mind in its countless practical struggles for fuller expression to adapt from emergency to emergency the available historical materials of the language to the more accurate processes of thought that became necessary in its growing intellectual life. Alongside of these involved structures are simpler forms of expression which in their first beginnings belong to the earliest stages of language growth. There is still preserved in old saws a very primitive type of complex sentence which is verbless and conjunctionless and yet as complete in its expression as a modern complex sentence with its highly developed hypotactic form: **Ende gut, alles gut!** = **Wenn das Ende gut ist, so ist alles gut. Neuer Arzt, neuer Kirchhof!** = **Wo ein neuer Arzt ist, da ist ein neuer Kirchhof.** Where the thought is not intricate the older type is still in use. In general, however, these old constructions have not in large numbers come down to us in their original form but have very often undergone considerable change, frequently under the influence of the younger clause structures, and hence in their present form are comparatively modern creations, which have long been developing into convenient terser types of expression alongside of the more intricate clause formations. These simpler types of expression are treated in the following articles alongside of the fuller and more precise clause formations. They are given under the caption of *abridgment* under the various kinds of clauses treated below and are often elsewhere spoken of as abridged or contracted forms. Altho these abridged clauses are in their original form older than the fuller clause structures and hence in a historical sense cannot be said to be abridged from them the terms "abridged" or "contracted" are not inappropriate, for the compacter structures have long been under the influence of the fuller more involved structures and in contrast to their fuller form are now felt as abridgments or contractions. English has gone much farther than German in preserving these old forms and developing

them into types of expression capable of wide use. Particularly terse and forceful is the predicate appositive construction, where the participle and its modifiers form an abridged clause in which the participle is the logical predicate and the subject of the principal proposition the logical subject, the clause as a whole indicating some adverbial relation, as time, cause, manner, &c., which can only be determined from the connection, as this relation is not formally expressed in the clause itself: Time: Going down town (= when I was going down town) I met an old friend. Having finished my work (= after I had finished my work) I went to bed. Cause: Being sick (= as I was sick) I stayed at home. This is the old attributive or appositional thing type of sentence structure described in **250.** *a* (2nd par.) and **252.** 1. *b. Note.* The thought is not expressed accurately by means of intricate grammatical form but is merely suggested by placing the participle alongside of the subject of the principal proposition. As German has in large measure abandoned this old construction for the more accurate fuller clause the English-speaking student should be on his guard here. Additional details on German usage here are given in **182. 1.** E. *Note.* The old attributive type of clause structure is also very common in English where the person implied in a subjective genitive or a possessive adjective (originally a gen. of a pers. pronoun, here still with the force of a subject. gen.) is the logical subject and the governing gerund the logical predicate: *I am opposed to your* or *John's going to his house* **Ich bin dagegen, daß du zu ihm gehst,** or **daß Hans zu ihm geht.** English and German usage at this point is treated in detail in the following articles, also in **182.** 1. B. *a.* Quite similar to the old attributive type of clause structure just described is the development of modifiers of the verb, especially the prepositional infinitive constructions, into terse forceful types of expression with the value of a subordinate clause, as illustrated in **269.** 3, **272.** C. *g*, **281.** *b. Note* (2nd par.). The outline of German usage here is given in **185.** A. II. 2. As English allows a much more liberal use of the infinitive than German the English-speaking student must again be on his guard. On the other hand, the abridged clause in the form of a prepositional phrase is very common in both German and English: **Er ist bei schönem Wetter angekommen** *He arrived in beautiful weather.* **Er sagte es mit Tränen in den Augen** *He said it with tears in his eyes.* The first noun in each prepositional phrase is the subject of the abridged clause. The attributive adjective or participle *before* the noun or the prepositional phrase *after* the noun, as **in den Augen** *in his eyes* in the second example, is the logical predicate of the clause, the preposition introducing the abridged clause is the sign of subordination to the principal verb. In German differing from English the sign of subordination to the principal verb is sometimes indicated by the genitive form of the noun instead of a preposition placed before the noun: **Schwankenden Schrittes erschien der alte Mann auf der Schwelle** *With tottering steps the old man appeared on the threshold.*

Subject Clause.

269. 1. The subject clause performs the function of the subject of the sentence: **Wer leicht glaubt** (= **Der Leichtgläubige**), **wird leicht betrogen.**

The subject clause is usually introduced by the conjunctions **daß** *that, since,* **seit** or **seitdem** *since,* **als** *when,* **ob** *whether,* **wenn** *if, when,* **weil** *because,* by the relatives **wer** (**156**), **was** (**153.** 1. (2)), **der** (**130.** 2. *b*, **151.** 3. C, and **156**), **die, das, wie, worüber, worauf,** &c., and in indirect questions by some interrogative pronoun or adverb: **Daß der Mond auf die Witterung Einfluß übt, ist eine verbreitete Ansicht. Es sind schon viele Jahre, daß ich hier wohne. Es ist viele Jahre her, daß** (or **seit** or **seitdem**) **ich ihn gesehen habe. Es sind vergangene Zeiten, als für dynastische Zwecke kleine Heere von Berufssoldaten ins Feld zogen** (Moltke). **Ob sie kommen werden, steht dahin** (remains to be seen). **Es ist erfreulich, wenn man wohlerzogene Kinder sieht** (= **Der Anblick wohlerzogener Kinder ist erfreulich**). **Die Lichtenstein tut vornehm und ernst; das macht aber, weil der gestrenge Herr Vater da ist** (Riehl). **Wer Schlösser**

in die Luft erbaut, wird billig als ein Tor verlacht. Kein Lärm, keine Erschütterung war es, was (153. 1. (2)) mich geweckt hatte, sondern ein Qualm unerträglich verpesteter Luft (Suttner's *Die Waffen nieder!*, iv). **Die (130. 2.** *b*) **so redeten, wußten sehr wohl, daß sie bis zu einem gewissen Grade die öffentliche Meinung ihres Volkes und Heeres hinter sich hatten. Eine Lust ist's, wie er alles weckt und stärkt und neu belebt um sich herum. Worüber der eine sich ärgert, das freut den anderen. Worin er sich auszeichne, ist schwer zu sagen. Es ist nicht bekannt, woher diese Krankheit zu uns gekommen.** The predicate word often introduces the sentence, as explained in *b* (2nd par.): **Mein einziger Trost ist, daß es den anderen nicht besser geht. Seine Antwort [war], er fürchte sich nicht. Tatsache ist, daß er schon da ist.**

a. There often stands in the principal proposition when it is preceded by the subject clause a demonstrative, which points to the preceding subordinate clause, and in a word sums up its contents, thus binding the two propositions more firmly together: **Worüber der eine sich ärgert, das freut den anderen. Wen der Neid zu stürzen denkt, der wird erst von ihm erhoben.** This demon. is usually necessary if its correlative in the subordinate clause is an adverb or a pronoun in a different case, as in the two sentences just given.

b. Anticipative Subject **es.** Often the sentence is introduced by the anticipative subject **es, das,** or **eines,** which points to a following subject clause, which is the real subject of the sentence: **Es ist zweifelhaft, ob er noch lebt. Es kann nicht fehlen, daß er daran gedacht** He must have thought of it. **Und das ist das Schrecklichste, daß einem die Welt so zu ist** (Fontane's *Effi*, XXXII). **Mag auch Entwickelung und Ausgang des Krieges in Ostasien noch gänzlich unabsehbar sein — eines ist heute schon sicher: Der erste Kanonenschuß in Ostasien hat in der ganzen Welt . . . das stärkste Echo erweckt** (*Neue Zürcher Zeitung*, Feb. 22, 1904). Of course **es** follows the verb in questions: **Ist es denn so nötig, daß er sich entfernt?** For the omission of **es** see **251.** I. 2. B. *Note.*

The **es,** pronounced with falling intonation—here indicated by a period—, is much used when the predicate is placed at the beginning of the sentence for emphasis: **Möglich** or **Eine Möglichkeit ist es., daß er morgen kommt.** On the other hand, when the predicate is placed at the beginning of the sentence, not for emphasis but in order that the subject clause may take the emphatic end position the anticipative **es** drops out, as the position of the unstressed predicate in the first place and the rising intonation—here indicated by a raised period—after the verb pointing forward indicate that the emphatic subject will follow: **Möglich** or **Eine Möglichkeit ist·, daß er morgen kommt. Eine andere Frage ist·, ob auf die Erklärung, die Lloyd George in seiner Rede abgegeben hat, bereits fest gebaut werden kann** (*Berliner Tageblatt*, May 14, 1921). If the predicate is a noun or an uninflected neuter demonstrative referring back to a preceding noun, an *inflected* demonstrative pronounced with rising intonation is often used as an anticipative subject pointing forward to the following emphatic subject clause: **Eine Möglichkeit ist die·, daß er morgen kommt. Mein Haupteinwand gegen ihn ist der·, daß er so selbstisch ist. Es gibt doch nur einen Termin für das Erscheinen eines Buches und das ist der·, wenn es fertig ist.** See also **251.** I. 2. B. *Note* and II. B. *a. aa. Note.*

When the subject clause thus stands at the end and there is a predicate adjective, noun, adverb, or prepositional phrase in the first place, we often find in the principal proposition the old verbless appositional type of sentence described in **252.** 1. *b. Note*: **Möglich [ist], daß das ganze Gerüste meiner Schlüsse ein bestandloses Traumbild gewesen** (Schiller). **Gewinn genug [ist es], wenn wir nur soviel erreichen! Vergebens [war es], daß ich durch Hin- und Hergehen mich zu erwärmen suchte** (Spielhagen). **Zum größten Glück, daß ich ihm aus den Augen kam.** After **nicht** in the first place **daß** is often replaced by **als ob,** as explained in 2. *b* (2nd par.) below, or now also often by **weil** thus indicating that the subject clause is developing into a causal clause: **Heute gibt es wenige gute Dichter, nicht daß** (or **als ob,** or **weil**) **sich heutzutage etwa so viel weniger Gutes fände als früher, nein, nur das Mittelmäßige, Überflüssige und Elende hat sich in einer Weise vermehrt, daß es jammervoll ist.** The **daß** that follows **kaum** in the first place has become so closely associated with it that both words are now felt as a temporal conjunction so that the subject clause has developed into a clause of time: **Schon dreht sich der Boden vor Wonne mit mir, | kaum daß ich die Schwelle betrat** (Mörike).

c. Omission of **daß.** The connective **daß** is often omitted in subject clauses and the normal or the inverted word-order employed, especially when **es** is used in the main proposition as an anticipative subject: **Es ist besser, du gehst,** or **daß du gehst. Schulze, heißt es, hat einen Ruf nach Berlin. Denn ist es zu leugnen? Der Übermut der fremden Lehrer hat sich täglich erhöht** (Goethe's *Egmont*, 1). Sometimes when the anticipative **es** is omitted in accordance with older usage: **Du bist, scheint mir, verstimmt. Im Gegenteil, ist mir viel lieber, Sie bleiben** (Wildenbruch's *Der unsterbliche Felix*, 3, 6). Especially, however, when a predicate word introduces the sentence in order that the subject may be withheld until the end for the purpose of making it more emphatic: **Wahr ist, der Vater hätt' früher g'scheit sein und nicht erlauben sollen, daß die Resel und der Toni von Kind auf beständig mitsammen herumrennen** (Ebner-Eschenbach's *Die Resel*, p. 160). **Das Natürlichste ist, du fragst ihn selbst. Sie sind beide sehr geschickte Leute; das macht, sie kommen von Sachsen** (E. von Handel-Mazzetti's *Jesse und Maria*, p. 25). For further particulars concerning the omission of **es** see **251.** I. 2. B. *Note* and II. B. *a. aa. Note.*

The **daß** should not, however, be omitted if it is needed to make the thought clear, i.e. to indicate the oneness of the words in the subject clause and maintain the integrity of the group as a distinct grammatical element in contradistinction to other elements in the sentence: **Es ist ein Vorurteil, daß in der allgemeinen Verbreitung der elementaren Kenntnisse das Altertum hinter unserer Zeit wesentlich zurückgestanden habe** (Mommsen's *Römische Geschichte*, III, chap. 14). The omission of **daß** in this sentence would bring a prep. phrase next to the noun **Vorurteil**, which at the first glance might lead us to seek for a connection between these two elements instead of connecting the phrase with the words that follow, where it properly belongs. The **daß** here points out the oneness of the following group of words.

There is often also another reason for the use of **daß**. The transposed word-order according to **284.** I. 3. *a* must be used after verbs expressing mere feeling: **Es tut mir sehr leid, daß du dich gekränkt fühlst** (not **du fühlst dich gekränkt**).

2. *Mood.* The mood of the subject clause is:

a. Indicative when it is desired to represent the statement as a fact: **Es ist mehr als wahrscheinlich, daß der Torf aus abgestorbenen Pflanzenteilen entsteht.**

b. The mood is the potential (**168.** II. G. *a.* (**1**); **169.** 2. G. *a.* (**1**)), the volitive (**168.** I. 2. E. *a.* (**1**)), the sanguine and the unreal subjunctive of wish and the subjunctive of modest wish (**168.** I. 2. E. *b.* (**1**); **169.** 1. A), or the subjunctive of indirect discourse (**170** and **171**) or indirect question: **Es läßt sich nicht bezweifeln, daß er es tun könnte** (potential subj.) There is no doubt that he could do it. **Es geziemt dem Manne, daß er auch das Schwerste willig tue** (volitive subj.; hence the will of the speaker). **Daß du an unserer Freude teilnehmest** (sanguine subj. of wish), **ist unser inniger Wunsch. Mir wäre besser, ich wäre** (unreal subjunctive of wish; **169.** 1. A) **nie geboren! Es ist noch ungewiß, ob diese Nachricht sich bestätige** (subj. of indirect question). **Wer den Brief abgesandt habe, ist noch nicht ermittelt worden.** Other examples are given in the examples referred to above.

To emphasize the idea of appearance, mere subjectivity, mere semblance, or unreality **als ob** with transposed word-order or simple **als** with question order often replaces **daß**. A good example to illustrate a subjective view is given in **168.** II. G. *a.* (**1**). The idea of appearance is often found in **als ob** after **vorkommen**: **Es kommt mir vor, als ob er löge.** Unreality: **Damals kam es mir vor, als ob ich verloren wäre.** Modest or cautious statement: **Es kommt mir vor, als ob du unrecht hättest.** Compare **272.** A. *a*, C. *d*, D. *b*, **276.** A.

c. Also the imperative mood, or the simple infinitive or the perfect participle used with the force of the imperative: **„Kehre um!“ schallte es ihm entgegen. Unser Wahlspruch, der Gambettas wie der meinige, war: „Nie davon sprechen, immer daran denken!“** (*Hamburger Nachrichten*, Nov. 18, 1904). **Unsere Haltung kann nur diese sein: kühl abwarten, an uns herankommen lassen, keine Liebenswürdigkeiten, keine Avancen!** (ib., March 31, 1906). **Frisch mitten durchgegriffen, das ist besser** (Schiller's *Die Piccolomini*, 1, 2). **Hier heißt es, den Geldbeutel offen, Karst und Spaten genommen und graben und abermals graben und zum letztenmal graben!** (Lauff's *Frau Aleit*, p. 348).

3. *Abridged Form.* Clauses introduced by **daß** can be abridged by substituting the infinitive construction, or a simple noun for the clause form if its subject is **man**, or is identical with or implied in some dependent word of the principal proposition: **Daß man vorsichtig sei, ist ratsam;** or **Vorsichtig zu sein ist ratsam;** or **Vorsicht ist ratsam. Hier ist das Schwerste, daß man seine Pflicht tue,** or **seine Pflicht zu tun. Sich abfinden, Mutter, ist Menschenlos** (Hauptmann's *Michael Kramer*, I.). **Es ist die Pflicht treuer Untertanen, daß sie das Vaterland schützen;** or **Das Vaterland zu schützen, ist treuer Untertanen Pflicht. Es war dumm von Ihnen, es zu sagen,** or **daß Sie es sagten. Es ist mein sehnlichster Wunsch, zu gehen.** When the subject of the subordinate clause is not identical with or implied in some dependent word of the principal proposition a full clause must be employed in German, while in English *for* with the prepositional infinitive can be used: **Es ist mein sehnlichster Wunsch, daß Sie gehen** My most ardent desire is for you to go. **Es ist unmöglich, daß ein Streit zwischen unseren beiden Ländern je entstehe** It is impossible for there ever to be any conflict between our two countries. This English construction originated in such sentences as *It would be better for me to go at once* and *For me the best plan would be to go at once,* which corresponds closely to the German: **Es wäre besser für mich, sogleich zu gehen** and **Für mich wäre das Beste, sogleich zu gehen.** The *for me* and **für mich** represent an older dative of reference (**258.** 3. A, 2nd par.) and hence originally modified the sentence as a whole and had grammatically nothing to do with the infinitive. As, however, there is in such sentences a close logical relation between the pronoun or noun after *for* and the infinitive, the pronoun or the noun usually serving as the logical subject of the infinitive, noun or pronoun and infinitive have come in English to be felt as forming together a subordinate clause introduced by *for*, just as in case of German infinitive clauses introduced by **um zu**, as described in **281**, *b. Note*, 2nd par. Thus *for* and the following noun or pronoun became entirely detached from the principal proposition, so that the infinitive could freely take as subject any noun or pronoun whatever without regard to whether it corresponded to the original dative construction in the principal proposition or not: *Your plan for me to go doesn't please me* **Ihr Plan, daß ich gehen sollte, gefällt mir nicht.** This infinitive *for*-clause arose in English in the fourteenth century and has become very productive since, so that it is now regularly used where the infinitive *to*-clause cannot be employed, i.e. where the subject of the principal proposition and that of the infinitive clause are not identical, as illustrated in **271.** I. *c*, **271.** II. 6, **272.** C. *g* and D. *c*, **277.** 2. *b*, **279.** *d*, **281.** *b. Note*, 2nd par. In German there are no traces of a development in this direction. In English the infinitive construction is often here in the subject relation

and often elsewhere replaced by the gerund: *Having done one's duty is a consolation in misfortune* **Seine Schuldigkeit getan zu haben ist ein Trost im Unglück.** Compare **182.** 1. B. *a.* (**1**).

The regular subject clause with a conjunction followed by a nominative subject and a finite verb is often replaced by the old appositional type of clause described in **268.** 4, which consists here of a subject in the absolute nominative followed by a predicate in the form of an appositive adjective or participle: **Einige Schurken weniger im Lande würde der Welt nichts schaden.** See **265.** B. *b.* (**2**), last par.

4. *Word-order.* As can be seen by the illustrative sentences, the word-order is usually the normal or the inverted, or, in case there is a connective, the transposed. The question order is also found: **Ist es möglich: liebt sie mich?** (K. F. Meyer).

5. For the case where several subject clauses have the same relative in common, see **272.** C. *c.*

Predicate Clause.

270. 1. The predicate clause performs the function of a predicate noun or adjective: **Widerwärtigkeiten sind für die Seele, w a s d e r S t u r m f ü r d i e L u f t i s t** (= **Läuterungsmittel**).

The predicate clause is introduced by the relative **wer, was, der, die, das** (never **welcher**), the relative adverbs **wozu, &c.,** and the conjunctions **wie, daß: Wir sind selten, was wir sein sollten. Ich bin nicht, der ich zu sein scheine. Seid, wozu die herrliche Natur Euch machte. Er ist, wie er ist. Alles** [**ist**], **wie Sie gewünscht haben. Das heißt, wir müssen morgen fort,** or **daß wir morgen fortmüssen. Das Essen war so, daß man es nicht genießen konnte.**

2. *Mood.* The mood is usually as in the preceding sentences the indicative, but sometimes the subjunctive, especially the potential subjunctive (**168.** II. F. *b*; **169.** 2. F. *b*), is found: **Wer der Dichtkunst Stimme nicht vernimmt, ist ein Barbar, er sei, w e r e r s e i.**

3. *Abridgment.* Predicate clauses cannot usually be abridged except, as in the first sentence in 1, by substituting some noun for the clause. On the other hand, in certain set expressions the infinitive is common: **Es ist mit ihm nicht auszukommen** *There* (formerly *it*) *is no getting along with him.* Compare **185.** A. I. 1. *b.* (**2**). (**3**). The perfect infinitive (**185.** B. II. *b*) is also common in set expressions, usually however without **zu: Das heißt recht den Nagel auf den Kopf getroffen** [**haben**] *That is hitting the nail on the head.* Also the present infinitive without **zu** may be used here after **sein** and **heißen: Sich allein leben heißt gar nicht leben** *To live for one's self is the same as not to live at all.* See **185.** B. I. 1. *b.* Notice that in the English translation of such sentences we must sometimes use the gerund instead of the infinitive. Compare **182.** 1. B. *a.* (**2**).

Adjective Clause.

271. Adjective clauses fall into two classes—attributive substantive clauses and attributive adjective clauses:

I. Attributive substantive clauses are for the most part either appositive or prepositional clauses: **Die Gewißheit, daß wir ewig leben werden, tröstet uns. Die Hoffnung, daß wir uns wiedersehen** (= **auf Wiedersehen**), **erleichtert die Trennung. Seine Angst** (**darüber**), **er könnte nie etwas erreichen, hat ihn furchtbar gequält. Seine innere Auflehnung dagegen, daß er doch schließlich weichen müsse, hat ihn sehr verbittert.** In examples like the last one the clause is evidently a prepositional clause. The two preceding examples may be similarly construed, but other interpretations are possible, for the clause in both examples may represent an older genitive, once common, or it may now be felt as an appositional clause. In the first example the clause is evidently an appositional clause. This interpretation often becomes very natural: **In allem Wandel menschlicher Zustände bleibt doch ein Naturgesetz unverändert: daß der Tag für den Lernbegierigsten und Fleißigsten doch eben nur 24 Stunden hat. Verzeihe mir die runde Frage: was willst du hier?** There is an old form of the appositional clause which has become so changed that the original construction is no longer felt. In this old form, as in **268.** 4, appositional clauses have often developed into adverbial clauses, here especially into clauses of result. Originally such a clause stood in apposition with a post-positive article of the governing noun. Thus **Er hat das Alter, daß er für sich selbst reden kann** was originally: **Er hat Alter, das: er kann für sich selbst reden.** In course of time **das** (now **daß**) became a stereotyped form, so that it can now be used even if the governing noun is masc. or fem., and also when an indefinite article, demonstrative, or adverb is used: **Sie haben ja hier einen Qualm, daß man ersticken möchte.** Such clauses may now be classed as adverbial clauses of quality or degree. For further examples see **276.** D; **277.** 2.

Attributive substantive clauses are usually introduced by **daß** (see **238.** 2. *d*), **weil** (sometimes used with the force of **daß**), **als,** or **als ob,** or **als wenn** (see *a* below), or the interrogative pronouns or particles, such as **was, wer, ob, wo, wie, wann, weshalb, weswegen, warum,** &c.: **Die Behauptung, daß die Erde sich drehe, setzte Galilei manchen Verfolgungen aus. Aus dem ganz einfachen Grunde, weil** (instead of **daß**) **der kluge König schon seine Maßregeln genommen** (Heine). **Wem ein offener Sinn für die Schönheiten der Natur verliehen ist, dessen** (**268.** 2. *a*) **Leben wird reich an Freuden sein. Immer wieder dazwischen waren ihre Gedanken abgeirrt, denn sie hatte Angst, was da kommen möchte. Die Ungewißheit, ob sein Sohn glücklich aus dem Kriege heimkehren werde, ließ ihm keine Ruhe. Können Sie mir Nachricht geben, wo er sich aufhält? Erst im Unglück gelangt man zu der Einsicht, wie schwer ein Freund in der Not wiegt. Die Hoffnung, daß wir ihm helfen werden, verleiht ihm Mut. Ich habe noch nicht die Ursache erfahren, warum** (or **weshalb,** or **weswegen,** or **derentwegen**) **dies geschehen ist. Sein Verzicht darauf, daß er zuerst rede, hat allgemein befriedigt.**

a. Mood. The mood is usually indicative, but the subjunctive often occurs, especially the subjunctive of indirect discourse in clauses modifying a preceding noun, as in the sentence above beginning **Die Behauptung,** or in clauses explaining a preceding prepositional adverb as in the last sentence of the examples given above, also the subjunctive of indirect question (see sentences above beginning with **Immer** and **Die Ungewißheit**). See also **168.** II. G. *b*; **169.** 2. G. *b*; **168.** I. 2. B. (**1**). Also the subjunctive of modest or cautious statement is common here. See **169.** 2. G. *b*. Instead of **daß** the conjunction **als** (with question order) or **als ob** or **als wenn** (with transposed order) is often used with a past or a present tense form of the subjunctive to give expression to the idea of non-reality or mere subjectivity. Examples are given in **168.** II. G. *b* (2nd par.); **169.** 2. G. *b* (2nd par.); **238.** 2. *d. Note.* Also the imperative mood or a simple infinitive with the force of an imperative may be used: **Dieser P. P. hat nur einen Gedanken: jung sein! Mitmachen mit der Jugend!** (Wildenbruch's *Der unsterbliche Felix,* 1, 5).

b. When the thought or feeling of someone is reported indirectly, **daß** is often dropped, and the subordinate clause has the order of a principal proposition: **Im Altertum war die Ansicht des Thales, die Erde sei eine große, auf dem Wasser schwimmende Scheibe, eine weit verbreitete.**

c. Abridgment. Clauses introduced by **daß** may, when no ambiguity would arise, be replaced by the infin. construction: **Jetzt ist der Zeitpunkt da, von diesen Papieren öffentlichen Gebrauch zu machen** (= **daß man von diesen Papieren öffentlichen Gebrauch mache**). A predicate nom. remains in the nom. in the contracted clause: **Er hatte das Lob, ein schöner Mann zu sein** (Freytag's *Rittmeister,* chap. vi). Where, however, the subject of the clause is other than the general or indefinite **man** or a person implied in the subject of the principal proposition the clause form must be retained in German, while in English *for* with the prepositional infinitive may be used: **Ihr Plan, selbst zu gehen, gefällt mir nicht** *Your plan to go yourself doesn't please me,* but **Ihr Plan, daß ich gehen sollte, gefällt mir nicht** *Your plan for me to go doesn't please me.* For the origin of English usage here see **269.** 3. In English the infinitive here may be replaced by a gerund, which requires as subject a person implied in a possessive adjective or a genitive if the subject of the clause is different from the person implied in the subject of the principal proposition, but has no subject expressed if it is the same as the person implied in the subject of the principal proposition: *Your plan of my* or *John's going doesn't please me* **Ihr Plan, daß ich** or **Hans gehen sollte, gefällt mir nicht,** but *Your plan of going yourself doesn't please me* **Ihr Plan, selbst zu gehen, gefällt mir nicht.** See **272.** C. *g* for further remarks on the gerund.

II. *Attributive Adjective Clause.* The attributive adjective clause was originally an appositive to the governing noun as the substantive clause in **I,** but it is no longer felt as such. Originally a **der, welcher,** or **so** stood in the principal proposition after the governing noun pointing as a demonstrative to the following appositional clause. These words are now felt as pronouns standing in the subordinate clause pointing *backward* to the governing noun, i.e. are now felt as relative pronouns. See **154.** *Note,* **130.** 3, **153.** 5. *Note.* This clause is now usually introduced by the relatives **der, welcher, was** (**153.** 1. (**1**), (**3**)), **desgleichen,** or **dergleichen** (**161.** 2), or by a relative adverb, such as **so** (**153.** 5), **wie** (**153.** 3. B and C. *f*), **als** (**153.** 3. C. *a*), **wo, worin, worunter,** &c., which are sometimes separated when compound (see **153.** 2, toward end): **Die Stätte,**

die ein guter Mann betrat, ist eingeweiht. Man war sehr unschlüssig über die Art, wie der Krieg geführt werden sollte. For the use of different relatives see articles **150–154**, where this subject, so difficult for foreigners, is treated at considerable length and many illustrative sentences are given. The conjunction **daß** is also used relatively. See **153.** 3. C. *e*.

1. As in English, the relative pronoun must agree with its antecedent in gender and number, while its case is determined by the office it performs in the clause.

a. Synesis of gender. If the antecedent is a common neut., fem., or masc. noun representing a male or female the relative is usually neut., fem., or masc. according to grammatical gender, but if the antecedent is the diminutive of a proper name the relative has, as a rule, natural gender. For fuller explanation see **263.** I. 1, 2, 3, 4, 5, 6.

Synesis of number. For usage here see **263.** II. 2, last paragraph.

b. The relatives **das** and **welches** were earlier in the period employed like **das** (**129.** 2. C. (**1**)) as the subject of the clause, remaining unchanged for all genders and numbers. See **151.** 1. *g*.

c. The relative is in the pl., altho its antecedent is in the sing., if it refers to the antecedent, not as to an individual, but as to a class or genus: **Das gebräuchlichste Gewand ist ein blauer Samtrock, von denen 20 auf einen von Tuch kommen** The most common garment is a blue velvet coat, of which there are 20 to one of cloth.

d. In English the relative often agrees incorrectly with some word closely connected with the antecedent instead of agreeing with the antecedent itself, as this word lies nearer the thought and feeling of the speaker or writer than the grammatical antecedent: *That is one of the most valuable books that has appeared in any language.* This incorrect construction is much less common in German: **So viel steht fest, daß unsere heimischen Kartoffelklöße eines der wunderbarsten Gerichte vorstellen, das die Welt kennt** (H. Seidel's *Thüringische Kartoffelklöße*).

e. A peculiar kind of attraction called *trajection* often takes place in relative clauses. This consists in conforming the relative pronoun or adverb to the construction required in the following dependent clause instead of to that required in its own clause: **Er besitzt das Buch, aus welchem du meinst, daß er viel lernen kann** instead of **Er besitzt das Buch, von welchem du meinst, daß er daraus viel lernen kann.** This construction is very common with Luther and Lessing, and is still sometimes used especially in clauses introduced by **wo** or **wie** to avoid a clumsy circumlocution: **Er ging in eine Restauration, wo er wußte, daß er seinen Freund treffen werde** instead of: **Er ging in eine Restauration, von der er wußte, daß er seinen Freund dort treffen werde. Denn ein Geist hat nicht fleisch vnd bein | wie jr** (**ihr**) **sehet das** (**daß**) **| ich habe** (Luke xxiv. 39) instead of **Ein Geist hat nicht Fleisch und Bein, von denen ihr seht, daß ich sie habe.**

2. If the relative has the same case in a number of successive clauses dependent upon the same word, it may be expressed in the first clause and understood in the others, or for rhetorical effect it may be retained in all: **Ich sandte ihm einen Mann, welcher in die Sache eingeweiht war, die Gegend genau kannte und sich bei einer früheren Gelegenheit zuverlässig gezeigt hatte.** If the relative be in the gen. it is usually repeated with each clause: **Aber einem romantischen Volke war eine Religion angemessen, deren prächtiger Pomp die Sinne gefangen nimmt, deren geheimnisvolle Rätsel der Phantasie einen unendlichen Raum eröffnen, deren vornehmste Lehren sich durch malerische Formen in die Seele einschmeicheln.** See also **272.** C. *c*. For the rhetorical repetition of the relative see **152. 2.**

3. If the relative in adjective clauses has a different case in a number of successive clauses dependent upon the same word, it is now usually repeated each time with its proper case form, tho many exceptions can be found in a careless style and in earlier periods where the influence of the grammarian was not so strong as to-day: **Das Schloß war schon mit mehreren Unglücklichen belegt, denen man nicht helfen, die man nicht erquicken konnte.** Either **der** or **welcher** can here be used, but they do not usually alternate with each other. See **152.** 2. Also **was** is employed here, but with a different shade of meaning, as explained in **153. 1.** The differentiation is not always carried out. See **153. 1.** (**1**) (last par.) and *a* and *b* thereunder.

a. Violations of this rule are not infrequent even in the best authors when the relative has the same form for different cases: **Dieses Anerbieten, das ich für kein leeres Kompliment halten durfte und für mich höchst reizend war** (Goethe). To-day when the grammatical conscience is so aroused such violations are becoming less frequent in choice language, but the relative was is still sometimes used but once even by good writers: **Ich muß zu dem übergehen, was hiermit zusammenhängt und ich dir vorzulegen habe** (G. Keller). The repetition of **was** is now felt as choicer German. Other seeming short cuts sometimes occur: **Es mag kommen zu was** (for

dem was) es will. Sie war unbekümmert um was (for **das was**) **nicht ihre nächste Sorge war.** Such sentences are curious survivals of older usage, where **was** and **wer** were not relative pronouns but indefinites belonging to the principal proposition, as explained in **154.** *Note.*

b. Very frequently we find in the best authors and in the language of the common people a personal, possessive, or demonstrative pronoun, or demonstrative adverb, or **derselbe** in the second of two relative clauses instead of the grammatically correct relative pronoun or adverb, a construction common also in M.H.G. hence old, usually found where the construction in the clause is different from that of the preceding clause hence often employed as a convenient means of avoiding the reconstruction of the clause: Goethe: **Die Elemente sind als kolossale Gegner zu betrachten, mit denen wir ewig zu kämpfen haben und sie nur durch die höchste Kraft des Geistes bewältigen** (instead of **die wir nur durch die höchste Kraft des Geistes bewältigen**). Schiller: **Sprüche, die der Wandersmann verweilend liest und ihren Sinn bewundert** (instead of **deren Sinn er bewundert**). Tieck: **Etwas Innigeres, welches er nicht verstand, jedoch bald einmal die Erklärung desselben von seinem Freunde zu hören hoffte.** Mommsen: **eine schändliche Gewalttat, vor der jedermann schauerte und sich dabei der furchtbaren Herrschaft des Schreckens erinnert. Wir bestellen bei unserem Meister Silberschmied einen neuen Becher, an dem er keinen Gewinn zu nehmen verspricht, sondern ihn so wertvoll als möglich liefert** (Keller's *Züricher Novellen,* II. 28). The attitude of the literary language is at present not as favorable to this construction as formerly.

c. Often we find a relative in one clause, but do not discover in the following clause, which is co-ordinate with it, a relative expressed or understood: **Darauf wagte Anton den Hals des Schwarzen zu streicheln, was der Pony wohlwollend aufnahm und seinerseits dem Fremdling die Rocktaschen beroch** (Freytag). In such sentences which cannot be translated literally the second clause has the word-order of a subordinate clause and a subject in common with the first clause, but there is no relative pronoun or conjunction that connects it to the main proposition, and it is in fact logically an independent statement. This construction, not infrequent in M.H.G. and later in the classical period and still common in the language of the common people but at present not so frequent in the literary language, is an ungrammatical but convenient way of adding to a preceding clause an additional proposition containing the same subject, without formally constructing a new sentence or a grammatical subordinate clause.

4. *Mood.* The mood is usually the indicative, but also the subjunctive is found, especially the subjunctive of indirect discourse, the optative subjunctive (for examples see **168.** I. 2. D. *a* and *b*), the potential subjunctive in all its uses, especially, however, that one known as the *subjunctive of modest or cautious statement,* which softens the broad, sweeping negative statement of the principal proposition: **Die Regierung der Vereinigten Staaten beschwerte sich über die Landung sovieler Armen, welche manche europäische Regierung fortschicke** (subj. of indirect discourse). **Sie grübelte über die Worte, die er zu ihr sprechen könnte** (potential subj.), **und über ihre Antworten. Noch nie ist eine Unwahrheit gesprochen worden, die nicht früher oder später nachteilige Folgen gehabt hätte** (subj. of cautious statement). For other illustrative examples of the potential subjunctive see **168.** II. C. *a, b,* F. *a;* **169.** 2. C, F. *a.* In elevated diction the *sanguine subjunctive of purpose* (see **168.** I. 2. B. (**3**)) is sometimes found: **Ihr wünscht euch einen tugendhaften Sohn, der eures Hauptes heil'ge Locken ehre** (Schiller). The *unreal subjunctive of purpose* is quite common. See **169.** 1. C. (**3**).

5. For the person of the verb in relative clauses, see **151.** 3. B. *a, b, c.*

6. *Abridgment.* A relative clause can only be abridged when the relative is the subject of the clause. Its contracted form is usually that of an appositive noun, adj., or part.: **Die Römer, [welche] ein tapferes und mächtiges Volk [waren], haben einst die Herrschaft über den halben Erdkreis besessen. Ein Morgen, [der] rot und golden [war], hat uns den Mai gebracht. Gott lohnt Gutes, [das] hier getan [wird], auch hier noch. Eine Sache, [die] zu oft gesagt [wird], tut den Ohren weh.**

In English, however, the clause can often be abridged to an infinitive phrase where the subject of the clause is the indefinite *one* or the antecedent of the relative, where in general the German employs the clause form: *He is not a man to trifle with* **Er ist kein Mann, mit dem man spaßen kann.** *He is the man to go* **Er ist der Mann, der gehen sollte** (or **müßte**). For other details of usage here see **185.** A. I. 2. *a.* (**3**), also **180.** B. *d.*

Where the subject of the infinitive is other than the indefinite **man** or the antecedent of the relative the preposition *for* must be used with the infinitive: *This is the man for you to send* **Das ist der Mann, den Sie schicken sollten** (or **müßten**). Compare **269.** 3.

7. *Descriptive Relative Clauses.* Propositions which are in form dependent adjective clauses, being introduced by **was** (referring to the thought as a whole), a relative pronoun (**der** or **welcher**), or a relative adverb (**wofür,** &c.), are often in fact independent propositions, as they do not limit the antecedent, but add an independent thought, hence are often employed as a convenient means of making an additional remark which has an important bearing upon the principal statement: **Sie versprachen, ihm in allen Nöten beizustehen, was sie auch getreulich ausführten. Mit dem notwendigen Geldumtausche kam der Wechselhandel auf, der den Niederländern eine neue fruchtbare Quelle des Reichtums eröffnete. Wir nahmen den Weg über den Berg, wodurch wir eine Stunde ersparten.** For fuller discussion of this common construction see **153.** 1. (**3**) and **153.** 2. A. (**1**). For the common use of a descriptive relative clause introduced by **als** *when* see **275.** *a.*

8. *Word-order.* The attributive adjective clause usually has the transposed word-order, but explanatory clauses which are not introduced by a connective have normal word-order:

Der Unglückliche — es war Chatillon — klammerte sich einen Augenblick mit Händen und Füßen an das Gesims (K. F. Meyer). **Friedrich — er war damals etwa zehn Jahre alt, aber schon sehr groß und stark — machte mit uns sehr weite und anstrengende Touren.** Such explanatory clauses with normal word-order are distinguished as subordinate clauses by their more rapid enunciation.

Object Clause.

272. Object clauses are divided into *genitive, dative, accusative,* and *prepositional* clauses:

A. *Genitive clause.* The genitive clause is usually introduced by **daß** (see **240.** *a*), and the interrogatives **was, ob, wie,** &c., and can be used to replace any gen., whether it be the object of a verb or an adjective: **Ich erinnere mich nicht, daß ich dies gesagt habe** (= **dieser Worte**). **Der Träge ist nicht wert, daß man ihn unterstütze. Ich erinnere mich nicht mehr genau, ob er sich dieses scharfen Ausdrucks bediente.** Often representing the old genitive of cause: **Ich freue mich riesig, daß du gekommen bist. Es wundert mich, daß er das Wort übel genommen hat,** or **Daß er das Wort übel genommen hat, wundert mich.** Compare **238.** 3. E. *c.* After a **deshalb, deswegen,** or **um deswillen** in the principal proposition the conjunction **weil** has become more common here than **daß: Was endlich das von Professor Laband angeführte Beispiel, betreffend die Ausweisung der Engländer aus Hamburg, betrifft, so ist es um deswillen beweisunkräftig, weil der Hamburger Senat so wenig wie eine andere Bundesregierung solche Torheiten begehen wird** (*Hamburger Nachrichten,* June 7, 1906).

From a modern point of view many such examples may be classed as prepositional clauses, as the genitive is now often replaced by a prepositional phrase: **Ich freue mich dessen** or **darüber.**

If the subordinate clause precedes there is usually a demonstrative in the principal proposition referring back to the subordinate clause: **Was du für recht hältst, dessen brauchst du dich nicht zu schämen.**

a. Mood. The mood is usually indic., but, as in the following sentences, the subjunctive of indirect discourse or indirect question, and the potential subjunctive, may be used: **Karl V. von Spanien konnte sich rühmen, die Sonne gehe** (subj. of indirect discourse) **in seinem weiten Reiche nicht unter. Er erinnerte sich, er habe es früher gesagt. Er war ungewiß, wo er mehr Ansehen hätte** (unreal potential form of the subj. of indirect question), **ob in dem Feld, ob in dem Kabinette. Er war nicht gewiß, ob er es tun könnte** (same kind of subj. as in the preceding sentence). **Ich erinnere mich nicht, daß ich ihm einen Besuch gemacht hätte** (unreal potential; very common after a negative proposition).

To give the idea of mere subjectivity or more commonly the idea of unreality **daß** is sometimes replaced by the conjunction **als ob** with transposed word-order or simple **als** with question order, as so often found in clauses of manner (**168.** II. B, **169.** 2. B, **276.** A): **welchen seine Gegner anklagten, als habe er Geld von den Juden empfangen** (Heine). **Welcher Eure Schwester fälschlich angeklagt, als hätte sie ihr Ehebett befleckt** (Schikaneder). This usage was more common here and in C. *d* a little earlier in the period than at present, but it is still common in adjective clauses (**168.** II. G. *b* and **169.** 2. G. *b*) and is not infrequent in subject (**269.** 2. *b*) and prepositional phrase (**272.** D. *b*) clauses, and in clauses of manner (**276.** A).

b. Tense. The idiomatic use of tenses in indirect discourse demands especial care, and hence this subject has been described at length in article **171.** 2.

c. Omission of **daß.** When the thought or feeling of someone is reported indirectly **daß** is often dropped, and the subordinate clause has the order of a principal proposition, as in the first two sentences in *a* above. The **daß** cannot be omitted after a negative, as in the first and second sentences in A, nor after a verb of feeling, as in the example in A which contains the verb **freuen.** For an explanation of this usage see **284.** I. 3. *a.* The use of **daß** is also regulated by the principle described in C. *f* below.

d. Abridgment. Those clauses which are introduced by **daß** may be replaced by the infinitive construction, provided the subject of the clause is identical with the subject or object of the principal proposition: **Ich bin nicht wert, daß ich dir die Schuhriemen auflöse;** or **Ich bin nicht wert, dir die Schuhriemen aufzulösen. Ich erinnere mich nicht, daß ich ihm einen Besuch gemacht habe** or **hätte** (see *a*, above, last sentence); or **Ich erinnere mich nicht, ihm einen Besuch gemacht zu haben.**

B. *Dative Clause.* This dative clause performs the function of a noun or adjective-substantive which is the dat. object of a verb or adjective: **Wer keinen Rat annimmt** (= **dem Eigensinnigen**), **dem kann nicht geholfen werden.** They are usually introduced by a relative pronoun or adverb, or by **daß** and

wenn: Wer sich nicht nach der Decke streckt, dem bleiben die Füße unbedeckt. Daß es dazu werde (i.e. **daß das Ergebnis der Wissenschaft Gemeingut werde**), **dem dient meine Arbeit** (Wilamowitz-Moellendorff's *Griechische Tragödien*, II. p. 4). **Es resultiert also ein Spannungszustand, hervorgerufen durch gegeneinander arbeitende Muskeln, vergleichbar dem, wenn ich die Bewegung einer Hand durch das Entgegenhalten der zweiten hemme** (E. Herzog in *Die Neueren Sprachen*, April 1905).

a. There are few dat. clauses which do not have in the principal proposition a demonstrative or other pronominal adjective in the dat. referring to the contents of the subordinate clause: **Was mir unrecht scheint, dem versage ich meine Beistimmung.** Only when the relative itself is in the dat., can the demon. be dropped: **Der Arzt hilft, wem er helfen kann.**

b. Mood. The mood is usually indic., but sometimes the subjunctive, especially the *concessive* (**168.** I. 2. A) subjunctive, is used: **Nimmermehr enthülle das Geheimnis, wem es auch sei.**

c. Non-omission of **daß.** If the clause is not introduced by a relative pronoun, a conjunction, as **daß** and **wenn** in the last two sentences in B, *must* be used. The conjunction here cannot be omitted as so often elsewhere, as it is needed to preserve the oneness of the words in the clause. Compare with C. *f* below and **284.** I. 3. *a*.

d. Abridgment. Such clauses may often be clumsily abridged by substituting an adjective or participial substantive with its modifiers for the clause form. Thus the second sentence in B, above, becomes **Dem sich nicht nach der Decke Streckenden bleiben die Füße unbedeckt.**

C. *Accusative Clause.* The accusative clause performs the function of a noun in the acc., object of some verb or adjective: **Ich weiß nicht, wo er sich befindet** (= **den Ort seines gegenwärtigen Aufenthalts**). After verbs which govern two accusatives, one of the person and one of the thing, either the object of the person or the object of the thing may be replaced by a clause: **Lehre, die dir folgen wollen** (= **deine Jünger**), **deine Wege. Lehre mich, was du von ihm gelernt hast** (=**die von ihm empfangene Wissenschaft**). Accusative clauses are usually introduced by **daß** or sometimes **weil** instead of the more common **daß** when the idea of cause is present, sometimes by **wie** (= **daß**) after verbs of *perceiving* and *relating*, sometimes by **wenn** *if, when,* often by relative pronouns and adverbs, and in indirect questions by the interrogative particles **ob, wann, wo, wie, warum, weshalb,** &c., or the interrogative pronouns **wer, was** and the interrogative adjectives **welch, was für ein, ein wie** (**134.** 3): **Wir versicherten ihm, daß wir bereit seien, ihm zu helfen. Und führen zur Ursache an, weil** (instead of the more common **daß**) **eine große Begebenheit darin erschöpft ist** (Schiller's *Briefe*, 1, 435). **Ich sah, wie** (= **daß**) **er auf und abging. Das nenne ich erfreulich, wenn man wohlerzogene Kinder sieht. Was Hände bauten, können Hände stürzen. Ich will doch sehen, wie** (here interrog. particle used to introduce an indirect question) **es ablaufen wird. Er fragte, weshalb ich nicht gekommen sei** (direct: **Weshalb sind Sie nicht gekommen**). **Ich weiß nicht, mit wem er am meisten umgeht.**

a. Often the neut. **es, eines,** or a demonstrative pronoun in the principal proposition serves as an anticipative object pointing to the following subordinate clause, which as an appositive explains it, and is in fact the real object: **Ich mag's und will's nicht glauben, daß mich der Max verlassen kann** (Schiller). **Ich weiß es, daß er nicht Wort hält. Sagt mir nur eins: ob er im Bann ist** (Hauptmann's *Der arme Heinrich*, 2, 1). **Eines nur entbehr' ich mit Kummer: daß ich nicht mehr vom frühesten Morgen | für ihn schaffen darf** (Fulda's *Der Talisman*, 2, 4). **Diese Ansicht vertreten wir und weiter die: daß es nicht nur das gute Recht, sondern auch die Pflicht und Schuldigkeit der Regierung erheischt, Staat und Gesellschaft davor zu sichern, daß usw.** (*Hamburger Nachrichten*, Feb. 27, 1907). When the subordinate clause precedes, a demonstrative may stand in the principal proposition pointing back to the subordinate clause: **Was du heute tun kannst, das verschiebe nicht auf morgen.** The demonstrative **das** here may be omitted, but where the subordinate clause begins with **wer** the demonstrative *must* be used in the principal proposition: **Wer das getan hat, den bestrafen wir.**

b. Attraction. Here and elsewhere in substantive clauses a relative is sometimes attracted into the case of the preceding demonstrative, which is then, however, always understood and never formally expressed: **Sie eilt durch den Hof zum Toresgang, dem Wanderer zu bieten Schutz und Rast, und [den,] wen's** (for **wer es**) **auch sei, zu wärmen und zu laben** (Redwitz's *Amaranth*).

Sometimes, especially in early N.H.G., and still in the language of the common people, the opposite construction is found, namely, a noun or pronoun is attracted into the case of a following relative: **Ein König | der die Armen trewlich** (**treulich**) **richtet | des thron wird ewiglich bestehen** (Proverbs xxix. 14).

c. If several consecutive subject, accusative or adjective clauses have the relative **was** in common it need only be used once, when the relative is in the same case in the different clauses. If the relative is in different cases in the different clauses it should be repeated. If, however, the relative should happen to have the same form for two different cases, it is sometimes used but once, a usage once common but now infrequent in choice prose: **Was geschieht und ich nicht hindern kann** (Lessing). **Und was wir sind und haben, hat in ihm** (i.e. **dem Christentum**) **seine Wurzel und Kraft** (Spielhagen's *Was will das werden?*, I, chap. IX). The repetition of **was** in the second clause is now preferred in choice language.

d. Mood. The mood is usually indicative, but the subjunctive of *indirect discourse* and *indirect question* is frequently found. To give the idea of mere subjectivity or more commonly the idea of unreality **daß** is sometimes replaced by the conjunction **als ob** with transposed word-order or simple **als** with question order, as so often found in clauses of manner (**168.** II. B and **169.** 2. B): **gleichsam um zu zeigen, als hätte die bessere Regung schon von Anbeginn bestanden** (Gutzkow). This usage was more common here and in A. *a* a little earlier in the period than at present, but it is still common in adjective clauses (**168.** II. G. *b*, **169.** 2. G. *b*) and is not infrequent in subject (**269.** 2. *b*) and prepositional phrase (**272.** D. *b*) clauses, and in clauses of manner (**276.** A).

Also the imperative mood is used, or here as elsewhere instead of the imperative proper the perfect participle or the present infinitive: **Ich sah ihn an, und mein Blick mochte ihm erwidern: Erzähle! Nicht immer alten Fummel** (dress of poor material or an old dress) **tragen, hat dein Sohn gesagt** (Georg Hirschfeld's *Nebeneinander*, p. 15).

e. Tense. The idiomatic use of tenses in indirect discourse demands especial care, and hence this subject has been discussed at length in **171.** 2.

f. Omission of **daß** *and* **ob**. When the thought or feeling of someone is reported indirectly **daß** is often dropped, and the subordinate clause has the order of the principal proposition: **Fichte behauptet, der Mensch könne, was er wolle, und wenn er sage, er könne nicht, so wolle er nicht. Ich fürchte, Ihr Sohn wird nicht versetzt** (to a mother anxious about her son's promotion). **Er ist, glaube ich, davon überzeugt. Den Brackenburg solltest du in Ehren halten, sag' ich dir** (Goethe's *Egmont*, 3). As in **269.** 1. *c* the **daß** should not be omitted if it is necessary to make the thought clear, i.e. to indicate the oneness of the words in the object clause and maintain its integrity as a distinct grammatical element in contradistinction to the other elements in the sentence: **Die Erfahrung bewies, daß die römische Symmachie trotz ihrer scheinbar loseren Fügung gegen Pyrrhos zusammenhielt wie eine Mauer aus Felsenstücken** (Mommsen's *Römische Geschichte*, III, chap. 1). If the **daß** were omitted in this sentence it would bring **die römische Symmachie** next to the verb, which might at the first glance lead us to seek for a grammatical relation between these two elements instead of connecting the noun with the words that follow.

There are often also other reasons for the use of **daß**. The transposed order is used after negatives: **Ich glaube nicht, daß du recht hast. Daß** is regularly employed after a demonstrative, as after **die** in the third sentence from the last in *a* above. For an explanation of this usage see **284.** I. 3. *a*.

The connective is always omitted in direct quotations: **Das Volk rief: Es lebe der Kaiser.—Viel [ist] erreicht! durfte er sich gestehen** (Ebner-Eschenbach's *Der Kreisphysikus*, p. 19).

In indirect questions **ob** is sometimes in lively language omitted and the word-order of a direct question employed: **Manchmal waren es welche, mit denen ich nie ein Wort gewechselt, ich konnte nicht wissen, waren sie klug oder dumm unter dem reizenden Lärvchen, schlummerte in den Tiefen ihrer Seelen etwas, oder waren sie seelenlos wie jene Fabelwesen der Sage** (Ompteda's *Herzeloide*, p. 2). Of course the full question form is employed if it is desired to relate directly: **Es wollte ihr kaum gelingen, „Mann, Mann! was gibt es, Andreas?" hinunterzurufen** (G. Ebers's *Die Frau Bürgermeisterin*, p. 242).

g. Abridgment. An acc. clause can be abridged only when its subject is identical with the subject or sometimes the object (expressed or understood) of the principal proposition. The clause may then be abridged to an infin. with **zu** or a single noun: **Ich hoffe, ihn noch heute zu sehen. Ich bitte, daß Sie gehen,** or **Ich bitte Sie, zu gehen. Ich rate Ihnen, daß Sie vorsichtig seien;** or **Ich rate Ihnen Vorsicht;** or **Ich rate Ihnen, vorsichtig zu sein. Das macht es ihm und mir unmöglich, es zu tun.** Originally the infinitive was only a modifier of the verb, but in course of time a close relation developed between it and the subject or object of the principal verb, so that the infinitive and the subject or object of the principal proposition came to be felt as an abridged clause, in which the subject or object of the principal proposition was the logical subject and the infinitive the logical predicate. This construction has become thoroly established where the subject of the infinitive is the subject of the principal proposition, often also when the subject of the infinitive is an accusative or dative object of the principal verb. In German the infinitive has not spread beyond these limits, while in English it is used with an accusative subject after verbs of wishing, desiring, believing, imagining, knowing, expecting, reporting, representing, where the accusative in a strict sense cannot be construed as the object of the principal verb: *I desire, expect*, &c., *him to go.* As illustrated in **185.** B. 1. 5, German also formerly employed the infinitive here, but as it was not deeply rooted it was entirely replaced by a full clause: **Ich wünsche, erwarte, daß er gehe.** Aside from the list of verbs just given English expression now has the simple rule here that the *to*-form of the infinitive is used when its subject is the subject or object of the principal verb and that elsewhere, according to **269.** 3, *for* is placed before the *to*-form: *I planned to go myself* **Ich plante, selbst zu gehen,** but *I planned for him to go* **Ich plante, daß er gehe.** With certain groups of verbs, however, we regularly find the simple infinitive instead of the prepositional form. See **185.** B. I. 2. *a, b, c, d, e*. In English we often find the gerund instead of the prepositional infinitive. The gerund has as subject the person implied in a possessive adjective or a genitive: I remember *his* or *John's* saying it. On mere formal grounds, i.e. on account of the lack of an s-genitive in a number of the most common pronouns, *this, these, any, several, all, both, two, three,* &c., and on account of the ambiguity of this form in nouns, the singular and plural genitive sounding alike to the ear, there is a tendency in colloquial speech to use the accusative as the subject of the gerund: I remember *one, several, all* of them, *the lad* (acc. sing.), *the lads* (acc. pl.) saying it. German requires in all these cases a full clause: **Ich erinnere mich, daß der Junge es gesagt hat.** If the subject of the gerund is the subject of the principal proposition, it is suppressed: I planned going myself **Ich plante selbst zu gehen.** The gerundial construction belongs to the old attributive or appositional type of clause described in **268.** 4.

h. The principal verb or the principal proposition is often suppressed so that the subordinate clause becomes the bearer of the thought: **Sie aber mit immer wachsender Angst: „Denken Sie an Ihre Frau! an Ihre Tochter!"** (P. Heyse's *Geteiltes Herz*, p. 29). **Laura — daß das Kind nur recht, recht was Gutes bekommt** (Wildenbruch's *Der unsterbliche Felix*, 3, 7) Laura, see to it that, or I desire that, &c. See also **169.** I. A.

D. *Prepositional Clause.* This clause performs the function of a prepositional object: **Die Eltern freuen sich d a r ü b e r, d a ß i h r e K i n d e r F o r t s c h r i t t e m a c h e n** (= **über die Fortschritte ihrer Kinder**). This clause is introduced by **daß** (see **240.** *a*), **als ob** (see *b* below), **ob,** and the relative and interrogative pronouns, or the relative or interrogative adverbs **womit,** &c.: **Es bleibt da'bei, daß wir reisen. Es fehlt viel da'ran, daß ich zufrieden sein könnte. Es ist da'für gesorgt, daß die Bäume nicht in den Himmel wachsen. Er hat es da'hin gebracht, daß er nicht mehr für seinen Unterhalt arbeiten muß. Ob du der klügste seist, da'ran ist wenig gelegen. Das erinnert mich da'ran, wa'rum ich dich jetzt habe rufen lassen. Es fehlte ihm da'zu, daß er ein Staatsmann hätte sein können, der scharfe, klare Blick in die Zukunft.** This clause is sometimes, especially earlier in the period and still in colloquial language, also introduced by other conjunctions instead of the regular **daß,** namely by **wenn** to indicate a condition, **indem** means, **damit** purpose, and **weil** cause: **Das Vertrauen eines Kranken kann nur da'durch erschlichen werden, wenn** (usually **daß**) **man seine eigene Sprache gebraucht** (Schiller). **Du hast doch nichts da'gegen, wenn** (usually **daß**) **ich heute abend zum Gottesdienst gehe? Daß man nur da'durch Kenner wird, indem** (usually **daß**) **man den einseitigen Enthusiasmus verliert** (Tieck). **Marianel benützte diese Gelegenheit schon deshalb, damit** (usually **daß,** but of course **damit** is used if **deshalb** is suppressed) **sie jedes hingeworfene Wörtlein aufhaschen möge** (Holtei). **Das kommt da'her, weil sie ihn liebt. Das kommt da'von, Herr Förster, weil** (usually **daß**) **ich früher Totengräber gewesen bin** (Baumbach's *Das Habichtsfräulein*, III). After **da'rum, da'her, deshalb, deswegen, um deswillen** (**129.** 2. *a*), however, it has become the rule to use **weil** to indicate cause, so that **darum daß, daher daß, deshalb daß, deswegen daß, um deswillen daß** are characteristic of older German. This is development in the direction of more accurate expression. Such clauses with **weil** are now causal clauses (**278**).

The conjunction **daß** cannot usually be dropped after the demonstrative adverbs **da'bei, da'her,** &c. For an explanation of this usage see **284.** I. 3. *a.*

a. In the principal proposition there is usually a demon. prepositional adverb, **da'rüber, da'für, da'bei, da'durch,** &c., **deshalb, deswegen, um'hin** (very common before abridged clauses), **da'her, da'hin,** &c., pointing to the following clause. The demonstrative prepositional adverb, however, often drops out: **Ich konnte nicht in Zweifel [darüber] sein, wem ich es zu danken hätte** (K. F. Meyer). If the subordinate clause precedes, either a demon. adverb or pronoun can stand in the principal clause: **Was dieser Zeuge beim ersten Verhör ganz Unglaubliches angegeben hatte, auf dêm** (or **'darauf**) **bestand er jetzt.**

b. Mood. The mood is usually indic., but various forms of the optative and the potential subjunctive are also used: **Alle rieten ihm dazu, daß er das Amt trotz der damit verbundenen Schwierigkeiten annehme. Er denkt darüber nach, wie er fortkomme.** Other examples with explanation in **168.** II. G. *a.* (**2**). Instead of **daß** the conjunction **als ob** or simple **als** is often used with a present or past tense form of the subjunctive to give expression to the idea of mere subjectivity or unreality: **Das möge nicht dahin mißverstanden werden, als sei eine bloße Hypothese von Haeckel** (name) **in unwissenschaftlicher Weise als richtig angenommen worden** (A. Koelsch in *Frankfurter Zeit.*, Feb. 15, 1914). **Der Minister verwahrte sich dagegen, als ob er mit Schließung der Universität gedroht hätte** (*Hamburger Nachrichten*, Nov. 23, 1904) protested against the charge that, &c. Compare **272.** A. *a*, C. *d.*

c. Abridgment. If the clause is introduced by **daß,** it is more often abridged to an infin. with **zu** when the subject of the principal proposition and that of the subordinate clause are identical, and sometimes when the subjects are not identical, provided no ambiguity may arise: **Ich kann nicht umhin, dir meine Freude darüber auszudrücken. Er hat die größte Lust dazu, uns auf unserer Reise zu begleiten.** Where the preposition (**zu, auf,** &c. in the **dazu, darauf,** &c.) means direction, inclination, as in this sentence, the infinitive with **zu** is still the rule. But where the **zu** in the **dazu** means purpose or result the new form **um zu** is now more common before the infinitive than the older simple **zu,** as the **um** brings out more clearly the idea of purpose or result, indeed brings out this idea so clearly that in many expressions the **dazu** in the principal proposition is omitted: **Es gehörte die ganze Unabhängigkeit und Energie . . . der Herzogin da'zu, um nicht an dem Unternehmen zu scheitern** (Rodenberg). **Um das fertig zu machen, da'zu gehört noch Arbeit. Es fehlt mir nur an mir, um recht beglückt zu sein** (Goethe). **Pompejus fehlte keine Bedingung, um nach der Krone zu greifen, als die erste von allen: der eigene königliche Mut** (Mommsen's *Römische Geschichte,* V, chap. 3). **Es fehlte ihm, um Staatsmann zu sein, der scharfe, klare Blick in die Zukunft** (Dürckheim). **Das Ministerium besaß nicht die nötige Kühnheit, um den König von seinem Eigensinn abzuwenden** (id.). **Der folgende Tag wurde benützt, um die Stadt kennen zu lernen** (id.). If **dazu** stands in the principal proposition as in the example from Rodenberg the **um** is not needed before the infinitive, but even here the trend of usage is toward the employment of **um: Die Bücher sind da'zu da, um gelesen zu werden.** Compare **281.** *b. Note.* Altho **um zu** with the infinitive is quite freely used to express purpose or result the infinitive with simple **zu** can only take the place of a prepositional clause denoting direction when the subject of the clause is identical with the subject of the principal proposition: **Ich warte darauf, ihn beim Verlassen des Hauses abzufangen.** In English, however, after verbs that take a prepositional object, such as *to count upon,* &c., instead of a clause with a nominative subject we may use the prepositional infinitive with an accusative subject, where German requires the clause form with a nominative subject: I am counting upon him to do it **Ich rechne darauf, daß er es tue.** In many common expressions containing the preposition *for* following a verb, as *to hope for, to wait for* the *for* is not a preposition at all but a conjunction introducing an infinitive for-clause, as explained in **269.** 3: *He is still hoping to be able to do it soon* **Er hofft noch darauf, es bald tun zu können,** but *I am still hoping for him to go soon* **Ich hoffe noch darauf, daß er bald gehe.** The *for* is used in English here as so often elsewhere when the subject of the infinitive is not identical with the subject of the principal proposition. After real prepositions English often employs a gerund instead of an infinitive. In this construction the logical subject of the gerund is the person implied in a possessive adjective or a genitive: *I am counting on his* or *John's doing it* **Ich rechne darauf, daß er** or **Hans es tue.** For further remarks on the gerund see C. *g*.

Adverbial Clause.

273. 1. An adverbial clause performs the function of an adverbial element: **Biege den Baum, s o l a n g e e r n o c h j u n g i s t** (= **früh,** or **in seiner Jugend**), or in older form: **Biege den Baum so lange, als er noch jung ist.** Such a clause is the result of a long development. Originally **so lange** was in the principal proposition the **so** pointing forward to the following appositional clause which explains **so lange.** The appositive clause is introduced here as appositives often elsewhere by **als** (originally **all so**). Gradually **so lange** became more closely related to the following clause and finally became a part of it and **als** as a superfluous element disappeared. In many sentences the appositive clause is introduced by **daß: Er schwankte so, daß ich ihn nicht mehr halten konnte.** Other words than **so** often point forward to the following appositional clause, such as **der** (**271.** I), **ein** (**271.** I), **solch,** &c.: **Ich setzte ein solches Mißtrauen in ihn, daß ich ihn beobachten ließ.** Thus different forms with different shades of meaning have gradually developed.

a. The adverbial clause is introduced by a subordinate conjunction (full list of them in **238.** 3). In the principal proposition a demon. adverb often points to the adverbial clause: **Wo viel Licht [ist], da ist viel Schatten.**

b. The mood and tense of the adverbial clause are subject to the general rules for mood and tense.

c. Adverbial clauses may often be abridged, especially when the subject of the principal proposition and that of the subordinate clause are identical. The abridged form is either that of an infin. phrase, or an appositive noun, adj. or participle: **Der Knabe besucht die Schule, d a m i t e r s i c h n ü t z l i c h e K e n n t n i s s e e r w e r b e;** or **u m s i c h n ü t z l i c h e K e n n t n i s s e z u e r w e r b e n. O b g l e i c h e r S i e g e r w a r;** or **O b g l e i c h S i e g e r, mußte er doch das Schlachtfeld räumen. W e i l e r k r a n k u n d e l e n d w a r;** or **K r a n k u n d e l e n d,**

sehnte er sich nach dem Tode. Wenn sie zu weit getrieben wird; or **Zu weit getrieben, verfehlt die Strenge ihres weisen Zwecks. Während ich das bei mir dachte**; or **Dies bei mir denkend, schlief ich ein.**

Note. This adverbial apposition is especially frequent in case of a substantive or adjective preceded by the conjunction **als**. Such a noun may be used instead of a clause to express the following adverbial relations: 1. Time: **Cicero entdeckte als Konsul die Verschwörung des Catilina.** 2. Manner: **Er lebte als Christ.** 3. Degree (containing a restriction): **Als** (in so far as) **Tier gehört der Mensch der Erde an, als Geist einer höheren Welt.** 4. Cause or reason: **Als treuer Diener wollte uns Joseph nicht verlassen. Mein Freund hat als enterbt jetzt keine Mittel mehr.** 5. Condition: **Wer dir als Freund nicht nützen kann, kann als Feind dir schaden.** 6. Concession: **Als Anfänger behandelt er die Sache doch mit Meisterschaft.** 7. Purpose or end: **Er zog seinen Freund als Mitarbeiter heran.**

2. Adverbial clauses are subdivided into classes corresponding to those of adverbial elements—clauses of *place, time, manner, degree, cause, condition and exception, concession, purpose* or *end, means*.

Clause of Place.

274. A clause of place indicates the place where the action of the principal verb occurs (for conjunctions see **238.** 3. A): **Nicht überall, wo Wasser ist, sind Frösche; aber wo man Frösche hört, ist Wasser. Woher der befruchtende Regen strömt, (daher) stürzt auch der verheerende Blitzstrahl. Wohin das Christentum drang, da erloschen vor ihm alle Leichenbrände. Dorthin wendet euch, von wannen alle Hilfe kommt** (Uhland). **Wol dem | der nicht wandelt im Rat der Gotlosen | Noch tritt auff den Weg der Sünder | Noch sitzt da die Spötter sitzen** (Ps. i. 1).

a. The demonstratives **da, dort, daher, dorther, dahin, dorthin** often stand in the principal proposition, as can be seen from the above examples.

b. The mood in these clauses is usually the indicative, but a past tense form of the subjunctive is not infrequent. See **169.** 2. I.

c. Abridgment. These clauses cannot usually be abridged, except sometimes by substituting a simple adverb: **Wohin ich blicke,** (or **Überall**) **redest du mit Wohltat mir und Güte zu** (Seume). On the other hand, however, short pithy form is still very common in the old verbless, appositional type of sentence described in **252.** 1. *b. Note*: **Viel Feind', viel Ehr'! = Wo viele Feinde sind, da ist viel Ehre. Viele Köpfe, viele Sinne!**

Clause of Time.

275. A temporal clause limits the time of the action of the principal verb, which is thus represented as taking place simultaneously with, or before, or after that of the temporal clause (for conjunctions see **238.** 3. B): **Ich erschrak, als ich ihn sah. Es schließt** (historical present) **sich hinter ihm und als er sich umwendet, um von dem Schließer Auskunft zu erhalten, weist ihn dieser mit höhnischen Worten hinweg** (E. Martin's *Wolframs von Eschenbach Parzival*, II, p. xxiii). **Kaum erblickte er mich, als** (see *a*) **er auf mich zueilte. Ich lag schon in tiefem Schlafe, als** (see *a*) **ich plötzlich durch ein Geräusch geweckt wurde. Ich war soeben** (or **gerade**) **im Begriff zu dir zu gehen, als** (see *a*) **du mir zuvorkamst. Noch war ich nicht daheim, als** (see *a*) **das Gewitter ausbrach** (Paul's *Deutsche Grammatik*, IV, p. 325). **Was wir gemeinhin Ehre nennen, das ist wohl nichts weiter als der Schatten, den wir werfen, wenn die Sonne der öffentlichen Achtung uns bescheint** (Sudermann's *Die Ehre*, 2, 11). **Wenn sich der Winter nähert, verlassen uns die Zugvögel. Wenn Sie fertig sind, möchte ich gern mit Ihnen sprechen. Ach, da ich irrte, hatt' ich viel Gespielen, da ich dich** (**die Wahrheit**) **kenne, bin ich fast allein** (Goethe). **Das Eisen muß geschmiedet werden, weil** (now **während** or **indem**) **es glüht** (Schiller's *Die Piccolomini*, 3, 2). **Seit** (or **seitdem**) **er auf das Land gezogen ist, habe ich ihn nicht wieder gesehen,** but in **Es ist viele Jahre her, seit** (**seitdem,** or **daß**) **ich ihn gesehen habe** the conjunction introduces a subject clause, not a clause of time. **Solange die Nationen ein gesondertes Dasein führen, wird es Streitigkeiten geben, welche nur mit den Waffen geschlichtet werden können** (Moltke). **Im Unterhause erklärte Grey, daß England so lange nicht in amtlichen Verkehr mit Serbien trete, solange die Offiziere, welche an der**

Ermordung des Königspaares teilgenommen, nicht aus ihren offiziellen Stellungen entfernt worden wären (*Neue Zürcher Zeit.*, April 14, 1906). **Die Führer wissen ganz gut, daß sie so lange vergebens kämpfen, als sie mit ihrer Opposition allein stehen** (*Hamburger Nachrichten*, Oct. 29, 1904). **Man kann meist so lange nicht genügend über eine Tat urteilen, als man die Beweggründe dazu nicht kennt. Ich bin wie der Lehrling beim Konditor gewesen, den man Zuckerzeug naschen läßt, bis daß er sich den Magen daran verdirbt** (Wildenbruch's *Der unsterbliche Felix*, 3, 5). **Sie gelobten einander, sich nicht zu unterwerfen, bis nicht** (see **223.** XI. B. *a.* (**3**)) **der unterste Stein zu oberst gekommen wäre** (Ranke's *D. Gesch. im Z. d. R.*, IV, 538). **Der Krug geht zum Brunnen, bis er bricht. Bis du nach Rom zurückkommst, ist die längst Großmutter** (Sudermann's *Johannes*, 1, 1). **Ich habe so lange keine Ruhe, bis ich mich von dér Seite gereinigt habe. In Rußland dauert das Soldatische des heimkehrenden Reservisten in der Haltung kaum so lange, als bis die alte mitgebrachte Soldatenmütze aufgetragen ist** (*Hamb. Nachr.*, Oct. 29, 1904). **Ihr Anhang . . . . . wird nicht ehe** (now usually **eher**) **zu bändigen sein, bis wir sie vor den Augen der Welt zu nichte gemacht . . . . haben** (Goethe's *Götz*, 3, 1), a blending of **. . . wird nicht eher zu bändigen sein, als bis wir usw.** and **. . . wird nicht zu bändigen sein, bis wir usw. Ich hab' dein Wort, du wirst nicht eher handeln, | bevor du mich, mich selber überzeugt** (Schiller's *Die Piccolomini*, 5, 1), a blending of **Du wirst nicht eher handeln, als bis du mich usw.** and **Du wirst nicht handeln, bevor du mich usw. Nicht eher, als bis** (after **nicht eher** more common than simple **bis** or **bevor**) **er sie von Weindünsten taumeln sah, gab er ihnen die Schrift zur Unterzeichnung** (Schiller). **Man muß nicht eher fliegen wollen, als bis einem die Flügel gewachsen sind. 's wird keiner bös, der nicht, bevor er's ward, erst gut gewesen** (Grillparzer). **Man pflegt in einem wichtigen Werke zu blättern, ehe man es ernstlich zu lesen anfängt** (Lessing). **Sie ist so bescheiden und so dankbar, sie hat gesagt, sie könnte keinen Bissen zu sich nehmen, ehe sie nicht** (**223.** XI. B. *a.* (**3**)) **dem Hausherrn, der sie so gütig aufgenommen, gedankt hätte** (Wildenbruch's *Der unsterbliche Felix*, 3, 6). **Dort (in Griechenland) nur standen Musen und Grazien auf, wenn** (now **während**; see **238.** 3. B. *a*) **das neblichte** (now **neblige**) **Lappland, kaum Menschen, niemals ein Genie gebiert** (Schiller). **Sie (die Zitherspielerin) war eine schlanke Blondine, da** (now **während**) **jene (die Harfenspielerin) dunkelbraunes Haar schmückte** (Goethe).

a. Principal Proposition instead of a Subordinate Clause. As the subordinate clause introduced by **als** is in fact a descriptive relative clause (**271.** II. 7) and hence has the force of an independent proposition, it is often replaced by a principal proposition introduced by **so** or **und**: **Kaum war der König am jenseitigen Ufer des Rheins gelandet, so überfiel ihn ein Haufen spanischer Reiter** (Schiller). **Kaum ist der edle Prinz von Samarkand begraben, und schon ein neues Todesopfer naht** (id.). Similarly instead of **nicht lange — bis** we often find co-ordination in accord with older usage described in **267.** 4: **So dauerte es nicht lange und er befand sich mit allen in Betracht kommenden Faktoren des Wiener Kunstlebens auf dem gespanntesten Fuße** (Eduard Engels in *Velhagen und Klasings Monatshefte*, April 1905, p. 154).

b. Mood. The indicative and subjunctive are employed according to the rules generally observed for their use. See **169.** 1. C. (**3**) and 2. I. After the conj. **bis** notice that the verb depending upon a verb in a past tense form is in the subjunctive, to indicate the continuance of an action up to a certain point in the future with doubtful result: **Sie wollten ausharren, bis der Entsatz käme** They desired to wait till relief might come. The subjunctive is usually in a past tense form, but occasionally the subjunctive of a present tense form is found in accordance with older usage. See **168.** I. 2. B. (**3**)). If the governing verb is in a present tense form the dependent verb is in the indicative, altho the subjunctive was common here in early N.H.G.: **Sie wollen warten, bis der Entsatz kommt. Ich will das Schwert hinder (hinter) sie schicken | bis das (daß) aus mit jnen (ihnen) sey (sei)** — Jeremiah ix. 16. The use of the indic. after a present tense form here shows that the tendency at present is to look at the action as actually completed, while in earlier periods it was regarded as only contemplated or desired.

c. Abridgment. These clauses can usually be abridged only when their subject is identical with that of the principal proposition. The clause then may become a participle, adjective, or substantive appositive: **Und indem ich dies bei mir dachte**, or **Und dies bei mir denkend, schlief ich ein. Wenn er kaum einer Gefahr entronnen ist**, or **Kaum einer Gefahr entronnen, stürzt er sich in die andere. Daß er in den Sitzungen, wenn behufs der Abstimmung aus dem leichten Schlummer geweckt, zu sagen pflegte** (Bismarck). **Still und eingezogen lebt er für sich, redet nur gefragt**

(J. Minor's *Fragmente vom ewigen Juden*, p. 2). **Als er arm war,** or **Arm, hatt' er sich noch satt gegessen; seitdem er reich geworden,** or **Reich, hungert er bei halbem Essen. Und so saß er (, nachdem er) eine Leiche (geworden,) eines Morgens da** (Schiller). In the abridged clause the time relations can only be gathered from the context as they are not usually expressed, but in modern literature a conjunction is sometimes employed as in the full clause form: **gefühlt bevor erblickt** (Wieland's *Idr.* 2, 40, 7). **Der Keim war welk, bevor entfaltet** (A. Grün's *Werke*, 4, 288). The perfect participle of transitive verbs has passive force except in case of reflexives, which have active force but suppress regularly the reflexive object: [sich] **Zur Wirtin gewendet sagte sie usw.** (Auerbach's *Dorfgeschichten*, 8, p. 39). It has active force also in case of intransitives, but it can only be used of such intransitives as are conjugated with **sein**, as in the second example. In all these examples we have the old attributive or appositional type of clause structure described in **268.** 4. The participle, adjective, or substantive appositive is the logical predicate of the clause and the subject of the principal proposition the logical subject. English has gone much farther than German in developing this old type of clause. In English it is very common in the form of a prepositional phrase, in which the subject of the principal proposition is the logical subject, a verbal noun, especially the gerund, the logical predicate, and the preposition a particle to indicate the ideas of time and subordination to the principal proposition: After having played an hour he began to work **Nachdem er eine Stunde gespielt hatte, fing er an zu arbeiten.**

Sometimes when the temporal clause has a different subject from that of the principal proposition it can be abridged, but usually only by substituting a prep. phrase for the clause: **Wenn die Not am größten ist, so ist Gottes Hilfe am nächsten,** or **In der größten Not ist Gottes Hilfe am nächsten.**

Sometimes the absolute accusative construction has the force of a temporal clause. See **265.** B. *b.* (**1**).

Sometimes in lively style an absolute nominative takes the place of a clause of time: **Eine Stunde, dann ist alles vorbei! Nicht ganz acht Monate, so war sie eine Leiche. Acht Tage später und Brüssel öffnete dem Sieger die Tore.** Often in popular speech: **Keine halbe Pfeife Toback, so habens (= haben Sie) den See** (Storm, 2, 36) Before you smoke half a pipeful of tobacco you'll reach the lake.

A verbless temporal clause is often contained in the old verbless appositional type of sentences described in **252.** 1. *b. Note*: **Gesagt, getan = Sobald es gesagt war, wurde es getan.**

Clause of Manner.

276. A clause of manner describes the manner of the action of the principal verb. This clause may define the action in each of the four following ways:

A. *Comparison and Manner Proper.* The action of the principal verb is compared with that in the subordinate clause. The clause is introduced by the conjunctions enumerated in **238.** 3. C. *a.* In **239** these conjunctions are treated at length, where also illustrative sentences are given which show the use of the moods. For moods see also **168.** II. B. *a*, *b* and **169.** 2. B. *a*, *b*.

In such sentences as **Er sieht aus, als [er aussehen würde] wäre er krank,** or **als wenn** or **als ob er krank wäre** the final clause is in fact a conditional clause that modifies the verb in the clause of comparison. In such conditional clauses **ob,** cognate with English *if* and earlier in the period a common conditional conjunction also in German, has been preserved in its old function. But the peculiar use of mood and tense in such clauses, as illustrated in **168.** II. B, indicates that the clause is now sometimes felt as indirect discourse rather than as a condition.

When **so** stands in the principal proposition pointing forward to a following appositional or explanatory clause this clause is usually introduced by **daß**: **Die Entwickelung verläuft nun einmal so, daß neben der Steigerung der Ausdrucksfähigkeit und des geistigen Gehalts einer Sprache eine gewisse Abschleifung der Formschwierigkeit einhergeht** (W. Fischer's *Die deutsche Sprache von heute*, p. 56). The **daß** may be omitted and the clause assume normal word-order, **So kann man vom Tiere aussagen: es verstehe, aber nicht: es habe Verstand** (Vischer's *Ästh.*, 2, 111). To convey the idea of mere subjectivity or unreality **daß** is often replaced here by **als ob** with transposed word-order or simple **als** with question order, as so often found in clauses of manner (**168.** II. B and **169.** 2. B): **So wollen wir das nicht so verstehen, als ob jede andere Aussprache tadelnswert wäre** (W. Fischer's *Die deutsche Sprache von heute*, p. 123.) Where the **so** of the principal proposition points forward to a following **wie**-clause it is often dropped: **Er handelt immer so, wie es sein Vorteil erheischt,** or **Er handelt, wie es sein Vorteil erheischt. Er schilderte das Ereignis, wie folgt** He described the event *as* (for older *all so*) *follows*, originally He described the event *all so*: (*it*, i.e. the description) *follows*. In English the *as* has been transferred from the principal to the subordinate proposition. The German development is exactly the same, but the older **als** (from older **all so**) has been replaced by **wie.** In both German and English the subordinate clause may precede: **Wie man's treibt, so geht's** As you make your bed, so must you lie on it, or As you sow, so will you reap.

a. Abridgment. The clause can often be abridged when the verb is common to both propositions: **Sie liebte ihn, wie eine Mutter ihren Sohn** [**liebt**]. Often also when the verb is not common to both propositions in case of appositive participles: **Die Schar drang langsam vor, als ob den Widerstand der Gegner scheuend** (Grillparzer). **Der kommt mir grade gepfiffen** (in apposition with **mir**) (Lauff's *Frau Aleit*, p. 251) = **als ob ich ihm grade gepfiffen hätte.**

Er kam wie hereingeschneit = wie wenn er hereingeschneit wäre. Er kam wie gerufen. Der Rock sitzt wie angegossen. In clauses of manner proper the present participle is quite common when its subject is the subject of the principal proposition: **Sie kam singend, weinend, lachend in das Haus.** In case of all these participial constructions we have to do with the old attributive or appositional type of clause described in **268.** 4. In this old type, as explained in **252.** 1. *b. Note*, the whole sentence may be verbless. **Wie gewonnen, so zerronnen** Easy come, easy go.

The English contraction *as if to* for *as if he would* is rendered by **wie um zu: Der Esel fing an, seine Ohren zu schwenken und seine wehmütige Stimme erschallen zu lassen, wie um den Kameraden an der Kette zu trösten** (Boßhart's *Die Barettlitochter*, p. 15).

B. *Attendant Circumstance.* The action of the principal verb is accompanied by some attendant circumstance which is contained in the subordinate clause. The clause is introduced by the conjunctions in **238.** 3. C. *b*: **Indem er sich mit dem Rücken an den Baum lehnte, verteidigte er sich tapfer gegen die an Zahl überlegenen Feinde. Das Tier zog sich zurück, indem es mich fortwährend unverwandt anblickte. Er ging an mir vorüber, ohne daß er mich grüßte. Außerdem daß** (or **abgesehen davon daß**) **sie eine reiche Erbin ist, ist sie auch schön und liebenswürdig.**

Instead of a principal proposition and a subordinate clause we often find two principal propositions connected by **und: Er ging an mir vorüber und grüßte mich nicht.** For explanation and force of this construction see **267.** 4 (3rd par.).

a. Abridgment. The clause may be abridged by substituting a participle or a prepositional infinitive for the clause form, provided the subject of the clause and that of the principal proposition are identical: **Er grüßte, i n d e m e r s i c h t i e f v e r b e u g t e,** or **s i c h t i e f v e r b e u g e n d. Er ging an mir vorüber, ohne mich zu grüßen.** A prepositional phrase may often take the place of the clause: **Ein größerer Haufe marschierte in der Richtung der Klosterwiese, um, m i t V e r m e i d u n g e i n e s G e f e c h t e s** (= **indem er ein Gefecht vermied**), **die dort sich versammelnden andern Ritter zur Seite zu locken** (Riehl's *Der Dachs auf Lichtmeß*). **Unter heftigem Weinen** (or **heftig weinend**) **drückte er mir die Hand. Er sang bei geöffnetem Fenster** He sang with the window open, *not* by the open window. **Er ging ohne Erlaubnis aus.**

Instead of a full clause we often find the absolute accusative construction. See **265.** B. *b.* (**1**).

C. *Alternative Agreement.* The action of the principal proposition is in alternative agreement with that of the subordinate clause (for conjunctions see **238.** 3. C. *c*): **Danach einer tut, danach es ihm geht** (proverb; for word-order see **288.** B. *d*). **Das Herz überströmt von Handlungen, von bösen und guten, nachdem** (now **je nachdem**) **der Urquell trüb ist oder hell.** (Klopstock, 9, 18). **Nach Ihnen ist viel Nachfrage und ich antworte, je nachdem die Menschen sind** (Goethe). **Wir werden gelobt oder getadelt, je nachdem wir fleißig oder träge sind. Je nachdem du ausmißt, wird dir wieder eingemessen.**

D. *Result.* The action of the principal verb is followed by a result which is contained in the subordinate clause (for conjunctions see **238.** 3. C. *d*; for the origin of the **daß** clause see **271.** I). Exs.: **Handle auch im Verborgenen so, daß es jedermann sehen könnte. Er sprach mit solchen Gebärden, daß alles** (everybody) **lachte. Die Feinde haben derartige Maßregeln getroffen, daß jeder Rückzug unmöglich wird. Das Verhältnis war nicht dérărt** or **dér Ărt, daß es Johanna große Verlegenheit verursacht hätte. Er hat einen** (see **271.** I) **Charakter, daß man sich von ihm nichts Gutes versehen kann. Es war eine derartige Beleidigung, daß eine Versöhnung unmöglich ist. Er ist nicht der Mann danach, daß er sich das Errungene wehrlos aus den Händen winden ließe. Er hat es danach gemacht, daß wir ihn hassen müssen. Wie viele Eltern gehen dem Vergnügen nach, anstatt daß** (*instead of*, i.e. *so that they do not*) **sie für die Erziehung ihrer Kinder sorgen! Anstatt daß es ihm eingefallen wäre zu arbeiten, vertrödelte er den ganzen Tag. Ich schlich ihm nach, ohne daß er sich umsah. Er erfocht einen glänzenden Sieg, ohne daß er viel Menschenleben geopfert hätte. Ich habe selten geschlafen, daß ich nicht geträumt hätte. Ich denke an den Verlust nicht mehr, geschweige daß ich denselben gegen deinen Bruder erwähnen sollte. Die Bauern saßen da, ohne einander anzusehen, geschweige daß sie zusammen geredet hätten. Weit entfernt, daß man den Feldherrn unterstützt hätte, ward sogar der Sold der Truppen verschwendet. Rauh liegt in der Runde das Bergland, kaum daß auf den Klippen die Föhre dürftige Nahrung findet. Jetzt ging alles wieder seinen alten Weg, kaum daß einer mehr des Abwesenden gedachte** or **gedacht hätte** (cautious statement).

We often find a simple **daß** or **so daß** in the subordinate clause without any corresponding **so, derartig,** &c., in the principal proposition, so that the result is represented as a result pure and simple without the modal idea of manner: **Der Kanzleirat ließ die Feder fallen, daß auf dem vor ihm liegenden Bogen ein großer Klecks entstand** (Baumbach's *Der Schwiegersohn*, VII). **Wo waren meine Sinne, daß ich diesen Ton nicht sogleich verstand? Fräulein Frieda, Sie sehen aus — daß sich ein alter Knasterbart, wie ich, in Sie verlieben könnte. Er schwankte, so daß ich ihn nicht mehr halten konnte. Er schwankte so, daß ich usw.** gives the modal idea. The simple **daß**-clause is older than the form with **so daß.**

The clause of result sometimes assumes the form of a relative clause: **Ein solcher Kampf steht uns bevor, wobei es sich verlohnt** (= **daß es sich dabei verlohnt**), **im vollen Kriegesschmucke zu erscheinen** (Uhland). Often in descriptive (**271. II.** 7) relative clauses: **Hans ist endlich angekommen, weshalb** (or **weswegen,** or **infolge dessen,** all three = **so daß**) **wir alle sehr glücklich sind,** or in the form of a principal proposition: **deshalb** (or **deswegen,** or **infolge dessen**) **sind wir alle sehr glücklich.**

In poetry and choice prose the clause of result that follows a negative proposition is often positive altho the meaning requires a negative word, but in this case it should be noted that **daß** is omitted and the clause has the form of a principal proposition: **Denn niemals kehrt' er heim, er bracht' euch etwas** (Schiller's *Tell*, 4, 3). **In der Stadt entsteht kein gemeinnütziges Werk, sie steht als die reiche Frau mit der offenen Hand dazu, sie zeichnet dafür den ersten großen Beitrag** (Heer's *Felix Notvest*, p. 289). For historical explanation see **168.** II. E. *a. Note.* In plain prose this construction is replaced by **ohne daß.**

The idea of result is often found in clear attributive form, especially in the form of a relative clause: **Es gibt keinen, der nicht seine Fehler hätte.**

a. Mood. The mood of the clause is indic. if it is desired to represent the statement as a result that has been actually attained, but the subjunctive to indicate that the statement is merely conceived. See **168.** II. D, H; **169.** 2. D, H. *c.*

b. Abridgment. Clauses introduced by **anstatt daß** and **ohne daß** may be abridged to the infin. construction if the subject of the clause is identical with that of the principal proposition: **Sie schweigen, anstatt daß sie sich beklagen,** or **anstatt sich zu beklagen. Er leistete das Menschenmögliche, ohne den geringsten Erfolg zu haben** *He accomplished as much as is possible for men without meeting with the least success.* See also **185.** A. II. 2. *a* and *Note* 2 thereunder. For the development of the infinitive clause with **ohne** and **anstatt** see **281.** *b. Note* (2nd par.). As can be seen by the translation of the last German sentence English employs the gerund here, the old attributive or appositive type of clause structure described in **268. 4.** It has a wider field of usefulness here than the German infinitive, for it is also employed when its subject is not identical with that of the principal verb. Its logical subject is then the person implied in a possessive adjective or a genitive: *I left the room without his* or *John's seeing me.* For further remarks upon the gerund see **272.** *C. g.* Clauses introduced by simple **daß** (with a preceding **so ein, kein, solch, derartig** in the principal proposition) are in recent literature very often abridged to an infinitive with **um zu** instead of simple **zu,** as **um** brings out the idea of end, result more clearly: **Aristoteles sagt, daß eine Stadt so gebaut sein müsse, um die Menschen zugleich sicher und glücklich zu machen. Es wäre ein Anblick, um Engel weinen zu machen** (Goethe's *Götz*, 4, 1). **Es ist, um sich die Haare auszuraufen** (Raabe's *Frau Salome*, chap. vi) = **Die Verhältnisse sind derart, daß man sich die Haare ausraufen möchte. Es ist kein Wetter, um noch länger hier in der Nacht darüber zu beratschlagen** (id., *Der Dräumling*, xxviii). **Es war recht ein Fleckchen Erde, um sich allein mit seinen Gedanken darin zu befinden, und wiederum doch auch, um sich nicht allein hier aufzuhalten, sondern sonst jemandem einen Mitgenuß daran zu vergönnen** (Jensen's *Die Schatzsucher*, p. 80). **Doch warum meinten Sie vorhin, das sei kein Thema, um es mit mir zu erörtern?** (id., *Die Katze*, p. 99). Sometimes also with **zu** instead of **um zu** in accordance with older usage: **Er ist kein solcher Narr, dies zu glauben.** Usually so after **danach: Der Physikus war nicht der Mann danach, sich das Errungene wehrlos aus den Händen winden zu lassen** (Enking's *Warum schwieg sie nicht?*). See also **281.** *b. Note.*

Clause of Degree.

277. Clauses of degree define the degree or intensity of that which is predicated in the principal proposition. The degree can be expressed in the following ways: —

1. *Comparison.* It is expressed in the form of a comparison:

A. Signifying a degree equal to that of the principal proposition:

a. Expressing a simple comparison (for conjunctions see **238.** 3. D. 1. A. *a*): **Er ist ebenso gelehrt als [er] bescheiden [ist]. Sein Wort bedeutet so'viel wie ein Eid [bedeutet].** When the verb of the clause is the same as that of the principal proposition it is usually, as in the preceding sentence, understood. See also **239.** 3. Concerning the subjunctive mood here see **169.** 2. H. *a.*

b. Expressing a proportionate agreement (for conjunctions see **238.** 3. D. 1. A. *b*): **Je mehr das Alter wächst, je** (now more commonly **desto** or **um so**) **schwerer wird das Sorgen** (Günther). **Je mehr [Geld] ihr habt, je mehr bringt ihr durch** (Hauptmann's *Und Pippa tanzt*, 1). **Je eher, je** (still more common than **desto** or **um so** in short, pithy sayings) **lieber** the sooner, the better. **Je mehr du dich ärgerst, desto** (or **um so,** or less commonly **um desto**) **mehr freuen sich deine Feinde. Wir können aber auch im allgemeinen behaupten, um so** (instead of the more common **je**) **mehr Sorgfalt auf die Erlernung der künstlichen Sprache verwendet wird, um so näher kommt man darin der Norm, namentlich in allen denjenigen Punkten, die sich schriftlich fixieren lassen** (H. Paul's *Prinzipien der Sprachgeschichte*, chap. xxiii). **Je nachdem der Meister ist, wird aus dem Block ein Trog oder eine Bildsäule. Je nachdem die Arbeit ist, nach dem wird der Lohn sein. Seine Hoffnung stieg in eben dem Maße** (or **Verhältnisse**)**, wie seine Gesundheit wiederkam.** In old saws the sentence is still often verbless as explained in **252.** 1. *b. Note*: **Darnach die Arbeit [ist], darnach [ist] der Lohn.**

c. Expressing the extent or a restriction (for conjunctions see **238.** 3. D. 1. A. *c*): **Manche böse Tat ist in'sofern zu entschuldigen, als sie nicht in böser Absicht getan wird. Der Gelehrte ist nur in'sofern ein Gelehrter, inwie'fern er in der Gesellschaft beachtet wird** (Fichte). **Er strengte sich sō séhr an, als er konnte. Jeder Mensch gilt in der Welt nur sō víel, als er sich gelten macht. Er legte ihr sō víel vor, als er finden konnte. Er ehrt die Wissenschaft, so'fern sie nutzt. So'weit ich über seine Handlungsweise urteilen kann, halte ich sie für gerecht,**

Dieser Schriftsteller hat ein, so'weit sich das nach dem Absatz beurteilen läßt, brauchbares Buch verfaßt. Er ordnete die am Boden liegenden Blätter, so'gut es in der Schnelligkeit gehen wollte. Sie drückte, so'fest sie konnte, ihr Ohr an eine Ritze. Er bemüht sich, so'sehr er kann. Ich tue, so'viel ich kann. Zunächst einigte man sich wenigstens sò wéit, daß an der vierjährigen Dauer der Grundschule unbedingt festgehalten werden solle (**168.** II. G. *a.* (**2**)). The clause can also be in the form of a substantive relative clause introduced by **das,** now written **daß** as it has been taken for a conjunction: **So weit ging weder mein Auftrag, daß** (= **soweit** *so far as*) **ich wüßte, noch mein Eifer.** We often use **was** here to express the extent or restriction: **Da lief er, was er konnte. Sie suchte, was an ihr lag, die Tücke des Schicksals wieder gutzumachen. Was mich** (**den Vorfall,** &c.) **anbelangt** or **betrifft, so irrst du dich.** Instead of a clause containing the verbs **(an)betreffen** or **anbelangen** we often find a prepositional phrase, and sometimes the absolute present participle: **Was sein Alter anbetrifft,** or **in Betreff** or **betreffs seines Alters,** or **sein Alter betreffend.** Concerning the subjunctive mood here see **169.** 2. H. *b*.

Note. In clauses introduced by an **als** or **wie** that follows **so'viel** the subject may often be the partitive genitive of a pronoun or the subject of the clause may be suppressed in accordance with older usage (see **251.** II. A. *d*): **Bringen Sie so'viele Bücher, als** (or **wie**) **deren auf dem Tische liegen,** or **als auf dem Tische liegen.** See also **255.** II. 1. H. *c* (2nd par.). We also find here the old verbless type of sentence described in **252.** 1. *b. Note*: **Soviel Köpfe, soviel Sinne.**

B. Following a comparative (for conjunctions see **238.** 3. D. 1. B): **Es ist schicklicher, daß ein zärtlicher Charakter Augenblicke des Stolzes hat, als daß ein stolzer von der Zärtlichkeit sich fortreißen läßt** (Lessing). **. . . von all der Pracht und Schönheit der Welt nicht mehr sehen, als [als] ob man blind wäre** (Spielhagen, 13, 139), or more accurately **nicht mehr sehen, denn** (**239.** 6, 2nd par.) **als ob usw. Sie dachte nicht anders, als er sage es bloß zum Spaß. Was kann ich aber von Savignys Vorlesungen anders sagen, als daß sie mich aufs gewaltigste ergriffen und auf mein ganzes Leben und Studieren entschiedenen Einfluß erlangten** (Jakob Grimm). **Denke ich natürlich nicht anders, als Ihnen ist etwas passiert** (Wildenbruch's *Der unsterbliche Felix*, 4, 1). **Er benimmt sich nicht anders, als [als] ob er das einzige Wesen in der Welt wäre,** or more accurately **nicht anders, denn** (**239.** 6, 2nd par.) **als ob er . . . wäre,** or more smoothly, dropping **nicht anders: Er benimmt sich, als ob er . . . wäre. Wir können von jenen keinen andern Grund angeben, warum sie uns gefallen, als weil** (usually **als daß**) **sie einen ganz angenehmen Eindruck auf unsere Organe machen** (Wieland). **Kein Naturereignis wird von der Jugend freudiger begrüßt als der Schnee [begrüßt wird].** When the clause has the same verb as the principal proposition the verb of the clause, as in the preceding example, can be understood. Especially the subject or the object of the clause is often omitted. See **251.** II. A. *d*. When the subject of the principal proposition and that of the subordinate clause are identical, the subordinate clause can be abridged to an infinitive clause: **Ich konnte nicht anders, als ihm zuzustimmen.** See also **239.** 1. *a* and **279.** *e*.

a. Negative after a Comparative. In early N.H.G. **kein** (see **139.** 3. *e. Note* 2) = **irgend ein** *any* was used: **Denn das wort Gottes ist lebendig vnd krefftig | vnd scherffer | denn kein zweischneidig Schwert** (Hebrews iv. 12). This usage remained after a comparative up to the close of the eighteenth century and later, but it must have soon become identified with the negative **kein,** as it became the custom quite early in the period under French influence to use a pleonastic negative after a comparative. In the classic period this usage is still common, not only in case of **kein,** but of the other negatives also: **Es ging besser, als wir nicht dachten** (Goethe). At present rare: **Im Reisewagen hab' ich an meines Königlichen Herren Seite seine Art und sein Wesen in Stunden sicherer erkennen können, wie ich es hier in Jahren nicht vermöchte** (Otto Erler's *Struensee*, p. 22). See **223.** XI. B. *a.* (**2**).

b. Use of **daß.** The **daß** cannot be omitted when the thought as a whole is important: **Das Kind kriecht viel mehr, als daß es aufrecht geht** *The child is rather creeping than walking upright*, but **Das Kind kriecht viel mehr, als es aufrecht geht** *The child creeps more frequently than it walks upright*, where the attention is called more to the verbs than to the thought as a whole.

2. *Result.* Expressing a result (for conjunctions see **238.** 3. D. 2; for the origin of the **daß**-clause see **271.** I): **Die Luft ist sò stíll, daß das Rauschen des fernen Baches herüberdringt. Dein Vater ist noch nicht sò rúhig, daß er die tägliche Anwesenheit eines Freundes ertragen könnte. Er war sò wéich gestimmt, daß er fast geweint hätte** (**169.** 2. H. *c*). **Ich blieb so lange, daß ich den Zug versäumte. Er ärgerte sich so sehr, daß er krank wurde. Er hat die** (see **271.** I) **Gewandtheit im Reden, daß niemand es mit ihm aufnehmen kann. Er hat eine** (see **271.** I) **Stimme, daß man ihn überall im Saal deutlich hören kann. Ich setzte ein solches Mißtrauen in ihn, daß ich ihn beobachten ließ. Es war nicht so dunkel, daß er nicht alles sehen konnte. Er hat den Jungen derartig** (or **derart**) **gehauen, daß er nicht gehen kann. In jedem jungen Jahre steht hier** (i.e. in Nice) **eine Persönlichkeit im mittelsten Mittelpunkt, die nach allen Regeln der Kunst derart verrissen und verschandmäult wird, bis kein Faden mehr an ihrem ganzen Leibe bleibt** (F. F. von Conring in *Hamburger Nachrichten*, Jan. 28, 1905). **In den nächsten zwei Büchern, dem VII. und VIII., verlieren wir Parzival fast völlig aus den Augen, kaum daß er gelegentlich im Hintergrund auftaucht** (E. Martin's *Wolframs von Eschenbach Parzival*, II, p. xxiv). **Selbstverständlich kann es mit dieser Zahl nicht allzu genau genommen werden, da die Erdbebenforschung sich nicht genügend auf alle Länder verbreitet hat, als daß jedes Erdbeben zur Beobachtung käme** (*Hamburgischer Correspondent*, May 5, 1905). **Er ist zu stolz, als daß** (less commonly **um daß**) **er diese Beleidigung verzeihen könnte. Die Nachrichten lauteten zu schön, als daß** (now rarely **um daß**) **wir sie hätten glauben können. Meine Sünde ist größer, als daß sie mir könnte vergeben werden.** Notice that the force of the subordinate clause introduced by **als daß** is negative. If the clause is to have affirmative force the negative **nicht** must be used: **Er denkt zu edel, als daß er nicht die Wahrheit sagte.** A nega-

tive clause following a negative proposition has affirmative force. Sometimes the subordinate clause after a negative proposition has affirmative instead of the usual negative form, but in this case it should be noted that **daß** is omitted and the subordinate clause has the form of a principal proposition: **Nichts ist so fein gesponnen, es kommt doch an die Sonnen** (prov.). **So schau dir deine Springebächlein an: | da ist kein Wässerlein so dünn und klein, | es will und muß ins Menschenland hinein** (Hauptmann's *Die versunkene Glocke*, 1). The history of this construction is the same as that described in **276.** D (next to the last par.).

Instead of a clause of result we sometimes find an independent proposition: **Er ist so lieb, man kann ihm nicht böse sein. So still wurde es dann, man hätte im Saale das Weben einer Spinne hören können.** In lively expression of feeling we often have instead of a subordinate clause a principal proposition with question order: **Ich bin so müde, kann ich doch nicht mit euch spazieren!** In a calm reasoning mood we can connect these two principal propositions by the co-ordinating illative conjunction **daher: Ich bin sehr müde, daher kann ich nicht mitgehen.** In a narrative mood we can connect these two propositions by **und: Ich war sehr müde und konnte nicht mitgehen.** For meaning and force of these paratactic constructions see **267.** 4 (3rd par.).

a. Mood. The mood of the clause is indic. if it is desired to represent the statement as a result that has been actually attained, but the potential subjunctive to indicate that the statement is possible, or to make a statement modestly or cautiously. See **169.** 2. D, H. *c*; **168.** II. D.

b. Abridgment. To express a simple result where the subject of the subordinate clause is the indefinite **man** or is identical with the subject or often some dependent word in the principal proposition the subordinate clause is usually abridged to the infinitive with **zu,** usually so after **so** + an adjective or adverb, or elsewhere now more commonly with **um zu** when it is desired to bring out prominently the idea of result: **Sei so gut, mir deinen Regenschirm zu leihen. Man ging so weit, uns zu schimpfen. Sie gehen zu langsam, als daß Sie Ihren Freund einholen könnten,** but in the abridged form the **als,** tho common in the eighteenth century is now replaced by **um,** or sometimes simple **zu** is used: **Sie gehen zu langsam, Ihren Freund einzuholen,** or now more commonly **um** (or in the eighteenth century **als**) **Ihren Freund einzuholen. Es wäre keiner sicher genug, daß man ihn als Boten schicken könnte, or um ihn als Boten zu schicken. Die Zeit macht uns kühl genug, um alle irdischen Freuden nichtig zu finden. Weil sie nicht so viel Flachs haben, um ihre Weibsleute mit Spinnen zu beschäftigen. Eben zur rechten Zeit traf er ein, um den Verzagten Mut einzuflößen. Der häufige und vertraute Verkehr mit einem Manne von der unwiderstehlichen Liebenswürdigkeit Cäsars tat das Übrige, um den Bund der Interessen in einen Freundschaftsbund umzugestalten** (Mommsen's *Römische Geschichte*, V, chap. vi). **Die Bewachung des Gefangenen wurde derart verschärft, um ihm jeden weiteren Versuch zum Entkommen als zwecklos erscheinen zu lassen. Der allgemeine Wohlstand hat sich so gehoben, um auch eine Aufbesserung der Beamtenstellungen zu fordern. Der Rat war zu dringend und einleuchtend, um nicht befolgt zu werden.** See also **281.** *b. Note.* In English *for* with the prepositional infinitive can be quite freely used where the subjects are not identical, where in German the clause form must often be employed: She was not near enough for him to discern the expression of her face **Sie war nicht nahe genug, daß er ihren Gesichtsausdruck sehen konnte.** Modern life is too full of difficult problems for writers to ignore them **Das moderne Leben ist zu voll von schwierigen Problemen, als daß Schriftsteller sie übersehen dürften.** There were too many for the boat to hold them **Es waren zu viele, als daß das Boot sie hätte fassen können.** Compare **269.** 3 and **185.** A. II. 2. *a* and *Note* 2 thereunder.

Clause of Cause.

278. The subordinate clause contains the cause or reason, the principal proposition the result or conclusion (for conjunctions see **238.** 3. E): **Der Walfisch kann nur kleine Tiere verschlingen, weil sein Schlund sehr eng ist. Philipp II. zitterte knechtisch vor Gott, weil Gott das einzige war, wovor er zu zittern hatte. Mancher unterläßt nur deshalb eine böse Handlung, weil er die Folgen fürchtet. Das Merkwürdigste ist die Fortsetzung der „Kritischen Nachrichten," nicht weil** (or **nicht als ob,** or **nicht als wenn**) **sie besondere Merkwürdigkeiten enthielten, sondern weil sie so lustig zu lesen sind. Der Herr wusch sich allemal die Hände, bevor er ans Quartettgeigen ging, nicht weil** (or **nicht als ob,** or **nicht als wenn**) **sie schmutzig gewesen wären, sondern wie zu einer symbolischen Reinigung. Der Müßiggang verkürzt notwendig unser Leben, indem er uns schwächer macht. Ich wil nu gerne sterben | nach dem** (temporal and causal) **ich dein angesicht gesehen habe** (Gen. xlvi. 30). **Nachdem** (temporal and causal) **auch Piccolomini sich nicht wieder sehen läßt, fällt die Decke von Wallensteins Augen** (Schiller's *G. d. d. K.*, II. 4). **Nachdem** (= **weil**) **das Protokoll der Generalversammlung mit Rücksicht auf den Umstand, daß dasselbe von den Verifikatoren beglaubigt werden muß, erst später veröffentlicht werden muß, teilen wir kurz die gefaßten Beschlüsse mit** (Austrian newspaper). **Da alle Zeugen in ihren Aussagen übereinstimmen, so wird die Sache wohl sich so verhalten. Du solltest so schwere Gedanken nicht in dir aufkommen**

lassen, da du doch mit mehr Genugtuung als viele andere auf dein vergangenes Leben und auf die Gegenwart blicken kannst (R. Huch's *Vita somnium breve*, I, p. 56). **Können umbrische Schädel erhalten sein, da doch die Umbrer ihre Leichen verbrannten?** (*Beilage zur Allgemeinen Zeit.*, 1904, p. 250). **Ehrwürdiger, ich bitte dich, mir zu verzeihen und mich nicht zu senden, anerwogen ich, wie du weißt, der einfältigste und unwissendste bin von allen** (Ertl's *Die Stadt der Heiligen*). **In Anbetracht, daß er noch so jung ist, entschuldigten wir ihn. Ich ärgere mich, daß** (see **238.** 3. E. *c*) **du das getan hast. Er hätte es nicht sagen sollen, zumal er wußte, daß es mir nachteilig sein kann. Nun er reich ist, hat er Freunde. Dieses Übel ist desto** (or **um so,** sometimes **um desto**) **lästiger, als** (also **da** or **weil**) **es nur durch eine schmerzliche Operation geheilt werden kann. Da'von bist du krank geworden, daß du nach dem schnellen Laufe kaltes Wasser getrunken. Man erkennt einen seichten Menschen leicht da'ran, daß er viel Unnützes schwätzt.** As the genitive or a prepositional phrase may denote a cause, the genitive and prepositional phrase clauses treated in **272.** A and D often belong also here: (genitive clause) **Ich freue mich, daß es Ihnen wohl geht.** For examples of such a prepositional phrase clause see sentence above beginning with **Da'von,** and also the last two sentences in **272.** D. The subordinate clause above introduced by **da'ran daß** may also be regarded as a clause of means (**282**).

When an inference from some known fact is placed before the statement of fact the latter appears in the light of a clause of cause: **Er muß blind gewesen sein, daß** (or **weil**) **er es nicht gesehen hat.** Often in abridged form: **Er muß blind sein, das nicht zu sehen.**

The idea of cause sometimes finds expression in an attributive element, either in the form of an attributive adjective or a relative clause: **Der gráusame Mánn achtete nicht auf das Flehen des Unglücklichen** (= **der Mann achtete nicht auf das Flehen des Unglücklichen, weil er grausam war**). **Das Kind, das ja noch zu jung ist, hat einen Vormund erhalten** (= **das Kind hat einen Vormund erhalten, da es ja noch zu jung ist**). See **255.** I. *c*, VII. *a*.

A subject clause following **nicht** now often has the force of a causal clause, as illustrated in **269.** 1. *b*, 3rd par.

A principal proposition instead of a subordinate clause: **ich gehe nicht mit, ich habe Zahnschmerzen** (= **weil ich Zahnschmerzen habe**). **Zurück! Du rettest den Freund nicht mehr** (= **da du den Freund nicht mehr retten kannst**), **so rette das eigene Leben. In unsrer Provinz singen wir, was wir wollen. Das macht, daß Graf Egmont unser Statthalter ist** (= **weil Graf Egmont unser Statthalter ist**) (Goethe's *Egmont*). Compare **267.** 4.

a. *Mood.* We usually find here the indic. For the subjunctive here see **169.** 2. J.

b. *Abridgment.* A causal clause introduced by **weil** or **da** can sometimes be abridged to a participle, adjective, noun, or prepositional phrase, when the subject of the principal proposition and that of the subordinate clause are identical: **Er ist, weil durch Tapferkeit hervorragend, or weil tapfer** (= **weil er durch Tapferkeit hervorragt, or weil er tapfer ist**), **des Sieges gewiß. Die Feinde baten, durch die Niederlage gebeugt** (= **weil sie durch die Niederlage gebeugt waren**), **um Frieden. Ein geborener Herrscher regierte er (Cäsar) die Gemüter der Menschen, wie der Wind die Wolken zwingt** (Mommsen's *Römische Geschichte*, V, chap. ii). **Im Besitz von Talienwan und Dalny können die Japaner ihre Verstärkungen und den Belagerungstrain landen, der für den Angriff auf Port Arthur nötig wird** (*Neue Zürcher Zeitung*, June 9, 1904) Since the Japanese are in possession of, &c. **Da aus Französelei entstanden, ist „Es hat" statt „Es gibt" unbedingt zu verwerfen** (Eduard Engel's *Gutes Deutsch*, p. 220). In all these sentences the abridgments are examples of the old attributive or appositional type of clause structure described in **268.** 4. The subject of the principal proposition is the logical subject of the clause, the participle, adjective, noun, or prepositional phrase is the logical predicate. The ideas of cause and subordination to the principal proposition do not find here a formal expression in the clause itself but are merely suggested by the context and the placing of the clause alongside of the principal proposition. English has gone much farther than German in the development of this old type of clause. In English the logical subject here is often the person implied in a possessive adjective or a genitive, the logical predicate the governing noun, usually a gerund: *Owing to* (or *on account of* or *because of*) *his* or *John's bringing me word so late I couldn't go* **Da er or Hans mir so spät Bescheid brachte, konnte ich nicht mehr gehen.** For further remarks on the gerund see **272.** *C. g.* Sometimes the accusative absolute construction has the force of a clause of cause. See **265.** B. *b.* (**1**).

Clause of Condition or Exception.

279. This clause states the condition upon which the action of the principal proposition hinges, or adds an exception, i.e. a fact or proviso that qualifies in some particular respect the preceding statement (for conjunctions see **238.** 3. F.). A marked feature in the development since early N.H.G. is the gradual replacement of the conjunctions **ob** *if*, indicating uncertainty, **so** *if*, originally a demonstrative pointing to the following clause, for the most part also **wo** *if* originally a relative, *where, in case that* by the conjunction **wenn** *if*, originally temporal, *when*, while in English *if*, cognate with **ob**, is still the most common form here. **Ob** is, however, still common in conditional clauses which follow **als,** as illustrated in **276.** A (2nd par.). In connection with other particles it is also still widely used in concessive clauses which have developed out of older conditional clauses: **obgleich, obschon,** &c. In object clauses simple **ob** still has the old idea of uncertainty: **Ich weiß nicht, ob er kommen wird.** Examples of conditional sentences: **Vnd ob jemand sündiget | So haben wir einen Fursprecher bey dem Vater** (I John II. 1). **Das alles wil ich dir geben | So du niederfellest | vnd mich anbetest** (Matth. iv. 9). **Wo diese werden schweigen | so werden die Steine schreien** (Luke xix. 40). **Wir mußten uns resignieren, wo nicht für immer, doch für eine gute Zeit. In diesem Jahre, wo nicht noch vorher. Will er es tun, so ist es gut, wo nicht, so mag er es bleiben lassen. Mein Onkel sucht ein Haus, das vor der Stadt, wo möglich, inmitten eines großen Gartens liege. Wenn das Fleisch eingesalzen und geräuchert ist, geht es nicht in Fäulnis über. Wenn alle Menschen gut wären, so bedürfte es keiner Strafgesetze. Eine, wenn ich nicht irre, französische Familie hat die neue Wohnung gemietet. Ich komme morgen, wenn es überhaupt möglich ist. Vnd wiltu also mit mir thun | so erwürge mich lieber | habe ich anders gnade fur deinen Augen funden | das ich nicht mein vnglück so sehen müsse** (Numbers xi. 15). **Ja dieser Widerwille, wenn ich anders mein Gefühl sorgfältig untersucht habe, ist gänzlich von der Natur des Ekels** (Lessing). **Wenn anders es möglich ist, so schreibe mir. Er verspricht zu kommen, vorausgesetzt daß das Wetter es erlaubt. Ich werde es ihm geben, vorausgesetzt, daß er tue, was er versprochen hat. Wofern er fleißig sein wollte, würde er Bedeutendes leisten. Alles ist verloren, wenn nicht ein schnelles Mittel zur Hand ist. Im Falle daß,** or **falls er morgen noch Fieber hat, muß er im Bette liegen bleiben. Ordnen Sie an — falls jemand komme — daß er nicht vorgelassen werde** (Suttner's *Im Berghause*, p. 47). **Schreiben Sie sofort, falls** (or **im Falle daß,** or **auf den Fall daß**) **dies geschehe** (or **geschähe**). **Und als der alte Herr sich auf sein Sofa gestreckt hatte und sie ihn gut zugedeckt und ihm die Birne der elektrischen Klingel auf das Tischchen an seiner Seite hingelegt, falls** (for use in case that) **er etwas brauche, schlich sie verstohlen davon** (Ompteda's *Cäcilie von Sarryn*, chap. II). **Er soll es hören, doch daß er nicht davon spricht. Ich billige alles, außer daß er nicht selbst kommen will. Ich kann nicht hineinkommen, außer wenn Sie das Tor öffnen. Das hübsche Berghaus hat sicher ein Gastzimmer, und darin will ich mich — außer Sie jagen mich gewaltsam hinaus — volle drei Tage festsetzen** (Suttner's *Im Berghause*, p. 26). **Ich tue es nicht, außer er bitte mich darum** (Fritsch's *German Grammar*, p. 486). **Ganz bestimmt werde ich kommen, außer ich wäre tot** (Felix Schwarzenberg). **Ich bin ganz zufrieden mit ihm, nur daß er etwas langsam arbeitet,** or. according to **236, nur arbeitet er etwas langsam,** or **er arbeitet nur etwas langsam. Das Reiten wäre hübsch, nur daß man leicht Hals und Bein bricht. Wir könnten es schon tun, nur daß er dann verloren wäre. Es ginge schon, nur daß er nicht will. Ich seh' es gern, das steht dir frei, nur daß es gefällig sei** (Goethe's *Faust*, Studierzimmer). **Niemand hat gesprochen, als er** (or **außer ihm**). **Keiner als er hätte das tun können. Kein anderer als er hat es getan. Wer anders als er hätte es tun können? Er nahm nichts anderes, als was ihm gehörte. Er liebte nichts als ihn. Tue alles andere eher als das!,** or **Tue alles andere, nur nicht das! Aus welchem andern Grunde sandte ich einen Eilboten, als**

damit ihr möglichst rasch die Nachricht erhieltet? Ich konnte meine Empfindung mit nichts ausdrücken, als dadurch daß ich das Kind von der Erde nahm und es lebhaft küßte. Wodurch denn sind wir groß geworden, als daß (more commonly **als dadurch daß**) **wir gingen mit dem Sturm des Volks?** (Immermann). **Sie sieht keine Rettung, als sie muß das Kind entfernen** (Goethe), or more commonly with **daß: Es ist nichts anderes möglich, als daß du nachgibst. Es fehlt nichts, als daß du nicht da bist,** or **als daß du da wärst** (subjunctive of modest wish; see **169.** 1. A, 3rd par.). **Du rettest nicht den Sohn, als wenn du weichst** (Grillparzer's *Argonauten*, 4). **Du hast's ja selber zu tragen! Kein anderer wie du!** (Halbe's *Das tausendjährige Reich*, p. 45). **Wem wohl, denn ihr** (i.e. **der Frau**), **verdankt er des Liedes Keim?** (Otto Brahm in *Die neue deutsche Rundschau*, Dec. 1906, p. 1420). **Ich tue es nicht, ohne daß ich seine Erlaubnis habe. Er sprach nie, ohne daß er gefragt worden wäre. Es sei denn daß ich aus Gründen der heiligen Schrift oder mit klaren und hellen Gründen überwiesen werde, sonst kann und will ich nicht widerrufen** (Luther). **Ich werde es nicht tun, es sei denn, daß er mich darum bitte** (or **bittet**), or **es sei denn, er bitte** (or **bittet**) **mich darum. Ich lasse dich nicht, du segnest mich denn** (Gen. xxxii. 26, revised ed.). **Ich werde es nicht tun, er bitte mich denn darum. Das werde ich nie glauben, er müßte es mir denn selbst sagen. Ich gehe sicher morgen, ich müßte denn sehr krank werden. Die jungen Mädchen und Frauen gehen bis nach der Geburt des ersten Kindes vollkommen nackt, höchstens daß sie bisweilen eine dünne Schnur um die Hüften tragen** (Hutter's *Wanderungen und Forschungen*, p. 421).

a. The adverb **so** is in these sentences very often found in the principal proposition, as in the first example above.

b. The conditional clause is usually introduced by a conditional or qualifying conjunction, but it may assume other forms: (**1**) Instead of the transposed word-order the question order is often used if the conjunction **wenn** is omitted. See **237.** 1. A. *b*, and also *Note* 2 thereunder. (**2**) The clause may for especial emphasis be replaced by an imperative, in which case **so** is usually found in the principal proposition: **Sprich ja oder nein, so bin ich zufrieden.** The volitive subjunctive can also be used like the imperative. See **168.** I. 2. C. *a*, *b*. **Dürfen** and **sollen** with dependent infinitive are often used with similar force: **Man darf nur vom Wolfe reden, so kommt er. Er soll nur kommen, ich werde ihm schon heimleuchten.** (**3**) Instead of a conditional clause and a conclusion we often find two independent propositions connected by a co-ordinating conjunction, **und, oder, sonst,** or **dann: Sei im Besitze und du wohnst im Recht** Possession is nine points of the law. **Wir wollen Frieden machen, und alles ist gut** Let us make peace and all will be well. **Du tust das, oder du bekommst Prügel,** or **sonst bekommst du Prügel = Wenn du das nicht tust, bekommst du Prügel. Es muß anhaltend regnen, dann tritt oft Hochwasser ein = Wenn es anhaltend regnet, tritt oft Hochwasser ein.** (4) The absolute construction is often used here instead of a subordinate clause. For examples see **265.** B. *a.* and *b.* (**1**). (**5**) The conditional idea is sometimes found in the form of a relative clause: (**1**) In the form of a clause with the conditional relative **wer** as subject, as illustrated in **159**; (**2**) In the form of a subject clause: **Wer jung heiratet,** or **Jung geheiratet lebt lang**; (**3**) In the form of an attributive adjective clause: **Ein Bettler, der etwa kommt, wird abgewiesen! Ein Junge, der das täte, würde ausgelacht.** See **255.** VII. *a.*

c. Mood. When the supposition is real the verb of the conditional clause is in the indic.: **Wenn ich stumm blieb, geschah es nur, weil ich über ein Rätsel nachgrübelte** If I remained silent (and I actually did so) it was because I was pondering over an enigma. If the case is only a supposed one, but one that can easily happen, the indic. is now used, or to indicate a little more uncertainty the past subjunctive of **sollen** with the infin. of the verb: **Ich gehe fort, wenn er kommt** *I shall go away if he comes*, or **Ich gehe fort, wenn er kommen sollte** *I shall go away if he should come.* See **168.** II. E. The present subjunctive could be used instead of the indicative in earlier periods, but it now only survives in the volitive constructions in *b.* (**2**) and in the potential construction with **denn** (**168.** II. E. *a*) or **es sei denn daß** (**168.** II. E. *a* and *c*) and **außer** (**168.** II. E. *d*).

The past tense forms of the subjunctive may be used here to denote unreality. This unreal potential subjunctive is very common in **wenn**-clauses if the condition is a mere conception of the mind, or is represented as in conflict with fact. The use of the moods and tenses in such unreal conditional sentences is explained at length in **169.** 2. A. (**1**). *a* and E. The past tense forms of the subjunctive are often used after **ohne daß** to make a statement modestly or cautiously. The present tense of the subjunctive is sometimes found in clauses of exception to represent the statement as only conceived, but the indicative is in many cases more common, as the statement is felt as true, or the past subjunctive may be used instead of the indicative for the sake of modesty: **So bleibt nichts übrig, als daß man seine Kräfte zusammennehme, zusammennimmt,** or **zusammennähme.** For the mood after **nur daß** see **168.** I. 2. C. *b.*

d. Abridgment. When the subject of the principal proposition and that of the subordinate clause are identical the conditional clause introduced by **wenn** can be abridged to an appositional participle: **Auch die Schwachen werden mächtig, wenn sie verbunden sind,** or **Verbunden werden auch die Schwachen mächtig. Ob sie** (i.e. die Rede) **mir, gehört** (= **wenn sie von mir gehört worden wäre**), **ebenso imponiert hätte?** (Spielhagen's *Frei geboren*, p. 170). **Das wäre besser verschwiegen (wenn es verschwiegen worden wäre). Das wäre eben so gut unterblieben (wenn es unterblieben wäre). Das ist leicht gesagt, aber schwer getan,** where **leicht** and **schwer** were originally the predicates and **gesagt** and **getan** predicate appositives, i.e. easy if spoken but difficult if performed, but **leicht** and **schwer** are now often felt as adverbs, i.e. That is easily said but performed with difficulty, after the analogy of **Das ist bald gesagt** That is soon said. The present participle is less commonly used as an abridged conditional clause: **Wissend nur kann ich dir raten.** The participle is often used absolutely (**265.** B. *a*): **Davon abgesehen ist das Buch zu empfehlen.** Often the conjunction **wenn** alone or **wenn** or **falls** in connection with a predicate adjective or the negative **nicht** represents the subordinate clause: **Gab's eine Schuld? Wenn** (*if so*), **dann war sie auf beide Seiten verteilt** (Ponten's *Jungfräulichkeit*, p. 501). **Die neueste, wenn wahr, erschütternde Nachricht. Eine Abordnung der Soldatenwehr betonte . . . , man werde, falls nötig, den Kommandanten Wels** (name) **noch im Laufe der Nacht mit Gewalt befreien** (*Neue Zürcher Zeit.*, Dec. 27, 1918).

The subordinate clause is sometimes contracted to the infinitive with **zu** when the subject of the clause is identical with the subject or an object of the principal verb: **Du tätest besser, nach Frankreich zu gehen** (Goethe). **Es kann uns wenig Heil erblühn, um eine Tote zu streiten** (Uhland). **Eins muß er dazu mitbringen, um es irgendwo erträglich zu finden. Ich tue es nicht, ohne seine Erlaubnis zu haben.** Sometimes when the subjects are not identical: **Den Namen nur zu hören, steigt das Blut in den Kopf** (Wildenbruch's *Kaiser Heinrich*, 2, 3). Quite often when the subject to be supplied is the indefinite or general **man: „Wie weit ist das nächste Dorf?" „Eine halbe Stunde zu fahren, dreiviertel zu gehen"** (Karl Busse's *Die schöne Andrea*). **Der Komödiendichter schien, nach seinem schlichten Anzug zu urteilen, kein Günstling des Plutos zu sein.** In English the infinitive construction with *for* is much used where the subjects are not identical, where in German the clause form is usually employed: I should be glad for Mary to come **Ich freute mich, wenn Marie käme.** Compare **269.** 3.

In lively style an absolute nominative often takes the place of a conditional clause: **Noch ein Schritt, so ist er verloren. Einige Schritte weiter, und Sie hätten den Mann bemerken müssen.**

Sometimes we find a prepositional phrase instead of the conditional clause: **Ohne ihn** (= **wenn er nicht gewesen wäre**) **war ich verloren. Sie sagen, bei ungelöster Schnur kommen die Erdmännchen und spinnen am Rocken** (Freytag's *Rittmeister*, 5) They say that if the band is not taken off the wheel, &c.

Sometimes an attributive adjective modifying the subject takes the place of the conditional clause: **Ein wahrer Freund hätte anders gehandelt** (= **Ein Freund hätte anders gehandelt, wenn er wahr gewesen wäre**). In English we often find the gerund, an example of the old attributive or appositional type of clause described in **268.** 4. Its subject is the person implied in a possessive adjective or a genitive: *Write me in case of his* or *John's coming* **Schreibe mir, falls er** or **Hans kommt.** For further remarks on the gerund see **272.** C. *g*.

A verbless conditional clause is often contained in the old verbless appositional type of sentence described in **252.** 1. *b. Note*: **Ende gut, alles gut** = **Wenn das Ende gut ist, so ist alles gut.**

e. Elliptical Forms. The subordinate clause is often suppressed: **Hättest du ihn nehmen mögen, Anna? [wenn du an meiner Stelle gewesen wärest].** The principal proposition is frequently omitted: **Wenn du es nur getan hättest!** For other examples see **169.** 1. A, **169.** 2. E. *Note* 4. **Als, wie** and **denn** are in this category most commonly found in elliptical sentences, where the construction in the subordinate clause follows closely that of the principal proposition: **Ich habe nichts getan als [ich habe] eine Krisis beschleunigt. Heute kann sie nichts [tun] als [sie kann] weinen. Sie tut nichts als [sie tut] weinen. Ich habe nicht anders [tun können] als [ich habe] es glauben können,** but where **können** is felt as an independent verb rather than as an auxiliary the infinitive takes **zu: Ich habe nicht anders gekonnt, als es zu glauben.** Similarly **Ich konnte nicht anders als ihm zustimmen,** but **Ich konnte nicht anders, als ihm zuzustimmen** (felt as a subordinate clause dependent upon the independent verb **konnte**). **Und da ich nun einmal nichts [zu tun weiß] wie [ich] zu lieben weiß** (Sudermann's *Die drei Reiherfedern*, 3, 10). Sometimes the infinitive depends upon a noun understood, which is suppressed as it has just been mentioned in the principal proposition: **Sie haben keine andere Wahl, als [die Wahl] die Tatsache anzuerkennen.** The use of **als, wie, denn** in all these examples indicates that the clause has developed out of a comparative clause (**277.** 1. B) and in a formal sense is still a comparative clause.

Concessive Clause.

280. The concessive clause contains a conceded statement, which, tho it is naturally in contrast or opposition to that of the principal proposition, is nevertheless unable to destroy the validity of the latter (for conjunctions see **238.** 3. G). As can be seen by the common use of the conjunctions **wenn** and **ob** (once widely employed in conditional clauses) and often also by the question word-order in connection with the past subjunctive, as illustrated in **237.** 1. A. *b. Note* 2, the concessive clause has in large measure developed out of the conditional clause. But the frequent use of relative pronouns and adverbs, demonstrative forms such as **so**, **trotzdem**, &c., indicate that important materials have been derived from other sources. Examples: **Vnd ob ich Alber** (now **albern**) **bin mit reden | So bin ich doch nicht alber in dem** (now **der**) **erkentnis** (2. Cor. xi. 6). **Irrtum ist Irrtum, ob ihn der größte Mann, ob ihn der kleinste beging. Ob die Sonne scheint oder** (or **oder ob**) **der Regen in Strömen herabgießt, er macht seinen Spaziergang. Ob es nahe sei oder weit, gehe ich. Und wird dir Guts geschehen, ob du auch wohl ein Sünder bist** (Luther). **Wiewohl du solches in deinem Herzen verbirgest, so weiß ich doch, daß du des gedenkest** (id.). **Ob man gleich über den erfochtenen Sieg das Tedeum anstimmte, so gestand doch Wallenstein selbst seine Niederlage. Obgleich die Alpen höher sind als die Pyrenäen, so lassen sie sich doch leichter überschreiten. Dieser, obgleich er noch wenig gemalt hat, weltberühmte Künstler hat große Einnahmen. Obschon** (or **wennschon**) **er reich ist** (conceded fact), or **Ob** (or **wenn**) **er schon reich ist, ist er doch unglücklich. Obgleich** (or **wenngleich**) **Karl es mir gesagt hat** (fact), **glaube ich es nicht**, but **Wenngleich** (or **wennschon**, or **auch wenn**, or **und wenn**, or **selbst wenn**, but not **obgleich** or **obschon**) **Karl es sagte** (mere assumption), **so glaubte ich es doch nicht. Ich komme, auch wenn es schneit** (assumption), but **obgleich** (**obwohl**, &c.) **es schneit** (fact). **So** (or **wie**) **wichtige Gründe der Minister auch vorbringen mochte, der König achtete nicht auf seine Worte. So sehr ich auch bat, er blieb bei seiner abschlägigen Antwort. Es muß doch heraus, wie** (or **so**) **gern ich es auch noch länger verschwiege. Für jede Seelenwunde, wie** (or **so**) **tief sie brennt, hat Zeit, die große Trösterin, den wahren Balsam. Wie** (or **so**) **Verbrecher** (pred. noun with the force of an adj.) **dieser Mensch auch ist, so zeigt er doch Spuren besserer Gesinnung. Welch tapfer Haupt auch dieser Helm bedeckt** (**hat**), **er kann kein würdigeres zieren** (Schiller). **Trotzdem er schon seit längerer Zeit sehr unwohl war, erfüllte er doch noch immer die Pflichten seines Amtes mit der größten Pünktlichkeit. Die Menschen Ho′mers, unbeschadet dessen, daß sie bereits auf den Schultern ungezählter Generationen stehen, erscheinen uns doch wie die Kinder, die Prometheus eben geformt hat** (Wilamowitz-Moellendorff's *Griechische Tragödien*, II, p. 14). **Hier könnt' ich meine Seele von mir hauchen, so mild und leise wie das Wiegenkind . . ., da** (now **da doch**) **fern von dir ich rasend toben würde** (A. W. Schlegel). **Du duldest die Strafe eines Schlemmers, da doch niemand ehrlicher gefastet hat als du** (Riehl). **Oft lobt man einen Gegenstand, während man von dessen Unwert überzeugt ist. Er geht stets zu Fuße, während er doch die schönsten Pferde im Stalle stehen hat. Wenn** (now **da doch** or **obschon**) **ich in Wien nie ins Theater ging, ging ich beinahe täglich in Paris** (Grillparzer).

a. The adversative particle **doch** is frequently used for emphasis in the principal proposition.

b. The clause is usually introduced by a concessive conjunction, but it may assume other forms: (**1**) The clause may be replaced by a proposition with normal or question order with the verb in the indicative or subjunctive. See **237**. 1. A. *d* and **168**. I. 2. A. (**2**) The imperative may take the place of the clause: **Sei noch so dumm, es gibt doch jemand, der dich für weise hält.** (**3**) A proposition with question order and a verb in the indic. or subjunc. may be used instead of the subordinate clause, as explained in **237**. 1. A. *b*. *Note* 2. (**4**) Instead of a concessive clause and a principal proposition we sometimes find two principal propositions connected by a co-ordinating conjunction, **und doch**, **aber**, **dennoch**, **trotz′dem**, often with **zwar** in the first proposition when **aber**, **dennoch**, or **trotzdem** follows: **Du könntest dich jeden Tag vollstopfen und** [**könntest**] **doch mager bleiben** = **Auch wenn du dich jeden Tag vollstopftest, könntest du doch mager bleiben. Wir sind zwar arm**, or **Zwar sind wir arm, aber wir sind doch nicht unglücklich**, or **dennoch** or **trotzdem sind wir nicht unglücklich.** For explanation and force of this construction see **267**. 4 (3rd par.). (**5**) The concessive idea sometimes finds expression in an attributive element, either in the form of an attributive adjective or a relative clause: **Diese álte Fráu putzt sich noch gern!** (= **Diese Frau putzt sich noch gern, obgleich sie alt ist**). **Der Unglückliche, der doch so bedürftig ist, konnte keine Unterstützung erhalten** (= **Der Unglückliche konnte keine Unterstützung erhalten, obgleich er so bedürftig ist**). See **255**. I. *c*. (**6**) The absolute accusative and nominative constructions sometimes take place of the concessive clause. See **265**. B. *a*. *b*. (**1**), (**2**). Compare *c* below.

c. Mood. The indic. is usually used if the clause is introduced by a conjunction. Sometimes, however, the subjunctive is employed. See **168**. I. 2. A. *a*, 2nd paragraph. If the clause is introduced by an interrogative pronoun or interrogative adverb the subjunctive is also still quite common, tho the indic. is often found, and always when describing past events the results of which are now definitely known: **Wie dem auch sei** (or **sein mag**), **es wird sich alles zum Besten wenden. Wie strafbar auch des Fürsten Zwecke waren, die Schritte, die er öffentlich getan, verstatteten noch eine milde Deutung.** If the conceded statement is not represented as an actual fact, but only as possible or impossible, or contrary to fact, the unreal potential subjunctive is used, see **169.** 1. B. If the conjunction is dropped the moods are used as described in *b* above. See also **168.** I. 2. A.

d. Abridgment. If the subject of the subordinate clause and that of the principal proposition are identical the clause may be abridged to an appositional participle, adjective, or noun, or an adverb, but more commonly retains here the conjunction (**obgleich** or **obwohl**): **Obwohl er vom Schicksal gebeugt ist**, or **Obwohl vom Schicksal gebeugt, strebt der Gute empor. Er kommt wohl nicht und wenn já, so kann er doch nur sehr spät kommen.** Sometimes the conjunction is suppressed: **Pünktlich sonst in seinem Dienste, war er jetzt von der Regel abgewichen** (Immermann).

Sometimes in colloquial language when the subjects are not identical abridgment occurs: **Den 2. März bestieg ich den Vesuv, obgleich bei trübem und umwölktem Gipfel** (Goethe). **Ob wahr, ob unwahr** (or **Ob wahr oder unwahr**), **man glaubt's. Man schaffe mir den Frevler tot oder lebendig** (or **ob tot, ob lebendig**) **herbei!** Zawisch: **Der Sieg ist unser, glaubt mir das, Herr Kanzler!** Kanzler: **Und wenn auch! was ist noch damit gewonnen?** (Grillparzer's *Ottokar*, 3). **Schlafen wird er nicht mehr; und wenn** [**er auch noch schläft**], **so weck' ich ihn** (Hoffmann's *Wider den Kurfürsten*, chap. viii). [**Na, du hast ja den Jungen gehörig bearbeitet. Er hat trotzig erklärt, er wolle so schnell als möglich ins Institut. Er tut's wohl dir zuliebe.**] **„Und wenn," warf Henrik ein, „Hauptsache muß doch wohl für dich sein, daß du deinen Zweck erreicht hast"** (Maria Janitschek's *Einer Mutter Sieg*, xiii).

English often employs the gerund here after *in spite of*, *despite*: *In spite of his* or *John's being so diligent the teacher has not praised him* **Trotzdem er** or **Hans so fleißig gewesen ist, hat ihn der Lehrer nicht gelobt.** For further remarks on the gerund see **272.** C. *g*.

Clause of Purpose.

281. The *clause of purpose* or *final clause*, as it is often called, states the purpose or direct end of the action of the principal proposition (for conjunctions see **238.** 3. H): **Er soll schnell machen, daß er nicht zu spät kommt. Darum bin ich euch entgegengeeilt, daß ich euch warnen könnte. Daß die Hand gesichert bleibe, faßt man Kohlen an mit Zangen. Da warf Konradin seinen Handschuh vom Blutgerüste herab, damit er dem König Peter von Aragonien gebracht werde.**

The clause of purpose is often used in elliptical sentences corresponding to the common elliptical infinitive construction in *b* (2nd par.): **Daß ich es nicht vergesse,** [**will ich dir sagen,**] **gestern war dein Bruder bei mir. Daß ich es kurz sage, ich will nicht.**

The idea of purpose often finds expression in other grammatical forms, such as object, subject, attributive substantive, relative clauses, and temporal clauses after **bis** and **ehe**. See **168.** I. 2. B. (**1**), (**3**), **169.** 1. C. (**1**), (**3**).

a. Mood. The subjunctive was always used here in oldest German as it alone could represent the statement as a clause of purpose, i.e. as something only planned or desired. After distinctive conjunctions had come into use here, such as **auf daß** and the now more common **damit** (**240.** *a*), the subjunctive was no longer absolutely necessary to indicate purpose and was gradually in colloquial speech after present tense forms displaced by the indicative. A more accurate description of usage and of the forces at work here is given in **168.** I. 2. B. *b*; **169.** 1. C. (**2**).

b. Abridgment. The final clause is in common prose usually contracted to an infin. with **zu** or **um zu** wherever no ambiguity can arise: **Er trank ein Glas Wein, um sich zu erwärmen** (much more common than **daß er sich erwärme**). See also **185.** A. II. 2. *a*.

The abridged form is very common in elliptical sentences where some such words as **so sage ich** are understood: **Die Wahrheit zu gestehen,** [**so sage ich**] **ich weiß es nicht. Er ist ein seltsamer Mensch,** [**so drücke ich mich aus**] **um nicht zu sagen ein Narr. Um es kurz zu sagen, ich will nicht.** As the infinitive in such sentences does not stand in relation to any other word that is formally expressed it is often called an absolute infinitive.

Note on Historical Development of the Infinitive Clause of Purpose. In Luther's time **um zu** was not yet widely used, but it is now much more common than the simple **zu**. The increasing use of **um zu** instead of **zu** is quite natural. Altho **zu** often expresses the idea of purpose when used with nouns, as described in **229.** 2 under **zu**, II. 1. B. *f*, it is so often used with the infinitive as the subject or object of a verb that the original idea of purpose is no longer vividly felt. The prep. **um** brings out this idea clearly. Tho **um zu** originally was limited to clauses of purpose, it has in accordance with one of the common meanings of **um** also spread to clauses of result, as mentioned in **272.** D. *c*, **276.** D. *b*, and **277.** 2. *b*, and even to adjective clauses, as mentioned in **255.** IV. 2. *a*. This favorite construction has to the alarm of the grammarians spread much beyond its old historic boundaries and is now used with especial frequency to add to a statement about a person or thing some item concerning their later fate, lot, or conduct: **Sie schieden, um sich nie wiederzusehen** They parted never to see one another again. **Dann lachte wohl der kindliche Frohsinn auf, um bald wieder desto schwerer niedergedrückt zu werden.** This censured construction corresponds closely to the use of the infinitive with *to* in similar expressions in English. The infinitive with *to* in English and **um zu** in German are here employed to denote a result which is the natural outcome of events or plans independent of the action described in the principal proposition, while they elsewhere denote a result as the effect of the activity or state indicated in the governing proposition. While the use of *to* and **um zu** here is contrary to the general principle observed in clauses of result, it should be regarded as a valuable modification and extension of this principle which should be encouraged rather than discouraged, as it is one of the tersest and most expressive constructions known to either language.

The first examples of a double prepositional infinitive to express purpose are found in the classical literature of the M.H.G. period: Die herȥogin lost uf den stric, durch die schrift uȥ ȥe lesenne an dem seile (Wolfram's *Titurel*, 154. 4) The duchess untied the chord in order to read to the end the writing on it, lit. untied the chord on account of the writing, in order to read on the chord to the end. The two prepositional phrases *durch die schrift* and *ze lesenne* both modify the verb *lost uf*. Instead of *durch* the preposition *um* soon became more common. Still later the noun after the preposition *um* came to be felt as the object of the following infinitive and the *um* was construed as a connective introducing a contracted clause of purpose, as first seen in Low German: Dat is gescheen umme tho beholdende de vriheid dusser stat (*Berichte und Aktenstücke über die Ereignisse in Lübeck von* 1405–1408, 404. 19) **Dies ist geschehen, um die Freiheit dieser Stadt zu behaupten.** In this old document of the fifteenth century it can be clearly seen that *um* is no longer a preposition governing a following noun, for its stands before the prepositional infinitive. This development may possibly have taken place earlier, but it is impossible to prove it as the *um* usually stood before the substantive as in the original construction, where moreover it normally still stands. The occasional position of the *um* immediately before the prepositional infinitive indicates that the change has taken place. The construction was at first little used and did not become common before the middle of the seventeenth century. This long period of development is explained by the simple fact that *um* did not originally belong to the infinitive clause as a whole but to only one word in it, namely the substantive which followed it. It often requires many centuries for an entirely new syntactical structure to become established. Here the prepositional infinitive and the words associated with it slowly acquired the force of a subordinate clause of purpose with the distinctive conjunction *um*, which distinguished it from other kinds of subordinate clauses. It also differs from other subordinate clauses in that instead of a finite verb it has as verbal predicate a prepositional infinitive with a subject which has to be supplied from the context of the principal proposition. Thus tho slow to become established this construction has at length by virtue of its distinct form and pithy terseness become a decided favorite. In dialect other prepositions are used as conjunctions instead of **um**, as for instance **for** in Alsatian corresponding to older English *for*, as in Are ye come out as against a thief with swords and staves for to take me? (Matth. xxvi. 55): **siine Exame gemacht fore Doktor zu wäre** (= **werden**) (Karl Bernhard's *Straßburjer Wibble*, 33). In English *for* is still quite common here where the subject of the infinitive is not identical with the subject of the principal proposition: The lad pulled at his mother for her to take notice of him **Der Junge zupfte an der Mutter, damit sie auf ihn aufmerksam werde.** Compare **269. 3.** When the subject of the infinitive is the same as that of the principal proposition English uses *in order* here as a conjunction: I arose early in order to get the work done before noon. Quite similar to the infinitive clause of purpose with a distinctive conjunction, **um** in German and *for* and *in order* in English, is the German infinitive clause of manner with the conjunctions **ohne** and **anstatt**: **Er verschwand, ohne ein Wort zu sagen. Man erzählte ihm, anstatt ihn erzählen zu lassen.** The infinitive with **ohne** first appeared in the fourteenth century, and was used much in the same way as **um** as described above. The infinitive with **anstatt** is modern and has arisen under the influence of the infinitive with **um** and **ohne.** The English infinitive *for*-clause has a similar development. See **269. 3.**

Clause of Means.

282. The clause of means indicates the means by which the effect mentioned in the principal proposition is produced: **Da'durch daß du ihm trotzest, wirst du gar nichts von ihm erreichen. Ich erkannte ihn da'ran, daß er hinkte. Ihm gelang die Flucht aus dem Gefängnis, in'dem er die Wächter bestach.** For the conjunctions used see **238. 3. I.** In a formal sense many of these clauses are prepositional clauses, so that they may be classed under **272. D.**

a. Abridgment. The clause of means is sometimes contracted to an appositional participial clause: **Mich am Stricke festhaltend, rettete ich mich ans Ufer** *Holding on to the rope firmly I came safe to the shore.* This is the attributive or appositional type of clause structure described in **268. 4.** English has gone much farther than German in developing this old type of clause. In English it is often found in prepositional phrases in which the person implied in a possessive adjective or a genitive is the logical subject, the governing gerund the logical predicate, and the preposition the sign of subordination to the principal verb: *By his* or *John's holding the ladder firmly I succeeded in climbing on to the roof* **Dadurch daß er or Hans die Leiter festhielt, gelang es mir, auf das Dach zu steigen.** German is often similar to English when the subject of the principal verb serves as the subject of the gerund: By holding on to the rope firmly I came safe to the shore **Durch Festhalten am Stricke rettete ich mich ans Ufer.** For further remarks on the gerund see **272. C. *g*.**

Word-Order.

283. The German word-order presents peculiar difficulties to the English-speaking student. One of the first things to learn is that word-order in a German sentence is intimately connected with accent. In German words are removed from their usual position and placed at the beginning of the sentence when they become emphatic, while in English we may accent words heavily without changing their position. The next important position in a German sentence is at the end. The least emphatic words are usually found near the middle of the sentence, and further on the words receive more stress as they approach the end. Also considerations of euphony influence word-order. Short, light objective or adverbial elements precede longer, heavier ones. Opposed to this freedom of placing words according to their logical or emotional importance, or the requirements of euphony, &c., are certain mere formal grammatical principles which have developed certain fixed types. Hence the whole subject must be studied in detail.

284. I. In German there are three word-orders: the verb in the second place, the verb in the first place, the verb in the last place.

1. *Verb in the Second Place.* This word-order may assume two different forms. The subject may stand in the first place with the verb in the second place: **Der Vater liebt den Sohn.** This form is called *normal order.* If any other word for emphasis, or to establish a nearer relation with what goes on before, or because it lies nearer in thought, stand in the first place, the verb still maintains the second place, followed usually by the subject in the third place: **Auf Sonnenschein folgt Regen.** This order is called *inverted.*

a. This division into normal and inverted order is now quite general, but not altogether scientific. In earlier periods there is no difference whatever between these two orders. The subject or any word in the predicate could for emphasis, or to establish a nearer relation with what went on before, or because it lay nearer in thought, stand in the first place, followed later by the verb, which in oldest German often stood in the final position in the sentence and only as a result of a long development, as described in 3. *a* below, became established in the second place immediately after the subject or the stressed object or adverb introducing the sentence. By reason of its importance the subject stood so often in the first place that this position has become functional, i.e. it now normally stands in the first place even tho it is unimportant and unstressed. The older order of things, however, is often still in force. The subject still takes its place at the head of the sentence when it becomes emphatic, especially the interrogatives, **wer, welcher,** &c., or a noun which has important modifiers: **Alle wirkliche Kunst beruht auf der individuellen Freiheit und dem fröhlichen Lebensgenuß** (Mommsen's *Römische Geschichte,* III, chap. xiv). The subject is also brought forward to establish a nearer relation with what goes on before, especially in case of demonstrative pronouns. Even the weakly accented personal pronoun establishes the connection with what precedes: **Willst du nicht deinen Kaffee trinken, Tantchen? Er wird ganz kalt** (Sudermann's *Fritzchen,* 5). This personal pronoun is in a contrast still accented, and then it stands at the head of the sentence in a double capacity — as an emphatic word and to establish a connection with what precedes: **Herr, ér hatte es leicht! Ér ging von hinnen, aber dír ließ er als Erbe das halb zerstörte Reich** (Sudermann's *Teja,* 11).

These original ideas which once characterized the normal word-order are now often little felt or not felt at all, as this word-order has developed a different force. It has become the form of expression suited to the mind in its normal condition of steady activity and easy movement, from which it only departs under the stress of emotion or for logical reasons, or in conformity to fixed rules. Thus where there are several subordinate clauses connected by **und, oder,** &c., there is often, especially in colloquial speech, a tendency after the conjunction to return to the normal order: **Stünd' Agamemnons Sohn dir gegenüber, | und du verlangtest, was sich nicht gebührt: | so hat usw.** (Goethe's *Iphigenie,* 5, 3). **Wenn Sie einen [Jungen] erwischen und haun ihm 'n paar 'runter, dann werden sie's wohl lassen** (Ilse Leskien's *Schuld,* p. 3). **Wer einen solchen Schritt unternimmt und den, Gott sei Dank! immer noch fest gefügten Bau der Kirche zertrümmern will und hat sich nicht besser alles vorher überlegt, der kann sich nur lächerlich machen.** In much the same manner the inverted order is often replaced by the normal: **Als er zurückkam, war sein Gesicht stark verweint und er schloß sich mehrere Stunden in sein Zimmer ein** (Schubin's *Boris Lensky,* x). The normal order is also now usually employed where in earlier periods the question order was used, i.e. the verb was placed at the head of the sentence for especial emphasis in accordance with its importance in individual cases or in ballads and epics in accordance with the general importance which attaches to the verb in narrative and descriptive style. In a somewhat veiled form this older usage is still quite common in the literary language. The expletive es is placed at the beginning of the sentence as a grammatical subject followed immediately by the verb so that the verb is still the first word of real importance. For full treatment of this point see **251.** II. B. *a. bb, b.*

The first place is not the only emphatic position for the subject. It may be made prominent by being reserved for the important position at the end of the sentence. For fuller treatment of this point see **251.** II. B. *a. cc.*

2. *Verb in the First Place.* This is the usual order of a question that requires an affirmative or negative answer, and may be called *question order:* **Ist der Knabe fleißig?**

a. In earlier periods the verb, just as still an object or an adverb, stood in the first place whenever it was emphatic, or in order to establish a nearer relation with what went on before, or because it lay nearest in thought. This older order of things survives in wishes, in expressions of will containing an imperative and often in those containing a volitive subjunctive, also in questions that require yes or no for an answer, in all of which cases the verb is brought forward because of its importance to the thought and is consequently stressed: **Käme er doch! Reiche mir das Buch! Hol' ihn der Teufel! Rette sich, wer kann! Reisen Sie dieses Jahr wieder nach Karlsbad?** Compare **50.** A. 3. *c* and **168.** I. 1. B. *a.* In older periods this position and stress of the verb were also common in certain types of the declarative sentence where the verb is important to the thought. In literary German this order in declarative sentences is now restricted to definite groups of cases, which are given in **287.** B. In popular and colloquial language, however, the earlier freedom of placing a verb at the beginning of even a declarative sentence is still quite common. See **251.** II. B. *b*, also **286.** A. *c*.

3. *Verb in the Last Place.* This is the order of a subordinate clause, and is usually called *transposed order*: **Die Sterne erscheinen uns deswegen so klein, weil sie so weit von uns entfernt sind.**

a. Historical Development of the Word-order. In the oldest as well as modern German and English the verb could stand in the *second* place between subject and object, but in older English and in oldest and modern German it can also stand in the *second* place after an adverb or object. In the oldest period it also often in both languages stood in the *first* place in emphatic statement and narrative, and survivals of this usage still often occur in German in emphatic statements and ballads, as indicated in **287.** B (**7**) and (**8**), but in the *normal* declarative sentence the verb stood at the end, almost regularly so in oldest English and quite commonly so in oldest German, indicating a still greater regularity in pre-Germanic. This was in conformity with a general principle of the older normal word-order that modifiers of a word should precede it. This old word-order with the verb at the end preceded by its modifiers corresponds to the order found in old group-words (**247.** 2. *a*), where the governing word stands at the end preceded by its modifiers. This old word-order was based upon a mere grammatical principle. As the modifiers were not originally inflected they could only be felt as modifiers by having a fixed position. Thus they always preceded the governing verb. This old order was later in the inflectional period often disturbed by reserving for the end the important modifier or modifiers of the verb, in order to create the feeling of suspense and thus increase the emphasis. As the verb was thus not the center of attention and was often weakly stressed it gradually settled into the weakly stressed position after the subject or the strongly accented object or adverb which often introduces the sentence. Besides this rhythmical principle there was also a psychological force active in establishing the verb in this position. The verb contains the basal idea of the predication, so that there was often, especially in long sentences, a tendency to bring it near the subject in order that subject and predicate together might at the outset make clear the general line of thought and thus relieve the tension somewhat and make it possible to concentrate the attention upon the important details which were to be presented later. In course of time this position of the verb became fixed, so that the originally *emphatic* order became the new *normal* or *inverted* order as they exist to-day. In English the tendency to place the subject before and in the vicinity of the verb is very much stronger and more universal than in German, for it almost invariably takes place in all declarative sentences in both the principal proposition and the subordinate clause, but in English it has never been an absolute requirement that the verb should follow the subject *immediately* as in German, as in **Hans tut es oft,** in English *John often does it.* In English the tendency to place the subject before the verb and thus indicate the grammatical relations by means of the word-order manifested itself in early times and century after century became stronger and stronger, so that the distinctive case forms of nouns and adjectives gradually as useless inflections disappeared in whole or in part. In German the case forms have been largely preserved as they are still often needed to make clear the grammatical relations. Here also the older normal word-order with the verb at the end of the sentence still survives in poetry. See **288.** B. *c*. It has also been preserved in prose and poetry in the subordinate clause. The main reason for the preservation of the old order here seems to be that the subordinate clause had the same word-order and stress as a compound or old group-word (**247.** 2) — stressed verbal element preceded by a still stronger stressed modifier — and gradually developed into a somewhat similar speech unit with the same fixed word-order and stress. The free stressing of important words in the principal proposition by placing them in important positions has gradually associated with the normal or inverted order the idea of *positive assertion* with the emphasis upon certain words, while the set word-order and stress of the subordinate clause arouses the idea of a compact unit, a thought, an impression, or a feeling as a *whole* without special reference to particular words: **Noch héute geht er** and **Ich bestéhe darauf, noch héute geht er,** but **Ich bestehe darauf, daß er noch heute geht** *I insist upon it that,* &c., where **darauf** points to the thought of the following clause as a whole. After negatives and verbs expressing mere feeling the normal or inverted word-order with their idea of positive assertion and definite emphasis upon certain words often cannot be used at all: **Ich glaube, heute geht noch ein Zug,** but **Ich glaube kaum, daß heut noch ein Zug geht** and **Ich bin keineswegs überzeugt, daß du recht hast. Ich freue mich riesig, daß du gekommen bist** (not **du bist gekommen**). **Es tut mir sehr leid, daß du dich gekränkt fühlst** (not **du fühlst dich gekränkt**). In **Ich weiß, du bist ein braver Junge** there is in the subordinate clause with normal word-order the warmth of positive assertion, while in **Ich weiß, daß du ein braver Junge bist** we feel in the subordinate word-order the tone slightly cooler, i.e. we feel the utterance as a calm objective statement of a fact, a thought as a whole. In the transposed order the verb is never weakly stressed as often in normal and inverted order, but always distinctly stressed as the verbal element in old group-words, as **Kópfverlètzung,** altho often with a little less force than other words yet with an unmistakable accent as the subordinate clause, like an old group-word, is felt as a thought as a whole, a fact, an essential element of which is the idea contained in the verbal element: **Minìster Gérber tritt** (weakly stressed) **am 1. Oktober in den Rúhestand,** but **Ich wundere mich, daß Minister Gerber in den Rúhestand trìtt** (distinctly stressed). **Wo wohnt** (weakly stressed) **der neue Bűrgermeister?** but **Nein, wo der neue Bűrgermeister wòhnt!** (distinctly stressed), as the attention is not directed to any word in particular but to the thought as a whole, namely surprise that the mayor would reside in such a house. As in the last example German often employs the transposed order in independent propositions to represent the utterance, not as an assertion with certain important details, but as a mere thought or impression as a whole. Likewise in giving a definite command to be carried out at once we say: **Schlíeße mir die Haustür** with distinct emphasis upon the imperative to indicate immediate action, but to impress the thought as a whole upon someone's mind we say: **Daß du mir heute abend die Háustür schlìeßt!** In directing a question to someone we say: **Wie heißt denn dein Brúder?** If, however, the question is not understood we do not usually repeat the exact words but reproduce the thought as a whole in transposed order: **Wie dein Bruder heißt?**

II. These different word-orders are discussed somewhat in detail in the following articles, but a number of still smaller details can only be learned from practical acquaintance with the language. The word-order, as it is, has only after a long period of development assumed its present form. Earlier usage is still reflected occasionally in poetry and elevated language in general, as is mentioned below and in **237**, in the treatment of transposed word-order.

Normal Order.

I. General Statement.

285. 1. *Order of Words.* This order is, first the subject with all its modifiers, then the simple verb or in compound tenses the auxiliary, followed by the modifiers of the verb: **Goethe, der am 28. August 1749 auf die Welt kam, hat im geistigen Leben Deutschlands gewirkt, wie eine gewaltige Naturerscheinung im physischen gewirkt hätte.**

2. Normal order is found:

a. In independent declarative sentences: **Ich trage immer die Schuhe vorn eckig** I always wear square-toed shoes. A declarative sentence often has the force of a command: **Ich habe Hunger = Gib mir zu essen.**

b. In questions in which the interrogative word or phrase is itself the subject of the sentence: **Wer kommt denn alles?** Who all are coming? **Wessen Hut liegt auf dem Tische?** This form of questions is often used to express a wish: **Wer von euch hilft mir?**

c. Often in other interrogative sentences, which are distinguished from declarative sentences only by the rising inflection or in print by the punctuation: **Und Sie haben das im Ernste geglaubt?** And you really believed that? Such sentences usually express doubt or surprise. In connection with **nicht wahr** *is he not, has he not, is she not, has she not, must you not*, &c., which may introduce the sentence or close it, this order is much used in questions which confidently expect an affirmative answer: **Es ist heute schönes Wetter, nicht wahr?** It is fine weather to-day, isn't it? **Nicht wahr, sie kann schön singen?** She can sing beautifully, can't she?

d. In wishes the normal order may be used. See **168.** I. 1. B. *a*.

e. In commands which are expressed by the indicative. See **177.** I. B. *b*. *c*.

f. The normal order is also sometimes used in subordinate clauses. See **237.** 1. A. *a*, *d*, *f*, and *Note* 1 under *b*.

II. Detailed Statement.

A. *Word-order of the Subject.* The general rule for the position of the modifiers of the subject is that adjectives and participles precede, an adjective clause, an adverb (see B. *a*. *Note* (**1**), (**2**), (**3**), (**4**), below), or prep. phrase follow, an appositive or genitive either precedes or follows the subject: **Ein edler Mann wird durch ein gutes Wort der Frauen weit geführt. Ein Glaube, welchem die Werke fehlen, ist ein toter Glaube. Der Durst nach Ruhm verleitet manche auf falsche Wege. Das Schloß des Kaisers bei Potsdam ist sehr schön.**

a. The position of an appositive is described in **255.** II. 1. G. *a*, III. 1. A, B, and that of a genitive is treated in **255.** II. 1. The appositive noun, which represents an older partitive genitive, may precede the governing noun or pronoun, and often stands at the head of the sentence, whether it modifies the subject or an object. See **255.** II. 1. H. *a.*

b. The adjective and participle sometimes stand after the subject. See **104.** 2. B. *a* and *b*; **111.** 9; **137.** 1. *a.*

c. All modifiers of an attributive adjective or participle must stand before it: **Der gegen seinen Beschützer für die empfangenen Wohltaten in hohem Grade dankbare Knabe übernahm freudig den gefährlichen Auftrag. Das auf dem Tische liegende Buch.** When, however, such adjectives and participles follow the governing noun the adjective or participle may either stand *after* their modifiers, or *before* them if the modifiers are to be made prominent: **dieser Mann, auf seinen Rang so stólz,** or **so stolz auf seinen Ráng.**

d. An adverb or prepositional phrase that modifies the subject usually follows it, but sometimes it precedes. See **255.** IV. 2 and VI.

e. An appositional noun, adjective, or participle, which precedes the subject, not as an attributive modifier, but as the equivalent of an adverbial clause, must like adverbs cause inversion: **Ein geborener Herrscher** (= **weil er ein geborener Herrscher war**), **regierte er die Gemüter der Menschen, wie der Wind die Wellen zwingt.**

B. *Word-order of the Predicate.* The personal part of the verb follows the logical subject. The general rule for the word-order of the modifiers of the verb is that the important words gravitate towards the end of the sentence and the less important, as personal or reflexive (see **218.** 1. *a*) pronouns, stand near the verb. The following points should be carefully mastered:

a. The verb, or in compound tenses the auxiliary, must follow the logical subject *immediately*, and hence no adverbial expressions or clauses must be allowed to stand between subject and verb as in English: **Ich besuche ihn oft** I often visit him. **Die Griechen wälzten, damit ihre eigene Schwäche verdeckt bliebe, alle Schuld des Verlustes auf ihn** The Greeks, in order that their own weakness might remain concealed, threw all blame for the loss upon him.

Note. To this important rule there must be added, however, a few exceptions: (**1**) Often a few adverbial expressions, as **nur** *only*, **wenigstens** *at the least*, **jedenfalls** *at any rate*, **für meine Person,** or **für meinen Teil,** or **meinesteils** *for my part*, and the concessive terms **freilich** *to be sure*, **in der Tat** *indeed*, **wie ich zugeben muß** *as I must confess* &c., modify not the verb, but only the subject, and hence may follow it, and thus stand between subject and verb: **Ich wenigstens habe nichts gesehen** *I for my part have seen nothing.* (**2**) A few adverbs as **besonders** *especially*, **vorzüglich** *particularly*, **vor allem** *above all*, &c., especially emphasize the subject, and may follow it: **Dein Bruder besonders hat sich in der letzten Zeit gegen mich sehr freundlich bewiesen.** (**3**) Partitive and adversative conjunctions or adverbs, as **einerseits** on the one hand, **ander**(**er**)**seits** on the other hand, **aber, indessen, jedoch** however, **dagegen, hingegen** on the other hand, &c., which represent the subject as sharing in an action or as being in contrast to another subject, may follow the subject: **Seine Kränklichkeit einerseits, seine Trägheit anderseits waren ihm ein großes Hindernis. Alle waren über den frechen Mordanfall auf den Fürsten außer sich, dieser im Gegenteil** (or **hingegen**) **verlor keinen Augenblick die Fassung.** (**4**) Sometimes adverbs or adverbial phrases, tho true adverbial elements in form, are felt as the equivalent of adj. modifiers, and follow the subject: **Das Haus da** (= **das da steht**) **gehört mir** The house there belongs to me. **Die Treibjagd am 3. Januar** (= **die am 3. Januar stattfand**) **brachte über hundert Menschen auf die Beine.** (**5**) A clause sometimes stands before the verb when it refers to the thought contained in the predicate as a whole rather than to the verb itself: **Der Tunnel** (literary society in Berlin in the years 1827–77), **was nicht gleichgültig war und deshalb hier mit erwähnt werden mag, besaß auch ein nicht unbeträchtliches Vermögen** (Fontane). (**6**) A phrase, clause, or sentence is often inserted parenthetically between subject and verb: **Die Stiftungsfeste, wie gesagt** (*as already mentioned*), **waren gut. Dein Bruder, wenn du es durchaus wissen willst, hat das Geld genommen; er, um frei von der Leber zu sprechen, ist der Dieb. Der Knabe — Wilhelm hieß er — antwortete: Ich weiß es nicht.**

b. In sentences containing a compound tense and also those containing a separable prefix or a predicate adjective, the grammatically important word of the predicate, i.e. *participle*, *infinitive*, *separable prefix*, *predicate adjective* or *noun*, usually stands at the end of the sentence, as this word-order has become functional. For fuller treatment of this important word-order see **215.** II. 1. A. This word-order is observed even where the participle is used instead of a past tense. See **183.** 1. G. Besides the points discussed in **215.** II. 1. A, the following additional details should be noted:

aa. Auxiliary infinitives stand after perf. participles, altho less heavily stressed: **Sie dürften sich geírrt hàben** You have probably made a mistake. **Wir müssen wohl beide zugleich darauf gekómmen sèin** We must have both hit upon that idea at the same time. A dependent infinitive, however, precedes a participle: **Ich habe ihn kómmen gesèhen.**

bb. The predicate noun, adjective, or participle is followed by a perf. participle or infinitive altho the latter are less heavily stressed: **Er ist ein tüchtiger Mánn gewòrden. Sie ist schón gewèsen. Sie wird ihnen náhe blèiben. Er wird ein tüchtiger Mánn gewòrden sein** He has probably become a good, solid man. Here belongs the predicate participle in the passive voice, which must always be followed by the participle or infinitive of **werden: Der Schüler ist gelóbt**

wòrden. Er wird gelóbt wèrden. For further details concerning the word-order and stress here see **215.** II. 1. A (3rd par.); **178.** 2. B. *c* and *e*.

If, however, the predicate be a clause, the participle or infinitive precedes: **Die nächste Folge hiervon war gewesen, daß sich die Bildung einer deutschen politischen Hegemonie in diesem Nordwesten nicht hatte vollziehen können** (Lamprecht's *Deutsche Geschichte*, 7. 2, p. 649).

cc. The infinitive or participle which stands regularly at the end of the sentence must be preceded by its modifiers: **Ich kann Ihnen keine bestimmte Antwort geben. Er hat einen Streit angefangen.** For the explanation of the word-order in all these cases see **215.** II. 1. A (3rd par.). If, however, the infinitive or participle is modified by an infinitive with **zu** or by a clause it must usually precede these modifiers: **Ich muß Sie bitten, mir einen Regenschirm zu leihen. Ich möchte gern wissen, was dies ist. Das Kind hat angefangen, Französisch zu lernen. Ich hab's erfahren, was Hungern ist.** Where, however, the infinitive with **zu** is so closely related in thought to the governing infinitive or participle that it is felt as forming a group with it, it precedes the governing word: **Ich werde zu árbeiten hàben. Sie haben sich nicht davon zu befréien gewùßt. Er hat es nicht zu tún vermòcht.**

Unemphatic dative objects, especially unstressed personal pronouns and the reflexive **sich,** may introduce the clause in German, while in English the *subject* of the infinitive must have the first place in the clause: **Er ließ dem Armen durch einen Diener Brot geben** *He ordered some bread to be given to the poor fellow.* **Laß dir dás** (or also **dás dir**) **eine Warnung sein.**

dd. A single adverb, a genitive, or dative modifying a predicate adjective, or participle must precede it, but a phrase or longer expression may also follow it, a clause usually so: **Er ist dort gebürtig** He is a native of that place. **Er ist der deutschen Sprache mächtig** He can speak and understand German. **Verstellung ist der offenen Seele fremd.** But: **Er ist aus dem südlichen Frankreich gebürtig,** or **Er ist gebürtig aus dem südlichen Frankreich. Er ist darüber sehr erfreut,** but **Ich bin sehr erfreut, daß er sich meiner erinnert.** A modifying phrase usually follows when some word in the phrase is modified by other words: **Der Augenblick war daher möglichst ungünstig gewählt für den nochmals gemachten Versuch, gütlich zwischen den Parteien zu vermitteln.**

ee. A participle which has the form of an infinitive may stand at the end of a sentence or before the dependent infinitive and its modifiers; see **178.** 2. B. *c*.

ff. Sometimes in both normal and question order other words can follow an infinitive or participle contrary to the general rule that infinitive and participle must stand at the end. This exceptional order was common in older German, and it is not infrequent in the vigorous prose of our own time whenever it seems best for sake of emphasis to place some important modifier of the verb at the end of the sentence, altho in general the word-order has become stereotyped: **Hast du die Schmerzen gelindert je des Beladenen?** (Goethe). **Sie haben Ihr Lebensglück geopfert um meinetwillen** (Sudermann's *Heimat*, 4, 5). Often a word is withheld to the end to create the feeling of suspense: **Ich werde euch etwas Neues erzählen — von Fritz.** Sometimes in colloquial language unimportant words follow the infinitive or participle: **Ich behaupte, auf wen dein Vater einwirkt, der kann gar nie gänzlich verflachen im Leben** (Hauptmann's *Michael Kramer*, 1, p. 26).

On the other hand, this irregular feature is a regular characteristic feature of the German spoken by Jews who have not eradicated all traces of Hebrew or other foreign influence from their language: **Die Papiere sind gewesen in unsrer Stadt, einer hat sie gekriegt von einem alten sterbenden Bettler, und ist geworden ein mächtiger Mann** (Veitel Itzig in Freytag's *Soll und Haben*, chap. i). This order is also found in the German of Poles, Frenchmen, Englishmen, and other foreigners: **Ich aber sage, Herr Pfarrer, diese Sünde kann nicht verziehen werden in Ewigkeit, denn er hat sich nicht nur selbst erniedrigt zum Tier, er hat auch andre hineingezogen in seinen Fall und hat sie betrogen um ihr zeitliches und ewiges Heil** (the Polish chaplain in Halbe's *Jugend*, p. 96). Compare also the German of Riccaut in Lessing's *Minna von Barnhelm*, 4, 2. See likewise **215.** II. 1. A. *a. Note.*

gg. The preceding remarks refer to the usual position of participle, infinitive, separable prefix, predicate adjective, or noun. A certain logical emphasis always lies in all these grammatical functions, even tho there may be no especial stress upon the individual words, and hence the regularity with which we find these words in their position at the close of the sentence. However, if any *especial* emphasis be placed upon the individual words in these functions, they are placed at the head of the sentence: **Schön ist das Wetter heute nicht. Gegeben habe ich ihm das Buch nicht, sondern nur geliehen. Schreiben hätte er doch wenigstens gekonnt.** The separable prefix only rarely thus introduces the sentence, and that usually in poetry, preferring as a rule to stand at the end of the sentence: **Zurücke bleibt der Knappen Troß** (Schiller). See **215.** II. 1. A. *e* for the manner of writing the prefix here.

hh. If an infinitive or participle belongs to several propositions it is usually in normal, inverted, and question order found in its proper position in the last of the propositions, and understood with the others: **Er (Cäsar) hat diese beiden großen Aufgaben nicht bloß nebeneinander, sondern eine durch die andere gelöst** (Mommsen's *Römische Geschichte*, V, chap. ii). Participle or infinitive, however, is often found in the first proposition and understood with the others: **Hätt' ich hingehen sollen und ihn anzeigen?** (Halbe's *Der Strom*, p. 69).

c. Order of Objects. The general rule is, here as elsewhere in the predicate, that the known and hence less important and unaccented word comes first, and the newly introduced word, to which the attention is to be especially called, and which consequently bears the accent, follows. A longer, heavier word often for the sake of euphony follows a shorter word. The following applications of these points are to be especially noted, but it must be borne in mind that these positions, tho the common ones, are not absolute, and hence will change at once when the relative importance and accent of the objects change.

aa. If there are two acc. objects, one of the person and one of the thing, the object of the thing will follow if it is a noun, but will precede if it is a pronoun, as it already will have been referred to, and hence is the less important word: **Der Lehrer lehrte den Schüler** (or **ihn,** if the person has been mentioned) **den richtigen Ausdruck.** But: **Ich weiß den richtigen Ausdruck nicht. Lehre ihn mich.** Of course the pronominal object of the thing may follow when it becomes the more important or a longer, heavier word: **Der Schüler lernt den richtigen Ausdruck. Der Lehrer lehrt ihn denselben** (instead of **ihn ihn**).

There can also be two objects of another kind, the first one the object of the principal verb, the following one the object of the dependent infinitive: **Die Sage läßt Zeus den Kronos entthronen.** The word-order here has gradually become fixed, as without a set order the thought would often be obscured. In accordance with the older freedom of position here, however, we still often find the object of the infinitive before the object of the principal verb, especially in case of pronominal objects: **Man durfte es ihn natürlich nicht merken lassen** (Beyerlein's *Jena oder Sedan?*, I).

Note. The contracted form of **es** often by way of exception follows a pronominal acc. of the person when no especial emphasis of the person is involved: **Ich weiß das Richtige nicht. Lehre es mich** or **Lehre mich's.** The contractions **ihn's** and **uns's**, however, are not used, and hence here the regular forms **es ihn** and **es uns** must be employed.

bb. When there are two objects, a dat. and an acc., the dat. precedes if the acc. is a noun or any pronoun other than a personal or reflexive pronoun: **Ich schrieb meinem Freund** (or **ihm**) **einen Brief** (or **dies**). **Seine Mittel erlaubten ihm dies.**

Note. Of course the dat. follows when it becomes more prominent than the acc., especially when it is modified by a clause: **Franz reichte seinem Bruder den Bríef,** but **Franz reichte den Brief seinem Brúder. Ich empfehle diesen Knaben meinem Freunde, der sich gewiß seiner annehmen wird.**

cc. Of two objects, a dat. and an acc., the acc. precedes if it is a *personal* or *reflexive* pronoun: **Heute früh brachte die Post einen Brief aus China für Ta** (name). **Ich gab ihn ihm** (Heyking's *Briefe, die ihn nicht erreichten*). **Ich sagte es ihm. Er nahm ihn sich zum Muster. Ein Scherz, wie er ihn sich oft erlaubt. Er entzog sich mir.**

Note. The following exceptions are common: **(1)** The contracted form of **es** often follows the dat., especially the datives **mir, dir, sich: Gib es mir,** or **Gib mir's. (2)** The ethical dative (**258.** 3. *C*), which is usually weakly accented, can stand before the acc. of a pronoun: **Schilt ihn mir,** or **mir ihn nicht, den lieben Jungen! (3)** Of course the dat. follows the acc. if it is the more important and emphatic of the two: **Ich bedarf eines Rates von Ihnen. Wollen Sie mir ihn geben?** Here both the dat. and the acc. object have already been brought to the attention of the person addressed, but the thing represented by the acc. is the point towards which the attention is more particularly directed. Notice in the following sentences the shifting of position according to fine shades of meaning: **Ach bleib nur, Lotte! Ich bringe dir ihn** (i.e. **den Kaffee**) **schon** (Beyerlein's *Dämon Othello*, 1, 5). **Die** (i.e. **die Blumen**) **will ich mir aber alle aufheben, und wenn sie verwelkt sind, presse ich sie mir** (ib., 1, 5). **Ach was, dumm! — Kind! Das wäre schlimm! Bin ich doch selbst dein Lehrer gewesen und hab' dich mir herangezogen, so wie ich dich haben wollte** (ib., 1, 7).

dd. If there are an accusative and a prepositional or genitive object, the acc. precedes: **Er schrieb einen Brief an seinen Freund. Der König zieh den Herzog des Verrates.**

ee. The preceding rules for the position of objects must of course be set aside if one of the objects is an interrogative or relative pronoun, for these must always stand at the beginning of the sentence: **Was schreiben Sie Ihrem Freund?**

d. Order of Adverbs. Here as elsewhere in the predicate the rule holds that the unimportant words stand nearest the personal part of the verb, and the important ones gravitate towards the end of the sentence. Adverbs usually observe the following order: *Time, Place, Manner, Cause, Purpose*: **Er kehrt heute von Paris mit seinem Freunde wegen Familienverhältnisse und zur Regelung seiner Geschäfte zurück.** An adverb of degree stands at or near the end of the sentence, usually following objects and other adverbs: **Er fördert diese Woche die Arbeit sehr. Ich weiche heute hier unter diesen Verhältnissen von meinem Vorhaben keinen Schritt zurück.** The following details should be carefully noted:

aa. For the sake of euphony a short word often precedes a heavier one or a phrase, altho according to the usual rule it would follow it: **Ich reiste gern nach Paris.**

bb. Of several adverbs the more general precede the more specific: **Wir reisen morgen früh um sechs Uhr 50 Minuten ab. Der Polizist fand den Betrunkenen auf der Fahrstraße im Drecke liegen.** Of course the word of more general meaning follows if it is to be made emphatic: **Ich beauftragte ihn, meinem Kutscher zu sagen, er möge sich um acht Uhr morgens zur Weiterfahrt bereit halten.**

cc. As the idea of place is important with verbs of rest, arrival, and departure there is a strong tendency to make here the position of an adverb of time before an adverb of place functional even where the idea of time is more important: **Er war vierzehn Tage hier. Er ist vor vierzehn Tagen hier angekommen. Ich ging aufs Feld und blieb den lieben langen Tag da.** Even here time follows place if its importance is quite marked: **Diese steinerne Bank mit den Greifenköpfen war hier vorhín nicht gestanden** (Thomas Mann's *Königliche Hoheit*, p. 84). With other verbs this order is the rule if the element of time is more important than that of place: **Ich ging aufs Feld und grub da den lieben langen Tag.**

dd. Position of Negatives. Originally **nicht** was an adverbial accusative of degree (see **145.** *g. Note* 2) and like an adverb of degree it still often stands at or near the end of the sentence following objects and other adverbs: **Du hast den Segen der Arbeit nicht. Willst du den Segen der Arbeit nicht haben?** As **nicht** is only lightly stressed there is a strong tendency for it to-day to seek the place before a stressed word: **Hans will nicht Soldát werden,** but **Hans will Soldat nicht wérden, er ist es schon. Ich kann über deinen Unsinn nicht láchen,** but **Ich kann nicht über deinen Únsinn lachen.** There is sometimes fluctuation between older usage with **nicht** at the end and the newer tendency to place it before a stressed word: Mason **sträubt sich gegen** means **als Einzahl, aber der gute Sprachgebrauch unterstützt ihn darín nicht** (Gustav Krüger's *Schwierigkeiten des Englischen*, p. 132), or according to the new rhythmical principle **unterstützt ihn nicht darín.**

Quite similar is the use of **nie** and **niemals.**

ee. A single adverb modifying another must stand before it: **Er ist sehr alt.**

e. Order when there are both Adverbs and Objects. Of the modifiers of the verb, adverbial elements are of less importance as a rule than noun objects and hence precede them, but pronominal objects precede adverbial elements: **Der Fürst verlieh aus Dankbarkeit dem Feldherrn diese Würde. Sie sprechen vollkommen gut Deutsch. Er überträgt mit schneller Besonnenheit seinem Adjutanten die Verfolgung der Feinde. Er sagte es mir gestern mit großer Freude.** An adverbial modifier usually precedes a prepositional object: **Er spricht oft von ihm, von seinem Sohne.**

aa. Adverbs of place usually follow an accusative or dative object, but precede a prepositional object: **Wir konnten das Buch nirgends im Hause finden,** but **Die warten hier in der Nähe auf euren Wink.**

bb. Of course emphasis can reverse the usual order of objects and adverbs. Especially in short sentences adverbs of time and manner often stand after objects: **Ich sah diesen Herrn gestern. Er spricht von ihm oft. Ich trinke den Kaffee sehr gern.** Even a personal pronoun follows an adverb if it is more prominent and is followed by an accented word: **Er befand sich im Himmel, sagte die Mutter, und erwartete dort sie alle.**

C. *Order of Adjective Modifiers.* The adjective modifiers of any noun whether in the subject or predicate have exactly the same word-order as the modifiers of the subject (see A): **Kein Dichter oder Denker hat nach Luthers Zeiten einen in soviel Richtungen gleichzeitig wirkenden, vier aufeinanderfolgende Generationen volldurchdringenden Einfluß gehabt als Goethe** (Hermann Grimm's *Goethe*, Einleitung).

a. For the cases where the adjective follows its governing noun see **104.** 2. B. *a* and *b*; **111.** 9; **137.** 1. *a.*

b. The pronominals **dies-, jen-, all-** precede possessives, as in English. Formerly also **beid-** had precedence here. See **139.** 1. *d. Note* 2. (**5**).

Inverted Order.

286. In this word-order the predicate, an object, an adverbial word, phrase, or clause, or the expletive **es**, occupies the first place, the verb stands in the second place, and the subject then follows immediately or at an interval of several words. If the subject is a personal pronoun or the indefinite **man** it must follow the verb immediately: **Dann beruhigte er sich. Oft muß man sich selber helfen.** This rule has become perfectly rigid for personal pronouns, so that they must follow the verb immediately when used as subject even tho they are heavily stressed: **Heute mußt dú ihn besuchen.** Aside from personal pronouns heavier and more prominent pronominal subjects follow weaker pronominal objects: **Dann kann mir dás alles nichts nützen. Dann neigten sich béide vor dem Könige. Manchmal erkannten mich éinige.** Substantival subjects usually follow pronominal objects because they are heavier and more important: **Hinter uns schloß sich ein undurchdringlicher Wall der empörten Menge.** In German it would be impossible to place the light object **sich** after the heavy and important subject **ein undurchdringlicher Wall.** When, on the other hand, the predicate is heavy and important the reflexive as a part of the predicate sometimes follows the subject: **Als Gottlieb Bänsch sich zum Einsteigen in Bewegung setzte, hing Männchen sich mit beiden Händen an seine**

Hand (Wildenbruch's *Der Letzte*, p. 57). The position of the reflexive here after the subject is becoming more common in recent literature, but the old position before the subject is still the more common one. When both subject and object are nouns the usual order is subject — object: **Endlich besiegte der Ritter den Türken.** Altho this rule is quite firm in modern usage it is not yet perfectly rigid, for the subject may still follow the substantival object when it becomes prominent, as in the following example from Mommsen's *Römische Geschichte*, III, p. 240: **Damals wohnten die Kelten in offenen Flecken, jetzt umgaben ihre Ortschaften wohlgefügte Mauern.** This order differs from the normal order in that some word from the predicate, or the expletive **es**, takes the first place and the subject takes the position after the verb, or in compound tenses after the auxiliary. In other respects the position of the words is in general retained as in normal order.

Compare older English: Now has he land and beefs (Shakespeare's *Henry IV*, Second Part, 3, 2). This older usage sometimes still survives after accented words that are closely connected with the verb in thought, as a predicate noun or adjective, a negative or restrictive word or phrase, strongly stressed *so* or *such*, and sometimes accented adverbs of time or place: *Most gráteful were they for my offer. Nówhere does he say anything on this point. He quickened his pace and só did I. Only ónce did he deviate from this principle.* In general, however, there has not been for many centuries a live feeling for this old construction as it was destroyed long ago by the newer principle of always putting the subject before the verb, as explained in **284.** I. 3. *a.*

The leading points as to the use of this order and the particulars concerning the word-order are as follows:

A. *Use of Inverted Order.* This order is used:

a. Just as in English, as the usual form for a question introduced by an interrogative word which is not the subject of the verb: **Was gibt es Neues? Warum kommt er? Wie geht's?** The same form is also often used in exclamations: **Wie schön ist das Wetter! Was hat er schon durchgemacht!** This exclamatory form is an old type of sentence out of which questions with the same word-order have probably developed, differentiating themselves from exclamations as in English by a different tone. In these exclamations we sometimes find the transposed word-order instead of the inverted, as they have been influenced by the exclamatory type described in **288.** B. *b*: **Wie schön das Wetter ist! Was er schon durchgemacht hat!** Instead of the inverted or the transposed word-order here we still have the old verbless type of sentence (**250.** *a*): **Wie schön!**

The interrogative word stands in the first place in accordance with the old Germanic principle that the emphatic word stands first in the sentence. The interrogative word is even brought forward from the subordinate clause to the beginning of the principal proposition just as in English: **Wo wollen Sie, daß ich anfangen soll?** (Lessing), now more commonly **Wo soll ich anfangen?**, as Germans are beginning to avoid the old construction, which is still common in English.

b. The inverted order is used whenever for some rhetorical reason a word or an expression is brought forward from the predicate and placed at the head of the sentence, and hence its use is a matter of style. Words are thus in general brought forward for the following reasons. (**1**) A word or words containing a reference to a preceding sentence or connected with it in thought are naturally brought forward, so that that which is stated in the one sentence and is now known may become the sure foundation for the next, upon which the thought can be further built up and enlarged: **Er war zwar ein großer Redner, Schriftsteller und Feldherr, aber jedes davon ist er nur geworden, weil er ein vollendeter Staatsmann war.** Here **jedes davon,** referring as it does to the foregoing words **Redner, Schriftsteller, Feldherr,** serves nicely as a foundation upon which to build a new thought. In older German such words were often brought forward from the subordinate clause to the beginning of the principal proposition: **Auf alle diese Fragen wird Ihnen Ihr Herz sagen, daß Sie mir die Antwort**

schuldig sind (H. v. Kleist's *Werke*, 5, 310, 5), now more commonly **Daß Sie mir auf alle diese Fragen Antwort schuldig sind, wird Ihnen Ihr Herz sagen.** (**2**) Words take the first place which lie nearest in thought, especially such as give us a general idea of the situation, so that the mind may be prepared for that which follows: **Tief unten zu unseren Füßen lag wie im bangen Traume die Stadt Freiburg mit ihren zerstreuten, matt schimmernden Lichtern.** In older German such words were often brought forward from the subordinate clause to the beginning of the principal proposition: **Auch auf dem Theater glaube ich, daß sie Glück machen werde** (Goethe's *Briefe*, 20, 195, 5), now **Auch auf dem Theater, glaube ich, wird sie Glück machen.** (**3**) Any word or words may for especial emphasis be brought forward from the predicate and be placed at the beginning of the proposition: **Er hat sehr vieles unternommen, gelúngen ist ihm nichts. Éingewirkt auf ihn kann es (das lebensvolle Landschaftsbild) freilich in diesen frühesten Jahren noch nicht haben** (Otto Harnack's *Schiller*, p. 6). **Bis der Löwe kommen wird, und — kómmen wird er** (Ludwig's *Makkabäer*, 1). **Man mag Cornelius heute verehren oder gleichgültig an ihm vorübergehen: lében tut** (**251.** II. B. *a. bb*, 2nd paragraph) **er und überlében wird er viele noch** (Hermann Grimm in *Deutsche Rundschau*, May 1896, p. 255). For other examples of this emphatic position for the perfect participle and the infinitive see **251.** II. B. *a. bb*, 3rd par. On the other hand, the infinitive sometimes stands at the beginning of the proposition not for emphasis but in order that the auxiliary may come into the unusual and hence emphatic position at or near the end of the sentence: **Wer sollte helfen? Ihr Vater? Ach, Unsinn! Aber geholfen werden múßte! Múßte!** (Hans Hoffmann's *Iwan der Schreckliche*, chap. VII). A verb in a simple tense cannot, like a participle or an infinitive, be put in the first place for emphasis. See B. *b* below. The dative and accusative can be brought forward from the predicate: **Nicht mír gab er das Buch, er gab es meinem Bruder. Den Váter liebt der Sohn** and **Die Franzósen schlug Wellington,** but not **Sogar Konstantinopel** (acc.) **hat Hamburg** (nom.) **überflügelt,** as the case forms are not clear and consequently **Konstantinopel** would be construed as nominative in accordance with the normal form of statement. The inverted order, however, can be freely used even where the case forms are not clear, provided the thought would not thereby be endangered: **Die ältere Ánsicht vertrat mit großer Bestimmtheit Kräuter** (name), **auch Braune** (name) (Wilmanns's *Deutsche Grammatik*, I, p. 81). Still other elements are brought forward: **Dort unter dem Báum sitzt er. Schön ist sie nicht, gút ist sie. Gar kein Kerl! Ein Lúmp ist er.** This order is usually required in German when the subject is **es** and the predicate a personal pronoun. See **251. I. 3.** Also in questions some word can for emphasis be placed at the head of the sentence, followed by inverted order: **Und d á s dulden Sie?** The question is not here detected by the order, but by the rising inflection of the voice. The tendency to place an accented word at the beginning of the sentence is much stronger in popular speech than in the literary language. Thus often in dialect an object or an adverbial element that belongs to the subordinate clause is placed at the beginning of the sentence: **Einen freien Platz ist nicht ausgemacht, daß du bekommst** (Renward Brandstetter's *Das schweizerische Lehngut im Romontschen*, p. 81). **Aus Breslau war ich froh, daß ich naus war** (L. Hanke's *Die Wortstellung im Schlesischen*, p. 23). Of these different uses (**1**) and (**3**) distinguish themselves by a stronger accent. The former, however, is often without stress, since the word used is a mere formal introduction to the principal proposition, as illustrated in **268.** 2. *a.* (**4**) Instead of a word or phrase, as in the preceding cases, a full or contracted clause may for the same reasons precede the verb, or the main sentence may be found within the body of the subordinate clause. In both of these cases inversion in the principal proposition is the rule: **Was möglich war, hat er geleistet. Um den Arzt zu holen, fuhr er schnell nach der Stadt. „Lauf nur," sagte ich, „lauf!"**

c. This order is also used to emphasize the subject or a verb in a simple tense, in which cases the sentence is usually introduced by **es,** followed immediately by the verb and still later by the subject. See **251.** II. B. *a. bb, cc.* In this construction, however, the word-order is only formally inverted. It is in reality that of a question, as the verb in fact stands in the first place. The **es** which precedes the verb has no accent and no logical force and hence does not count, serving here merely as a *formal* introduction to the sentence. This introductory **es**, however, is quite serviceable, as it *formally* distinguishes this emphatic form of the declarative sentence from the interrogative form. In popular language this **es** is often dropped. See **251.** II. B. *b.*

On the other hand, when an object, an adverbial element, or a predicate word introduces the proposition and the subject stands last for emphasis, the **es** is not employed as the introductory word clearly marks the declarative form of statement: **Das nämlich tun und müssen tun die schwächeren Menschen, die nicht an sich halten können** (Ricarda Huch's *Ausbreitung und Verfall der Romantik*, p. 150). **Gegen Abend begegnete mir noch etwas Wunderliches.** For other interesting examples see **251.** I. 2. B. *Note* and II. B. *a. aa. Note.* This form of statement is often used when both the introductory element and the subject near the end or in the final position are to be made prominent: **Für Líeblosigkeit kann sie das Géld nicht entschädigen** (Hauptmann's *Einsame Menschen*, p. 67). **Selbst die Hånde gedrückt hatten ihm éinige Menschen, die er kaum kannte** (R. H. Bartsch's *Die Haindlkinder*, p. 302).

B. *Particulars of the Inverted Word-order*:

a. If an object, or an adverbial word, phrase, or clause introduces the sentence, the subject usually follows the verb immediately, or is separated from it by unimportant words, but also, as in the following sentences, the subject may stand near the end of the sentence, especially when it contains the new and hence important element in the sentence, and is therefore to be emphasized: **Bei den Griechen und Römern trat sehr früh an die Stelle des Gaues als die Grundlage der politischen Einheit der Mauerring.** Emphasis often requires the subject to be placed last when it consists of a list of things or a series of clauses: **Entmündigt kann werden: 1. wer in Folge von Geisteskrankheit oder Geistesschwäche seine Angelegenheiten nicht zu besorgen vermag; 2. wer durch Verschwendung sich oder seine Familie der Gefahr des Notstandes aussetzt; 3. wer in Folge von Trunksucht usw.** (*Bürgerliches Gesetzbuch*, § 5). See also A. *c* (2nd par.) above.

On the other hand, an unaccented pronominal subject must follow the verb immediately: **Heute hat sie es dem Vater überreicht.**

b. If it is desired to emphasize the *subject* or a *verb in a simple tense* we most commonly employ the inverted order, introducing the sentence with **es.** This important construction is explained in **251.** II. B. *a. bb. cc.* From another standpoint this word-order may be regarded as the *normal* order, as the grammatical subject **es** stands in the first place. From still another point of view it is the *question* order, as explained in A. *c* above, and also in **284.** I. 1. *a*, 2nd par., toward end.

c. The emphatic object or adverbial element is usually placed in the important position at the beginning of the sentence. When, however, an unemphatic sentence adverb introduces the sentence the emphatic object or adverb follows as closely as possible and thus stands in the first place after the verb, for the verb *must* stand in the second place: **Vielleicht stellt auch mír sich noch einiges anders** (Konrad Zwierzina in *Zeitschrift für das deutsche Altertum*, 45, p. 393).

d. It is a peculiarity of German that after a subordinate clause, especially one of cause (reason, condition, concession), the following principal proposition is often introduced by **so,** which sums up in one word the substance of the preceding clause and by its adverbial form calls attention to the fact that inversion must follow: **Wenn der Mensch keinen Genuß mehr in der Arbeit findet und bloß arbeitet, um so schnell wie möglich zum Genuß zu gelangen, so ist es nur ein Zufall, wenn er kein Verbrecher wird.** This use of **so** is, as in the preceding example, more common after long subordinate clauses, but must also be used sometimes in shorter sentences where the principal proposition and the subordinate clause have the same word-order, as it is here necessary to distinguish the principal proposition from the subordinate clause: **Kann ich, so komme ich.** Here the relation of the propositions would not be clear without the use of **so,** as both propositions have the same order. In poetry, however, the **so** is often even here dispensed with: **Ehrt den König seine Würde, | ehret uns der Hände Fleiß** (Schiller).

e. If any adverb or adverbial element, or a predicate noun or adjective, belongs to two coordinate sentences connected by **und** or **oder,** it usually causes inversion only in the first proposition, the second standing in normal order: **Dann ziehen sich Bruder und Schwester zurück, und Sonje eilt die Treppe hinauf. Schön ist sie nicht, und sie wird es nie werden.** In case the subjects of the different propositions refer to the same person, the subject is quite commonly suppressed in the second proposition. For examples see **251.** II. A. *e.* Sometimes, however, the force of the word introducing the first proposition is felt, and inversion in the next proposition results: **Schön war sie (die Stadt Kiel) niemals, ist sie auch nicht geworden und wird sie nie werden** (Jensen). **Trotz dieser gewagtesten aller Lagen wurde die Stellung genommen, wurde gesiegt, wurde der Feind eingeschlossen** (Generaloberst Graf Schlieffen at the unveiling of the Moltke statue in Berlin, Oct. 25, 1905).

In case an object is common to several propositions it is usually expressed in the first, and repeated in the form of a pronoun in the second, which has normal word-order: **Das weiß ich und die ganze Stadt weiß es.** Sometimes, however, the object is expressed but once, namely, in the first proposition, in which case the second must have inverted order, as the force of the object introducing the first proposition is felt: **Verpflichtungen hat jeder Gastgeber gegen seine Gäste, und daß ich die meinigen kenne, weiß ich und weiß die Welt** (Raabe's *Der Dräumling*, xxvi). See also **251.** II. A. *e* (toward end).

f. If a sentence is introduced by certain co-ordinating conjunctions, the order remains normal, while on the other hand it becomes inverted if introduced by others. This matter is discussed in articles **233–237.**

g. The following words or classes of words may introduce a sentence without causing inversion: (**1**) Exclamations do not usually influence the word-order, as they are felt as standing outside of the structure of the sentence: **Na, das wird was Schönes geben!** Plague on it, that will make a pretty mess! (**2**) The affirmative adverb **ja** and negative **nein: Nein! ich geh' nicht in die Stadt.** (**3**) The adverbs **nun** in the one meaning *well*, **gewiß** *certainly*, and a number of concessive adverbs, adverbial conjunctions (for which see **235.** A. *c*, and **236**), adverbial clauses, and also independent sentences with the force of adverbs, do not always cause inversion, as they are felt as independent remarks bearing upon the sentence rather than as modifiers of the predicate; **allerdings** it must be admitted, **freilich** to be sure, **immerhin** at any rate, at all events, **zwar** it is true, **in der Tat** indeed, **wie ich zugeben muß** as I must confess, **ich gestehe es** I acknowledge it, &c. Exs.: **Nun, ich werde zum Vater kommen** (Benedix's *Doktor Treuwald*, 1, 4). **Gewiß, man muß auch schweigen können** (Fontane's *Effi*, ix). **Allerdings, ich habe es nicht selbst gesehen, aber ich glaube es.** In M.H.G., for the same reason, the word-order in the principal proposition was not usually influenced by a preceding clause as in the present period, where a preceding clause is felt as modifying the principal verb as any other adverbial element and hence influences the word-order in the following proposition. As a survival of older usage the normal order is still usually found after a concessive clause or a pair of concessive clauses, except after a single concessive clause introduced by a conjunction, **obgleich,** &c., stating an *actual fact*: **Sei es nun recht oder nicht,** or **Mag es recht oder nicht recht sein, ich werde es nicht tun. Wie betrübt ich auch war, ich mußte lächeln. Ob wir gewinnen, ob wir verlieren, die Zukunft wird es zeigen.** But **Obgleich er von meiner Unschuld überzeugt war, machte er mir doch Vorwürfe.** After concessive clauses which have developed out of conditional clauses, however, we sometimes find normal order as after a concessive clause, sometimes inverted order as after a conditional clause: **Wenn du auch noch so sehr klagtest, er würde** or **würde er sich doch nicht rühren lassen** (Paul's *Deutsche Syntax*, II. p. 316). After a clause of purpose the order is often normal as the utterance is in fact an object clause after a verb of saying understood: **Daß ich es kurz sage,** or **Um es kurz zu sagen, [sage ich dir], ich will nicht.** All the above mentioned adverbs and adverbial expressions, with the exception of the short concessive sentences and the concessive and purpose clauses, may also cause inversion, as they are also often felt as modifiers of the predicate: **Allerdings habe ich es nicht selbst gesehen, aber ich glaube es.** After the adverbs which are followed by normal order, the voice pauses somewhat, while after those which are followed by inverted order there is no such distinct pause, as the adverb is felt as belonging closely to the following verb. (**4**) A number of adverbs as **nur** only, **vielleicht** perhaps, **besonders,** especially, **dagegen, hingegen** on the contrary, **selbst** even, **schon** even, &c., modify, not the predicate, but only the subject, or some part of it, and hence can stand before (and also after) the subject without causing inversion: **Vielleicht der zuverlässigste Messer der steigenden Kultur ist das Gefühl der Zusammengehörigkeit der Nation** (Mommsen's *Römische Geschichte*, V, chap. vii). Sometimes inversion takes place after such words, but then with a different meaning, as inversion is a sign that the adverb modifies the verb and not the subject: **Wenigstens mein Bruder behauptet es** *My brother* AT LEAST (I do not know whether anybody else does) *asserts it*, but **Wenigstens behauptet es mein Bruder** *My brother asserts it* AT LEAST (I do not know whether his statement is true). (**5**) After a conditional clause the following principal proposition sometimes as in older usage remains in normal order: **Gerhard merkte nicht, wie arg er seine Frau vernachlässigte; hätte er's gemerkt, er würde es nicht gemacht haben** (Riehl's *Der stumme Ratsherr*, I). **Kämest du** (originally **Kämest du!**, an unreal subjunction of wish), **ich würde mich freuen** (Sommer's *Vergleichende Syntax*, p. 105). The subordinate clause here was originally often an independent sentence, either an independent wish, as in the last example, or an independent question, as nicely illustrated by the example from Luther given in **237. 1. A.** ***b. Note*** **2, hence it often still does not influence the order of the principal proposition.**

Question Order.

287. A. In this order the personal part of the verb stands in the first place, the subject usually stands in the second place, always if it is a personal pronoun, and the other parts are arranged in general as in normal order: **Muß ich mich rechts oder links wenden?** The pronoun must be repeated with each verb: **Gehst du oder kommst du?** Are you going or coming? The position of the personal pronoun used as *subject* after the verb has become functional and is not at all regulated by emphasis. The personal pronoun *must* stand immediately after the verb even if it is strongly accented and should come to stand before an unaccented personal pronoun, altho usually the accented personal pronoun follows the unaccented one: **Muß ích ihm helfen?** If the subject is a noun or a pronoun other than a personal pronoun it can for emphasis be placed toward the end of the sentence: **Kennt den Mann der Váter oder die Mútter? Gibt's der Vater dem Knáben?**, but **Gibt's dem Knaben der Váter oder die Mútter? Kann mich das ein Mä́dchen fragen?** Can a *girl* ask me such a question as that? **Wundert dich dás?** As in these sentences, the subject is quite commonly separated from the verb by unaccented pronouns, providing it is itself not an unaccented personal pronoun. However, if the pronominal *objects* are to be made emphatic, they should follow the subject: **Gehen die Streitigkeiten anderer dich an?** Notice that in German **nicht** cannot follow immediately the personal part of the verb as often *not* in English: **Kommt er heute nicht?** Isn't he coming to-day? In general its position is much the same as in normal order. See **285.** II. B. *d. dd.* If an infinitive is to be made emphatic it cannot, of course, in normal or question order stand in the first place. If it depends upon a participle it can be emphasized by being placed after the participle: **Habt ihr von eurem Tale her je einen Felsen gesehen sich neigen?** (Sudermann's *Johannes*, 2, 1).

Note. In many cases in colloquial speech the word-order is only seemingly the question order as an object or adverb must be supplied in thought immediately before the verb: suppressed object: **„Und ich wette, Sie haben wieder einen Eierkuchen gebacken."** [Das] **„Hab' ich auch"** [getan] (Fontane). Suppressed adverb: Kurt (unter erneuten Küssen): **Nun?** Eva: **Ich rufe!** Kurt: **Umso besser!** [Dann] **Wissen's alle** (delle Grazie's *Sphinx*).

B. This order is found: (**1**) In all independent interrogative sentences which are not introduced by an interrogative pronoun, adjective, or adverb: **Wollen Sie wohl dies für mich tun?** Here there is a marked rising of the voice toward the end of the sentence as in English, but in the following uses the voice falls toward the end of the sentence, except, however, in the cases mentioned in (**2**) and (**4**). In the conditional and concessive clauses there mentioned the voice rises slightly toward the end of the clause. See **237.** 1. A. *b. Note* 2. The question form is often used to express a wish: **Hilft mir einer von euch?** Often also with the force of a declarative sentence to state something confidently: **Hab' ich nicht recht gehabt? Bin ich etwa dein Sklave?** For the use of the question form in various shades of imperative meaning see **177.** I. B. *b. c.* On the other hand, in ordinary questions we often instead of the question order employ the transposed word-order, in which case the sentence is introduced by **ob: Ob er wohl wiederkommen wird?** When for some reason or another a question is repeated the transposed word-order is the rule. See **284.** I. 3. *a* (toward end). (**2**) In conditional clauses not introduced by a conjunction. For examples see **237.** 1. A. *b.* (**3**) In clauses introduced by **als** *as if*. See **237.** 1. A. *c.* (**4**) In concessive clauses not introduced by a conjunction: **Ist es gleich Nacht, so leuchtet unser Recht.** See **280.** *b.* (**1**) and (**3**). (**5**) In independent sentences containing the volitive subjunctive and the sanguine and the unreal subjunctive of wish. See **168.** I. 1. A, B. *a*, and **169.** 1. A. (**6**) In imperative sentences: **Lassen Sie diese Schüssel herumgehen.** (**7**) The question order is often used to make a statement in a stronger, more lively manner, especially when accompanied by the adverb **doch, aber** or **ja** (for historical explanation see **251.** II. B. *b*): **Hab' ich den Markt und die Straßen doch nie so einsam gesehen! | Ist doch die Stadt wie gekehrt!** (Goethe's *H. und D.*, I. 1–2). **Ist dás schö́n!** How beautiful that is! **Weiß ich doch, woran ich bin!** I know what I am about! **Ist dás ein Wétter! Wird dér Áugen machen! Wird's der Úlrich gút kriegen! Setzen Sie sich hier ins Warme. Müssen Sie frieren in dem kalten Deutschland!** (Sudermann's *Die Ehre*, 2, 8). **Diese hatte abermals eine neue Toilette an. Weiß der liebe Himmel, wo die alle herkommen!** (Ompteda's *Herzeloide*, p. 58). **Hab' ich ihn gestern verhauen!** (K. Brugmann's *Der Ursprung des Scheinsubjekts* es, p. 45) I tell you I gave him a good thrashing yesterday! **Bist du aber schmutzig!** (id.). How dirty you are! **War der Mensch zornig!** I tell you the fellow was mad! **Wußten wir es ja alle!** Why, we all knew that! **Hat das aber Mühe gekostet!** I tell you that cost a good deal of trouble. Compare older English: Fab.: Is't so saucy? Sir And.: Ay, *is't*, I warrant him: do but read (Shakespeare's *Twelfth Night*, 3, 4). For other German examples see **251.** II. B. *b.* Such sentences often contain the idea of cause, adding an explanation or the self-evident reason for the preceding statement: **Er kann es nicht bestreiten, hatten es doch alle gesehen.** In a more formal style free from lively feeling the causal idea is here usually expressed by a principal clause with normal word-order introduced by the conjunction **denn.** Similarly instead of a principal proposition introduced by the illative conjunction **da'rum** or **da'her** *for that reason, therefore* we often find in lively language the question order: **Ich bin so müde, kann ich doch nicht mit euch spazieren gehen!** (**8**) In poetry and colloquial speech the question order is frequently found in lively narrative style: **Sah ein Knab' ein Röslein steh'n, | Röslein auf der Heiden, | war so jung und morgenschön, | lief er schnell, es nah zu seh'n, | sah's mit vielen Freuden** (Goethe). See also **251.** II. B. *b.* (**9**) After the conjunction **und** to emphasize the verb or the subject. See **251.** II. B. *b.* The *question* order after **und** is sometimes apparently used where in fact the order is the *inverted*, as an adverb or an object which has been previously employed is understood. See **286.** B. *e.*

Transposed Order.

288. A. In this order the clause is introduced by a subordinating conjunction, or a relative or interrogative pronoun or adverb, and ends with the personal part of the verb, the remaining elements having about the same arrangement as in normal and inverted order: **Seine Freunde fürchteten, daß es ihm zu schwer werden würde.** As in the preceding sentence, the subject usually stands at the head of the clause, always if it is a relative or interrogative pronoun, commonly so also in case of **man** or a personal pronoun. As the subordinate clause is usually presented dispassionately as a compact unit it does not in a marked degree show in the word-order the influence of logical consideration or strong emotion, but it nevertheless often contains touches of logic and feeling as shown by the tendency for important words to follow unimportant ones and for emphatic words to stand near the beginning or the end of the clause. Where the subject is a noun or pronoun other than those just mentioned it is quite commonly preceded by an unaccented pronominal or reflexive object: **Er sah mich verwundert an, vielleicht, weil ihm der fremde Akzént aufgefallen war. Ich liebte ihn auch, wie ihn álle lieben.** The unaccented pronoun has been firm here in the initial position since the oldest historic period. On the other hand, when the verb is more prominent than the subject there is a tendency to remove the reflexive to a position after the subject and nearer the verb to which it belongs: **Daß das Pflänzchen sich áuswächst, während wir leben, das dürfen wir nicht hoffen** (Hauptmann's *Einsame Menschen*, p. 88). Of course, the reflexive stands near the end of the clause immediately before the verb when it is itself emphatic: **Sie wußte instinktiv, daß solch ein Herr Sohn und Österreicher oft lieber sích sélbst gehört als einem Berufe** (R. H. Bartsch's *Die Haindlkinder*, p. 23). The subject may also be preceded by adverbial elements: **Wie heutzutage in unserer und durch unsere Weltliteratur die Gegensätze der zivilisierten Nationen aufgehoben sind, so hat die griechische Dichtkunst das dürftige und egoistische Stammgefühl zum hellenischen Volksbewußtsein und dieses zum Humanismus umgewandelt** (Mommsen's *Römische Geschichte*, I, chap. xv). Sometimes a subject noun for especial emphasis stands after an object noun: **In Deutschland, wo den Frieden die Armée beschützt, wird der Plan der Abrüstung schwerlich allzuviel Anklang finden** (Georg Edward in 1906). Altho adverbial elements or an object may thus introduce the subordinate clause, as they lie nearer in thought or give a general idea of the situation preparing the mind for what follows, or in order that the subject may for a time be suspended and thus become conspicuous, they only occasionally take this position that they themselves may be rendered emphatic, as in the following sentence: **Der Wert seiner Publikation beruht allein auf den drei Schriftstücken, von denen**

das míttlere wir nur durch ihn kennen (Reinhold Steig in *Euphorion*, vol. XII, p. 247). The predicate noun, adjective, infinitive, or perfect participle, however, cannot, as in the inverted order, for special emphasis be placed at the beginning of the clause, nor can they take the emphatic position at the end. The infinitive and participle stand next to the end before the personal part of the verb, the predicate adjective or noun stand before the personal part of the verb in case of a simple tense, and before the different parts of the verb in case of a compound tense. In case of an infinitive, however, dependent upon a modal auxiliary which has been attracted into the form of an infinitive, the real infinitive can for emphasis, as in the principal proposition, stand near the beginning of the clause: **Nicht weil sie ihn schützen hätten können, o nein!** (R. H. Bartsch's *Die Haindlkinder*, p. 209). **Man sagt, daß Österreich „zerfiel." Nein: es war gar nichts mehr da, das erst noch „zerfällen" hätte können** (Hermann Bahr in *Preußische Jahrbücher*, 1921, p. 1). On the other hand, the modifiers of the verb have toward the end of the clause the same freedom of position as in the principal proposition: **Er wartete, bis er zu Hause den Sóhn traf, or bis er den Sohn zu Háuse traf,** according to the accent.

a. Note especially that a clause or infinitive phrase which is dependent upon another dependent clause is more likely to follow the pronominal subject of the governing dependent clause than to precede it as in English: **Er behauptete, daß er, anstatt die Versammlung aufzulösen, einen Antrag machen wolle** He stated that instead of dissolving the assembly he would make a proposal. **Wenn er, nachdem man seine Aussage bezweifelte, wieder fragen sollte usw.** If, upon their doubting his statement, he asked again, &c.

B. This order is used:

a. In subordinate clauses. There are, however, exceptions, which are stated in **237.** I. A, B, C, D; **269.** 4; **271.** II. 8.

b. In lively questions and exclamations which are introduced by a subordinate conjunction: **[Ich wundere mich] Daß er immer noch nicht kommt! [ich wünschte] Daß er doch bald käme! Wenn er nur bald käme! [wäre es gut, or würde ich mich freuen]. Wenn ich es nur gewußt hätte! [wäre ich gekommen]. „Kennen Sie diesen Menschen?"** [Sie fragen mich] **„Ob ich ihn kenne!"** (spoken in tone of surprise). **[ich möchte es gern wissen] Ob's jedem Mädchen so ist, das eine Braut werden soll, wie mir?** After the analogy of such examples sentences introduced by an interrogative pronoun or adverb sometimes have the transposed word-order instead of the inverted: **Was der Junge doch fährt!** (Goethe's *H. und D.*). **Wo er wohl jetzt ist?** Compare **286.** A. *a.*

c. In poetry frequently also in principal propositions, for sake of rime or meter, as a survival of the older *normal* order (see **284.** I. 3. *a*): **Der alte Schmied den Bart sich streicht: | „Das Schwert ist nicht zu schwer noch leicht"** (Uhland's *Das Schwert*). Also in old saws: **Willenskraft Wege schafft.**

d. In early N.H.G., when **je** and **danach** introduce both the principal proposition and the subordinate clause, the principal proposition sometimes has transposed order for the sake of a parallelism between the two propositions, and this older usage survives in poetry and proverbs: **Je mehr er aber verbot, je mehr sie es ausbreiteten** (Mark vii. 36). **Danach einer tut, danach es ihm geht** (prov.). **Je — je** is now largely replaced by **je** (with transposed order) — **desto** or **um so** (with inverted order): **Je mehr der Vorrat schmolz, desto** (or **um so**) **schrecklicher wuchs der Hunger.** Transposed order in both propositions for the sake of the parallelism is now quite rare: **Desto zahlreicher so eine Grablegung gehandhabt wird, je umfänglicher die Offertorien fließen** (Hauptmann's *Die Weber*, 3, p. 50).

C. For the position of an auxiliary which is common to two or more subordinate clauses see **237.** 1. E.

INDEX OF GERMAN WORDS, SUFFIXES, SOUNDS, &C.

The figures in this index refer to pages, those employed in the body of the Grammar, however, refer to articles. The abbreviations here used are: pron. for pronunciation; orthog. for orthography; decl. for declension; compar. for comparison; grad. for gradation, i.e. the principal parts of a strong or irregular verb; syn. for syntax, i.e. influence upon the syntactical structure of the sentence, government of case, &c. Other contractions are given in alphabetical order in the two indexes below.

INDEX OF SUBJECTS